# Judaism A to Z

*170 chapters in alphabetical order*

## Saul Silas Fathi

508 West 26th Street KEARNEY, NE 68848
402-819-3224
info@medialiteraryexcellence.com

# TABLE OF CONTENTS

# A Jewish History

**Jewish history** (or the **history of the Jewish people**) is the history of the Jews, and their religion and culture, as it developed and interacted with other peoples, religions and cultures. Jewish ancestry is traced back to the Biblical patriarchs **Abraham, Isaac and Jacob** who lived in Canaan around the 18th century BCE. Historically, Jews had descended mostly from the **Tribe of Judah and Simeon,** and partially from the other Israelite tribes, especially of **Binyamin** and **Levi,** who had all together formed the ancient **Kingdom of Judah** and the ancient **Kingdom of Israel.**

## Time periods in Jewish history

The history of the Jews and Judaism can be divided into five periods: (1) ancient Israel before Judaism, from the beginnings to 586 BCE; (2) the beginning of Judaism in the 6th and 5th centuries BCE; (3) the formation of rabbinic Judaism after the destruction of the Second Temple in 70 CE; (4) the age of rabbinic Judaism, from the ascension of Christianity to political power under the emperor **Constantine the Great** in 312 CE to the end of the political hegemony of Christianity in the 18th century, and (5), the age of diverse Judaism, from the French and American Revolutions to the present.

## Ancient Israelites (to 586 BCE)

The history of the early Jews, and their neighbors, is mainly that of the **Fertile Crescent** and east coast of the Mediterranean Sea. It begins among those people who occupied the area lying between the **Nile, Tigris** and the **Euphrates** rivers, was a meeting place of civilizations. According to the Jewish sacred writings, which became the **Hebrew Bible**, Jews are descended from the ancient people of Israel who settled in the land of Canaan between the eastern coast of the Mediterranean Sea and the Jordan River.

Ancient Hebrew writings describe the "**Children of Israel**" as descendants of common ancestors, including **Abraham**, his son **Isaac**, and Isaac's son **Jacob**. Religious literature suggests that the nomadic travels of the Hebrews centered around Hebron in the first centuries of the second millennium BCE, apparently leading to the establishment of the **Cave of the Patriarchs** as their burial site in Hebron. The Children of Israel consisted of **twelve tribes**, each descended from one of the Jacob's twelve sons, **Reuven, Shimon, Levi, Yehuda, Yissachar, Zevulun, Dan, Gad, Naftali, Asher, Yosef, and Benyamin.**

Religious texts tell the story of Jacob and his twelve sons, who left Canaan during a severe famine and settled in Goshen of northern Egypt. While in Egypt their descendants were said to be enslaved by the government led by the Egyptian Pharaoh. **After some 400 years of slavery**, YHWH, the God of Israel, sent the Hebrew prophet **Moses** of the tribe of **Levi** to release the Israelites from bondage. According to the Bible, the Hebrews miraculously emigrated out of Egypt (an event known as the Exodus), and returned to their ancestral homeland in Canaan. This event marks the formation of Israel as a political nation in Canaan, in 1400 BCE. The culture of the earliest Israelite settlement is Canaanite, their cult-objects are those of the Canaanite good **El,** the pottery remains in the local Canaanite tradition, and the alphabet used is early Canaanite.

According to the Bible, after their emancipation from Egyptian slavery, the people of Israel wandered around and lived in the Sinai desert for a span of **forty years** before conquering Canaan in 1400 BCE under the command of **Joshua**. While living in the desert, according to the Biblical writings, the nation of Israel received the **Ten Commandments** at Mount Sinai from **YHWH**, carried by Moses.

This marked a beginning for normative Judaism, and contributed to the formation of the first Abrahamic religion. After entering Canaan, **portions of the land were given to each of the twelve tribes of Israel.** For several hundred years, the Land of Israel was organized into a confederacy of twelve tribes ruled by a series of Judges. After that, notes the Bible, came the Israelite monarchy. In 1000 BCE, the monarchy was established under **Saul**, and continued under **King David** and his son, **Solomon**. During the reign of David, the already existing city of Jerusalem became the national and spiritual capital of Israel Solomon built the **First Temple** on Mount Moriah in Jerusalem. However, the tribes were fracturing politically.

Upon his death, a civil war erupted between the ten northern Israelite tribes, and the tribes of Judah (Simeon was absorbed into Judah) and Benjamin in the south. The nation split into the **Kingdom of Israel** in the north, and the **Kingdom of Judah** in the south. Israel was conquered by the Assyrian ruler **Tiglath-Pileser III** in the 8th century BCE. There is no commonly accepted historical record of the fate of the ten northern tribes, sometimes referred to as the **Ten Lost Tribes** of Israel.

## Babylonian captivity (c. 587-518 BCE)

After revolting against the new dominant power and an ensuing siege, the **Kingdom of Judah** was conquered by the Babylonian army in **587 BCE** and the **First Temple** was destroyed. The elite of the kingdom and many of their people were exiled to Babylon, where the religion developed outside their traditional temple. Others fled to Egypt. After the fall of Jerusalem, Babylonia (modern day Iraq), would become the focus of Judaism for more than a thousand years. The first Jewish communities in Babylonia started with the exile of the Tribe of Judah to the Babylon by **Jehoiachin** in 597 BCE, as well as after the **destruction of the Temple in Jerusalem in 586 BCE.**

Many more Jews migrated to Babylon in 135 CE after the **Bar Kokhba** revolt and in the centuries after, Babylonia, where some of the largest and most prominent Jewish cities and communities were established, became the center of Jewish life all the way up to the 13th century. By the first century, Babylonia already held a speedily growing population of an estimated 1,000,000 Jews, which increased to an estimated 2 million between the years 200 CE – 500 CE, both by natural growth and by immigration of more Jews from the Land of Israel, making up about 1/6 of the world Jewish population at that era.

It was there that they would write the **Babylonian Talmud** in the languages used by the Jews of ancient Babylonia – **Hebrew** and **Aramaic**. The Jews established Talmudic Academies in Babylonia, also known as the **Geonic Academies**, which became the center for Jewish scholarship and the development of Jewish law in Babylonia from roughly 500 CE to 1038 CE. The two most famous academies were the **Pumbedita Academy** and the **Sura Academy**.

Major Yeshivot was also located at **Neharde**a and **Mahuza**. After a few generations and with the conquest of Babylonia by the **Persian Empire**, some adherents led by prophets **Ezra** and **Nehemiah**, returned to their homeland and traditional practices.

## Post-exilic period (c. 538-332 BCE)

Following their return to Jerusalem and with Persian approval and financing, **construction of the Second Temple in 516 BCE** was completed under the leadership of the last three Jewish Prophets **Haggai, Zechariah and Malachi**. After the death of the last Jewish prophet and while still under Persian rule, the leadership of the Jewish people passed into the hands of five successive generations of **zugot ("pairs of")** leaders. They flourished first under the Persians and then under the Greeks. As a result the **Pharisees** and **Sadducees** were formed. Under the Persians then under the Greeks, Jewish coins were minted in Judea as Yehud coinage.

## Hellenistic period (c. 332-110 BCE)

In 332 BCE, the Persians were defeated by **Alexander the Great** of Macedon. After his demise, and the division of Alexander's empire among his generals, the **Seleucid Kingdom** was formed. Greek culture was spread eastwards by the Alexandrian conquests. During this time, currents of Judaism were influenced by Hellenistic philosophy developed from the 3$^{rd}$ century BCE, notably the Jewish diaspora in Alexandria, culminating in the compilation of the **Septuagint.**

## The Hasmonean Kingdom (110-63 BCE)

A deterioration of relationship between Hellenized Jews and orthodox Jews led the Seleucid king **Antiochus IV Epiphanes** to impose decrees banning certain Jewish religious rites and traditions. Consequently, the orthodox Jews revolted under the leadership of the **Hasmonean family (also known as the Maccabees)**. This revolt eventually led to the formation of an independent Jewish kingdom, known as the **Hasmonaean Dynasty**, which lasted from 165 BCE to 63 BCE.

The Hasmonean Dynasty eventually disintegrated as a result of civil war between the sons of **Salome Alexandra, Hyrcanus II and Aristobulus II**. The people, who did not want to be governed by a king but by theocratic clergy, made appeals in this spirit to the Roman authorities. A Roman campaign of conquest and annexation, led by **Pompey**, soon followed.

## Roman rule in the land of Israel (63 BCE-324 CE)

Judea had been an independent Jewish kingdom under the Hasmoneans, but was **conquered by the Roman general Pompey in 63 BCE** and reorganized as a client state. Later, **Herod the Great** was appointed **"King of the Jews"** by the Roman Senate, supplanting the Hasmonean dynasty. Some of his offspring held various positions after him, known as the **Herodian dynasty**. After the **Census of Quirinius** in 6 CE, the Roman province of Judaea was formed as a satellite of Roman Syria under the rule of a prefect (as was roman Egypt) until 41 CE, then procurators after 44 CE.

The empire was often callous and brutal in its treatment of its Jewish subjects; see Anti-Judaism in the pre-Christian Roman Empire. In 66 CE, the Jews began to revolt against the Roman rulers of Judea. The revolt was defeated by the future Roman emperors **Vespasian** and **Titus**. In the Siege of Jerusalem in **70 CE, the Romans destroyed much of the Temple in Jerusalem** and, according to some accounts, plundered artifacts from the temple, such as the **Menorah**, Jews continued to live in their land in significant numbers, the **Kitos War** of 115-117 CE notwithstanding, until **Julius Severus** ravaged Judea while putting down the **Bar Kokhba revolt** of 132-136 CE. 985 villages were destroyed and most of the Jewish population of central Judaea was essentially wiped out, killed, sold into slavery, or forced to flee. Banished from Jerusalem, except for the day of **Tisha B'Av**, the Jewish population now centered on Galilee and initially in Yavne. Jerusalem was renamed **Aelia Capitolina** and Judea was renamed **Syria Palestina**, to spite the Jews by naming it after their ancient enemies, the **Philistines.**

## The diaspora

The Jewish diaspora began with the Assyrian conquest and continued on a much larger scale with the Babylonian conquest, in which the **Tribe of Judah** was exiled to Babylonia along with the dethroned King of Judah, **Jehoiachin**, in the 6th Century BCE, and was taken into captivity in 597 BCE. The exile continued after the **destruction of the First Temple in Jerusalem in 586 BCE.** Many more Jews migrated to Babylon in 135 CE after the **Bar Kokhba revolt** and in the centuries after.

Many of the Judean Jews were sold into slavery while others became citizens of other parts of the Roman Empire. The **Book of Acts** in the New Testament, as well as other Pauline texts, makes frequent reference to the large populations of Hellenized Jews in the cities of the roman world. Of critical importance was the development of the interpretations of the **Torah** found in the *Mishnah* and *Talmud.*

## Late Roman period in the Land of Israel

In spite of the failure of the **Bar Kokhba revolt**, a significant number of Jews remained in the Land of Israel. The completion of the *Mishnah*, the system of *niqqud*, and the compilation of the Jerusalem Talmud are examples. In this period the *tannaim* and *amoraim* were active, rabbis who organized and debated the Jewish oral law. The decisions and opinions of the *tannaim* are contained in the **Mishnah, Beraita, Tosefta**, and various Midrash compilations. The Mishnah was completed shortly after 200 CE, probably by **Judah HaNasi**. The commentaries of the *amoraim* upon the Mishnah are compiled in the *Jerusalem Talmud*, which was completed around 400 CE, probably in Tiberias.

In 359 CE **Hillel II** created the Hebrew calendar based on the lunar year. Until then, the entire Jewish community outside the land of Israel depended on the calendar sanctioned by the **Sanhedrin**; this was necessary for the proper observance of the Jewish holy days. As the religious persecutions continued, **Hillel** determined to provide an authorized calendar for all time to come. In 363, shortly before launching his campaign against the Sassanid Empire, **Julian II**, the last pagan Roman Emperor, allowed the Jews to return to **"holy Jerusalem which you have for many years longed to see rebuilt"** and to rebuild the Temple. But, Julian's campaign against the Persians failed and he was killed in battle on June 26, 363. The Temple was not rebuilt.

## Middle Ages: Jews of Babylonia (219-1250)

After the fall of Jerusalem, Babylonia (modern day Iraq), would become the focus of Judaism for more than a thousand years.

The first Jewish communities in Babylonia started with the exile of the **Tribe of Judah** to Babylon by Jehoiachin in **597 BCE** as well as after the **destruction of the Temple in Jerusalem in 586 BCE.** The **Talmudic Yeshiva Academies** became a main part of Jewish culture and education, and Jews continued on establishing **Yeshiva Academies** in Western and Eastern Europe, North

Africa, and in the centuries later on to America and other countries around the world where Jews lived in the Diaspora.

These Talmudic Yeshiva academies of Babylonia followed the era of the **Amoraim ("expounders")** – the sages of the Talmud who were active (both in the Land of Israel and in Babylon) during the end of the era of the sealing of the Mishnah and until the times of the sealing of the **Talmud** (220 CE-500 CE), and following the **Savoraim ("reasoners")**- the sages of Beth midrash (Torah study places) in Babylon from the end of the era of the **Amoraim** (5th century) and until the beginning of the era of the **Geonim.**

The Geonim were the presidents of the two great rabbinical colleges of **Sura** and **Pumbedita**, and were the generally-accepted spiritual leaders of the worldwide Jewish community in the early medieval era, in contrast to the **Resh Galuta** (Exilarch) who wielded secular authority over the Jews in Islamic lands. According to traditions, the **Resh Galuta** was descendants of Judean kings, which is why the kings of **Parthia** would treat them with much honor.

The academies were founded in pre-Islamic Babylonia under the **Zoroastrian Sassanid Dynasty** and were located not far from the Sassanid capital of **Ctesiphon**, which at that time was the largest city in the world. After the conquest of Persia in the 7th Century, the academies subsequently operated for four hundred years under the Islamic caliphate.

## Byzantine period in the land of Israel (324-638)

Jews were also widespread throughout the Roman Empire, and this carried on to a lesser extent in the period of Byzantine rule in the central and eastern Mediterranean. The militant and exclusive Christianity and caesaropapism of the **Byzantine Empire** did not treat Jews well, and the condition and influence of diaspora Jews in the Empire declined dramatically.

It was official Christian policy to **convert Jews to Christianity**, and the Christian leadership used the official power of Rome in their attempts. In 351 CE the Jews revolted against the added pressures of their Governor, **Constantius Gallus**. Gallus put down the revolt and destroyed the major cities in the Galilee area where the revolt had started. In the beginning of the 5th century, the **Emperor Theodosius** issued a set of decrees establishing official persecution against Jews. Jews were not allowed to own slaves, build new synagogues, hold public office or try cases between a Jew and a non-Jew.

Intermarriage between Jew and non-Jew was made a capital offense, as was a Christian converting to Judaism. Theodosius did away with the **Sanhedrin** and abolished the post of **Nazi.** Under the **Emperor Justinian**, the authorities further restricted the civil rights of Jews, and threatened their religious privileges. The emperor interfered in the internal affairs of the synagogue, and forbade, for instance, the use of the Hebrew language in divine worship.

Those who disobeyed the restrictions were threatened with corporal penalties, exile, and loss of property. The Jews who resisted the Byzantine **General Belisarius** in his campaign against the Vandals, were **forced to embrace Christianity, and their synagogue was converted to a church.**

The **Muslim Caliphate** ejected the Byzantines from the **Holy Land** within a few years of their victory at the **Battle of Yarmouk** in 636. The size of the Jewish community in the **Byzantine Empire** was not affected by attempts by some emperors (most notably Justinian) to forcibly convert the Jews of Anatolia to Christianity, as these attempts met with very little success. Much of the Jewish population of Constantinople remained in place after the conquest of the city by **Mehmet II.**

Sometime in the 7<sup>th</sup> or 8<sup>th</sup> century, the **Khazars**, a Turkic tribe, (who for some three centuries (ca. 650-965) dominated the vast area extending from the **Volga-Don** steppe lands to the eastern Crimea and the northern Caucasus), seem to have converted to Judaism. Perhaps in the 4<sup>th</sup> century, the **Kingdom of Semien**, a Jewish nation in modern **Ethiopia** was established, lasting until the 17<sup>th</sup> century.

## Islamic period in the land of Israel (638-1099)

In 638 CE the Byzantine Empire lost control of the Levant. The **Arab Islamic Empire** under **Caliph Omar** conquered Jerusalem and the lands of **Mesopotamia, Syria, Palestine and Egypt**. Under the various regimes, the Jews suffered massacres and fled the inland villages toward the coast. They were subsequently induced to return inland after the coastal towns had been destroyed.

During the **Fatimid** period, many Jewish officials served in the regime. At the time of the Arab conquest in the 7<sup>th</sup> century CE, the majority of the population was Jewish. During this time Jews were lived in thriving communities all across ancient Babylonia. In the Geonic period (650-1250 CE), the Babylonian **Yeshiva Academies** were the chief centers of Jewish learning, the Geonim (meaning either "**Splendor" or Geniuses**") who were the heads of these schools, were recognized as the highest authorities in Jewish law.

## Jewish Golden Age (711-1031)

The **Golden Age** of Jewish culture in Spain coincided with the Middle Ages in Europe, a period of Muslim rule throughout much of the **Iberian Peninsula**. During that time, Jews were generally accepted in society and Jewish religious, cultural, and economic life blossomed. A period of tolerance thus dawned for the Jews of the Iberian Peninsula, whose number was considerably augmented by immigration from Africa in the wake of the Muslim conquest.

Especially after 912, during the reign of **Abd-ar-Rahman III** and his son, **Al-Hakam II**, the Jews prospered, devoting themselves to the service of the Caliphate of Cordoba, to the study of the sciences, and to commerce and industry, especially to trading in silk and slaves, in this way promoting the prosperity of the country. Jewish economic expansion was unparalleled. In Toledo, Jews were involved in translating Arabic texts to the romance languages, as well as translating Greek and Hebrew texts into Arabic. Jews also contributed to botany, geography, medicine, mathematics, poetry and philosophy.

**'Abd al-Rahman's** court physician and minister was **Hasdai ben Isaac ibn Shaprut**, the patron of Menahem ben Saruq, dunash ben Labrat, and other Jewish scholars and poets. Jewish thought during this period flourished under famous figures such as **Samuel Ha-Nagid, Moses ibn Ezra, Solomon ibn Gabirol Judah Halevi** and **Moses Maimonides**.

During 'Abd al-Rahman's term of power, the scholar **Moses ben Enoch** was appointed rabbi of Cordoba, and as a consequence al-Andalus became the center of Talmudic study, and Cordoba the meeting-place of Jewish savants. **The Golden Age ended with the invasion of the Reconquista and the invasion of the Almohades.** The major Jewish presence in Iberia continued until the Jews were forcibly expelled en masse due to the **edict of expulsion by Christian Spain in 1492 and a similar decree by Christian Portugal in 1496.**

## Crusaders period in the land of Israel (1099-1260)

In 1099, Jews helped the Arabs to defend Jerusalem against the **Crusaders**. When the city fell, the Crusaders gathered many Jews in a synagogue and set it on fire. Jews were not allowed to hold land during the Crusader period. **Maimonides** wrote that in 1165 he visited Jerusalem and went to the **Temple Mount**, where he prayed in the **"great, holy house"**. In 1141 **Yehuda Halevi** issued a call to Jews to immigrate to the land of Israel and took on the long journey himself. After a stormy passage from **Cordoba**, he arrived in **Egyptian Alexandria**, where he was enthusiastically greeted by friends and admirers.

## Mamluk period in the land of Israel (1260-1517)

In the years 1260-1516, the land is Israel was part of the empire of the **Mamluks**, who ruled first from Turkey, then from Egypt. War, uprisings, bloodshed and destruction followed the Maimonides. Jews suffered persecution and humiliation. **Nahmanides** is recorded as settling in the Old City of Jerusalem in 1267. He moved to **Acre**, where he was active in spreading Jewish learning, which was at that time neglected in the **Holy Land.**

He gathered a circle of pupils around him, and people came in crowds, even from the district of the Euphrates, to hear him. **Karaites** were said to have attended his lectures, among them **Aaron ben Joseph the Elder**. He later became one of the greatest Karaite authorities.

**Nahmanides** died after reaching seventy-six, and his remains were interred at Haifa, by the grave of **Yechiel of Paris.** Yechiel had immigrated to Acre in 1260, along with his son and a large group of followers. There he established the Talmudic academy *Midrash haGadol d'Paris*. He is believed to have died there between 1265 and 1268. In 1488 **Obadiah ben Abraham**, commentator on the Mishnah, arrived in Jerusalem; this marked a new period of return for the Jewish community in the land.

## Spain, North Africa, and the Middle East

During the Middle Ages, Jews were generally better treated by Islamic rulers than Christian ones. Despite second-class citizenship, Jews played prominent roles in Muslim courts, and experienced a **"Golden Age" in Moorish Spain about 900-1100**. Riots resulting in the deaths of Jews did however occur in North Africa through the centuries and especially in Morocco, Libya and Algeria, where eventually Jews were forced to live in ghettos. During the 11th century, Muslims in Spain conducted pogroms against the Jews.

During the Middle Ages, the governments of Egypt, Syria, Iraq and Yemen enacted decrees ordering the **destruction of synagogues**. At certain times, Jews were forced to convert to Islam or face death in some parts of **Yemen, Morocco and Baghdad**. The **Almohads**, who had taken control of much of Islamic Iberia by 1172. They treated the *dhimmis* harshly. They expelled both

Jews and Christians from Morocco and Islamic Spain. Faced with the choice of death or conversion, many Jews emigrated. Some, such as the family of **Maimonides**, fled south and east to the more tolerant Muslim lands.

## Europe
**"Jews accounted for 10% of the total population of the roman Empire. By that ratio, if other factors had not intervened, there would be 200 million Jews in the world today, instead of g like 15 million."** Between 800 and 1100, an estimated 1.5 million Jews lived in Christian Europe. In relations with the Christian society, the Jews were protected by kings, princes and bishops, because of the crucial services they provided in three areas: financial, administrative and medical.

By 1300, the friars and local priests stages the **Passion Plays** during **Holy Week**, which depicted Jews (in contemporary dress) killing Christ, according to Gospel accounts. Around 1500, Jews found relative security and a renewal of prosperity in present-day Poland. **After 1300, Jews suffered more discrimination and persecution in Christian Europe.**

Jews became imperials "*servi camerae*", the property of the King, who might present them and their possessions to princes or cities. Jews were frequently massacred and exiled from various European countries. The persecution hit its first peak during the Crusades. In the **First Crusade** (1096) flourishing Jewish communities on the Rhine and the Danube were utterly destroyed. In the **Second Crusade** (1147) the Jews in France were subject to frequent massacres. They were also subjected to attacks by the **Shepherds' Crusades** of 1251 and 1320.

The Crusades were followed by massive expulsions, including (in 1290) the banishing of all English Jews; in 1396 100,000 Jews were expelled from France; and in 1421, thousands were expelled from Austria. Over this time many Jews in Europe, either fleeing or being expelled, migrated to Poland, where they prospered into another **Golden Age.**

## Early Modern period
The established paradigm has been one in which **Ashkenazic Jews** entered modernity through a self-conscious process of westernization led by **"highly atypical, Germanized Jewish intellectuals"**. **Haskalah** gave birth to the **Reform** and **Conservative** movements and planted the seeds of Zionism while at the same time encouraging cultural assimilation into the countries in which Jews resided. **Hasidic Judaism** was spreading as a movement that preached a world view almost opposed to the Haskalah. In the 1990s, the concept of the "**Port Jew**" has been suggested as an "**alternate path to modernity**" that was distinct from the **European Haskalah.**

## Court Jew
**Court Jews** were Jewish bankers or businessmen who lent money and handled the finances of some of the Christian European noble houses. They lent money to nobles and in the process gained social influence. Noble patrons of court Jews employed them as financiers, suppliers, diplomats and trade delegates. In return for their services, court Jews gained social privileges, including up to noble status for themselves and could live outside the Jewish ghettos.

From medieval times, court Jews could amass personal fortunes and gained political and social influence. Sometimes they were the only Jews who could interact with the local high society and present petitions of the Jews to the ruler. Due to the precarious position of Jews, some nobles could just ignore their debts. **If the sponsoring noble died, his Jewish financier could face exile or execution.**

## Iberia

During the **European Renaissance**, the worst of the expulsions occurred following the Reconquista of Andalus, as the Moorish or Arab Islamic government of Spain was known. With the ejection of the last Muslim rulers from Grenada in **1492, the Spanish Inquisition followed and the entire Spanish population of around 200,000 Sephardic Jews was expelled**. This was followed by expulsions in 1493 in Sicily (37,000 Jews) and Portugal in 1496. The expelled Spanish Jews fled mainly to the **Ottoman Empire**, Holland, and North Africa, others migrating to Southern Europe and the Middle East.

## Ottoman Empire

During the Classical Ottoman period (1300-1600), the Jews, together with most other communities of the empire, enjoyed a certain level of prosperity. Compared with other Ottoman subjects, they were the predominant power in commerce and trade as well in diplomacy and other high offices. In the 16th century especially, the Jews were the most prominent under the *millets,* the apogee of Jewish influence could arguably be the appointment of **Joseph Nasi** to **Sanjak-bey** (*governor*, a rank usually only bestowed upon Muslims) of the island of Naxos.

At the time of the **Battle of Yarmuk** when the Levant passed under Muslim Rule, thirty Jewish communities existed in **Haifa, Sh'chem, Hebron, Ramleh, Gaza, Jerusalem**, and many in the north. Safed became a spiritual center for the Jews and the **Shulchan Aruch** was compiled there as well as many Kabbalistic texts. The first Hebrew printing press and the first printing in Western Asia began in 1577. Jews lived in the geographic area of Asia Minor for more than 2,400 years. Muslim governments that displaced and succeeded rule from **Constantinople**. **For much of the Ottoman period, Turkey was a safe haven for Jews fleeing persecution.**

## Poland-Lithuania

In the 17th century, there were many significant Jewish populations in Western Europe. The relatively tolerant **Poland had the largest Jewish population in Europe** that dated back to 13th century. The calm situation there ended when Polish and Lithuanian Jews were slaughtered in the hundreds of thousands by the **Cossacks** during **Chmielnicki uprising** (1648) and by the Swedish wars (1655). The last ban on Jews (by the English) was revoked in 1654, but periodic expulsions from individual cities still occurred, and Jews were often restricted from land ownership, or forced to live in ghettos.

## The European Enlightenment and Haskalah (18th century)

During the period of the **European Renaissance** and **Enlightenment,** significant changes occurred within the Jewish community. The **Haskalah** movement paralleled the wider **Enlightenment,** as Jews began in the 18th century to campaign for emancipation from restrictive laws and integration into the wider European society. Haskalah gave birth to the **Reform** and **Conservative** movements and planted the seeds of Zionism while at the same time **encouraging cultural assimilation into the countries in which Jews resided.**

At around the same time another movement was born, one preaching almost the opposite of Haskalah, **Hasidic Judaism**, Hasidic Judaism began in the 18th century by **Rabbi Israel Baal Shem Tov,** and quickly gained a following with its more exuberant, mystical approach to religion. The outside world was changing, and debates began over the potential emancipation of the Jews, granting them equal rights. The first country to do so was France, during the **French Revolution** in 1789.

## Hasidic Judaism

**Hasidic Judaism** is a branch of **Orthodox Judaism** that promotes spirituality and joy through the popularization and internalization of Jewish mysticism as the fundamental aspects of the Jewish faith. Hasidism comprises part of contemporary Judaism **Ultra-Orthodox**, alongside the previous Talmudic Lithuanian-Yeshiva approach and the Oriental Sephardi tradition.

It was founded in 18th-century Eastern Europe by **Rabbi Israel Baal Shem Tov** as a reaction against overly legalistic Judaism. The emphasis on the **Immanent Divine** presence in everything gave new value to prayer and deeds of kindness, alongside Rabbinic supremacy of study, and replaced historical mystical (**kabbalistic**) and ethical (**musar**) asceticism and admonishment with optimism, encouragement, and daily fervor.

This populist emotional revival accompanied the elite ideal of nullification of paradoxical **Divine Panentheism,** through intellectual articulation of inner dimensions of mystical thought. The adjustment of Jewish values sought to add to required standards of ritual observance, while relaxing others where inspiration predominated. Its communal gatherings celebrate soulful song and storytelling as forms of mystical devotion.

## 19th century

Though persecution still existed, emancipation spread throughout Europe in the 19th century. **Napoleon** invited Jews to leave the Jewish ghettos in Europe and seek refuge in the newly created tolerant political regimes that offered equality under **Napoleonic Law**. Despite increasing integration of the Jews with secular society, a new form of anti-Semitism emerged, based on the ideas of race and nationhood rather than the religious hatred of the Middle Ages.

This form of anti-Semitism held that Jews were a separate and inferior race from the **Aryan** people of Western Europe, and led to the emergence of political parties in France, Germany, and Austria-Hungary that campaigned on a platform of rolling back emancipation. This form of anti-Semitism emerged frequently in European culture, most famously in the **Dreyfus trial in France**.

These persecutions, along with state-sponsored pogroms in Russia in the late 19th century, led a number of Jews to believe that they would only be safe in their own nation. **Over 2 million Jews arrived in the United States between 1890 and 1924,** most from Russia and Easter Europe. A similar case occurred in the southern tip of the continent, specifically in the countries of Argentina and Uruguay.

## 20th century: Modern Zionism

During the 1870s and 1880s the Jewish population in Europe began to more actively discuss immigration back to Israel and the re-establishment of the **Jewish Nation** in its national homeland, fulfilling the biblical prophecies relating to **Shivat Tzion**. In 1882 the first Zionist settlement – **Rishon LeZion** – was founded by immigrants who belong to the **"Hovevei Zion"** movement.

The Zionist movement was founded officially after the **Kattowitz convention (1884)** and the **World Zionist Congress** (1897), and it was **Theodor Herzl** who began the struggle to establish a state for the Jews. After the First World War, it seemed that the conditions to establish such a state had arrived: The United Kingdom captured Palestine form the Ottoman Empire, and the Jews received the promise of a **"National Home"** from the British in the form of the **Balfour Declaration of 1917, given to Chaim Weizmann**.

In 1920 the **British Mandate of Palestine** began and the pro-Jewish **Herbert Samuel** was appointed High Commissioner in Palestine, the Hebrew University of Jerusalem was established and several big Jewish immigration waves to Palestine occurred. The Arab inhabitants of Palestine were not fond of the increasing Jewish immigration however, and began to oppose Jewish settlement and the pro-Jewish policy of the British government by violent means.

Arab gangs began performing violent acts and murders on convoys and on the Jewish population. After the 1920 Arab riots and 1921 Jaffa riots, the Jewish leadership in Palestine believed that the British had no desire to confront local Arab gangs over their attacks on Palestinian Jews. Believing that they could not rely on the British administration for protection from these gangs, the Jewish leadership created the **Haganah** organization to protect their farms and Kibbutzim. Major riots occurred during the 1929 Palestine riots and the 1936-1939 Arab revolt in Palestine.

Due to the increasing violence the United Kingdom gradually started to backtrack from the original idea of a Jewish state and to speculate on a binational solution or an Arab state that would have a Jewish minority. The Jews of Europe and the United States gained success in the fields of the science, culture and the economy. Among those generally considered the most famous were scientist **Albert Einstein** and philosopher **Ludwig Wittgenstein**. In the Soviet Union, many Jews were involved in the **October Revolution** and belonged to the communist party.

## The Holocaust

In 1933, with the rise to power of **Adolf Hitler** and the Nazi party in Germany, the Jewish situation became more severe. Economic crises, racial anti-Semitic laws, and a fear of an upcoming war led many Jews to flee from Europe to Palestine, to the United States and to the Soviet Union.

In 1939 **World War II** began and until 1941 Hitler occupied almost all of Europe, including Poland – where millions of Jews were living at that time – and France. In 1941, following the invasion of the Soviet Union, the **Final Solution** began, an extensive organized operation on an unprecedented scale, aimed at the annihilation of the Jewish people. This genocide, in which approximately **six million Jews** were murdered methodically and with horrifying cruelty, is known as **The Holocaust or *Shoah*** (Hebrew term). In Poland, more than one million Jews were murdered in gas chambers at the **Auschwitz** concentration camp alone. After the war, efforts were increased to establish a Jewish state in Palestine.

## The establishment of the State of Israel

In 1945 the Jewish resistance organizations in Palestine unified and established the **Jewish Resistance Movement.** The movement began attacking the British authority. The Jewish Agency backed Weizmann's recommendation to cease activities, a decision reluctantly accepted by the **Haganah**, but not by the **Irgun** and the **Lehi. The British authorities decided to let the United Nations decide upon the fate of Palestine.**

On November 29, 1947, the United Nations General Assembly adopted **Resolution 181** (II) recommending partitioning Palestine into an Arab state, a Jewish state and the City of Jerusalem. The Jewish leadership accepted the decision but the **Arab League** and the leadership of Palestinian Arabs opposed it. Following a period of civil war the 1948 Arab-Israeli War started. After the last soldiers of the British mandate left Palestine, **David Ben-Gurion proclaimed on May 14, 1948, the establishment of a Jewish state in Eretz Israel** to be known as the State of Israel. In 1949 the war ended and the state of Israel started building the state and absorbing massive waves of hundreds of thousands of Jews from all over the world.

Since 1948, Israel has been involved in a series of major military conflicts, including the 1956 Suez Crisis, 1967 Six-Day War, 1973 Yom Kippur War, 1982 Lebanon War, and 2006 Lebanon War, as well as a nearly constant series of ongoing minor conflicts.

## 21<sup>st</sup> century

Today (2014), Israel is a parliamentary democracy with a population of over 9 million people, of whom about 6 million are Jewish.

# A SHORT HISTORY OF THE JEWS OF IRAQ

One can say that the first Jew was an Iraqi Jew. Of course he was out first patriarch who was born in Ur, a city south of Mesopotamia, which is now called Iraq. So **Abraham** (± 1900 B.C.) was a citizen of great civilization and culture.

**In 586 BCE**, king **Nebuchadnezzar** destroyed our first temple and razed the whole city of Jerusalem to the ground, one of the events we still commemorate on **Tisha b'Av** (the ninth day of Av in the Hebrew calendar). The Jews were dispersed mostly to Persia and Babylonia. The opportunity to return arrived at **538 BCE** (after 48 years) when **Cyrus** of Persia issued the famous decree permitting the Jews to return to Jerusalem and rebuild their Temple. About 40,000 people returned.

It was there that the occupations of merchant, trade, finance, and banker were introduced to Jewry— professions we continue to favor to this day. Our ancestors in Palestine had been peasants, settlers, cattle breeders, and traders. Following the **Bar Kokhba** rebellion in 135 CE, Roman repression succeeded in driving the community out of Palestine into poverty and decline.

By the third century, the Jews had prospered and flourished. Babylon (Babel) had become the center of Jewish scholarship. Their most influential contribution was the **Babylonian Talmud** (Oral Law). They built many **Yeshivas**, the most famous being **Sura, Nehadrea**, and **Pumbeditha**. They prospered and flourished twelve-hundred years before the Muslim conquest.

In the first half of the seventh century, after the death of the prophet **Mohammed**, his followers invaded Mesopotamia. The Jewish population under Islam was tolerated as **"The people of the Book,"** which means believers in one God. They were designated **Dhimmis**, protected people of special covenant with the Muslims. Islam offered them protection and religious autonomy at economic and political cost. They were politically second-class citizens and had to pay a special toll tax. The state was defined in religious terms and, therefore, excluded the Jews (and non-Muslims).

**Hulagu, grandson of Genghis Khan the Mongol, took Baghdad in 1258**. Anti-Jewish resentment among the Muslims grew more as the Babylonian Jewish center fell into a period of deep slumber, and the glory of the Jewish people faded. The Jews were almost not heard from at that time. And Babylonia, which had hosted a peak of population of two million Jews, had little Jewish population left. Baghdad is a Persian name consisting of two words: *bagh,* which means a garden, and *dad,* which is the past tense of the verb **"to give."** Baghdad, therefore, means *a garden-given gift.*

The **Ottomans came in 1534**. Life for the Jewish community under the Ottoman Turks was for the most part tolerable and hospitable to growth. They were the ones who welcomed the **Spanish exiles in 1492,** in what is known as the Inquisition. By the middle of the sixteenth century, the Jewish community of Baghdad began to reassert its existence. There were 6,000 Jews living in Baghdad alone in the first quarter of the nineteenth century. Jews, however, were subjected to the whims of the local *walis* (governors).

In 1808, **Sultan Mahmud II** instituted reforms that were salutary to the Jews. There were rebirths of some commerce, Rabbinic scholarship, and **Torah** study. In 1840, some Yeshivot were opened for the first time in five centuries.

The Jews lived very well under the **Ottoman Empire**, which lasted more than four hundred years. The Turks lost their empire after WWI and Iraq became part of the **British Empire**. In 1932 the British gave Iraq independence. The first king was **King Faisal I** who was friendly with the Jews and had no racial discrimination to Jews, Muslims, Christians, or other ethnic groups. The Jews prospered and some held very high political and financial jobs in the government. For example, **Sir Sasson Heskell** was the first Jewish financial minister who had negotiated the revenues of oil with the British and asked for gold instead of pound paper currency.

**The Jews, who numbered about 1.8 million**, were the elite and well-educated. There were prominent doctors, senators, lawyers, and rabbis. The chief rabbi was the famous **Hakham Ezra Dangoor,** who opened the first printing company, which was used to print all Hebrew books, as well as Arabic texts books. Everything suddenly changed for the worse beginning just before WWII. With the rise of **Communism, Zionism, Nationalism**, and **Nazism**, the Iraqi Jews felt them all with torture and pain. **Radio Berlin** started to broadcast poisonous propaganda against the Jews to the Iraqi people.

In April 1941, a pro-Nazi coup d'état occurred against the pro-British government. May 1941 was a dark month in the history of the Jews. On the feast of Shavout, the first and second of June, a horrible pogrom (called **Farhood**) took place where more than two hundred innocent Jews were murdered, and women and young girls were raped.

From that day on, the Jews felt no security. Some of them escaped illegally to Iran. The Jewish Agency seized the opportunity to encourage immigration to the **Holy Land** by forming what was called a *Tnu'a*—a movement. After a relative calm came executions, terror, and firing. The Jews were seen as being associated with Israel, which had defeated Iraq in the war of independence. Jewish life in Iraq was no longer tenable.

When Jews started to emigrate illegally, laws of surrender of Iraqi nationality were promulgated. That meant that Jews could renounce their citizenship and leave the country for an **"unknown destination"** (the word Israel could never be mentioned). The majority of Jews registered to leave fearing the unknown future after the expiration of the law, which was valid for only one year. The government froze all the assets of the departing Jews, and in one day they became penniless. Israel played a part in this exodus, which was called **Operation Ezra** and **Nehemiah**, named after the leaders of the Babylonian Jews who led them to Israel under the Persians in 539 BCE. Only about six thousand Jews were left in Iraq in 1952. Today none is left.

> *By the rivers of Babylon—there we sat and also wept*
> *When we remembered Zion*
> *On the willows with it we hung our lyres*
> *For there our captors requested words of song from us*
> *Without (playing) joyous (music)*

*"Sing for us from Zion's song!*
*"How can we sing the song of God upon alien soil?"*
*If I forget you, O Jerusalem, let my right hand forget its skill*
*Let my tongue adhere to my palate if I fail to recall you*
*If I fail to elevate Jerusalem above my foremost joy*

# Abraham the Patriarch

**Abraham**, originally **Abram**, is the **common patriarch of the three Abrahamic religions**. In Judaism, he is the founding father of the **Covenant**, the special relationship between the Jewish people and God; in Christianity, he is the prototype of all believers, Jewish or Gentile; and in Islam he is seen as a link in the chain of prophets that begins with **Adam** and culminates in **Muhammad**. The narrative in **Genesis** revolves around the themes of posterity and land. **Abraham** is called by God to leave the house of his father **Terah** and settle in the land originally given to **Canaan** but which God now promises to Abraham and his progeny. Various candidates are put forward who might inherit the land after Abraham; and, while promises are made to **Ishmael** about founding a great nation, **Isaac**, Abraham's son by his half-sister Sarah, inherits God's promises to Abraham.

Abraham purchases a tomb (**Cave of the Patriarchs**) at Hebron to be Sarah's grave, thus establishing his right to the land; and, in the second generation, his heir Isaac is married to a woman from his own kin, thus ruling the **Canaanites** out of any inheritance. Abraham later marries **Keturah** and has six more sons; but, on his death, when he is buried beside Sarah, it is Isaac who receives **"all Abraham's goods"**, while the other sons receive only **"gifts" (Genesis 25:5–8).**

The Abraham story cannot be definitively related to any specific time, and it is widely agreed that the patriarchal age, along with the exodus and the period of the judges, is a late literary construct that does not relate to any period in actual history. A common hypothesis among scholars is that it was composed in the early Persian period **(late 6th century BCE)** as a result of tensions between Jewish landowners who had stayed in Judah during the Babylonian captivity and traced their right to the land through their **"father Abraham"**, and the returning exiles who based their counter-claim on **Moses** and the **Exodus** tradition.

## Biblical account / Origins and calling

Terah, the ninth in descent from Noah, was the father of three sons: Abram, Nahor, and Haran. In his youth, **Abram worked in Terah's idol shop. Haran was the father of Lot, and thus Lot was Abram's nephew**. Haran died in his native city, Ur of the Chaldees. **Abram married Sarah (Sarai), who was barren.** Terah, with Abram, Sarai, and Lot, then departed for Canaan, but settled in a place named Haran, where Terah died at the **age of 205**.

God had told Abram to leave his country and kindred and go to a land that he would show him, and promised to make of him a great nation, bless him, make his name great, bless them that bless him, and curse them who may curse him. **Abram was 75 years old** when he left **Haran** with his wife **Sarai**, his nephew **Lot**, and the substance and souls that they had acquired, and traveled to Shechem in Canaan.

### *Abraham and Lot's conflict*

When they came back to the **Bethel** and **Hai** area, Abram's and Lot's sizable herds occupied the same pastures. This became a problem for the herdsmen who were assigned to each family's cattle. Lot chose to go eastward to the plain of Jordan where the land was well watered everywhere as far as **Zoar**, and he dwelled in the cities of the plain toward **Sodom**. Abram went south to **Hebron** and settled in the plain of Mamre, where he built another altar to worship God.

## Chedorlaomer / *Battle of Siddim*

During the rebellion of the Jordan River cities against Elam, Abram's nephew, Lot, was taken prisoner along with his entire household by the invading Elamite forces. The Elamite army came to collect the spoils of war, after having just defeated the king of Sodom's armies. Lot and his family, at the time, were settled on the outskirts of the **Kingdom of Sodom** which made them a visible target.

Once Abram received this news, he immediately assembled **318 trained servants**. Abram's force headed north in pursuit of the **Elamite** army, who were already worn down from the **Battle of Siddim.** When they caught up with them at **Dan, Abram** devised a battle plan by splitting his group into more than one unit, and launched a night raid. Not only were they able to free the captives, Abram's unit chased and **slaughtered the Elamite King Chedorlaomer at Hobah,** just north of Damascus. They freed Lot, as well as his household and possessions, and recovered all of the goods from **Sodom** that had been taken.

## Covenant of the pieces

The voice of the Lord came to Abram in a vision and repeated the promise of the land and descendants as numerous as the stars. Abram and God made a covenant ceremony, and God told of the future bondage of Israel in Egypt. **God described to Abram the land that his offspring would claim: the land of the Kenites, Kenizzites, Kadmonites, Hittites, Perizzites, Rephaims, Amorites, Canaanites, Girgashites, and Jebusites.**

## *Hagar and Hagar in Islam*

Abram and Sarai tried to make sense of how he would become a progenitor of nations, because after 10 years of living in Canaan, no child had been born. **Sarai then offered her Egyptian handmaiden, Hagar, to Abram with the intention that she would bear him a son.** After Hagar found she was pregnant, she began to despise her mistress, Sarai. Sarai responded by mistreating Hagar, and Hagar fled into the wilderness. An angel spoke with Hagar at the fountain on the way to **Shur.** She was told to call her son **Ishmael.** Hagar then called God who spoke to her **"El-Roi",** **("Thou God seest me:" KJV).**

From that day onward, the well was called **Beer-lahai-Roi, ("The well of him that liveth and seeth me." KJV margin).** She then did as she was instructed by returning to her mistress in order to have her child. **Abram was 86 years of age when Ishmael was born.**

## Sarah

Thirteen years later, **when Abram was 99 years of age**, God declared Abram's new name: **"Abraham"** – **"a father of many nations".** Abraham then received the instructions for the covenant, of which **circumcision** was to be the sign. God declared Sarai's new name: **"Sarah",** blessed her, and told Abraham, **"I will give thee a son also of her".** Abraham laughed, and **"said in his heart, 'Shall a *child* be born unto him that is a hundred years old? And shall Sarah, that is ninety years old, bear?'"** Immediately after Abraham's encounter with God, he had his **entire household of men, including himself (age 99) and Ishmael (age 13), circumcised.**

## Abraham's plea / *Sodom and Gomorrah and Lot*

They walked over to the peak that overlooked the 'cities of the plain' to discuss the fate of **Sodom** and **Gomorrah** for their detestable sins that were so great, it moved God to action. Because Abraham's nephew was living in Sodom, God revealed plans to confirm and judge these cities. Then Abraham turned to God and pleaded decrement ally with Him (from fifty persons to less) that **"if there were at least ten righteous men found in the city, would not God spare the city?"** For the sake of ten righteous people, God declared that he would not destroy the city.

When the two visitors got to Sodom to conduct their report, they planned on staying in the city square. However, Abraham's nephew, Lot, met with them and strongly insisted that these two **"men"** stay at his house for the night. A rally of men stood outside of Lot's home and demanded that they bring out his guests so that they may **"know"** (v.5) them. **However, Lot objected and offered his virgin daughters who had not "known"** (v.8) **man to the rally of men instead.**

They rejected that notion and sought to break down Lot's door to get to his male guests, thus confirming the wickedness of the city and portending their imminent destruction. Early the next morning, Abraham went to the place where he stood before God. He **"looked out toward Sodom and Gomorrah"** and saw what became of the cities of the plain, where not even **"ten righteous" (v.18:32)** had been found, as **"the smoke of the land went up as the smoke of a furnace."**

## Isaac

As had been prophesied in Mamre the previous year, **Sarah became pregnant and bore a son to Abraham, on the first anniversary of the covenant of circumcision. Abraham was "a hundred years old",** when his son whom he named **Isaac was born; and he circumcised him when he was eight days old**. For Sarah, the thought of giving birth and nursing a child, at such an old age, also brought her much laughter, as she declared, **"God hath made me to laugh, so that all that hear will laugh with me."** Isaac continued to grow and on the day he was weaned, Abraham held a great feast to honor the occasion. During the celebration, however, **Sarah found Ishmael mocking**; an observation that would begin to clarify the birthright of Isaac.

## *Ishmael in Islam § the sacrifice*

Ishmael was fourteen years old when Abraham's son Isaac was born to Sarah. When she found Ishmael teasing Isaac, Sarah told Abraham to send both Ishmael and Hagar away. She declared that Ishmael would not share in Isaac's inheritance. Abraham was greatly distressed by his wife's words and sought the advice of his God. God told Abraham not to be distressed but to do as his wife commanded. **God reassured Abraham that "in Isaac shall seed be called to thee." He also said that Ishmael would make a nation, "because he is thy seed".** Early the next morning, Abraham brought Hagar and Ishmael out together. He gave her bread and water and sent them away. The two wandered in the wilderness of **Beersheba** until her bottle of water was completely consumed.

In a moment of despair, she burst into tears. After God heard the boy's voice, an angel of the Lord confirmed to **Hagar** that he would become a great nation, and will be **"living on his sword"**. A well of water then appeared so that it saved their lives. As the boy grew, he became a skilled archer living in the wilderness of Paran. **Eventually his mother found a wife for Ishmael from her home country, the land of Egypt.**

## Binding of Isaac

At some point in Isaac's youth, **Abraham was commanded by God to offer his son up as a sacrifice in the land of Moriah.** The patriarch traveled three days until he came to the mount that God told him of. He then commanded the servants to remain while he and Isaac proceeded alone into the mount. Isaac carried the wood upon which he would be sacrificed. Along the way, Isaac asked his father where the animal for the burnt offering was, to which Abraham replied **"God will provide himself a lamb for a burnt offering".** Just as Abraham was about to sacrifice his son, he was interrupted by the angel of the Lord, and he saw behind him a **"ram caught in a thicket by his horns",** which he sacrificed instead of his son. For his obedience he received another promise of numerous descendants and abundant prosperity. **After this event, Abraham went to Beersheba.**

## Later years / *Abraham's family tree*

**Sarah died, and Abraham buried her in the Cave of the Patriarchs (the "cave of Machpelah"),** near Hebron which he had purchased along with the adjoining field from **Ephron** the Hittite. After the death of Sarah, Abraham took another wife, **a concubine named Keturah,** by whom he had six sons: **Zimran, Jokshan, Medan, Midian, Ishbak,** and **Shuah.** According to the Bible, reflecting the change of his name to **"Abraham"** meaning **"a father of many nations".** Abraham lived to see his son marry **Rebekah. He died at age 175, and was buried in the cave of Machpelah by his sons Isaac and Ishmael.**

## Religious overview

**Abraham is given a high position of respect in three major world faiths, Judaism, Christianity and Islam.** In Judaism he is the founding father of the Covenant, the special relationship between the Jewish people and God – a belief which gives the Jews a unique position as the **Chosen People of God.**

## Judaism

In Jewish tradition, Abraham is called *Avraham Avinu* **"our father Abraham,"** signifying that he is both the biological progenitor of the Jews and the father of Judaism, the first Jew. In Jewish legend, God created heaven and earth for the sake of the merits of Abraham.

## Christianity

Abraham does not loom as large in Christianity as he does in Judaism and Islam. **It is Jesus as the Jewish Messiah who is central to Christianity,** and the idea of a divine **Messiah** is what separates Christianity from the other two religions. In **Romans 4, the covenant becomes one of faith, not obedience.**

## *Abraham in Islam*

**Islam regards Abraham as a link in the chain of prophets that begins with Adam and culminates in Muhammad. Ibrahim is mentioned in 35 chapters of the Quran, more often than any other biblical personage apart from Moses.** He is called both **a** *hanif* **(monotheist)** and *Muslim* (one who submits), and Muslims regard him as a prophet and patriarch, the **archetype of the perfect Muslim,** and the revered reformer of the **Kaaba** in Mecca.

In Islam, Abraham holds an exalted position among the **Major Prophets** and he is referred to as **"Ibrahim Khalilullah",** meaning **"Abraham the Beloved of Allah".** Ibrahim was also mentioned in Quran as **"Father of Muslims"** and the role model for the community.

# Alhambra Decree: Jewish Expulsion

The **Alhambra Decree** (also known as the **Edict of Expulsion**; Spanish: *Decreto de la Alhambra, Edicto de Granada*) was an edict issued on 31 March 1492, by the joint Catholic Monarchs of Spain (**Isabella I** of Castile and **Ferdinand II** of Aragon) ordering the expulsion of practicing Jews from the Kingdoms of Castile and Aragon and its territories and possessions by 31 July of that year. The primary purpose was to **eliminate their influence on Spain's large Converso population and ensure they did not revert to Judaism.**

**Over half of Spain's Jews had converted** as a result of the religious persecution and pogroms which occurred in 1391, and as such were not subject to the **Decree** or to expulsion. A further number of those remaining chose to avoid expulsion as a result of the edict. As a result of the Alhambra decree and persecution in prior years, **over 200,000 Jews converted to Catholicism and between 40,000 and 100,000 were expelled.**

The edict was formally and **symbolically revoked on 16 December 1968**, following the **Second Vatican Council** and a full century after Jews had once more been allowed to openly practice their religion in Spain and synagogues had been allowed to be used as places of worship under **Spain's Laws of Religious Freedom**. In 1924, the regime of **Primo de Rivera** granted Spanish citizenship to the entire Sephardic Jewish diaspora.

In 2014, the government of Spain passed a law allowing dual citizenship to Jewish descendants who apply, in order to **"compensate for shameful events in the country's past."** Thus, Sephardi Jews who are descendants of those Jews expelled from Spain due to the **Alhambra Decree**, and can prove it, can **"become Spaniards without leaving home or giving up their present nationality."**

## Background: *History of the Jews in Spain*

Beginning in the 8th century, Muslims had conquered and settled most of the Iberian Peninsula. Jews, who had lived in these regions since Roman times, were considered "**People of the Book**" and given special status and often thrived. The tolerance of the **Muslim Moorish** rulers of **Al-Andalus** compared to the repressive **Visigothic kingdom** which preceded them led to Jewish enclaves in **Muslim Iberian** cities flourishing as places of learning and commerce. Although **Jews never enjoyed equal status to Muslims**, in some Taifas, such as Granada, Jewish men were appointed to very high offices, including **Grand Vizier**.

The *Reconquista,* the gradual reconquest of **Muslim Iberia** by the Christian kingdoms, was driven by a powerful religious motivation: to reclaim Iberia for Christendom following the **Umayyad** conquest of **Hispania** centuries before. By the 14th century, most of the Iberian

Peninsula (present-day Spain and Portugal) had been conquered by the Christian kingdoms of Castile, Aragon, León, Galicia, Navarre, and Portugal.

# Angels

An **angel** is a supernatural being in various **Circum-Mediterranean religions**. Abrahamic religions often depict them as benevolent celestial intermediaries between God (Or Heaven) and humanity. Other roles include protectors and guides for humans, and servants of God. Some angels have specific names (such as **Gabriel or Michael**) or titles (such as **seraph** or **archangel**). Humans have also used "**angel**" to describe various spirits and figures in other religious traditions. The theological study of angels is known as "**angelology**". Those expelled from Heaven are called **fallen angels**, distinct from the heavenly host. **Angels in art are usually shaped like humans of extraordinary beauty. They are often identified In Christian artwork with bird wings, halos, and divine light.**

## Abrahamic religions / Judaism

The term מלאך (*mal'āḵ*) is also used in other books of the **Tanakh**. Depending on the context, the Hebrew word may refer to a human messenger or to a supernatural messenger. A human messenger might be a prophet or priest, such as **Malachi, "my messenger"**. Examples of a supernatural messenger are the **"Malak YHWH,"** who is either a messenger from God, an aspect of God (such as the **Logos**), or God himself as the messenger (the **"theophanic angel."**)

**Daniel** is the first biblical figure to refer to individual angels by name, mentioning **Gabriel** (God's primary messenger) in **Daniel 9:21** and **Michael** (the holy fighter) in **Daniel 10:13**. In **Daniel 7**, Daniel receives a dream-vision from God. As Daniel watches, the **Ancient of Days** takes his seat on the throne of heaven and sits in judgement in the midst of the heavenly court an like a son of man approaches the **Ancient One** in the clouds of heaven and is given everlasting kingship.

**"In the postexilic period, with the development of explicit monotheism, these divine beings— the 'sons of God' who were members of the Divine Council—were in effect demoted to what are now known as 'angels', understood as beings created by God, but immortal and thus superior to humans."** This conception of angels is best understood in contrast to demons and is often thought to be **"influenced by the ancient Persian religious tradition of Zoroastrianism, which viewed the world as a battleground between forces of good and forces of evil, between light and darkness."** One of these is *hāśāṭān*, a figure depicted in (among other places) the **Book of Job.**

**Philo of Alexandria** identifies the angel with the **Logos** inasmuch as the angel is the immaterial voice of God. The angel is something different from God himself, but is conceived as God's instrument. Four classes of ministering angels minister and utter praise before the **Holy One**, blessed be He.

**Metatron** is considered one of the highest of the angels in **Merkabah** and Kabbalist mysticism and often serves as a scribe; he is briefly mentioned in the **Talmud** and figures prominently in Merkabah mystical texts. **Michael**, who serves as a warrior and advocate for Israel (**Daniel 10:13**), is looked upon particularly fondly. **Gabriel** is mentioned in the **Book of Daniel** (**Daniel 8:15–17**) and briefly in the **Talmud,** as well as in many **Merkabah** mystical texts. There is no evidence in Judaism for the worship of angels.

According to **Kabbalah**, there are four worlds and our world is the last world: the world of action (**Assiyah**). Angels exist in the worlds above as a **'task' of God**. They are an extension of God to produce effects in this world. After an angel has completed its task, it ceases to exist. The angel is in effect the task. This is derived from the book of **Genesis** when **Abraham** meets with three angels and **Lot** meets with two. The task of one of the angels was to inform Abraham of his coming child. The other two were to save Lot and to destroy **Sodom** and **Gomorrah**.

Jewish philosopher **Maimonides** explained his view of angels in his *Guide for the Perplexed* **II: 4 and II** ... This leads **Aristotle** in turn to the demonstrated fact that God, glory and majesty to Him, does not do things by direct contact. God burns things by means of fire; fire is moved by the motion of the sphere; the sphere is moved by means of a disembodied intellect, these intellects being the 'angels which are near to Him', through whose mediation the spheres move ... thus totally disembodied minds exist which emanate from God and are the intermediaries between God and all the bodies here in this world.

## Individuals /Angelology".

- **Michael** (archangel) (translation: *who is like God?*), kindness of God, and stands up for the children of mankind
- **Gabriel** (archangel) (translation: *God is my strength*), performs acts of justice and power
- **Jophiel** (translation: *Beauty of God*), expelled Adam and Eve from the Garden of Eden holding a flaming sword and punishes those who transgress against God.
- **Raphael** (archangel) (translation: *It is God who heals*), God's healing force
- **Uriel** (archangel) (translation: *God is my light*), leads us to destiny
- **Samael** (archangel) (translation: *Venom of God*), angel of death—see also Malach HaMavet (translation: *the angel of death*)
- **Sandalphon** (archangel) (translation: *bringing together*), battles Samael and brings mankind together

### *Christian angelic hierarchy*

The Christian concept of an angel characterized the angel as a messenger of God. Later came identification of individual angelic messengers: **Gabriel, Michael, Raphael, and Uriel**.

According to **St. Augustine**, "'Angel' is the name of their office, not of their nature. If you seek the name of their nature, it is 'spirit'; if you seek the name of their office, it is 'angel': from what they are, 'spirit', from what they do, 'angel'

The angels are represented throughout the Christian Bible as spiritual beings intermediate between God and men: **"You have made him  a little less than the angels ..."** (**Psalms 8:4–5**). Christians believe that angels are created beings, based on (**Psalms 148:2–5; Colossians 1:16**): **"praise ye Him, all His angels: praise ye Him, all His hosts ... for He spoke and they were made. He commanded and they were created ..."**. The First Vatican Council (1869) repeated this declaration in *Dei Filius*, the "**Dogmatic constitution on the Catholic faith**".

**Thomas Aquinas** (13th century) relates angels to Aristotle's metaphysics in his ***Summa contra Gentiles, Summa Theologica***, and in ***De substantiis separatis***, a treatise on angelology. Although angels have greater knowledge than men, they are not omniscient, as **Matthew 24:36** points out.

## Interaction

The New Testament includes many interactions and conversations between angels and humans. For instance, three separate cases of angelic interaction deal with the births of **John the Baptist** and **Jesus Christ**. In **Luke 1:11**, an angel appears to **Zechariah** to inform him that he will have a child despite his old age, thus proclaiming the birth of John the Baptist. In **Luke 1:26** the Archangel Gabriel visits the **Virgin Mary** in the Annunciation to foretell the birth of Jesus Christ. Angels then proclaim the birth of Jesus in the **Adoration** of the shepherds in **Luke 2:10.**

According to **Matthew 4:11**, after Jesus spent 40 days in the desert, **"...the Devil left him and, behold, angels came and ministered to him."** In **Luke 22:43** an angel comforts Jesus Christ during the Agony in the Garden. In **Matthew 28:5** an angel speaks at the empty tomb, following the **Resurrection** of Jesus and the rolling back of the stone by angels.

Pope John Paul II emphasized the role of angels in Catholic teachings in his 1986 address titled **"*Angels Participate In History Of Salvation*"**, in which he suggested that modern mentality should come to see the importance of angels.

According to the Vatican's Congregation for Divine Worship and Discipline of the Sacraments, **"The practice of assigning names to the Holy Angels should be discouraged, except in the cases of Gabriel, Raphael and Michael whose names are contained in Holy Scripture."**

# Antisemitism

**Antisemitism** (also spelled **anti-Semitism** or **anti-Semitism**) is prejudice, hatred of, or discrimination against Jews for reasons connected to their Jewish heritage. A person who holds such positions is called an **"anti-Semite".** It is a form of racism. The term was coined in the late 19th century in Germany

**Antisemitism** may be manifested in many ways, ranging from expressions of hatred of or discrimination against individual Jews to organized violent attacks by mobs, state police, or even military attacks on entire Jewish communities. Notable instances of persecution include the pogroms which preceded the **First Crusade in 1096, the expulsion from England in 1290, the massacres of Spanish Jews in 1391, the persecutions of the Spanish Inquisition, the expulsion from Spain in 1492, Cossack massacres in Ukraine, various pogroms in Russia, the Dreyfus affair, the Holocaust, official Soviet anti-Jewish policies and the Jewish exodus from Arab and Muslim countries.**

## Evolution of usage
In the aftermath of the **Kristallnacht** pogrom in 1938, German propaganda minister **Goebbels** announced: **"The German people is anti-Semitic. It has no desire to have its rights restricted or to be provoked in the future by parasites of the Jewish race."**

## A category of social anti-Semitism.
- **Religious** (Jew as Christ-killer),
- **Economic** (Jew as banker, usurer, money-obsessed),
- **Social** (Jew as social inferior, "pushy," vulgar, therefore excluded from personal contact),
- **Racist** (Jews as an inferior "race"),
- **Ideological** (Jews regarded as subversive or revolutionary),
- **Cultural** (Jews regarded as undermining the moral and structural fiber of civilization).

## Religious antisemitism
Liturgical exclusion of Jewish converts (the case of Christianized *Marranos* or Iberian Jews in the late 15th century and 16th century convicted of secretly practicing Judaism or Jewish customers).

## Economic antisemitism
Linking Jews and money underpins the most damaging and lasting Anti-Semitic canards. Antisemites claim that Jews control the world finances, a theory promoted in the fraudulent **Protocols of the Elders of Zion**, and later repeated by **Henry Ford** and his Dearborn Independent.

## Racial antisemitism
Racial antisemitism is prejudice against Jews as a racial/ethnic group, rather than Judaism as a religion. Racial antisemitism is the idea that the Jews are a distinct and inferior race compared to their host nations. In the late 19th century and early 20th century, it gained mainstream acceptance. It more specifically claimed that Northern Europeans, or **"Aryans"**, were superior. In the early 19th century, **Ethnonationalism** usually excluded the Jews from the national community as an alien race.

## Conspiracy theories
Holocaust denial and Jewish conspiracy theories are also considered a form of antisemitism. Zoological conspiracy theories have been propagated by the Arab media and Arabic language websites.

## New antisemitism
Starting in the 1990s, some scholars have advanced the concept of new antisemitism, coming simultaneously from the left, the right, and radical Islam, which tends to focus on opposition to the creation of a Jewish homeland in the State of Israel.

## History
**The roots of economic antisemitism in early Christianity**.
1.  Pre-Christian anti-Judaism in ancient Greece and Rome which was primarily ethnic in nature
2.  Christian antisemitism in antiquity and the Middle Ages which was religious in nature and has extended into modern times
3.  Traditional Muslim antisemitism which was nuanced in that Jews were a protected class
4.  Political, social and economic antisemitism of Enlightenment and post-Enlightenment Europe which laid the groundwork for racial antisemitism
5.  Racial antisemitism that arose in the 19th century and culminated in Nazism
6.  Contemporary antisemitism which has been labeled by some as the New Antisemitism

## Ancient world
The first clear examples of anti-Jewish sentiment can be traced back to **Alexandria** in the 3rd century BCE. Alexandria was home to the largest Jewish diaspora community in the world at the time and the **Septuagint**, a Greek translation of the Hebrew Bible, was produced there. One of the earliest anti-Jewish edicts, promulgated by **Antiochus IV Epiphanes** in about 170-167 BCE, sparked a revolt of the **Maccabees** in Judea.

The ancient Jewish philosopher **Philo of Alexandria** describes an attack on Jews in Alexandria in 38 CE in which thousands of Jews died. There are examples of Hellenistic rulers desecrating the Temple and bagging Jewish religious practices, such as circumcision, **Shabbat** observance, study of Jewish religious books, etc. **Jews accounted for 10% of the total population of the Roman Empire.** When Christianity became the state religion of the Roman Empire, attitudes toward the Jews worsened.

## Persecutions in the middle Ages
From the 9th century CE, the medieval Islamic world classified Jews (and Christians) as *dhimmi,* and allowed them to practice their religion more freely than they could do in medieval Christian Europe. Under Islamic rule, there was a **Golden age** of Jewish culture in Spain that lasted until at least the 11th century, when several Muslim pogroms against Jews took place on the **Iberian Peninsula.** Several decrees ordering the destruction of synagogues were also enacted in **Egypt, Syria, Iraq** and **Yemen** from the 11th century. Jews were also forced to convert to Islam or face death. Faced with the choice of either death or conversion, many Jews and Christians emigrated.

During the middle Ages in Europe there was persecution against Jews in many places, with blood libels, expulsions, forced conversions and massacres. The persecution hit its first peak during the **Crusades**. In the Second Crusade (1147) the Jews in Germany were subject to several massacres. In 1290, the banishing of all English Jews, and in 1396, the expulsion of 100,000 Jews in France; and in 1421 the expulsion of thousands from Austria.

As the **Black Death** epidemics devastated Europe in the mid-14th century **annihilating more than half of the population,** Jews were used as scapegoats. Rumors spread that they caused the disease by deliberately poisoning wells. Hundreds of Jewish communities were destroyed. Although **Pope Clement VI** tried to protect them by issuing the 6 July 1348 **Papal bull,** several months later, **900 Jews were burned alive in Strasbourg**

## Enlightenment
In 1744, **Frederick II of Prussia** limited the number of Jews allowed to live in Breslau to only ten so-called **"protected"** Jewish families and encouraged a similar practice in other Prussian cities. The **Dreyfus Affair** was an infamous anti-Semitic event of the late 19th century and early 20th century. **Alfred Dreyfus**, a Jewish artillery captain in the French Army, was accused in 1894 of passing secrets to the Germans. Dreyfus was convicted and sentenced to life imprisonment on **Devil's Island**.

## 20th century
American Jews had amounted to less than 1% of America's total population, but by 1930 Jews formed about 3.5%. The lynching of **Leo Frank** by a mob of prominent citizens in Marietta, Georgia in 1915 turned the spotlight on anti-Semitism in the United States. The case was also used to build support for the renewal of the **Ku Klux Klan**.

In Germany the **National Socialist** regime of **Adolf Hitler**, which came to power on 30 January 1933, instituted repressive legislation denying the Jews basic civil rights. It instituted a pogrom on the night of 9-10 November 1938, dubbed *Kristallnacht,* in which Jews were killed, their property destroyed and their synagogues torched.

The **Third Reich** forced Jews into ghettos in Warsaw, Krakow, Lvov, Lublin and Radom. After the invasion of the Soviet Union in 1941 a campaign of mass murder, conducted by the **Einsatzgruppen**, culminated between 1942 and 1945 by systematic genocide: the **Holocaust**. **Eleven million Jews** were targeted for extermination by the Nazis, and some six million were eventually killed. Antisemitism was commonly used as an instrument for personal conflicts in the Soviet Union, starting from conflict between **Joseph Stalin** and **Leon Trotsky** and continuing through numerous conspiracy-theories spread by official propaganda.

A 2007 survey by the Anti-Defamation League **(ADL)** concluded that 15% of Americans hold anti-Semitic views. The belief that Jews have too much power was considered a common anti-Semitic view by the ADL, and that they are **responsible for the death of Jesus of Nazareth**. The 2007 survey also found that 29% of foreign-born Hispanics and 32% of African-Americans hold strong anti-Semitic beliefs.

## The Netherlands

The Netherlands has the second highest incidence of anti-Semitic incidents in the European Union. According to Centre for Information and Documentation on Israel (CIDI). There are approximately 52,000 Dutch Jews. According to the **Anne Frank Foundation**, actual anti-Semitic incidents increased from 19 in 2010 to 30 in 2011.

## United Kingdom

In November 2010, the **BBC's** investigative program *Panorama* reported that Saudi national textbooks advocating antisemitism were being used in Islamic religious programs attended by 5,000 British schoolchildren in the United Kingdom. **In the textbooks, Jews were described as looking like monkeys and pigs.**

## Sweden

After Germany and Austria, Sweden has the highest rate of anti-Semitic incidents in Europe. 5% of the entire adult population and 39% of the Muslim population, harbor strong and consistent anti-Semitic views. In 2009, a synagogue that served the Jewish community in Malmo was set ablaze, Jewish cemeteries were repeatedly desecrated; worshipers were abused. Members of the Swedish Parliament have attended **anti-Israel rallies** where the Israeli flag was burned while the flags of **Hamas** and **Hezbollah** were waved, and the rhetoric was often anti-Semitic.

## Middle East

Antisemitism is deeply ingrained and institutionalized in **"Arab nations in modern times."** Muslim clerics in the Middle East have frequently referred to **Jews as descendants of apes and pigs,** which are conventional epithets for Jews and Christians. **They call for the destruction of Israel by Iran or by Hamas.**

## Saudi Arabia

The website of the **Saudi Arabian Supreme Commission for Tourism** initially stated that Jews would not be granted tourist visas to enter the country. One Saudi Arabian government newspaper suggested that hatred of all Jews is justifiable. Saudi textbooks still call Jews apes demand that students avoid and not befriend Jews; claim that Jews worship the devil; and encourage Muslims to engage in Jihad to vanquish Jews. **The Protocols of the Elders of Zion** is taught as historical fact. The texts described Jews and Christians as enemies of Muslim believers.

# Anusim (Conversos/Marranos)

**Anusim** (Hebrew: אֲנוּסִים, meaning **"Coerced"**) is a legal category of Jews in *halakha* (Jewish law) who were forced to abandon Judaism against their will, typically while forcibly converted to another religion. The term **"Anusim"** is most properly translated as the **"coerced**" or **"forced "**.

## Etymology

The term Anusim derives from the Talmudic phrase *averah b'ones* meaning **"a forced transgression."** In Modern Hebrew, the word *ones* is mainly used to mean rape. The term *anús* is used in contradistinction to *meshumad* , which means a person who has voluntarily abandoned the practice of Jewish law in whole or part. The forced converts were also known as *cristianos nuevos* (Spanish) or *cristãos-novos* (Portuguese); *Converso or Marrano*, which had and still has today a pejorative connotation in Spanish.

## Meaning

**The two most common descriptions are:**
- *"Min"*, or an apostate of Judaism, for a Jew who basically denies the existence of God; and
- *"Meshumad"*, literally **"self-destroyed"** or a heretic to Judaism, for a Jew who deliberately rebels against the observance of Jewish law.

The main difference between a *min,* **a** *meshumad*, and the *Anusim* is that the act of abandonment of Judaism is voluntary for a *min* and a *meshumad*, while for the *Anusim* it is not. In more recent times, the term **Anusim** has also been used to describe **Reverse Marranos,** that is, Haredi Jews who are religious on the outside, but are not necessarily practicing in private.

## History of use

The term *Anusim* became more frequently used after the forced conversion to Christianity of Ashkenazi Jews in Germany at the end of the 11th century. Following the mass forced conversion of Sephardi Jews (those Jews with extended histories in Spain and Portugal, known jointly as Iberia, or **"Sepharad"** in Hebrew) of the 15th and 16th centuries, the term **"Anusim"** became widely used by Spanish rabbis and their successors for the following 600 years, henceforth becoming associated with Sephardic history.

The **Mashhadi Jews of Persia (modern Iran)**, who converted to Islam in the public eye, but secretly practiced Judaism at home. They lived dual-religious lives, being fully practicing Muslims in public life, and fully practicing Jews at home.
- **"Conversos"**, meaning "**converts** " in Spanish, Portuguese, Catalan and Ladino (Judaeo-Spanish).

30

- **"New Christians"**, or *cristianos nuevos* in Spanish, and *cristãos novos* in Portuguese (Catalan: *cristians nous*), which also encompasses converts from Islam.
- **"Crypto-Jews"**, and
- **"Marranos"**, a term which refers to those Conversos which practiced Judaism in secret and, as a result, were targeted by the **Spanish Inquisition**.

## In rabbinic literature

The subject of Anusim has a special place in rabbinic literature. In normal circumstances, a person who abandons Jewish observance, or part of it, is classified as a *meshumad*. Such a person is still counted as a Jew for purposes of lineage, but is under a disability to claim any privilege pertaining to Jewish status: for example, he **should not be counted in a minyan**, that is, a quorum for religious services.

*Anusim*, by contrast, not only remain Jews by lineage but continue to count as fully qualified Jews for all purposes. Since the act of the original abandonment of the religion was done against the Jew's will, the Jew under force may remain a kosher Jew, as long as the *anús* keeps practicing Jewish law to the best of his/her abilities under the coerced condition. In this sense, **"kosher"** is the rabbinic legal term applied to a Jew who adheres to rabbinic tradition and is accordingly not subject to any disqualification.

## Rabbinic legal opinions

Indeed, when it comes to lineage, all the people of Israel are brethren. We are all the sons of one father, the rebels (*reshaim*) and criminals, the heretics (*meshumadim*) and forced ones (*Anusim*), and the proselytes (*gerim*) who are attached to the house of Jacob. **All these are Israelites**.

# The Arab-Israeli Conflict

On July 1949, Israel had signed armistice agreement with the Arab countries that had invaded in 1948, but as a result the Palestinians, who had fled their homes during the fighting were deprived of any prospect of immediate return.  In their refugee camps, mostly in Lebanon and the area on the West Bank of the Jordan, they became the responsibility of the **United Nations Relief and Works Agency (UNRWA),** which operated programs to relieve their plight.

## Continued fighting

Bitterness between Israel and Arab countries broke out into open warfare on a number of further occasions.  In 1956, the Israelis joined in the **Anglo-French** operation to occupy the **Suez Canal** after its nationalization by Egyptian president Nasser, and they briefly occupied much of the strategic Sinai Desert.

In May 1967, a mutual defense pact between **Egypt, Lebanon, and Syria** looked likely to turn into an invasion of Israel, which provoked the Israelis to a pre-emptive strike.  In the ensuing **Six Days' War,** the Israelis destroyed much of the **Egyptian Air Force** on the ground and made large territorial gains in the Sinai from Egypt, took much of the **West Bank** (including East Jerusalem) from Jordan, and seized parts of the **Golan Heights** from Syria.

These areas became known as the **Occupied Territories**.  In 1973, Egypt and Syria launched an attack on Israel on **Yom Kippur** – the Jewish Day of Atonement – when they knew much of the Israeli military would be at religious observances.  The Arab forces made significant early advances, but the Israeli **Defense Force** (IDF) struck back, pushing their opponents back beyond the 1967 lines.  After the conflict, Israel was left with small territorial gains in the Golan Heights; the Arabs with nothing.

## The PLO

Resorting to terrorist and guerrilla tactics, in 1964 the Palestinians founded the **Palestine Liberation Organization** (PLO), which for the next 40 years aimed to help Palestinians realize their hopes of restoring some of their 1948 losses.

Under the leadership of **Yasser Arafat** from 1969, the PLO sponsored guerrilla raids on Israeli and military targets.  It also hijacked international aircraft and murdered members of the **Israeli Olympic team** at the 1972 Munich games.  Setbacks occurred when Jordan expelled militant Palestinians in 1970, and when PLO fighters were pushed out of Lebanon in 1985-88.

## Moves for peace

Israel evacuated the Sinai in 1979 following the **Camp David Accords**, signed by presidents **Sadat** of Egypt and **Begin** of Israel, but hopes for a more permanent settlement proved illusory.  In 1987, a low-level insurrection broke out among the **Palestinians in Gaza** and in the other **Occupied Territories**, eventually leading the Israeli government to soften its reluctance to negotiate with the Palestinian leadership.  This led to the **Oslo Accords** of September 1993, which allowed the creation of a **Palestinian Authority** – led by **Yasser Arafat** – and the Palestinians' gradual assumption of power over much of the **Occupied Territories**.

However, opposition from extremists on both sides frittered away the chance for lasting peace. Suicide bombers from the radical **Islamist Hamas** movement struck several times in Israel in 1993-95, and on November 4, 1995, a Jewish extremist killed the Israeli Prime Minister **Yitzhak Rabin**. A new Palestinian intifada, or uprising, erupted in the fall of 2000, and since then, peace processes have offered the Palestinians less and less.

The Israeli government has sponsored settlements on formerly Palestinian land and built a security wall isolating those Palestinian enclaves it does not seek to control directly. **Radicalism** has flourished on the Palestinian side, with **Hamas** taking power in **Gaza** in 2007. The 75-year Arab-Israeli conflict looks set to continue for a long time yet.

## Oil and politics

The awareness among oil-producing nations that they could use the threat of cutting off oil exports as an economic weapon became much stronger after the foundation of the State of Israel in 1948, with one major oil embargo being put into place since then. Outside powers have also sought to exert political or direct military influence over oil-producing nations in a bid to ensure vital fuel supplies.

## The 1973 oil crisis

An oil embargo formed part of the Arab response to the **Six Days' War** with Israel in 1967, but was largely ineffective due to a lack of solidarity between the oil-producing countries. This led to the foundation, in 1968 of the **Organization of Arab Petroleum Exporting Countries** (OAPEC), a body whose purpose was to coordinate and control the use of oil as a political weapon.

The **Yom Kippur War** of 1973 saw OAPEC flex its political muscles for the first time, as **Saudi Arabia** and **Egypt** put an embargo on shipments of crude oil to Western nations that were providing aid to Israel; this tripled world oil prices and sent the world into recession. But the oil weapon has never again been used to such conspicuous effect: some members have always been tempted – by the higher profits that could be made – into sidestepping any restrictions or embargo.

In the early 21$^{st}$ century, control of energy reserves and the means of their transmission remains an area of supreme concern for industrialized powers. **Russia** (which has massive natural gas fields) has become increasingly ready to threaten to cut off supplies or raise prices to countries whose foreign policies are not to its taste.

**The only long-term solution for the Israeli-Palestinian conflict is the eventual establishment of a Palestinian State.**

# Archangels

An **archangel** / is an angel of high rank. The word **"archangel"** itself is usually associated with the Abrahamic religions, but beings that are very similar to archangels are found in a number of religious traditions. The English word *archangel* is derived from the Greek (*arch-* + *angel*, literally **"chief angel"** or **"angel of origin"**). It appears only twice in the New Testament in the phrase "with the voice of the archangel, and with the trumpet call of God" (1 Thessalonians 4:16) and in relation to **'the *archangel* Michael'** (Jude 9). The corresponding but different Hebrew word in the Hebrew Scripture (Old Testament) is found in two places as in **"Michael, one of the *chief princes*"** (Dan 10:13) and in **"Michael, the *great prince*"** (Dan 12:1).

## Description

**Michael and Gabriel are recognized as archangels in Judaism, Islam, the Baha'i Faith, and by most Christians.** Some Protestants consider Michael to be the only archangel. Raphael—mentioned in the deuterocanonical **Book of Tobit**—is also recognized as an archangel in the Catholic and Orthodox churches. **Gabriel**, **Michael**, and **Raphael** are venerated in the Roman Catholic Church.

The named archangels in Islam are **Jibrael, Mikael, Israfil**, and **Azrael.** Jewish literature, such as the **Book of Enoch**, also mentions **Metatron** as an archangel, called the **"highest of the angels"**, though the acceptance of this angel is not canonical in all branches of the faith. Some branches of the faiths mentioned have identified a group of seven Archangels, but the named angels vary, depending on the source. **Gabriel, Michael**, and **Raphael** are always mentioned, but most commonly include **Uriel,** who is mentioned in *2 Esdras.* In Zoroastrianism, sacred texts allude to the six great **Amesha Spenta** (literally **"Bounteous/Holy Immortals"**) of Ahura Mazda.

## In Zoroastrianism / *Amesha Spenta*

To maintain equilibrium, **Ahura Mazda** engaged in the first act of creation, distinguishing his **Holy Spirit Spenta Mainyu,** the Archangel of righteousness. Ahura Mazda also distinguished from himself six more **Amesha Spentas,** who, along with **Spenta Mainyu,** aided in the creation of the physical universe. The **Amesha Spentas** were charged with protecting these holy lands and through their emanation, also believed to align each respective population in service to God.

**The Amesha Spentas (Amesha meaning eternal and Spenta meaning brilliance and beneficence) as attributes of God are:**
1. **Spenta Mainyu** (Phl. Spenamino): lit. "Bountiful Spirit"
2. **Asha Vahishta** (Phl. Ardwahisht): lit. "Highest Truth"
3. **Vohu Mano** (Phl. Vohuman): lit. "Righteous Mind"
4. **Khshathra Vairya** (Phl. Shahrewar): lit. "Desirable Dominion"
5. **Spenta Armaiti** (Phl. Spandarmad): lit. "Holy Devotion"

6. **Haurvatat** (Phl. Hordad): lit. "Perfection or Health"
7. **Ameretat** (Phl. Amurdad): lit. "Immortality"

## In Judaism

The Hebrew Bible uses the term (*malakhi Elohim*; **Angels of God**), The Hebrew word for angel is **"Malach,"** which means messenger, for the angels (*malakhi Adonai*; **Angels of the Lord**) are God's messengers to perform various missions - e.g. **'angel of death'**; (*b'nei elohim*; **sons of God**) and (*ha-q'doshim*; **the holy ones**) to refer to beings traditionally interpreted as *angelic messengers.*

References to angels are uncommon in Jewish literature except in later works such as the **Book of Daniel,** though they are mentioned briefly in the stories of **Jacob** and **Lot** (who was warned by angels of the impending destruction of the cities of **Sodom** and **Gomorrah**). Daniel is the first biblical figure to refer to individual angels by name. It is therefore widely speculated that Jewish interest in angels developed during the Babylonian captivity.

**Metatron** is considered one of the highest of the angels in **Merkavah** and Kabbalist mysticism and often serves as a scribe. He is briefly mentioned in the **Talmud**, and figures prominently in **Merkavah** mystical texts. **Michael**, who serves as a warrior and advocate for Israel, is looked upon particularly fondly. **Gabriel** is mentioned in the **Book of Daniel** and briefly in the **Talmud**, as well as many **Merkavah** mystical texts.

In the **Kabbalah there are ten archangels**, each assigned to one sephira: **Metatron, Raziel (other times Jophiel), Tzaphkiel, Tzadkiel, Khamael, Raphael, Haniel, Michael, Gabriel, and Sandalphon.** Chapter 20 of the **Book of Enoch** mentions seven holy angels who watch, that often are considered the seven archangels: **Michael, Raphael, Gabriel, Uriel, Saraqael, Raguel, and Remiel.** The Life of Adam and Eve lists the archangels as well: **Michael, Gabriel, Uriel, Raphael and Joel.** Medieval Jewish philosopher **Maimonides** made a Jewish angelic hierarchy.

## In Christianity

The New Testament makes over a hundred references to angels, but uses the word **"archangel"** only twice, at **Thessalonians 4:16 ("For the Lord himself shall descend from heaven with a shout, with the voice of the archangel, and with the trump of God: and the dead in Christ shall rise first", KJV)** and **Jude 1:9 ("Yet Michael the archangel, when contending with the devil he disputed about the body of Moses, durst not bring against him a railing accusation, but said, The Lord rebuke thee", KJV).**

## Roman Catholic

**In Roman Catholicism, three are honored by name:**
- **Gabriel** ("God is my strength")

- **Michael** ("Who is like God?")
- **Raphael** ("It is God who heals")

The latter of these identifies himself in Tobit 12:15[NAB] thus: **"I am Raphael, one of the seven angels who stand and serve before the Glory of the Lord."** The **Fourth Book of Esdras**, which mentions the angel **Uriel** (and also the **"archangel"** Jeremiel), was popular in the West and was frequently quoted by Church Fathers, especially **Ambrose**, but was never considered part of the Catholic biblical canon.

## Eastern Orthodox

**Eastern Orthodox Tradition** mentions **"thousands of archangels"**; however, only seven archangels are venerated by name. **Uriel** is included, and the other three are most often named **Selaphiel, Jegudiel**, and **Barachiel** (an eighth, **Jeremiel**, is sometimes included as archangel).

Every Monday throughout the year is dedicated to the Angels, with special mention being made in the church hymns of Michael and Gabriel. In Orthodox iconography, each angel has a symbolic representation:

- *Michael* in the Hebrew language means "Who is like God?" or "Who is equal to God?" Michael has been depicted from earliest Christian times as a commander, who holds in his right hand a spear with which he attacks Lucifer/Satan, and in his left hand a green palm branch. At the top of the spear, there is a linen ribbon with a red cross. The Archangel Michael is especially considered to be the Guardian of the Orthodox Faith and a fighter against heresies.
- *Gabriel* means "God is my strength" or "Might of God". He is the herald of the mysteries of God, especially the Incarnation of God and all other mysteries related to it. He is depicted as follows: In his right hand, he holds a lantern with a lighted taper inside, and in his left hand, a mirror of green jasper. The mirror signifies the wisdom of God as a hidden mystery.
- *Raphael* means "It is God who heals" or "God Heals". Raphael is depicted leading Tobit (who is carrying a fish caught in the Tigris) with his right hand and holding a physician's alabaster jar in his left hand.
- *Uriel* means "God is my light", or "Light of God" (II Esdras 4:1, 5:20). He is depicted holding a sword in his right hand, and a flame in his left.
- *Sealtiel* means "Intercessor of God". He is depicted with his face and eyes lowered, holding his hands on his bosom in prayer.
- *Jegudiel* means "Glorifier of God". He is depicted bearing a golden wreath in his right hand and a triple-thonged whip in his left hand.
- *Barachiel* means "Blessed by God". He is depicted holding a white rose in his hand against his breast.
- *Jerahmeel* means "God's exaltation". He is venerated as an inspirer and awakener of exalted thoughts that raise a person toward God (II Esdras 4:36). As an *eighth*, he is sometimes included as an archangel.

## Protestant

The Protestant Bible provides names for three angels: "**Michael the archangel**", the angel **Gabriel,** who is called **"the man Gabriel"** in **Daniel 9:21** and third **"Abaddon"/"Apollyon"** in **Revelation 9:11**. Within Protestantism, the Anglican and Methodist tradition recognizes four angels as archangels: **Michael the Archangel, Raphael the Archangel, Gabriel the Archangel**, and **Uriel the Archangel**. In this case, in addition to the aforementioned angels, **Chamuel, Jophiel** and **Zadkiel** are also depicted.

## *Islamic view of angels*

**In Islam, the mentioned archangels in the Quran and Sunnah include:**

- **Gabriel** (Jibrail or Jibril in Arabic). Gabriel is said to be the archangel responsible for transmitting God's revelations to all prophets, including revealing the Quran to Muhammad and inducing him to recite it. Various hadiths (traditions) mention his role in delivering messages from "God the Almighty" to the prophets.
- **Michael** (Mikail in Arabic). Michael is often depicted as the archangel of mercy who is responsible for bringing rain and thunder to Earth.
- **Raphael** (Israfil in Arabic). Mentioned in the Quran as the angel of the trumpet responsible for signaling the coming of Judgment Day.
- **Azrael** (Azra'il in Arabic, also called Malak al-Maut, literally "angel of death"). Mentioned in the Quran as the angel of death.
- **Maalik** (literally: owner). Mentioned in the Quran as the angel of Fire/Hell.
- **Riḍwan** (literally: pleasure). Mentioned in the Sunnah as the angel of paradise/heaven.

## Cultural references

In art, archangels are sometimes depicted with larger wings. Some of the more commonly represented archangels are **Gabriel, Michael, Raphael**, and **Uriel. "Before me Raphael; Behind me Gabriel; On my right hand Michael; On my left hand Auriel ..."**

# Ark of the Covenant

The **Ark of the Covenant**, also known as the **Ark of the Testimony**, is a chest described in the **Book of Exodus** as containing the Tablets of Stone on which the **Ten Commandments** were inscribed. According to some traditional interpretations of the **Book of Exodus**, **Book of Numbers**, and the Letter to the Hebrews, the Ark also contained **Aaron's rod**, a jar of manna and the first Torah scroll as written by Moses; however, the first of the **Books of Kings** says that at the time of King Solomon, **the Ark contained only the two Tablets of the Law**. According to the Book of Exodus, the Ark was built at the command of God, in accordance with the instructions given to Moses in Mount Sinai, God was said to have communicated with Moses **"from between the two cherubim"** on the Ark's cover.

The biblical account relates that about a year after the Israelites' exodus from Egypt, the Ark was created according to the pattern given Moses by God when Israel was encamped at the foot of **Mount Sinai**. Thereafter the gold plated, acacia chest was carried by the Levites some 2,000 cubits in advance of the people when on the march or before the Israelite army, the host of fighting men.

When the Ark was **borne by Levites** into the bed of the Jordan, the waters parted as God had parted the waters of the **Red Sea**, opening a pathway for the entire host to pass through (**Josh. 3:15-16; 4:7-18**). The walls of the city of **Jericho** were shaken to the ground with no more than a shout from the army after the Ark of the Covenant was paraded round them for seven days by Levites. **Seven priests sounding seven trumpets of rams' horns (Josh. 6:4-20)**.

### Biblical account: Construction and description
According to the **Book of Exodus**, Yahweh instructed Moses on Mount Sinai during his 4-day stay upon the mountain within the thick cloud and darkness where God was (**Ex. 19:20; 24:18**) and he was shown the pattern for the tabernacle and furnishings of the Ark to be made of **Shittim** wood to house the **Tablets of Stone**. Moses instructed **Bezalel** and **Oholiab** to construct the ark (**Exodus 31**). The Book of Exodus gives detailed instructions on how the Ark is to be constructed.

### Mobile vanguard
After its creation by Moses, the Ark was carried by the Israelites during their 40 years of wandering in the desert. Whenever the Israelites camped, the Ark was placed in a special and sacred tent, called the **Tabernacle**. When the Israelites, led by **Joshua** toward the **Promised Land**, arrived at the banks of the River Jordan, the Ark was carried in the lead preceding the people and was the signal for their advance (**Joshua 3:3, 6**). During the crossing, the river grew dry as soon as the feet of the priests carrying the Ark touched its waters, and remained so until the priests – with the Ark – left the river after the people had passed over (**Josh. 3:15-17); 4:10, 11, 18**).

In the **Battle of Jericho**, the Ark was carried round the city once a day for seven days, preceded by the armed men and seven priests sounding seven trumpets of rams' horns (**Josh. 6:4-15**). On the seventh day, the seven priests sounding the seven trumpets of rams' horns before the Ark compassed the city seven times and with a great shout, Jericho's wall fell down flat and the people took the city (**Josh. 6:16-20**).

## Capture by the Philistines

The Ark is next spoken of as being in the Tabernacle at Shiloh during Samuel's apprenticeship (**1 Sam. 3:3).** After the settlement of the Israelites in Canaan, the Ark remained in the Tabernacle at Gilgal for a season before being removed to **Shiloh** until the time of **Eli**, between 300 and 400 years **(Jeremiah 7:12),** when it was carried into the field of battle, so as to secure, as they had hoped, victory to the Hebrews. The Ark was taken by the Philistines **(1 Sam. 4:3-11)** who subsequently sent it back after retaining it for seven months **(1 Sam. 4:7, 8)** because of the events said to have transpired. After their first defeat at **Eben-ezer**, the Israelites had the Ark brought from Shiloh, and welcomed its coming with great rejoicing.

In the second battle, the Israelites were again defeated, and the Philistines captured the Ark **(1 Sam. 4:3-5, 10, 11).** The news of its capture was at once taken to Shiloh by a messenger **"with his clothes rent, and with earth upon his head."** The old priest, **Eli**, fell dead when he heard it. Explained as **"The glory was departed Israel"** in reference to the loss of the Ark **(1 Sam. 4:12-22).** The Philistines took the Ark to several places in their country, and at each place misfortune befell them **(1 Sam. 5:1-6), (1 Sam. 6:5).** After the Ark had been among them for seven months, the Philistines, on the advice of their diviners, returned it to the Israelites.

## In the days of King David

At the beginning of his reign, **King David** removed the Ark from Kirjath-jearim amid great rejoicing. David, in fear, carried the Ark aside into the house of **Obed-Edom the Gittite**, instead of carrying it on to **Zion**, and there it stayed three months **(2 Samuel 6:1-11; 1 Chronicles 13:1-13).** On hearing that God had blessed **Obed-Edom** because of the presence of the Ark in his house, David had the Ark brought to Zion by the Levites. **(2 Sam. 6:12-16, 20-22; 1 Chron. 15).**

In Zion, David put the Ark in the tabernacle he had prepared for it, offered sacrifices, distributed food, and blessed the people and his own household **(2 Sam. 6:17-20; 1 Chron. 16:1-3; 2 Chron. 1:4).** The Levites were appointed to minister before the Ark **(1 Chron. 16:4)**, David's plan of building a temple for the Ark was stopped at the advice of God **(2 Sam. 7:1-17; 1 Chron. 17:1-15; 28:2, 3).** And when David fled from Jerusalem at the time of Absalom's conspiracy, the Ark was carried along with him until he ordered **Zadok** the priest to return it to Jerusalem **(2 Sam. 15:24-29).**

## In Solomon's Temple

When **Abiathar** was dismissed from the priesthood by **King Solomon** for having taken part in Adonijah's conspiracy against David, his life was spared because he had formerly borne the Ark **(1 Kings 2:26)**, Solomon worshipped before the Ark after his dream in which God promised him wisdom **(1 Kings 3:15).** During the construction of **Solomon's Temple**, a special inner room, named **Kodesh Hakodashim** (Holy of Holies), was prepared to receive and house the Ark **(1 Kings 6:19)**; and when the Temple was dedicated, **the Ark – containing the original tablets of the Ten Commandments** – was placed therein **(1 Kings 8:6-9).** **King Josiah** also had the Ark put in the Temple **(2 Chron. 35:3)**

**The Babylonian Conquest and aftermath**

In 597 BC, the Babylonians destroyed Jerusalem and Solomon's Temple. There is no record of what became of the Ark in the **Books of Kings** and Chronicles, but the Greek 3$^{rd}$ **Book of Ezra (1 Esdras)** suggests that Babylonians:

> **"…took all the holy vessels of the Lord, both great and small, and the ark of God, and the king's treasures, and carried them away into Babylon". (1 Esdras 1:54).**

**Jewish Tanakh**

The Ark is first mentioned in the **Book of Exodus**, and then numerous times in **Deuteronomy, Joshua, Judges, 1 Samuel, 11 Samuel, 1 Kings, 1 Chronicles, 11 Chronicles, Psalms** and **Jeremiah.** In the Book of Jeremiah, it is referenced by Jeremiah, who, speaking in the days of Josiah (**Jer. 3:16**), prophesied a future time, possibly the end of days, when the Ark will no longer be talked about or be made again:

> *"And it shall be that when you multiply and become fruitful in the land, in those days – the word of the LORD – they will no longer say, 'The Ark of the Covenant of the LORD' and it will not come to mind; they will not mention it, and will not recall it, and it will not be used anymore."*

**Rashi** comments on this verse that **"The entire people will be so imbued with the spirit of sanctity that God's Presence will rest upon them collectively, as if the congregation itself was the Ark of the Covenant."**

# Armageddon (Judeo-Christian)

**Armageddon** (Late Latin: *Armagedon*) will be the site of a battle during the end times. The word **"Armageddon"** appears in the **Greek New Testament Revelation 16:16**. Megiddo was the location of battles going back to 15<sup>th</sup> century BC. Modern Megiddo is a town off the southern tip of the **Sea of Galilee** in the Kishon River area, Israel.

## Christianity
According to Christian interpretation, **the Messiah will return to earth and defeat the Antichrist (the "beast") and Satan the Devil in the Battle Armageddon**. Then **Satan** will be put into the **"bottomless pit"** or abyss for 1,000 years, known as the Millennium. Fire will come down from God and devour **Gog and Magog** after the Millennium. The Devil, death, hell, and those not found written in the **Book of Life** are then thrown into **Gehenna** (The Lake of Fire burning with Brimstone).

Within dispensational premillennialists writing, Christians will be summoned to Heaven by Christ at the **Rapture,** occurring before a **"Great Tribulation"** prophesied in Matthew 24-25; Mark 13 and Luke 21. The Tribulation is described in the **book of Revelation**. The Mormons believe that there will be increasing war, earthquakes, hurricanes, and man-made disasters prior to the **Second Coming**.

## Dispensationalism
The Dispensational viewpoint interprets biblical prophecy literally and expects that the fulfillment of prophecy will also be literal, depending upon the context of scripture. After the destruction of the Beast at the **Second Coming of Jesus, the promised Kingdom is set up, in which Jesus and the Saints will rule for a 1,000 years.**

## Jehovah's Witnesses
The armies of heaven will eradicate all who oppose the **kingdom of God** and its rule, wiping out all wicked humans on Earth, leaving only righteous mankind. The armies of heaven, commanded by **Jesus Christ**, will then destroy all forms of human government and then **Jesus with a selected 144,000 will rule Earth for 1,000 years.** Those who follow **Satan** are destroyed, along with him, leaving the Earth, and humankind at peace with God forever, **free of sin and death.**

## Seventh-day Adventist
The teachings of the **Seventh-day Adventist** Church state that the terms **"Armageddon", "Day of the Lord" and "The Second Coming of Christ"** all describe the same event. They teach that the righteous will be taken to heaven while the rest of humanity will be destroyed, leaving **Satan** with no one to tempt and effectively **"bound."**

## Ahmadiyya
In **Ahmadiyya**, Armageddon is viewed as a spiritual battle or struggle in the present age between the forces of good, i.e. righteous ness, purity and virtue, and the forces of evil. The final struggle between the two comes as satanic influence is let loose with the emergence of **Gog and Magog**. **Satan** gathers all his powers, and uses all his methods to mislead people, introducing an age where

iniquity, promiscuity, atheism, and materialism abound. **Apocalypse**; it is characterized by the **assembling of mankind under one faith, Islam.**

## End Time: Judaism

In Judaism, the term **"end of days"** is a reference to the **Messianic Age**, and includes an in-gathering of the exiled diaspora, the coming of the *mashiach, olam haba*, and resurrection of the Tsadikim. The Messianic Age will follow, and will be an era of global peace, free of strife, and conductive to knowledge of the creator. In the **Talmud**, the Midrash, and the **Kabbalah (Zohar), the messiah must arrive before the year 6000 from the time of creation, or before the year 2240 CE. The seventh millennium begins with the year 6000 AM, and is the latest time the Messiah can come.**

## Zoroastrianism

Zoroastrian eschatology is the oldest in recorded history, with beliefs paralleling and predating the framework of the major Abrahamic faiths. **By the year 500 BC**, a fully developed concept of the end of the world was established in **Zoroastrianism**. A **Manichaean battle** between the righteous and wicked will be followed by the **Frashokereti**. On earth, the Saoshyant will arrive as the final savior of mankind, and bring about the resurrection of the dead. **Bodies will become so light as to cast no shadow. All humanity will speak a single language, and belong to a single nation with no orders.**

## Islam

There are three periods before the **Day of Judgment**, also known as *ahsratu's-sa'ah* or *alamatu qiyami's-sa-ah.* The first period began with the death of **Muhammad**. The second began with the passing of all his Companions, and ended a thousand years later. Another event of the second period was the **Tartar invasion, occurring 650 years after Muhammad.** Following the second, the third and final period will be heralded by the appearance of the **Mahdi**. The dead will stand in a grand assembly, awaiting a scroll detailing their righteous deeds, sinful acts and ultimate judgment. **Muhammad will be the first to be resurrected.**

## Buddhism: Maitreya

Buddha described his teachings disappearing **five thousand years** from when he preached them, corresponding approximately to the year 2000. This will be a period of greed, lust, poverty, ill will, violence, murder, impiety, physical weakness, sexual depravity and societal collapse, and even the **Buddha** himself will be forgotten.

## Baha'i Faith

The inception of the **Baha'i Faith** coincides with **Millerite** prophecy pointing to the year **1844**. They also believe the Battle of Armageddon has passed and that the mass martyrdom anticipated during the *End Times* had already passed within the historical context of the Baha'i Faith. Baha'is expects their faith to be eventually embraced by the masses of the world, ushering in a golden age.

**There is no agreement between them as to when this will take place.**

# Ashkenazi Jews

**Ashkenazi Jews**, also known as **Ashkenazic Jews** or simply **Ashkenazim** (Hebrew: Ashkenazi a Jewish diaspora population who coalesced as a distinct community in the **Holy Roman Empire around the end of the first millennium**. The traditional diaspora language of Ashkenazi Jews is **Yiddish**, with Hebrew used only as a sacred language until relatively recently. Throughout their time in Europe, Ashkenazim have made many important contributions to philosophy, scholarship, literature, art, music, and science.

Ashkenazim originate from the Jews who settled along the **Rhine River**, in Western Germany and Northern France. There they became a distinct diaspora community with a unique way of life that adapted traditions from **Babylon and the Land of Israel.** The eminent **French *Rishon* Rabbi Shlomo Itzhaki** (Rashi) would have a significant impact on the Jewish religion.

In the late Middle Ages, the majority of the Ashkenazi population shifted steadily eastward, moving out of the **Holy Roman Empire** into the **Pale of Settlement** (comprising parts of present-day **Belarus, Latvia, Lithuania, Moldova, Poland, Russia**, and **Ukraine**). In the course of the late 18th and 19th centuries, those Jews who remained in or returned to the German lands experienced a cultural reorientation; under the influence of the **Haskalah** and the struggle for emancipation, as well as the intellectual and cultural ferment in urban centers, they gradually abandoned the use of **Yiddish**, while developing new forms of Jewish religious life and cultural identity.

The genocidal impact of the **Holocaust** (the mass murder of approximately six million Jews during World War II) devastated the Ashkenazim and their culture, affecting almost every Jewish family. Immediately prior to the **Holocaust**, the number of Jews in the world stood at approximately 16.7 million. Ashkenazi Jews, oscillating **between 10 million and 11.2 million.**

**Ashkenazi Jews** are popularly contrasted with **Sephardi Jews** (also called Sephardim), who descend from Jews who settled in the **Iberian Peninsula**, and **Mizrahi Jews**, who descend from Jews who remained in the **Arab Middle East.**

## Etymology
In **Jeremiah 51:27**, Ashkenaz figures as one of **three kingdoms** in the far north, the others being **Minni** and **Ararat**, perhaps corresponding to **Urartu**, called on by God to resist Babylon. In the Yoma tractate of the **Babylonian Talmud** the name Gomer is rendered as *Germania*, which elsewhere in rabbinical literature was identified with **Germanikia** in northwestern Syria, but later became associated with *Germania.*

In the 10th-century *History of Armenia* of **Yovhannes Drasxanakertc'i** (1.15) Ashkenaz was associated with **Armenia,** as it was occasionally in Jewish usage, where its denotation extended at times to **Adiabene, Khazaria, Crimea** and areas to the east. His contemporary **Saadia Gaon** identified Ashkenaz with the *Saquliba* or Slavic territories, and such usage covered also the lands of tribes neighboring the Slavs, and Eastern and Central Europe.

Sometime in the early medieval period, the Jews of central and Eastern Europe came to be called by this term. In conformity with the custom of designating areas of Jewish settlement with biblical names, **Spain** was denominated *Sefarad* (Obadiah 20), France was called *Tsarefat* **(1 Kings 17:9)**, and Bohemia was called the *Land of Canaan.*

By the high medieval period, Talmudic commentators like **Rash**i began to use *Ashkenaz/Eretz Ashkenaz.* Rashi uses *leshon Ashkenaz* (Ashkenazi language) to describe German speech, and Byzantium and Syrian Jewish letters referred to the **Crusaders** as Ashkenazim. Given the close links between the Jewish communities of France and Germany following the **Carolingian** unification, the term Ashkenazi came to refer to both the Jews of medieval Germany and France.

# Babylonian Captivity

The **Babylonian captivity** or **Babylonian exile** is the period in Jewish history during which a number of **Judahites** of the ancient **Kingdom of Judah** were captives in Babylonia. After the **Battle of Carchemish** in 605 BCE, **Nebuchadnezzar**, the king of Babylon, besieged Jerusalem, resulting in tribute being paid by **King Jehoiakim**.

Jehoiakim refused to pay tribute in Nebuchadnezzar's fourth year, which led to another siege in Nebuchadnezzar's seventh year, culminating with the death **of Jehoiakim** and the exile of **King Jeconiah**, his court and many others; Jeconiah's successor **Zedekiah** and others were exiled in Nebuchadnezzar's eighteenth year; a later deportation occurred in Nebuchadnezzar's twenty-third year.  These deportations are dated to 597 BCE for the first, with others dated at 587/586 BCE, and 582/581 BCE respectively.

After the fall of Babylon to the Persian king **Cyrus the Great** in 539 BCE (after 58 years), exiled Judeans were permitted to return to Judah. According to the biblical book of **Ezra, construction of the second temple in Jerusalem began around 516 BCE. It stood until it was destroyed again by the Romans in 70 AD.**

Although Jerusalem was utterly destroyed, other parts of Judah continued to be inhabited during the period of the exile. The return of the exiles was a gradual process rather than a single event, and many of the deportees or their descendants did not return.

## Biblical accounts of the exile:

In the late 7th century BCE, the **kingdom of Judah** was a client state of the **Assyrian Empire**. In the last decades of the century, Assyria was overthrown by Babylon, an Assyrian province. **Egypt**, fearing the sudden rise of the **Neo-Babylonian Empire**, seized control of Assyrian territory up to the **Euphrates River** in Syria, but Babylon counter-attacked. In the process **Josiah,** the king of Judah, was killed in a battle with the Egyptians at the **Battle of Megiddo** (609 BC). After the defeat of Pharaoh Necho's army by the Babylonians at Carchemish in 605 BCE, **Jehoiakim** began paying tribute to **Nebuchadnezzar II** of Babylon. Some of the young nobility of Judah (such as **Daniel, Shadrach, Meshach, and Abednego**) were taken to Babylon.

In the following years, the court of Jerusalem was divided into two parties, in support of **Egypt** and **Babylon**. After Nebuchadnezzar was defeated in battle in 601 BCE by Egypt, Judah revolted against Babylon, culminating in a three-month siege of Jerusalem beginning in late 598 BCE.

**Jehoiakim**, the king of Judah, died during the siege and was succeeded by his son **Jehoiachin** (also called **Jeconiah**) at the age of eighteen. The city fell on 2 Adar (March 16) 597 BCE, and **Nebuchadnezzar pillaged Jerusalem and its Temple** and took Jeconiah, his court and other prominent citizens (including the prophet **Ezekiel**) back to Babylon. Jehoiakim's uncle **Zedekiah** was appointed king in his place, but the exiles in Babylon continued to consider Jeconiah as their **Exilarch**, or rightful ruler.

Despite warnings by **Jeremiah** and others of the pro-Babylonian party, **Zedekiah** revolted against Babylon and entered into an alliance with **Pharaoh Hophra**. Nebuchadnezzar returned, defeated the Egyptians, and again besieged Jerusalem, resulting in the **city's destruction in 587 BCE**. **Zedekiah** and his sons were captured, **the sons were executed in front of Zedekiah, who was then blinded and taken to Babylon** with many others (Jer 52:10-11). Judah became a Babylonian province, called **Yehud**, putting an end to the independent **Kingdom of Judah**. Rabbinic sources place the date of the **destruction of the First Temple at 423 BCE**.

By the end of the second decade of the 6th century, in addition to those who remained in Judah, there were significant Jewish communities in Babylon and in Egypt; this was the beginning of the later numerous Jewish communities living permanently outside Judah in the **Jewish Diaspora.**

According to the **book of Ezra**, the Persian **Cyrus the Great** ended the exile in 538 BCE, the year after he captured Babylon. The exile ended with the return under **Zerubbabel the Prince** and **Joshua the Priest** and their construction of the **Second Temple in the period 521–516 BCE.**

Nebuchadnezzar and the Babylonian forces returned in 588/586 BCE and rampaged through Judah, leaving clear archaeological evidence of destruction in many towns and settlements there. Archaeological finds from Jerusalem testify that virtually **the whole city within the walls was burnt to rubble in 587 BCE and utterly destroyed.** At most 25% of the population had been deported to Babylon, with the remaining 75% staying in Judah. As part of the **Persian Empire**, the former Kingdom of Judah became the province of Judah (*Yehud Medinata*) with different borders, covering a smaller territory.

## Significance in Jewish history:

In the Hebrew Bible, the captivity in Babylon is presented as a punishment for idolatry and disobedience to **Yahweh** in a similar way to the presentation of Israelite slavery in Egypt followed by deliverance. The **Babylonian Captivity** had a number of serious effects on Judaism and Jewish culture. For example, the current Hebrew alphabet was adopted during this period, replacing the **Paleo-Hebrew alphabet**. Most frequently the term "**Babylon**" meant the diaspora prior to the destruction of the **Second Temple.**

# Balfour Declaration

The **Balfour Declaration** was a public statement issued by the British government in 1917 during World War I announcing support for the establishment of a **"national home for the Jewish people"** in Palestine, then an Ottoman region with a small minority Jewish population. **It read:**

**"His Majesty's government view with favor the establishment in Palestine of a national home for the Jewish people, and will use their best endeavors to facilitate the achievement of this object, it being clearly understood that nothing shall be done which may prejudice the civil and religious rights of existing non-Jewish communities in Palestine, or the rights and political status enjoyed by Jews in any other country.** "The declaration was contained in a letter dated 2 November 1917 from the United Kingdom's Foreign Secretary **Arthur Balfour** to **Lord Rothschild,** a leader of the British Jewish community, for transmission to the Zionist Federation of Great Britain and Ireland. The text of the declaration was published in the press on 9 November 1917.

Immediately following their declaration of war on the **Ottoman Empire** in November 1914, the British War Cabinet began to consider the future of Palestine; within two months a memorandum was circulated to the Cabinet by a Zionist Cabinet member, Herbert Samuel, proposing the support of Zionist ambitions in order to enlist the support of Jews in the wider war. A Committee was established in April 1915 by British Prime Minister **H. H. Asquith** to determine their policy toward the Ottoman Empire including Palestine. Asquith, who had favored post-war reform of the Ottoman Empire, resigned in December 1916; his replacement **David Lloyd George**, favored partition of the Empire.

The first negotiations between the British and the Zionists took place at a conference on 7 February 1917 that included **Sir Mark Sykes** and the Zionist leadership. Subsequent discussions led to Balfour's request, on 19 June, that **Rothschild** and **Chaim Weizmann** submit a draft of a public declaration. Further drafts were discussed by the British Cabinet during September and October, with input from Zionist and anti-Zionist Jews but with no representation from the local population in Palestine.

By late 1917, in the lead up to the **Balfour Declaration**, the wider war had reached a stalemate, with two of Britain's allies not fully engaged: The United States had yet to suffer a casualty, and the Russians were in the midst of a revolution with **Bolsheviks** taking over the government. A stalemate in southern Palestine was broken by the **Battle of Beersheba** on 31 October 1917. The release of the final declaration was authorized on 31 October; the preceding Cabinet discussion had referenced perceived propaganda benefits amongst the worldwide Jewish community for the Allied war effort.

The opening words of the declaration represented the first public expression of support for Zionism by a major political power. The term **"national home"** had no precedent in international law, and was intentionally vague as to whether a Jewish state was contemplated. The second half of the declaration was added to satisfy opponents of the policy, who had claimed that it would otherwise prejudice the position of the local population of Palestine and encourage antisemitism worldwide by **"stamping the Jews as strangers in their native lands"**.

The declaration called for safeguarding the civil and religious rights for the Palestinian Arabs, who composed the vast majority of the local population. The British government acknowledged in 1939 that the local population's views should have been taken into account, and recognized in 2017 that the declaration should have called for protection of the **Palestinian Arabs'** political rights. The declaration had many long-lasting consequences. It is considered a principal cause of theongoing Israeli–Palestinian conflict, often described as the world's most intractable conflict.

## Background / Early British support

French influence had grown in Palestine and the wider Middle East, and its role as protector of the Catholic communities began to grow, just as Russian influence had grown as protector of the Eastern Orthodox in the same regions. This left Britain without a sphere of influence, and thus a need to find or create their own regional **"protégés"**.

These political considerations were supported by a sympathetic evangelical Christian sentiment towards the **"restoration of the Jews"** to Palestine among elements of the mid-19th-century British political elite – most notably **Lord Shaftesbury**. The British Foreign Office actively encouraged Jewish emigration to Palestine, exemplified by **Charles Henry Churchill's** 1841–1842 exhortations to **Moses Montefiore**, the leader of the British Jewish community.

## Early Zionism

Zionism arose in the late 19th century in reaction to anti-Semitic and exclusionary nationalist movements in Europe. Romantic nationalism in Central and Eastern Europe had helped to set off the **Haskalah,** or "Jewish Enlightenment". The 1881–1884 **anti-Jewish pogroms in the Russian Empire** encouraged the growth of the latter identity, resulting in the formation of the **Hovevei Zion** pioneer organizations, the publication of **Leon Pinsker's** *Auto-emancipation*, and the first major wave of Jewish immigration to Palestine – **retrospectively named the "First Aliyah"**.

In 1896, **Theodor Herzl,** a Jewish journalist living in Austria-Hungary, published the foundational text of political Zionism, *Der Judenstaat* **("The Jews' State" or "The State of the Jews"),** in which he asserted that the only solution to the **"Jewish Question"** in Europe, including growing anti-Semitism, was the establishment of a state for the Jews. A year later, Herzl founded the

**Zionist Organization,** which at its first congress called for the establishment of **"a home for the Jewish people in Palestine secured under public law".**

Herzl died in 1904, 44 years before the establishment of State of Israel, the Jewish state that he proposed, without having gained the political standing required to carry out his agenda. Zionist leader **Chaim Weizmann**, later President of the World Zionist Organization and first President of Israel, moved from Switzerland to the UK in 1904 and met **Arthur Balfour** – who had just launched his 1905–1906 election campaign after resigning as Prime Minister – in a session arranged by **Charles Dreyfus,** his Jewish constituency representative. Earlier that year, Balfour had successfully driven the **Aliens Act** through Parliament with impassioned speeches regarding the need to restrict the wave of immigration into Britain from Jews fleeing the Russian Empire.

During this meeting, he asked what Weizmann's objections had been to the 1903 **Uganda Scheme** that Herzl had supported to provide a portion of British East Africa to the Jewish people as a homeland. Weizmann responded that he believed the English are to London as the Jews are to Jerusalem.

In January 1914 Weizmann first met Baron Edmond de Rothschild, a member of the French branch of the Rothschild family and a leading proponent of the Zionist movement, in relation to a project to build a Hebrew university in Jerusalem. This connection was to bear fruit later that year when the Baron's son, James de Rothschild, requested a meeting with Weizmann on 25 November 1914, to enlist him in influencing those deemed to be receptive within the British government to their agenda of a **"Jewish State"** in Palestine.

**Ottoman Palestine**

The year 1916 marked four centuries since Palestine had become part of the Ottoman Empire, also known as the **Turkish Empire**. For most of this period, the Jewish population represented a small minority, approximately 3% of the total, with Muslims representing the largest segment of the population, and Christians the second. Ottoman government in Constantinople began to apply restrictions on Jewish immigration to Palestine in late 1882, in response to the start of the First Aliyah earlier that year. In 1901 the Sublime Porte (the Ottoman central government) gave Jews the same rights as Arabs to buy land in Palestine and the percentage of Jews in the population rose to 7% by 1914.

# World War I / 1914–16

In July 1914 war broke out in Europe between the **Triple Entente** (Britain, France, and the Russian Empire) and the Central Powers (Germany, Austria-Hungary, and, later that year, the Ottoman Empire). The British Cabinet first discussed **Zionism** at a meeting on 9 November 1914. At the meeting **David Lloyd George**, then Chancellor of the Exchequer, **"referred to the ultimate destiny of Palestine".**

Samuel circulated a memorandum entitled *The Future of Palestine* to his Cabinet colleagues. The memorandum stated: **"I am assured that the solution of the problem of Palestine which would be much the most welcome to the leaders and supporters of the Zionist movement throughout the world would be the annexation of the country to the British Empire".**

## 1915–16: *McMahon–Hussein Correspondence and Sykes–Picot Agreement*

The Cabinet document states that Palestine was included in the McMahon pledge to the Arabs, whereas the **White Paper** states that it **"has always been regarded"** as being excluded. In late 1915 the British High Commissioner to Egypt, Henry McMahon, exchanged ten letters with **Hussein bin Ali**, Sharif of Mecca, in which he promised Hussein to recognize Arab independence **"in the limits and boundaries proposed by the Sherif of Mecca"** in return for Hussein launching a revolt against the Ottoman Empire. The pledge excluded **"portions of Syria"**. In the decades after the war, the extent of this coastal exclusion was hotly disputed since Palestine lay to the southwest of Damascus and was not explicitly mentioned.

The **Arab Revolt** was launched on June 5th, 1916, on the basis of the *quid pro quo* agreement in the correspondence. However, less than three weeks earlier the governments of the United Kingdom, France, and Russia secretly concluded the **Sykes–Picot Agreement,** which Balfour described later as a **"wholly new method"** for dividing the region, after the 1915 agreement **"seems to have been forgotten".** Picot was a French diplomat and former consul-general in Beirut.

Their agreement defined the proposed spheres of influence and control in Western Asia should the **Triple Entente** succeed in defeating the Ottoman Empire during World War I, dividing many Arab territories into British- and French-administered areas. The January draft noted Christian and Muslim interests, and that **"members of the Jewish community throughout the world have a conscientious and sentimental interest in the future of the country."**

## 1916–17: Change in British Government

Lloyd George and **Balfour,** appointed as his Foreign Secretary, favoured a post-war partition of the Ottoman Empire as a major British war aim, whereas **Asquith** and his Foreign Secretary, Sir Edward Grey, had favoured its reform.

The recapture of the Sinai for British-controlled Egypt, and, with the capture of El Arish in December 1916 and Rafah in January 1917, the arrival of British forces at the southern borders of the Ottoman Empire. Following two unsuccessful attempts to capture Gaza between 26 March and 19 April, a six-month stalemate in Southern Palestine began; the Sinai and Palestine Campaign would not make any progress into Palestine until 31 October 1917.

## 1917: British-Zionist formal negotiations

Following the change in government, Sykes was promoted into the War Cabinet Secretariat with responsibility for Middle Eastern affairs. On 7 February 1917, Sykes, claiming to be acting in a private capacity, entered into substantive discussions with the Zionist leadership. The previous British correspondence with **"the Arabs"** was discussed at the meeting. At this point the Zionists were still unaware of the **Sykes-Picot Agreement**, although they had their suspicions. One of Sykes' goals was the mobilization of Zionism to the cause of British suzerainty in Palestine.

## Late 1917: Progress of the wider war

Although the United States declared war on Germany in the spring of 1917, it did not suffer its first casualties until 2 November 1917, at which point President Woodrow Wilson still hoped to avoid dispatching large contingents of troops into the war. The Russian forces were known to be distracted by the ongoing **Russian Revolution** and the growing support for the **Bolshevik** faction. Russia only withdrew after the final stage of the revolution on **7 November 1917**.

## Approvals / April to June: Allied discussions

Balfour met Weizmann at the Foreign Office on 22 March 1917; two days later, Weizmann described the meeting as being **"the first time I had a real business talk with him"**. Weizmann explained at the meeting that the Zionists had a preference for a British protectorate over Palestine, as opposed to an American, French or international arrangement; Balfour agreed, but warned that **"there may be difficulties with France and Italy"**. Prior to 1917, the British had led the fighting on the southern border of the Ottoman Empire alone, given their neighboring Egyptian colony and the French preoccupation with the fighting on the Western Front that was taking place on their own soil.

Italy's participation in the war, which began following the April 1915 Treaty of London, did not include involvement in the Middle Eastern sphere until the April 1917 **Agreement of Saint-Jean-de-Maurienne;** at this conference, Lloyd George had raised the question of a British protectorate of Palestine and the idea **"had been very coldly received"** by the French and the Italians.

Before travelling to the Middle East, Picot, via Sykes, invited Nahum Sokolow to Paris to educate the French government on Zionism. Sokolow was granted an audience with **Pope Benedict XV** on 6 May 1917. Sokolow's notes of the meeting stated that the Pope expressed general sympathy and support for the Zionist project. **"Generally speaking"** he was not opposed to the legitimate claims of the Jews.

## June and July: Decision to prepare a declaration

The Prime Minister, the Foreign Secretary, and the Parliamentary Under-Secretary of State for Foreign Affairs, Lord Robert Cecil – were all in favor of Britain supporting the Zionist movement; on the same day Weizmann had written to Graham to advocate for a public declaration.

Six days later, at a meeting on 19 June, Balfour asked Lord Rothschild and Weizmann to submit a formula for a declaration. Over the next few weeks, a 143-word draft was prepared by the Zionist negotiating committee. The Foreign Office draft was strongly opposed by the Zionists, and was discarded. Following further discussion, a revised – and at just 46 words in length, much shorter – draft declaration was prepared and sent by Lord Rothschild to Balfour on 18 July. It was received by the Foreign Office, and the matter was brought to the Cabinet for formal consideration.

## September and October: American consent and War Cabinet approval

The decision to release the declaration was taken by the **British War Cabinet on 31 October 1917**. This followed discussion at four **War Cabinet** meetings (including the 31 October meeting) over the space of the previous two months. These included the views of government ministers, war allies – notably from **President Woodrow Wilson** – and in October, formal submissions from six Zionist leaders and four non-Zionist Jews. British officials asked **President Wilson** for his consent on the matter on two occasions – first on 3 September, when he replied the time was not ripe, and later on 6 October, when he agreed with the release of the declaration.

Emir Faisal, King of Syria and Iraq, made a formal written agreement with Zionist leader **Chaim Weizmann,** which was drafted by **T.E. Lawrence**, whereby they would try to establish a peaceful relationship between Arabs and Jews in Palestine. The 3 January 1919 **Faisal–Weizmann Agreement** was a short-lived agreement for Arab–Jewish cooperation on the development of a Jewish homeland in Palestine. Faisal did treat Palestine differently in his presentation to the Peace Conference on 6 February 1919. The agreement was never implemented. In a subsequent letter **written in English by Lawrence for Faisal's signature, he explained:**

**"We feel that the Arabs and Jews are cousins in race, suffering similar oppression at the hands of powers stronger than themselves, and by a happy coincidence have been able to take the first step toward the attainment of their national ideals together. We Arabs, especially the educated among us, look with deepest sympathy on the Zionist movement...We will do our best, in so far as we are concerned, to help them through; we will wish the Jews a most hearty welcome home."**

Referring to his 1922 White Paper, Churchill later wrote that **"there is nothing in it to prohibit the ultimate establishment of a Jewish State."** And in private, many British officials agreed with the Zionists' interpretation that a state would be established when a Jewish majority was achieved. When Chaim Weizmann met with Churchill, Lloyd George and Balfour at Balfour's home in London on 21 July 1921, Lloyd George and Balfour assured Weizmann **"that by the Declaration they had always meant an eventual Jewish State,"** according to Weizmann minutes of that meeting.

## Scope of the national home "in Palestine"

The declaration did not include any geographical boundaries for Palestine. Following the end of the war, three documents – the declaration, the **Hussein-McMahon Correspondence** and the **Sykes-Picot Agreement** – became the basis for the negotiations to set the boundaries of Palestine. **Balfour Declaration as published in *the Times*, 9 November 1917**

The declaration spurred an unintended and extraordinary increase in the number of adherents of American Zionism; in 1914 the 200 American Zionist societies comprised a total of 7,500 members, which grew to 30,000 members in 600 societies in 1918 and 149,000 members in 1919.

## Opposition in Palestine

**The most popular Palestinian Arab newspaper, *Filastin (La Palestine)*, published a four-page editorial addressed to Lord Balfour in March 1925.** The local Christian and Muslim community of Palestine, who constituted almost 90% of the population, strongly opposed the declaration. **"We have noticed yesterday a large crowd of Jews carrying banners and over-running the streets shouting words which hurt the feeling and wound the soul. We Arabs, Muslim and Christian, have always sympathized profoundly with the persecuted Jews and their misfortunes in other countries... but there is wide difference between such sympathy and the acceptance of such a nation... ruling over us and disposing of our affairs".**

## Broader Arab response

Hussein **"would not accept an independent Jewish State in Palestine".** The Sykes–Picot **Agreement** was not a formal treaty. Hussein, in 1921, stated that he could not be expected to **"affix his name to a document assigning Palestine to the Zionists and Syria to foreigners."** Hussein continued in his refusal to recognize the **Balfour Declaration** or any of the Mandates that he perceived as being his domain.

### Allies and Associated Powers

The French and the Italians made clear their dislike of the **"Zionist cast of the Palestinian mandate"** and objected especially to language that did not safeguard the **"political"** rights of non-Jews, accepting claim that "in the British language all ordinary rights were included in **"civil rights".**

In 1922, Congress officially endorsed America's support for the **Balfour Declaration** through the passage of the **Lodge-Fish Resolution**, notwithstanding opposition from the State Department. Professor **Lawrence Davidson**, of West Chester University, whose research focuses on American relations with the Middle East, argues that **President Wilson** and Congress ignored democratic values in favor of **"biblical romanticism"** when they endorsed the declaration. He points to an organized pro-Zionist lobby in the United States, which was active at a time when the country's small Arab American community had little political power.

## Central Powers

The publication of the Balfour Declaration was met with tactical responses from the Central Powers. In 1922, German anti-Semitic theorist Alfred Rosenberg in his primary contribution to Nazi theory on Zionism, *Der Staatsfeindliche Zionismus* (**"Zionism, the Enemy of the State"**), accused German Zionists of working for a German defeat and supporting Britain and the implementation of the **Balfour Declaration**, in a version of the stab-in-the-back myth. Adolf Hitler took a similar approach in some of his speeches from 1920 onwards.

## The Holy See / *Pope Benedict XV and Judaism*

With the advent of the declaration and the British entry into Jerusalem on 9 December, the Vatican reversed its earlier sympathetic attitude to Zionism and adopted an oppositional stance that was to continue until the early 1990s. Following the issuance of the **Churchill White Paper** in June 1922, the **House of Lords** rejected a Palestine Mandate that incorporated the **Balfour Declaration** by 60 votes to 25, following a motion issued by Lord Islington.

## Historiography

**Lloyd George and Balfour remained in government until the collapse of the coalition in October 1922.** The authors of the declaration were Balfour, Sykes, Weizmann, and Sokolow. Following the 1936 general strike that was to degenerate into the 1936–1939 **Arab Revolt** in Palestine, the most significant outbreak of violence since the Mandate began, a **British Royal Commission** was appointed to investigate the causes of the unrest. Completed its 404-page report after six months of work in June 1937, publishing it a month later. American Zionism was still in its infancy; in 1914 the **Zionist Federation** had a small budget of about $5,000 and only 12,000 members, despite an American Jewish population of three million.

## Long-term impact

The declaration had two indirect consequences, the emergence of a Jewish state and a chronic state of conflict between Arabs and Jews throughout the Middle East. It has been described as the **"original sin"** with respect to both Britain's failure in Palestine and for wider events in Palestine.

Starting in 1920, intercommunal conflict in **Mandatory Palestine** broke out, which widened into the regional Arab–Israeli conflict, often referred to as the world's **"most intractable conflict"**. The **"dual obligation"** to the two communities quickly proved to be untenable; the British subsequently concluded that it was impossible for them to pacify the two communities in Palestine by using different messages for different audiences.

Following the 1936–1939 Arab revolt in Palestine, and as worldwide tensions rose in the buildup to World War II, the British Parliament approved the **White Paper of 1939** – their last formal statement of governing policy in **Mandatory Palestine** – declaring that Palestine should not become a Jewish State and placing restrictions on Jewish immigration. Whilst the British considered this consistent with the **Balfour Declaration's** commitment to protect the rights of non-Jews, many Zionists saw it as a repudiation of the declaration.  This policy lasted until the British surrendered the Mandate in 1948.

# Banu Nadir Jewish tribe

The **Banu Nadir** were a Jewish tribe who lived in northern Arabia until the 7th century at the oasis of Medina. The tribe challenged **Muhammad** as the leader of Medina, planned along with allied nomads to attack **Muhammad** and were expelled from Medina as a result. The **Banu Nadir** then planned the **battle of the Trench** together with the **Quraysh**. They later participated in the **battle of Kaybar.**

## Early history

In early Medina, in addition to the **Banu Nadir,** there were two other major Jewish tribes: the **Banu Qurayza** and the **Banu Qaynuqa**. They were joined earlier by two non-Jewish Arab tribes from Yemen, **Banu Aus and Khazraj**. Like other Medinese Jews, **Banu Nadir** bore Arabic names, but spoke a distinct dialect of Arabic. They earned their living through agriculture, money lending, and trade in weapons and jewels, maintaining commercial relations with Arab merchants of Mecca. Their fortresses were located half a day's march to the south of Medina. **Banu Nadir** were wealthy and lived in some of the best lands in Medina.

## Tribal warfare

When the two Arabian tribes of **Aws** and **Khazraj** went to war against each other in the **Battle of Bu'ath** in 617, the three Jewish tribes split on different sides of the war. The **Banu Nadir**, led by **Ka'ab ibn al-Ashraf and Huyayy ibn Akhtab**, and the **Banu Qurayza** fought with the **Aus,** while the **Banu Qaynuqa** were allied with the tribe of **Khazraj**. The latter were defeated after a long and arduous battle.

## Arrival of Muhammad

**Muhammad** was invited to Medina to broker a peace between the warring tribes, and in **September 622** he arrived with a group of his followers, who were given shelter by members of the indigenous community known as the **Ansar**. Amongst his first actions were the construction of the first mosque in Medina, as well as obtaining residence with **Abu Ayyub al-Ansari**. He then set about the establishment of a pact, known as the **Constitution of Medina**, between the Muslims, the **Ansar,** and the various Jewish tribes of Medina to regulate the matters of governance of the city, as well as the extent and nature of inter-community relations. The conditions of the pact included boycotting **Quraysh**, abstinence from **"extending any support to them"**, assistance of one another if attacked by a third party, as well as *"defending Medina, in case of a foreign attack"*.

## Reaction to the expulsion of the Banu Qaynuqa

When **Muhammad** expelled the Jewish tribe of the **Banu Qaynuqa**, the **Banu Nadir** did not get involved, viewing the conflict as another example of tribal struggle. The conflict led to a ruling that such future action by any of the other parties under the **Constitution of Medina** would constitute a voiding of their benefits under the system.

## Assassination of Ka'ab ibn al-Ashraf

After the **Battle of Badr**, one of the **Banu Nadir's chiefs Ka'ab ibn al-Ashraf**, went to the **Quraysh** in order to lament the loss at **Badr** and to incite them to take up arms to regain lost honor. This was in contravention of the Constitution of Medina, of which the tribe led by **Ka'ab ibn al-Ashraf** was a signatory, which prohibited them from "**extending any support**" to the tribes of Mecca, namely **Quraysh**. Some sources suggest that during his visit to Mecca, **Ka'ab concluded a treaty with Abu Sufyan,** stipulating cooperation between the **Quraysh** and Jews against **Muhammad**.

Other historians cite that **Ka'ab ibn al-Ashraf,** who was also a gifted poet, wrote a poetic eulogy commemorating the slain **Quraysh** notables; later, he also wrote erotic poetry about Muslim women, which the Muslims found offensive. This poetry influenced so many that this too was considered directly against the **Constitution of Medina, a** *crime* **Muhammad called upon his followers to kill Ka'ab**.

**Muhammad ibn Maslamah** offered his services, collecting four others. **Muhammad ibn Maslamah** and the others enticed **Ka'ab** out of his fortress on a moonlit night, and killed him in spite of his vigorous resistance. The Jews were terrified at his assassination, and as the historian **ibn Ishaq** put it "**...there was not a Jew who did not fear for his life**".

## Expulsion from Medina

After defeat by the **Quraysh** at the **Mount Uhud** in March, 625, the **Banu Nadir** challenged **Muhammad** as the leader of Medina. In July of the same year, two men were killed during skirmish in which the Muslims were involved. As a result, **Muhammad** went to the **Nadir**, asking them to make a contribution towards the **blood money** of two men killed. Initially most of the **Nadir**, except **Huyayy ibn Akhtab**, were inclined to accept **Muhammad**'s request. The **Nadir**, then postponed the contribution until later that day.

**Muhammad** left the locality immediately accusing the **Banu Nadir** of plotting to assassinate him. According to other sources, the **Banu Nadir** invited **Muhammad** to their habitations for a religious debate, to which **Muhammad** accepted. **Muhammad** also accepted the condition that he bring no more than three men with him. On his way he was notified by a **Banu Nadir** convert to Islam of an assassination attempt at the debate.

**Muhammad** besieged the **Banu Nadir**. He ordered them to surrender their property and leave Medina within ten days. The tribe at first decided to comply, but "**certain people of Medina who were not Believers of Muhammad sent a message to the Banu al-Nadir, saying, 'Hold out,**

and defend yourselves; we shall not surrender you to Muhammad. If you are attacked we shall fight with you and if you are sent away we shall go with you."

**Huyayy ibn Akhtab decided to put up resistance**, hoping also for help from the **Banu Qurayza**, despite opposition within the tribe. The **Nadir** were forced to surrender after the siege had lasted for 14 days, when the promised help failed to materialize and when **Muhammad** ordered the burning and felling of their palm-trees. Under the conditions of surrender, the **Banu Nadir could only take with them what they could carry on camels with the exception of weapons.**

Most of **Banu Nadir** found refuge among the Jews of **Kaybar**, while others immigrated to Syria. According to **Ibn Ishaq**, the chiefs of **Nadir** who went to **Kaybar** were **Sallam b. Abu'l-Huqayq, Kenana ibn al-Rabi and Huyayy b. Akhtab.** When these chiefs arrived in **Kaybar**, the Jewish inhabitants of **Kaybar** became subject to them.

**Muhammad** divided their land between his companions who had emigrated with him from Mecca. Until then, the emigrants had to rely upon the Medinese sympathizers for financial assistance. **Muhammad reserved a share of the seized land for himself**, which also made him financially independent. Upon expulsion of the **Banu Nadir**, **Muhammad** is said to have received a revelation of the **Surah al-Hashr.**

## *Battle of the Trench: 627*

A number of Jews who had formed a party against **Muhammad**, including **Sallam b. Abu'l-Huqayq, Kenana ibn al-Rabi and Huyayy b. Akhtab**, the chiefs of **Nadir** who had gone to **Kaybar**, together with two chiefs from the **tribe of B. Wa 'ili** went to **Quraysh** and invited them to form a coalition against **Muhammad** so that they might get rid of him altogether. Then they persuaded the tribe of **Ghaftan** to join the battle against **Muhammad**.

**Banu Nadir** promised half the date harvest of **Kaybar** to nomadic tribes if they would join the battle against Muslims. **Abu Sufyan**, the military leader of **Quraysh**, with the financial help of **Banu Nadir** had mustered a force of size 10,000 men. **Muhammad** was able to prepare a force of about 3000 men.

Muslims had dug a trench wherever Medina lay open to cavalry attack. The idea is credited to a **Persian convert to Islam, Salman the Persian**. The siege of Medina began on March 31, 627 and lasted for two weeks. **Abu Sufyan's** troops were unprepared for the fortifications they were confronted with, and after an ineffectual siege lasting several weeks, the coalition decided to go home. The Qur'an discusses this battle in verses **Qur'an 33:9-33:27**.

## Battle of Kaybar: 628

**In 628, Muhammad attacked Kaybar**. Later, **Muhammad** sent a delegation under **Abdullah bin Rawaha** to ask another chief of the **Banu Nadir, Usayr (Yusayr) ibn Zarim**, to come to Medina along with other **Nadir** leaders to discuss the two groups' political relations. Among whom were **Abdullah bin Unays**, an ally of **Banu Salima**, a clan hostile to the Jews.

When they came to him they spoke to him and treated him saying that if he would come to **Muhammad** he would give him an appointment and honor him. They kept on at him until he went with them with a number of Jews. **Abdullah bin Unays** mounted him on his beast until when he was in **al-Qarqara**, about six miles from **Kaybar**, **al-Yusayr** changed his mind about going with them.

**Abdullah** perceived his intention as he was preparing to draw his sword so he rushed at him and struck him with his sword cutting off his leg. **Al-Yusayr** hit him with a stick of **shauhat wood** which he had in his hand and wounded his head. All **Muhammad**'s emissaries fell upon the thirty Jewish companions and killed them except one man who escaped on his feet.

**Abdullah bin Unays** is the assassin who volunteered and got permission to **kill Banu Nadir's Sallam ibn Abu al-Huqayq** at a previous night mission in **Kaybar**.

**Muhammad** and his followers attacked **Kaybar** in May/June 628 after the **Treaty of Hudaybiyyah**. Although the Jews put up fierce resistance, the lack of central command and preparation for an extended siege sealed the outcome of the battle in favor of the Muslims. When all but two fortresses were captured, the Jews negotiated their surrender. The terms required them to hand over one-half of the annual produce to the Muslims, while the land itself became the collective property of the Muslim state.

# Banu Qaynuqa Jewish Tribe

The **Banu Qaynuqa** was one of the three main Jewish tribes living in the 7th century of **Medina**, now in Saudi Arabia. In 624, the great-grandfather of **Banu Qaynuqa** tribe is **Qaynuqa** ibn Amchel ibn Munshi ibn Yohanan ibn Benjamin ibn Saron ibn Naphtali ibn Hayy ibn Moses and they are descendant of Manasseh ibn Joseph ibn Jacob ibn Isaac son of Abraham. They were expelled during the Invasion of **Banu Qaynuqa**, after breaking the treaty known as the **Constitution of Medina.**

## Background

In the 7th century, the **Banu Qaynuqa** were living in two fortresses in the south-western part of the city of **Yathrib**, now **Medina**, having settled there at an unknown date. Although the **Banu Qaynuqa** bore mostly Arabic names, they were both ethnically and religiously Jewish. They owned no land, earned their living through commerce and craftsmanship, including goldsmithery. The marketplace of **Yathrib** was located in the area of the town where the **Qaynuqa** lived. The **Banu Qaynuqa** were allied with the local Arab tribe of **Kazraj** and supported them in their conflicts with the rival Arab tribe of **Aws.**

## Arrival of Muhammad

In September 622, **Muhammad** arrived at **Yathrib** now called as **Medina** with a group of his followers, who were given shelter by members of all indigenous tribes of the city who came to be known as the **Ansar**. He proceeded to set about the establishment of a pact, known as the **Constitution of Medina**, between the Muslims, the **Ansar**, and the various Jewish tribes of **Yathrib** to regulate the matters of governance of the city, as well as the extent and nature of inter-community relations. Conditions of the pact, according to traditional Muslim sources, included boycotting the **Quraysh**, abstinence from **"extending any support to them"**, assistance of one another if attacked by a third party, as well as **"defending Medina, in case of a foreign attack"**. The nature of this document as recorded by **Ibn Ishaq** and transmitted by **Ibn Hisham** is the subject of dispute among modern historians many of whom maintain that this **"treaty"** is possibly a collage of agreements, oral rather than written, of different dates, and that it is not clear when they were made or with whom.

## Expulsion: *Invasion of Banu Qaynuqa*

In March 624, Muslims led by **Muhammad** defeated the Meccans of the **Banu Quraysh** tribe in the **Battle of Badr**. **Ibn Ishaq** writes that a dispute broke out between the Muslims and the **Banu Qaynuqa** (the allies of the **Kazraj** tribe) soon afterwards. When a Muslim woman visited a jeweler's shop in the **Qaynuqa** marketplace, **she was molested**. The goldsmith, a Jew, pinned her clothing such that, upon getting up, she was stripped naked. A Muslim man coming upon the resulting commotion killed the shopkeeper in retaliation. A mob of Jews from the **Qaynuqa** tribe then pounced on the Muslim man and killed him. This escalated to a chain of revenge killings, and enmity grew between Muslims and the **Banu Qaynuqa**.

Traditional Muslim sources view these episodes as a violation of the **Constitution of Medina**. **Muhammad** himself regarded this as *casus belli*. Western historians, however, do not find in these events the underlying reason for **Muhammad's** attack on the **Qaynuqa**. The precise circumstances of the alleged violation of the **Constitution of Medina** are not specified in the sources. Available sources do not elucidate the reasons for the expulsion of the **Qaynuqa**. **Muhammad** turned against the **Qaynuqa** because as artisans and traders, the latter were in close contact with Meccan merchants.

The Jews had assumed a contentious attitude towards **Muhammad** and as a group possessing substantial independent power, they posed a great danger. **Muhammad** strengthened by the victory at **Badr,** soon resolved to eliminate the Jewish opposition to himself. **Muhammad** decided to move against the Jews of **Medina** after being strengthened in the wake of the **Battle of Badr. Muhammad** then approached the **Banu Qaynuqa**, gathering them in the market place and addressing them as follows,

" *O Jews, beware lest God bring on you the like of the retribution which he brought on Quraysh. Accept Islam, for you know that I am a prophet sent by God. You will find this in your scriptures and in God's covenant with you.*"

**To which the tribe replied,**

" *Muhammad, do you think that we are like your people? Do not be deluded by the fact that you met a people with no knowledge of war and that you made good use of your opportunity. By God, if you fight us you will know that we are real men!*"

This response was a declaration of war. According to the Muslim tradition, the verses **3:10-13 of the Qur'an** were revealed to **Muhammad** following the exchange. **Muhammad** then besieged the **Banu Qaynuqa** for fourteen or fifteen days, according to **ibn Hisham**, after which **the tribe surrendered unconditionally**. It was certain, that there were some sort of negotiations. At the time of the siege, the **Qaynuqa had a fighting force of 700 men, 400 of whom were armored.** **Muhammad** could not have besieged such a large force so successfully without **Qaynuqa's** allies' support. After the surrender of **Banu Qaynuqa, Abdullah ibn Ubayy,** the chief of a section of the clan of **Khazraj** pleaded for them. **According to Ibn Ishaq:**

**Abd-Allah ibn Ubayy** was attempting to stop the expulsion, and **Muhammad's** insistence was that the **Qaynuqa** must leave the city, but was prepared to be lenient about other conditions; **Ibn Ubayy** argument was that presence of **Qaynuqa** with 700 fighting men can be helpful in the view of the expected Meccan onslaught. Because of this interference and other episodes of his discord with **Muhammad, Abdullah ibn Ubayy** earned for himself the title of the leader of hypocrites (*munafiqun*) in the Muslim tradition.

## Aftermath: *Invasion of Banu Qaynuqa*

The **Banu Qaynuqa** left first for the Jewish colonies in the **Wadi al-Kura**, north of **Medina**, and from there to **Der'a** in Syria, west of **Salkhad.** In the course of time, they assimilated with the Jewish communities, pre-existing in that area, strengthening them numerically.

**Muhammad divided the property of the Banu Qaynuqa, including their arms and tools, among his followers, taking for the Islamic state a fifth share of the spoils for the first time.** Some members of the tribe chose to stay in **Medina** and convert to Islam.

One man from the **Banu Qaynuqa, Abdullah ibn Salam, became a devout Muslim**. Although some Muslim sources claim that he converted immediately after **Muhammad**'s arrival to **Medina**, modern scholars give more credence to the other Muslim sources, which indicate that 8 years later, 630, as the year of **ibn Salam's** conversion.

# Banu Qurayza Jewish Tribe

The **Banu Qurayza** (**Quraiza, Qurayzah, Quraytha,** and **Koreiza**) were a Jewish tribe which lived in northern Arabia, at the oasis of **Yathrib** (now known as **Medina**), until the 7th century, when their conflict with **Muhammad** led to their extermination. Jewish tribes reportedly arrived in **Hijaz** in the wake of the Jewish-Roman wars. However, in the 5th century, the **Banu Aws** and the **Banu Khazraj**, two Arab tribes that had arrived from Yemen, gained dominance. When these two tribes became embroiled in conflict with each other, the Jewish tribes, now clients or allies of the **Arabs,** fought on different sides, the **Qurayza** siding with the **Aws.**

In 622, the Islamic prophet **Muhammad** arrived at **Yathrib** from **Mecca** and reportedly established a pact between the conflicting parties. While the city found itself at war with **Muhammad**'s native Meccan tribe of the **Quraysh**, tensions between the growing numbers of Muslims and the Jewish communities mounted. In 627, when the **Quraysh** and their allies besieged the city in the **Battle of the Trench**, the **Qurayza** entered into negotiations with the besiegers. Subsequently, the tribe was charged with treason and besieged by the Muslims commanded by **Muhammad**. The **Banu Qurayza** eventually surrendered and all the men, apart from a few who converted to Islam, **were beheaded, while the women and children were enslaved.**

## Early history

Just like the other Jews of **Yathrib**, the **Qurayza** claimed to be of Israelite descent and observed the commandments of **Judaism**, but adopted many Arab customs and intermarried with Arabs. They were dubbed the **"priestly tribe"** (*kahinan* in Arabic from the Hebrew **kohanim**). In the 5th century CE, the **Qurayza** lived in **Yathrib** together with two other major Jewish tribes: **Banu Qaynuqa and Banu Nadir** . Jews arrived in **Hijaz** in the wake of the **Jewish-Roman wars;** the **Qurayza** settled in Mahzur, a Wadi in Al Harrah.

The Jews introduced agriculture to **Yathrib**, growing date palms and cereals, and this cultural and economic advantage enabled the Jews to dominate the local Arabs politically. **Al-Waqidi** wrote that the **Banu Qurayza** were people of high lineage and of properties, **"whereas we were but an Arab tribe who did not possess any palm trees nor vineyards, being people of only sheep and camels."**

## Account of the king of Himyar

**Ibn Ishaq** tells of a conflict between the last **Yemenite King of Himyar** and the residents of **Yathrib**. When the king was passing by the oasis, the residents killed his son, and the Yemenite ruler threatened to exterminate the people and cut down the palms. According to **Ibn Ishaq**, he was stopped from doing so by two rabbis from the **Banu Qurayza**, who implored the king to spare the oasis because it was the place **"to which a prophet of the Quraysh would migrate in time**

to come, and it would be his home and resting-place". The Yemenite king thus did not destroy the town and **converted to Judaism**.

He took the rabbis with him, and in Mecca, they reportedly recognized the **Ka'aba** as a temple built by Abraham and advised the king **"to do what the people of Mecca did: to circumambulate the temple, to venerate and honor it, to shave his head and to behave with all humility until he had left its precincts."**

## Arrival of the Aws and Khazraj

The situation changed after two Arab tribes named **Banu Aws** and **Banu Khazraj** arrived to **Yathrib** from Yemen. At first, these tribes were clients of the Jews, but toward the end of the **5th century CE**, they revolted and became independent. Most modern historians accept the claim of the Muslim sources that after the revolt, the Jewish tribes became clients of the **Aws** and the **Khazraj**.

Eventually, the **Aws** and the **Khazraj** became hostile to each other. They had been fighting possibly for around a hundred years before 620 and at least since 570s. The **Banu Nadir** and the **Banu Qurayza** were allied with the **Aws**, while the **Banu Qaynuqa** sided with the **Khazraj**. There are reports of the constant conflict between **Banu Qurayza** and **Banu Nadir**, the two allies of **Aws**, yet the sources often refer to these two tribes as **"brothers"**. **Aws** and **Khazraj** and their Jewish allies fought a total of four wars. The last and bloodiest altercation was the **Battle of Bu'ath**.

The **Qurayza** appear as a tribe of considerable military importance: they possessed large numbers of weaponry, as upon their surrender 1,500 swords, 2,000 lances, 300 suits of armor, and 500 shields were later seized by the Muslims. The **Qurayza** were addressed as *Ahlu al-halqa* ("people of the weapons") by the **Quraysh** and that these weapons **"strengthened their position and prestige in the tribal society"**.

## Muhammad's *Migration to Medina*

The continuing feud between the **Aws** and the **Khazraj** was probably the chief cause for several emissaries to invite **Muhammad** to **Yathrib** in order to adjudicate in disputed cases. After his arrival in 622, **Muhammad** established a compact, the **Constitution of Medina**, which committed the Jewish and Muslim tribes to mutual cooperation. The nature of this document as recorded by **Ibn Ishaq** and transmitted by **Ibn Hisham** is the subject of dispute among modern historians, many of whom maintain that this **"treaty"** is possibly a collage of agreements, of different dates, and that it is not clear when they were made.

Aside from the general agreements, the chronicles by **Ibn Ishaq** and **al-Waqidi** contain a report that after his arrival, **Muhammad** signed a special treaty with the **Qurayza** chief **Ka'ab ibn**

**Assad. Ibn Ishaq** gives no sources, while **al-Waqidi** refers to **Ka'b ibn Malik of Salima**, a clan hostile to the Jews, and **Mummad ibn Ka'b**, the son of a **Qurayza** boy who was sold into slavery in the aftermath of the siege and subsequently became a Muslim. The Jews knew **"of the penalty for breaking faith with Muhammad"**.

The Jews were bound by the aforementioned general agreement and by their alliance to the two Arab tribes not to support an enemy against **Muhammad**. The **Qurayza** were aware of the two parts of a pact made between **Muhammad** and the Jewish tribes in the confederation according to which **"Jews having their religion and the Muslims having their religion excepting anyone who acts wrongfully and commits crime/acts treacherously/breaks an agreement, for he but slays himself and the people of his house."**

During the first few months after **Muhammad**'s arrival in **Medina**, the **Banu Qurayza** were involved in a dispute with the **Banu Nadir**: The more powerful **Nadir** rigorously applied **Lex Talionis** against the **Qurayza** while not allowing it being enforced against themselves. Further, the blood money paid for killing a man of the **Qurayza** was only half of the blood-money required for killing a man of the **Nadir**, placing the **Qurayza** in a socially inferior position.

The **Qurayza** called on **Muhammad** as arbitrator, who delivered the **surah 5:42-45** and judged that the **Nadir** and **Qurayza** should be treated alike in the application of **Lex Talionis** and raised the assessment of the **Qurayza** to the full amount of blood money.

Tensions quickly mounted between the growing numbers of Muslims and Jewish tribes, while **Muhammad** found himself at war with his native Meccan tribe of the **Quraysh**. In 624, after his victory over the Meccans in the **Battle of Badr**, **Banu Qaynuqa** threatened **Muhammad**'s political position and assaulted a Muslim woman which led to their expulsion from **Medina** for breaking the peace treaty of **Constitution of Medina**. The **Qurayza** remained passive during the whole **Qaynuqa** affair.

Soon afterwards, **Muhammad** came into conflict with the **Banu Nadir**. He had one of the **Banu Nadir** 's chiefs, the **poet Ka'ab ibn al-Ashraf**, assassinated and after the **Battle of Uhud** accused the tribe of treachery and plotting against his life and expelled them from the city. The **Qurayza** remained passive during this conflict, because of the **blood money** issue related above.

## Battle of the Trench

In 627, the Meccans, accompanied by tribal allies as well as the **Banu Nadir** - who had been very active in supporting the Meccans - marched against **Medina** - the Muslim stronghold - and laid siege to it. It is unclear whether their treaty with **Muhammad obliged the Qurayza to help him defend Medina,** or merely to remain neutral, according to **Ramadan**, they had signed an agreement of mutual assistance with **Muhammad**.

The **Qurayza** did not participate in the fighting, because they were offended by attacks against Jews in **Muhammad**'s preaching - but lent tools to the town's defenders. The **Banu Qurayza** helped the defense effort of **Medina** by supplying spades, picks, and baskets for the excavation of the defensive trench the defenders of **Medina** had dug in preparation. The **Banu Qurayza "seem to have tried to remain neutral"** in the battle but later changed their attitude when a Jew from **Khaybar** persuaded them that **Muhammad** was sure to be overwhelmed and though they did not commit any act overtly hostile to **Muhammad**, they entered into negotiations with the invading army.

During the siege, the **Qurayza** readmitted **Huyayy ibn Akhtab**, the chief of the **Banu Nadir** whom **Muhammad** had exiled and who had instigated the alliance of his tribe with the besieging **Quraysh** and **Ghatafan** tribes. **Akhtab** persuaded the **Qurayza** chief **Ka'ab ibn Assad** to help the Meccans conquer **Medina**. **Ka'ab** was, account, initially reluctant to break the contract and argued that **Muhammad** never broke any contract with them or exposed them to any shame, but decided to support the Meccans after **Huyayy** had promised to join the **Qurayza** in **Medina** if the besieging army would return to Mecca without having killed **Muhammad**. **Huyayy tore into pieces the agreement between Ka'ab and Muhammad.**

Rumors of this one-sided renunciation of the pact spread and were confirmed by **Muhammad**'s emissaries, **Sa'd ibn Mua'dh** and **Sa'd ibn Ubadah**, leading men of the **Aws** and **Khazraj** respectively. **Sa'ad ibn Mua'dh** reportedly issued threats against the **Qurayza** but was restrained by his colleague. As this would have allowed the besiegers to access the city and thus meant the collapse of the defenders' strategy, **Muhammad** became anxious about their conduct and sent some of the leading Muslims to talk to them; the result was disquieting.

"**Muhammad** sent **Nuaym ibn Masud**, a well-respected elder of the **Ghatafan** who had secretly converted to Islam, to go to **Muhammad**'s enemies and sow discord among them. **Nuaym** went to the **Qurayza** and advised them to join the hostilities against **Muhammad** only if the besiegers provide hostages from among their chiefs. He then hurried to the invaders and warned them that if the **Qurayza** asked for hostages, it is because they intended to turn them over to the **Medina**n defenders.

When the representatives of the **Quraysh** and the **Ghatafan** came to the **Qurayza**, asking for support in the planned decisive battle with **Muhammad**, the **Qurayza** indeed demanded hostages. The representatives of the besiegers refused, breaking down negotiations and resulting in the **Banu Qurayza** becoming extremely distrustful of the besieging army. The **Qurayza** did not take any actions to support them until the besieging forces retreated. Thus the threat of a second front against the defenders never materialized.

## Siege and surrender

After the Meccans' withdrawal, **Muhammad** then led his forces against the **Banu Qurayza** neighborhood. He had been asked to do so by the angel **Gabriel**. The **Banu Qurayza** retreated into their stronghold and endured the siege for 25 days. As their morale waned, **Ka'ab ibn Assad** suggested three alternative ways out of their predicament: **embrace Islam; kill their own children and women, then rush out for a charge to either win or die; or make a surprise attack on the Sabbath**. The **Banu Qurayza accepted none of these alternatives**. Instead they asked to confer with **Abu Lubaba**, one of their allies from the **Aws**.

**Abu Lubaba** felt pity for the women and children of the tribe who were crying and when asked whether the **Qurayza** should surrender to **Muhammad**, advised them to do so. However he also **"made a sign with his hand toward his throat, indicating that at the hands of the Prophet would be slaughter"**. The next morning, the **Banu Qurayza** surrendered and the Muslims seized their stronghold and their stores. **The men - number between 400 and 900 - were bound and placed under the custody of one Muhammad ibn Maslamah, who had killed Ka'ab ibn al-Ashraf, while the women and children - numbering about 1,000 - were placed under Abdullah ibn Sallam, a former rabbi who had converted to Islam.**

## Demise of the Banu Qurayza

The circumstances of the **Qurayza**'s demise has been related by **Ibn Ishaq** and other Muslim historians who relied upon his account. The **Qurayza** surrendered to **Muhammad**'s judgement - a move was classifies as unconditional. The **Aws**, who wanted to honor their old alliance with the **Qurayza**, asked **Muhammad** to treat the **Qurayza** leniently as he had previously treated the **Qaynuqa** for the sake of **Ibn Ubayy**.

**Muhammad** then suggested to bring the case before an arbitrator chosen from the **Aws**, to which both the **Aws** and the **Qurayza** agreed to. **Muhammad** then appointed **Sa'ad ibn Mua'dh** to decide the fate of the Jewish tribe. The tribe agreed to surrender on the condition of a Muslim arbitrator of their choosing. According to **Khadduri** (also cited by **Abu-Nimer**), **"both parties agreed to submit their dispute to a person chosen by them"** in accordance with the Arabian tradition of arbitration. The **Qurayza** surrendered on the condition that **"their fate was decided by their allies, the Bani Aws"**.

During the **Battle of the Trench**, he had been one of **Muhammad**'s emissaries to the **Qurayza** and now was dying from a wound he had received later in the battle. When **Sa'ad** arrived, his fellow **Aws** pleaded for leniency towards the **Qurayza** and on his request pledged that they would abide by his decision. He then decreed that **"the men should be killed, the property divided, and the women and children taken as captives"**. **Muhammad** approved of the ruling, calling it **similar to God's judgment**.

67

Sa'ad dismissed the pleas of the **Aws**, because being close to death and concerned with his afterlife, he put what he considered **"his duty to God and the Muslim community"** before tribal allegiance. **Muhammad** deviated from his earlier, more lenient treatment of prisoners as this was seen **"as sign of weakness if not madness"**, the Muslims wanted to deter future treachery by setting an example with severe punishment.

Sa'ad feared that if expelled, the **Qurayza** would join the **Nadir** in the fight against the Muslims. **Muhammad** chose Sa'd so as not to pronounce the judgment himself, after the precedents he had set with the **Banu Qaynuqa** and the **Banu Nadir**: **"Sa`ad took the hint and condemned the adult males to death and the hapless women and children to slavery."**

## Ibn Ishaq describes the killing of the Banu Qurayza men as follows:

**"Then they surrendered, and the apostle confined them in Medina in the quarter of d. al-Harith, a woman of B. al-Najjar. Then the apostle went out to the market of Medina and dug trenches in it. Then he sent for them and struck off their heads in those trenches as they were brought out to him in batches. Among them was the enemy of Allah Huyayy b. Akhtab and Ka`b b. Assad their chief. There were 600 or 700 in all, though some put the figure as high as 800 or 900."**

**Huyayy** was brought out wearing a flowered robe in which he had made holes about the size of the finger-tips in every part so that it should not be taken from him as spoil, with his hands bound to his neck by a rope.

When he saw the apostle he said, **"By God, I do not blame myself for opposing you, but he who forsakes God will be forsaken."** Then he went to the men and said, **"God's command is right. A book and a decree, and massacre have been written against the Sons of Israel."** Then he sat down and his head was struck off.

Several accounts note **Muhammad**'s companions as executioners, **Ali** and **Al-Zubayr** in particular, and that each clan of the **Aws** was also charged with killing a group of **Qurayza** men. This was done in order to avoid the risk of further conflicts between **Muhammad** and the **Aws**. **Muhammad** wanted to distance himself from the events and, had he been involved, he would have risked alienating some of the **Aws**. It is also reported that one woman, who had thrown a millstone from the battlements during the siege and killed one of the Muslim besiegers, was also beheaded along with the men.

The spoils of battle, including the enslaved women and children of the tribe, were divided up among the Islamic warriors that had participated in the siege and among the emigrees from Mecca. **Mohammad collected one-fifth of the booty, which was then redistributed to the Muslims in need, as was customary.** As part of his share of the spoils, **Muhammad** selected one of the women, **Rayhana**, for himself and took her as part of his booty. **Muhammad** offered to free and marry her and she accepted his proposal. **She is said to have later become a Muslim.** Some of the women and children of the **Banu Qurayza** who were enslaved by the Muslims were later bought by Jews, in particular the **Banu Nadir**.

## Analysis

Muslim jurists have looked upon **Surah 8:55-58** as a justification of the treatment of the **Banu Qurayza**, arguing that the **Qurayza** broke their pact with **Muhammad**, and thus **Muhammad** was justified in repudiating his side of the pact and killing the **Qurayza** en masse. In the 8th and early 9th century many Muslim jurists, such as **Ash-Shafii,** based their judgments and decrees supporting collective punishment for treachery on the accounts of the demise of the **Qurayza**, with which they were well acquainted.

The **Banu Qurayza** were killed not because of their faith but for **"treasonable activities against the Medinan community"**. **"no important clan of Jews was left in Medina".** Prior to Islam, the annihilation of an adversary was never an aim of war.

# Bar Kokhba Revolt

The **Bar Kokhba** revolt 132-136 CE; (Hebrew: **bar kokhba**) against the **Roman Empire**, was the third major rebellion by the Jews of **Judaea Province** being the last of the **Jewish-Roman Wars**. **Simon bar Kokhba**, the commander of the revolt, was acclaimed as a **Messiah**, a heroic figure who could restore Israel. The revolt established an independent state of Israel over parts of Judea for over two years, but a Roman army made up of six full legions with auxiliaries and elements from up to six additional legions finally crushed it.

The Romans then **barred Jews from Jerusalem, except to attend Tisha B'Av**. Although Jewish Christians hailed **Jesus as the Messiah** and did not support **Bar Kokhba**, they were barred from Jerusalem along with the rest of the Jews. The rebellion is also known as **The Third Jewish-Roman War or The Third Jewish Revolt,** though some historians relate it as **Second Jewish Revolt,** not counting the **Kitos War,** 115-117 CE.

**Background**

After the failed **Great Jewish Revolt in 70 CE**, the Roman authorities took measures to suppress the rebellious province of Iudaea. Instead of a procurator, they installed a praetor as a governor and stationed an entire legion, the **X Fretensis**. Because the **Great Revolt of 70 CE** had resulted in the destruction of Jerusalem, the **Council at Yavne** provided spiritual guidance for the Jewish nation, both in Judea and throughout the **Jewish Diaspora**. The tensions continued to build up in the consequence of the **Kitos War**, the second large-scale Jewish insurrection in the Eastern Mediterranean, which final stages were fought in Judaea.

Multiple reasons have been offered for the beginning of the **Bar Kokhba** revolt. One interpretation is that in 130 CE, **Emperor Hadrain** visited the ruins of the temple. At first sympathetic towards the Jews, **Hadrain** promised to rebuild the temple, but the Jews felt betrayed when they found out that his intentions were to build a temple dedicated to **Jupiter** upon the ruins of the **Second Temple**.

An additional legion, the **VI Ferrata**, was stationed in the province to maintain order, and the works commenced in 131 CE after the governor of Judaea **Tineius Rufus** performed the foundation ceremony of **Aelia Capitolina**, the city's projected new name. **"Ploughing up the Temple"** was a religious offence that turned many Jews against the Roman authorities.

The tensions grew higher when **Hadrain** abolished circumcision (**brit milah**), which he, a Hellenist, viewed as mutilation. Subsequently, it is known that a Roman coin inscribed **Aelia Capitolina** was issued in 132, right with the revolt beginnings.

## Revolt

The Jewish sage **Rabbi Akiva** (alternatively Akiba) indulged the possibility that **Simon Bar Kosiba (Bar Kokhba)** could be the Jewish **Messiah**, and gave him the surname "**Bar Kokhba**" meaning **"son of a star"** in the Aramaic language, from the **Star Prophecy** verse from **Numbers 24:17: "There shall come a star out of Jacob".**

At this time, Jewish Christians were still a minor sect of Judaism, and most historians believe that it was this messianic claim in favor of **Bar Kokhba** alienated many of them, who believed that the true **Messiah** was Jesus, and sharply deepened the schism between Jews and messianic Jews. The Jewish leaders carefully planned the second revolt to avoid numerous mistakes that had plagued the first Great Jewish Revolt sixty years earlier. In 132, a revolt led by **Bar Kokhba** quickly spread from **Modi'in** across the country, cutting off the Roman garrison in Jerusalem.

## Roman reaction

The outbreak took the Romans by surprise. **Hadrain** called his general **Sextus Julius Severus** from Britain, and troops were brought from as far as the **Danube**. The size of the Roman army amassed against the rebels was much larger than that commanded by **Titus** sixty years earlier. Roman losses were very heavy **XXII Deiotariana** was disbanded after serious losses. In addition, some argue that **Legio IX Hispana** disbandment in the mid-2nd century could also have been a result of this war.

The struggle lasted for three years before the revolt was brutally crushed in the summer of 135 CE. After losing Jerusalem, **Bar Kokhba** and the remnants of his army withdrew to the fortress of **Betar**, which also subsequently came under siege. The **Talmud** also relates that for seventeen years the Romans did not allow the Jews to bury their dead in **Betar.**

## "The Era of the redemption of Israel"

A sovereign State of Israel was restored for two and a half years that followed. The functional public administration was headed by **Simon Bar Kokhba**, who took the title **Nasi Israel** (prince [lord, president] of Israel). The **"Era of the redemption of Israel"** was announced, contracts were signed and coins were minted in large quantity in silver and copper with corresponding inscriptions (all were struck over foreign coins).

## Outcome of the war

According to **Cassius Dio, 580,000 Jews were killed, and 50 fortified towns and 985 villages razed. Cassius Dio** claimed that "**Many Romans, moreover, perished in this war. Hadrain** attempted to root out Judaism, which he saw as the cause of continuous rebellions. He prohibited the **Torah law** and the **Hebrew calendar**, and executed Judaic scholars. The sacred scroll was ceremonially burned on the **Temple Mount**. At the former Temple sanctuary, he installed two statues, one of **Jupiter**, another of himself. In an attempt to erase any memory of Judea or Ancient

Israel, he wiped the name off the map and replaced it with **Syria Palaestina** (after the Philistines, the ancient enemies of the Jews).

Similarly, he re-established Jerusalem but now as the Roman pagan polis of **Aelia Capitolina**, and Jews were forbidden from entering it, except on the day of **Tisha B'Av**. According to a **Rabbinic Midrash** (the Ten Martyrs), in addition to **Bar Kokhba** the Romans executed ten leading members of the **Sanhedrin**. The Rabbinic account describes agonizing tortures: **Rabbi Akiba** was flayed, **Rabbi Ishmael** had the skin of his head pulled off slowly, and **Rabbi Hanania** was burned at a stake, with wet wool held by a Torah scroll wrapped around his body to prolong his death.

By destroying association of Jews to Judea and forbidding the practice of Jewish faith, **Hadrain** aimed to root out a nation that engaged heavy casualties on the Empire. Yet, **Hadrain**'s death in 138 CE marked a significant relief to the surviving Jewish communities. **Rabbinic Judaism** had already become a portable religion, centered around synagogues, and the Jews themselves kept books and **dispersed throughout the Roman world and beyond**.

**Long-term consequences and historic importance**
Constantine I allowed Jews to mourn their defeat and humiliation once a year on **Tisha B'Av** at the **Western Wall**. Jews remained scattered for close to two millennia. Modern historians have come to view the **Bar-Kokhba Revolt** as being of decisive historic importance. The massive destruction and loss of life occasioned by the revolt has led some scholars to date the beginning of the **Jewish Diaspora** from this date. They note that, unlike the aftermath of the **First Jewish-Roman War** chronicled by **Josephus**, the majority of the Jewish population of Judea was either killed, exiled, or sold into slavery after the **Bar-Kokhba Revolt**, and Jewish religious and political authority was suppressed far more brutally. After the revolt the Jewish religious center shifted to the **Babylonian** Jewish community and its scholars.

Judea would not be a center of Jewish religious, cultural, or political life again until the modern era, though Jews continued to live there and important religious developments still occurred there. In Galilee, the **Jerusalem Talmud** was compiled in the 2nd 4th centuries. Eventually, Safed became known as a center of Jewish learning, especially **Kabbalah** in the 15th century.

In the centuries after Bar Kochba and **Hadrain**, some of the most significant creations of the Jewish spirit were produced in Palestine. It was there that the Mishnah was completed and the **Jerusalem Talmud** was compiled, and the bulk of the community farmed the land. In the post-rabbinical era, however, the **Bar-Kokhba Revolt** became a symbol of valiant national resistance. The Zionist youth movement **Betar** took its name from **Bar-Kokhba**'s traditional last stronghold, and **David Ben-Gurion**, Israel's first prime minister, took his Hebrew last name from one of **Bar-Kokhba**'s generals.

**Further relations between the Jews and the Roman Empire**

In 351-352 CE, the Jews launched yet another revolt, provoking once again heavy retribution. In 438 CE, when the **Empress Eudocia** removed the ban on Jews' praying at the Temple site, the heads of the Community in Galilee issued a call **"to the great and mighty people of the Jews" which began: "Know that the end of the exile of our people has come!"**

During the 5th and the 6th centuries, a series of **Samaritan** insurrections broke out across the **Palaestina Prima** province. Especially violent were the third and the fourth revolts, which resulted in almost entire annihilation of the **Samaritan** community. It is likely that the **4th Samaritan Revolt** was joined by the Jewish community, which had also suffered a brutal suppression of Israelite (Mosaic) religion.

In the belief of restoration to come, the Jews made an alliance with the **Persians** who invaded **Palaestina Prima** in 614, fought at their side, overwhelmed the Byzantine garrison in Jerusalem, and for five years governed the city. However, their autonomy was brief: with the withdrawal of Persian forces, Jews surrendered to Byzantine forces in 625 CE and were consequently massacred by them in 629 CE. The **Byzantine** (Eastern Roman Empire) control of the region was finally lost to the **Muslim Arab** armies in 637 CE, when **Umar ibn al-Khattab** completed the conquest of **Akko.**

# Bar and Bat Mitzvah

**Bar-mitzvah** is a Jewish coming of age ritual for boys. **Bat-mitzvah** is a Jewish coming of age ritual for girls. The plural is *B'Nai mitzvah* for boys, and *b'not mitzvah* (Ashkenazi pronunciation: *b'nos mitzvah*) for girls.

According to Jewish law, when a **Jewish boy is 13 years old**, he becomes accountable for his actions and becomes a **bar-mitzvah**. A girl becomes a **bat-mitzvah at the age of 12 according to Orthodox and Conservative Jews, and at the age of 13 according to Reform Jews.** Before the child reaches **bar-mitzvah** age, parents hold the responsibility for their child's actions. After this age, the boys and girls bear their own responsibility for Jewish ritual law, tradition, and ethics, and are able to participate in all areas of Jewish community life.

Traditionally, the father of the bar-**mitzvah** gives thanks to God that he is no longer punished for the child's sins. In addition to being considered accountable for their actions from a religious perspective, a **thirteen-year-old male** may be counted towards an Orthodox prayer quorum and may lead prayer and other religious services in the family and the community.

**Bar-mitzvah** is mentioned in the **Mishnah (Ethics of the Fathers, 5:21)** and in the **Talmud**. In some classic sources, the age of 13 appears for instance as the age from which **males must fast on the Day of Atonement, while females fast from the age of 12. The age of B'nai mitzvah roughly coincides with physical puberty.** The bar or bat mitzvah ceremony is usually held on the first Shabbat after a boy's thirteenth and a girl's twelfth birthday (or thirteenth in Reform congregations).

## Etymology

*Bar* **is a Jewish Babylonian Aramaic word meaning "son" while** *bat* **means "daughter" in Hebrew, and** *mitzvah* **means "commandment" or "law" (plural:** *mitzvot***). Thus** *bar-mitzvah* **and** *bat-mitzvah* **literally translate to "son of commandment" and "daughter of commandment".** However, in rabbinical usage, the word *bar* means **"under the category of"** or **"subject to".** *Bar mitzvah* therefore translates to **"who is subject to the law".** Although the term is commonly used to refer to the ritual itself, in fact, the phrase originally refers to the person.

## History

The modern method of celebrating becoming a **bar-mitzvah** did not exist in the time of the Hebrew Bible, **Mishnah** or **Talmud**. Early rabbinic sources specify 13 as the age at which a boy becomes a legal adult; however, **the celebration of this occasion is not mentioned until the Middle Ages.**

# Bereavement in Judaism

**Bereavement in Judaism** (Hebrew: *avelut*; mourning) is a combination of *Minhag* and *mitzvah* derived from Judaism's classical **Torah** and rabbinic texts. The details of observance and practice vary according to each Jewish community.

## Mourners

In Judaism, the principal mourners are the first-degree relatives: parent, child, sibling, and spouse. There are some customs that are unique to an individual mourning a parent. **Halachos** concerning mourning do not apply to those under thirteen years of age. **Also, *Halachos* of mourning do not apply when the deceased is aged 30 days or less.**

## Upon receiving news of the passing

Upon receiving the news of the passing, the following blessing is recited: Transliteration: ***Barukh atah Adonai Eloheinu Melech ha'olam, Dayan ha-Emet.*** Translation: **"Blessed are You, Lord, our God, King of the universe, the Judge of Truth."** There is also a custom of rending one's clothes at the moment one hears news of a passing. Another prevalent custom is to tear at the funeral so that the procedure is done properly.

## Terminology and timing

- **Petira** - passing
- **Shomayr** - watcher (the body should not be left alone/unwatched). **Shmira** means watching.
- **Chevra Kadisha** - burial society. Chevra kadisha
- **Kria** - tearing. Timing varies by custom. At times deferred to funeral chapel or at the cemetery. Keriah
- **Onayn** - generally the day when the news is heard; before burial. Aninut
- **Tahara** - purification (by water) of the body Preparing the body — Taharah
- **Levaya** - The funeral service. The word means escort(ing). Funeral service
- **Hesped** - Eulogy. Eulogies
- **Kvura** - burial. Burial
- **Aveil** (plural *Aveilim*) - mourner(s).
- **Aveilut** - mourning (there are different levels, based on who & timing): Mourning Avelut
- **Shiva** - seven days, from the Hebrew word for seven. Begins day of burial. Shiva
- **Shloshim** - 30 days, starting from the day of burial. Shloshim – Thirty days
- **Yud Bais Chodesh** - means 12 months, for a parent. Yud Bais means 12. Chodesh means month. Shneim Asar Chodesh – Twelve months
- **Matzevah** - means monument. Matzevah (Unveiling of the tombstone)
- **Yahrzeit** - is Yiddish for anniversary of the (Hebrew/Jewish) date of passing. Annual remembrances

- **Kaddish** - said by a mourner (or by someone else, on behalf of ...) Memorial through prayer

## Chevra Kadisha

The *chevra kadisha* ("holy society") is a Jewish burial society usually consisting of volunteers, men and women, who prepare the deceased for proper Jewish burial. Their job is to ensure that the body of the deceased is shown proper respect, ritually cleansed, and shrouded. Many local *chevra kadishas* in urban areas are affiliated with local synagogues, and they often own their own burial plots in various local cemeteries. Some Jews pay an annual token membership fee to the *chevra kadisha* of their choice, so that when the time comes, the society will not only attend to the body of the deceased as befits Jewish law, but will also ensure burial in a plot that it controls at an appropriate nearby Jewish cemetery.

If no gravediggers are available, then it is additionally the function of the male society members to ensure that graves are dug. In Israel, members of *chevra kadishas* consider it an honor to not only prepare the body for burial but also to dig the grave for a fellow Jew's body, particularly if the deceased was known to be a righteous person. Many burial societies hold one or two annual fast days and organize regular study sessions to remain up to date with the relevant articles of Jewish law. In addition, most burial societies also support families during the **Shiva** (traditional week of mourning) by arranging prayer services, preparing meals, and providing other services for the mourners.

## Preparing the body — Taharah

There are three major stages to preparing the body for burial: washing (*rechitzah*), ritual purification (*Taharah*), and dressing (*halbashah*). The term *Taharah* is used to refer both to the overall process of burial preparation, and to the specific step of ritual purification. Prayers and readings from **Torah**, including **Psalms, Song of Songs, Isaiah, Ezekiel, and Zechariah** are recited. After the closing of the casket, the *chevra* asks forgiveness of the deceased for any inadvertent lack of honor shown to the deceased in the preparation of the body for burial.

There is no viewing of the body and no open casket at the funeral. Sometimes the immediate family pay their final respects before the funeral. In Israel caskets are not used at all, with the exception of military and state funerals. Instead, the body is carried to the grave wrapped in a *tallit* and placed directly in the earth. In the **Diaspora**, in general, a casket is only used if required by local law. From death until burial, it is traditional for guards or watchers (*shomrim*) to stay with the deceased. It is traditional to recite **Psalms (*Tehillim*)** during this time.

## Funeral service

The Jewish funeral consists of a burial, also known as an interment. Cremation is forbidden. Burial is considered to allow the body to decompose naturally, therefore embalming is forbidden. Burial is intended to take place in as short an interval of time after death as possible. **Displaying of the body prior to burial does not take place.**

## *Shiva* – Seven days

The first stage of *avelut* is *Shiva* (Hebrew: **"seven"**), a week-long period of grief and mourning. Observance of *Shiva* is referred to by English-speaking Jews as **"sitting *Shiva"*.** During this period, mourners traditionally gather in one home and receive visitors.

When they get home, the mourners refrain for a week from showering or bathing, wearing leather shoes or jewelry, or shaving. In many communities, mirrors in the mourners' home are covered since they should not be concerned about their personal appearance. It is customary for the mourners to sit on low stools or even the floor, symbolic of the emotional reality of being **"brought low" by the grief**. The meal of consolation *seudat hav (ra'ah)*, the first meal eaten on returning from the funeral, traditionally consists of hard-boiled eggs and other round or oblong foods.

This is often credited to the Biblical story of **Jacob** purchasing the birthright from **Esau** with stewed lentils **(Genesis 25:34);** it is traditionally stated that Jacob was cooking the lentils soon after the death of his grandfather **Abraham**. During this seven-day period, family and friends come to visit or call on the mourners to comfort those **(*"Shiva* calls")**. It is considered a great *mitzvah* (commandment) of kindness and compassion to pay a home visit to the mourners. Traditionally, no greetings are exchanged and visitors wait for the mourners to initiate conversation. The mourner is under no obligation to engage in conversation and May, in fact, completely ignore his/her visitors.

Visitors will traditionally take on the hosting role when attending a **Shiva**, often bringing food and serving it to the mourning family and other guests. The mourning family will often avoid any cooking or cleaning during the Shiva period; those responsibilities become those of visitors.

**"The Omnipresent will comfort you (pl.) among the mourners of Zion and Jerusalem"**
Depending on their community's customs, others may also add such wishes as: **"You should have no more *tza'ar* (distress)"** or **"You should have only *simchas* (celebrations)"** or **"we should hear only *besorot tovot* (good tidings) from each other"** or **"I wish you a long life"**. Traditionally, prayer services are organized in the house of mourning. It is customary for the family to lead the services themselves.

## Mourner's Kaddish

**Kaddish Yatom** (*Heb. lit. "Orphan's Kaddish"*) or the **"Mourner's" Kaddish**, is said at all prayer services, as well as at funerals and memorials. Customs for reciting the Mourner's Kaddish vary markedly among various communities. In many **Ashkenazi** synagogues, particularly Orthodox ones, it is customary that everyone in the synagogue stands. **In Sephardi synagogues,**

**most people sit for most sayings of Kaddish.** In many non-Orthodox **Ashkenaz** ones, the custom is that only the mourners themselves stand and chant, while the rest of the congregation sits, chanting only responsively.

## Halakha (Jewish law) forbids cremation.

An ancient historian described as **"a distinguishing characteristic"** that **"Jews buried, rather than burned, their dead."** Judaism stresses burial in the earth (included entombment, as in caves) as a religious duty of laying a person's remains to rest. This, as well as the belief that the human body is created in the image of the divine and is not to be vandalized before or after death, teaches the belief that it was necessary to keep the whole body intact in burial, in anticipation of the eventual resurrection of the dead in the messianic age.

Nevertheless, some Jews who are not religiously adherent, or who have attached to an alternative movement or religious stream that does not see some or all the laws of the **Torah** as binding upon them, have chosen cremation, either for themselves prior to death, or for their loved ones, a choice made in 2016 by more than 50% of non-Jews in the United States.

## *Religious views of suicide.*

As **Judaism considers suicide to be a form of murder**, a Jew who commits suicide is denied some important after-death privileges: No eulogies should be given for the deceased, and burial in the main section of the Jewish cemetery is normally not allowed.

In recent times, most people who die by suicide have been deemed to be the unfortunate victims of depression or of a serious mental illness. Under this interpretation, their act of **"self-murder"** is not deemed to be a voluntary act of self-destruction, but rather the result of an involuntary condition. They have therefore been looked upon as having died of causes beyond their control.

Additionally, the **Talmud (in Semakhot, one of the minor tractates)** recognizes that many elements of the mourning ritual exist as much for the living survivors as for the dead, and that these elements ought to be carried out even in the case of the suicide.

Furthermore, if reasonable doubt exists that the death may not have been suicide or that the deceased might have changed her mind and repented at the last moment (e.g., if it is unknown whether the victim fell or jumped from a building, or if the person falling changed her mind mid-fall), the benefit of the doubt is given and regular burial and mourning rituals take place. Lastly, **the suicide of a minor is considered a result of a lack of understanding ("Da'at"), and in such a case, regular mourning is observed.**

# The Bible Code

The **Bible Code**, also known as the **Torah code**, is a purported set of secret messages encoded within the **Hebrew** text of the **Torah**. This *hidden code* has been described as a method by which specific letters from the text can be selected to reveal an otherwise obscured message. Although **Bible Code**s have been postulated and studied for centuries, the subject has been popularized in modern times by **Michael Drosnin's** book *The Bible Code* and the movie *The Omega Code*. (**The Bible contains 807,300 words**).

Many examples have been documented in the past. One cited example is that by taking every 50$^{th}$ letter of the **Book of Genesis** starting with the first raw, the **Hebrew** word **"Torah"** is spelled out. The same happens in the **Book of Exodus**. Modern computers have been used to search for similar patterns and more complex variants, and it has been published as a **"challenging puzzle"** in a peer-reviewed academic journal in 1994. Proponents hold that it is exceedingly unlikely such sequences could arise by chance, while skeptics and opponents hold that such sequences do often arise by chance, as demonstrated on other **Hebrew** and English texts.

## Overview

Contemporary discussion and controversy around one specific encryption method became widespread in 1994 when **Doron Witztum, Eliyahu Rips and Yoav Rosenberg** published a paper, **"Equidistant Letter Sequences in the Book of Genesis"**, in the scientific journal *Statistical Science*. The paper, which was presented by the journal as a **"challenging puzzle"**, presented strong statistical evidence that biographical information about famous rabbis and encoded in the text of the **Book of Genesis**, centuries before those rabbis lived. Since then the term **"Bible Codes"** has been popularly used to refer specifically to information encrypted via this **ELS** method. This is based on a belief that the **Torah** is unique among biblical texts in that it was given directly to mankind (via Moses) in *exact letter-by-letter sequence* and in the original **Hebrew** language.

## Equidistant Letter Sequence method

The primary method by which purportedly meaningful messages have been extracted is the *Equidistant Letter Sequence* (**ELS**). Often more than one **ELS** related to some topic can be displayed simultaneously in an *ELS letter array*. This is produced by writing out the text in a regular grid with exactly the same number of letters in each line, then cutting out a rectangle. **Bible Code**s proponents usually use a **Hebrew Bible** text. For religious reasons, most Jewish proponents use only the **Torah (Genesis-Deuteronomy).**

## ELS extensions

Once a specific word has been found as an **ELS**, it is natural to see if that word is part of a longer **ELS** consisting of multiple words. Code pioneers **Haralick and Rips** have published an example of a longer, extended **ELS**, which reads, **"Destruction I will call you; cursed is Bin Laden and revenge is to the Messiah."** **ELS** extensions that form phrases or sentences are of interest. It follows from the basics of probability theory that the longer the extended **ELS**, the less likely it is to be the result of chance.

## History

Jewish culture has a long tradition of interpretation, annotation, and commentary regarding the **Bible**, leading to both exegesis and eisegesis (drawing meaning from and imposing meaning on the texts). The **Bible Code** can be viewed as a part of this tradition, albeit one of the more controversial parts. Throughout history, many Jewish and later Christian, scholars have attempted to find hidden or coded messages within the **Bible**'s text, notably including **Isaac Newton**. **(Although religious, Newton did not believe in the concept of Trinity)**.

The 13th-century Spanish Rabbi **Bachya ben Asher** may have been the first to describe **ELS** in the **Bible**. His four-letter example related to the traditional zero-point of the **Hebrew** calendar. At this point many examples were found by the Slovak Rabbi **Michael Ber Weissmandl** and published by his students after his death in 195. Nevertheless, the practice remained known only to a few until the early 1980s, when some discoveries of an Israeli school teacher **Avraham Oren** came to the attention of the mathematician **Eliyahu Rips** at the **Hebrew University** of Jerusalem. Rips then took up the study together with his religious studies partners **Doron Witztum** and **Alexander Rotenberg**, and several others.

**Rips** and **Witztum** designed computer software for the **ELS** technique and subsequently found many examples. About 1985, they decided to carry out a formal test, and the **"Great rabbis' experiment"** was born. This experiment tested the hypothesis that **ELS**'s of the names of famous rabbinic personalities and their respective birth and death dates form a more compact arrangement than could be explained by chance. Their definition of **"compact"** was complex but, roughly, two **ELS**s were compactly arranged if they can be displayed together in a small window. When **Rips** *et al.* carried out the experiment, the data was measured and found to be statistically significant, supporting their hypothesis.

The **"great rabbis' experiment"** went through several iterations, and was eventually published in 1994, in the peer-reviewed journal *Statistical Science*. Prior to publication, the journal's editor, **Robert Kass**, subjected the paper to three successive peer reviews by the journal's referees, who according to Kass were **"baffled"**. Though still skeptical, none of the reviewers had found any flaws. Understanding that the paper was certain to generate controversy, it was presented to readers in the context of a **"challenging puzzle."**

Another experiment, in which the names of the famous rabbis were matched against the places of their births and deaths (rather than the dates), was conducted in 1997 by **Harold Gans**, former Senior Cryptologic Mathematician for the **United States National Security Agency**. Again, the results were interpreted as being meaningful and thus suggestive of a more than chance result. These **Bible Code**s became known to the public primarily due to the American journalist **Michael Drosnin**, whose book *The Bible Code* (Simon and Schuster, 1997) was a best-seller in many countries. **Rips** issued a public statement that he did not support **Drosnin's** work or conclusions; even **Gans** has said that although the book states that **the codes in the Torah can be used to predict future events:** *This is absolutely unfounded.*

*There is no scientific or mathematical basis for such a statement, and the reasoning used to come to such a conclusion in the book is logically flawed.* In 2002, **Drosnin** published a second book on the same subject, called *Bible Code II; the Countdown*. The Jewish outreach group **Aish-**

**HaTorah** employs **Bible Code**s in their Discovery Seminars to persuade secular Jews of the divinity of the **Torah** and to encourage them to trust in its traditional Orthodox teachings. Use of **Bible Code** techniques also spread into certain Christian circles, especially in the United States. The main early proponents were **Yaakov Rambsel**, **who is a Messianic Jew**, and **Grant Jeffrey**. Another **Bible Code** technique was developed in 1997 by **Dean Coombs** (also Christian). Various pictograms are claimed to be formed by words and sentences using **ELS.**

Since 2000, physicist **Nathan Jacobi**, an agnostic Jew, and engineer **Moshe Aharon Shak**, an orthodox Jew, claim to have discovered hundreds of examples of lengthy, extended **ELS**s. The number of extended **ELS**'s at different lengths is compared with those expected from a non-encoded text, as determined by a formula from **Markov** chain theory.

**Criticism**
The primary objection advanced against **Bible Code**s is that information theory does not prohibit **"noise"** from appearing to be sometimes meaningful. Although the probability of an **ELS** in a random place being a meaningful word is small, there are so many possible starting points and skip patterns that many such words can be expected to appear, depending on the details chosen for the experiment, and that it is possible to **"tune"** an **ELS** experiment to achieve a result which appears to exhibit patterns that overcome the level of noise.

**Criticism of the original paper**
In 1999, four authors, the Australian mathematician **Brendan McKay**, the Israeli mathematicians **Dror Bar-Natan and Gil Kalai,** and the Israeli psychologist **Maya bar-Hillel** (collectively known as **"MBBK"**) published a paper in *Statistical Science*, in which they argue that the case of Witztum, Rips and Rosenberg (WRR) is **"fatally defective, indeed that their result merely reflects on the choices made in designing their experiment and collecting the data for it."** The **MBBK** paper was reviewed anonymously by four professional statisticians prior to publication. In the introduction to the paper, **Robert Kass**, the Editor of the Journal who previously had described the **WRR** paper as a **"challenging puzzle"** wrote that **"considering the work of McKay, Bar-Natan, Kalai and Bar-Hillel as a whole it indeed appears as they conclude, that the puzzle has been solved"**.

From these observations, **MBBK** created an alternative hypothesis to explain the **"puzzle"** of how the codes were discovered, **MBBK's** claim, in essence, was that the **WRR** authors had cheated **MBBK** went on to describe the means by which the cheating might have occurred, and demonstrate the tactic as presumed. The MBBK paper argued that the **ELS** experiment is extraordinarily sensitive to very small changes in the spellings of appellations, and that the **WRR** result **"merely reflects on the choices made in designing their experiment and collecting the data for it."** Psychologist and **MBBK** co-author **Maya Bar-Hillel** subsequently summarized the MBBK view that the WRR paper was a hoax, an intentionally and a carefully designed **"magic trick"**.

**Replies to MBBK's criticisms**
**Harold Gans** has argued that **MBBK's** hypothesis implies a conspiracy between **WRR** and their co-contributors to fraudulently tune the appellations in advance. **Gans** argues that the conspiracy must include **Doron Witztum, Eliyahu Rips, and S.Z. Havlin**, because all of them say that

**Havlin** compiled the appellations independently. **Gans** argues further that such a conspiracy must include the multiple rabbis who have written a letter confirming the accuracy of Havlin's list. Finally, argues **Gans**, such a conspiracy must also include the multiple participants of the cities experiment conducted by **Gans** (which includes **Gans** himself). **Gans** concludes that **"the number of people necessarily involved in [the conspiracy] will stretch the credulity of any reasonable person."**

**Brendan McKay** has replied that he and his colleagues have never accused **Havlin** or **Gans** of participating in a conspiracy. The **WRR** authors issued a series of responses regarding of the claims of **MBBK**, including the claim that no such tuning did or even could have taken place. Using **MBBK's** alternates, the results **WRR** returned showed equivalent or better support for the existence of the codes, and so challenged the **"wiggle room"** assertion of **MBBK**. In 2006, seven new **Torah** Codes papers were published at the **18ᵗʰ International Conference on Pattern Recognition (ICPR'06).**

**Robert Aumann**, a notable game theorist and winner of the **Nobel Prize in Economics in 2005**, has followed the **Bible Code** research and controversy for many years. He wrote: **"Though the basic thesis of the research seems wildly improbable, for many years I thought that an ironclad case had been made for the codes; I did not see how 'cheating' could have been possible"… "A priori, the thesis of the Codes research seems wildly improbable…Research conducted under my own supervision failed to confirm the existence of the codes – though it also did not establish their non-existence. So I must return to my a priori estimate, that the Codes phenomenon is improbable".**

### Criticism of Michael Drosnin

Journalist **Drosnin's** books have been criticized by some who believe that the **Bible Code** is real but that it cannot predict the future. On **Drosnin's** claim of Rabin's death, **Drosnin** wrote in his book **"The Bible Code"** (published in 1997) on page 120; **"Yigal Amir could not be found in advance".** This is very telling in that dangerous period of Israeli politics from the **Oslo Accords of 1993** to the assassination of **Yitzhak Rabin** on November 4, 1995. Another message (p. 71) supposedly contains a **"complete"** description of the terrorist bombing of a bus in Jerusalem on February 25, 1996.

**Drosnin** also made a number of claims and alleged predictions that have since failed. Among the most important, **Drosnin** clearly states in his book **"The Bible Code II"**, published on December 2, 2002, that there was to be a **World War** involving an **"Atomic Holocaust"** that would allegedly be the end of the world. Another claim **Drosnin** makes in **"The Bible Code II"** is that the nation of Libya would develop weapons of mass destruction that they would then be given to terrorists who would then use them to attack the West (specifically the United States). In reality **Libya** improved relations with the West in 2003 and gave up all their existing weapons of mass destruction programs.

A final claim **Drosnin** made in **"The Bible Code II"** was that Palestinian Authority leader **Yasser Arafat** would allegedly be assassinated by being shot to death by gunmen which **Drosnin** specifically stated would be from the **Palestinian Hamas** movement. This prediction by **Drosnin** also failed, as **Yasser Arafat** died on November 11, 2004 of what was later declared to be natural causes (specifically a stroke brought on by an unknown infection).

Some accuse him of factual errors, claiming that he has much support in the scientific community, mistranslating **Hebrew** words to make his point more convincing, and using the **Bible** without proving that other books do not have similar codes. Responding to an explicit challenge from **Drosnin**, who claimed that other texts such as *Moby-Dick* would not yield **ELS** results comparable to the **Torah**, **McKay** created a new experiment that was tuned to find many **ELS** letter arrays in *Moby-Dick* that relate to modern events, including the assassination of **Martin Luther King, Jr**. He also found a code relating to the **Rabin assassination**, containing the assassin's first and last name and the university he attended, as well as the motive **("Oslo", relating to the Oslo accords).**

In his television series ***John Saran vs. God,*** Australian television personality **John Saran** and **McKay** again demonstrated the **"tuning"** technique, demonstrating that these techniques could produce **"evidence"** of the **September 11** terrorist attacks on New York in the lyrics of **Vanilla Ice's** repertoire. **McKay** and others claim that in the absence of an objective measure of quality and an objective way to select test subjects it is not possible positively to determine whether any particular observation is significant or not. For that reason, most of the serious effort of the skeptics has been focused on the scientific claims of **Witztum, Rips and Gans.**

**Bible**: **Torah**: **Five books of Moses: 807,300 words. Tanach: 24 books**.

### Predictions in the Bible Code:

Napoleon Bonaparte, World-War-I & World-War-II, Hitler and Nazism, Atom Bombs on Hiroshima and Nagasaki, 1948 establishment of the State of Israel, The Hijackers of 9/11/2001, Princess Dianna, and many more…

# Biblical prophets

In Christianity the figures widely recognized as prophets are those mentioned as such in the **Hebrew Bible** and the canonical **New Testament**. It is believed that prophets are called or chosen by God.

The main list below consists of only those individuals that have been clearly defined as prophets, either by explicit statement or strong contextual implication, along with the Biblical reference to their office.

In **Roman Catholicism**, prophets are recognized as having received either **Public** or **Private Revelation.** Public Revelation is part of the "**deposit of faith**", which refers to the entire revelation of **Jesus Christ** passed to successive generations in the forms of sacred scripture (the Bible) and sacred tradition.

The secondary list consists of those individuals who are recorded as having had a visionary or prophetic experience, but without a history of any major or consistent prophetic calling. A final list contains the names of those described in the **Bible** as prophets, but who either misused this gift or were fraudulent.

## Main list by alphabetical order
### A
- Aaron (Exodus 7:2)
- Abraham (Genesis 20:7)
- Agabus (Acts 21:10)
- Agur (Book of Proverbs 30:1)
- Ahijah (1 Kings 11:29)
- Amos (Amos 7:14-15)
- Anna (Luke 2:36)
- Asaph (2 Chronicles 29:30)
- Azariah (2 Chronicles 15:8)

### B
- Barnabas (Acts 13:1)

### D
- Daniel (Matthew 24:15)
- David (Hebrews 11:32)
- Deborah (Judges 4:4)

### E
- Elijah (1 Kings 18:36)
- Elisha (2 Kings 9:1)
- Enoch (Jude 1:14)

- Ezekiel (Ezekiel 1:3)
- Ezra (Book of Ezra)

## G

- Gad (1 Samuel 22:5)
- Gideon (Judges 6 through 8)

## H

- Habakkuk (Habakkuk 1:1)
- Haggai (Haggai 1:1)
- Hanani (2 Chronicles 16:7)
- Hosea (Book of Hosea 1:1)
- Huldah (2 Kings 22:14)

## I

- Iddo (2 Chronicles 13:22)
- Isaiah (2 Kings 19:2)

## J

- Jacob (Genesis 28:11-16)
- Jehu (1 Kings 16:7)
- Jeremiah (Jeremiah 20:2)
- Joel (Acts 2:16)
- John the Baptist (Luke 7:28)
- John of Patmos (Revelation 1:1)
- Jonah (2 Kings 14:25)
- Joshua (Joshua 1:1)
- Judas Barsabbas (Acts 3:15)

## L

- Lucius of Cyrene (Acts 13:1)

## M

- Malachi (Malachi 1:1)
- Manahen (Acts 13:1)
- Micah (Micah 1:1)
- Micaiah (1 Kings 22:9)
- Miriam (Exodus 15:20)
- Moses (Deuteronomy 34:10)

## N

- Nahum (Nahum 1:1)
- Nathan (2 Samuel 7:2)
- Noah (Genesis 7:1)

## O

- Obadiah (Obadiah 1:1)
- Oded (2 Chronicles 28:9)

## P

- Philip the Evangelist (Acts 8:26) Note: His four daughters also prophesied (Acts 21:8, 9)
- Paul the Apostle (Acts of the Apostles 9:20)

**S**

- Samuel (1 Samuel 3:20)
- Shemaiah (1 Kings 12:22)
- Silas (Acts 15:32)
- Simeon Niger (Acts 13:1)

**T**

- Two Witnesses (Revelation 11:3)

**U**

- Urijah (Jeremiah 26:20)

**Z**

- Zechariah, son of Berechiah (Zechariah 1:1)
- Zechariah, son of Jehoiada (2 Chronicles 24:20)
- Zephaniah (Zephaniah 1:1)

## Secondary list

- Eldad (Numbers 11:26)
- Eliezer (2 Chronicles 20:37)
- Elisabeth, mother of John the Baptist (Luke 1:41)
- Elihu(Job 32-35)
- Jahaziel (2 Chronicles 20:14)
- Joseph (Genesis 37:5 - 11)
- Joseph, foster father of Jesus (Matthew 1:20)
- Mary, mother of Jesus (Luke 1:26-28)
- Medad (Numbers 11:26)
- King Nebuchadnezzar of Babylon (Daniel 2:1)
- King Saul (1Samuel 10:10)
- Simeon of Jerusalem (Luke 2:25, 26)
- King Solomon (1Kings 3:5)
- The seventy elders of Israel (Numbers 11:25)

- Zechariah, father of John the Baptist (Luke 1:67)

## False prophets

- Ahab (Jeremiah 29:21)
- Antichrist (1 John 2:18-19)
- Azur (Jeremiah 28:1)
- Elymas (a.k.a. Bar-Jesus) (Acts 13:6-12)
- Hananiah (Jeremiah 28:5)
- Jezebel (Revelation 2:20) (not to be confused with the Jezebel of the Old Testament)
- The false prophet of the Book of Revelation (16:13, 19:20, 20:10)

- Noadiah (Nehemiah 6:14)
- Simon Magus (Acts 8:9–24)
- Zedekiah (Jeremiah 29:21)

# Biblical Stories: From Abraham to Jesus

## 1. Genesis (Creation):

The **Genesis creation narrative** is the creation myth of both Judaism and Christianity. God, creates the world in six days, then rests on, blesses and sanctifies the seventh day, the **Sabbath**. God creates by spoken command (**"Let there be..."**), and names the elements of the cosmos as he creates them. **Yahweh**, the personal name of god, shapes the first man from dust, places him in the **Garden of Eden**. The man names the animals, signifying his authority within God's creation, and God creates the first woman, **Eve,** from the man's body. **Genesis 1** consists of eight of creation over six days. Man is created to rule over the whole of creation as God's regent. In **Genesis 1:27 "God created the human in his own image...male and female he created them"**. Creation is followed by rest. Rest is both disengagement, as the work of creation is finished, but also engagement, as the deity is now present in his temple to maintain a secure and ordered cosmos.

## Adam and Eve:

**Adam** is a prominent figure in **Abraham**ic religions. He is the first man created by God in **Judaism, Christianity**, and **Islam**. **"Male and female created He them; and blessed them, and called their name Adam..."** Genesis 2 records that God first formed Adam out of **"dust of the ground"** and then **"breathed into his nostrils the breath of life",** causing him to **"become a living soul"** (**Genesis 2:7**), God then placed **Adam** in the Garden of Eden, giving him the commandment that **"Of every tree of the garden thou mayest freely eat: But of the tree of the knowledge of good and evil, thou shalt not eat of it: for in the day that thou eatest thereof thou shalt surely die"**. God then noted that **"It is not good that the man should be alone"** (**Genesis 2:18**). He then brought every **"beast of the field and every fowl of the air"** before Adam and had Adam name all the animals, so God caused **"a deep sleep to fall upon Adam"** and took one of his ribs, and from that rib, formed a woman (**Genesis 2:21-22**) subsequently named Eve.

## Expulsion from the Garden of Eden:

**Adam** and **Eve** were subsequently expelled from the **Garden of Eden**, were ceremonially separated from God, and lost their innocence after they broke God's law about not eating of the fruit of the tree of knowledge of good and evil. This occurred after the serpent (understood to be Satan in many Christian traditions) told **Eve** that eating of the tree would result not in death, but in **Adam** and **Eve's** eyes being opened, resulting in their begin **"as gods, knowing good and evil"** (**Gen. 3:6**).

As a result, both immediately become aware of the fact that they are naked, and thus cover themselves with garments made of fig leaves (**Gen. 3:7**). As a result of their breaking God's law, the couple was removed from the garden (**Gen. 3:23**) and both receive a curse. Adam's curse is contained in **Gen. 3:17-19: "in sorrow that thou eat of it all the days of thy life; In the sweat of thy face shalt thou eat bread, till thou return unto the ground; for out of it wast thou taken: for dust thou art, and unto dust shalt thou return"**.

## 2. Cain and Abel:

**Cain and Abel** are two sons of **Adam** and **Eve**. **Cain** is a crop farmer and his younger brother **Abel** is a shepherd. **Cain** committed the first murder by killing his brother, after God has rejected his offerings of produce, but accepted the animal sacrifices brought by **Abel**. The Lord had regard for **Abel** and his offering, but He did not have regard for **Cain** and his offering. **Cain** was furious, and he was downcast. **Cain** said to his brother **Abel**, "Let's go out to the field." And while they were in the field, **Cain** attacked his brother **Abel** and killed him. (**Genesis 4:1-8**). Then the Lord said to **Cain**, **"Where is your brother Abel?" "I know not,"** he replied, **"Am I my brother's keeper?" "Your brother's blood cries out to Me from the ground! If you work the land, it will never again give you its yield. You will be a restless wanderer on the earth."**

## 3. Noah and the Great Flood:

The biblical story of **Noah** is contained in **chapters 6-8 in the book of Genesis**, where he saves his family (his wife, three sons, and their wives) and representatives of all the animals from the flood by constructing an ark. **Noah** was the son of **Lamech**. In his five hundredth year **Noah** had three sons, Shem, Ham, and Japheth. In his six hundredth year God was saddened at the wickedness of mankind, sent a great deluge to destroy all life, but instructed **Noah**, a man **"righteous in his generation,"** to build an ark and save a remnant of life from the Flood. After the Flood **"Noah was the first tiller of the soil"**. **Noah died 350 years after the Flood, at the age of 950.**

## 4. Sodom and Gomorrah:

**Sodom and Gomorrah** were cities mentioned in the **Book of Genesis**. Divine Judgment by **Yahweh** was then passed upon **Sodom** and **Gomorrah** along with two neighboring cities that were completely consumed by fire and brimstone. **Sodom** and **Gomorrah** have become synonymous with impenitent sin and their fall with a proverbial manifestation of God's wrath. **Sodom** and **Gomorrah** have also been used as metaphors for vice and **homosexuality** viewed as a deviation. Used in so-called **sodomy laws** to describe a sexual **"crime against nature"** consisting of oral or anal, either homosexual or heterosexual. The Bible indicates they were located near the **Dead Sea (Genesis 14:1-3). (Found in Jorden)**

In **Genesis 18** the two angels received the hospitality of **Abraham** and **Sarah**, his wife; God reveals to **Abraham** that he will destroy **Sodom** and **Gomorrah**, because their cry is great, **"and because their sin is very grievous. Two of the angels of God procedure to Sodom and are met by Abraham's nephew Lot who convinces the angels to lodge with him, and they eat with his family (Genesis 19:4-5). But before they lay down, the men of the city surrounded the house; and they called to Lot, Where are the men who came to you tonight? Bring them out to us, that we may know them (k now them: Can have intercourse with them)".**

In response, **Lot** refuses to give his guests to the inhabitants of **Sodom** and instead, offers them his two virgin daughters to **"do to them whatever you like." (Genesis 19:8)**. Then, (not having found even 10 righteous people in the city) the angels command Lot to gather his family and leave, revealing that they were sent to destroy **Sodom** and **Gomorrah**. As **Sodom** and **Gomorrah** are destroyed by **Yahweh** with fire and brimstone, **Lot's** wife looks back at the city and she becomes a pillar of salt.

## Lot and his daughters:

With the loss of his wife, Lot decided that it would be best to retreat to the mountains. There, he and his daughters found a suitable cave to dwell in. The oldest daughter, concerned about preserving the family line, suggested to her younger sister that since there were no men around, it was their duty to preserve the bloodline by taking advantage of their father. The daughters then got their father so drunk they were able to have intercourse with him. **Genesis 19:33-35**. As a result of their intercourse with their father, a child was born to each of them. **(Biblical Incest?)**

## 5. Abraham and Monotheism:

**Abraham** whose birth name was **Abram**. His sons were **Ishmael** and Isaac. **Abraham** is the forefather of many tribes, including the **Ishmael**ites, Israelites, Midianites and Edomites. **Abraham** was a descendant of **Noah**'s son, Shem. **Abraham** first appears in the book of Genesis as Abram, until he is renamed by God in Genesis 17:5. The Hebrew Bible places **Abraham**'s birth 1,948 years after the Creation. Abram married Sarai, who was barren. Terah, with Abram, Sarai and Lot, then departed for Canaan, but settled in a place named Haran, where Terah died at the age of 205. **(Genesis 11:27-11:32)**

## Abram's calling & Covenant:

God then told Abram to "go" from his country and his father's house for a land that He would show him, promising to make of him "a great nation", bless him, make his name great, bless those who blessed him, and curse those who cursed him, (Genesis 12:1-3). There God appeared to Abram to tell him that he would give the land to his heirs, and Abram built an altar to God. Abram then moved to the hill country east of Bethel and built an altar to God there and invoked God by name, and journeyed toward the Negev Desert. There was a severe famine in the land of Canaan, so that Abram and Lot and their households, travelled south to Egypt (Genesis 12:10-13). Abram went to Hebron and settled in the plain of Mamre, where he built another altar to worship God. (Genesis 13:1-18). **(Why was he not given the 10 Commandments?)**

## Abram and Hagar:

Abram and Sarai were trying to make sense of how he would become a progenitor of nations since it had already been 10 years of living in Canaan, and still no child had been born from Abram's seed. Sarai then offered her Egyptian handmaid, **Hagar**, for Abram to consort with so that she may have a child by her, as a wife. Abram consented and had sexual intercourse with **Hagar**. (Genesis 6:1-6). Abram was eighty-six years of age when **Ishmael** was born. **(Genesis 16:7-16).**

## Abraham and Sarah:

**Genesis 15 & 17:** Abram is now ninety-nine when God declares Abram's new name: **"Abraham, a father of many nations."** Every male must be circumcised otherwise it was a breach of contract. Then God declared Sarai's new name: "Sarah" and blessed her. Immediately after Abram's encounter with his God, he had his entire household of men, including himself and **Ishmael**, circumcised. **(Genesis 17:1-27).**

## Abraham and Ishmael:

**Abraham** was fond of his son **Ishmael** who had grown up to be fourteen years old when his son Isaac was born. Now that **Sarah** had finally borne her own child, she could no longer stand the sight of either **Hagar** or **Ishmael**. Sarah told **Abraham** to send the two of them away. She declared that **Ishmael** would not share in Isaac's inheritance. God reassured **Abraham** that **"in Isaac shall seed be called to thee."** (Genesis 21:12) He also said that **Ishmael** would make a nation, "because he is they seed", too. (**Genesis 21:9-13**). Early the next morning, **Abraham** brought **Hagar** and **Ishmael** out together.

He gave her bread and water and sent them away. The boy then called to God and upon hearing him, an angel of God confirmed to **Hagar** that he would become a great nation. A well of water then appeared so that it saved their lives. Eventually his mother found a wife for **Ishmael** from her native country, the land of Egypt. (**Genesis 21:14-21**). **(About 2,600 years later, Muhammad names Ishmael the father of the Arab People.)**

## Abraham and Isaac:
At some point in **Isaac's** youth, **Abraham** was commanded by God to offer his son **Isaac** up as a sacrifice in the land of **Moriah**. Just as **Abraham** was about to sacrifice his son, he was prevented by an angel, and given on that spot a ram which he sacrificed in place of his son. **(Isn't this too much to ask for?)**

## 6. Moses and Exodus:
The **Book of Exodus** is the second book of the **Hebrew Bible**, and of the five books of the **Torah** (the **Pentateuch**). The book tells how the children of Israel leave slavery in Egypt through the strength of **Yahweh**, the god who has chosen Israel as his people. Led by their great prophet **Moses** they journey through the wilderness to **Mount Sinai**, where **Yahweh** promises them the land of **Canaan (the "Promised Land")** in return for their faithfulness. Israel enters into a covenant with **Yahweh** who gives them their laws and instructions for the **Tabernacle**, the means by which he will dwell with them and lead them to the land. Egypt's Pharaoh, fearful of the Israelites' numbers, orders that all their newborn boys be thrown into the **Nile**. A **Levite** woman saves her baby by setting him adrift on the river in an **Ark** of bulrushes.

Pharaoh's daughter finds the child, names him **Moses**, and brings him up as her own. But **Moses** is aware of his origins, and one day, when grown, he kills an Egyptian overseer who is beating a Hebrew slave and has to flee into **Midian**. There he marries the daughter of Jethro the priest of Midian, and encounters God in a burning bush. **Moses** asks God for his name; God replies **"I AM that I AM"**. God tells **Moses** to return to Egypt and lead the Hebrews into Canaan, the land promised to **Abraham**. **(Moses was an Egyptian Prince, how could he has written the Torah in Hebrew?)**

**Moses** and his brother **Aaron** return to Egypt, but Pharaoh refuses to release the Hebrew slaves. **Yahweh** causes a series of ten plagues to strike Egypt. The **Exodus** begins. God destroys the Egyptian army at the crossing of the **Red Sea (Yam Suf)** and the Israelites celebrate **Yahweh**'s victory. God calls **Moses** up the mountain to receive a set of stone tablets containing the law, and he and **Joshua** go up, leaving **Aaron** in charge. God gives **Moses** instructions for the construction of the tabernacle so that God can dwell permanently amongst his chosen people.

**Aaron** is appointed as the first **High Priest**, and the priesthood is to be hereditary in his line. God gives **Moses** the two stone tablets containing these instructions, written by God's own finger. **Moses** comes down from the mountain, smashes the stone tablets in anger, and commands the Levites to massacre the unfaithful Israelites. God commands **Moses** to make two new tablets on which **He** will personally write the words that were on the first tablets. **Moses** ascends the mountain, God dictates the **Ten Commandments** (the Ritual Decalogue), and **Moses** writes them on the tablets. The **Tabernacle** is the place where God is physically present, where, through the priesthood; Israel could be in direct, literal communion with him. God punishes **Moses** and deprives him from entering the **Promised Land**. **(The Laws of the Babylonian Hammurabi)**

## Joshua and the conquest of Canaan:

**Joshua** (Hebrew: Yehoshua), is a minor figure in the **Torah**, being one of the spies for Israel **(Numbers 13-14)** and in few passages as **Moses'** assistant. He became the leader of the Israelite tribes after the death of **Moses**; **(Numbers 13:16)** and he was born in Egypt prior to the **Exodus**. **(Numbers 13:1-16)** After the death of **Moses**, he led the Israelite tribes in the conquest of Canaan, and allocated the land to the tribes. According to **Joshua 24:29**, **Joshua** died at the age of 110. As **Moses'** apprentice, he accompanied **Moses** part of the way when he ascended Mount Sinai to receive the **Ten Commandments**. **(Exodus 32:17)** He was one of the twelve spies sent by **Moses** to explore and report on the land of Canaan **(Numbers 13:16-17)**, **(Numbers 1`4:23-24**. According to **Joshua** 1:1-9, **Moses** appointed **Joshua** to succeed him as leader of the Israelites. **(General?)**

## 7. Babylonian captivity:

The **Babylonian captivity** (or **Babylonian exile**) was the period in Jewish history during which the Jews of the ancient **Kingdom of Judah** were captives in Babylon – conventionally 587-538 BCE. In 599 BCE, **Nebuchadnezzar II** of Babylon laid siege to Jerusalem, and **Jehoiakim**, the King of Judah, died in 598 BCE with the siege still under way. He was succeeded by his son **Jeconiah,** aged either eight or eighteen. The city fell about three months later, on 2 Adar (March 16) 597 BCE and **Nebuchadnezzar** pillaged Jerusalem and its **Temple** and took **Jeconiah** and his court and other prominent citizens (including the prophet **Ezekiel**) back to Babylon. Jehoikim brother **Zedekiah** was appointed king in his place, but the exiles in Babylon continued to consider Jeconiah as their Exilarch, or rightful ruler. **(49 years later)**

**Nebuchadnezzar** returned, defeated the Egyptians, and again besieged Jerusalem. The city fell in 587. **Nebuchadnezzar** destroyed the city wall and the **Temple**, and **Zedekiah** was blinded, and taken to Babylon, together with many others. Judah became a Babylonian province, called **Yehud Medinata**, putting an end to the independent **Kingdom of Judah**. The forced exile ended in 538/7 BCE after the fall of Babylon to the Persian king **Cyrus the Great**, who gave the Jews permission to return to **Yehud** province and to rebuild the **Second Temple**, 520-515 BCE.

The return by the Jews to Yehud under **Zerubbabel** and **Joshua** the High Priest. The current Hebrew script was adopted during this period, replacing the traditional Israelite script. This period saw the last high-point of Biblical prophecy in the person of **Ezekiel,** followed by the emergence of the central role of the **Torah** in Jewish life; it was edited and redacted during this time, and saw the beginning of the canonization of the Bible, which provided a central text for Jews. **(First Diaspora of the Jewish people)**

## 8. Jesus of Nazareth:

**Jesus of Nazareth** is the central figure of Christianity. Most Christian denominations venerate him as God the Son incarnated and believe that he rose from the dead after being crucified. Most critical historians agree that **Jesus was a Galilean Jewish Rabbi** who was regarded as a teacher and healer in Judaea, that he was baptized by **John the Baptist**, and that he was crucified in Jerusalem on the orders of the Roman Prefect, **Pontius Pilate**, on the charge of **sedition against the Roman Empire**. (**As King of the Jews**). Christians traditionally believe that **Jesus** was born of a virgin, performed miracles, founded the Church, rose from the dead, and ascended into heaven, from which he will return.

The majority of Christians worship **Jesus** as the incarnation of God the Son, and **"the Second Person of the Blessed Trinity"**. Christian scholars today present **Jesus** as the awaited **Messiah** promised in the Old Testament and as God. Judaism rejects assertions that **Jesus** as the awaited Messiah, arguing that he did not fulfill the Messianic prophecies in the **Tanakh**. In Islam, **Jesus** is considered one of God's important prophets, a bringer of scripture, and the product of a virgin birth, but **not to have experienced crucifixion**. **Islam** and the **Baha'i Faith** use the title **"Messiah"** for **Jesus**, but do not teach that he was God incarnate, not the Son of God. **(Circumcised on the 8 day, Bar-Mitzvah at 12-13= Jewish Covenant).**

## Chronology:

Roman involvement in Judaea began around 63 BC/BCE and by AC Judaea had become a Roman province. From 26-37 AC **Pontius Pilate** was the governor of Roman Judaea. In its **Nativity** account, the **Gospel of Matthew** associates the birth of **Jesus** with the reign of **Herod the Great**, who is generally believed to have died around 4 BC. As per the writings of **Josephus,** it has been estimated that around 27-29 AC, **Jesus** was **"about thirty years of age"**. Most scholars thus estimate the year 28 AC to be roughly the 32$^{nd}$ birthday of **Jesus** and the birth year of **Jesus** to be around 6-4 BC. Although Christian feasts related to the **Nativity** have had specific dates (**December 25 for Christmas**) there is no historical evidence for the exact day or month of the birth of **Jesus**. (**The New Testament is based on the Gospels of 4 people who never met Jesus: Matthew, Mark, Luke, and John; New Testament = 27 books; Jesus left nothing in his own writing).**

## Years of ministry estimates:

According to **Josephus** the temple reconstruction was started by **Herod the Great** in the 15$^{th}$-18$^{th}$ year of his reign at about the time that **Augustus** arrived in Syria. Temple expansion and reconstruction was ongoing, and it was in constant reconstruction until it was **destroyed in 70 AC by the Romans.** Both the gospels and Josephus refer to **Herod Antipas** killing **John the Baptist.**

## Year of death estimates:

All four canonical **Gospels** report that **Jesus** was crucified in **Calvary** during the prefecture of **Pontius Pilate**, the Roman prefect who governed Judaea from 26 to 36 AC. The late 1$^{st}$ century Jewish historian **Josephus,** writing in *Antiquities of the Jews* (c. 93 AC), also state that **Pilate ordered the execution of Jesus.**

## The five major milestones:

The five major milestones in the gospel narrative of the life of **Jesus** are his **Baptism. Transfiguration, Crucifixion, Resurrection** and **Ascension**, and **John 14:10** positions them as the revelations of **God the Father**. Both gospels state that **Jesus** was begotten not by **Joseph**, but by God. Both accounts **trace Joseph back to King David and from there to Abraham.**

## Nativity:

According to **Luke** and **Matthew**, **Jesus** was born to **Joseph** and **Mary**, his betrothed, in Bethlehem. Both support the doctrine of the **Virgin Birth** in which **Jesus** was miraculously conceived in his mother's womb by the **Holy Spirit**, when his mother was still a virgin. In **Luke 1:31-38 Mary** learns from the angel Gabriel that she will conceive and bear a child called **Jesus** through the action of the Holy Spirit. In **Luke 2:1-7**, **Mary** gives birth to **Jesus** and, having found no place in the inn, places the newborn in a manger. **King Herod** hears of **Jesus'** birth from the **Wise Men** and tries to kill him by massacring all the male children in Bethlehem under the age of two (**the Massacre of the Innocents**). Before the massacre, **Joseph** is warned by an angel in his dream and the family flees to Egypt and remains there until **Herod's death** (4 BC), after which they leave Egypt and settle in **Nazareth.**

## Ministry:

**Luke 3:23** states that **Jesus** was **"about 30 years of age"** at the start of his ministry. The gospel accounts place the beginning of **Jesus'** ministry in the countryside of Judaea, near the River Jordan. **Jesus'** ministry begins with his **Baptism by John the Baptist (Matthew 3, Luke 3)**, and ends with the **Last Supper** with his disciples (**Matthew 26, Luke 22**) in Jerusalem. **(Was this His pre-destination?)**

## Betrayal, arrest, trial, and death:

The description of the last week of the life of **Jesus** (often called the **Passion Week**) occupies about one third of the narrative in the Canonical gospels. The narrative for that week starts by a description of the final entry into Jerusalem, and ends with his crucifixion. After the supper, **Jesus** is betrayed with a kiss, and is arrested. **Jesus** is first questioned by the **Sanhedrin**, and then tried by **Pontius Pilate**, the Roman governor of Judea. After the scourging of **Jesus** and his mocking as the King of the Jews, **Pilate orders the crucifixion**.

## Last supper:

In the **New Testament**, the **Last Supper** is the final meal that **Jesus** shares with his twelve apostles in Jerusalem before his crucifixion. The **Last Supper** is mentioned in all four Canonical Gospels. In all four gospels, during the meal, **Jesus** predicts that one of the **Apostles** will betray him. In **Matthew 26:23-25** and **John 13:26-27** Judas is specifically singled out as the traitor. In all four Gospels **Jesus** predicts that **Peter** will deny knowledge of him. The Gospel of John provides the only account of **Jesus** washing his disciples' feet before the meal.

## Crucifixion and burial:

After the trials, **Jesus** made his way to **Calvary** (the path is traditionally called via **Dolorosa**). Once at **Calvary (Golgotha)**, **Jesus** was offered wine mixed with gall to drink – usually offered as a form of painkiller. The soldiers then crucified **Jesus** and cast lots for his clothes. Above **Jesus'** head on the cross was the inscription **King of the Jews**, and the soldiers and those passing by mocked him about the title. **Jesus** was crucified between two convicted thieves. In **Luke 23:34** he states: **"Father, forgive them; for they know not what they do"**.

## Christian views:

Almost all Christian groups regard **Jesus** as the **"Savior and Redeemer"**, as the Messiah (Greek: *Christos*; English: Christ) prophesied in the **Old Testament**, who, through his life, death, and resurrection, restored humanity's communion with God in the blood of the **New Covenant.** His death on a cross is understood as the redemptive sacrifice; the source of humanity's salvation and the atonement for sin, which had entered human history through the sin of Adam.

That foreshadows the resurrection of humanity at the end of time, when **Christ** will come again to judge the living and the dead, resulting in either entrance into heaven or damnation. Christians profess **Jesus** to be the only **Son of God**, **the Lord**, and **the eternal Word**, who became man in the incarnation, so that those who believe in him might have eternal life. Most Christian denominations believe in some form of the doctrine of the **Trinity**, i.e., that **Jesus, as the second person of the Trinity, is fully God.**

## Jewish and Islamic views:

According to Jewish tradition, there were no more prophets after **Malachi,** who lived centuries before **Jesus** and delivered his prophesies about 420 BC. In Islam, **Jesus** is considered to be a **Messenger of God** and the **Messiah** who was sent to guide the Children of Israel with the Gospel. **Jesus** is seen in Islam as a precursor to **Prophet Muhammad**, and is believed by Muslims to have foretold the latter's coming. According to the **Qur'an,** believed by Muslims to be God's final revelation, **Jesus** was born to **Mary** as the result of **virginal conception**, and was given the ability to perform miracles. (**He was neither crucified nor was he the Son of God**).

# Blood Libels

**Blood libel** (also **blood accusation**) is an accusation that Jews kidnapped and murdered the children of Christians in order to use their blood as part of their religious rituals during Jewish holidays.

Blood libels typically say that Jews require human blood for the baking of **matzos for Passover**, although this element was allegedly absent in the earliest cases which claimed that then-contemporary Jews reenacted the crucifixion. The accusations often assert that the blood of the children of Christians is especially coveted, and, historically, blood libel claims have been made in order to account for the otherwise unexplained deaths of children.

In Jewish lore, blood libels were the impetus for the creation of the **Golem of Prague** by **Rabbi Judah Loew ben Bezalel** in the 16th century. Altogether, there have been about 150 recorded cases of blood libel (not to mention thousands of rumors) that resulted in the arrest and killing of Jews throughout history, most of them in the Middle Ages. In almost every case, **Jews were murdered, sometimes by a mob, sometimes following torture and a trial.**

The supposed torture and human sacrifice alleged in the blood libels run contrary to the teachings of Judaism. According to the **Bible**, God commanded **Abraham in the Binding of Isaac** to sacrifice his son, but ultimately provided a ram as a substitute. The **Ten Commandments** in the **Torah forbid murder**. In addition, the use of blood (human or otherwise) in cooking is prohibited by the kosher dietary laws (**kashrut**). Blood from slaughtered animals may not be consumed, and must be drained out of the animal and covered with earth (**Lev 17:12-13**). Furthermore, **consumption of human flesh would violate kashrut.**

While animal sacrifice was part of the practice of ancient Judaism, the **Tanakh** (Old Testament) and Jewish teachings portray human sacrifice as one of the evils that separated the pagans of Canaan from the Hebrews (**Deut 12:31, 2 Kings 16:3**). Jews were prohibited from engaging in these rituals and were punished for doing so (**Ex 34:15, Lev 20:2, Deut 18:12, Jer 7:31**). In fact, ritual cleanliness for priests prohibited them from even being in the same room as a human corpse (**Lev 21:11**).

## History
The earliest versions of the accusation involved Jews crucifying Christian children at **Easter /Passover** because of a prophecy.

## Possible precursors
There are two records of ancient stories about Jewish acts of sacrifice that have been linked to the later blood libel stories of the medieval era. The first is in the writings of the **Graeco-Egyptian**

author **Apion**, who claimed that Jews sacrificed Greek victims in their temple. This accusation is known from **Josephus'** rebuttal of it in *Against Apion*. Apion states that when **Antiochus Epiphanes** entered the temple in Jerusalem, he discovered a Greek captive who told him he was being fattened for sacrifice. Every year, **Apion** claimed, the Jews would sacrifice a Greek and consume his flesh, at the same time swearing eternal hatred to Greeks.

## Origins in England

In England in 1144, Jews of Norwich were accused of ritual murder after a boy, **William of Norwich,** was found dead with stab wounds in the woods. William's hagiographer, **Thomas of Monmouth,** claimed that every year there is an international council of Jews at which they choose the country in which a child will be killed during **Easter,** because of a Jewish prophecy that states that the killing of a Christian child each year will ensure that the Jews will be restored to the **Holy Land.**

**King Henry III**, on reaching Lincoln at the beginning of October, refused to carry out the promise of **John of Lexington**, and had **Copin** executed and 91 of the Jews of Lincoln seized and sent up to London, where 18 of them were executed. Within a few decades, Jews would be **expelled from all of England in 1290** and not allowed to return until 1657.

## Continental Europe

The first known case outside England was in **Blois, France, in 1171**. This was the site of a blood libel accusation against the town's entire Jewish community that led to around **31 Jews being burned to death.** The child's body was never found, and all the Jews who lived in Blois were killed for the alleged ritual murder.

On 17 January 1670 **Raphael Levy**, a member of the Jewish community of Metz, was executed on charges of the ritual murder of a peasant child who had gone missing in the woods outside the village of Glatigny on 25 September 1669, the eve of **Rosh Hashanah.**

## Views of the Catholic Church

The attitude of the **Roman Catholic Church** towards these accusations and the cults venerating children supposedly killed by Jews has varied over time. The Papacy generally opposed them, although it had problems in enforcing its opposition.

In 1911, the *Dictionnaire apologétique de la foi catholique*, an important French Catholic encyclopedia, published an analysis of the blood libel accusations. Other contemporary Catholic sources (notably the Jesuit periodical *La Civiltà Cattolica*) promoted the blood libel as truth.

## Papal pronouncements

- **Pope Innocent IV** took action against the blood libel: "5 July 1247 **"Mandate to the prelates of Germany and France to annul all measures adopted against the Jews on account of the ritual murder libel, and to prevent accusation of Arabs on similar charges**" (The Apostolic See and the Jews, Documents: 492–1404).

- **Pope Gregory X** (1271–1276) issued a letter which criticized the practice of blood libels and forbade arrests and persecution of Jews based on a blood libel, *unless which we do not believe they be caught in the commission of the crime.*
- **Pope Paul III**, in a bull of 12 May 1540, made clear his displeasure at having learned, through the complaints of the Jews of Hungary, Bohemia and Poland, that their enemies, looking for a pretext to lay their hands on the Jews' property, were falsely attributing terrible crimes to them, in particular that of killing children and drinking their blood.
- **St. Pius V** in the bull *Hebraeorum gens sola* (26 February 1569), by which he expelled Jews from all the cities of the Papal States except Rome and Ancona, made multiple accusations of wrong-doing against the Jews, including usury, theft, receiving stolen goods, pimping, divination and magic. He did not mention the blood libel.
- **Pope Benedict XIV** wrote the bull *Beatus Andreas* (22 February 1755) in response to an application for the formal canonization of the 15th-century Andreas Oxner, a folk saint alleged to have been murdered by Jews "**out of hatred for the Christian faith**". Benedict did not dispute the factual claim that Jews murdered Christian children, and in anticipating that further cases on this basis would be brought appears to have accepted it as accurate, but decreed that in such cases beatification or canonization would be inappropriate.

## Views of Muslims

In late 1553 or 1554, **Suleiman the Magnificent**, the reigning Sultan of the Ottoman Empire, issued a firman (royal decree) formally **denouncing blood libels against the Jews**.

In 1983**, Mustafa Tlass** wrote and published *The Matzah of Zion*, which is a treatment of the **Damascus affair** of 1840 that repeats the ancient "**blood libel**", that Jews use the blood of murdered non-Jews in religious rituals such as baking Matza bread. In this book, he argues that the true religious beliefs of Jews are "**black hatred against all humans and religions**," and that no Arab country should ever sign a peace treaty with Israel.

In 2003, the Egyptian newspaper *Al-Ahram* published a series of articles by **Osama El-Baz,** a senior advisor to then **Egyptian President Hosni Mubarak**. Among other things, Osama El-Baz explained the origins of the blood libel against the Jews. He said that Arabs and Muslims have never been anti-Semitic, as a group, but accepted that a few Arab writers and media figures attack Jews "**on the basis of the racist fallacies and myths that originated in Europe**". He urged people not to succumb to "**myths**" such as the blood libel.

However, the blood libel was featured in a scene in the **Syrian TV series *Ash-Shatat,*** shown in 2003, while in 2013 the Israeli website *Arutz Sheva* reported cases of Israeli Arabs asking "**where Jews find the Christian blood they need to bake Matza**".

# Book of Daniel

The **Book of Daniel** is a 2nd-century BC biblical apocalypse combining a prophecy of history with an eschatology (a portrayal of end times) which is both cosmic in scope and political in its focus. In more mundane language, it is **"an account of the activities and visions of Daniel, a noble Jew exiled at Babylon,"** its message being that just as the God of Israel saved **Daniel** and his friends from their enemies, so he would save all of Israel in their present oppression.

In the Hebrew Bible it is found in the *Ketuvim* **(writings)**, while in **Christian Bibles** it is grouped with the Major Prophets. The book divides into two parts, a set of six court tales in **chapters 1–6** followed by four apocalyptic visions in **chapters 7–12**. The deuterocanon contains three additional stories: **the Song of the Three Holy Children, Susanna, and Bel and the Dragon.**

The book's influence has resonated through later ages, from the **Dead Sea Scrolls** community and the authors of the gospels and Revelation, to various movements from the 2nd century to the **Protestant Reformation** and modern millennialist movements—on which it continues to have a profound influence.

## ☑ Structure / Divisions

The Book of **Daniel** is divided between the court tales of **chapters 1–6** and the apocalyptic **visions of 7–12**, and between the Hebrew of **chapters 1 and 8–12** and the **Aramaic of chapters 2–7**. The division is reinforced by the chiastic arrangement of the Aramaic chapters (see below), and by a chronological progression in chapters 1–6 from Babylonian to Median times, and from Babylonian to Persian in **chapters 7–12**. Various suggestions have been made by scholars to explain the fact that the genre division does not coincide with the other two, but it appears that the language division and concentric structure of **chapters 2–6** are artificial literary devices designed to bind the two halves of the book together.

## Chiastic structure in the Aramaic section

There is a clear chiasm (a concentric literary structure in which the main point of a passage is placed in the centre and framed by parallel elements on either side in **"ABBA"** fashion) in the chapter arrangement of the Aramaic section. The following is taken from Paul Redditt's **"Introduction to the Prophets"**:

A1 (2:4b-49) – A dream of four kingdoms replaced by a fifth
B1 (3:1–30) – **Daniel**'s three friends in the fiery furnace
C1 (4:1–37) – **Daniel** interprets a dream for **Nebuchadnezzar**
C2 (5:1–31) – **Daniel** interprets the handwriting on the wall for Belshazzar
B2 (6:1–28) – **Daniel** in the lions' den
A2 (7:1–28) – A vision of four world kingdoms replaced by a fifth

## Introduction in Babylon (chapter 1)

In the third year of **King Jehoiakim**, God allows Jerusalem to fall into the power of **Nebuchadnezzar II**, king of Babylon. Young Israelites of noble and royal family, **"without physical defect, and handsome,"** versed in wisdom and competent to serve in the palace of the king, are taken to Babylon to be taught the literature and language of that nation. Among them are **Daniel** and his three companions, who refuse to touch the royal food and wine. Their overseer fears for his life in case the health of his charges deteriorates, but **Daniel** suggests a trial and the four emerge healthier than their counterparts from ten days of nothing but vegetables and water. They are allowed to continue to refrain from eating the king's food, and to **Daniel** God gives insight into visions and dreams. When their training is done **Nebuchadnezzar** finds them **'ten times better'** than all the wise men in his service and therefore keeps them at his court, where **Daniel** continues until the first year of **King Cyrus**.

## Nebuchadnezzar's dream of four kingdoms (chapter 2) / *Daniel 2*

In the second year of his reign **Nebuchadnezzar** has a dream. When he wakes up, he realizes that the dream has some important message, so he consults his wise men. Wary of their potential to fabricate an explanation, the king refuses to tell the wise men what he saw in his dream. Rather, he demands that his wise men tell him what the content of the dream was, and then interpret it. **When the wise men protest that this is beyond the power of any man, he sentences all, including Daniel and his friends, to death.**

**Daniel** receives an explanatory vision from God: **Nebuchadnezzar** had seen an enormous statue with a head of gold, breast and arms of silver, belly and thighs of bronze, legs of iron, and feet of mixed iron and clay, then saw the statue destroyed by a rock that turned into a mountain filling the whole earth. **Daniel** explains the dream to the king: the statue symbolized four successive kingdoms, starting with **Nebuchadnezzar**, all of which would be crushed by God's kingdom, which would endure forever. **Nebuchadnezzar acknowledges the supremacy of Daniel's god, raises Daniel over all his wise men, and places Daniel and his companions over the province of Babylon.**

## The fiery furnace (chapter 3) / *Shadrach, Meshach, and Abednego*

**Daniel**'s companions **Shadrach, Meshach, and Abednego** refuse to bow to King **Nebuchadnezzar**'s golden statue and are thrown into a fiery furnace. **Nebuchadnezzar** is astonished to see a fourth figure in the furnace with the three, one **"with the appearance like a son of the gods."** So the king called the three to come out of the fire, and blessed the God of Israel, and decreed that any who blasphemed against him should be torn limb from limb.

## Nebuchadnezzar's madness (chapter 4) / *Daniel 4*

**Nebuchadnezzar** recounts a dream of a huge tree that is suddenly cut down at the command of a heavenly messenger. **Daniel** is summoned and interprets the dream. The tree is **Nebuchadnezzar**

himself, who for seven years will lose his mind and live like a wild beast. All of this comes to pass until, at the end of the specified time, **Nebuchadnezzar** acknowledges that "heaven rules" and his kingdom and sanity are restored.

## Belshazzar's feast (chapter 5) / *Belshazzar's feast / Fall of Babylon*

**Belshazzar** and his nobles blasphemously drink from sacred Jewish temple vessels, offering praise to inanimate gods, until a hand mysteriously appears and writes upon the wall. The horrified king summons **Daniel**, who upbraids him for his lack of humility before God and interprets the message: Belshazzar's kingdom will be given to the Medes and Persians. **Belshazzar rewards Daniel and raises him to be third in the kingdom, and that very night Belshazzar is slain and Darius the Mede takes the kingdom.**

## Daniel in the lions' den (chapter 6)

Darius elevates **Daniel** to high office, exciting the jealousy of other officials. Knowing of **Daniel**'s devotion to his God, his enemies trick the king into issuing an edict forbidding worship of any other god or man for a 30-day period. **Daniel** continues to pray three times a day to God towards Jerusalem; he is accused and **King Darius**, forced by his own decree, throws **Daniel** into the lions' den. But God shuts up the mouths of the lions, and the next morning Darius rejoices to find him unharmed. The king casts **Daniel**'s accusers into the lions' pit together with their wives and children to be instantly devoured, while he himself acknowledges **Daniel**'s God as he whose kingdom shall never be destroyed.

## Vision of the beasts from the sea (chapter 7) / *Daniel 7 / Four kingdoms of Daniel*

In the first year of **Belshazzar Daniel** has a dream of four monstrous beasts arising from the sea. The fourth, a beast with ten horns, devours the whole earth, treading it down and crushing it, and a further small horn appears and uproots three of the earlier horns. The Ancient of Days judges and destroys the beast, and **"one like a son of man"** is given everlasting kingship over the entire world. A divine being explains that the four beasts represent four kings, but that **"the holy ones of the Most High"** would receive the everlasting kingdom. The fourth beast would be a fourth kingdom with ten kings, and another king who would pull down three kings and make war on the "holy ones" for **"a time, two times and a half,"** after which the heavenly judgement will be made against him and the **"holy ones"** will receive the everlasting kingdom.

## Vision of the ram and goat (chapter 8) / *Daniel 8*

In the third year of **Belshazzar Daniel** has vision of a ram and goat. The ram has two mighty horns, one longer than the other, and it charges west, north and south, overpowering all other beasts. A goat with a single horn appears from the west and destroys the ram. The goat becomes very powerful until the horn breaks off and is replaced by four lesser horns. A small horn that grows very large, it stops the daily temple sacrifices and desecrates the sanctuary for two thousand three hundred **"evening and mornings"** (which could be either 1150 or 2300 days) until the temple is cleansed. The angel Gabriel informs him that the ram represents the **Medes** and **Persians**, the goat is Greece, and the **"little horn"** is a wicked king.

## Vision of the Seventy Weeks (chapter 9) / *Prophecy of Seventy Weeks*

In the first year of **Darius the Mede**, **Daniel** meditates on the word of Jeremiah that the desolation of Jerusalem would last seventy years; he confesses the sin of Israel and pleads for God to restore Israel and the **"desolated sanctuary"** of the Temple. The angel **Gabriel** explains that the **seventy years stand for seventy "weeks" of years (490 years)**, during which the Temple will first be restored, then later defiled by a **"prince who is to come,"** **"until the decreed end is poured out."**

## Vision of the kings of north and south (chapters 10–12) / *Daniel's final vision*

**Daniel** 10: In the third year of **Cyrus Daniel** sees in his vision an angel (called **"a man"**, but clearly a supernatural being) who explains that he is in the midst of a war with the **"prince of Persia"**, assisted only by **Michael, "your prince." The "prince of Greece"** will shortly come, but first he will reveal what will happen to **Daniel**'s people.

**Daniel** 11: A future king of Persia will make war on the king of Greece, a **"mighty king"** will arise and wield power until his empire is broken up and given to others, and finally the king of the south (identified in verse 8 as Egypt) will go to war with the **"king of the north."** After many battles (described in great detail) a **"contemptible person"** will become king of the north; this king will invade the south two times, the first time with success, but on his second he will be stopped by **"ships of Kittim."** He will turn back to his own country, and on the way his soldiers will desecrate the **Temple**, abolish the daily sacrifice, and set up the abomination of desolation. He will defeat and subjugate Libya and Egypt, but **"reports from the east and north will alarm him,"** and he will meet his end **"between the sea and the holy mountain."**

**Daniel** 12: At this time **Michael** will come. It will be a time of great distress, but all those whose names are written will be delivered. **"Multitudes who sleep in the dust of the earth will awake, some to everlasting life, others to shame and everlasting contempt; those who are wise will shine like the brightness of the heavens, and those who lead many to righteousness, like the stars for ever and ever."** In the final verses the remaining time to the end is revealed: **"a time, times and half a time"** (three years and a half). **Daniel** fails to understand and asks again what will happen, and is told: **"From the time that the daily sacrifice is abolished and the abomination that causes desolation is set up, there will be 1,290 days. Blessed is the one who waits for and reaches the end of the 1,335 days."**

## Historical background

The visions of **chapters 7–12** reflect the crisis which took place in **Judea in 167–164 BC when Antiochus IV Epiphanes, the Greek king of the Seleucid Empire, threatened to destroy traditional Jewish worship in Jerusalem.** When **Antiochus** came to the throne in 175 BC the

Jews were largely pro-Seleucid. The **High Priestly** family was split by rivalry, and one member, Jason, offered the king a large sum to be made **High Priest**. **Jason** also asked—or more accurately, paid—to be allowed to make Jerusalem *a polis*, or Greek city. This meant, among other things, that city government would be in the hands of the citizens, which meant in turn that citizenship would be a valuable commodity, to be purchased from **Jason**. None of this threatened the Jewish religion, and the reforms were widely welcomed, especially among the Jerusalem aristocracy and the leading priests. Three years later **Jason** was deposed when another priest, **Menelaus**, offered **Antiochus** an even larger sum for the post of **High Priest**.

**Antiochus invaded Egypt twice, in 169 BC with success**, but on the second incursion, in late 168 BC, he was forced to withdraw by the Romans. Jason, hearing a rumor that **Antiochus** was dead, attacked Menelaus to take back the High Priesthood. **Antiochus** drove Jason out of Jerusalem, **plundered the Temple**, and introduced measures to pacify his Egyptian border by imposing complete **Hellenization**: **the Jewish Book of the Law was prohibited and on 15 December 167 BC and "abomination of desolation",** probably a Greek altar, was introduced into the Temple. With the Jewish religion now clearly under threat a resistance movement sprang up, led by the **Maccabee** brothers, and over the next three years it won sufficient victories over **Antiochus** to take back and purify the Temple.

The crisis which the author of **Daniel** addresses is the **defilement of the altar in Jerusalem in 167 BC** (first introduced in **chapter 8:11**): the daily offering which used to take place twice a day, at morning and evening, stopped, and the phrase **"evenings and mornings"** recurs through the following chapters as a reminder of the missed sacrifices. But whereas the events leading up to the **sacking of the Temple in 167 BC** and the immediate aftermath are remarkably accurate, the predicted war between the Syrians and the Egyptians **(11:40–43)** never took place, and the prophecy that **Antiochus would die in Palestine (11:44–45) was inaccurate (he died in Persia).** The obvious conclusion is that the account must have been completed near the end of the reign of **Antiochus** but before his **death in December 164 BC**, or at least before news of it reached Jerusalem, and the consensus of modern scholarship is accordingly that the book dates to the period **167-163 BCE.**

## Authorship

**Daniel** is one of a large number of Jewish apocalypses, all of them pseudonymous. The stories of the first half are considered legendary in origin, and the visions of the second the product of anonymous authors in the **Maccabean** period (2nd century BC).

Although the entire book is traditionally ascribed to **Daniel** the seer, **chapters 1–6** are in the voice of an anonymous narrator, except for chapter 4 which is in the form of a letter from king **Nebuchadnezzar**; only the second half (**chapters 7–12**) is presented by **Daniel** himself, introduced by the anonymous narrator in **chapters 7 and 10**. The real author/editor of **Daniel** was probably an educated Jew, knowledgeable in Greek learning, and of high standing in his own community. The book is a product of **"Wisdom"** circles, but the type of wisdom is mantic (the discovery of heavenly secrets from earthly signs) rather than the wisdom of learning—the main source of wisdom in **Daniel** is God's revelation.

It is possible that the name of **Daniel** was chosen for the hero of the book because of his reputation as a wise seer in Hebrew tradition. **Ezekiel,** who lived during the Babylonian exile, mentioned him in association with **Noah** and **Job (Ezekiel 14:14)** as a figure of legendary wisdom **(28:3),** and a hero named **Daniel** (more accurately **Daniel,** but the spelling is close enough for the two to be regarded as identical) features in a late 2nd millennium myth from Ugarit. **"The legendary Daniel, known from long ago but still remembered as an exemplary character ... serves as the principal human 'hero' in the biblical book that now bears his name"; Daniel** is the wise and righteous intermediary who is able to interpret dreams and thus convey the will of God to humans, the recipient of visions from on high that are interpreted to him by heavenly intermediaries.

## Dating

**The prophecies of Daniel are accurate down to the career of Antiochus IV Epiphanes, king of Syria and oppressor of the Jews, but not in its prediction of his death:** the author seems to know about **Antiochus'** two campaigns in Egypt (169 and 167 BC), **the desecration of the Temple (the "abomination of desolation"),** and the fortification of the **Akra** (a fortress built inside Jerusalem), but he seems to know nothing about the reconstruction of the Temple or about the actual circumstances of **Antiochus' death in late 164 BC. Chapters 10–12** must therefore have been **written between 167 and 164 BC.** There is no evidence of a significant time lapse between those chapters and **chapters 8 and 9, and chapter 7** may have been written just a few months earlier again.

Further evidence of the book's date is in the fact that **Daniel** is excluded from the **Hebrew Bible's** canon of the prophets, which was closed around 200 BC, and the **Wisdom of Sirach**, a work dating from around 180 BC, draws on almost every book of the Old Testament except **Daniel**, leading scholars to suppose that its author was unaware of it. **Daniel** is, however, quoted in a section of the **Sibylline Oracles** commonly dated to the middle of the 2nd century BC, and was popular at **Qumran** at much the same time, suggesting that it was known from the middle of that century.

Theologian **David Malick** has put forward a list of arguments for why he believes **Daniel** was written long before the 2nd century BC date. His arguments come in five parts: **first**, that **Daniel** would have needed time to have been canonized; **second**, the language used looks like it is from an earlier era; **third**, that the style and content of the book could have been earlier than the 2nd century BC; **fourth**, that **"he reason the development of history seems to stop with Antiochus IV Epiphanes is not necessarily because that was when the writer lived; it is probably for**

**literary/theological reasons, he best foreshadows the Antichrist to come";** and **fifth,** that his prophecy of future kingdoms goes beyond the Greek empire (which would make the book prophecy whether it was written in 160s BC or an earlier date).

## Manuscripts

The Book of **Daniel** is preserved in the 12-chapter **Masoretic Text** and in two longer Greek versions, the original Septuagint version, c. 100 BC, and the later **Theodotion** version from c. 2nd century AD. Both Greek texts contain three additions to **Daniel**: The **Prayer of Azariah** and **Song of the Three Holy Children**; the story of **Susannah and the Elders**; and the story of **Bel and the Dragon**. Theodotion is much closer to the **Masoretic Text** and became so popular that it replaced the original **Septuagint** version in all but two manuscripts of the Septuagint itself. The Greek additions were apparently never part of the Hebrew text.

**Eight copies of the Book of Daniel, all incomplete, have been found at Qumran, two in Cave 1, five in Cave 4, and one in Cave 6.** Between them, they preserve text from eleven of **Daniel**'s twelve chapters, and the twelfth is quoted in the **Florilegium** (a compilation scroll) **4Q174**, showing that the book at Qumran did not lack this conclusion. **All eight manuscripts were copied between 125 BC (4QDan$^c$) and about 50 AD (4QDan$^b$),** showing that **Daniel** was being read at Qumran only about 40 years after its composition. All appear to preserve the 12-chapter Masoretic version rather than the longer Greek text. None reveal any major disagreements against the Masoretic, and the four scrolls that preserve the relevant sections **(1QDan$^a$, 4QDan$^a$, 4QDan$^b$, and 4QDan$^d$)** all follow the bilingual nature of **Daniel** where the book opens in Hebrew, switches to **Aramaic at 2:4b, then reverts to Hebrew at 8:1.**

## Meaning, symbolism and chronology

The message of the **Book of Daniel** is that, just as the God of Israel saved **Daniel** and his friends from their enemies, so he would save all Israel in their present oppression. The book is filled with monsters, angels, and numerology, drawn from a wide range of sources, both biblical and non-biblical, that would have had meaning in the context of 2nd-century Jewish culture, and while Christian interpreters have always viewed these as predicting events in the **New Testament—"the Son of God", "the Son of Man", Christ and the Antichrist**—the book's intended audience is the Jews of the 2nd century BC. The following explains a few of these predictions, as understood by modern biblical scholars.

- The *four kingdoms* and the *little horn* (**Daniel** 2 and 7): The concept of four successive world empires stems from Greek theories of mythological history; most modern interpreters agree that the four represent Babylon, the Medes, Persia and the Greeks, ending with Hellenistic Seleucid Syria and with Hellenistic Ptolemaic Egypt. The symbolism of four metals in the statue in chapter 2 comes from Persian writings, while the four **"beasts from the sea" in chapter 7 reflect Hosea 13:7–8**, in which God threatens that he will be to Israel like a lion, a leopard, a bear or a wild beast. The consensus among scholars is that the four beasts of **chapter 7**, like the metals of **chapter 2**, symbolize

Babylon, Media, Persia and the Seleucids, with **Antiochus IV (reigned 175–164 BC)** as the **"small horn"** that uproots three others (**Antiochus** usurped the rights of several other claimants to become king of the Seleucid Empire).

- The *Ancient of Days* and the *one like a son of man* (**Daniel 7**): The portrayal of God in **Daniel 7:13** resembles the portrayal of the Canaanite god El as an ancient divine king presiding over the divine court. The **"Ancient of Days"** gives dominion over the earth to **"one like a son of man"**, and then in **Daniel 7:27** to **"the people of the holy ones of the Most High"**, whom scholars consider the son of man to represent. These people can be understood as the *maskilim* (**sages**), or as the Jewish people broadly.

- *The ram and he-goat* (**Daniel 8**) as conventional astrological symbols represent Persia and Syria, as the text explains. The **"mighty horn"** stands for **Alexander the Great (reigned 336–323 BC)** and the "four lesser horns" represent the four principal generals (Diadochi) who fought over the Greek empire following Alexander's death. The **"little horn"** again **represents Antiochus IV. The key to the symbols lies in the description of the little horn's actions**: he ends the continual burnt offering and overthrows the Sanctuary, a clear reference to **Antiochus'** desecration of the Temple.

- The *anointed ones* and the *seventy years* (**Chapter 9**): **Daniel** reinterprets Jeremiah's **"seventy years"** prophecy regarding the period Israel would spend in bondage to Babylon. From the point of view of the Maccabean era, Jeremiah's promise was obviously not true— the gentiles still oppressed the Jews, and the **"desolation of Jerusalem"** had not ended. **Daniel** therefore reinterprets the **seventy years as seventy "weeks" of years, making up 490 years.** The 70 weeks/490 years are subdivided, with seven **"weeks"** from the **"going forth of the word to rebuild and restore Jerusalem"** to the coming of an **"anointed one"**, while the final **"week"** is marked by the violent death of another **"anointed one"**, probably the **High Priest Onias III** (ousted to make way for Jason and murdered in 171 BC), and the profanation of the Temple. The point of this for **Daniel** is that the period of gentile power is predetermined, and is coming to an end.

- *Kings of north and south*: **Chapters 10 to 12** concern the war between these kings, the events leading up to it, and its heavenly meaning. In **chapter 10 the angel (Gabriel?)** explains that there is currently a war in heaven between **Michael**, the angelic protector of Israel, and the **"princes" (angels)** of Persia and Greece; then, in **chapter 11**, he outlines the human wars which accompany this—the mythological concept sees standing behind every nation a god/angel who does battle on behalf of his people, so that earthly events reflect what happens in heaven. The wars of the **Ptolemies ("kings of the south")** against the **Seleucids ("kings of the north")** are reviewed down to the career of **Antiochus the Great (Antiochus III (reigned 222–187 BC), father of Antiochus IV),** but the main focus is **Antiochus IV**, to whom more than half the chapter is devoted. The accuracy of these predictions lends credibility to the real prophecy with which the passage ends, the death of **Antiochus**—which, in the event, was not accurate.

- *Predicting the end-time* (**Daniel 8:14 and 12:7–12**): Biblical eschatology does not generally give precise information as to when the end will come, and **Daniel's** attempts to specify the number of days remaining is a rare exception. **Daniel** asks the angel how long the **"little horn"** will be triumphant, and the angel replies that the Temple will be reconsecrated after **2300 "evenings and mornings" have passed (Daniel 8:14).** The angel is counting the two daily sacrifices, so the period is **1150 days from the desecration in December 167. In chapter 12** the angel gives three more dates: the desolation will last **"for a time, times and half a time"**, or a year, two years, and a half a year **(Daniel 12:8);** then that the "**desolation**" will last for 1290 days (**12:11**); and finally, 1335 days (**12:12**). Verse **12:11** was presumably added after the lapse of the 1150 days of chapter 8, and **12:12** after the lapse of the **number in 12:11.**

# Book of Enoch

The **Book of Enoch** is an ancient Jewish religious work, ascribed by tradition to **Enoch**, the great-grandfather of Noah. It is not part of the biblical canon as used by Jews, apart from Beta Israel. Most Christian denominations and traditions may accept the **books of Enoch** as having some historical or theological interest. It is regarded as canonical by the **Ethiopian Orthodox Tewahedo Church** and **Eritrean Orthodox Tewahedo Church**, but not by any other Christian groups. It is wholly extant only in the Ge-ez language, with Aramaic fragments from the **Dead Sea Scrolls** and a few Greek and Latin fragments. No Hebrew version is known to have survived its author was **Enoch**, before the biblical Flood. The text was also utilized by the community that originally collected the **Dead Sea Scrolls**.

## Content

The first part of the **Book of Enoch** describes the fall of the **Watchers**, the angels who fathered the **Nephilim**. The remainder of the book describes **Enoch**'s visits to heaven in the form of travels, visions and dreams, and his revelations. **The book consists of 5 major Ferons:**

- **The Book of the Watchers** (1 **Enoch** 1-36)
- **The Book of Parables** of **Enoch** (1 **Enoch** 37-71) (also called the Similitudes of **Enoch**)
- **The Astronomical Book** (1 **Enoch** 72-82) (also called the Book of the Heavenly Luminaries or Book of Luminaries)
- **The Book of Dream Vision** (1 **Enoch** 83-90) (also called the Book of Dreams)
- **The epistle of Enoch** (1 **Enoch** 91-108)

## Canonicity: Judaism

Although evidently widely known during the development of the Hebrew Bible canon, **1 Enoch** was excluded from both the formal canon of the **Tanakh** and the typical canon of the **Septuagint** and, therefore, also from the writings known today as the **Deuterocanon**. The content, particularly detailed descriptions of fallen angels, would also be a reason for rejection from the Hebrew canon at this period, that angels sinned and revolted from God.

## Christianity

By the 4th century, the **Book of Enoch** was mostly excluded from Christian canons, and it is now regarded as scripture by only the **Ethiopian Orthodox Church** and the **Eritrean Orthodox Church.**

## References in the New Testament

**Enoch** is referred to as a historical person and prophet, and quoted, in **Jude 1:14-15**

**And Enoch also, the seventh from Adam, prophesied of these, saying, Behold, the Lord cometh with ten thousands of his saints, To execute judgment upon all, and to convict all that are ungodly among which ungodly sinners have spoken against him.**

Other Jewish groups, most notably those living in **Qumran** near the **Dead Sea**, also used and valued 1 **Enoch**, but we do not find it grouped with the scriptural scrolls.

## Reception

The **Book of Enoch** was considered as scripture in the epistle of **Barnabas (16:4)** and by many of the early **Church Fathers**, such as **Athenagoras, Clement of Alexandria**, the **Book of Enoch** had been rejected by the Jews because it contained prophecies pertaining to **Christ**.

## The Church of Jesus Christ of Latter-day Saints

The Church of Jesus Christ of Latter-day Saints (**LDS Church**) does not consider 1 **Enoch** to be part of its standard canon, though it believes that the *original* book of **Enoch** was an inspired book.

## Ethiopic

The most extensive witnesses to the **Book of Enoch** exist in the **Ge-ez** language. Thought to be more ancient and more similar to the Greek versions.

## Aramaic

Eleven Aramaic-language fragments of the **Book of Enoch** were found in cave 4 of **Qumran I** 1948 and are in the care of the **Israel Antiquities Authority**. It was also partly damaged, with the ink blurred and faint.

## History:

### Second Temple period

The 1976 publication by **Milik** of the results of the paleographic dating of the **Enoch**ic fragments found in **Qumran** made a breakthrough. According to this scholar, who studied the original scrolls for many years, the oldest fragments of the **Book of Watchers** are dated to 200-150 BC. Since the **Book of Watchers** shows evidence of multiple stages of composition, it is probable that this work was extant already in the 3rd century BC. The same can be said about the **Astronomical Book**.

It was no longer possible to claim that the core of the book of **Enoch** was composed in the wake of the **Maccabean Revolt** as a reaction to Hellenization. Some scholars speak even of an "**Enoch**ic **Judaism**" from which the writers of Qumran scrolls were descended. Margaret Barker argues, **"Enoch is the writing of a very conservative group whose roots go right back to the time of the First Temple"**.

It is probable that the Qumran community gradually lost interest in the **Book of Enoch**. The relation between 1 **Enoch** and the Essenes was noted even before the discovery of the **Dead Sea Scrolls**. The main peculiar aspects of the not-Qumranic units of 1 **Enoch** are the following:

- a Messiah called **"Son of Man"**, with divine attributes, generated before the creation, who will act directly in the final judgment and sit on a throne of glory (**1 Enoch 46:1-4, 48:2-7, 69:26-29**)
- The sinners usually seen as the wealthy ones and the just as the oppressed (a theme we find also in the Psalms of Solomon).

# Book of Esther

The **Book of Esther**, also known in Hebrew as **"the Scroll"** (*Megillah*), is a book in the third section (*Ketuvim*, **"Writings"**) of the Jewish *Tanakh* (the Hebrew Bible) and in the Christian Old Testament. It is one of the five **Scrolls** (*Megillot*) in the Hebrew Bible. It relates the story of a Hebrew woman in Persia, **born as Hadassah but known as Esther, who becomes queen of Persia** and thwarts a genocide of her people. The story forms the core of the Jewish festival of **Purim**, during which it is read aloud twice: once in the evening and again the following morning. **The books of Esther and Song of Songs are the only books in the Hebrew Bible that do not explicitly mention God.**

## Setting and structure

The biblical **Book of Esther** is set in the Persian capital of **Susa** (*Shushan*) in the third year of the reign of the **Persian king Ahasuerus**. The name *Ahasuerus* is equivalent to *Xerxes* (both deriving from the **Persian** *Khshayārsha*), and **Ahasuerus** is usually identified in modern sources as **Xerxes I**, who ruled between 486 and 465 BC, as it is to this monarch that the events described in **Esther** are thought to fit the most closely.

Assuming that **Ahasuerus** is indeed **Xerxes I**, the events described in **Esther** began around the years 483–482 BC, and concluded in March 473 BC. Classical sources such as **Josephus**, the Jewish commentary *Esther Rabbah* and the Christian theologian **Bar-Hebraeus**, as well as the Greek Septuagint translation of **Esther**, instead identify **Ahasuerus** as either **Artaxerxes I** (reigned 465 to 424 BC) or **Artaxerxes II** (reigned 404 to 358 BC).

On his accession however **Artaxerxes II** lost Egypt to pharaoh **Amyrtaeus**, after which it was no longer part of the Persian Empire. In his *Historia Scholastica* Petrus Comestor identified **Ahasuerus** (**Esther** 1:1) as **Artaxerxes III** (358–338 BC) who reconquered Egypt.

## Structure

The **Book of Esther** consists of an introduction (or exposition) in **chapters 1 and 2**; the main action (complication and resolution) in **chapters 3 to 9:19**; and a conclusion in **9:20–10:3**. The plot is structured around banquets (*mishteh*), a word that occurs twenty times in **Esther** and only 24 times in the rest of the Hebrew bible. This is appropriate given that **Esther** describes the origin of a Jewish feast, the feast of **Purim**, but **Purim** itself is not the subject and no individual feast in the Book is commemorated by **Purim**.

The book's theme, rather, is the reversal of destiny through a sudden and unexpected turn of events: the Jews seem destined to be destroyed, but instead are saved. In literary criticism such a reversal is termed **"peripety",** and while on one level its use in **Esther** is simply a literary or aesthetic device, on another it is structural to the author's theme, suggesting that the power of God is at work behind human events.

## Summary

**King Ahasuerus**, ruler of the **Persian Empire**, holds a lavish **180-day banquet**, initially for his court and dignitaries and afterwards a **seven day banquet** for all inhabitants of the capital city, Shushan. **(Esther 1:1-9.)** On the seventh day of the latter banquet, **Ahasuerus** orders the queen, **Vashti**, to display her beauty before the guests by coming before them wearing only her crown. **(1:10-11.)** She refuses, infuriating **Ahasuerus**, who on the advice of his counselors removes her from her position as an example to other women who might be emboldened to disobey their husbands**. (1:12-19.) A decree follows that "that every man should bear rule in his own house." (1:20-22.)**

**Ahasuerus** then makes arrangements to choose a new queen from a selection of beautiful young women from throughout the empire. **(2:1-4.)** among these women is a Jewish orphan named **Esther**, who was raised by her cousin or uncle, **Mordecai. (2:5-7.)** She finds favor in the King's eyes, and is **crowned his new queen, but does not reveal her Jewish heritage. (2:8-20).** shortly afterwards, **Mordecai** discovers a plot by two courtiers, **Bigthan and Teresh, to assassinate Ahasuerus**. The conspirators are apprehended and hanged, and **Mordecai**'s service to the King is recorded. **(2:21-23.)**

**Ahasuerus appoints Haman as his viceroy. (3:1.) Mordecai**, who sits at the palace gates, falls into **Haman**'s disfavor, as he refuses to bow down to him. **(3:2-5.) Haman** discovers that **Mordecai** refused to bow on account of his Jewishness, and in **revenge plots to kill not just Mordecai, but all the Jews in the empire. (3:6.)** He obtains **Ahasuerus'** permission to execute this plan, against payment of ten thousand talents of silver, and casts lots **("Purim")** to choose the date on which to do this—the thirteenth of the month of Adar. **(3:7-12.) A royal decree is issued throughout the kingdom to slay all Jews on that date. (3:13-15.)**

When **Mordecai** discovers the plan, he goes into mourning and implores **Esther** to intercede with the King. **(4:1-5)** But she is afraid to present herself to the King unsummoned, an offense punishable by death. **(4:6-12.)** Instead, she directs **Mordecai** to have all Jews fast for three days for her, and vows to fast as well. **(4:15-16.)** on the third day she goes to **Ahasuerus**, who stretches out his sceptre to her to indicate that she is not to be punished. **(5:1-2.)** She invites him to a feast in the company of **Haman. (5:3-5.)** during the feast, she asks them to attend a further feast the next evening. **(5:6-8.)** Meanwhile, **Haman** is again offended by **Mordecai** and, at his wife's suggestion, has a gallows built to hang him. **(5:9-14.)**

That night, **Ahasuerus** cannot sleep, and orders the court records be read to him. **(6:1.)** He is reminded that **Mordecai** interceded in the previous plot against his life, and discovers that

**Mordecai** never received any recognition. **(6:2-3.)** Just then, **Haman** appears to request the King's permission to hang **Mordecai**, but before he can make this request, **Ahasuerus** asks **Haman** what should be done for the man that the King wishes to honor. **(6:4-6.)** Assuming that the King is referring to **Haman** himself, **Haman** suggests that the man be dressed in the King's royal robes and led around on the King's royal horse, while a herald calls: **"See how the King honors a man he wishes to reward!"** **(6:7-9.)** to his surprise and horror, the King instructs **Haman** to do so to **Mordecai. (6:10-11.)**

Immediately after, **Ahasuerus** and **Haman** attend **Esther**'s second banquet. The King promises to grant her any request, and she reveals that she is Jewish and that **Haman** is planning to exterminate her people, including her. **(7:1-6.)** Overcome by rage, **Ahasuerus** leaves the room; meanwhile **Haman** stays behind and begs **Esther** for his life, falling upon her in desperation. **(7:7.)** The King returns in at this very moment and thinks **Haman** is assaulting the queen; this makes him angrier and he **orders Haman hanged on the very gallows that Haman had prepared for Mordecai. (7:8-10.)**

Unable to annul a formal royal decree, the King instead adds to it, **permitting the Jews to arm and defend themselves on the day chosen for their annihilation. (8:1-14.)** On 13 Adar, **Haman**'s ten sons and 500 other men are killed in Shushan. **(9:1-12.)** upon hearing of this **Esther** requests it be repeated the next day, whereupon 300 more men are killed. **(9:13-15.) Over 75,000 people are slaughtered by the Jews, who are careful to take no plunder. (9:16-17.)** **Mordecai** and **Esther** send letters throughout the provinces instituting an annual commemoration of the Jewish people's redemption, in a holiday called **Purim (lots). (9:20-28.)** **Ahasuerus** remains very powerful and continues his reign, with **Mordecai** assuming a prominent position in his court. **(10:1-3.)**

## Authorship and date

The *Megillat Esther* **(Book of Esther) became the last of the 24 books of the Tanakh to be** canonized by the **Sages of the Great Assembly**. According to the **Talmud**, it was a redaction by the **Great Assembly** of an original text by **Mordecai**. It is usually dated to the **4th century BC.** Shemaryahu Talmon, however, suggests that "**the traditional setting of the book in the days of Xerxes I cannot be wide off the mark."**

The Greek **Book of Esther**, included in the **Septuagint**, is a retelling of the events of the **Hebrew Book of Esther** rather than a translation and records additional traditions which do not appear in original Hebrew version, in particular the identification of **Ahasuerus** with **Artaxerxes** and details of various letters. It is dated around the **late 2nd to early 1st century BC.** The Coptic and Ethiopic versions of **Esther** are translations of the Greek rather than the Hebrew **Esther**.

A Latin version of **Esther** was produced by Jerome for the **Vulgate**. It translates the Hebrew **Esther** but interpolates translations of the Greek **Esther** where the latter provides additional material. **Several Aramaic Targums of Esther** were produced in the Middle Ages of which two survive – the *Targum Rishon* (**"First Targum"**) and *Targum Sheni* ("**Second Targum**") dated c. 500–1000 AD. These were not Targums (**"translations"**) in the true sense but like the Greek **Esther** are retellings of events and include additional legends relating to **Purim**. There is also a 16th-century recension of the *Targum Rishon*, sometimes counted as *Targum Shelishi* (**"Third Targum").**

The **Book of Esther** falls under the **category of Ketuvim, one of three parts of the Jewish canon**. Written to explain the origin of the Jewish holiday of **Purim**.

# Book of Genesis

The **Book of Genesis** is the first book of the **Hebrew Bible (the Tanakh)** and the **Christian Old Testament**. The basic narrative expresses the central theme: God creates the world (along with creating the first man and woman) and appoints man as his regent, but man proves disobedient and God destroys his world through the **Flood**. The new post-Flood world is equally corrupt, but God does not destroy it, instead calling one man, **Abraham, to be the seed of its salvation.**

At God's command **Abraham** descends from his home into the land of Canaan, given to him by God, where he dwells as a sojourner, as does his son Isaac and his grandson **Jacob**. Jacob's name is changed to **Israel,** and through the agency of his son **Joseph**, the children of Israel descend into Egypt, 70 people in all with their households, and God promises them a future of greatness. **Genesis** ends with Israel in Egypt, ready for the coming of **Moses** and the **Exodus**.

The book's author or authors appear to have structured it around then **"toledot"** sections (the **"these are the generations of…"** phrases), but modern commentators see it in terms of a **"primeval history"**. In Judaism, the theological importance of **Genesis** centers on the covenants linking God to his chosen people and the people to the **Promised Land** Christianity has interpreted **Genesis** as the prefiguration of certain cardinal Christian beliefs, primarily the need for salvation (the hope or assurance of all Christians) and the redemptive act of **Christ** on the Cross as the fulfillment of covenant promises as the **Son of God**. Tradition credits **Moses** as the author of **Genesis**, as well as **Exodus, Leviticus, Numbers** and most of **Deuteronomy**, but modern scholars increasingly see them as a product of the 6th and 5th centuries BC.

## Structure
**Genesis** appears to be structured around the recurring phrase *elleh toledot*, meaning **"these are the generations,"** with the first use of the phrase referring to the **"generations of heaven and earth"** and the remainder marking individuals – **Noah**, the **"sons of Noah"**, **Shem**, etc., down to **Jacob**. The **"patriarchal history"** recounts the events of the major **patriarchs Abraham, Isaac and Jacob,** to whom God reveals himself and to whom the promise of descendants and land is made, while the story of **Joseph** serve to take the Israelites into Egypt in preparation for the next book, **Exodus.**

## Summary
**God creates the world in six days and consecrates the seventh as a day of rest**. God creates the first humans **Adam** and **Eve** and all the animals in the **Garden of Eden** but instructs them not to eat the fruit of the tree of knowledge of good and evil. A talking serpent, portrayed as a deceptive creature or trickster, entices **Eve** into eating it anyway, and she entices **Adam**, whereupon God curses them and throws them out in the **fall of man**. **Eve bears two sons, Cain and Abel**. Cain kills Abel after God accepts Abel's offering, but not Cain's. God then curses Cain. **Eve bears another son, Seth, to take Abel's place.**

After many generations of **Adam** have passed from the lines of **Cain** and **Seth**, the world becomes corrupted by the sin of man and **Nephilim**, and God determines to wipe out mankind. First, he instructs the righteous **Noah** and his family to build a huge boat and put examples of all the animals on it.

Then God sends a great flood to wipe out the rest of the world. When the waters recede, God promises that he will not destroy the world a second time with water with the rainbow as the symbol of his promise. But upon seeing mankind cooperating to build a great tower city, the **Tower of Babel, God divides humanity with many languages and sets them apart with confusion.**

God instructs **Abram** to travel from his home in Mesopotamia to the land of **Canaan**. There God makes a covenant with **Abram** promising that his descendants shall be as numerous as the stars. But that people will suffer oppression in a foreign land for four hundred years, after which they will inherit the land **"from the river of Egypt to the great river, the river Euphrates."**

**Abram's name is changed to Abraham and that of his wife Sarai to Sarah**, and circumcision of all males is instituted as the sign of the covenant. Because Sarah is old, she tells **Abraham** to take her Egyptian handmaiden, **Hagar**, as a second wife. Through **Hagar, Abraham** father's **Ishmael.**

God resolves to destroy the city of **Sodom** and **Gomorrah** for the sins of its people. **Abraham** protests and gets God to agree not to destroy the city if **10 righteous men** can be found. Angels save **Abraham**'s nephew **Lot** and his family but his wife looks back on the destruction against their command and is turned into a pillar of salt. Lot's daughters, concerned that they are fugitives who will never find husbands, get him drunk to become pregnant by him, and give birth to the ancestors of the **Moabites and Ammonites.**

**Abraham** and **Sarah** go to the foreign land of **Gerar**, pretending to be brother and sister (they are half-siblings). The King of Gerar takes Sarah for his wife, but God warns him to return here, and he obeys. God sends Sarah a son to be named **Isaac**, through whom the covenant will be established. **At Sarah's insistence, Ishmael and his mother Hagar are driven out into the wilderness, but God saves them and promises to make Ishmael a great nation.**

God tests **Abraham** by demanding that he sacrifice **Isaac**. As **Abraham** is about to lay the knife upon his son, God restrains him, promising him numberless descendants. On the death of Sarah, **Abraham** purchases **Machpelah** (believed to be modern for a family tomb and sends his servant to Mesopotamia to find among his relations a wife for **Isaac**, and **Rebekah** as chosen. Other children are born to **Abraham** by another wife, **Keturah**, among whose descendants are the Midianites, and he dies in a prosperous old age and is buried in his tomb at **Hebron**.

**Isaac's wife Rebecca gives birth to the twins Esau, father of the Edomites, and Jacob.** Through deception, Jacob becomes the heir instead of Esau and gains his father's blessing. He flees to his uncle where he prospers and earns his two wives, **Rachel** and **Leah**. Jacob's name is changed to **Israel**, and by his wives and their handmaidens he has twelve sons, the ancestors of the **twelve tribes** of the Children of Israel, and a daughter, **Dinah**. Joseph, Jacob's favorite son, is sold into slavery in Egypt by his jealous brothers. But Joseph prospers, after hardship, with God's guidance of interpreting **Pharaoh's** dream of upcoming famine. He is then reunited with his father and brothers, who don't recognize him but who plead for food.

After much manipulation, he reveals himself and lets them and their households into Egypt, where Pharaoh assigns to them the **land of Goshen**. Jacob calls his sons to his bedside and reveals their future before he dies. **Joseph** lives to an old age and exhorts his brethren, if God should lead them out of the country, to take his bones with them.

### Composition / Origins

There are four major textual witnesses to the **book of Genesis**: the **Masoretic text**, the **Samaritan Pentateuch,** the **Septuagint**, and **fragments of Genesis** found at **Qumran**. The Qumran group provides the oldest manuscripts but covers only a small proportion of the book. For much of the 20$^{th}$ century most scholars agreed that the **five books of the Pentateuch – Genesis, Exodus, Leviticus, Numbers and Deuteronomy** – came from four sources, the Yahwist, the Elohist, the Deuteronomist and the Priestly source, each telling the same basic story, and joined together by various editors. Since the 1970s there has been a revolution in scholarship.

Scholars in the first half of the 20$^{th}$ century came to the conclusion that the **Yahwist** was produced in the monarchic period, specifically at the court of Solomon, and the **Priestly** work in the middle of the 5$^{th}$ century BC (**the author was even identified as Ezra**), but more recent thinking is that the **Yahwist** was written either just before or during the Babylonian exile of the 6$^{th}$ century, and the Priestly final edition was made late in the **Exilic** period or soon after.

The Persians, after their **conquest of Babylon in 538 BC**, agreed to grant Jerusalem a large measure of local autonomy within the empire, but required the local authorities to produce a single law code accepted by the entire community. The Persian promise of greatly increased local autonomy for all provided a powerful incentive to cooperate in producing a single text.

### Promises to the ancestors

The **patriarchs**, or ancestors, are **Abraham**, **Isaac** and **Jacob**, with their wives (Joseph is normally excluded). The promise itself has three parts: offspring, blessings, and land. The fulfillment of the promise to each patriarch depends on having a male heir, and the story is constantly complicated by the fact that each prospective mother – **Sarah, Rebekah** and **Rachel** – is barren. The ancestors, however, retain their faith in God and God in each case gives a son – **in Jacob's case, twelve sons, the foundation of the chosen Israelites.**

### God's chosen people

The first covenant is between God and all living creatures, and is marked by the sign of the rainbow; the second is with the descendants of **Abraham** (Ishmaelites and others as well as Israelites), and its sign is circumcision, and the last, which doesn't appear until the book of **Exodus**, is with Israel alone, and its sign is **Sabbath**. Each covenant is mediated by a great leader (Noah, **Abraham**, **Moses**), and at each stage God progressively reveals himself by his name (**Elohim with Noah, El Shaddai with Abraham, Yahweh with Moses).**

# Book of Isaiah

The **Book of Isaiah** is the first of the Latter Prophets in the **Hebrew Bible** and the first of the Major Prophets in the **Christian Old Testament**. It is identified by a superscription as the words of the **8th-century BCE** prophet **Isaiah ben Amoz**, but there is extensive evidence that much of it was composed during the **Babylonian captivity** and later.

While virtually no scholars today attribute the entire book, or even most of it, to one person, the book's essential unity has become a focus in more recent research. **Isaiah 1–33** promises judgment and restoration for **Judah, Jerusalem** and the nations, and **chapters 34–66** presume that judgment has been pronounced and restoration follows soon. It can thus be read as an extended meditation on the destiny of Jerusalem into and after the **Exile.**

The **Deutero-Isaian** part of the book describes how God will make Jerusalem the centre of his worldwide rule through a royal savior (a **messiah**) who will destroy her oppressor (**Babylon**); this messiah is the Persian **king Cyrus the Great**, who is merely the agent who brings about **Yahweh's** kingship. **Isaiah** speaks out against corrupt leaders and for the disadvantaged, and roots righteousness in God's holiness rather than in Israel's covenant. **Isaiah 44:6** contains the first clear statement of monotheism: **"I am the first and I am the last; beside me there is no God"**. This model of monotheism became the defining characteristic of **post-Exilic Judaism**, and the basis for Christianity and Islam.

**Isaiah** was one of the most popular works among Jews in the **Second Temple period (c. 515 BCE – 70 CE)**. In Christian circles, it was held in such high regard as to be called **"the Fifth Gospel",** and its influence extends beyond Christianity to English literature and to Western culture in general, from the libretto of **Handel's Messiah** to a host of such everyday phrases as **"swords into ploughshares"** and **"voice in the wilderness".**

## Structure

The **Isaiah** scroll, the oldest surviving manuscript of **Isaiah**: found among the **Dead Sea Scrolls** and dating from about **150 to 100 BCE**, it contains almost the whole **Book of Isaiah** and is substantially identical with the modern Masoretic text.

The scholarly consensus which held sway through most of the 20th century saw three separate collections of oracles in the book of **Isaiah**. A typical outline based on this understanding of the book sees its underlying structure in terms of the identification of historical figures who might have been their authors:

- **1–39: Proto-Isaiah, containing the words of the original Isaiah;**
- **40–55: Deutero-Isaiah, the work of an anonymous Exilic author;**
- **56–66: Trito-Isaiah, an anthology of about twelve passages.**

While one part of the consensus still holds – virtually no contemporary scholar maintains that the entire book, or even most of it, was written by one person – this perception of **Isaiah** as made up of three rather distinct sections underwent a radical challenge in the last quarter of the 20th century. The newer approach looks at the book in terms of its literary and formal characteristics, rather than authors, and sees in it a two-part structure divided between **chapters 33 and 34:**

- 1–33: **Warnings of judgment and promises of subsequent restoration for Jerusalem, Judah and the nations;**
- 34–66: **Judgment has already taken place and restoration is at hand.**

## Summary

Seeing **Isaiah** as a two-part book **(chapters 1–33 and 34–66)** with an overarching theme leads to a summary of its contents like the following:

- The book opens by setting out the themes of judgment and subsequent restoration for the righteous. God has a plan which will be realized on the **"Day of Yahweh"**, when Jerusalem will become the centre of his worldwide rule. On that day all the nations of the world will come to **Zion** (Jerusalem) for instruction, but first the city must be punished and cleansed of evil. Israel is invited to join in this plan. **Chapters 5–12** explain the significance of the Assyrian judgment against Israel: righteous rule by the Davidic king will follow after the arrogant Assyrian monarch is brought down. **Chapters 13–27** announce the preparation of the nations for **Yahweh**'s world rule; **chapters 28–33 announce that a royal savior (a messiah) will emerge in the aftermath of Jerusalem's punishment and the destruction of her oppressor.**
- The oppressor (now identified as **Babylon** rather than Assyria) is about to fall. **Chapters 34–35** tell how **Yahweh** will return the redeemed exiles to Jerusalem. **Chapters 36–39** tell of the faithfulness of **King Hezekiah** to **Yahweh** during the Assyrian siege as a model for the restored community. **Chapters 40–54** state that the restoration of **Zion** is taking place because **Yahweh**, the creator of the universe, has designated the **Persian king Cyrus the Great** as the promised messiah and temple-builder. **Chapters 55–66** are an exhortation to Israel to keep the covenant. God's eternal promise to David is now made to the people of Israel/Judah at large. The book ends by enjoining righteousness as the final stages of God's plan come to pass, including the pilgrimage of the nations to **Zion** and the realization of **Yahweh's kingship.**

The older understanding of this book as three fairly discrete sections attributable to identifiable authors leads to a more atomized picture of its contents, as in this example:

- **Proto-Isaiah/First Isaiah (chapters 1–39):**
  - 1–12: Oracles against Judah mostly from **Isaiah**'s early years;
  - 13–23: Oracles against foreign nations from his middle years;
  - 24–27: The **"Isaiah Apocalypse"**, added at a much later date;
  - 28–33: Oracles from **Isaiah**'s later ministry
  - 34–35: A vision of **Zion**, perhaps a later addition;
  - 36–39: Stories of **Isaiah**'s life, some from the **Book of Kings**

- **Deutero-Isaiah/Second Isaiah (chapters 40–54), with two major divisions, 40–48 and 49–54,** the first emphasizing Israel, the second **Zion** and Jerusalem:
    - An introduction and conclusion stressing the power of God's word over everything;
    - A second introduction and conclusion within these in which a herald announces salvation to Jerusalem;
    - Fragments of hymns dividing various sections;
    - The role of foreign nations, the fall of **Babylon**, and the rise of **Cyrus** as God's chosen one;
    - Four **"Servant Songs"** personalizing the message of the prophet;
    - Several longer poems on topics such as God's power and invitations to Israel to trust in him;
- Trito-**Isaiah**/Third **Isaiah (chapters 55–66):**
    - A collection of oracles by unknown prophets in the years immediately after the return from **Babylon.**

## Composition / Authorship

While it is widely accepted that the book of **Isaiah** is rooted in a historic prophet called **Isaiah**, who lived in the **Kingdom of Judah** during the **8th century BCE**, it is also widely accepted that this prophet did not write the entire book of **Isaiah**. The observations which have led to this are as follows:

- **Historical situation: Chapters 40–55** presuppose that Jerusalem has already been destroyed (they are not framed as prophecy) and the **Babylon**ian exile is already in effect – they speak from a present in which the Exile is about to end. **Chapters 56–66** assume an even later situation, in which the people are already returned to Jerusalem and the rebuilding of the Temple is already under way.
- **Anonymity: Isaiah**'s name suddenly stops being used after **chapter 39.**
- **Style**: There is a sudden change in style and theology after **chapter 40**; numerous key words and phrases found in one section are not found in the other.

The composition history of **Isaiah** reflects a major difference in the way authorship was regarded in ancient Israel and in modern societies; the ancients did not regard it as inappropriate to supplement an existing work while remaining anonymous. While the authors are anonymous, it is plausible that all of them were priests, and the book may thus reflect **Priestly** concerns, in opposition to the increasingly successful reform movement of the **Deuteronomists.**

## Historical context

The historic **Isaiah ben Amoz** lived in the Kingdom of Judah during the reigns of four kings from the mid to late **8th-century BCE**. During this period, Assyria was expanding westward from its origins in modern-day northern **Iraq** towards the Mediterranean, destroying first **Aram** (modern Syria) in **734–732 BCE**, then the **Kingdom of Israel in 722–721**, and finally subjugating **Judah in 701. Proto-Isaiah** is divided between verse and prose passages, and a currently popular theory is that the verse passages represent the prophecies of the original 8th-century **Isaiah**, while the prose sections are **"sermons"** on his texts composed at the court of **Josiah** a hundred years later, at the end of the 7th century.

The **conquest of Jerusalem by Babylon and the exile of its elite in 586 BCE** ushered in the next stage in the formation of the book. **Deutero-Isaiah** addresses himself to the Jews in exile, offering them the hope of return. This was the period of the meteoric rise of Persia under its king **Cyrus the Great – in 559 BCE** he succeeded his father as ruler of a small vassal kingdom in modern eastern Iran, by 540 he ruled an empire stretching from the Mediterranean to Central Asia, and in **539 he conquered Babylon. Deutero-Isaiah**'s predictions of the imminent fall of **Babylon** and his glorification of **Cyrus** as the deliverer of Israel date his prophecies to **550–539 BCE**, and probably towards the end of this period.

**The Persians ended the Jewish exile, and by 515 BCE the exiles, or at least some of them, had returned to Jerusalem and rebuilt the Temple.** The return, however, was not without problems: the returnees found themselves in conflict with those who had remained in the country and who now owned the land, and there were further conflicts over the form of government that should be set up. This background forms the context of **Trito-Isaiah**.

## Themes / Overview

**Isaiah** is focused on the main role of Jerusalem in God's plan for the world, seeing centuries of history as though they were all the single vision of the 8th-century prophet **Isaiah. Proto-Isaiah** speaks of Israel's desertion of God and what will follow: **Israel will be destroyed by foreign enemies**, but after the people, the country and Jerusalem are punished and purified, a holy remnant will live in God's place in **Zion**, governed by God's chosen king (**the messiah**), under the presence and protection of God;

**Deutero-Isaiah** has as its subject the liberation of Israel from captivity in **Babylon** in another **Exodus**, which the God of Israel will arrange using **Cyrus**, the Persian conqueror, as his agent; **Trito-Isaiah** concerns Jerusalem, the Temple, the **Sabbath**, and Israel's salvation. (More explicitly, it concerns questions current among Jews living in Jerusalem and Palestine in the post-Exilic period about who is a God-loving Jew and who is not).

## Holiness, righteousness, and God's plan

God's plan for the world is based on his choice of Jerusalem as the place where he will manifest himself, and of the **line of David** as his earthly representative – a theme that may possibly have been created through Jerusalem's reprieve from **Assyrian attack in 701 BCE**. God is **"the holy one of Israel";** justice and righteousness are the qualities that mark the essence of God, and Israel has offended God through unrighteousness. **Isaiah** speaks out for the poor and the oppressed and against corrupt princes and judges, but unlike the prophets **Amos and Micah** he roots righteousness not in Israel's covenant with God but in God's holiness.

## 2nd Temple Judaism (515 BCE – 70 CE)

**Isaiah** was one of the most popular works in the period between the foundation of the **Second Temple c. 515 BCE and its destruction by the Romans in 70 CE.** Isaiah's "shoot will come up from the stump of Jesse" is alluded to or cited in the **Psalms of Solomon** and various apocalyptic works including the **Similitudes of Enoch, 2 Baruch, 4 Ezra**, and the third of the Sibylline oracles, all of which understood it to refer to a/the messiah and the messianic age. **Isaiah 6,** in which **Isaiah** describes his vision of God enthroned in the **Temple**, influenced the visions of God in works such as the **"Book of the Watchers"** section of the **Book of Enoch**, the **Book of Daniel** and others, often combined with the similar vision from the **Book of Ezekiel**. A very influential portion of **Isaiah** was the four so-called **Songs of the Suffering Servant from Isaiah 42, 49, 50 and 52**, in which God calls upon his servant to lead the nations (the servant is horribly abused, sacrifices himself in accepting the punishment due others, and is finally rewarded).

Some **Second Temple** texts, including the **Wisdom of Solomon** and the Book of Daniel identified the Servant as a group – "the wise" who **"will lead many to righteousness" (Daniel 12:3)** – but others, notably the **Similitudes of Enoch**, understood it in messianic terms. The earliest Christians, building on this second tradition, interpreted **Isaiah 52:13–53:12**, the fourth of the songs, as a **prophecy of the death and exaltation of Jesus, a role which Jesus himself accepted according to Luke 4:17–21.**

## Christianity

The **Book of Isaiah** has been immensely influential in the formation of **Christianity**, from the **devotion to the Virgin Mary** to anti-Jewish polemic, medieval passion iconography, and modern Christian feminism and liberation theology. The regard in which **Isaiah** was held was so high that the book was frequently called **"the Fifth Gospel"**, the prophet who spoke more clearly of Christ and the Church than any others. Its influence extends beyond the Church and Christianity to English literature and to Western culture in general, from the libretto of **Handel's Messiah** to a host of such everyday phrases as **"swords into ploughshares"** and **"voice in the wilderness"**.

The **Gospel of John** quotes **Isaiah 6:10** and states that **"Isaiah said this because he saw Jesus' glory and spoke about him."** Isaiah makes up **27 of the 37 quotations** from the prophets in the Pauline epistles, and takes pride of place in the Gospels and in **Acts of the Apostles. Isaiah 7:14**, where the prophet is assuring **king Ahaz** that God will save Judah from the invading armies of Israel and Syria, forms the basis for **Matthew 1:23's doctrine of the virgin birth, while Isaiah 40:3–5's** image of the exiled Israel led by God and proceeding home to Jerusalem on a newly constructed road through the wilderness was taken up by **all four Gospels and applied to John the Baptist and Jesus.**

# Book of Job

The **Book of Job** is one of the Writings of the **Hebrew Bible**, and the first poetic book in the Christian Old Testament. Addressing the theme of God's justice in the face of human suffering – or more simply, **"Why do the righteous suffer?"** – It is a rich theological work setting out a variety of perspectives.

## Structure
The **Book of Job** consists of a prose prologue and epilogue narrative framing poetic dialogues and monologues. Recent trends have tended to concentrate on the book's underlying editorial unity.

## Prologue on earth and in heaven
The prologue on earth shows the righteous **Job** blessed with wealth and sons and daughters. The scene shifts to heaven, where God asks **Satan** (*ha-satan*, literally **"the accuser"**) for his opinion of **Job** 's piety. **Satan** answers that **Job** is pious only because God has blessed him; if God were to take away everything that **Job** had, then he would surely curse God. God gives **Satan** permission to take **Job** 's wealth and kill all of his children and servants, but **Job** nonetheless praises God: **"Naked I came out of my mother's womb, and naked shall I return: the Lord has given, and the Lord has taken away; blessed be the name of the Lord."** God allows **Satan** to afflict his body with boils. **Job** sits in ashes, and his wife prompts him to **"curse God, and die,"** but Job answers: **"Shall we receive Good from God and shall we not receive evil?"**

## Job 's opening monologue and dialogues between Job and his three friends
**Job** laments the day of his birth; he would like to die, but even that is denied him. The friends do not waver in their belief that **Job** 's suffering is a punishment for sin, for God causes no one to suffer innocently, and they advise him to repent and seek God's mercy. **Job** responds with scorn: **a just God would not treat him so harshly**, patience in suffering is impossible, and the Creator should not take his creatures so lightly, to come against them with such force. The dialogues of **Job** and his friends are followed by a poem (the **"hymn to wisdom"**) on the inaccessibility of wisdom: **"Where is wisdom to be found?"** it asks, and concludes that it has been hidden from man (**chapter 28**). **Job** contrasts his previous fortune with his present plight, an outcast, mocked and in pain. He protests his innocence, lists the principles he has lived by, and demands that God answer him.

## Two speeches by God
God speaks from a whirlwind. They contrast **Job** 's weakness with divine wisdom and omnipotence: **"Where were you when I laid the foundations of the earth?"** **Job** makes a brief response, but God's monologue resumes, never addressing **Job** directly. In 42:1-6 **Job** makes his final response, confessing God's power and his own lack of knowledge **"of things beyond me which I did not know"**. Previously he has only heard, but now his eyes have seen God, and **"therefore I retract/and repent of dust and ashes."**

## Epilogue
**Job** is restored to health, riches and family, and lives to see his children to the fourth generation.

## Authorship, language, texts

Ascribed by Jewish tradition to Moses, it is generally agreed by scholars that the book comes from the period between the **7th and 4th centuries BCE**, with the 6th century as the most likely date for a variety of reason. According to the 6th-century prophet **Ezekiel**, **Job** was a man of antiquity renowned for his righteousness.

The language of **Job** stands out for its conservative spelling and for its exceptionally large number of words and forms not found elsewhere in the **Bible**. The 12th century Jewish scholar Ibn Ezra concluded that the book must have been written in some other language and translated into Hebrew, and many later scholars down to the 20th century looked for an **Aramaic, Arabic or Edomite** original. The book exists in a number of forms: the **Hebrew Masoretic Text**, which underlies many modern **Bible** translations; the Greek Septuagint made in Egypt in the last centuries BCE; and **Aramaic and Hebrew manuscripts found among the Dead Sea Scrolls**.

## Job and the wisdom tradition

**Job**, Ecclesiastes and the **Book of Proverbs** belong to the genre of wisdom literature, sharing a perspective that they themselves call the **"way of wisdom"**. Wisdom means both a way of thinking and a body of knowledge gained through such thinking, as well as the ability to apply it to life. It is attainable in part through human effort and in part as a gift from God, but never in its entirety – except by God. Wisdom literature was not confined to the **Bible**, or to Israel. Several texts from ancient Mesopotamia and Egypt offer parallels to **Job**. Their existence suggests that he was the recipient of a long tradition of reflection on the existence of inexplicable suffering.

## Themes

**Job** is an investigation of the problem of divine justice. This problem, known in theology as theodicy, can be rephrased as a question: **"Why do the righteous suffer?"** The conventional answer in ancient Israel was that God rewards virtue and punishes sin (the principle known as **"retributive justice")**. The biblical concept of righteousness was rooted in the covenant-making God who had ordered creation for communal well-being, and the righteous were those who invested in the community, showing special concern for the poor and needy (see **Job**'s description of his life in chapter 31), wicked, who were selfish and greedy.

The book begins with the frame narrative, giving the reader an omniscient **"God's eye perspective"** which introduces **Job** as a man of exemplary faith and piety, **"blameless and upright"**, who **"fears God"** and **"shuns evil",** and the reader sees that God himself bears responsibility for **Job**'s suffering. In the poetic dialogues **Job**'s friends see his suffering and assume he must be guilty, since God is just. **Job**, knowing he is innocent, concludes that God must be unjust. He retains his piety throughout the story (belying **Satan**'s suspicion that his righteousness is due to the expectation of reward), but makes clear from his first speech that he agreed with his friends that **God should and does reward righteousness.**

**Chapter 28**, the Hymn to Wisdom, introduces another theme, divine wisdom. The hymn does not place any emphasis on retributive justice, stressing instead the inaccessibility of wisdom. Wisdom cannot be discovered or purchased, it says; God alone knows the meaning of the world, and he grants it only to those who live in reverence before him. God possesses wisdom because he grasps the complexities of the world (**Job 28:240-26**). When God finally speaks he neither explains the reason for **Job's** suffering. **Job** then confesses his lack of wisdom, meaning his lack of understanding of the workings of the cosmos and of the ability to maintain it. In the concluding part of the frame narrative God restores and increases his prosperity, indicating that the divine policy on retributive justice remains unchanged.

## History of interpretation
In the **Second Temple period (500 BCE – 70 CE) Job** began being transformed into something more patient and steadfast, with his suffering a test of virtue and a vindication of righteousness for the glory of God, but it was the tradition taken up by the **New Testament Epistle** of James, which presented **Job** as one whose patience and endurance should be emulated by believers (**James 5:7-11**). Jewish interpretation of **Job** was initially positive. He was seen as a righteous Gentile who acknowledged God. Very early, however, Christianity began interpreting **Job 19:23-29** (verses concerning a **"redeemer"** whom **Job** hopes can save him from God) as a prophecy of Christ, although the major view among scholars is that **Job** 's **"redeemer"** is either an angelic being or God himself.

Saint Augustine recorded that **Job** had prophesied the coming of **Christ,** and Gregory the Great offered him as a model of right living worthy of respect. The medieval Jewish scholar Maimonides declared his story a parable, and the medieval Christian **Thomas Aquinas** wrote a detailed commentary declaring it true history. In the **Reformation Martin Luther** explained how **Job's** confession of sinfulness and worthlessness underlay his saintliness and **John Calvin's Job** demonstrated the doctrine of the resurrection and the ultimate certainty of divine justice.

## Liturgical use
There are some Jews, particularly the **Spanish and Portuguese Jews**, who do hold public readings of **Job** on the **Tisha B'Av fast** (a day of mourning over the destruction of the **First and Second Temples** and other tragedies). The **Eastern Orthodox Church** reads from **Job** and Exodus during **Holy Week**. The Roman Catholic Church reads from **Job** during Matins in the first two weeks of September and in the **Office of the Dead**, and in the revised Liturgy of the Hours **Job** is read during the **Eighth and Ninth Weeks in Ordinary Time.**

## In Islam and Middle Eastern folk tradition
**Job** (Arabic Ayyub) is one of the 25 prophets mentioned by name in the Qur'an, where he is lauded as a steadfast and upright worshipper (**Q.38:44**). His story has the same basic outline as in the **Bible**, although the three friends are replaced by his brothers, and his wife stays by his side. In Lebanon the **Muwahideen (or Druze)** community has a shrine built in the Shouf area that allegedly contains **Job's** tomb. **There is also a tomb of Job outside the city of Salalah in Oman.**

# Book of Lamentations

The **Book of Lamentations** (Hebrew: *'Eikhah*, from its incipit meaning **"how"**) is a collection of poetic laments for the destruction of Jerusalem. In the Hebrew Bible it appears in the **Ketuvim ("Writings")**, beside the **Song of Songs, Book of Ruth, Ecclesiastes and the Book of Esther (the Megillot or "Five Scrolls"),** although there is no set order; in the Christian Old Testament it follows the **Book of Jeremiah**, as the prophet **Jeremiah** is its traditional author. **Jeremiah**'s authorship is no longer generally accepted, although it is generally accepted that the **destruction of Jerusalem by Babylon in 586 BC** forms the background to the poems.

The book is partly a traditional **"city lament"** mourning the desertion of the city by God, its destruction, and the ultimate return of the divinity, and partly a funeral dirge in which the bereaved bewails and addresses the dead. The tone is bleak: **God does not speak**, the degree of suffering is presented as undeserved, and expectations of future redemption are minimal.

The book is traditionally recited on the fast day of **Tisha B'Av ("Ninth of Av")**, mourning the **destruction of both the First Temple and the Second**; in Christianity it is traditionally read during **Tenebrae** of the **Holy Triduum**.

## Structure
**"Jeremiah Lamenting the Destruction of Jerusalem" (Rembrandt)**
**Lamentations** consists of five distinct poems, corresponding to its **five chapters**. The first four are written as acrostics – **chapters 1, 2**, and 4 each have 22 verses, corresponding to the 22 letters of the Hebrew alphabet, the first lines beginning with the first letter of the alphabet, the second with the second letter, and so on. Chapter 3 has 66 verses, so that each letter begins three lines, and the fifth poem is not acrostic but still has 22 lines. Unlike standard alphabetical order, the middle chapters in **Lamentations** have the letter **Pe** (the 17th letter) comes before **Ayin** (the 16th). The first chapter uses standard alphabetical order.

## Summary
The book consists of **five separate poems**. In the first **(chapter 1),** the city sits as a desolate weeping widow overcome with miseries. In **Chapter 2** these miseries are described in connection with national sins and acts of God. **Chapter 3** speaks of hope for the people of God: the chastisement would only be for their good; a better day would dawn for them. **Chapter 4** laments the ruin and desolation of the city and temple, but traces it to the people's sins. **Chapter 5** is a prayer that Zion's reproach may be taken away in the repentance and recovery of the people.

## Composition
**Lamentations** has traditionally been ascribed to **Jeremiah**, probably on the grounds of the reference in **2 Chronicles 35:25** to the prophet composing a lament on the **death of King Josiah**,

but there is no reference to **Josiah** in the book and no reason to connect it to **Jeremiah**. The language fits an **Exilic date (586–520 BCE)**, and the poems probably originated from Judeans who remained in the land. Scholars are divided over whether they are the work of one or multiple authors.

One clue pointing to multiple authors is that the gender and situation of the first-person witness changes – the narration is feminine in the first and second lamentation, and masculine in the third, while the fourth and fifth are eyewitness reports of Jerusalem's destruction; conversely, the similarities of style, vocabulary, and theological outlook, as well as the uniform historical setting, are arguments for one author.

## Themes

**Lamentations** combines elements of the *qinah*, a funeral dirge for the loss of the city, and the **"communal lament"** pleading for the restoration of its people. It reflects the view, traceable to Sumerian literature of a thousand years earlier, that the destruction of the holy city was a punishment by God for the communal sin of its people.

Beginning with the reality of disaster, **Lamentations** concludes with the bitter possibility that God may have finally rejected Israel **(chapter 5:22)**. Sufferers in the face of grief are not urged to a confidence in the goodness of God; in fact God is accountable for the disaster. The poet acknowledges that this suffering is a just punishment, still God is held to have had choice over whether to act in this way and at this time.

Hope arises from a recollection of **God's past goodness**, but although this justifies a cry to God to act in deliverance, there is no guarantee that he will. **Repentance** will not persuade God to be gracious, since he is free to give or withhold grace as he chooses. In the end, the possibility is that God has finally rejected his people and may not again deliver them: if God is predictable, then God is just a tool of humans. Nevertheless, it also affirms confidence that the mercies of **Yahweh (the God of Israel)** never end, but are new every morning **(3:22–33)**.

## Later interpretation and influence

The Book of **Lamentations** is recited annually by Jews on **Tisha b'Av** (Ninth of Av), the anniversary of the destruction of both of the **Jewish Temples**.

In Western Christianity, readings (often chanted) and choral settings of extracts from the book are used in the Lenten religious service known as **Tenebrae** (Latin for *darkness*). In the Church of England, readings are used at Morning and Evening Prayer on the Monday and Tuesday of **Holy Week,** and at Evening Prayer on **Good Friday.** In the **Coptic Orthodox Church**, the book's third chapter is chanted on the twelfth hour of the **Good Friday Service** that commemorates the burial of **Jesus.**

# Book of Ruth

The **Book of Ruth** (abbreviated **Rth**) (Hebrew: , *Megilath Ruth*, **"the Scroll of Ruth"**, one of the **Five Megillot**) is included in the third division, or the **Writings (Ketuvim)**, of the **Hebrew Bible**; in most Christian canons it is treated as a history book and placed between **Judges** and **1 Samuel**, as it is set **"in the days when the judges judged"**,

The book tells of **Ruth's** accepting the God of the Israelites as her God and the **Israelite** people as her own. In **Ruth 1:16–17**, **Ruth** tells **Naomi**, her Israelite mother-in-law, **"Where you go I will go, and where you stay I will stay. Your people will be my people and your God my God. Where you die I will die, and there I will be buried. May the Lord deal with me, be it ever so severely, if even death separates you and me."** The book is held in esteem by Jews who fall under the category of **Jews-by-choice**, as is evidenced by the considerable presence of **Boaz** in rabbinic literature. The **Book of Ruth** also functions liturgically, as it is read during the **Jewish holiday of Shavuot ("Weeks")**.

## The book is structured in four chapters:

**Act 1: Prologue and Problem: Death and Emptiness (1:1–22)**
- Scene 1: Setting the scene **(1:1–5)**
- Scene 2: **Naomi** returns home **(1:6–18)**
- Scene 3: Arrival of **Naomi** and **Ruth** in Bethlehem **(1:19–22)**

**Act 2: Ruth Meets Boaz, Naomi's Relative, on the Harvest Field (2:1–23)**
- Scene 1: **Ruth** in the field of **Boaz (2:1–17)**
- Scene 2: **Ruth** reports to **Naomi (2:18–23)**

**Act 3: Naomi Sends Ruth to Boaz on the Threshing Floor (3:1–18)**
- Scene 1: **Naomi** Reveals Her Plan **(3:1–5)**
- Scene 2: **Ruth** at the threshing-floor of **Boaz (3:6–15)**
- Scene 3: **Ruth** reports to **Naomi (3:16–18)**

**Act 4: Resolution and Epilogue: Life and Fullness (4:1–22)**
- Scene 1: **Boaz** with the men at the gate **(4:1–12)**
- Scene 2: A son is born to **Ruth (4:13–17)**

## Genealogical appendix (4:18–22)

## Summary

During the time of the judges when there was a famine, an Israelite family from **Bethlehem – Elimelech,** his wife **Naomi**, and their sons **Mahlon and Chilion** – emigrated to the nearby country of Moab. **Elimelech** died, and the sons married two Moabite women: **Mahlon** married **Ruth** and **Chilion** married **Orpah**.

After about ten years, the two sons of **Naomi** also died in **Moab (1:4)**. **Naomi** decided to return to **Bethlehem**. She told her daughters-in-law to return to their own mothers and remarry. **Orpah** reluctantly left; however, **Ruth** said, **"Do not urge me to leave you, to turn back and not follow you. For wherever you go, I will go; wherever you lodge, I will lodge; your people shall be my people, and your God my God. Where you die, I will die, and there I will be buried. Thus and more may the Lord do to me if anything but death parts me from you." (Ruth 1:16–17 NJPS)**.

The two women returned to **Bethlehem** at the beginning of the barley harvest, and in order to support her mother-in-law and herself, **Ruth** went to the fields to glean. As it happened, the field she went to belonged to a man named **Boaz,** who was kind to her because he had heard of her loyalty to her mother-in-law. **Ruth** told **Naomi** of **Boaz's** kindness, and she gleaned in his field through the remainder of barley and wheat harvest.

**Boaz** was a close relative of **Naomi**'s husband's family. He was therefore obliged by the Levirate law to marry **Mahlon's widow**, **Ruth**, in order to carry on his family's inheritance. **Naomi** sent **Ruth** to the threshing floor at night and told her to go where he slept, and **"uncover his feet and lie down. He will tell you what you are to do." (3:4). Ruth did so.**

**Boaz** asked her who she was, and she replied: **"I am your handmaid Ruth. Spread your robe over your handmaid, for you are a redeeming kinsman" (3:9 NJPS).** **Boaz** blessed her and agreed to do all that is required, and he noted that, **"all the elders of my town know what a fine woman you are" (3:11 NJPS)**. He then acknowledged that he was a close relative, but that there was one who was closer, and she remained in submission at his feet until she returned into the city in the morning.

Early that day, **Boaz** went to the city gate to meet with the other male relative before the town elders. The relative is not named: **Boaz** addresses him as *ploni almoni*, literally **"so and so"**. The unnamed relative is unwilling to jeopardize the inheritance of his own estate by marrying **Ruth**, and so relinquished his right of redemption, thus allowing **Boaz** to marry **Ruth**. They transferred the property and redeemed it, ratified by the nearer kinsman taking off his shoe and handing it over to **Boaz**. **Ruth 4:7** notes for later generations.

**Boaz and Ruth were then married and have a son**. The women of the city celebrate **Naomi**'s joy, for **Naomi** found a redeemer for her family name, and **Naomi** takes the child and places it in her bosom. The child is named **Obed**, who we discover is **"the father of Jesse, the father of David" (Ruth 4:13–17), that is, the grandfather of King David.**

The book concludes with an appendix which traces the Davidic genealogy all the way back from **Perez**, **"whom Tamar bore to Judah"**, through to **Obed**, down to **David.**

## Composition

The book does not name its author. It is traditionally ascribed to the prophet **Samuel**, but **Ruth**'s identity as a non-Israelite and the stress on the need for an inclusive attitude towards foreigners suggests an origin in the fifth century BC, when intermarriage had become controversial (as seen in **Ezra 9:1 and Nehemiah 13:1**). A substantial number of scholars therefore date it to the Persian period **(6th–4th centuries BC)**. The genealogy that concludes the book is believed to be a post-exilic Priestly addition, as it adds nothing to the plot; nevertheless, it is carefully crafted and integrates the book into the history of Israel running from **Genesis to Kings**.

## Levirate marriage and the "redeemers"

The **Book of Ruth** illustrates the difficulty of trying to use laws given in books such as Deuteronomy as evidence of actual practice. **Naomi** plans to provide security for herself and **Ruth** by arranging a Levirate marriage with **Boaz**. She instructs **Ruth** to uncover **Boaz**'s feet after he has gone to sleep and lie down. When **Boaz** wakes up, surprised to see a woman at his feet, **Ruth** explains she wants him to redeem (and thus marry) her. Many modern commentators see sexual allusions in this part of the story, arguing that **'feet' is a euphemism for genitals.**

Since there was no heir to inherit **Elimelech's land**, custom required a close relative (usually the dead man's brother) to marry the widow of the deceased in order to continue his family line **(Deuteronomy 25:5–10)**. This relative was called the **go'el**, the **"kinsman-redeemer"**. As **Boaz** is not **Elimelech's** brother, nor is **Ruth** his widow, scholars refer to the arrangement here as **"Levirate-like"**. A complication arises in the story: another man is a closer relative to **Elimelech** than **Boaz** and has first claim on **Ruth**.

It is resolved through the custom that required land to stay in the family: a family could mortgage land to ward off poverty, but the law required a kinsman to purchase it back into the family **(Leviticus 25:25ff)**. **Boaz** meets the near kinsman at the city gate (the place where contracts are settled); the kinsman first says he will purchase **Elimelech's** (now **Naomi**'s) land, but, upon hearing he must also take **Ruth** as his wife, withdraws his offer. **Boaz** thus becomes **Ruth** and **Naomi**'s **"kinsman-redeemer."**

## Mixed marriage

The book can be read as a political parable relating to issues around the time of **Ezra and Nehemiah (the 4th century BCE)**. The realistic nature of the story is established from the start through the names of the participants: the husband and father is **Elimelech**, meaning **"My God is King"**, and his wife is **Naomi**, **"Pleasing"**, but after the deaths of her sons **Mahlon**, **"Sickness"**, and **Chilion**, **"Wasting"**, she asks to be called **Mara**, **"Bitter"**. The reference to Moab raises questions, since in the rest of the biblical literature it is associated with hostility to Israel, sexual perversity, and idolatry, and **Deuteronomy 23:3–6 excluded an Ammonite or a Moabite from "the congregation of the LORD; even to their tenth generation"**.

Despite this, **Ruth the Moabite married a Judahite** and even after his death still regarded herself a member of his family; she then married another Judahite and bore him a son who became an ancestor of **David**. Contrary to the message of **Ezra–Nehemiah**, where marriages between Jewish men and non-Jewish women were broken up, **Ruth** teaches that **foreigners who convert to Judaism can become good Jews,** foreign wives can become exemplary followers of Jewish law, and there is no reason to exclude them or their offspring from the community.

## Contemporary interpretations

Scholars have increasingly explored **Ruth** in ways which allow it to address contemporary issues. Feminists, for example, have recast the story as one of the dignity of labor and female self-sufficiency, and even as a **model for lesbian relations**, while others have seen in it a celebration of the relationship between strong and resourceful women. Others have criticized it for its underlying, and potentially exploitative, acceptance of a system of patriarchy in which a **woman's worth can only be measured through marriage and child-bearing**. Others again have seen it as a book that champions outcast and oppressed peoples.

# Brothers of Jesus

The New Testament describes **James, Joseph (Joses), Judas (Jude)**, and **Simon** as **brothers of Jesus** (Greek: translit. 'Brothers'). Also mentioned, but not named, are **sisters of Jesus**. Some scholars argue that these brothers, especially **James**, held positions of special honor in the early Christian church.

Catholic, Assyrian, Eastern Orthodox and Oriental Orthodox believe in the **perpetual virginity of Mary,** as did the Protestant leaders **Martin Luther, Huldrych Zwingli, John Wesley** and their respective movements; **John Calvin** believed that it was possible that **Mary** remained a virgin but believed the scriptural evidence was inconclusive. Those who hold this belief reject the claim that **Jesus** had biological siblings and maintain that these brothers and sisters received this designation because of their close association with the nuclear family of **Jesus**, as either children of **Joseph** from a previous marriage, or as nephews of either **Mary** or **Joseph**.

The literal translation of the words **"brother" and "sister"** is an objective problem, because of the very little number of quotations, and their polysemy in the family of Semitic languages. In the 3rd century, biological relatives on account of their connection with the nuclear family of **Jesus**, without explicit reference to brothers or sisters, were called the *Desposyni,* from the Greek δεσπόσυνοι, plural of δεσπόσυνος, meaning **"of or belonging to the master or lord".** The term was used by **Sextus Julius Africanus**, a writer of the early 3rd century.

## Jesus' brothers and sisters
**The Gospel of Mark 6:3 and the Gospel of Matthew 13:55–56 state that James, Joses (or Joseph), Jude and Simon were the brothers of Jesus, the son of Mary.** The same verses also mention unnamed sisters of **Jesus**. Another verse in the **Epistle to the Galatians 1:19** mentions seeing **James, "the Lord's brother"**, and none other of the apostles except **Peter**, when **Paul** went to Jerusalem after his conversion. The **"brothers of the Lord"** are also mentioned, alongside (but separate from) **Cephas** and the apostles in **1 Corinthians 9:5**, in which it is mentioned that they had wives. Some scholars claim that **Jesus'** relatives may have held positions of authority in the Jerusalem area until **Trajan** excluded Jews from the new city that he built on its ruins.

That the brothers were children of both **Mary** and **Joseph** was held by some people of the early centuries; *The Oxford Dictionary of the Christian Church* claimed that **Tertullian (c. 160 – c. 225)** was one of them. The 3rd-century **Antidicomarianites ("opponents of Mary")** maintained that, when **Joseph** became **Mary**'s husband, he was a widower with six children, and that he had normal marital relations with **Mary**, but they later held that **Jesus** was not born of these relations. **Bonosus** was a bishop who in the late 4th century held that **Mary** had other children after **Jesus**, for which the other bishops of his province condemned him. **Jovinian**, and various Arian teachers such as **Photinus** held a similar view.

## Degree of consanguinity between Jesus and his brothers

The New Testament names **James the Just, Joses, Simon, and Jude** as the brothers (Greek *adelphoi*) of **Jesus (Mark 6:3, Matthew 13:55, John 7:3, Acts 1:13, 1 Corinthians 9:5)** Aramaic and Hebrew inclined to use circumlocutions to point out blood relationships, calling some people **"brothers of Jesus"** would not have always implied the same biological mother. Scholars and theologians, who assert this view, point out that **Jesus was called "*the* son of Mary" rather than "*a* son of Mary" in his hometown (Mark 6:3).**

## Relationship of Jesus' brothers to Mary

By the 3rd century, the doctrine of the **perpetual virginity of Mary** had become well established; important early Christian theologians such as **Hippolytus (170–235), Eusebius (260/265–339/340)** and **Epiphanius(c. 310/320–403)** defended it. The early church had not accepted that **Mary** had any children apart from **Jesus. Eusebius and Epiphanius** held that these men were Joseph's sons from (an unrecorded) former marriage. Epiphanius adds that **Joseph** became the father of **James** and his three brothers (Joses, Simeon, Judah) and two sisters (a **Salome** and a **Mary**) or (a **Salome** and an **Anna**) with **James** being the elder sibling. **James** and his siblings were not children of Mary but were Joseph's children from a previous marriage. **Joseph**'s first wife died; many years later, at the age of eighty, **"he took Mary (mother of Jesus)".** According to **Epiphanius** the Scriptures call them **"brothers of the Lord"** to confound their opponents. **Origen (184–254)** also wrote that **"according to the Gospel of Peter the brethren of Jesus were sons of Joseph by a former wife, whom he married before Mary".**

The apocryphal *History of Joseph the Carpenter*, written in the 5th century and framed as a biography of **Joseph** dictated by **Jesus**, describes how **Joseph had with his first wife four sons and two daughters.** His sons' names were **Judas, Justus, James**, and **Simon**, and the names of the **two daughters were Assia and Lydia. Years after his first wife died, he took Mary.** Therefore, the brothers of **Jesus** would be the children of **Joseph** by his first wife. The **Protoevangelium of James** explicitly claims that **Joseph** was a widower, with children, at the time that **Mary** is entrusted to his care.

**The *Catholic Encyclopedia*, citing the texts contained in the apocryphal writings, writes that: When forty years of age, Joseph married a woman called Melcha or Escha by some, Salome by others; they lived forty-nine years together and had six children, two daughters and four sons, the youngest of whom was James (the Less, "the Lord's brother").** A year after his wife's death, as the priests announced through Judea that they wished to find in the tribe of Juda a respectable man to espouse **Mary, then twelve to fourteen years of age. Joseph, who was at the time ninety years old,** went up to Jerusalem among the candidates; a miracle manifested the choice God had made of **Joseph**, and two years later the **Annunciation** took place.

## Absence of Jesus' brothers

There are some events in scripture where brothers or sisters of **Jesus** are not shown, e.g. when **Jesus** was lost in the **Temple** and during his crucifixion. This is argued to support the view that **"brothers"** of **Jesus** are not blood brothers or siblings, although some reject this.

**Luke 2:41–51** reports the visit of **Mary**, **Joseph**, and **Jesus** to the Temple in Jerusalem when **Jesus** was 12 years old but does not mention any siblings. Luke sought to minimize the importance of **Jesus'** family by whatever means possible, editing **James** and **Jesus'** brothers out of the Gospel record.

The **Gospel of John** records the sayings of **Jesus** on the cross, i.e. the pair of commands **"Woman, behold your son!" and "Behold, thy mother!" (John 19:26–27),** then states that **"from that hour the disciple took her unto his own home"**. Since the era of the **Church Fathers** this statement has been used to reason that **after the death of Jesus there was no other biological children to look after Mary, and she had to be entrusted to the disciple.**

It would have been against Jewish custom for **Jesus** to give his mother to the care of the disciple if **Mary** had other living sons, because the eldest son would always take responsibility for his mother.

**Pope John Paul II** also said that the command **"Behold your son!"** was the entrustment of the disciple to **Mary** in order to fill the maternal gap left by the death of her only son on the cross. There are difficulties in this interpretation: it ignores both the fact that **Jesus'** brothers opposed his claims, and the position of honor of **John**, the beloved disciple.

# Camp David Accords

The **Camp David Accords** were signed by Egyptian President **Anwar El Sadat** and Israeli Prime Minister **Menachem Begin** on 17 September 1978, following twelve days of secret negotiations at **Camp David**. The two framework agreements were signed at the White House, and were witnessed by United States President **Jimmy Carter**. The second of these frameworks (*A Framework for the Conclusion of a Peace Treaty between Egypt and Israel*) led directly to the 1979 **Egypt-Israel Peace Treaty**. Due to the agreement, **Sadat and Begin received the shared 1978 Nobel Peace Prize.**

Had presented three main objectives for Arab-Israeli peace: Arab recognition of Israel's right to exist in peace. Israel's withdrawal from occupied territories gained in the **Six Day War** through negotiating efforts with neighboring Arab nations to ensure that Israel's security would not be threatened and securing an **undivided Jerusalem**.

The **Camp David Accord**s were the result of 14 months of diplomatic efforts by Egypt, Israel, and the United States that began after **Jimmy Carter** became President. Upon assuming office on January 20, 1977, President **Carter** moved to rejuvenate the Middle East peace process that had stalled throughout the 1976 presidential campaign in the United States. The **Yom Kippur War** further complicated efforts to achieve the objectives written in **United Nations Security Council Resolution 242.**

Israel's Prime Minister **Yitzak Rabin** and his successor, **Menachem Begin**, were both skeptical of an international conference. **Begin** had not been opposed to returning the Sinai, but a major future obstacle was his firm refusal to consider relinquishing control over the **West Bank**.

### Begin Initiative
Secretary of State **Cyrus Vance** travelled to the Middle East to obtain firsthand confirmation of the agreement between Israel and Egypt. The plan was that Israel agreed on 6 August to return the land to Egypt **Sadat**'s then waning popularity would be greatly enhanced as a result of such an achievement.

### Sadat Initiative
President **Anwar El Sadat** came to feel that the Geneva track peace process was more show than substance. His frustration boiled over, and after clandestine preparatory meetings between Egyptian and Israeli officials, unknown even to the **NATO** countries, in November 1977, **Sadat became the first Arab leader to visit Israel.**

On 9 November 1977, President **Sadat** startled the world by announcing to parliament his intention to go to Jerusalem and speak before the **Knesset.** Shortly afterward, the Israeli government cordially invited him to address the Knesset. Ten days after his speech, **Sadat** arrived for the groundbreaking three-day visit, which launched the first peace process between Israel and an Arab state. **Sadat** had no ideological base, which made him politically inconsistent. In **Sadat**'s Knesset speech he talked about his views on peace, the status of Israel's occupied territories, and the Palestinian refugee problem.

**Begin** also saw many reasons why bilateral talks would be in his country's best interests. Israel felt Egypt could help protect Israel from other Arabs and Eastern Communists. **Carter**'s people apparently had no inkling of the secret talks in Morocco between **Dayan** and **Sadat**'s representative, **Hassan Tuhami** that paved the way for **Sadat**'s initiative. The basic message of **Sadat**'s speech at the Knesset was the request for the implementation of **Resolutions 242 and 338.**

## Egyptian-Israeli talks

His trip to Jerusalem signaled a major reorientation of Cairo's place in the global scheme of things, from the Soviet to the American camp. **Carter** could not thwart the Israeli-Egyptian peace push. An Israeli-Egyptian working summit was scheduled for 25 December in **Ismailiya, near the Suez Canal.**

Both leaders converged on **Camp David** for 13 days of tense and dramatic negotiations from 5 to 17 September 1978. **Carter**'s advisers insisted on the establishment of an Egyptian-Israeli agreement which would lead to an eventual solution to the Palestine issue. **Carter** felt they were not **"aiming high enough"** and was interested in the establishment of a written **"land for peace"** agreement with Israel returning the Sinai Peninsula and West Bank.

**Begin** and **Sadat** had such mutual antipathy toward one another that they only seldom had direct contact; **Begin** and **Sadat** were **"literally not on speaking terms."** The issues of Israeli settlement withdrawal from the Sinai and the status of the West Bank created what seemed to be an impasse. Consequently, the 13 days marking the **Camp David Accords** were considered a success. The Israeli delegation had a stable of excellent talent in **Ministers Dayan** and **Weizman** and legal experts **Dr. Meir Rosenne and Aharon Barak**.

## Framework for Peace in the Middle East

*The agreed basis for a peaceful settlement of the conflict between Israel and its neighbors is United Nations Security Council Resolution 242, in all its parts.* The framework itself consists of 3 parts. The first part of the framework was to establish an autonomous self-governing authority in the West Bank and the Gaza strip and to fully implement **Resolution 242.**

The Accords recognized the **"legitimate rights of the Palestinian people"**; a process was to be implemented guaranteeing the full autonomy of the people within a period of five years. The Accords did not mention the Golan H eights, Syria, or Lebanon. **The fate of Jerusalem was deliberately excluded from this agreement.** The framework merely concerned autonomy of the inhabitants of West Bank and Gaza. It neither mentions the status of Jerusalem, nor the **Palestinian Right of Return**.

## UN Rejection of the Middle East Framework

The **UN General Assembly** rejected the Framework for Peace in the Middle East, because the agreement was concluded without participation of **UN** and **PLO** and did not comply with the Palestinian right of return, of self-determination and to national independence and sovereignty. On 6 December 1979, the **UN condemned in Resolution 34/70** all partial agreements and separate treaties that did not meet the Palestinian rights and comprehensive solutions to peace; it condemned Israel's continued occupation and demanded withdrawal from all occupied territories.

All such partial agreements and separate treaties were strongly condemned. The part of the **Camp David Accord**s regarding the Palestinian future and all similar ones were declared invalid.

**Framework Peace Treaty Egypt and Israel**
The second framework outlined a basis for the peace treaty six months later, in particular deciding the future of the **Sinai Peninsula**. Israel agreed to withdraw its armed forces from the Sinai, evacuate its 4,500 civilian inhabitants, and restore it to Egypt in return for normal diplomatic relations with Egypt, guarantees of freedom of passage through the **Suez Canal** and other nearby waterways (such as the Straits of Tiran), and a restriction on the forces Egypt could place on the **Sinai Peninsula**, especially within 20-40 km from Israel.

With the withdrawal, Israel also returned **Egypt's Abu-Rudeis oil fields** in western Sinai, which contained long term, commercially productive wells. The agreement also resulted in the United States committing to several billion Dollars-worth of annual subsidies to the governments of both Israel and Egypt, subsidies which continue to this day.

**Consequences**
President **Anwar Sadat's** signing of the **Camp David Accord**s on 17 September 1978 and his shared 1978 **Nobel Peace Prize** with Israeli Prime Minister **Menachem Begin** led to his assassination by dissatisfied Islamic extremists from within Egypt. The group was outraged over the president's decision to make peace with Israel.

On 6 October 1981 President **Anwar Sadat** was assassinated by members of the Egyptian Islamic Jihad during the annual victory parade held in Cairo to celebrate Egypt's crossing of the Suez Canal. He was airlifted to a military hospital where, despite the efforts of 11 doctors and surgeons, he died just 2 hours after arriving. In total, 11 were killed from collateral gunfire and 28 were injured. Among the wounded were Vice President **Hosni Mubarak**, Irish Defense Minister **James Tully**, and four U.S. military liaison officers.

> **"The normalization of relations [between Israel and Egypt] went into effect in January 1980. Ambassadors were exchanged in February. In March 1980 regular airline flights were inaugurated. Egypt also began supplying Israel with crude oil".**

Egypt was subsequently suspended from the **Arab League** from 1979 until 1989. When the **Camp David Accord**s were signed, Jordan's **King Hussein** saw it as a slap to the face. Like the **Rabat Summit Resolution**, the **Camp David Accord**s circumscribed Jordan's objective to reassert its control over the West Bank. Jordan could not risk accepting the Accords without the support from powerful Arab neighbors, like Iraq, Saudi Arabia, and Syria.

The **Camp David Accord**s also prompted the disintegration of a united Arab front in opposition to Israel. Many of the Arab nations blamed Egypt for not putting enough pressure on Israel to deal with the Palestinian problem in a way that would be satisfactory to them. **The 1994 Israel-Jordan Treaty of Peace has not fully normalized relations with Israel.**

# Celibacy

**Celibacy is the state of voluntarily being unmarried, sexually abstinent, or both, usually for religious reasons.** The term celibacy is applied only to those for whom the unmarried state is the result of a sacred vow, act of renunciation, or religious conviction. Celibacy has existed in one form or another throughout history, in virtually all the major religions of the world, and views on it have varied. **Ancient Judaism was strongly opposed to celibacy.** Similarly, the Romans viewed it as an aberration and legislated fiscal penalties against it, with the sole exception granted to the **Vestal Virgins**. Christians in the Middle Ages and in particular Catholics believed that celibacy was a prerequisite for religious office (**clerical celibacy**).

Protestantism saw a reversal of this trend in the West and the **Eastern Orthodox Church** never adopted it. The Islamic attitudes toward celibacy have been complex as well; **Muhammad** denounced it, but some **Sufi** orders embrace it. **Classical Hindu** culture encouraged asceticism and celibacy in the later stages of life, after one has met his societal obligations. **Jainism** and **Buddhism** have been influenced by Hinduism in this respect. It was not well received in **China**, for example, where other religions movements such as **Daoism** were opposed to it. A somewhat similar situation existed in **Japan**, where the **Shinto** tradition also opposed celibacy. In most native African and American Indian religious traditions, celibacy have been viewed negatively as well.

## Abstinence and celibacy

The words *abstinence* and *celibacy* are often used interchangeably. Sexual abstinence, also known as *continence*, is abstaining from some or all aspects of sexual activity, often for some limited period of time.

## Buddhism

The rule of celibacy in the Buddhist religion, whether **Mahayana or Theravada**, has a long history. Celibacy was advocated as an ideal rule of life for all monks and nuns by **Gautama Buddha, except for Japan**. In Japan, celibacy was an ideal among Buddhist clerics for hundreds of years. But violations of clerical celibacy were so common for so long that, finally, **in 1872, state laws made marriage legal for Buddhist clerics**. Subsequently, ninety percent of Buddhist monks/clerics married. **Gautama**, later known as the **Buddha**, is known for his renunciation of his wife, **Princess Yasodhara**, and son, **Rahula**. Later on both his wife and son joined the ascetic community and are mentioned in the Buddhist texts to have become enlightened.

## Brahma Kumaris

In the religious movement of **Brahma Kumaris**, celibacy is also promoted for peace and to defeat power of lust and to prepare for life in **forthcoming Heaven on earth for 2,500 years** when children will be created by the power of the mind even for householders to like holy brother and sister. In this belief system, **celibacy is given the utmost importance**. It is said that, as per the direction of the **Supreme God** those lead a pure and celibate life will be successfully able to conquer the surging vices. Those with the power of celibacy are eligible to claim a bright future of **Golden Age of heaven/Paradise**. It is said that the craving for sex and impure thoughts are the reason for the whole trouble in the universe today.

## Christianity

In **Matthew 19:11-12** Jesus says, **"All men cannot receive this saying, save they to whom it is given. For there are some eunuchs, which were so born from their mother's womb: and there are some eunuchs, which were made eunuchs of men: and there be eunuchs, which have made themselves eunuchs for the kingdom of heaven's sake. He that is able to receive it, let him receive it."**

Restriction of divorcee was based on the necessity of protecting the woman and her position in society, not necessarily in a religious context, but an economic context. It was the custom at the time Jesus lived for priests of some ancient gods and goddesses to be castrated. In the pre-Christian period **Vestals,** who served the virgin goddess of the hearth, were obliged to forgo marriage, and so were some priests and servants of some ancient deities such as **Isis. Jewish priests are allowed to marry. However, they were not allowed to marry a prostitute or a widow (Leviticus 21:7, 8, 14 and 15).**

**There is no commandment in the New Testament that Jesus' disciples have to live in celibacy.** The general view on sexuality among the early **Jewish Christians** was quite positive. Jesus himself does not speak in negative terms of the body in the **New Testament. Saint Peter, also known as Simon Peter, the Apostle was married. Paul the Apostle, also known as Saul of Tarsus, was also married.** In his early writings, **Paul the Apostle** described marriage as a social obligation that has the potential of distracting from Christ.

Sex, in turn, is not sinful but natural, and sex within marriage is both proper and necessary. **"Husbands love your wives even as Christ loved the church. Husbands should love their wives as their own bodies"** (Ephesians 5:25-28). **Paul** encouraged both celibate and marital lifestyles among the members of the **Corinthian** congregation, regarding celibacy as the preferable of the two:

> **It is good for a man not to touch a woman. Nevertheless, to avoid fornication, let every man have his own wife, and let every woman have her own husband. Let the husband render unto the wife due benevolence: and likewise also the wife unto the husband.**

**Paul the Apostle** emphasized the importance of overcoming the desires of the flesh and saw the state of celibacy being superior to the marriage. In the **Catholic Church,** a consecrated virgin is a woman who has been consecrated by the church to a life of **perpetual virginity** in the service of God. According to most Christian thought, **the first sacred virgin was Mary**, the mother of Jesus, who was **consecrated by the Holy Spirit during the Annunciation**.

## Desert Fathers

The **Desert Fathers** were Christian hermits, and ascetics who had a major influence on the development of Christianity and celibacy. **Paul of Thebes** is often credited with being the first hermit monk to go to the desert, but it was **Anthony the Great** who launched the movement that became the **Desert Fathers**. They chose a life of extreme asceticism. By the time of **Anthony's** death, there were so many men and women living in the desert in celibacy.

According to the later **St. Jerome (347-420)** celibacy is a moral virtue, consisting of living in the flesh, but outside the flesh, and so being not corrupted by it (*vivere in carne praeter carnem*). Celibacy excludes not only libidinous acts, but also sinful thoughts or desires of the flesh. In the Catholic, Orthodox and Oriental Orthodox traditions, bishops are required to be celibate. In the Eastern Christian traditions, priests and deacons are allowed to be married, yet have to remain celibate if they are unmarried at the time or ordination.

## Augustinian view

In the early Church higher clerics lived in marriages. **Augustine of Hippo was one of the first to develop a theory that sexual feelings were sinful and negative.** **Augustine** taught that the original sin of Adam and Eve. The first couple disobeyed God, who had told them not to eat of the **Tree of the knowledge of good and evil (Gen. 2:17).** The sin of Adam is inherited by all human beings. **Augustine** taught that **Original Sin** was transmitted by concupiscence, which he regarded as the passion of both, soul and body, making humanity a *Massa damnata* (mass of perdition, condemned crowd) and much enfeebling, though not destroying, the freedom of the will.

He believed that the serpent approached **Eve** because she was less rational and lacked self-control. **Augustine** believed sin entered the world because man (the spirit) did not exercise control over woman (the flesh).

## After Augustine

It remains a matter of **Canon Law** that priests may not own land and therefore cannot pass it on to legitimate or illegitimate children. The land belongs to the Church through the local diocese as administered by the **Local Ordinary** (usually a bishop), who is often an *ex officio* corporation sole. **The Protestant Reformation rejected celibate life and sexual continence for preachers.** Many evangelicals prefer the term **"abstinence" to "celibacy."** There are also many Pentecostal churches which practice celibate ministry. The **Pentecostal Mission** is a church spread worldwide which strictly forbids its ministers to marry.

## Catholic Church

During the first three or four centuries, no law was promulgated prohibiting clerical marriage. Celibacy was a matter of choice for bishops, priests, and deacons. **1 Timothy 4:1 "For everything created by God is good and nothing is to be rejected when received with thanksgiving. For it is made holy by the invocation of God in prayer".** Statutes forbidding clergy from having wives were written beginning with the **Council of Elvira (306). The Apostolic Constitutions (c 400) excommunicated a priest or bishop who left his wife 'under the pretense of piety'"** (Mansi, 1:51).

**"The Second Lateran Council (1139) seems to have enacted the first written law making sacred orders a diriment impediment to marriage for the universal Church."** Celibacy was first required of some clerics in 1123 at the **First Lateran Council.** Because clerics resisted it, the celibacy mandate was restated at the **Second Lateran Council (1139)** and the **Council of Trent (1545-64).** The earliest decree in which the children [of clerics] were declared to be slaves and never to be enfranchised [freed] seems to have been a canon of the **Synod of Pavia in 1018.** Similar penalties were promulgated against wives and concubines. **Mandatory celibacy for priests continues to be a contested issue even today.**

In the **Roman Catholic Church**, the **Twelve Apostles** are considered to have been the first priests and bishops of the Church. Others are the call to be sexually continent in **Matthew 19** to be a caution for men who were too readily divorcing and remarrying. The view of the Church is that celibacy is a reflection of life in Heaven, a source of detachment from the material world which aids in one's relationship with God. Celibacy is designed to **"consecrate themselves with undivided heart to the Lord and to "the affairs of the Lord, they give themselves entirely to God and to men.**

In contrast, **Saint Peter, whom the Church considers its first Pope, was married** given that he had a mother-in-law whom Christ healed (Matthew 8). Mandatory priestly celibacy is not *doctrine* of the Church (such as the belief in the Assumption of Mary) but a matter of discipline, like the use of the vernacular (local) language in **Mass** or **Lenten fasting** and **abstinence. The Easter Catholic Churches ordain both celibate and married men.**

## Celibate homosexual Christians

Some **homosexual Christians** choose to be celibate due to their faith's teachings on homosexuality. In 2014 the **American Association of Christian Counselors** amended its code of ethics to eliminate the promotion of conversion therapy for homosexuals and encouraged them to be celibate instead.

## Hinduism

In Hinduism, celibacy is usually associated with the *sadhus* **("holy men"),** ascetics who withdraw from society and renounce all worldly ties. The purpose of practicing *brahmacharya* is to keep a person focused on the purpose in life, the things that instill a feeling of peace and contentment.

## Islamic perspective

Islamic attitudes toward celibacy have been complex. **Muhammad denounced it;** however some Sufi orders embrace it. **Islam does not promote celibacy; rather it condemns premarital sex and extramarital sex.** In fact, according to Islam, marriage enables one to attain the highest form of righteousness within this sacred spiritual bond and is as such to be sought after and desired. The Qur'an (57:27) states, **"But the Monasticism which they invented for themselves. We did not prescribe for them but only to please God therewith, but that they did not observe it with the right observance."**

**Celibacy was practiced by women saints in Sufism.** Celibacy was debated along with women's roles in Sufism in medieval times. Celibacy, poverty, meditation, and mysticism within an ascetic context along with worship centered around Saint's tombs were promoted by the **Qadiri Sufi order among Hui Muslims in China. In China, unlike other Muslim sects, the leaders (Shaikhs) of the Qadiriyya Sufi order are celibate.**

## Meher Baba

The spiritual teacher **Meher Baba** stated that **"For the spiritual aspirant a life of strict celibacy is preferable to married life, if restraint comes to hi easily without undue sense of self-repression. Promiscuity in sex gratification is bound to land the aspirant in a most pitiful and dangerous chaos of ungovernable lust."**
**Ancient Greece and Rome**

In Sparta and many other Greek cities, failure to marry was grounds for loss of citizenship, and could be prosecuted as a crime. Both **Cicero** and **Dionysius** of Halicarnassus stated that **Roman law forbade celibacy.**

# Chabad

**Chabad**, also known as **Lubavitch**, **Habad** and **Chabad-Lubavitch** , is an Orthodox Jewish, **Hasidic movement**. Chabad is today one of the world's best known **Hasidic movements** and is well known for its outreach. **It is one of the largest Hasidic groups and Jewish religious organizations in the world.**

Founded in 1775 by **Rabbi Schneur Zalman of Liadi**, the name **"Chabad"** is a Hebrew acronym for *Chochmah, Binah, Da'at* : **"Wisdom, Understanding, and Knowledge",** which represent the intellectual underpinnings of the movement. The name **Lubavitch** is the Yiddish name of the **Polish–Lithuanian Commonwealth village Lubowicze (Lyubavichi)** now in Russia, where the movement's leaders lived for over 100 years. **In the 1930s, the sixth Rebbe of Chabad, Rabbi Yosef Yitzchak Schneersohn**, moved the center of the Chabad movement from Russia to Poland. After the outbreak of World War Two, the sixth Rebbe moved the center of the movement to the United States.

In 1951**, Rabbi Menachem Mendel Schneerson** became the seventh **Chabad Rebbe**. The seventh Rebbe transformed the movement into one of the largest and most widespread Jewish movements in the world today. Under **Rabbi Menachem Mendel's** leadership, the movement established a network of more than **3,600 institutions** that provide religious, social and humanitarian needs in over **1,000 cities**, spanning **100 countries** and all 50 American states**.** Chabad institutions provide outreach to unaffiliated Jews and humanitarian aid, as well as religious, cultural and educational activities at Chabad-run community centers, synagogues, schools, camps, and soup kitchens.

The movement is thought to number between **40,000 and 200,000 adherents**. In 2005 the Jerusalem Center for Public Affairs reported that up to one million Jews attend Chabad services at least once a year. **In 2013, Chabad forecast that their Chanukah activities would reach up to 8,000,000 Jews in 80 countries worldwide.**

## History

The Chabad movement was established in the town of **Liozna**, Grand Duchy of Lithuania (present day **Belarus**), in 1775, by **Rabbi Shneur Zalman of Liadi**, a student of **Rabbi Dovber ben Avraham**, the **"Maggid of Mezritch"**, **the successor to Hasidism's founder, Rabbi Israel Baal Shem Tov**. Since 1940, the movement's center has been in the Crown Heights neighborhood of Brooklyn. In the early 1900s, Chabad-Lubavitch legally incorporated itself under **Agudas Chasidei Chabad ("Association of Chabad Hasidim").**

## Leadership

The Chabad movement has been led by a succession of Hasidic rebbes. The main line of the movement, **Chabad-Lubavitch, has had seven rebbes in total.** Rabbi Shneur Zalman of Liadi (1745–1812), founded the Chabad movement in the town of Liozna. **Rabbi Dovber Schneuri** (1773–1827), son of **Rabbi Shneur Zalman**, led the Chabad movement in the town of Lyubavichi (Lubavitch). **Rabbi Menachem Mendel Schneersohn** (1789–1866), a grandson of **Rabbi Shneur Zalman** and son-in-law of **Rabbi Dovber. Rabbi Shmuel Schneersohn** (1834–1882), was the seventh and youngest son of **Rabbi Menachem Mendel. Rabbi Shalom Dovber Schneersohn** (1860–1920), Shmuel's second son, succeeded his father as Rebbe. **Rabbi Yosef Yitzchak Schneersohn** (1880–1950), the only son of **Sholom Dovber**, succeeded his father as Rebbe of Chabad. **Rabbi Menachem Mendel Schneerson** (1902–1994), son-in-law of **Rabbi Yosef Yitzchak**, and a great-grandson of the third Rebbe of Lubavitch, assumed the title of Rebbe one year after his father-in-law's death.

## Oppression and resurgence in Russia

The Chabad movement was subject to government oppression in Russia. The Russian government, first under the **Czar**, later under the **Bolsheviks**, imprisoned all but one of the **Chabad Rebbes**. The Bolsheviks also imprisoned, exiled and executed a number of Chabad Hasidim. Since the dissolution of the Soviet Union in 1991, **Chabad is not persecuted by the Russian government**.

## *Chabad philosophy*

Chabad Hasidic philosophy focuses on religious and spiritual concepts such as God, the soul, and the meaning of the Jewish commandments. Classical Judaic writings and Jewish mysticism, especcially the **Zohar** and the **Kabbalah** of **Rabbi Isaac Luria**, are frequently cited in Chabad works. Chabad philosophy is rooted in the teachings of **Rabbis Yisroel ben Eliezer,** (the **Baal Shem Tov,** founder of Hasidism) and **Dovber ben Avraham**, the **"Maggid of Mezritch"** (Rabbi Yisroel's successor). **Rabbi Shneur Zalman's** teachings formed the basis of Chabad philosophy.

## Tanya

*Sefer HaTanya*, Shneur Zalman's magnum opus, is the first schematic treatment of Hasidic moral philosophy and its metaphysical foundations. The original name of the first book is *Sefer Shel Beinonim,* the *Book of the Intermediates. Sefer Shel Beinonim* analyzes the inner struggle of the individual and the path to resolution.

## "Chabad"

According to **Shneur Zalman's** seminal work *Tanya*, the intellect consists of three interconnected processes: *Chochma* **(wisdom)**, *Bina* **(understanding), and** *Da'at* **(knowledge).** While other branches of Hasidism focused primarily on the idea that **"God desires the heart,"** Shneur

**Zalman** argued that God also desires the mind, and that the mind is the **"gateway"** to the heart. **Shneur Zalman** taught that the emotions must be led by the mind, and thus the focus of Chabad thought was to be **Torah** study and prayer rather than **esotericism** and song. As a Talmudist, **Shneur Zalman** endeavored to place **Kabbalah** and Hasidism on a rational basis. In *Tanya,* he defines his approach as *moach shalit al halev* **(Hebrew: "the brain ruling the heart").**

## Demographics

Demographic accounts on the Chabad movement vary. Chabad adherents are often reported to number some **200,000 persons**. Some scholars have pointed to the lack of quantitative data to back this claim, and some place the number of Chabad followers at around **40,000** but note that the number may be higher if the non-Hasidic Jews who join Chabad synagogues are included as well. An estimate places Chabad's followers in the US at around **18,600**. The estimate is drawn from existing data on the **Montreal Chabad** community, and Chabad day school figures.

## Student body in the United States

The report findings of studies on Jewish day schools and supplementary Jewish education in the United States show that the student body currently enrolled in some **295 Chabad schools exceeds 20,750.**

## Institutions

As of 2007 there are **3,300 Chabad institutions** around the world. As of 2006 there were Chabad centers in **75 countries**. Listed on the Chabad movement's online directory are around **1,350 Chabad institutions**. In total, according to its directory, Chabad maintains a presence in **950 cities around the world**: 178 in Europe, 14 in Africa, 200 in Israel, 400 in North America, 38 in South America, and about 70 in Asia (excluding Israel, including Russia).

## Controversies

Several movement-wide controversies have occurred in Chabad's **200-year history**. Two major leadership succession controversies occurred in the 1800s, one took place in the 1810s following the death of the movement's founder, the other occurred in the 1860s following the death of the third Rebbe. The movement's other major controversy is **Chabad Messianism**, which began in the 1990s. Chabad Messianism appears to be among the most frequently cited controversies within the Orthodox Jewish community.

## *Chabad Messianism*

In the late 1980s, the Rebbe called for his followers to become involved in outreach activities with the purpose of bringing about the **Jewish Messianic Age**. Some Chabad Hasidim**, called** *mashichists,* **"have not yet accepted the Rebbe's passing"** and even after his death regard him as the (living) **'King Messiah' and 'Moses of the generation'.**

# The Chosen People

Throughout history, various groups of people have considered themselves to be **chosen people** by a deity for a purpose, such as to act as the deity's agent on earth. In monotheistic faiths references to God are used in constructs such as **"God's Chosen People"**. The phenomenon of a **"chosen people"** is particularly common in the Israelite tradition, where it originally referred to the Israelites—in fact Jews refer to this as a burden to spread the message of one God.

Some claims of chosenness are based on parallel claims of Israelite ancestry, as is the case for the Christian Identity and **Black Hebrew** sects—both which claim themselves (and not Jews) to be the **"true Israel"**. Others claim a **"spiritual"** chosenness, including most Christian denominations, who traditionally believe the church has replaced Israel as the **People of God**.

## Jews as the chosen people

In Judaism, **"chosenness"** is the belief that the Jews, via descent from the ancient Israelites, are the chosen people, i.e. chosen to be in a covenant with God. The idea of the Israelites being chosen by God is found most directly in the **Book of Deuteronomy** as the verb *bahar*, and is alluded to elsewhere in the **Hebrew Bible** using other terms such as **"holy people"**. Much is written about these topics in rabbinic literature.

The three largest Jewish denominations—**Orthodox Judaism, Conservative Judaism and Reform Judaism**—maintain the belief that the Jews have been chosen by God for a purpose. Sometimes this choice is seen as charging the Jewish people with a specific mission—to be a light unto the nations, and to exemplify the covenant with God as described in the **Torah.**

## Christianity / *Supersessionism and People of God* / Seventh-day Adventism Mormonism

In **Mormonism**, all **Latter Day Saints** are viewed as covenant, or chosen, people because they have accepted the name of **Jesus Christ** through the ordinance of baptism. In contrast to **Supersessionism**, **Latter Day Saints** do not dispute the **"chosen"** status of the Jewish people. Most practicing Mormons receive a patriarchal blessing that reveals their lineage in the **House of Israel.**

This lineage may be blood related or through **"adoption;"** therefore, a child may not necessarily share the lineage of her parents (but will still be a member of the tribes of Israel). It is a widely held belief that most members of the faith are in the tribe of **Ephraim** or the tribe of **Manasseh**.

## Christian Identity

The **Christian Identity** movement sees the **Anglo-Saxon, Germanic, Nordic** and kindred peoples of the world as both the descendants of the ancient Israelites and the physical descendants of **Abraham, Isaac and Jacob**. Christian Identity, though not organized as a religion, comprises certain individuals, churches and some prison gangs with a white supremacist theology that promotes a racial interpretation of Christianity.

**Christian Identity** beliefs were primarily developed and promoted by two authors who regarded Europeans as the **"chosen people"** and Jews as the cursed offspring of **Cain**. White supremacist sects and gangs later adopted many of these teachings.

## Rastafari

Based on Jewish biblical tradition and Ethiopian legend via **Kebra Nagast**, Rastas believe that Israel's **King Solomon**, together with **Ethiopian Queen of Sheba**, conceived a child which began the Solomonic line of kings in Ethiopia, rendering the Ethiopian people as the true children of Israel, and thereby chosen. Reinforcement of this belief occurred when **Beta Israel**, Ethiopia's ancient **Israelite First Temple** community, were rescued from Sudanese famine and brought to Israel during **Operation Moses in 1985.**

## Unification Church

**Sun Myung Moon** taught that Korea is the chosen nation, selected to serve a divine mission and was **"chosen by God to be the birthplace of the leading figure of the age"** and was the birthplace of **"Heavenly Tradition",** ushering in God's kingdom.

## Nation of Islam

The **NOI** teaches that black people constitute a nation and that through the institution of the Atlantic slave trade they were systematically denied knowledge of their history, language, culture, and religion and, in effect, lost control of their lives. **Founder Elijah Muhammad** called for the establishment of a separate nation for black Americans and the adoption of a religion based on the worship of **Allah** and on the belief that blacks were his chosen people.

# Circumcision (Judaism & Islamic)

**Circumcision** is the removal of the foreskin from the human penis. After that, a device may be placed, and then the foreskin is cut off. Topical or locally injected anesthesia is sometimes used to reduce pain and physiologic stress. For adults and children, general anesthesia is an option, and the procedure may be performed without a specialized circumcision device.

The procedure is most often an elective surgery performed on babies and children, for religious or cultural reasons. In other cases it may be done as a treatment for certain medical conditions or for preventative reasons. It is contraindicated in cases of certain genital structure abnormalities or poor general health.

No major medical organization recommends either universal circumcision of all males or banning the procedure. Ethical and legal questions regarding informed consent and human rights have been raised over the circumcision of babies and children for non-medical reasons; for these reasons the procedure is controversial.

Male circumcision reduces the risk of **HIV** infection among heterosexual men in sub-Saharan Africa. The effectiveness of using circumcision to prevent **HIV** in the developed world is unclear, however there is some evidence that circumcision reduces **HIV** infection risk for men who have sex with men. Circumcision is also associated with reduced rates of cancer-causing forms of human papillomavirus **(HPV), UTIs**, and cancer of the penis.

**Studies of other sexually transmitted infections also suggest that circumcision is protective, including for men who have sex with men.** Bleeding, infection, and the removal of either too much or too little foreskin are the most common complications cited. **Circumcision does not appear to have a negative impact on sexual function.**

**An estimated one-third of males worldwide are circumcised.** The procedure is most common among **Muslims** and **Jews** (among whom it is near-universal for religious reasons), and in parts of Southeast Asia, and Africa. In the United States rates of circumcision decreased from 64% in 1979 to 58% in 2010. The origin of circumcision is not known with certainty; **the oldest documented evidence for it comes from ancient Egypt.** It is part of religious law in Judaism and is an established practice in Islam, Coptic Christianity, and the Ethiopian Orthodox Church. The word circumcision is from Latin *circumcidere*, meaning **"to cut around"**.

## Other infections

**Studies evaluating the effect of circumcision on the rates of other sexually transmitted infections have generally, found it to be protective.** A 2006 meta-analysis found that circumcision was associated with lower rates of **syphilis, chancroid** and possibly genital **herpes**.

A 2010 review found that circumcision reduced the incidence of **HSV-2** (herpes simplex virus, type 2) infections by 28%.

## Urinary tract infections

**A UTI affects parts of the urinary system including the urethra, bladder, and kidneys. There is about a one percent risk of UTIs in boys under two years of age, and the majority of incidents occur in the first year of life.** There is a plausible biological explanation for the reduction in **UTI** risk after circumcision. As these bacteria are a risk factor for **UTI**s, circumcision may reduce the risk of **UTI**s through a decrease in the bacterial population.

## Cancers

**Circumcision has a protective effect against the risks of penile cancer in men, and cervical cancer in the female sexual partners of heterosexual men.** Penile cancer is rare, with about 1 new case per 100,000 people per year in developed countries, and higher incidence rates per 100,000 in sub-Saharan Africa (for example: 1.6 in Zimbabwe, 2.7 in Uganda and 3.2 in Swaziland).

## Women's health

A 2017 systematic review found consistent evidence that male circumcision prior to heterosexual contact was associated with a decreased risk of cervical cancer, cervical dysplasia, HSV-2, chlamydia, and syphilis among women.

## Sexual effects

**The highest quality evidence indicates that circumcision does not decrease the sensitivity of the penis, harm sexual function or reduce sexual satisfaction.** A 2017 systematic review and meta-analysis found that circumcision did not affect **premature ejaculation**.

## Rate of male circumcision by country

**Circumcision is one of the world's most widely performed procedures. Approximately 37% to 39% of males worldwide are circumcised,** about half for religious or cultural reasons. It is most often practiced between infancy and the early twenties. The **WHO** estimated in 2007 that 664,500,000 males aged 15 and over were circumcised (30–33% global prevalence), almost 70% of whom were Muslim. Circumcision is most common in the Muslim world, Israel, South Korea, the United States and parts of Southeast Asia and Africa. It is relatively rare in Europe, Latin America, parts of Southern Africa and Oceania and most of Asia.

Prevalence is near-universal in the Middle East and Central Asia. Non-religious circumcision in Asia, outside of the Republic of Korea and the Philippines, is fairly rare, and prevalence is generally low (less than 20%) across Europe. Estimates for individual countries include Taiwan at 9% and Australia 58.7%. Prevalence in the United States and Canada is estimated at 75% and 30%

respectively. Prevalence in Africa varies from less than 20% in some southern African countries to near universal in North and West Africa.

## Middle East, Africa and Europe

Evidence suggests that circumcision was practiced in the Arabian Peninsula by the 4th millennium BCE, when the Sumerians and the Semites moved into the area that is modern-day Iraq. The earliest historical record of circumcision comes from Egypt, in the form of an image of the circumcision of an adult carved into the tomb of **Ankh-Mahor at Saqqara**, dating to about 2400–2300 BCE. Circumcision was done by the Egyptians possibly for hygienic reasons, but also was part of their obsession with purity and was associated with spiritual and intellectual development. Though secular scholars consider the story to be literary and not historical, circumcision features prominently in the **Hebrew Bible**. The narrative in **Genesis chapter 17 describes the circumcision of Abraham and his relatives and slaves**. In the same chapter, Abraham's descendants are commanded to circumcise their sons on the **eighth day of life** as part of a covenant with God.

In addition to proposing that circumcision was taken up by the Israelites purely as a religious mandate, scholars have suggested that Judaism's patriarchs and their followers adopted circumcision to make penile hygiene easier in hot, sandy climates; as a rite of passage into adulthood; or as a form of blood sacrifice.

**Alexander the Great** conquered the Middle East in the 4th century BCE, and in the following centuries ancient Greek cultures and values came to the Middle East. The Greeks abhorred circumcision, making life for circumcised Jews living among the Greeks (and later the Romans) very difficult. **Antiochus Epiphanes** outlawed circumcision, as did **Hadrian**, which helped cause the **Bar Kokhba revolt.**

A narrative in the Christian Gospel of Luke makes a brief mention of the **circumcision of Jesus**, but the subject of physical circumcision itself is not part of the received teachings of Jesus. **Paul the Apostle** reinterpreted circumcision as a spiritual concept, arguing the physical one to be unnecessary for Gentile converts to Christianity. Although it is not explicitly mentioned in the **Quran** (early 7th century CE), **circumcision is considered essential to Islam**, and it is nearly universally performed among Muslims.

**Genghis Khan** and the following **Yuan Emperors in China** forbade Islamic practices such as halal butchering and circumcision. This led Chinese Muslims to eventually take an active part in rebelling against the Mongols and installing the more tolerant Ming Dynasty.

## Judaism / *Brit Milah*

**Circumcision is very important to most branches of Judaism, with over 90% of male adherents having the procedure performed as a religious obligation.** The basis for its observance is found in the Torah of the Hebrew Bible, in Genesis chapter 17, in which a **covenant of circumcision is made with Abraham and his descendants.** Jewish circumcision is part of the *brit Milah* ritual, to be performed by a specialist ritual circumciser, a *mohel*, on the eighth day of a newborn son's life, with certain exceptions for poor health.

## Islam / *Khitan (circumcision)*

Although there is some debate within Islam over whether it is a religious requirement, **circumcision (called *Khitan*) is practiced nearly universally by Muslim males.** Islam bases its practice of circumcision on the **Genesis 17** narrative, the same Biblical chapter referred to by **Jews.** The procedure is not explicitly mentioned in the **Quran,** however, it is a tradition established by **Islam's prophet Muhammad directly (following Abraham),** and so its practice is considered a *Sunnah* (prophet's tradition) and is very important in **Islam.**

**It may be done from soon after birth up to about age 15; most often it is performed at around six to seven years of age.** The timing can correspond with the boy's completion of his recitation of the whole Quran, with a coming-of-age event such as taking on the responsibility of daily prayer or betrothal. **Circumcision is recommended for, but is not required of, converts to Islam.**

## *Religious male circumcision § In Christianity*

**The New Testament chapter Acts 15 records that Christianity did not require circumcision.** In 1442 the Catholic Church banned the practice of religious circumcision in the 11th Council of Florence and currently maintains a neutral position on the practice of non-religious circumcision. **Coptic Christians practice circumcision as a rite of passage. The Ethiopian Orthodox Church calls for circumcision.**

The **American Academy of Pediatrics** (2012) recommends that neonatal circumcision in the United States be covered by third-party payers such as Medicaid and insurance. A 2014 review that considered reported benefits of circumcision such as reduced risks from **HIV, HPV, and HSV-2** stated that circumcision is cost-effective in both the United States and Africa and may result in health care savings.

However, a 2014 literature review found that there are significant gaps in the current literature on male and female sexual health that need to be addressed for the literature to be applicable to North American populations.

# Conservative Judaism

**Conservative Judaism** (known as **Masorti Judaism** outside North America) is a Jewish religious movement that regards the authority of Jewish law and tradition as emanating primarily from the assent of the people through the generations, more than from divine revelation. It therefore views Jewish law, or *Halakha*, as both binding and subject to historical development.

The conservative rabbinate employs modern historical-critical research, rather than only traditional methods and sources, and lends great weight to its constituency, when determining its stance on matters of practice. The movement considers its approach as the authentic and most appropriate continuation of *Halakhic* discourse, maintaining both fealty to received forms and flexibility in their interpretation. It also eschews strict theological definitions, lacking a consensus in matters of faith and allowing great pluralism.

While regarding itself as the heir of **Rabbi Zecharias Frankel's** 19th-century positive-historical school in Europe, **Conservative Judaism** fully institutionalized only in the United States during the mid-20th century. Its largest center today is in North America, where its main congregational arm is the **United Synagogue** of **Conservative Judaism**, and the New York–based Jewish Theological Seminary of America operates as its largest rabbinic seminary. Globally, affiliated communities are united within the umbrella organization **Masorti Olami. Conservative Judaism** is the third-largest Jewish religious movement worldwide, estimated to represent close to 1.1 million people, including over **600,000 registered adult congregants** and many non-member identifiers.

## Theology: Attitude

**Conservative Judaism**, from its earliest stages, was marked by ambivalence and ambiguity in all matters theological. **Rabbi Zecharias Frankel**, considered its intellectual progenitor, believed the very notion of theology was alien to traditional Judaism. He was often accused of obscurity on the subject by his opponents, both **Reform** and **Orthodox**. The American movement largely espoused a similar approach, and its leaders mostly avoided the field. Only in 1985 did a course about **Conservative** theology open in the Jewish **Theological Seminary of America** (JTS ). The hitherto sole major attempt to define a clear credo was made in 1988, with the Statement of Principles *Emet ve-Emunah* (Truth and Belief), formulated and issued by the **Leadership Council of Conservative Judaism**.

The introduction stated that **"lack of definition was useful"** in the past but a need to articulate one now arose. The platform provided many statements citing key concepts such as God, revelation and Election, but also acknowledged that a variety of positions and convictions existed within its ranks, eschewing strict delineation of principles and often expressing conflicting views. In a 1999 special edition of *Conservative Judaism* dedicated to the matter, leading **rabbis Elliot N. J**

**Dorf and Gordon Tucker** stated that **"the great diversity"** within the movement **"makes the creation of a theological vision shared by all neither possible nor desirable".**

## God and eschatology

**Conservativ Judaism** largely upholds the theistic notion of a personal God. *Emet ve-Emunah* stated that **"we affirm our faith in God as the Creator and Governor of the universe. His power called the world into being; His wisdom and goodness guide its destiny."** Concurrently, the platform also noted that His nature was **"elusive"** and subject to many options of belief. A naturalistic conception of divinity, regarding it as inseparable from the mundane world, once had an important place within the movement, especially represented by **Mordecai Kaplan**. After Kaplan's **Reconstructionism** fully coalesced into an independent movement, these views were marginalized.

A similarly inconclusive position is expressed toward other precepts. Most theologians adhere to the **Immortality of the Soul**, but while references to the Resurrection of the Dead are maintained, English translations of the prayers obscure the issue. In *Emet,* it was stated that death is not tantamount to the end of one's personality. Relating to the Messianic ideal, the movement rephrased most petitions for the restoration of the Sacrifices into past tense, rejecting a renewal of animal offerings, though not opposing a **Return to Zion** and even a **New Temple**. The 1988 platform announced that **"some"** believe in classic eschatology, but dogmatism in this matter was **"philosophically unjustified"**. The notions of Election of Israel and God's covenant with it were basically retained as well.

## Revelation

**Conservative** conception of **Revelation** encompasses an extensive spectrum. **Zecharias Frankel** himself applied critical-scientific methods to analyze the stages in the development of the **Oral Torah,** pioneering modern study of the Mishnah. He regarded the **Beatified Sages** as innovators who added their own, original contribution to the canon, not merely as expounders and interpreters of a legal system given in its entirety to Moses on Mount Sinai. Yet he also vehemently rejected utilizing these disciplines on the **Pentateuch**, maintaining it was beyond human reach and wholly celestial in origin. **Frankel** never elucidated his beliefs, and the exact correlation between human and divine in his thought is still subject to scholarly debate.

A similar negative approach toward **Higher Criticism**, while accepting an evolutionary understanding of **Oral Law**, defined **Rabbi Alexander Kohut, Solomon Shechter** and the early generation of American **Conservative Judaism**. When **JTS** faculty began to embrace Biblical criticism in the 1920s, they adapted a theological view consistent with it: an original, verbal revelation did occur at Sinai, but the text itself was composed by later authors. The latter, classified by **JDorf** as a relatively moderate metamorphosis of the old one, is still espoused by few traditionalist right-wing **Conservative rabbis**, though it is marginalized among senior leadership.

A small but influential segment within the **JTS** and the movement adhered, from the 1930s, to **Mordecai Kaplan's** philosophy that denied any form of revelation but viewed all scripture as a purely human product. Along with other Reconstructionist tenets, it dwindled as the latter consolidated into a separate group. **Kaplan's** views and the permeation of Higher Criticism gradually swayed most **Conservative** thinkers towards a non-verbal understanding of theophany, which has become dominant in the 1970s. This was in sync with the wider trend of lowering rates of Americans who accepted the Bible as the **Word of God**.

**JDorf** categorized the proponents of this into two schools. One maintains that God projected some form of message which inspired the human authors of the **Pentateuch** to record what they perceived. The other is often strongly influenced by **Franz Rosenzweig** and other existentialists, but also attracted many **Objectivists** who consider human reason paramount. The second school states that God conferred merely his presence on those he influenced, without any communication, and the experience drove them to spiritual creativity.

While they differ in the theoretical level surrounding revelation, both practically regard all scripture and religious tradition as a human product with certain divine inspiration—providing an understanding that recognizes **Biblical Criticism** and also justifies major innovation in religious conduct. The first doctrine, advocated by such leaders as **rabbis Ben-Zion Bokser** and **Robert Gordis**, largely imparted that some elements within Judaism are fully divine but determining which would be impractical, and therefore received forms of interpretation should be basically upheld.

Exponents of the latter view, among them rabbis Louis Jacobs and **Neil Gillman**, also emphasized the encounter of God with the Jews as a collective and the role of religious authorities through the generations in determining what it implied. The stress on the supremacy of community and tradition, rather than individual consciousness, defines the entire spectrum of **Conservative thought.**

## Ideology

The **Conservative** mainstay was the adoption of the historical-critical method in understanding Judaism and setting its future course. In accepting an evolutionary approach to the religion, as something that developed over time and absorbed considerable external influences, the movement distinguished between the original meaning implied in traditional sources and the manner they were grasped by successive generations, rejecting belief in an unbroken chain of interpretation from God's original Revelation, immune to any major extraneous effects. This evolutionary perception of religion, while relatively moderate in comparison with more radical modernizers— the scholarship of the **Positive-Historical** school, for example, sought to demonstrate the continuity and cohesiveness of Judaism over the years—still challenged **Conservative leaders.**

They regarded tradition and received mores with reverence, especially the continued adherence to the mechanism of **Religious Law** (*Halakha*), opposing indiscriminate modification, and emphasized they should be changed only with care and caution and remain observed by the people. **Rabbi Louis Ginzberg**, summarizing his movement's position, wrote:

We may now understand the apparent contradiction between theory and practice... One may conceive of the origin of **Sabbath** as the professor at university would, yet observe the smallest detail known to strict **Orthodox**y... The sanctity of the **Sabbath** reposes not upon the fact that it was proclaimed on Sinai, but on the fact that it found for thousands of years its expression in Jewish souls. It is the task of the historian to examine the beginnings and developments of customs and observances; practical Judaism, on the other hand, is not concerned with origins but regards the institutions as they have come to be.

This discrepancy between scientific criticism and insistence on heritage had to be compensated by a conviction that would forestall either deviation from accepted norms or laxity and apathy. A key doctrine which was to fulfil this capacity was the collective will of the Jewish people. **Conservative** s lent great weight in determining religious practice, both in historical precedent and as a means to shape present conduct. **Zecharias Frankel** pioneered this approach; as **Michael A. Meyer** commented, **"the extraordinary status which he ascribed to the ingrained beliefs and practices of the community is probably the most original element of his thought."** He turned it into a source of legitimacy for both change and preservation, but mostly the latter.

The basic moderation and traditionalism of the majority among the people were to guarantee a sense of continuity and unity, restraining the guiding rabbis and scholars who at his age were intent on reform but also allowing them manoeuvrability in adopting or discarding certain elements. **Solomon Shechter** espoused a similar position. He turned the old rabbinic concept of **K'lal Yisrael**, which he translated as "Catholic Israel", into a comprehensive worldview.

For him, the details of divine Revelation were of secondary significance, as historical change dictated its interpretation through the ages notwithstanding: **"The centre of authority is actually removed from the Bible"**, he surmised, **"and placed in some living body... in touch with the ideal aspirations and the religious needs of the age, best able to determine... This living body, however, is not represented by... Priesthood, or Rabbihood, but by the collective conscience of Catholic Israel."**

The scope, limits and role of this corpus were a matter for contention in **Conservative** ranks. **Shechter** himself used it to oppose any major break with either traditionalist or progressive elements within American Jewry of his day, while some of his successors argued that the idea became obsolete due to the great alienation of many from received forms, that had to be countered by innovative measures to draw them back.

The **Conservative** rabbinate often vacillated on to which degree may the non-practicing, religiously apathetic strata be included as a factor within Catholic Israel, providing impulse for them in determining religious questions; even avant-garde leaders acquiesced that the majority could not serve that function. Right-wing critics often charged that the movement allowed its uncommitted laity an exaggerated role, conceding to its demands and successively stretching *halakhic* boundaries beyond any limit.

The **Conservative** leadership had limited success in imparting their worldview to the general public. While the rabbinate perceived itself as bearing a unique, original conception of Judaism, the masses lacked much interest, regarding it mainly as a compromise offering a channel for religious identification that was more traditional than **Reform** Judaism yet less strict than **Orthodox**y.

Only a low percentage of **Conservative** congregants actively pursue an observant lifestyle: in the mid-1980s, **Charles Liebman** and **Daniel J. Elazar** calculated that barely 3 to 4 per cent held to one quite thoroughly. This gap between principle and the public, more pronounced than in any other Jewish movement, is often credited at explaining the decline of the **Conservative movement**. While some 41 per cent of American Jews identified with it in the 1970s, it had shrunk to an estimated 18 per cent (and 11 per cent among those under 30) in 2013.

## Jewish law: *Conservative Halakha*

Fidelity and commitment to *Halakha*, while subject to criticism as disingenuous both from within and without, were and remain a cornerstone doctrine of **Conservative Judaism**. The movement views the legalistic system as normative and binding, and believes Jews must practically observe its precepts, like **Sabbath**, dietary ordinances, ritual purity, daily prayer with phylacteries and the like. Concurrently, examining Jewish history and rabbinic literature through the lens of academic criticism, it maintained that these laws were always subject to considerable evolution, and must continue to do so.

*Emet ve-Emunah* titled its chapter on the subject with "The Indispensability of **Halakha**", stating that **"*Halakha* in its developing form is an indispensable element of a traditional Judaism which is vital and modern."** **Conservative Judaism** regards itself as the authentic inheritor of a flexible legalistic tradition, charging the **Orthodox** with petrifying the process and **Reform** with abandoning it.

The tension between "**tradition and change**"—which were also the motto adopted by the movement since the 1950s—and the need to balance them were always a topic of intense debate within **Conservative Judaism**. In its early stages, the leadership opposed pronounced innovation, mostly adopting a relatively rigid position. **Mordecai Kaplan's Reconstructionism** raised the demand for thoroughgoing modification without much regard for the past or *Halakhic* considerations, but senior rabbis opposed him vigorously. Even in the 1940s and 1950s, when **Kaplan's** influence grew, his superiors **rabbis Louis Ginzberg**, **Louis Finkelstein** and **Saul Lieberman** espoused a very conservative line.

Since the 1970s, with the strengthening of the liberal wing within the movement, the majority in the **Rabbinic Assembly** opted for quite radical reformulations in religious conduct, but rejected the **Reconstructionist** *Non-Halakhic* approach, insisting that the legalistic method be maintained. The *Halakhic* commitment of **Conservative Judaism** has been subject to much criticism, from within and without.

Right-wing discontents, including the **Union for Traditional Judaism** which seceded in protest of the 1983 resolution to ordain women rabbis—adopted at an open vote, where all **JTS** faculty regardless of qualification were counted—contested the validity of this description, as well as progressives like **Rabbi Neil Gillman**, who exhorted the movement to cease describing itself as *Halakhic* in 2005, stating that after repeated concessions, **"Our original claim has died a death by a thousand qualifications... It has lost all factual meaning."**

The main body entrusted with formulating rulings, **Responsa** and statues is the **Committee on Jewish Law and Standards (CJLS)**, a panel with 25 voting legalistic specialists and further 11 observers. There is also the smaller *Va'ad ha-Halakha* (Law Committee) of Israel's **Masorti Movement**. Every **Responsa** must receive a minimum of six voters to be considered an official position of the **CJLS**. **Conservative Judaism** explicitly acknowledges the principle of *halakhic* pluralism, enabling the panel to adopt more than one resolution in any given subject. The final authority in each **Conservative** community is the local rabbi, the *Mara D'Atra* (Lord of the Locality, in traditional terms), enfranchised to adopt either minority or majority opinions from the **CJLS** or maintain local practice.

Thus, on the issue of **admitting openly homosexual rabbinic candidates**, the Committee approved two resolutions, one in favor and one against; the **JTS** took the lenient position, while the **Seminario Rabinico Latinoamericano** still adheres to the latter. Likewise, while most **Conservative** synagogues approved of egalitarianism for women in religious life, some still maintain traditional gender roles and do not count females for prayer quorums.

## Characteristics

The **Conservative** treatment of *Halakha* is defined by several features, though the entire range of its *Halakhic* discourse cannot be sharply distinguished from either the **Traditional** or **Orthodox** one. **Rabbi David Golinkin**, who attempted to classify its parameters, stressed that quite often rulings merely reiterate conclusions reached in older sources or even **Orthodox** ones. For example, in the details of preparing **Sabbath** ritual enclosures, it draws directly on the opinions of the *Shulchan Aruch* and **Rabbi Hayim David HaLevi**. Another tendency prevalent among the movement's rabbis, yet again not particular to it, is the adoption of the more lenient positions on the matters at question—though this is not universal, and **Responsa** also took stringent ones not infrequently.

A more distinctive characterization is a greater proclivity to base rulings on earlier sources, in the *Rishonim* or before them, as far back as the Talmud. **Conservative** decisors frequently resort to less canonical sources, isolated **Responsa** or minority opinions. They demonstrate more fluidity in regards to established precedent and continuum in rabbinic literature, mainly those by the later authorities, and lay little stress on the perceived hierarchy between major and minor legalists of the past. They are far more inclined to contend (*machloket*) with old rulings, to be flexible towards custom or to wholly disregard it.

This is especially expressed in less hesitancy to rule against or notwithstanding the major codifications of Jewish Law, like *Mishneh Torah*, *Arba'ah Turim* and especially the *Shulchan Aruch* with its **Isserles Gloss** and later commentaries. **Conservative** authorities, while often relying on the *Shulchan Aruch* themselves, criticize the **Orthodox** for relatively rarely venturing beyond it and overly canonizing **Rabbi Joseph Karo's** work. In several occasions, **Conservative** rabbis discerned that the *Shulchan Aruch* ruled without firm precedent, sometimes deriving his conclusions from the *Kabbalah*.

An important example is the ruling of **Rabbi Golinkin**—contrary to the majority consensus among the *Acharonim* and the more prominent *Rishonim*, but based on many opinions of the lesser *Rishonim* which is derived from a minority view in the Talmud—that the Sabbatical Year is not obligatory in present times at all (neither *de'Oraita* nor *de'Rabanan*) but rather an act of piety. Ethical considerations and the weight due to them in determining *halakhic* issues, mainly to what degree may modern sensibilities shape the outcome, are subject to much discourse. **Right-Wing** decisors, like **Rabbi Joel Roth**, maintained that such elements are naturally a factor in formulating conclusions, but may not alone serve as a justification for adopting a position. The majority, however, basically subscribed to the opinion evinced already by **Rabbi Seymour Siegel** in the 1960s, that the cultural and ethical norms of the community, the contemporary equivalents of **Talmudic** *Aggadah*, should supersede the legalistic forms when the two came into conflict and there was a pivotal ethical concern.

**Rabbi Elliot J Dorf** concluded that in contrast to the **Orthodox**, **Conservative Judaism** maintains that the juridical details and processes mainly serve higher moral purposes and could be modified if they no longer do so: **"In other words, the *Aggadah* should control the *Halakha*."**

The liberal **Rabbi Gordon Tucker**, along with **Gillman** and other progressives, supported a far-reaching implementation of this approach, making **Conservative Judaism** much more *Aggadic* and allowing moral priorities an overriding authority at all occasions. This idea became very popular among the young generation, but it was not fully embraced either. In the 2006 resolution on homosexuals, the **CJLS** chose a middle path: they agreed that the ethical consideration of human dignity was of supreme importance, but not sufficient to uproot the express Biblical prohibition on not to lie with mankind as with womankind (traditionally understood as banning full anal intercourse).

**All other limitations, including on other forms of sexual relations, were lifted**. A similar approach is manifest in the great weight ascribed to sociological changes in deciding religious policy. The **CJLS** and the **Rabbinical Assembly** members frequently state that circumstances were profoundly transformed in modern times, fulfilling the criteria mandating new rulings in various fields (based on general talmudic principles like *Shinui ha-I'ttim*, **"Change of Times"**). This, along with the ethical aspect, was a main argument for revolutionizing the role of women in religious life and embracing egalitarianism.

The most distinctive feature of **Conservative** legalistic discourse, in which it is conspicuously and sharply different from **Orthodox**y, is the incorporation of critical-scientific methods into the process. Deliberations almost always delineate the historical development of the specific issue at hand, from the earliest known mentions until modern times.

This critical approach is central to the movement, for its historicist underpinning stresses that all religious literature has an original meaning relevant in the context of its formulation. This meaning may be analyzed and discerned, and is distinct from the later interpretations ascribed by traditional commentators. Decisors are also far more prone to include references to external scientific sources in relevant fields, like veterinarian publications in *Halakhic* matters concerning livestock.

**Conservative** authorities, as part of their promulgation of a dynamic *Halakha*, often cite the manner in which the sages of old used rabbinic statutes (*Takkanah*) that enabled the bypassing of prohibitions in the **Pentateuch**, like the *Prozbul* or *Heter I'ska*. In 1948, when employing those was first debated, **Rabbi Isaac Klein** argued that since there was no consensus on leadership within Catholic Israel, formulation of significant *takkanot* should be avoided. Another proposal, to ratify them only with a two-thirds majority in the **RA**, was rejected.

New statues require a simple majority, 13 supporters among the 25 members of the **CJLS**. In the 1950s and 1960s, such drastic measures—as **Rabbi Arnold M. Goodman** cited in a 1996 writ allowing members of the priestly caste to marry divorcees, **"Later authorities were reluctant to assume such unilateral authority... fear that invoking this principle would create the proverbial slippery slope, thereby weakening the entire *halakhic* structure... thus imposed severe limitations on the conditions and situations where it would be appropriate"**—were carefully drafted as temporal, emergency ordinances (*Horaat Sha'ah*), grounded on the need the avoid a total rift of many nonobservant Jews.

Later on, these ordinances became accepted and permanent on the practical level. The **Conservative** movement issued a wide range of new, thoroughgoing statues, from the famous 1950 responsum that allowed driving to the synagogue on the **Sabbath** and up to the 2000 decision to ban rabbis from inquiring about whether someone was a *mamzer,* de facto abolishing this legal category.

## Rulings and policies

The **RA** and **CJLS** reached many decisions through the years, shaping a distinctive profile for **Conservative** practice and worship. In the 1940s, when the public demanded mixed seating of both sexes in synagogue, some rabbis argued there was no precedent but obliged on the ground of dire need (**Eth la'asot),** others noted that archaeological research showed no partitions in ancient synagogues. **Mixed seating became commonplace in almost all congregations**.

In 1950, it was ruled that using electricity (that is, closure of an electrical circuit) did not constitute kindling a fire unto itself, not even in incandescent bulbs, and therefore was not a forbidden labour and could be done on the **Sabbath**. On that basis, while performing banned labors is of course forbidden—for example, video recording is still constituted as writing—switching lights and other functions are allowed, though the **RA** strongly urges adherents to keep the sanctity of the **Sabbath** (refraining from doing anything that may imitate the atmosphere of weekdays, like loud noise reminiscent of work).

The need to encourage arrival at synagogue also motivated the **CJLS**, during the same year, to issue a temporal statue allowing driving on that day, for that purpose alone; it was supported by decreeing that the combustion of fuel did not serve any of the acts prohibited during the construction of the Tabernacle, and could therefore be classified, according to their interpretation of the Tosafists' opinion, as **"redundant labor"** (*Sh'eina Tzricha L'gufa*) and be permitted.

The validity of this argument was heavily disputed within the movement. In 1952, members of the priestly caste were allowed to marry divorcees, conditioned on forfeiture of their privileges, as termination of marriage became widespread and women who underwent it could not be suspected of unsavory acts. In 1967, the ban on priests marrying converts was also lifted. In 1954, the issue of *agunot* (women refused divorce by their husbands) was largely settled by adding a clause to the prenuptial contract under which men had to pay alimony as long as they did not concede.

In 1968, this mechanism was replaced by a retroactive expropriation of the bride price, rendering the marriage void. In 1955, more girls were celebrating **Bat Mitzvah** and demanded to be allowed ascents to the **Torah**, the **CJLS** agreed that the ordinance under which women were banned from this due to respect for the congregation (*Kvod ha'Tzibur*) was no longer relevant. In 1972 it was decreed that rennet, even if derived from unclean animals, was so transformed that it constituted a wholly new item (*Panim Chadashot ba'u l'Khan*) and therefore all hard cheese could be considered kosher.

The 1970s and 1980s saw the emergence of women's rights on the main agenda. Growing pressure led the **CJLS** to adopt a motion that females may be counted as part of a quorum, based on the argument that only the *Shulchan Aruch* explicitly stated that it consist of men. While accepted, this was very controversial in the Committee and heavily disputed. A more complete solution was offered in 1983 by **Rabbi Joel Roth**, and was also enacted to allow women rabbinic ordination.

Roth noted that some decisors of old acknowledged that women may bless when performing positive time-bound commandments (from which they are exempted, and therefore unable to fulfill the obligation for others), especially citing the manner in which they assumed upon themselves the **Counting of the Omer**. He suggested that women voluntarily commit to pray thrice a day et cetera, and his **Responsa** was adopted. Since then, female rabbis were ordained at **JTS** and other seminaries.

In 1994, the movement accepted **Judith Hauptman's** principally egalitarian argument, according to which equal prayer obligations for women were never banned explicitly and it was only their inferior status that hindered participation. In 2006, openly gay rabbinic candidates were also to be admitted into the **JTS**. In 2012, a commitment ceremony for same-sex couples was devised, though not defined as *kiddushin*. In 2016, the rabbis passed a resolution supporting transgender rights.

**Conservative Judaism** in the United States held a relatively strict policy regarding intermarriage. Propositions for acknowledging Jews by patrilineal descent, as in the **Reform** movement, were overwhelmingly dismissed. Unconverted spouses were largely barred from community membership and participation in rituals; clergy are banned from any involvement in interfaith marriage on pain of dismissal. However, as the rate of such unions rose dramatically, **Conservative** congregations began describing gentile family members as *K'rov Yisrael* (Kin of Israel) and be more open toward them. The **Leadership Council of Conservative Judaism** stated in 1995: **"we want to encourage the Jewish partner to maintain his/her Jewish identity, and raise their children as Jews."**

Despite the centralization of legal deliberation on matters of Jewish law in the **CJLS** individual synagogues and communities must, in the end, depend on their local decision-makers. The rabbi in his or her or their community is regarded as the *Mara D'Atra*, or the local *Halakhic* decisor. Rabbis trained in the reading practices of **Conservative** Jewish approaches, historical evaluation of Jewish law and interpretation of Biblical and Rabbinic texts may align directly with the **CJLS** decisions or themselves opine on matters based on precedents or readings of text that shine light on congregants' questions.

So, for instance, a rabbi may or may not choose to permit video streaming on Shabbat despite a majority ruling that allows for use of electronics. A local *Mara D'Atra* may rely on the reasoning found in the majority or minority opinions of the **CJLS** or have other textual and halakhic grounds, i.e., prioritizing Jewish values or legal concepts, to rule one way or another on matters of ritual, family life or sacred pursuits. This balance between a centralization of *Halakhic* authority and maintaining the authority of local rabbis reflects the commitment to pluralism at the heart of the **Movement**.

## Organization and demographics

The term *Conservative Judaism* was used, still generically and not yet as a specific label, already in the 1887 dedication speech of the **Jewish Theological Seminary of America** by **Rabbi Alexander Kohut**. By 1901, the **JTS** alumni formed the **Rabbinical Assembly**, of which all ordained **Conservative** clergy in the world are members. As of 2010, there were 1,648 rabbis in the **RA**. In 1913, the **United Synagogue of America**, renamed the **United Synagogue of Conservative Judaism** in 1991, was founded as a congregational arm of the **RA**. The movement established the **World Council of Conservative Synagogues** in 1957.

Offshoots outside North America mostly adopted the Hebrew name "**Masorti**", traditional', as did the Israeli **Masorti Movement**, founded in 1979, and the **British Assembly of Masorti Synagogues**, formed in 1985. The **World Council** eventually changed its name to "**Masorti Olami**", **Masorti** International. Besides the **RA**, the international **Cantors Assembly** supplies prayer leaders for congregations worldwide.

The **United Synagogue of Conservative Judaism**, covering the United States, Canada and Mexico, is by far the largest constituent of **Masorti Olami**. While most congregations defining themselves as "**Conservative are affiliated with the USCJ**, some are independent. While accurate information of Canada is scant, it is estimated that some third of religiously affiliated Canadian Jews are **Conservative**. In 2008, the more traditional Canadian Council of **Conservative Synagogues** seceded from the parent organization. It numbered seven communities as of 2014.

According to the **Pew Research Center** survey in 2013, 18 per cent of Jews in the United States and in 2020 13 per cent identified with the movement, making it the second largest in the country. **Steven M. Cohen** calculated that as of 2013, 962,000 U.S. Jewish adults considered themselves **Conservative**: 570,000 were registered congregants and further 392,000 were not members in a synagogue but identified. In addition, Cohen assumed in 2006 that 57,000 unconverted non-Jewish spouses were also registered (12 per cent of member households had one at the time): 40 per cent of members intermarry.

Beyond North America, the movement has little presence—in 2011, **Rela Mintz Geffen** appraised there were only 100,000 members outside the U.S. (and the former figure including Canada).

"**Masorti AmLat**", the MO branch in Latin America, is the largest with 35 communities in Argentina, 7 in Brazil, 6 in Chile and further 11 in the other countries. The British Assembly of **Masorti Synagogues** has 13 communities and estimates its membership at over 4,000. More than 20 communities are spread across Europe, and there are 3 in Australia and 2 in Africa. The **Masorti Movement** in Israel incorporates some 70 communities and prayer groups with several thousand full members.

## History: Positive-Historical School

The final schism between Frankel and the **Orthodox** occurred after the 1859 publication of his *Darke ha-Mishna* (Ways of the Mishna). He heaved praise on the **Beatified Sages**, presenting them as bold innovators, but not once affirmed the divinity of the **Oral Torah**. On the ordinances classified as Law given to Moses at Sinai, he quoted **Asher ben Jehiel** that stated several of those were only apocryphally dubbed as such; he applied the latter's conclusion to all, noting they were **"so evident *as if* given at Sinai"**. **Hirsch** branded **Frankel** a heretic, demanding he announce whether he believed that both the **Oral** and **Written Torah** were of celestial origin.

**Rabbis Benjamin Hirsch Auerbach**, **Solomon Klein** and others published more complaisant tracts, but also requested an explanation. Rapoport marshaled to Frankel's aid, assuring that his words were merely reiterating ben **Jehiel's** and that he would soon release a statement that will belie Hirsch's accusations. But then the Chancellor of Breslau issued an ambiguous defence, writing that his book was not concerned with theology and avoiding giving any clear answer. Now even Rapoport joined his critics.

**Hirsch** succeeded, severely tarnishing **Frankel's** reputation among most concerned. Along with fellow **Orthodox Rabbi Azriel Hildesheimer**, Hirsch launched a protracted public campaign through the 1860s. They ceaselessly stressed the chasm between an **Orthodox** understanding of *Halakha* as derived and revealed, applied differently to different circumstances and subject to human judgement and possibly error, yet unchanging and divine in principle—as opposed to an evolutionary, historicist and non-dogmatic approach in which past authorities were not just elaborating but consciously innovating, as taught by **Frankel. Hildesheimer** often repeated that this issue utterly overshadowed any specific technical argument with the **Breslau School** (the students of which were often more lenient on matters of head covering for women, **Chalav Yisrael** and other issues).

**Hildesheimer** was concerned that Jewish public opinion perceived no practical difference between them; though he cared to distinguish the observant acolytes of **Frankel** from the **Reform** camp, he noted in his diary: **"How meager is the principal difference between the Breslau School, who don silk gloves at their work, and Geiger who wields a sledgehammer."** In 1863, when Breslau faculty member **Heinrich Graetz** published an article where he appeared to doubt the Messianic belief, **Hildesheimer** immediately seized upon the occasion to prove once more the dogmatic, rather than practical, divide. He denounced **Graetz** as a heretic.

The **Positive-Historical School** was influential, but never institutionalized itself as thoroughly as its opponents. Apart from the many graduates of Breslau, **Isaac Noah Mannheimer, Adolf Jellinek and Rabbi Moritz Güdemann** led the central congregation in Vienna along a similar path. In **Jellinek's** local seminary, **Meir Friedmann** and **Isaac Hirsch Weiss** followed Frankel's moderate approach to critical research. The rabbinate of the liberal **Neolog** public in Hungary, which formally separated from the **Orthodox**, was also permeated with the "**Breslau spirit**". Many of its members studied there, and its **Jewish Theological Seminary of Budapest** was modeled after it, though the assimilationist congregants cared little for rabbinic opinion.

## Jewish Theological Seminary

Jewish immigration to the United States bred an amalgam of loose communities, lacking strong tradition or stable structures. In this free-spirited environment, a multitude of forces was at work. As early as 1866, **Rabbi Jonas Bondi** of New York wrote that a Judaism of the **"golden middleway, which was termed Orthodox by the left and heterodox or reformer by the right"** developed in the new country. The rapid ascendancy of **Reform Judaism** by the 1880s left few who opposed it, merely a handful of congregations and ministers remained outside the Union of **American Hebrew Congregations**. These included **Sabato Morais** and **Rabbi Henry Pereira Mendes** of the elitist Sephardi congregations, along with rabbis **Bernard Drachman** (ordained at Breslau, though he regarded himself as **Orthodox**) and **Henry Schneeberger**.

## A third movement

The boundaries between **Orthodox** and **Conservative Judaism** in America were institutionalized only in the aftermath of World War II. The 1940s saw the younger generation of **JTS** graduates less patient with the prudence of the **CJL** and Talmud faculty in face of popular demand. **Kaplan's Reconstructionism**, while its fully committed partisans were few, had much influence. The majority among recent alumni eschewed the epithet **"Orthodox"** and tended to employ **"Conservative"** exclusively. Succeeding **Shechter's** direct disciples who headed the **RA, JTS** and United Synagogue in the interwar period, a new strata of activist leaders was rising.

In 1946, a committee chaired by Gordis issued the ***Sabbath and Festival Prayerbook***, the first clearly **Conservative** liturgy: references to the sacrificial cult were in the past tense instead of a petition for restoration, and it rephrased blessings such as **"who hast made me according to thy will"** for women to **"who hast made me a woman"**.

**Chancellor Louis Finkelstein (left), the dominant leader of JTS from 1940 to 1972.**
The postwar decades were a time of immense growth for the **Conservative movement**. Most of the 500,000 decommissioned Jewish GIs left the densely populated immigrant neighbourhoods of

the East Coast, moving to suburbia. They were Americanized but still retained traditional sentiments, and **Reform Judaism** was too radical for most. The **United Synagogue of America** offered Jewish education for children and a familiar religious environment which was also comfortable and not strict. It expanded from 350 communities by 1945 to 832 by 1971, becoming the largest denomination, with some 350,000 dues-paying member households (1.5 million people) at synagogues and over 40 per cent of American Jewry identifying with it in polls, adding an estimated million more non-registered supporters.

In 1962, the young Rabbi Marshall Meyer founded the **Seminario Rabinico Latinoamericano** in Buenos Aires, which would serve as the basis for **Conservative** expansion in South America. **In 1979, four communities formed the Israel Masorti Movement.**

Female ordination was a matter of great friction until 1983, when **Rabbi Joel Roth** devised a solution that entailed women voluntarily accepting the obligation to pray regularly. The leadership passed it not by scholarly consensus but via a popular vote of all **JTS** faculty, including non-specialists. Two years later, the first **JTS** -ordained female rabbi, **Amy Eilberg**, was admitted into the **RA. David Weiss Halivni**, professor of the Talmud faculty, claimed that Roth's method must have required waiting until a considerable number of women did prove sufficient commitment.

**LGBT** acceptance replaced it as the main source of contention between the declining right wing and the liberal majority. A first attempt was rebuffed in 1992 by a harsh responsum written by Roth. The retirement of **Chancellor Ismar Schorsch**, a staunch opponent, allowed the **CJLS** to endorse a motion which still banned anal intercourse but not any other physical contact, and allowed the ordination of openly **LGBT** rabbis, in 2006. **Masorti** affiliates in South America, Israel and Hungary objected severely. The **Seminario** is yet to accept the resolution, while several Canadian congregations seceded from the **United Synagogue** in 2008 to form an independent union in protest of the slide to the left. Since the 2013 Pew survey, which assessed that only 18 per cent of American Jews identify with it, **Conservative** leadership is engaged in attempting to solve **Conservative Judaism**'s demographic crisis.

# Converso (Crypto-Judaism)

A *converso* (Spanish: ; Portuguese: ; feminine form *conversa*), **"convert",** was a Jew who converted to Catholicism in Spain or Portugal, particularly during the 14th and 15th centuries, or one of his or her descendants. **The majority of Spain's Jews converted to Christianity as a result of the pogroms in 1391**. To safeguard the Old Christian population and make sure that *converso* **"New Christians"** were true to their new faith, **the Holy Office of the Inquisition** was established in Spain in 1478.

The Catholic monarchs **Ferdinand and Isabella** expelled those remaining openly practicing Jews by the **Alhambra decree of 1492**, following the **Christian *Reconquista*** (reconquest) of **Spain**. However, even a significant proportion of these remaining practicing Jews chose to join the already large *converso* community rather than face exile. *Conversos* who did not fully or genuinely embrace Catholicism, but continued to practice Judaism in secrecy, were referred to as *judaizantes* **("Judaizers")** and pejoratively as *marranos* **("swine").**

New Christian converts of Muslim origin were known as *moriscos*. Unlike Jewish *Conversos, moriscos* were subject to an edict of expulsion even after their conversion to Catholicism, which was implemented severely in Valencia and in Aragón and less so in other parts of Spain. *Conversos* played a vital role in the **1520–1521 Revolt of the Comuneros**, a popular uprising and civil war centered on Castile's region against the imperial pretensions of the Spanish monarchy.

## History

**Ferrand Martinez,** Archdeacon of Écija, directed a 13-year anti-Semitic campaign that began in 1378. **Martinez** used a series of provocative sermons, through which he openly condemned the Jews with little to no opposition. IIe rallied non-Jews against the Jews by creating a constant state of fear through riots. **Martinez's** efforts led to a series of outbreaks on 4 June 1391, where **several synagogues in Seville were burned to the ground and churches were erected in their place.** Amidst this outbreak, many Jews fled the country, some converted to Christianity in fear, and some were sold to Muslims. **Martinez** set in motion the largest forced mass conversion of Jews in Spain.

The new converts, most of whom were forced, due to their large numbers, were victims of a new problem. A problem that temporarily solved the Jewish presence in Spain, however, led to the creation of a new group that was neither completely Catholic or Jewish.

**The Conversos**, who were now fully privileged citizens, competed in all aspects of the economic sphere. This resulted in a new wave of racial anti-Semitism that was targeted at the **Conversos**. This anti-Semitism evolved into small and large riots in Toledo, 1449, that now oppressed not the Jews by the Christians, but the New Christians (**Conversos**) by the Old Christians. Thus, the

Crown established a **National Inquisition in 1478**, that would test the loyalty and purity of a newly baptised Christian (converso). Due to continued oppression, some Jews and **Conversos** fled Spain, others created a community to ensure the survival of Judaism in the **Iberian Peninsula**, although outwardly practicing Christianity.

## Perpetuation of Jewish heritage

**Conversas** played a pivotal role in keeping Jewish traditions alive by observing many Jewish holidays like Shabbat. **Conversas** cooked and baked traditional Jewish dishes in honor of the **Sabbath** (starting on Friday sundown), **Yom Kippur**, and other religious holidays. During festivals like **Sukkot** and **Passover**, **Conversas** participated by giving clothing articles and ornaments to Jewish women, attending a **seder**, or obtaining a baking matzah.

**Conversas** ensured that their household maintained similar dietary regulations as their Jewish counterparts, by eating only kosher birds and other animals. **Conversas** also financially contributed to the growth of the Jewish/Converso community and synagogue. The Jewish community and the **Conversos** exchanged books and knowledge, Jews taught **Conversos** how to read to ensure constant growth of their Jewish heritage. To take a stance against the church and its principles, some **Conversos** performed professional work even on Sundays. The traditional Jewish **Purim** was kept by the **Conversos** in the disguise of a Christian holiday, they named it **"Festival of Santa Esterica".**

## Description

*Conversos* were subject to suspicion and harassment from both what was left of the community they were leaving and that which they were joining. Both Christians and Jews called them *tornadizo* **(renegade). James I, Alfonso X** and **John I** passed laws forbidding the use of this epithet. This was part of a larger pattern of royal oversight, as laws were promulgated to protect their property, forbid attempts to convert them back to Judaism or the **Muslim** faith, and regulate their behavior, preventing their cohabitation or even dining with Jews, lest they convert back.

**Conversos** did not enjoy legal equality. **Alfonso VII** prohibited the **"recently converted"** from holding office in Toledo. They had supporters and bitter opponents in the Christian secular of general acceptance, yet they became targets of occasional pogroms during times of social tension (as during an epidemic and after an earthquake). **They were subject to the Spanish and Portuguese inquisitions.**

While **"pure blood"** (so-called *limpieza de sangre*), free of the **"taint"** of non-Christian lineage, would come to be placed at a premium, particularly among the nobility, in a 15th-century defence of *Conversos*, **Bishop Lope de Barrientos** would list what Roth calls **"a veritable 'Who's Who' of Spanish nobility"** as having *converso* members or being of *converso* descent. He pointed out that given the near-universal conversion of Iberian Jews during Visigothic times, **"who among the Christians of Spain could be certain that he is not a descendant of those *Conversos*?"**

With advances in science able to trace individuals' ancestry via their **DNA**, according to a widely publicized study (December 2008) in the ***American Journal of Human Genetics***, modern Spaniards (and Portuguese) have an average admixture of **19.8 percent** from ancestors originating in the Near East during historic times (i.e. Phoenicians, Carthaginians, Jews and **Levantine Arabs**) – compared to 10.6 percent of North African – Berber admixture.

This proportion could be as high as **23%** in the case **of Latin Americans**, however, according to a study published in Nature Communications. The possibly higher proportion of significant Jewish ancestry in the Latin American population could stem from increased emigration of **Conversos** to the **New World** to avoid persecution by the **Spanish Inquisition**.

## By country / In Italy

Specific groups of **Conversos** left Spain and Portugal after the **Spanish Inquisition in 1492**, in search for a better life. They left for other parts of Europe, especially Italy, where they were inevitably looked at with suspicion and harassment, both in their old and new communities. Subsequently, many **Conversos** who arrived in Italian cities did not openly embrace their Judaism, since they were tempted by the advantages they could seek in the Christian world.

The first three cities to accept the **Conversos** who openly converted back to Judaism, were **Florence, Ferrara**, and **Ancona**. Most of these **Conversos** appeared after 1536 from Portugal, and most lived in Florence. In 1549, **Duke Cosimo de' Medici** allowed the Portuguese **Conversos** to trade and reside within Florence. Most of the re-converted Jews lived in the ghetto of Florence, and by 1705 there were 453 Jews in the city.

**Conversos** arrived to Ferrara in 1535, and were able to assimilate with their neighbors, perform circumcisions, and return openly to Judaism, due to the **Lettres Patentes** issued by **Duke Ercole II.** After the plague in 1505 and the eventual fall of Ferrara in 1551, many of these Jews relocated North towards the economically stable ports in Venice. Venice slowly became a center for **Conversos** who either stopped temporarily on their way to **Turkey** or stayed permanently as residents in the ghetto Jewish community port.

Venetian leaders were convinced to openly accept **Conversos** to practice Judaism because they recognized that if **Conversos** were not welcome in Venice, they would take their successful trades to the country's economic rival of Turkey. A Portuguese converso in Venice, named **Abraham de Almeda**, connected strongly with Christianity, however, turned to the Jewish members of his family when in need of financing for moral support. As a result, many of the **Conversos** during this period struggled with their Christian and Jewish identities.

**Conversos** in the city of Ancona faced difficult lives living under the pope and eventually fled to Ferrara in 1555. Portuguese **Conversos** in Ancona were falsely misled that they were welcome to Ancona and that they could openly convert back to Judaism. **Their fate was overturned by the succeeding pope, Pope Paul IV**. The **Conversos** in Ancona faced traumatic emotional damage after the pope imprisoned 102 **Conversos** who refused to reside in the ghetto and wear badges to distinguish themselves. In 1588, when the duke granted a charter of residence in return for the **Conversos** building up the city's economy, they refused, due to accumulated scepticism.

# Covenant (Biblical)

The **Hebrew Bible** makes reference to a number of **covenants with God (YHWH).** The **Noahic Covenant** (in Genesis), which is between God and all living creatures, as well as a number of more specific covenants with individuals or groups. Biblical covenants include those with **Abraham,** the whole Israelite people, the Israelite priesthood, and the **Davidic** lineage of kings.

In the **Book of Jeremiah, verses 31:30–33 predict "a new covenant" that God will establish with "the house of Israel".** Most Christians believe this **New Covenant** is the **"replacement"** or **"final fulfilment"** of the Old Covenant described in the Old Testament and as applying to the **People of God.**

## Ancient Near Eastern treaties

There are two major types of covenants in the **Hebrew Bible**, including the obligatory type and the promissory type. The obligatory covenant is more common with the **Hittite** peoples, and deals with the relationship between two parties of equal standing. **God** rewarded **Abraham, Noah,** and **David** in his covenants with them. As part of his covenant with **Abraham**, God has the obligation to keep **Abraham**'s descendants as God's **chosen people** and be their God. God is the party taking upon the curse if he does not uphold his obligation.

## Terminology of covenants

Phrases about having a **"whole heart"** or having **"walked after me with all his heart"** strongly parallels with **Neo-Assyrian** grant language, such as **"walked with royalty"**. In **Jeremiah**, God uses prophetic metaphor to say that **David** will be adopted as a son. Babylonian contracts often expressed **Fathership** and sonship in their grants to actually mean a king to vassal relationship. **Abraham** kept God's charge in **Genesis 26: 4–5: "I will give to your descendants all these lands...in as much as Abraham obeyed me and kept my charge, my commandments, my rules and my teachings."**

## Dissolving covenant form

The loosely bound tribes merged under the Mosaic covenant to legitimize their unity. They believed that to obey the law was to obey God. They also believed that the king was put into power as a result of God's benefaction, and that this accession was the fulfillment of God's promise of dynasty to **David**. A conflict arose between those who believed in the **Davidic covenant**, and The **Mosaic covenant** were almost entirely forgotten.

## Edenic covenant

The **Edenic covenant** applies to all of humanity. It can be found in **Genesis 1:28-30**. In this passage, God gives mankind the mandate to procreate and God gives mankind dominion over the earth and all the animals.

## Noahic covenant / *Seven Laws of Noah*

The **Noahic covenant** applies to all of humanity and all other living creatures. In this covenant with all living creatures, God promises never again to destroy all life on Earth by flood and creates the rainbow as the sign of this **"everlasting covenant between God and every living creature of all flesh that is on the earth"**.

## Abrahamic covenant / *Covenant of the pieces*

The covenant found in **Genesis 12–17** is known as the ***Brit bein HaBetarim***, the"**Covenant Between the Parts**" in Hebrew, and is the basis for **brit milah (covenant of circumcision)** in Judaism. The covenant was for **Abraham** and his seed, or offspring, both of natural birth and adoption.

With **Abraham** multiple promised lands were given to his innumerable descendants **(Gen 15:18-21; 17:1-9, 19; 22:15-18; 26:2-4, 24; 28; 35:9-13; Gal 3; Abr 2:6-11)**, and circumcision marking them as a peculiar people set apart **(Gen 17:10-13)**.

In **Genesis 12–17** three covenants can be distinguished based on the differing **Jahwist, Elohist** and **Priestly** sources. In **Genesis 12 and 15**, God grants **Abraham** land and a multitude of descendants but does not place any stipulations (meaning it was unconditional) on **Abraham** for the covenant's fulfillment.

## Genesis 17 contains the covenant of circumcision (conditional).

1. To make of **Abraham** a great nation and bless **Abraham** and make his name great so that he will be a blessing, to bless those who bless him and curse him who curses him and all peoples on earth would be blessed through **Abraham**.
2. To give **Abraham**'s descendants all the land from the river of Egypt to the Euphrates. Later, this land came to be referred to as the **Promised Land** or the Land of Israel.
3. To make **Abraham** the father of many nations and of many descendants and give **"the whole land of Canaan"** to his descendants. Circumcision is to be the permanent sign of this everlasting covenant with **Abraham** and his male descendants and is known as the ***brit milah***.

There are many similarities between **Genesis 15** and the **Abba-El** deed. In **Genesis 15** and similarly in the **Abba-El** deed, it is the superior party who places himself under oath. The oaths in both. The animals that are slaughtered in the covenant in **Genesis 15** are considered a sacrificial offering.

## Mosaic covenant / *Ten Commandments, 613 commandments, and Law of Moses*

**The Mosaic covenant** made with **Moses** and the Israelite people at Horeb-Sinai, which is found in **Exodus 19–24** and the book of **Deuteronomy**, contains the foundations of the written Torah and the **Oral Torah**. In this covenant, God promises to make the Israelites his treasured possession among all people and **"a kingdom of priests and a holy nation"**, if they follow God's commandments. God gives Moses the **Ten Commandments (Exod 24:8).**

Like the treaties, the **Ten Commandments** begins with **Yahweh's** identification and what he had done for Israel **("who brought you out of the land of Egypt"; Ex 20:2)** as well as the stipulations commanding absolute loyalty (**"You shall not have other gods apart from me"**). God gave the children of Israel the **Shabbat** as the permanent sign of this covenant.

## Davidic covenant / *David § Jerusalem and the Davidic covenant*

The royal covenant was made with **David (2 Sam 7)**. It promised to establish his dynasty forever while acknowledging that its original royal-covenant promises had been given to the ancestor of the whole nation, **Abraham.**

The **Davidic covenant** establishes **David** and his descendants as the kings of the united monarchy of Israel (which included Judah). The **Davidic covenant** is an important element in **Jewish messianism** and Christian theology. The messiah is believed to be a future Jewish king from the **David**ic line, who will be anointed with holy anointing oil, gather the Jews back into the Land of Israel, usher in an era of peace, build the **Third Temple**, have a male heir, re-institute the **Sanhedrin** and rule the Jewish people during the **Messianic Age.**

The tablets of the **Ten Commandments** were kept in the **Ark of the Covenan**t, and this became the symbol of the Israelite nation, and of God's presence with His people. Thus when **King David** wanted to establish Jerusalem as his own capital city he brought the **Ark** there **(2 Sam 6).**

## Christian view of Davidic covenant

Christian theologians maintain that the **David**ic covenant deserves an important place in determining the purposes of God and that its exegesis confirms the doctrine of a future reign of Christ on earth. While Jewish theologians have always held that Jesus did not fulfill the expectations of a Jewish messiah, **Dispensational** biblical theologians are almost unanimous that **Jesus will fully fulfill the Davidic covenant**, the provisions of which list as:
1. **David** is to have a child, yet to be born, who shall succeed him and establish his kingdom.
2. A son (Solomon) shall build the temple instead of **David**.
3. The throne of his kingdom shall be established forever.

4. The throne will not be taken away from him (**Solomon**) even though his sins justify chastisement.
5. **David**'s house, throne, and kingdom shall be established forever (**2 Samuel 7:16**).

## New covenant (Christian)

The **New Covenant** is a biblical interpretation originally derived from a phrase in the **Book of Jeremiah,** in the Hebrew Scriptures. It is often thought of as an eschatological **Messianic Age** or world to come and is related to the biblical concept of the **Kingdom of God.**

Christians believe that the **New Covenant** was instituted at the **Last Supper** as part of the **Eucharist**, which in the **Gospel of John** includes the **New Commandment**. A connection between the **Blood of Christ** and the **New Covenant** is seen in most modern English translations of the New Testament with the saying: **"this cup that is poured out for you is the new covenant in my blood".**

Christians see Jesus as the mediator of this **New Covenant**, and that his blood, shed at his crucifixion is the required blood of the covenant. **"A bond in blood sovereignly administered by God".** It has been theorized that the **New Covenant** is the **Law of Christ** as spoken during his **Sermon on the Mount.**

## Islamic view

The Mosaic covenant is referred to in a number of place in the **Quran** [Quran 2:63][Quran 2:83-84][Quran 2:93][Quran 4:154] as a reminder for the Jews, of whom two tribes inhabited **Medina** at the time of **Muhammad**. The verses also mention particular commandments of the Decalogue and, in God's words, admonishes the Jews for being insolent about it and displaying violence against the prophets [Quran 4:155][Quran 5:70].

The Quran also states how God cursed the Children of Israel and made them suffer for breaking the covenant [Quran 4:155][Quran 5:13] while also mentioning other covenants such a prophetic covenant with the Israelites in **Quran 3:81**, the Noahic and **Abraham**ic covenants in **Quran 33:7**, and in **Quran 5:14** and **Quran 7:169** a covenant made with the followers of Jesus , who likewise failed to observe it following their own desires.

# Crypto-Jewish

**Crypto-Judaism** is the secret adherence to Judaism while publicly professing to be of another faith; practitioners are referred to as **"Crypto-Jews"** (origin from Greek **kryptos**, 'hidden'). The term is especially applied historically to European Jews who – outwardly or forcedly – professed Catholicism, also known as **Anusim or Marrano**. The phenomenon is especially associated with early modern Spain, following the June 6, 1391 Anti-Jewish pogroms and the **expulsion of the Jews in 1492.**

## Europe

Officially, Jews who converted in Spain in the 14th and 15th centuries were known as **Cristianos Nuevos (New Christians),** but were commonly called *conversos*. **Spain** and **Portugal** passed legislation restricting their rights in the mother countries and colonies. Despite the dangers of the **Inquisition**, many *conversos* continued to secretly and discreetly practice Jewish rituals.

In the Balearic Islands, numerous *conversos,* also called **Chuetas,** publicly professed Roman Catholicism but privately adhered to Judaism after the **Alhambra decree of 1492** and during the **Spanish Inquisition**. They are among the most widely known **Crypto-Jews**. In Greece **"Romaniote Jews"** have been present for a little more than two thousand years. In the after math of the **Holocaust**, a large percentage of the surviving community emigrated to Israel or the United States.

Some of the Jewish followers of **Sabbatai Zevi (Sabbateans)** formally converted to **Islam**, and later followers of **Jacob Frank ("Frankists")** formally converted to Christianity, but maintained aspects of their versions of **Messianic Judaism**. **Crypto-Jews** persisted in Russia and Eastern European countries influenced by the Soviet Union after the rise of Communism with the **Russian Revolution of 1917.**

Since the end of Communism, many people in former Soviet states, including descendants of Jews, have publicly taken up the faith of their families again. The **"Belmonte Jews"** of Portugal, dating from the 12th century, maintained strong secret traditions for centuries. They and their practices were discovered only in the 20th century. Their rich **Sephardic** tradition of **Crypto-Judaism** is unique. Only recently did they contact other Jews. Some now profess **Orthodox** Judaism, although many still retain their centuries-old traditions.

## Before the Spanish Inquisition

One of the earliest conversions happened a century after the Fall of Rome and was in **Clermont-Ferrand**. After a member of the Jewish community in **Clermont-Ferrand** became a Jewish Christian and was persecuted by other members of the community for doing so, the cavalcade in which he was marching persecuted his persecutors in turn. The Jews who preferred exile left for **"Marseilles. In 582 the Frankish King Chilperic compelled numerous Jews to adopt Christianity**. Again the **anusim** were not wholehearted in their conversion.

The **Clermont-Ferrand** conversions preceded the first forced conversions in Iberia by 40 years, and the first one in Iberia happened in 516 due to **Visigoth monarch Sisibut:**

**Persistent attempts to enforce conversion were made in the seventh century by the Visigoths in Spain after they had adopted the Roman Catholic faith. Comparatively mild legal measures were followed by the harsh edict issued by King Sisbut in 616, ordering the compulsory baptism of all Jews.**

The final conversions in Iberia (which had Al-Andalus) prior to 1492 (with the 1492 ones being effected by ones that began in 1391) happened in the 1100s and were Muslim-forced conversions. The final ones outside of Iberia before 1492 happened in Italy in the 1200s and spread as far as Apulia, where the **Anusim Italqim** assimilated to the point of not being recognized as Jewish (as was later observed). **"Their forefathers were Jews who adopted Christianity 150 years ago, rather from compulsion than of their own free will.'"**

## Asia
There are, or have been, several communities of **Crypto-Jews** in Muslim lands. The ancestors of the **Daggatuns** in Morocco probably kept up their Jewish practices a long time after their nominal adoption of Islam. In Iran, a large community of **Crypto-Jews** lived in **Mashhad**, near Khorassan, where they were known as **"Jedid al-Islam"**, who was mass-converted to Islam around 1839 after the **Allahdad** events. Most of this community left for Israel in 1946, but some have converted into Muslims and live in Iran today.

## Early colonial period – 16<sup>th</sup> century
However, **Portugal in 1497 issued a similar decree that effectively converted all remaining Jewish children, making them wards of the state unless the parents also converted**. Therefore, many of the early crypto-Jewish migrants to Mexico in the early colonial days were technically first to second generation Portuguese with Spanish roots before that. The number of such Portuguese migrants was significant enough that **the label of "Portuguese" became synonymous with "Jewish" throughout the Spanish colonies.**

During this time, the administration initiated the **Mexican Inquisition** to ensure the Catholic orthodoxy of all migrants into Mexico. The **Mexico Inquisition** was also deployed in the traditional manner to ensure orthodoxy of converted indigenous peoples. The first victims of burnings or **autos de fe** of the Mexican Inquisition was indigenous converts convicted of heresy or **Crypto-Jews** convicted of relapsing into their ancestral faith. Except for the province of Nuevo Leon, initiation of the **Blood Purity Laws** reduced the migration of **Conversos**.

## Nuevo Leon – 1590s to early 17<sup>th</sup> century
The governor, his immediate family members, and others of his entourage were called to appear before the Inquisition in Mexico City. They were arrested and jailed. The governor subsequently died in jail, while his family members were rehabilitated. One of these was **Anna Carvajal**, a niece of the Governor. She and others were later again taken captive and **sentenced to burning at the stake for relapsing.**

The governor's nephews changed their name to **Lumbroso**. One of these was **Joseph Lumbroso**, also known as **Luis de Carvajal** el Mozo, who is said to have circumcised himself in the desert to conform to Jewish law. His memoirs, letters and inquisition record survive. When Governor

**Carvajal** was in office, the city of Monterrey became a destination for other **Crypto-Jews** feeling the pressure of the Mexican Inquisition in the south of the territory.

## Current times

According to a December 2008 study published in the **American Journal of Human Genetics**, 19.8 percent of modern Spaniards (and Portuguese) have **DNA** reflecting Sephardic Jewish ancestry, compared to 10.6 percent having **DNA** reflecting Moorish ancestors. Estimate that much earlier migrations, **5,000 to 10,000 years ago** from the Eastern Mediterranean might also have accounted for the Sephardic estimates.

Recent genetic research, however, has shown that many Latinos of the **American Southwest** may be descended from **Anusim (Sephardic Jews who converted to Roman Catholicism).** In northern Mexico, Monterrey, the capital city of the state of **Nuevo Leon**, which shares a border with Texas, is said to contain descendants of **Crypto-Jews**. Many Jewish symbols can be found on cemetery headstones I Northern New Mexico, alongside Catholic crosses. **Today there are about 40,000 Mexican Jews, both Ashkenazi and Sephardi.**

## Famous Crypto-Jews

- **Dona Gracia Mendes Nasi** was a 16th-century international banker who created an escape network that saved thousands of **Crypto-Jews** from the Inquisition. She was also a patron of (Jewish) writers, and a diplomat on behalf of her people, who also attempted to start a modern state of Israel.
- **Luis de Carvajal** was the governor of the state of Nuevo Leon, a northern Mexico province in which the restriction against immigration from converses was relaxed in order to encourage migration to the peril-fraught frontier. He was responsible for bringing a significant group of crypto-Jewish converses living in Portugal since the Expulsion of 1492.
- **Luis de Carvajal el Mozo** was the nephew of Jose Luis Carvajal y de la Cueva, the only crypto-Jew of the Spanish colonial era whose memoirs have been preserved.
- **Antonio Fernandez Carvajal** was a Portuguese merchant in London, "like other Marranos in London, Carvajal prayed at the Catholic chapel of the Spanish ambassador, while simultaneously playing a leading role in the secret Jewish community, which met at the clandestine synagogue at Creechurch Lane."
- Some scholars of Judaic studies believe that **Miguel de Cervantes** may have been a crypto-Jew or of crypto-Jewish descent.
- **Rodrigo Lopez**, a converso who fled from Portugal to England and became physician to Queen Elizabeth I.

# Dead Sea Scrolls

The **Dead Sea Scrolls** are a collection of **972 texts** discovered between 1947 and 1956 at *Khirbet Qumran* in the West Bank. They were found on the northwest shore of the **Dead Sea**, from which they derive their name. The texts are of great historical, religious and linguistic significance because they include the earliest known surviving manuscripts of works later included in the **Hebrew Bible** canon, along with extra-biblical manuscripts which preserve evidence of the diversity of religious thought in the **Second Temple Judaism**.

The texts are written in **Hebrew, Aramaic, Greek**, and **Nabataean**, mostly on parchment, but with some written on papyrus and bronze. The manuscripts have been dated to various ranges between **408 BCE and 318 CE**. Bronze coins found on the site form a series beginning with **John Hyrcanus** (135-104 BCE) and continuing until the **First Jewish-Roman War (66-73 CE)**.

The scrolls have traditionally been identified with the ancient Jewish sect called the **Essenes**, although some recent interpretations have challenged this association and argue that the scrolls were penned by priests in Jerusalem, **Zadokites**, or other unknown Jewish groups. The **Dead Sea Scrolls** are divided into three groups; copies of texts from the **Hebrew Bible**, which comprise roughly 40% of the identified scrolls, texts from the **Second Temple Period** like the **Book of Enoch, Jubilees, the Book of Tobit, the wisdom of Sirach, Psalms 152-155, etc.**, that ultimately were not canonized in the Hebrew Bible, which comprise roughly 30% of the identified scrolls, **the war Scroll, the Pesher on Habakkuk** and **The Rule of the Blessing, which comprise roughly 30% of the identified scrolls.**

## Discovery
The **Dead Sea Scrolls** were discovered in a series of **twelve caves** around the site known as **Wadi Qumran near the Dead Sea** in what is now the West Bank between 1946 and 1956 by the Bedouin people and archeologists.

## Initial discovery (1946-1947)
The initial discovery, by Bedouin shepherd **Muhammed Edh-Dhib**, his cousin **Jum'a Muhammed,** and **Khalil Musa,** took place between November 1946 and February 1947. The shepherds discovered **7 scrolls** housed in jars in a cave at what is now known as the **Qumran** site.

In 1947 the original seven scrolls caught the attention of **Dr. John C. Trever**, of the **American Schools of Oriental Research (ASOR),** who compared the script in the scrolls to that of **The Nash Papyrus**, the oldest biblical manuscript then known, and found similarities between them. In March the **1948 Arab-Israeli War** prompted the move of some of scrolls to Beirut, Lebanon for safekeeping. On 11 April 1948, **Miller Burrows**, head of the **ASOR**, announced the discovery of the scrolls in a general press release.

## Search for the Qumran caves (1948-1949)
Early in September 1948, **Bishop Mar** brought **Professor Ovid R. Sellers**, the new Director of **ASOR**, some additional scroll fragments that he had acquired. By the end of 1948, nearly two years after their discovery, scholars had yet to locate the original cave where the fragments had been found. In early 1948, the government of Jordan gave permission to the **Arab Legion** to

search the area where the original **Qumran** cave was thought to be. Consequently, Cave 1 was rediscovered on 28 January 1949.

## Qumran caves rediscovery and new scroll discoveries (1949-1951)

The rediscovery of **Cave 1** prompted the initial excavation of the site from 15 February to 5 March 1949 by the **Jordanian Department of Antiquities.** The excavation was led by **Lancaster Harding,** director of the **Palestine Archaeological Museum.** The Cave 1 site yielded discoveries of additional **Dead Sea Scroll** fragments, linen cloth, jars, and other artifacts.

## Excavations of Qumran (1951-1956)

In November 1951, **Roland de Vaux** and his team from the **ASOR** began a full excavation of **Qumran.** In February 1952, the Bedouin people discovered 30 fragments in what was to be designated **Cave 2.** These included fragments of **Jubilees and Ben Sira** written in Hebrew. The following month, the **ASOR** team discovered **Cave 3** and **the Copper Scroll.** Between September and December 1952 the fragments and scrolls of Caves 4, 5, and 6 were subsequently discovered by the **ASOR** teams. Between 1953 and 1956, **Roland de Vaux** led four more archaeological expeditions in the area to uncover scrolls and artifacts. The last cave, **Cave 11**, was discovered in 1956 and yielded the last fragments to be found in the vicinity of **Qumran.**

## Origin

**There has been much debate about the origin of the Dead Sea Scrolls.** The dominant theory remains that the scrolls were the product of a sect of Jews living at nearby **Qumran** called the **Essenes.** The **Qumran**-Essene theory holds that the scrolls were written by the **Essenes,** or by another Jewish sectarian group, residing at **Khirbet Qumran.** They composed the scrolls and ultimately hid them in the nearby caves during the **Jewish Revolt** sometime between 66 and 68 CE. **The site of Qumran was destroyed and the scrolls never recovered.**

## Christian Origin Theory

Spanish Jesuit **Jose O'Callaghan Martinez** has argued that one fragment (7Q5) preserves a portion of text from the **New Testament Gospel of Mark 6:52-53**. In recent years, **Robert Eisenman** has advanced the theory that some scrolls describe the early Christian community. **Eisenman** also attempted to relate the career of **James the Just and Paul the apostle** to some of these documents.

## Jerusalem Origin Theory

Some scholars have argued that the scrolls were the product of Jews living in Jerusalem, who hid the scrolls in the caves near **Qumran** while fleeing from the Romans during the **Roman's destruction of Jerusalem in 70 CE.**

# Dhimmi (Jizya)

A **Dhimmi "the people of the *Dhimma*"**) is a historical term referring to non-Muslim citizens of an Islamic state. **Dhimma** allows rights of residence in return for taxes. They were excused or excluded from specific duties assigned to Muslims and otherwise equal under the laws of property, contract and obligation. Under **Sha'aria Law**, **Dhimmis** status was originally afforded to Jews, Christians and Sabians. The protected religions later came to include **Zoroastrians, Mandaeans, Hindus and Buddhists.**

## The "Dhimma contract"

As monotheists, Jews and Christians have traditionally been considered **"People of The Book,"** and afforded a special status known as *dhimmi* derived from a theoretical contract – **"Dhimma"** or **"residence in return for taxes"**. Eventually, the largest school of Islamic scholarship applied this term to all non-Muslims living in Islamic lands outside the sacred area surrounding Mecca, Saudi Arabia.

By the 18th century, however, **Dhimmis** frequently attended the **Ottoman Muslim courts**, where cases were taken against them by Muslims, or they took cases against Muslims or other **Dhimmis**. Oaths sworn by **Dhimmis** in these courts were tailored to their beliefs. Religious minorities were also free to do whatever they wished in their own homes, provided they did not publicly engage in **illicit sexual activity** in ways that could threaten public morals. **However, the classical Dhimmi contract is no longer enforced.**

## The Dhimma contract and sha'aria law

The **Dhimma** contract is an integral part of traditional Islamic **sha'aria law**. From the 9th century AD, the power to interpret and refine law in traditional Islamic societies was in the hands of the **Scholars (ulema)**. The wide variety of forms of government, systems of law, attitudes toward modernity and interpretations of **sha'aria** are a result of the ensuing drives for independence and modernity in the Muslim world. Muslim states, sects, schools of thought and individuals differ as to exactly what sha'aria law entails. Islamic law is, therefore, **Polynormative** and despite several cases of regression in recent years, the trend is towards modernization and liberalization.

## The end of the Dhimma contract

The collection of the **jizya tax** from non-Muslims was widespread throughout the history of Islam. In the mid-19th century, the **Ottoman Empire** significantly relaxed the restrictions and taxes placed on its non-Muslim residents under **Ottomanism**. These relaxations occurred gradually as part of the **Tanzimat Reform Movement**, which began in 1839 with the accession of the **Ottoman Sultan Abd-ul-Majid I**. On February 18, 1856, the **Hatt-i Humayan** edict was issued, building upon the 1839 edict. For example, **the jizya tax was abolished and non-Muslims were allowed to join the army.**

## Dhimmi communities

The **Dhimmis** communities had their own chiefs and judges, with their own family, personal and religious laws. **"Muslims guaranteed freedom of worship and livelihood, provided that they remained loyal to the Muslim state and paid a poll tax"**. However, **Dhimmis** faced social and symbolic restrictions, and a pattern of stricter, then more lax, enforcement developed over time.

From an Islamic legal perspective, the pledge of protection granted **Dhimmis** the freedom to practice their religion and spared them forced conversions. The Arabs generally established garrisons outside towns in the conquered territories, and had little interaction with the local **Dhimmis** populations for purposes other than the collection of taxes.

## Christians

In 1095 AD, **Pope Urban II** urged western European Christians to come to the aid of the Christians of Palestine. The subsequent **Crusades** brought Roman Catholic Christians into contact with Orthodox Christians. When the Arab East came under Ottoman rule in the 16th century AD, Christian populations and fortunes rebounded significantly. By the 19th century AD European pressure had removed all **Dhimma** restrictions on Ottoman religious minorities.

## Jews

Accustomed to survival in adverse circumstances after many centuries of discrimination and persecution within the **Roman Empire**, both pre-Christian and Christian, Jews saw the Islamic conquests as just another change of rulers, this time for the better. **Jews were less dangerous and more loyal to the Muslim regime. "Jews in Islam were well integrated into the economic life of the larger society"** and that they were allowed to practice their religion more freely than they could do in Christian Europe.

## Hindus and Buddhists

By the 10th century, the **Turks of Central Asia** had brought Islam to the mountains north of the Indic plains. It was not long before they swept south across the **Punjab**. The Indus basin held a substantial Buddhist population in addition to the ruling Hindu castes, and **most converted to Islam over the next two centuries**. At the end of the 12th century, the Muslims advanced quickly into the Ganges plain. By the 15th century, Islamic and Hindu civilization had evolved in a complementary manner, with the **Muslims taking the role of a ruling caste in Hindu society.**

In the 16th century A D, India came under the influence of the **Mughals (Mongols), Babar**, a ruler of the **Mongol Timuri Empire**, established a foothold in the North which paved the way for the further expansion by his successors. Until it was eclipsed by European hegemony in the 18th century, the **Timuri Moghul Emperors** oversaw a period of coexistence and tolerance between Hindus and Muslims. The emperor **Akbar** has been described as a **Universalist. The entire subcontinent fell under European colonial rule during the 18th century.**

## Hadith

A hadith by Muhammad, **"Whoever killed a *Mu'ahid* (a person who is granted the pledge of protection by the Muslims) shall not smell the fragrance of Paradise though its fragrance can be smelt at a distance of forty years (of travelling)".**

## Constitution of Medina

A precedent for the **Dhimma** contract was established with the agreement **between the Islamic Prophet Muhammad and the Jews of Khaybar, an oasis near Medina.** Khaybar was the first territory attacked and conquered by Muslims. When the Jews of **Khaybar** surrendered to Muhammad after a siege, Muhammad allowed them to remain in Khaybar in return for handing over to the Muslims one half their annual produce. The **Constitution of Medina**, a formal agreement between Muhammad and all of the significant tribes and families of Medina (including Muslims, Jews and pagans), declared that non-Muslims in the *Ummah* had the following rights:

1. The security (**Dhimma**) of God is equal for all groups.
2. **Non-Muslim** members have equal political and cultural rights as Muslims. They will have autonomy and freedom of religion.
3. **Non-Muslims** will take up arms against the enemy of the Ummah and share the cost of war. There is to be no treachery between the two.
4. **Non-Muslims** will not be obliged to take part in religious wars of the Muslims.

## Pact of Umar

Academic historians believe the **Pact of Umar** in the form it is known today was a product of later jurists who attributed it to the venerated caliph **Umar I** in order to lend greater authority to their own opinions. At least some of the clauses of the pact mirror the measures first introduced by the **Umayyad caliph Umar II** or by the early **Abbasid caliphs**.

## Restrictions

Jews and Christians living under early Muslim rule were considered **Dhimmis**; a status that was later also extended to other non-Muslims like Hindus and guaranteed their personal safety and security of property, in return for paying tribute and acknowledging Muslim rule. They were also **exempted from the zakaat tax paid by Muslims**. The **Dhimmis** communities living in Islamic states had their own laws independent from the **Sha'aria Law**, such as the Jews who had their own *Halakha* courts. **Muslim tolerance of unbelievers was far better than anything available in Christendom, until the rise of secularism in the 17th century".**

In modern sense the **Dhimmis** would be described as second class citizens. Although **Dhimmis** were allowed to perform their religious rituals, they were obliged to do so in a manner not conspicuous to Muslims. Display of non-Muslim religious symbols, such as crosses or icons, was prohibited on buildings and on clothing (unless mandated as part of *distinctive clothing*).

Loud prayers were forbidden, as were the ringing of church bells or the trumpeting of **shofars**. They were also not allowed to build or repair churches without Muslim consent. Moreover, **Dhimmis** were not allowed to seek converts among Muslims. In the **Mamluk Egypt**, where non-Mamluk Muslims were not allowed to ride horses and camels, **Dhimmis** were prohibited even from riding donkeys inside cities. **Sometimes, Muslim rulers issued regulations requiring Dhimmis to attach distinctive signs to their houses.**

Most of the restrictions were social and symbolic in nature, and a pattern of stricter, then more lax, enforcement developed over time. The major financial disabilities of the **dhimmi** were the **jizya** poll tax and the fact **Dhimmis** and Muslims could not inherit from each other, which would create incentive to convert if someone from the family was already converted.

## Jizya tax

Payment of the *jizya* obligated Muslim authorities to protect **Dhimmis** in civil and military matters. **Sura 9:29** stipulates that *jizya* be exacted from non-Muslims as a condition required for jihad to cease. Failure to pay the *jizya* could result in the pledge of protection of a dhimmi's life and property becoming void, with the **Dhimmis** facing the alternatives of conversion, enslavement or death (or imprisonment). In some places, for example Egypt, **the obligations of the Jizya tax created economic incentives for Christians to convert to Islam.**

Most Islamic scholars agree that *jizya* must be levied only upon adult males and additional taxes were to be levied against **Dhimmis** who travelled on business. There are varying opinions among scholars as to how much of a burden *jizya* was. *Jizya* and *kharaj* were a crushing burden for the non-Muslim peasantry who eked out a bare living in a subsistence economy. The additional taxation on non-Muslims was a critical factor that drove many **Dhimmis** to leave their religion and accept Islam. **Dhimmi**s were sometimes recruited for military operations. **In such cases, they were exempted from *jizya* for the year of service.**

## Administration of law

The **Dhimmis** communities living in Islamic states usually had their own laws independent from the Sha'aria law, such as the Jews who had their own *Halakha* courts. **Dhimmi**s were allowed to operate their own courts following their own legal systems. **Dhimmi**s often took cases relating to marriage, divorce or inheritance to the Muslim courts so these cases would be decided under sha'aria law.

**Muslim men could generally marry Dhimmis women who are considered "People of the Book,"** however, Islamic jurists rejected the possibility any non-Muslim man might marry a Muslim woman. Similar position existed under the law of **Byzantine Empire**, according to which **a Christian could marry a Jewish woman, but a Jew could not marry a Christian woman under pain of death.**

Muslims and Jews were sometimes partners in trade, with the Muslim taking days off on Fridays and Jews taking off on Saturdays.

# Jewish Diaspora

**The Jewish diaspora (Hebrew: *Tfoot'za*) or Exile (Hebrew: *Galat*) refers to the dispersion of Israelites and later Jews out of what is considered their ancestral homeland (the Land of Israel).** In terms of the Hebrew Bible, the term **"Exile"** denotes the fate of the Israelites who were taken into exile from the **Kingdom of Israel** during the 8th century BCE and from the **Kingdom of Judah** during the 6th century BCE. **While in exile, the Judahites became to be known as "Jews".**

It continued with the exile of a portion of the population of the **Kingdom of Judah in 597 BCE with the Babylonian exile. The Babylonian exile ended after 70 years with Cyrus'** declaration that the exited Jews would be allowed to return to Jerusalem and build the **Second Temple.** The Jews revolted against the Roman Empire in **66 CE** during the period known as the **First Jewish-Roman War which culminated in the destruction of Jerusalem in 70 CE.** During the siege, **the Romans destroyed the Second Temple** and most of Jerusalem. This event marked the beginning of the Roman exile, also called **Edom** exile Jewish leaders and elite were exiled, killed or sold into slavery.

**In 132 CE, the Jews under Bar Kokhba rebelled against Hadrian.** In 135 CE, Hadrian's army defeated the Jewish armies and Jewish independence was lost. **As punishment Hadrian changed the name of Jerusalem to Aelia Capitolina,** turned it into a pagan city and banned the Jews from living there. **Judea and Samaria was renamed by Hadrian to Syria Palestina.** Throughout much of Jewish history, most of the Jews had lived in the **Diaspora**.

## Origins of the term

The Modern Hebrew concept of **Tefutzot, "scattered",** was introduced in the 1930s by the Jewish-American Zionist academic **Simon Rawidowicz**, who to some degree argued for the acceptance of the Jewish presence outside of the Land of Israel as a modern reality and an inevitability.

## Pre-Roman diaspora

**In 722 BCE, the Assyrians, under Sargon II, successor to Shalmaneser V, conquered the Kingdom of Israel, and many Israelites were deported to Mesopotamia.** After the overthrow of the kingdom of Judah in 586 BC by **Nebuchadnezzar II** of Babylon and the deportation of a considerable portion of its inhabitants to Mesopotamia, the Jews had two principal cultural centers Babylonia and the land of Israel.

**The poorest, but most fervent of the exiles returned to Judah/the Land of Israel, during the reign of the Achaemenids.** There with the reconstructed Temple in Jerusalem as their center, they organized themselves into a community animated by a remarkable religious ardor and a tenacious attachment to the **Torah** as the focus of its identity.

After numerous vicissitudes, and especially owing to internal dissensions in the **Seleucid** dynasty on the one hand and to the interested support of the pre-Roman Empire, pre-autocratic Roman Republic on the other, the cause of **Jewish independence finally triumphed Under the Hasmonean princes**, who were at first high priests and then kings, the Jewish state displayed even a certain luster and annexed several territories. **In 63 BC Pompeii invaded Jerusalem**, the Jewish people lost their political sovereignty and independence and **Gabinius** subjected the Jewish people to tribute.

## Early diaspora populations
According to the ancient Jewish historian **Josephus**, the next densest Jewish population after the Land of Israel and Babylonia was in Syria, particularly in **Antioch**, and Damascus, where **10,000 to 18,000 Jews were massacred during the great insurrection.** The ancient Jewish philosopher **Philo** gives the number of Jewish inhabitants in Egypt as one million, one-eighth of the population. The Jews in the Egyptian diaspora were on a par with their Ptolemaic counterparts and close ties existed for them with Jerusalem.

To judge by the accounts of **wholesale massacres in 115 BCE, the number of Jewish residents in Cyrenaica, Cyprus, and Mesopotamia was also large.** At the commencement of the reign of **Caesar Augustus**, there were over 7,000 Jews in Rome. Many sources say that the Jews constituted a full one-tenth (10%) of the population of the ancient city of Rome itself.

**The Jewish population of Asia Minor numbered 45,000 adult males, for a total of at least 180,000 persons.** The dispersal of Judean Jews from the Land of Israel and their expulsion from Jerusalem after the **revolt of CE 66-70 (The First Jewish-Roman War, known as the Great Revolt)** and the **revolt of 132-135 (the Second Jewish-Roman War, known as the Bar Kokhba Revolt).**

## Roman destruction of Judea
**Roman rule, which began in 63 BCE, continued until a revolt from CE 66-70**, a Jewish uprising to fight for independence, was eventually crushed after four years, culminating in the **capture of Jerusalem and the burning and destruction of the Temple**, the center of the national and religious life of the Jews throughout the world. **Jerusalem was also destroyed.** The Jewish **Diaspora** at the time of the Temple's destruction, according to **Josephus**, was in **Parthia (Persia), Babylonia (Iraq), Arabia**, as well as some Jews beyond the Euphrates and in Adiabene (Kurdistan). In **Josephus'** own words, he had informed **"the remotest Arabians"** about the destruction.

The complete destruction of Jerusalem and the settlement of several Greek and Roman colonies in Judah/Judaea and the Land of Israel (and the c hanging of its name to **Palestina and of Jerusalem's name to Aelia Capitolina)**, indicated the intention of the Roman government to prevent the political regeneration of the Jewish nation and sever the connection to their homeland. Nevertheless, forty years later the Jews put forth efforts to recover their former freedom.

With Israel exhausted they strove to establish commonwealths on the ruins of **Hellenism in Cyrene, Cyprus, Egypt, and Mesopotamia.** These efforts were suppressed by **Trajan** (115-117 CE), and under the **Emperor Hadrian** the same fate befell the attempt of the Jews of Israel in a new uprising to regain their independence (133-135 CE). Under the name **"Aelia Capitolina"**, a Roman colony and entirely pagan city **Jews were forbidden entrance on pain of death**, except for the day of **Tisha B'Av**. Yet despite the decree there has been an almost **continual Jewish presence in Jerusalem for 3,300 years.**

## Dispersion of the Jews in the Roman Empire

Following the **1ˢᵗ century Great Revolt and the 2ⁿᵈ century Simon Bar Kokhba revolt**, the destruction of Judaea exerted a decisive influence upon the dispersed Jewish people throughout the world. Many Jews entered the **Diaspora** as slaves after the **destruction of the Temple in 70 CE and 135 CE**. Many of these slave populations may have served as the basis of later European Jewish communities.

After the **Bar Kokhba Revolt of 132-135 CE** the Romans engaged in mass executions and enslavement, and destroyed large numbers of Judaean towns, forbidding Jews from settling in Jerusalem or its environs (**Dio Cassius, Roman History 69, 12-14**), there was no further Jewish government or overarching legal system thereafter in Judaea, this effectively turned the expatriate Jews of the **Diaspora into a permanently exiled people without a national homeland.**

It was at this time that Judaea became normatively known as **Syria Palestina**. The name reflected both the large scale killing of Jews during the suppression of the **2ⁿᵈ Jewish revolt**, and a Roman policy, first pagan, then Christian, to alienate Jews from the Land of Israel and Judaea, **ensuring that no Jewish temple, Jerusalem or state ever rose again.**

**Hadrian encouraged non-Jews to settle the land**. Although Jews maintained their presence in Palestine, they became disposed and dispersed people. After the revolt, the Jewish religious center shifted to the Babylonian Jewish community and its scholars. **The destruction of the Second Temple was responsible for a seismic change in communal Jewish self-perception and of their place in the world.**

## Post-Roman period Jewish populations

During the middle Ages, due to increasing geographical dispersion and re-settlement, Jews divided into distinct regional groups which today are generally addressed according to two primary geographical groupings the **Ashkenazi** of Northern and Eastern Europe, and the **Sephardic** Jews of Iberia (Spain and Portugal). North Africa and the Middle East. These groups have parallel histories sharing many cultural similarities as well as a series of **massacres, persecutions and expulsions, such as the expulsion from Spain in 1492. The expulsion from England in 1290 and the expulsion from Arab countries in 1948-1973).**

## Classic period: Jews and Samaritans

After the **Persian conquest of Babylon in 539 BCE** Judah (Hebrew: Yehuda) became a province of the Persian Empire. This status continued into the following Hellenistic period, when Yehud became a disputed province of Ptolemaic Egypt and Seleucid Syria. **In the early part of the 2ⁿᵈ century BCE, a revolt against the Seleucids led to the establishment of an independent Jewish kingdom under the Hasmonean dynasty.** The Hasmoneans adopted a deliberate policy of imitating and reconstituting the **Davidic kingdom,** and as part of this forcibly converted to Judaism their neighbors in the Land of Israel. The Babylonian Jewish community, though maintaining permanent ties with the Hasmonean and later Herodian kingdoms, evolved into a separate Jewish community, which during the Talmudic period assembled its own practices, the **Babylonian Talmud. The Babylonian Jewry is considered to be the predecessor of most Mizrahi Jewish communities.**

## Ashkenazi Jews

**Modern Ashkenazi Jews are the descendants of Jews who migrated into northern France and lower Germany around 800-1000 CE, later migrating into Eastern Europe.** Many Ashkenazi Jews also have mixed Sephardic origins, as a result of exiles from Spain, first during Islamic persecutions (11$^{th}$-12$^{th}$ centuries) and later during Christian reconquest (13$^{th}$-15$^{th}$ centuries) and the **Spanish Inquisition (15$^{th}$-16$^{th}$ centuries).**

## Sephardic Jews

**Sephardim are Jews whose ancestors lived in Spain or Portugal.** Some 300,000 Jews resided in Spain before the Spanish Inquisition in the 15$^{th}$ century, when the **Reyes Catolicos** reconquered Spain from the Arabs and **ordered the Jews to convert to Catholicism, leave the country or face execution without trial.** The Jews were expelled from Spain in 1492 in the wake of the **Alhambra Decree.** Sephardic Jews subsequently migrated to North Africa (Maghreb), Christian Europe (Netherlands, Britain, France and Poland), throughout the Ottoman Empire and even the newly discovered Latin America. **In the Ottoman Empire, the Sephardim mostly settled in the European portion of the Empire.**

A large population of **Sephardic** refugees who fled via the Netherlands as **Marranos** settled in Hamburg and Altona Germany in the early 16$^{th}$ century, eventually appropriating Ashkenazic Jewish rituals into their religious practice. Other Sephardim remained in Spain and Portugal as **Anusim** (forced converts to Catholicism), which would also be the fate for those who had migrated to Spanish and Portuguese ruled Latin America Sephardic Jews evolved to form most of North Africa's Jewish communities of the modern era, as well as the bulk of the Turkish, Syrian, Galilean and Jerusalemite Jews of the Ottoman period.

## Genetic analysis

Modern DNA studies have provided evidence that most of the world's Jews, Palestinians, Syrians and Lebanese, have a common ancestral lineage in the **Levant**, which can be traced to a common ancestral population that inhabited the Middle East some **four thousand years ago. Maternally, both Jews and Samaritans have had very low rates of intermarriage with local or host populations.**

The **Ashkenazi** population expanded through a series of bottlenecks – events that squeeze a population down to small numbers - perhaps as it migrated from the Middle East after the **destruction of the Second Temple in 70 CE** to Italy, reaching the Rhine Valley in the 10$^{th}$ century. The four major Ashkenazi maternal lineages and most of the minor maternal lineages had a prehistoric European source, rather than a Near Eastern or Caucasian one. These findings 'point to a **significant role for the conversion of women in the formation of Ashkenazi communities'.**

# The Dreyfus Affair

The **Dreyfus Affair** (French: *l'affaire Dreyfus*, was a political scandal that divided the **Third French Republic** from 1894 until its resolution in 1906. The affair remains as one of the most notable examples of a complex miscarriage of justice and antisemitism.

The scandal began in **December 1894** with the treason conviction of **Captain Alfred Dreyfus**, a young Alsatian French artillery officer of **Jewish descent.** Sentenced to life imprisonment for allegedly communicating French military secrets to the **German Embassy** in Paris, **Dreyfus** was imprisoned on **Devil's Island** in French Guiana, where he spent nearly five years.

Evidence came to light in 1896—primarily through an investigation instigated by **Georges Picquart**, head of counter-espionage—identifying a **French Army** major named **Ferdinand Walsin Esterhazy** as the real culprit. After high-ranking military officials suppressed the new evidence, a military court unanimously acquitted **Esterhazy** after a trial lasting only two days. The Army then accused **Dreyfus** with additional charges based on falsified documents. Word of the military court's framing of **Dreyfus** and of an attempted cover-up began to spread, a vehement open letter published in a Paris newspaper in January 1898 by writer **Émile Zola**. Activists put pressure on the government to reopen the case.

In 1899, **Dreyfus** was returned to France for another trial. The intense political and judicial scandal that ensued divided French society between those who supported **Dreyfus** (now called **"Dreyfusards"),** such as **Sarah Bernhardt, Anatole France, Henri Poincaré and Georges Clemenceau,** and those who condemned him (the anti-**Dreyfusards**), such as **Édouard Drumont**, the director and publisher of the antisemitic newspaper *La Libre Parole*.

The new trial resulted in another conviction and a **10-year sentence**, but **Dreyfus** was given a pardon and set free. Eventually all the accusations against **Dreyfus** were demonstrated to be baseless. In 1906, **Dreyfus** was exonerated and reinstated as a major in the **French Army**. He served during the whole of World War I, ending his service with the rank of lieutenant-colonel. **He died in 1935**. The affair from 1894 to 1906 divided France deeply and lastingly into two opposing camps: the pro-Army, mostly **Catholic "anti-Dreyfusards"** and the anticlerical, pro-republican **Dreyfusards.** It embittered French politics and encouraged radicalization.

## Summary
At the end of 1894 a French army captain named **Alfred Dreyfus**, a graduate of the **École Polytechnique** and a Jew of Alsatian origin, was accused of handing secret documents to the Imperial German military. After a closed trial, he was found guilty of treason and sentenced to prison for life. He was deported to **Devil's Island**. At that time, the opinion of the French political class was unanimously unfavorable towards **Dreyfus**.

Certain of the injustice of the sentence, the family of the Captain, through his brother **Mathieu,** worked with the journalist **Bernard Lazare** to prove his innocence. Meanwhile Colonel **Georges Picquart**, head of counter-espionage, found evidence in March 1896 indicating that **the real traitor was Major Ferdinand Walsin Esterhazy.** The General Staff, however, refused to reconsider its judgment and transferred Picquart to North Africa.

In July 1897 **Dreyfus**' family contacted the President of the Senate **Auguste Scheurer-Kestner** to draw attention to the tenuousness of the evidence against **Dreyfus**. Scheurer-Kestner reported three months later that he was convinced of the innocence of **Dreyfus** and also persuaded **Georges Clemenceau,** a former MP and then a newspaper reporter. In the same month, **Mathieu Dreyfus** complained to the **Ministry of War** against Esterhazy.

**Esterhazy** was acquitted of treason charges (afterwards shaving his moustache and fleeing France), and **Émile Zola** published his **"J'accuse...!"** a **Dreyfusard** declaration that rallied many intellectuals to **Dreyfus**' cause. France became increasingly divided over the case, and the issue continued to be hotly debated until the end of the century. Antisemitic riots erupted in more than twenty French cities. There were several deaths in Algiers.

Despite the intrigues of the army to quash the case, the first judgment against **Dreyfus** was annulled by the **Supreme Court** after a thorough investigation and a new court-martial was held in 1899. Despite increasingly robust evidence to the contrary, **Dreyfus** was convicted again and sentenced to ten years of hard labor, though the sentence was commuted due to extenuating circumstances. Exhausted by his deportation for four long years, **Dreyfus** accepted the presidential pardon granted by **President Émile Loubet**. It was only in 1906 that his innocence was officially recognized through a decision without recourse by the **Supreme Court**. Rehabilitated, **Dreyfus** was reinstated in the army with the rank of **Major** and participated in the **First World War**. He died in 1935.

The implications of this case were numerous and affected all aspects of French public life. It was during the affair that the term intellectual was coined. The affair engendered numerous antisemitic demonstrations, which in turn affected emotions within the Jewish communities of Central and Western Europe. These demonstrations affected the international movement of **Zionism** by persuading one of its founding fathers, **Theodor Herzl**, that the Jews must leave Europe and establish their own state.

## Military

The **Dreyfus** Affair occurred in the context of the annexation of **Alsace** and **Moselle** by the Germans, an event that fed the most extreme nationalism. The traumatic defeat in 1870 seemed far away, but a vengeful spirit remained. Many participants in the **Dreyfus** Affair were Alsatian. The military required considerable resources to prepare for the next conflict, and it was in this spirit that the **Franco-Russian Alliance**, which some saw as **"against nature"**, of 27 August 1892 was signed.

The arms race created an acute atmosphere of intrigue in French counter-espionage from 1890. One of the missions of the section was to spy on the **German Embassy** at Rue de Lille in Paris to thwart any attempt to transmit important information to the Germans. This was especially critical since several cases of espionage had already hit the headlines of newspapers, which were fond of sensationalism. Thus in 1890 the archivist **Boutonnet** was convicted for selling plans of shells that used **melinite.**

The German military attaché in Paris in 1894 was **Count Maximilian von Schwartzkoppen**, who developed a policy of infiltration which appears to have been effective. In the 1880s Schwartzkoppen had begun an affair with an Italian military attache, Lieutenant Colonel Count Alessandro Panizzardi. While neither had anything to do with **Dreyfus**, their intimate and erotic correspondence (e.g. **"Don't exhaust yourself with too much buggery."),** which was obtained by the authorities, lent an air of truth to other documents that were forged by prosecutors to lend retroactive credibility to **Dreyfus**'s conviction as a spy.

The letters, real and fake, provided a convenient excuse for placing the entire **Dreyfus** dossier under seal, given that exposure of the liaison would have 'dishonored' Germany and Italy's military and compromised diplomatic relations. As **homosexuality** was, like **Judaism**, then often perceived as a sign of national degeneration, recent historians have suggested that combining them to inflate the scandal may have shaped the prosecution strategy. This is what led to the origins of the **Dreyfus** Affair.

**Social/The social context was marked by the rise of nationalism and of antisemitism**. The growth of antisemitism, virulent since the publication of *Jewish France* by Édouard **Drumont** in 1886 (150,000 copies in the first year), went hand in hand with the rise of clericalism. Antisemitism did not spare the military, which practiced hidden discrimination with the **"cote d'amour"** (a subjective assessment of personal acceptability) system of irrational grading, encountered by **Dreyfus** in his application to the Bourges School. The French Army as a whole was relatively open to individual talent. At the time of the **Dreyfus** Affair there were an estimated 300 Jewish officers in the army (about 3 per cent of the total), of whom 10 were generals.

Hatred of Jews was now public and violent, driven by a firebrand (Drumont) who demonized the Jewish presence in France. Jews in metropolitan France in 1895 numbered about 80,000 (40,000 in Paris alone), who were highly integrated into society; an additional 45,000 Jews lived in Algeria. The launch of *La Libre Parole* with a circulation estimated at 200,000 copies in 1892. The antisemitism circulated by *La Libre Parole*, as well as by *L'Éclair, Le Petit Journal, La Patrie*, *L'Intransigeant* and *La Croix*, drew on antisemitic roots in certain **Catholic circles.**

## The trial of 1894: The beginning: Acts of espionage

The origin of the **Dreyfus** Affair, although fully clarified since the 1960s. **Dreyfus was innocent of any crime or offence.**

## Discovery of the Bordereau

The staff of the **Military Intelligence Service** (SR) worked around the clock to spy on the German Embassy in Paris. A confidential French military documents regarding the newly developed 120 calibre artillery piece were about to be sent to a foreign power.

## The search for the author of the bordereau

This catch seemed of sufficient importance for the head of the **"Statistical Section"**, the **Mulhousian Jean Sandherr**, to inform the Minister of War, **General Auguste Mercier**. He immediately initiated two secret investigations, one administrative and one judicial. To find the culprit, using simple though crude reasoning, the circle of the search was arbitrarily restricted to suspects posted to, or former employees of, the **General Staff** – necessarily a trainee artillery officer.

The ideal culprit was identified: Captain **Alfred Dreyfus**, a graduate of the École Polytechnique and an artillery officer, **of the Jewish faith** and of Alsatian origin, coming from the republican meritocracy. These origins were not, however, exceptional because these officers were favored by France for their knowledge of the German language and culture. There was also antisemitism in the offices of the General Staff. In particular, **Dreyfus** was at that time the only Jewish officer to be recently passed by the General Staff.

## Expertise in writing

To condemn **Dreyfus**, the writing on the bordereau had to be compared to that of the Captain. There was nobody competent to analyze the writing on the General Staff. **Dreyfus** was therefore **"the probable author"** of the bordereau in the eyes of the General Staff. **General Mercier** believed he had the guilty party, but he exaggerated the value of the affair, which took on the status of an affair of state during the week preceding the arrest of **Dreyfus**.

## The arrest

On 13 October 1894, without any tangible evidence and with an empty file, **General Mercier** summoned Captain **Dreyfus** for a general inspection in **"bourgeois clothing"**, i.e. in civilian clothes. In the morning of 15 October 1894 Captain **Dreyfus** underwent this ordeal but admitted nothing. **Du Paty** even tried to suggest suicide by placing a revolver in front of **Dreyfus**, but he refused to take his life, saying he **"wanted to live to establish his innocence"**. The hopes of the military were crushed. Nevertheless Du Paty **de Clam** still arrested the captain, accused him of conspiring with the enemy, and told him that he would be brought before a court-martial. **Dreyfus was imprisoned at the Cherche-Midi prison in Paris.**

## The enquiry and the first military court

Totally illegally, **Dreyfus** was placed in solitary confinement in prison, where **Du Paty** interrogated him day and night in order to obtain a confession, which failed. The captain was morally supported by the first **Dreyfusard**, **Major Forzinetti**, commandant of the military prisons of Paris.

On 29 October 1894 the affair was revealed in an article in *La Libre Parole*, the antisemitic newspaper owned by **Édouard Drumont**. On 1 November 1894 Alfred's brother, **Mathieu Dreyfus**, became aware of the arrest after being called urgently to Paris. He became the architect of the arduous fight for the liberation of his brother. Without hesitation, and retained the distinguished criminal lawyer **Edgar Demange**.

## The enquiry

On 3 November 1894 General Saussier the Military governor of Paris reluctantly gave the order for an enquiry. **"This is a proof of guilt because Dreyfus made everything disappear"**. The complete lack of neutrality of the indictment led to **Émile Zola** calling it a **"monument of bias"**.On 4 December 1894 **Dreyfus** was referred to the first **Military Court** with the empty file. The secrecy was lifted and Demange could access the file for the first time. The prosecution rested completely on the writing on a single piece of paper, the bordereau, on which experts disagreed, and on vague indirect testimonies.

## The trial: "Closed Court or War!" / *Trial and conviction of Alfred Dreyfus*

On 8 November 1894, General Mercier declared **Dreyfus** guilty in an interview with *Le Figaro*. He repeated himself on 29 November 1894 in an article by Arthur Meyer in *Le Gaulois*, **which in fact condemned the indictment against Dreyfus and asked, "How much freedom will the military court have to judge the defendant?"**

The trial opened on 19 December 1894 at one o'clock and a closed court was immediately pronounced. Detailed discussions on the bordereau showed that Captain **Dreyfus** could not be the author. **Dreyfus** was indeed a very patriotic officer highly rated by his superiors, very rich and with no tangible reason to betray France. The fact of **Dreyfus**'s Jewishness was used only by the right-wing press and was not presented in court.

He argued that leaks betraying the **General Staff** had been suspected to exist since February 1894 and that **"a respectable person"** accused Captain Dreyfus. He swore on oath that the traitor was **Dreyfus**, pointing to the crucifix hanging on the wall of the court. **Dreyfus** was apoplectic with rage and demanded to be confronted with his anonymous accuser, which was rejected by the General Staff.

## Transmission of a secret dossier to the judges

Military witnesses at the trial alerted high command about the risk of acquittal. For this eventuality the Statistics Section had prepared a file containing, in principle, four **"absolute"** proofs of the guilt of Captain **Dreyfus** accompanied by an explanatory note. The Statistics Section knew that the letter could not be attributed to **Dreyfus** and if it was, it was with criminal intent.

## Conviction, degradation, and deportation

On 22 December 1894, after several hours of deliberation, the verdict was reached. Seven judges unanimously convicted **Alfred Dreyfus** of collusion with a foreign power, to the maximum penalty under section **76 of the Criminal Code:** *permanent exile in a walled fortification* (prison), the cancellation of his army rank and military degradation. **Dreyfus** was not sentenced to death, as it had been abolished for political crimes since 1848. Antisemitism peaked in the press and occurred in areas so far spared. **Jean Jaurès** regretted the lightness of the sentence in an address to the House and wrote, **"A soldier has been sentenced to death and executed for throwing a button in the face of his corporal. So why leave this miserable traitor alive?"**

On 5 January 1895, the ceremony of degradation took place in the Morlan Court of the Military School in Paris. While the drums rolled, **Dreyfus** was accompanied by four artillery officers, who brought him before an officer of the state who read the judgment. A Republican Guard adjutant tore off his badges, thin strips of gold, his stripes, cuffs and sleeves of his jacket.

Witnesses report the dignity of **Dreyfus**, who continued to maintain his innocence while raising his arms: **"Innocent, Innocent! Vive la France! Long live the Army"**. The Adjutant broke his sword on his knee and then the condemned **Dreyfus** marched at a slow pace in front of his former companions. An event known as **"the legend of the confession"** took place before the degradation. On 17 January 1895, he was transferred to the prison on **Île de Ré** where he was held for over a month.

On 21 February 1895, he embarked on the ship Ville de Saint-Nazaire. The next day the ship sailed for **French Guiana**. On 12 March 1895, after a difficult voyage of fifteen days, the ship anchored off the **Îles du Salut. Dreyfus** stayed one month in prison on **Île Royale** and was transferred to **Devil's Island** on 14 April 1895.

## Truth on the march (1895–1897)

**Mathieu Dreyfus**, the elder brother of Alfred, was convinced of his innocence. He was the chief architect of the rehabilitation of his brother and spent his time, energy and fortune to gather an increasingly powerful movement for a retrial in December 1894.

## The discovery of the real culprit: Picquart "going to the enemy"

In March 1896 Picquart, who had followed the **Dreyfus** Affair from the outset, now required to receive the documents stolen from the German Embassy directly without any intermediary. He discovered a document called the **"petit bleu"**: a telegram that was never sent, written by von Schwartzkoppen and intercepted at the German embassy at the beginning of March 1896.

On seeing letters from Esterhazy, Picquart realized with amazement that his writing was exactly the same as that on the **"bordereau"**, which had been used to incriminate **Dreyfus**. Picquart diligently conducted an enquiry in secret without the consent of his superiors. The enquiry demonstrated that **Esterhazy** had knowledge of the elements described by the **"bordereau"** and that he was in contact with the German embassy. **It was established that the officer sold the Germans many secret documents, whose value was quite low.**

Picquart communicated the results of his investigation to the General Staff, which opposed him under **"the authority of the principle of already judged"**. After this, everything was done to oust him from his position, with the help of his own deputy, **Major Henry**. It was primarily the upper echelons of the Army that did not want to admit that **Dreyfus**'s conviction could be a grave miscarriage of justice.

## The denunciation of Esterhazy and the progress of Dreyfusism

Picquart tried to convince his seniors to react in favor of **Dreyfus**, but the General Staff seemed deaf. The General Staff, still suspected Picquart of causing leaks. This was the beginning of the Picquart affair, a new conspiracy by the General Staff against an officer.

Parallel to the investigations of Picquart, the defenders of **Dreyfus** were informed in November 1897 that the identity of the writer of the "bordereau" was Esterhazy. Mathieu **Dreyfus** had a reproduction of the bordereau published by *Le Figaro*. A banker, Castro, formally identified the writing as that of **Esterhazy**, who was his debtor, and told **Mathieu**. The **Dreyfus** Affair occupied more and more discussions, something the political world did not always recognize. **Jules Méline** declared in the opening session of the National Assembly on 7 December 1897, **"There is no Dreyfus affair. There is not now and there can be no Dreyfus affair."**

## Trial and acquittal of Esterhazy

General Georges-Gabriel de Pellieux was responsible for conducting an investigation. The militarist press rushed to the rescue of Esterhazy with an unprecedented antisemitic campaign. The **Dreyfusard** press replied with strong new evidence in its possession. **Georges Clemenceau**, in the newspaper *L'Aurore*, asked, "Who protects Major Esterhazy? The law must stop sucking up to this ineffectual Prussian disguised as a French officer. **Why is an honest soldier such as Lieutenant-Colonel Picquart discredited, overwhelmed, dishonored? If this is the case we must speak out!"**

The trial was not normal: the civil trial Mathieu and Lucy **Dreyfus** requested was denied, and the three handwriting experts decided the writing in the bordereau was not Esterhazy's. Esterhazy was acquitted unanimously the next day after just three minutes of deliberation. With all the cheering, it was difficult for Esterhazy to make his way toward the exit, where some 1,500 people were waiting. The acquittal of Esterhazy therefore brought about a change of strategy for the **Dreyfusards**. In response to the acquittal, large and violent riots by anti-**Dreyfusards** and anti-Semites broke out across France, respecting neither property nor people.

Outraged by the acquittal of **Esterhazy**, **Zola** decided to strike a blow. He published a 4,500-word article on the front page of *L'Aurore* in the form of an open letter to President Félix Faure (Clemenceau thought up the headline *J'Accuse…!*). With a typical circulation of 30,000, the newspaper distributed nearly 300,000 copies that day. It denounced all those who had conspired against **Dreyfus**, including the minister of war and the General Staff. His trial forced a new public review of both the **Dreyfus** and **Esterhazy** affairs. Thanks to the national and international success of **Zola**'s brilliant coup, a trial became inevitable.

## The trial of Zola

**General Billot**, Minister of War, filed a complaint against **Zola** and **Alexandre Perrenx**, the manager of *L'Aurore,* to be heard at the Assises of the Seine from 7 to 23 February 1898. The minister referred to only three passages of **Zola**'s article, eighteen lines out of hundreds. He accused **Zola** of having written that the court martial had committed **"unlawful acts by order"**. The trial opened in an atmosphere of extreme violence—**Zola** had been the object of **"the most shameful attacks"** as well as important support and congratulations.

## Lawyer for the defense and the President of the Court, Delegorgue

**Zola** was sentenced to one year in prison and a fine of 3,000 francs, which was the maximum penalty. This harshness was due to the atmosphere of violence surrounding the trial. **"The excitement of the audience and the exasperation of the crowd in front of the courthouse were so violent that one could fear the worst excesses if the jury acquitted Mr. Zola"**. However, the **Zola** trial was rather a victory for the **Dreyfusards**. Even more than the **Dreyfus** Affair the **Zola** affair resulted in a regrouping of intellectual forces into two opposing camps.

## Henry unmasked, the case is rekindled

Anti-Semitism made considerable progress and riots were common throughout the year 1898. The majority was moderate, though a parliamentary group in the House was anti-Semitic. Nevertheless the cause of the **Dreyfusards** was restarted. Godefroy Cavaignac, the new minister of war and a fierce supporter of anti-revisionism, definitely wanted to prove the guilt of **Dreyfus** and from there **"wring the neck"** of Esterhazy, whom he considered **"a pathological liar and blackmailer"**. Cavaignac decided to investigate—in his office, with his assistants—and retrieved the secret file, which now contained 365 items.

On 7 July 1898 during a questioning in the House, Cavaignac reported three items **"overwhelming among a thousand"**, two of which had no connection with the case. The other was the **"faux Henry"**. Picquart declared in *Le Temps* to the council president, **"I am in a position to establish before a court of competent jurisdiction that the two documents bearing the date of 1894 could not be attributed to Dreyfus and that the one that bears the date of 1896 had all the characteristics of a fake,"** which earned him eleven months in prison.

The request for review filed by **Lucie Dreyfus** could not be rejected. Yet Cavaignac said **"less than ever!"**, but the president of the council, Henri Brisson, forced him to resign. Brisson remained convinced that **Dreyfus** was guilty and made a statement disparaging and offensive to **Dreyfus** at the Rennes trial. The government transferred the case to the Supreme Court for its opinion on the past four years of proceedings.

## The appeal on the judgment of 1894

On 9 February 1899, the Criminal Division submitted its report by highlighting two important facts: it was certain Esterhazy used the same paper as the bordereau and the secret file was completely void. These two major events alone destroyed all proceedings against **Alfred Dreyfus**.

## The trial in Rennes 1899

**Alfred Dreyfus** was in no way aware of what was happening thousands of kilometres from him. On 5 June 1899 **Alfred Dreyfus** was notified of the decision of the Supreme Court on the judgement of 1894.

On 9 June 1899 he left **Devil's Island**, heading to France, but locked in a cabin as if guilty, even though he no longer was. After five years of imprisonment, he was on his native soil, but he was immediately locked up from 1 July 1899 in the military prison in Rennes. He was remanded on 7 August 1899 before the military court of the Breton capital.

General Mercier, champion of the anti-**Dreyfusards**, intervened constantly in the press to confirm the accuracy of the first judgement: **Dreyfus** was surely guilty. **Esterházy**, who admitted authorship of the bordereau, was in exile in England. He and du Paty were both excused. All the General Staff testified against **Dreyfus** without providing any proof. They stubbornly considered null and void the confessions of Henry and Esterhazy.

## New conviction

On 9 September 1899 the court rendered its verdict: **Dreyfus was convicted of treason, but "with extenuating circumstances"** (by five votes to two) and sentenced to ten years' imprisonment and a further degradation. Many **Dreyfusards** were frustrated by this final act. Public opinion welcomed this conclusion indifferently. **Alfred Dreyfus** himself who was instead pardoned to be able to still seek acquittal.

## Reactions

Two of the seven judges voted for acquittal. They refused to yield to the implied military order. In an apostrophe for the army, Galliffet announced: **"The incident is closed"**.

## Rehabilitation, 1900–1906 / *Resolution of the Dreyfus Affair*

Preferring to avoid a third trial the government decided to pardon **Dreyfus** by a decree signed by **President Émile Loubet** on 19 September 1899 after much hesitation. **Dreyfus** was not found innocent. The rehabilitation process was not completed until six years later without sparkle or passion.

## Death of Zola

On 29 September 1902 **Zola**, who was the initiator of *The Affair* and the first of the intellectual **Dreyfusards**, died, and asphyxiated by fumes from his chimney. His wife, **Alexandrine**, narrowly escaped. It was a shock for the **Dreyfusard** clan. Before recalling the struggle undertaken by **Zola** for justice and truth is it possible for me to keep silent about those men bent on the destruction of an innocent man and who, after feeling lost, was saved and overwhelmed with the desperate audacity of fear?

**How to depart from your sight then I have a duty to show you**
**Zola rises up weak and disarmed against them?**
**Can I hide their lives?**
**It would silence his heroic righteousness.**
**Can I hide their crimes?**
**That would conceal his virtue.**
**Can I silence the insults and calumnies which they have pursued?**
**It would silence his reward and honors.**
**Can I hide their shame?**
**It would silence his glory.**
**No, I will speak.**
**Envy him: he honored his country and the world by a vast and a great act.**
**Envy him, his destiny and his heart gave out the greatest.**
**It was a moment of human conscience.**

In 1953, the newspaper **Liberation** published a death-bed confession by a Parisian roofer that he had murdered **Zola** by blocking the chimney of his house.

## The semi-rehabilitation / Legal rehabilitation

The years 1904 and 1905 were devoted to different legal phases before the Supreme Court. The report showed that the writing was certainly by **Esterhazy** and that the latter had also confessed subsequently. General Sebert, maintained **"it is highly unlikely that an artillery officer could write this missive"**.

On 9 March 1905 Attorney-General Baudouin delivered an 800-page report in which he demanded the convictions be quashed without further reference to another court and denounced the army. It was not until 12 July 1906 that the Supreme Court unanimously cancelled the judgment without reference to the military trial at Rennes in 1899 and pronounced **"the end of the rehabilitation of Captain Dreyfus"**.

The Court focused on the legal aspects only and observed that **Dreyfus** did not have a duty to be returned before a **Military Court** for the simple reason that it should never have taken place due to the total absence of charges: Whereas in the final analysis of the accusation against **Dreyfus** nothing remains standing and setting aside the judgment of the Military Court leaves nothing that can be considered to be a crime or misdemeanor; therefore by applying the final paragraph of **Article 445** no reference to another court should be pronounced.

## Subsequent career

**Dreyfus was reinstated in the army with the rank of artillery major by law on 13 July 1906**. After serving for a year as commander of the artillery depot at Fort Neuf de Vincennes, Major **Dreyfus** retired in June 1907; a decision taken in part because of recurrent tropical fevers and chronic fatigue arising from the strain of his imprisonment.

As a reserve officer **Dreyfus** participated in the **First World War of 1914–1918**, serving as head of the artillery depot at a fortified camp near Paris and commander of a supply column. In 1917 he saw frontline service at the Chemin des Dames and Verdun. Having been named as a Chevalier of the Legion of Honor at the time of his reinstatement in 1906, **Dreyfus** was promoted to the rank of officer of the Legion of Honor in 1919. **Dreyfus** died on 12 July 1935 at the age of seventy-five years. His funeral cortège passed through ranks assembled for **Bastille Day** celebrations at the **Place de la Concorde** and he was buried in Montparnasse Cemetery.

## Consequences of the Dreyfus Affair

According to **Katrin Schultheiss,** a modern historian: **"The enduring significance of the Dreyfus Affair ... lies in its manifest embodiment of multiple narratives and multiple strands of historical causality. It shows how longstanding beliefs and tensions can be transformed ... into a juggernaut that alters the political and cultural landscape for decades. In the interest of increasing our understanding ... the complexities of that transformation should be recognized and analyzed rather than packaged for moral or political usefulness."**

## Social consequences

This antisemitism was reinforced by the crisis of the separation of church and state in 1905, which probably led to its height in France. Antisemitic actions were permitted on the advent of the **Vichy** regime, which allowed free and unrestrained expression of racial hatred. At the end of the war the monstrosity of the **Final Solution** was known by all and even today the expression of antisemitism is revealed from time to time through declarations of nationalist parties, which are all the more startling that they have become rarities.

## International consequences

The shock of the **Dreyfus** Affair also affected the Zionist movement **"which found fertile ground for its emergence"**. The Austro-Hungarian journalist **Theodor Herzl** appeared profoundly moved by the **Dreyfus** affair, which followed his debut as a correspondent for the *Neue Freie Presse* of Vienna and was present at the degradation of **Dreyfus** in 1895. **"The Affair ... acted as a catalyst in the conversion of Herzl"**. Before the wave of antisemitism that accompanied the degradation **Herzl** was **"convinced of the need to resolve the Jewish question"**, which became **"an obsession for him"**.

The **Dreyfus** Affair shook **Herzl**'s view on the world, and he became completely enveloped in a tiny movement **calling for the restoration of a Jewish State within the biblical homeland in Israel. Herzl** quickly took charge in leading the movement. **He organized on 29 August 1897, the First Zionist Congress in Basel and is considered the "inventor of Zionism as a real political movement". Theodor Herzl wrote in his diary (1 September 1897):**

**On 29 November 1947, a little over fifty years after the First Zionist Congress, the United Nations voted in favor to partition Palestine into a Jewish State.** The following year the state of Israel was established. Consequently, the **Dreyfus** Affair is seen as a turning point in Jewish history and as **the beginning of the Zionist movement**.

## Other related events / Commission of sculpture

In 1985, **President François Mitterrand** commissioned a statue of **Dreyfus** by sculptor Louis Mitelberg. It was to be installed at the École Militaire but the Minister of Defense refused to display it there, even though **Alfred Dreyfus** had been rehabilitated into the Army and fully exonerated in 1906. A replica is located at the entrance of **Paris's Museum of Jewish Art and History**, housing the **Fond Dreyfus**, more than three thousand historical documents donated by the grandchildren of Captain **Dreyfus**.

## Centennial commemoration

On 12 July 2006 President Jacques Chirac held an official state ceremony marking the centenary of **Dreyfus**'s official rehabilitation. This was held in the presence of the living descendants of both Émile **Zola** and **Alfred Dreyfus**. Chirac stated that **"the combat against the dark forces of** intolerance and hate is never definitively won", and called **Dreyfus "an exemplary officer" and a "patriot who passionately loved France".**

# Ebionites (Jewish-Christian)

Ebionites (derived from Hebrew *ebyonim, ebionim*, meaning **'the poor' or 'poor ones'**) as a term refers to a Jewish Christian sect who were vegetarians, viewed poverty as holy, believed in ritual ablutions, and rejected animal sacrifices. They existed during the early centuries of the **Common Era.**

The **Ebionites** embraced an **Adoptionist Christology**, thus **understanding Jesus of Nazareth as a mere man** who, by virtue of his righteousness, was chosen by God to be the last true prophet who heralds the coming **Kingdom of God on Earth. A majority of the Ebionites rejected as heresies the proto-orthodox Christian beliefs in Jesus's divinity and virgin birth.** They maintained that **Jesus** was the natural son of Joseph and Mary who became the Messiah because he obeyed the Jewish law.

Accordingly, the **Ebionites** insisted on the necessity of following the **Written Law of Moses** alone **(without the Oral Law);** used one, some or all of the Jewish–Christian gospels, such as the *Gospel of the Ebionites,* as additional scripture to the Hebrew Bible; and revered **James the Just** as an exemplar of righteousness and the **true successor to Jesus (rather than Peter)**, while rejecting **Paul** as a false apostle and an apostate from the Law. The **Church Fathers** consider the **Ebionites** identical with other Jewish Christian sects, such as the **Nazarenes.**

## ☑ Name
Origen wrote **"for Ebion signifies 'poor' among the Jews, and those Jews who have received Jesus as Christ are called by the name of Ebionites." Tertullian** was the first to write against a heresiarch called **Ebion.**

## History / Emergence
The earliest reference to a sect that might fit the description of the later **Ebionites** appears in **Justin Martyr's** *Dialogue with Trypho* **(c. 140)**. Justin distinguishes between Jewish Christians who observe the **Law of Moses** but do not require its observance upon others and those who believe the **Mosaic Law** to be obligatory on all. **Irenaeus** (c. 180) was probably the first to use the term *Ebionites* to name a sect he labeled heretical **"Judaizers"** for **"stubbornly clinging to the Law"**.

Epiphanius of Salamis (c. 310–320 – 403) gives the most complete account in his **heresiology called** *Panarion,* **denouncing eighty heretical sects, among them the Ebionites**. According to the **Encyclopædia Britannica**, the Ebionite movement **"may have arisen about the time of the destruction of the Jewish Temple in Jerusalem (70 CE)."** The *Book of Elchasai*, which may not have had anything to do with the **Ebionites. Paul** talks of his collection for the **"poor** among the saints" in the Jerusalem church, but this is generally taken as meaning the poorer members of the church rather than a schismatic sect.

Other sects mentioned are the Carpocratians, the **Cerinthians, the Elcesaites, the fourth century Nazarenes and the Sampsaeans,** most of whom were Jewish Christian sects who held gnostic or other views rejected by the **Ebionites**.

There is no evidence linking the origin of the later sect of the **Ebionites** with the **First Jewish-Roman War of 66–70 CE** or with the Jerusalem church led by James. They were led by Simeon of Jerusalem (d. 107) and during the **Second Jewish-Roman War of 115–117**, they were persecuted by the Jewish followers of **Bar Kochba** for refusing to recognize his messianic claims. From these places, they dispersed and went into Asia (Turkey), Rome and Cyprus.

## Disappearance

After the end of the **First Jewish–Roman War**, the importance of the Jerusalem church began to fade. Jewish Christianity became dispersed throughout the Jewish diaspora in the **Levant,** where it was slowly eclipsed by **Gentile Christianity,** which then spread throughout the Roman Empire without competition from Jewish Christian sects. Once the Jerusalem church was eliminated during the **Bar Kokhba revolt in 135**, the **Ebionites** gradually lost influence and followers. Following the defeat of the rebellion and the expulsion of all Jews from Judea, Jerusalem became the Gentile city of **Aelia Capitolina**.

The **Ebionites** are still attested, if as marginal communities, down to the 7th century. The **Ebionites** survived much longer and identify them with a sect encountered by the historian **Abd al-Jabbar ibn Ahmad around the year 1000**. The **"Book of the Travels"** of Rabbi Benjamin of Tudela, a rabbi from Spain. The 12th century Muslim historian **Muhammad al-Shahrastani** mentions Jews living in nearby **Medina** and **Hejaz** who accepted **Jesus** as a prophetic figure and followed traditional Judaism, rejecting mainstream Christian views.

## Views and practices / Judaism, Gnosticism and Essenism

Most patristic sources portray the **Ebionites** as Jews who zealously followed the **Written Law alone** (without the Oral Law), revered Jerusalem as the holiest city and restricted table fellowship only to Gentiles who converted to Judaism. **Epiphanius of Salamis** stated that the **Ebionites** engaged in excessive ritual bathing, possessed an angelology which claimed that the **Christ is an angel of God** who was incarnated in **Jesus** when he was adopted as the son of God during his baptism, denied parts of the **Law** deemed obsolete or corrupt, opposed animal sacrifice, practiced Jewish vegetarianism and celebrated a commemorative meal annually on or around **Passover** with unleavened bread and water only, in contrast to the daily **Christian Eucharist**.

Regarding the **Ebionites** specifically, a number of scholars have different theories on how the **Ebionites may have developed from an Essene Jewish messianic sect**.

# Ecclesiastes (Koheleth)

**Ecclesiastes**, (Hebrew: *Koheleth, Qoheleth*) is one of 24 books of the Tanakh or Hebrew Bible, where it is classified as one of the *Ketuvim* (or "Writings"). **Koheleth** (meaning "**Gatherer**", but traditionally translated as "**Teacher**" or "**Preacher**"). This anonymous work was probably composed in the last part of the 3$^{rd}$ century BC. The author, introducing himself as "**son of David, king in Jerusalem**" (i.e., **Solomon**) discusses the meaning of life and the best way to live. He proclaims all the actions of man to be inherently *hevel*, meaning "**vain**" or "**futile**", ("**mere breath**"), as both wise and foolish end in death.

**Koheleth** clearly endorses wisdom as a means for a well-lived earthly life. In light of this senselessness, one should enjoy the simple pleasures of daily life, such as eating, drinking, and taking enjoyment in one's work, which are gifts from the hand of God. "**Fear God, and keep his commandments; for that is the whole duty of everyone**" **(12:13). Ecclesiastes** has had a deep influence on Western literature **Abraham Lincoln** addressing Congress in 1862. "**Ecclesiastes is the greatest single piece of writing I have ever known. Verse 1:1 is a superscription, the ancient equivalent of a title page: it introduces the book as "the words of Koheleth, son of David, king in Jerusalem."**

## Summary
The ten-verse introduction in verses **1:2-11** are the words of the frame narrator; they set the mood for what is to follow: **Koheleth's message is that all is meaningless.** After the introduction come the words of **Koheleth.** As king he has experienced everything and done everything, but nothing is ultimately reliable. **Death levels all.** The only good is to partake of life in the present, for enjoyment is from the hand of God. Everything is ordered in time and people are subject to time in contrast to God's eternal character.

The world is filled with injustice, which only God will adjudicate God and humans do not belong in the same realm and it is therefore necessary to have a right attitude before God. People should enjoy, but should not be greedy; no-one knows what is good for humanity; **righteousness and wisdom escape us. Koheleth reflects on the limits of human power: all people face death, and death is better than life, but we should enjoy life when we can.** The world is full of risk: he gives advice on living with risk, both political and economic. Mortals should take pleasure when they can, for a time may come when no one can. **Koheleth's** words finish with imagery of nature languishing and humanity marching to the grave. "**For God will bring every deed to judgment.**"

## Title, date and author
*Koheleth*, meaning something like "**one who convenes or addresses an assembly**". The presence of Persian loan-words and Aramaisms points to a date no earlier than about 450 BCE, while the latest possible date for its composition is 180 BCE, when another Jewish writer, **Ben Sira,** quotes from it. Also unresolved is whether the author and narrator of **Koheleth** is one and the same person. The question, however, has no theological importance.

## Genre and setting

**Ecclesiastes** has taken its literary form from the Middle Eastern tradition of the fictional autobiography, in which a character, often a king, relates his experiences and draws lessons from them, often self-critical: **Koheleth** likewise identifies himself as a king, speaks of his search for wisdom, relates his conclusions, and recognizes his limitations. **Ecclesiastes** differs from the other biblical Wisdom books in being deeply skeptical of the usefulness of Wisdom itself. He may also have been influenced by Greek philosophy, specifically the schools of **Stoicism**, which held that all things are fated, and **Epicureanism**, which held that happiness was best pursued through the quiet cultivation of life's simpler pleasures.

## Canonicity

God who reveals and redeems, who elects and cares for a chosen people – are absent from it, which gives it tone that **Koheleth** had lost his faith in his old age. Yet another suggestion is that **Ecclesiastes** is simply the most extreme example of a tradition of skepticism, but none of the proposed examples match **Ecclesiastes** for a sustained denial of faith and doubt in the goodness of God. **Martin A. Shields** in his 2006 book *The End of Wisdom: A Reappraisal of the Historical and Canonical Function of Ecclesiastes.* Scholars disagree about the themes of **Ecclesiastes**. Is it positive and life-affirming, or deeply pessimistic? Is **Koheleth** coherent or incoherent, insightful or confused, orthodox or heterodox? Is the ultimate message of the book to copy **Koheleth**, the wise man, or to avoid his errors? **"The dead are better off than the living"** (4:2) vs. **"a living dog is better off than a dead lion" (9:4)).**

The subjects of **Ecclesiastes** are the pain and frustration engendered by observing and meditating on the distortions and inequities pervading the world, the uselessness of human deeds, and the limitations of wisdom and righteousness. The **phrase "under the sun"** appears thirty times in connection with these observations, all this co-exists with a firm belief in God, whose power, and justice and unpredictability are sovereign. Life has no meaning or purpose: the wise man and the man who does not study wisdom will both die and be forgotten: **man should be reverent ("Fear God"), but in this life it is best to simply enjoy God's gifts.**

## Judaism

In Judaism, **Ecclesiastes** is read either on **Shemini Atzeret** (by Yemenites, Italians, some Sepharadim, and the medieval French Jewish rite) or on the Shabbat of the Intermediate **Days of Sukkot** (by Ashkenazim), by telling the listeners that, without God, **life is meaningless.**

## Influence on Western literature

**Ecclesiastes** has had a deep influence on Western literature. It contains several phrases that have resonated in British and American culture, such as **"nothing new under the sun," "a time to be born and a time to die,"** and **"vanity of vanities; all is vanity."** **Abraham Lincoln** quoted **Ecclesiastes** 1:4 in his address to the reconvening Congress on December 1, 1862, during the darkest hours of the American Civil War: **"One generation passeth away, and another generation cometh: but the earth abideth forever.'...Our strife pertains to ourselves – to the passing generations of men; and it scan without convulsion be hushed forever with the passing of one generation."**

# El Shaddai (God)

**El Shaddai** (Hebrew: שַׁדַּי אֵל) or just **Shaddai** is one of the names of the God of Israel. *El Shaddai* is conventionally translated into English as ***God Almighty (Deus Omnipotens*** in Latin), but its original meaning is unclear.

The translation of *El* **as "God" or "Lord"** in the **Ugaritic/Canaanite** language is straightforward, as **El** was the supreme god of the ancient Canaanite religion. The literal meaning of *Shaddai,* however, is the subject of debate. The form of the phrase *El Shaddai* fits the pattern of the divine names in the **Ancient Near East**, exactly as is the case with names like **"'El Olam", "'El Elyon"** or **"'El Betel"**. As such, *El Shaddai* **can convey several different semantic relations between the two words, among them:**

- *El* of a place called *Shaddai*
- *El* possessing the quality of *shaddai*
- *El* who is also known by the name *Shaddai*

## Occurrence

**The name *Shaddai* appears 48 times in the Bible, seven times as "El Shaddai" (five times in Genesis, once in Exodus, and once in Ezekiel).**

In Genesis 17:1, **"When Abram was ninety-nine years old the Lord appeared to Abram and said to him, 'I am *El Shaddai*; walk before me, and be blameless,'** Similarly, in Genesis 35:11 God says to Jacob, **"I am El Shaddai: be fruitful and multiply; a nation and a company of nations shall be of thee, and kings shall come out of thy loins".** According to Exodus 6:2–3, *Shaddai* was the name by which God was known to **Abraham, Isaac, and Jacob.**

In the vision of Balaam recorded in the **Book of Numbers 24:4 and 16**, the vision comes from **Shaddai** along with **El**. The name *Shaddai* is often used in parallel to **El** later in the **Book of Job.** In the Septuagint *Shaddai* or *El Shaddai* was often translated just as **"God"** or **"my God"**, and in at least one passage (**Ezekiel 10:5**) it is transliterated. In other places (such as **Job 5:17**) it is translated **"Almighty"** and this word is used in other translations as well (such as the **King James Bible).**

## Shaddai related to wilderness or mountains

"El Shaddai" means "God of the Wilderness" and originally would not have had a doubled "d". The word is related to the word "śadé" meaning "the (uncultivated) field", the area of hunting. Another theory is that **Shaddai** is a derivation of a Semitic stem that appears in the **Akkadian shadû ("mountain")**. According to this theory, God is seen as inhabiting a holy mountain, a concept not unknown in ancient West Asian mythology and also evident in the **Syriac Christian** writings of **Ephrem the Syrian**, who places Eden on an inaccessible mountaintop.

The term **"El Shaddai"** may mean **"god of the mountains"**, referring to the Mesopotamian divine mountain. This could also refer to the Israelite camp's stay at **biblical Mount Sinai where God gave Moses the Ten Commandments**. The term was **"one of the patriarchal names for the Mesopotamian tribal god"**, presumably meaning of the tribe of Abram. In Exodus 6:3, **El Shaddai** is identified explicitly with the **God of Abraham and with YHWH. The term "El Shaddai" appears chiefly in Genesis.**

## Shaddai meaning destroyer

**The root word "*shadad*" means to plunder, overpower, or make desolate**. This would give **Shaddai** the meaning of **"destroyer"**, representing one of the aspects of God, and in this context it is essentially an epithet. The meaning may go back to an original sense which was **"to be strong"** as in the Arabic **"*shadid*" "strong"**. The termination **"*ai*"**, typically signifying the first person possessive plural, functions as a pluralis excellentiae like other titles for the Hebrew deity, **Elohim ("gods") and Adonai ("my lords")**.

## Shaddai as a toponym

It has been speculated that the tell in Syria called **Tell eth-Thadeyn ("tell of the two breasts")** was called **Shaddai** in the Amorite language. It has been conjectured that **El Shaddai** was therefore the **"God of Shaddai"** and that the inclusion of the Abrahamic stories into the Hebrew Bible may have brought the northern name with them.

## Shaddai meaning breasts

It has been speculated that **Shaddai** comes from the root **"*shad*" "breast"**. El Shaddai is considered by some to be the feminine aspect of the Hebrew God, while **YHWH** is the masculine. **Shaddai in the later Jewish tradition / God that said "enough"**

The noun containing the **dagesh** is the Hebrew word *dai* meaning **"enough, sufficient, sufficiency"**. This is the same word used in the **Passover Haggadah, Dayeinu**, which means **"It would have been enough for us."** The song **Dayeinu** celebrates the various miracles God performed while liberating the Israelites from Egyptian servitude. The **Talmud** explains it this way, but says that **"Shaddai"** stands for **"Mi she'Amar Dai L'olamo"** – **"He who said 'Enough' to His world."**

*I am El Shaddai* (**Genesis 35:11**)? I am he who said to the world **"enough!"**. *He reproaches the sea and makes it dry; and all the rivers makes desolate* (**Nahum 1:4**). This account has two parallel variants with some minute changes. One appears in **Bereshit Rabbah 5:8**, where **Shaddai** stops the world from expanding and in **46:3** where he limits the earth and heavens. The divine plan of drawing the borders between mind and matter, keeping the balance between his right and left hand or as an early manifestation of the **kabbalistic idea of *tzimtzum*.**

It is possible to discern two basic essences engaged in the opposition: the active, dividing agent and passive amorphous matter. Moreover, each of the recalled accounts has strong cosmological undertones, what suggests assuming the comparative perspective. **Shaddai** limiting the expansionist outburst of the world fits well the pattern of the so-called *chaoskampf* – an initial divine battle followed by the triumph of the young and vivacious deity, subjugating the hostile, usually aquatic monster and building the palace or creating the cosmos.

Babylonian **Marduk and Tiamat, Ugaritic Baal and Yam, Egyptian Ra and Apep**, etc. Not only does the Hebrew Bible recall the cosmic battle numerous times, especially in **Psalms** (e.g., **77:16–17; 89:10**) and Prophets (e.g. **Isaiah 51:9–10; Ezekiel 32:13**) but also plays with this ancient motif reiterating it to convey a specific meaning. **Yahveh** blowing the waters of the flood in **Genesis 8:1** to make place for the new creation or dividing the **Sea of Reeds in Exodus 14–15** to let the Hebrews walk to the other side and start a new national existence – all of these may be read as the retellings of the initial cosmogonic conflict.

**"El Shaddai"** may also be understood as an allusion to the singularity of deity, **"El"**, as opposed to **"Elohim"** (plural), being sufficient or enough for the early patriarchs of Judaism. To this was later added the Mosaic conception of the **Tetragrammaton YHWH**, meaning a god who is sufficient in himself, that is, a self-determined eternal being qua being, for whom limited descriptive names cannot apply.

This may have been the meaning the Hebrew phrase **"ehyeh asher ehyeh"** (which translates as **"I will be that which I will be"**) and which is how God describes himself to Moses in **Exodus 3:13–15.** This phrase can be applied to the **Tetragrammaton YHWH**, which can be understood as an anagram for the three states of being: past, present and future, conjoined with the conjunctive Hebrew letter **vav.**

## Apotropaic usage of the name "Shaddai"

The name **"Shaddai"** often appears on the devices such as amulets or dedicatory plaques, which could be understood as apotropaic: **male circumcision, mezuzah and tefillin.** According to the biblical chronology it is **El Shaddai** who ordains the custom of circumcision in **Genesis 17:1** and, as is apparent in **Midrash Tanhuma Tzav 14** the *brit milah* itself is the inscription of the part of the name on the body:

**The Holy, blessed be he, has put his name on so they would enter the Garden of Eden.** It is **"Shaddai".** *shin* he put in the nose, *dalet* – on the hand, whereas *yod* on the {circumcised} . There is an angel {appointed} in the Garden of Eden who picks up every son of which is circumcised and brings him {there}. Therefore it hints at a demon (**Heb. *shed***), which brings him down to **Gehenna.**

Analogous is the case with mezuzah – a piece of parchment with two passages from the Book of Deuteronomy, curled up in a small encasement and affixed to a doorframe. *Shomer daltot Yisrael* ("the guardian of the doors of Israel") or *shomer dirot Yisrael* ("the guardian of the dwellings of Israel"). The name "Shadday" can also be found on tefillin – a set of two black leather boxes strapped to head and arm during the prayers.

## Biblical translations

The Septuagint (and other early translations) sometimes translate "Shaddai" as "(the) Almighty". It is often translated as "God", "my God," or "Lord". However, in the Greek of the Septuagint translation of Psalm 91.1, "Shaddai" is translated as "the God of heaven".

"Almighty" is the translation of "Shaddai" followed by most modern English translations of the Hebrew Scriptures, including the popular New International Version and Good News Bible.

"El Shaddai" as "Almighty God" is inaccurate. The N.J.B. leaves it untranslated as "Shaddai", and makes footnote suggestions that it should perhaps be understood as "God of the Mountain" from the Akkadian "shadu", or "God of the open wastes" from the Hebrew "sadeh" and the secondary meaning of the Akkadian word. The translation in the Concordant Old Testament is 'El Who-Suffices' (Genesis 17:1).

## Use by Bunyan

God is referred to as "Shaddai" throughout the 1682 Christian allegorical book, *The Holy War* by John Bunyan.

# Eschatology (End Times)

**Eschatology** is a part of theology concerned with the final events of history, or the ultimate destiny of humanity. This concept is commonly referred to as the **"end of the world"** or **"end times"**. The *Oxford English Dictionary* defines eschatology as **"the part of theology concerned with death, judgment, and the final destiny of the soul and of humankind"**.

In the context of mysticism, the term refers metaphorically to the end of ordinary reality and to reunion with the **Divine**. Most modern eschatology and **Apocalypticism,** both religious and secular, involve the violent disruption or destruction of the world; whereas Christian and Jewish eschatologies view the end times as the consummation or perfection of God's creation of the world, albeit with violent overtures, such as the **Great Tribulation**.

According to some ancient Hebrew worldviews, reality unfolds along a linear path **the world began with God and is ultimately headed toward God's final goal for creation, the world to come.** Groups claiming *imminent* eschatology are also referred to as **Doomsday cults**.

## Religion / Baha'i

**In Baha'i belief, creation has neither a beginning nor an end**. In **Baha'i** belief, human time is marked by a series of progressive revelations in which successive messengers or prophets come from God. The coming of each of these messengers is seen as the **Day of Judgment** to the adherents of the previous religion, who may choose to accept the new messenger and enter the **"heaven"** of belief, or denounce the new messenger and enter the **"hell"** of denial.

In this view, the terms **"heaven"** and **"hell"** are seen as symbolic terms for the person's spiritual progress and their nearness to or distance from God. In **Baha'i** belief, the coming of **Bahá'u'lláh,** the founder of the **Baha'i** Faith, signals the fulfilment of previous eschatological expectations of Islam, Christianity and other major religions.

## Christianity

Christian eschatology is the study concerned with the ultimate destiny of the individual soul and the entire created order, based primarily upon biblical texts within the Old and New Testament. Christian eschatology looks to study and discuss matters such as death and the afterlife, Heaven and Hell, the **Second Coming of Jesus**, the resurrection of the dead, the **Rapture, the Tribulation, Millennialism**, **the end of the world, the Last Judgment, and the New Heaven and New Earth in the world to come.**

In the Old Testament, apocalyptic eschatology can be found notably in **Isaiah 24–27, Isaiah 56–66, Joel, Zechariah 9–14** as well as closing chapters of **Daniel,** and **Ezekiel.** In the New

Testament, applicable passages include **Matthew 24, Mark 13, the parable of "The Sheep and the Goats"** and in the **Book of Rebelation**

The **Second Coming of Christ is the central event in Christian eschatology** within the broader context of the fullness of the **Kingdom of God. Most Christians believe that death and suffering will continue to exist until Christ's return**. The **Book of Rebelation is at the core of Christian eschatology**. The study of **Rebelation** is usually divided into four interpretative methodologies or hermeneutics. In the Futurist approach, **Rebelation** is treated mostly as unfulfilled prophecy taking place in some yet undetermined future. In the Preterist approach, **Rebelation** is chiefly interpreted as having prophetic fulfillment in the past, principally the events of the first century CE.

In the Historicist approach, **Rebelation** provides a broad view of history, and passages in **Rebelation** are identified with major historical people and events. This is view the Jewish scholars held, along with the early Christian church, and Reformers such as **Martin Luther, John Calvin, John Wesley, and Sir Isaac Newton,** and many others.

## *Hindu eschatology*

Contemporary Hindu eschatology is linked in the **Vaishnavite** tradition to the figure of **Kalki**, the tenth and last avatar of **Vishnu** before the age draws to a close who will reincarnate as **Shiva** and simultaneously dissolve and regenerate the universe. **Most Hindus believe that the current period is the Kali Yuga, the last of four *Yuga* that make up the current age.** Each period has seen successive degeneration in the moral order, to the point that in the **Kali Yuga** quarrel and hypocrisy are the norm.

**In Hinduism, time is cyclic, consisting of cycles or "kalpas". Each kalpa lasts 4.1 – 8.2 billion years, which is one full day and night for Brahma, who in turn will live for 311 trillion, 40 billion years.** Some Shaivites hold the view that **Shiva is incessantly destroying and creating the world.**

## *Islamic eschatology*

**Islamic eschatology is documented in the sayings of the Prophet Muhammad, regarding the Signs of the Day of Judgement.** The Prophet's sayings on the subject have been traditionally divided into **Major and Minor Signs**. He spoke about several **Minor Signs** of the approach of the **Day of Judgment, including:**

- **Abu Hurairah reported that Muhammad said: "If you survive for a time you would certainly see people who would have whips in their hands like the tail of an ox. They would get up in the morning under the wrath of God and they would go into the evening with the anger of God."**
- **Abu Hurairah narrated that Muhammad said, "When honesty is lost, then wait for the Day of Judgment." It was asked, "How will honesty be lost, O Messenger of God?"**

He said, "**When authority is given to those who do not deserve it, then wait for the Day of Judgment.**"

- '**Umar ibn al-Khattāb**, in a long narration, relating to the questions of the angel **Gabriel**, reported: "**Inform me when the Day of Judgment will be.**" He remarked: "**The one who is being asked knows no more than the inquirer.**" He said: "**Tell me about its indications.**" He said: "**That the slave-girl gives birth to her mistress and master, and that you would find barefooted, destitute shepherds of goats vying with one another in the construction of magnificent buildings.**"
- "**Before the Day of Judgment there will be great liars, so beware of them.**"
- "**When the Most Wicked member of a tribe becomes its ruler, and the most worthless member of a community becomes its leader, and a man is respected through fear of the evil he may do, and leadership is given to people who are unworthy of it, expect the Day of Judgment.**"

Regarding the **Major Signs**, a Companion of the Prophet narrated: "**Once we were sitting together and talking amongst ourselves when the Prophet appeared. He asked us what it was we were discussing. We said it was the Day of Judgment. He said: 'It will not be called until ten signs have appeared: Smoke, Dajjal (the Antichrist), the creature (that will wound the people), the rising of the sun in the West, the Second Coming of Jesus, the emergence of Gog and Magog, and three sinkings (or cavings in of the earth): one in the East, another in the West and a third in the Arabian Peninsula.'**"

## *Jewish eschatology*

Jewish eschatology is concerned with events that will happen in the end of days, according to the Hebrew Bible and Jewish thought. **This includes the ingathering of the exiled diaspora, the coming of the Jewish Messiah, afterlife, and the revival of the dead Tzadikim. In Judaism, the end times are usually called the "end of days"** (*aḥarit ha-Yamim,*), a phrase that appears several times in the **Tanakh**.

The idea of a messianic age has a prominent place in Jewish thought and is incorporated as part of the end of days. **Judaism addresses the end times in the Book of Daniel** and numerous other prophetic passages in the Hebrew Scriptures, and also in the **Talmud**, particularly **Tractate Avodah Zarah**.

## Zoroastrianism / *Frashokereti*

**Frashokereti is the Zoroastrian doctrine of a final renovation of the universe when evil will be destroyed, and everything else will then be in perfect unity with God (Ahura Mazda).**

The doctrinal premises are **(1) good will eventually prevail over evil; (2) creation was initially perfectly good, but was subsequently corrupted by evil; (3) the world will ultimately be restored to the perfection it had at the time of creation; (4) the "salvation for the individual** depended on the Sum of thoughts, words and deeds, and there could be no intervention, whether compassionate or capricious, by any divine being to alter this." Thus, each human bears the responsibility for the fate of his own soul, and simultaneously shares in the responsibility for the fate of the world.

## Futures studies and transhumanism
### Astronomy / *Future of Earth, Future of an expanding universe, and Ultimate fate of the universe*

Occasionally the term "**physical eschatology**" is applied to the long-term predictions of astrophysics. **The Sun will turn into a red giant in approximately 6 billion years**. Life on Earth will become impossible due to a rise in temperature long before the planet is actually swallowed up by the Sun. Even later, **the Sun will become** a **white dwarf.**

# Evil

**Evil**, in a colloquial sense, is the opposite of good, the word being an efficient substitute for the more precise but religion-associated word **"wickedness."** As defined in philosophy it is the name for the psychology and instinct of individuals which selfishly but often necessarily defends the personal boundary against deadly attacks and serious threats.

Often, **Evil** denotes profound immorality, but typically not without some basis in the understanding of the human condition, where strife and suffering (cf. Hinduism) are the true roots of **Evil**. In certain religious contexts, **Evil has been described as a supernatural force.** Definitions of **Evil** vary, as does the analysis of its motives. However, elements that are commonly associated with **Evil** involve unbalanced behavior involving **anger, revenge, fear, hatred, psychological trauma, expediency, selfishness, ignorance, or neglect.**

In cultures with an **Abrahamic religious** backdrop, **Evil** is usually perceived as the dualistic antagonistic binary opposite to good, (possibly following Persia's **Zoroastrian** influence) in which good should prevail and **Evil** should be defeated. In cultures with **Buddhist** spiritual influence, both good and **Evil** are perceived as part of an antagonistic duality that it must be overcome through achieving *Nirvana.*

## Chinese moral philosophy / *Confucian Ethics, Confucianism and* Taoist Ethics
As with **Buddhism, in Confucianism or Taoism** there is no direct analogue to the way *good and Evil* are opposed although reference to *demonic influences* common in **Chinese folk religion**. **Evil** would correspond to wrong behavior. Still less does it map into **Taoism**, in spite of the centrality of dualism in that system, but the opposite of the cardinal virtues of **Taoism**, compassion, moderation, and humility can be inferred to be the analogue of **Evil** in it.

## European philosophy / Spinoza
1. **By good**, I understand that which we certainly know is useful to us.
2. **By Evil**, on the contrary, I understand that which we certainly know hinders us from possessing anything that is good.

## Nietzsche
**Friedrich Nietzsche**, in a **rejection of the Judeo-Christian morality**, addresses this in two works *Beyond Good and Evil* and **Morals where** he essentially says that the natural, functional non-good has been socially transformed into the religious concept of **Evil** by the slave mentality of the weak and oppressed masses who resent their masters (the strong).

## Psychology / Carl Jung

**Carl Jung**, in his book *Answer to Job* and elsewhere, depicted **Evil** as the *dark side of God*. People tend to believe **Evil** is something external to them, because they project their shadow onto others. Jung interpreted the story of Jesus as an account of God facing his own shadow. The subject of God, and what **Jung** saw as the **dark side of God**, was a lifelong preoccupation. An emotional and theoretical struggle with the core nature of deity is evident in Jung's earliest fantasies and dreams, as well as in his complex relationships with his father (a traditional minister), his mother (who had a strong spiritual-mystical dimension), and the Christian church itself.

## Philip Zimbardo

In 2007, **Philip Zimbardo** suggested that people may act in **Evil** ways as a result of a collective identity. This hypothesis, based on his previous experience from the Stanford prison experiment, was published in the book *The Lucifer Effect: Understanding How Good People Turn Evil.*

## Baha'i Faith

The Baha'i asserts that **Evil** is non-existent and that it is a concept reflecting lack of good, just as cold is the state of no heat, darkness is the state of no light, forgetfulness the lacking of memory, ignorance the lacking of knowledge. All of these are states of lacking and have no real existence. Thus, **Evil does not exist and is relative to man**. `Abdu'l-Bahá, son of the founder of the religion, in Some Answered Questions states:

**"Nevertheless a doubt occurs to the mind—that is, scorpions and serpents are poisonous. Are they good or Evil, for they are existing beings? Yes, a scorpion is Evil in relation to man; a serpent is Evil in relation to man; but in relation to themselves they are not Evil, for their poison is their weapon, and by their sting they defend themselves."** Thus, **Evil** is more of an intellectual concept than a true reality. Since God is good, and upon creating creation he confirmed it by saying it is Good (**Genesis 1:31**) **Evil** cannot have a true reality.

## Ancient Egyptian Religion

**Evil** in the religion of **Ancient Egypt** is known as **Isfet**, "disorder/violence". It is the opposite of Maat, **"order"**, and embodied by the serpent god Apep, who routinely attempts to kill the sun god **Ra** and is stopped by nearly every other deity. **Isfet** is not a primordial force, but the consequence of free will and an individual's struggle against the non-existence embodied by **Apep**, as evidenced by the fact that it was born from Ra's umbilical cord instead of being recorded in the religion's creation myths.

## Buddhism / *Buddhist Ethics*

The primal duality in Buddhism is **between suffering and enlightenment**, so the good vs. **Evil** splitting has no direct analogue in it. One may infer however from the general teachings of the Buddha that the catalogued causes of suffering are what correspond in this belief system to '**Evil**. Practically this can refer to 1) the **three selfish emotions—desire, hate and delusion**; and 2) to their expression in physical and verbal actions. **See** *ten unvirtuous actions in Buddhism*. Specifically, *Evil* means whatever harms or obstructs the causes for happiness in this life, a better rebirth, liberation from samsara, and the true and complete enlightenment of a **Buddha (samyaksambodhi)**.

"What is **Evil**? Killing is **Evil**, lying is **Evil**, slandering is **Evil**, abuse is **Evil**, and gossip is **Evil**: envy is **Evil**, hatred is **Evil**, to cling to false doctrine is **Evil**; all these things are **Evil**. And what is the root of **Evil**? **Desire is the root of Evil**, illusion is the root of **Evil**." **Gautama Siddhartha, the founder of Buddhism, 563–483 BC.**

## Hinduism

In Hinduism, the concept of **Dharma** or righteousness clearly divides the world into good and **Evil**, and clearly explains that wars have to be waged sometimes to establish and protect Dharma, this war is called **Dharmayuddha**. This division of good and **Evil** is of major importance in both the Hindu epics of **Ramayana and Mahabharata**. However, the main emphasis in Hinduism is on bad action, rather than bad people. The Hindu holy text, the **Bhagavad Gita**, speaks of the balance of good and **Evil**. When this balance goes off, divine incarnations come to help to restore this balance.

## Sikhism

In adherence to the core principle of **spiritual evolution**, the Sikh idea of **Evil** changes depending on one's position on the path to liberation. At the beginning stages of spiritual growth, good and **Evil** may seem neatly separated. However, once one's spirit evolves to the point where it sees most clearly, the idea of **Evil** vanishes and the truth is revealed. In his writings **Guru Arjan** explains that, because God is the source of all things, what we believe to be **Evil** must too come from God. And **because God is ultimately a source of absolute good, nothing truly Evil can originate from God.**

Nevertheless, **Sikhism**, like many other religions, does incorporate a list of **"vices"** from which suffering, corruption, and abject negativity arise. These are known as the **Five Thieves**, called such due to their propensity to cloud the mind and lead one astray from the prosecution of righteous action. **These are:**
- **Moh**, or Attachment
- **Lobh**, or Greed
- **Karodh**, or Wrath

- **Kaam**, or Lust
- **Ahankar**, or Egotism

One who gives in to the temptations of the **Five Thieves** is known as **"Manmukh",** or someone who lives selfishly and without virtue. Inversely, the "**Gurmukh**, who thrive in their reverence toward divine knowledge, rise above vice via the practice of the high virtues of **Sikhism**. These are:
- **Sewa**, or selfless service to others.
- **Nam Simran**, or meditation upon the divine name.

## *Islamic views on sin*

**There is no concept of absolute Evil in Islam.** Within Islam, it is considered essential to believe that **all comes from God**, whether it is perceived as good or bad by individuals; and things that are perceived as *Evil or bad* are either natural events (natural disasters or illnesses) or caused by humanity's free will. Much more **the behavior of beings with free will,** then they disobey God's orders, harming others or putting themselves over **Allah** or others, is considered to be **Evil**.

A typical understanding of **Evil** is reflected by **Al-Ash`ari** founder of **Asharism**. Since God is omnipotent and nothing can exist outside of God's power, God's will determine, whether or not something is **Evil**. According to the **Ahmadiyya** understanding of Islam, **Evil** does not have a positive existence in itself and is merely the lack of good, just as darkness is the result of lack of light.

## Judaism / *Satan in Judaism*

**In Judaism, Evil is not real, it is per se not part of God's creation, but comes into existence through man's bad actions.** Human beings are responsible for their choices. However, Jews and non-Jews have the **free will** to choose good (life in olam haba) or bad (**death in heaven**). (**Deuteronomy 28:20**) Judaism stresses obedience to **God's 613 commandments** of the Written **Torah** and the collective body of Jewish religious laws expounded in the **Oral Torah and Shulkhan Arukh**. In Judaism, there is no prejudice in one's becoming good or **Evil** at the time of birth, since full responsibility comes with **Bar and Bat Mitzvah, when Jewish boys become 13, and girls become 12 years old.**

## *DEvil in Christianity*

**Evil according to a Christian worldview is any action, thought, or attitude that is contrary to the character or will of God.** There is no moral action given in the Bible that is contrary to God's character or God's will. Therefore, **Evil** in a Christian worldview is contrasted by and in conflict with God's character or God's will. **This Evil shows itself through deviation from the character or will of God.**

In the **Old Testament**, **Evil** is understood to be an opposition to God as well as something unsuitable or inferior such as the leader of the fallen angels **Satan.** The Dominican theologian, **Thomas Aquinas,** who in *Summa Theologica* defines **Evil** as the absence or privation of good. In Mormonism, mortal life is viewed as a test of faith, where one's choices are central to the Plan of Salvation. **Evil** is that which keeps one from discovering the nature of God. It is believed that one must choose not to be **Evil** to return to God.

**Christian Science** believes that **Evil** arises from a misunderstanding of the goodness of nature. Christian Scientists argue that even the most *Evil* person does not pursue **Evil** for its own sake, but from the mistaken viewpoint that he or she will achieve some kind of good thereby.

## Zoroastrianism

In the originally Persian religion of **Zoroastrianism, the world is a battleground between the god Ahura Mazda (also called Ormazd) and the malignant spirit Angra Mainyu (also called Ahriman).** The final resolution of the struggle between good and **Evil** was supposed to occur on a day of Judgement, in which all beings that have lived will be led across a bridge of fire, and those who are **Evil** will be cast down forever.

## Specifics

The **Nazis,** during World War II, considered genocide to be acceptable, as did the **Hutu Interahamwe** in the Rwandan genocide. Universalists consider **Evil** independent of culture, and wholly related to acts or intents. Thus, while the ideological leaders of **Nazism** and the Hutu Interahamwe accepted (and considered it moral) to commit genocide, the belief in genocide as *fundamentally* or *universally* **Evil** holds that those who instigated this genocide are actually **Evil**.

**Hitler** considered it a moral duty to destroy Jews because he saw them as the root of all of Germany's ills and the violence associated with communism. **Osama bin Laden** found it moral to kill all Christians and Jews because he saw Islam as under attack by Western and US influence, accusing the US and Israel of forming a **Crusader-Zionist** alliance to destroy Islam. He therefore considered non-Muslims and **Shiite Muslims Evil** people intent on destroying Islamic purity and therefore heretic.

## Philosophical questions / *Ethics*

Views on the nature of **Evil** belong to the branch of philosophy known as ethics - which in modern philosophy is subsumed into three major areas of study:
1. **Meta-ethics**, that seeks to understand the nature of ethical properties, statements, attitudes, and judgments.
2. **Normative ethics**, investigates the set of questions that arise when considering how one ought to act, morally speaking.

3.  **Applied ethics**, concerned with the analysis of particular moral issues in private and public life.

## Necessary Evil

**Martin Luther** believed that occasional minor **Evil** could have a positive effect. Martin Luther argued that there are cases where a little **Evil** is a positive good. He wrote, **"Seek out the society of your boon companions, drink, play, talk bawdy, and amuse yourself. One must sometimes commit a sin out of hate and contempt for the DEvil, so as not to give him the chance to make one scrupulous over mere nothings ..."** This approach to politics was put forth by **Niccolò Machiavelli, a 16th-century Florentine writer who advised politicians "... it is far safer to be feared than loved."**

# Exilarchs (Babylonian Judaism)

**Exilarch** (Hebrew: *Rosh Galut*, "**head of the exile**", "**leader of the captives**") refers to the leaders of the Diaspora Jewish community In Babylon following the deportation of **King Jeconiah and his court into Babylonian exile after the first fall of Jerusalem in 597 BCE** and augmented after the further deportations following the **destruction of the kingdom of Judah in 587 BCE**. The people in exile were called *golah* (**Jeremiah 28:6**) or *galut* (Jeremiah 29:22).

The first historical documents referring to it date from the time when Babylon was part of the **Parthian Empire**. The office lasted to the middle of the 6$^{th}$ century, under different regimes (the Arsacids and Sassanids). **Exilarch**s continued to be appointed through the 11$^{th}$ century. Under Arab rule, **Muslims treated the Exilarch with great pomp and circumstance**.

## Development and organization
The history of the **Exilarch**ate falls naturally into two periods, separated by the beginning of the Arabic rule in Babylonia. Nothing is known about the office before the 2$^{nd}$ century.

The *golah,* the Jews living in compact masses in various parts of **Babylon**, tended gradually to unite and create an organization, and that this tendency, together with the high regard in which the descendants of the **house of David** living in Babylon were held, brought it about that a member of this house was recognized as **"head of the *golah*"** and hence became an established political institution, first of the **Arsacid** and then of the **Sassanid** empire.

## Biblical and rabbinic
**Exilarch**s listed in the **Second Book of Kings**, the **Books of Chronicles** and in the **Seder Olam Zutta,** some possibly legendary, are:
- Jeconiah or Jehoiachin, according to the chronology of the **Exilarch**ate, the last of the Davidic kings of Judah. After a reign of only three months and ten days, Jeconiah's reign came to an end by Babylonian intervention, and Jeconiah and the elite of Judah were taken into Babylonian exile in 597 BCE as part of the first deportation, Jeconiah continued to be regarded as the legitimate king of Judah by the Jews in Babylon. His family line was followed by subsequent **Exilarch**s.
- Cuneiform records dated to 592 BCE mention Jeconiah and his five sons as recipients of food rations in Babylon. In any event, all the sons of **Jehoiachin's** successor on the throne of Judah, Zedekiah, were killed by Nebuchadnezzar II after the fall of Jerusalem and destruction of the Temple in 586 BCE. (**2 Kings 25:7**)
- Shealtiel, son of Jehoiachin (**1 Chronicles 3:17**)
- Zerubbabel, son of Pedaiah, who was a son of Jehoiachin (**1 Chronicles 3:17-19**) ('attr(href)'), **Haggai 1:1** ('attr(href)') and is mentioned as a governor of the Persian Yehud Province. According to the *Seder Olam Zutta*, Zerubbabel was the son of Shealtiel.
- Meshullam, son of Zerubbabel (**1 Chronicles 3:19**)
- Hananiah, son of Zerubbabel (**1 Chronicles 3:19**)
- Berechiah, son of Zerubbabel (**1 Chronicles 3:19-20**)
- Hasadiah, son of Hananiah (**1 Chronicles 3:21**)
- Jesaiah, son of Hananiah (**1 Chronicles 3:21**)

- Obadiah, son of Hananiah (**1 Chronicles 3:21**)
- Shemaiah, son of Shecaniah, who was a son of Hananiah (**1 Chronicles 3:21-22**)
- Shechaniah, son of Hananiah (**1 Chronicles 3:21**). According to the *Seder Olam Zutta*, Shechaniah was the son of Shemaiah, and lived at the time of the destruction of the Second Temple. However, this is unlikely, since the Second temple wasn't destroyed until over 500 years after the days of Zerubbabel.
- Hezekiah, son of Nereiah, who was the son of Shemaiah (**1 Chronicles 3:22-23**)
- Akkub, son of Elioenai, who was a son of Heriah, who was a son of Shemaiah (**1 Chronicles 3:22-24**)

**David ben Zakkai** was the last **Exilarch** to play an important part I history. His son Judah survived him only by seven months. At the time of Judah's death, he left a twelve-year-old son, whose name is unknown. The only later **Exilarch** whose name is recorded is Hezekiah, an **Exilarch** who in 1038 also became *gaon* of Pumbedita, but was imprisoned and tortured to death in 1040. He was the last **Exilarch** and the last *gaon.*

## Karaite
**Karaite princes beginning in the 8th century, after the time of David ben Judah:**
- Anan ben David, son of David ben Judah (**ca 715 – ca 795 or 811?**), considered to be a major founder of the Karaite movement
- Saul ben Anan, son of Anan ben David, 8th century
- Josiah, son of Anan ben David
- Jehoshaphat ben Saul, son of Saul ben Anan, early 9th century
- Boaz ben Jehoshaphat, son of Jehoshaphat ben Saul, mid-9th century
- David ben Boaz, son of Boaz ben Jehoshaphat, 10th century
- Solomon ben David, son of David ben Boaz, late 10th and early 11th centuries
- Hezekiah ben Solomon, son of Solomon ben David, 11th century
- Hasdai ben Hezekiah, son of Hezekiah ben Solomon, 11th and 12th centuries
- Solomon ben Hasdai, son of Hasdai ben Hezekiah. During his reign many Karaite communities were destroyed by the Seljuks.

## Traced to Jehoiachin
Tradition has it that the first **Exilarch** was **Jehoiachin, a king of Judah carried off to captivity in Babylonia in 597 BCE.** A chronicle from about the year 800 – the **Midrashic** *Seder 'Olam Zuta* – fills up the gaps in the early history of the **Exilarch**. The captive king's advancement at Evil-Merodach's court – with which the narrative of the **Second Book of Kings** closes (**2 Kings 25:27** was apparently regarded by the author of the *Seder 'Olam Zuta* as the origin of the **Exilarch**ate. A list including generations of the descendants of the king is given in **1 Chronicles 3:17.**

# Exodus

**The Exodus**, (from Greek *exodos*, **"going out"**) is the founding myth of Israel; its message is that the Israelites were delivered from slavery by **Yahweh** and therefore belong to him through the Mosaic covenant. It tells of the enslavement of the Israelites in Egypt following the **death of Joseph**, their departure under the leadership of **Moses**, the revelations of Sinai, and their wanderings in the wilderness up to the borders of **Canaan**. The exodus story is told in the books of **Exodus, Leviticus, Numbers and Deuteronomy**, and their overall intent was to demonstrate God's actions in history, to recall Israel's bondage and salvation, and to demonstrate the fulfillment of Israel's covenant.

The archeological evidence does not support the story told in the **Book of Exodus** and most archaeologists have therefore abandoned the investigation of **Moses** and the **Exodus** as **"a fruitless pursuit"**. The traditions behind it are older and can be traced in the writings of the 8th century BCE prophets. **"Presumably an original Exodus story lies hidden somewhere inside all the later revisions and alterations, but centuries of transmission have long obscured its presence, and its substance, accuracy and dates are now difficult to determine.** It is recounted daily in Jewish prayers and celebrated in the festival of **Pesach.**

## Origins of the Exodus story
Numbers and Deuteronomy is the best-known account of the **Exodus**, there are over 150 references throughout the Bible. The earliest mentions are in the **prophets Amos** (possibly) and **Hosea** (certainly), both active in 8th century BCE Israel.

## Cultural significance
The exodus is remembered daily in Jewish prayers and celebrated each year at the feast of **Passover**. The Hebrew name for this festival, *Pesach*, refers to God's instruction to the Israelites to prepare **unleavened bread as they would be leaving Egypt in haste, and to mark their doors with the blood of slaughtered sheep so that the "Angel" or "the destroyer" tasked with killing the f first-born of Egypt would "pass over" them**. Jewish tradition has preserved national and personal reminders of this pivotal narrative in daily life.

## Historicity: Numbers and logistics
According to **Exodus 12:37-38**, the Israelites numbered **"about six hundred thousand men on foot, besides women and children,"** plus many non-Israelites and livestock. **Numbers 1:46 gives a more precise total of 603,550 men aged 20 and up. The 600,000, plus wives, children, the elderly, and the "mixed multitude"** of non-Israelites would have numbered some 2 million people, compared with an entire Egyptian population in 1250 BCE of around 3 to 3.5 million. No evidence has been found that indicates Egypt ever suffered such a demographic and economic catastrophe or that the Sinai desert ever hosted (or could have hosted) these millions of people and their herds.

## Anachronisms
Pharaoh's fear that the Israelites might ally themselves with foreign invaders seems unlikely in the context of the late 2nd millennium, when Canaan was part of an Egyptian empire and Egypt faced

no enemies in that direction, but does make sense in a 1<sup>st</sup> millennium context, when Egypt was considerably weaker and faced invasion first from the **Persians** and later from **Seleucid** Syria.

## Chronology

The number seven was sacred to God in Judaism, and so the Israelites arrive at Sinai, where they will meet God, at the beginning of the seventh week after their departure from Egypt, while the erection of the **Tabernacle**, God's dwelling-place among his people, occurs in the year **2666** after God creates the world, two-thirds of the way through a four-thousand-year era which culminates in or around the re-dedication of the **Second Temple in 164 BCE.**

## Route

The crossing of the **Red Sea** has been variously placed at the Pelusic branch of the Nile, anywhere along the network of **Bitter Lakes** and smaller canals that formed a barrier toward eastward escape, the **Gulf of Suez** (SSE of Succoth) and the **Gulf of Aqaba** (S. of Ezion-Geber), or even on a lagoon on the Mediterranean coast. The biblical Mt. Sinai is identified in Christian tradition with **Jebel Musa** in the south of the **Sinai Peninsula**, but this association dates only from the 3<sup>rd</sup> century CE and **no evidence of the Exodus has been found there.**

## Date

Attempts to date the **Exodus** to a specific century have been inconclusive. **1 Kings 6:1** says that the **Exodus occurred 480 years before the construction of Solomon's Temple**; this would imply an **Exodus** c. 1446 BCE, during **Egypt's Eighteenth Dynasty**. However, it is widely recognized that the number in **1 Kings** is symbolic, representing twelve generations of forty years each. There are also major archaeological obstacles in dating the **Exodus** to the **Eighteenth Dynasty.** Canaan at the time was a part of the Egyptian empire, so that the Israelites would in effect be escaping from Egypt to Egypt.

**William F. Albright**, the leading biblical archaeologist of the mid-20<sup>th</sup> century, proposed an alternative 13<sup>th</sup> century date of around **1250-1200 BCE** for the **Exodus** event and the entry into Canaan described in the **Book of Joshua.** Albright's theory enjoyed popularity at the time. **"Joshua"** cities, including **Hazor, Lachish, Megiddo** and others, have destruction and transition layers around 1250-1145 BCE, others, including Jericho, have none or were uninhabited during this period. The forty years of wilderness wanderings are also full of inconsistencies and anachronisms. A **"powerful collective memory of the Egyptian occupation of Canaan and the enslavement of its population"** during the 13<sup>th</sup> and 12<sup>th</sup> centuries.

## Extra-biblical accounts

The earliest non-Biblical account of the **Exodus** is in the writings of the Greek author **Hecataeus** of **Abdera**, who arrived in Egypt c. 320 BCE. The most famous is by the Egyptian historian Manetho (3<sup>rd</sup> century BCE), known from two quotations by the 1<sup>st</sup> century CE Jewish historian Josephus.

# Expulsions of Jews

In Jewish history, Jews have experienced numerous mass expulsions or ostracism by various local authorities and have sought refuge in other countries. The Land of Israel was always regarded by Jews as the Jewish homeland, though throughout most of Jewish history they were barred from the land. After its establishment in 1948, the State of Israel adopted the **1950 Law of Return** restoring Israel as the Jewish homeland and making it the place of refuge for **Jewish refugees** at the time and into the future.

This law was intended to encourage Jews to return to their homeland in Israel. After 1970 the **Jackson–Vanik amendment** accorded those Jewish emigrants from the Soviet bloc countries who desired to enter the United States refugee status combined with federal assistance in the initial stages of their resettlement.

## 722 BCE

The Assyrians led by **Shalmaneser** conquered the (Northern) Kingdom of Israel and sent the Israelites into captivity at **Khorasan**. Ten of **twelve Tribes of Israel** are considered lost; but these tribes are not considered Jewish, rather than Samaritan. These tribes have been living since then near the city of Nablus in what is today the West Bank.

## 597 BCE

The Babylonian captivity. In 537 BCE the Persians, who conquered Babylon two years earlier, allowed Jews to return and rebuild Jerusalem and the Second Temple.

## 70

The defeat of the **Great Jewish Revolt**. Masses of Jews were sold to slavery across the Roman Empire, many fled. The Second Temple was destroyed.

## 119

Large Jewish communities of **Cyrus**, Cyrene and Alexandria become extinct after the Jewish defeat in Kitos War against Rome. This event caused a major demographic shift in the Levant and North Africa. According to Eusebius of Caesarea the outbreak of violence left Libya depopulated to such an extent that a few years later new colonies had to be established there by the emperor Hadrian just to maintain the viability of continued settlement.

## 135

The Romans defeated **Bar Kokhba's revolt.** Emperor Hadrian expelled hundreds of thousands Jews from Judea, wiped the name off the maps, replaced it with Syria Palaestina, forbade Jews to set foot in Jerusalem.

## 629

The entire Jewish population of Galilee is massacred or expelled, following the Jewish rebellion against Byzantium.

## 7th century

Muhammad expelled Jewish tribes **Banu Qaynuqa and Banu Nadir** from Medina, The Banu Qurayza tribe was slaughtered and the Jewish settlement of Khaybar was ransacked. All three tribes previously had a peace treaty with Muhammad, but they broke the treaty and sided with the opposition.

## 1095 – mid-13th century

The waves of Crusades destroyed hundreds of Jewish communities in Europe and in the Middle East, including Jerusalem.

## Mid-12th century

The invasion of Almohads brought to end the Golden age of Jewish culture in Spain. Among other refugees was Maimonides, who fled to Morocco, then Egypt, then Eretz Israel.

## 1276

Jews expelled from Upper Bavaria.
Expulsions of Jews in Europe from 1100 to 1600

## 12th–14th centuries

France. The practice of expelling the Jews accompanied by confiscation of their property, followed by temporary readmissions for ransom, was used to enrich the crown: expulsions from Paris by **Philip Augustus in 1182**, from France by Louis IX in 1254, by Charles IV in 1322, by Charles V in 1359, by Charles VI in 1394.

## 13th century

The influential philosopher and logician **Ramon Llull (1232-1315)** called for expulsion of all Jews who would refuse conversion to Christianity. Some scholars regard Llull's as the first comprehensive articulation, in the Christian West, of an expulsionist policy regarding Jews.

## 1288

Naples issues first expulsion of Jews in Southern Italy.

## 1290

King Edward I of England issues the Edict of Expulsion for all Jews from England. The policy was reversed after 365 years in 1655 by Oliver Cromwell.

## 1293

Destruction of most of the Jewish communities in the Kingdom of Naples.

## 1392

Jews expelled from Bern, Switzerland. Although between 1408 and 1427 Jews were again residing in the city, the only Jews to appear in Bern subsequently were transients, chiefly physicians and cattle dealers.

## 1442

Jews again expelled from Upper Bavaria.

## 1478

Jews expelled from Passau.

## 1491

Jews of Ravenna expelled, synagogues destroyed.

## 1492

Ferdinand II and Isabella I issued the **Alhambra decree**, General Edict on the Expulsion of the Jews from Spain (approx. 200,000), from Sicily (1493, approx. 37,000), from Portugal (1496) from Calabria Italy1554. It is important to note that this event happened on **Tisha B'Av**, as with many other events in Jewish history.

## 1495

Charles VIII of France occupies Kingdom of Naples, bringing new persecution against the Jews, many of whom went there as refugees from Spain. See 1510.

## 1496

Jews expelled from Portugal

## 1499

Jews expelled from Nuremberg.

## 1510

Jews expelled from Naples.

## 1519

Jews expelled from Regensburg.

## 1547
Jews expelled from Naples.

## 1551
All remaining Jews expelled from the duchy of Bavaria. Jewish settlement in Bavaria ceased until toward the end of the 17th century, when a small community was founded in Sulzbach by refugees from Vienna.

## 1569
Pope Pius V expels the Jews from the Papal States, with the exception of Ancona and Rome.

## 1593
**Pope Clement VIII** expels the Jews living in all the Papal States, except Rome, Avignon and Ancona. Jews are invited to settle in Leghorn, the main port of Tuscany, where they are granted full religious liberty and civil rights, by the Medici family, who want to develop the region into a center of commerce.

## 1597
Nine hundred Jews expelled from Milan.

## 1654
The fall of the Dutch colony of Recife in Brazil to the Portuguese prompted the first group of Jews to flee to North America.

## 1701–1714
War of the Spanish Succession. After the war, Jews of Austrian origin were expelled from Bavaria, but some were able to acquire the right to reside in Munich.

## 1744–1790s
The reforms of Frederick II, Joseph II and Maria Theresa sent masses of impoverished German and Austrian Jews east.

## 1933–1957
**First Batch of Refugee children arrive in England from Germany. Buchenwald survivors arrive in Haifa.**

The German **Nazi** persecution started with the **Nazi** boycott of Jewish businesses in 1933, reached a first climax during *Kristallnacht* in 1938 and culminated in the Holocaust of European Jewry. The British Mandate of Palestine prohibited Jewish emigration to **Mandatory Palestine**. The

**1938 Evian Conference**, the 1943 Bermuda Conference and other attempts failed to resolve the problem of Jewish refugees, a fact widely used in **Nazi** propaganda (see also **MS *St. Louis***). Many German and Austrian Jewish refugees from **Nazi**sm immigrated to Britain where many were well treated, but many weren't and many fought for Britain in the **Second World War**. After WW-II eastern European **Holocaust** survivors migrated to the allied controlled part of Europe as the Jewish society to which most of them belonged did not exist anymore. Often they were lone survivors consumed by the often futile search for other family and friends, and often unwelcome in the towns from which they came. They were known as displaced persons (also known as **Sh'erit ha-Pletah**) and placed in displaced persons camps, most of which were by 1951 closed. **The last camp Föhrenwald was closed in 1957.**

## 1947–1972

Iraqi Jews displaced 1951. The Exodus bringing in refugees. In the course of the operation "**Magic Carpet**" (1949–1950), the entire community of Yemenite Jews (called Teimanim, about 49,000) immigrated to Israel. The Jewish exodus from Arab and Muslim countries, in which the combined population of Jewish communities of the Middle East and North Africa (excluding Israel) was reduced from about 900,000 in 1948 to less than 8,000 today, and approximately 600,000 of whom became citizens of Israel.

The history of the exodus is politicized, given its proposed relevance to a final settlement Israeli-Palestinian peace negotiations. When presenting the history, those who view the Jewish exodus as equivalent to the 1948 Palestinian exodus, such as the Israeli government and **NGOs** such as **JJAC** and **JIMENA**, emphasize "**push factors**", such as cases of anti-Jewish violence and forced expulsions,[5] and refer to those affected as **"refugees"**.

Those who argue that the exodus does not equate to the Palestinian exodus emphasize "**pull factors**", such as the actions of local Jewish Agency for Israel officials aiming to fulfil the **One Million Plan**, highlight good relations between the Jewish communities and their country's governments, emphasize the impact of other push factors such as the decolonization in the Maghreb and the Suez War and **Lavon Affair in Egypt**, and argue that many or all of those who left were not refugees.

Then **UNHCR** announced in February 1957 and in July 1967, that these Jews who had fled from Arab countries "may be considered prima facie within the mandate of this office," so according them in international law, as bona fide refugees.

## 1947

Egypt passed the **Companies' Law**. This law required that no less than 75% of employees of companies in Egypt must be Egyptian citizens. This law strongly affected Jews, as only about 20%

of all Jews in Egypt were Egyptian citizens. The rest, although in many cases born in Egypt and living there for generations, did not hold Egyptian citizenship.

## 1948

State of Israel established. Antisemitism in Egypt strongly intensified. On May 15, 1948, emergency law was declared, and a royal decree forbade Egyptian citizens to leave the country without a special permit. This was applied to Jews. Hundreds of Jews were arrested and many had their property confiscated. In June through August 1948, bombs were planted in Jewish neighborhoods and Jewish businesses looted. About 250 Jews were killed or wounded by the bombs. **Roughly 14,000 Jews left Egypt between 1948 and 1950**.

## 1949

Jordan occupies and then annexes the **West Bank** – largely allotted by the **1947 UN Partition of Palestine** to an Arab state, proposal rejected by the Arab leadership – and conducts large scale discrimination and persecution of all non-Muslim residents – Jewish, Christian (of many denominations), Druze, Circassian, etc. – and forces Arabization of all public activity, including schools and public administration.

## 1954

**Gamal Abdel Nasser** seizes power in Egypt. **Nasser** immediately arrested many Jews who were tried on various charges, mainly for Zionist and communist activities. Jews were forced to donate large sums of money to the military. Strict supervision of Jewish enterprises was introduced; some were confiscated and others forcibly sold to the government.

## 1956

**Suez Crisis. Roughly 3,000 Egyptian Jews** were interned without charge in four detention camps. The government ordered thousands of Jews to leave the country within a few days, and they were not allowed to sell their property, nor to take any capital with them. The deportees were made to sign statements agreeing not to return to Egypt and transferring their property to the administration of the government. The **International Red Cross** helped about 8,000 stateless Jews to leave the country, taking most of them to Italy and Greece. Most of the Jews of Port Said (about 100) were smuggled to Israel by Israel Agents. The system of deportation continued into 1957. Other Jews left voluntarily, after their livelihoods had been taken from them, until only 8,561 were registered in the 1957 census. The Jewish exodus continued until there were about 3,000 Jews left as of in 1967.

## 1967

**Six Day War.** Hundreds of Egyptian Jews arrested, suffering beatings, torture, and abuse. Some were released following intervention by foreign states, especially Spain, and were permitted to leave the country. Libyan Jews, who numbered approximately 7,000, were subjected to pogroms in which 18 were killed, prompting a mass exodus that left fewer than 100 Jews in Libya.

## 1970

Less than 1,000 Jews still lived in Egypt in 1970. They were given permission to leave but without their possessions. As of 1971, only 400 Jews remained in Egypt. As of 2013, only a few dozen Jews remain in Egypt.[14]

## 1960s–1989

Due to the 1968 Polish political crisis thousands of Jews were forced by the communist authorities to leave Poland.

## 1962

Jews flee Algeria as result of OAS violence. The community feared that the proclamation of independence would precipitate a Muslim outburst. By the end of July 1962, 70,000 Jews had left for France and another 5,000 for Israel. It is estimated that some 80% of Algerian Jews settled in France.

## 1965

Situation of Jews in Algeria rapidly deteriorates. By 1969, fewer than 1,000 Jews remain. By the 1990s, the numbers had dwindled to approximately 70.

## 1970s–1990s

State-sponsored persecution in the Soviet Union prompted hundreds of thousands of Soviet Jews to flee; most went to Israel or came to the United States on refugee status.

# False prophets

In religion, a **false prophet** is one who falsely claims the gift of prophecy or divine inspiration, or who uses that gift for evil ends. Often, someone who is considered a **"true prophet"** by some people is simultaneously considered a **"false prophet"** by others, even within the same religion as the **"prophet"** in question.

## Christianity

Throughout the New Testament, there are warnings of both false prophets and **false Messiahs**, and believers are adjured to be vigilant. The following verses **(Matthew 7:15–23)** are from the **Sermon on the Mount:**

**"Watch out for false prophets. They come to you in sheep's clothing, but inwardly they are ferocious wolves. By their fruit you will recognize them. Do people pick grapes from thorn bushes, or figs from thistles? Likewise every good tree bears good fruit, but a bad tree bears bad fruit. A good tree cannot bear bad fruit, and a bad tree cannot bear good fruit. Every tree that does not bear good fruit is cut down and thrown into the fire. Thus, by their fruit you will recognize them."**

In the **Gospel of Luke**, **Jesus** brought out an ethical application for his disciples using the analogy of false prophets in the Old Testament: **"Woe to you when all men speak well of you, for that is how their fathers treated the false prophets" (Luke NIV).**

In the **Acts of the Apostles,** Paul and Barnabas encountered a false prophet named **Elymas Bar-Jesus** on the island of Cyprus. **"They traveled through the whole island until they came to Paphos. There they met a Jewish sorcerer and false prophet named Bar-Jesus, who was an attendant of the proconsul, Sergius Paulus. The proconsul, an intelligent man, sent for Barnabas and Saul because he wanted to hear the word of God.** Then **Saul**, who was also called **Paul**, filled with the **Holy Spirit**, looked straight at Elymas and said, **'You are a child of the devil and an enemy of everything that is right! You are full of all kinds of deceit and trickery. Will you never stop perverting the right ways of the Lord? Now the hand of the Lord is against you. You are going to be blind, and for a time you will be unable to see the light of the sun.'**

**The Second Epistle of Peter** makes a comparison between false teachers and false prophets and how the former will bring in false teachings, just like the false prophets of old:

**"But there were also false prophets among the people, just as there will be false teachers among you. They will secretly introduce destructive heresies, even denying the sovereign Lord who bought them – bringing swift destruction on themselves. Many will follow their**

shameful ways and will bring the way of truth into disrepute. In their greed these teachers will exploit you with stories they have made up. Their condemnation has long been hanging over them, and their destruction has not been sleeping" (2 Peter NIV).

The **First Epistle of John** warns those of the Christian faith to test every spirit because of these false prophets: **"Dear friends, do not believe every spirit, but test the spirits to see whether they are from God, because many false prophets have gone out into the world. This is how you can recognize the Spirit of God: Every spirit that acknowledges that Jesus Christ has come in the flesh is from God, 3 but every spirit that does not acknowledge Jesus, that spirit is not from God. This is the spirit of the antichrist, which you have heard is coming and even now is already in the world"** (1 John NIV).

## The False Prophet of Revelation
One well-known **New Testament** false prophet is the false prophet mentioned in the **Book of Revelation**. The Apocalypse's false prophet is the **agent of the Beast**, the **Antichrist**, and he is ultimately cast with the **Beast** into the lake of "**fire and brimstone**" (Revelation KJV).

## *Prophets of Islam and List of Mahdi claimants*
**The Quran portrays Muhammad as the Seal of the Prophets**, which is understood by mainstream **Sunni** and **Shia** Muslims to mean that anyone who claims to be a new prophet after him is a false prophet. All mainstream Muslim scholars' perspectives from both Sunni and Shia sects do not see the second coming of the Messiah as the coming of a new prophet, as the **Islamic Messiah Jesus** had already been an existing prophet, and will rule by the Qur'an and **Sunnah of Muhammad**, bringing no new revelation or prophecy.

## Thawban ibn Kaidad narrated that Muhammad said;
"There will be 30 Dajjal among my Ummah. Each one will claim that he is a prophet; but I am the last of the Prophets (Seal of the Prophets), and there will be no Prophet after me."
— *Related by Ahmad ibn Hanbal as a sound hadith.*

**Abu Hurairah narrated that Muhammad said;**
"The Hour will not be established until two big groups fight each other whereupon there will be a great number of casualties on both sides and they will be following one and the same religious doctrine, until about 30 Dajjal appear, and each of them will claim that he is Allah's Apostle..."
— *Sahih al-Bukhari, Volume 9, Book 88: Afflictions and the End of the World, Hadith Number 237.*

**Muhammad also stated that the last of these Dajjal would be the False Messiah, al-Masih ad-Dajjal (Antichrist):**

"Verily by Allah, the Last Hour will not come until 30 Dajjal will appear and the final one will be the One-eyed False Messiah."
— *Related by Imam Ahmed and Imam Tabarani as a sound hadith.*

Anas ibn Malik narrated that Muhammad said;
"There is never a prophet who has not warned the Ummah of that one-eyed liar; behold he is one-eyed and your Lord is not one-eyed. Dajjal is blind of one eye on his forehead are the letters k. f. r. (Kafir) between the eyes of the Dajjal which every Muslim would be able to read."
— *Sahih Muslim, Book 41: The Book Pertaining to the Turmoil and Portents of the Last Hour, Chapter 7: The Turmoil Would Go Like The Mounting Waves of the Ocean, Ahadith 7007-7009.*

**Imam Mahdi,** the redeemer according to Islam, will appear on Earth before the Day of Judgment. at the time of the **Second Coming of Christ, the Prophet 'Isa** (**Jesus** Christ son of Mary) will kill al-Masih ad-Dajjal (The Antichrist). **Muslims believe that both Jesus and Mahdi will rid the world of wrongdoing, injustice and tyranny, ensuring peace and tranquility.**

## *Prophets in Judaism, Nevi'im, and Jewish Messiah claimants*

**Jesus is rejected in Judaism as a failed Jewish Messiah claimant and a false prophet. "If a prophet, or one who foretells by dreams, appears among you and announces to you a miraculous sign or wonder, and if the sign or wonder of which he has spoken takes place, and he says, 'Let us follow other gods' (gods you have not known) 'and let us worship them,' you must not listen to the words of that prophet or dreamer. The Lord your God is testing you to find out whether you love him with all your heart and with all your soul. It is the Lord your God you must follow, and him you must revere. Keep his commands and obey him; serve him and hold fast to him. That prophet or dreamer must be put to death, because he preached rebellion against the Lord your God, who brought you out of Egypt and redeemed you from the land of slavery; he has tried to turn you from the way the Lord your God commanded you to follow. You must purge the evil from among you" (Deuteronomy 13:1– 5 NIV).**

The **Books of Kings** records a story where, under duress from Ahab, the prophet **Micaiah** depicts God as requesting information from his heavenly counsel as to what he should do with a court of false prophets. **This depiction is recorded in 1 Kings 22:19–23: "Micaiah continued, 'therefore hear the word of the Lord: I saw the Lord sitting on his throne with all the host of heaven standing around him on his right and on his left. And the Lord said, "Who will entice Ahab into attacking Ramoth Gilead and going to his death there?"**

The penalty for false prophecy, including speaking in the name of a god other than **YHWH** or speaking presumptuously in **YHWH's** name, **is capital punishment**. Likewise, if a prophet makes a prophecy in the name of **YHWH** that does not come to pass, that is another sign that he is not commissioned of **YHWH** and that the people need not fear the false prophet.

# Farhood (Iraq June 1, 1941)

**Farhud** refers to the pogrom or "**violent dispossession**" carried out against the Jewish population of Baghdad, Iraq, on **June 1-2, 1941** during the Jewish holiday of **Shavnot.** The riots occurred in a power vacuum following the collapse of the pro-Nazi government of **Rashid Ali** while the city was in a state of instability. Before British and Transjordanian forces arrived, around **175 Jews had been killed and 1,000 injured.** Looting of Jewish property took place and **900 Jewish homes were destroyed.** By 1951, 110,000 Jews – 80% of Iraqi Jewry – had emigrated from the country, most to Israel. The **Farhud** has been called the "**forgotten pogrom of the Holocaust**" and "**the beginning of the end of the Jewish community of Iraq**", a community that had existed for 2,600 years.

The Jews lived in the land of Babylon for more than 2,500 years following the Babylonian captivity. **There had been at least two earlier comparable pogroms in the modern history of Iraqi Jews, in Basra in 1776 and in Baghdad in 1828.** There were many instances of violence against Jews during their long history in Iraq, as well as numerous enacted decrees ordering the destruction of synagogues in Iraq, and some forced conversion to Islam.

After the **Ottoman Empire** was defeated in the First World War, the **League of Nations** granted the mandate of Iraq to Britain. After **King Ghazi** who inherited the throne of **Faisal I**, died in a 1939 car accident, Britain installed 'Abd al-Ilah** as Iraq's governing regent. By 1941, the approximately **150,000 Iraqi Jews** played active roles in many aspects of Iraqi life, including farming, banking, commerce and the government bureaucracy.

## Events preceding the Farhood: Propaganda

Between 1932 and 1941, the German embassy in Iraq, headed by **Dr. Fritz Grobba**, significantly supported anti-Semitic and fascist movements. Intellectuals and army officers were invited to Germany as guests of the Nazi party, and anti-Semitic material was published in the newspapers. The German embassy purchased the newspaper *Al-alam Al-arabi* ("**The Arab world**") which published, in addition to anti-Semitic propaganda, a translation of *Mein Kampf* in Arabic. The German embassy also supported the establishment of **Al-Fatwa**, a youth organization based upon the model of the **Hitler Youth**.

## The Golden Square coup

Michael Eppel, in his book *"The Palestinian Conflict in Modern Iraq"* blames the **Farhud** on the influence of German ideology on the Iraqi people, as well as extreme nationalism, both of which were heightened by the **Golden Square coup**:

In 1941, a group of pro-Nazi Iraqi officers, known as the **"Golden Square"** and led by **General Rashid Ali**, overthrew **Regent Abdul Ilah** on April 1 after staging a successful coup. Iraq's new government then was quickly involved in confrontation with the British over the terms of the military treaty forced on Iraq at independence. The treaty gave the British unlimited rights to base troops in Iraq and transit troops through Iraq. The British arranged to land large numbers of soldiers from India in Iraq to force the country to show its intentions.

Iraq refused to let them land and confrontation afterward occurred both near Basra in the south and to the west of Baghdad near the British base complex and airfield. The Germans dispatched a group of **26 heavy fighters** to aid in a futile air attack on the British airbase at **Habbaniya** which accomplished nothing. **Winston Churchill** sent a telegram to **President Franklin D. Roosevelt,** warning him that if the Middle East fell to Germany, victory against the Nazis would be a **"hard, long and bleak proposition"** given that **Hitler** would have access to the oil reserves there. The telegram dealt with the larger issues of war in the Middle East rather than Iraq exclusively.

**On May 25, Hitler issued his *Order 30*, stepping up German offensive operations: *"The Arab Freedom Movement in the Middle East is our natural ally against England. In this connection special importance is attached to the liberation of Iraq…I have therefore decided to move forward in the Middle East by supporting Iraq."***

On May 30, the British-organized force called *Kingcol* led by **Brigadier J.J. Kingstone** reached Baghdad, causing the **"Golden Square"** and their supporters to escape via Iran to Germany. *Kingcol* included some elements of the **Arab Legion** led by **Major John Bagot Glubb** known as **Glubb Pasha.**

On May 31, **Regent Illah** prepared to fly back into Baghdad to reclaim his leadership. To avoid the reality of a British-organized countercoup, the regent entered Baghdad without a British escort.

## Anti-Semitic actions preceding the Farhood

**Sami Michael**, a witness to the **Farhud**, testified: **"Anti-Semite propaganda was broadcast routinely by the local radio and Radio Berlin in Arabic. Various anti-Jewish slogans were written on walls on the way to school, such as "Hitler was killing the Jewish germs".** Shops owned by Muslims had 'Muslim' written on them, so they would not be damaged in the case of anti-Jewish riots." **Shalom Darvish**, the secretary of the Jewish community in Baghdad, testified that several days before the **Farhud**, the homes of Jews were marked with a red palm print (**"Hamsa"),** buy **al-Futuwa** youth.

Two days before the **Farhud, Yunis al-Sabawi**, a government minister that proclaimed himself the governor of Baghdad, summoned **Rabbi Sasson Khaduri**, the community leader, and recommended to him that Jews stay in their homes for the next three days as a protective measure. An investigative committee later found that Yunis had the intent of killing the Jews, although his rule of Baghdad lasted only a few hours, to be seized by a public security committee. During the fall of the **Rashid Ali** government, false rumors were circulated that Jews used mirrors to signal the **Royal Air Force.**

## Farhud (June 1-2, 1941)

According to the Iraqi government and British sources, violence started when a delegation of Iraqi Jews, sent to meet the **Regent Abdullah** arrived at the palace of flowers (**Qasr al Zuhur**) and was attacked by the mob as they crossed **Al Khurr Bridge**. Violence in **Al Rusafa** and **Abu Sifyan** districts followed, and got worse the next day, when Iraqi policemen joined in on the attacks on the Jewish community. Shops belonging to Jews were buried and a synagogue was destroyed.

However, **Prof. Zvi Yehuda** alleges that the event leading to the riots was anti-Jewish incitement in the **Jami-Al-Gaylani** mosque, and that violence was premeditated **Prof. Yehuda** points to eyewitness testimonials and analyzes the different methods of operation to support his claim.

Only at the afternoon of June 2, two days into the riots, British forces quelled the violence by imposing a curfew and shooting violators on sight. An investigation conducted by the journalist **Tony Rocca** of the London Sunday Times attributes the delay to a personal decision by the British ambassador of the time (**Kinahan Cornwallis**), who did not execute orders received from London and refused pleas by his officers to act against the riots. Other testimonies suggest that the British delayed their entry into Baghdad for 48 hours because they wanted passions in the city to boil over and had an interest in a clash between Jews and Muslims.

The precise number of victims as unclear: Some sources say that about **180 Jews were killed** and about 240 were wounded, 586 Jewish-owned businesses were looted and 00Jewish houses were destroyed. Other accounts state that nearly **200 Jews were killed and over 2,000 injured, while 900- Jewish homes and hundreds of Jewish-owned shops destroyed and looted**. Bernard Lewis writes that according to the "**official**" statistics 600 Jews were killed and 240 injured, but the unofficial estimates were much higher. The Israeli-based **Babylonian Heritage Museum** maintains that in addition to 180 identified victims; about 600 unidentified victims were buried in a mass grave. An estimate published in **Haaretz** newspaper cites 180 killed and 700 wounded.

## Aftermath: Legal Action

In some accounts the *Farhud* marked the turning point for Iraq's Jews who, following this event, were targeted for violence, persecution, boycotts, confiscations, and near complete expulsion in 1951. Historians such as **Orit Bashkin**, however, see the pivotal moment for the Iraqi Jewish community much later, in 1948, as systematic persecution of the Jews did not begin in earnest until the height of the **Arab-Israeli conflict**.

Rather than being a turning point, the **Farhud** marks the start of a process of politicization of the Iraqi Jews in the 1940's. In the direct aftermath of the **Farhud**, many joined the **Iraqi Communist Party** in order to protect the Jews of Baghdad, yet they did not want to leave the country and rather sought to fight for better conditions in Iraq itself. After the **Farhud**, the ICP saw a massive influx of new members, and organized rallies against the Iraqi government became more frequent.

At the same time the course of the Iraqi government which had taken over after the **Farhud** reassured the Iraqi Jewish community, as ringleaders of the **coup d'état** and the riots were imprisoned or hanged and normal life soon returned to Baghdad, which saw a marked betterment of its economic situation during **World War II**. It was only after the Iraqi government initiated a policy shift towards the Iraqi Jews in 1948, curtailing their civil rights and firing many Jewish state employees, that the **Farhud** began to be regarded as more than just an outburst of violence instigated by foreign influences, namely Nazi propaganda.

Once **Shafiq Ades** was executed on October 23, 1948 for allegedly selling weapons to Israel, after a short show trial and despite the fact he was an outspoken anti-Zionist, anti-Jewish violence in Iraq had become institutionalized and as such the **Farhud** could no longer be dismissed as an isolated incident. After the execution of **Ades**, staying in Iraq was no longer an option for most Iraqi Jews, and once the opportunity presented itself to leave the country, they left the country.

And aiding the massive logistical effort that it took to organize **Operation Ezra** and **Nehemiah**, the airlift of Iraqi Jews to Israel, were the young generations of Iraqi Jews which had joined the **ICP** and Zionists after the **Farhud**.

It is estimated that in 2003, the Iraqi Jewish population numbered less than 100. In 2008 the Iraqi Jewish population dwindled to an estimated 7 people. (80+ years old, refusing to leave and wanting to be buried with their ancestor in Baghdad.)

# Final Solution to the Jewish question

The **Final Solution** (German: *Endlösung*) or the **Final Solution to the Jewish Question** (German: *die Endlösung der Judenfrage*, pronounced was a Nazi plan for the extermination of the Jews during World War II. The "Final Solution of the Jewish Question" was the Nazi code name for the plan to murder all Jews within reach, and was not limited to the European continent. It culminated in the **Holocaust** which saw the **killing of 90 percent of Jewish Poles, and two-thirds of the Jewish population of Europe.**

The program evolved during the first 25 months of war leading to the attempt at **"murdering every last Jew in the German grasp**." Most historians agree, that the **Final Solution** cannot be attributed to a single decision made at one particular point in time. In 1940, following the Fall of France, **Adolf Eichmann devised the Madagascar Plan** to move Europe's Jewish population to the French colony; but the plan was abandoned for logistical reasons mainly due to a naval blockade. There were also preliminary plans to **deport Jews to Palestine and Siberia**. The Jewish victims were sent on death trains to centralized extermination camps built for the purpose of systematic implementation of the **Final Solution**.

## Background

The term **"Final Solution"** was a euphemism used by the Nazis to refer to their plan for the annihilation of the Jewish people. From **gaining power in January 1933** until the outbreak of war in September 1939, the Nazi persecution of the Jews in Germany was focused on intimidation, expropriating their money and property, and encouraging them to emigrate. According to Nazi Party policy statement, the Jews, were the only **"alien people in Europe"**.

In 1936 the **Bureau of Romani Affairs** in Munich was taken over by the **Interpol** and renamed as the **Center for Combating the Gypsy Menace**. Introduced at the end of 1937, the **"final solution of the Gypsy Question"** entailed roundups, expulsions, and incarceration of Romani in concentration camps built at Dachau, Buchenwald, Flossenbürg, Mauthausen, Natzweiler, Ravensbruck, Taucha and Westerbork until this point in time. After the **Anschluss** with Austria in 1938, special offices were established in Vienna and Berlin to **"facilitate"** Jewish emigration without covert plans for their forthcoming annihilation.

The outbreak of war and the invasion of Poland brought a population of **3.5 million Polish Jews** under the control of the Nazi and Soviet security forces, and marked the start of a far more savage persecution, including mass killings. Jews were forced into hundreds of makeshift ghettos pending other arrangements. Two years later, with the launch of **Operation Barbarossa against the USSR,** in late June 1941 the German top echelon began to pursue **Hitler's** new anti-Semitic plan to eradicate rather than expel Jews.

*Reichsführer-SS* **Heinrich Himmler** became the chief architect of a new plan, which came to be called "**the Final Solution to the Jewish Question**". On 31 July 1941, *Reichsmarschall* **Hermann Goring** wrote to **Reinhard Heydrich** (**Himmler**'s deputy and chief of the **RSHA**), instructing **Heydrich** to submit concrete proposals for the implementation of the projected new goal.

The extermination of Jews was carried out in two major operations. With the onset of **Operation Barbarossa** launched from occupied Poland in June 1941, mobile killing units of the **SS** and **Orpo** were dispatched to Soviet controlled territories of eastern Poland and further into the Soviet republics for the express purpose of killing all Jews, both Polish and Soviet.

During the massive chase after the fleeing **Red Army**, **Himmler** himself visited Białystok in the beginning of July 1941 and requested that, **"as a matter of principle any Jew"** behind **the German-Soviet frontier "was to be regarded as a partisan"**. By August 1941, all Jewish men, women, and children were shot. In the second phase of annihilation, the Jewish inhabitants of central, western, and south-eastern Europe were transported by **Holocaust trains to camps with newly-built gassing facilities.**

Massacres of about one million Jews occurred before plans for the **Final Solution** were fully implemented in 1942, but it was only with the decision to annihilate the entire Jewish population that extermination camps such as **Auschwitz II Birkenau and Treblinka** were fitted with permanent gas chambers to kill large numbers of Jews in a relatively short period of time.

The plans to exterminate all the Jews of Europe was formalized at the SS's guesthouse on the Wannsee near Berlin on 20 January 1942. The conference was chaired by **Heydrich** and attended by 15 senior officials of the **Nazi Party** and the German government. At the conference, **Heydrich** indicated that approximately **11,000,000 Jews** in Europe would fall under the provisions of the **"Final Solution"**.

A copy of the minutes of this meeting was found by the Allies in March 1947; it was too late to serve as evidence during the first **Nuremberg Trial** but was used by prosecutor **General Telford Taylor** in the subsequent **Nuremberg Trials**. The **Wannsee Conference Protocol**, which documented the co-operation of various German state agencies in the **SS-led Holocaust**, as well as some 3,000 tons of original German records captured by Allied armies, including the **Einsatzgruppen** reports, which documented the progress of the mobile killing units assigned, among other tasks, to kill Jewish civilians during the attack on the Soviet Union in 1941.

## Phase one: killing squads of Operation Barbarossa

The Nazi invasion of the Soviet Union codenamed **Operation Barbarossa**, which commenced on 22 June 1941, set in motion a **"war of destruction"** which quickly opened the door to systematic mass murder of European Jews. **For Hitler, Bolshevism was merely "the most recent and most nefarious manifestation of the eternal Jewish threat"**. On 3 March 1941, **Wehrmacht** Joint Operations Staff Chief **Alfred Jodl** repeated **Hitler**'s declaration that the **"Jewish-Bolshevik intelligentsia would have to be eliminated"** and that the forthcoming war would be a confrontation between two completely opposing cultures.

In May 1941, **Gestapo** leader **Heinrich Müller** wrote a preamble to the new law limiting the jurisdiction of military courts in prosecuting troops for criminal actions because: **"this time the troops will encounter an especially dangerous element from the civilian population, therefore, have the right and obligation to secure themselves."**

**Himmler** assembled a force of about 3,000 men from **Security Police, Gestapo, Kripo, SD, and the Waffen-SS,** as the so-called **"special commandos of the security forces"** known as the *Einsatzgruppen,* to eliminate both communists and Jews in occupied territories. These forces were supported by 21 battalions of **Orpo Reserve Police** under **Kurt Daluege**, adding up to 11,000 men. Barbarossa is a war of annihilation against **Bolshevism**, and that his battalions would proceed ruthlessly against all Jews, regardless of age or sex. By July, significant numbers of women and children were being killed behind all front lines not only by the Germans but also by the local Ukrainian and Lithuanian auxiliary forces.

In late August 1941, the *Einsatzgruppen* **killed 23,600 Jews in the Kamianets-Podilskyi** massacre. A month later, the largest mass shooting of Soviet Jews took place on 29–30 September in the ravine of **Babi Yar**, near Kiev, where more than **33,000 Jewish people of all ages were systematically machine-gunned.** In mid-October 1941, **HSSPFSouth**, under the command of **Friedrich Jeckeln**, had reported the indiscriminate killing of more than 100,000 people.

By the end of December 1941, before the **Wannsee Conference**, over 439,800 Jewish people had been murdered, and the **Final Solution** policy in the east became common knowledge within the SS. Entire regions were reported **"free of Jews"** by the *Einsatzgruppen.* Within two years, the **total number of shooting victims in the east had risen to between 618,000 and 800,000 Jews.**

### *Bezirk Bialystok* and *Reichskommissariate Ostland*

On Friday, 27 June 1941, the **Reserve Police Battalion** 309 arrived in the city and set the Great Synagogue on fire with hundreds of Jewish men locked inside. The burning of the synagogue was followed by a frenzy of killings both inside the homes around the Jewish neighborhood of Chanajki, and in the city park, lasting until night time. The next day, some 30 wagons of dead bodies were taken to mass graves. In two days of 5–7 August in occupied Pińsk where over 12,000 Jews died at the hands of **Waffen SS,** not the *Einsatzgruppen*. An additional 17,000 Jews perished there in a ghetto uprising crushed a year later with the aid of **Belarusian Auxiliary Police.**

The subject of the **Holocaust** in Lithuania has been analyzed by **Konrad Kweit** from **USHMM** who wrote: **"Lithuanian Jews were among the first victims of the Holocaust . The Germans carried out the mass executions signaling the beginning of the 'Final Solution'."** About 80,000 Jews were killed in Lithuania by October (including in formerly Polish Wilno) and about 175,000 by the end of 1941 according to official reports.

## *Reichskommissariate Ukraine*

Within one week from the start of Operation Barbarossa, **Heydrich** issued an order to his *Einsatzkommandos* for the **on-the-spot execution of all Bolsheviks**, interpreted by the SS to mean all Jews. One of the first indiscriminate massacres of men, women, and children in *Reichskommissariate Ukraine* took the lives of over 4,000 Polish Jews in occupied Luck on 2–4 July 1941, murdered by *Einsatzkommandos* 4a assisted by the **Ukrainian People's Militia.**

Within the Soviet Union proper, between 9 July 1941 and 19 September 1941 the city of Zhytomyr was made *Judenfrei* in three murder operations conducted by German and Ukrainian police in which **10,000 Jews perished**. In the Kamianets-Podilskyi massacre of 26–28 August 1941 some 23,600 Jews were shot in front of open pits (including 14,000–18,000 people expelled from Hungary). After an incident in Bila Tserkva in which 90 small children left behind had to be shot separately, Blobel requested that Jewish mothers hold them in their arms during mass shootings. Long before the conference at **Wannsee, 28,000 Jews** were shot by **SS** and **Ukrainian** military in Vinnytsia on 22 September 1941, followed by the 29 September **massacre of 33,771 Jews at Babi Yar.**

In Dnipropetrovsk, on 13 October 1941 some 10,000–15,000 Jews were shot. In Chernihiv, 10,000 Jews were put to death and only 260 Jews were spared. In mid-October, during the Krivoy-Rog massacre of 4,000–5,000 Soviet Jews the entire Ukrainian auxiliary police force actively participated. In the first days of January 1942 in Kharkiv, 12,000 Jews were murdered, but smaller massacres continued in this period on daily basis in countless other locations. In August 1942 in the presence of only a few German SS men over 5,000 Jews were massacred in **Polish Zofjówka** by the **Ukrainian Auxiliary Police** leading to the town's complete sweep from existence.

## *District Galizien*

The killings continued uninterrupted. On 12 October 1941 in Stanisławów, some 10,000–12,000 Jewish men, women, and children were shot at the Jewish cemetery by the German uniformed SS-men and **Ukrainian Auxiliary Police** during the so-called **"Bloody Sunday"** *(de)*. The shooters began firing at 12 noon and continued without stopping by taking turns.

The conference at Wannsee gave impetus to the so-called *second sweep* of the **Holocaust** by the bullet in the east. Between April and July 1942 in Volhynia, 30,000 Jews were murdered in death pits with the help of dozens of newly formed **Ukrainian** *Schutzmannschaft*. Owing to good relations with the **Ukrainian** *Hilfsverwaltung*, these auxiliary battalions were deployed by the SS also in **Russia Center**, Russia south, and in Byelorussia; each with about 500 soldiers divided into three companies.

They participated in the **extermination of 150,000 Volhynia Jews alone, or 98 percent of the Jewish inhabitants of the entire region.** In July 1942 the Completion of the **Final Solution** in the General Government territory which included *Distrikt Galizien*, was ordered personally by **Himmler**. He set the initial deadline for 31 December 1942.

## Phase two: deportations to killing centers

When in 1941 the **Wehrmacht** forces attacked the Soviet positions in eastern Poland during the initially successful **Operation Barbarossa**, the killings of Jews from the **Łódź Ghetto** in the *Warthegau* district began in early December 1941 with the use of gas vans at the **Kulmhof extermination camp.** The deceptive guise of **"Resettlement in the East"** organized by **SS** Commissioners, was also tried and tested at Chełmno.

Construction work on the first killing center at **Bełżec** in occupied Poland began in October 1941, three months before the Wannsee Conference. More Jews were killed at Treblinka than at any other Nazi extermination camp apart from **Auschwitz**. By the time the mass killings of **Operation Reinhard** ended in 1943, roughly two million Jews in German-occupied Poland had been murdered.

The total number of people killed in 1942 in **Lublin/Majdanek, Bełżec, Sobibor**, and **Treblinka** was **1,274,166** by Germany's own estimation, not counting **Auschwitz** II **Birkenau** nor *Kulmhof*. Their bodies were buried in mass graves initially. Although other methods of extermination, such as the cyanic poison **Zyklon B**, were already being used at other Nazi killing centers such as **Auschwitz**, the *Aktion Reinhard* camps used lethal exhaust gases from captured tank engines.

In two weeks of July 1942 the **Slonim Ghetto** revolt crushed with the help of **Latvian, Lithuanian and Ukrainian** *Schutzmannschaft* **cost the lives of 8,000–13,000 Jews.** The second largest mass shooting (to that particular date) took place in late October 1942 when the insurgency was suppressed in the **Pińsk Ghetto**; over 26,000 men, women and children were shot with the aid of **Belarusian Auxiliary Police** before the ghetto's closure. During the suppression of the **Warsaw Ghetto Uprising** (the largest single revolt by Jews during World War II), 13,000 Jews were killed in action before May 1943.

The **Holocaust** trains run by the *Deutsche Reichsbahn* and several other national railway systems delivered condemned Jewish captives from as far as Belgium, Bulgaria, France, Greece, Hungary, Italy, Moravia, Netherlands, Romania, Slovakia, and even Scandinavia.

On 19 October 1943, five days after the prisoner revolt in Sobibor, **Operation Reinhard** was terminated by **Odilo Globocnik** on behalf of **Himmler**. The camps responsible for the killing of nearly 2,700,000 Jews were soon closed. The operation was followed by the single largest German massacre of Jews in the entire war carried out on 3 November 1943; with approximately 43,000 prisoners shot one-by-one simultaneously in three nearby locations by the **Reserve Police Battalion 101** hand-in-hand with the **Trawniki** men from **Ukraine**.

## Auschwitz II Birkenau

Until mid-June 20,000 Silesian Jews were killed there using **Zyklon B.** In July 1942 Bunker II became operational. **In August, another 10,000-13,000 Polish Jews from Silesia perished, along with 16,000 French Jews declared 'stateless', and 7,700 Jews from Slovakia.**

The infamous **'Gate of Death'** at **Auschwitz** II for the incoming freight trains was built of brick and cement mortar in 1943, and the three-track rail spur was added. **Until mid-August, 45,000 Thessaloniki Jews were murdered in a mere six months, including over 30,000 Jews** from Sosnowiec (Sosnowitz) and Bendzin Ghettos. The spring of 1944 marked the beginning of the last phase of the **Final Solution at Birkenau**. The new big ramps and sidings were constructed, and two freight elevators were installed inside **Crematoria II** and **III** for moving the bodies faster. In May 1944 **Auschwitz**-Birkenau became the site of one of the two largest mass murder operations in modern history following the *Großaktion Warschau* deportations of the **Warsaw Ghetto** inmates to **Treblinka** in 1942. It is estimated that until July 1944 approximately **320,000 Hungarian Jews were gassed** at **Birkenau** in less than eight weeks. The entire operation was photographed by the SS.

## Historiographic debate about the decision

**Hitler** made numerous chilling predictions regarding the **Holocaust** of the Jews of Europe prior to the beginning of World War II. During a speech given on 30 January 1939, on the sixth anniversary of his accession to power, **Hitler** said:

**Today I will once more be a prophet: If the international Jewish financiers in and outside Europe should succeed in plunging the nations once more into a world war, then the result will not be the Bolshevization of the earth, and thus the victory of Jewry, but the annihilation of the Jewish race in Europe! — Adolf Hitler, 1939**

An estimate of **5.1 million as the total number of Jews killed. Over 800,000; open-air shootings: over 1,300,000; extermination camps: up to 3,000,000.** Poland was home to the largest Jewish population in the world. **Germany's declaration of war on the United States on December 11, 1941,** meant that holding European Jews hostage to deter the US from entering the conflict was now pointless.

When **Himmler** addressed senior **SS** personnel and leading members of the regime in the **Posen** speeches on October 4, 1943, he used **"the fate of the Jews as a sort of blood bond to tie the civil and military leadership to the Nazi cause."**

**"I'm referring to the evacuation of the Jews, the extermination of the Jewish people. Most of you will know what it's like to see 100 corpses side by side or 500 corpses or 1,000 of them. This is an unwritten—never to be written—and yet glorious page in our history".**

# Frankism

**Frankism** was a Jewish religious movement of the 18th and 19th centuries, centered on the leadership of the **Jewish Messiah claimant Jacob Frank,** who lived from 1726 to 1791. **Frank** rejected religious norms, and said his followers were obligated to transgress as many moral boundaries as possible. At its height it claimed perhaps **500,000 followers**, primarily Jews living in Poland and other parts of Eastern Europe.

## About

Unlike traditional Judaism, which provides a set of detailed guidelines called **"halakha"** that are scrupulously followed by observant Jews and regulate many aspects of life, **Frank** claimed that **"all laws and teachings will fall"** and – following **antinomianism** – asserted that the most important obligation of every person was the transgression of every boundary. **Frankism** is commonly associated with the **Sabbateans,** a religious movement that identified the 17th-century **Jewish rabbi Sabbatai Zevi as the Messiah.**

Like **Frank**ism, the earlier forms of **Sabbateanism** believed that at least in some circumstances, **antinomianism** was the correct path. Zevi himself would perform actions that violated traditional Jewish taboos, such as eating foods that were forbidden by **kashrut (Jewish dietary laws)** and celebrating prescribed fast days as feast days. In **Frankism**, orgies featured prominently in ritual.

In traditional **Sabbatean doctrine, Zevi** – and often his followers – claimed to be able to liberate the sparks of holiness hidden within what seemed to be evil. **Frank**'s theology asserted that the attempt to liberate the sparks of holiness was the problem, not the solution. Rather, **Frank** claimed that the **"mixing" between holy and unholy was virtuous. Netanel Lederberg** claims that **Frank** had a **Gnostic philosophy** wherein there was a **"true God"** whose existence was hidden by a **"false God."**

This **"true God"** could allegedly only be revealed through a total destruction of the social and religious structures created by the **"false God,"** thus leading to a thorough **antinomianism.** For **Frank**, the very distinction between good and evil is a product of a world governed by the **"false God." Lederberg** compares **Frank**'s position to that of **Friedrich Nietzsche.**

## After Jacob Frank

After **Jacob Frank's death in 1791**, his daughter Eve, who had been declared in 1770 to be the **incarnation of the Shekhinah**, the dwelling of the divine presence, continued to lead the movement with her brothers.

# Garden of Eden

The Garden of Eden (Hebrew, *Gan 'Edhen*; Arabic: *Jannat 'Adn*) is in the Bible's Book of Genesis as being the place where the first man, Adam, and his wife, Eve, lived after they were created by God. (Gen. 2:8). This garden forms part of the **Genesis** creation narrative and theodicy of the Abrahamic religions, often being used to explain the origin of sin and mankind's wrongdoings. The **Genesis** creation narrative relates the geographical location of both **Eden** and the garden to **four rivers (Pishon, Gihon, Tigris, Euphrates), and three regions (Havilah, Assyria, and Kush).** There are hypotheses that place **Eden** at the headwaters of the Tigris and Euphrates (northern Mesopotamia), in Iraq (Mesopotamia), Africa, and the Persian Gulf.

## The story from Genesis

God charges **Adam** to tend the garden in which they live, and specifically **commands Adam not to eat from the Tree of Knowledge of Good and Evil.** **Eve** is questioned by the serpent concerning why she avoids eating from this tree. She says that even if she touches the fruit she will die. The serpent responds that she will not surely die, rather she and her husband would **"be as gods, knowing good and evil,"** and persuades **Eve** to eat from the **Tree of Knowledge of Good and Evil.** **Eve** eats and gives the fruit to **Adam**, who also eats. At this point the two become aware, **"to know good and evil,"** evidenced by an **awareness of their nakedness. God expels them from Eden,** to keep **Adam** and **Eve** from also partaking of the **Tree of Life**.

## Geography

The Book of **Genesis** does not state a physical geographic location for the **Garden of Eden**, but ideally it is **"the Garden of God" or divine home (Ezek 31:8-9).** Also, all of the world's major rivers flow out of the divine home. **Genesis 2:10-14** names the **Garden of Eden** as the source of four rivers, the **Tigris and Euphrates, great waterways of Mesopotamia, and the Pishon and Gihon.**

## In Jewish Eschatology

In the rabbinic literatures of the **Talmud** and the Jewish **Kabbalah**, the scholars agree that there are two types of spiritual places called *Garden in Eden*. The first is rather terrestrial, of abundant fertility and luxuriant vegetation, known as the *"lower Gan Eden"*. The second is envisioned as being celestial, the habitation of righteous, Jewish and non-Jewish, immortal souls, known as the *"higher Gan Eden"*. The **Rabbanim** differentiate between **Gan** and **Eden**. **Adam** is said to have dwelt only in the Gan. **Whereas Eden is said never to be witnessed by any mortal eye.**

# Gehenna

**Gehenna** or **Gehinnom** (literally translated as **"Valley of Hinnom"**) is thought to be a small valley in Jerusalem. In the Hebrew Bible, **Gehenna** was initially where some of the **kings of Judah sacrificed their children by fire. Thereafter, it was deemed to be cursed (Book of Jeremiah 7:31, 19:2–6).**

In rabbinic literature, **Gehenna** is also a destination of the wicked. **Gehinnom is not Hell**, but originally a grave and in later times a sort of purgatory where one is judged based on one's life's deeds, or rather, where one becomes fully aware of one's own shortcomings and negative actions during one's life. The **Kabbalah** explains it as a **"waiting room"** (commonly translated as an **"entry way"**) for all souls (not just the wicked). The overwhelming majority of rabbinic thought maintains that people are not in **Gehinnom** forever; the longest that a Jew can be there is said to be 11 months (unless he is a fully wicked person, in which case 12 months). This is different from the more neutral **Sheol/Hades**, the abode of the dead, although the **King James Version of the Bible** misleadingly translates both with the Anglo-Saxon word *hell.*

**In the King James Version of the Bible, the term appears 13 times in 11 different verses as Valley of Hinnom, Valley of the son of Hinnom or Valley of the children of Hinnom.** The **Valley of Hinnom** is the modern name for the valley surrounding Jerusalem's Old City, including **Mount Zion**, from the west and south. It meets and merges with the **Kidron Valley**, the other principal valley around the **Old City**, near the southeastern corner of the city.

## Etymology

English **"Gehenna"** represents the Greek *Geenna* found in the New Testament, a phonetic transcription of Aramaic *Gēhannā* , equivalent to the Hebrew *Ge Hinnom*, literally **"Valley of Hinnom"**. This is known in the Hebrew Bible as *Gei Ben-Hinnom*, literally the **"Valley of the son of Hinnom"**, and in the Talmud as *Gehinnom*.

## Geography

The exact location of the **Valley of Hinnom** is disputed. The **Tyropoeon** lay within the city walls and child sacrifice would have been practiced outside the walls of the city. In (1992) the **Wadi ar-Rababi**, which fits the description of **Joshua that Hinnom** valley ran east to west and lay outside the city walls. The valley began at **En-rogel. If the modern Bir Ayyub is En-rogel, then Wadi ar-Rababi, which begins there, is Hinnom.**

## Archaeology / *Tophet*

Child sacrifice at other **Tophets** contemporary with the Bible accounts (700–600 BCE) of the reigns of **Ahaz and Manasseh** have been established, such as the bones of children sacrificed at the **Tophet** to the **goddess Tanit** in Phoenician Carthage, and also child sacrifice in ancient Syria-

Palestine. Yet, the biblical words in the **Book of Jeremiah** describe events taking place in the seventh century in the place of **Ben-hinnom**: **"Because they have forsaken Me and have made this an alien place and have burned sacrifices in it to other gods, that neither they nor their forefathers nor the kings of Judah had ever known, and because they have filled this place with the blood of the innocent and have built the high places of Baal to burn their sons in the fire as burnt offerings to Baal, a thing which I never commanded or spoke of, nor did it ever enter My mind; therefore, behold, days are coming,"** declares the LORD, **"when this place will no longer be called Topheth or the valley of Ben-hinnom, but rather the valley of Slaughter"**.

No archaeological evidence such as mass children's graves has been found. The site would also have been disrupted by the actions of Josiah **"And he defiled Topheth, which is in the valley of the children of Hinnom, that no man might make his son or his daughter to pass through the fire to Molech." (2 Kings 23)**. Scholars have attempted to argue that the Bible does not portray actual child sacrifice, but only dedication to the **god by fire**; however, they are judged to have been **"convincingly disproved"**.

## The concept of Gehinnom / Hebrew Bible

The oldest historical reference to the valley is found in **Joshua 15:8, 18:16** which describe tribal boundaries. The next chronological reference to the valley is at the time of **King Ahaz of Judah** who sacrificed his sons there according to **2 Chron. 28:3**. The same is said of **Ahaz'** grandson Manasseh in **33:6**. Debate remains as to whether the phrase **"cause his children to pass through the fire"** referred to a religious ceremony in which the **moloch** priest would walk the child between two lanes of fire, or to literal child sacrifice; throwing the child into the fire.

The **Book of Isaiah** does not mention **Gehenna** by name, but the **"burning place"** 30:33 in which the Assyrian army is to be destroyed, may be read **"Topheth"**, and the final verse of **Isaiah** which concerns of those that have rebelled against God, **Isaiah 66:24**.

It is recorded that Josiah destroyed the shrine of Molech on Topheth to prevent anyone sacrificing children there in **2 Kings 23:10**. Despite **Josiah's** ending of the practice, Jeremiah also included a prophecy that Jerusalem itself would be made like **Gehenna** and **Topheth (19:2–6, 19:11–14).**

A final purely geographical reference is found in **Neh. 11:30** to the exiles returning from Babylon camping from Beersheba to Hinnom. Frequent references to '**Gehenna**' are also made in the books of **Meqabyan**, which are considered canonical in the **Ethiopian Orthodox Tewahedo Church**.

## Targums

The ancient Aramaic paraphrase-translations of the **Hebrew Bible** known as **Targums** supply the term **"Gehinnom"** frequently to verses touching upon resurrection, judgment, and the fate of the wicked. This may also include addition of the phrase **"second death"**, as in the final chapter of the **Book of Isaiah**, where the Hebrew version does not mention either **Gehinnom or the Second Death**, whereas the **Targums** add both. In this the **Targums** are parallel to the **Gospel of Mark** addition of **"Gehenna" to the quotation of the Isaiah verses describing the corpses "where their worm does not die"**.

## Rabbinical Judaism

**Gehenna** is considered a purgatory-like place where the wicked go to suffer until they have atoned for their sins. It is stated in most Jewish sources that the maximum amount of time a sinner can spend in **Gehenna** is one year. The Mishnah names seven Biblical individuals who do not get a share in **Olam Ha-Ba: Jeroboam, Ahab, Menasseh, Doeg the Edomite, Ahitophel, Balaam, and Gehazi.** According to the opinion of **Rabbi Yehuda, Menasseh** got a share in **Olam Ha-Ba.** The worst part of **Gehenna** is called **Tzoah Rotachat.**

He maintained that in this loathsome valley fires were kept burning perpetually to consume the filth and cadavers thrown into it. There is neither archaeological nor literary evidence in support of this claim, in either the earlier intertestamental or the later rabbinic sources. Also, **Lloyd R. Bailey's "Gehenna: The Topography of Hell"** from 1986 holds a similar view.

The use of this area for tombs continued into the first centuries BCE and CE. By 70 AD, the area was not only a burial site but also a place for cremation of the dead with the arrival of the **Tenth Roman Legion**, who were the only group known to practice cremation in this region. In time it became deemed to be accursed and an image of the place of destruction in Jewish folklore. Eventually the Hebrew term **Gehinnom** became a figurative name for the place of spiritual purification for the wicked dead in Judaism. The period of purification or punishment is limited to only 12 months and every **Sabbath** day is excluded from punishment. After this the soul will move on to **Olam Ha-Ba** (the world to come), be destroyed, or continue to exist in a state of consciousness of remorse. **Gehenna** became a metonym for **"Hell"** due to its morbid prominence in Jewish religious texts.

**Maimonides** declares, in his **13 principles of faith**, that the descriptions of **Gehenna**, as a place of punishment in rabbinic literature, were pedagogically motivated inventions to encourage respect of the **Torah** commandments by mankind, which had been regarded as immature. **Instead of being sent to Gehenna, the souls of the wicked would actually get annihilated.**

## Christianity (New Testament)

The Christian Bible refers to **Gehenna** as a place where both soul (Greek: psyche) and body could be destroyed (**Matthew 10:28**) in **"unquenchable fire"** (**Mark 9:43**). Christian usage of **Gehenna** often serves to admonish adherents of the religion to live pious lives. **Examples of Gehenna in the Christian New Testament include:**

- **Matthew 5:22**: "....whoever shall say, 'You fool', shall be guilty enough to go into **Gehenna**."
- **Matthew 5:29**: "....it is better for you that one of the parts of your body perish, than for your whole body to be thrown into **Gehenna**."
- **Matthew 5:30**: "....better for you that one of the parts of your body perish, than for your whole body to go into **Gehenna**."
- **Matthew 10:28**: "....rather fear Him who is able to destroy both soul and body in **Gehenna**."
- **Matthew 18:9**: "It is better for you to enter life with one eye, than with two eyes to be thrown into the **Gehenna**...."
- **Matthew 23:15**: "Woe to you, scribes and Pharisees, hypocrites, because you... make one proselyte...twice as much a child of **Gehenna** as yourselves."
- **Matthew 23:33**, to the Pharisees: "You serpents, you brood of vipers, how shall you to escape the sentence of **Gehenna**?"
- **Mark 9:43**: "It is better for you to enter life crippled, than having your two hands, to go into **Gehenna** into the unquenchable fire."
- **Mark 9:45**: "It is better for you to enter life lame, than having your two feet, to be cast into **Gehenna**."
- **Mark 9:47**: "It is better for you to enter the Kingdom of God with one eye, than having two eyes, to be cast into **Gehenna**."
- **Luke 12:5**: "....fear the One who, after He has killed has authority to cast into **Gehenna**; yes, I tell you, fear Him."

**Another book to use the word *Gehenna* in the New Testament is James:**
- **James 3:6: "And the tongue is a fire,...and sets on fire the course of our life, and is set on fire by Gehenna."**

## Translations in Christian Bibles

The **Book of Revelation** describes **Hades** being cast into the lake of fire **(Revelation 20:14).** In the New Testament, the New International Version, New Living Translation, **New American Standard Bible** (among others) all reserve the term **"hell"** for the translation of **Gehenna** or Tartarus.

## Translations without a distinction:

Many modern Christians consider **Gehenna** to be a place of eternal punishment. Annihilationist Christians, however, imagine **Gehenna** to be a place where **"sinners"** are tormented until they are eventually destroyed, soul and all.

## Quran

The name given to Hell in Islam, ***Jahannam,*** directly derives from **Gehenna. The Quran contains 77 references to the Islamic interpretation of Gehenna** but does not mention **Sheol/Hades** (abode of the dead), and instead uses the word **'Qabr'**, meaning grave).

# Gemara

The **Gemara** (also transliterated **Gemora**, **Gemarah**, from Hebrew גמרא, from the Aramaic verb *Gamar*, **study**) is the component of the **Talmud** comprising rabbinical analysis of and commentary on the **Mishnah**. After the **Mishnah** was published by **Judah the Prince** (c. 200 CE), the work was studied exhaustively by generation after generation of rabbis in Babylonia and the Land of Israel. Their discussions were written down in a series of books that became the **Gemara**, which when combined with the **Mishnah** constituted the **Talmud**.

There are two versions of the **Gemara**. The **Jerusalem Talmud** (**Talmud Yerushalmi**) was compiled by scholars of the Land of Israel, primarily of the academies of Tiberias and Caesarea, and was published between **about 350–400 CE**. The **Talmud Bavli** was published about 500 CE by scholars of Babylonia, primarily of the academies of **Sura, Pumbedita, and Mata Mehasia**. By convention, a reference to the "**Gemara**" or "**Talmud**," without further qualification, refers to the Babylonian version. **The main compilers were Revina and Rav Ashi.**

## Gemara and Mishnah

The **Gemara** and the **Mishnah** together make up the **Talmud**. The **Talmud** thus comprises two components: the **Mishnah** – the core text; and the *Gemara* – analysis and commentary which "completes" the **Talmud**. The rabbis of the **Mishnah** are known as *Tannaim* (sing. *Tanna* תנא). The rabbis of the **Gemara** are referred to as *Amoraim* (sing. *Amora* אמורא).

Because there are two **Gemara**s, there are in fact two **Talmud**s: the Jerusalem **Talmud** (Hebrew: תלמוד ירושלמי, "**Talmud Yerushalmi**"), and the Babylonian **Talmud** (Hebrew: תלמוד בבלי, "**Talmud Bavli**"), corresponding to the Jerusalem **Gemara** and the Babylonian **Gemara**; both share the same **Mishnah**. The **Gemara** is mostly written in Aramaic, the Jerusalem **Gemara** in Western Aramaic and the Babylonian in Eastern Aramaic, but both contain portions in Hebrew. Sometimes the language changes in the middle of a story.

## Origins of the word

In a narrow sense, the word *Gemara* refers to the mastery and transmission of existing tradition, as opposed to *sevara*, which means the deriving of new results by logic. Both activities are represented in the "**Gemara**" as a literary work. The term "**Gemara**" for the activity of study is far older than its use as a description of any text: thus **Pirke Avot** (Ch.5), a work long preceding the recording of the **Talmud**, recommends starting "**Mishnah**" at the age of 10 and "**Gemara**" at the age of 15.

## The *Sugya*

The analysis of the *Amoraim* is generally focused on clarifying the positions, words and views of the *Tannaim*. These debates and exchanges form the "**building-blocks**" of the **Gemara**; the name for such a passage of **Gemara** is a *sugya* (סוגיא; **plural** *sugyot*). A *sugya* will typically comprise a detailed proof-based elaboration of the **Mishna**. Every aspect of the **Mishna**ic text is treated as a subject of close investigation. This analysis is aimed at an exhaustive understanding of the **Mishna**'s full meaning.

In the **Talmud**, a *sugya* is presented as a series of responsive hypotheses and questions – with the **Talmud**ic text as a record of each step in the process of reasoning and derivation. The **Gemara** thus takes the form of a dialectical exchange (by contrast, the *Mishnah* states concluded legal opinions – and often differences in opinion between the **Tannaim**. There is little dialogue). The disputants here are termed the *makshan* (questioner, "**one who raises a difficulty**") and *tartzan* (answerer, "**one who puts straight**").

The **Gemara** records the semantic disagreements between *Tannaim* and *Amoraim*. Some of these debates were actually conducted by the *Amoraim,* though many of them are hypothetically reconstructed by the **Talmud**'s redactors. (Often imputing a view to an earlier authority as to how he may have answered a question: "**This is what Rabbi X could have argued** ...") Rarely are debates formally closed.

## Argumentation and debate

The distinctive character of the **Gemara** derives largely from the intricate use of argumentation and debate, described above. In each *sugya*, either participant may cite scriptural, **Mishna**ic and **Amoraic** proof to build a logical support for their respective opinions. The process of deduction required to derive a conclusion from a **proof text** is often logically complex and indirect.

**"Confronted with a statement on any subject, the Talmudic student will proceed to raise a series of questions before he satisfies himself of having understood its full meaning."** This analysis is often described as "**mathematical**" in approach; Adin Steinsaltz makes the analogy of the *Amoraim* as scientists investigating the **Halakha**, where the **Tanakh, Mishnah**, **Tosefta** and midrash are the phenomena studied.

## Proof texts

Proof texts quoted to corroborate or disprove the respective opinions and theories will include:
- verses from the Tanakh: the exact language employed is regarded as significant;
- other *Mishnayot*: cross-references to analogous cases, or to parallel reasoning by the *Tanna* in question;
- *Baraitot* בראתא – uncodified **Mishna**yot which are also sources of halakha (lit. outside material; sing. Beraita ברייתא);
  - references to opinions and cases in the Tosefta (תוספתא);
  - references to the Halakhic Midrash (Mekhilta, Sifra and Sifre);
- Cross-references to other *sugyot*: again to analogous cases or logic.

## Questions addressed

The actual debate will usually center on the following categories:

## Language

Why does the **Mishna** use one word rather than another? If a statement is not clear enough, the **Gemara** seeks to clarify the **Mishna**'s intention.

## Logic

Exploring the logical principles underlying the **Mishnah**'s statements, and showing how different understandings of the **Mishnah**'s reasons could lead to differences in their practical application. What underlying principle is entailed in a statement of fact or in a specific instance brought as an illustration? If a statement appears obvious, the **Gemara** seeks the logical reason for its necessity. It seeks to answer under which circumstances a statement is true, and what qualifications are permissible. All statements are examined for internal consistency.

## Legal

Resolving contradictions, perceived or actual, between different statements in the **Mishnah**, or between the **Mishnah** and other traditions; e.g., by stating that: two conflicting sources are dealing with differing circumstances; or that they represent the views of different Rabbis. Do certain authorities differ or not? If they do, why do they differ? If a principle is presented as a generalization, the **Gemara** clarifies how much is included; if an exception, how much is excluded.

## Biblical exposition

Demonstrating how the **Mishnah**'s rulings or disputes, derive from interpretations of Biblical texts. The **Gemara** will often ask where in the Torah the **Mishnah** derives a particular law. See **Talmud**ic hermeneutics.

# Geonim of Babylon

*Geonim* (Hebrew: גאונים;) ; also transliterated *Gaonim- singular Gaon*) were the presidents of the two great **Babylonian, Talmudic Academies of Sura and Pumbedita**, in the **Abbasid Caliphate**, and were the generally accepted spiritual leaders of the Jewish community worldwide in the early medieval era, in contrast to the *Resh Galuta* **(Exilarch)** who wielded secular authority over the Jews in Islamic lands.

*Geonim* is the plural of גאון (*Gaon'*), which means **"pride" or "splendor"** in Biblical Hebrew and since the 19th century **"genius"** as in modern Hebrew. As a title of a Babylonian college president it meant something like **"His Excellency"**.

The *Geonim* played a prominent and decisive role in the transmission and teaching of Torah and Jewish law. They taught **Talmud** and decided on issues on which no ruling had been rendered during the period of the **Talmud**. The **Geonim** were also spiritual leaders of the Jewish community of their time.

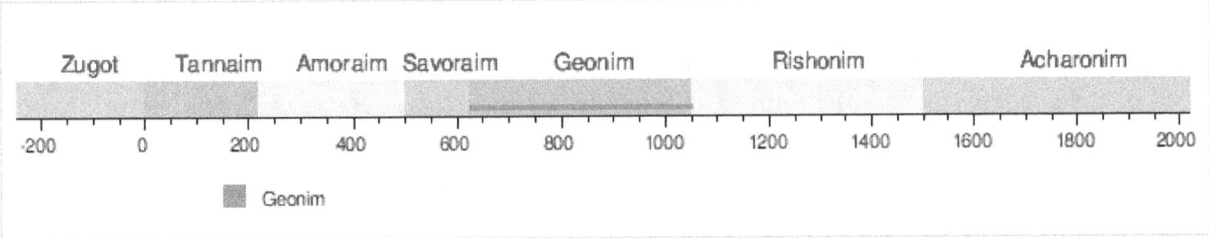

## Era
The period of the **Geonim began in 589 CE (Hebrew date: 4349),** after the period of the **Sevora'im**, and ended in 1038 (Hebrew date: 4798). The first **Gaon** of **Sura**, according to **Sherira Gaon**, was **Mar Rab Mar**, who assumed office in 609. The last **Gaon of Sura** was **Samuel ben Ḥofni**, who died in 1034 CE; the last **Gaon of Pumbedita** was **Hezekiah Gaon**, who was tortured to death by fanatics of the **Buyid Dynasty** in 1040; hence the activity of the **Geonim** covers a period of nearly 450 years.

There were two major Geonic academies, one in **Sura** and the other in **Pumbedita**. The Sura academy was originally dominant, but its authority waned towards the end of the Geonic Period and the Pumbedita **Gaon**ate gained ascendancy.

## Role in Jewish life
The **Geonim** officiated, in the last place, as directors of the academies, continuing as such the educational activity of the **Amoraim and Saboraim**. For while the **Amoraim**, through their interpretation of the **Mishnahh**, gave rise to the **Talmud**, and while the Saboraim definitively

edited it, the **Geonim**'s task was to interpret it; for them it became the subject of study and instruction, and they gave religio-legal decisions in agreement with its teachings.

During the Geonic period the Babylonian schools were the chief centers of Jewish learning; the **Geonim**, the heads of these schools, were recognized as the highest authorities in Jewish law. Despite the difficulties which hampered the irregular communications of the period, Jews who lived even in most distant countries sent their inquiries concerning religion and law to these officials in **Babylonia.**

In the latter centuries of the Geonic period, from the middle of the tenth to the middle of the eleventh, their supremacy lessened, as the study of the **Talmud** received care in other lands. The inhabitants of these regions gradually began to submit their questions to the heads of the schools in their own countries. Eventually they virtually ceased sending their questions to **Babylonian Geonim**.

## The title "Gaon"

The title of **Gaon** came to be applied to the heads of the two Babylonian academies of **Sura and Pumbedita**, though it did not displace the original title of *Rosh Yeshivah Ge'on Ya'akov* (Hebrew, head of the academy, pride of Jacob). The Aramaic term used was *Resh metivta*. The title **Gaon** properly designated the office of head of the academy. The title became popular in use around the end of the 6th century. As the academies of **Sura** and **Pumbedita** were invested with judicial authority, the **Gaon** officiated as supreme judge.

The organization of the Babylonian academies recalled the ancient Sanhedrin. In many **Responsa** of the **Geonim**, members of the schools are mentioned who belonged to the **"great Sanhedrin"**, and others who belonged to the **"small Sanhedrin"**. In front of the presiding **Gaon** and facing him were seated seventy members of the academy in seven rows of ten persons each, each person in the seat assigned to him, and the whole forming, with the **Gaon**, the so-called **"Great Sanhedrin"**. **Gaon** Amram calls them in a responsum (**"Responsa der Geonim"**) the **"ordained scholars who take the place of the Great Sanhedrin"**. (A regular ordination (**"semikhah"**) is of course not implied here: that did not exist in Babylonia, only a solemn nomination taking place.)

**Gaon** Ẓemaḥ refers in a responsum to **"the ancient scholars of the first row, who take the place of the Great Sanhedrin"**. The seven masters, or **"allufim"** and the **"Haberim"**, the three most prominent among the other members of the college, sat in the first of the seven rows. Nine Sanhedrists were subordinated to each of the seven **Allufim**, who probably supervised the instruction given during the entire year by their subordinates. The members of the academy who were not ordained sat behind the seven rows of **Sanhedrists**.

## Works of the Geonim / *History of Responsa: Geonim*

Early in the Geonic era, the majority of the questions asked them were sent from Babylonia and the neighboring lands. Jewish communities in these regions had religious leaders who were somewhat acquainted with the **Talmud**, and who could on occasion visit the Jewish academies in Babylon. A literature of questions and answers developed, known as the **Responsa** literature.

The questions were usually limited to one or more specific cases, while the **Responsum** to such a query gave a ruling, a concise reason for it, together with supporting citations from the **Talmud**, and often a refutation of any possible objection. More discursive were the **Responsa** of the later **Geonim** after the first half of the 9th century, when questions began to be sent from more distant regions, where the inhabitants were less familiar with the **Talmud**, and were less able to visit the Babylonian academies, then the only seats of **Talmud**ic learning.

The later **Geonim** did not restrict themselves to the **Mishnahh** and **Talmud**, but used the decisions and **Responsa** of their predecessors, whose sayings and traditions were generally regarded as authoritative. These **Responsa** of the later **Geonim** were often essays on **Talmud**ic themes, and since a single letter often answered many questions, it frequently became book-length in size. Two important examples of such books are the **Siddur of Amram Gaon**, addressed to the Jews of Spain in response to a question about the laws of prayer, and the **Epistle of Sherira Gaon**, which sets out the history of the **Mishnahh** and the **Talmud** in response to a question from Tunisia.

Some of the **Responsa** that have survived are in their original form, while others are extant only as quotations in later works. Many have been found in the **Cairo Geniza**.

**Examples of Responsa collections are:**
- *Halakhot Pesukot min ha-Geonim* (Brief Rulings of the **Geonim**): Constantinople 1516
- *Sheelot u-Teshuvot me-ha-Geonim*: Constantinople 1575
- *Shaare Tzedek* (Gates of Justice), edited by Nissim ben Hayyim: Salonica 1792, containing 533 **Responsa** arranged according to subject and an index by the editor
- *Teshuvot Ha-Geonim*, ed. Mussafia: Lyck 1864
- *Teshuvot ha-Geonim: Shaare Teshuvah* with commentary *Iyye ha-Yam* by Israel Moses Hazan: Livorno 1869; linked here
- *Shaare Teshuvah ha-Shalem*, ed. Leiter: New York 1946
- *Teshuvot Geone Mizrach u-Ma'arav*, ed. Mueller: Berlin 1888
- Lewin, B. M., *Otzar ha-Geonim: Thesaurus of the **Gaon**ic Responsa and Commentaries Following the Order of the **Talmud**ic Tractates* (13 vols): Haifa 1928
- Assaf, Simhah, *Teshuvot ha-Geonim*: Jerusalem 1927 (second volume 1942).

## Other works

**Individual Geonim often composed treatises and commentaries. Three handbooks on Jewish law are:**

- Halakhot Pesukot of Yehudai **Gaon** (not to be confused with the **Responsa** collection of the same name): this was the basis of many other abridgments
- She'iltot of Achai **Gaon**
- Halakhot Gedolot, by Simeon Kayyara.

The most notable author among the **Geonim** was Saadia **Gaon**, who wrote Biblical commentaries and many other works: he is best known for the philosophical work **Emunoth ve-Deoth.**

## *Yarchei Kalla*

Two months of the year were denoted as *Yarchei kallah*, or **"months of the bride"** (referring to the **Talmud**) – the Hebrew months of **Adar and Elul**. During this time, foreign students assembled in the academy for common study.

During the first three weeks of the *Yarchei kallah* the scholars seated in the first row reported on the **Talmud** treatise assigned for study during the preceding months; in the fourth week the other scholars and also some of the pupils were called upon. Discussions followed, and difficult passages were laid before the **Gaon**, who also took a prominent part in the debates, and freely reproved any member of the college who was not up to the standard of scholarship. At the end of the *Yarchei kallah* the **Gaon** designated the **Talmud**ic treatise which the members of the assembly were obliged to study in the months intervening until the next gathering took place. The students who were not given seats were exempt from this task, being free to choose a subject for study according to their needs.

During the *Yarchei kallah*, the **Gaon** laid before the assembly a number of the questions that had been sent in during the year from all parts of the **Diaspora**. The requisite answers were discussed, and were finally recorded by the secretary of the academy according to the directions of the **Gaon**. At the end of the *Yarchei kallah* the questions, together with the answers, were read to the assembly, and the answers were signed by the **Gaon**. A large number of the Geonic **Responsa** originated in this way; but many of them were written by the respective **Geonim** without consulting the Kallah assemblies convened in the spring.

## Individual Geonim
- Achai **Gaon** (died c. 761)
- Amram **Gaon** (died 875)
- Dodai ben Nahman, **Gaon** of the **Talmud**ic academy at Pumbedita (761–764)
- Hai **Gaon** (939–1038)
- Saadia **Gaon** (882 or 892 – 942)
- Sherira **Gaon** (906–1006)

**Chananel Ben Chushiel** (Rabbeinu Chananel) (990–1053) and Nissim **Gaon** (990–1062) of Kairouan, though not holders of the office of **Gaon**, are often ranked among the **Geonim**. Others, perhaps more logically, consider them as constituting the first generation of Rishonim. **Maimonides** (1135–1204) sometimes uses the term **"Geonim"** in an extended sense, to mean **"leading authorities",** regardless of what country they lived in.

# Gods in Judaism

The name of **God** most often used in the Hebrew Bible is the **Tetragrammaton (YHYH)**. Owing to the Jewish tradition viewing the divine name as too sacred to be uttered it was replaced vocally in the synagogue ritual by the Hebrew word *Adonai* ("My Lord"), which was translated as *Kyrios* ("Lord") in the **Septuagint**, the Greek version of the Hebrew scriptures. It is frequently anglicized as **Yahweh or Jehovah** and written in most English editions of the Bible as **"The LORD"**.

**Rabbinic Judaism describes seven names** which are so holy that, once written, should not be erased: **YHYH** and **El ("God")**, **Eloah ("God")**, **Elohim ("Gods")**, **Shaddai ("Almighty")**, **Ehyeh ("I Will Be")**, and **Tzevaot (" Hosts")**. Other names are considered mere epithets or titles reflecting different aspects of **God**, but *Khumra* sometimes dictates special care such as the writing of **"G-d"** instead of **"God"** in English or saying **Ṭēt-Vav (טו, lit. "9-6")** instead of **Yōd-Hē (יה, lit. "10-5"** but also **"Jah")** for the **number fifteen in Hebrew**.

- **Seven names of God**
  - 1.1 YHYH
  - 1.2 **El**
  - 1.3 **Eloah**
  - 1.4 **Elohim**
  - 1.5 **Elohai**
  - 1.6 **El** Shaddai
  - 1.7 Tzevaot
  - 1.8 Jah

- **2Other names and titles**
  - 2.1 Adonai
  - 2.2 Adoshem
  - 2.3 Baal
  - 2.4 Ehyeh Asher ehyeh
  - 2.5 **Elah**
  - 2.6 **El** Roi
  - 2.7 **Elyon**
  - 2.8 Eternal One
  - 2.9 HaShem
  - 2.10 Shalom
  - 2.11 Shekhinah

## Seven names of God

The seven names of **God** that, once written, cannot be erased because of their holiness are the **Tetragrammaton, El, Elohim, Eloah, Elohai, El Shaddai, and Tzevaot.** In addition, the name **Jah**—because it forms part of the Tetragrammaton—is similarly protected. It is considered **"Tzevaot"** a common name and that **"Elohim"** was. All other names, such as **"Merciful"**, **"Gracious" and "Faithful",** merely represent attributes that are also common to human beings.

## YHYH

### *Tetragrammaton, Yahweh, and Lord § Religion*

The name of **God** used most often in the Hebrew Bible is **YHYH**, also known as the Tetragrammaton (Greek for **"four-letter "**). Hebrew is an **abjad**, so the word's letters **Yōd, He, Vav**, He are usually taken for consonants and expanded to Yahweh in English. In modern Jewish culture, it is accepted as **forbidden to pronounce the name the way that it is spelled**. In prayers it is pronounced Adonai, and in discussion is usually said as **HaShem**, meaning **"The Name"**.

The **Masoretic Text** uses vowel points of **Adonai or Elohim** (depending on the context) marking the pronunciation as *Yəhōwāh.* The Tetragrammaton first appears in Genesis and occurs 6,828 times in total in the Stuttgart edition of the Masoretic Text. It is thought to be an archaic third-person singular imperfect tense of the verb **"to be" (i.e., " was being").** This agrees with the passage in Exodus where **God** names Himself as **"I Will Be What I Will Be"** using the first-person singular imperfect tense.

Rabbinical Judaism teaches that the name is forbidden to all except the **High Priest**, who should only speak it in the **Holy of Holies** of the Temple in Jerusalem on **Yom Kippur**. As the Temple has not been rebuilt since its destruction in 70 A.D., most modern Jews never pronounce **YHYH** but instead read **Adonai ("My Lord")** during prayer and while reading the **Torah** and as **HaShem ("The Name")** at other times. Most English translations of the Bible write **"the Lord"** for YHYH and **"the Lord God", "the Lord God"** or **"the Sovereign Lord"** for Adonai YHYH instead of transcribing the name.

### El / *El (deity) § Hebrew Bible*

**El** appears in Ugaritic, Phoenician and other 2nd and 1st millennium bce texts both as generic **"god"** and as the head of the divine pantheon. In the **Hebrew Bible El** appears very occasionally alone **(e.g. Genesis 33:20,** *el elohe Yisrael*, **"El the God of Israel",** and Genesis 46:3, *Ha'El elohe abika*, **"El the God of thy father"),** but usually with some epithet or attribute attached **(e.g.** *El Elyon,* **"Most High El",** *El Shaddai,* **"El of** *Shaddai*", *El `Olam* **"Everlasting El",** *El Hai,* **"Living El",** *El Ra'i* **"El my Shepherd", and** *El Gibbor* **"El of Strength"),** in which cases it can be understood as the generic **"god"**.

## Eloah / *Elohim* § *Etymology*

A common name of **God** in the Hebrew Bible is **Elohim.** Despite the *-im* ending common to many plural nouns in Hebrew, the word *Elohim* when referring to **God** is grammatically singular, and takes a singular verb in the Hebrew Bible. It is cognate to the *'lhm* found in Ugaritic, where it is used for the pantheon of Canaanite gods, the children of **El** and conventionally vocalized as **"Elohim".**

It is, however, either *communicative* (including the attendant angels: so at all events in **Isaiah 6:8** and **Genesis 3:22**), or according to others, an indication of *the fullness of power and might* implied. It is best explained as a plural of *self-deliberation*. The use of plural as possible evidence to suggest an evolution in the formation of early Jewish conceptions of monotheism.

## Elohai

**Elohai** or **Elohei ("My God")** is a form of **El**ohim along with the first-person singular pronoun enclitic. It appears in the names **"God of Abraham"** (*Elohai Avraham*); **"God of Abraham, Isaac, and Jacob"** (*Elohai Avraham, Elohai Yitzchak ve Elohai Ya'aqov*); and **"God of Sarah, Rebecca, Leah, and Rachel"** (*Elohai Sara, Elohai Rivka, Elohai Leah ve Elohai Rakhel*).

## El Shaddai

**El Shaddai**, is one of the names of **God** in Judaism, with its etymology coming from the influence of the **Ugaritic** religion on modern Judaism. **El Shaddai** is conventionally translated as **"God Almighty".**

## Tzevaot

**Tzevaot, Tsebaoth** or Sabaoth, lit. **"Armies")** appears in reference to armies or armed hosts of men in **Exodus and Isaiah** but is not used as a divine epithet in the Torah, Joshua, or Judges. In the First Book of Samuel, David uses the name **YHYH Tzevaot** and immediately glosses it as **"the God of the armies of Israel"**. The same name appears in the prophets along with **YHYH Elohe Tzevaot, Elohey Tzevaot, and Adonai YHYH Tzevaot.** These are usually translated in the King James Version as the **"Lord of Hosts"** or **"Lord God of Hosts".**

## Other names and titles / Adonai

Adonai **("My Lords")** is the plural form of *adon* **("Lord")** along with the first-person singular pronoun enclitic. As with **Elohim, Adonai's** grammatical form is usually explained as a plural of majesty. In the Hebrew Bible, it is nearly always used to refer to **God** (**approximately 450 occurrences**). **Adonai** itself has come to be too holy to say for Orthodox Jews, leading to its replacement by **HaShem ("The Name").**

**Deuteronomy 10:17** has the proper name *Yahweh* alongside the superlative constructions **"God of gods"** *elohe ha-elohim* and **"Lord of lords"** *adōnê ha-adonim* (KJV: **"For the LORD your God is God of gods, and Lord of lords"**).

## Adoshem

Up until the mid-twentieth century, the use of the word *Adoshem* combining the first two syllables of **"Adonai"** with the last syllable of **"Hashem"** was quite common. In the prayer **"Shema Yisrael"** with the words *Shema Yisrael Adoshem Eloheinu Adoshem Eḥad* instead of *Shema Yisrael Adonai Eloheinu Adonai Eḥad*.

## Baal

Baal , properly Ba'al, meant **"owner"** and, by extension, **"lord", "master", and "husband"** in Hebrew and the other Northwest Semitic languages. It and **Baali ("My Lord")** were treated as synonyms of Adon and Adonai. The name became particularly associated with the **Canaanite storm god Ba'al** and was gradually avoided as a title for **Yahweh**. The prophet **Hosea** in particular reproached the Israelites for continuing to use the term.

## Ehyeh Asher ehyeh / *I Am that I Am*

*Ehyeh Asher ehyeh* is the first of three responses given to Moses when he asks for **God**'s name in the **Book of Exodus**. Although *Ehyeh Asher ehyeh* is generally rendered in English **"I am that I am"**, better renderings might be **"I will be what I will be"** or **"I will be who I will be"**, or **"I shall prove to be whatsoever I shall prove to be"** or even **"I will be because I will be"**.

## Elah

**Elah (Aramaic: "Elim")** is the Aramaic word for God. The origin of the word is uncertain and it may be related to a root word, meaning **"reverence"**. **Elah** is found in the Tanakh in the **books of Ezra, Jeremiah (Jer 10:11,** the only verse in the entire book written in Aramaic), and **Daniel.** Elah is used to describe both pagan gods and the Jews' **God**. The word **'Elah -** is also an Arabic word which means god. The name is etymologically related to **Allah** used by Muslims**.**

- **Elah Yisrael**, **God** of Israel (Ezra 5:1)
- **Elah Yerushelem**, **God** of Jerusalem (Ezra 7:19)
- **Elah Shemaya**, **God** of Heaven (Ezra 7:23)
- **Elah-avahati**, **God** of my fathers, (Daniel 2:23)
- **Elah Elahin**, **God** of gods (Daniel 2:47)

## El Roi

In the **Book of Genesis, Hagar** is said to use this name for **God** who spoke to her through his angel. In Hebrew, her phrase **"El Roi"** is taken as an epithet of **God ("God of Seeing")** although the King James Version translates it as a statement: **"Thou God seest me."**

## Elyon

**The name Elyon occurs in combination with El, YHYH, Elohim and alone**. It appears chiefly in poetic and later Biblical passages. The Modern Hebrew adjective **"`Elyon"** means **"supreme"** (as in **"Supreme Court"**) or **"Most High"**. *El Elyon* has been traditionally translated into English as **'God Most High'**.

## Eternal One

**"The Eternal One"** is increasingly used, particularly in **Reform and Reconstructionist** communities seeking to use gender-neutral language. In the Torah, *Hashem El Olam* **("the Everlasting God") is used at Genesis 21:33 to refer to God.**

## HaShem

It is common Jewish practice to restrict the use of the names of **God** to a liturgical context. In casual conversation some Jews, even when not speaking Hebrew, will call **God** *HaShem* (השם), which is Hebrew for **"the Name" (cf. Leviticus 24:11 and Deuteronomy 28:58).** Likewise, when quoting from the Tanakh or prayers, some pious Jews will replace *Adonai* with *HaShem*. A popular expression containing this phrase is *Baruch HaShem*, meaning **"Thank God" (literally, "Blessed be the Name").**

## Shalom

Talmudic authors, ruling on the basis of Gideon's name for an altar **("YHVH-Shalom", according to Judges 6:24),** write that **"the name of God is 'Peace'"** (*Pereq ha-Shalom*, Shab. **10b);** consequently, a Talmudic opinion (*Shabbat*, 10b) asserts that one would greet another with the word *shalom (*help info*)* in order for the word not to be forgotten in the exile.

## Shekhinah

*Shekhinah*) help·info is the presence or manifestation of **God** which has descended to **"dwell"** among humanity. The term never appears in the Hebrew Bible; later rabbis used the word when speaking of **God** dwelling either in the **Tabernacle** or amongst the people of Israel. The root of the word means **"dwelling". Of the principal names of God, it is the only one that is of the feminine gender in Hebrew grammar.** Some believe that this was the name of a female counterpart of **God.**

**The Arabic form of the01 word "***Sakinah* **is also mentioned in the Quran**. This mention is in the middle of the narrative of the choice of **Saul** to be king and is mentioned as descending with the **Ark of the Covenant.**

## Kabbalistic use

**One of the most important names is that of the Ein SOF ("Endless"), which first came into use after CE 1300.** By spelling these four names out with the names of the Hebrew letters this new **forty-five letter long name** is produced. Spelling the letters in **(YHYH)** by itself gives each letter in Hebrew is given a value, according to **gematria**, and the value of is also 45. The seventy-two-fold name is derived from three verses in **Exodus 14:19–21.** Each of the verses contains 72 letters. Some regard this name as the **Shem hamphorasch.** The **Proto-Kabbalistic book** *Sefer Yetzirah* describe how **the creation of the world was achieved by manipulation of these 216 sacred letters that form the names of God.**

## Erasing the name of God

From this it is understood that one should not erase or blot out the name of **God**. The words **"God" and "Lord"** are written by some Jews as **"G-d" and "L-rd"** as a way of avoiding writing any name of **God** in full out. This issue is most controversial in the context of the motto of the United States, **"In God We Trust"**, which has been minted or printed without hyphenation since its first appearance in 1864. According to **Talmudic Tractate** *Rosh Hashana*, Jews in the times of the **Hasmonean Kingdom** were **"weaned off"** the practice of writing the name of Heaven by the Sages, an event that was commemorated as a holiday on the **third of Tishrei**, a date now dedicated to the **Fast of Gedaliah.**

# Golden Age (Spain)

**The golden age of Jewish culture in Spain coincided with the Middle Ages in Europe, a period of Muslim rule throughout much of the Iberian Peninsula**. During intermittent periods of time, Jews were generally accepted in society and Jewish religious, cultural, food, and economic life blossomed.

The nature and length of this "**Golden Age**" has been a subject of much debate, as there were at least **three Golden Ages** interrupted by periods of oppression of Jews and non-Jews. A few scholars give the **start of the Golden Age as 711–718, the Muslim conquest of Iberia**. Others date it from 912, during the rule of **Abd-ar-Rahman III**. The end of the age is variously given as 1031, when the Caliphate of Cordoba ended; 1066, **the date of the Granada massacre; 1090**, when the Almoravids invaded; or the mid-12th century, when the Almohads invaded.

## The nature of the Golden Age

Having invaded the areas throughout Southern Spain, and coming to rule in a matter of seven years, Islamic rulers were confronted with many questions relating to the implementation of **Islamic Rule on a non-Islamic society**. The coexistence of Muslims, Jews, and Christians during this time is revered by many writers. **Al-Andalus was a key center of Jewish life during the early Middle Ages,** producing important scholars and one of the most stable and wealthy Jewish communities and a relatively educated society for the Muslim occupiers and their Jewish collaborators, as well as some **Christians who openly collaborated with the Muslims and Jews.**

**Maria Rosa Menocal**, a specialist in Iberian literature at Yale University claims that **"tolerance was an inherent aspect of Andalusian society"**. Menocal's 2003 book, *The Ornament of the World*, argues that the Jewish dhimmis living under the Caliphate, while allowed fewer rights than Muslims, were still better off than in the Christian parts of Europe. Jews from other parts of Europe made their way to *Al-Andalus*. **Bernard Lewis** takes issue with this view, calling it ahistorical and exaggerated. He argues that Islam traditionally did not offer equality nor even pretend that it did, arguing that it would have been both a **"theological as well as a logical absurdity."** However, also Lewis states:

**"Generally, the Jewish people were allowed to practice their religion and live according to the laws and scriptures of their community. Jews were allowed certain freedoms but, like their Christian counterparts, were prohibited from having administrative authority over Muslims except in a few cases."**

**Mark Cohen**, Professor of Near Eastern Studies at Princeton University, in his *Under Crescent and Cross*, calls the idealized interfaith utopia a **"myth"** that was first promulgated by Jewish historians such as **Heinrich Graetz** in the 19th century as a rebuke to Christian countries for their treatment of Jews. This myth was met with the "**counter-myth**" of the "**neo-lachrymose conception of Jewish-Arab history**" by **Bat Yeor** and others, which also "**cannot be maintained in the light of historical reality**".

## Birth of the Golden Age

**Prior to 581, the Jews experienced a Golden Age under the Arian Visigoth occupiers of Spain.** The Visigoths were mainly indifferent towards Jews and allowed them to grow and prosper. After the **Visigoths joined the Catholic Church**, they placed ever greater economic burdens on the Jewish population, and later persecuted them severely. **It is possible that Jews welcomed the Muslim Arab and mainly Berber conquerors in the 8th century.**

A period of tolerance dawned for the Jews of the **Iberian Peninsula**, whose number was considerably augmented by immigration from North Africa in the wake of the Muslim conquest. North African Jewish immigrants and immigrants from the Middle East bolstered the Jewish population, and made **Muslim Spain probably the biggest center of contemporary Jews**. Especially after 912, during the reign of **Abd-ar-Rahman III** and his son, **Al-Hakam II**, the Jews prospered culturally, and some notable figures held high posts in the **Caliphate of Cordoba**. Jewish philosophers, mathematicians, astronomers, poets, and rabbinical scholars, composed highly rich cultural and scientific work.

Many devoted themselves to the study of the sciences and philosophy, composing many of the most valuable texts of **Jewish Philosophy**. **Jews took part in the overall prosperity of Muslim Al-Andalus.** Jewish economic expansion was unparalleled. In Toledo after the **Christian reconquest in 1085**, Jews were involved in translating Arabic texts to the romance languages in the so-called **Toledo School of Translators**, as they had been previously in translating Greek and Hebrew texts into Arabic. Jews also contributed to botany, geography, medicine, mathematics, poetry and philosophy.

'**Abd al-Rahman**'s court physician and minister was **Hasdai ibn Shaprut**, the patron of **Menahem ben Saruq, Dunash ben Labrat, and other Jewish scholars and poets.** In following centuries, Jewish thought flourished under famous figures such as **Samuel Ha-Nagid, Moses ibn Ezra, Solomon ibn Gabirol, Judah Halevi and Moses Maimonides**. During 'Abd al-Rahman's term of power, the scholar **Moses ben Enoch** was appointed rabbi of Córdoba, and as a consequence Al-Andalus became the center of Talmudic study, and Córdoba the meeting-place of Jewish savants.

This was a time of partial Jewish autonomy. As "**dhimmis**", or "**protected non-Muslims**", Jews in the Islamic world paid the **Jizya**, which was administered separately from the **zakat** paid by Muslims. The **Jizya** has been viewed variously as a head tax, as payment for non-conscription in the military (**as non-Muslims were normally prohibited from bearing arms or receiving**

**martial training),** or as a tribute. Jews had their own legal system and social services. Monotheist religions of the people of the book were tolerated but conspicuous **displays of faith, such as bells and processions, were discouraged.**

Comparing the treatment of Jews in the medieval Islamic world and medieval Christian Europe, **the Jews were far more integrated in the political and economic life of Islamic society**, and usually faced far less violence from Muslims, though there were some instances of persecution in the Islamic world as well from the 11th century. The Islamic world classified Jews (and Christians) as *dhimmi* and allowed them to practice their religion more freely than they could do in **Christian Europe**.

Other authors criticize the modern notion of **Al-Andalus** being a tolerant society of equal opportunities for all religious groups as a "**myth**". Jews were living in an uneasy coexistence with Muslims and Catholics, and the relationship between these groups was more often than not marked by segregation and mutual hostility. **In the 1066 Granada massacre of the entire Jewish population** of the city, the Jewish death toll was higher than in the much publicized **Christian Pogroms** in the **Rhineland** slightly later. The notable Jewish philosopher **Moses Maimonides (1135–1204)** was forced to flee from **Al-Andalus** to avoid conversion by the Almohads. **In Letter to Yemen, Maimonides wrote:**

**"Dear brothers, because of our many sins Hashem has cast us among this nation, the Arabs, who are treating us badly. They pass laws designed to cause us distress and make us despised. ... Never has there been a nation that hated, humiliated and loathed us as much as this one."**

## End of the Golden Age

With the death of **Al-Hakam II Ibn Abd-ar-Rahman in 976**, the Caliphate began to dissolve, and the position of the Jews became more precarious under the various smaller Kingdoms. The **first major persecution was the 1066 Granada massacre**, which occurred on 30 December, when a Muslim mob stormed the royal palace in Granada, **crucified Jewish vizier Joseph ibn Naghrela and massacred most of the Jewish population of the city.** "**More than 1,500 Jewish families, numbering 4,000 persons, fell in one day**." This was the first persecution of Jews on the Peninsula under Islamic rule.

**Manuscript page by Maimonides, one of the greatest Jewish scholars of Al Andalus, born in Córdoba. Arabic language in Hebrew letters**

Beginning in 1090 the situation deteriorated further with the invasion of the **Almoravids**, a puritan Muslim sect from Morocco. Even under the Almoravids, some Jews prospered (although far more so under **Ali III**, than under his father **Yusuf ibn Tashfin**). Among those who held the title of **"vizier" or "nasi"** in Almoravid times were the poet and physician **Abu Ayyub Solomon ibn al-Mu'allam, Abraham ibn Meir ibn Kamnial, Abu Isaac ibn Muhajar, and Solomon ibn Farusal.**

**The Almoravids, were ousted from the peninsula in 1148**; however, the peninsula was again invaded, by the even more puritanical Almohads. During the reign of these Berber dynasties, many Jewish and even Muslim scholars left the Muslim-controlled portion of Iberia for the city of Toledo, which had been reconquered in 1085 by Christian forces.

The major Jewish presence in Iberia continued until the **Jews were forcibly expelled en masse due to the edict of expulsion by Christian Spain in 1492 and a similar decree by Christian Portugal in 1496.**

## Notable figures

- Abu al-Fadl ibn Hasda, philosopher, vizier at Zaragoza
- Abu Ruiz ibn Dahari fought in the war against the Almohads.
- Amram ben Isaac ibn Shalbib, scholar and diplomat in the service of Alfonso VI of Castile
- Bahya ibn Paquda, philosopher and author of *Chovot ha-Levavot*
- Bishop Bodo-Eleazar; according to the *Jewish Encyclopedia*, "a convert to Judaism ... ... went to Córdoba, where he is said to have endeavored to win proselytes for Judaism from among the Spanish Christians."
- Dunash ben Labrat (920–990), poet
- Isaac ibn Albalia, astronomer and rabbi at Granada
- Jehiel ben Asher, poet
- Jekuthiel ibn Hasan, king's minister at Zaragoza, fell from favor, executed
- Joseph ibn Hasdai, poet, father of Abu al-Fadl ibn Hasdai
- Joseph ibn Migash, diplomat for Granada
- Maimonides, rabbi, physician, and philosopher
- Menahem ben Saruk
- Nahmanides
- Solomon Ibn Gabirol, poet and philosopher
- Moses ben Enoch[citation needed]
- Yehuda Halevi, poet and philosopher
- Abraham ibn Ezra, rabbi and poet
- Moses ibn Ezra, philosopher and poet
- Benjamin of Tudela, traveler and explorer
- Samuel Ha-Nagid ibn Nagrela, king's minister and poet
- Hasdai ibn Shaprut, royal physician and statesman
- Judah ben Saul ibn Tibbon

# *Halakha*

*Halakha* ( Hebrew: Sephardic: also transliterated as *Halacha, Halakhah, Halakhah or halocho*) (**Ashkenazic:** ) is the collective body of Jewish religious laws derived from the **Written and Oral Torah**. **Halakha** is based on biblical laws or **"commandments"** (*mitzvot*) (**traditionally numbered as 613),** subsequent Talmudic and Rabbinic law, and the customs and traditions compiled in the many books, one of the most famous of which is the 16th-century *Shulkhan Aruch* (literally **"Prepared Table").**

*Halakha* is often translated as **"Jewish Law",** although a more literal translation might be **"the way to behave"** or **"the way of walking".** *Halakha* guides not only religious practices and beliefs, but also numerous aspects of day-to-day life. Since the **Jewish Enlightenment (***Haskalah***)** and Jewish emancipation many have come to view the *halakha* as less binding in day-to-day life. Some differences in *halakha* itself are found among **Ashkenazi, Mizrahi, Sephardi, Yemenite.**

## ⌐ Etymology and terminology

*Halakha* does not include the parts of the Torah not related to commandments. *Halakha* **constitutes the practical application of the 613** *mitzvot* **("commandments")** in the Torah, as developed through the **Mishnah** and the **Talmud** (the "Oral Torah") and as codified in the Mishneh Torah **("Recapitulation of the Torah")** or Shulkhan **("Code of Law").** *Halakha* **has been developed throughout the generations since before 500 BCE.**

## The 613 mitzvot / *Mitzvah § Mitzvot and Jewish law*

*Halakha* **comprises the practical application of the 613** *mitzvot* **in the Torah. u shall")** *mitzvot* **and 365 negative ("thou shall not")** *mitzvot,* supplemented by **seven** *mitzvot* legislated by the Rabbis of antiquity. **Commandments are divided into positive and negative commands,** which are treated differently in terms of divine and human punishment. (**613 commandments).**

**Maimonides'** *Mishneh Torah* **divides the laws into 14 sections.** The codification efforts that culminated in the *Shulkhan Aruch* divide the law into four sections, including only laws that do not depend on being physically present in the Land of Israel.

## Sin

Judaism regards the **violation of the commandments, the** *mitzvot,* **to be a sin**. The generic Hebrew word for any kind of sin is *aveira* **("transgression").** Based on the Tanakh (Hebrew Bible) Judaism describes **three levels of sin:**

- **Pesha** – an "intentional sin"; an action committed in deliberate defiance of God's commandments
- *Avon* – a "sin of lust or uncontrollable emotion, committed against one's will, and is not in line with one's true inner desires". It is a sin done knowingly, but not done to defy God

- *Chet* – an "unintentional sin"

Judaism understands that the vast majority of people, aside from those who are termed *Tzadikim* and those termed *Tzadikim gemurim* (Hebrew: **"the righteous"** and **"the completely righteous"**), will succumb to sin in their lives. The punishments included **execution, corporal punishment, incarceration, and excommunication.** However, since the fall of the **Second Temple**, executions have been forbidden.

## Gentiles and Jewish law

The **Seven Laws of Noah**, also referred to as the **Noahide Laws** or the **Noachide Laws**, are a set of imperatives which, according to the Talmud, were given by God as a binding set of laws for the "**children of Noah**" – that is, all of humanity.

## Sources and process

In antiquity, the *Sanhedrin* functioned essentially as the **Supreme Court** and legislature (in the US judicial system) for Judaism, and had the power to administer binding law, including both received law and its own Rabbinic decrees, on all Jews—rulings of the Sanhedrin became *halakha*. That court ceased to function in its full mode in 40 CE. In some cases, the Sages allowed the temporary violation of a prohibition in order to maintain the Jewish system as a whole.

## Historical analysis

The **seven middot** (literally **"measurements"**, and referring to behavior) of Hillel and the **thirteen of Ishmael** are earlier than the time of Hillel himself, who was the first to transmit them. According to **Akiba**, the divine language of the Torah is distinguished from the speech of men by the fact that in the former no word or sound is superfluous.

## Views today / *Talmud § Present day*

Orthodox Judaism holds that *halakha* **is the divine law as laid out in the Torah (five books of Moses),** Rabbinical laws, Rabbinical decrees and customs combined. **Deuteronomy 17:11.** Conservative Judaism holds that *halakha* is normative and binding. Humanistic Jews value the Torah as a historical, political, and sociological text written by their ancestors. They do not believe **"that every word of the Torah is true, or even morally correct, just because the Torah is old".**

## Differences between Orthodox and Conservative Judaism

Orthodox Jews maintain *halakha* is derived from the divine law of the Torah (Bible), Rabbinical laws, Rabbinical decrees and customs combined. Conservative Jews have varied views regarding the origin of the Torah and its authority today, and believe it can be continuously reinterpreted.

## Orthodox Judaism

Orthodox Jews believe that **halakha** is a religious system whose core represents the revealed will of God. The regulations were transmitted orally until shortly after the **destruction of the Second Temple**. The most widely accepted codes of Jewish law are known as **Mishneh Torah** and the **Shulkhan**. **Haredi Jews** generally hold that even *Minhagim* (customs) must be retained and existing precedents cannot be reconsidered.

## Conservative Judaism / *Conservative halakha*

One view held by **Conservative Judaism** is that while God is real, the Torah is not the word of God in a literal sense. Traditional Jewish law is still seen as binding. The Talmudic concept of *Kavod HaBriyot* permits lifting Rabbinic decrees (as distinct from carving narrow exceptions) on grounds of human dignity, and used this principle in a December 2006 opinion lifting all Rabbinic prohibitions on **homosexual** conduct (the opinion held that only **male-male anal sex** was forbidden by the Bible and that this remained prohibited).

**"We cannot conceive of God sanctioning undeserved suffering ... When a law of Torah conflicts with morality, when the law is 'unpleasant,' we are committed to find a way to address the problem... We are willing to do explicitly what was largely implicit in the past, namely, to make changes when needed on moral grounds." "We should acknowledge that God's law is beyond our authority to eliminate".**

## Codes of Jewish law

There are many formal codes of Jewish law that have developed over the past two thousand years. The Torah and the Talmud are not formal codes of law - they are sources of law.

## The major works in the codification of Jewish law:

- **The Mishnah**, composed by Rabbi Judah the Prince, in 200 CE, as a basic outline of the state of the Oral Law in his time. This was the framework upon which the Talmud was based; the Talmud's dialectic analysis of the content of the **Mishna** (*Gemara*; completed c. 500) became the basis for all later halakhic decisions and subsequent codes.
- **Codifications by the Geonim** of the halakhic material in the Talmud. An early work, *She'iltot* ("Questions") by Achai of Shabcha (c. 752), discusses over **190** *mitzvot* – exploring and addressing various questions on these. The first legal codex proper, *Halakhot Pesukot* ("Decided Laws"), by Yehudai Gaon (c. 760), rearranges the Talmud passages in a structure manageable to the layman. (It was written in vernacular Aramaic, and subsequently translated into Hebrew as *Hilkhot Riu*). *Halakhot Gedolot* ("Great Law Book").
- The *Hilchot* of *the Rif*, **Rabbi Isaac Alfasi** (1013–1103), summations of the legal material in the Talmud. Alfasi transcribed the Talmud's halakhic conclusions verbatim, without the surrounding deliberation; he also excludes all Aggadic (non-legal, homiletic) matter. The *Hilchot* soon superseded the Geonic codes.

- The **Mishneh Torah by Maimonides** (1135–1204). This work encompasses the full range of Talmudic law; it is organized and reformulated in a logical system – in 14 books, 83 sections and 1000 chapters – with each *halakha* stated clearly. It also includes a section on Metaphysics and fundamental beliefs. It is within the tradition of **Saadia Gaon**.) It is the main source of practical *halakha* for many Yemenite Jews – mainly **Baladi and Dor Daim** – as well as for a growing community referred to as *talmidei haRamban.*

- **The work of *the Rosh***, Rabbi Asher ben Jehiel (1250?/1259?–1328), an abstract of the Talmud, concisely stating the final halakhic decision and quoting later authorities, notably Alfasi, Maimonides, and the Tosafists. This work superseded Rabbi Alfasi's and has been printed with almost every subsequent edition of the Talmud.

- The ***Sefer Mitzvot Gadol*** (The "SeMaG") of Rabbi Moses ben Jacob of Coucy (first half of the 13th century, Coucy, Northern France). "SeMaG" is organized around the 365 negative and the 248 positive commandments, separately discussing each of them according to the Talmud (in light of the commentaries of Rashi and the Tosafot) and the other codes existent at the time. ***Sefer Mitzvot Katan*** ("SeMaK") by **Isaac ben Joseph** of Corbeil is an abridgement of the *SeMaG*, including additional practical *halakha*, as well as Aggadic and ethical material.

- **"The Mordechai"** – by Mordecai ben Hillel, d. Nuremberg 1298 – serves both as a source of analysis, as well of decided law. Mordechai considered about 350 halakhic authorities, and was widely influential, particularly amongst the Ashkenazi and Italian communities. Although organized around the *Hilchot* of *the Rif*, it is, in fact, an independent work. It has been printed with every edition of the Talmud since 1482.

- **The Arba'ah Turim** (*The Tur*, lit. "The Four Columns") by Rabbi Jacob ben Asher (1270–1343, Toledo, Spain). This work traces the *halakha* from the Torah text and the Talmud through the Rishonim, with the *Hilchot* of Alfasi as its starting point. **Ben Asher** followed Maimonides's precedent in arranging his work in a topical order. The code is divided into four main sections.
  - **Orach Chayim:** "The Way of Life" worship and ritual observance in the home and synagogue, through the course of the day, the weekly Sabbath and the festival cycle.
  - **Yoreh De'ah: "Teach Knowledge"** assorted ritual prohibitions, dietary laws and regulations concerning menstrual impurity.
  - **Even Ha'ezer: "The Rock of the Helpmate"** marriage, divorce and other issues in family law.
  - **Choshen Mishpat: "The Breastplate of Judgment"** The administration and adjudication of civil law.

- The **Beit Yosef, and the Shulkhan Aruch of Rabbi Yosef Karo** (1488–1575). The ***Beit Yosef*** is a huge commentary on the *Tur* in which Rabbi Karo traces the development of each law from the Talmud through later Rabbinical literature (examining thirty-two authorities, beginning with the Talmud and ending with the works of Rabbi Israel Isserlein). The **Shulkhan Aruch** is, in turn, a condensation of the ***Beit Yosef*** – stating each ruling simply (literally translated, ***Shulkhan Aruch*** means "set table"); this work follows the chapter divisions of the **Tur.**

The Shulkhan Aruch, together with its related commentaries, is considered by many to be the most authoritative compilation of *halakha* since the Talmud. In writing the Shulkhan Aruch, **Rabbi Karo** based his rulings on three authorities – **Maimonides, Asher ben Jehiel (Rosh), and Isaac Alfasi (Rif);** he considered *the Mordechai* in inconclusive cases. Sephardic Jews, generally, refer to the Shulkhan Aruch as the basis for their daily practice.

- The works of **Rabbi Moshe Isserles** ("**Rema**"; Kraków, Poland, 1525 to 1572). Rema noted that the *Shulkhan Aruch* was based on the Sephardic tradition, and he created a series of glosses to be appended to the text of the Shulkhan Aruch for cases where Sephardi and Ashkenazi customs differed (based on the works of Yaakov Moelin, Israel Isserlein, and Israel Bruna). The glosses are called *Hamapah,* the "Tablecloth" for the "Set Table". Isserles' *Darkhei Moshe* is similarly a commentary on the Tur and the Beit Yosef.

- The *Levush Malkhut* ("Levush") of Rabbi Mordecai Yoffe (c. 1530–1612). A ten volume work, five discussing *halakha* at a level "midway between the two extremes: the lengthy Beit Yosef of Karo on the one hand, and on the other Karo's Shulkhan Aruch together with the Mappah of Isserles, which is too brief", that particularly stresses the customs and practices of the Jews of Eastern Europe. The Levush was exceptional among the codes, in that it treated certain *Halakhot* from a Kabbalistic standpoint.

- The **Shulkhan of Rabbi Shneur Zalman of Liadi** (c. 1800) was an attempt to recodify the law as it stood at that time– incorporating commentaries on the Shulkhan Aruch, and subsequent Responsa – and thus stating the decided *halakha*, as well as the underlying reasoning.

  It is the basis of practice for **Chabad-Lubavitch** and other Hasidic groups, and is quoted as authoritative by many subsequent works, Hasidic and non-Hasidic alike. *Likutey Halakhot* (c. 1800; 'Collected Laws'), also a Hasidic work, follows the order of topics in the **Shulkhan Aruch**, explaining them in the light of Breslover teachings. It was written by **Nathan of Breslov** as based on the teachings of his *Rebbe,* **Nachman of Breslov.**

- Works structured directly on the **Shulkhan Aruch**, providing analysis in light of Acharonic material and codes. The Mishnah Berurah of Rabbi Yisroel Meir ha-Kohen, (the "**Chofetz Chaim**", Poland, 1838–1933) is a commentary on the "**Orach Chayim**" section of the Shulkhan Aruch, discussing the application of each *halakha* in light of all subsequent Acharonic decisions.

  It has become the authoritative halakhic guide for much of Orthodox Ashkenazic Jewry in the postwar period. Aruch HaShulchan by **Rabbi Yechiel Michel Epstein** (1829–1888) is a scholarly analysis of *halakha* through the perspective of the major Rishonim..

  Kaf HaChaim on Orach Chayim and parts of Yoreh De'ah, by the Sephardi sage **Yaakov Chaim Sofer**(Baghdad and Jerusalem, 1870–1939) is similar in scope, authority and approach to the Mishnah Berurah. Yalkut Yosef, by Rabbi Yitzhak Yosef, is a voluminous, widely cited and contemporary work of *halakha*, based on the rulings of **Rabbi Ovadia Yosef.**

- "**Layman oriented**" digests of *halakha*. The *Kitzur Shulkhan Aruch* of Rabbi **Shlomo Ganzfried** (Hungary 1804–1886), based on the very strict Hungarian customs of the 19th

272

century, became immensely popular after its publication due to its simplicity. **The Ben Ish Chai by Yosef Chaim** (Baghdad, 1832–1909) is a corresponding Sephardi work.

# Hasidic Judaism

**Hasidism, Hasidic Judaism (Hebrew: "piety")**, is a Jewish religious group. It arose as a spiritual revival movement in contemporary **Western Ukraine during the 18th century**, and spread rapidly throughout Eastern Europe. **Israel Ben Eliezer, the "Baal Shem Tov"**, is regarded as its founding father, and his disciples developed and disseminated it. **Present-day Hasidism is a sub-group within Ultra-Orthodox ("Haredi") Judaism**, and is noted for its religious conservatism and social seclusion. Its members adhere closely both to **Orthodox** Jewish practice, including the use of the **Yiddish** language, are nowadays associated almost exclusively with **Hasidism**.

Hasidic thought draws heavily on **Lurianic Kabbalah**, and, to an extent, is a popularization of it. Teachings emphasize **God's immanence in the universe**, the need to cleave and be one with him at all times, the devotional aspect of religious practice, and the spiritual dimension of corporeality and mundane acts. *Hasidim*, the adherents of **Hasidism**, are organized in independent sects known as "**courts**" or dynasties, each headed by its own hereditary leader, a *Rebbe*. There are several "**courts**" with many thousands of member households each, and hundreds of smaller ones. As of 2016, there were over **130,000** Hasidic households worldwide, **about 5% of the global Jewish population**.

## ☑ Etymology

The terms *Hasid* and *Hasidut*, meaning "**pietist**" and "**piety**", have a long history in Judaism. Adam himself is honored with the title in tractate **Eruvin** 18b by **Rabbi Meir: "Adam was a great *Hasid*, having fasted for 130 years."** The first to adopt the epithet collectively were apparently the *Hasidim* in **Second Temple** period Judea, known as **Hasideans**, who perhaps served as the model for those mentioned in the **Talmud**.

In 12th-century Rhineland, or *Ashkenaz* in Jewish parlance, another prominent school of ascetics named themselves *Hasidim*; to distinguish them from the rest, later research employed the term **Ashkenazi Hasidim**. In the 16th century, when **Kabbalah** spread, the title also became associated with it. **Jacob ben Hayyim Zemah** wrote in his glossa on **Isaac Luria's** version of the **Shulkhan Aruch** that, **"One who wishes to tap the hidden wisdom, must conduct himself in the manner of the Pious."** The movement founded by **Israel Ben Eliezer** in the 18th century adopted the term *Hasidim* in the original connotation.

## Hasidic philosophy / Distinctions

The difficulty of separating the movement's philosophy from that of its main inspiration, **Lurianic Kabbalah**, and determining what was novel and what merely a recapitulation, also baffled historians. Ascribed all perceptions to so-called **"Neo-Hasidic"** writers and thinkers, like **Martin Buber**. The **"Neo-Hasidic"** interpretation influenced even scholarly discourse to a great degree, but had a tenuous connection with reality.

# Immanence

The most fundamental theme underlying all Hasidic theory is the **immanence of God in the universe**, often expressed in a phrase from **Tikunei haZohar**, *Leit Atar panuy mi-néya* (Aramaic: **"no site is devoid of Him"**). In the beginning, in order to create the world, God contracted (*Tzimtzum*) his omnipresence, the **Ein Sof**, leaving a Vacant Void (*Khalal panui*), bereft from obvious presence and therefore able to entertain free will, contradictions and other phenomena seemingly separate from God himself. The infinite **Ein Sof** cannot manifest in the **Vacant Void**, and must limit itself in the guise of measurable corporeality that may be perceived.

**Shneur Zalman of Liadi**, in his commentary **Torah or** on **Genesis 28:21**, who wrote that *"this is the purpose of Creation, from Infinity to Finitude, so it may be reversed from the state of Finite to that of Infinity"*. God progressively diminished himself into the world through the various dimensions, or **Sephirot**. *"Reality lost its static nature and permanent value, now measured by a new standard, seeking to expose the Godly, boundless essence, manifest in its tangible, circumscribed opposite."*

**One major derivative of this philosophy is the notion of** *devekut*, **"communion"**. As God was everywhere, connection with him had to be pursued ceaselessly as well, in all times, places and occasions. Closely linked with the former is **Bitul ha-Yesh, "Negation of the Existent",** or of the **"Corporeal".** Superficial observance of the universe by the **"eyes of the flesh"** (*Einei ha-Basar*) purportedly reflects the reality of all things profane and worldly, a true devotee must transcend this illusory façade and realize that there is nothing but God.

The true divine essence of man – **the soul** – may then ascend and return to the upper realm, where it does not possess an existence independent from God. This ideal is termed **Hitpashtut ha-Gashmi'yut, "the expansion (or removal) of corporeality"**. It is the dialectic opposite of God's contraction into the world. To be enlightened and capable of **Bitul ha-Yesh**, pursuing the pure spiritual aims and defying the primitive impulses of the body, one must overcome his inferior **"Bestial Soul",** connected with the **Eyes of the Flesh**. Hasidic masters exhorted their followers to **"negate themselves"**, paying as little heed as they could for worldly concerns, and thus, to clear the way for this transformation.

Another implication of this dualism is the notion of **"Worship through Corporeality"**, *Avodah be-Gashmi'yut*. According to Lurianic doctrine, the netherworld was suffused with divine sparks, concealed within **"husks"**, *Qliphoth*. The glints had to be recovered and elevated to their proper place in the cosmos. **"Materiality itself could be embraced and consecrated".** The complementary opposite of corporeal worship, or the elation of the finite into infinite, is the concept of **Hamshacha, "drawing down" or "absorbing", and specifically,** *Hamschat ha-Shefa*, **"absorption of effluence"**. Yet another reflection of the **Ein-Yesh** dialectic is pronounced in the **transformation of evil to goodness** and the relations between these two poles and other contradicting elements.

# Haskalah

The *Haskalah*, often termed as the **Jewish Enlightenment** (Hebrew: Literally, **"wisdom"**, **"erudition"** or **"education"**), was an intellectual movement among the Jews of Central and Eastern Europe, with a certain influence on those in Western Europe and the Muslim world. It arose as a defined ideological worldview during the 1770s, and its last stage ended around 1881, with the rise of Jewish nationalism.

The **Haskalah** pursued two complementary aims. It sought to preserve the Jews as a separate, unique collective, and it pursued a set of projects of cultural and moral renewal, including a revival of Hebrew for use in secular life, which resulted in an increase in Hebrew found in print. Concurrently, it strove for an optimal integration in surrounding societies. The *Haskalah* promoted rationalism, liberalism, freedom of thought, and enquiry, and is largely perceived as the Jewish variant of the general **Age of Enlightenment.**

The *Haskalah* fulfilled an important, though limited, part in the modernization of Central and Eastern European Jews. Its activists, the *Maskilim*, exhorted and implemented communal, educational and cultural reforms in both the public and the private spheres. Definitions.

## Literary Circle

The **Haskalah** was multifaceted, with many loci which rose and dwindled at different times and across vast territories. The name *Haskalah* became a standard self-appellation in 1860, when it was taken as the motto of the Odessa-based newspaper *Ha-Melitz*, but derivatives and the title *Maskil* for activists were already common in the first edition of *Ha-Meassef* from 1 October 1783: its publishers described themselves as *Maskilim*. While Maskilic centres sometimes had loose institutions around which their members operated, the movement as a whole lacked any such. In spite of that diversity, the *Maskilim* shared a sense of common identity and self-consciousness. They were anchored in the existence of a shared literary canon, which began to be formulated in the very first **Maskilic** locus at Berlin. Its members, like **Moses Mendelssohn, Naphtali Hirz Wessely, Isaac Satanow and Isaac Euchel**, authored tracts in various genres that were further disseminated and re-read among other **Maskilim**. Each generation, in turn, elaborated and added its own works to the growing body.

The **Maskilim** researched and standardized grammar, minted countless neologisms and composed poetry, magazines, theatrical works and literature of all sorts in Hebrew. Historians described the movement largely as a **Republic of Letters**, an intellectual community based on printing houses and reading societies.

The **Maskilim**'s attitude toward Hebrew, as noted by **Moses Pelli**, was derived from Enlightenment perceptions of language as reflecting both individual and collective character. They turned to Hebrew as their primary creative medium. They turned to the Bible as a source and standard, emphatically advocating what they termed "**Pure Hebrew Tongue**" (*S'fat E'ver tzacha*) and lambasting the Rabbinic style of letters, which mixed it with Aramaic as a single "**Holy Tongue**" and often employed loanwords from other languages. Some activists, however, were not averse to using Mishnaic and Rabbinic forms.

They also preferred the **Sephardi** pronunciation, considered more prestigious, to the **Ashkenazi** one, which was linked with the Jews of Poland, who were deemed backward. During a century of activity, the **Maskilim** produced a massive contribution, forming the first phase of modern Hebrew literature. In 1755, **Moses Mendelssohn** began publishing *Qohelet Musar* "**The Moralist**", regarded as the beginning of modern writing in Hebrew and the very first journal in the language. Between 1789 and his death, **Naphtali Hirz Wessely** compiled *Shirei Tif'eret* "**Poems of Glory**", an eighteen-part epic cycle concerning **Moses** that exerted influence on all neo-Hebraic poets in the following generations.

**Joseph ha-Efrati Troplowitz** was the **Haskalah**'s pioneering playwright, best known for his 1794 epic drama *Melukhat Sha'ul* "**Reign of Saul**", which was printed in twelve editions by 1888. **Judah Leib Ben-Ze'ev** was the first Modern Hebrew grammarian, and beginning with his 1796 manual of the language, he authored books which explored it and were vital reading material for young **Maskilim** until the end of the 19th century. **Solomon Löwisohn** was the first to translate Shakespeare into Hebrew.

The central platforms of the **Maskilic "Republic of Letters"** were its great periodicals, each serving as a locus for contributors and readers during the time it was published. The first was the Königsberg (and later Berlin)-based *Ha-Meassef*, launched by **Isaac Abraham Euchel** in 1783 and printed with growing intervals until 1797. The Russian *Haskalah* was robust enough to lack any single platform. Its members published several large magazines, including the Vilnius-based *Ha-Karmel* (1860–1880), *Ha-Tsefirah* in Warsaw and more, though the probably most influential of them all was *Ha-Melitz*, launched in 1860 at Odessa by **Aleksander Zederbaum**.

**Reforming movement**

While the partisans of the *Haskalah* were much immersed in the study of sciences and Hebrew grammar, this was not a profoundly new phenomenon, and their creativity was a continuation of a long, centuries-old trend among educated Jews. The potential of "**Words of Peace and Truth**" was fully realized later, by the second generation of the movement in Berlin and other radical *Maskilim*, who openly and vehemently denounced the traditional authorities. The *Maskilim* generated an upheaval which – though by no means alone – broke the sway held by the rabbis and the traditional values over Jewish society.

The more extreme and ideologically bent came close to the **universalist** aspirations of the radical **Enlightenment**, of a world freed of superstition and backwardness in which all humans will come together under the liberating influence of reason and progress. The reconstituted Jews, these radical *Maskilim* believed, would be able to take their place as equals in an enlightened world. The **Maskilim** perceived those as remnants of medieval discrimination. They criticized various traits of Jewish society, such as child marriage – traumatized memories from unions entered at the age of thirteen or fourteen are a common theme in **Haskalah** literature – the use of anathema to enforce community will and the concentration on virtually only religious studies.

In 1778, partisans of the movement were among the founders of the Berlin Jewish Free School, or *Hevrat Hinuch Ne'arim* (Society for the Education of Boys), the first institution in **Ashkenazi** Jewry that taught general studies in addition to the reformulated and reduced traditional curriculum. Far less **Talmud,** considered cumbersome and ill-suited for children, was taught; elements considered superstitious, like *midrashim*, were also removed. Matters of faith were taught in rationalistic spirit, and in radical circles also in a sanitized manner.

In the linguistic field, the *Maskilim* wished to replace the dualism which characterized the traditional Ashkenazi community, which spoke Judaeo-German and its formal literary language was Hebrew, with another: a refined Hebrew for internal usage and the local vernacular for external ones. They almost universally abhorred Judaeo-German, regarding it as a corrupt dialect and another symptom of Jewish destitution – the movement pioneered the negative attitude to **Yiddish** which persisted many years later among the educated – though often its activists had to resort to it for lack of better medium to address the masses.

In matters of faith (which were being cordoned off into a distinct sphere of **"religion"** by modernization pressures) the movement's partisans, from moderates to radicals, lacked any uniform coherent agenda. The main standard through which they judged Judaism was that of rationalism. Their most important contribution was the revival of Jewish philosophy, rather dormant since the Italian Renaissance, as an alternative to mysticist *Kabbalah* which served as almost the sole system of thought among **Ashkenazim** and an explanatory system for observance. Rather than complex allegorical exegesis, the *Haskalah* sought a literal understanding of scripture and sacred literature.

The rejection of *Kabbalah*, often accompanied with attempts to refute the ancientness of the *Zohar,* were extremely controversial in traditional society; apart from that, the *Maskilim* had little in common. Many of the Jewish enlightened were traumatized by their own experiences, either of assertive mothers or early marriage, often conducted at the age of thirteen. Bitter memories from those are a common theme in *maskilic* autobiographies. They insisted that men become economically productive while confining their wives to the home environment but also granting them proper religious education, a reversal of what was customary among Jews, copying Christian attitudes at the time.

## Transitory phenomena

The *Haskalah* was also mainly a movement of transformation, straddling both the declining traditional Jewish society of autonomous community and cultural seclusion and the beginnings of a modern Jewish public. Everything connected with the *Haskalah* was dualistic in nature. The Jewish Enlighteners pursued two parallel agendas: they exhorted the Jews to acculturate and harmonize with the modern state, and demanded that the Jews remain a distinct group with its own culture and identity. Sliding away from this precarious equilibrium, in any direction, signified also one's break with the **Jewish Enlightenment**.

Virtually all *Maskilim* received old-style, secluded education, and were young **Torah** scholars before they were first exposed to outside knowledge (from a gender perspective, the movement was almost totally male-dominated; women did not receive sufficient tutoring to master Hebrew).For generations, **Mendelssohn's Bible** translation to German was employed by such young initiates to bridge the linguistic gap and learn a foreign language, having been raised on Hebrew and **Yiddish** only. The children of these activists almost never followed their parents; they rather went forward in the path of acculturation and assimilation. *Haskalah* was, by and large, a unigenerational experience.

A tiny minority of writers was concerned with the latter. The *Haskalah* sought to introduce a different bilingualism: renovated, refined Hebrew for internal matters, while **Yiddish** was to be eliminated; and national vernaculars, to be taught to all Jews, for external ones. Upon the demise of Jewish Enlightenment in Eastern Europe, authors abandoned the *maskilic* paradigm not toward assimilation but in favor of exclusive use of Hebrew and **Yiddish**.

Those who abandoned the optimistic, liberal vision of the Jews (albeit as a cohesive community) integrating into wider society in favor of full-blown Jewish nationalism or radical, revolutionary ideologies which strove to uproot the established order like Socialism, also broke with the *Haskalah*. Hostile view was promulgated by nationalist thinkers and historians, from **Peretz Smolenskin, Ahad Ha'am, Simon Dubnow** and onwards. It was once common in Israeli historiography.

The government had no interest in the visions of renaissance which the **Enlightened** so fervently cherished. It demanded the Jews to turn into productive, loyal subjects with rudimentary secular education, and no more. Indeed, the great cultural transformation which occurred among the *Parnassim* (affluent communal wardens) class – they were always more open to outside society, and had to tutor their children in secular subjects, thus inviting general Enlightenment influences – was a precondition of *Haskalah.*

The term *Haskalah* became synonymous, among friends and foes alike and in much of early Jewish historiography, with the sweeping changes that engulfed Jewish society (mostly in Europe) from the late 18th century to the late 19th century. In many regions the *Haskalah* had no effect at all.

## Origins

As long as the Jews lived in segregated communities, and as long as all social interaction with their gentile neighbors was limited, the rabbi was the most influential member of the Jewish community. In addition to being a religious scholar and "**clergy**", a rabbi also acted as a civil judge in all cases in which both parties were Jews. Rabbis sometimes had other important administrative powers, together with the community elders. The rabbinate was the highest aim of many Jewish boys, and the study of the Talmud was the means of obtaining that coveted position, or one of many other important communal distinctions.

The example of **Moses Mendelssohn** (1729–86), a Prussian Jew, served to lead this movement, which was also shaped by **Aaron Halle-Wolfssohn** (1754–1835) and **Joseph Perl** (1773–1839). Mendelssohn's extraordinary success as a popular philosopher and man of letters revealed hitherto unsuspected possibilities of integration and acceptance of Jews among non-Jews. **Mendelssohn** also provided methods for Jews to enter the general society of Germany. The *Biur,* or grammatical commentary, prepared under Mendelssohn's supervision, was designed to counteract the influence of traditional rabbinical methods of exegesis. Together with the translation, it became, as it were, the primer of **Haskalah**.

Language played a key role in the **Haskalah** movement, as Mendelssohn and others called for a revival of Hebrew and a reduction in the use of **Yiddish**. The result was an outpouring of new, secular literature, as well as critical studies of religious texts. Julius Fürst along with other German-Jewish scholars compiled Hebrew and Aramaic dictionaries and grammars.

The movement is often referred to as the *Berlin Haskalah*. Reference to Berlin in relation to the **Haskalah** movement is necessary because it provides context for this episode of Jewish history. Subsequently, having left Germany and spreading across Eastern Europe, the *Berlin Haskalah* influenced multiple Jewish communities who were interested in non-religious scholarly texts and insight to worlds beyond their Jewish enclaves.

**Isaac Baer Levinsohn** (1788–1860) became known as the "**Russian Mendelssohn**". Joseph Perl's (1773–1839) satire of the Hasidic movement, "**Revealer of Secrets**" (Megalleh Temirim), is said to be the first modern novel in Hebrew. It was published in Vienna in 1819 under the pseudonym "**Obadiah ben Pethahiah**".

## Effects

The **Haskalah** also resulted in the creation of a secular Jewish culture, with an emphasis on Jewish history and Jewish identity, rather than on religion. One commentator describes these effects as **"The emancipation of the Jews brought forth two opposed movements: the cultural assimilation, begun by Moses Mendelssohn, and Zionism, founded by Theodor Herzl in 1896."**

Even within orthodoxy, the **Haskalah** was felt through the appearance, in response, of the **Mussar Movement** in Lithuania, and *Torah im Derech Eretz* in Germany. **"Enlightened"** Jews sided with gentile governments, in plans to increase secular education and assimilation among the Jewish masses, which brought them into acute conflict with the orthodox, who believed this threatened the traditional Jewish lifestyle – which had up until that point been maintained through segregation from their gentile neighbors – and Jewish identity itself.

Groups of Reform Jews, including the **Society of the Friends of Reform** and the **Association for the Reform of Judaism** were formed, because such groups wanted, and actively advocated for, a change in Jewish tradition, in particular, regarding rituals like circumcision. The Orthodox Jews were actively against these reformers because they viewed changing Jewish tradition as an insult to God and believed that fulfillment in life could be found in serving God and keeping his commandments. The effect of **Haskalah** was that it gave a voice to plurality of views, while the orthodoxy preserved the tradition, even to the point of insisting on dividing between sects.

Another important facet of the **Haskalah** was its interests to non-Jewish religions. **Moses Mendelssohn** criticized some aspects of Christianity, but depicted **Jesus** as a Torah-observant rabbi, who was loyal to traditional Judaism. Mendelssohn explicitly linked positive Jewish views of **Jesus** with the issues of Emancipation and Jewish-Christian reconciliation.

# Hasmonean Dynasty

The **Hasmonean dynasty (Hebrew: Ḥashmuna'im)** was a ruling dynasty of Judea and surrounding regions during classical antiquity. **Between c. 140 and c. 116 BCE** the dynasty ruled semi-autonomously from the **Seleucids** in the region of Judea. **From 110 BCE, with the Seleucid Empire disintegrating**, the dynasty became fully independent, expanded into the neighboring regions of Samaria, Galilee, Iturea, Perea, and Idumea, and took the title **"basileus"**. Some modern scholars refer to this period as an **independent kingdom of Israel.**

The dynasty was established under the leadership of **Simon Maccabaeus**, two decades after his brother **Judah the Maccabee ("*Y'hudah HaMakabi*")** defeated the Seleucid army during the **Maccabean Revolt**. According to the first book of *The Jewish War* by Jewish historian **Flavius Josephus** (37 CE–c. 100), **Antiochus IV** moved to assert strict control over the Seleucid satrapy of Coele Syria and Phoenicia after his successful invasion of Ptolemaic Egypt was turned back by the intervention of the **Roman Republic**.

He sacked Jerusalem and its **Temple**, suppressing Jewish and Samaritan religious and cultural observances, and imposed Hellenistic practices. The ensuing **revolt by the Jews (167 BCE)** began a period of Jewish independence potentiated by the steady collapse of the **Seleucid Empire** under attacks from the rising powers of the **Roman Republic** and the **Parthian Empire**.

In 63 BCE, the kingdom was invaded by the Roman Republic, broken up and set up as a Roman client state. **Hyrcanus II** and **Aristobulus II**, Simon's great-grandsons, became pawns in a proxy war between **Julius Caesar and Pompey the Great. The deaths of Pompey (48 BCE) and Caesar (44 BCE),** and the related **Roman Civil Wars** temporarily relaxed Rome's grip on the **Hasmonean** kingdom, allowing a brief reassertion of autonomy backed by the **Parthian Empire**. This short independence was rapidly crushed by the Romans under **Mark Antony** and **Octavian.**

**The dynasty had survived for 103 years before yielding to the Herodian dynasty in 37 BCE.** The installation of **Herod the Great** (an Idumean) as **king in 37 BCE** made Judea a Roman client state and marked the end of the **Hasmonean** dynasty. **Herod the Great** tried to bolster the legitimacy of his reign by marrying a **Hasmonean** princess, **Mariamme**, and planning to drown the last male **Hasmonean** heir at his Jericho palace. In 44 CE, Rome installed the rule of a Roman procurator side by side with the rule of the **Herodian kings (specifically Agrippa I 41–44 and Agrippa II 50–100).**

## Background

The lands of the former Kingdom of Israel and **Kingdom of Judah (722–586 BCE)**, had been occupied in turn by Assyria, Babylonia, the Achaemenid Empire, and **Alexander the Great's**

**Hellenic Macedonian empire (330 BCE).** The entire region was heavily contested between the successor states of Alexander's empire, the **Seleucid Empire** and Ptolemaic Egypt, during the **six Syrian Wars** of the 3rd–1st centuries BCE: **"After two centuries of peace under the Persians, the Hebrew state found itself once more caught in the middle of power struggles between two great empires. Between 319 and 302 BC, Jerusalem changed hands seven times."**

**Under Antiochus III, the Seleucids wrested control of Israel from the Ptolemies for the final time, defeating Ptolemy V Epiphanes at the Battle of Panium in 200 BCE.** It was in Antioch that the Jews first made the acquaintance of **Hellenism** and of the more corrupt sides of Greek culture; and it was from Antioch that Judea henceforth was ruled.

## Historical sources

The origin of the **Hasmonean** dynasty is recorded in the books **1 Maccabees and 2 Maccabees**, covering the period from 175 to 134 BCE during which time the **Hasmonean** dynasty became semi-independent from the Seleucid empire but had not yet expanded far outside of Judea. The other primary source for the **Hasmonean** dynasty is the first book of *The Wars of the Jews* by the Jewish historian **Josephus, (37–shortly after 100 CE).** Josephus' account is the only primary source covering the history of the **Hasmonean** dynasty during the period of its expansion and independence between **110 to 63 BCE**.

## Seleucid rule over Israel / Hellenization

Generally, the Jews accepted foreign rule when they were only required to pay tribute, and otherwise allowed to govern themselves internally. When the **High Priest Simon II** died in 175 BCE, conflict broke out between supporters of his son **Onias III** (who opposed Hellenization and favored the Ptolemies) and his son **Jason** (who favored Hellenization and the Seleucids). The **Tobiads**, a philo-Hellenistic party, succeeded in placing Jason into the powerful position of **High Priest.**

## Antiochus IV against Jerusalem

In **168 BCE**, after successfully invading the Ptolemaic kingdom of Egypt (apparently without Jewish support), **Antiochus IV** was pressured by the **Roman Republic** to withdraw. Returning toward Antioch, the troops of Antiochus sacked Jerusalem and removed the sacred objects from the Jerusalem **Temple**, slaughtering an unknown, but large, number of Jews.

His government set up an idol of **Zeus** on the **Temple** Mount, which Jews considered to be desecration of the Mount; it also forbade both circumcision and possession of Jewish scriptures, on pain of death. According to Josephus, **"He compelled the Jews to dissolve the laws of their country, and to keep their infants uncircumcised, and to sacrifice swine's flesh upon the**

**altar**." He also outlawed observance of the Sabbath and the offering of sacrifices at the Jerusalem **Temple**.

## Maccabean Revolt

The author of the **First Book of Maccabees** regarded the Maccabean revolt as a rising of pious Jews against the Seleucid king who had tried to eradicate their religion and against the Jews who supported him. The author of the **Second Book of Maccabees** presented the conflict as a struggle between **"Judaism" and "Hellenism",** words that he was the first to use. Modern scholarship tends to the second view.

According to **I and II Maccabees**, the priestly family of **Mattathias** (Mattisyahu/Mattitiyahu in Hebrew), which came to be known as the *Maccabees*, called the people forth to holy war against the Seleucids. Mattathias' sons Judah (Yehuda), Jonathan (Yonoson/Yonatan), and Simon (Shimon) began a military campaign, initially with disastrous results: **one thousand Jewish men, women, and children were killed** by Seleucid troops because they refused to fight, even in self-defense, on the **Sabbath**. Other Jews then reasoned that they must fight when attacked, even on the Sabbath.

**In 164 BCE, Judah captured Jerusalem** and the **Temple** in Jerusalem was freed and re-consecrated: **"After having recovered Jerusalem, Judah ordered the Temple to be cleansed, a new altar to be built in place of the desecrated one, and new holy vessels to be made.**" The celebratory festival of Hanukkah is instituted: **"When the fire had been kindled anew upon the altar and the lamps of the candlestick lit, the dedication of the altar was celebrated for eight days amid sacrifices and songs."** Antiochus IV died that same year, and was ultimately succeeded by **Demetrius I Soter**, the nephew whose throne he had usurped. Bacchides subdued Jerusalem and returned to his King.

## From revolt to independence / Judah and Jonathan

After five years of war and raids, Judah sought an alliance with the Roman Republic to remove the Greeks: **"In the year 161 BCE he sent Eupolemus the son of Johanan and Jason the son of Eleazar, 'to make a league of amity and confederacy with the Romans.'"** A Seleucid army under General Nicanor was defeated by Judah (**ib. 7:26–50**) at the **Battle of Adasa**, with **Nicanor** himself killed in action. Bacchides now established the Hellenes as rulers in Israel; and upon Judah's death, the persecuted patriots, under **Jonathan**, brother of Judah, fled beyond the Jordan River. **(ib. 9:25–27).**

Jonathan and Simeon, now more experienced in guerilla warfare, thought it well to retreat farther, and accordingly fortified in the desert a place called **Beth-hogla**; there they were besieged several days by Bacchides. Jonathan offered the rival general a peace treaty and exchange of prisoners of war. Bacchides readily consented and even took an oath of nevermore making war upon Jonathan.

He and his forces then vacated Israel. The chief source, 1 Maccabees, says that with this **"the sword ceased in Israel"**, and in fact nothing is reported for the five following years **(158–153 BCE)**.

## Seleucid civil conflict

**Ptolemy VI of Egypt** (reigned 163–145 BCE), and Ptolemy's co-ruler **Cleopatra II** of Egypt were deteriorating, and they supported a rival claimant to the Seleucid throne. **Jonathan** gladly accepted these terms, took up residence at Jerusalem in 153 BCE, and began fortifying the city.

Jonathan became the official leader of his people, and officiated at the **Feast of Tabernacles of 153 BCE** wearing the High Priest's garments. The Hellenistic party could no longer attack him without severe consequences.

## Hasmoneans under Demetrius and Diodotus

In 145 BCE, the **Battle of Antioch** resulted in the final defeat of **Alexander Balas** by the forces of his father-in-law **Ptolemy VI**. Ptolemy himself, however, was among the casualties of the battle. In consideration of a present of 300 talents the entire country was exempted from taxes, the exemption being confirmed in writing. Jonathan in return lifted the siege of the Acra and left it in Seleucid hands.

## Simon assumes leadership

When **Diodotus Tryphon** was about to enter Judea at Hadid, he was confronted by the new Jewish leader, Simon, ready for battle. Tryphon, avoiding an engagement, demanded one hundred talents and Jonathan's two sons as hostages, in return for which he promised to liberate Jonathan. Although Simon did not trust **Diodotus Tryphon**, he complied with the request so that he might not be accused of the death of his brother.

But **Diodotus Tryphon** did not liberate his prisoner; angry that Simon blocked his way everywhere and that he could accomplish nothing, he executed Jonathan at Baskama, in the country east of the Jordan. Jonathan was buried by Simeon at Modin. Nothing is known of his two captive sons. **One of his daughters was an ancestor of Josephus**.

**Simon** assumed the leadership **(142 BCE),** receiving the double office of High Priest and prince of Israel. The leadership of the **Hasmonean**s was established by a resolution, adopted in 141 BCE, at a large assembly **"of the priests and the people and of the elders of the land, to the effect that Simon should be their leader and High Priest forever, until there should arise a faithful prophet"** (1 Macc. 14:41).

**Simon**, having made the Jewish people semi-independent of the Seleucid Greeks, reigned from 142 to 135 BCE and formed the **Hasmonean** dynasty, finally capturing the citadel in 141 BCE. The Roman Senate accorded the new dynasty recognition c. 139 BCE, when the delegation of Simon was in Rome. Simon led the people in peace and prosperity, until in February 135 BCE, he was assassinated at the instigation of his son-in-law **Ptolemy, son of Abubus**, who had been named governor of the region by the Seleucids. **Simon's eldest sons, Mattathias and Judah, were also murdered.**

## Hasmonean expansion and civil war

**In c. 135 BCE, John Hyrcanus**, Simon's third son, assumed the leadership and ruled as high priest (Kohen Gadol) and took a Greek **"regnal name"** in an acceptance of the Hellenistic culture of his Seleucid suzerains. Within a year of the death of Simon, **Seleucid King Antiochus VII Sidetes** attacked Jerusalem. For the next two decades of his reign, **Hyrcanus** continued, like his father, to rule semi-autonomously from the Seleucids.

The Seleucid empire had been disintegrating in the face of the **Seleucid–Parthian Wars** and in 129 BCE **Antiochus VII** Sidetes was killed in Media by the forces of **Phraates II** of Parthia, permanently ending Seleucid rule east of the Euphrates. In **116 BCE**, a civil war between Seleucid half-brothers **Antiochus VIII Grypus** and **Antiochus IX Cyzicenus** broke out, resulting in a further breakup of the already significantly reduced kingdom. This provided opportunity for semi-independent Seleucid client states such as Judea to revolt. In 110 BCE, **John Hyrcanus** carried out the first military conquests of the newly independent **Hasmonean Kingdom**, raising a mercenary army to capture Madaba and Schechem, significantly increasing his regional influence.

Upon Hyrcanus' death, however, **Aristobulus** jailed his mother and three brothers, including Alexander Jannaeus, and allowed her to starve there. By this means he came into possession of the throne, but died one year later after a painful illness in 103 BCE. In 87 BCE, according to **Josephus**, following a **six-year civil war** involving Seleucid king Demetrius III Eucaerus, **Hasmonean** ruler Alexander Jannaeus **crucified 800 Jewish rebels in Jerusalem.**

The **Hasmoneans** lost the territories acquired in Transjordan during the 93 BC **Battle of Gadara**, where the Nabataeans ambushed Jannaeus and his forces in a hilly area. Jannaeus returned to fierce Jewish opposition in Jerusalem after his defeat. **Alexander** was followed by his wife, **Salome Alexandra**, who reigned from **76–67 BCE. She was the only *regnant* Jewish Queen**.

## Pharisee and Sadducee factions

During the **Hasmonean** period, the Sadducees and Pharisees functioned primarily as political parties. Alexander was succeeded by his widow, **Salome Alexandra**, whose brother was **Shimon ben Shetach,** a leading Pharisee. The conflict between Hyrcanus and **Aristobulus** culminated in a civil war that ended when the **Roman general Pompey captured Jerusalem in 63 BCE** and inaugurated the Roman period of Jewish history.

## Civil war

**Alexander Jannaeus'** son, **Hyrcanus II**, had scarcely reigned three months when his younger brother, **Aristobulus II**, rose in rebellion. The greatest part deserted Hyrcanus, and went over to **Aristobulus**. **Hyrcanus** took refuge in the citadel of Jerusalem, but the capture of the **Temple** by **Aristobulus** II compelled Hyrcanus to surrender. That **Aristobulus** should be king, and Hyrcanus should resign, but retain all the rest of his dignities, as being the king's brother. **Aristobulus** ruled from **67–63 BCE**). From **63–40 BCE**, the government was in the hands of **Hyrcanus II** as High Priest and Ethnarchs, although effective power was in the hands of his adviser **Antipater the Idumaean.**

## Intrigues of Antipater

**Antipater** saw clearly that it would be easier to reach the object of his ambition, the control of Judea, under the government of the weak Hyrcanus than under the warlike and energetic **Aristobulus**. **Honi**, ordered to curse the besieged, prayed: **"Lord of the universe, as the besieged and the besiegers both belong to Thy people, I beseech Thee not to answer the evil prayers of either."** According to Josephus, the besiegers kept the enormous price of one thousand drachmas they had asked for the lamb.

## Roman intervention / Pompey the Great

While this civil war was going on the Roman general **Marcus Aemilius Scaurus** went to Syria to take possession, in the name of **Gnaeus Pompeius Magnus,** of the kingdom of the Seleucids. But when Pompey came to Syria (**63 BCE**), Pompey, who had just been awarded the title **"Conqueror of Asia"** due to his decisive victories in Asia Minor over Pontus and the **Seleucid Empire**, had decided to bring Judea under the rule of the Romans. **Aristobulus II** entrenched himself in the fortress of Alexandrium; but, soon realizing the uselessness of resistance, surrendered at the first summons of the Romans, and undertook to deliver Jerusalem to them.

The patriots, however, were not willing to open their gates to the Romans, and a siege ensued which ended with the capture of the city. Pompey entered the **Holy of Holie**s; this was only the second time that someone had dared to penetrate into this sacred spot. Judaea had to pay tribute to Rome and was placed under the supervision of the Roman governor of Syria: **"In 63 BC, Judaea became a protectorate of Rome. Coming under the administration of a governor, Judaea was allowed a king; the governor's business was to regulate trade and maximize tax revenue."**

## Pompey and Caesar

**Julius Caesar** initially supported **Aristobulus** against **Hyrcanus** and **Antipater**. Between the weakness of Hyrcanus and the ambition of **Aristobulus**, Judea lost its independence. **Aristobulus**

was taken to Rome a prisoner, and **Hyrcanus** was reappointed High Priest, but without political authority. When, in **50 BCE**, it appeared that **Julius Caesar** was interested in using **Aristobulus** and his family as his clients to take control of Judea from **Hyrcanus** and **Antipater**.

However, Pompey's pawns soon had occasion to turn to the other side. When **Pompey** was murdered, **Antipater** led the Jewish forces to the help of Caesar, who was hard pressed at Alexandria. Joppa was restored to the **Hasmonean** domain, Judea was granted freedom from all tribute and taxes to Rome, and the independence of the internal administration was guaranteed.

Hyrcanus' restoration as ethnarch in **47 BCE** coincided with Caesar's appointment of Antipater as the first Roman Procurator, allowing Antipater to promote the interests of his own house: **"Caesar appointed Hyrcanus to be high priest, and gave Antipater what principality he himself should choose, leaving the determination to himself; so he made him procurator of Judea." Caesar was assassinated in 44 BCE** and unrest and confusion spread throughout the Roman world, including Judaea. **Antipater the Idumean** was assassinated by a rival, **Malichus**, in 43 BCE, but Antipater's sons managed to kill **Malichus** and maintain their control over Judea and their father's puppet **Hasmonean**, **Hyrcanus.**

## Parthian invasion, Antony, Augustus

After **Julius Caesar was murdered in 44 BCE**, **Quintus Labienus**, a Roman republican general and ambassador to the Parthians, sided with Brutus and Cassius in the **Liberators' civil war**; after their defeat Labienus joined the Parthians and assisted them in invading Roman territories in 40 BCE.

**Antigonus,** whose Hebrew name was **Mattathias**, bore the double title of king and High Priest for only three years, as he had not disposed of **Herod**, the most dangerous of his enemies. **Herod** fled into exile and sought the support of **Mark Antony**. **Herod** was designated **"King of the Jews"** by the Roman Senate in 40 BCE: After the Parthians' defeat, **Herod** was victorious over his rival in **37 BCE**. **Antigonus** was delivered to **Antony** and executed shortly thereafter. The Romans assented to **Herod**'s proclamation as **King of the Jews**, bringing about the end of the **Hasmonean** rule over Judea.

## Herod and the end of the dynasty

**Aristobulus III**, grandson of **Aristobulus** II through his elder son **Alexander**, was briefly made high priest, but was soon executed (36 BCE) due to **Herod**'s jealousy. His sister **Mariamne** was married to **Herod**, but fell victim to his notorious jealousy. Her sons by **Herod**, **Aristobulus** IV and Alexander, were in their adulthood also executed by their father. **Hyrcanus II** had been held by the Parthians since **40 BCE**. For four years, until **36 BCE**, he lived amid the Babylonian Jews, who paid him every mark of respect. As the last remaining **Hasmonean**, **Hyrcanus** was too dangerous a rival for **Herod**. In the year 30 BCE, charged with plotting with the King of Arabia, **Hyrcanus** was condemned and executed.

## Jewish nationalism

The fall of the **Hasmonean Kingdom** marked an end to a century of Jewish self-governance, but Jewish nationalism and desire for independence continued under Roman rule, beginning with the **Census of Quirinius** in 6 and leading to a series of **Jewish-Roman wars** in the 1st–2nd centuries, including the **Great Revolt** (AD 66–73), the Kitos War (115–117), and **Bar Kokhba's** revolt (132–135).

Roman legions under **Vespasian and Titus** besieged and destroyed Jerusalem, looted and burned **Herod**'s **Temple** (in the year 70 A.D.) and Jewish strongholds (notably Gamla in 67 and Masada in 73), and enslaved or massacred a large part of the Jewish population. Many Jews were scattered after losing their state or were sold into slavery throughout the empire.

## Jewish religious scholarship

Jewish tradition holds that the claiming of kingship by the later **Hasmonean**s led to their eventual downfall, since that title was only to be held by descendants of the line of **King David**.

# Hebrew Bible

**Hebrew Bible or Hebrew Scriptures (Latin: *Biblia Hebraica*) is the term used by biblical scholars to refer to the *Tanakh* (Hebrew: Latin: *Thanach*),** the canonical collection of Jewish texts, which is the common textual source of several canonical editions of the **Christian Old Testament.** They are composed mainly in Biblical Hebrew, with some passages in **Biblical Aramaic** (in the books of **Daniel, Ezra** and a few others). (**24 books = 783,137 words**). Hebrew Bible refers to the **Jewish Biblical Canon.** In its Latin form, *Biblia Hebraica*, it traditionally serves as a title for printed editions of the **Masoretic Text.**

## Additional difficulties

All of these formulations, except some forms of **Dual-covenant theology**, are objectionable to mainstream Judaism and to many Jewish scholars and writers, for whom there is **one eternal covenant between God and the Israelites, and who therefore reject the term "Old Testament" as a form of antinomianism.** Lutheranism and Protestant denominations that follow the **Westminster Confession of Faith** accept the entire Jewish canon as the Old Testament without additions, however in translation they sometimes give preference to the Septuagint rather than the **Masoretic Text**; for example, **Isaiah 7:14.**

In terms of language, **"Hebrew"** refers to the original language of the books, but it may also be taken as referring to the Jews of the **Second Temple** era and Jewish diaspora, and their descendants, who preserved the transmission of the **Masoretic Text** up to the present day. The Hebrew Bible includes small portions in **Aramaic** (mostly in the books of **Daniel** and **Ezra**), written and printed in **Aramaic square-script, which was adopted as the Hebrew alphabet after the Babylonian exile.**

## *Dating the Bible and Development of the Hebrew Bible canon*

The books that constitute the Hebrew Bible developed over roughly a millennium. The oldest texts seem to come from the **11th or 10th centuries BCE**, whilst most of the other texts are somewhat later. Since the 19th century, most biblical scholars have agreed that the **Pentateuch** (the **first five books of Scriptures**) consists of four sources which have been woven together.

These four sources are J **(Yahwist), D (Deuteronomist), E (Elohist) and P (Priestly)** sources. **They were combined to form the Pentateuch sometime in the 6th century BCE.** This theory is now known as the **documentary hypothesis,** and has been the dominant theory for the past two hundred years. The Deuteronomist credited with the Pentateuch's book of Deuteronomy is also said to be the source of the books of **Joshua, Judges, Samuel, and Kings** and also in the **book of Jeremiah.**

# The Hebrews

**Hebrews (Modern Hebrew *'Ivrim, 'Ivriyyim*;) is a term appearing 34 times within 32 verses of the Hebrew Bible.** While the term was not an ethnonym, it is mostly taken as synonymous with the Semitic-speaking Israelites, especially in the pre-monarchic period when they were still nomadic.

By the time of the Roman Empire, Greek *Hebraios* could refer to the Jews in general, as **Strong's Hebrew Dictionary** puts it **"any of the Jewish Nation"** and at other times more specifically to the Jews living in Judea. In Early Christianity, the Greek term refers to Jewish Christians as opposed to the gentile Christians and **Judaizers (Acts 6:1 among others)**. With the revival of the Hebrew language and the emergence of the **Hebrew Yishuv**, the term has been applied to the Jewish people of this re-emerging society in Israel or anything associated with it.

## Etymology

The definitive origin of the term **"Hebrew"** remains uncertain. The Biblical **term *Ivri*** meaning **"to traverse" or "to pass over",** is usually rendered as *Hebrew* in English, from the ancient Greek and the Latin *Hebraeus*. The Biblical word *Ivri* has the plural form *Ivrim, or Ibrim*.

**Genesis 10:21 refers to Shem, the elder brother of Ham and Japheth and thus the first-born son of Noah, as the father of the sons of Eber (עבר), which may have a similar meaning.** Some authors argue that *Ibri* denotes the descendants of the biblical **patriarch Eber,** son of Shelah, a great-grandson of Noah and an ancestor of Abraham, hence the occasional Anglicization *Eberites*.

Some scholars argue that the name **"Hebrew"** is related to the name of **those seminomadic Habiru people recorded in Egyptian inscriptions of the 13th and 12th centuries BCE as having settled in Egypt.** Other scholars rebut this, proposing that the Hebrews are mentioned in older texts of the **3rd Intermediate Period of Egypt** (15th century BCE) as **Shasu of *Yhw*.**

## Synonym for "Israelites" who is a Jew?

In the Hebrew Bible, the term **"Hebrew"** is normally used by Israelites when speaking of themselves to foreigners, or is used by foreigners when speaking about Israelites. In fact, the Torah in *Parashat Lekh Lecha* (**"go!" or "leave!" literally "go for you"**) calls Abraham *Avram Ha-Ivri* ("Abram the Hebrew"), which translates literally as **"Abram the one who stands on the other side."**

**Israelites are defined as the descendants of Jacob, son of Isaac, grandson of Abraham.** Eber, an ancestor of Jacob (seven generations removed), is a distant ancestor of many people, including the **Israelites, Ishmaelites, Edomites, Moabites, Ammonites, Midianites and Qahtanites.** According to the **Jewish Encyclopedia** the terms **"Hebrews"** and **"Israelites"** usually describe the same people, stating that they were called Hebrews before the conquest of the Land of Canaan and Israelites afterwards.

## Use as synonym for "Jews"

By the Roman period, "**Hebrews**" could be used to designate the Jews, who use the Hebrew language. **The Epistle to the Hebrews was probably written for Jewish Christians**. In some modern languages, including Armenian, Greek, Italian, Romanian, and many Slavic languages, the name *Hebrews* survives as the standard ethnonym for Jews, but in many other languages in which there exist both terms, it is considered derogatory to call modern Jews "**Hebrews**".

## Use in Zionism

Beginning in the late 19th century, the term "**Hebrew**" became popular among secular Zionists; in this context the word alluded to the transformation of the Jews into a strong, independent, self-confident secular national group (**"the New Jew"**) sought by classical Zionism. This use died out after the establishment of the state of Israel, when "**Hebrew" was replaced with "Jew" or "Israeli"**.

# The Real Hero of the Yom Kippur War

The history books say that Israeli intelligence broken down in the 1970s and allowed the Arabs to launch a simultaneous sneak attack in 1973. The invasion on Yom Kippur, Israel's most holy day, caught the entire country unawares.

Some of the **"old spies"** make gagging noises when presented with this version of history. Others pretend to be convulsed with laughter. **Kissinger** was a military incompetent, whose petty intrigues and dabbling in covert operations nearly caused the destruction of Israel.

- In order to curry favor with the Arabs, the **White House** ordered the National Security Agency to suppress information that a sneak attack against Israel would take place on October 6, 1973.
- **Kissinger**'s strategy was to let Israel get "bloodied" a bit and then force both sides to the peace table.
- The man who saved Israel from **Kissinger**'s blunders was the White House chief of staff, **Alexander Haig.**
- The man who became the scapegoat for **Kissinger**'s blunders was the **CIA** counterintelligence chief, **James Jesus Angleton**.

Israel's old nemesis, **Nasser**, was dead, but his successor, **Anwar Sadat**, was not considered an improvement by Prime Minister **Gold Meir**, who recalled his pro-Nazi stance during World War II as evidence of his hatred for Jews. But **Sadat** was more than just another Nazi in Arab clothing. He was a brilliant politician. In fact, **Sadat**'s initiative was a missed opportunity, a tragic blunder. If **Sadat** could not persuade Israel to negotiate for the return of Egyptian land, he would force Israel to meet his terms.

**Sadat** had turned to the Soviets for military support. The Soviets had taken the Arab military commanders under their wing and explained that it was the lack of Egyptian intelligence security, not the failure of Soviet arms, which accounted for the 1967 debacle. Hundreds of **Soviet Military Intelligence** (the **GRU**) agents poured into Israel. Between 1967 and 1973 the **GRU** had penetrated Israel's most secret communications channels, identified Israeli sources in Arab countries, and probed for weak points in Israeli electronic surveillance.

After 1967 the Israelis had grown overconfident. The **Mossad** was blinded. Arab agents were equipped with the best communications gear available – ironically, American-made satellite communication sets developed by the **NSA.** For the first time, the Israelis could not listen in to Arab war plans. In 1972 **Sadat** threw the Soviets out and told both superpowers that they had squandered his peace initiatives. **He would redeem Egyptian honor by force of arms.** No one took him seriously. They should have anticipated that Saudi Arabian oil was crucial to American interests, and that President **Sadat** of Egypt was putting immense pressure on **King Faisal**, head of the Saudi royal family.

Not that there was any real political difference between the two leaders – both were Arab nationalists. In fact, **King Faisal was even more emphatic than Sadat about the need to destroy the State of Israel.**

The Wahhabi tradition of ignorant racism was alive and well. In 1973, Faisal announced that he was changing his mind about an oil embargo. For a start, the oil marketplace had changed radically. The United States was already dependent o Saudi oil, twelve years before the previously predicted date of 1985. **Sadat**'s repudiation of **Nasser**'s pro-Soviet stance also weighed heavily in the king's deliberations.

The Saudis geared up for economic war against the Jews' patrons in the West. The oil men could see billions of dollars of profits going down the drain, and all because of Israel. This time the king meant business. He took the propaganda offensive in a series of media interviews that made it clear that by supporting Israel, the United States was placing its oil supplies at risk.

On August 23, 1973, **Sadat** told Faisal that he intended to attack Israel. The king promised his support, financially and by way of the **"oil weapon."** A few days later the powerful Saudi oil minister, **Sheik Ahmed Yamani**, began dropping hints to the oil companies about a cutback in production that would affect the United States. The United States must change its policy of supporting Israel or suffer the consequences.

This time they got their message through: Bashing Jews was good for business. The **Nixon** administration realized that a new policy was needed to avert a potential disaster. By the fall of 1973 U.S. consumers were on the brink of panic, and gas prices had begun their steep rise. The Organization of Petroleum Exporting Countries (**OPEC**) demanded a new deal from the oil companies, and a showdown was set for October 6, in Vienna.

The companies chose **John J. McCloy** as their lawyer to push their case for a counter-cartel against the Arabs. **McCloy** was not well disposed to Israeli interests. As previously discussed, **McCloy** was the U.S. official during World War II who ordered, in writing, that no American planes be diverted to bomb the gas chambers and t hen released **Nazi war criminals imprisoned at Nuremberg.**

However, the American response for a countercartel was too little too late. The Moslem world had been preparing secretly for battle. When the Egyptian army began its military buildup in the Sinai, the **CIA** passed a new estimate to the Israelis on September 26 that war was growing more likely. By the end of the first week of October, everyone was relaxed. **The Israelis were blissfully ignorant of the storm building around them.**

On October 1 only ten people in Egypt knew that their training exercise was about to be converted into a genuine attack. On October 3 the date and hour of the attack was agreed upon with the Syrians: 2:00 P.M. October 6. The Syrians then briefed their Soviet advisers. **It was the best-kept secret in the Arab world.**

On October 3 and 4 the **NSA** decoded several messages from the Soviet embassy about the evacuation of personnel. By October 4 the **NSA** knew beyond a shadow of a doubt that an attack on Israel would take place on the afternoon of October 6. **The Nixon White House ordered the NSA to sit on the information. "We knew where. We were told to shut up and let it happen."** American intelligence was helping Israel's enemies in time of war. The Israeli mobilization plan requires sixteen hours to call up its reserves for war.

In wartime, everyone in Israel uses their own cars to transport hitchhiking soldiers to their positions. This quaint mobilization plan works well, with sixteen hours' notice. **Eight hours' warning causes chaos in Israel. Two hours' notice is a disaster.** One **NSA** official later confirmed publicly that he knew of the planned attack on Israel by Syria and Egypt thirty hours before the United States notified Israel. The **NSA**'s warning was not circulated to the Israelis or to other members the U.S. intelligence community.

On the same day Israeli intelligence continued to rate the risk of attack as a **"very low probability."** In fact, only the **NSA** knew that the Arab version of **Pearl Harbor** was about to happen. Dozens of summaries based on electronic intercepts were sent on a restricted channel to the **Nixon** White House. As one source admitted, **Nixon's staff had at least two days' advance warning that an attack was coming on October 6.**

*But no one in the Nixon White House warned the Jews until the last few hours on the day of the attack.* **Nixon** certainly had a motive for revenge. As previously discussed, **Nixon** was well aware that, apart from **J. Edgar Hoover**, only the Israelis knew enough about his past to cause him major political damage.

As the **Watergate** tape-recordings show, **Nixon** was terribly afraid of the Jews. He made lists of his enemies and kept track of **Jewish Americans** in his administration. **Nixon** knew that Jews didn't vote for him anyway. During September and October 1973 the **Nixon** White House turned a blind eye toward **Sadat**'s plans for a consolidated sneak attack against the Jews. **Not one word of the NSA's information leaked out until the morning of the attack.** Egypt and Syria had attacked Israel, and the Yom Kippur War had started.

If Israel wanted American support, **Kissinger** warned, it could not even begin to mobilize until the Arabs invaded. No general mobilization was issued after the warning from the United States. The cabinet was still in emergency session when the attack came. Prime Minister **Gold Meir** was supposedly the person who overruled all entreaties from **Defense Minister Moshe Dayan** for immediate offensive action. **She cited Kissinger's threats as the major reason.**

The Israeli front-line units were crushed as the Egyptian army used high-powered water cannon to blast down Israeli sand forts and then cross the Suez. In the north, Syrian tank brigades obliterated significant sections of the Israeli battle line within hours. **Kissinger** was conveniently absent on the day the war broke out, sitting **"incommunicado at the Waldorf Astoria in New York".**

**Kissinger** had set up the Jews. He sat on the **NSA**'s information, disappeared on the day of the invasion, and waited three days before convening the **Security Council** at the UN. **Kissinger** was eager that Israel should be forced to comply with **UN Resolution 242**, which would reverse all the territorial gains that Israel had made in 1967.

Instead of rushing arms to Israel, Defense Secretary **James Schlesinger** cautioned that the United States had to keep a **"low profile in order not to create an Arab reaction"** in the oil markets. The outbreak of hostilities gave the Arabs at the Vienna oil negotiations a great morale boost.

**The oil companies offered a 15 percent price increase**, but the Arabs wanted to double their take. The time was ripe to squeeze the West. Any country that helped Israel in the war faced an oil embargo. The oil men wanted their political masters to abandon the Jews.

The economy and national security of the United States were at stake. The Israeli ambassador called **Kissinger** hourly to complain: **"These delays are costing lives. Who's playing games?"** By Monday, October 8, the third day of the war, the American games had cost Israel heavily. Several thousand soldiers had died, more in the first day then had died in the entire 1967 war. **Over 500 tanks were destroyed**. The Israeli air force had been crippled by **Soviet SAM** missiles. At the start of the war, the Israelis had had only a seven-day supply of ammunition for some units.

For once **Moshe Dayan** was despondent. He said sadly: **"The situation is desperate. Everything is lost. We must withdraw."** The end of Israel seemed imminent and **Meir**'s friend made plans for the two of them to commit suicide. Only when Israeli ammunition was almost exhausted did the Americans act. The war had been going for six days, and the Arabs continued to inflict huge casualties on the Jews. The secret architect of this **"let Israel come out ahead, but bleed"** strategy was none other than **Henry Kissinger**.

But six days into the **Yom Kippur War**, the White House was beginning to realize that it might be much worse than a small **"nosebleed"** for the Jews. On October 12 **Nixon** received **Meir's** desperate plea for assistance. The Soviets had started a massive resupply operation to Syria and Egypt; without a similar response from the United States for the Jews, **Israel would surely be destroyed.**

**Henry Kissinger** allegedly told **Nixon**, in no uncertain terms, that the country could not stand by and allow Israel to be defeated by Soviet arms. When Prime Minister **Meir** secretly wrote to **Nixon "warning that Israel was being overwhelmed and might soon be destroyed,"** Washington gave her some comfort. The Americans told the Israelis they could have supplies for the war, as long as it was done secretly.

The arms were to be shipped by plane, and only at night. **Nixon** personally leaned on **Portugal** to supply a refueling base in the Azores, and the operations were timed to land in Israel under cover of darkness. The American cargo planes landed in broad daylight on October 14. The very next day, October 15, the Israelis did exactly that, launching a successful counteroffensive that threw back the Egyptians just as they seemed likely to destroy Israel.

The man they blame for betraying Israel in 1973 is **Henry Kissinger**. Many of the American comments about **Kissinger** are unprintable. He was an intelligence professional for the **Dalles** brothers. In fact, **Allen Dalles** thought quite highly of him. In 1946-47, just as **Dalles** was putting together his **OPC** network to recruit e x-Nazi **"freedom fighters,"** Captain **Kissinger** suddenly became a civilian instructor at the intelligence school in Germany, which coincidentally also became a cover for **OPC** agents.

The 1947 version of the army's ***Consolidated Orientation and Guidance Manual*** listed the various war criminals living in the U.S. zone, indexed them by atrocity, and cross-referenced them to their various employers in Western intelligence. This top-secret manual was considered basic reference for intelligence officers at the time **Kissinger** was teaching intelligence courses. If **Kissinger** knew about the **OPC**'s Nazi recruiting, he kept his mouth shut.

In 1952 **Kissinger** became a consultant for the **National Security Council's Psychological Strategy Board,** which supported **Dalles**' entire program of covert paramilitary operations. This office consulted on the employment of Nazis as **"freedom fighters"** behind the Iron Curtain for the rest of the **Eisenhower-Nixon** administration. In 1954 **Nelson Rockefeller** took over as Cold War coordinator for the White House. Shortly thereafter **Kissinger** was promoted to consultant to the **NSC's "highest policy-making board for implementing clandestine operations against foreign governments."**

By the time **Nixon** ran for president in 1968, **Kissinger** was an old professional in spy work. A few days after the election, **Nixon** asked him to head his **NSC**, setting up a new organization **"to exclude the CIA from the formulation of policy."**

**Kissinger** has always denied involvement with **Dalles' Nazis**. From the Israeli point of view, **Kissinger** might as well have been an Arab. Israeli intelligence remembered that it was **Kissinger** who told them not to mobilize and wait for the Arabs to fire the first shot. **It was Kissinger who went into hiding on the first day of the war.**

Instead of standing by the only democracy in the Middle East, **Kissinger had sold the Jews out for Arab oil.** Then, as the new secretary of state, he wanted to take the credit for **"peace"** negotiations in which Israel would have to give back the territory it had won in 1967. The problem was incompetence, not bigotry. His aim was to let the Jews win the war, but to wound them a little in the process. However, **his scheme nearly destroyed Israel.**

The Soviets, who had completely penetrated Israeli communications, were relaying to the Arabs the despair within the inner circle of **Gold Meir**'s advisers. With Soviet prompting, other Arab nations had jumped into the war. **Two Iraqi tank divisions, with 30,000 men and 1,200 armed vehicles, had suddenly appeared on the Golan Heights.**

Just as President **Nixon** was considering **Meir**'s desperate plea, which reached him on October 12, Israel had some help from the White House chief of staff, General **Alexander Haig**. **Haig** held up the oil companies' letter recommending a price increase for Arab oil producers for several crucial days. **Haig**'s action helped Israel, by allowing time for **Meir**'s dramatic plea to have its effect on **Nixon** and for the cold hard facts of the Arab and Soviet threats to sink in at the White House.

But Al **Haig** did much more for Israel. In fact, he was **making policy behind Kissinger's back**. Defense Secretary **Schlesinger** had dragged his feet too long on military supplies. The U.S. airlift did not even commence until Sunday, October 14. **Haig** realized that there was a good chance that the Israeli Army would be crushed before the bulk of the supplies reached the front. The logistics loop was too long. On Saturday, October 6, **Alexander Haig** told Israeli intelligence that there was a new weapon that could stop the Arab tank onslaught. If they could get a team to the United States, he would give it to them.

The U.S. Army had just developed the **tube-launched, optically tracked, wire-guided (TOW) missile** and so far had shared it only with Britain and West Germany. The **TOW** could be fired from a foxhole and destroy a moving tank three kilometers away. As the missile was flying, it unreeled three kilometers of cable behind it, connected to a steering telescope. As the enemy tank moved, trying to get away from the missile, the missile followed, even up and downhill. **The "kill ratio" for the TOW was 97 percent**.

The Israeli captains and majors had long hair, mustaches, and wore hippie-style civilian clothes. The Israelis disappeared the next day for training. The Israelis were back in Israel by October 14, just in time to repulse a massive Egyptian armored attack in the Sinai. It was the turning point of the war. Al **Haig** was stripping every **TOW** missile off the eastern seaboard of the United States and from Germany and shipping them to Israel.

A number of histories of the **Yom Kippur War** have made a great deal of the **Israeli threat to use the atomic bomb.** On the other hand, four thousand **TOW** missiles could make quite an impact. They did just that. Al **Haig**'s missiles arrived in time to blunt the next Egyptian offensive. The opening of the final Egyptian assault on Israel turned into a rout as the Arabs' tank force was cut to ribbons. **Haig** had saved **Kissinger**'s reputation by giving Israel the **TOW** s. **If the vital Mitla Pass had fallen, Israel's fate would have been sealed.**

It is no coincidence that **the Israelis put their atomic bombs back in to storage on October 14**, the day the **TOW** s were first tried out in Israel. On October 15 the Israeli army counterattacked, crossed the **Suez Canal**, and began to drive toward Cairo. By October 16 the Soviet premier flew to Cairo and advised **Sadat** to call for a cease-fire. **The Israelis kept quiet about the TOW missiles.**

As a young Army captain in the late 1940s, **Haig** had served briefly in **General Gehlen's Nazi** base and hated what he saw. **Gehlen**'s recruitment of Nazis as Cold War **"freedom fighters,"** the revival of anti-Semitism, and programs aimed directly at the new State of Israel, and was sickened by the hypocrisy and cynicism of his superiors.

As cogently argued by **Len Colodny** and **Robert Gettlin**, it was **Haig** who became **"Deep Throat"** in the Watergate Affair. **Haig** vehemently denies that he was the source of the leaks against **Nixon**. Bad intelligence about Soviet actions and intentions probably caused **Kissinger** to hit the panic button and put American forces on full alert.

**Seymour Hersh** documented that it was **Kissinger** himself who first leaked word to the Egyptians that Israel had three nuclear missiles. The Arabs were not impressed. **They had a more powerful weapon: oil.** On October 16 the Arab members of OPEC unilaterally announced a 70 percent oil price rise. They threatened the president with an oil embargo unless the American resupply of Israel was stopped, but **Nixon**, to his credit, refused to back down. **Nixon** and **Kissinger** argued that the supplies to Israel were anti-Soviet, not anti-Arab. **Nixon** made some gratuitous comments about **Kissinger**'s Jewish origins and pledged **Kissinger**'s absolute neutrality.

In fact, Iraq wanted to nationalize all U.S. interests in the Middle East. On October 19 **Nixon** announced a **$2.2 billion military aid package for Israel**. The Arab response was entirely predictable to everyone except **Kissinger**. **Libya** immediately announced a total embargo on the United States. **Saudi Arabia** had done likewise. Further, the Saudi cutback in production was increased from 5 to 10 percent each month, and then to 20. **Once again the House of Saud was trying to blackmail an American president over Israel.**

As usual, profit triumphed over principle and **Aramco** cut off oil supplies to the U.S. Navy. Washington actually had to turn to London to ask if it could supply the **Sixth Fleet**, much as Britain had been forced to turn to the United States in 1956. For a few hours on October 25, it even seemed as if the two superpowers were squaring off for a nuclear confrontation, but then **Kissinger pressured the Jews to allow the Arab armies to retreat unmolested**. The cease-fire held. By October 26 the **Yom Kippur War** was over. Soon thereafter Israel and Egypt began their first direct talks in a quarter of a century.

The first priority for the White House was to find a scapegoat for the failure to give Israel timely intelligence. By throwing **James Angleton** to the wolves, the White House could kill two investigations with one stone. **Golda Meir** wanted to know why their trusted source, **James Jesus Angleton**, had not given them any warning of the Arab attack. It was perhaps fitting that **Angleton**'s failure helped end his longstanding liaison with Israel. **His iron grip on the CIA's Israeli desk was being questioned.**

**Schlesinger** later told **Angleton**'s biographers, **Tom Mangold**, that **"he was unhappy at the intimacy that had developed . . . between the Counterintelligence chief and the Israelis"**. However, after only five months in the job, **Schlesinger** left the **CIA** and became defense secretary in July 1973. **Angleton**'s control of the Israeli account was given a reprieve while **William Colby**, the new **CIA** head.

**Angleton** had become quite obsessive and paranoid and, although only 66, was long overdue for retirement. **Angleton** became the major fall guy for all the failures of U.S. intelligence during the 1973 war. **Angleton** resisted all attempts at his removal in a most ferocious manner. **Perhaps Colby feared that Angleton like James Forrestal, would have committed suicide.**

In December 1974 **Colby** finally acted. After twenty-three years of officially holding the Israeli account, and nearly thirty since he first seized de factor control over it with his **Zionist intelligence forgery**, Angleton was removed as the Israeli liaison. **Colby** transferred responsibility for Israeli matters to the **Near East Division**. A few days after **Angleton** lost his last remaining job as head of counterintelligence.

After his death in 1986, his friends in Israeli intelligence gathered to dedicate a memorial to the memory. There was hardly a Jew in the American government whom **Angleton** had not bugged.

**Angleton's secret files on the Jews** were discovered during the investigation of **Operation Chaos.** Later it was revealed that **Angleton** also was instrumental in using **Chaos** to spy on both the Israeli embassy in Washington and domestic Jewish groups. This covert operation involved the **CIA** buying a trash collection company to collect the garbage of both the Israeli embassy and the **B'Nai Brith** for intelligence purposes.

The **Nixon** White House was a circle of snakes swallowing each other's tails. When the dust had finally settled on the 1973 war, **Nixon had resigned**. **Angleton** had been fired, **Kissinger** was discredited, but **Israel had received more arms in three months than from all previous U.S. presidents combined.**

**Casualties**

Israel suffered between 2,521 and 2,800 killed in action. An additional 7,250 to 8,800 soldiers were wounded. Some 293 Israelis were captured. Approximately **400 Israeli tanks were destroyed**. Another 600 were disabled but returned to service after repairs. The **Israeli Air Force lost 102 airplanes:** 32 F-4s, 53 A-4s, 11 Mirages and 6 Super Mysteres. Two helicopters, a Bell 205 and a CH-53, were also lost.

Egypt and Syria never disclosed official figures with the **Insight Team** of the London *The Sunday Times* combined Egyptian and Syrian losses of 16,000 killed, and yet another source citing a figure of some 15000 dead and 35,000 wounded. U.S. estimates placed Egyptian casualties at 13,000. Iraq lost 278 killed and 898 wounded, while Jordan suffered 23 killed and 77 wounded. Some 8,372 Egyptians, 392 Syrians, 13 Iraqis and 6 Moroccans were taken prisoner.

Arab tank losses amounted to 2,250. 400 of these fell into Israeli hands in good working order and were incorporated into Israeli service. Between 341 and 514 Arab aircraft were shot down. Arab naval vessels, including 10 missile boats, were sunk for no Israeli losses.

# Herod the Great

Herod (*Hordus*, Tiberian: *Hōreḏōs*, 74/73 BCE – 4 BCE), also known as **Herod the Great** and **Herod I**, was a Roman client king of Judea, referred to as the **Herodian kingdom**. The history of his legacy has polarized opinion, as he is known for his colossal building projects throughout Judea, including his expansion of the **Second Temple** in Jerusalem (**Herod's Temple**), the construction of the port at **Caesarea Maritima**, the fortress at **Masada**, and **Herodium**. Vital details of his life are recorded in the works of the 1st century CE Roman–Jewish historian **Josephus**.

**Herod** also appears in the **Christian Gospel of Matthew** as the ruler of Judea who orders the **Massacre of the Innocents** at the time of the birth of **Jesus**. Despite his successes, including singlehandedly forging a new aristocracy from practically nothing, he has still garnered criticism from various historians. His reign polarizes opinion amongst scholars and historians, some viewing his legacy as evidence of success, and some as a reminder of his tyrannical rule.

Upon **Herod's death,** the Romans divided his kingdom among three of his sons and his sister— **Archelaus** became **ethnarch of the tetrarchy of Judea, Herod Antipas** became **tetrarch of Galilee and Peraea, Philip** became tetrarch of territories north and east of the Jordan, and **Salome I** was given a toparchy including the cities of Jabneh, Ashdod, and Phasaelis.

## Biography

It is generally accepted that **Herod** was born around 73 BCE in **Idumea, south of Judea**. He was the second son of **Antipater the Idumaean**, a high-ranking official under ethnarch **Hyrcanus II**, and Cypros, a Nabatean. **Herod's** father was by descent an **Edomite**, descendants of **Esau**, whose ancestors had converted to Judaism. **Herod was raised as a Jew**.

A loyal supporter of **Hyrcanus II**, **Antipater** appointed his son **Herod** governor of Galilee in 47 BCE, when **Herod** was either about 25 or 28 years old. His elder brother, **Phasael,** was appointed governor of Jerusalem. **Herod** enjoyed the backing of Rome, but his brutality was condemned by the **Sanhedrin.**

In 41 BCE, **Herod** and his brother **Phasael** were named as tetrarchs by the Roman leader **Mark Antony.** They were placed in this role to support **Hyrcanus II**. Later, **Antigonus,** Hyrcanus' nephew, took the throne from his uncle with the help of the Parthians. **Herod** fled to Rome to plead with the Romans to restore **Hyrcanus II** to power. The Romans had a special interest in Judea because their general **Pompey the Great** had conquered Jerusalem in 63 BCE, thus placing the region in the Roman sphere of influence.

In Rome, **Herod** was unexpectedly appointed **King of the Jews** by the Roman Senate. **Josephus** puts this in the year of the consulship of **Calvinus** and **Pollio** (40 BCE), but Appian places it in 39 BCE. **Herod** went back to Judea to win his kingdom from **Antigonus**. Toward the end of the campaign against **Antigonus**, **Herod** married the granddaughter of **Hyrcanus II**, **Mariamne** (known as **Mariamne I**), who was also a niece of **Antigonus**. **Herod** did this in an attempt to secure his claim to the throne and gain some Jewish favor. However, **Herod** already had a wife, **Doris**, and a young son, **Antipater**, and chose therefore to banish **Doris** and her child.

After three years of conflict, **Herod** and the Romans finally captured Jerusalem and **Herod** sent **Antigonus** for execution to **Marc Antony**. **Herod** took the role as sole ruler of Judea and the title of *basileus* (**"king"**) for himself, ushering in the **Herod**ian **Dynasty** and ending the **Hasmonean Dynasty**. **Josephus** reports this as being in the year of the consulship of **Agrippa** and **Gallus** (37 BCE), but also says that it was exactly 27 years after Jerusalem fell to **Pompey**, which would indicate 36 BCE. **Cassius Dio** also reports that in 37 BCE **"the Romans accomplished nothing worthy of note"** in the area. According to **Josephus**, **Herod** ruled for 37 years, 34 of them after capturing Jerusalem.

As some believe **Herod**'s family were converts to Judaism, his religious commitment was questioned by some elements of Jewish society. When **John Hyrcanus** conquered the region of Idumaea (the Edom of the Hebrew Bible) in 140–130 BCE, he required all **Idumaeans** to obey Jewish law or to leave; most **Idumaeans** thus converted to Judaism, which meant that they had to be circumcised, and many had intermarried with the Jews and adopted their customs. While **Herod** publicly identified himself as a Jew and was considered as such by some, this religious identification was undermined by the decadent lifestyle of the **Herodians**, which would have earned them the antipathy of observant Jews. **Herod later executed several members of his own family, including his wife Mariamne I and 3 sons.**

## Reign in Judea

**Herod**'s rule marked a new beginning in the history of Judea. Judea had been ruled autonomously by the **Hasmonean** kings from 140 BCE until 63 BCE. The **Hasmonean** kings retained their titles, but became clients of Rome after the **conquest by Pompey in 63 BCE**. **Herod** overthrew the **Hasmonean Antigonus** in a three-year-long war between 40 and 37 BCE, ruled under Roman overlordship until his death ca. 4 BCE, and officially passed on the throne to his sons, thus establishing his own, so-called **Herodian dynasty.**

**Herod** was granted the title of **"King of Judea"** by the Roman Senate. As such, he was a vassal of the Roman Empire, expected to support the interests of his Roman patrons. Nonetheless, just when **Herod** obtained leadership in Judea, his rule faced two threats. The first threat came from his mother-in-law **Alexandra**, who sought to regain power for her family, the **Hasmonean**s, whose dynasty **Herod** had overthrown in 37 BCE. In the same year, **Cleopatra** married the Roman leader **Antony**. Recognizing Cleopatra's influence over **Antony**, **Alexandra asked Cleopatra for aid in making Aristobulus III the High Priest.**

As a member of the **Hasmonean** family, **Aristobulus III** might partially repair the fortunes of the **Hasmonean**s if made **High Priest**. Alexandra's request was made, but **Cleopatra** urged **Alexandra** to leave Judea with **Aristobulus III** and visit **Antony**. **Herod** received word of this plot, and feared that if **Antony** met **Aristobolus III** in person he might name **Aristobulus III** King of Judea.

This concern induced **Herod**, in 35 BCE, to order the assassination of **Aristobulus**, ending this first threat to **Herod**'s throne. The marriage of 37 BCE also sparked a power struggle between Roman leaders **Octavian**, who would later be called **Augustus**, and **Antony.**

**Herod**, owing his throne to Rome, had to pick a side, and he chose **Antony**. In 31 BCE at **Actium**, **Antony** lost to **Octavian**, posing a second threat to **Herod**'s rule. **Herod** had to regain **Octavian**'s support if he was to keep his throne. At Rhodes in 31 BCE, **Herod**, through his ability to keep Judea open to Rome as a link to the wealth of Syria and Egypt, and ability to defend the frontier, convinced **Octavian** that he would be loyal to him. **Herod** continued to rule his subjects as he saw fit. Despite the autonomy afforded to **Herod** in his internal reign over Judea, restrictions were placed upon him in his relations with other kingdoms.

**Herod**'s support from the Roman Empire was a major factor in enabling him to maintain his authority over Judea. There have been mixed interpretations concerning **Herod**'s popularity during his reign. In *The Jewish War*, **Josephus** characterizes **Herod**'s rule in generally favorable terms, and gives **Herod** the benefit of the doubt for the infamous events that took place during his reign. However, in his later work, *Jewish Antiquities*, **Josephus** emphasizes the tyrannical authority that many scholars have come to associate with **Herod**'s reign.

**Herod**'s despotic rule has been demonstrated by many of his security measures aimed at suppressing the contempt his people, especially Jews, had towards him. For instance, it has been suggested that **Herod** used secret police to monitor and report the feelings of the general populace towards him. He sought to prohibit protests, and had opponents removed by force. He had a bodyguard of 2,000 soldiers. **Josephus** describes various units of **Herod**'s personal guard taking part in **Herod**'s funeral, including the *Doryphnoroi*, and a **Thracian**, Celtic (probably Gallic) and Germanic contingent.

While the term *Doryphnoroi* does not have an ethnic connotation, the unit was probably composed of distinguished veteran soldiers and young men from the most influential Jewish families. **Thracians** had served in the Jewish armies since the **Hasmonean** dynasty, while the Celtic contingent were former bodyguards of **Cleopatra** given as a gift by **Augustus** to **Herod** following the **Battle of Actium**. The Germanic contingent was modeled upon Augustus's personal bodyguard, the *Germani Corporis Custodes*, responsible for guarding the palace.

**Herod** spent lavish sums on his various building projects and generous gifts to other dominions, including Rome itself. His buildings were very large, ambitious projects. **Herod** was responsible for the construction of the **Temple Mount**, a portion of which remains today as the **Western Wall**. In addition, **Herod** also used the latest technology in hydraulic cement and underwater construction to build the harbor at **Caesarea**. While **Herod**'s zeal for building transformed Judea, his motives were not selfless.

Although he built fortresses (**Masada, Herod**ium, **Alexandrium, Hyrcania, and Machaerus**) in which he and his family could take refuge in case of insurrection, these vast projects were also intended to gain the support of the Jews and improve his reputation as a leader. **Herod** also built **Sebaste** and other pagan cities because he wanted to appeal to the country's substantial pagan population.

In order to fund these projects, **Herod** utilized a **Hasmonean** taxation system that heavily burdened the Judean people. Nevertheless, these enterprises brought employment and opportunities for the people's provision. In some instances, **Herod** took it upon himself to provide for his people in times of need, such as during a severe famine that occurred in 25 BCE.

Although he made many attempts at conforming to traditional Jewish laws, there were more instances where **Herod** was insensitive, which constitutes one of the major Jewish complaints towards **Herod** as highlighted in **Jewish Antiquities**. In Jerusalem, **Herod** introduced foreign forms of entertainment, and erected a golden eagle at the entrance of the **Temple**, which suggested a greater interest in the welfare of Rome than of Jews. **Herod**'s taxes garnered a bad reputation - his constant concern for his reputation led him to make frequent, expensive gifts, increasingly emptying the kingdom's coffers, and such lavish spending upset his Jewish subjects. The two major Jewish sects of the day, the **Pharisees** and the **Sadducees**, both showed opposition to **Herod**.

The Pharisees were discontented because **Herod** disregarded many of their demands with respect to the **Temple**'s construction. The **Sadducees**, who were closely associated with priestly responsibilities in the **Temple**, opposed **Herod** because he replaced their high priests with outsiders from **Babylonia** and **Alexandria**, in an effort to gain support from the Jewish Diaspora. **Herod**'s outreach efforts gained him little, and at the end of his reign anger and dissatisfaction were common amongst Jews. Heavy outbreaks of violence and riots followed **Herod**'s death in many cities, including Jerusalem, as pent-up resentments boiled over. The scope of the disturbances sparked hopes that the Jews of Judea might someday overthrow the Roman overlords, hopes reawakened decades later in the outbreak of the **Great Revolt of 70 CE**.

## Architectural achievements / *Herodian architecture*

**Herod**'s most famous and ambitious project was the expansion of the **Second Temple** in Jerusalem. **Herod**'s rebuilding of the **Second Temple** in Jerusalem was done so that he would **"have a capital city worthy of his dignity and grandeur"** and with this reconstruction **Herod** hoped to gain more support from the Jews. Recent findings suggest that the **Temple Mount** walls and **Robinson's Arch** may not have been completed until at least 20 years after his death, during the reign of **Herod Agrippa II.**

In the 18th year of his reign (20–19 BCE), **Herod rebuilt the Temple** on **"a more magnificent scale".** Although work on out-buildings and courts continued for another 80 years, the new **Temple** was finished in a year and a half. To comply with religious law, **Herod employed 1,000 priests as masons** and carpenters in the rebuilding. The finished temple, which was destroyed in 70 CE, is sometimes referred to as **Herod**'s **Temple**. Today, only the four retaining walls remain standing, including the **Western Wall**. These walls created a flat platform (the **Temple Mount**) upon which the **Temple** was then constructed.

**Herod**'s other achievements include the development of water supplies for Jerusalem, building fortresses such as Masada and **Herodium,** and founding new cities such as **Caesarea Maritima** and the enclosures of **Cave of the Patriarchs** and **Mamre** in Hebron. He and **Cleopatra** owned a monopoly over the extraction of asphalt from the **Dead Sea**, which was used in shipbuilding. He leased copper mines on Cyprus from the Roman emperor.

## New Testament references / *Massacre of the Innocents*

**Herod** appears in the Gospel according to **Matthew**, which describes an event known as the **Massacre of the Innocents**. According to this account, after the birth of **Jesus**, some magi from the East visited **Herod** to inquire the whereabouts of **"the one having been born king of the Jews"**, because they had seen his star in the east (or, according to certain translations, at its rising) and therefore wanted to pay him homage. **Herod**, as King of the Jews, was alarmed at the prospect of a usurper. **Herod** assembled the chief priests and scribes of the people and asked them where the **"Anointed One"** (the **Messiah**) was to be born.

They answered, in Bethlehem, citing **Micah 5:2**. **Herod** therefore sent the magi to Bethlehem, instructing them to search for the child and, after they had found him, to **"report to me, so that I too may go and worship him"**. However, after they had found **Jesus**, they were warned in a dream not to report back to **Herod**. Similarly, **Joseph** was warned in a dream that **Herod intended to kill Jesus, so he and his family fled to Egypt**. When **Herod** realized he had been outwitted, he gave orders to **kill all boys of the age of two** and under in Bethlehem and its vicinity. **Joseph and his family stayed in Egypt until Herod's death**, then moved to Nazareth in Galilee to avoid living under **Herod**'s son **Archelaus.**

Regarding the **Massacre of the Innocents**, although **Herod** was guilty of many brutal acts including the killing of his wife, brother-in-law, three of his sons, 300 military leaders, and many others, as recorded by firsthand sources, contemporary sources including **Herod**'s friend and personal historian, **Nicolas of Damascus**, did not leave behind records of the massacre. "**Josephus** wrote for a Greco-Roman audience, which would have little concern for infant deaths. Greeks regularly practiced infanticide as a kind of birth control, particularly in Sparta, while the Roman father had the right not to lift his baby off the floor after birth, letting it die".

**Macrobius** (ca. AD 400), one of the last pagan writers in Rome, in his book **Saturnalia**, wrote: **"When it was heard that, as part of the slaughter of boys up to two years old, Herod, king of the Jews, had ordered his own son to be killed, he remarked, 'It is better to be Herod's pig than his son'".** This was a reference of how **Herod**, as a Jew, would not kill pigs, but had three of his sons, and many others, killed.

Besides killing his enemies, **Herod** he had no qualms in killing family members and friends as well. **Herod** would not have given a second thought about killing a handful of babies in a small, obscure village south of Jerusalem in order to keep his throne secure for himself, or his sons, even if it was one of the last dastardly deeds he committed before he died. The killing **"wholly in keeping with all that we know of him."**

## Death

**Herod** died in Jericho, after an excruciatingly painful, putrefying illness of uncertain cause, known to posterity as **"Herod's Evil"**. **Josephus** states that the pain of his illness led **Herod** to attempt suicide by stabbing, and that the attempt was thwarted by his cousin.

Most scholarship concerning the date of **Herod**'s death follows, which revised a traditional death date of 1 BCE to **4 BCE**. Two of **Herod**'s sons, **Archelaus** and **Philip the Tetrarch**, dated their rule from **4 BCE**, though **Archelaus** apparently held royal authority during **Herod**'s lifetime. **Philip's** reign would last for 37 years, until his death in the 20th year of **Tiberius** (34 CE), which implies his accession as 4 BCE. **In Josephus' account, Herod's death was preceded by a lunar eclipse and followed by Passover.**

Scholars agree **Herod** suffered throughout his lifetime from depression and paranoia. **Josephus** stated that **Herod** was so concerned that no one would mourn his death, that he commanded a large group of distinguished men to come to Jericho, and he gave an order that they should be killed at the time of his death so that the displays of grief that he craved would take place; but his son **Archelaus** and his sister **Salome** did not carry out this wish.

## Successors

**Augustus** respected the terms of **Herod**'s will, which stipulated the division of **Herod's kingdom** among three of his sons. Augustus recognized **Herod**'s son **Herod Archelaus** as ethnarch of Judea, Samaria, and Idumea to 6 CE, referred to as the tetrarchy of Judea. **Augustus** then judged Archelaus incompetent to rule, removed him from power, and combined the provinces of Samaria, Judea proper, and Idumea into Iudaea province. This enlarged province was ruled by a prefect until the year 41. As to **Herod**'s other sons, **Herod Antipas** was tetrarch of Galilee and Peraea from **Herod**'s death to 39 CE; Philip became tetrarch of territories north and east of the Jordan.

## Herod's tomb

The location of **Herod**'s tomb is documented by **Josephus**, who writes, **"And the body was carried two hundred furlongs, to Herodium, where he had given order to be buried."** Lower **Herod**ium consists of the remains of a large palace, a race track, service quarters, and a monumental building whose function is still a mystery. Perhaps, it is **Herod**'s mausoleum. Next to it is a pool, almost twice as large as modern Olympic-size pools.

On May 7, 2007, an Israeli team of archaeologists of Hebrew University, led by **Netzer**, announced they had discovered the tomb. The site is located at the exact location given by **Josephus**, atop tunnels and water pools, at a flattened desert site, halfway up the hill to **Herod**ium, 12 kilometers (7.5 mi) south of Jerusalem. **The tomb contained a broken sarcophagus but no remains of a body.**

## Opinion of his reign

According to contemporary historians, **Herod** the Great **"is perhaps the only figure in ancient Jewish history who has been loathed equally by Jewish and Christian posterity"**, depicted both from Jews and Christians as a tyrant and bloodthirsty ruler. The study of **Herod**'s reign includes polarizing opinions on the man himself. Modern critics have described him as **"the evil genius of the Judean nation"**, and as one who would be **"prepared to commit any crime in order to gratify his unbounded ambition."**

His extraordinary spending spree is cited as one of the causes of the serious impoverishment of the people he ruled, adding to the opinion that his reign was exclusively negative. **Herod**'s religious policies gained a mixed response from the Jewish populace. Although **Herod considered himself king of the Jews,** he let it be known that he also represented the non-Jews living in Judea, building temples for other religions outside of the Jewish areas of his kingdom.

Many Jews questioned the authenticity of **Herod**'s Judaism on account of his Idumean background and his infamous murders of members of his family. However, he generally respected traditional Jewish observances in his public life. For instance, he minted coins without human images to be used in Jewish areas and acknowledged the sanctity of the **Second Temple** by employing priests in the construction of the **Temple**.

**Herod**'s sensitivity towards Jewish traditions in his private life with the presence of around **40 ritual baths or *mikvehs*** found in several of his palaces. These *mikvehs* were known for being used in Jewish purity rituals during this time where Jewish people could submerge themselves in these pools and purify their bodies without the presence of a priest. There is some speculation as to whether or not these baths were actual *mikvehs* as they have also been identified as stepped *frigidarium* or Roman cold-water baths; however, several historians have identified these baths as a combination of both types.

While it has been proven that **Herod** showed a great amount of disrespect towards the Jewish religion. The presence of these ritual baths shows that **Herod** found ritual purity important enough in his private life to place a large number of these baths in his palaces despite his several connections to gentiles and pagan cults. These baths also show that the combination of the Roman *frigidarium* and the Jewish *mikvehs* suggests that **Herod** sought for there to be some type of combination between the Roman and Jewish cultures as he enjoyed the purity of Jewish tradition and the comfort of Roman luxury simultaneously.

However, he was also praised for his work, being considered the greatest builder in Jewish history, and one who **"knew his place and followed rules."** In fact, what is left of his building ventures are now popular tourist attractions in the Middle East, which many have come to cherish as both a historical and religious area.

## Chronology / *Herodian kingdom* / 30s BCE
- **39–37 BCE** – Roman war against Antigonus. After the conquest of Jerusalem and victory over Antigonus, Mark **Antony** executes him.
- **36 BCE** – **Herod** makes his 17-year-old brother-in-law, Aristobulus III, high priest, fearing that the Jews would appoint Aristobulus III as **"King of the Jews"** in his place.
- **35 BCE** – Aristobulus III is drowned at a party on **Herod**'s orders.
- **32 BCE** – The war against Nabatea begins, with victory one year later.
- **31 BCE** – Judea suffers a devastating earthquake. **Octavian** defeats Mark **Antony**, so **Herod** switches allegiance to **Octavian**, later known as Augustus.
- **30 BCE** – **Herod** is shown great favor by **Octavian**, who at Rhodes confirms him as King of Judea.

## 20s BCE
- 29 BCE – **Josephus** writes that **Herod** had great passion and also great jealousy concerning his wife, Mariamne I. She learns of **Herod**'s plans to murder her, and stops sleeping with him. **Herod** puts her on trial on a charge of adultery. His sister, Salome I, was chief witness against her. Mariamne I's mother Alexandra made an appearance and

incriminated her own daughter. Historians say her mother was next on **Herod**'s list to be executed and did this only to save her own life. **Mariamne** was executed, and Alexandra declared herself Queen, stating that **Herod** was mentally unfit to serve. **Josephus wrote that this was Alexandra's strategic mistake; Herod executed her without trial.**

- **28 BCE** – **Herod** executed his brother-in-law Kostobar (husband of Salome, father to Berenice) for conspiracy. Large festival in Jerusalem, as **Herod** had built a theatre and an amphitheater.
- **27 BCE** – An assassination attempt on **Herod** was foiled. To honor Augustus, **Herod** rebuilt Samaria and renamed it Sebaste.
- **25 BCE** – **Herod** imported grain from Egypt and started an aid program to combat the widespread hunger and disease that followed a massive drought. He also waives a third of the taxes. **Herod** began construction on Caesarea Maritima and its harbor.
- **23 BCE** – **Herod** built a palace in Jerusalem and the fortress **Herod**ion (**Herod**ium) in Judea. He married his third wife, Mariamne II, the daughter of the priest Simon Boethus; immediately **Herod**es deprived **Jesus** the son of Phabet of the high priesthood and conferred that dignity on Simon.
- **22 BCE** – The Roman emperor Augustus granted him the regions Trachonitis, Batanaea, and Auranitis to the northeast.
- **Circa 20 BCE** – Expansion started on the **Temple** Mount; **Herod** completely rebuilt the Second **Temple** of Jerusalem.

## 10s BCE
- Circa 18 BCE – **Herod** traveled for the second time to Rome.
- 14 BCE – **Herod** supported the Jews in Anatolia and Cyrene. Owing to the prosperity in Judaea he waived a quarter of the taxes.
- 13 BCE – **Herod** made his first-born son Antipater (his son by Doris) first heir in his will.
- 12 BCE – **Herod** suspected his sons from his marriage to Mariamne I, Alexander and Aristobulus, of threatening his life. He took them to Aquileia to be tried. Augustus reconciled the three.
- **Herod** supported the financially strapped Olympic Games and ensured their future. **Herod** amended his will so that Alexander and Aristobulus rose in the royal succession, but Antipater would be higher in the succession.
- **Circa 10 BCE** – The newly expanded temple in Jerusalem was inaugurated. War against the Nabateans began.

## First decade BCE
- **9 BCE** –Caesarea Maritima was inaugurated. Owing to the course of the war against the Nabateans, **Herod** fell into disgrace with Augustus. **Herod** again suspected Alexander of plotting to kill him.
- **8 BCE** – **Herod** accused his sons Alexander and Aristobulus of high treason. **Herod** reconciled with Augustus, who also gave him the permission to proceed legally against his sons.

- **7 BCE** – The court hearing took place in Berytos (Beirut) before a Roman court. His sons Alexander and Aristobulus were found guilty and executed. The succession changed so that Antipater was the exclusive successor to the throne. In second place the succession incorporated (**Herod**) Philip, his son by Mariamne II.
- **6 BCE** – **Herod** proceeded against the Pharisees.
- **5 BCE** – Antipater was brought before the court charged with the intended murder of **Herod**. **Herod**, by now seriously ill, named his son (**Herod**) Antipas (from his fourth marriage with Malthace) as his successor.
- **4 BCE** – Young disciples smashed the golden eagle over the main entrance of the **Temple** of Jerusalem after the **Pharisee** teachers claimed it was an idolatrous Roman symbol. **Herod** arrested them, brought them to court, and sentenced them. **Augustus approved the death penalty for Antipater. Herod then executed his son, and again changed his will**: **Archelaus** (from the marriage with Malthace) would rule as ethnarch over the tetrachy of Judea, while **Antipas** (by Malthace) and **Philip** (from the fifth marriage with Cleopatra of Jerusalem) would rule as tetrarchs over Galilee and Peraea (Transjordan), also over **Gaulanitis** (Golan), **Trachonitis** (Hebrew: Argob), **Batanaea** (now Ard-el-Bathanyeh) and **Panias**. **Salome I** was also given a small toparchy in the Gaza region. **As Augustus did not confirm his will, no one received the title of King; however, the three sons were granted rule of the stated territories.**

It is very probable that **Herod** had more children, especially with the last wives, and also that he had more daughters, as female births at that time were often not recorded.

# Theodor Herzl

**Theodor Herzl** ( Hungarian: *Herzl Tivadar*; Hebrew name given at his brit Milah **Binyamin Ze'ev** also known in Hebrew as חוֹזֵה הַמְדִינָה, *Chozeh HaMedinah*, lit. **"Visionary of the State"**; 2 May 1860 – 3 July 1904) was an Austro-Hungarian journalist, playwright, political activist, and writer who was the father of modern political **Zionism**. **Herzl** formed the **Zionist Organization** and promoted Jewish immigration to Palestine in an effort to form a Jewish state. Though he died before its establishment, he is **known as the father of the State of Israel**.

While **Herzl** is specifically mentioned in the **Israeli Declaration of Independence** and is officially referred to as **"the spiritual father of the Jewish State"**, i.e. the visionary who gave a concrete, practicable platform and framework to political **Zionism**, he was not the first Zionist theoretician or activist; scholars, many of them religious such as rabbis **Yehuda Bibas, Zvi Hirsch Kalischer** and **Judah Alkalai**, promoted a range of proto-Zionist ideas before him.

## ⌐ Early life

**Theodor Herzl** was born in the *Tabakgasse (Dohány utca* in Hungarian), a street in the Jewish quarter of Pest (now eastern part of Budapest), Kingdom of Hungary(now Hungary), to a secular Jewish family. His father's family were originally from **Zimony** (today **Zemun, Serbia**). He was the second child of **Jeanette** and **Jakob Herzl**, who were German-speaking, assimilated Jews. It is believed **Herzl** was of both Ashkenazi and Sephardic lineage predominately through his paternal line and to a lesser extent through the maternal line. He also claimed to be a direct descendent of the famous Greek Kabbalist **Joseph Taitazak**.

Jakob **Herzl** (1836–1902), **Herzl**'s father, was a highly successful businessman. **Herzl** had one sister, **Pauline**, a year older than he was, who died suddenly on 7 February 1878, of typhus. **Theodor** lived with his family in a house next to the Dohány Street Synagogue (formerly known as **Tabakgasse Synagogue**) located in Belváros, the inner city of the historical old town of Pest, in the eastern section of Budapest.

As a youth, **Herzl** aspired to follow in the footsteps of **Ferdinand de Lesseps**, builder of the **Suez Canal,** but did not succeed in the sciences and instead developed a growing enthusiasm for poetry and the humanities. This passion later developed into a successful career in journalism and a less-celebrated pursuit of play righting.

As a young man, **Herzl** was an ardent Germanophile who saw the Germans as the best *Kulturvolk* (cultured people) in Central Europe and embraced the German ideal of *Bildung,* whereby reading great works of literature by **Goethe** and **Shakespeare** could allow one to appreciate the beautiful things in life, and thus become a morally better person (the *Bildung* theory tended to equate beauty with goodness). Through *Bildung,* **Herzl** believed that Hungarian Jews such as himself could shake off their **"shameful Jewish characteristics"** caused by long centuries of impoverishment and oppression, and become civilized Central Europeans, a true *Kulturvolk* along the German lines.

In 1878, after the death of his sister, **Pauline**, the family moved to Vienna, Austria-Hungary, and lived in the 9th district, Alsergrund. **At the University of Vienna, Herzl studied law**. As a young law student, **Herzl** became a member of the German nationalist *Burschenschaft* (fraternity) Albia, which had the motto *Ehre, Freiheit, Vaterland* (**"Honor, Freedom, Fatherland"**). He later resigned in protest at the organization's antisemitism.

After a brief legal career in the University of Vienna and Salzburg, he devoted himself to journalism and literature, working as a journalist for a Viennese newspaper and a correspondent for *Neue Freie Presse*, in Paris, occasionally making special trips to London and Istanbul. He later became literary editor of *Neue Freie Presse*, and wrote several comedies and dramas for the Viennese stage. His early work did not focus on Jewish life. It was of the feuilleton order, descriptive rather than political.

## Zionist intellectual and activist

As the Paris correspondent for *Neue Freie Presse*, **Herzl** followed the **Dreyfus** affair, a political scandal that divided the **Third French Republic** from 1894 until its resolution in 1906. It was a notorious antisemitic incident in France in which a Jewish French army captain was falsely convicted of spying for Germany. **Herzl** was witness to mass rallies in Paris following the **Dreyfus** trial. There has been some controversy surrounding the impact that this event had on **Herzl** and his conversion to **Zionism**.

**Herzl** himself stated that the **Dreyfus** case turned him into a Zionist and that he was particularly affected by chants of **"Death to the Jews!"** from the crowds. This had been the widely held belief for some time. However, some modern scholars now believe that due to little mention of the **Dreyfus** affair in **Herzl**'s earlier accounts and a seemingly contrary reference he made in them to shouts of **"Death to the traitor!"** that he may have exaggerated the influence it had on him in order to create further support for his goals.

The **Dreyfus** influence was a myth that **Herzl** did not feel necessary to deflate and that he also believed that **Dreyfus** was guilty. Another modern claim is that, while upset by antisemitism evident in French society, **Herzl**, like most contemporary observers, initially believed in **Dreyfus'** guilt and only claimed to have been inspired by the affair years later when it had become an international cause célèbre and that, rather, it was the rise to power of the antisemitic demagogue **Karl Lueger** in Vienna in 1895 that seems to have had a greater effect on **Herzl**, before the pro-**Dreyfus** campaign had fully emerged.

It was at this time that **Herzl** wrote his play **"The New Ghetto,"** which shows the ambivalence and lack of real security and equality of emancipated, well-to-do Jews in Vienna. The protagonist is an assimilated Jewish lawyer who tries unsuccessfully to break through the social ghetto enforced on Western Jews.

**Herzl** was initially **"fanatically devoted to the propagation of Jewish-German 'Liberal' assimilationist doctrine"**. However, **Herzl** came to reject his early ideas regarding Jewish emancipation and assimilation and to believe that the Jews must remove themselves from Europe.

**Herzl** grew to believe that antisemitism could not be defeated or cured, only avoided, and that the only way to avoid it was the establishment of a Jewish state. In June 1895, he wrote in his diary: **"In Paris, as I have said, I achieved a freer attitude toward anti-semitism ... Above all, I recognized the emptiness and futility of trying to 'combat' anti-semitism."**

**Herzl**'s editors of **Neue Freie Presse** refused any publication of his Zionist political activities. A mental clash gripped **Herzl**, between the craving for literary success and a desire to act as a public figure. Around this time, **Herzl** started writing pamphlets about **'A Jewish State'**. **Herzl** claimed that these pamphlets resulted in the establishment of the **Zionist Movement**, and they did play a large role in the movement's rise and success. His testimony before the **British Royal Commission** reflected his fundamental, romantic liberal view on life as the **'Problem of the Jews'**.

Beginning in late 1895, **Herzl** wrote *Der Judenstaat* (*The State of the Jews*), which was published February 1896 to immediate acclaim and controversy. The book argued that the Jewish people should leave Europe if they wished to, either for **Argentina** or, preferably, for **Palestine**, their historic homeland. The Jews possessed a nationality; all they were missing was a nation and a state of their own. Only through a Jewish state could they avoid antisemitism, express their culture freely and practice their religion without hindrance.

**Herzl**'s ideas spread rapidly throughout the Jewish world and attracted international attention. Supporters of existing Zionist movements, such as the **Hovevei Zion**, immediately allied themselves with him, but establishment Jewry vilified him and considered his ideas as a threat to their attempts at integration and a **rebellion against God**.

### A philosophy for a homeland: In *Der Judenstaat* he writes:
**"The Jewish question persists wherever Jews live in appreciable numbers. Wherever it does not exist, it is brought in together with Jewish immigrants. We are naturally drawn into those places where we are not persecuted, and our appearance there gives rise to persecution. This is the case, and will inevitably be so, everywhere, even in highly civilized countries—see, for instance, France—so long as the Jewish question is not solved on the political level."**

**The book concludes:**

Therefore, I believe that a wondrous generation of Jews will spring into existence. The **Maccabeans will rise again**. Let me repeat once more my opening words: The Jews who wish for a State will have it. We shall live at last as free men on our own soil, and die peacefully in our own homes. The world will be freed by our liberty, enriched by our wealth, magnified by our greatness. And whatever we attempt there to accomplish for our own welfare, will react powerfully and beneficially for the good of humanity.

## Diplomatic liaison with the Ottomans

**Herzl** began to energetically promote his ideas, continually attracting supporters, Jewish and non-Jewish. **Herzl "mapped out for himself the role of martyr ... as the Parnell of the Jews".** On 10 March 1896, **Herzl** was visited by **Reverend William Hechler**, the Anglican minister to the British Embassy in Vienna. Hechler had read **Herzl's** *Der Judenstaat*, and the meeting became central to the eventual legitimization of **Herzl** and **Zionism**. **Herzl** later wrote in his diary, **"Next we came to the heart of the business. I said to him: (Theodor Herzl to Rev. William Hechler) I** must put myself into direct and publicly known relations with a responsible or non-responsible ruler – that is, with a minister of state or a prince.

**Then the Jews will believe in me and follow me. The most suitable personage would be the German Kaiser."** Hechler arranged an extended audience with **Frederick I, Grand** Duke of Baden, in April 1896. The Grand Duke was the uncle of the German Emperor **Wilhelm II**. Through the efforts of Hechler and the Grand Duke, **Herzl** publicly met **Wilhelm II** in 1898. The meeting significantly advanced **Herzl's** and **Zionism's** legitimacy in Jewish and world opinion.

In May 1896, the English translation of *Der Judenstaat* appeared in London as *The Jewish State*. **Herzl** had earlier confessed to his friend **Max Bodenheimer** that he **"wrote what I had to say without knowing my predecessors, and it can be assumed that I would not have written it had I been familiar with the literature"**.

In Istanbul, Ottoman Empire, 15 June 1896, **Herzl** saw an opportunity. With the assistance of **Count Filip Michał Newleński**, a sympathetic Polish émigré with political contacts in the Ottoman Court, **Herzl** attempted to meet **Sultan Abdulhamid II** in order to present his solution of a Jewish State to the Sultan directly. He failed to obtain an audience but did succeed in visiting a number of highly placed individuals, including the **Grand Vizier**, who received him as a journalist representing the *Neue Freie Presse*.

**Herzl** presented his proposal to the **Grand Vizier**: **"The Jews would pay the Turkish foreign debt and attempt to help regulate Turkish finances if they were given Palestine as a Jewish homeland under Turkish rule".** Prior to leaving Istanbul, 29 June 1896, Newleński obtained for **Herzl** a symbolic medal of honor. The medal, the **"Commander's Cross of the Order of the**

**Medjidie",** was a public relations affirmation for **Herzl** and the Jewish world of the seriousness of the negotiations. Five years later, 17 May 1901, **Herzl** did meet with **Sultan Abdulhamid II**, but the Sultan refused **Theodor Herzl**'s offer to consolidate the Ottoman debt in exchange for a charter allowing the Zionists access to Palestine.

Returning from Istanbul, **Herzl** traveled to London to report back to the **Maccabeans**, a proto-Zionist group of established English Jews led by **Colonel Albert Goldsmid**. In November 1895 they received him with curiosity, indifference and coldness. Israel Zangwill bitterly opposed **Herzl**, but after Istanbul, **Goldsmid** agreed to support **Herzl**. In London's East End, a community of primarily Yiddish speaking recent **Eastern European Jewish** immigrants, **Herzl** addressed a mass rally of thousands on 12 July 1896 and was received with acclaim. They granted **Herzl** the mandate of leadership for **Zionism**. Within six months this mandate had been expanded throughout Zionist Jewry: **the Zionist movement grew rapidly.**

## A World Congress

In 1897, at considerable personal expense, he founded the Zionist newspaper *Die Welt* in Vienna, Austria-Hungary, and planned the **First Zionist Congress** in Basel, Switzerland.

He was elected president of the Congress (a position he held until his death in 1904), and in 1898 he began a series of diplomatic initiatives to build support for a Jewish country. He was received by **Wilhelm II** on several occasions, one of them in Jerusalem, and attended the **Hague Peace Conference,** enjoying a warm reception from many statesmen there.

His work on Auto-emancipation was pre-figured by a similar conclusion drawn by Marx's friend **Moses Hess**, in *Rome and Jerusalem* (1862). **Pinkser** had never yet read it, but was aware of the distant and far off **Hibbat Zion**. **Herzl**'s philosophical instruction highlighted the weaknesses and vulnerabilities. To **Herzl** each dictator or leader had a nationalistic identity, even down to the Irish from **Wolfe Tone** onwards.

He was drawn to the mawkishness of Judaism rendered distinctively as German. But he remained convinced that Germany was the center *(Hauptsitz)* of antisemitism rather than France. In a much quoted aside he noted **"If there is one thing I should like to be, it is a member of old Prussian nobility".** **Herzl** appealed to the nobility of Jewish England - the **Rothschilds, Sir Samuel Montagu,** later cabinet minister, to the Chief Rabbis of France and Vienna, the railroad magnate, **Baron Hirsch.**

He fared best with **Israel Zangwill**, and **Max Nordau**. They were both well-known writers or 'men of letters'—imagination that engenders understanding. Hirsch's correspondence led nowhere. **Baron Albert Rothschild had little to do with the Jews. Herzl** was disliked by the bankers *(Finanzjuden)* and detested them. **Herzl** was defiant of their social authority. He also shared Pinkser's pessimistic opinion that the Jews had no future in Europe; that they were too antisemitic to tolerate because each country in Europe had tried antisemitic assimilation. In Berlin they said *Juden Raus* in a well-worn phrase.

**Herzl** therefore advocated a mass exodus from Europe to the *Judenstaat.* Pinkser's manifesto was a cry for help; a warning to others *Mahnruf*, a call for attention to their plight. **Herzl**'s vision was less about mental states of Jewry, and more about delivering prescriptive answers about land. "The idea that i have developed is a very old one; it is the restoration of the Jewish State" was a follow-up of Pinkser's early weaker version *Mahnruf and seine Stammesgenossen von einem nassichen Juden.*

## Herzl, Zionism and the Holy Land

**Herzl** visited Jerusalem for the first time in October 1898. He deliberately coordinated his visit with that of **Wilhelm II** to secure what he thought had been prearranged with the aid of **Rev. William Hechler**, public world power recognition of himself and **Zionism**. **Herzl** and **Wilhelm II** first met publicly on 29 October, at **Mikveh Israel**, near present-day Holon, Israel. It was a brief but historic meeting. He had a second formal, public audience with the emperor at the latter's tent camp on Street of the Prophets in Jerusalem on 2 November 1898. The **English Zionist Federation,** the local branch of the **World Zionist Organization was founded in 1899 that Herzl had established in Austria in 1897.** In 1902–03, **Herzl** was invited to give evidence before the **British Royal Commission** on **Alien Immigration**.

His appearance brought him into close contact with members of the British government, particularly with **Joseph Chamberlain**, then secretary of state for the colonies, through whom he negotiated with the Egyptian government for a charter for the settlement of the Jews in **Al 'Arish** in the Sinai Peninsula, adjoining southern Palestine.

In 1903, **Herzl** attempted to obtain support for the Jewish homeland from **Pope Pius X**, an idea broached at **6th Zionist Congress**. Palestine could offer a safe refuge for those fleeing persecution in Russia. Cardinal Rafael Merry Del Val ordained that the Church's policy was explained non possumus on such matters, decreeing that as long as the **Jews denied the divinity of Christ**, the Catholics could not make a declaration in their favor. The pogroms included 47 Jews murdered at Kishinev, and hundreds more injured, their property looted and destroyed.

The delegates to the Congress backed **Herzl**'s line of argument. A vociferous minority of opposition came from those who thought adoption of a **Ugandan Plan** over Palestine was a sell-out. Still later the East African Scheme failed, dying with **Herzl** himself. It was taken off the agenda in 1905. Yet another nationalistic splinter group with Zionist aspirations, in England called the **Jewish Territorial Association (JTO)** was founded.

After the failure of that scheme, which took him to Cairo, he received, through **Leopold Greenberg**, an offer (August 1903) from the British government to facilitate a large Jewish settlement, with autonomous government and under British suzerainty, in **British East Africa**. At the same time, the Zionist movement was threatened by the Russian government. Accordingly, **Herzl** visited St. Petersburg and was received by **Sergei Witte**, then finance minister, and **Viacheslav Plehve**, minister of the interior, the latter placing on record the attitude of his government toward the Zionist movement. On that occasion **Herzl** submitted proposals for the amelioration of the Jewish position in Russia.

He published the Russian statement, and brought the British offer, commonly known as the **"Uganda Project"**, before the **Sixth Zionist Congress** (Basel, August 1903), carrying the majority (295:178, 98 abstentions) on the question of investigating this offer, after the Russian delegation stormed out. In 1905 the **6th Zionist Congress**, after investigations, decided to decline the British offer and firmly committed itself to a Jewish homeland in Palestine. A *Heimstatte*—a homeland for the Jewish people in Palestine secured by public law.

## Death and burial

**Herzl** did not live to see the rejection of the **Uganda** plan. At 5 p.m. 3 July 1904, in Edlach, a village inside Reichenau and der Rax, Lower Austria, **Theodor Herzl**, having been diagnosed with a heart issue earlier in the year, **died of cardiac sclerosis**. A day before his death, he told the **Reverend William H. Hechler: "Greet Palestine for me. I gave my heart's blood for my people."**

His will stipulated that he should have the poorest-class funeral without speeches or flowers and he added, **"I wish to be buried in the vault beside my father, and to lie there till the Jewish people shall take my remains to Israel"**. Nevertheless, some six thousand followed **Herzl**'s hearse, and the funeral was long and chaotic.

Despite **Herzl**'s request that no speeches be made, a brief eulogy was delivered by **David Wolffsohn**. **Hans Herzl**, then thirteen, read the *Kaddish*. In 1949, his remains were moved from Vienna to be reburied on the top of **Mount Herzl in Jerusalem, named in his memory.**

## Legacy and honors

**Herzl Day** (Hebrew: יום הרצל) is an Israeli national holiday celebrated annually on the tenth of the Hebrew month of Iyar, to commemorate the life and vision of **Zionist leader Theodor Herzl**.

## Family

**Herzl**'s grandfathers, both of whom he knew, were more closely related to traditional Judaism than were his parents. In **Zemun (Zemlin),** his grandfather **Simon Loeb Herzl "had his hands on"** one of the first copies of **Judah Alkalai's** 1857 work prescribing the **"return of the Jews to the**

318

**Holy Land and renewed glory of Jerusalem"**. Contemporary scholars conclude that **Herzl**'s own implementation of modern **Zionism** was undoubtedly influenced by that relationship. **Herzl**'s grandparents' graves in Semlin can still be visited. **Alkalai** himself witnessed the rebirth of Serbia from **Ottoman** rule in the early and mid-19th century and was inspired by the **Serbian** uprising and subsequent re-creation of Serbia.

In 25 June 1889, he married **Julie Naschauer**, daughter of a wealthy Jewish businessman in Vienna. The marriage was unhappy, although three children were born to it: **Paulina, Hans** and **Margaritha** (Trude). **Herzl** had a strong attachment to his mother, who was unable to get along with his wife. These difficulties were increased by the political activities of his later years, in which his wife took little interest. His daughter **Paulina** suffered from mental illness and drug addiction. She died in 1930 at the age of 40 of a heroin overdose.

His only son **Hans** was given a secular upbringing and **Herzl** notably refused to allow him to be circumcised. After **Herzl**'s early death, Hans successively converted and became a **Baptist**, then a **Catholic**, and flirted with other **Protestant** denominations. He sought a personal salvation for his own religious needs and a universal solution, as had his father, to Jewish suffering caused by antisemitism. **Hanz Herzl voluntarily had himself circumcised 29 May 1905; Hans shot himself to death on the day of his sister Paulina's funeral; he was 39 years old.**

## Hans left a suicide note explaining his reasons.

**"A Jew remains a Jew, no matter how eagerly he may submit himself to the disciplines of his new religion, how humbly he may place the redeeming cross upon his shoulders for the sake of his former coreligionists, to save them from eternal damnation: a Jew remains a Jew ... I can't go on living. I have lost all trust in God. All my life I've tried to strive for the truth, and must admit today at the end of the road that there is nothing but disappointment. Tonight I have said Kaddish for my parents—and for myself, the last descendant of the family. There is nobody who will say Kaddish for me, who went out to find peace—and who may find peace soon ... My instinct has latterly gone all wrong, and I have made one of those irreparable mistakes, which stamp a whole life with failure. Then it is best to scrap it."**

In 2006 the remains of Paulina and Hans were moved from Bordeaux, France, and reburied not far from their father on **Mt. Herzl**. Paulina and Hans had little contact with their young sister, "**Trude**" (Margarethe, 1893–1943). She married **Richard Neumann**, a man 17 years her elder. Neumann lost his fortune in the **Great Depression**. The Nazis sent **Trude** and **Richard** to the **Theresienstadt** concentration camp where they died. Her body was burned. (Her mother, who died in 1907, was cremated. Her ashes were lost by accident.)

At the request of his father **Richard Neumann**, Trude's son **(Herzl's only grandchild), Stephan Theodor Neumann**, (1918–1946) was sent for his safety to England in 1935 to the Viennese

Zionists and the **Zionist Executive** in Israel based there. The Neumanns deeply feared for the safety of their only child as violent Austrian antisemitism expanded. In England he read extensively about his grandfather. **Zionism** had not been a significant part of his background in Austria, but **Stephan became an ardent Zionist**, was the only descendant of **Theodor Herzl** to have become one. Anglicizing his name to **Stephen Norman**, during World War II, Norman enlisted in the British Army rising to the rank of **Captain in the Royal Artillery**.

In late 1945 and early 1946 he took the opportunity to visit the **British Mandate of Palestine "to see what my grandfather had started."** He wrote in his diary extensively about his trip. What most impressed him was the **"look of freedom"** on the faces of the children, which were not like the sallow look of those from the concentration camps of Europe. He wrote upon leaving Israel, **"My visit to Israel is over ... It is said that to go away is to die a little. And I know that when I went away from Erez Israel, I died a little. But sure, then, to return is somehow to be reborn. And I will return."** Norman planned to return to Israel following his military discharge. **The Zionist Executive** had worked for years through **Dr. L. Lauterbach** to get Norman to come to Israel as a symbol of **Herzl**'s returning.

**Operation Agatha of 29 June 1946**, precluded that possibility: British military and police fanned out throughout Israel and arrested Jewish activists. About 2,700 individuals were arrested. On 2 July 1946, Norman wrote to -**Kahn Mrs. Stybovitz** in Haifa. Her father, Jacob Kahn, had been a good friend of **Herzl** and a well-known Dutch banker before the war. Norman wrote, **"I intend to go to Israel on a long visit in the future, in fact as soon as passport & permit regulations permit. But the dreadful news of the last two days have done nothing to make this easier."** He never did return to Israel.

Norman was buried by the Jewish Agency in Washington, D.C. His tombstone read simply, 'Stephen **Theodor**e Norman, Captain Royal Artillery British Army, Grandson of **Theodor Herzl**, 21 April 1918 − 26 November 1946'. **"You will be amazed at the Jewish Youth in Palestine ... they have the look of freedom."**

## Writings
**Herzl**'s solution was the creation of a Jewish state. In the book he outlined his reasoning for the need to reestablish the historic Jewish state. **"The idea I have developed in this pamphlet is an ancient one: It is the restoration of the Jewish State ..."**

**"We are a people—one people.**
**"We have sincerely tried everywhere to merge with the national communities in which we live, seeking only to preserve the faith of our fathers. It is not permitted us. "Oppression and persecution cannot exterminate us. No nation on earth has endured such struggles and sufferings as we have. Jew-baiting has merely winnowed out our weaklings; the strong**

among us defiantly return to their own whenever persecution breaks out ..." "Wherever we remain politically secure for any length of time, we assimilate. I think this is not praiseworthy ..." "Israel is our unforgettable historic homeland ..."

"The Jews who will it shall achieve their State. We shall live at last as free men on our own soil, and in our own homes peacefully die. The world will be liberated by our freedom, enriched by our wealth, magnified by our greatness. And whatever we attempt there for our own benefit will redound mightily and beneficially to the good of all mankind."

**Herzl** also envisioned the future Jewish state to be a "third way" between capitalism and socialism, with a developed welfare program and public ownership of the main natural resources. Along with many other progressive Jews of the day, such as **Emma Lazarus, Louis Brandeis**, **Albert Einstein, and Franz Oppenheimer, Herzl** desired to enact the land reforms proposed by the American political economist **Henry George**. Specifically, they called for a land value tax.

"It is founded on the ideas which are a common product of all civilized nations ... It would be immoral if we would exclude anyone, whatever his origin, his descent, or his religion, from participating in our achievements. For we stand on the shoulders of other civilized peoples ... What we own we owe to the preparatory work of other peoples. Therefore, we have to repay our debt. There is only one way to do it, the highest tolerance. Our motto must therefore be, now and ever: 'Man, you are my brother.'"

*"If you will it, it is no dream."* a phrase from **Herzl**'s book *Old New Land*, became a popular slogan of the Zionist movement—the striving for a **Jewish National Home in Israel**.

"Matters of faith were once and for all excluded from public influence ... Whether anyone sought religious devotion in the synagogue, in the church, in the mosque, in the art museum, or in a philharmonic concert, did not concern society. That was his private affair." Herzl wanted to win over non-Jewish opinion for **Zionism**.

# The Holocaust

The **Holocaust**, also known as the **Shoah** (Hebrew: "**the catastrophe**") was a genocide in which **Adolf Hitler's Nazi** Germany and its collaborators killed about **six million Jews**. The victims included **1.5 million children** and represented about two-thirds of the nine million Jews who had resided in Europe. Killings took place throughout **Nazi** Germany and German-occupied territories (1933 ~ 1945).

From 1941 to 1945, Jews were systematically murdered in one of the deadliest genocides in history. Every arm of Germany's bureaucracy was involved in the logistics and the carrying out of the genocide. Other victims of **Nazi** crimes included ethnic Poles, Soviet citizens and Soviet POWs, other Slavs, Romans, Communists, homosexuals, Jehovah's Witnesses and the mentally and physically disabled. A network of about **42,500 facilities** in Germany and German-occupied territories were used to concentrate victims for slave labor, mass murder, and other human rights abuses. Over **200,000 people are estimate to have been Holocaust perpetrators.**

The persecution and genocide were carried out in stages, culminating in what **Nazis** termed the **"Final Solution to the Jewish Question"**, an agenda to exterminate Jews in Europe. Initially the German government passed laws to exclude Jews from civil society, most prominently the **Nuremberg Laws of 1935**. **Nazis** established a network of concentration camps starting in 1933 and ghettos following the outbreak of **World War II** in 1939. Victims were being regularly transported by freight trains to extermination camps where, if they survived the journey, most were systematically killed in gas chambers. This continued until the **end of World War II in Europe in May 8th, 1945.**

Jewish armed resistance was limited. The most notable exception was the **Warsaw Ghetto Uprising of 1943**, when thousands of poorly-armed Jewish fighters held the **Waffen-SS** at bay for four weeks. An estimated **20-30,000 Jewish partisans** actively fought against the **Nazis** and their collaborators in Eastern Europe.

## Etymology and use of the term
The biblical word *shoah* (also transliterated *sho'ah* and *shoa*), meaning **"calamity"** became the standard Hebrew term for the **Holocaust** as early as the 1940s, especially in Europe and Israel. The **Nazis** used the phrase **"Final Solution to the Jewish Question"** and the formula **"Final Solution"** has been widely used as a term for the genocide of the Jews.

## Institutional collaboration
Every arm of Germany's bureaucracy was involved in the logistics that led to the genocides. As prisoners entered the death camps, they were made to surrender all personal property which was catalogued and tagged before being sent to Germany to be reused or recycled. **German National Bank helped launder valuables stolen from the victims.**

## Ideology and scale
The killings were systematically conducted in virtually all areas of German-occupied territory in what are now 35 separate European countries. It was at its most severe in Central and Easter

Europe, which had more than seven million Jews in 1939. About **five million Jews were killed there,** including three million in occupied Poland and over one million in the Soviet Union. Anyone with three or four Jewish grandparents was to be exterminated without exception. The **Nazis** envisioned the extermination of the Jews worldwide, not only in Germany proper, **unless their grandparents had converted before 18 January 1871.**

## Extermination camps

The use of extermination camps (also called **"death camps"**) equipped with gas chambers for the systematic mass extermination of peoples was an unprecedented feature of the **Holocaust**. These were established at **Auschwitz, Belzec, Chelmno, Jasenovac, Majdanek, Maly Trostenets, Sobibor, and Treblinka.**

## Medical experiments

A distinctive feature of **Nazi** genocide was the extensive use of human subjects in **"medical" experiments**. The most notorious of these physicians was **Josef Mengele**, who worked in **Auschwitz**. His experiments included placing subjects in pressure chambers, testing drugs on them, freezing them, attempting to change eye color by injecting chemicals into children's eyes, and amputations and other surgeries. **Mengele** worked extensively with Romani children. He would bring them sweets and toys and personally take them to the gas chamber. **They would call him "Onkel (Uncle) Mengele".**

## Development and execution: Origins

Anti-Semitism was incorporated into the platforms of the mainstream political parties. **The National Socialist German Workers' Party (Nazi Party; NSDAP)** was founded in 1920 as an offshoot of the *volkisch* movement and adopted their anti-Semitism. Many Germans did not accept that their country had been defeated in battle, giving rise to the **Stab-in-the back myth**. The myth insinuated that it was disloyal politicians, chiefly Jews and Communists, who orchestrated Germany's surrender.

By the time the **Nazis** came to power in 1933, a tendency already existed in the German social policy to save the racially **"valuable"** while seeking to rid society of the **racially "undesirable"**. **Hitler** states in *Mein Kampf* that he first became an anti-Semite in Vienna. In *Mein Kampf,* he announced his intention of removing them from Germany's political, intellectual, and cultural life. **Hitler** had by now viewed **Marxism as a Jewish doctrine** and proclaimed he was fighting against **"Jewish Marxism"**.

These pogroms became known as *Kristallnacht* (**"Crystal Night" or "Night of Broken Glass"**). Jews were attacked and Jewish property was vandalized. Over 7,000 Jewish shops and more than 1,200 synagogues were damaged or destroyed. 30,000 were sent to concentration camps, including **Dachau, Sachsenhausen, Buchenwald, and Oranienburg.** German Jewry was made collectively responsible for restitution of the material damage of the pogroms, and furthermore had to pay an **"atonement tax"** of more than a billion Reichsmarks.

## Resettlement and deportation

**Nazi** bureaucrats also developed plans to deport Europe's Jews to Siberia. Palestine was the only location to which any **Nazi** relocation plan succeeded in producing significant results, via an agreement begun in 1933 between the **Zionist Federation** of Germany and the **Nazi** government, the **Haavara Agreement**. This agreement resulted in the transfer of about 60,000 German Jews and $100 million from Germany to Palestine, until the outbreak of World War II.

Diplomatic efforts were undertaken to convince the other colonial powers, primarily the United Kingdom and France, to accept expelled Jews in their colonies. Areas considered for possible resettlement included British Palestine, Italian Abyssinia, British Rhodesia, French Madagascar, and Australia.

Of these areas, **Madagascar** was the most seriously discussed. **Heydrich** called the **Madagascar Plan** a **"territorial final solution"**; it was a remote location, and the island's unfavorable conditions would hasten deaths. **Hitler** approved in 1938 and **Adolf Eichmann's** office carried out resettlement planning, but abandoned it once the mass killing of Jews had begun in 1941.

**In 1935, Hitler** introduced the **Nuremberg Laws**, which prohibited "**Aryans**" from having sexual relations or marriages with Jews, although this was later extended to include **"Gypsies, Negroes or t heir bastard offspring"**. Stripped German Jews of their citizenship and deprived them of all civil rights. **The "final solution" (*Endlosung*) became the standard Nazi euphemism for the extermination of the Jews.**

Intellectuals were among the first Jews to leave. **Albert Einstein** was visiting the US on 30 January 1933. He returned to Ostende in Belgium, never to set foot in Germany again, and calling events there a **"psychic illness of the masses"**; he was expelled from the **Kaiser Wilhelm Society** and the **Prussian Academy of Sciences**, and his citizenship was rescinded. When Germany annexed Austria in 1938, **Sigmund Freud** and his family fled from Vienna to England.

## Kristallnacht (1938)
On 7 November 1938, Jewish minor **Herschel Grunspan** assassinated **Nazi** German diplomat **Ernst vom Rath** in Paris. The **Nazis** used this incident a pretext to go beyond legal repression to large-scale physical violence against Jewish Germans. These pogroms became known as *Kristallnacht* (**"Crystal Night"** or **"Night of Broken Glass"**). Jews were attacked and Jewish property was vandalized; **over 7,000 Jewish shops and more than 1,200 synagogues.**

## Early measures: In German-occupied Poland
Germany's invasion of Poland in September 1939 increased the urgency of the **"Jewish Question"**. Poland was home to about three million Jews (nearly nine percent of the Polish population) in centuries-old communities, two-thirds of whom fell under **Nazi** control and Poland's capitulation. In September 1939, **Himmler** appointed **Reinhard Heydrich** chief of the **Reich Main Security Office**. Here many thousands died from maltreatment, disease, starvation, and exhaustion, but there was still no program of systematic killing.

**Hermann Goring**, who had overall control of the German war industry, and the Germany army's **Economics Department**, argued that the enormous Jewish labor force assembled in the General Government area (more than a million able-bodied workers), was an asset too valuable to waste, particularly with Germany failing to secure rapid victory over the **Soviet Union**.

## In other occupied countries

When Germany occupied Norway, the Netherlands, Luxembourg, Belgium, and France in 1940, and Yugoslavia and Greece in 1941, Jews were removed from economic and cultural life and were subject to various restrictive laws, but physical deportation did not occur in most places before 1942.

## In North Africa

Though the vast majority of the Jews affected and killed during **Holocaust** were of Ashkenazi descent, Sephardi and Mizrahi Jews suffered greatly as well. **In the 1930s, the Fascist Italian regime passed anti-Semitic laws** barring Jews from government jobs and government schools, and required them to stamp "**Jewish race**" into their passports. But this was not enough to deter Jews from Libya, as 25 % of Tripoli's population was Jewish, and it had over 44 synagogues.

In 1942, the **Nazis** occupied Benghazi's Jewish Quarter and deported more than 2,000 Jews to **Nazi** labor camps. By the end of WWII, about one-fifth of those who were sent away had perished. Several forced labor camps for Jews were established in Libya the camp held almost 2,600 inmates, of whom 562 died of weakness, hunger, and disease.

Tunisia, the only North African country to come under direct **Nazi** occupation, had 100,000 Jews when the **Nazis** arrived in November 1942. During their six months of occupation, the **Nazis** imposed anti-Semitic policies in Tunisia, including **forcing Jews to wear the Yellow Star**, fines, and property confiscation. Some 5,000 Tunisian Jews were subjected to forced labor, and some were deported to European death camps. **More than 2,500 Tunisian Jews died in slave labor camps during the German occupation.**

### General Government and Lublin reservation (Nisko plan)

On 28 September 1939, Germany gained control over the Lublin area through the German-Soviet agreement in exchange for Lithuania. During 1940 and 1941, the murder of large numbers of Jews in German-occupied Poland continued, and the deportation of Jews to the General Government was undertaken. By December 1939, 3.5 million Jews were crowded into the General Government area.

## Concentration and labor camps (1933-1945)

The **Third Reich** first used concentration camps as places of incarceration. And though death rates were high – with a mortality rate of 50% - they were not designed to be killing center. By 1942, six large camps were built in Poland solely for mass killing. It is estimated that the Germans established **15,000 camps** and sub-camps in the occupied countries, mostly in Eastern Europe. Extermination through labor was a policy of systematic extermination – camp inmates would literally be worked to death, or worked to physical exhaustion, when they would be gassed or shot. Some camps tattooed prisoners with an identification number on arrival.

## Ghettos (1939-1945)

The ghettos' inhabitants were sent to extermination camps. Germany required each ghetto to be run by a *Judenrat* (Jewish council). The first order establishing a council is contained in a 29 September 1939 letter from **Heydrich** to the heads of the *Einsatzgruppen*. The Germans required councils to confiscate property, organize forced labor, and, finally, facilitate deportations to extermination camps.

**On 14 October 1942, the entire council of Byaroza committed suicide** rather than cooperate with the deportations. The **Warsaw** Ghetto was the largest, with 380,000 people; the **Lodz** Ghetto was second, holding 160,000. Between 1940 and 1942, starvation and disease, especially typhoid, killed hundreds of thousands. Over 43,000 Warsaw ghetto residents, or one in ten of the total population, died in 1941.

**Himmler** ordered the start of the deportations on 19 July 1942. 300,000 people from Warsaw alone were transported in freight trains to the **Treblinka** extermination camp. Many other ghettos were completely depopulated.

## Pogroms (1939-1942)

The Iasi pogrom in Romania on 30 June 1941, in which as many as 14,000 Jews were killed by Romanian residents and police. Some 6,000 Polish Jews were murdered in the streets between June 30 and July 29, 1941, on top of 3,000 arrests and mass shootings by *Einsatzgruppe C.* 300 Jews were burned to death in a locked barn by local Poles, which were preceded by German execution of 40 Jewish men at the same location.

## Death squads (1941-1943)

**Germany's invasion of the Soviet Union in June 1941** opened a new phase in the **Holocaust**. Even before the invasion of the Soviet Union, German troops had been indoctrinated with **anti-Bolshevik, anti-Semitic and anti-Slavic ideology** via movies, radio, lectures, books and leaflets. **Hitler** on 30 March 1941 described the war with the Soviet Union as a **"war of annihilation"**. The Soviet territories occupied by early 1942, including all of Belarus, Estonia, Latvia, Lithuania, Ukraine, and Moldova and most Russian territory west of the line **Leningrad-Moscow-Rostov,** contained about three million Jews at the start of the war.

Many of the collaborators enlisted in the **Waffen-SS** participated in the killings of Jews. In Lithuania, Latvia, and western Ukraine locals were deeply involved in the murder of Jews from the very beginning of the German occupation. To the south, **Ukrainians killed about 24,000 Jews.** Some Ukrainians went to Poland where they served as concentration and death-camp guards. The large-scale killings of Jews in the occupied Soviet territories was assigned to **SS** formations called *Einsatzgruppen* (**"task groups"**), which were under **Heydrich's** overall command.

**"The *Einsatzgruppen* had the mission to protect the rear of the troops by killing the Jews, gypsies, Communist functionaries, active Communists, and all persons who would endanger the security."** The most notorious massacre of Jews in the Soviet Union was at a ravine called **Babi Yar** outside Kiev, where 33,771 Jews were killed in a single operation on 29-30 September 1941. A mixture of **SS**, SD, and Security Police, assisted by Ukrainian police, carried out the killings.

On 29 September Kiev's Jews gathered by the cemetery as ordered, expecting to be loaded onto trains. The crowd was large enough that most of the men, women, and children could not have known what was happening until it was too late; by the time they heard the machine gun fire, there was no chance to escape. All were driven down a corridor of soldiers, in groups of ten, and shot. **A truck, driver described the scene:**

> **Once undressed, they were led into the ravine which was about 150 meters long and 30 meters wide and a good 15 meters deep…The corpses were literally in layers. A police marksman came along and shot each Jew in the neck with a submachine gun…**

### *Wehrmacht* played a key role in the Holocaust: New methods of mass murder
Starting in December 1939, the **Nazis** introduced new methods of mass murder by using gas. In the **Sachsenhausen** concentration camp, larger vans holding up to 100 people were used from November 1941, using the engine's exhaust rather than a cylinder. These gas vans were developed and run under supervision of the **SS** and were used to kill about **500,000 people**, primarily Jews, but also Romani and others.

### Wannsee Conference and the Final Solution (1942-1945)
Reinhard **Heydrich** convened the **Wannsee Conference on 20 January 1942** in Berlin's Wannsee suburb. **Heydrich** announced that the emigration policy was superseded by a policy of evacuating Jews to the east. This was seen to be only a temporary solution leading up to a final solution that would involve some **11 million Jews** living not only in territories then controlled by Germany, but in major countries in the rest of the world including the UK and the US. **"The Jews were to be annihilated by a combination of forced labor and mass murder."** In some camps, such as Auschwitz, those fit for work would be kept alive for a while, but eventually all would be killed.

### German public
**"The road to Auschwitz was built by hate, but paved with indifference"**. The majority of the anti-**Nazi** national –conservatives were anti-Semitic. The vast majority of **Holocaust** victims, prior to their deportation to concentration camps, were either unaware of the fate that awaited them or were in denials; they honestly believed that they were to be resettled.

### Extermination camps
During 1942, in addition to Auschwitz, five other camps were designated as extermination camps (*Vernichtungslager*) for the carrying out of the Reinhard plan. Three new camps were built for the sole purpose of killing large numbers of Jews as quickly as possible, at **Belzec, Sobibor and Treblinka,** but **Auschwitz** was the most radically transformed in terms of systematic killing. A seventh camp, at **Maly Trostinets in Belarus**, was also used for this purpose.

### Approx. number killed at each extermination camp

| Camp name | Killed |
|---|---|
| Auschwitz II | 1,000,000 |
| Belzec | 600,000 |
| Chelmno | 320,000 |
| Jasenovac | 97,000 |

| Majdanek | 360,000 |
|---|---|
| Maly Trostinets | 65,000 |
| Sobibor | 250,000 |
| Treblinka | 870,000 |
| **Total** | **3,562,000** |

There were another few **"concentration"** camps, such as the Mauthausen-Gusen concentration camp in pre-war Austria, which were designed as Extermination through labor camps.

## Gas chambers

At the extermination camps with gas chambers all the prisoners arrived by train. Sometimes entire trainloads were sent straight to the gas chambers, but usually the camp doctor on duty subjected individuals to selections, where a small percentage were deemed fit to work in the salve labor camps; the majority were taken directly from the platforms to a reception area where all their clothes and other possessions were seized by the **Nazis** to help fund the war. They were then herded naked into the gas chambers. Usually they were told these were **showers or delousing chambers**, and there were signs outside saying **"baths" and "sauna."**

Once the chamber was full, the doors were screwed shut and solid pellets of **Zyklon-B** were dropped into the chambers through vents in the side walls, releasing **toxic HCN, or hydrogen cyanide.** Those inside died within 20 minutes; about one-third of the victims died immediately. The gas was then pumped out, the bodies were removed. Gold fillings in their teeth were extracted with pliers by dentist prisoners, and women's hair was cut. At first, the bodies were buried in deep pits and covered with lime, but between September and November 1942, on the orders of **Himmler**, they were dug up and burned. **Children of tender years were invariably exterminated, since by reason of their youth they were unable to work.**

## Jewish resistance

The most well-known example of Jewish armed resistance was the **Warsaw Ghetto Uprising of January 1943**, when thousands of poorly armed Jewish fighters held the **SS** at bay for four weeks before being crushed by overwhelmingly superior forces. 13,000 Jews were killed, 57,885 were deported and gassed according to German figures.

An estimated 20,000 to 30,000 Jewish partisans actively fought the **Nazis** and their collaborators in Eastern Europe. As many as **1.4 million Jewish soldiers fought in the Allied armies**, including 500,000 in the Red Army, 550,000 in the U.S. Army, 100,000 in the Polish army and 30,000 in the British army. About 200,000 Jewish soldiers serving in the Red Army died in the war. Although Jews made up only one percent of the French population, they made up fifteen to twenty percent of the **French Resistance.**

## Climax

**Reinhard Heydrich was assassinated on Prague in June 1942** by soldiers from Czechoslovakia's army-in-exile on a clandestine mission codenamed **Operation Anthropoid.** During 1943 and 1944, the extermination camps worked at a furious rate to kill the hundreds of thousands of people shipped to them by rail from almost every country within the German sphere of influence. By the spring of 1944, up to 8,000 people were being gassed every day at Auschwitz. **About 42,000 Jews were shot during the Operation Harvest Festival on 3-4 November 1943.**

By 1944, it was evident to most Germans not blinded by **Nazi** fanaticism that Germany was losing the war. But the power of **Himmler** and the **SS** within the German Reich was too great to resist. On o19 March 1944, **Hitler** ordered the military occupation of Hungary, and **Eichmann** was dispatched to Budapest to supervise the **deportation of Hungary's 800,000 Jews**. More than half of them were shipped to Auschwitz after the occupation. The commandant, **Rudolf Hoss,** said at his trial that he killed 400,000 Hungarian Jews in three months.

## "Blood for Goods"
There were unofficial negotiations in Istanbul between **Himmler**'s agents, British agents, and representatives of Jewish organizations; at one point an attempt by **Eichmann to exchange one million Jews for 10,000 trucks** – the so-called **"blood for goods"** proposal – but there was no real possibility of such a deal being struck on this scale.

## Escapes, publication of existence (April-June 1944)
By 9 October 1942, British radio had broadcast news of gassing of Jews to the Netherlands. Between 15 and 27 May 1944, 100,000 Hungarian Jews had arrived at **Birkenau**, and had been killed at an unprecedented rate, with human fat being used to accelerate the burning. Before and during World War II, T**he** *Times* had maintained a strict policy in their news reporting and editorials to minimize reports on the **Holocaust**. *The New York Times* **had deliberately suppressed news of the Third Reich's persecution and murder of Jews.**

## Death marches (1944-1945)
By mid-1944, the **Final Solution** had largely run its course. Auschwitz itself was closed as the Soviets advanced through Poland. The last 13 prisoners, all women, were killed in Auschwitz II on 25 November 1944. The gas chambers were dismantled, the crematoria dynamited, mass graves dug up and the corpses cremated. Local commanders continued to kill Jews, and to shuttle them from camp to camp by forced **"death marches"** until the last weeks of the war. Those who lagged behind or fell were shot. Around 250,000 Jews died during these marches.

Nine days before the Soviets arrived at Auschwitz, the **SS** marched 60,000 prisoners out of the camp toward Wodzislaw away, where they were put on freight trains to other camps. Around 15,000 died on the way. **Elie Wiesel and his father, Shlomo, were among the marchers.**

## Liberation
The first major camp to be directly encountered by Allied troops, **Majdanek**, was discovered by the advancing Soviets on 23 July 1944. **Chelmno** was liberated by the Soviets on 20 January 1945. **Auschwitz** was liberated, also by the Soviets, on 27 January 1945; **Buchenwald** by the Americans on 11 April; **Bergen-Belsen** by the British on 15 April; **Dachau** by the Americans on 29 April; **Ravensbruck** by the Soviets on the same day; **Mauthausen** by the Americans on 5 May; and **Theresienstadt** by the Soviets on 8 May. **Treblinka, Sobibor, and Belzec** were never liberated, but were destroyed by the **Nazis** in 1943.

7,600 inmates were found in **Auschwitz**, including 180 children who had been experimented on by doctors. Some 60,000 prisoners were discovered at **Bergen-Belsen** by the British 11th Armored Division, 13,000 corpses lay unburied, and another 10,000 died from typhus or malnutrition over the following weeks.

## Victims

The total number of victims is just under **six million** – around 78 percent of the 7.3 million Jews in occupied Europe at the time. The figure most commonly used is the six million attributed to **Adolf Eichmann**, a senior **SS** official.

Broader definitions include the two to **three million Soviet POWs who died** as a result of mistreatment due to **Nazi** racial policies, two million non-Jewish ethnic Poles who died due to the conditions of **Nazi** occupation, 90,000-220,000 **Romani**, 270,000 mentally and physically disabled killed in Germany's eugenics program, 80,000-200,000 **Freemasons**, 20,000-25,000 **Slovenes**, 5,000-15,000 **homosexuals**, 2,500-5,000 **Jehovah's Witnesses** and 7,000 **Spanish Republicans**, bringing the death toll to around **11 million.** The broadest definition would include six million Soviet civilians who died as a result of war-related famine and disease, raising the death toll to **17 million**.

# Homosexuality in Judaism

The subject of **homosexual behavior and Judaism** dates back to the **Torah.** The book of **Vayikra** (Leviticus) is traditionally regarded as classifying sexual intercourse between males as a *to'eivah* (something abhorred or detested) that can be subject to **capital punishment** by the currently nonexistent **Sanhedrin** under *halakha* **(Jewish law).**

**Traditionally, Judaism has understood homosexual male *intercourse* as contrary to Judaism, and this opinion is still maintained by Orthodox Judaism.** On the other hand, **Reconstructionist** Judaism and **Reform Judaism** do not hold this view and allow homosexual intercourse and same-sex marriage. **Conservative Judaism's Committee on Jewish Law and Standards**, which until December 2006 held the same position as **Orthodoxy**, recently issued multiple opinions under its philosophy of pluralism, liberalizing its view of **homosexual sex** and relationships while continuing to regard **certain sexual acts as prohibited**.

## Homosexuality in the Hebrew Bible

The traditional viewpoint is that the *Torah* mentions homosexuality twice in the book of **Leviticus** (JPS): **Lev. 18:22 "Thou shalt not lie with mankind, as with womankind; it is detestable." Lev. 20:13 "And if a man lie with mankind, as with womankind, both of them have committed a detestable act: they shall surely be put to death; their blood shall be upon them."**

## Deuteronomy 23:18 tells followers:

The story of **Ruth** and **Naomi** in the *Book of Ruth* is also occasionally interpreted as the story of a **lesbian couple**, while the biblical description of the relationship between **David** and **Jonathan** in the *Book of Kings* is sometimes interpreted as male **homosexual love**.

## Applicability of Biblical death penalty

Like many similar commandments, the stated punishment for willful violation was the **death penalty,** though minors under 13 years of age were exempt from this as from any other penalty (Sanh. 54a). The **Jewish Oral Law** states that **capital punishment would only be applicable if two men were caught in the act of anal sex,** if there were two witnesses to the act, or the willing party, in case of rape — subsequently acknowledged the warning but continued to engage in the prohibited act anyway.

**In fact, there is no account of capital punishment, in regards to this law, in Jewish history.** Rabbinic tradition understands the **Torah**'s system of capital punishment to **not be in effect for the past approximately 2,000 years, in the absence of a Sanhedrin and Temple.** Classical rabbinic Jewish sources do not specifically mention that **homosexual *attraction* is inherently sinful.** If he does **teshuva (repentance)**—i.e., he ceases his forbidden actions, regrets what he has done, apologizes to God, and makes a binding resolution never to repeat those actions, he is seen to be **forgiven by God**.

## Lesbian sexual activity

Why lesbianism is not explicitly prohibited in the Bible has become a matter of interpretation. **Religious rules that apply to men automatically apply to women.** Sexual liaisons between women are, however, viewed as forbidden by most rabbis. **"Do not follow the ways of Egypt where you once lived, nor of Canaan, where I will be bringing you. Do not follow any of their customs." (Leviticus 18:3).** The **Talmud** prohibits any activity which it defines as **mesolelot or tribalism** (women rubbing genitals together). It was doubtful whether this activity removed their status as a virgin or made them a harlot. **Talmudic law limits the penalty for lesbianism to flagellation rather than the death penalty.**

## Same-sex marriage in the Midrash and the Talmud

The **Babylonian Talmud** is one of the few ancient religious texts that makes reference to same-sex marriage: **"Non-Jews accepted upon themselves thirty mitzvot [divinely ordered laws] but they only abide by three of them: the first one is that they do not write marriage documents for male couples, the second one is that they don't sell dead [human] meat by the pound in stores and the third one is that they respect the Torah."**

## Orthodox Jewish views

**Orthodox Judaism generally prohibits homosexual conduct. Orthodox Judaism puts male-male anal sex in the category of** *yehareg ve'al ya'avor*, **"die rather than transgress".** Biblically-prohibited acts (including murder, idolatry, adultery, and incest). Similarly, some consider lesbianism a martyrdom-demanding transgression if only based upon the principle of *abizrayhu*. **According to the Talmud, homosexual acts are forbidden between non-Jews as well**, and this is included among the sexual restrictions of the **Noachide laws**. The entry *Homosexuality* in the *Encyclopedia Judaica* (Keter Publishing), describes the traditional opinion on homosexuality in this way:

**"Jewish law [...] rejects the view that homosexuality is to be regarded merely as a disease or as morally neutral.... Jewish law holds that no hedonistic ethic, even if called "love", can justify the morality of homosexuality any more than it can legitimize adultery or incest".**

## 2008 Israeli Document of Principles (Hod)

**"Anal intercourse between men (Isur Mishkav Zakhar) is what is forbidden in the Torah, and not the homosexual orientation. ...One can advise a person who is interested in doing so, to consult a certified professional mental health worker, on condition that complete information is provided about the type of treatment, its chances of success and its risks. No treatment should be seen as either ultimate or exclusive. Homosexual activity (as opposed to**

the homosexual orientation itself) is prohibited absolutely by the Torah... Every Jewish person should try to keep all the commandments and should do everything he or she can to be as observant of the Torah as possible".

## Statement by Rabbis Schachter, Willig, Rosensweig, and Twersky (2010)

In 2010, TorahWeb.org published a brief position statement entitled "Torah View on Homosexuality". Reads: ... Prohibited homosexual activity includes any non-platonic physical contact; even *yichud* (seclusion) with someone of the same gender is forbidden for homosexually active individuals. ... ... **Homosexual behavior is absolutely prohibited and constitutes an abomination. They should be encouraged to seek professional guidance.**

## July 2010 public statement by some leaders

On July 22, 2010, a **"Statement of Principles on the Place of Jews with a Homosexual Orientation in Our Community"** was released. The statement makes it clear that **homosexual activity is still prohibited, saying interalia that "Halakhah sees heterosexual marriage as the ideal model and sole legitimate outlet for human sexual expression"; "Halakhic Judaism views all male and female same-sex sexual interactions as prohibited".**

## Ex-gay organizations

**JONAH** is a Jewish ex-gay organization that focuses on **"prevention, intervention, and healing of the underlying issues causing same-sex attractions."** It is a world-wide organization, with the majority of its membership in the United States, Israel, Canada and Europe. In 2012, the **Rabbinical Council of America (RCA),** a professional association of more than 1,000 Orthodox rabbis around the world, sent an open email to its members that **it no longer supported reparative therapy generally, or JONAH specifically.**

In November 2016 dozens of **LGBT** activists protested in Jerusalem against comments reportedly made by the city's chief rabbi **Rabbi Shlomo Amar,** who reportedly told an Israeli newspaper that **gay people were an "abomination" and homosexuality a "cult."** Masorti synagogues in Europe and Israel, which have historically been somewhat more traditional than the American movement, continue to maintain a complete ban on homosexual and bisexual conduct, clergy, and unions. The Masorti movements in Argentina, Hungary, and the United Kingdom have indicated that they **will not admit or ordain openly gay/lesbian/bisexual rabbinical students.** The Masorti Movement's Israeli seminar also rejected a change in its view of the status of homosexual conduct, stating that **"Jewish law has traditionally prohibited homosexuality."**

## Reform Judaism

The **Reform Judaism** movement, the largest branch of **Judaism in North America,** has rejected the traditional view of Jewish Law on homosexuality and bisexuality. As such, **they do not prohibit ordination of openly gay, lesbian, and bisexual people as rabbis and cantors.** In 1977, the **Central Conference of American Rabbis (CCAR)**, which is the Union for Reform Judaism's principal body, adopted a resolution calling for legislation **decriminalizing homosexual acts between consenting adults,** and calling for an end to discrimination against gays and lesbians.

The committee endorsed the view that **"all Jews are religiously equal regardless of their sexual orientation."** The **Central Conference of American Rabbis** support the right of gay and lesbian couples to share fully and equally in the rights of civil marriage, and that the **CCAR** oppose governmental efforts to ban gay and lesbian marriage. In 2003, **Women of Reform Judaism** issued a statement describing their support for human and civil rights and the struggles of the bisexual and transgender communities. In 2014, the **CCAR** joined a lawsuit challenging North Carolina's ban on **same-sex marriage**, which is America's first faith-based challenge to same-sex marriage bans.

## Reconstructionist Judaism

**The Reconstructionist movement sees homosexuality and bisexuality as normal expressions of sexuality and welcomes gays, bisexuals, and lesbians into Reconstructionist communities to participate fully in every aspect of community life.** In 2007, the **Reconstructionist Rabbinical Association** elected as President **Rabbi Toba Spitzer,** the first openly **LGBT** person chosen to head a rabbinical association in the United States. In 2013, the **Reconstructionist Rabbinical Association** elected as President **Rabbi Jason Klein**, the first openly gay man chosen to head a national rabbinical association of one of the major Jewish denominations in the United States.

## Jewish Renewal

The **Jewish Renewal movement ordains people of all sexual orientations as rabbis and cantors**. In 2005, **Eli Cohen** became the first openly gay rabbi ordained by the **Jewish Renewal Movement,** followed by **Chaya Gusfield** and **Rabbi Lori Klein** in 2006, who became the two first openly lesbian rabbis ordained by the Jewish Renewal movement. **"We welcome and recognize the sanctity of every individual regardless of sexual orientation or gender identity**.

## Humanistic Judaism

In 2004 the **Society for Humanistic Judaism** issued a resolution supporting **"the legal recognition of marriage and divorce between adults of the same sex,"** and affirming **"the value of marriage between any two committed adults with the sense of obligations, responsibilities, and consequences thereof."**

## LGBT-affirmative activities

Jewish **LGBT** rights advocates and sympathetic clergy have created various institutions within Jewish life to accommodate gay, lesbian, bisexual and transgender parishioners. **Beth Chayim Chadashim,** established in 1972 in West Los Angeles, was the world's first explicitly-gay-and-lesbian-centered synagogue recognized by the **Reform** Jewish community. In October 2012 **Rainbow Jews**, an oral history project showcasing the lives of Jewish bisexual, lesbian, gay, and transgender people in the United Kingdom from the 1950s until the present, was launched. It is the United Kingdom's first archive of Jewish bisexual, lesbian, gay, and transgender history.

# Humanistic Judaism

**Humanistic Judaism (Hebrew: יהדות הומניסטית *Yahadut Humanistit*) is a Jewish movement that offers a nontheistic alternative in contemporary Jewish life**. It defines Judaism as the cultural and historical experience of the Jewish people. Its philosophical foundation includes the following ideas:

## Origins

In its current form, **Humanistic Judaism was founded in 1963 by Rabbi Sherwin Wine**. As a rabbi trained in Reform Judaism, with a small secular, non-theistic congregation in Michigan, Wine developed a Jewish liturgy that reflected his and his congregation's philosophical viewpoint by emphasizing Jewish culture, history, and identity along with Humanistic ethics, while **excluding all prayers and references to God**.

**In 1969, these congregations and others were united organizationally under the umbrella of the Society for Humanistic Judaism (SHJ).** The Society for **Humanistic Judaism** has 10,000 members in 30 congregations spread throughout the United States and Canada. **The International Institute for Secular Humanistic Judaism was founded in 1986**. It was established in Jerusalem in 1985 and currently has two centers of activity: one in Jerusalem and the other in Lincolnshire, IL. **Rabbi Adam Chalom** is the North American dean.

## Principles of belief and practice

**Humanistic Judaism** presents a far more radical departure from traditional Jewish religion than **Mordecai Kaplan** (co-founder of Reconstructionist Judaism) ever envisioned. **Kaplan** redefined God and other traditional religious terms so as to make them consistent with the naturalist outlook, and continued to use traditional prayer language. Wine rejected this approach as confusing.

**Humanistic Judaism** was developed as a possible solution to the problem of retaining Jewish identity and continuity among non-religious. Wine believed that secular Jews who had rejected theism would be attracted to an organization that provided all the same forms and activities as, for example, Reform temples, but which **expressed a purely Secular Humanistic viewpoint**. The **International Institute for Secular Humanistic Judaism**, which is sponsored by the Society for **Humanistic Judaism** and the Congress of Secular Jewish Organizations, trains rabbis and other leaders in the United States and in Israel.

## Jewish identity and intermarriage

Within **Humanistic Judaism**, Jewish identity is largely a matter of self-identification. Rabbis and other trained leaders officiate at intermarriages between Jews and non-Jews, and the **Humanistic Judaism** movement, unlike the **Conservative** and **Orthodox** Jewish denominations, does not take any position or action in opposition to intermarriage, rather it affirms that **"Intermarriage is an American Jewish reality—a natural consequence of a liberal society in which individuals have the freedom to marry whomever they wish...that intermarriage is neither good nor bad, just as we believe that the marriage of two Jews, in itself, is neither good nor bad. The moral worth of a marriage always depends on the quality of the human relationship—on the degree of mutual love and respect that prevails."**

## Egalitarianism

**Humanistic Judaism is egalitarian with respect to gender and gender identification, Jewish status, and sexual orientation.** Brit shalom (baby-naming ceremonies), similar for boys and girls, are performed rather than the **brit millah**.

**Humanistic Judaism ordains both men and women as rabbis, and its first rabbi was a woman, Tamara Kolton, who was ordained in 1999.** They issued a statement in 2011 condemning the passage of the **"No Taxpayer Funding for Abortion Act"** by the U.S. House of Representatives, which they called **"a direct attack on a woman's right to choose"**.

In 2013 they issued a resolution stating in part, "Therefore, be it resolved that: The **Society for Humanistic Judaism wholeheartedly supports the observance of Women's Equality Day** on August 26 to commemorate the anniversary of the passage of the **Nineteenth Amendment** to the U.S. Constitution allowing women to vote.

In 2004, the Society for **Humanistic Judaism** issued a resolution supporting **"the legal recognition of marriage and divorce between adults of the same sex"** and affirming **"the value of marriage between any two committed adults with the sense of obligations, responsibilities, and consequences thereof"**.

337

# Ishmael

**Ishmael** is a figure in the Hebrew Bible and the **Qur'an**, and was **Abraham**'s first born child according to Jews, Christians and Muslims. **Ishmael** was born of **Abraham**'s marriage to **Sarah**'s handmaiden **Hagar**. According to the Genesis account, he died at the age of 137 **(Genesis 25:17)**.

## Birth of Ishmael

In Genesis 16, the birth of **Ishmael** was planned by the **Patriarch Abraham's** first wife, who at that time was known as **Sarai.** She and her husband Abram (**Abraham**), sought a way to have children in order to fulfill **Yahweh**'s covenant that was established in **Genesis 15**. Since **Sarah** had yet to bear Abram a child, her idea was to offer her Egyptian handmaiden **Hagar** to Abram, so that they could have a child by her. Abram consented to a marital arrangement taking **Hagar** as his second wife when he was in his late **85th year of age**.

**Genesis 16:7-16** describes the naming of **Ishmael**, and **Yahweh**'s promise to **Hagar** concerning **Ishmael** and his descendants. The blessing that this child's father was promised was that Abram's descendants would be as numerous as the dust of the earth. The promise would be extended to this child, who would be named **Ishmael**. When **Ishmael** was born, **Abram was 86 years old.**

## Inheritance rights

When he was 13 years old, **Ishmael was circumcised** at the same time as all other males in **Abraham**'s house becoming a part of the covenant in a mass covenant. This occurred because his father **Abram** was inaugurated as **Abraham at the age of 99** and then initiated into the covenant by having himself and his entire household circumcised (**Genesis 17**).

At the time of the covenant, **Yahweh** informed **Abraham** that his wife **Sarah** would give birth to a son, which he was instructed to name Isaac. **Yahweh** told **Abraham** that He would establish his covenant through Isaac (Genesis 16). One year later, **Ishmael**'s half-brother Isaac was born by **Abraham** to his first wife **Sarah**.

**Sarah** asked **Abraham** to expel **Ishmael** and his mother. **Abraham** only agreed when God told his that is was through Isaac that **Abraham**'s offspring would **"be reckoned"**, and that He would "make **Ishmael** into a nation" too, since he was a descendant of **Abraham (Genesis 21:11-13).**

The Lord's covenant also made clear **Ishmael** was not to inherit **Abraham**'s house and that Isaac would be the instrument of the covenant. **Ishmael**'s father gave him and his mother a supply of bread and water and sent them away. **"And God heard the voice of the lad"** and sent his angel to tell **Hagar, "Arise, life up the lad, and hold him in thine hand; for I will make him a great nation."** And God **"opened her eyes, and she saw a well of water"**, from which she drew to save **Ishmael**'s life and her own. **"And God was with the lad; and he grew, and dwelt in the wilderness, and became an archer." (Genesis 21:14-21).**

## Descendants

After roaming the wilderness for some time, **Ishmael** and his mother settled in the **Desert of Paran,** where he became an expert in archery. Eventually, his mother found him a wife from the land of Egypt. They had 12 sons who became 12 tribal chiefs throughout the regions from Havilah to Shur (from Assyria to the border of Egypt.) **Ishmael** also appeared with Isaac at the burial of **Abraham**. **Ishmael died at the age of 137**.

## Deuterocanonical references

The book of Jubilees places the location and identity of the **Ishmael**ites as the Arab peoples residing in Arab territories.

## World views

Islamic traditions consider **Ishmael** to be the ancestor of Arab people. The **Prophet Muhammad** was of these Arabs. However, many modern Arabs also believe their tribes and houses to be of Isaac's blood line, in particular in Southern Palestine.

## Jewish views

Judaism has generally viewed **Ishmael** as wicked though repentant. In the **Midrash Genesis Rabbah** also say that **Ishmael**'s mother **Hagar** was the Pharaoh's daughter, thereby making **Ishmael** the grandson of the Pharaoh. This could be why **Genesis 17:20** refers to **Ishmael** as the father of 12 mighty princes. **According to Genesis 21:21, Hagar married Ishmael to an Egyptian woman.**

## Islamic view

**Ishmael** is recognized as an important prophet and patriarch of Islam. Muslims believe that **Ishmael** was the firstborn of **Abraham**, born to him from his second wife **Hagar**. **Ishmael** is recognized by Muslims as the ancestor of several prominent Arab tribes and being the forefather of Muhammad. Muslims also believe that **Muhammad was the descendant of Ishmael that would establish a great nation, as promised by God in the Old Testament.**

## Ishmael in the Qur'an

**Ishmael** is mentioned over ten times in the **Qur'an**, often alongside other patriarchs and prophets of ancient times. **Ishmael** is mentioned closely with his father **Abraham**: **Ishmael** stands alongside **Abraham** in their attempt to set up the **Ka'aba** in Mecca as a place of monotheistic pilgrimage (**II: 127-129**). In the narrative of the near-sacrifice of **Abraham**'s son, the son is not named and, although the general interpretation is that it was Ishmael, **Tabari maintained that it was Isaac.**

## Ishmael in Muslim literature

According to Muslim tradition, **Ishmael** was buried in **Al-Hijrd**, inside the Sacred Mosque. **Sarah** asked **Abraham** to marry her Egyptian handmaiden **Hagar** because she herself was barren. **Hagar** soon bore **Ishmael**, who was the first son of **Abraham**. After **Sarah** gave birth to her own son, Isaac, tension arose between the two women. **Abraham** took **Hagar** and **Ishmael** to the desert himself, where he left them and returned to his household. God helped them by making spring water gush forth from the **Zamzam well**, so both mother and son could rejuvenate themselves. To commemorate the bravery of **Hagar** and **Ishmael**, Muslims run between the Safa and Marwah hills during Hajj.

On one of his visits to Mecca, **Abraham** is said to have asked his son to help him build the requested **Ka'aba**. Islamic traditions hold that the **Ka'aba** was first built by Adam and that **Abraham** and **Ishmael** rebuilt the **Ka'aba** on the old foundations. **Ishmael** was considered the ancestor of the Northern Arabs and Muhammad was linked to him through the lineage of the patriarch **Adnan.**

# The Israelites

The **Israelites** (Hebrew: *Bnei Yisra'el*) were a confederation of Iron Age **Semitic-speaking tribes** of the ancient Near East, who inhabited a part of Canaan during the periods. According to the religious narrative of the **Hebrew Bible,** the Israelites' origin is traced back to the Biblical patriarchs and matriarchs **Abraham and his wife Sarah, through their son Isaac and his wife Rebecca, and their son Jacob who was later called Israel, whence they derive their name, with his wives Leah and Rachel.**

The Israelites and their culture, according to the modern archaeological account, did not overtake the region by force, but instead branched out of the indigenous Canaanite peoples later cementing as monotheistic—religion centered on **Yahweh, one of the Ancient Canaanite deities**.

In the Hebrew Bible the term *Israelites* is used interchangeably with the term *Twelve Tribes of Israel*. Israelites, and Jews are not interchangeable in all instances. "Israelites" (Yisraelim) refers specifically to the direct descendants of any of the sons of the **patriarch Jacob (later called Israel),** and his descendants as a people are also collectively called "Israel", including converts to their faith in worship of the god of Israel, **Yahweh.**

"**Hebrews**" (ʿIvrim) on the contrary is used to denote the Israelites' immediate forebears who dwelt in the land of Canaan. "**Jews**" (Yehudim) is used to denote the descendants of the Israelites' who coalesced when the **Tribe of Judah** absorbed the remnants of various other Israelite tribes. Thus, **Abraham was a Hebrew but he was not technically an Israelite nor was he a Jew,** but Jacob was both a Hebrew and the first Israelite but not a Jew, while **King David** (as a member of the Tribe of Judah) was all three, a **Hebrew**, an **Israelite**, and a **Judahite** (Yehudi, Jew). **A Samaritan, on the contrary, while being both a Hebrew and an Israelite, is not a Jew.**

## Etymology
**The name *Israel* first appears in the Hebrew Bible in Genesis 32:29**. It refers to the renaming of Jacob, who, according to the Bible, wrestled with an angel, who gave him a blessing and renamed him *Israel* because he had **"striven with God and with men, and have prevailed"**. The **Hebrew Bible etymologizes the name as from *yisra* "to prevail over" or "to struggle/wrestle with", and *el*, "God, the divine".** The name *Israel* first appears in non-biblical sources c. 1209 BCE, in an inscription of the Egyptian pharaoh **Merneptah**. The inscription is very brief and says simply: **"Israel is laid waste and his seed is not".**

## Historical Israelites
The name **Israel** first appears c. 1209 BCE, at the end of the **Late Bronze Age** and the very beginning of the period archaeologists and historians call **Iron Age I,** on the **Merneptah** Stele raised by the **Egyptian Pharaoh Merneptah**. Over the next two hundred years (the period

of Iron Age I) the number of highland villages increased from 25 to over 300 and the settled population doubled to 40,000.

A state began to emerge there in the 9th century, and from 850 BCE onwards a series of inscriptions are evidence of a kingdom which its neighbors refer to as the **"House of David."** After the **destruction of the Israelite kingdoms of Samaria and Judah in 720 and 586 BCE** respectively, the concepts of Jew and Samaritan gradually replaced Judahite and Israelite. When the Jews returned from the **Babylonian captivity**, the **Hasmonean** kingdom was established in present-day Israel, consisting of three regions which were **Judea, Samaria**, and the **Galilee**.

In the pre-exilic **First Temple Period** the political power of Judea was concentrated within the tribe of Judah, Samaria was dominated by the tribe of **Ephraim** and the **House of Joseph**, while the Galilee was associated with the tribe of **Naphtali**, the most eminent tribe of northern Israel. The Galilee was populated by northern tribes of Israel, but following the Babylonian exile the region became Jewish.

In 120 BCE the **Hasmonean king Yohanan Hyrcanos** I destroyed the Samaritan temple on **Mount Gerizim**, due to the resentment between the two groups over a disagreement of whether **Mount Moriah** in Jerusalem or Mount Gerizim in Shechem was the actual site of the **Aqedah**, and the chosen place for the **Holy Temple**, a source of contention that had been growing since the two houses of the former united monarchy first split asunder in 930 BCE and which had finally exploded into warfare.

190 years after the destruction of the **Samaritan Temple** and the surrounding area of Shechem, the Roman general and future emperor **Vespasian** launched a military campaign to crush the Jewish revolt of 66 CE, which resulted in the **destruction of the Jewish Temple in Jerusalem in 70 CE by his son Titus, and the subsequent exile of Jews from Judea and the Galilee in 135 CE following the Bar Kokhba revolt.**

Jacob and his sons are forced by **famine** to go down into Egypt, although Joseph was already there, as he had been sold into slavery while young. When they arrive they and their families are 70 in number, but within four generations they have increased to **600,000 men** of fighting age, and the Pharaoh of Egypt, alarmed, first enslaves them and then orders the death of all male Hebrew children.

**A woman from the tribe of Levi hides her child**, places him in a woven basket, and sends him down the **Nile River**. He is named **Mosheh, or Moses**, by the Egyptians who find him. **At the age of forty Moses kills an Egyptian**, after he sees him beating a Hebrew to death, and escapes as a fugitive into the Sinai desert, where he is taken in by the Midianites and **marries Zipporah, the daughter of the Midianite priest Jethro. The God of Israel calls to Moses from the fire and**

**reveals his name, Yahweh** and tells Moses that he is being sent to Pharaoh to bring the people of Israel out of Egypt.

# Jehovah (Abrahamic God)

**Jehovah** (a Latinization of the Hebrew יְהֹוָה, one vocalization of the **Tetragrammaton** (**YHWH**), the proper name of the God of Israel in the **Hebrew Bible** and one of the seven names of God in Judaism.

The historical vocalization of the **Tetragrammaton** at the time of the redaction of the **Torah** (6th century BCE) is most likely **Yahweh**. The historical vocalization was lost because in **Second Temple** Judaism, during the 3rd to 2nd centuries BCE, the pronunciation of the **Tetragrammaton** came to be avoided, being substituted with **Adonai** ("**my Lord**"). The Hebrew vowel points of *Adonai* were added to the **Tetragrammaton** by the **Masoretes**, and the resulting form was transliterated around the 12th century as *Yehowah*. The derived forms *Iehouah* and *Jehovah* first appeared in the 16th century.

"**Jehovah**" was introduced to the English-speaking world by **William Tyndale** in his translation of **Exodus 6:3**, and was taken up in very limited fashion (the **King James** Version has it only four times as an independent name plus three times in compound terms). The **Watchtower Society's New World Translation** uses "**Jehovah**" throughout the Old Testament.

## Pronunciation

Most scholars believe "**Jehovah**" (also transliterated as "**Yehowah**") to be a hybrid form derived by combining the Latin letters *JHVH* with the vowels of *Adonai*. Others say that it is the pronunciation *Yahweh* that is testified in both Christian and pagan texts of the early Christian era. Some **Karaite** Jews, as proponents of the rendering *Jehovah*, state that although the original pronunciation **of** יהוה has been obscured by disuse of the spoken name according to **oral Rabbinic law. "The English form *Jehovah* is quite simply an Anglicized form of Yehovah.**"

## Introduction into English

The earliest available Latin text to use a vocalization similar to *Jehovah* dates from the 13th century. The *Brown-Driver-Briggs Lexicon* suggested that the pronunciation *Jehovah* was unknown until 1520 when it was introduced by **Galatinus**, who defended its use. In English it appeared in **William Tyndale's** translation of the Pentateuch (**"The Five Books of Moses"**) published in 1530 in Germany, where **Tyndale** had studied since 1524.

The *Authorized King James Version*, which used "**Jehovah**" in a few places, most frequently gave "**the LORD**" as the equivalent of the **Tetragrammaton**. The *New World Translation of the Holy Scriptures* of Jehovah's Witnesses in 1961. (Exodus 6:3–6)  **Hebrew vowel points**

The translation of the "**Dead Sea Scrolls**", have acknowledged the general agreement among scholars that the original pronunciation of the Tetragrammaton was probably *Yahweh*, and that the vowel points now attached to the Tetragrammaton were added to indicate that *Adonai* was to be read instead, as seen in the alteration of those points after prefixes.

## Proponents of pre-Christian origin

18th-century theologian **John Gill** puts forward the arguments of 17th-century **Johannes Buxtorf II** and others in his writing, *A Dissertation Concerning the Antiquity of the Hebrew Language, Letters, Vowel-Points and Accents.* He argued for an extreme antiquity of their use, rejecting the idea that the vowel points were invented by the **Masoretes.**

He argued that throughout this history the **Masoretes** did not invent the vowel points and accents, but that they were delivered to Moses by God at Sinai, citing Karaite authorities **"all our wise men with one mouth affirm and profess that the whole law was pointed and accented, as it came out of the hands of Moses, the man of God."**

Gill quoted Elia Levita, who said, **"There is no syllable without a point, and there is no word without an accent. "if anyone could convince him that his opinion was contrary to the book of Zohar, he should be content to have it rejected."** The 1602 Spanish Bible (Reina-Valera/Cipriano de Valera) used the name *Iehova* and gave a lengthy defense of the pronunciation *Jehovah* in its preface.

## Proponents of later origin

The **Dead Sea Scrolls**, discovered in 1946 and dated from 400 BC to 70 AD, include texts from the **Torah** or **Pentateuch** and from other parts of the Hebrew Bible, and have provided documentary evidence that, in spite of claims to the contrary, the original Hebrew texts were in fact written without vowel points.

# Jesus of Nazareth

**Jesus of Nazareth Born 7-2 BCE)**, commonly referred to as **Jesus Christ** or simply as **Jesus** or **Christ**, is the central figure of Christianity. Most Christian denominations venerate him as **God the Son incarnated** and believe that he rose from the dead after being crucified. The principal sources of information regarding Jesus are the **four canonical gospels**. Most critical historians agree that Jesus was a **Galilean Jewish Rabbi** who was regarded as a teacher and healer in Judaea, that he was baptized by **John the Baptist**, and that he was crucified in Jerusalem on the orders of the **Roman Prefect, Pontius Pilate**, on the charge of sedition against the Roman Empire.

Christians traditionally believe that Jesus was **born of a virgin**, performed miracles, founded the Church, rose from the dead, and ascended into heaven, from which he will return. The majority of **Christians worship Jesus as** the **incarnation of God the Son**, and **"the Second Person of the Blessed Trinity"**. Christian scholars today present Jesus as the awaited **Messiah** promised in the Old Testament and as God, arguing that he fulfilled many Messianic prophecies of the **Old Testament.** Judaism rejects assertions that Jesus was the awaited Messiah, arguing that he did not fulfill the Messianic prophecies in the **Tanakh, being related to King David, among others.**

In Islam, **Jesus** (Islamic usage, Isa) is considered **one of God's important prophets**, a bringer of scripture, and the product of a **virgin birth**, but not to have experienced crucifixion. Islam and the **Baha'i Faith** use the title **"Messiah"** for Jesus, but do not teach that he was God incarnate.

## Etymology of name
**"Jesus"** is a transliteration, a Hellenization of the Hebrew (**Joshua**) or Hebrew-Aramaic, meaning **"Yahweh delivers (or rescues)"**. The name Jesus appears to have been in use in Judaea at the time of the birth of Jesus. In the New Testament, in **Luke 1:26-33** the angel **Gabriel** tells **Mary** to name her child Jesus, and in **Matthew 1:21** an angel tells **Joseph** to name the child Jesus. The statement in **Matthew 1:21 "you shall call his name Jesus, for he will save his people from their sins"** associates salvific attributes to the name Jesus in Christian theology. "Christ" is derived from the Greek, meaning **"the anointed one"**. In **Matthew 16:16**, Apostle **Peter's** profession: **"You are the Christ"** identifies Jesus as the Messiah.

## Chronology
The estimation of the year of death of Jesus places his lifespan around the beginning of the 1<sup>st</sup> century AD/CE, in the geographic region of Roman Judaea. Roman involvement in Judaea began around 63 BC/BCE and by 6 AD/CE Judaea had become a Roman province. From 26-37 CE/AD **Pontius Pilate** was the governor of Roman Judaea.

## Year of birth estimates
In its Nativity account, the **Gospel of Matthew** associates the birth of Jesus with the reign of **Herod the Great**, who is generally believed to have died around 4 BC/BCE. **Matthew 2:1** states that: **"Jesus was born in Bethlehem of Judaea in the days of Herod the king"** and **Luke 1:5** mentions the reign of Herod shortly before the birth of Jesus. Matthew also suggests that Jesus may have been as much as two years old at the time of the visit of the **Magi** and hence even older at the time of Herod's death, 4 BC. Most scholars generally assume a date of birth between 6 and

4 BCE. The statement in **Luke 3:23** that Jesus was **"about 30 years of age"** at the start of his ministry.

By combining information from **John 2:13** and **John 2:20** with the writings of **Josephus**, it has been estimated that around 27-29 AD/CE, Jesus was **"about thirty years of age"**. Although Christian feasts related to the Nativity have had specific dates (e.g. **December 25** for Christmas) there is no historical evidence for the exact day or month of the birth of Jesus.

## Years of ministry estimates

From the **Gospel of Luke** with historical data about **Emperor Tiberius** yields a date around 28-29 AD/CE, while a second independent approach based on statements in the **Gospel of John**. A third method uses the date of the death of **John the Baptist** and the marriage of **Herod Antipas** to Herodias based on the writings of **Josephus**, and correlates it to **Matthew 14:4**. Given that Tiberius began his reign in 14 AD/CE, this yields a date about 28-29 AD/CE.

According to **Josephus** (Ant 15.380) the temple reconstruction was started by **Herod the Great** in the $15^{th}$-$18^{th}$ year of his reign at about the time that **Augustus** arrived in Syria (Ant 15.354). Temple expansion and reconstruction was ongoing, and it was in constant reconstruction until it was destroyed in 70 AD by the Romans. Although both the gospels and Josephus refer to Herod Antipas killing **John the Baptist**, they differ on the details, e.g. whether this act was a consequence of the marriage of **Herod Antipas** and Herodias, as indicated in **Matthew 14:4**, or a pre-emptive measure by Herod which possibly took place before the marriage, as Josephus suggests in **Ant 18.5.2**.

## Year of death estimates

All four canonical Gospels report that **Jesus was crucified in Calvary** during the prefecture of **Pontius Pilate**, the Roman prefect who governed Judaea from 26 to 36 CE/AD. The late $1^{st}$ century Jewish historian **Josephus**, writing in *Antiquities of the Jews* (*c.* 93 AD/CE), also state that **Pilate ordered the execution of Jesus**. The estimation of the date of the conversion of Paul places the death of Jesus before this conversion, which is estimated at around 33-36 CE/AD. **Isaac Newton's** method relied on the relative visibility of the crescent of the new moon and he suggested the date as Friday, April 23, 34 AD.

## Life and teachings in the New Testament

The canonical gospels, **Matthew, Mark, Luke, and John**, are the main sources for the biography of Jesus' life. The Acts of the Apostles **(10:37-38) and 19:4)** refers to the early ministry of Jesus and its anticipation by John the Baptist.

## The four gospel accounts

Three of the four canonical gospels, namely **Matthew, Mark, and Luke**, are known as the *Synoptic Gospels*. The presentation in the fourth canonical Gospel, i.e. the **John**, differs from these three in that it has more of a thematic nature rather than a narrative format. It is impossible to find any direct literary relationship between the synoptic gospels and the **Gospel of John**.

As stated in **John 21:25** the gospels do not claim to provide an exhaustive list of the events in the life of Jesus.

## Key elements and the five major milestones

The five major milestones in the gospel narrative of the life of Jesus are his **Baptism, Transfiguration, Crucifixion, Resurrection and Ascension**. Parables represent a major component of the teachings of Jesus in the gospels, forming approximately one third of his recorded teachings, and **John 14:10** positions them as the revelations of **God the Father**.

## Genealogy

Matthew begins his **gospel in 1:1** with the genealogy of Jesus, and presents it before the account of the birth of Jesus, while Luke discusses the genealogy in chapter 3, after the Baptism of Jesus in **Luke 3:22** when the voice from Heaven addresses Jesus and identifies him as the Son of God.

At that point Luke traces Jesus' ancestry through **Adam** to God. While Luke traces the genealogy upwards towards Adam and God, Matthew traces it downwards towards Jesus. Both gospels state that **Jesus was begotten not by Joseph, but by God**. Both accounts trace Joseph back to **King David** and from there to Abraham. Luke traces the genealogy through Mary while Matthew traces it through Joseph.

## Nativity

According to Luke and Matthew, Jesus was born to Joseph and Mary, his betrothed, in Bethlehem. Both support the doctrine of the **Virgin Birth** in which Jesus was miraculously conceived in his mother's womb by the **Holy Spirit**, when his mother was still a virgin. Luke is the only Gospel to provide an account of the birth of John the Baptists, and uses it to draw parallels between the births of John and Jesus. In **Luke 1:31-38** Mary learns from the angel **Gabriel** that she will conceive and bear a child called Jesus through the action of the **Holy Spirit**.

When Mary is due to give birth, she and Joseph travel from Nazareth to Joseph's ancestral home in Bethlehem to register in the census of **Quirinius**. In **Luke 2:1-7**, Mary gives birth to Jesus and, having found no place in the inn, places the newborn in a manger. An angel visits the shepherds and sends them to adore the child in **Luke 2:22.** After presenting Jesus at the Temple, Joseph and Mary return home to Nazareth.

Following his betrothal to Mary, Joseph is troubled in **Matthew 1:19-20** because Mary is pregnant, but in the first of Joseph's three dreams an angel assures him not to be afraid to take Mary as his wife, because her child was conceived by the **Holy Spirit. King Herod** hears of Jesus' birth from the **Wise Men** and tries to kill him by massacring all the male children in Bethlehem under the age of two (**the Massacre of the Innocents**). Before the massacre, Joseph is warned by an angel in his dream and the family **flees to Egypt** and remains there until Herod's death, in 4 AD, after which they leave Egypt and settle in Nazareth to avoid living under the authority of Herod's son and successor **Archelaus.**

## Baptism and temptation

In the gospels, the accounts of the **Baptism of Jesus** are always preceded by information about **John the Baptist** and his ministry.

As he baptized people in the area of the **River Jordan** about the time of the commencement of the ministry of Jesus. In **Acts 10:37-38**, Apostle Peter refers to how the ministry of Jesus followed "**the baptism which John preached**". In the Antiquities of the Jews **(18.5.2)** 1ˢᵗ century historian **Flavius Josephus** also wrote about John the Baptist and his eventual death in Perea.

In **Matthew 3:14**, upon meeting Jesus, the Baptist states: "**I need to be baptized by you.**" However, Jesus persuades John to baptize him nonetheless. This is one of two cases in the gospels where a voice from **Heaven** calls Jesus **"Son"**, the other being in the **Transfiguration** of Jesus episode. The Temptation of Jesus is narrated in the three Synoptic gospels after his baptism. In these accounts, as in **Matthew 4:1-11** and **Luke 4:1-13**, Jesus goes to the desert for forty days to fast. While there, **Satan** appears to him and tempts him in various ways, e.g. asking Jesus to show signs that he is the **Son of God** by turning stone to bread, or offering Jesus worldly rewards in exchange for worship. Jesus rejects every temptation and when Satan leaves, angels appear and minister to Jesus.

## Ministry

**Luke 3:23** states that Jesus was "**about 30 years of age**" at the start of his ministry. The end of his ministry is estimated to be in the range 30-36 AD/CE. The three Synoptic gospels refer to just one **Passover** during his ministry, while the **Gospel of John** refers to three Passovers, suggesting a period of about three years.

Jesus' ministry begins with his Baptism by **John the Baptist (Matthew 3, Luke 3)**, and ends with the **Last Supper** with his disciples **(Matthew 26, Luke 22)** in Jerusalem. The *Early Galilean ministry* begins when Jesus goes back to Galilee from the Judean desert after rebuffing the temptation of **Satan**. This period includes the **Sermon on the Mount**, one of the major discourses of Jesus. The *Final Galilean ministry* includes the Feeding the 5000 and Walking on water episodes, both in **Matthew 14**. At the end of this period, the Gospel of John includes the Raising **of Lazarus** episode.

The *Final ministry in Jerusalem* is sometimes called the *Passion Week* and begins with Jesus' triumphal entry into Jerusalem on **Palm Sunday**. In that week Jesus drives the money changers from the Temple, and **Judas** bargains to betray him. This period includes the **Olivet Discourse** and the **Second Coming Prophecy** and culminates in the **Last Supper**, at the end of which Jesus prepares his disciples for his departure in the **Farewell discourse**. The accounts of the ministry of Jesus generally end with the **Last Supper.**

## Teachings and preachings

The New Testament equates the words of Jesus with divine revelation, with **John the Baptists** stating in **John 3:34**: "**he whom God hath sent speaketh the words of God**". In Matthey 11:27 Jesus claims divine knowledge, stating: "**No one knows the Son except the Father and no one knows the Father except the Son**", asserting the mutual knowledge he has with the Father.

## Proclamation as Christ and Transfiguration

At the beginning of the final journey to Jerusalem which ends in the Passion and **Resurrection** of Jesus. Peter's Confession beings as a dialogue between Jesus and his disciples in **Matthew 16:13, Mark 8:27 and Luke 9:18. Jesus** unequivocally **declares himself to be both Christ and the Son of God.** The account of the Transfiguration of Jesus appears in **Matthew 17:1-9, Mark 9:2-8, Luke 9:28-36.** At that point the **prophets Elijah and Moses** appear and Jesus begins to talk to them. A bright cloud appears around them, and a voice from the cloud states: **"This is my beloved Son, with whom I am well pleased; listen to him"**.

## Final week: betrayal, arrest, trial, and death

The description of the last week of the life of Jesus (often called the **Passion Week**) occupies about one third of the narrative in the **Canonical gospels**. The narrative for that week starts by a description of the final entry into Jerusalem, and ends with his crucifixion. One of his disciples, **Judas Iscariot**, decides to betray Jesus for **thirty pieces of silver**. After the supper, Jesus is betrayed with a kiss while he is in agony in the garden, and is arrested. After his arrest, Jesus is abandoned by most of his disciples, and **Peter denies him three times**, as Jesus had predicted during the **Last Supper.**

Jesus is first questioned by the **Sanhedrin**, and then tried by **Pontius Pilate**, the Roman governor of Judea. After the scourging of Jesus, and his mocking as the **King of the Jews**, Pilate orders the crucifixion. The final week that begins with his entry into Jerusalem, concludes with his crucifixion and burial on that Friday. The New Testament accounts then describe the resurrection of Jesus three days later, on the Sunday following his death.

## Final entry into Jerusalem

In the four Canonical Gospels, Jesus' Triumphal entry into Jerusalem takes place at the beginning of the last week of his life, a few days before the **Last Supper**, marking the beginning of the **Passion** narrative. In the three **Synoptic Gospels**, entry into Jerusalem is followed by the Cleansing of the Temple episode, in which Jesus expels the **money changers** from the Temple, accusing them of turning the Temple to a den of thieves through their commercial activities.

## Last supper

In the New Testament, the **Last Supper** is the final meal that Jesus shares with his twelve apostles in Jerusalem before his crucifixion. The Last Supper is mentioned in all four Canonical Gospels, and **Paul's First Epistle** to the **Corinthians (11:23-26)**, which was likely written before the Gospels, also refers to it. In all four gospels, during the meal, Jesus predicts that one of the Apostles will betray him. In **Matthew 26:23-25** and **John 13:26-27 Judas** is specifically singled out as the traitor.

In **1 Corinthians 11:23-26** Apostle Paul provides the theological underpinnings for the use of the Eucharist, stating: **"This cup is the new covenant in my blood; do this, whenever you drink it, in remembrance of me."** In all four Gospels Jesus predicts that Peter will deny knowledge of him, stating that Peter will disown him three times before the rooster crows the next morning. The Gospel of John provides the only account of Jesus washing his disciples' feet before the meal.

## Trials by the Sanhedrin, Herod and Pilate

In the narrative of the four **Canonical Gospels** after the betrayal and arrest of Jesus, he is taken to the **Sanhedrin**, a Jewish judicial body. Jesus is tried by the Sanhedrin, mocked and beaten and is condemned for making claims of being the **Son of God**. He is then taken to **Pontius Pilate** and the Jewish elders ask Pilate to judge and condemn Jesus—accusing him of claiming to be the **King of the Jews**. After questioning, **Pilate then orders Jesus' crucifixion.**

In **Mark 14:61** the high priest then asked Jesus: **"Are you the Christ, the Son of the Blessed? And Jesus said, I am"** at which point the high priest tore his own robe in anger and accused Jesus of blasphemy. In **22:70** when asked: **"Are you then the Son of God**?" Jesus answers: **"You say that I am"** affirming the title Son of God. In John **18:36** Jesus states: **"My kingdom is not of this world",** but does not directly deny being the King of the Jews.

Pilate then writes **"Jesus of Nazareth, King of the Jews"** as a sign to be affixed to the cross of Jesus. Pilate publicly washes his hands of responsibility, yet orders the crucifixion in response to the demands of the crowd. The trial by Pilate if followed by the flagellation episode, the soldiers mock Jesus as the **King of Jews** by putting a purple robe (that signifies royal status) on him, place a **Crown of Thorns** on his head, and beat and mistreat him in **Matthew 27:29-30, Mark 15:17-19 and John 19:2-3**. Jesus is then sent to Calvary for crucifixion.

## Crucifixion and burial

After the trials, Jesus made his way to Calvary (the path is traditionally called **via Dolorosa**). Once at Calvary (**Golgotha**), Jesus was offered wine mixed with gall to drink. Matthew's and Mark's Gospels state that he refused this. The soldiers then crucified Jesus and cast lots for his clothes. Above Jesus' head on the cross was the inscription **King of the Jews.** Jesus was crucified between two convicted thieves. In **Luke 23:34** Jesus says: **"Father, forgive them; for they know not what they do".**

The Roman soldiers did not break Jesus' legs, as they did to the other two men crucified (breaking the legs hastened the crucifixion process), as Jesus was dead already. One of the soldiers pierced the side of Jesus with a lance and water flowed out. Following Jesus' death on Friday, **Joseph of Arimathea** asked the permission of Pilate to remove the body. The body was removed from the cross, was wrapped in a clean cloth and buried in a new rock-hewn tomb, with the assistance of **Nicodemus**.

## Resurrection and ascension

The New Testament accounts of the resurrection and ascension of Jesus, state that the first day of the week after the crucifixion (typically interpreted as a Sunday), his followers encounter him **risen from the dead**, after his tomb is discovered to be empty. In the four Canonical Gospels, when the tomb of Jesus is discovered empty, in **Matthew 28:5, Mark 16:5, Luke 24:4 and John 20:12** his resurrection is announced and explained to the followers who arrive there early in the morning. All four accounts include **Mary Magdalene** and three include Mary the mother of Jesus. After the discovery of the empty tomb, the Gospels indicate that Jesus made a series of appearances to the disciples. The final post-resurrection appearance in the Gospel accounts is when Jesus ascends to Heaven where he remains with God the Father and the Holy Spirit.

**Luke 24:51** states that Jesus **"was carried up into heaven".** **1 Peter 3:22** describes Jesus as being on **"the right hand of God, having gone into heaven"**.

## Title attributions

Two of the key titles used for Jesus in the New Testament are Christ and Son of God. The statement by **Apostle Peter in Matthew 16:16** ("**you are the Christ, the Son of the living God**"). However, scholars still debate if Jesus was making a claim to divinity in these statements. **While the Gospel**

**of John frequently uses the Son of God title, the Gospel of Luke emphasizes Jesus as a prophet**. Many modern scholars believe that Jesus never made a claim to divinity.

## Language, race and appearance

Jesus grew up in Galilee and much of his ministry took place there. The languages spoken in Galilee and Judea during the 1st century AD/CE include **Aramaic, Hebrew and Greek**, with Aramaic being the predominant language. Aramaic was the mother tongue of virtually all women in Galilee and Judea. Most scholars support the theory that **Jesus spoke Aramaic** and that he may have also spoken Hebrew and Greek.

Old Testament references about the coming Messiah have been projected forward to form conjectures about the appearance of Jesus on theological, rather than historical grounds; e.g. **Isaiah 53:2** which refers to the coming Messiah as **"no beauty that we should desire him"** and **Psalm 45:2-3**. By the 20th century, theories had also been proposed that Jesus was of black African descent, e.g. based on the argument that Mary his mother was a descendant of black Jews.

## Analysis of the gospels

The **Gospel of Thomas**, a collection of 114 sayings of Jesus, predates the four orthodox gospels, and believe it may have been composed around mid-1st century.

## Jewish religious movements in Jesus' day

Some scholars theorize that Jesus was an Essene, or close to them. **Zealots** were a revolutionary party opposed to Roman rule, one of those parties that, according to **Josephus** inspired the fanatical stand in Jerusalem that led to its destruction in the year 70 AD/CE.

## Mythical view

One viewpoint is that there was no real historical figure Jesus and that he was invented by Christians. Another viewpoint is that there was a person called Jesus, but much of the teachings and miracles attributed to him were either invented or symbolic references. Yet another view holds that the Jesus portrayed in the gospels is a composite character constructed from multiple people over a period of time.

## Christian views

Almost all Christian groups regard Jesus as the "**Savior and Redeemer**", as the (English: Christ) prophesied in the Old Testament, who, through his life, death, and resurrection, restored humanity's communion with God in the blood of the New Covenant. His death on a cross is understood as the redemptive sacrifice: the source of humanity's salvation and the atonement for sin, which had entered human history through the sin of Adam. Christians profess that Jesus suffered death by crucifixion, and rose bodily from the dead in the definitive miracle that foreshadows the resurrection of humanity at the end of time, when **Christ will come again** to judge the living and the dead, resulting in either entrance into heaven or damnation.

Christians profess Jesus to be the only **Son of God**, the Lord, and the eternal Word who became man in the incarnation, so that those who believe in him might have eternal life. They hold that he was born of the **Virgin Mary** by the power of the **Holy Spirit** in an event described as the miraculous virgin birth or incarnation. Most Christian denominations believe in some form of the doctrine of the Trinity, i.e. that Jesus, as the second person of the Trinity, is **fully God**.

## Jewish views

Judaism, rejects the idea of Jesus being God, or a person of a Trinity, or a mediator to God. Judaism holds that Jesus is not the **Messiah**, arguing that he had not fulfilled the Messianic prophecies in the **Tanakh** nor embodied the personal qualifications of the Messiah. According to Jewish tradition, there were no more prophets after Malachi, who lived centuries before Jesus.

## Islamic views

In Islam, Jesus is considered to be a Messenger of God and the Messiah who was sent to guide the Children of Israel with the Gospel. Jesus is seen in Islam as a precursor to **Prophet Muhammad,** and is believed by Muslims to have foretold the latter's coming. In the **Qur'an**, Jesus is referred to as *Isa Ibn E Maryam* (Jesus the son of Mary) and Jesus is mentioned by name more times than Muhammad. According to the Qur'an, Jesus was born to Mary as the result of **virginal conception**, and was given the ability to perform miracles.

## Baha'i views

Baha'i Faith, founded in 19th-century Persian, considers Jesus, along with Muhammad, the Buddha, Krishna, and Zoroaster, and other messengers of the great religions of the world to be **Manifestations of God (or prophets), with both human and divine stations.** God's will is revealed to mankind progressively as mankind matures and is better able to comprehend the purpose of God in creating humanity. In the **Book of Certitude**, Baha'u'llah claims that these messengers have two natures: **divine and human**. Baha'is believe that Baha'u'llah is, in both respects, the return of Jesus.

## Buddhist views

Some Buddhists, including **Tanzin Gyatso**, the 14th century **Dalai Lama** regard Jesus as a bodhisattva who dedicated his life to the welfare of human beings. The 14th century Zen master **Gasan Jōseki** indicated that the sayings of Jesus in the Gospels were written by an enlightened man.

# Jewish Holidays

**Jewish holidays**, also known as **Jewish festivals** or *Yamim Tovim* (Hebrew: lit. 'Good Days', in transliterated Hebrew ), are holidays observed in Judaism and by Jews throughout the Hebrew calendar. They include religious, cultural and national elements, derived from three sources: **biblical *mitzvot* ("commandments"); rabbinic mandates; Jewish history and the history of the State of Israel.** Jewish holidays occur on the same dates every year in the **Hebrew calendar**, but the dates vary in the **Gregorian**.

## ⌐ General concepts / Groupings
**Certain terms are used very commonly for groups of holidays.**

- The Hebrew-language term *Yom Tov*, sometimes referred to as "**festival day**," usually refers to the **six biblically-mandated festival dates** on which all activities prohibited on **Shabbat** are prohibited, except for some related to food preparation. These include the first and seventh days of **Passover**, **Shavuot**, both days of **Rosh Hashanah**, first day of Sukkot, and Shemini Atzeret. By extension, outside the Land of Israel, the second-day holidays known under the rubric *Yom tov sheni shel galuyot* (literally, **"Second Yom Tov of the Diaspora"**)—including Simchat **Torah**—are also included in this grouping. **The tradition of keeping two days of Yom Tov in the diaspora has existed since roughly 300 BCE.**
- The English-language term High Holy Days (or High Holidays) refers to **Rosh Hashanah** and **Yom Kippur** collectively. Its Hebrew analogue, *Yamim Nora'im* ("Days of Awe", is more flexible: it can refer just to those holidays, or to the **Ten Days of Repentance**, or to the entire penitential period, starting as early as the beginning of Elul, and (more rarely) ending as late as **Shemini Atzeret**.
- The term Three Pilgrimage Festivals ( *shalosh regalim*) refers to **Passover**, **Shavuot** and Sukkot. Within this grouping Sukkot normally includes Shemini Atzeret and Simchat **Torah**.

## Terminology used to describe holidays
*Shabbat* Ashkenazi pron. from Yiddish *shabbos*), or Sabbath, is referred to by that name exclusively. Similarly, *Rosh Chodesh* (ראש חודש) is referred to by that name exclusively.

- *Yom tov* (Ashkenazi pron. from Yid. *yontif*) (*lit.,* "good day"): See "Groupings" above.
- *Moed* ("**festive season**"), plural *moadim* (מועדים), refers to any of the Three Pilgrimage Festivals of **Passover**, **Shavuot** and Sukkot. When used in comparison to *Yom Tov*, it refers to Chol HaMoed, the intermediate days of **Passover** and Sukkot.
- *Ḥag or chag* ("**festival**"), plural *chagim* (חגים), can be used whenever *yom tov* or *moed* is. It is also used to describe **Hanukkah** and **Purim**, as well as *Yom Ha'atzmaut* (Israeli Independence Day) and *Yom Yerushalayim* (Jerusalem Day).
- *Ta'anit* , or, less commonly, *tzom* (צום), refers to a *fast*. These terms are generally used to describe the rabbinic fasts, although *tzom* is used liturgically to refer to **Yom Kippur** as well.

354

## "Work" on Sabbath and biblical holidays / *Melacha*

The most notable common feature of **Shabbat** and the biblical festivals is the requirement to refrain from *melacha* on these days. *Melacha* is most commonly translated as **"work"**; perhaps a better translation is **"creative-constructive work"**. Strictly speaking, *Melacha* is defined in Jewish law *(Halakha)* **by 39 categories of labor** that were used in constructing the **Tabernacle** while the Jews wandered in the desert. As understood traditionally and in **Orthodox Judaism:**

- On **Shabbat** and **Yom Kippur** all *melacha* is prohibited.
- On a Yom Tov (other than **Yom Kippur**) which falls on a weekday, not **Shabbat**, most *melacha* is prohibited. Some *melacha* related to preparation of food is permitted.
- On weekdays during Chol HaMoed, *melacha* is not prohibited *per se*. However, *melacha* should be limited to that required either to enhance the enjoyment of the remainder of the festival or to avoid great financial loss.
- On other days, there are no restrictions on *melacha.*

In principle, Conservative Judaism understands the requirement to refrain from *melacha* in the same way as Orthodox Judaism. In practice, Conservative rabbis frequently rule on prohibitions around *melacha* differently from Orthodox authorities. Still, there are a number of Conservative/ Masorti communities around the world where Sabbath and Festival observance fairly closely resembles Orthodox observance.

**Shabbat** and holiday work restrictions are always put aside in cases of *pikuach nefesh*, which is saving a human life. At the most fundamental level, if there is any possibility whatsoever that action must be taken to save a life, **Shabbat** restrictions are set aside immediately, and without reservation. Where the danger to life is present but less immediate, there is some preference to minimize violation of **Shabbat** work restrictions where possible.

## Second day of biblical festivals / *Yom tov sheni shel galuyot*

The **Torah** specifies a single date on the Jewish calendar for observance of holidays. Nevertheless, festivals of biblical origin other than **Shabbat** and **Yom Kippur** are observed for two days outside the land of Israel, and **Rosh Hashanah** is observed for two days even inside the land of Israel. Dates for holidays on the Jewish calendar are expressed in the **Torah** as **"day x of month y."** Accordingly, the beginning of *monthly* needs to be determined before the proper date of the holiday on *day x* can be fixed.

Months in the Jewish calendar are lunar, and originally were thought to have been proclaimed by the blowing of a *shofar*. Later, the Sanhedrin received testimony of witnesses saying they saw the new crescent moon. Then the **Sanhedrin** would inform Jewish communities away from its meeting place that it had proclaimed a new moon. The practice of observing a second festival day stemmed from delays in disseminating that information.

- ***Rosh Hashanah***. Because of holiday restrictions on travel, messengers could not even leave the seat of the Sanhedrin until the holiday was over. Inherently, there was no possible way for anyone living away from the seat of the Sanhedrin to receive news of the proclamation of the new month until messengers arrived *after the fact*. Accordingly, the practice emerged that **Rosh Hashanah** was observed on both possible days, as calculated from the previous month's start, everywhere in the world.

- ***Three Pilgrimage Festivals***. Sukkot and **Passover** fall on the 15th day of their respective months. This gave messengers two weeks to inform communities about the proclamation of the new month. Normally, they would reach most communities within the land of Israel within that time, but they might fail to reach communities farther away (such as those in Babylonia or overseas). Consequently, the practice developed that these holidays be observed for one day within Israel, but for two days (both possible days as calculated from the previous month's start) outside Israel. This practice is known as ***yom tov sheni shel galuyot*, "second day of festivals in exile communities"**.

**For Shavuot**, calculated as the fiftieth day from **Passover**, the above issue did not pertain directly, as the "**correct**" date for **Passover** would be known by then. Nevertheless, the Talmud applies the same rule to **Shavuot**, and to the Seventh Day of **Passover** and Shemini Atzeret, for consistency. **Yom Kippur** is not observed for two days anywhere because of the difficulty of maintaining a fast over two days.

**Shabbat** is not observed based on a calendar date, but simply at intervals of seven days. Accordingly, there is never a doubt of the date of **Shabbat**, and it need never be observed for two days. Adherents of Reform Judaism and Reconstructionist Judaism generally do not observe the second day of festivals, although some do observe two days of **Rosh Hashanah**.

## Holidays of biblical and rabbinic (Talmudic) origin
*Theories concerning possible non-Jewish sources for biblical holidays are beyond the scope of this article. Please see individual holiday articles, particularly Shabbat (History)*.

## Shabbat—the Sabbath
Jewish law *(Halakha)* accords *Shabbat* the status of a holiday, a day of rest celebrated on the seventh day of each week. Jewish law defines a day as ending at either sundown or nightfall, when the next day then begins. Thus,

- **Shabbat** begins just before sundown Friday night. Its start is marked by the lighting of **Shabbat** candles and the recitation of Kiddush over a cup of wine.
- **Shabbat** ends at nightfall Saturday night. Its conclusion is marked by the prayer known as Havdalah.

**In many ways, *halakha* (Jewish law) sees *Shabbat* as the most important holy day in the Jewish calendar.**

- It is the first holiday mentioned in the Tanakh (Hebrew Bible), and God was the first one to observe it (Genesis).

- The **Torah** reading on *Shabbat* has more sections of *parshiot* (**Torah** readings) than on **Yom Kippur** or any other Jewish holiday.
- The prescribed penalty in the **Torah** for a transgression of *Shabbat* prohibitions is death by stoning (Exodus 31), while for other holidays the penalty is (relatively) less severe.
- Observance of **Shabbat** is the benchmark used in *Halakha* to determine whether an individual is a religiously observant, religiously reliable member of the community.

## Rosh Chodesh—The New Month

**Rosh Chodesh** (lit., **"head of the month"**) is a minor holiday or observance occurring on the first day of each month of the Jewish calendar, as well as the last day of the preceding month if it has thirty days.

- **Rosh Chodesh** observance during at least a portion of the period of the prophets could be fairly elaborate.
- Over time there have been varying levels of observance of a custom that women are excused from certain types of work.
- Fasting is normally prohibited on Rosh Chodesh.

Beyond the preceding, current observance is limited to changes in liturgy. In the month of Tishrei, this observance is superseded by the observance of **Rosh Hashanah**, a major holiday.

*Related observances:*
- The date of the forthcoming **Rosh Chodesh** is announced in synagogue on the preceding Sabbath.
- There are special prayers said upon observing the waxing moon for the first time each month.

## Rosh Hashanah: The Jewish New Year / Selichot

The month of **Elul** that precedes **Rosh Hashanah** is considered to be a propitious time for repentance. For this reason, additional penitential prayers called **Selichot** are added to the daily prayers, except on **Shabbat**. **Sephardi Jews** add these prayers each weekday during Elul. **Ashkenazi Jews** recite them from the last Sunday (or Saturday night) preceding **Rosh Hashanah** that allows at least four days of recitations.

## Rosh Hashanah
- Erev **Rosh Hashanah** (eve of the first day): 29 Elul
- **Rosh Hashanah**: 1–2 Tishrei

According to oral tradition, **Rosh Hashanah** (lit., **"Head of the Year"**) is the Day of Memorial or Remembrance (*Yom HaZikaron*), and the **Day of Judgment** (*Yom HaDin*). God appears in the role of King, remembering and judging each person individually according to his/her deeds, and making a decree for each person for the following year. The holiday is characterized by one specific mitzvah: blowing the *shofar*. According to the **Torah**, this is the first day of the seventh month of the calendar year, and marks the beginning of a ten-day period leading up to **Yom Kippur**. According to one of two Talmudic opinions, the creation of the world was completed on **Rosh Hashanah**.

Morning prayer services are lengthy on **Rosh Hashanah**, and focus on the themes described above: majesty and judgment, remembrance, the birth of the world, and the blowing of the *shofar*. Ashkenazi Jews recite the brief *Tashlikh* prayer, a symbolic casting off of the previous year's sins, during the afternoon of **Rosh Hashanah**. The Bible specifies **Rosh Hashanah** as a one-day holiday, but it is traditionally celebrated for two days, even within the Land of Israel. (**See** *Second day of biblical festivals,* **above**.)

## Four New Years

The **Torah** itself does not use any term like "**new year**" in reference to **Rosh Hashanah**. The Mishnah in **Rosh Hashanah** specifies four different "**New Year's Days**" for different purposes:

- **1 Tishrei** (conventional "**Rosh Hashanah**"): "**new year**" for calculating calendar years, sabbatical-year *(shmita)* and jubilee cycles, and the age of trees for purposes of Jewish law; and for separating grain tithes.
- **15 Shevat** (Tu Bishvat): "**new year**" for trees–*i.e.,* their current agricultural cycle and related tithes.
- **1 Nisan**: "**new year**" for counting months and major festivals and for calculating the years of the reign of a Jewish king
  - In biblical times, the day following 29 Adar, Year 1 of the reign of ___, would be followed by 1 Nisan, Year 2 of the reign of ___.
  - In modern times, although the Jewish calendar year number changes on **Rosh Hashanah**, the months are still numbered from Nisan.
  - The three pilgrimage festivals are always reckoned as coming in the order **Passover-Shavuot-Sukkot**. This can have religious law consequences even in modern times.
- 1 Elul (**Rosh Hashanah** LaBehema): "new year" for animal tithes.

## Aseret Yemei Teshuva—Ten Days of Repentance

The first ten days of Tishrei (from the beginning of Rosh Hashana until the end of **Yom Kippur**) are known as the **Ten Days of Repentance (***Aseret Yemei Teshuva***)**. During this time, in anticipation of **Yom Kippur**, it is "exceedingly appropriate" for Jews to practice *teshuvah* (literally **"return"**), an examination of one's deeds and repentance for sins one has committed against other people and God. This repentance can take the form of additional supplications, confessing one's deeds before God, fasting, self-reflection, and an increase of involvement with, or donations to, charity.

# Yom Kippur—Day of Atonement

- **Erev Yom Kippur: 9 Tishrei**
- Yom Kippur: 10 Tishrei (begins at sunset)

**Yom Kippur** is the holiest day of the year for Jews. Its central theme is atonement and reconciliation. This is accomplished through prayer and complete fasting—including abstinence from all food and drink (including water)—by all healthy adults. Bathing, wearing of perfume or cologne, wearing of leather shoes, and sexual relations are some of the other prohibitions on **Yom Kippur**—all of them designed to ensure one's attention is completely and absolutely focused on the quest for atonement with God. **Yom Kippur** is also unique among holidays as having work-related restrictions identical to those of **Shabbat**. The fast and other prohibitions commence on 10 Tishrei at sunset—sunset being the *beginning* of the day in Jewish tradition.

A traditional prayer in Aramaic called *Kol Nidre* (**"All Vows"**) is traditionally recited just before sunset. Although often regarded as the start of the **Yom Kippur** evening service—to such a degree that *Erev Yom Kippur* ("**Yom Kippur** Evening") is often called **"Kol Nidre"** (also spelled **"Kol Nidrei"**)—it is technically a separate tradition. This is especially so because, being recited before sunset, it is actually recited on 9 Tishrei, which is the day *before* **Yom Kippur**; it is not recited on **Yom Kippur** itself (on 10 Tishrei, which begins *after* the sun sets).

The words of **Kol Nidre** differ slightly between Ashkenazic and Sephardic traditions. In both, the supplicant prays to be released from all personal vows made to God during the year, so that any unfulfilled promises made to God will be annulled and, thus, forgiven. Only vows between the supplicant and God are relevant. Vows made between the supplicant and other people remain perfectly valid, since they are unaffected by the prayer.

A *Tallit* (four-cornered prayer shawl) is donned for evening and afternoon prayers–the only day of the year in which this is done. In traditional Ashkenazi communities, men wear the *kittel* throughout the day's prayers. The prayers on **Yom Kippur** evening are lengthier than on any other night of the year. Once services reconvene in the morning, the services (in all traditions) are the longest of the year. Two highlights of the morning prayers in traditional synagogues are the recitation of *Yizkor*, the prayer of remembrance, and of liturgical poems *(piyyutim)* describing the temple service of **Yom Kippur**.

Two other highlights happen late in the day. During the *Minchah* prayer, the *haftarah* reading features the entire **Book of Jonah**. Finally, the day concludes with *Ne'ilah*, a special service recited only on the day of **Yom Kippur**. **Ne'ilah** deals with the closing of the holiday, and contains a fervent final plea to God for forgiveness just before the conclusion of the fast. **Yom Kippur** comes to an end with the blowing of the *shofar*, which marks the conclusion of the fast. It is always observed as a one-day holiday, both inside and outside the boundaries of the Land of Israel.

**Yom Kippur** is considered, along with 15th of Av, as the happiest days of the year **(Talmud Bavli—Tractate Ta'anit)**.

## Sukkot—Feast of Booths (or Tabernacles)

- **Erev Sukkot: 14 Tishrei**
- Sukkot: 15–21 Tishrei (22 outside Israel)
- **The first day of Sukkot is (outside Israel, first two days are) full** *yom tov,* **while the remainder of Sukkot has the status of Chol Hamoed, "intermediate days".**

*Sukkot* (*sukkōt*) or *Succoth* is a seven-day festival, also known as the **Feast of Booths,** the **Feast of Tabernacles**, or just Tabernacles. It is one of the **Three Pilgrimage Festivals (***shalosh regalim***)** mentioned in the Bible. Sukkot commemorates the years that the Jews spent in the desert on their way to the **Promised Land**, and celebrates the way in which God protected them under difficult desert conditions. Jews are commanded to "**dwell**" in booths during the holiday. This generally means taking meals, but some sleep in the *Sukkah* as well, particularly in Israel. There are specific rules for constructing a *Sukkah.*

Along with dwelling in a *Sukkah*, the principal ritual unique to this holiday is use of the Four Species: *lulav* (palm), *hadass* (myrtle), *aravah* (willow) and *etrog* (citron). The seventh day of the Sukkot is called Hoshanah Rabbah, the "**Great *Hoshanah"*** (singular of *Hoshanot* and the source of the English word hosanna). The climax of the day's prayers includes seven processions of *Hoshanot* around the synagogue. This tradition mimics practices from the Temple in Jerusalem. Many aspects of the day's customs also resemble those of **Rosh Hashanah** and **Yom Kippur**. Hoshanah Rabbah is traditionally taken to be the day of the **"delivery"** of the final judgment of **Yom Kippur**, and offers a last opportunity for pleas of repentance before the holiday season closes.

## Shemini Atzeret and Simchat Torah

- **Shemini Atzeret: 22 Tishrei (combined with Simchat Torah in Israel)**
- **Simchat Torah outside Israel: 23 Tishrei**

The holiday of Shemini Atzeret immediately follows the conclusion of the holiday of Sukkot. The Hebrew word *shemini* means **"eighth**", and refers to its position on **"the eighth day"** of Sukkot, actually a seven-day holiday.

The main notable custom of this holiday is the celebration of *Simchat Torah*, meaning **"rejoicing with the Torah"**. This name originally referred to a special **"ceremony"**: the last weekly **Torah** portion is read from **Deuteronomy**, completing the annual cycle, and is followed immediately by the reading of the first chapter of **Genesis**, beginning the new annual cycle. Services are especially joyous, and all attendees, young and old, are involved. This ceremony so dominates the holiday that in Israel, where the holiday is one day long, the whole holiday is often referred to as *Simchat*

*Torah*. Outside Israel, the holiday is two days long; the name *Shemini Atzeret* is used for the first day, while the second is normally called *Simchat Torah*.

## Hanukkah—Festival of Lights

- **Erev Hanukkah: 24 Kislev**
- **Hanukkah: 25 Kislev–2 or 3 Tevet**

The story of **Hanukkah** is preserved in the books of the First and Second Maccabees. These books are not part of the **Tanakh** (Hebrew Bible), they are apocryphal books instead. The miracle of the one-day supply of olive oil miraculously lasting eight days is first described in the **Talmud (Shabbat 21b)**, written about 600 years after the events described in the books of Maccabees.

**Hanukkah** marks the defeat of **Seleucid Empire** forces that had tried to prevent the people of Israel from practicing Judaism. Judah Maccabee and his brothers destroyed overwhelming forces, and rededicated the Temple in Jerusalem. The eight-day festival is marked by the kindling of lights—one on the first night, two on the second, and so on—using a special candle holder called a *Hanukkiah*, or a *Hanukkah menorah.*

Religiously, **Hanukkah** is a minor holiday. Except on **Shabbat**, restrictions on work do not apply. Aside from the kindling of lights, formal religious observance is restricted to changes in liturgy. **Hanukkah** celebration tends to be informal and based on custom rather than law. Three widely practiced customs include:

- Consumption of foods prepared in oil, such as potato pancakes or *sufganiyot*, commemorating the miracle of oil
- Playing the game of dreidel (called a *sevivon* in Hebrew), symbolizing Jews' disguising of illegal **Torah** study sessions as gambling meetings during the period leading to the Maccabees' revolt
- Giving children money, especially coins, called **Hanukkah gelt**. However, the custom of giving presents is of far more recent, North American, origin, and is connected to the gift economy prevalent around North American Christmas celebrations.

## Tu Bishvat—New Year of the Trees

- **Tu Bishvat: 15 Shevat**

**Tu Bishvat** (lit., "**fifteenth of Shevat**", as ט״ו is the number **"15"** in Hebrew letters), is the new year for trees. It is also known as (*Ḥag ha-Ilanot*, Festival of Trees), or (*Rosh ha-Shanah la-Ilanot*, **New Year for Trees**). According to the Mishnah, it marks the day from which fruit tithes are counted each year. Starting on this date, the biblical prohibition on eating the first three years of fruit (*orlah*) and the requirement to bring the fourth year fruit *(neta revai)* to the Temple in Jerusalem were counted.

During the 17th century, **Rabbi Yitzchak Luria** of Safed and his disciples created a short **seder,** called *Hemdat ha-Yamim,* reminiscent of the **seder** that Jews observe on **Passover,** that explores the holiday's Kabbalistic themes. This **Tu Bishvat seder** has witnessed a revival in recent years. More generally, **Tu Bishvat** is celebrated in modern times by eating various fruits and nuts associated with the Land of Israel. Traditionally, trees are planted on this day. Many children collect funds leading up to this day to plant trees in Israel.

## Purim—Festival of Lots

- **Fast of Esther: normally 13 Adar**
- **Purim: 14 Adar**
- **Shushan Purim: 15 Adar**
- **In leap years on the Hebrew calendar, the above dates are observed in the Second Adar *(Adar Sheni). The 14th and 15th of First Adar* (Adar Rishon) *are known as* Purim Katan**

## Purim Katan

*Purim Katan* (lit., "**small Purim**") is observed on the 14th and 15th of First Adar in leap years. These days are marked by a small increase in festivity, including a prohibition on fasting, and slight changes in the liturgy.

## Purim and Shushan Purim

**Purim** commemorates the events that took place in the Book of Esther. The principal celebrations or commemorations include:

- The reading of the *Megillah.* Traditionally, this is read from a scroll twice during **Purim**— once in the evening and again in the morning. Ashkenazim have a custom of making disparaging noises at every mention of Haman's name during the reading.
- The giving of *Mishloakh Manot*, gifts of food and drink to friends and neighbors.
- The giving of *Matanot La'evyonim*, gifts to the poor and the needy.
- The **Purim** meal (*Se'udat Purim* or *Purim Se'udah*). This meal is traditionally accompanied by consumption of alcohol, often heavy, although Jewish sages have warned about the need to adhere to all religious laws even in a drunken state.

Several customs have evolved from these principal commemorations. One widespread custom to act out the story of **Purim.** The **Purim** spiel, or **Purim** play, has its origins in this, although the *Purim* spiel is not limited to that subject. Wearing of costumes and masks is also very common. These may be an outgrowth of **Purim** plays, but there are several theories as to the origin of the custom, most related in some way to the "**hidden**" nature of the miracles of **Purim.**

**Purim** carnivals of various types have also become customary. In Israel there are festive parades, known as *Ad-D'lo-Yada*, in the town's main street. The largest and most renowned is in Holon.

Most Jews celebrate **Purim** on 14 Adar, the day of celebration after the Jews defeated their enemies. Because Jews in the capital city of **Shushan** fought with their enemies an extra day, **Purim** is celebrated a day later there, on the day known as, **Shushan Purim**. This observance was expanded to **"walled cities"**, which are defined as cities **"walled since the time of Joshua"**. In practice, there are no Jews living in **Shushan** (Shush, Iran), and **Shushan Purim** is observed fully only in Jerusalem. Cities like Safed and Tiberias also partially observe **Shushan Purim**. Elsewhere, **Shushan Purim** is marked only by a small increase in festivity, including a prohibition on fasting, and slight changes in the liturgy.

## Pesach—Passover
- **Erev Pesach and Fast of the Firstborn, ("Ta'anit Bechorot"): 14 Nisan**
- **Pesach (Passover): 15–21 Nisan (outside Israel 15–22 Nisan)**
- **The first day and last day of Passover (outside Israel, first two and last two days) are full *yom tov*, while the remainder of Passover has the status of *Chol Hamoed*, "intermediate days".**
- **Pesach Sheni (second Passover): 14 Iyar**

## Month of Nisan
As a rule, the month of Nisan is considered to be one of extra joy. Traditionally, throughout the entire month, **Tahanun** is omitted from the prayer service, many public mourning practices (such as delivering a eulogy at a funeral) are eliminated, and voluntary fasting is prohibited. However, practices sometimes vary.

## Eve of Passover and Fast of the Firstborn
**The day before Passover (*Erev Pesach*, lit., "Passover eve") is significant for three reasons:**
- It is the day that all of the involved preparations for **Passover**, especially elimination of leavened food, or *chametz*, must be completed. In particular, a formal search for remaining *chametz* is done during the evening of **Erev Pesach**, and all remaining *chametz* is finally destroyed, disposed of or nullified during the morning of Erev **Pesach**.
- It is the day observed as the **Fast of the Firstborn**. Jews who are firstborn fast, in remembrance of the tenth plague, when **God killed the Egyptian firstborn**, while sparing the Jewish firstborn. This fast is overridden by a ***seudat mitzvah***, a meal celebrating the fulfillment of a commandment; accordingly, it is almost universal for firstborn Jews to attend such a meal on this day so as to obviate their need to fast.
- During the era of the Temple in Jerusalem, the ***Korban Pesach***, or sacrifice of the **Paschal Lamb**, was carried out the afternoon of 14 Nisan in anticipation of its consumption on **Passover** night.

When **Passover** starts on Sunday, and the eve of **Passover** is therefore **Shabbat**, the above schedule is altered.

## Passover

**Passover** *(Pesach)*, also known liturgically as *("Ḥag haMatzot"*, the **"Festival of Unleavened Bread")**, is one of the **Three Pilgrimage Festivals (*shalosh regalim*)** mentioned in the **Torah**. **Passover** commemorates the Exodus, the liberation of the Israelite slaves from Egypt. No *chametz* (leavened food) is eaten, or even owned, during the week of **Passover**, in commemoration of the biblical narrative in which the Israelites left Egypt so quickly that their bread did not have enough time to rise. Observant Jews go to great lengths to remove all *chametz* from their homes and offices in the run-up to **Passover**.

Along with the avoidance of *chametz*, the principal ritual unique to this holiday is the **seder**. The *seder*, meaning **"order"**, is an ordered ritual meal eaten on the first night of **Passover**, and outside Israel also on the second night. This meal is known for its distinctive ritual foods—matzo (unleavened bread), maror (bitter herbs), and four cups of wine—as well as its prayer text/handbook/study guide, the **Haggadah**. Participation in a **Passover Seder** is one of the most widely observed Jewish rituals, even among less affiliated or less observant Jews.

**Passover lasts seven days in Israel, and eight days outside Israel**. The holiday of the last day of **Passover** (outside Israel, last two days) commemorates the **Splitting of the Red Sea**; according to tradition this occurred on the seventh day of **Passover**.

## Pesach Sheni

*Pesach Sheni* (**"Second Passover"**) is a day prescribed in the **Torah** to allow those who did not bring the Paschal Lamb offering *(Korban Pesach)* a second chance to do so. Eligibility was limited to those who were distant from Jerusalem on **Passover**, or those who were ritually impure and ineligible to participate in a sacrificial offering.

## Lag Ba'Omer

- **Lag Ba'Omer: 18 Iyar**

*Lag Ba'Omer:* is the 33rd day in the Omer count (is the number 33 in Hebrew). By Ashkenazi practice, the semi-mourning observed during the period of Sefirah is lifted *on* **Lag Ba'Omer, while Sefardi practice is to lift it *at the end of* Lag Ba'Omer.**

**Lag Ba'Omer** is identified as the *Yom Hillula (yahrzeit)* of Rabbi **Shimon bar Yochai**, one of the leading *Tannaim* (teachers quoted in the Mishna) and ascribed author of the core text of Kabbalah, the Zohar. Customary celebrations include bonfires, picnics, and bow and arrow play by children. Boys sometimes receive their first haircuts on **Lag Ba'Omer**, while Hasidic rebbes hold *tishes* in honor of the day.

In Israel, **Lag Ba'Omer** is associated with the **Bar Kokhba revolt** against the Roman Empire. In Zionist thought, the plague that decimated **Rabbi Akiva's** 24,000 disciples is explained as a veiled reference to the revolt; the 33rd day representing the end of the plague is explained as the day of **Bar Kokhba's** victory. The traditional bonfires and bow-and-arrow play were thus reinterpreted as celebrations of military victory. In this vein, the order originally creating the Israel Defense Forces was issued on **Lag Ba'Omer** 1948, 13 days after Israel declared independence.

## Shavuot—Feast of Weeks—Yom Ha Bikurim

- Erev **Shavuot**: 5 Sivan
- **Shavuot**: 6 (and outside Israel: 7) Sivan

*Shavuot* , the Feast of Weeks, is one of the three pilgrimage festivals (*Shalosh regalim*) ordained in the **Torah**. Different from other biblical holidays, the date for **Shavuot** is not explicitly fixed in the **Torah**. Instead, it is observed on the day following the 49th and final day in the counting of the Omer. In the current era of the fixed Jewish calendar, this puts the date of **Shavuot** as 6 Sivan. In Israel and in **Reform Judaism**, it is a one-day holiday; elsewhere, it is a two-day holiday extending through 7 Sivan.

According to Rabbinic tradition, codified in the **Talmud** at **Shabbat** 87b, the **Ten Commandments** were given on this day. In the era of the Temple, there were certain specific offerings mandated for **Shavuot**, and **Shavuot** was the first day for bringing of **Bikkurim** to the Temple. Other than those, there are no explicit *mitzvot* unique to **Shavuot** given in the **Torah** (parallel to matzo on **Passover** or Sukkah on **Sukkot**).

Nevertheless, there are a number of widespread customs observed on **Shavuot**. During this holiday the **Torah** portion containing the **Ten Commandments** is read in the synagogue, and the biblical **Book of Ruth** is read as well. It is traditional to eat dairy meals during **Shavuot**. In observant circles, all night **Torah** study is common on the first night of **Shavuot**, while in Reform Judaism, **Shavuot** is the customary date for **Confirmation ceremonies.**

## Mourning for Jerusalem: Seventeenth of Tammuz and Tisha B'Av

The three-week period starting on 17 Tammuz and concluding after **Tisha B'Av** has traditionally been observed as a period of mourning for the destruction of Jerusalem and the Holy Temple there. The **Mishnah** cites five negative events that happened on 17 Tammuz. This fast is observed like other minor fasts (**Tzom Gedalia** ). When this fast-falls out on **Shabbat**, its observance is postponed until Sunday.

**Orthodox Judaism** continues to maintain the traditional prohibitions. In **Conservative Judaism**, the **Rabbinical Assembly's Committee** on Jewish Law and Standards has issued several **responsa** (legal rulings) which hold that the prohibitions against weddings in this timeframe are deeply held traditions, but should not be construed as binding law. Rabbis within Reform Judaism and Reconstructionist Judaism hold that **halakha** (Jewish law) is no longer binding and follow their individual consciences on such matters.

## Tisha B'Av—Ninth of Av

- **Tisha B'Av: 9 Av**

*Tisha B'Av* is a major fast day and day of mourning. A Midrashic tradition states that the spies' negative report concerning the **Land of Israel** was delivered on **Tisha B'Av**. Consequently, the day became auspicious for negative events in Jewish history. Most notably, both the **First Temple**, originally built by King Solomon, and the **Second Temple** of Roman times were destroyed on **Tisha B'Av**. Other calamities throughout Jewish history are said to have taken place on Tisha B'Av, including **King Edward I's edict** compelling the Jews to leave England (1290) and the **Jewish expulsion from Spain in 1492**.

Tisha B'Av is a major fast. It is a 25-hour fast, running from sundown to nightfall. As on **Yom Kippur**, not only are eating and drinking prohibited, but also bathing, anointing, marital relations and the wearing of leather shoes. The **Book of Lamentations** is read in the synagogue, while in the morning lengthy *kinot*, poems of elegy, are recited. From evening until noon mourning rituals resembling those of **shiva** are observed, including sitting on low stools or the floor; after noon those restrictions are somewhat lightened, in keeping with the tradition that Messiah will be born on **Tisha B'Av.**

## Israeli/Jewish national holidays and days of remembrance

As a general rule, the biblical Jewish holidays (Sabbath, **Rosh Hashanah**, **Yom Kippur**, **Passover**, **Shavuot**, **Sukkot** and **Purim**) are observed as public holidays in Israel. **Chanukah** is a school holiday, but businesses remain open. Between the creation of the State of Israel in 1948 and the aftermath of the **Six-Day War**, the Knesset, generally in consultation with the **Chief Rabbinate** of Israel, established four national holidays or days of remembrance:

- *Yom HaShoah*: Holocaust Remembrance Day
- *Yom Hazikaron*: Memorial Day
- *Yom Ha'atzmaut*: Israel Independence Day
- *Yom Yerushalayim*: Jerusalem Day

The status of these days as *religious* events is not uniform within the Jewish world. Non-Orthodox, Religious Zionist and Modern Orthodox Jewish religious movements accept these days as *religious* as well as *national* in nature.

**More recently, the Knesset established two additional holidays:**
- *Yom HaAliyah*: **Aliyah Day**
- **A day to commemorate the expulsion of Jews from Arab lands and Iran**

## Yom HaShoah—Holocaust Remembrance Day

- **Yom HaShoah: (nominally) 27 Nisan**

*Yom HaShoah* (lit. **"Holocaust Day"**) is a day of remembrance for victims of the Holocaust. Its full name is *Yom Hazikaron LaShoah v'LiGevurah* (lit. **"Holocaust and Heroism Remembrance Day")**, and reflects a desire to recognize martyrs who died in active resistance to the Nazis alongside those who died as passive victims. Its date, 27 Nisan, was chosen because it commemorates the **Warsaw Ghetto uprising**, the best known of the armed Jewish uprisings. Outside Israel, Jewish communities observe **Yom HaShoah** in addition to or instead of their countries' **Holocaust Memorial Days**. Probably the most notable commemoration is the March of the Living, held at the site of **Auschwitz-Birkenau,** attended by Jews from all parts of the world.

## Yom Hazikaron—Memorial Day

- **Yom Hazikaron: (nominally) 4 Iyar**

*Yom Hazikaron* (lit. **"Memorial Day"**) is a day of remembrance of the fallen of Israel's wars. During the first years of Israel's independence, this remembrance was observed on **Yom Ha'atzmaut (Independence Day)** itself. However, by 1951, the memorial observance was separated from the festive celebration of Independence Day and moved to its current date, the day before Yom Ha'atzmaut.

The public observances conclude with the service at the military cemetery on **Mount Herzl** that serves as the transition to **Yom Ha'atzmaut**. Outside Israel, **Yom HaZikaron** observances are often folded into **Yom Ha'atzmaut** celebrations. Within Israel, **Yom Hazikaron** is always the day before **Yom Ha'atzmaut**, but that date moves to prevent violation of Sabbath prohibitions during the ceremonies of either day. See following section for details.

## Yom Ha'atzmaut—Israel Independence Day

- **Yom Ha'atzmaut: (nominally) 5 Iyar**

*Yom Ha'atzmaut* is Israel's **Independence Day**. Observance of this day by Jews inside and outside Israel is widespread, and varies in tone from secular (military parades and barbecues) to religious. Although Israel's independence was declared on a Friday, the Chief Rabbinate has long been mindful of the possibility of **Yom Ha'atzmaut** (and **Yom Hazikaron**) observances leading to violation of Sabbath prohibitions.

## Yom Yerushalayim: Jerusalem Day

- **Yom Yerushalayim: 28 Iyar**

**Jerusalem Day** marks the 1967 reunification of Jerusalem under Israeli control during the **Six-Day War.** This marked the first time in 19 years that the **Temple Mount** was accessible to Jews, and the first time since the destruction of the **Second Temple** 1900 years earlier that the **Temple Mount** was under Jewish political control. As with **Yom Ha'atzmaut**, celebrations of **Yom Yerushalayim** range from completely secular (including hikes to Jerusalem and a large parade through downtown Jerusalem) to religious.

## Yom HaAliyah—Aliyah Day

- **Yom HaAliyah: 10 Nisan**

**Aliyah Day** is an Israeli national holiday celebrated annually on the tenth of Nisan. The day was established to acknowledge Aliyah, immigration to the Jewish state, as a core value of the State of Israel, and honor the ongoing contributions of **Olim** (immigrants) to Israeli society. Immigration to Israel is a recognized religious value of Judaism, sometimes referred to as the **Gathering of Israel**. The date chosen for **Yom HaAliyah**, 10 Nisan, has religious significance: it is the day on which Joshua and the Israelites crossed the **Jordan River** at Gilgal into the Promised Land. It was thus the first documented "**mass Aliyah**". God instructs Abraham to leave his home and his family and go up to the Land of Israel.

## Day to commemorate the expulsion of Jews from Arab lands and Iran

- **Day to Mark the Departure and Expulsion of Jews from the Arab Countries and Iran: 30 November (on the Gregorian calendar)**

The Knesset established this observance in 2014. The purpose of this observance is to recognize the collective trauma of **Mizrahi Jews** during the period around the establishment of the State of Israel. Many **Mizrachi Jews** felt that their own suffering was being ignored, both in comparison to the suffering of European Jewry during the **Holocaust** and in comparison to the **Palestinian Nakba**.

# Jewish life in Arab Countries

**Islamic rules for non-Muslims: Omar's Edict (The 2nd Caliph):**
**People of the Book** must stand in respect to the Muslim. They must turn around and find another road to walk through. They were not permitted to ride horses. They had to ride donkeys. They were required to ride their donkey's side saddle. They were not allowed to build their houses higher than the Muslims houses. Muslims were always supposed to be above the non-Muslims. **A Jewish or Christian man was not permitted to marry a Muslim woman. A Muslim man could marry a Christian or Jewish woman.**

**People of the Book** were not allowed to drink alcohol in front of Muslims. Christians were not allowed to let Muslims see the pigs they were raising. Christians and Jews were not allowed to bury their dead during the daylight where a Muslim might see, they were not allowed to cry for their dead in public. In the synagogues or churches, people were not allowed to raise their voices loud enough to be heard outside the building. **People of the Book** could not celebrate in public. They were not allowed to try to convert Muslims away from Islam. They were prohibited from holding high positions in the Islamic government. They were prohibited from serving in the Islamic military. **The Iraqi Jews are the oldest Jewish community in the world. (My book "Full Circle: Escape from Baghdad and the return", was dubbed "The Schindler's list of the Sephardim").**

Non-Muslims were not allowed to help anyone declare war against Muslims. They were not permitted to carry weapons. They could not testify against a Muslim in court. A Muslim could not be killed because of a Christian or a Jew. **Muhammad** said in Hadith, **"A Muslim believer cannot be killed for an infidel".** They had to wear special clothing and special colors that identified them as non-Muslims. **Christians wore blue; Jews wore yellow**. Christian women had to wear a sash around their waist. Christian and Jewish women had to wear shoes of different colors. In other words, the left shoe had to be a different color than the right shoe. Christians were not permitted to enter any public place without wearing a large cross around their necks.

Leaders among Christians and Jews were responsible for enforcing these rules. **An angry mob of Arabs in Spain killed five thousand Jews because they felt the Jews had too much political power (1066).** Arab mobs killed thousands of Jews throughout Morocco (1465). In the city of Fez, only eleven Jews were alive. Mass murders, destruction of synagogues and forced conversion to Islam. Some of the worst persecution of Jews at the hands of Muslim authorities occurred in Egypt from 996 to 1301. Starting in 1006, the Muslim leader of Egypt gave the Jews and Christians two options: accept Islam or leave Egypt. He went to the Jewish community in Cairo and burned down the entire neighborhood. Next he took all the Jews that were left and banished them to an area south of Cairo.

# A SHORT HISTORY OF THE JEWS OF IRAQ

One can say that the first Jew was an Iraqi Jew. **Abraham** was our first patriarch who was born in Ur, a city in south of Mesopotamia, now called Iraq (1900 B.C.). In 586 BCE, the Babylonian king **Nebuchadnezzar destroyed our first temple** and razed the whole city of Jerusalem to the ground. The Jews were dispersed throughout Persian and Babylonia. In 538 BCE (after 48 years) **Cyrus the Great** of Persia re-conquered the entire area and issued a decree permitting the Jews to return to Jerusalem and rebuild their second Temple.

About 40,000 people returned, led by The **Great Gaon, Ezra the Scribe**. Babylon (Babel) had become the center of Jewish scholarship. Their most influential contribution was the Babylonian **Talmud** (Oral Law), which became a road map for the Jews worldwide. They built many Yeshivas, the most famous being **Sura, Nehadrea**, and **Pumbeditha.**

In the first half of the seventh century ACE, following the death of the prophet **Muhammad in 632 A.D.**, his followers invaded Mesopotamia (Iraq). The Jewish population under Islam was tolerated as "The **People of the Book**", believers in one God. They were designated **Dhimmis**, protected people of special covenant with the Muslims. They were politically second-class citizens and had to pay a special **Poll tax**. **The Ottomans came in 1534**. Life for the Jewish community under the Ottoman Turks was tolerable and hospitable to growth. They welcomed the **Spanish Jews exiled in 1492**, throughout their empire.

**The Turks lost their empire after WWI** and Iraq became part of the **British Empire**. In 1932 the British granted Iraq independence, but remained in Iraq till the late 1950's. The Jews, who numbered about **1.8 million**, were the elite and well-educated. There were prominent doctors, senators, lawyers, and rabbis. The chief was the famous **Hakham Ezra Dangoor**, who opened the first printing company, which was used to print all Hebrew books, as well as Arabic text books.

Everything changed for the worse beginning with WWII, with the rise of Communism, Zionism, Nationalism, and Nazism. **Radio Berlin** started to broadcast poisonous propaganda against the Jews to the Arab world. On **June 1st, 1941**, a pro-Nazi coup d'état occurred against the pro-British government. **May & June 1941 were dark months in the history of the Iraqi Jews**. A horrible pogrom (called **Farhud**) took place where more than two hundred innocent Jews were murdered, women and young girls were raped and Jewish businesses burnt to the ground.

From that day on, the Jews felt no security. Some escaped illegally to Iran. After a relative calm came executions, terror, and firing. The Jews were seen as being supporters of the State of Israel, which had defeated the Iraqi army in the war of independence (1948-49). Jewish life in country for an **"unknown destination"** (the word Israel could never be mentioned). About **120,000 Jews registered to leave**. The government froze all the assets; in one day they became penniless. Israel played an important role in this exodus, called **Operation Ezra** and **Nehemiah** (named after the Prophets of the Babylonian Jews who led them to Israel under the Persians in 539 BCE). Only about six thousand Jews were left in Iraq in 1952. Today no Jews remain in Iraq (zero).

*"By the rivers of Babylon – there we sat and also wept. When we remembered Zion on the willows with it we hung our lyres. For there our captors required words of song from*

*us. Without (playing) joyous (music), "Sing for us from Zion's song! "How can we sing the song of God upon alien soil?" If I forget you, O Jerusalem, let my right hand forget its skill. Let my tongue adhere to my palate if I fail to recall you, if I fail to elevate Jerusalem above my foremost joy".*

Prospects for peace between Israel and the Palestinians are most unlikely in the immediate future. Neither **Natanyahu** nor **Abbas** are capable of signing a peace agreement without fearing assassination. (Remember **Sadat** and **Rabin**). It is left to future generations; resulting in a peaceful **Palestinian State**.

Jerusalem is the greatest obstacle to peace between Israel and the Palestinians: It is the Capital of the State of Israel since 1948 (Actually going back to **King David**, 3,000 years ago), but, because of **Al-Aqsa Mosque**, the 3<sup>rd</sup> holiest place in Islam (situated on top of the Temple Mount), the Palestinians insist on naming Jerusalem their capital.

# The Jewish–Roman Wars

The **Jewish–Roman wars** were a series of large-scale revolts by the Jews of the Eastern Mediterranean against the Roman Empire **between 66 and 135 CE**. While the **First Jewish–Roman War (66–73 CE)** and the **Bar Kokhba revolt (132–136 CE)** were nationalist rebellions, striving to restore an independent Judean state, the Kitos War was more of an ethno-religious conflict, mostly fought outside Judea Province. Hence, some sources use the term Jewish-Roman Wars to refer only to the **First Jewish–Roman War (66–73 CE)** and the **Bar Kokhba revolt (132–135 CE), while others include the Kitos War (115–117 CE) as one of the Jewish–Roman wars.**

The Jewish–Roman wars had a dramatic impact on the Jewish people, turning them from a major population in the Eastern Mediterranean into a scattered and persecuted minority. The Jewish–Roman wars are often cited as a disaster to Jewish society. The events also had a major impact on Judaism, after the central worship site of **Second Temple Judaism, the Second Temple in Jerusalem, was destroyed by Titus' troops.** Although having a sort of autonomy in Galilee until the 4th century and later a limited success in establishing the short-lived **Sasanian Jewish autonomy in Jerusalem in 614–617 CE, Jewish dominance in parts of the Southern Levant was regained only in the mid-20th century, with the founding of the modern state of Israel in 1948 CE.**

## Background / *Jacob and Simon uprising and Alexandria pogroms*

Following increasing Roman domination of the Eastern Mediterranean, the client kingdom of the **Herodian Dynasty** had been officially merged into the **Roman Empire** in the year 6 CE with the creation of the Roman province of Judea. The transition of the **Tetrarchy of Judea** into a Roman province immediately brought a great deal of tensions and a Jewish uprising by Judas of Galilee erupted right away as a response to the **Census of Quirinius.**

Although initially pacified (the years between 7 and 26 CE being relatively quiet), the province continued to be a source of trouble under **Emperor Caligula** (after 37 CE). The cause of tensions in the east of the Empire was complicated, involving the spread of Greek culture, Roman law, and the rights of Jews in the Empire. **Caligula** did not trust the prefect of Roman Egypt, **Aulus Avilius Flaccus.** Flaccus had been loyal to **Tiberius**, had conspired against **Caligula**'s mother and had connections with Egyptian separatists. In 38 CE, **Caligula** sent **Agrippa** to Alexandria unannounced to check on **Flaccus**. According to **Philo**, the visit was met with jeers from the Greek population, who saw **Agrippa as the king of the Jews.**

**Flaccus** tried to placate both the Greek population and **Caligula** by having statues of the emperor placed in Jewish synagogues. As a result, extensive religious riots broke out in the city. **Caligula** responded by removing **Flaccus** from his position and executing him. In 39 CE, Agrippa accused **Herod Antipas**, the tetrarch of Galilee and Perea, of planning a rebellion against Roman rule with the help of Parthia. **Herod Antipas confessed and Caligula exiled him. Agrippa was rewarded with his territories.**

Riots again erupted in Alexandria in 40 CE between Jews and Greeks. Jews were accused of not honoring the emperor. Disputes occurred also in the city of Jamnia. Jews were angered by the erection of a clay altar and destroyed it. In response, **Caligula** ordered the erection of a statue of himself in the **Temple of Jerusalem**, a demand in conflict with Jewish monotheism. In this context, **Philo** wrote that **Caligula "regarded the Jews with most especial suspicion, as if they were the only persons who cherished wishes opposed to his".**

The governor of Roman Syria, **Publius Petronius**, fearing civil war if the order were carried out, delayed implementing it for nearly a year. **Agrippa** finally convinced **Caligula** to reverse the order. However, only **Caligula**'s death at the hands of Roman conspirators in 41 CE prevented a full-scale war in Judaea, that might have well spread to the entire Eastern Roman Empire.

**Caligula**'s death did not stop the tensions completely and in 46 CE an insurrection led by two brothers, the Jacob and Simon uprising, broke out in Judea province. The revolt, mainly in the Galilee, began as sporadic insurgency; when it climaxed in 48 CE it was quickly put down by Roman authorities. **Both Simon and Jacob were executed**.

### Sequence / The Jewish–Roman wars include the following:
- **First Jewish–Roman War (66–73 CE)** — also called the First Jewish Revolt or the Great Jewish Revolt, spanning from the 66 CE insurrection, through the 67 CE fall of the Galilee, the destruction of Jerusalem and the **Second Temple** and institution of the Fiscus Judaicus in 70 CE, and finally the fall of Masada in 73 CE.
- **Kitos War (115–117 CE)** — known as the "**Rebellion of the Exile**" and sometimes called the Second Jewish–Roman War.
- **Bar Kokhba revolt (132–136 CE)** — also called the Second Jewish–Roman War (when Kitos War is not counted), or the Third (when the Kitos War is counted).

## History / First Jewish–Roman War

The **First Jewish–Roman War** began in the year 66 CE, originating in the Greek and Jewish religious tensions, and later escalated due to anti-taxation protests and attacks upon Roman citizens. In response to the Roman **plunder of the Second Jewish Temple and the execution of up to 6,000 Jews in Jerusalem,** a full-scale rebellion erupted. The Roman military garrison of Judaea was quickly overrun by rebels, while the pro-Roman **king Agrippa II** together with Roman officials fled Jerusalem.

As it became clear the rebellion was getting out of control, **Cestius Gallus**, the legate of Syria, brought the Syrian army, based on **XII Fulminata** and reinforced by auxiliary troops, to restore order and quell the revolt. Despite initial advances, the **Syrian Legion** was ambushed and defeated by Jewish rebels at the **Battle of Beth Horon with 6,000 Romans massacred** and the *Legio Aquila* lost – a result that shocked the Roman leadership. The experienced and unassuming general **Vespasian** was then tasked with crushing the rebellion in Judaea province. His son **Titus** was appointed second-in-command. **Vespasian** was given four legions and assisted by forces of **King Agrippa II**. In 67 CE he invaded Galilee.

While avoiding a direct attack on the reinforced city of Jerusalem which was packed with the main rebel force, Titus' forces launched a persistent campaign to eradicate rebel strongholds and punish the population.

Within several months **Vespasian** and **Titus** took over the major Jewish strongholds of Galilee and finally overran Jotapata under command of **Yosef ben Mattitiyahu,** following a **47-day siege**. Meantime in Jerusalem, an attempt by Sicarii leader **Menahem** to take control of the city failed, resulting in his execution. A peasant leader **Simon Bar-Giora** was ousted from the city by the new moderate Judean government and **Ananus ben Ananus** began reinforcing the city. Driven from Galilee, **Zealot rebels** and thousands of refugees arrived in Judea, creating political turmoil in Jerusalem. Zealots were at first sealed in the Temple compound.

However, confrontation between the mainly **Sadducee Jerusalemites** and the mainly Zealot factions of the Northern Revolt under the command of **John of Giscala** and **Eleazar ben Simon** became evident. With Edomites entering the city and fighting on the side of the Zealots, **Ananus ben Ananus** was killed and his forces suffered severe casualties. **Simon Bar Giora**, commanding 15,000 troops, was then invited into Jerusalem by the Sadducee leaders to stand against the Zealots, and quickly took control over much of the city. Bitter infighting between factions of **Bar Giora, John and Elazar** followed through the year 69 CE.

After a lull in the military operations, owing to civil war and political turmoil in Rome, **Vespasian** returned to Rome and was accepted as the new **Emperor** in 69 CE. With **Vespasian's** departure, Titus besieged the center of rebel resistance in Jerusalem in early 70 CE. While the first two walls of Jerusalem were breached within three weeks, a stubborn stand prevented the Roman Army from breaking the third and thickest wall.

Following a brutal **seven-month siege**, in which Zealot infighting resulted in the burning of the entire food supply of the city to enhance **"fighting to the end",** the Romans finally succeeded in breaching the weakened Jewish forces in the summer of 70 CE. Following the fall of Jerusalem, **Titus** left for Rome, while **Legion X** *Fretensis* **defeated the remaining Jewish strongholds later on, finalizing the Roman campaign in Masada in 73/74 CE.**

## Kitos War

The Kitos War (115–117 CE) also known as *mered ha'galuyot* or *mered ha'tfutzot* (Rebellion of the exile) is the name given to the second of the **Jewish–Roman wars**. The **Kitos War** consisted of major revolts by diasporic Jews in Cyrene (Cyrenaica), Cyprus, Mesopotamia and Aegyptus, which spiraled out of control, resulting in a widespread slaughter of Roman citizens and others (200,000 in Cyrene, 240,000 in Cyprus according to **Cassius Dio**) by the Jewish rebels. The rebellions were finally crushed by Roman legionary forces, chiefly by the Roman general **Lusius Quietus,** whose nomen later gave the conflict its title, as **"Kitos"** is a later corruption of **Quietus**.

## Bar Kokhba Revolt

The **Bar Kokhba revolt (132–136 CE),** (Hebrew:  or *mered bar Kokhba*), was the third major rebellion by the Jews of Judaea Province and Eastern Mediterranean against the Roman Empire and the last of the **Jewish–Roman wars. Simon bar Kokhba, the commander of the revolt, was acclaimed as a Messiah**, a heroic figure who could restore Israel. The revolt established an independent state of Israel over parts of Judea for more than two years, but a Roman army made up of six full legions with auxiliaries and elements from up to six additional legions finally crushed it.

**The Romans then barred Jews from Jerusalem, except to attend Tisha B'Av.** Although Jewish Christians hailed Jesus as the **Messiah** and did not support **Bar Kokhba**, they were barred from Jerusalem along with the rest of the Jews. The war and its aftermath helped differentiate Christianity as a religion distinct from Judaism (see also Split of early Christianity and Judaism). The rebellion is also known as **The Third Jewish–Roman War or The Third Jewish Revolt,** though some historians relate it as **Second Jewish Revolt,** not counting the **Kitos War, 115–117 CE.**

## Aftermath

Due to the **First Jewish-Roman War**, the destruction of the **Second Temple** ushered in a major time of dramatic reformation in religious leadership, causing the face of Judaism to change. The **Second Temple** served as the centralized location from which the ruling groups **Sadducees** and the **Pharisees** maintained Judaism, with rivaling Essenes and Zealots being largely in opposition. With the destruction of the temple, the major ruling group lost their power - the Sadducees, who were the priests, directly lost their localized power source and were rendered obsolete.

Due to this, only one group was left with all the power - the **Pharisees**, who were the rabbinic group. The rabbinic groups' power did not derive from the temple or from military prowess, which enabled their power to spread among synagogues to different communities. This changed the way Judaism was practiced on a daily basis, which included changing from sacrificing animals to praying in order to worship God. **Rabbinic Judaism** became a religion centered  around synagogues, and the Jews themselves dispersed throughout the Roman world and beyond.

With the **destruction of Jerusalem**, important centers of Jewish culture developed in the area of Galilee and in Babylonia and work on the Talmud continued in these locations. Before **Vespasian's** departure, the Pharisaic sage and **Rabbi Yohanan ben Zakkai** obtained his permission to establish a Judaic school at Yavne. **Zakkai** was smuggled away from Jerusalem in a coffin by his students. **This school later became a major center of Talmudic study (see Mishnah).**

**Hadrian (emperor 117-138 CE) attempted to completely root out Judaism**, which he saw as the cause of continuous rebellions. He prohibited the **Torah** and the Hebrew calendar and executed Judaic scholars. **The sacred scroll was ceremonially burned on the Temple Mount. At the former Temple sanctuary he installed two statues, one of Jupiter, another of himself.** In an attempt to erase any memory of Judea or Ancient Israel, he wiped the name off the map and replaced it with **Syria Palaestina**, supplanting earlier terms, such as Judaea. Similarly, he re-established Jerusalem, this time as the Roman polis of **Aelia Capitolina**, and **Jews were barred from entering the city, except on the fast day of Tisha B'Av.**

The **Jewish–Roman wars** had a dramatic impact on the Jews, turning them from a major population in the Eastern Mediterranean into a scattered and persecuted minority. The Jewish–Roman wars are often cited as a disaster to Jewish society. The defeat of the Jewish revolts altered the Jewish population and enhanced the importance of Jewish diaspora, essentially moving the demographic center of Jews from Judea to Galilee and Babylon, with minor communities across the Mediterranean.

Although having a sort of autonomy in the Galilee until the 4th century and later a limited success in establishing the short-lived **Sasanian** Jewish autonomy in Jerusalem in 614–617 CE, Jewish dominance in parts of the **Southern Levant** was regained only in the mid-20th century, with **the founding of the modern state of Israel in 1948 CE.**

# Jews and Monotheism

**In 586 B.C.E., King Nebuchadnezzar II**, ruler of the might **Babylonian Empire** and earthly agent of the **High God Marduk – king of the gods** – broke through the walls of Jerusalem, sacked the capital of the kingdom of Israel, and **burned the Jewish temple to the ground**. Thousands of Jews were put to the sword; the few who survived – especially the educated elite, the priests, the military, and the royals – were sent into exile in a transparent attempt to put an end to Israel as a nation. **And if Israel no longer existed, then neither did its god, Yahweh.**

In fact, warfare in the **Ancient Near East** was considered less a battle of armies than a contest between gods. The Babylonians conquered Israel not in the name of **Nebuchadnezzar**, their king, but in the name of **Marduk**, their god. The Israelites had the same agreement with their god. It was **Yahweh** who ruled Israel, and thus **Yahweh** whose task it was to defend it. Indeed, **Yahweh** was often charged with planning, commanding, and executing those battles on Israel's behalf.

**"David inquired of Yahweh, "Shall I go up against the Philistines? Will you give them into my hand?' Yahweh said to David . . . 'You shall not go up; go around to their rear and come upon them opposite the balsam trees'" (2 Samuel 5:19-23).** When **Yahweh** helped the Israelites crush the Philistines, it proved that the Israelite god was more powerful than the **Philistine god, Dagon**. But when the Babylonians destroyed the Israelites, the theological conclusion was that Marduk, the god of Babylon, was more powerful than **Yahweh**.

For a great many Israelites, the destruction of their temple – the **House of Yahweh** – signaled more than the end of their national ambitions. It meant the end of their religion. They had no choice but to surrender to the new reality. They adopted Babylonian names, studied Babylonian scriptures, and began worshipping Babylonian gods. Perhaps Israel's destruction and exile were part of **Yahweh**'s divine plan all along. Perhaps **Yahweh** was punishing the Israelites for believing in Marduk in the first place. *Perhaps there was no Marduk.*

The GOD who would come to be known as **Yahweh** made his first appearance in the form of a **burning bush**. **"This is my name forever,"** Yahweh tells the prophet **Moses, "and this is how I will be remembered from generation to generation" (Exodus 3:15).** The Israelites who, a few generations earlier, had followed the descendants of the patriarch **Abraham** into the land of Egypt, had grown so numerous and powerful that they were stripped of their wealth and freedom and forced into slavery. So, feared were they in Egypt that the **pharaoh himself commanded that every newborn Israelite son be drowned in the Nile.**

Yet somehow this one child was spared. His parents, descendants of **Levite priests**, placed him in a papyrus basket when he was only three months old and sent it floating among the reeds on the riverbank. The pharaoh's daughter found him there. She took pity on the boy, brought him into her house, and raised him as **Egyptian royalty**.

One day, after he was grown, **Moses** went out among the people and witnessed for himself the crushing labor enforced upon the Israelites. He saw an Egyptian master beating an Israelite slave and, in a fit of rage, he **killed the Egyptian**. Fearing for his life, **Moses** fled Egypt for what the Bible calls **"the land of Midian."**

There he met a "**priest of Midian**," who welcomed him into his home and tribe, **giving him his own daughter**, **Zipporah**, **in marriage**. Late one afternoon, as he was tending his father-in-law's flock, **Moses** herded them beyond the wilderness, to the foot of a sacred Midianite place known as "**the mountain of god**." It was there that he came across the mysterious deity who introduced himself as **Yahweh.**

In the **book of Exodus**, it seems clear that the location of "**the mountain of god**" is in northeastern Sinai. But in **Deuteronomy** and elsewhere in the Bible, the mountain where **Moses** meets **Yahweh** is located **near Seir, in southern Transjordan.** The Midianites were a loose federation of non-Semitic, desert-dwelling people whose homeland was I northwestern Arabia – not in the Sinai Peninsula, nor near Transjordan. **Moses's father-in-law is named Reuel in Exodus 2:18, and Jethro just a few verses later (Exodus 3:1).**

The problem is that **no archaeological evidence has ever been unearthed to indicate the presence of Israelites in ancient Egypt**. The Egyptians regularly employed slave labor, the role and social status of a slave fell into one of three categories: slaves who had been captured in war, slaves who had sold themselves into slavery in order to pay a debt, and slaves who were, like indentured servants, duty bound to the state for a set period of time. The Israelites fit into none of these categories. **The Egyptians were, at the time, the largest, wealthiest, most militarily potent empire the world had ever known (Exodus 1:9-10).**

**Yahweh's origins are an enigma**. The name does not appear in any of the god lists of the **Ancient Near East,** an extraordinary omission considering the thousands of deities included in these lists. There are, however, two hieroglyphic references to **Yahweh** in **Nubia dating to the New Kingdom** period – one at the temple **built by Akhenaten's father, Amenhotep III, in the fourteenth century B.C.E.,** the other at a temple **built by Rameses II** in the thirteenth century B.C.E. – that mention something called **"the land of the nomads of Yahweh."**

So then, **Moses**, who had married into a Midianite tribe, came across a **Midianite deity (Yahweh)** while under the employ of a Midianite priest (his father-in-law) in the land of Midian. But the story doesn't end there. Because the first task that this Midianite god gives to **Moses** is to return to Egypt, free the Israelite slaves from bondage, and shepherd them back to their home in the **Land of Canaan: "Thus will you say to the children of Israel, 'Yahweh, the god of your fathers, the god of Abraham, the god of Isaac, and the god of Jacob, has sent me to you'" (Exodus 3:15).**

This claim would have come as something of a surprise to **Abraham, Isaac, and Jacob. These biblical patriarchs did not worship a Midianite desert deity called Yahweh. They worshipped an altogether different god – a Canaanite deity they knew as** *El*. The Pentateuch – the first five books of the Bible (**Genesis, Exodus, Leviticus, Numbers, and Deuteronomy**) – is actually a composite work stitched together from various sources spanning a period of hundreds of years. There are, for instance, two separate creation stories written by two different hands: **Genesis chapter 1, in which man and woman are created together and simultaneously, and Genesis chapter 2, the much more popular Adam and Eve story, in which Eve is made from Adam's rib.**

There are also two different flood narratives, conflicting account in which **the flood lasts either forty days (Genesis 7:17) or one hundred fifty days (Genesis 7:24);** the animals are brought aboard the **Ark** in either seven pairs of male and female (**Genesis 7:2**) or just one pair of every kind (**Genesis 6:19**); and the flood begins either seven days after Noah enters the **Ark** (**Genesis 7:10**) or immediately after he boards with his kin **(Genesis 7:11-13).**

Biblical scholars have managed to identify at least four different written sources that make up the bulk of the early books in the Bible. These are named the *Yahwist, or J, source* (*j* is pronounced as *y* in German), which dates to the tenth or ninth century B.C.E. and runs through large parts of Genesis, Exodus, and Numbers; the *Elohist*, or E, source, which dates to the eighth or seventh century B.C.E. and is mostly confined to Genesis and parts of Exodus; the *Priestly*, or P, source, which was written either during or immediately after the **Babylonian Exile in 586 B.C.E.** and is primarily a reworking of the J and E material; and finally, the *Deuteronomist,* or D, source, which runs from the book of Deuteronomy through **First and Second Kings** and can be dated to somewhere between the seventh and fifth centuries B.C.E.

The **Elohist** material, which was probably written by a priest from northern Israel, refers to Mount Sinai as Mount Horeb (**Exodus 3:1**) and calls the Canaanites "Amorites", which often portray God in uncannily anthropomorphic ways: He creates the world through trial and error, forgetting to craft a mate for Adam (**Genesis 2:18**); he strolls through the Garden of Eden, enjoying the evening breeze (**Genesis 3:8**); and at one point, he loses track of his creation, **Adam and Eve, unable to find them when they hide among the trees. "Where are you?" Yahweh shouts into the night air (Genesis 3:9).**

However, the primary difference between the **Yahwist** and **Elohist** sources in the Pentateuch is that God is called by a different name in each. **The god of the Elohist is *El* or *Elohim*** (the plural form of **El**). **"After these things, God [Elohim] tested Abraham" (Genesis 22:1).** In contrast, the god of the Yahwist tradition is known as *Yahweh*, usually rendered in English Bibles as the *Lord,* spelled with all capital letters: **"The LORD [Yahweh] said, 'Surely I have seen the misery of my people who are in Egypt'" (Exodus 3:7).**

Although the **Yahwist material is about a hundred years older than the Elohist**, the Elohist tradition represents the older deity. In fact, while we know next to nothing about the origins of **Yahweh** save that he was likely a Midianite god, **El** is one of the best-known and most well-documented deities in the **Ancient Near East.**

**El was the High God of Canaan**. Known as the **Creator of Created Things** and the Ancient of Days**,** El also functioned as one of Canaan's chief fertility gods. Seated on his heavenly throne, **El** presided over a divine council of Canaanite gods that included **Asherah, the Mother Goddess and El's consort**; **Baal,** the young storm god known as the **Rider of the Clouds**; **Anat**, the warrior deity; **Astarte**, also called **Ishtar**; and a host of other, lower deities. **El was also unquestionably the original god of Israel.** Indeed, the very word *Israel* means **"El perseveres."**

The early Israelites worshipped **El** by many names – **El Shaddai, or El of the Mountains (Genesis 17:1); El Olam, or El Everlasting (Genesis 21:33); El Roy, or El Who Sees (Genesis**

16:13); and **El Elyon**, or **El Most High (Genesis 14:18-24)**, to name a few. The influence of Canaanite theology runs deep in the Bible, in the early history of Israel **(c. 1200-1000 B.C.E.).**

**There was no single group called the Canaanites**; (the southern Levant, comprising parts of modern-day Syria, Lebanon, Jordan, and Israel-Palestine). Many scholars now believe that the Israelites were of Canaanite stock. Both groups were comprised of West Semitic peoples who spoke a similar language, shared a similar script, and held in common similar rites and rituals, leading to **dozens of Canaanite loan words in the Hebrew language**, most of them pertaining to religious matters. And, of course, they shared the same god: **El.**

**By no stretch of the imagination could the early Israelites be considered monotheistic.** At best, they practiced *monolatry,* meaning they worshipped one god. **El**, without necessarily denying the existence of the other gods in the Canaanite pantheon, especially **Baal and Asherah** and, to a lesser degree, **Anat. King Saul**, the first king of Israel, even named two of his sons after the god **Baal – Eshbaal and Meribbaal** – alongside the son he named after **Yahweh**: *Yehonatan*, **or Jonathan**.

The early Israelites likely viewed their god **El** pretty much the same way the Canaanites viewed **El**: as the chief deity presiding over a divine assembly of lower deities, just as **Enlil, or Amun-Re, or Marduk, or Zeus**, or any other High God would. But their allegiance was to the god after whom they were named: **El.**

It was this same **El** with whom the patriarch Abraham, who lived most of his life in the land of Canaan and who was steeped in Canaanite culture and religion (if not a Canaanite himself), made a covenant in exchange for a promise of fertility – which was, after all, one of **El**'s primary functions: **"I am *El Shaddai*; walk before me, and be blameless. . . I will make you exceedingly fruitful; and I will make nations of you and kings shall come from you" (Genesis 17:1, 6).**

It was **El** who asked **Abraham** to sacrifice his son, Isaac, as a test of his loyalty and faith; **El** who renewed the covenant with Isaac's son, Jacob: **"You will no longer be called Jacob, rather your name will be Israel" (Genesis 35:10).** And it was in the name of this same **El** – the **"El of your father" (Genesis 49:25)** – that Jacob passed the covenant on to his own son, Joseph, where generations later his descendants would come into contact with a hitherto unknown Midianite god who called himself **Yahweh. The god of Abraham, El, and the god of Moses, Yahweh, gradually merged** to become the sole, singular deity that we now know as God.

After that first encounter with **Yahweh** in the desert, **Moses** returned to Egypt with a message for the Israelites: The god of their forefathers – of Abraham, Isaac, Jacob, and Joseph – had heard their cry and would soon liberate them from bondage. They continued to exhibit little loyalty to this unknown god. As **Moses** stood atop **"the mountain of god"** to receive a new covenant from **Yahweh (the Ten Commandments),** meant to supplant Abraham's covenant with **El**, the Israelites down below had already reverted to the worship of Abraham's god, fashioning for themselves an idol in the shape of a **golden calf – the primary symbol of El.**

**"I am Yahweh. I appeared to Abraham, Isaac, and Jacob as *El Shaddai*, but by my name Yahweh I did not make myself known to them" (Exodus 6:2-3).** In the northern regions of

Canaan, the Israelites who had been living in the land for generations worshipped **El** as their High God while also acknowledging, and on occasion worshipping, the other gods of Canaan. We can catch a glimpse of this gradual process in the so-called **Song of Moses in the book of Deuteronomy:**

> *When Elyon gave the nations their inheritance,*
> *When he separated the sons of man,*
> *He fixed the borders of the people in accordance with the*
> *Number of the gods;*
> *Yahweh's own portion was his people.*
> *DEUTERONOMY 32:8-9*

This extraordinary passage not only affirms Israel's recognition of other gods under **El**'s rule, it clearly casts **Yahweh** as one of those gods, that **Yahweh**'s gift was the nation of Israel. When the nation of Israel became the kingdom of Israel around **1050 B.C.E.**, the merging of **Yahweh** and **El** was reinforced. Even their names were occasionally fused together as *Yahweh-El* or *Yahweh-Elohim*. **"My son, give glory to the *Lord God* [Yahweh-Elohim] of Israel; give thanks to him and tell me what you have done" (Joshua 7:19).**

And as happened in Babylon, Assyria, Egypt, and elsewhere, as the nature of the rule of men on earth changed, so, too, did the rule of the gods in heaven to match; in other words, **Politicomorphism**. Thus, the desert deity worshipped by nomads in the Sinai was elevated to the top of the Israelite pantheon as king of heaven and ruler of all other gods. **"Yahweh has established his throne in the heavens and his kingdom rules over all" (Psalms 103:19).**

**Yahweh essentially became the patron god of the Israelite kings.** A temple was built in Jerusalem, and the new national god was placed there in the form of the **Ark of the Covenant** – **Moses**'s covenant, that is. As with Marduk, Ashur, Amun-Re, and all the other **High Gods**, the higher **Yahweh** ascended in Israel's pantheon, the more he absorbed the qualities and attributes of the other gods.

> *Let the heavens praise your wonders, O Yahweh,*
> *and your faithfulness in the assembly of the holy ones.*
> *Who in the sky can be compared to Yahweh?*
> *Who among the sons of god is like Yahweh,*
> *A god feared in the council of the holy ones,*
> *Greater and more fearful than any of those who surround him?*
> *PSALMS 89:5-7; SEE ALSO PSALMS 82, 97, AND 99*

**Yahweh** began to embody the imagery of the **storm god Baal**, the Rider of the Clouds, becoming **"the one who makes the clouds his chariot, the one who rides upon the wings of the wind" (Psalms 104:3).** "You rule over the raging sea," the Psalmist sings; **"when its waves rise, you still them" (Psalms 89:9).**

**Yahweh even took on the female traits of the goddess Asherah, particularly her maternal, nurturing characteristics, as when Yahweh cries out like a woman giving birth" (Isaiah**

42:14). "Listen to me house of Jacob and all of the remnants of the house of Israel," Yahweh says, "those who have been born from my belly, those who were carried in my womb? (Isaiah 46:3).

**The Israelites did not deny the existence of other deities**. The monarchy itself neither discouraged nor encouraged the worship of other gods; they merely focused their worship on their own national god. **"Who is like you, Yahweh, among the gods? Who is like you, glorious in holiness, awesome doer of deeds, worker of wonders? (Exodus 15:11).**

Again, this is not monotheism. **The Israelites had a difficult time envisioning Yahweh as the sole god in the universe. They thought Yahweh was merely the *best* god in the universe. "For you, Yahweh, are most high over all the earth; you are greatly exalted over all the gods"** (Psalms 97:9). They viewed **Yahweh** as king and ruler over the other gods: the *highest* god, the *strongest* god – the *god of gods*. **"Thus, says Yahweh, the King of Israel and its redeemer . . . 'I am the first and the last; *besides me there are no gods*'"** (Isaiah 44:6).

The introduction of monotheism among the Jews was, in other words, a means of rationalizing Israel's catastrophic defeat at the hands of the Babylonians. The cognitive dissonance created by the Exile required a dramatic, hitherto unworkable religious framework to make sense of the experience. It was better to devise a single vengeful god full of contradictions than to give up that god and thus their very identity as a people. **"I am Yahweh, and there is no other. I form light and create darkness, I make peace and create evil. I, Yahweh, am the maker of all these things"** (Isaiah 45:6-7).

The very testament of faith in Judaism, known as the **Shema ("Hear O Israel, Yahweh is our god, Yahweh is *one*"),** was composed after this transformational moment in Israelite history, as was most of what we know today as the **Hebrew Bible, or Old Testament**.

The God that ultimately arises from the **Babylonian Exile** is not the abstract deity that Akhenaten had worshipped. It is not the pure animating spirit that Zarathustra imagined. It is not the formless substance of the universe written about by Greek philosophers. **This was a new kind of God, both singular and personal**. A solitary God with no human form who nevertheless made humans in his image. **An eternal, indivisible God who exhibits the full range of human emotions and qualities, good and bad.**

# Jews, as enemies of Islam (Qur'an)

"You will surely find that the people with the most enmity towards the believers are the Jews and the polytheists." (**Qur'an 5:82**).

- "Fight against those to whom the Scriptures were given, who believe not in Allah nor in the Last Day, who forbid not what Allah and His apostle have forbidden, and follow not the true faith, until they pay the tribute out of hand and are humbled! (**Qur'an 9:29**).

- "O you who believe! Take not the Jews and the Christians as friends. They are friends to one another. Whoever of you befriends them is one of them. Allah does not guide the people who do evil." (**Qur'an 5:51**).

- The Quran says that Jews love the present life of this world and do not care about things of eternity. "And verily, you will find the Jews the greediest of mankind for life" (**Qur'an 2:96**).

- Allah would bless Jews and Christians who practiced the teachings of their holy books, "Verily, we did send down the Taurat to Musa. (Qur'an **5:44, 46-47**).

-"And whoever seeks a religion other than Islam, it will never be accepted of Him, and in the hereafter he will be one of the losers". (**Qur'an 3:85**).

- "O you who believe! Take not as friends the people who incurred the wrath of Allah. Surely, they have despaired of the hereafter. (**Qur'an 60:13**).

- The earlier revelation said that the Jews were Allah's chosen people (**Qur'an 2:47**).

-Allah transformed Jews into monkeys and pigs as punishment for their wrong doing. "We said to them, "Be you monkeys, despised and rejected". (**Qur'an 7:166, 2:65**).

- "O Muhammad, never will the Jews nor the Christians be pleased with you till you follow their religion". (**Qur'an 2:120**).

- The Quran says that Jews start wars and cause trouble on earth. "Every time they kindled the fire of war, Allah extinguished it, …and they ever strive to make mischief on the earth"
(**Qur'an 5:64, 5-67**).

- Previously, Muhammad instructed his followers to face Jerusalem to pray. In January 624 he changed direction to face Mecca. "Turn your face in the direction of al Masjid al-Haram that is indeed the truth from your Lord". (**Qur'an 2:149**).

- The Quran says that Allah and Allah's people will curse the Jews until Judgment Day.
(**Qur'an 2:159**).

- Muhammad told the horrible fate of "those (Jews) who incurred the curse of Allah and His wrath, and those of whom He transformed into monkeys and swine." (**Qur'an 5:60**). As his armies approached the fortifications of the Qurayzah, Muhammad addressed them "You brothers of monkeys, has God disgraced you and brought his vengeance upon you?"

-The Qur'an says that Allah transformed the Sabbath-breaking Jews into pigs and monkeys. Has been sent to Banu Qurayza to shake their castles and strike terror to their hearts. The Muslims laid siege to the Qurayzah strongholds for 25 days. (**Qur'an 2-62, 5-59-60**).

- The Qur'an' explicitly denounced the Jews (**Qur'an 5:64**).

- Muhammad: "The last hour would not come unless the Muslims will fight against the Jews and the Muslims would kill them until the Jews would hide themselves behind a stone or a tree."

- "Patience, patience all ye Jews: Muhammad's military is on their way back to you."

- Muhammad: "O ye who believe! Take not the Jews and the Christians for your friends and protectors. They are but friends and protectors to each other."

- Muhammad, to the Jews of Banu Nadir, after the Battle of Uhud: "Leave my country and do not live with me. You have intended treachery."

- The remaining Jews of Medina were next to receive the wrath of Muhammad. The massacre of the Jewish Qurayzah tribe. The abuse of the women of the Mustaliq tribe.

- The Qaynuqa Jews replied with disdain, infuriating the Prophet. Muhammad's forces laid siege to the Qaynuqa until they offered him unconditional surrender. Muhammad wanted to have all the men of the tribe put to death.

- Muhammad: "O you brothers of apes, has Allah shamed you and brought down His vengeance upon you?"

- The men of Qurayza were beheaded in the central marketplace of medina, and their bodies thrown into large open trenches. Between 600 and 900 men were slain. Only two or three saved their lives through conversion.

- The Quran: "The hour had drawn near." So until the day of resurrection comes, committed Muslims are fighting an "unfinished battle" against the Jews.

- "By God, we will offer them only the sword, until God judges between us and them".

- The second choice was to kill their wives and children, "leaving no encumbrances behind us". -
"He then killed their men and distributed their women, children and property among the Muslims. He exiled all the remaining Jews from Medina."

- Safiyya bint Huyayy (Jewish): Was the daughter of Huyayy bin Akhtab, who had induced the Banu Quraysh Jews to repudiate their alliance with Muhammad. Muhammad had killed Huyayy along with the rest of the men of the Qurayzah. Safiyya's husband was Kinana ibn Rabi, who had just been tortured and killed by the warriors of jihad. She was a stunning beauty: "We have not seen the like of her among the captives of war."

- Muhammad: "Take any slave girl other than her from the captives." Muhammad then freed her and married her himself, since she agreed to convert to Islam.

# Kabbalah & Zohar

The **Zohar** (Hebrew: lit. *Splendor* or *Radiance*) is the foundational work in the literature of Jewish mystical thought known as **Kabbalah**. It is a group of books including commentary on the mystical aspects of the **Torah (the five books of Moses)** and scriptural interpretations as well as material on mysticism, mythical cosmogony, and mystical psychology.

The **Zohar** contains a discussion of the nature of God, the origin and structure of the universe, the nature of souls, redemption, the relationship of **Ego** to **Darkness** and **"true self"** to **"The Light of God"**, and the relationship between the **"universal energy"** and man. Its scriptural exegesis can be considered an esoteric form of the Rabbinic literature known as **Midrash**, which elaborates on the **Torah**.

The **Zohar** is mostly written in what has been described as an exalted, eccentric style of **Aramaic**. Aramaic was the day-to-day language of Israel in the **Second Temple period (539 BCE – 70 CE)**, was the original language of large sections of the biblical books of **Daniel** and **Ezra**, and is the main language of the **Talmud. The Zohar first appeared in Spain in the 13th century,** and was published by a Jewish writer named **Moses de Leon.**

**De Leon** ascribed the work to **Shimon bar Yochai ("Rashbi"),** a rabbi of the 2nd century during the roman persecution who, according to Jewish legend, hid in a cave for thirteen years studying the **Torah** and was inspired by the **Prophet Elijah** to write the **Zohar**. This accords with the traditional claim by adherents that **Kabbalah** is the concealed part of the **Oral Torah**.

While the traditional majority view in irreligious Judaism has been that the teachings of **Kabbalah** were revealed by God to Biblical figures such as **Abraham** and **Moses** and were then transmitted orally from the Biblical era until its redaction by **Shimon ben Yochai**. The purpose of the **Zohar** is to help the Jewish people through and out of the **Exile** and to infuse the **Torah** and mitzvoth (Judaic commandments) with the wisdom of **Kabbalah** for its Jewish readers.

## Etymology
In the Bible the word **"Zohar"** appears in the vision of **Ezekiel Chapter 8 Verse 2** and is usually translated as meaning radiance or light. It appears again in **Daniel Chapter 12 Verse 3, "The wise ones will shine like the radiance of the firmament".**

The **Zohar** spread among the Jews with remarkable swiftness. Scarcely fifty years had passed since its appearance in Spain before it was quoted by many Kabbalists, including the Italian mystical writer **Menahem Recanati** and by **Todros Abulafia**. Certain Jewish communities, however, such as the **Dor Daim**, Andalusian (Western Sefardic or Spanish and Portuguese Jews), and some Italian communities, never accepted it as authentic.

## Late Middle Ages
By the 15th century, its authority in the Spanish Jewish community was such that **Joseph ibn Shem-Tov** drew from it arguments in his attacks against **Maimonides**, and even representatives of non-mystical Jewish thought began to assert its sacredness and invoke its authority in the decision of some ritual questions and which was held in contrast to the view of **Maimonides** and

his followers, who regarded man as a fragment of the universe whose immortality is dependent upon the degree of development of his active intellect.

The **Zohar** instead declared Man to be the lord of the creation, whose immortality is solely dependent upon his morality. Conversely, **Elijah Delmedigo** (c. 1458 – c. 1493), in his ***Bechinat ha-Dat*** endeavored to show that the **Zohar** could not be attributed to **Shimon bar Yochai**. Believers in the authenticity of the **Zohar** countered that the lack of references to the work in Jewish literature were because **bar Yochai** did not commit his teachings to writing but transmitted them orally to his disciples over generations until finally the doctrines were embodied in the **Zohar**.

They found it unsurprising that **bar Yochai** should have foretold future happenings or made references to historical events of the post-Talmudic period. The authenticity of the **Zohar** was accepted by such 16$^{th}$ century Jewish luminaries as **R'Yosef Karo (d. 1575), R' Moses Isserles (d. 1572), and r' Solomon Luria (d. 1574),** who wrote that Jewish law (**Halacha**) follows thee **Zohar**, except where **the Zohar is contradicted by the Babylonian Talmud**.

## Enlightenment period

The influence of the **Zohar** and the **Kabbalah** in **Yemen**, where it was introduced in the 17$^{th}$ century, give rise to the ***Dor Daim*** movement, whose adherents believed that the core beliefs of Judaism were rapidly diminishing in favor of the mysticism of the **Kabbalah**. The ***Dor Daim*** movement, led by **Rabbi Yihyah Qafih**, emerged as a recognizable force in the later part of the 19$^{th}$ century, and considered the Kabbalists to be irrational, anti-scientific, and anti-progressive in attitude.

Especially controversial were the views of the **Dor Daim** on the **Zohar**, as presented in ***Milhamoth Hashem*** (Wars of the Lord), written by **Rabbi Qafih** A group of Jerusalem rabbis published an attack on **Rabbi Qafih** under the title of ***Emunat Hashem*** (Faith of the Lord), and measures were taken to ostracize members of the movement. In the **Ashkenazi** community of Easter Europe, later religious authorities including the **Vilna Gaon** (d. 1797) and **Rabbi Shneur Zalman of Liadi** (d. 1812) (The Baal Ha Tanya) believed in the authenticity of the **Zohar**.

## Contemporary religious view

Most of Orthodox Judaism holds that the teachings of **Kabbalah** were transmitted from teacher to teacher, in a long and continuous chain, from the Biblical era until its redaction by **Shimon ben Yochai**. Many (most?) accept fully the claims that the **Kabbalah**'s teachings are in essence a revelation from God to the Biblical patriarch **Abraham, Moses** and other ancient figures, but were never printed and made publicly available until the time of the **Zohar**'s medieval publication.

The greatest acceptance of this sequence of events is held within **Haredi Judaism**. Some claim the tradition that Rabbi Shimon wrote that the concealment of the **Zohar** would last for exactly **1200 years** from the time of destruction of the **Holy Temple** in Jerusalem. **The Temple of Jerusalem was destroyed in 70 CE** and so before revealing the **Zohar** in 1270, **Moses De Leon** uncovered the manuscripts in a cave in Israel.

Within Orthodox Judaism the traditional view that **Shimon bar Yochai** was the author is maintained. This has also been pointed out by **R' David Luria** in his work **"Kadmus Safer Ha'Zohar."** The **Zohar**'s major opponent **Elijah Delmedigo** refers to the **Zohar** as having existed for **"only"** 300 years. Even he agrees that it was extant before the time of **R' Moses De Leon**. It is impossible to accept that **R' Moshe De Leon** managed to forge a work of the scope of the **Zohar** (1700 pages) within a period of six years as **Scholem** claims.

A comparison between The **Zohar** and **De Leon's** others works show major stylistic differences. Although he made us of his manuscript of the **Zohar**, many ideas presented in his works contradict or ignore ideas mentioned in the **Zohar**. (**Luria** also points this out). An ancient manuscript that refers to a book **Sod Gadol** that seems to in face be the **Zohar**.

Belief in the authenticity of the **Zohar** among Orthodox Jewish movements can be seen in various forms online today. Featured on **Chabad.org** is the multi-part article. *The Zohar's Mysterious Origins* by **Moshe Miller**. The **Zohar** figures prominently in the mysticism of Chabad.

## Modern critical views

In the mid-20th century, the Jewish historian **Gershom Scholem** contended that **de Leon** himself was the most likely author of the **Zohar**. **Yeshayahu Leibowitz**, noted professor of philosophy at the Hebrew University of Jerusalem, claimed that **"It is clear that the Zohar was written by de Leon as it is clear that Theodore Herzl wrote *Medinat HaYehudim* (The Jewish State)."**

In the **Encyclopaedia Judaica** article written by Professor **Gershom Scholem** of the Hebrew University of Jerusalem there is an extensive discussion of the sources cited in the **Zohar**. Academic studies of the **Zohar** show that many of its ideas are based in the **Talmud**, various works of **Midrash**, and earlier Jewish mystical works. His main sources were the Babylonian Talmud.

The author of the **Zohar** drew upon the bible commentaries written by medieval rabbis, including **Rashi, Abraham ibn Ezra, David Kimhi** and even authorities as late as **Nahmanides** and **Maimonides**. The **Zohar** draws upon early mystical texts such as the **Sefer Yetzirah** and the **Bahir**, and the early medieval writings of the **Hasidei Ashkenaz**. **Scholem** saw this dualism of good and evil within the Godhead as a kind of **"gnostic"** inclination within **Kabbalah**, and as a predecessor of the *Sitra Ahra* (the other, evil side) in the **Zohar**. The main text of the Castile circle, the **Treatise on the Left Emanation**, was written by **Jacob ha-Cohen** in around 1265.

## Contents

The *Tikunei haZohar* was first printed in Mantua in 1557. The main body of the **Zohar** was printed in Cremona in 1558 (a one-volume edition), in Mantua in 1558-1560 (a three-volume edition), and in Salonika in 1597 (a two-volume edition). Each of these editions included somewhat different texts.

## Zohar

The earlier part of the **Zohar**, also known as *Zohar 'Al haTorah* (**Zohar** on the **Torah**) or *Midrash Rashbi*, contains several smaller **"books,"** as described below.

This book was published in three volumes: Volume I on *Bereishit* (Genesis), Volume 2 on *Shemot* (Exodus) and Volume 3 on *Viyikra, Bamidbar* and *Devarim* (Leviticus, Numbers, and Deuteronomy).

## Sifra diTzni'uta/Book of the Hidden

This small "book, **"three pages long, (Volume 2, *parashat Teruma* pages 176b-179a) – the name of which, "Book of the Hidden,"** attests to its veiled and cryptic character – is considered by some an important and concentrated part of the **Zohar**. Its enumerations and anatomical references are reminiscent of the *Sefer Yetzirah*, the latter being *remazim* (hints) of divine characteristics. **It has five chapters.** Intrinsically it includes, according to Rashbi, the foundation of **Kabbalah**, which is explained at length in the **Zohar** and in the books of **Kabbalah** after it.

## *Idra Rabba*/The Great Assembly

The *Idra Rabba* is found in the **Zohar** Vol. 3, *parashat Nasso* (pp. 127b-145a), and its name means, **"The Great Assembly."** "*Idra*" is a sitting-place of sages, usually circular, and the word "*Rabba*/Great" differentiates this section from the section *Idra Zuta*, which was an assembly of fewer sages that occurred later.

**Idra Rabba** contains the discussion of nine of Rashbi's friends, who gathered together to discuss great and deep secrets of **Kabbalah**. The nine are: **Rabbi Elazar his son, Rabbi Abba, Rabbi Yehuda, Rabbi Yossi bar Yaakov, Rabbi Yitzchak, Rabbi Chezkiyah bar Rav, Rabbi Chiyya, Rabbi Yossi and Rabbi Yisa.** As described in the Idra Rabba, before the Idra disjourned, three of the students died: **Rabbi Yossi bar Yaakov, Rabbi Chezkiyah bar Rav,** and **Rabbi Yisa**. As it is told, these students filled up with Godly light and therefore journeyed to the eternal world after their deaths. The remaining students saw their friends being carried away by angels.

## *Ra'aya Meheimna*/The Faithful Shepherd

The book *Ra'aya Meheimna*, the title of which means "**The Faithful Shepherd,**" and which is by far the largest **"book"** included in the book of the **Zohar**, is what Moshe, the "**Faithful Shepherd,**" teaches and reveals to Rashbi and his friends, who include **Tannaim** and **Amoraim**. In this assembly of **Holy Friends**, which took place in the **Beit Midrash** of Rabbi **Shimon bar Yochai**, secrets of and revelations on mitzvot of the **Torah** are explained and clarified – roots and deep meanings of mitzvot.

Several great rabbis and sages have tried to find the *Ra'aya Mehimna,* which originally is a vast book on all the **613 mitzvot**, and arrange it according the order of positive commandments and negative commandments, and even print it as a book on its own. The language of *Midrash haNe'elam* is sometimes Hebrew, sometimes **Aramaic**, and sometimes both mixed. Unlike the body of the **Zohar**, its **drashas** are short and not long. Also, the topics it discusses – the work of Creation, the nature the soul, the days of **Mashiach**, and *Olam Haba* – are not of the type found in the **Zohar**, which are the nature of God, the emanation of worlds, the **"forces"** of evil, and more.

The commentary of **Rav Yiba Saba** regarding transmigration of souls, and punishments of the body in the grave. It is found in the **Zohar Vol. 2**, *parashat Mishpatim* (pp. 94a-114a).

### *Zohar Chadash*/The New Zohar

After the book of the **Zohar** was printed (in Mantua and in Cremona, in the Jewish years 5318-5320 or 1558-1560? CE), many more manuscripts were found which included paragraphs which pertained to the **Zohar** in their content and which had not been included in printed editions. The manuscripts pertained also to all parts of the **Zohar**, some were similar to **Zohar** on the **Torah**, some were similar to the inner parts of the **Zohar** (*Midrash haNe'elam, Sitrei Otiyot* and more), and some pertained to **Tikunei Ha'Zohar.**

### Tikunei haZohar/Rectifications of the Zohar

*Tikunei haZohar*, which was printed as separate book, includes seventy commentaries called **"Tikunim"** (lit. Repairs) and an additional eleven Tikkunim. Each of the seventy **Tikunim** of Tikunei ha**Zohar** begins by explaining the word **"Bereishit"** (בראשית), and continues by explaining other verses, mainly in parashat **Bereishit**, and also from the rest of **Tanakh**. And all this is in the way of **Sod**, in commentaries that reveal the hidden and mystical aspects of the **Torah**.

### Parts of the Zohar, Summary of Rabbinic View

The traditional Rabbinic view is that most of the **Zohar** and the parts included in it (i.e. those parts mentioned above) were written and compiled by **Rabbi Shimon bar Yochai**, but some parts preceded Rashbi and he used them (such as *Sifra deTzni'uta*; see above), and some parts were written or arranged in generations after Rashbi's passing (for example, **Tannaim** after Rashbi's time are occasionally mentioned).

However, aside from the parts of the **Zohar** mentioned above, in the **Zohar** are mentioned tens of earlier sources which Rashbi and his **Chevra Kadisha** had, and they were apparently the foundation of the Kabbalistic tradition of the **Zohar**. In the Jewish view this indicates more, that the teaching of the Sod in the book of the **Zohar** was not invented in the **Tannaic** period, but rather it is a tradition from ancient times which Rashbi and his **Chevbraya Kadisha** used and upon which they built and founded their **Kabbalah, and also that its roots are in the Torah that was given by Hashem to Moshe on Sinai.**

### Viewpoint and Exegesis, Rabbinic View

According to the **Zohar**, the moral perfection of man influences the ideal world of the **Sefirot**; for although the Sefirot accept everything from the **Ein Sof** (Heb. **infinity**), the **Tree of Life** itself is dependent upon man he alone can bring about the divine effusion. This concept is somewhat akin to the concept of **Tikkun Olam**. The dew that vivifies the universe flows from the just.

By the practice of virtue and by moral perfection, many may increase the out pouring of heavenly grace. Even physical life is subservient to virtue. This, says the **Zohar**, is indicated in the words **"for the Lord God had not caused it to rain" (Gen. 2:5)**, which means that there had not yet been beneficent action in heaven, because man had not yet been created to pray for it. **The Zohar assumes four kinds of Biblical text exegesis, from the literal to the more mystical:**
1. The simple, literal meaning of the text: *Peshat*
2. The allusion or hinted/allegorical meaning: *Remez*
3. The rabbinic comparison through sermon or illustration and metaphor: *Derash*
4. The secret/mysterious/hidden meaning: *Sod*

The initial letters of these words (**P,R,D,S**) form together the word **PaRDeS** ("**paradise /orchard**"), which became the designation for the **Zohar**'s view of a fourfold meaning of the text, of which the mystical sense is considered the highest part.

## Viewpoint, Academic Views

These polarities must be conjoined (have *yihud*, "**union**") to maintain the harmony of the cosmos. Idel characterizes this metaphysical point of view as **"ditheism,"** holding that there are two aspects to God, and the process of union as **"theoeroticism."**

The oneness of God is perceived in androgynous terms as the pairing of **male and female.** Just as, in the case of the **original Adam, woman was constructed from man**, and their carnal cleaving together was portrayed as becoming one flesh, so the ideal for kabbalists is the reconstitution of what is called the **male androgyne.** Much closer in spirit to some ancient Gnostic dicta, we understand the eschatological ideal in traditional kabbalah to have been the female becoming male.

## Influence: Judaism

The **Zohar** was lauded by many rabbis because it opposed religious formalism, stimulated one's imagination and emotions, and for many people helped reinvigorate the experience of prayer. In many places prayer had become a mere external religious exercise, while prayer was supposed to be a means of transcending earthly affairs and placing oneself in union with God. Many classical rabbis, especially **Maimonides**, viewed all such beliefs as a violation of Judaic principles of faith.

**Shabbat**, the Jewish Sabbath, began to be looked upon as the embodiment of God in temporal life and every ceremony performed on that day was considered to have an influence upon the superior world. In the 17$^{th}$ century, it was proposed that only Jewish men who were at least 40 years old could study **Kabbalah**, and by extension read the **Zohar**, because it was believed to be too powerful for those less emotionally mature and experienced.

## Neo-Platonism

Founded in the 3$^{rd}$ century CE by **Plotinus**, The Neoplatonist tradition has clear echoes in the **Zohar**, as indeed in many forms of mystical spirituality, whether Jewish, Christian or Muslim. The concept of creation by successive emanations of God in particular is characteristic of Neoplatonist thought. In both Kabbalistic and Neoplatonist systems, the Logos, or **Divine Wisdom,** is the primordial archetype of the universe and mediates between the divine idea and the material world.

## Christian mysticism

According to the *Jewish Encyclopedia*, the enthusiasm felt for the **Zohar** was shared by many Christian scholars, all of whom believed that the book contained proofs of the truth of Christianity, such as the fall and redemption of man, and the dogma of the **Trinity**, which seems to be expressed in the **Zohar**. According to the *Jewish Encyclopedia*, this and other similar doctrines found in the **Zohar** are now known to be much older than Christianity, but the Christian scholars who were led by the similarity of these teachings to certain Christian dogmas deemed it their duty to propagate the **Zohar**.

However, fundamental to the **Zohar** are descriptions of the absolute Unity and uniqueness of God, in the Jewish understanding of it, rather than a trinity or other plurality. One of the most common phrases in the **Zohar** is *"raza d'yichuda"* **"the secret of his Unity"** which describes the Oneness of God as completely indivisible, even in spiritual terms. For example, says:

> **Elijah opened and said: "Master of the worlds! You are One, but not in number. You are He Who is Highest of the High, Most Hidden of the Hidden; no thought can grasp You at all…And there is no image or likeness of You, inside or out…And aside from You, there is no unity on High or Below. And You are acknowledged as the Cause of everything and the Master of everything…And You are the completion of them all. Blessed is God forever, amen and amen!**

The meaning of the three heads of **Keter**, according to the kabbalists, has extremely different connotations from ascribing validity to any compound or plurality of God, even if the compound is viewed as unified. In **Kabbalah**, while God is an absolutely simple (non-compound), infinite Unity beyond grasp, as described in Jewish philosophy by **Maimonides**, through His Kabbalistic manifestations such as the **Sephirot** and the **Shekhinah** (Divine Presence), we relate to the living dynamic Divinity that emanates, **enclothes**, is revealed in, and incorporates, the multifarious spiritual and physical plurality of **Creation within the Infinite Unity.**

Creation is plural, while **God is Unity**. The spiritual role of Judaism is to reach the level of perceiving the truth of the paradox, that all is One, spiritual and physical **Creation** being nullified into absolute **Divine Monotheism**.

The relationship between God's absolute **Unity** and **Divine** manifestations, may be compared to a man in a room – there is the man himself, and his presence and relationship to others in the room. In Hebrew, this is known as the **Shekhinah**. It is also the concept of God's Name – it is His relationship and presence in the world towards us. The **Wisdom** in kabbalistic terms refers to the **Shekhinah, the Divine Presence.**

This is known as perceiving the **Shekhinah** through a blurry, cloudy lens. This means to say, although we see **God's Presence** (not God Himself) through natural occurrences, it is only through a blurry lens; as opposed to miracles, in which we clearly see and recognize God's presence in the world. **The Holy Ancient One refers to God Himself, Who is imperceivable.**

Within the descending **Four Worlds of Creation**, each successive realm perceives Divinity less and apparent independence more. The highest realm *Atziluth-Emanation*, termed the **"Realm of Unity,"** is distinguished from the lower three realms, termed the **"Realm of Separation,"** by still having no self-awareness; absolute Divine Unity is revealed and Creation is mollified in its source.

The **lower three Worlds** feel progressive degrees of independence from God. Where lower Creation can mistake the different Divine emanations as plural, **Atziluth** feels their non-existent unity in God. All such forms when traced back to their source in God's infinite light, return to their state of absolute Oneness. This is the consciousness of **Atziluth**. In **Kabbalah**, this perception is considered subconsciously innate to the souls of Israel, rooted in **Atzilut.**

There is an alternative notion of three in the **Zohar** that are One, **"Israel, the Torah and the Holy One Blessed Be He are One. As Judaism innately perceives the absolute Monotheism of God. In a Kabbalistic phrase, one prays "to Him, not to His attributes."** Accordingly, in the Kabbalistic view, the non-Jewish belief in the **Trinity**, as well as the beliefs of all religions, has parallel, supernal notions within **Kabbalah** from which they ultimately exist in the process of **Creation.**

In normative Christian theology, as well as the declaration of the **First Council of Nicaea**, God is declared to be **"one".** Declarations such as **"God is three"** or **"God is two"** are condemned in later counsels as entirely heretical and idolatrous. The beginning of the essential declaration of belief for Christians, The **Nicene Creed** (somewhat equivalent to **Maimonides'** 13 principles of Faith), starts with the **Shema** influenced declaration that **"We Believe in One God... Like Judaism, Christianity asserts the absolute monotheism of God".**

Unlike the **Zohar**, Christianity interprets the coming of the **Messiah** as the arrival of the true immanence of God. Like the **Zohar** the Messiah is believed to be the bringer of **Divine Light**: **"The Light (the Messiah) shineth in the Darkness and the Darkness has never put it out,"** yet the Light, although being God, is separable within God since no one has seen God in flesh: **"for no man has seen God..." (John 1).**

It is through the belief that **Jesus Christ** is the Messiah, since God had vindicated him by raising him from the dead, that Christians believe that Jesus is paradoxically and substantially God, despite God's simple undivided unity. The belief that **Jesus Christ** is **"God from God, Light from Light"** is assigned as a mystery and weakness of the human mind affecting and effecting our comprehension of him.

## Zohar Study (Jewish View)

Although some rabbis since the **Shabbetai Tzvi** debacle still maintain that one should be married and forty years old in order to study **Kabbalah**, since the time of **Baal Shem Tov** there has been relaxation of such stringency, and many maintain that it is sufficient to be married and knowledgeable in **halakhah** and hence permitted to study **Kabbalah** and by inclusion. In any case the aim of such caution is to not become caught up in **Kabbalah** to the extent of departing from reality or **halakhah.**

# Kaddish (Aramaic)

**Kaddish** (*Qaddish* Aramaic: **"holy"**; alternative spellings: **Qaddish**, **Kaddish**) is a hymn of praises to God found in the Jewish prayer service. The central theme of the *Kaddish* is the magnification and sanctification of God's name.

The term **"Kaddish"** is often used to refer specifically to **"The Mourner's Kaddish"**, said as part of the mourning rituals in Judaism in all prayer services, as well as at funerals (other than at the grave site – see below *Kaddish ahar Hakk'vurah*) and memorials. When mention is made of **"saying Kaddish"**, this unambiguously refers to the rituals of mourning. **Mourners say Kaddish to show that despite the loss they still praise God.**

**The opening words of this prayer are inspired by Ezekiel 38:23**, a vision of God becoming great in the eyes of all the nations. The central line of the **Kaddish** in Jewish tradition is the congregation's response: **(Yehei shmëh rabba mevarakh lealam ulalmey almaya, "May His great name be blessed forever, and to all eternity")**, a public declaration of God's greatness and eternality.

This response is an Aramaic translation of the Hebrew **(Blessed be His name, whose glorious kingdom is forever)**, which is to be found in the Jerusalem Targum (**Genesis 49:2 and Deuteronomy 6:4)**, and is similar to the wording of **Daniel 2:20.**

The Mourners, Rabbis and Complete **Kaddish** end with a supplication for peace (**"Oseh Shalom..."),** which is in Hebrew, and is somewhat similar to the **Bible Job 25:2**. Along with the **Shema** and **Amidah**, the **Kaddish** is one of the most important and central elements in the Jewish liturgy. **Kaddish cannot be recited alone. Along with some prayers, it can only be recited with a minyan of ten Jews.**

## History and background

**"The Kaddish is in origin a closing doxology to an Aggadic discourse."** Most of it is written in Aramaic, which, at the time of its original composition, was the lingua franca of the Jewish people. It is not composed in the vernacular Aramaic, however, but rather in a **"literary, jargon Aramaic"** that was used in the academies, and is identical to the dialect of the **Targum**.

The oldest version of the **Kaddish** is found in the **Siddur of Rab Amram Gaon, c. 900**. **"The first mention of mourners saying Kaddish at the end of the service is in a 13th century halakhic writing by Isaac ben Moses of Vienna, the *Or Zarua* (literally "Light is sown").** The **Kaddish** at the end of the service became designated as **Kaddish Yatom** or Mourner's **Kaddish** (literally, **"Orphan's Kaddish"**).

All versions of the **Kaddish** begin with the *Hatzi Kaddish* (there are some extra passages in the **Kaddish** after a burial or a **siyum**). The longer versions contain additional paragraphs, and are often named after distinctive words in those paragraphs. The **Half Kaddish** is used to punctuate divisions within the service: for example, before **Barechu,** between the **Shema** and the **Amidah** and following readings from the Torah.

The *Kaddish d'Rabbanan* is used after any part of the service that includes extracts from the **Mishnah** or the **Talmud**, as its original purpose was to close a study session. *Kaddish Titkabbal* originally marked the end of the service, though in later times extra passages and hymns were added to follow it.

The Jewish Encyclopedia's article on **Kaddish** mentions an additional type of **Kaddish**, called **"Kaddish Yahid",** or **"Individual's Kaddish".** This is included in the **Siddur of Amram Gaon,** but is a meditation taking the place of **Kaddish** rather than a **Kaddish** in the normal sense.

## Recent additions to Oseh Shalom

In some recent prayer books, for example, the **American Reform Machzor**, line 36 is replaced with:

**"This effort to extend the reach of Oseh Shalom to non-Jews is said to have been started by the British Liberal Jewish movement in 1967, with the introduction of *v'al kol bnai Adam* ("and upon all children of Adam");** these words continue to be used by some in the UK. NOTE: The phrase (ben Adam) pl. (bnai Adam) literally means **"son of Adam"** or **"son of man"** but in Hebrew usage the phrase is taken to mean **"human."**

## Customs

The **Kaddish**, as used in the services on special days is chanted. There are different melodies in different Jewish traditions and within each tradition the melody can change according to the version, the day it is said and even the position in the service; many mourners recite it slowly and contemplatively.

- **Virtual Cantor's Kaddish Shalem for Shabbat Mussaf**
- **Virtual Cantor's Hatzi Kaddish for Yom Kippur**

**In Sephardi synagogues the whole congregation sits for Kaddish, except:**
- **During the Kaddish immediately before the Amidah, where everyone stands;**
- **During the Mourner's Kaddish, where those reciting it stand and everyone else sits.**

In **Ashkenazi** synagogues, the custom varies. Very commonly, in both Orthodox and Reform congregations, everyone stands; but in some (especially many Conservative and Hasidic) synagogues, most of the congregants sit. Sometimes, a distinction is made between the different forms of **Kaddish**, or each congregant stands or sits according to his or her own custom. The

Mourner's **Kaddish** is often treated differently from the other variations of **Kaddish** in the service, as is the **Half Kaddish before the maftir.**

Those standing to recite the **Kaddish** bow, by widespread tradition, at various places. Generally: At the first word of the prayer, at each *Amen,* at *Yitbarakh,* at *Brikh hu*, and for the last verse (*Oseh shalom*).

For *Oseh shalom* it is customary take three steps back (if possible) then bow to one's left, then to one's right, and finally bow forward, as if taking leave of the presence of a king, in the same way as when the same words are used as the concluding line of the **Amidah.**

## Minyan requirement

**Masekhet Soferim,** an eighth-century compilation of Jewish laws regarding the preparation of holy books and public reading, states (Chapter 10:7) that **Kaddish may be recited only in the presence of a minyan (at least 10 men).** While the traditional view is that **"if Kaddish is said in private, then by definition it is not Kaddish,"** some alternatives have been suggested, including the *Kaddish L'yachid* (**"Kaddish for an individual"**), attributed to ninth-century **Gaon Amram bar Sheshna,** and the use of **kavanah** prayer, asking heavenly beings to join with the individual **"to make a minyan of both Earth and heaven".**

## Mourner's Kaddish: *Bereavement in Judaism*

"Mourner's Kaddish" is said at all prayer services and certain other occasions. It is written in Aramaic. It takes the form of **Kaddish Yehe Shelama Rabba,** and is traditionally recited several times, most prominently at or towards the end of the service, after the **Aleinu** and/or closing Psalms and/or (on the Sabbath) **Ani'im Zemirot.**

Following the death of a parent, child, spouse, or sibling it is customary to recite the Mourner's **Kaddish in the presence of a congregation daily for thirty days, or eleven months in the case of a parent, and then at every anniversary of the death.** The "mourner" who says the **Kaddish** will be any person present at a service who has the obligation to recite **Kaddish** in accordance with these rules.

Customs for reciting the Mourner's **Kaddish** vary markedly among various communities. In **Sephardi** synagogues, the custom is that all the mourners stand and chant the **Kaddish** together. In **Ashkenazi** synagogues, the earlier custom was that one mourner be chosen to lead the prayer on behalf of the rest, though most congregations have now adopted the Sephardi custom. In many **Reform** synagogues, the entire congregation recites the Mourner's **Kaddish** together.

This is sometimes said to be for those victims of the **Holocaust** who have no one left to recite the Mourner's **Kaddish** on their behalf. In some congregations **(especially Reform and Conservative**

**ones),** the Rabbi will read a list of the deceased who have a **Yahrzeit** on that day (or who have died within the past month), and then ask the congregants to name any people they are mourning for.

Some synagogues try to multiply the number of times that the Mourner's **Kaddish** is recited, for example, reciting a separate Mourner's **Kaddish** after both **Aleinu** and then each closing **Psalm**. Other synagogues limit themselves to one Mourner's **Kaddish** at the end of the service.

**Saying the Mourner's Kaddish was mostly prohibited for Orthodox Jewish women, but is now becoming more common.** In 2013 the Israeli Orthodox rabbinical organization **Beit Hillel** issued a halachic ruling which allows women, for the first time, to say the **Kaddish** in memory of their deceased parents.

It is important to note that **the Mourner's Kaddish does not mention death at all, but instead praises God**. Though the **Kaddish** is often popularly referred to as the **"Jewish Prayer for the Dead,"** that designation more accurately belongs to the prayer called **"El male rachamim"**, **which specifically prays for the soul of the deceased**. Written in Aramaic, the Mourner's **Kaddish** is the prayer traditionally recited in memory of the dead, although it makes no mention of death. It is included in all three daily prayer services.

**Mourner's Kaddish in English Translation:**
"Glorified and sanctified be God's great name throughout the world which he has created according to His will. May he establish His kingdom in your lifetime and during your days, and within the life of the entire House of Israel, speedily and soon, and say **Amen**…

May His great name be blessed forever and to all **Eternity**. Blessed and praised, glorified and exalted, extolled and honored, adored and lauded be the name of the Holy one, blessed be He, beyond all the blessings and hymns, praises and consolations that are ever spoken in the world; and say **Amen**… May there be abundant peace from heaven, and life, for us and for all Israel; and say **Amen**… He who creates peace in His celestial heights, may He create peace for us and for all Israel; and say **Amen**. "

# Kashrut (Judaism)

*Kashrut* (also *kashruth* or *kashrus*,) is a set of Jewish religious dietary laws. Food that may be consumed according to *halakha* (Jewish law) is deemed **kosher** meaning **'fit' for consumption'**. Among the numerous laws of *kashrut* are prohibitions on the consumption of certain animals (such as pork and shellfish), mixtures of meat and milk, and the commandment to slaughter mammals and birds according to a process known as *shechita*.

Most of the basic laws of *kashrut* are derived from the **Torah's Books of Leviticus and Deuteronomy.** Their details and practical application, however, are set down in the oral law (eventually codified in the **Mishnah and Talmud**) and elaborated on in the later rabbinical literature. **Currently, about a sixth of American Jews or 0.3% of the American population fully keep kosher.** The **Seventh-day Adventist Church**, a Christian denomination, has a health message that expects adherence to the kosher dietary laws.

## ⌐ Explanations / Philosophical

Jewish philosophy divides the **613 commandments** (or *mitzvot*) **into three groups**—laws that have a rational explanation and would probably be enacted by most orderly societies (*mishpatim*), **The dietary laws were given as a demonstration of God's authority, and man must obey without asking why**. However, **Maimonides** believed that Jews were permitted to seek out reasons for the laws of the Torah.

The Torah prohibits **"seething the kid (goat, sheep, calf) in its mother's milk"**. While the Bible does not provide a reason, it has been suggested that the practice was perceived as cruel and insensitive. **Hasidic Judaism** believes that everyday life is imbued with channels connecting with Divinity, the *activation* of which it sees as helping the **Divine Presence** to be drawn into the physical world. Hasidism argues that the food laws are related to the way such channels, termed *sparks of holiness*, interact with various animals.

These *sparks of Holiness* are released whenever a Jew manipulates any object for a *holy reason* (which includes eating); however, not all animal products are capable of releasing their *sparks of holiness*. Signs are expressed in the biblical categorization of ritually *clean* and ritually *unclean*.

The purpose of *kashrut* was to help Jews maintain a distinct and separate existence from other peoples; the effect of the laws was to prevent socialization and intermarriage with non-Jews, preventing Jewish identity from being diluted. **One of the earliest is that of Maimonides in *The Guide for the Perplexed*.**

**Biblically prohibited foods include:**

- **Non-kosher animals and birds**: mammals require certain identifying characteristics (cloven hooves and being ruminants), while birds require a tradition that they can be consumed. Fish require scales and fins (thus excluding catfish, for instance). All invertebrates are non-kosher apart from certain types of locust, on which most communities lack a clear tradition. No reptiles or amphibians are kosher.
- **Carrion (*nevelah*):** meat from a kosher animal that has not been slaughtered according to the laws of *shechita*. This prohibition includes animals that have been slaughtered by non-Jews.
- **Injured (*terefah*):** an animal with a significant defect or injury, such as a fractured bone or particular types of lung adhesions.
- **Blood (*dam*):** The blood of kosher mammals and fowl is removed through salting, with special procedures for the liver, which is very rich in blood.
- **Particular fats (*chelev*):** particular parts of the abdominal fat of cattle, goats and sheep must be removed by a process called *nikkur*.
- **The twisted nerve (*gid hanasheh*):** the sciatic nerve, as according to Genesis 32:32 the patriarch Jacob's was damaged when he fought with an angel, may not be eaten and is removed by *nikkur*.
- **A limb of a living animal (*ever min ha-chai*):** According to Jewish law, God forbade Noah and his descendants to consume flesh torn from a live animal. Hence, Jewish law considers this prohibition applicable even to non-Jews, and therefore, a Jew may not give or sell such meat to a non-Jew.
- **Untithed food (*tevel*):** produce of the Land of Israel requires the removal of certain tithes, which in ancient times were given to the Kohanim (priests), Levites and the poor (*terumah*, *maaser Rishon* and *maasar ani* respectively) or taken to the Old City of Jerusalem to be eaten there (*maaser sheni*).
- **Fruit during the first three years (*orlah*):** according to Leviticus 19:23, fruit from a tree in the first three years after planting may not be consumed (both in the Land of Israel and the diaspora). This applies also to the fruit of the vine—grapes, and wine produced from them.
- **New grain (*Chadash*):** the Bible prohibits newly grown grain (planted after Passover the previous year) until the second day of Passover; there is debate as to whether this law applies to grain grown outside the Land of Israel.
- **Wine of libation (*yayin nesekh*):** wine that may have been dedicated to idolatrous practices.

**A 2013 survey found that 22% of American Jews surveyed claimed to keep kosher in the home**.

# King David

(Biblical Hebrew: **"beloved one"**) was, according to the Hebrew Bible, the third king of the United Kingdom of Israel. David probably lived c. 1000 BCE.

David ascended the throne as the king of Judah in 885 BCE. The Tel Dan stele, an Aramaic-inscribed stone erected by a king of Aram-Damascus in the late 9th/early 8th centuries BCE to commemorate a victory over two enemy kings, contains the phrase *bytdwd* , which is translated as **"House of David"** by most scholars. The **Mesha Stele**, erected by **King Mesha** of Moab in the 9th century BCE, may also refer to the "**House of David**".

In the biblical narrative of the **Books of Samuel,** David is described as a young shepherd and harpist who gains fame and becomes a hero by killing **Goliath**. He becomes a favorite of **Saul,** the first king of Israel, but is forced to go into hiding when Saul suspects that David is trying to take his throne. After Saul and his son **Jonathan** are killed in battle, David is anointed king by the tribe of Judah and eventually all the tribes of Israel. He conquers Jerusalem, makes it the capital of a united Israel, and brings the **Ark of the Covenant** to the city.

He commits adultery with **Bathsheba** and arranges the death of her husband, **Uriah the Hittite**. David's son **Absalom** later tries to overthrow him, but David returns to Jerusalem after Absalom's death to continue his reign. David desires to build a **Temple to Yahweh**, but he is denied because of the bloodshed in his reign. He dies at age 70 and chooses **Solomon,** his son with Bathsheba, as his successor instead of his eldest son **Adonijah**. David is honored as an ideal king and the forefather of the future **Hebrew Messiah** in Jewish prophetic literature and many psalms are attributed to him.

Early Christians interpreted the life of **Jesus of Nazareth** in light of references to the Hebrew Messiah and to David; Jesus is described as being directly descended from David in the **Gospel of Matthew and the Gospel of Luke. In the Quran and hadith.** David is described as an Israelite king as well as a prophet of Allah.

## Biblical account

The **First Book of Samuel** and the **First Book of Chronicles** both identify David as the son of **Jesse**, the Bethlehemite, the youngest of eight sons. He also had at least two sisters: **Zeruiah,** whose sons all went on to serve in David's army, and **Abigail**, whose son **Amasa** served in Absalom's army, Absalom being one of David's younger sons. The Book of Ruth claims David as the great-grandson of **Ruth, the Moabite, by Boaz.**

According to **1 Samuel 17:25**, King Saul said that he would make whoever killed **Goliath** a very wealthy man, give his daughter to him and declare his father's family exempt from taxes in Israel.

Saul offered David his oldest daughter, **Merab**, a marriage David respectfully declined. Saul then gave Merab in marriage to **Adriel the Meholathite**. Having been told that his younger daughter Michal was in love with David, Saul gave her in marriage to David. Saul became jealous of David and tried to have him killed. David escaped.

His daughter **Tamar,** by **Maachah**, is raped by her half-brother **Amnon**. David fails to bring Amnon to justice for his violation of Tamar, because he is his firstborn and he loves him, and so **Absalom** (her full brother) murders Amnon to avenge Tamar.

## Narrative

God is angered when Saul, Israel's king, unlawfully offers a sacrifice and later disobeys a divine command both to kill all of the **Amalekites** and to destroy their confiscated property. Consequently, God sends the prophet **Samuel** to anoint a shepherd, David, the youngest son of Jesse of Bethlehem, to be king instead.

After God sends an evil spirit to torment Saul, his servants recommend that he send for a man skilled in playing the lyre. David enters Saul's service as one of the royal armour-bearers and plays the lyre to soothe the king.

War comes between Israel and the Philistines, and the giant **Goliath** challenges the Israelites to send out a champion to face him in single combat. David declares that he can defeat Goliath. Refusing the king's offer of the royal armour, he kills Goliath with his sling.

All Israel loves David, but his popularity causes Saul to fear him (**"What else can he wish but the kingdom?"**). Saul plots his death, but Saul's son **Jonathan**, one of those who loves David, warns him of his father's schemes and David flees. He goes first to **Nob**, where he is fed by the priest **Ahimelech** and given Goliath's sword. David sees that he is in danger there. He goes to seek refuge with the king of Moab.

**Jonathan** meets with David again and confirms his loyalty to David as the future king. Returning from battle with the Philistines, Saul heads to **Ein Gedi** in pursuit of David and enters the cave where, as it happens, David and his supporters are hiding, **"to attend to his needs"**. David realises he has an opportunity to kill Saul, but this is not his intention: he secretly cuts off a corner of Saul's robe, and when Saul has left the cave he comes out to pay homage to Saul as the king and to demonstrate, using the piece of robe, that he holds no malice towards Saul. The two are thus reconciled and Saul recognizes David as his successor.

In 1 Samuel 27:1–4, David begins to doubt Saul's sincerity, and reasons that the king will eventually make another attempt on his life. Jonathan and Saul are killed in battle with the

Philistines, and after hearing of their deaths, David travels to Hebron, where he is anointed king over Judah.

With the death of Saul's son, the elders of Israel come to Hebron and David is anointed king over all of Israel. He conquers Jerusalem, previously a Jebusite stronghold, and makes it his capital. He brings the **Ark of the Covenant** to the city, intending to build a temple for God, but the prophet **Nathan** forbids it, prophesying that the temple would be built by one of David's sons. Nathan also prophesies that God has made a covenant with the house of David stating, **"Your throne shall be established forever"**. David wins additional victories over the Philistines, Moabites, Edomites, Amalekites, Ammonites and king Hadadezer of Aram-Zobah.

During a siege of the Ammonite capital of Rabbah, David remains in Jerusalem. He spies a woman, **Bathsheba**, bathing and summons her; she becomes pregnant. The text in the Bible does not explicitly state whether Bathsheba consented to sex. David calls her husband, **Uriah the Hittite**, back from the battle to rest, hoping that he will go home to his wife and the child will be presumed to be his. Uriah does not visit his wife, however, so David conspires to have him killed in the heat of battle. David then marries the widowed Bathsheba.

In response, Nathan prophesies the punishment that will fall upon him, stating **"the sword shall never depart from your house."** Absalom's forces are routed at the battle of the Wood of Ephraim, and he is caught by his long hair in the branches of a tree where, contrary to David's order, he is killed by Joab, the commander of David's army.

David laments the death of his favourite son: **"O my son Absalom, my son, my son Absalom! Would I had died instead of you, O Absalom, my son, my son!"** until Joab persuades him to recover from **"the extravagance of his grief"** and to fulfill his duty to his people. David returns to Gilgal and is escorted across the River Jordan and back to Jerusalem by the tribes of Judah and Benjamin. David dies at the age of 70 after reigning for 40 years, and on his deathbed counsels **Solomon** to walk in the ways of God and to take revenge on his enemies.

# King Saul

(Hebrew: שָׁאוּל, **"asked/prayed for"**) was, according to the Hebrew Bible, the first monarch of the United Kingdom of Israel. His reign, traditionally placed in the late 11th century BC, marked the transition of Israel and Judah from a scattered tribal society ruled by various judges to organized statehood.

The historicity of Saul and the **United Kingdom of Israel** is not universally accepted, as what is known of both comes exclusively from the Hebrew Bible. According to the text, he was anointed as king of the Israelites by **Samuel**, and reigned from **Gibeah**. Saul is said to have **commited suicide when he "fell on his sword" during a battle with the Philistines at Mount Gilboa**, in which three of his sons were also killed. Saul's son **Ish-bosheth** succeeded him on the throne and was later murdered by his own military leaders, and then his son-in-law **David** became king.

## Biblical account

The biblical accounts of Saul's life are found in the **Books of Samuel.** According to the Hebrew text of the Bible, Saul reigned for two years, but Biblical commentators generally agree that the text is faulty and that a reign of 20 or 22 years is more probable. In the New Testament book of **Acts 13:21**, the **Apostle Paul** indicates that Saul's reign lasted for forty years.

According to the Hebrew Bible, Saul was the son of **Kish,** of the family of the **Matrites**, and a member of the tribe of **Benjamin**, one of the twelve Tribes of Israel. Saul married **Ahinoam**, daughter of **Ahimaaz**, with whom he sired at least five sons **(Jonathan, Abinadab, Malchishua, Ishvi and Ish-bosheth) and two daughters (Merab and Michal).** Saul also had a concubine named **Rizpah,** daughter of **Aiah**, who bore him two sons, **Armoni and Mephibosheth.**

Saul died at the Battle of Mount Gilboa, and was buried in Zelah, in the region of Benjamin. Three of Saul's sons – Jonathan, Abinadab, and Malchishua – died with him at Mount Gilboa. At David's request Abner had Michal returned to David. Ish-bosheth reigned for two years, but after the death of Abner, was killed by two of his own captains.

During a famine, God told king David that the famine happened because of how Saul treated the **Gibeonites**. The Gibeonites told David that only the death of seven sons of Saul would compensate them for losing their livelihood after the priests at **Nob** were killed under Saul's orders. David then granted the Gibeonites the jurisdiction to individually execute Saul's surviving two sons and five of Saul's grandsons (the sons of Merab and Adriel). The Gibeonites killed all seven, and hung up their bodies at the sanctuary at Gibeah. For five months their bodies were hung out in the elements. Finally, David had the bodies taken down and buried in the family grave at **Zelah** with the remains of Saul and their half-brother **Jonathan**. **Michal** was childless.

## Anointed as king

The **First Book of Samuel** gives three accounts of Saul's rise to the throne in three successive chapters:

- Saul is sent with a servant to look for his father's strayed donkeys. Leaving his home at Gibeah, they eventually arrive at the district of **Zuph,** at which point Saul suggests abandoning their search. Saul's servant tells him that they happen to be near the town of Ramah, where a famous *seer* dwells, and suggests that they should consult him first. The *seer* (later identified by the text as Samuel) offers hospitality to Saul and later anoints him in private.

- A popular movement having arisen to establish a centralized monarchy like other nations, Samuel assembles the people at **Mizpah** in Benjamin to appoint a king, fulfilling his previous promise to do so. Samuel organizes the people by tribe and by clan. Using the **Urim** and **Thummim**, he selects the tribe of **Benjamin**, from within the tribe selecting the **clan of Matri**, and from them selecting Saul. After having been chosen as monarch, Saul returns to his home in Gibeah, along with a number of followers. However, **some of the people are openly unhappy with the selection of Saul.**

- The **Ammonites**, led by **Nahash**, lay siege to **Jabesh-Gilead**. Under the terms of surrender, **the occupants of the city are to be forced into slavery and have their right eyes removed.** Instead they send word of this to the other tribes of Israel, and the tribes west of the Jordan assemble an army under Saul. **Saul leads the army to victory over the Ammonites,** and the people congregate at Gilgal where they acclaim Saul as king and he is crowned. **Saul's first act is to forbid retribution against those who had previously contested his kingship.**

## Saul among the prophets

Having been anointed by Samuel, Saul is told of signs indicating that he has been **divinely appointed.** The last of these is that Saul will be met by an ecstatic group of prophets leaving a *high place* and playing the lyre, tambourine, and flutes. Saul encounters the ecstatic prophets and joins them. Later, **Saul sends men to pursue David,** but when they meet a group of ecstatic prophets playing music, they are overcome by the Spirit of God and join in giving prophetic words. Saul sends more men, but they too join the prophets. **Eventually, Saul himself goes and also joins the prophets.**

## Military victories

After relieving the siege of **Jabesh-Gilead**, Saul conducts military campaigns against the Moabites, Ammonites, Edomites, Aram Rehob and the kings of Zobah, the Philistines, and the Amalekites. A biblical summary states that **"wherever he turned, he was victorious".**

In the second year of his reign, King Saul, his son **Jonathan**, and a small force of a few thousand Israelite soldiers defeated a massive Philistine force of 3,000 chariots, 6,000 horsemen, and more than 30,000 infantry in the pass of **Michmash**.

## Rejection

Several years after Saul's victory against the Philistines at **Michmash Pass**, Samuel instructs Saul to make war on the **Amalekites** and to **"utterly destroy"** them including all their livestock in fulfilment of a mandate set out:

*When the Lord your God has given you rest from all your enemies on every hand, in the land that the Lord your God is giving you as an inheritance to possess, you shall blot out the remembrance of Amalek from under heaven; do not forget.*

Having forewarned the **Kenites** who were living among the **Amalekites** to leave, Saul goes to war and defeats the Amalekites. **Saul kills all the men, women, children and poor quality livestock, but leaves alive the king, Agag, and best livestock**. When Samuel learns that Saul has not completely obeyed his instructions so that he could plunder the livestock for self-gain, he informs Saul that God has rejected him as king. As Samuel turns to go, Saul seizes hold of his garments and tears off a piece; **Samuel prophesies that the kingdom will likewise be torn from Saul**. Samuel then kills Agag himself. Samuel and Saul each return home and never meet again after these events.

## Saul and David

After Samuel tells Saul that God has rejected him as king, **David, a son of Jesse**, from the tribe of Judah, enters the story: from this point on Saul's story is largely the account of his increasingly troubled relationship with David.

- Samuel heads to Bethlehem, ostensibly to offer sacrifice and invited Jesse and his sons. Dining together, Jesse's sons are brought one by one to Samuel, each being rejected; at last, Jesse sends for David, the youngest, who is tending sheep. When brought to Samuel, **David is anointed by him in front of his other brothers.**
- In **1 Samuel 16:25-23**, Saul is troubled by an evil spirit sent by God. He requests soothing music, and a servant recommends David the son of Jesse, who is renowned for his skills as a harpist and other talents:

*A son of Jesse the Bethlehemite, who is skillful in playing, a mighty man of valor, a man of war, prudent in speech, and a handsome person; and the Lord is with him*

When word of Saul's needs reaches Jesse, he sends David, who had been looking after Jesse's flock, with gifts as a tribute, and **David is appointed as Saul's armor bearer**. With Jesse's permission he remains at court, playing the harp as needed to calm Saul during his troubled spells.

- The **Philistines** return with an army to attack Israel, and the Philistine and Israelite forces gather on opposite sides of a valley. The Philistine's champion **Goliath** issues a challenge for single combat, but none of the Israelite accept. David is described as a young shepherd who happens to be delivering food to his three eldest brothers in the army, and he hears Goliath's challenge. David speaks mockingly of the Philistines to some soldiers; his speech is overheard and reported to Saul, who summons David and appoints David as his champion. **David easily defeats Goliath with a single shot from a sling**. At the end of the passage, Saul asks his general, Abner, who David is.

Saul offered his elder daughter Merab as a wife to the now popular David, after his victory over Goliath, but David demurred. David distinguishes himself in the Philistine wars. Upon David's return from battle, the women praise him in song:

***Saul has slain his thousands and David his tens of thousands***
Implying that David is the greater warrior. Saul fears David's growing popularity and henceforth views him as a rival to the throne. Saul's son Jonathan and David become close friends. Jonathan recognizes David as the rightful king, and **"made a covenant with David, because he loved him as his own soul."** Jonathan even gives David his military clothes, symbolizing David's position as successor to Saul.

On two occasions, Saul threw a spear at David as he played the harp for Saul. David becomes increasingly successful and Saul becomes increasingly resentful. Now Saul actively plots against David. **Saul offered his other daughter, Michal in marriage to David**. David initially rejects this offer also, claiming he is too poor. David obtains 200 foreskins and is consequently married to Michal. Jonathan arranges a short-lived reconciliation between Saul and David and for a while David served Saul **"as in times past"** until **"the distressing spirit from the Lord"** re-appeared.

Saul sends assassins in the night, but Michal helps him escape, tricking them by placing a household idol in his bed. David flees to Jonathan, who arranges a meeting with his father. Saul warns him that his love of David will cost him the kingdom, furiously throwing a spear at him. The next day, Jonathan meets with David and tells him Saul's intent. The two friends say their goodbyes, and David flees into the countryside. **Saul later marries Michal to another man.**

## Battle of Gilboa and the death of King Saul
The **Philistines** make war again, assembling at **Shunem**, and Saul leads his army to face them at **Mount Gilboa**. Before the battle he goes to consult a medium or witch at **Endor**. The medium, tells him that God has fully rejected him, will no longer hear his prayers, has given the kingdom to David and that the next day he will lose both the battle and his life. Saul collapses in fear, and the medium restores him with food in anticipation of the next day's battle. The defeated Israelites flee from the enemy and Saul asks his armour bearer to kill him, but the armour bearer refuses,

and so Saul falls upon his own sword. David has the Amalekite put to death, advancing the theme that David will never kill the Lord's anointed king **(1 Samuel 24, 26)**.

The victorious Philistines recover Saul's body as well as those of his three sons who also died in the battle, decapitate them and display them on the wall of **Beth-shan**. But at night the inhabitants of **Jabesh-Gilead** retrieve the bodies for cremation and burial. Later on, David takes the bones of Saul and of his son Jonathan and buries them in **Zela**, in the tomb of his father. *Saul died for his unfaithfulness which he had committed against the Lord, because he did not keep the word of the Lord, and also because he consulted a medium for guidance.*

# King Solomon

Solomon (Hebrew: שְׁלֹמֹה, *Shlomoh)*, also called **Jedidiah** (**Hebrew** *Yedidyah*), was, according to the Hebrew **Bible**, **Qur'an**, and Hadiths, a fabulously wealthy and wise king of Israel who succeeded his father, **King David**. The conventional dates of **Solomon**'s reign are circa **970 to 931 BCE**, normally given in alignment with the dates of **David**'s reign. He is described as the third king of the **United Monarchy**, which would break apart into the northern Kingdom of Israel and the southern Kingdom of Judah shortly after his death. Following the split, his patrilineal descendants ruled over Judah alone. According to the **Talmud**, **Solomon is one of the 48 = prophets**. In the **Qur'an**, he is considered a major prophet, and Muslims generally refer to him by the Arabic variant **Sulayman, son of David**.

The Hebrew **Bible** credits him as the builder of the **First Temple** in Jerusalem, beginning in the fourth year of his reign, using the vast wealth he and his father had accumulated. He dedicated the temple to **Yahweh**, the God of Israel. He is portrayed as great in wisdom, wealth and power beyond either of the previous kings of the country, but also as a king who sinned. His sins included idolatry, marrying foreign women and, ultimately, turning away from **Yahweh**, and they led to the Kingdom's being torn in two during the reign of his son **Rehoboam**.

**Solomon** is the subject of many other later references and legends, most notably in the 1st-century apocryphal work known as the Testament of **Solomon**. In the New Testament, he is portrayed as a teacher of wisdom excelled by **Jesus,** and as arrayed in glory, but excelled by **"the lilies of the field"**. In later years, in mostly non-biblical circles, **Solomon** also came to be known as a magician and an exorcist, with numerous amulets and medallion seals dating from the Hellenistic period invoking his name.

## Biblical account

The life of **Solomon** is primarily described in the second **Book of Samuel**, and by **1 Chronicles and 1 Kings**. His two names mean **"peaceful" and "friend of God",** both appropriate to the story of his rule.

## Chronology

The conventional dates of **Solomon**'s reign are derived from biblical chronology and are set from **c. 970 to 931 BCE.** Regarding the **David**ic dynasty, to which **King Solomon** belongs, its chronology can be checked against datable Babylonian and Assyrian records at a few points, and these correspondences have allowed archaeologists to date its kings in a modern framework. According to the most widely used chronology, based on that by **Old Testament** professor Edwin R. Thiele, the death of **Solomon** and the division of his kingdom would have occurred in the spring of **931 BCE**.

## Childhood

**Solomon** was born in Jerusalem, **the second born child of David and his wife Bathsheba, widow of Uriah the Hittite.** The first child (unnamed in that account), a son conceived **adulterously during Uriah's lifetime**, had died as a punishment on account of the death of Uriah by **David**'s order. **Solomon had three named full brothers born to Bathsheba: Nathan, Shammua, and Shobab, besides six known older half-brothers born of as many mothers.**

The biblical narrative shows that **Solomon** served as a peace offering between God and **David**, due to his adulterous relationship with Bathsheba. In an effort to hide this sin, for example, he sent the woman's husband to battle, hoping that he would be killed there. After he died, **David** was finally able to marry his wife. As punishment, the first child, who was conceived during the adulterous relationship, died. **Solomon was born after David was forgiven.**

It is this reason why his name, which means peace, was chosen. Some historians cited that **Nathan the Prophet** brought up **Solomon** as his father was busy governing the realm. This could also be attributed to the notion that the prophet held great influence over **David** because he knew of his adultery, which was considered a grievous offense under the **Mosaic Law**. It was only during **Absalom's** rebellion when **Solomon** started spending more time at **David**'s side.

## Succession and administration

**According to the First Book of Kings, when David was old, "he could not get warm". "So they sought a beautiful young woman throughout all the territory of Israel, and found Abishag the Shunamite, and brought her to the king. The young woman was very beautiful, and she was of service to the king and attended to him, but the king knew her not."** While **David** was in this state, court factions were maneuvering for power. **David**'s heir apparent, **Adonijah**, acted to have himself declared king, but was outmaneuvered by **Bathsheba** and the prophet **Nathan**, who convinced **David** to proclaim **Solomon** king according to his earlier promise (not recorded elsewhere in the biblical narrative), despite **Solomon** being younger than his brothers.

**Solomon**, as instructed by **David**, began his reign with an extensive purge, including his father's chief general, **Joab**, among others, and further consolidated his position by appointing friends throughout the administration, including in religious positions as well as in civic and military posts. It is said that **Solomon ascended to the throne when he was only about fifteen. Solomon** greatly expanded his military strength, especially the cavalry and chariot arms. He founded numerous colonies, some of which doubled as trading posts and military outposts.

Trade relationships were a focus of his administration. In particular he continued his father's very profitable relationship with the Phoenician **king Hiram I** of Tyre (see 'wealth' below); they sent out joint expeditions to the lands of **Tarshish** and **Ophir** to engage in the trade of luxury products, importing gold, silver, sandalwood, pearls, ivory, apes and peacocks. **Solomon is considered the most-wealthy of the Israelite kings named in the Bible**.

## Wisdom

**Solomon** was the Biblical king most famous for his wisdom. In **1 Kings** he sacrificed to God, and God later appeared to him in a dream asking what **Solomon** wanted from God. **Solomon** asked for wisdom. Pleased, God personally answered **Solomon**'s prayer, promising him great wisdom because he did not ask for self-serving rewards like long life or the death of his enemies.

Perhaps the best known story of his wisdom is the Judgment of **Solomon**; **two women each lay claim to being the mother of the same child**. **Solomon** easily resolved the dispute by commanding the child to be cut in half and shared between the two. One woman promptly renounced her claim, proving that she would rather give the child up than see it killed. **Solomon** declared the woman who showed compassion to be the true mother, entitled to the whole child.

**Solomon was traditionally considered the author of several biblical books, "including not only the collections of Proverbs, but also of Ecclesiastes and the Song of Solomon and the later apocryphal book the Wisdom of Solomon."**

## Wealth / *Solomon's Temple*

According to the Hebrew **Bible**, the Israelite monarchy gained its highest splendor and wealth during **Solomon**'s **reign of 40 years**. In a single year, according to **1 Kings 10:14**, **Solomon** collected tribute amounting to **666 talents (18,125 kilograms) of gold**. **Solomon** is described as surrounding himself with all the luxuries and the grandeur of an Eastern monarch, and his government prospered. He entered into an alliance with **Hiram I, king of Tyre,** who in many ways greatly assisted him in his numerous undertakings.

## Construction projects

For some years before his death, **David** was engaged in collecting materials for building a temple in Jerusalem as a permanent home for **Yahweh** and the **Ark of the Covenant**. **Solomon** is described as undertaking the construction of the temple, with the help of an architect, also named **Hiram**, and other materials, sent from **King Hiram of Tyre.**

After the completion of the temple, **Solomon** is described in the biblical narrative as erecting many other buildings of importance in Jerusalem. For 13 years, he was engaged in the building of a royal palace on **Ophel** (a hilly promontory in central Jerusalem). This complex included buildings referred to as:
- **The House of the Forest of the Lebanon**
- **The Hall or Porch of Pillars**
- **The Hall of the Throne or the Hall of Justice**

**As well as his own residence and a residence for his wife, Pharaoh's daughter.**

**Solomon** also constructed great works for the purpose of securing a plentiful supply of water for the city, and the **Millo** (Septuagint, *Acra*) for the defense of the city. However, excavations of Jerusalem have shown a distinct lack of monumental architecture from the era, and remains of neither the Temple nor **Solomon**'s palace have been found.

**Solomon** is also described as rebuilding cities elsewhere in Israel, creating the port of **Ezion-Geber**, and constructing Palmyra in the wilderness as a commercial depot and military outpost. Although the location of the port of **Ezion-Geber** is known, no remains have ever been found. More archaeological success has been achieved with the major cities **Solomon** is said to have strengthened or rebuilt, for example, **Hazor, Megiddo and Gezer**. These all have substantial ancient remains, including impressive six-chambered gates, and ashlar palaces; however, it is no longer the scholarly consensus that these structures date to the time, according to the **Bible**, when **Solomon** ruled.

According to the **Bible**, during **Solomon**'s reign, Israel enjoyed great commercial prosperity, with extensive traffic being carried on by land with Tyre, Egypt, and Arabia, and by sea with **Tarshish, Ophir, and South India**.

## Wives and concubines

According to the biblical account, **Solomon** had **700 wives and 300 concubines**. The wives were described as foreign princesses, including Pharaoh's daughter and women of Moab, Ammon, Edom, Sidon and of the Hittites. **His marriage to Pharaoh's daughter** appears to have cemented a political alliance with Egypt whereas he clung to his other wives and concubines **"in love"**.

The only wife mentioned by name is Naamah the Ammonite, **mother of Solomon's successor, Rehoboam**. The Biblical narrative notes with disapproval that **Solomon** permitted his foreign wives to import their national deities, building temples to **Ashtoreth** and **Milcom**.

In the branch of literary analysis that examines the **Bible**, called higher criticism, the story of **Solomon** falling into idolatry by the influence of Pharaoh's daughter and his other foreign wives is **"customarily seen as the handiwork of the 'Deuteronomistic historian(s)'"**, who are held to have written, compiled, or edited texts to legitimize the reforms of Hezekiah's grandson, King Josiah who reigned from ca **641 BCE to 609 BCE** (over 280 years after **Solomon**'s death according to **Bible** scholars). Scholarly consensus in this field holds that **"Solomon's wives/women were introduced in the 'Josianic'** (customarily Dtr) **edition of Kings as a theological construct to blame the schism on his misdeeds"**.

## Relationship with Queen of Sheba

In a brief, unelaborated, and enigmatic passage, the Hebrew **Bible** describes how the fame of **Solomon**'s wisdom and wealth spread far and wide, so much so that the queen of Sheba decided that she should meet him. The queen is described as visiting with a number of gifts including gold, spices and precious stones. When **Solomon** gave her **"all her desire, whatsoever she asked,"** she left satisfied **(1 Kings 10:10).**

Whether the passage is simply to provide a brief token, foreign witness of **Solomon**'s wealth and wisdom, or whether there is meant to be something more significant to the queen's visit is unknown; nevertheless the visit of the **Queen of Sheba** has become the subject of numerous stories.

Sheba is typically identified as Saba, a nation once spanning the Red Sea on the coasts of what are now **Eritrea, Somalia, Ethiopia** and **Yemen**, in Arabia **Felix**. In a Rabbinical account (e.g. Targum Sheni), **Solomon** was accustomed to ordering the living creatures of the world to dance before him (Rabbinical accounts say that **Solomon** had been given control over all living things by **Yahweh**), but one day upon discovering that the mountain-cock or hoopoe **(Aramaic name: *nagar Tura*)** was absent, he summoned it to him, and the bird told him that it had been searching for somewhere new (Colloquy of the **Queen of Sheba**).

The bird had discovered a land in the east, exceedingly rich in gold, silver, and plants, whose capital was called *Kitor* and whose ruler was the **Queen of Sheba**, and the bird, on its own advice, was sent by **Solomon** to request the queen's immediate attendance at **Solomon**'s court.

An Ethiopian account from the 14th century (*Kebra Nagast*) maintains that the **Queen of Sheba** had sexual relations with **King Solomon** and gave birth by the **Mai Bella** stream in the province of Hamasien, Eritrea. The Ethiopian tradition has a detailed account of the affair. The child was a son who went on to become **Manelik I, King of Axum**, and founded a dynasty that would reign as the first Jewish, then **Christian Empire of Ethiopia** for 2,900+ years (less one usurpation episode, an interval of c. 133 years until a legitimate male heir regained the crown) until **Haile Selassie was overthrown in 1974.**

**Manelik** was said to be a practicing Jew who was given a replica of the **Ark of the Covenant** by **King Solomon**; and, moreover, that the original was switched and went to Axum with him and his mother, and is still there, guarded by a single priest charged with caring for the artifact as his life's task.

The claim of such a lineage and of possession of the **Ark** has been an important source of legitimacy and prestige for the Ethiopian monarchy throughout the many centuries of its existence, and had important and lasting effects on Ethiopian culture as a whole. **The Ethiopian government**

**and church deny all requests to view the alleged ark**. Some classical-era Rabbis, attacking **Solomon**'s moral character, have claimed instead that the child was an ancestor of **Nebuchadnezzar II,** who destroyed **Solomon**'s temple some 300 years later.

## Sins and punishment

According to **1 Kings 11:4 Solomon**'s **"wives turned his heart after other gods",** their own national deities, to whom **Solomon** built temples, thus incurring divine anger and retribution in the form of the division of the kingdom after **Solomon**'s death **(1 Kings 11:9–13). 1 Kings 11** describes **Solomon**'s descent into idolatry, particularly his turning after Ashtoreth, the goddess of the Sidonians, and after Milcom, the abomination of the Ammonites. In **Deuteronomy 17:16–17,** a king is commanded not to multiply horses or wives, neither greatly multiply to himself gold or silver. **Solomon** sins in all three of these areas.

**Solomon collects 666 talents of gold each year (1 Kings 10:14),** a huge amount of money for a small nation like Israel. **Solomon** gathers a large number of horses and chariots and even brings in horses from Egypt. Just as **Deuteronomy 17** warns, collecting horses and chariots takes Israel back to Egypt. Finally, **Solomon marries foreign women, and these women turn Solomon to other gods.** According to **1 Kings 11:30–34 and 1 Kings 11:9–13**, it was because of these sins that **"the Lord punishes Solomon by removing 10 of the 12 Tribes of Israel from the Israelites. And the Lord was angry with Solomon**, because his heart had turned away from the Lord, the **God of Israel**, who had appeared to him twice and had commanded him concerning this thing that he should not go after other gods. But he did not keep what the Lord commanded. Therefore, the Lord said to **Solomon, "Since this has been your practice and you have not kept my covenant and my statutes that I have commanded you, I will surely tear the kingdom from you and will give it to your servant. Yet for the sake of David your father I will not do it in your days, but I will tear it out of the hand of your son. However, I will not tear away all the kingdom, but I will give one tribe to your son, for the sake of David my servant and for the sake of Jerusalem that I have chosen."**

## Enemies

Near the end of his life, **Solomon** was forced to contend with several enemies, including **Hadad of Edom, Rezon of Zobah**, and one of his officials named Jeroboam who was from the tribe of Ephraim.

## Death, succession of Rehoboam, and kingdom division

According to the Hebrew **Bible, Solomon** is the last ruler of a United Kingdom of Israel. **He dies of natural causes at around 60 years of age**. Upon **Solomon**'s death, **his son, Rehoboam, succeeds him**. However, ten of the Tribes of Israel refuse to accept him as king, splitting the United Monarchy in the northern Kingdom of Israel under Jeroboam, while Rehoboam continues to reign over the much smaller southern Kingdom of Judah. Henceforth the two kingdoms are never again united.

## Jewish scriptures

King **Solomon** is one of the central Biblical figures in Jewish heritage that have lasting religious, national and political aspects. As the builder of the **First Temple in Jerusalem** and last ruler of the united Kingdom of Israel before its division into the northern Kingdom of Israel and the southern Kingdom of Judah, **Solomon** is associated with the peak **"golden age"** of the independent Kingdom of Israel as well as a source of judicial and religious wisdom. According to Jewish tradition, **King Solomon wrote three books of the Bible:**

- *Mishlei* (Book of Proverbs), a collection of fables and wisdom of life
- *Kohelet* (Ecclesiastes), a book of contemplation and his self-reflection.
- *Shir ha-Shirim* (Song of Songs), an unusual collection of poetry interspersed with verse, whose interpretation is either literal (i.e., a romantic and sexual relationship between a man and a woman) or metaphorical (a relationship between God and his people).

The Hebrew word **"To Solomon"** (which can also be translated as "by **Solomon**") appears in the title of two hymns, 72 and 127, in the book of **Psalms (*Tehillim*)**, suggesting to some that **Solomon** wrote them.

## Apocryphal texts

Rabbinical tradition attributes the *Wisdom of Solomon* to **Solomon**, although this book was probably written in the 2nd century BCE. In this work, **Solomon** is portrayed as an astronomer. Other books of wisdom poetry such as the *Odes of Solomon* and the *Psalms of Solomon* also bear his name. The Jewish historian Eupolemus, who wrote about 157 BCE, included copies of apocryphal letters exchanged between **Solomon** and the kings of Egypt and Tyre.

The Gnostic *Apocalypse of Adam*, which may date to the 1st or 2nd century, refers to a legend in which **Solomon** sends out an army of demons to seek a virgin who had fled from him, perhaps the earliest surviving mention of the later common tale that **Solomon** controlled demons and made them his slaves. This tradition of **Solomon**'s control over demons appears fully elaborated in the early pseudo graphical work called the *Testament of Solomon* with its elaborate and grotesque demonology.

## *David: Historicity / Arguments against biblical description*

Historical evidence of King **Solomon** other than the biblical accounts has been so minimal that some scholars have understood the period of his reign as a **'Dark Age'** (Muhly 1998). The first-century Romano-Jewish scholar **Josephus** in *Against Apion*, citing Tyrian court records and Menander, gives a specific year during which King Hiram I of Tyre sent materials to **Solomon** for the construction of the Temple. However, no material evidence indisputably of **Solomon**'s reign has been found. **Yigael Yadin's** excavations at Hazor, Megiddo, Beit Shean and Gezer uncovered structures that he and others have argued date from **Solomon's** reign, but others, such as **Israel Finkelstein** and **Neil Silberman**, argue that they should be dated to the Omride period, more than a century after **Solomon**.

According to **Finkelstein** and **Silberman**, authors of *The Bible Unearthed: Archaeology's New Vision of Ancient Israel and the Origin of Its Sacred Texts*, at the time of the kingdoms of **David** and **Solomon**, Jerusalem was populated by only a few hundred residents or less, which is insufficient for an empire stretching from the Euphrates to **Eilath**. According to *The Bible Unearthed*, archaeological evidence suggests that the kingdom of Israel at the time of **Solomon** was little more than a small city state, and so it is implausible that **Solomon received tribute as large as 666 talents of gold per year**. Although both Finkelstein and Silberman accept that **David** and **Solomon** were real inhabitants of Judah about the 10th century BCE, they claim that the earliest independent reference to the **Kingdom of Israel is about 890 BCE, and for Judah about 750 BCE.**

They suggest that because of religious prejudice, the authors of the **Bible** suppressed the achievements of the Omrides (whom the Hebrew **Bible** describes as being polytheist), and instead pushed them back to a supposed golden age of Judaism and monotheists, and devotees of **Yahweh**. Some Biblical minimalists like **Thomas L. Thompson** go further, arguing that Jerusalem became a city and capable of being a state capital only in the mid-7th century. Likewise, Finkelstein and others consider the claimed size of **Solomon's** temple implausible.

## Arguments in favor of biblical description

These views are criticized by **William G. Dever**, and André Lemaire, among others. Lemaire states in *Ancient Israel: From Abraham to the Roman Destruction of the Temple* that the principal points of the biblical tradition of **Solomon** are generally trustworthy, although elsewhere he writes that he could find no substantiating archaeological evidence that supports the **Queen of Sheba's** visit to **king Solomon**, saying that the earliest records of trans-Arabian caravan voyages from Tayma and Sheba unto the Middle-Euphrates etc. occurred in the mid-8th century BCE, placing a possible visit from the **Queen of Sheba** to Jerusalem around this time – some 250 years later than the timeframe traditionally given for **king Solomon's** reign.

**Kenneth Kitchen** argues that **Solomon** ruled over a comparatively wealthy **"mini-empire"**, rather than a small city-state, and considers 666 gold talents a modest amount of money. Kitchen calculates that over 30 years, such a kingdom might have accumulated up to 500 tons of gold, which is small compared to other examples, such as the 1,180 tons of gold that Alexander the Great took from Susa. Similarly **Kitchen** and others consider the temple of **Solomon** a reasonable and typically sized structure for the region at the time. Dever states **"that we now have direct**

**Bronze and Iron Age parallels for every feature of the 'Solomonic temple' as described in the Hebrew Bible".**

## Middle way

Some scholars have charted a middle path between minimalist scholars like **Finkelstein**, **Silberman**, and **Philip Davies (who believes that "Solomon is a totally invented character")** on the one hand, and maximalist scholars like **Dever, Lemaire**, and **Kitchen** on the other hand. For instance, the archaeologist **Avraham Faust** has argued that biblical depictions of **Solomon** date to later periods and do overstate his wealth, buildings, and kingdom, but that **Solomon** did have an acropolis and ruled over a polity larger than Jerusalem. In particular, his archaeological research in regions near Jerusalem, like **Sharon**, finds commerce too great not to be supported by a polity and such regions probably were ruled loosely by Jerusalem. Scholars like **Lester Grabbe** also believe that there must have been a ruler in Jerusalem during this period and that he likely built a temple, although the town was quite small.

## Archaeology / General Observations

The archaeological remains that are considered to date from the time of **Solomon** are notable for the fact that Canaanite material culture appears to have continued unabated; there is a distinct lack of magnificent empire, or cultural development – indeed comparing pottery from areas traditionally assigned to Israel with that of the Philistines points to the latter having been significantly more sophisticated. However, there is a lack of physical evidence of its existence, despite some archaeological work in the area. This is not unexpected because the area was devastated by the Babylonians, then rebuilt and destroyed several times.

## Temple Mount in Jerusalem

Little archaeological excavation has been done around the area known as the **Temple Mount**, in what is thought to be the **foundation of Solomon's Temple**, because attempts to do so are met with protests by the Muslim authorities.

## Precious metals from Tarshish

The biblical passages that understand Tarshish as a source of **King Solomon**'s great wealth in metals – especially silver, but also gold, tin and iron **(Ezekiel 27)** – were linked to archaeological evidence from silver-hoards found in Phoenicia in 2013. The metals from Tarshish were reportedly obtained by **Solomon** in partnership with **King Hiram** of Phoenician Tyre **(Isaiah 23),** and the fleets of Tarshish-ships that sailed in their service, and the silver-hoards provide the first recognized material evidence that agrees with the ancient texts concerning **Solomon**'s kingdom and his wealth.

Possible evidence for the described wealth of **Solomon** and his kingdom was discovered in ancient silver-hoards, which were found in Israel and Phoenicia and recognized for their importance in

2003. The evidence from the hoards shows that the Levant was a center of wealth in precious metals during the reign of **Solomon** and **Hiram**, and matches the texts that say the trade extended from Asia to the Atlantic Ocean.

## Biblical criticism: Solomon's religiosity

From a critical point of view, **Solomon**'s building of a **temple for Yahweh** should not be considered an act of particular devotion to **Yahweh** because **Solomon** is also described as building places of worship for a number of other deities. Some scholars and historians argue that **Solomon**'s apparent initial devotion to **Yahweh**, described in passages such as his dedication prayer **(1 Kings 8:14–66),** were written much later, after Jerusalem had become the religious center of the kingdom, replacing locations such as **Shiloh** and **Bethel.**

Some scholars believe that passages such as these in the **Books of Kings** were not written by the same authors who wrote the rest of the text, instead probably by the Deuteronomist. Such views have been challenged by other historians who maintain that there is evidence that these passages in Kings are derived from official court records at the time of **Solomon** and from other writings of that time that were incorporated into the canonical **books of Kings.**

## Religious views / Judaism

King **Solomon** sinned by acquiring many foreign wives and horses because he thought he knew the reason for the Biblical prohibition and thought it did not apply to him. When **King Solomon** married the daughter of the Egyptian Pharaoh, a sandbank formed which eventually formed the **"great nation of Rome"** – the nation that destroyed the **Second Temple (Herod's Temple).** **Solomon** gradually lost more and more prestige until he became like a commoner. Some say he regained his status while others say he did not. In the end however, he is regarded as a righteous king and is especially praised for his diligence in building the **Temple**.

The **Seder Olam Rabba** holds that **Solomon's reign was not in 1000 BCE**, but rather in the 9th century BCE, during which time he built the **First Temple in 832 BCE**. However, the 1906 Jewish Encyclopedia gives the more common **date of "971 to 931 B.C.".**

## Christianity

Christianity has traditionally accepted the historical existence of **Solomon**, though some modern Christian scholars have also questioned at least his authorship of those biblical texts ascribed to him. Such disputes tend to divide Christians into traditionalist and modernist camps.

Of the two genealogies of Jesus given in the Gospels, **Matthew** mentions **Solomon**, but **Luke** does not. Some commentators see this as an issue that can be reconciled while others disagree. For instance, it has been suggested that Luke is using Joseph's genealogy and **Matthew** is using Mary's, but **Darrell Bock** states that this would be unprecedented, **"especially when no other single**

**woman appears in the line".** Other suggestions include the use by one of the royal and the other of the natural line, one using the legal line and the other the physical line, or that **Joseph was adopted**.

Jesus makes reference to **Solomon**, using him for comparison purposes in his admonition against worrying about your life. This account is recorded in **Matthew 6:29** and the parallel passage in **Luke 12:27.** In the Eastern Orthodox Church, **Solomon** is commemorated as a saint, with the title of **"Righteous Prophet and King".** His feast day is celebrated on the Sunday of the **Holy Forefathers (two Sundays before the Great Feast of the Nativity of the Lord).**

The staunchly Catholic **King Philip II of Spain** sought to model himself after **King Solomon**. Statues of **King David** and **Solomon** stand on either side of the entrance to the basilica of El Escorial, Philip's palace, and **Solomon** is also depicted in a great fresco at the center of **El** Escorial's library. Philip identified the warrior-king **David** with his own father **Charles V**, and himself sought to emulate the thoughtful and logical character which he perceived in **Solomon**. Moreover, the structure of the Escorial was inspired by that of **Solomon's Temple.**

## Islam

In Islamic tradition, **Solomon** is venerated as a **Prophet and a Messenger of God**, as well as a divinely appointed monarch, who ruled over the Kingdom of Israel. As in Judaism, Islam recognizes **Solomon** as the son of **King David**, who is also considered a Prophet and a King but, refuses the claim that **Solomon** turned to idolatry. One of the enslaved **Jinn** escaped his enslavement, instead, and took over his kingdom and posed as **Solomon**, while others thought indeed he became a ruthless king.

And they followed what the devils taught during the reign of **Solomon**. It was not **Solomon** who disbelieved, but it was the devils who disbelieved. They taught the people witchcraft and what was revealed in **Babil** (Arabic: Babylon) to the **two angels Harut and Marut**. They did not teach anybody until they had said **"We are a test, so do not lose faith."** But they learned from them the means to cause separation between man and his wife. But they cannot harm anyone except with God's permission. And they learned what would harm them and not benefit them. Yet they knew that whoever deals in it will have no share in the Hereafter. Miserable is what they sold their souls for, if they only knew.

The **Qur'an** ascribes to **Solomon** a great level of wisdom, knowledge and power. He knew the *Mantiq al-tayr* (Arabic: language of the birds). **Solomon** was also known in the Islam to have other supernatural abilities bestowed upon him by Allah, after a special request by **Solomon** himself, such as controlling the wind, ruling over the Jinn, including demons, and the hearing of distant speeches by ants:

"And to Solomon (We made) the wind (obedient): its early morning (stride) was a month's (journey), and its evening (stride) was a month's (journey); and We made a font of molten brass to flow for him; and there were Jinns that worked in front of him, by the leave of his Lord, and if any of them turned aside from Our command, We made him taste of the Penalty of the Blazing Fire." (34: 12) and "At length, when they came to a (lowly) valley of ants, one of the ants said: 'O ye ants, get into your habitations, lest Solomon and his hosts crush you (under foot) without knowing it.' – So he smiled, amused at her speech; and he said: 'O my *Rabb* (Arabic: Lord)!

So order me that I may be grateful for **Thy favors**, which Thou hast bestowed on me and on my parents, and that I may work the righteousness that will please Thee: and admit me, by **Thy Grace, to the ranks of Thy righteous Servants.'"** (27: 18–19). The Qur'an mentions Solomon 17 times.

## Baháii

In the **Baha'i Faith**, **Solomon** is regarded as one of the lesser prophets along with **David, Isaiah, Jeremiah, Ezekiel**, along with others. Baha'is see **Solomon** as a prophet who was sent by God to address the issues of his time. **Baha'ullah** wrote about **Solomon** in the *Hidden Words*. He also mentions **Solomon** in the *Tablet of Wisdom*, where he is depicted as a contemporary of **Pythagoras**.

## Legends / *One Thousand and One Nights*

A well-known story in the collection *One Thousand and One Nights* describes a genie who had displeased **King Solomon** and was punished by being locked in a bottle and thrown into the sea. Since the bottle was sealed with **Solomon**'s seal, the genie was helpless to free himself, until freed many centuries later by a fisherman who discovered the bottle. In other stories from the *One Thousand and One Nights*, protagonists who had to leave their homeland and travel to the unknown places of the world saw signs which proved that **Solomon** had already been there. Sometimes, protagonists discovered words of **Solomon** that were intended to help those who were lost and had unluckily reached those forbidden and deserted places.

## Angels and magic

According to the Rabbinical literature, on account of his modest request for wisdom only, **Solomon** was rewarded with riches and an unprecedented glorious realm, which extended over the upper world inhabited by the angels and over the whole of the terrestrial globe with all its inhabitants, including all the beasts, fowl, and reptiles, as well as the demons and spirits. His control over the demons, spirits, and animals augmented his splendor, the demons bringing him precious stones, besides water from distant countries to irrigate his exotic plants.

The beasts and fowl of their own accord entered the kitchen of **Solomon**'s palace, so that they might be used as food for him, and extravagant meals for him were prepared daily by each of his **700 wives and 300 concubines**, with the thought that perhaps the king would feast that day in her house.

## Seal of Solomon

A magic ring called the **"Seal of Solomon"** was supposedly given to **Solomon** and gave him power over demons or Jinn. The magical symbol said to have been on the **Seal of Solomon** which made it efficacious is often considered to be the *Star of David* though this emblem (also known as the **Shield of David**) is known to have been associated with Judaism only as recently as the 11th century CE while the five pointed star (pentagram) can be found on jars and other artifacts from Jerusalem dating back to at least the 2nd and 4th centuries BCE and is more likely to have been the emblem found on the ring purportedly used by **King Solomon** to control the Jinn or demons. **Asmodeus**, king of demons, was one day, according to the classical Rabbis, captured by **Benaiah** using the ring, and was forced to remain in **Solomon**'s service.

In one tale, **Asmodeus** brought a man with two heads from under the earth to show **Solomon**; the man, unable to return, married a woman from Jerusalem and had seven sons, six of whom resembled the mother, while one resembled the father in having two heads. After their father's death, the son with two heads claimed two shares of the inheritance, arguing that he was two men; **Solomon** decided that the son with two heads was only one man. The **Seal of Solomon**, in some legends known as the **Ring of Aandaleeb**, was a highly sought after symbol of power. In several legends, different groups or individuals attempted to steal it or attain it in some manner.

## Solomon and Asmodeus

One legend concerning Asmodeus (see: The Story of **King Solomon** and **Ashmedai**) goes on to state that **Solomon** one day asked **Asmodeus** what could make demons powerful over man, and Asmodeus asked to be freed and given the ring so that he could demonstrate; **Solomon** agreed but Asmodeus threw the ring into the sea and it was swallowed by a fish. Asmodeus then swallowed the king, stood up fully with one wing touching heaven and the other earth, and spat out **Solomon** to a distance of 400 miles.

The Rabbis claim this was a divine punishment for **Solomon's having failed to follow three divine commands**, and **Solomon** was forced to wander from city to city, until he eventually arrived in an Ammonite city where he was forced to work in the king's kitchens.

**Solomon** gained a chance to prepare a meal for the Ammonite king, which the king found so impressive that the previous cook was sacked and **Solomon** put in his place; the king's daughter, Naamah, subsequently fell in love with **Solomon**, but the family (thinking **Solomon** a commoner) disapproved, so the king decided to kill them both by sending them into the desert.

**Solomon** and the king's daughter wandered the desert until they reached a coastal city, where they bought a fish to eat, which just happened to be the one which had swallowed the magic ring.

**Solomon** was then able to regain his throne and expel **Asmodeus.** The element of a ring thrown into the sea and found back in a fish's belly also appeared in **Herodotus'** account of **Polycrates,** the tyrant of Samos from c. **538 BCE to 522 BCE.**

In another familiar version of the legend of the **Seal of Solomon**, Asmodeus disguises himself. In some myths, he's disguised as **King Solomon** himself, while in more frequently heard versions he's disguised as a falcon, calling himself **Gavyn** (Gavinn or Gavin), one of King **Solomon's** trusted friends. The concealed Asmodeus tells travelers who have ventured up to King **Solomon's** grand lofty palace that the **Seal of Solomon** was thrown into the sea. He then convinces them to plunge in and attempt to retrieve it, for if they do they would take the throne as king.

## Artifacts

Other magical items attributed to **Solomon** are his key and his Table. The latter was said to be held in Toledo, Spain during Visigoth rule and was part of the loot taken by **Tarik ibn Ziyad during the Umayyad Conquest of Iberia,** according to **Ibn Abd-el-Hakem's** *History of the Conquest of Spain*. The former appears in the title of the **Lesser Key of Solomon**, a grimoire whose framing story is **Solomon** capturing demons using his ring, and forcing them to explain themselves to him. In *The Book of Deadly Names*, purportedly translated from Arabic manuscripts found hidden in a building in Spain, the **"King of the Jinn" Fiqitush** brings **72 Jinn** before King **Solomon** to confess their corruptions and places of residence. **Fiqitush** tells **King Solomon** the recipes for curing such corruptions as each evil Jinn confesses.

## Angels

Angels also helped **Solomon** in building the Temple; though not by choice. The edifice was, according to rabbinical legend, miraculously constructed throughout, the large heavy stones rising and settling in their respective places of themselves. The general opinion of the Rabbis is that **Solomon** hewed the stones by means of a *Shamir,* a mythical worm whose mere touch cleft rocks. According to **Midrash Tehillim**, the **Shamir** was brought from paradise by **Solomon's** eagle; but most of the Rabbis state that **Solomon** was informed of the worm's haunts by **Asmodeus**.

The **Shamir** had been entrusted by the prince of the sea to the mountain rooster alone, and the rooster had sworn to guard it well, but **Solomon's** men found the bird's nest, and covered it with glass. When the bird returned, it used the **Shamir** to break the glass, whereupon the men scared the bird, causing it to drop the worm, which the men could then bring to **Solomon**.

## In the Kabbalah

Early adherents of the **Kabbalah** portray **Solomon** as having sailed through the air on a throne of light placed on an eagle, which brought him near the heavenly gates as well as to the dark mountains behind which the fallen angels *Uzza* and *Azzazel* were chained; the eagle would rest on the chains, and **Solomon**, using the magic ring, would compel the two angels to reveal every mystery he desired to know.

## The palace without entrance

According to one legend, while traveling magically, **Solomon** noticed a magnificent palace to which there appeared to be no entrance. He ordered the demons to climb to the roof and see if they could discover any living being within the building but they found only an eagle, which said that it was **700 years old**, but that it had never seen an entrance. An elder brother of the eagle, **900 years old**, was then found, but it also did not know the entrance.

The eldest brother of these two birds, which was 1,300 years old, then declared it had been informed by its father that the door was on the west side, but that it had become hidden by sand drifted by the wind. Having discovered the entrance, **Solomon** found an idol inside that had in its mouth a silver tablet saying in Greek (a language not thought by modern scholars to have **existed 1000 years before the time of Solomon**) that the statue was of *Shaddad, the son of 'Ad*, and that it **had *reigned over a million cities, rode on a million horses, had under it a million vassals and slew a million warriors*,** yet it could not resist the angel of death.

## Throne

**Solomon**'s throne is described at length in **Targum Sheni**, which is compiled from three different sources, and in two later **Midrash**. According to these, there were on the steps of the throne twelve golden lions, each facing a golden eagle. There were six steps to the throne, on which animals, all of gold, were arranged in the following order: on the first step a lion opposite an ox; on the second, a wolf opposite a sheep; on the third, a tiger opposite a camel; on the fourth, an eagle opposite a peacock, on the fifth, a cat opposite a cock; on the sixth, a sparrow-hawk opposite a dove. On the top of the throne was a dove holding a sparrow-hawk in its claws, symbolizing the dominion of Israel over the Gentiles. The first midrash claims that six steps were constructed because **Solomon foresaw that six kings would sit on the throne, namely, Solomon, Rehoboam, Hezekiah, Manasseh, Amon, and Josiah.**

There was also on the top of the throne a golden candelabrum, on the seven branches of the one side of which were engraved the names of the seven patriarchs **Adam, Noah, Shem, Abraham, Isaac, Jacob**, and **Job**, and on the seven of the other the names of **Levi, Kohath, Amram, Moses, Aaron, Eldad, Medad, and, in addition, Hur** (another version has Haggai). Above the candelabrum was a golden jar filled with olive-oil and beneath it a golden basin which supplied the jar with oil and on which the names of **Nadab, Abihu**, and **Eli** and his two sons were engraved. Over the throne, twenty-four vines were fixed to cast a shadow on the king's head.

By a mechanical contrivance the throne followed **Solomon** wherever he wished to go. Supposedly, due to another mechanical trick, when the king reached the first step, the ox stretched forth its leg, on which **Solomon** leaned, a similar action taking place in the case of the animals on each of the six steps. From the sixth step the eagles raised the king and placed him in his seat, near which a golden serpent lay coiled. When the king was seated the large eagle placed the crown on his head, the serpent uncoiled itself, and the lions and eagles moved upward to form a shade over him.

The dove then descended, took the scroll of the Law from the **Ark**, and placed it on **Solomon**'s knees. When the king sat, surrounded by the **Sanhedrin**, to judge the people, the wheels began to turn, and the beasts and fowls began to utter their respective cries, which frightened those who had intended to bear false testimony. Moreover, while **Solomon** was ascending the throne, the lions scattered all kinds of fragrant spices. After **Solomon**'s death, **Pharaoh Shishak**, when taking away the treasures of the Temple **(I Kings xiv. 26),** carried off the throne, which remained in Egypt until Sennacherib conquered that country.

After **Sennacherib's** fall Hezekiah gained possession of it, but when **Josiah** was slain by **Pharaoh Necho**, the latter took it away. However, according to rabbinical accounts, **Necho** did not know how the mechanism worked and so accidentally struck himself with one of the lions causing him to become lame; **Nebuchadnezzar,** into whose possession the throne subsequently came, shared a similar fate. The throne then passed to the Persians, whose **king Darius** was the first to sit successfully on **Solomon**'s throne after his death; subsequently the throne came into the possession of the Greeks and **Ahasuerus.**

## Freemasonry

Masonic rituals refer to **King Solomon** and the building of his Temple. Masonic Temples, where a Masonic Lodge meets, are an allegorical reference to **King Solomon's Temple**.

# The Kenesset

(Hebrew: הַכְּנֶסֶת, romanized: *HaKenesset* lit. **'gathering, assembly'**, is the unicameral legislature of Israel. As the supreme state body, the **Kenesset** is sovereign and thus, with the exception of checks and balances from the courts and local governments, has total control over the entirety of the Israeli government.

The **Kenesset** passes all laws, elects the president and prime minister (although the former is ceremonially appointed by the Prime Minister), approves the cabinet, and supervises the work of the government, among other things. In addition, the **Kenesset** elects the state comptroller. It also has the power to waive the immunity of its members, remove the president and the state comptroller from office, dissolve the government in a constructive vote of no confidence, and to dissolve itself and call new elections.

The prime minister may also dissolve the **Kenesset**. However, until an election is completed, the **Kenesset** maintains authority in its current composition. The **Kenesset** meets in Givat Ram, Jerusalem. Members of the **Kenesset** are elected nationwide through proportional representation.

## Name
The term "**Kenesset**" is derived from the ancient *Kenesset HaGdola* or "**Great Assembly**", which according to Jewish tradition was an assembly of **120 scribes, sages, and prophets**, in the period from the end of the Biblical prophets to the time of the development of Rabbinic Judaism – about two centuries ending c. 200 BCE. There is, however, no organisational continuity and aside from the number of members, there is little similarity, as the ancient **Kenesset** was a religious, completely unelected body. Members of the **Kenesset** are known in Hebrew as (*Haver HaKenesset*), if male, or (*Havrat HaKenesset*), if female.

## History
The **Kenesset** first convened on 14 February 1949 in Jerusalem following the 20 January elections, replacing the **Provisional State Council** which acted as Israel's official legislature from its date of **independence on 14 May 1948** and succeeding the **Assembly of Representatives** that had functioned as the Jewish community's representative body during the **Mandate Era**. Before the construction of its current location, the **Kenesset** met in Tel Aviv, before moving to the **Froumine** building in Jerusalem.

The **Kenesset** compound sits on a hilltop in western Jerusalem in a district known as **Sheikh Badr** before the 1948 Arab–Israeli War, now **Givat Ram**. The main building was financed by **James de Rothschild** as a gift to the State of Israel in his will and was completed in 1966. It was built on land leased from the **Greek Orthodox Patriarchate** of Jerusalem. Over the years, significant additions to the structure were constructed, however, these were built at levels below and behind the main 1966 structure as not to detract from the original assembly building's appearance.

Despite numerous motions of no confidence being tabled in the **Kenesset**, a government has only been defeated by one once, when **Yitzhak Shamir's** government was brought down on 15 March 1990 as part of a plot that became known as **"the dirty trick".**

However, several governments have resigned as a result of no-confidence motions, even when they were not defeated. These include the fifth government, which fell after **Prime Minister Moshe Sharett** resigned in June 1955 following the abstention of the **General Zionists** (part of the governing coalition) during a vote of no-confidence; the ninth government, which fell after **Prime Minister Ben-Gurion** resigned in January 1961 over a motion of no-confidence on the **Lavon Affair**; and the seventeenth government, which resigned in December 1976 after the **National Religious Party** (part of the governing coalition) abstained in a motion of no-confidence against the government.

## Timeline

- **14 February 1949**: First meeting of the Constituent Assembly, Jewish Agency, Jerusalem
- **16 February 1949**: Name "Kenesset" approved for the Constituent Assembly; number of members fixed at 120; the Kenesset starts convening in Tel Aviv (first as at what is now the Opera Tower, later at the San Remo Hotel in Tel Aviv)
- **26 December 1949 – 8** March 1950: Kenesset moved to Jerusalem; first convened at the Jewish Agency building
- **13 March 1950**: Kenesset moved to the Froumine House, in King George Street, Jerusalem
- **1950–1955**: Israeli government holds architectural competitions for the permanent Kenesset building. Ossip Klarwein's original design won the competition
- **1955**: Government approves plans to build the Kenesset in its current location
- **1957:** James de Rothschild informs Prime Minister David Ben-Gurion of his desire to finance the construction of the building
- **14 October 1958**: Cornerstone-laying for new Kenesset building
- **30 August 1966**: Dedication of new building (during the sixth Kenesset)
- **1981**: Construction of new wing begins
- **1992**: New wing opens
- **2001:** Construction starts on a large new wing that essentially doubles the overall floorspace of the Kenesset compound.
- 2007: New large wing opens

## Government duties

As the legislative branch of the Israeli government, the **Kenesset** passes all laws, elects the president, approves the cabinet, and supervises the work of the government through its committees. It also has the power to waive the immunity of its members, remove the president and the **State Comptroller** from office, and to dissolve itself and call new elections.

The **Kenesset** has *de jure* parliamentary supremacy, and can pass any law by a simple majority, even one that might arguably conflict with the **Basic Laws of Israel**, unless the basic law includes specific conditions for its modification; in accordance with a plan adopted in 1950, the **Basic Laws** can be adopted and amended by the **Kenesset**, acting in its capacity as a **Constituent Assembly.** The **Kenesset** itself is regulated by a **Basic Law** called "**Basic Law: the Kenesset**".

In addition to the absence of a formal constitution, and with no **Basic Law** thus far being adopted which formally grants a power of judicial review to the judiciary, the **Supreme Court** of Israel has since the early 1990s asserted its authority, when sitting as the **High Court** of Justice, to invalidate provisions of **Kenesset** laws it has found to be inconsistent with **Basic Law**. The **Kenesset** is presided over by a **Speaker** and **Deputy Speakers**, called the **Kenesset Presidium**, which currently consists of:

## Kenesset committees

**Kenesset** committees amend bills on various appropriate subjects. **Kenesset** members are assigned to committees, while chairpersons are chosen by their members, on recommendation of the **House Committee,** and their factional composition represents that of the **Kenesset** itself. Committees may elect sub-committees and delegate powers to them, or establish joint committees for issues concerning more than one committee.

To further their deliberations, they invite non-voting people, like government ministers, senior officials, and experts in the matter being discussed. Committees may request explanations and information from any relevant ministers in any matter within their competence, and the ministers or persons appointed by them must provide the explanation or information requested.

There are four types of committees in the **Kenesset. Permanent committees** amend proposed legislation dealing with their area of expertise, and may initiate legislation. However, such legislation may only deal with **Basic Laws** and laws dealing with the **Kenesset**, elections to the **Kenesset, Kenesset** members, or the **State Comptroller**. Special committees function in a similar manner to permanent committees, but are appointed to deal with particular manners at hand, and can be dissolved or turned into permanent committees.

Parliamentary inquiry committees are appointed by the plenum to deal with issues viewed as having special national importance. In addition, there are two types of committees that convene only when needed: the **Interpretations Committee**, made up of the Speaker and eight members chosen by the **House Committee**, deals with appeals against the interpretation given by the

Speaker during a sitting of the plenum to the **Kenesset** rules of procedure or precedents, and **Public Committees,** established to deal with issues that are connected to the **Kenesset**.

## Permanent committees:

- House Committee
- Finance Committee
- Economic Affairs Committee
- Foreign Affairs and Defense Committee
- Interior and Environment Committee
- Immigration, Absorption, and Diaspora Affairs Committee
- Education, Culture, and Sports Committee
- Constitution, Law, and Justice Committee
- Labour, Welfare, and Health Committee
- Science and Technology Committee
- State Control Committee
- Committee on the Status of Women

## Special committees:

- Committee on Drug Abuse
- Committee on the Rights of the Child
- Committee on Foreign Workers
- Israeli Central Elections Committee
- Public Petitions Committee

The other committees are the **Arrangements Committee** and the **Ethics Committee**. The **Ethics Committee** is responsible for jurisdiction over **Kenesset** members who violate the rules of ethics of the **Kenesset**, or are involved in illegal activities outside the **Kenesset**. Within the framework of responsibility, the **Ethics Committee** may place various sanctions on a member, but is not allowed to restrict a member's right to vote. The **Arrangements Committee** proposes the makeup of the permanent committees following each election, as well as suggesting committee chairs, lays down the sitting arrangements of political parties in the **Kenesset**, and the distribution of offices in the **Kenesset** building to members and parties.

## Caucuses

**Kenesset** members often join in formal or informal groups known as **"lobbies"** or **"caucuses"**, to advocate for a particular topic. There are hundreds of such caucuses in the **Kenesset**. The **Kenesset Christian Allies Caucus** and the **Kenesset Land of Israel Caucus** are two of the largest and most active caucuses.

## Membership

**The Kenesset numbers 120 members**, after the size of the **Great Assembly.** The subject of **Kenesset** membership has often been a cause for proposed reforms. Under the **Norwegian Law**, **Kenesset** members who are appointed to ministerial positions are allowed to resign and allow the next person on their party's list to take their seat. If they leave the cabinet, they are able to return to the **Kenesset** to take the place of their replacement.

## Kenesset elections

**The 120 members of the Kenesset** (MKs) are popularly elected from a single nationwide electoral district to concurrent four-year terms, subject to calls for early elections (which are quite common). **All Israeli citizens 18 years or older may vote** in legislative elections, which are conducted by secret ballot.

**Kenesset** seats are allocated among the various parties using the **D'Hondt** method of party list proportional representation. A party or electoral alliance must pass the election threshold of 3.25% of the overall vote to be allocated a **Kenesset** seat. Parties select their candidates using a closed list. Thus, **voters select the party of their choice, not any specific candidate**.

The electoral threshold was previously set at 1% from 1949 to 1992, then 1.5% from 1992 to 2003, and then 2% until March 2014 when the current threshold of 3.25% was passed (effective with elections for the 20th **Kenesset**). As a result of the low threshold, a typical **Kenesset has 10 or more factions represented**. With so many parties, it is nearly impossible for one party or faction to govern alone, let alone win a majority.

No party or faction has ever won the 61 seats necessary for a majority; the closest being the 56 seats won by the **Alignment** in the 1969 elections (the Alignment had briefly held 63 seats going into the 1969 elections after being formed shortly beforehand by the merger of several parties, the only occasion on which any party or faction has ever held a majority). **Every Israeli government has been a coalition of two or more parties.**

After an election, the president meets with the leaders of every party that won **Kenesset** seats and asks them to recommend which party leader should form the government. The president then nominates the party leader who is most likely to command the support of a majority in the **Kenesset** (though not necessarily the leader of the largest party/faction in the chamber). The prime minister-designate has 42 days to put together a viable coalition (extensions can be granted and often are), and then must win a vote of confidence in the **Kenesset** before taking office.

## Security

The **Kenesset** is protected by the **Kenesset** Guard, a protective security unit responsible for the security of the **Kenesset** building and **Kenesset** members. Guards are stationed outside the building to provide armed protection, and ushers are stationed inside to maintain order.

The **Kenesset** Guard also plays a ceremonial role, participating in state ceremonies, which includes greeting dignitaries on **Mount Herzl** on the eve of **Israeli Independence Day**.

## Public perception

A poll conducted by the **Israeli Democracy Institute** in April and May 2014 showed that while a majority of both Jews and Arabs in Israel are proud to be citizens of the country, both groups share a distrust of Israel's government, including the **Kenesset**. Almost three quarters of Israelis surveyed said corruption in Israel's political leadership was either **"widespread or somewhat prevalent"**. A majority of both Arabs and Jews trusted the **Israel Defense Forces**, the President of Israel, and the **Supreme Court** of Israel, but Jews and Arabs reported similar levels of mistrust, with little more than a third of each group claiming confidence in the **Kenesset**.

# Kol Nidre

**Kol Nidre (also known as Kol Nidrey or Kol Nidrei) is an Aramaic declaration recited in the synagogue before the beginning of the evening service on every Yom Kippur.** It is not a prayer. This dry legal formula and its ceremonial accompaniment have been charged with emotional undertones since the medieval period, creating a dramatic introduction to **Yom Kippur** on what is often dubbed **"Kol Nidrei night"**.

**It is written in Aramaic, not Hebrew.** Its name is taken from the opening words, meaning *all vows*. The formula proactively annuls any personal or religious oaths or prohibitions made upon oneself to God for the next year, so as to preemptively avoid the sin of breaking vows made to God which cannot be or are not upheld.

*Kol Nidrei* has had an eventful history, both in itself and in its influence on the legal status of the Jews. Introduced into the liturgy despite the opposition of some rabbinic authorities, it was attacked in the course of time by some rabbis and in the 19th century expunged from the prayer book by many communities of Western Europe.

## Form of the chant

Before sunset on the eve of **Yom Kippur ("Day of Atonement"),** the congregation gathers in the synagogue. The **Ark** is opened and two people take from it two **Torah Scrolls**. Then they take their places, one on each side of the cantor, and the three (symbolizing a **Beth Din** or rabbinical court) recite:

**"By the authority of the Court on High and by authority of the court down here, by the permission of One Who Is Everywhere and by the permission of this congregation, we hold it lawful to pray with sinners."**

The occasion is worthy of Divine clemency. This announcement was introduced by **Rabbi Meir of Rothenburg** (late 13th century), and endorsed by the **Maharil** (Rabbi **Yaakov ben Moshe Levi Moelin**, early 15th century). Their inclusion in the **Yom Kippur** service is a temporary expedient, and does not operate as a remission of their sins or rejoin them to the congregation. The cantor then chants the passage beginning with the words *Kol Nidre* with its touching melodic phrases, and, in varying intensities from pianissimo (quiet) to fortissimo (loud).

All vows we are likely to make, all oaths and pledges we are likely to take between this **Yom Kippur** and the next **Yom Kippur**, we publicly renounce. Let them all be relinquished and abandoned, null and void, neither firm nor established. Let our vows, pledges and oaths be considered neither vows nor pledges nor oaths.

The leader and the congregation then say together three times, **"May all the people of Israel be forgiven, including all the strangers who live in their midst, for all the people are in fault."** (Quoting Numbers 15:26.) The leader then says: **"O pardon the iniquities of this people, according to Thy abundant mercy, just as Thou forgave this people ever since they left Egypt."** And then the leader and congregation say together three times, **"The Lord said, 'I pardon them according to your words.'" (Quoting Numbers 14:20).** The Torah scrolls are then put back in the Ark, and the customary evening service begins.

The *Kol Nidrei* declaration can invalidate only vows that one undertakes on his own volition. It has *no* effect on vows or oath imposed by someone else, or a court. **Only the erroneously broken vows are annulled, that nobody might commit the sin of intentionally breaking vows.**

In the eleventh century **Rabbi Meir ben Samuel** (Rashi's son-in-law) changed the original wording of *Kol Nidre* so as to make it apply to the future instead of the past, that is, to vows that one might not be able to fulfill during the next year. This is the **Nusach Ashkenaz** version, the **Nusach Sefard** version still refers to the past year. **Kol Nidrei** is not a prayer, it makes no requests and is not addressed to God, and rather, it is a juristic declaration before the **Yom Kippur** prayers begin.

## Origin

The date of the composition of the declaration and its author are alike unknown; but it was in existence at the **Geonic period (589–1038 CE)**. **Jews were forced at sword's point to convert (either to Christianity or Islam) and that Kol Nidre was supposed to nullify that forced conversion.**

**"It is considered a fearsome sin for one to violate his vows and oaths and the Sages regard it as an extremely serious matter for one to approach the Days of Judgment, with such violation in hand."** Halakha allowed for the absolution from a vow (**'hattarat nedarim'**), which might be performed only by a scholar, or an expert on the one hand, or by a board of three Jewish laymen on the other.

## Adoption into the prayer services

The readiness with which vows were made and the facility with which they were annulled by the scribes gave the **Karaites** an opportunity to attack rabbinic Jews. **Yehudai Gaon of Sura** (760 CE), author of the *Halakot Pesukot*, forbade the study of the *Nedarim*, the Talmudic treatise on oaths. Thus the *Kol Nidre* **was discredited in both of the Babylonian academies and was not accepted by them. Amram Gaon** in his edition of the **Siddur** calls the custom of reciting the *Kol Nidre* a foolish one (**"Minhag shetut"**).

At one time it was widely believed that the *Kol Nidre* was composed by **Spanish "Marranos"**, Jews who were forced to convert to Christianity, yet who secretly maintained their original faith. **Kol Nidre** clearly predated the **Spanish Inquisition.** It may be that it was simply inspired by the Talmudic instructions about avoiding oaths.

According to the holy *Zohar*, Kol Nidre is recited on **Yom Kippur** because, at times, the Heavenly judgment is handed down as an **'avowed decree'** for which there can normally be no annulment. By reciting the **Kol Nidre** annulment of vows at this time, we are **asking of God that He favor us by annulling any negative decrees of judgment that await us, even though we are undeserving of such annulment.**

## Adoption into Yom Kippur services

Originally, the annulment of vows was performed on **Rosh Hashana**, the New Year, and ten days before **Yom Kippur**. The Talmud (*Nedarim* 23b) says, **"Who wished to cancel his vows of a whole year should arise on Rosh Hashanah and announce, 'All vows that I will pledge in the coming year shall be annulled.'"** The tribunal responds by reciting three times, **"May everything be permitted you, may everything be forgiven you, may everything be allowed you**.

So, from a time before the composition of **Kol Nidrei** there was a corresponding ritual intended for **Rosh Hashana**. It is believed that **Kol Nidrei** was added to the liturgy of **Yom Kippur**, ten days after Rosh Hashana, because that service is much more solemn, because the **Day of Atonement** is entirely attuned to the theme of repentance and remorse, **Yom Kippur** services are better attended.

## Text

The following provides the traditional Aramaic text, which (except for the one line connecting one Day of Atonement to another, as noted) is nearly identical in both **Ashkenaz** and **Sefardic** liturgies.

| Aramaic Text | English Gloss |
|---|---|
| כָּל נִדְרֵי, וֶאֱסָרֵי, וּשְׁבוּעֵי, וַחֲרָמֵי, וְקוֹנָמֵי, וְקִנּוּסֵי, וְכִנּוּיֵי, דְּנָדַרְנָא, וּדְאִשְׁתַּבַּעְנָא, וּדְאַחֲרַמְנָא עַל נַפְשָׁתָנָא. •מִיּוֹם כִּפּוּרִים שֶׁעָבַר עַד יוֹם כִּפּוּרִים זֶה, וּ־ ־• ◆מִיּוֹם כִּפּוּרִם זֶה עַד יוֹם כִּפּוּרִים הַבָּא עָלֵינוּ לְטוֹבָה.◆ בְּכֻלְּהוֹן אִחֲרַטְנָא בְהוֹן. כֻּלְּהוֹן יְהוֹן שָׁרָן, שְׁבִיקִין, שְׁבִיתִין, בְּטֵלִן וּמְבֻטָּלִין, לָא שְׁרִירִין, וְלָא קַיָּמִין. נִדְרָנָא לָא נִדְרֵי, וֶאֱסָרָנָא לָא אֱסָרֵי, וּשְׁבוּעָתָנָא לָא שְׁבוּעוֹת. | All vows, and prohibitions, and oaths, and consecrations, and *konams* and *konasi* and any synonymous terms, that we may vow, or swear, or consecrate, or prohibit upon ourselves, •from the previous Day of Atonement until this Day of Atonement and ...• ◆from this Day of Atonement until the Day of Atonement that will come for our benefit.◆ Regarding all of them, we repudiate them. All of them are undone, abandoned, cancelled, null and void, not in force, and |

| | not in effect. Our vows are no longer vows, and our prohibitions are no longer prohibitions, and our oaths are no longer oaths. |
|---|---|

## Explanation of terms and variants

The Hebrew version of **Kol Nidrei** set out in the Siddur of **Rav Amram Gaon** (ca. 870) uses the formula "**from the last ... to this ...**" **The Rinat Yisroel combines both**, "**from the last ... to this..., and from this....**", and similarly the Syrian and other Sefardic or Mizrahi traditions set forth in the **Orot Mahzor** and the Bagdadi version.

## Historical controversies / Use by Anti-Semites

The *Kol Nidrei* prayer has been used by non-Jews as a basis for asserting that an oath taken by a Jew may not be trusted. Many non-Jewish legislators considered it necessary to have a special form of oath administered to Jews (**"Oath More Judaico"**), and many judges refused to allow them to take a supplementary oath, basing their objections chiefly on this prayer.

## Jewish rebuttals

Rabbis have always pointed out that the dispensation from vows in *Kol Nidrei* refers only to those an individual voluntarily assumes for himself alone and in which no other persons or their interests are involved. The formula is restricted to those vows between man and God alone; they have no effect on vows made between one man and another. According to Jewish doctrine, the sole purpose of this prayer is to give protection from divine punishment in case of violation of the vow.

## Jewish opposition

**Five Geonim** (rabbinic leaders of medieval **Babylonian Jewry**) were against while only one was in favor of reciting the formula. Even so early an authority as **Saadia Gaon** (early 10th century) wished to restrict it to those vows extorted from the congregation in the synagogue in times of persecution (**"Kol Bo"**), and he declared explicitly that the **"Kol Nidre"** gave no absolution from oaths an individual took during the year.

# Kristallnacht

**Kristallnacht "Crystal Night"**, also referred to as the **Night of Broken Glass**, and *November pogrome*, was a pogrom (a series of coordinated attacks) against Jews throughout **Nazi** Germany and parts of Austria on **9-10 November 1938**, carried out by SA paramilitary forces and non-Jewish civilians, German authorities looked on without intervening. The name *Kristallnacht* comes from the shards of broken glass that littered the streets after Jewish-owned stores, buildings, and synagogues had their windows smashed.

At least **91** Jews were killed in the attacks, and **30,000** were arrested and incarcerated in concentration camps. Jewish homes, hospitals, and schools were ransacked, as the attackers demolished buildings with sledgehammers. **Over 1,000 synagogues were burned (95 in Vienna alone) and over 7,000 Jewish businesses destroyed or damaged**.

The pretext for the attacks was the assassination of the **German diplomat Ernst vom Rath by Herschel Grynszpan**, a German-born Polish Jew resident in Paris. *Kristallnacht* was followed by additional economic and political persecution of Jews, and is viewed by historians as part of **Nazi** Germany's broader racial policy, and the beginning of the **Final Solution and The Holocaust.**

## Early Nazi persecutions

In the 1920s, most German Jews were fully integrated into German society as German citizens. They served in the German army and navy and contributed to every field of German science, business and culture. Conditions for the Jews began to change after the appointment of **Adolf Hitler** (the leader of the **Nazi** group) as **Chancellor of Germany on 30 January 1933** and the assumption of power by **Hitler** after the **Reichstag fire**. From its inception, **Hitler**'s regime moved quickly to introduce anti-Jewish policies.

The **500,000 Jews in Germany, who accounted for only 0.76% of the overall population**, were singled out by the **Nazi** propaganda machine as an enemy within who were **responsible for Germany's defeat in the First World War** and for its subsequent economic difficulties, such as the 1920s hyperinflation and **Great Depression**. The subsequent **1935 Nuremberg Laws** stripped German Jews of their citizenship and forbade Jews to marry non-Jewish Germans.

The result of these laws was the exclusion of Jews from German social and political life. Hundreds of thousands emigrated, but as **Chaim Weizmann** wrote in 1936, "**The world seemed to be divided into two parts – those places where the Jews could not live and those where they could not enter.**" The international **Evian Conference**, on 6 July 1938, **more than 250,000 Jews had fled Germany and Austria**, which had been annexed by Germany in March 1938; more than 300,000 German and Austrian Jews were still seeking refuge and asylum from oppression.

**The Polish government threatened to extradite all Jews who were Polish citizens**, but would stay in Germany, thus creating a burden of responsibility on the German side. The immediate reaction by the **Gestapo** was to push the Polish Jews – 16,000 persons – over the borderline, but this measure failed due to the stubbornness of the Polish customs officers.

The report of the **Woodhead Commission** on the partition of the British Mandate of Palestine into a Jewish and an Arab State was presented to the British parliament and **published on November 9, the day of the *Kristallnacht*.**

## Expulsion of Polish Jews in Germany

In August 1938 the German authorities announced that residence permits for foreigners were being cancelled and would have to be renewed. This included German-born Jews of foreign origin. **Poland stated that it would not accept Jews of Polish origin after the end of October.**

In the so-called "**Polenaktion**", more than 12,000 Polish-born Jews, among them the philosopher and theologian **Rabbi Abraham Joshua Heschel**, and future literary critic **Marcel Reich-Ranicki**, were expelled from Germany on 28 October 1938, on **Hitler**'s orders. They were ordered to leave their homes in a single night, and were allowed only one suitcase per person to carry their belongings. As the Jews were taken away, their remaining possessions were seized as booty by both the **Nazi** authorities and by their neighbors.

Four thousand were granted entry into Poland, but the remaining 8,000 were forced to stay at the border. They waited there in harsh conditions to be allowed to enter Poland. Conditions in the refugee camps **"were so bad that some actually tried to escape back into Germany and were shot".**

## Shooting of vom Rath

Among those expelled was the family of **Sendel and Riva Grynszpan**, Polish Jews who had emigrated to Germany in 1911 and settled in Hanover, Germany. At the trial of **Adolf Eichmann in 1961**, **Sendel Grynszpan** recounted the events of their deportation from Hanover on the night of 27 October 1938: The streets were full of people shouting: *'Juden raus! Auf nach Palastina!'*" (**"Jews out, out to Palestine!"**). Their seventeen-year-old son **Herschel** was living in Paris with an uncle. **Herschel** received a postcard from his family from the Polish border, describing the family's expulsion. He received the postcard on 3 November 1938.

On the morning of **Monday, 7 November 1938**, he purchased a revolver and a box of bullets, then went to the German embassy and asked to see an embassy official. After he was taken to the office of **Ernst vom Rath**, **Grynszpan** fired five bullets at **Vom Rath**, two of which hit him in the abdomen. **Grynszpan** made no attempt to escape the French police and freely confessed to the shooting. In his pocket, he carried a postcard to his parents with the message, **"May God forgive me … I must protest so that the whole world hears my protest, and that I will do."**

The next day, the German government retaliated, barring Jewish children from German state elementary schools, indefinitely suspending Jewish cultural activities, and putting a halt to the publication of Jewish newspapers and magazines, including the three national German Jewish newspapers. **Their rights as citizens had been stripped.**

## Death of vom Rath

**Ernst vom Rath died of his wounds on November 9.** Word of his death reached **Hitler** that evening while he was with several key members of the **Nazi** party at a dinner commemorating the **1923 Beer Hall Putsch**. **Hitler** left the assembly abruptly without giving his usual address.

Propaganda Minister **Joseph Goebbels** delivered the speech, I his place. The chief party judge **Walter Bush** later stated that the message was clear; with these words **Goebbels had commanded the party leaders to organize a pogrom**.

**Heinrich Himmler** wrote, "I suppose that it is **Goebbels'** megalomania…and stupidity which are responsible for starting this operation now, in a particularly difficult diplomatic situation." Goebbels had personal reasons for wanting to bring about *Kristallnacht*. Goebbels had recently suffered humiliation for the ineffectiveness of his propaganda campaign during the **Sudeten crisis**. **Goebbels** needed a chance to improve his standing in the eyes of **Hitler**.

At 01:20 am on 10 November 1938, **Reinhard Heydrich** sent an urgent secret telegram to the **Sicherheitspolizei** (Security Police) and the Sturmabteilung (SA), containing instructions regarding the riots. **Police were instructed not to interfere with the riots unless the guidelines were violated.** Police were also instructed to seize Jewish archives from synagogues and community offices, and to arrest and detain **"healthy male Jews, who are not too old", for eventual transfer to concentration camps**.

## Riots

The timing of the riots varied from unit to unit. They were followed by the SA at 11 pm, and the **SS** at around 1:20 am. Most were wearing civilian clothes and were armed with sledgehammers and aces, and soon went to work on the destruction of Jewish property. Jewish businesses or dwellings could be destroyed but not looted; foreigners (even Jewish foreigners) were not to be the subjects of violence; and synagogue archives were to be transferred to the **Sicherheitsdienst** (SD). The men were also ordered to arrest as many Jews as the local jails would hold, **the preferred targets beings healthy young men.**

**The SA** shattered the storefronts of about 7,500 Jewish stores and businesses, hence the appellation *Kristallnacht* **(Crystal Night)**. Jewish homes were ransacked all throughout Germany. This pogrom damaged, and in many cases destroyed, about **200 synagogues**, many Jewish cemeteries, more than **7,000 Jewish shops, and 29 department stores**. Some Jews were beaten to death while others were forced to watch. More than **30,000 Jewish men were arrested** and taken to concentration camps; primarily **Dachau, Buchenwald, and Sachsenhausen**.

**The number of German Jews killed is uncertain**. It is thought that there were hundreds of suicides. Counting deaths in the concentration camps, **around 2,000-2,500 deaths were directly or indirectly attributable to the *Kristallnacht* pogrom.** A few non-Jewish Germans, mistaken for Jews, were also killed. The synagogues, some centuries old, were also victims of considerable violence and vandalism. Tombstones were uprooted and graves violated. Fires were lit, and prayer books, scrolls, artwork and philosophy texts were thrown upon them and precious buildings were either burned or smashed until unrecognizable.
After this, the **Jewish community was fined 1 billion reichsmarks. In addition, it cost 4 million marks to repair the windows.**

Events in recently annexed Austria were no less horrendous. Of the entire *Kristallnacht,* only the pogrom in Vienna was completed. Most of Vienna's 94 synagogues and prayer houses were partially or totally destroyed. People were subjected to all manner of humiliations, including being forced to scrub the pavements whilst being tormented by their fellow Austrians, some of whom had been their friends and neighbors.

Official figures released after the event by **Reinhard Heydrich** stated that 191 synagogues were destroyed, with 76 completely demolished; 100,000 Jews were arrested; three foreigners were arrested; 174 people were arrested for looting Jewish shops; and 815 Jewish businesses were destroyed.

### Concentration camps

The violence was officially called to a stop by **Goebbels on 11 November**, but violence continued against the Jews in the concentration camps. The 30,000 Jewish men who had been imprisoned during *Kristallnacht* were released over the next three months but, by then, more than 2,000 had died.

### Aftermath

**Hermann Goring** met with other members of the **Nazi** leadership on 12 November to plan the next steps after the riot, setting the stage for formal government action. In the transcript of the meeting, Goring said: **'I have received a letter written on the Fuhrer's orders requesting that the Jewish question be now, once and for all, coordinated and solved one way or another...** I should not want to leave any doubt, gentlemen, as to the aim of today's meeting. I implore competent agencies to take all measures for the elimination of the Jew from the German economy, and to submit them to me.'

The Jews were forced to pay *Judenvermogensabgabe*, a collective fine of one billion marks for the murder of **vom Rath** (equal to roughly $US 5.5 billion in today's currency), which was levied by the compulsory acquisition of 20% of all Jewish property by the state. **Six million Reichsmarks** of insurance payments for property damage due to the Jewish community were to be paid to the government instead as "**damages to the German Nation**".

In the ten months following **Kristallnacht, more than 115,000 Jews emigrated from the Reich**. The majority went to other European countries, the US and Palestine, and at least 14,000 made it to Shanghai, China. The **Nazi**s seized houses, shops, and other property the émigrés left behind. *At conference on the day after the pogrom, Hermann Goring said: "The Jewish problem will reach its solution if, in any time soon, we will be drawn into war beyond our border – then it is obvious that we will have to manage a final account with the Jews."*

# Lot's Daughters

**Lot's daughters** are four women, two unnamed people in the **Book of Genesis**, and two others, including **Paltith**, in the **Book of Jasher.** Only two daughters are mentioned in **Genesis 19**, while **Lot** and his family are in **Sodom**.

**Lot's wife turns into a pillar of salt**, but Lot and his daughters escape to **Zoar**, and end up living in a cave in the mountains. Lot's daughters realize that they are not going to find men to have sex with them, so that they may have children and continue the family line. **They get their father drunk, and over two consecutive nights have sex with him without his knowledge**. They both get pregnant. The older daughter gives birth to **Moab**, while the younger daughter gives birth to **Ammon.**

A number of commentators describe the actions of **Lot's** daughters as rape. **Esther Fuchs** suggests that the text presents Lot's daughters as the **"initiators and perpetrators of the incestuous 'rape'."** **Ilan Kutz** suggests that today it would be called **"drug rape"**, but concludes that it was actually **Lot** who abused his daughters, and this was covered up by the biblical narrators.

# Lucifer (Satan)

**Lucifer**, is a name that, refers to the **Devil** (Archangel) or to the planet **Venus** when appearing as the morning star. In the first sense the name is the rendering of the Hebrew **word הֵילֵל in Isaiah (Isaiah 14:12)** given in the **King James Version**. Meaning **"the morning star, the planet Venus"**, or, as an adjective, **"light-bringing"**. In the second sense, the morning star, *Lucifer* in Latin, was also personified and considered a **Greco-Roman pagan god**.

## In Isaiah 14:12

According to both Christian and Jewish exegesis, in the **Book of Isaiah, chapter 14**, the King of Babylon, **Nebuchadnezzar II**, conqueror of Jerusalem, is condemned in a prophetic vision by the prophet **Isaiah** and is called the "**Morning Star**" (planet Venus). Later Christian tradition came to use the Latin word for **"morning star"**, *Lucifer*, as the proper name **("Lucifer")** of the **Devil** as he was before his fall. As a result, **"Lucifer has become a by-word for Satan / the Devil in the church and in popular literature"**, as in **Dante Alighieri's** *Inferno*, John Milton's *Paradise Lost*.

## Literal meaning

The Abrahamic scriptural texts could be interpreted as a weak usurping of true kingly power, and a taunt at the failed regency of **Belshazzar**. For the unnamed **"king of Babylon"** a wide range of identifications have been proposed. They include a Babylonian ruler of the prophet **Isaiah's** own time the later **Nebuchadnezzar II**, under whom the Babylonian captivity of the Jews began, or **Nabonidus**, and the **Assyrian kings Tiglath-Pileser, Sargon II and Sennacherib**.

**Isaiah 14:12** is not the only place where the **Vulgate** uses the word *Lucifer*. It uses the same word four more times, in contexts where it clearly has no reference to a fallen angel: **2 Peter 1:19** (meaning **"morning star"**), Job 11:17 ("the light of the morning"), Job 38:32 ("the signs of the zodiac") and Psalms 110:3 ("the dawn"). **Sirach 50:6** (referring to the actual morning star), and **Revelation 2:28** (of uncertain reference) and **22:16** (referring to **Jesus**). In Latin, the word is applied to **John the Baptist** and is used as a title of **Jesus** himself in several early Christian hymns. The morning hymn *Lucis larger splendide* of **Hilary** contains the line: **"*Tu verus mundi Lucifer*"** (you are the true light bringer of the world).

The Latin word *Lucifer* is also used of **Jesus** in the **Easter Proclamation** prayer to God regarding the paschal candle: *Flammas eius Lucifer matutinus inveniat: ille, inquam, Lucifer, qui nescit occasum. Christus Filius tuus, qui, regressus ab inferis, humano generi serenus illuxit, et vivit et regnat in saecula saeculorum* (**"May this flame be found still burning by the Morning Star: the one Morning Star who never sets, Christ your Son, who, coming back from death's domain, has shed his peaceful light on humanity, and lives and reigns for ever and ever"**).

## Satan in Judaism

The Hebrew words הֵילֵל בֶּן-שָׁחַר (*Helel ben Shahar*, "day-star, son of the morning") in **Isaiah 14:12** are part of a prophetic vision against an oppressive king of Babylon. Jewish exegesis of **Isaiah 14:12–15** identified the king of Babylon as **Nebuchadnezzar II**. **Verse 20** says that this king of Babylon will not be **"joined with them in burial, because thou hast destroyed thy land, thou hast slain thy people; the seed of evil-doers shall not be named forever"**, but rather be cast out of the grave, while **"All the kings of the nations, all of them, sleep in glory, everyone in his own house"**.

## Apocrypha and pseudepigrapha

**"Christian explanations of the origin of evil linked Lk 10:18 with Isa 14 and eventually Gen. 3 so vs 4 could be a Christian interpolation... Jewish theology concentrated on Gen 6. and this is prominent in the Enoch cycle as in other apocalypses."**

## *Devil in Christianity*

**Christian writers applied the words of Isaiah 14:12 to Satan. The New Testament War in Heaven theme of Revelation 12:7-9**, in which the dragon **"who is called the devil and Satan … was thrown down to the earth"**, derives from the passage in Isaiah 14. **Tertullian** (c. 160 – c. 225), who wrote in Latin, also understood **Isaiah 14:14 ("I will ascend above the tops of the clouds; I will make myself like the Most High")**.

Linking **Isaiah 14:12** with **Luke 10:18 ("I saw Satan fall like lightning from heaven")**. Calvin said: **"The exposition of this passage, which some have given, as if it referred to Satan, has arisen from ignorance: for the context plainly shows these statements must be understood in reference to the king of the Babylonians."**

## Islamic account on the Devil

In Islam the Devil is known as **Iblīs or Shaytān** (Arabic: *shayāṭīn*). Iblis is banished from heaven for refusing to prostrate himself before **Adam**, which is similar to the earlier **3 Enoch, chapter 4**, in which all of the angels prostrate themselves before Enoch, an early descendant of Adam.

**Thus, he sins *after* the creation of man**. He asks God for seducing human to sin until judgment day as long Gods curse rest on him. God grants this request, and **Iblis** then swears revenge by tempting human beings and turning them away from God. God tells him that any humans who follow him will join him in the fire of hell at judgment day, but that **Iblis** will have no power over all mankind. **QS (17:63–65)** this story is cited multiple times in the **Qur'an** for different reasons.

## Anthroposophy

**Lucifer** represents an intellectual, imaginative, delusional, otherworldly force which might be associated with visions, subjectivity, psychosis and fantasy. **Lucifer, as a supersensible Being, had incarnated in China about 3000 years before the birth of Christ.**

# The Maccabees

The **Maccabees**, also spelled **Maccabees**, were the leaders of a Jewish rebel army that took control of Judea, which at the time had been a province of the **Seleucid Empire**. They founded the **Hasmonean Dynasty, which ruled from 164 BCE to 63 BCE**. They reasserted the Jewish religion, partly by forced conversion, expanded the boundaries of Judea by conquest and reduced the influence of Hellenism and **Hellenistic Judaism**.

## Background

In the 2$^{nd}$ century BCE, Judea lay between the **Ptolemaic Kingdom based in Egypt** and the Seleucid Empire based in Syria, kingdoms formed after the death of **Alexander the Great (356-323 BCE)**. Judea had been under Ptolemaic rule, but fell to the Seleucids around 200 BCE. The Hellenizing Jews built a gymnasium in Jerusalem, competed in international Greek games, **"removed their marks of circumcision and repudiated the holy covenant"**.

When **Antiochus IV Epiphanes (ca. 215-164 BCE)**, became ruler of the **Seleucid Empire** in 175 BCE, the **High Priest** in Jerusalem was **Onias III.** To **Antiochus**, the **High Priest** was merely a local governor within his realm who could be appointed or dismissed at will, while to orthodox Jews he was divinely appointed. **Jason**, the brother of **Onias**, bribed **Antiochus** to make him **High Priest** instead Jason abolished the traditional theocracy and constituted Jerusalem as a **Greek** *polis*. Menelaus then bribed **Antiochus** and was appointed **High Priest** in place of Jason. **Menelaus had Onias assassinated Menelaus' brother Lysimachus stole holy vessels from the Temple, causing riots that led to his death.**

Menelaus was arrested for **Onias'** murder, and was arraigned before **Antiochus**, but he bribed his way out of trouble. Jason subsequently drove out **Menelaus** and became **High Priest** again. **Antiochus pillaged the Temple**, attacked Jerusalem and **"led captive the women and children"**.

According to **I Maccabees**, he made possession of the **Torah** a capital offense and burned the copies he could find, and he banned many traditional Jewish and Samaritan religious practices; **ritual sacrifice was forbidden, Sabbaths and feasts were banned. Circumcision was outlawed, and mothers who circumcised their babies were killed along with their families.** Altars to Greek gods were set up and animals prohibited to Jews were sacrificed on them. **The idol of Olympian Zeus was placed on the altar of the Temple.**

## The revolt

In the narrative of *I Maccabees*, after **Antiochus** issued his decrees forbidding Jewish religious practice, a rural Jewish priest from Modiin, **Mattathias the Hasmonean**, sparked the revolt against the **Seleucid Empire** by refusing to worship the Greek gods. He and his **five sons** fled to the wilderness of Judah. After **Mattathias'** death about one year later in 166 BCE, his son **Judas Maccabee** led an army of Jewish dissidents to victory over the **Seleucid Dynasty** in guerrilla warfare, which at first was directed against Hellenizing Jews, of whom there were many. **The Maccabees destroyed pagan altars in the villages, circumcised boys and forced Jews into outlawry.**

The revolt involved many battles, in which the **Maccabean** forces gained notoriety among the Seleucid army for their use of guerrilla tactics. After the victory, the **Maccabees** entered Jerusalem in triumph and ritually cleansed the Temple, reestablishing traditional Jewish worship there and installing **Jonathan Maccabee as high priest**. A large Seleucid army was sent to quash the revolt, but returned to Syria on the death of **Antiochus** IV.

The Jewish festival of **Hanukkah** celebrates the re-dedication of the Temple following Judah Maccabee's victory over the **Seleucids**. According to Rabbinic tradition, the victorious **Maccabees** could only find a small jug of oil that had remained uncontaminated by virtue of a seal, and although it only contained enough oil to sustain the Menorah for one day, it miraculously lasted for eight days, by which time further oil could be procured.

## Maccabean rule

When the revolt began under the leadership of **Mattathias**, it was seen as a war for religious freedom to end the oppression of the Seleucids. However, as the **Maccabees** realized how successful they had been, many wanted to continue the revolt and conquer other lands with Jewish populations or to convert their peoples. This policy exacerbated the divide between the Pharisees and **Sadducees** under later **Hasmonean** monarchs such as **Alexander Jannaeus**.

Those who sought the continuation of the war were led by **Judah Maccabee**. On his death in battle in 160 BCE, Judah was succeeded as army commander by his younger brother, **Jonathan**, who was already **High Priest**. Jonathan made treaties with various foreign states, causing further dissent between those who merely desired religious freedom and those who sought greater power.

**In 142 BCE, Jonathan was assassinated by Diodotus Tryphon**, a pretender to the Seleucid throne, and was succeeded by **Simon Maccabee**, the last remaining son of **Mattathias**. **Simon** gave support to **Demetrius II Nicator**, the Seleucid king, and in return **Demetrius** exempted the **Maccabees** from tribute. Simon conquered the port of Joppa where the **Gentile** population were 'forcibly removed', the fortress of Gezer and expelled the garrison from the Acra in Jerusalem.

In 140 BCE, he was recognized by an assembly of the priests, leaders and elders as high priest, military commander and ruler of Israel. Their decree became the basis of the **Hasmonean Kingdom**. Although the **Maccabees** won autonomy, the region remained a province of the **Seleucid Empire** and **Simon** was required to provide troops to **Antiochus VII Sidetes**, the brother of **Demetrius II**. When **Simon** refused to give up the territory he had conquered, **Antiochus** took them by force.

**Simon was murdered in 134 BCE by his son-in-law Ptolemy**, and was succeeded as high priest and king by his son **John Hyrcanus I**. **Antiochus** conquered the entire district of Judea, but refrained from attacking the Temple or interfering with Jewish observances, Judea was freed from Seleucid rule on the **death of Antiochus in 129 BCE**.

**Independent Hasmonean rule lasted until 63 BCE**, when the Roman general Pompeus intervened in **Hasmonean** civil war, making it a client kingdom of Rome. **The Hasmonean Dynasty ended in 37 BCE** when the Idumean **Herod the Great** became king of Israel, designated

**"King of the Jews"** by the Roman Senate, effectively transforming the **Hasmonean** Kingdom into Herodian Kingdom – a client kingdom of Rome.

## Origin of name

The name Maccabee is often used as a synonym for the entire **Hasmonean Dynasty**, but the **Maccabees** proper were **Judah Maccabee** and his four brothers. One explanation of the name's origins is that it derives from the Aramaic "**makkaba**", "**the hammer**", in recognition of Judah's ferocity in battle.

## Modern perception

The author of the **First Book of Maccabees** regarded the **Maccabean** revolt as a rising of pious Jews against the Seleucid king who had tried to eradicate their religion and against the Jews who supported him. The author of the **Second Book of Maccabees** presented the conflict as a struggle between **"Judaism"** and **"Hellenism"**, words that he was the first to use.

# Maimonides

**Moshe ben Maimon** or **Musa ibn Maymun**, acronymed **Rambam** for ***"Rabbeinu Moshe Ben Maimon"***, **"Our Rabbi/Teacher Moses Son of Maimon")**, (and subsequently Latinized) **Moses Maimonides**, a preeminent medieval Sephardic Jewish philosopher and astronomer, became one of the most prolific and influential Torah scholars and physicians of the Middle Ages. Born in Cordova (present-day Spain), **Almoravid Empire** on Passover Eve, 1135 or 1138, he died in Egypt on December 12, 1204, whence his body was taken to the lower Galilee and buried in Tiberias. He worked as a **rabbi, physician, and philosopher** in Morocco and Egypt.

Although **Maimonides** rose to become the revered head of the Jewish community in Egypt, there were also vociferous critics of some of his writings, particularly in Spain. Nonetheless, he was posthumously acknowledged as among the foremost rabbinical arbiters and philosophers in Jewish history. His fourteen-volume *Mishmeh Torah* still carries significant canonical authority as a codification of **Talmudic law**. In the Yeshiva world, he is called sometimes **"ha Nesher ha Gadol"** (the great eagle) in recognition of his outstanding status as a ***bona fide*** exponent of the Oral Torah.

Aside from being revered by Jewish historians, **Maimonides** also figures very prominently in the history of Islamic and Arab sciences and is mentioned extensively in studies. Influenced by **Al-Farabi** (ca. 872-950/951), **Avicenna** (c. 980-1037), and his contemporary **Averroes** (1126-1198), he in his turn influenced other prominent Arab and Muslim philosophers and scientists. He became a prominent **philosopher and polymath in both the Jewish and Islamic worlds**.

## Biography

**Maimonides** was born in Cordoba during what some scholars consider to be the end of the golden age of Jewish culture in the Iberian Peninsula, after the first centuries of the Moorish rule. At an early age, he developed an interest in sciences and philosophy. He read those Greek philosophers accessible in Arabic translations, and was deeply immersed in the sciences and learning of Islamic culture. **Maimonides** was not known as a supporter of mysticism, although a strong intellectual type of mysticism has been discerned in his philosophy, wrote many of his works while travelling or in temporary accommodation. **Maimonides** studied Torah under his father **Maimon**, who had in turn studied under **Rabbi Joseph ibn Migash**, a student of Isaac Alfasi.

A Berber dynasty, the Almohads, conquered Cordoba in 1148, and abolished ***dhimmi*** status (i.e., state protection of life and wealth) in some of their territories. The loss of this protected status threatened the Jewish and Christian communities with conversion to Islam, death, or exile. Many Jews were forced to convert, but due to suspicion by the authorities of fake conversions, the new converts had to wear identifying clothing that set them apart and made them subject to public scrutiny.

**Maimonides'** family, along with most other Jews, chose exile. This forced conversion was ruled legally invalid under Islamic law when brought up by a rival in Egypt. For the next ten years, **Maimonides** moved about in southern Spain, eventually settling in Fes in Morocco. During this time, he composed his acclaimed commentary on the **Mishnah** in the years 1166-1168. Following this sojourn in Morocco, together with two sons, he sojourned in the **Holy Land**, before settling in **Fustat**, Egypt around 1168. While in Cairo, he studied in a yeshiva attached to a small synagogue (which now bears his name). In the **Holy Land**, he prayed at the **Temple Mount**.

**Maimonides** shortly thereafter was instrumental in helping rescue Jews taken captive during the **Christian King Amalric's** siege of the Egyptian town of Bilbays. He sent five letters to the Jewish communities of Lower Egypt asking them to pool money together to pay the ransom. The money was collected and then given to two judges sent to Palestine to negotiate with the Crusaders. The captives were eventually released. Following this triumph, the **Maimonides** family, hoping to increase their wealth, gave their savings to his brother, the youngest son **David ben Maimon**, a merchant. After a long arduous trip through the desert, however, **David** was unimpressed by the goods on offer there. Against his brother's wishes, **David** boarded a ship for India, since great wealth was to be found in the East. Before he could reach his destination, **David drowned at sea sometime between 1169 & 1170**.

Around 1171, **Maimonides** was appointed the *Nagid* of the Egyptian Jewish community. **Maimonides** assumed the vocation of physician, for which he was to become famous. He had trained in medicine in both Cordoba and in Fes. Gaining widespread recognition, he was appointed court physician to the **Grand Vizier Al Qadi al Fadil**, then to **Sultan Saladin**, after whose death he remained a physician to the royal family.

In his medical writings, **Maimonides** described many conditions, including **asthma, diabetes, hepatitis, and pneumonia.** He was knowledgeable about Greek and Arabic medicine, and followed the principles of **Humorism** in the tradition of **Galen**. Although he frequently wrote of his longing for solitude in order to come closer to God and to extend his reflections – elements considered essential in his philosophy to the prophetic experience – he gave over most of his time to caring for others. In 1173/4 **Maimonides** wrote his famous **Iggeret Teman (*Epistle to Yemen*)**. It has been suggested that his "**incessant travail**" undermined his own health and brought about his death at 69 (although this is a normal lifespan). His rabbinic writings are valued as fundamental and unparalleled resources for religious Jews today.

**Maimonides died on December 12, 1204** (20th of Tevet 4965) in Fustat. It is widely believed that he was briefly buried in the study room (**beit hamidrash**) of the synagogue courtyard, and that, soon after, in accordance with his wishes, his remains were exhumed and taken to Tiberias, where he was re-interred. The **Tomb of Maimonides** on the western shore of the Sea of Galilee in Israel marks his grave. **Maimonides** and his wife, the daughter of **Mishael ben Yeshayahu Halevi**, had one child who survived into adulthood, **Avraham**, who became recognized as a great scholar. He succeeded **Maimonides as Nagid** and as court physician at the age of eighteen. The office of Nagid was held by the **Maimonides** family for four successive generations until the end of the 14th century.

## Influence

**Maimonides'** **Mishneh torah** is considered by Jews even today as one of the chief authoritative codifications of Jewish law and ethics. It is still closely studied in rabbinic **yeshivot** (academies). But **Maimonides** was also one of the most influential figures in medieval Jewish philosophy. His brilliant adaptation of **Aristotelian** thought to Biblical faith deeply impressed later Jewish thinkers, and had an unexpected immediate historical impact. The intensity of debate spurred **Catholic**

**Church** interventions against "**heresy**" and a general confiscation of rabbinic texts. Maimonidean thought continues to influence traditionally observant Jews.

Because of his path-finding synthesis of **Aristotle** and Biblical faith, **Maimonides** had a fundamental influence on the great Christian theologian **Saint Thomas Aquinas**. Aquinas refers specifically to **Maimonides** in several of his works, including the *Commentary on the Sentences*.

## 13 principles of faith

In his commentary on the **Mishnah** (tractate Sanhedrin, chapter 10), **Maimonides** formulates his "**13 principles of faith**". They summarized what he viewed as the required beliefs of Judaism:

1. The existence of God.
2. God's unity and indivisibility into elements.
3. God's spirituality and incorporeality.
4. God's eternity.
5. God alone should be the object of worship.
6. Revelation through God's prophets.
7. The preeminence of Moses among the prophets.
8. The Torah that we have today is the one dictated to Moses by God.
9. The Torah given by Moses will not be replaced and that nothing may be added or removed from it.
10. God's awareness of all human actions and thoughts.
11. Reward of good and punishment of evil.
12. The coming of the Jewish Messiah.
13. The resurrection of the dead.

Today, Orthodox Judaism holds these beliefs to be obligatory. Two poetic restatements of these principles (*Ani Ma'amin* and *Yigdal*) eventually became canonized in many editions of the "**Siddur**" (Jewish prayer book).

## Legal works

With **Mishneh Torah**, **Maimonides** composed a code of Jewish law with the widest-possible scope and depth. It was still recognized as a monumental contribution to the systemized writing of Halakha. Throughout the centuries, it has been widely studied and its halakhic decisions have weighed heavily in later rulings. In response to those who would attempt to force followers of **Maimonides** and his *Mishneh Torah* to abide by the rulings of his own **Shulchan Aruch** or other later works, **Rabbi Yosef Karo** wrote: Who would dare force communities who follow the **Rambam** to follow any other decisor, early or late? **The Jews Pentateuch was divided into 53 sections according to the Persian style.**

## Charity (tzedakah)

One of the most widely referred to sections of the *Mishneh Torah* is the section dealing with tzedakah. **Maimonides** lists his famous **Eight Levels of Giving** (where the first level is most preferable and the eighth the least):

1. **Giving** an interest-free loan to a person in need; forming a partnership with a person in need; giving a grant to a person in need; finding a job for a person in need; so long as that loan, grant, partnership, or job results in the person no longer living by relying upon others.

2. **Giving tzedakah** anonymously to an unknown recipient via a person (or public fund) which is trustworthy, wise, and can perform acts of **tzedakah** with your money in a most impeccable fashion.
3. **Giving tzedakah** anonymously to a known recipient.
4. **Giving tzedakah** publicly to an unknown recipient.
5. **Giving tzedakah** before being asked.
6. **Giving** adequately after being asked.
7. **Giving** willingly, but inadequately.
8. **Giving "in sadness"** (giving out of pit): It is thought that **Maimonides** was referring to giving because of the sad feelings one might have in seeing people in need (as opposed to giving because it is a religious obligation). Other translations say "**Giving unwillingly**."

## Philosophy

Through the *Guide for the Perplexed* (which was initially written in Arabic as *Dalalat al-ha'irin*) and the philosophical introductions to sections of his commentaries on the **Mishna**, **Maimonides** exerted an important influence on the Scholastic philosophers, especially on **Albert the Great, Thomas Aquinas** and **Duns Scotus**. He was a Jewish Scholastic. Educated more by reading the works of Arab Muslim philosophers than by personal contact with Arabian teachers, he acquired an intimate acquaintance not only with Arab Muslim philosophy, but with the doctrines of **Aristotle**. **Maimonides** strove to reconcile Aristotelian philosophy and science with the teachings of the Torah. **Maimonides** is said to have been influenced by **Asaph ha-Jehoudi**, who was the first Hebrew medical writer.

## Negative theology

**Maimonides** primarily relied upon the science of **Aristotle** and the teachings of the **Talmud**, commonly finding basis in the former for the latter. In some important points, he departed from the teaching of **Aristotle**; for instance, he rejected the Aristotelian doctrine that God's provident care extends only to humanity, and not to the individual.

**Maimonides** was an adherent of **"negative theology"** (also known as **"Apophatic theology"**.) In this theology, one attempts to describe God through negative attributes. It can be said that God is not non-existent. We should not say that "**God is wise**"; but we can say that "**God is not ignorant**," i.e. We should not say that "**God is One**," but we can state that "**there is no multiplicity in God's being.**" The Scholastics agreed that no predicate is adequate to express the nature of God, but they did not say that no affirmative term could be applied to God. **Maimonides** suggested that when people give God anthropomorphic qualities, they do not explain anything more of what God is, because people cannot know the essence.

## Prophecy

He agrees with **"the Philosopher"** (**Aristotle**) in teaching that the use of logic is the "**right**" way of thinking. Here he rejects previous ideas (especially portrayed by **Rabbi Yehuda Halevi** in **"Hakuzari"**) that in order to become a prophet, God must intervene. **Maimonides** claims that any man has the potential to become a prophet (not just Jews) and that in fact it is the purpose of the human race.

## The problem of evil

**Maimonides** wrote on theodicy (the philosophical attempt to reconcile the existence of a God with the existence of evil). He took the premise that an omnipotent and good God exists. In his *Guide for the Perplexed*, **Maimonides** writes that all the evil that exists within human beings stems from their individual attributes, while all good comes from a universally shared humanity.

To justify the existence of evil, assuming God is both omnipotent and omnibenevolent, **Maimonides** postulates that one who created something by causing its opposite not to exist is not the same as creating something that exists; so evil is merely the absence of good. God did not create evil, rather **God created good, and evil exists where good is absent (Guide 3:10)**. Therefore, all good is divine invention, and evil both is not and comes secondarily.

**Maimonides** contests the common view that evil outweighs good in the world. Man, he reasons, is too insignificant a figure in God's myriad works to be their primary characterizing force, and so when people see mostly evil in their lives, they are not taking into account the extent of positive Creation outside of themselves. **Maimonides** believes that there are **three types of evil** in the world: **evil caused by nature, evil that people bring upon others**, and **evil man brings upon himself (Guide 3:12)**. To prevent the majority of evil which stems from harm we do to ourselves, we must learn how to ignore our bodily urges.

## Astrology

He responded that man should believe only what can be supported either by rational proof, by the evidence of the senses, or by trustworthy authority. He ridicules the concept that the fate of a man could be dependent upon the constellations; he argues that such a theory would rob life of purpose, and would make man a slave of destiny.

## True beliefs versus necessary beliefs

In *Guide for the Perplexed* Book III, Chapter 28, **Maimonides** draws a distinction between **"true beliefs,"** which were beliefs about God that produced intellectual perfection, and **"necessary beliefs,"** which were conducive to improving social order. God does not become angry with people, as God has no human passions; but it is important for them to believe God does, so that they desist from doing wrong.

## Resurrection, acquired immortality, and the afterlife

**Maimonides** distinguishes two kinds of intelligence in man, the one material in the sense of being dependent on, and influenced by, the body, and the other immaterial, that is, independent of the bodily organism. It is acquired as the result of the efforts of the soul to attain a correct knowledge of the absolute, pure intelligence of God.

The knowledge of God is a form of knowledge which develops in us the immaterial intelligence, and thus confers on man an immaterial, spiritual nature. This confers on the soul that perfection in which human happiness consists, and endows the soul with immortality. One who has attained a correct knowledge of God has reached a condition of existence, which renders him immune from all the accidents of fortune, from all the allurements of sin, and from death itself. Man is in a position to work out his own salvation and his immortality.

**Spinoza's** doctrine of immortality was strikingly similar. But **Spinoza** teaches that the way to attain the knowledge which confers immortality is the progress from sense-knowledge through scientific knowledge to philosophical intuition of all things *sub specie aeternitatis*, while **Maimonides** holds that the road to perfection and immortality is the path of duty as described in the Torah and the rabbinic understanding of the oral law.

Religious Jews believed in immortality in a spiritual sense, and most believed that the future would include a messianic era and a resurrection of the dead. Rabbinic works usually refer to this after life as *Olam Haba* (the World to come). Some rabbinic works use this phrase to refer to a messianic era, an era of history here on Earth; in other rabbinic works this phrase refers to a purely spiritual realm. Some Jews at this time taught that Judaism did not require a belief in the physical resurrection of the dead, as the afterlife would be a purely spiritual realm. They used **Maimonides'** works on this subject to back up their position.

Eventually, **Maimonides** felt pressured to write a treatise on the subject, the *"Ma'amar Tehiyyat Hametim"* **"The Treatise on Resurrection."** Chapter two of the treatise on resurrection refers to those who believe that the world to come involves physically resurrected bodies. **Maimonides** refers to one with such beliefs, as being an "utter fool" whose belief is **"folly"**.

**Maimonides** asserts that belief in resurrection is a fundamental truth of Judaism about which there is no disagreement, and that it is not permissible for a Jew to support anyone who believes differently. He cites **Daniel 12:2 and 12:13** as definitive proofs of physical resurrection of the dead when they state **"many of them that sleep in the earth shall awake, some to everlasting life and some to reproaches and everlasting abhorrence"**.

**Maimonides** believed that the resurrection was not permanent or general. In his view, God never violates the laws of nature. Rather, divine interaction is by way of angels, whom **Maimonides** often regards to be metaphors for the laws of nature, the principles by which the physical universe operates, or Platonic eternal forms. **Maimonides** describes angels that are actually created beings.

In this view, any dead who are resurrected must eventually die again. In this discussion **Maimonides** says nothing of a universal resurrection. All he says it is that whatever resurrection does take place, it will occur at an indeterminate time before the world to come, which he repeatedly states will be purely spiritual. **Maimonides** thus disassociated the resurrection of the dead from both the World to come and the **Messianic era**.

## Messianic era:

"....'**The days of the Messiah'** (i.e., the Messianic Era) is a timeframe in which the kingdom shall return to Israel, and they (i.e., the people of Israel) will return to the **Land of Israel**, and the king who shall stand-up will establish the place of his kingdom in **Zion**, whose name shall be extolled and it will reach unto the ends of the earth, being [even] greater than **Solomon's kingdom**, and the nations will enter a covenant of peace with him, and all lands shall serve him on account of the abundance of his righteousness, and for the wondrous things that shall be revealed through him; whosoever shall rise-up against him, the **Lord** will cut him off and deliver him into his hands. There is no difference between this world and the days of the **Messiah**, excepting only the subjugation of kingdoms'.

Now the greatest advantage at that time will be that we'll have rest from the subjugation of the wicked kingdom, which prevents us from performing that which God has enjoined unto us to do, while knowledge will be vastly increased, as it says" 'For the earth shall be filled with the knowledge of the **Lo-rd' (Isa. 11:9).** Meanwhile, battles and wars will come to an end, as it says: **'Nation shall not lift up a sword against nation' (Micha 4:3).**

## Maimonides and the Modernists

**Maimonides** remains one of the most widely debated Jewish thinkers among modern scholars. He has been adopted as a symbol and an intellectual hero by almost all major movements I modern Judaism, and has proven immensely important to philosophers such as **Leo Strauss**; and his views on the importance of humility have been taken up by modern humanist philosophers, including **Peter Singer.**

**Maimonides'** reconciliation of the philosophical and the traditional has given his legacy an extremely diverse and dynamic quality. **Judaic and philosophical works. Maimonides** composed works of Jewish scholarship, rabbinic law, philosophy, and medical texts. Most of **Maimonides'** works were written in Judeo-Arabic. However, the *Mishneh Torah* was written in Hebrew.

## Medical works

**Maimonides** wrote ten known medical works in Arabic that have been translated by the Jewish medical ethicist **Fred Rosner** into contemporary English.

## Treatise on logic

The **treatise on Logic** (Arabic: **Maqala Fi-sinat Al-Mantiq**) has been printed 17 times, including editions in Latin (1527), German (1805, 1822, 1833, 1828), French (1935), and English (1938), and in an abridged Hebrew form. The work illustrates the essentials of Aristotelian logic to be found in the teachings of the great Arabic philosophers such as **Avicenna** and, above all, **Al-Farabi, "the Second Master,"** the **"First Master"** being **Aristotle**. The work proceeds rationally trough a lexicon of philosophical terms to a summary of higher philosophical topics, in 14 chapters corresponding to **Maimonides'** birthdate of 14 Nissan. **The number 14 records in many of Maimonides' works.**

# Marranos (Crypto-Jews)

**Marranos** were Jews living in the **Iberian Peninsula** who converted or were forced to convert to Christianity during the Middle Ages yet continued to practice Judaism in secret. **"Marrano"** is now often considered offensive and **"Crypto-Jew"** is preferred in scholarly works. The term specifically refers to the accusation of **Crypto-Judaism**, whereas the term **Converso** was used for the wider population of Jewish converts to Catholicism whether or not they secretly still practiced Jewish rites. Converts from both Judaism and Islam were referred to by the even broader term **"New Christians"**.

The term "**Marrano**" came into later use in 1492 with the **Castilian Alhambra Decree**, which outlawed the practice of Judaism in Spain and required all remaining Jews to convert or leave. By then, the large majority of Jews in Spain had converted to Catholicism and **Conversos numbered hundreds of thousands.** They remained under the watchful eye of the **Spanish Inquisition** subject to suspicions of secret practice of Judaism by formal Catholics, also known as **"Marranism".**

## Etymology
One derives from Arabic *muḥarram*; meaning **"forbidden, anathematized".** *Marrano* in this context means **"swine"** or **"pig",** from the ritual prohibition against eating pork, practiced by both Jews and Muslims. However, as applied to **Crypto-Jews**, the term **Marrano** may also derive from the Spanish verb **"marrar"** meaning **"to deviate"** or "to err".

## Demographics
Under state pressure in the late 14th and early 15th century, **over half of Jews in the Iberian Peninsula converted to Christianity**, thus avoiding the **Decree of Expulsion** which affected Spain's remaining openly Jewish population in **1492**. A phylogeographic study in 2008 of 1,150 volunteer **Y-chromosome DNA haplo groups:** 20% of the tested Iberian population had haplo groups consistent with Sephardi ancestry.

## Portugal / *History of the Jews in Portugal*
**Some Portuguese *Conversos* or *cristãos-novos* continued to practice as Crypto-Jews**. Members had managed to survive more than four centuries without being fully assimilated into the **Old Christian** population. After the expulsion of Jews and Muslims from Spain **(1492)** and Portugal **(1497)**, *Conversos* continued to be suspect in times of social strain. In Lisbon in 1506, a months-long plague caused people to look for scapegoats. **The mob dragged *Converso* victims from their houses and killed some**. Within 48 hours, many "Conversos" were killed; by the third day all who could have escaped, often with the help of other Portuguese. The killing spree lasted from 19 to 21 April, in what came to be known as **the Lisbon Massacre**.

**King Manuel** severely punished those who took part in the killings. The ringleaders and the Dominicans who encouraged the riot were also executed. The foreigners who had taken part generally escaped punishment, leaving with their ships.

Spanish and Portuguese **Conversos** made financial sacrifices. None were successful in preventing Portugal from introducing the **Holy Office** in 1478. The *Conversos* suffered immensely both from mob violence and interrogation and testing by the **Inquisition**. At **Covilhã,** there were rumors that the people planned to massacre all the **New Christians** on one day.

## Spain / *History of the Jews in Spain*
Spanish political intrigues had earlier promoted the anti-Jewish policies which culminated in 1391, when **Regent Queen Leonora of Castile** gave the **Archdeacon of Ecija, Ferrand Martinez,** considerable power in her realm. Martinez gave speeches that led to violence against the Jews, and this influence culminated in the sack of the Jewish quarter of Seville on June 4, 1391. It is estimated that **200,000 Jews saved their lives by converting to Christianity** in the wake of these persecutions. Other Jews left the country altogether and around 100,000 openly practicing Jews remained.

**In 1449,** feelings rose against *Conversos*, breaking out in a riot at Toledo. Under Juan de la Cibdad, the **Conversos** opposed the mob, but were repulsed. They were executed with their leader. Nearly 20 years later in July 1467, another riot occurred where a mob attacked *Conversos* in Toledo. The conflagration spread so rapidly that **1,600 houses were consumed.** Both Old Christians and **Conversos** perished. **The brothers De la Torre were captured and hanged.** The government decreed that Jews and **Conversos** should remain in their neighborhood or leave the city. In 1473, attacks on **Conversos** arose in numerous other cities: At Segovia, there was a massacre (May 16, 1474).

## Inquisition
Tens of thousands of Jews were baptised in the three months before the deadline for expulsion, some 40,000 if one accepts the totals given by **Kamen**: These *Conversos* were the principal concern of the **Inquisition**; being suspected of continuing to practice Judaism. During 1492, about 12,000 **Conversos** entered Navarre from Aragon's repression, where they were allowed to remain. The most intense period of persecution of *Conversos* lasted until 1530. There was a rise in denunciations of *Conversos* in the last decade of the sixteenth century. At the beginning of the seventeenth century, some *Conversos* who had fled to Portugal began to return to Spain, fleeing the persecution of the **Portuguese Inquisition**, founded in 1536. **In 1691, 37 *Chuetas*, or *Conversos* of Majorca, were burned.**

## Converso-Jewish relations

The **Spanish Inquisition established in 1478**. The government issued an edict directing traditional Jews to live within a ghetto and be separated from *Conversos*. Despite the law, however, the Jews remained in communication with their **New Christian** brethren. These were the charges brought by the government of **Ferdinand II of Aragon and Isabella I of Castile against the Jews**. They constituted the grounds for their expulsion and banishment in 1492, so they could not subvert **Conversos. Jews who did not want to leave Spain had to accept baptism as a sign of conversion.**

## Conversos in Italy

Although the vast majority of **Spain's 250,000 *Conversos* abandoned Judaism** and simply assimilated into Spain's dominant Catholic culture, many of those continuing to secretly practice their former religion felt threatened and persecuted by the **Inquisition** which continued to actively persecute heresy. **Pope Paul III** received them at Ancona for commercial reasons. Two years later, **Pope Paul IV** issued orders to have all the *Conversos* in Italy be thrown into the prisons of the **Inquisition** which he had instituted. Sixty of them, who acknowledged the Catholic faith as penitents, were transported to the island of Malta; twenty-four, who adhered to Judaism, were **publicly burned (May 1556).**

## France / *History of the Jews in France*

About 3,000 Jews came to Provence after the **Alhambra Decree** expelled Jews from Spain in 1492. From 1484, one town after another had called for expulsion, but the calls were rejected by **Charles VIII.** However, **Louis XII,** in one of his first acts as king in 1498, issued a general expulsion order of the **Jews of Provence**. The order was renewed in 1500 and again in 1501. The Jews of Provence were given the option of conversion to Christianity and a number chose that option. However, after a short while –the king imposed a special tax, referred to as **"the tax of the neophytes."**

## Migrations

The vast majority of Spain's *Conversos*, remained in Spain and Portugal and were suspected of **"Marranism"** by the Spanish **Inquisition**. They constituted a significant portion of the over three thousand people executed for heresy by the Spanish **Inquisition**. The **New Christians** of Portugal breathed more freely when **Philip III** of Spain came to the throne. After a few years, however, the privilege was revoked, and the **Inquisition** resumed its activity. Migrations to Constantinople and Thessaloniki, where Jewish refugees had settled after the expulsion from Spain, as well as to Italy, Serbia, Romania, Bulgaria, Vienna, and Timisoara, continued into the middle of the 18th century.

## Today

By **Spanish Civil Code Art. 22.1**, the government created concessions for gaining citizenship to nationals of several countries and Sephardi Jews historically linked with Spain, allowing them to seek citizenship after five years rather than the customary ten required for residence in Spain. Later it was dropped to two years. In **2004, Shlomo Moshe Amar** traveled to Portugal to celebrate the centennial anniversary of the Lisbon synagogue **Shaare Tikvah**. During his stay, **Shlomo Moshe Amar** met descendants of Jewish families persecuted by the **Inquisition** who still practice Judaism **(Bnei Anusim) at the house of Rabbi Boaz Pash**.

# Masada & the Holocaust

Fortification in the Southern District of Israel, on top of an isolated rock plateau on the eastern edge of the Judaean Desert, overlooking the **Dead Sea**. **Herod the Great** built palaces for himself on the mountain and fortified **Masada** between 37 and 31 BCE. The Siege of **Masada** by troops of the Roman Empire towards the end of the **First Jewish-Roman war ended in the mass suicide of the 960 Jewish** rebels and their families holed up there.

## Geography

The cliffs on the east edge of **Masada** are about 1,300 feet (400 m) high and the cliffs on the west are about 300 feet (91 m) high; the natural approaches to the cliff top are very difficult. The top of the plateau is flat and rhomboid-shaped, about 1,800 feet (550 m) by 900 feet (270m). The fortress included storehouses, barracks, an armory, the palace, and cisterns that were refilled by rainwater. Three narrow, winding paths led from below up to fortified gates.

## History

Almost all historical information about **Masada** comes from the 1st-century Jewish Roman historian **Josephus**. Herod the Great captured it in the power-struggle that followed the death of father **Antipater**. It survived the siege of the **Parthian King Antigonus**. In 66 CE, a group of Jewish rebels, the **Sicarii**, overcame the Roman garrisoned **Masada** with the aid of a ruse. After the **destruction of the Second Temple in 70 CE**, additional members of the Sicarii fled Jerusalem and settled on the mountaintop.

From there they took no further part in the rebellion against Rome, but raided nearby villages including **Ein Gedi**, where, according to **Josephus**, they **massacred 700 women and children**. In 73 CE, the Roman governor of Judaea **Lucius Flavius** laid siege to **Masada**. The Roman legion surrounded **Masada**, and built a circumvallation wall and then a siege embankment against the western face of the plateau.

The ramp was complete in the spring of 73, after probably two to **three months of siege**, allowing the Romans to finally breach the wall of the fortress with a battering ram on April 16. Romans took the **X Legion** and a number of auxiliary units and Jewish prisoner of war, totaling some 15,000 troops in order to crush Jewish resistance at **Masada**. A giant siege tower with a battering ram was constructed and moved laboriously up the completed ramp. **The walls of the fortress were breached in 73 CE.** According to **Josephus**, when Roman troops entered the fortress, they discovered that **its 960 inhabitants had set all the buildings and the food storerooms ablaze and committed mass suicide.** Only two women and five children were found alive.

## Archaeology

The site of **Masada** was identified in 1842 and extensively excavated between 1963 and 1965 by an expedition led by Israeli archaeologist **Yigael Yadin**. The Roman ramp still stands on the western side and can be climbed on foot. Water cisterns two-thirds of the way up the cliff drain the nearby wadis by an elaborate system of channels, which explains how the rebels managed to conserve enough water for such a long time.

Inside the synagogue, an ostracon bearing the inscription *me'aser Cohen* (tithe for the priest) was found, as were fragments of two scrolls; parts of **Deuteronomy 33-34** and parts of **Ezekiel 35-38** (including the vision of the "**dry bones**"), found hidden in pits dug under the floor of a small room built inside the synagogue.

In the area in front of the northern palace, eleven small ostraca were recovered, each bearing a single name. One reads, "Ben Yair" and could be short for **Eleazar ben Ya'ir**, the commander of the fortress. It has been suggested that the other ten names are those of the men chosen by **Lot** to kill the others and then themselves, as recounted by **Josephus**.

The skeletal remains of 28 people were unearthed at **Masada**. The remains of a male 20-22 years of age, a female 17-18 and a child approximately 12 years old were found in the palace. The remains of two men and a full head of hair with braids belonging to a woman were also found in the bath house. The remains of 25 people were found in a cave at the base of the cliff. The remains are those of the Jewish **Zealots** who committed suicide during the siege of **Masada**, and all were reburied at **Masada** with full military honors on July 7, 1969.

The Chief of Staff of the Israel Defense Forces (IDF), **Moshe Dayan**, initiated the practice of holding the swearing-in ceremony of soldiers who have completed their **Tironut** (IDF basic training) on top of **Masada**. The ceremony ends with the declaration: "**Masada shall not fall again.**" The soldiers climb the **Snake Path** at night and are sworn in with torches lighting the background. **Masada was declared a UNESCO World Heritage Site in 2001.**

In 2007, a new museum opened at the site in which archaeological findings are displayed in a theatrical setting. A **2,000 year-old seed** discovered during archaeological excavations in the early 1960s was successfully germinated into a date plant. It was the oldest known germination, remaining so until a new record was set in 2012.

## The Nazis & the Holocaust

The **Holocaust**, also known as the **Shoah** (Hebrew: "**the catastrophe**") was a genocide in which **Adolf Hitler's Nazi Germany and its collaborators killed about six million Jews**. The victims included 1.5 million children and represented about two-thirds of the nine million Jews who had resided in Europe. Killings took place throughout Nazi Germany and German-occupied territories. A network of about **42,500 facilities** in Germany and German-occupied territories were used to concentrate victims for slave labor, mass murder, and other human rights abuses.

Over 200,000 people are estimate to have been **Holocaust perpetrators**. The persecution and genocide were carried out in stages, culminating in what Nazis termed the **"Final Solution to the Jewish Question",** an agenda to exterminate Jews in Europe. Jewish armed resistance was limited. The most notable exception was the **Warsaw Ghetto Uprising of 1943**, when thousands of poorly-armed Jewish fighters held the **Waffen-SS** at bay for four weeks. An estimated 20-30,000 Jewish partisans actively fought against the Nazis and their collaborators in Eastern Europe.

## Extermination camps

The use of extermination camps (also called **"death camps"**). These were established at **Auschwitz, Belzec, Chełmno, Jasenovac, Majdanek, Maly Trostenets, Sobibor, and Treblinka.**

## Medical experiments

A distinctive feature of Nazi genocide was the extensive use of human subjects in **"medical"** experiments. The most notorious of these physicians was Josef Mengele, who worked in **Auschwitz**. He would bring them sweets and toys and personally take them to the gas chamber. They would call him **"Onkel (Uncle) Mengele"**. In **Hitler**'s *Mein Kampf* he viewed Marxism as a Jewish doctrine and proclaimed he was fighting against **"Jewish Marxism"**. Of these areas, Madagascar was the most seriously discussed.

In 1935, **Hitler** introduced the Nuremberg Laws, which prohibited "**Aryans**" from having sexual relations or marriages with Jews, although this was later extended to include **"Gypsies, Negroes or t heir bastard offspring"** stripped German Jews of their citizenship and deprived them of all civil rights.

## Kristallnacht (1938)

On 7 November 1938, Jewish minor **Herschel Grunspan** assassinated Nazi German diplomat Ernst Vom Rath in Paris. These pogroms became known as *Kristallnacht* (**"Crystal Night"** or **"Night of Broken Glass"**). Jews were attacked and Jewish property was vandalized; over 7,000 Jewish shops and more than 1,200 synagogues.30, 000 were sent to concentration camps, including **Dachau, Sachsenhausen, Buchenwald, and Oranienburg**. The **Vichy** regime in occupied France actively collaborated in persecuting French Jews.

## In North Africa

In the 1930s, the Fascist Italian regime passed anti-Semitic laws barring Jews from government jobs and government schools, and required them to stamp **"Jewish race"** into their passports. Tunisia, the Nazis arrived in November 1942. The Nazis imposed anti-Semitic policies in Tunisia, including forcing Jews to wear the **Yellow Star**, fines, and property confiscation.

## Death squads (1941-1943)

Germany's invasion of the Soviet Union in June 1941 opened a new phase in the **Holocaust**. **Hitler** on 30 March 1941 described the war with the Soviet Union as a **"war of annihilation"**. The Soviet territories contained about 3,000,000 Jews at the start of the war. A mixture of SS, SD, and Security Police, assisted by Ukrainian police, carried out the killings.

## Approx. number killed at each extermination camp

| Camp name | Killed |
| --- | --- |
| Auschwitz II | 1,000,000 |
| Belzec | 600,000 |
| Chełmno | 320,000 |
| Jasenovac | 97,000 |
| Majdanek | 360,000 |

| Maly Trostinets | 65,000 |
|---|---|
| Sobibor | 250,000 |
| Treblinka | 870,000 |
| Total | 3,562,000 |

## Gas chambers

At the extermination camps with **gas chambers** all the prisoners arrived by train. Usually they were told these were showers or delousing chambers, and there were signs outside saying **"baths"** and **"sauna."** Solid pellets of **Zyklon-B** were dropped into the chambers through vents in the side walls, releasing toxic HCN, or hydrogen cyanide. As many as 1.4 million Jewish soldiers fought in the Allied armies, including 500,000 in the Red Army, 550,000 in the U.S. Army, 100,000 in the Polish army and 30,000 in the British army.

## Climax

**Reinhard Heydrich** was assassinated on Prague in June 1942 by soldiers from Czechoslovakia's army-in-exile. On 19 March 1944, **Hitler** ordered the military occupation of Hungary, and Eichmann was dispatched to Budapest to supervise the deportation of **Hungary's 800,000 Jews**. Commandant **Rudolf Hoss**, said at his trial that he killed 400,000 Hungarian Jews in three months.

## "Blood for Goods"

There were unofficial negotiations in Istanbul between Himmler's agents, British agents, and representatives of Jewish organizations; at one point an attempt by **Eichmann** to exchange one million Jews for 10,000 trucks – the so-called **"blood for goods"** proposal – but there was no real possibility of such a deal being struck on this scale. *The New York Times* had deliberately suppressed news of the **Third Reich's** persecution and murder of Jews.

## Death marches (1944-1945)

By mid-1944, the Final Solution had largely run its course. Local commanders continued to kill Jews, and to shuttle them from camp to camp by forced **"death marches"** until the last weeks of the war. Those who lagged behind or fell were shot. Around 250,000 Jews died during these marches. **Elie Wiesel** and his father, **Shlomo**, were among the marchers.

## Victims

**The total number of victims is just under six million – around 78 percent of the 7.3 million Jews in occupied Europe at the time.**

## Holocaust: Is a new one possible?

The State of Israel would not have formed without the **Holocaust**. It was a most unique momentin the history of the world to have enough sympathy for the Jewish people to propose the partition of Palestine between Arabs and Jews. Another **Holocaust** is not possible anywhere in the world as long as the State of Israel exists. No Arab country can destroy Israel without being destroyed itself.

But if ever another **Holocaust** is perpetrated on the Jewish people, the Jews will not climb **Masada** and commit a communal suicide, nor will they march silently into gas chambers. Like Samson, the Jews will bring the "**House**" down with them. The world should be put on notice:

**No Israel = No Middle East!!!**

# Mashhadi Jews

The **Jewish community of Mashhad**, Iran formed in the 1740s, when **Nadir Shah Afshar** called for the relocation of forty Jewish families **from Qazvin and Dilaman to Kalat**. Circumstances ultimately led these families to settle in Mashhad. Known for their integrity and loyalty, these trusted Jewish families were selected to protect **Nadir Shah's** treasures and jewels, spoils which he had taken from his Indian invasion. **He did not live long enough to witness the implementation of his proclamation.**

## Background

**Mashhadi** Jews living in the current Iranian diaspora remain steadfast in their community ties. Religion, community, and nationality are key components forming the identity of the **Mashhadi Jewish community.** The Jews of Mashhad gravitated towards professions that allowed their trade skills to flourish. They were avid merchants, navigating the ancient **Silk Road**. **Mashhadi Jews** were held with the highest regard by **Sunni Turkmen and Shiite Mashhadi** tradesmen, because of their reputation for **honorable and ethical business practices**. The perils of travel subjected **Mashhadi** traders to freezing temperatures, murderous bandits, and limited means of transportation.

Due to their occupations and the arduous conditions involved in their travels, **Mashhadi** men adopted a lifestyle which required spending several months to years on the road without their families. Modern **Mashhadi** men continue their forefathers' unique tradition of working as traveling merchants to support their families. **Mashhadi** women have likewise upheld their matriarchal tradition of creating family and community cohesiveness by nurturing home, family, and community relationships. Unlike their female predecessors, **modern Mashhadi women are exemplary businesswomen,** who are heirs to the savvy trade skills of their ancestors.

## History

The pivotal historic event that transformed an undefined group of Iranian Jews into an unfaltering community was the **Allahdad (means "God's Justice") of 1839**. Building social tensions and resentment and suspicion by **Shiite Muslims** of the Jewish inhabitants of Mashhad's **Eydgah ghetto**, culminated in an explosive event. A **blood Libel** on the commemoration day of a holy Muslim Imam led to a devastating pogrom. On the eve of **Mashhad's Allahdad (March 27, 1839), an estimated thirty-six Jews were killed and approximately seven Jewish girls were abducted to become Muslim child brides.** Within the next twenty-four hours, under the risk of death, approximately three hundred Jewish families made the pretense of **converting to Islam**, under the advisement of their community leaders. The term **Allahdad** was coined by the forced converts to relate their past sins with the calamity they were enduring.

Following the forced conversions, a number of Jewish families, unable to sustain the facade of Muslim faith, **escaped to Herat, Afghanistan**. Later on, from Afghanistan to Sub-Continent (Pakistan). **Very few Mashhadi converts permanently assimilated to Islam**. It is estimated that the remaining community members proceeded to live dual lives as **crypto-Jews** through the 1920s. During this time, the **Jadid-al-Islam** (a term meaning **"New Muslims"**) boasted of two known Sheikhs, fifty-seven known Hajjis, and twenty-one known Karbalais while **preserving their secret Jewish identities.**

**Mashhadi** families gradually migrated to Marv and surrounding areas of **Czarist Turkmenistan**, in an effort to escape persecution in Mashhad and look for better business opportunities in pre-communist Russia. The seemingly stable social and trade environment of Russia did not benefit them for long. **In the fall of 1917**, the **Russian revolution caused the first return of Mashhadi Jews, from Marv to Mashhad. Mashhadi**s who remained in Russia, fell prey to **Stalin's "purge of petit bourgeoisie"** and some members of the community were imprisoned. **In 1925, Reza Shah made an agreement with Stalin to exchange Iranian and Russian nationals.** The imprisoned **Mashhadi**s were released to return home, once again. A **second blood libel in 1946** led the disenchanted community's gradual relocation to the tolerant cities of Tehran and Jerusalem, joining the few **Mashhadi** families who already resided there.

**Within an eighty-year span, the Mashhadi community migrated at least five times to avoid persecution.** Throughout this short period they migrated from Mashhad to Herat, Mashhad to Russia and back, Mashhad to Jerusalem and Tehran, **ultimately fleeing during the Iranian Revolution of 1979. Mashhadi** communities now exist in Israel, New York, Milan, Hamburg, London and Pakistan. **In Pakistan, Mashhadi families are Muslims.** Some of them are Shia and some of them are Sunnis.

**Mashhadi** youth have assumed their predecessors' ethos of primarily socializing and marrying within their community. This once necessary survival mechanism has transitioned to a comfortable modus operandi for today's **Mashhadi**s. All perspectives undeniably credit the **Mashhadi** community for their fervor in upholding their Jewish heritage and traditions.

The resounding conclusion of the **Mashhadi** story is one that reflects their ability to protect their inherent Jewish religion. The unusual survival method of the **Mashhadi crypto-Jews** laid the foundation for a modern **Mashhadi** community who now safely and proudly practice Judaism.

## Timeline of Jews of Mashhad

**Iranian Jews are considered to be the descendants of the Assyrian 722 B.C. and Babylonian Exiles 586 B.C.** Within this diaspora, a smaller tribe of Jews evolved, due to their geographic setting in the city of Mashhad, and their robust community ties.

- 1650 – Safavid dynasty ruling in Iran calls to convert or kill all Iranian Jews

- 1739 – Nadir Shah of the Afsharid dynasty invades India.
- 1740 – Nadir Shah brings spoils back from his Indian invasion, in the form of treasures and jewels.
- 1746 – Nadir Shah orders the relocation of forty Jewish families from Qazvin to Khorasan province, for the purpose of guarding his acquired treasures and jewels. Nadir Shah holds a favorable disposition towards Jews.
- 1747 – Nadir Shah is assassinated. Persecution of Iranian Jews resumes. Seventeen of the forty original families move to Eydgah ghetto, Mashhad.
- 1750 – Seven of the original forty families proceed from Sabzavar and settle in Mashhad.
- 1755 – Sixteen of the original forty families proceed from Kalat and settle in Mashhad.
- 1839 – The Allahdad - the forced conversion of **Mashhadi** Jews to Islam - March 27, 1839 (12 Nissan 5599/11 Muharram 1255). **Mashhadi** (Anusim) live dual lives as crypto-Jews, through 1925
- 1840 – A number of Jewish families, unable to sustain the facade of Muslim faith, escaped to Herat, Afghanistan
- 1886 – Some **Mashhadi** Jewish families immigrate to Turkmenistan, Russia, through 1917.
- 1890 – Muslim **Mashhadi** attempts to expose secret Jewish burial proceedings of crypto-Jews. A potential pogrom is averted.
- 1890s – After completing the Hajj, some **Mashhadi** families make Aliya to Jerusalem, instead of returning from Mecca to Mashhad.
- 1901 – Haji Adonya HaCohen builds the first **Mashhadi** Jewish synagogue in Jerusalem, followed by Haji Yehezkel's synagogue, built in 1905.
- 1910s – Some **Mashhadi** Jews move to London
- 1918 – Russian Revolution and start of communism prompts the first wave of **Mashhadi** Jews to return from Marv to Mashhad.
- 1925 – Reza Shah permits freedom of religious practice in Iran. **Mashhadi**s begin to practice their Jewish faith openly
- 1946 – Second notable Blood Libel in Mashhad forces the now openly Jewish **Mashhadi** community to begin a decade-long migration to Tehran and Israel.
- 1940s – Some **Mashhadi** Jews move to United States, well through 1980s
- 1950s – Some **Mashhadi** Jews move to Germany and Italy.
- 1979 – Iranian revolution impels Iranian Jews to flee Iran
- 2010 – Over twenty-thousand **Mashhadi** Jews now reside in Israel, New York, Milan, Germany, and London.

# Markabah (Jewish Mysticism)

**Markabah/Merkavah mysticism** (or **Chariot mysticism**) is a school of early **Jewish mysticism, c. 100 BCE – 1000 CE,** centered on visions such as those found in the **Book of Ezekiel chapter 1**, or in the *Hekhalot* ("palaces") literature, concerning stories of ascents to the heavenly palaces and the **Throne of God.** The main corpus of the Merkavah literature was composed in the period 200–700 CE.

## Etymology

The noun *Markabah/Merkavah* **"thing to ride in, cart"** with the general meaning **"to ride".** The word **"chariot"** is found 44 times in the Masoretic text of the Hebrew Bible—most of them referring to normal chariots on earth, and although the concept of the **Markabah** is associated with **Ezekiel's vision (1:4–26), the word is not explicitly written in Ezekiel 1.** In English the Hebrew term *Markabah/Merkavah* relates to the **throne-chariot of God** in prophetic visions.

It is most closely associated with the vision in Ezekiel chapter 1 of the four-wheeled vehicle driven by four *hayyot* (**"living creatures"**), each of which has four wings and the four faces of a **man, lion, ox, and eagle (or vulture).**

## Ezekiel's vision of the chariot / *Angelology § Tanakh (Hebrew Bible)*

According to the verses in **Ezekiel**, his vision consists of a chariot made of many heavenly beings driven by the **"Likeness of a Man".** The base structure of the chariot is composed of four beings. These beings are called the **"living creatures".** The bodies of the creatures are **"like that of a human being",** but each of them has four faces, corresponding to the four directions the chariot can go (**East, South, North and West**). The faces are that of a **man, a lion, an ox** (later changed to a cherub in **Ezekiel 10:14**) and an **eagle.** Since there are four angels and each has four faces, there are a total of sixteen faces. Each of the *hayyot* angels also has four wings.

These wheel angels, which are described as **"a wheel inside of a wheel",** are called *"ophanim"* (lit. wheels, cycles or ways). The angel with the face of the man is always on the east side and looks up at the **"Likeness of a Man"** that drives the chariot. The **"Likeness of a Man"** sits on a throne made of sapphire.

The Bible later makes mention of a third type of angel found in the **Markabah** called *"seraphim"* (**lit. "Burning"**) angels. These angels appear like flashes of fire continuously ascending and descending. The chariot is in a constant state of motion, and the energy behind this movement runs according to this hierarchy. The movement of the *ophanim* is controlled by the **"Living creatures",** or *Hayyot,* while the movement of the *hayyot* is controlled by the *seraphim.* **The movement of all the angels of the chariot is controlled by the "Likeness of a Man" on the Throne.**

## Early Jewish Markabah mysticism

**There are distinguished four periods in early Jewish mysticism, developing from Isaiah's and Ezekiel's visions of the Throne/Chariot, to later extant Markabah mysticism texts:**

1. 800–500 BCE, mystical elements in Prophetic Judaism such as Ezekiel's chariot
2. Beginning c. 530s BCE, especially 300–100 BCE, Apocalyptic literature mysticism
3. Beginning c. 100 BCE, especially 1–130s CE, early Rabbinic **Markabah** mysticism referred to briefly in exoteric Rabbinic literature such as the *Pardes* ascent; also related to early Christian mysticism
4. c. 1–200 CE, continuing till c. 1000 CE, **Markabah** mystical ascent accounts in the esoteric **Markabah**-Hekhalot literature

## Rabbinic commentary

The earliest **Rabbinic Markabah** commentaries were exegetical expositions of the prophetic visions of God in the heavens, and the divine retinue of angels, hosts, and heavenly creatures surrounding God. **"Many have expounded upon the Markabah without ever seeing it."** One mention of the **Markabah** in the Talmud notes the importance of the passage:

**"A great issue—the account of the Merkavah; a small issue—the discussions of Abaye and Rava ."** The sages **Rabbi Yochanan Ben Zakkai** (d. c. 80 CE) and later, **Rabbi Akiva** (d. 135) were deeply involved in **Markabah** exegesis. **Rabbi Akiva** and his contemporary **Rabbi Ishmael ben Elisha** are most often the protagonists of later **Markabah** ascent literature.

## Prohibition against study

The Talmudic interdictions concerning **Markabah** speculation are numerous and widely held. Discussions concerning the **Markabah** were limited to **only the most worthy sages**, and admonitory legends are preserved about the dangers of overzealous speculation concerning the **Markabah**. **"Seek not out the things that are too hard for thee, neither search the things that are above thy strength. But what is commanded thee, think thereupon with reverence; for it is not needful for thee to see with thine eyes the things that are in secret."** It must be studied only by exemplary scholars.

Further commentary notes that the chapter-headings of *Ma'aseh Markabah* may be taught, as was done by **Rabbi Hiyya. Rabbi Zera** said that even the chapter-headings might be communicated only to a person who was head of a school and was cautious in temperament.

According to **Rabbi Ammi,** the secret doctrine might be entrusted only to one who possessed the five qualities enumerated in **Isaiah 3:3** (being experienced in any of five different professions requiring good judgement), and a certain age is, of course, necessary. A boy who recognized the meaning of חשמל (**Ezekiel 1:4**) was consumed by **fire (*Hagigah* 13b),** and the perils connected with the unauthorized discussion of these subjects are often described (***Hagigah* ii. 1; *Shab.* 80b).**

## Jewish development

A small number of texts unearthed at **Qumran** indicate that the **Dead Sea** community also engaged in **Markabah** exegesis. Recently uncovered Jewish mystical texts also evidence a deep affinity with the rabbinic **Markabah** homilies.

The **Markabah** homilies eventually consisted of detailed descriptions of multiple layered heavens (usually **Seven Heavens**), often guarded over by angels, and encircled by flames and lightning. Contemporary historians of Jewish mysticism usually date this development to the third century CE.

### *Maseh Markabah*

**Maseh Markabah (*Working of the Chariot*)** is the modern name given to a *Hekhalot* text, discovered by scholar **Gershom Scholem**. *Works of the Chariot* dates from late Hellenistic period, after the end of the **Second Temple period following the destruction of the Second Temple in 70 CE** when the physical cult ceased to function. It seems to have been an esoteric movement that grew out of the priestly mysticism already evident in the **Dead Sea Scrolls** and some apocalyptic writings.

The chariot and its accompanying angels are analogies for the various ways that God reveals himself in this world. Hasidic philosophy and **kabbalah** discuss at length what each aspect of this vision represents in this world, and how the vision does not imply that God is made up of these forms.

## Hekhalot literature

The main interests of **Hekhalot** literature are accounts of divine visions, mystical ascents into heaven and observance of the divine council, and the summoning and control of great angels, usually for the purpose of gaining insight into **Torah**. In their visions, these mystics would enter into the celestial realms and journey through the **seven stages** of mystical ascent: the **Seven Heavens** and seven throne rooms.

The *Hekalot Zutarti* in particular is concerned with the secret names of God and their powers: **This is His great name, with which Moses divided the great sea: This is His great name which turned the waters into high walls:**

In some texts, the mystic's interest extends to the heavenly music and liturgy, usually connected with the angelic adorations mentioned in **Isaiah 6:3.** The ultimate goal of the ascent varies from text to text. In some cases, it seems to be a **visionary glimpse of God**, to **"Behold the King in His Beauty"**. Others hint at **"enthronement"**, that the adept be accepted among the angelic retinue of God and be given an honored seat.

## Key texts
**The ascent texts are extant in four principal works, all redacted well after the third but certainly before the ninth century CE. They are: 1l**

1. *Hekhalot Zutartey* ("**The Lesser Palaces**"), which details an ascent of Rabbi Akiva;
2. *Hekhalot Rabbati* ("**The Greater Palaces**"), which details an ascent of Rabbi Ishmael;
3. *Ma'aseh Markabah* ("**Account of the Chariot**"), a collection of hymns recited by the "descenders" and heard during their ascent;
4. *Sepher Hekhalot* ("**Book of Palaces**", also known as *3 Enoch*), which recounts an ascent and divine transformation of the biblical figure Enoch into the archangel Metatron, as related by Rabbi Ishmael.

A fifth work provides a detailed description of the Creator as seen by the "**descenders**" at the climax of their ascent. The literal message of the work was repulsive to those who maintained **God's incorporeality; Maimonides** (d. 1204) wrote that the book should be erased and all mention of its existence deleted. It features a linguistic theory of creation in which **God** creates the universe by combining the 22 letters of the Hebrew alphabet, along with emanations represented by the ten numerals, or *Sefirot.*

## Hekhalot literature and "Four Entered *Pardes*"
The Babylonian Talmud's treatment of "**The Work of the Chariot**" in the presentation and analysis of such in the Gemara to tractate *Hagigah* of the Mishna. This portion of the Babylonian Talmud, which includes the famous "**four entered *pardes***" material, runs from 12b-iv (wherein the Gemara's treatment of the "**Work of Creation**" flows into and becomes its treatment of "**The Work of the Chariot**") to and into 16a-i. (All references are to the Artscroll pagination.)

However, in both the Jerusalem Talmud and the Babylonian Talmud the major players in this Chariot/Throne endeavor are, clearly, **Rabbi Akiva and Elisha ben Abuyah** who is referred to as "**Akher**". Neither Talmud presents Rabbi Ishmael as a player in **Markabah** study and practice.

Both Akiva and the "**Ishmaelic Akher**" traded upon the "**two-thrones**"/"**two-powers**"-in-Heaven motif in their respective **Markabah**-oriented undertakings. The text offers Justice and Charity (*ts'daqqa*) as the *middot* of God which are enthroned in Heaven.

In the "**four-entered-*pardes***" section of this portion of the Babylonian **Gemara** on tractate *Hagigah*, it is the figure of Akiva who seems to be lionized. For of the four he is the only one presented who ascended and descended "**whole**". The other three were broken, one way or another:

## The Markabah in later Jewish interpretations / Maimonides' explanation

**Maimonides'** philosophical 12th-century work *Guide for the Perplexed* is in part intended as an explanation of the passages *Ma'aseh Bereshit* and *Ma'aseh Markabah*. **Maimonides** explains basic mystical concepts via the Biblical terms referring to Spheres, elements and Intelligences.

"…We must, therefore, begin with teaching these subjects according to the capacity of the pupil, and on two conditions, first, that he be wise, i.e., that he should have successfully gone through the preliminary studies, and secondly that he be intelligent, talented, clear-headed, and of quick perception, that is, **"have a mind of his own",** as our Sages termed it…
— *Guide for the Perplexed, ch. XXXIII*

## The Four Worlds of Kabbalah

**Kabbalah relates the Markabah vision of Ezekiel and the Throne vision of Isaiah (Isaiah 6:1–8)** describing the *seraph* angels, to its comprehensive Four Worlds. The highest World, *Atziluth* ("Emanation"-Divine wisdom), is the realm of absolute Divine manifestation without self-awareness, metaphorically described in the vision as the likeness of a **Man** on the throne.

**The second World, *Beriah* ("Creation"—Divine understanding),** is the first independent root creation, the realm of the Throne, denoting God descending into Creation, as a king limits his true greatness and revealed posture when seated. The **World of *Beriah*** is the realm of the higher angels, the *Seraphim* **("burning" in ascent and descent as their understanding of God motivates self-annihilation).**

**The third World, *Yetzirah* ("Formation"—Divine emotions),** is the realm of archetypal existence, the abode of the main *Hayyot* angels ("alive" with divine emotion). They are described with faces of a lion, ox and eagle, as their emotional nature is instinctive like animals, and they are the archetypal origins of creatures in this World. **The lowest World, *Assiah* ("Action"—Divine rulership),** is the realm guided by the lower channels of the *Ophanim* (humble "ways" in realized creation). Isaiah prophesied in the era of Solomon's Temple, **Ezekiel's vision took place in the exile of Babylonian captivity.**

**"And they (the *Seraphim*) called one unto the other and said, Holy, holy, holy is the Lord of Hosts; the whole earth is full of His glory."**
— *Isaiah 6:3*

**Those over against them (the *Hayyot*) say, Blessed: "Blessed be the glory of the Lord from His place."**
— *Ezekiel 3:12*

468

And in Thy holy words it is written, saying: "The Lord shall reign forever, thy God, O Zion, unto all generations; Hallelujah."
— *Psalm 146:10*

The lower *Hayyot* ("living" angels) in *Yetzirah* (divine emotions) say, **"Blessed be the glory ... from His place"** of *Atziluth.* In Ezekiel's vision, the *Hayyot* have a central role in the **Markabah**'s channeling of the divine flow in creation.

## Hasidic explanation

Hasidic thought explains **Kabbalah** in terms of human psychology. Through this, the **Markabah** is a multi-layered analogy that offers insight into the nature of man, the ecosystem, the world, and teaches self-refinement. The four *Hayyot* angels represent the basic archetypes that **God** used to create the current nature of the world.

*Ophanim,* which means **"ways"**, are the ways these archetypes combine to create actual entities that exist in the world. However, in practice, everything in the world is some combination of all four, and the particular combination of each element that exist in each thing are its particular *Ophanim* or ways.

The 'man on the throne' in the vision of **Ezekiel** descriptively represents **God**, who is controlling everything that goes on in the world, and how all of the archetypes He set up should interact. The 'man on the throne', however, drives when the four angels connect their wings. This shows that there is really a higher power (God) telling these elements how to act.

A person should strive to be like a **Markabah**, that is to say, he should realize all the different qualities, talents and inclinations he has (his angels). Ultimately, we should strive to realize how all of the forces in the world, though they may seem to conflict, can unite when one knows how to use them all to fulfill a higher purpose; namely to serve **God**.

## Christianity / *Christian mysticism*

Early Christian theology and discourse was influenced by the Jewish **Markabah** tradition. Similarly. **Paul the Apostle**'s accounts of his conversion experience and his ascent to the heavens (**2 Corinthians 12:2–4**) as the earliest first person accounts we have of a **Markabah** mystic in Jewish or Christian literature.

In Christianity, the **man, lion, ox, and eagle** are used as symbols for the four evangelists (or gospel-writers), and appear frequently in church decorations. These Creatures are called **Zoë** (or the Tetramorph), and surround the throne of God in Heaven, along with twenty-four elders and seven spirits of God (**Revelation 4:1–11**). **Warnings against children or "excitable persons" reading the Ezekiel story exist in some translations.**

# Messianism

In Abrahamic religions, Messianism is the belief and doctrine that is centered on the advent of the messiah, who acts as the **chosen savior and leader of humanity by God**. Messianism originated from the Hebrew Bible (Christian Old Testament), in which a messiah is a Jewish monarch or **High Priest** traditionally anointed with holy anointing oil. In Judaism, the **Mashiach** will be a future Jewish king **from the line of David** and redeemer of the Jewish people and humanity.

In Christianity and Islam, **Jesus** is the messiah who is called the **Christ**, the savior and redeemer. Other religions have a Messianism-related concept, including the **Buddhist Maitreya**, the **Hindu Kalki**, the **Zoroastrian Saoshyant and** *He whom God shall make manifest* in Babism.

## Abrahamic religions: Judaism

*Messiah* ( *mashiah, moshiah, mashiach,* or *moshiach*, **("anointed ")** is a term used in the Hebrew Bible to describe priests and kings, who were traditionally anointed. For example, Cyrus the Great, the King of Persia, is referred to as **"God's anointed"** (**Messiah**) in the Bible.

In Jewish messianic tradition and eschatology, the term came to refer to a future **Jewish King from the Davidic line**, who will be "**anointed**" with holy anointing oil and rule the Jewish people during the Messianic Age.

Traditional Rabbinic teachings and current **Orthodox** thought hold that the **Messiah** will be an anointed one (**Messiah**), descended from his father through the **Davidic line of King David, who will gather the Jews back into the Land of Israel and usher in an era of peace.**

The most popular **Messiah** claimants were **Simon Bar Kokhba** in 2nd century Judea, **Nehemiah ben Hushiel** in the 7th century Sasanian Empire, **Sabbatai Zevi** in the 17th century Ottoman Empire (precursor to Sabbateans), **Jacob Frank** in 18th century Europe, **Shukr Kuhayl I** and **Judah ben Shalom** in 19th century Ottoman Yemen. There are those who currently identify the 20th century **Rabbi Menachem Mendel Schneerson** (the Lubavitcher Rebbe) as the Mashiach). Other denominations, such as **Reform Judaism**, perceive a **Messianic Age** when the world will be at peace, but do not agree that there will be a **Messiah** as the leader of this era.

## Christianity: *Christ, Christology, and Jesus*

In Christianity, the **Messiah** is called the Christ (/kraɪst/; Greek: , translit. *Khristós*, lit. 'Anointed one'; Hebrew: translit. *Māšîah,* **lit. 'Mashiach'**), the savior and redeemer who would bring salvation to the Jewish people and mankind. **"Christ"** is the Greek translation of **"Messiah"**, meaning **"Anointed one"**. The role of the Christ, the **Messiah** in Christianity, originated from the concept of the messiah in Judaism. Christians believe **Jesus** to be the Jewish messiah (Christ) of the Hebrew Bible and the **Christian Old Testament**.

Christians believe that the messianic prophecies were fulfilled in his mission, death, **Resurrection**, and Ascension to his Session on the heavenly throne, where "H**e sat down at the right hand of God, where he is now waiting until his enemies are made a footstool for his feet" (Heb 10:12-13 NET, quoting the Davidic royal Psalm 110:1)**.

Christians believe that the rest of the messianic prophecies will be fulfilled in the **Second Coming of Christ.** One prophecy, distinctive in both the Jewish and Christian concept of the messiah, is that a Jewish king from the Davidic line, who will be **"anointed"** with holy anointing oil, will be king of God's kingdom on earth, and rule the Jewish people and mankind during the Messianic Age and World to come.

One distinguishing characteristic of the Christian **Messiah**, is that **His Second Coming** is preceded by the arrival of a **false Messiah, the Anti-Christ, or "Alternate-Christ"**, **who enjoys universal reign for 3-1/2 years or 7 years**. In the **Book of Revelation**, the end of the present age culminates in man-made and natural catastrophes, through which divine judgment concludes with the arrival of the **Messianic Kingdom** expected by both Jews and Christians.

## Islam: *Jesus in Islam*

The word *Masih* (the Arabic word for "**Messiah**") literally means **"The anointed one"** and in Islam, *Isa Ibn Mariam, al-Masih* (the **Messiah, Jesus** son of Mary) is believed to have been anointed from birth by Allah with the specific task of being a prophet and a king. In Islam, **Mahdi** is believed to hold the task of establishing the truth and fighting against divisions of Islam uniting all sects before the return of **Jesus** who will kill the false messiah **al-Dajjal** (similar to the Antichrist in Christianity), who will emerge shortly before him in human form in the end of the times, claiming that he is the messiah.

Then **Jesus** will pray for the death of **Yajuj Majuj** who are an ancient tribe seal away from humanity who will rise to cause destruction. After he has destroyed **al-Dajjal Mahdi's** final task will be to become a just king and to re-establish justice. After the death of **Mahdi Jesus'** reign of the messianic King will begin bringing eternal peace and monotheism in the **world ending all religions besides Islam. Sahih al-Bukhari, 3:43:656: Narrated Abu Hurairah:**

"**Allah's Apostle said, "The Hour will not be established until the son of Mary (Mariam) (i.e. Jesus) descends amongst you as a just ruler, he will break the cross, kill the pigs, and abolish the Jizya tax. Money will be in abundance so that nobody will accept it (as charitable gifts)."**

## Other religions: Buddhism

**Maitreya is a bodhisattva** who in the Buddhist tradition is to appear on Earth, achieve complete enlightenment, and teach the pure dharma. According to scriptures, **Maitreya** will be a successor of the historic **Śākyamuni Buddha, the founder of Buddhism.** The prophecy of the arrival of Maitreya is found in the canonical literature of all Buddhist sects (**Theravada, Mahayana, and Vajrayana**) and is accepted by most Buddhists as a statement about an actual event that will take place in the distant future.

Though **Maitreya Buddha** appears in the canonical literature shared by many sects of **Buddhism**, Buddhists in different historical contexts have conceived of **Maitreya Buddha** in different ways. In early medieval Chinese **Buddhism**, for example, **Taoist** and Buddhist ideas combined to produce a particular emphasis on the messianic role of a **Bodhisattva** called **"Prince Moonlight."** Furthermore, the **Chinese Maitreyan** traditions were themselves marked by considerable diversity.

A certain **"canonical" Maitreyan** cult from the fourth to sixth centuries believed Maitreya to inhabit the **Tusita** heaven where Buddhists might be reborn in the very distant future. Another rival tradition, however, believed that Maitreya would appear in the imminent future in this world to provide salvation during a time of misery and decline. This latter form of **Maitreyan** belief was generally censored and condemned as heretical to the point that few manuscripts survive written by Buddhists sympathetic to this tradition. **Maitreya Buddha** continued to be an important figure in millenarian rebellions throughout Chinese history such as in the rebellions associated with the so-called **White Lotus Society.**

## Taoism

Around the 3rd century CE, religious **Taoism** developed eschatological ideas. A number of scriptures predict the end of the world cycle, the deluge, epidemics, and coming of the **Savior Li Hong** (not to be confused with the Tang personalities).

## Hinduism: *Kalki and List of avatar claimants*

In Hinduism, **Kalki** (Devanagari: also rendered by some as *Kalkin* and *Kalaki*) is the tenth and final **Maha Avatara** (great incarnation) of **Vishnu** who will come to end the present age of darkness and destruction known as **Kali Yuga.** The name **Kalki** is often a metaphor for eternity or time. The origins of the name probably lie in the Sanskrit word "*kalka*" which refers to dirt, filth, or foulness and hence denotes the **"destroyer of foulness," "destroyer of confusion," "destroyer of darkness,"** or **"annihilator of ignorance."**

## Zoroastrianism: *Saoshyant and Frashokereti*

According to Zoroastrian philosophy, redacted in the *Zand-i Vohuman Yasht*, **"at the end of thy tenth hundredth winter  the sun is more unseen and more spotted; the year, month, and day** are shorter; and the earth is more barren; and the crop will not yield the seed; and men become more deceitful and more given to vile practices. They have no gratitude. Honorable wealth will all proceed to those of perverted faith and a dark cloud makes the whole sky night and it will rain more noxious creatures than winter."

Saoshyant, the **Man of Peace**, battles the forces of evil. **"In the final battle with evil, the *yazata*s Airyaman and Atar will 'melt the metal in the hills and mountains, and it will be upon the earth like a river' (Bundahishn 34.18), but the righteous (*Ashavan*) will not be harmed."**

Eventually, **Ahura Mazda** will triumph, and his agent **Saoshyant** will resurrect the dead, whose bodies will be restored to eternal perfection, and whose souls will be cleansed and reunited with God. Time will then end, and **truth/righteousness (*Asha*)** and immortality will thereafter be everlasting.

## Rastafarianism

Rastafarians believe that **Emperor Haile Selassie was not killed by the Derg in Ethiopia's civil war**, but will return to save Earth, and in particular, people of African descent. This is a particularly interesting case, as **Selassie** is identified as the **Second Coming of Jesus, so the Rastafarian prophecy is effectively a second coming of the second coming.**

## John Frum

Some cargo cults believe in a messiah figure called **John Frum**. When **David Attenborough** asked one of its adherents if it was rational for them to be still waiting for Frum to re-appear after 50 years, he was told that Christianity had been waiting 2,000 years, so waiting for **Frum** was much more rational.

## Russian and Slavic Messianism

**Romantic Slavic Messianism** held that the Slavs, especially the Russians, suffer in order that other European nations, and eventually all of humanity, may be redeemed. This theme had a profound impact in the development of Pan-Slavism and Russian and Soviet imperialism; it also appears in works by the Polish Romantic poets **Zygmunt Krasiński** and **Adam Mickiewicz**, including the latter's familiar expression, **"*Polska Chrystusem narodów*"** ("Poland is the Christ of the nations").

# *Mezuzah*

A *Mezuzah* (Hebrew: מְזוּזָה "doorpost") is a piece of parchment called a *klaf* contained in a decorative case and inscribed with specific Hebrew verses from the Torah (**Deuteronomy 6:4–9 and 11:13–21**). These verses consist of the Jewish prayer *Shema Yisrael*, beginning with the phrase: **"Hear, O Israel, the Lord (is) our God, the Lord is One"**. In mainstream Rabbinic Judaism, a *Mezuzah* is affixed to the doorpost of Jewish homes to fulfill the mitzvah (Biblical commandment) to **"write the words of God on the gates and doorposts of your house"** (**Deuteronomy 6:9**).

The **klaf** parchment is prepared by a qualified scribe (**"*sofer stam*"**) who has undergone training, both in studying the relevant religious laws, and in the more practical parts i.e. carving the quill and practicing writing. The verses are written in black indelible ink with a special quill pen made either from a feather or, in what are now rare cases, a reed. The parchment is then rolled up and placed inside the case.

## Karaite and Samaritan Mezuzah

Karaite Judaism and Samaritanism have their own distinct traditions. In Karaite Judaism the Deuteronomic verse **"And you shall write them on the doorposts of your houses and your gates"** (**Deuteronomy 6:9; 11:20**) is interpreted to be a metaphor and not as referring to the **Rabbanite *Mezuzah***. Thus Karaites do not traditionally use *mezuzot*, but put up a little plaque in the shape of the two Tablets of the Law with the **Ten Commandments**. In Israel, where they might try not to make other Jews feel uncomfortable, many **Karaites** make an exception and place a **Mezuzah** on their doorpost as well. The Karaite version of the *Mezuzah* is fixed to the doorways of public buildings and sometimes to private buildings, too.

Samaritan Mezuzah in Israel, written exposed, in Samaritan Hebrew. This one reads, **"Blessed is the One who said: I will look with favor upon you, and make you fertile and multiply you; and I will maintain my covenant with you. (Leviticus 26:9) The LORD will open for you His bounteous store, the heavens, to provide rain for your land in season and to bless all your undertakings. (Deuteronomy 28:12)"**

The Samaritans interpret the Deuteronomic commandment to mean displaying any select text from the Samaritan version of the **Five Books of Moses**. This can contain a blessing or a particularly holy or uplifting message.

Nowadays a Samaritan *Mezuzah* is usually made of either marble, a wooden plate, or a sheet of parchment or high quality paper, on which they inscribe select verses from the **Samaritan Torah**. This they place either above the house door, or inside the house, in the entrance hall or at a prominent place on a large wall. These *mezuzot* are found in every Samaritan household as well as in the synagogue.

## Affixing the Mezuzah

According to *halakha*, the **Mezuzah** should be placed on the right side of the door or doorpost, in the upper third of the doorpost (i.e., approximately shoulder height), within approximately 3 inches (8 cm) of the doorway opening. Generally, *halakha* requires Jews living in the Diaspora (i.e., outside of the Land of Israel) to affix a *mezuzot* within 30 days of moving into a rented house or apartment.

Most Sephardic, Mizrahi and other non-Ashkenazi Jews affix the **Mezuzah** vertically, though Spanish and Portuguese Jews living in countries where the majority of Jews are Ashkenazim usually place it slanting. **"Blessed are You, Lord our God, King of the Universe, Who sanctified us with His *mitzvot*, and commanded us to affix a *Mezuzah*."** Whenever passing through the doorway, many people touch a finger to the **Mezuzah** as a way of showing respect to God in a simpler fashion than saying the prayer. Many people also kiss their finger before touching it to the **Mezuzah**.

## Mezuzah cases

The commandment to affix a **Mezuzah** is widely followed in the Jewish world, even by Jews who are not religiously observant. While the important part of the **Mezuzah** is the *klaf,* or the parchment, and not the case itself, designing and producing **Mezuzah** cases has been elevated to an art form over the ages. **Mezuzah** cases are produced from a wide variety of materials, from silver and precious metals, to wood, stone, ceramics, pewter, and even polymer clay. **Additional inscriptions: It is very customary to write two inscriptions on the back of the parchment:**

- The Hebrew word שדי (*Shaddai*)
- The phrase "כוזו במוכסז כוזו"

*Shaddai,* one of the biblical names of God, also serves here as an acronym for *Shomer Daltot Yisrael,* **"Guardian of Israel's doors"**. Many **Mezuzah** cases are also marked with the Hebrew letter ש (Shin), for *Shaddai.* According to the Sephardic custom (**minhag**), the phrase "כוזו במוכסז כוזו" is prohibited, and only the Hebrew word שדי (*Shaddai*) is to be written on the back of the **Mezuzah**. This follows the Shulchan Aruch and the writings of the Rambam.

## Amuletic usage of Mezuzah

The early Rabbinic sources explicitly witness the belief in the anti-demonic function of **Mezuzah**. The belief in the protective power of **Mezuzah** is prevalent in the modern times as well. In the 1970s after a series of terrorist attacks in **Ma'a lot**, the representatives of **Chabad-Lubavitch** started the campaign for the systematic checking of **Mezuzah**s. According to various pieces of sociological research, approximately three-quarter of adults in Israel believe that the **Mezuzah** literally guards their houses.

# *Midrash*

Midrash ( Hebrew: מִדְרָשׁ) is biblical exegesis by ancient Judaic authorities, using a mode of interpretation prominent in the **Talmud**. The term is also used of a rabbinic work that interprets Scripture in that manner.

Such works contain early interpretations and commentaries on the **Written Torah and Oral Torah** (spoken law and sermons), as well as non-legalistic rabbinic literature (*aggadah*) and occasionally Jewish religious laws (*halakha*), which usually form a running commentary on specific passages in the **Hebrew Scripture (*Tanakh*).**

**"Midrash",** especially if capitalized, can refer to a specific compilation of these rabbinic writings composed between 400 and 1200 CE. **"Midrash"** has three technical meanings: 1) Judaic biblical interpretation; 2) the method used in interpreting; 3) a collection of such interpretations.

## Etymology

The Hebrew word *Midrash* is derived from the root of the verb *darash* (דָּרַשׁ), which means **"resort to, seek, seek with care, enquire, require",** forms of which appear frequently in the Bible.

**The word *Midrash* occurs twice in the Hebrew Bible: 2 Chronicles 13:22 "in the *Midrash* of the prophet Iddo", and 24:27 "in the *Midrash* of the book of the kings".** Since the early Middle Ages the function of much of Midrashic interpretation has been distinguished from that of *peshat*, straight or direct interpretation aiming at the original literal meaning of a scriptural text.

## Midrash as genre

A definition of "Midrash" repeatedly quoted by other scholars: **"a type of literature, oral or written, which stands in direct relationship to a fixed, canonical text, considered to be the authoritative and revealed word of God by the Midrashist and his audience, and in which this canonical text is explicitly cited or clearly alluded to".**

While some scholars agree with the limitation of the term **"Midrash"** to rabbinic writings, others apply it also to certain **Qumran** writings, to parts of the **New Testament,** and of the Hebrew Bible (in particular the superscriptions of the Psalms, Deuteronomy, and Chronicles), and even modern compositions are called **Midrashim.**

## Midrash as method

Midrashic creativity reached its peak in the schools of **Rabbi Ishmael and Akiba**, where two different hermeneutic methods were applied. The first was primarily logically oriented, making inferences based upon similarity of content and analogy. The second rested largely upon textual scrutiny, assuming that words and letters that seem superfluous teach something not openly stated in the text.

## There are Midrash processes:
1. **paraphrase**: recounting the content of the biblical text in different language that may change the sense;
2. **prophecy**: reading the text as an account of something happening or about to happen in the interpreter's time;
3. **parable or allegory**: indicating deeper meanings of the words of the text as speaking of something other than the superficial meaning of the words or of everyday reality, as when the love of man and woman in the Song of Songs is interpreted as referring to the love between God and Israel or the Church as in Isaiah 5:1-6 and in the New Testament.

## Jewish Midrashic literature
Proposed is the term **"medieval Midrashim",** since the period of their production extended from the twilight of the rabbinic age to the dawn of the **Age of Enlightenment.**

## Halakhic Midrashim
*Midrash halakha* is the name given to a group of **Tannaitic** expositions on the **first four books of the Hebrew Bible.** These Midrashim, written in Mishnahic, this work is based on pre-set assumptions about the sacred and divine nature of the text, and the belief in the legitimacy that accords with rabbinic interpretation.

## Aggadic Midrashim
Midrashim which seek to explain the non-legal portions of the Hebrew Bible are sometimes referred to as *aggadah* or *Haggadah*. Aggadic discussions of the non-legal parts of Scripture are characterized by a much greater freedom of exposition than the halakhic Midrashim (**Midrashim on Jewish law**). These Aggadic explanations could be philosophical or mystical disquisitions concerning angels, demons, paradise, hell, the messiah, Satan, feasts and fasts, parables, legends, satirical assaults on those who practice idolatry, etc.

## An example of a Midrashic interpretation:
**"And God saw all that He had made, and found it very good. And there was evening, and there was morning, the sixth day." (Genesis 1:31)**—Midrash: *Rabbi Nahman said in Rabbi Samuel's name: "Behold, it was very good" refers to the Good Desire; "AND behold, it was very good" refers to the Evil Desire. Can then the Evil Desire be very good? That would be extraordinary! But without the Evil Desire, however, no man would build a house, take a wife and beget children; and thus said Solomon: "Again, I considered all labor and all excelling in work, that it is a man's rivalry with his neighbor." (Kohelet IV, 4).*

# Contemporary views

**Baruch 3:29-4:1** states that the divine wisdom is not available anywhere other than in the **Torah.**

# Mishnah

The **Mishnah** or **Mishna** (Hebrew: **"study by repetition"**, or **"to study and review"**, also **"secondary"**) is the first major written redaction of the Jewish oral traditions known as the **"Oral Torah"**.

It is also the first major work of Rabbinic literature. The **Mishnah** was redacted by **Judah the Prince** at the beginning of the third century CE in a time when, according to the **Talmud**, the persecution of the Jews and the passage of time raised the possibility that the details of the oral traditions of the Pharisees from the **Second Temple period (536 BCE – 70 CE) would be forgotten. Most of the Mishnah is written in Mishnaic Hebrew, while some parts are Aramaic.**

## Structure

The term **"Mishnah"** originally referred to a method of teaching by presenting topics in a systematic order, as contrasted with *Midrash*, which followed the order of the Bible. The *Mishnah* consists of **six orders** (*Sedarim*, singular *Seder*), each containing 7–12 tractates (*masechtot*, singular *Masekhet*; lit. "Web"), 63 in total. Each *Masekhet* is divided into chapters (*peraqim*, singular *pereq*) and then paragraphs (*Mishnayot*, singular *Mishnah*). Because of the division into six orders, the *Mishnah* is sometimes called 'Shas' (an acronym for *Shisha Sedarim* – the "six orders").

## The six orders are:
- *Zeraim* ("Seeds"), dealing with prayer and blessings, tithes and agricultural laws (11 tractates)
- *Moed* ("Festival"), pertaining to the laws of the Sabbath and the Festivals (12 tractates)
- *Nashim* ("Women"), concerning marriage and divorce, some forms of oaths and the laws of the nazirite (7 tractates)
- *Nezikin* ("Damages"), dealing with civil and criminal law, the functioning of the courts and oaths (10 tractates)
- *Kodashim* ("Holy things"), regarding sacrificial rites, the Temple, and the dietary laws (11 tractates) and
- *Tohorot* ("Purities"), pertaining to the laws of purity and impurity, including the impurity of the dead, the laws of food purity and bodily purity (12 tractates).

The **Babylonian Talmud (Hagigah 14a)** states that there were either six hundred or seven hundred orders of the **Mishnah. Hillel the Elder** organized them into six orders to make it easier to remember. There is also a tradition that **Ezra the scribe** dictated from memory not only the 24 books of the **Tanakh** but 60 esoteric books. The *Mishnah* **consist of 60 tractates. (The current total is 63, but Makkot was originally part of Sanhedrin.**

## Omissions

A number of important laws are not elaborated upon in the *Mishnah*. These include the laws of **Tzitzit, tefillin** (phylacteries), **mezuzot**, the holiday of **Hanukkah**, and the laws of conversion to Judaism.

## Mishnah, Gemara and Talmud

Rabbinic commentaries on the *Mishnah* from the next four centuries, done in the Land of Israel and in Babylonia, were eventually redacted and compiled as well. In themselves they are known as *Gemara*. The books which set out the *Mishnah* in its original structure, together with the associated *Gemara*, are known as **Talmuds**. Two Talmuds were compiled, the **Babylonian Talmud** (to which the term **"Talmud"** normally refers) and the **Jerusalem Talmud**. The *Gemara* is written primarily in Aramaic.

## Content and purpose

The *Mishnah* teaches the oral traditions by example, presenting actual cases being brought to judgment, usually along with the debate on the matter and the judgment that was given by a notable rabbi based on **halakha, mitzvot**, and spirit of the teaching **("Torah")** that guided his decision. It demonstrates a pragmatic exercise of the Biblical laws, which was much needed since the time when the **Second Temple was destroyed (70 CE)**.

## Oral law: *Oral Torah*

Before the publication of the *Mishnah*, Jewish scholarship and judgement were predominantly oral, as according to the **Talmud**, it was not permitted to write them down. Rabbis expounded on and debated the **Tanakh**, the Hebrew Bible, without the benefit of written works (other than the Biblical books themselves). The oral traditions were far from monolithic, and varied among various schools, the most famous of which were the **House of Shammai** and the **House of Hillel.**

After **First Jewish–Roman War in 70 CE, with the end of the Second Temple** Jewish center in Jerusalem, Jewish social and legal norms were in upheaval. The possibility was felt that the details of the oral traditions of the Pharisees from the **Second Temple period (530s BCE – 70 CE)** would be forgotten, so the justification was found to have these oral laws transcribed.

Over time, different traditions of the **Oral Law** came into being, raising problems of interpretation. According to the *Mevo Hatalmud* many rulings were given in a specific context, but would be taken out of it; or a ruling was revisited but the second ruling would not become popularly known. To correct this, **Judah the Prince** took up the redaction of the *Mishnah*.

## The Mishnah and the Hebrew Bible

According to Rabbinic Judaism, **the Oral Torah was given to Moses with the Torah at Mount Sinai or Mount Horeb** as an exposition to the latter. The accumulated traditions of the Oral Law, expounded by scholars in each generation from Moses onward, is considered as the necessary basis for the interpretation, and often for the reading, of the Written Law.

Jews sometimes refer to this as the **Masorah**, roughly translated as tradition. The resulting Jewish law and custom is called **halakha**. It is arranged in order of topics rather than in the form of a Biblical commentary. (In a very few cases, there is no scriptural source at all and the law is described as *Halakha leMoshe miSinai*, **"law to Moses from Sinai"**.) The *Midrash halakha,* by contrast, while presenting similar laws, does so in the form of a Biblical commentary and explicitly links its conclusions to details in the Biblical text. **These Midrashim often predate the Mishnah.**

## Rejection

Some Jews did not accept the codification of the oral law at all. **Karaite Judaism**, for example, recognized only the **Tanakh** as authoritative in *Halakha* **(Jewish religious law)** and theology. It vehemently rejected the codification of the **Oral Torah** in the **Mishnah** and **Talmud** and subsequent works of mainstream Rabbinic Judaism which maintained that the **Talmud was an authoritative interpretations of the Torah.**

**Karaites** maintained that all of the divine commandments handed down to Moses by God were recorded in the written Torah without additional **Oral Law** or explanation. The Karaites comprised a significant portion of the world Jewish population in the 10th and 11th centuries CE, and remain extant, although they currently number in the thousands.

## Authorship: *Tannaim*

The rabbis who contributed to the *Mishnah* are known as the *Tannaim,* of whom approximately 120 are known. The period during which the *Mishnah* was assembled spanned about 130 years, or five generations, in the first and second centuries CE. **Judah the Prince** is credited with the final redaction and publication of the *Mishnah. H*is grandson, **Judah II**, and the end of tractate **Sotah**, which refers to the period after Judah the **Prince's death.**

The Talmud refers to these differing versions as *Mishnah Rishonah* **("First Mishnah")** and *Mishnah Acharonah* **("Last Mishnah")**. There are also references to the **"Mishnah of Rabbi Akiva"**, suggesting a still earlier collection. Another possibility is that **Rabbi Akiva** and **Rabbi Meir** established the divisions and order of subjects in the **Mishnah**, making them the authors of a school curriculum rather than of a book.

## Manuscripts: Printed editions

The first printed edition of the **Mishnah** was published in Naples. There have been many subsequent editions, including the late 19th century **Vilna edition**, which is the basis of the editions now used by the religious public. Vocalized editions were published in Italy, culminating in the edition of **David ben Solomon Altaras,** publ. Venice 1737. **The Livorno editions are the basis of the Sephardic tradition for recitation.**

## Oral traditions and pronunciation

Jewish communities around the world preserved local melodies for chanting the **Mishnah,** and distinctive ways of pronouncing its words. Most vowelized editions of the **Mishnah** today reflect standard **Ashkenazic** vowelization, and often contain mistakes.

## Commentaries

- **In 1168, Maimonides (Rambam)** published a comprehensive commentary on the **Mishnah.** It was written in transliterated **Judeo-Arabic** (using Hebrew letters) and was one of the first commentaries of its kind. In it, **Rambam** condensed the associated Talmudical debates, and offered his conclusions in a number of undecided issues. Perhaps the most famous is his introduction to the tenth chapter of tractate **Sanhedrin** where he enumerates the **thirteen fundamental beliefs of Judaism.**
- **Rabbi Obadiah ben Abraham** of Bertinoro (15th century) wrote one of the most popular **Mishnah** commentaries. He draws on Maimonides' work but also offers Talmudical material (in effect a summary of the Talmudic discussion) largely following the commentary of **Rashi.** In addition to its role as a commentary on the **Mishnah,** this work is often referenced by students of Talmud as a review-text
- **Yomtov Lipman Heller** wrote a commentary called *Tosafot Yom Tov.* In the introduction Heller says that his aim is to make additions (tosafoth) to Bertinoro's commentary. It is sometimes compared to the **Tosafot** – discussions of **Babylonian Gemara** by French and German scholars of the 12th–13th centuries.
- **A prominent commentary** from the 19th century is *Tiferet Yisrael* by Rabbi Israel Lipschitz. It is subdivided into two parts, one more general and the other more analytical, titled *Yachin* and *Boaz* respectively (after two large pillars in the Temple in Jerusalem). He is widely accepted in the Yeshiva world. **The *Tiferet Yaakov* is an important gloss on the *Tiferet Yisrael.***

## As a historical source

According to the **Encyclopaedia Judaica** (Second Edition), it is accepted that **Judah the Prince** added, deleted, and re wrote his source material during the process of redacting the **Mishnah.** The **Mishnah** used in the Babylonian rabbinic community differing markedly from that used in the Palestinian one. These differences are shown in divergent citations of individual **Mishnah** passages in the **Talmud Yerushalmi** and the **Talmud Bavli.**

- Some scholars hold that many or most of the statements and events described in the **Mishnah** and Talmud usually occurred more or less as described, and that they can be used as serious sources of historical study.

# Mosaic Laws

The **Law of Moses,** also called the **Mosaic Law**, primarily refers to the **Torah or the first five books of the Hebrew Bible.** Traditionally believed to have been written by **Moses**, most academics now believe they had many authors.

## Terminology

The Law of **Moses** or Torah of **Moses ("Teachings of Moses")** is a biblical term first found in the **Book of Joshua 8:31–32**, where **Joshua** writes the Hebrew words of **"Torat Moshe "** on an altar of stones at **Mount Ebal**. The text continues:

**"And afterward he read all the words of the teachings, the blessings and cursings, according to all that is written in the book of the Torah** *(Joshua 8:34).***"**

The term occurs 15 times in the **Hebrew Bible**, a further 7 times in the New Testament, and repeatedly in **Second Temple** period, intertestamental, rabbinical and patristic literature.

The Hebrew word for the first five books of the **Hebrew Bible**, *Torah* (which means "**law**" and was translated into Greek as **"nomos"** or **"Law"**) refers to the same five books termed in English **"Pentateuch" (from Latinized Greek "five books," implying the five books of Moses).** According to some scholars, use of the name "Torah" to designate the "**Five Books of Moses**" of the **Hebrew Bible** is clearly documented only from the 2nd century BCE.

In modern usage, *Torah* **can refer to the first five books of the Tanakh** , as the **Hebrew Bible** is commonly called, to the instructions and commandments found in the 2nd to 5th books of the **Hebrew Bible**, and also to the entire **Tanakh** and even all of the **Oral Law** as well. Among English-speaking Christians the term **"The Law"** can refer to the whole Pentateuch including **Genesis**, but this is generally in relation to the New Testament where *nomos* **"the Law"** sometimes refers to all five books, including **Genesis.**

## Law in the Ancient Near-East

The **"Law of Moses"** in ancient Israel was different from other legal codes in the ancient Near East. This contrasts with the **Sumerian Code of Ur-Nammu** (c. 2100-2050 BCE), and the Babylonian **Code of Hammurabi** (c. 1760 BCE, of which almost half concerns contract law). However, the influence of the ancient Near Eastern legal tradition on the **Law** of ancient Israel is recognized and well documented. For example, the **Israelite Sabbatical Year** has antecedents in the **Akkadian** *mesharum* edicts granting periodic relief to the poor. Ancient Israel, before the monarchical period beginning with **David**, was set up as a theocracy, rather than a monarchy, although God is most commonly portrayed like a king.

## Hebrew Bible / Moses and authorship of the Law

According to the **Hebrew Bible**, **Moses** was the leader of early Israel out of Egypt; and traditionally the first five books of the **Hebrew Bible** are attributed to him. The law attributed to **Moses**, specifically the laws set out in the books of **Leviticus and Deuteronomy**, as a consequence came to be considered supreme over all other sources of authority (any king and/or his officials), and the Levites were the guardians and interpreters of the law.

The **Book of Deuteronomy (Deuteronomy 31:24–26)** records **Moses** saying, **"Take this book of the law, and put it by the side of the Ark of the Covenant of the LORD."** Similar passages referring to the Law include, for example, **Exodus 17:14, "And the LORD said unto Moses, Write this for a memorial in a book, and rehearse it in the ears of Joshua, that I will utterly blot out the remembrance of Amalek from under heaven;" Exodus 24:4, "And Moses wrote all the words of the LORD, and rose up early in the morning, and built an altar under the mount, and twelve pillars, according to the twelve tribes of Israel;" Exodus 34:27, "And the LORD said unto Moses, Write thou these words, for after the tenor of these words I have made a covenant with thee and with Israel;" and Leviticus 26:46 "These are the decrees, the laws and the regulations that the LORD established on Mount Sinai between himself and the Israelites through Moses."**

## Later references to the Law in the Hebrew Bible

The **Book of Kings** relates how a **"law of Moses"** was discovered in the Temple during the reign of **King Josiah (r. 641–609 BCE).** This book is mostly identified as an early version of the **Book of Deuteronomy,** perhaps chapters **5–26 and chapter 28** of the extant text. This text contains a number of laws, dated to the 8th century BCE **kingdom of Judah. Another mention of the "Book of the Law of Moses" is found in Joshua 8:30-31.**

## Content

The content of the Law is spread among the books of **Exodus, Leviticus**, and **Numbers**, and then reiterated and added to in Deuteronomy. This includes:

- The Ten Commandments
- Moral laws - on murder, theft, honesty, adultery, etc.
- Social laws - on property, inheritance, marriage and divorce,
- Food laws - on what is clean and unclean, on cooking and storing food.
- Purity laws - on menstruation, seminal emissions, skin disease and mildew, etc.
- Feasts - the Day of Atonement, Passover, Feast of Tabernacles, Feast of Unleavened Bread, Feast of Weeks etc.
- Sacrifices and offerings - the sin offering, burnt offering, whole offering, heave offering, Passover sacrifice, meal offering, wave offering, peace offering, drink offering, thank offering, dough offering, incense offering, red heifer, scapegoat, first fruits, etc.
- Instructions for the priesthood and the high priest including tithes.

- Instructions regarding the **Tabernacle**, and which were later applied to the Temple in Jerusalem, including those concerning the **Holy of Holies containing the Ark of the Covenant** (in which were the tablets of the law, Aaron's rod, the manna). Instructions and for the construction of various altars.
- Forward looking instructions for time when Israel would demand a king.

## Rabbinical interpretation

The content of the instructions and its interpretations, the **Oral Torah**, was passed down orally, excerpted and codified in Rabbinical Judaism, and in the **Talmud** were numbered as the **613 commandments**. The Law given to **Moses** at Sinai is a halakhic distinction.

Rabbinic Judaism asserts that **Moses** presented the laws to the Jewish people, and that **the laws do not apply to Gentiles** (including Christians), with the exception of the **Seven Laws of Noah,** which (it teaches) apply to all people.

## Christian interpretation

Most Christians believe that only parts dealing with the moral law (as opposed to ceremonial law) are still applicable, others believe that none apply, dual-covenant theologians believe that the **Old Covenant** remains valid only for Jews, and a minority have the view that **all parts still apply to believers in Jesus and in the New Covenant.**

# Moses & the Torah

**Moses** was a prophet according to the teachings of the Abrahamic religions. Unlike other religious figures such as **Buddha**, **Jesus**, and **Muhammad**, whose historical existences are well documented; scholarly consensus sees **Moses** as a legendary figure and not a historical person.

According to the **Hebrew Bible**, he was adopted by an Egyptian princess, and later in life became the leader of the Israelites and lawgiver, to whom the authorship of the **Torah**, or acquisition of the **Torah** from Heaven is traditionally attributed. Also called *Moshe Rabbenu* in Hebrew ("**Moses our Teacher**"), he is the most important prophet in Judaism. He is also an important prophet in Christianity, Islam, the **Bahá'í Faith**, and a number of other Abrahamic religions.

According to the **Book of Exodus**, **Moses** was born in a time when his people, the Israelites, an enslaved minority, were increasing in numbers and the **Egyptian Pharaoh** was worried that they might ally themselves with Egypt's enemies. **Moses**' Hebrew mother, **Jochebed**, secretly hid him when the **Pharaoh ordered all newborn Hebrew boys to be killed** in order to reduce the population of the Israelites. Through the Pharaoh's daughter (identified as **Queen Bithia** in the **Midrash**), the child was adopted as a foundling from the Nile river and grew up with the Egyptian royal family.

After killing an Egyptian slavemaster (because the slavemaster was smiting a Hebrew), **Moses** fled across the **Red Sea** to Midian, where he encountered **The Angel of the Lord**, speaking to him from within a burning bush on **Mount Horeb** (which he regarded as the Mountain of God).

God sent **Moses** back to Egypt to demand the release of the Israelites from slavery. **Moses** said that he could not speak eloquently, so God allowed **Aaron**, his brother, to become his spokesperson. After the **Ten Plagues**, **Moses** led the **Exodus** of the Israelites out of Egypt and across the Red Sea, after which they based themselves at **Mount Sinai**, where **Moses** received the **Ten Commandments**. After 40 years of wandering in the desert, **Moses** died within sight of the **Promised Land** on Mount Nebo. Jerome gives 1592 BCE, and James Ussher 1571 BCE as Moses' birth year. In the Book of Deuteronomy, **Moses** was called **"the man of God"**.

## Name

The Biblical account of **Moses**' birth provides him with a folk etymology to explain the ostensible meaning of his name. He is said to have received it from the Pharaoh's daughter: **"he became her son. She named him Moses (Moshe), saying, 'I drew him out (*meshitihu*) of the water.'"** This explanation links it to a verb *mashah*, meaning **"to draw out"**, which makes the Pharaoh's daughter's declaration a play on words. The princess made a grammatical mistake which is prophetic of his future role in legend, as someone who will "draw the people of Israel out of Egypt through the waters of the **Red Sea**."

Several etymologies have been proposed. An Egyptian root *msy*, "child of", has been considered as a possible etymology, arguably an abbreviation of a theophoric name, as for example in Egyptian names like **Thutmoses (Thoth created him)** and **Ramesses** (Ra created him), with the god's name omitted. **Abraham Yahuda**, based on the spelling given in the **Tanakh**, argues that it combines **"water"** or **"seed"** and **"pond, expanse of water"**, thus yielding the sense of **"child of the Nile"**

The Hebrew etymology in the Biblical story may reflect an attempt to cancel out traces of **Moses'** Egyptian origins. The Egyptian character of his name was recognized as such by ancient Jewish writers like **Philo of Alexandria** and **Josephus. Philo** linked Mōēsēs to the Egyptian (Coptic) word for water, while **Josephus**, in his Antiquities of the Jews, claimed that the second element, *-esês*, meant **'those who are saved'**.

The problem of how an Egyptian princess, known to **Josephus** as **Thermutis** (identified as **Tharmuth**) and in later Jewish tradition as Bithiah, could have known Hebrew puzzled medieval Jewish commentators like **Abraham ibn Ezra** and **Hezekiah ben Manoah**, known also as **Hizkuni. Hizkuni** suggested she either converted or took a tip from **Jochebed**.

## Biblical narrative / *The Exodus*
The Israelites had settled in the **Land of Goshen** in the time of **Joseph** and **Jacob**, but a new pharaoh arose who oppressed the children of Israel. At this time **Moses** was born to his father **Amram**, son of **Kehath the Levite**, who entered Egypt with Jacob's household; his mother was **Jochebed** (also Yocheved), who was kin to **Kehath. Moses** had one older (by seven years) sister, **Miriam**, and one older (by three years) brother, **Aaron.**

The Pharaoh had commanded that all male Hebrew children born would be drowned in the river Nile, but **Moses'** mother placed him in an ark and concealed the ark in the bulrushes by the riverbank, where the baby was discovered and adopted by Pharaoh's daughter, and raised as an Egyptian. One day after **Moses** had reached adulthood he killed an Egyptian who was beating a Hebrew. **Moses**, in order to escape the Pharaoh's death penalty, fled to **Midian** (a desert country south of Judah), where he married **Zipporah.**

There, on **Mount Horeb**, God appeared to **Moses** as a burning bush, revealed to **Moses** his name **YHWH** (probably pronounced **Yahweh**) and commanded him to return to Egypt and bring his chosen people (Israel) out of bondage and into the **Promised Land (Canaan)**. During the journey, God tried to kill **Moses** because he had not circumcised his son, but **Zipporah** saved his life. **Moses** returned to carry out God's command, but God caused the Pharaoh to refuse, and only after God had subjected Egypt to ten plagues did the Pharaoh relent. **Moses** led the Israelites to the border of Egypt, but there God hardened the Pharaoh's heart once more, so that he could destroy the Pharaoh and his army at the **Red Sea Crossing** as a sign of his power to Israel and the nations.

After defeating the **Amalekites** in Rephidim, **Moses** led the Israelites to biblical **Mount Sinai**, where he was given the **Ten Commandments** from God, written on stone tablets. However, since **Moses** remained a long time on the mountain, some of the people feared that he might be dead, so they made a statue of a golden calf and worshiped it, thus disobeying and angering God and **Moses**. **Moses**, out of anger, broke the tablets, and later ordered the elimination of those who had worshiped the golden statue, which was melted down and fed to the idolaters.

He also wrote the **Ten Commandments** on a new set of tablets. Later at **Mount Sinai**, **Moses** and the elders entered into a covenant, by which Israel would become the people of **YHWH**, obeying his laws, and **YHWH** would be their god. **Moses** delivered the laws of God to Israel, instituted the priesthood under the sons of **Moses'** brother **Aaron**, and destroyed those Israelites who fell away from his worship. In his final act at Sinai, God gave **Moses** instructions for the **Tabernacle**, the mobile shrine by which he would travel with Israel to the **Promised Land**.

From Sinai, **Moses** led the Israelites to the **Desert of Paran** on the border of **Canaan**. From there he sent twelve spies into the land. The spies returned with samples of the land's fertility, but warned that its inhabitants were giants. The people were afraid and wanted to return to Egypt, and some rebelled against **Moses** and against God. **Moses** told the Israelites that they were not worthy to inherit the land, and would wander the wilderness for forty years until the generation who had refused to enter **Canaan** had died, so that it would be their children who would possess the land.

When the forty years had passed, **Moses** led the Israelites east around the **Dead Sea** to the territories of **Edom** and **Moab**. There they escaped the temptation of idolatry, conquered the lands of **Og and Sihon in Transjordan**, received God's blessing through **Balaam** the prophet, and massacred the Midianites, who by the end of the **Exodus** journey had become the enemies of the Israelites due to their notorious role in enticing the Israelites to sin against God. **Moses was twice given notice that he would die before entry to the Promised Land: in Numbers 27:13,** once he had seen the **Promised Land** from a viewpoint on **Mount Abarim**, and again in **Numbers 31:1** once battle with the Midianites had been won.

On the banks of the Jordan River, in sight of the land, **Moses** assembled the tribes. After recalling their wanderings he delivered God's laws by which they must live in the land, sang a song of praise and pronounced a blessing on the people, and passed his authority to **Joshua**, under whom they would possess the land. **Moses** then went up **Mount Nebo** to the top of Pisgah, looked over the promised land of Israel spread out before him, and died, at the age of one hundred and twenty. More humble than any other man **(Num. 12:3)**, "there hath not arisen a prophet since in Israel like unto Moses, whom YHWH knew face to face" (Deuteronomy 34:10). The New Testament states that after **Moses'** death, **Michael the Archangel** and the Devil disputed over his body **(Epistle of Jude 1:9)**.

## Lawgiver of Israel

**Moses** is honored among Jews today as the **"lawgiver of Israel"**, and he delivers several sets of laws in the course of the four books. The first is the **Covenant Code (Exodus 20:19–23:33),** the terms of the covenant which God offers to the Israelites at biblical **Mount Sinai**. Embedded in the covenant are the Decalogue (the **Ten Commandments, Exodus 20:1–17**) and the **Book of the Covenant (Exodus 20:22–23:19).** The entire Book of Leviticus constitutes a second body of law, the **Book of Numbers** begins with yet another set, and the **Book of Deuteronomy** another. **Moses** has traditionally been regarded as the author of those four books and the **Book of Genesis,** which together comprise the **Torah**, the first section of the **Hebrew Bible**.

## Historicity

The modern scholarly consensus is that the figure of **Moses** is legendary, and not historical, although a **"Moses-like figure may have existed somewhere in the southern Transjordan in the mid-late 13th century B.C."** Certainly no Egyptian sources mention **Moses** or the events of **Exodus–Deuteronomy**, nor has any archaeological evidence been discovered in Egypt or the Sinai wilderness to support the story in which he is the central figure. The story of his discovery picks up a familiar motif in ancient Near Eastern mythological accounts of the ruler who rises from humble origins: Thus **Sargon of Akkad's** Akkadian account of his own origins runs;

**"My mother, the high priestess, conceived; in secret she bore me
she set me in a basket of rushes, with bitumen she sealed my lid
she cast me into the river which rose over me".**

The tradition of **Moses** as a lawgiver and culture hero of the Israelites may go back to the **7th-century BCE** sources of the Deuteronomist, which might conserve earlier traditions. **Kitchen** argued that there is a lack of factual evidence to deny his existence. **Martin Noth** called the Deuteronomic description of **Moses'** burial a **"lone historical tradition"**.

Despite the imposing fame associated with **Moses**, no source mentions him until he emerges in texts associated with the Babylonian exile. A theory developed by **Cornelius Tiele** in 1872, which had proved influential, argued that **Yahweh** was a Midianite god, introduced to the Israelites by **Moses**, whose father-in-law Jethro was a Midianite priest. It was to such a **Moses** that **Yahweh** reveals his real name, hidden from the Patriarchs who knew him only as **El Shaddai**.

**Manfred Görg** and **Rolf Krauss**, the latter in a somewhat sensationalist manner, have suggested that the **Moses** story is a distortion or transmogrification of the historical pharaoh **Amenmose** (c. 1200 BCE), who was dismissed from office and whose name was later simplified to *msy* (Mose).

The name **King Mesha of Moab** has been linked to that of **Moses**. Mesha also is associated with narratives of an exodus and a conquest, and several motifs in stories about him are shared with the

Exodus tale and that regarding Israel's war with **Moab (2 Kings 3)**. Moab rebels against oppression, like **Moses**, leads his people out of Israel, as **Moses** does from Egypt, and his first-born son is slaughtered at the wall of **Kir-hareseth** as the firstborn of Israel are condemned to slaughter in the **Exodus** story, **"an infernal Passover that delivers Mesha while wrath burns against his enemies"**.

An Egyptian version of the tale that crosses over with the **Moses** story is found in **Manetho** who, according to the summary in **Josephus**, wrote that a certain **Osarseph**, a **Heliopolitan priest**, became overseer of a band of lepers, when Amenophis, following indications by **Amenhotep**, son of **Hapu**, had all the lepers in Egypt quarantined in order to cleanse the land so that he might see the gods.

## Moses in Hellenistic literature

Non-biblical writings about Jews, with references to the role of **Moses**, first appear at the beginning of the Hellenistic period, **from 323 BCE to about 146 BCE**. Shmuel notes that **"a characteristic of this literature is the high honour in which it holds the peoples of the East in general and some specific groups among these peoples."**

**Moses** also appears in other religious texts such as the **Mishnah** (c. 200 CE), **Midrash** (200–1200 CE), and the **Qur'an (c. 610–653)**. The figure of Osarseph in Hellenistic historiography is a renegade Egyptian priest who leads an army of lepers against the pharaoh and is finally expelled from Egypt, changing his name to **Moses**.

## In Artapanus

The Jewish historian **Artapanus of Alexandria (2nd century BCE)**, portrayed **Moses** as a cultural hero, alien to the Pharaonic court. According to theologian **John Barclay**, the **Moses** of Artapanus **"clearly bears the destiny of the Jews, and in his personal, cultural and military splendor, brings credit to the whole Jewish people."**

Jealousy of **Moses'** excellent qualities induced **Chenephres** to send him with unskilled troops on a military expedition to Ethiopia, where he won great victories. After his return to Memphis, **Moses** taught the people the value of oxen for agriculture, and the consecration of the same by **Moses** gave rise to the **cult of Apis**. Finally, after having escaped another plot by killing the assailant sent by the king, **Moses** fled to Arabia, where he married the daughter of **Raguel**, the ruler of the district.

**Artapanus** goes on to relate how **Moses** returns to Egypt with **Aaron**, and is imprisoned, but miraculously escapes through the name of **YHWH** in order to lead the **Exodus**. This account further testifies that all Egyptian temples of Isis thereafter contained a rod, in remembrance of that used for **Moses' miracles**. He describes **Moses as 80 years old**, **"tall and ruddy, with long white hair, and dignified."**

## In Strabo

**Strabo**, a Greek historian, geographer and philosopher, in his *Geographica* (c. 24 CE), wrote in detail about **Moses**, whom he considered to be an Egyptian who deplored the situation in his homeland, and thereby attracted many followers who respected the deity.

An **Egyptian priest named Moses**, who possessed a portion of the country called the Lower Egypt, being dissatisfied with the established institutions there, left it and came to Judaea with a large body of people who worshipped the Divinity. **For God may be this one thing which encompasses us all, land and sea, which we call heaven, or the universe, or the nature of things....** By such doctrine **Moses** persuaded a large body of right-minded persons to accompany him to the place where Jerusalem now stands....

**"The Temple of Jerusalem continued to be surrounded by an aura of sanctity."** Strabo's **"positive and unequivocal appreciation of Moses' personality is among the most sympathetic in all ancient literature."** His portrayal of **Moses** is said to be similar to the writing of Hecataeus who **"described Moses as a man who excelled in wisdom and courage."** Egyptologist Jan Assmann concludes that Strabo was the historian **"who came closest to a construction of Moses' religion as monotheistic and as a pronounced counter-religion."** It recognized **"only one divine being whom no image can represent... the only way to approach this god is to live in virtue and in justice."**

## In Tacitus

The **Roman historian Tacitus (c. 56–120 CE)** refers to **Moses** by noting that the Jewish religion was monotheistic and without a clear image. His primary work, wherein he describes Jewish philosophy, is his *Histories* (c. 100), where, according to **Arthur Murphy**, as a result of the Jewish worship of one God, **"pagan mythology fell into contempt."** Tacitus states that, despite various opinions current in his day regarding the Jews' ethnicity, most of his sources are in agreement that there was an **Exodus** from Egypt. **Moses and the Jews wander through the desert for only six days, capturing the Holy Land on the seventh.**

## In Longinus

The Septuagint, the Greek version of the **Hebrew Bible**, influenced Longinus, who may have been the author of the great book of literary criticism, *On the Sublime*. The writer quotes Genesis in a **"style which presents the nature of the deity in a manner suitable to his pure and great being,"** however he does not mention **Moses** by name, calling him 'no chance person' but **"the Lawgiver" (thesmothete) of the Jews,"** a term that puts him on a par with Lycurgus and Minos.

## In Josephus

In **Josephus'** (37 – c. 100 CE) *Antiquities of the Jews*, Moses is mentioned throughout. For example **Book VIII Ch. IV**, describes Solomon's Temple, also known as the **First Temple**, at the time the **Ark of the Covenant** was first moved into the newly built temple:

When **King Solomon** had finished these works, these large and beautiful buildings, and had laid up his donations in the temple, and all this in the interval of seven years, and had given a demonstration of his riches and alacrity therein; ...he also wrote to the rulers and elders of the Hebrews, and ordered all the people to gather themselves together to Jerusalem, both to see the temple which he had built, and to remove the ark of God into it; and when this invitation of the whole body of the people to come to Jerusalem was everywhere carried abroad.

**The Feast of Tabernacles** happened to fall at the same time, which was kept by the Hebrews as a most holy and most eminent feast. So they carried the ark and the tabernacle which **Moses** had pitched, and all the vessels that were for ministration to the sacrifices of God, and removed them to the temple. ...Now the ark contained nothing else but those two tables of stone that preserved the **Ten Commandments**, which God spake to **Moses** in **Mount Sinai**, and which were engraved upon them...

## In Justin Martyr

The Christian saint and religious philosopher **Justin Martyr (103–165 CE)** drew the same conclusion as Numenius, according to other experts. Theologian **Paul Blackham** notes that Justin considered **Moses** to be **"more trustworthy, profound and truthful because he is *older* than the Greek philosophers."**

## Abrahamic religions / Judaism

Most of what is known about **Moses** from the Bible comes from the books of **Exodus, Leviticus, Numbers** and **Deuteronomy**. The majority of scholars consider the compilation of these books to go back to the Persian period, **538–332 BCE**, but based on earlier written and oral traditions. There is a wealth of stories and additional information about **Moses** in the Jewish apocrypha and in the genre of rabbinical exegesis known as **Midrash**, as well as in the primary works of the Jewish oral law, the **Mishnah** and the **Talmud**. **Moses** is also given a number of bynames in Jewish tradition. The Midrash identifies **Moses** as one of seven biblical personalities who were called by various names. **Moses had ascended to the first heaven until the seventh, even visited Paradise and Hell alive, after he saw the Divine vision in Mount Horeb.** Jewish tradition considers **Moses** to be the **greatest prophet who ever lived**. Despite his importance, Judaism stresses that **Moses** was a human being, and is therefore not to be worshipped. Only God is worthy of worship in Judaism. To Orthodox Jews, **Moses** is called *Moshe Rabbenu, `Eved HaShem, Avi haNeviim zya"a*: **"Our Leader Moshe, Servant of God, Father of all the Prophets (may his merit shield us, amen)"**. In the orthodox view, **Moses** received not only the **Torah**, but also the revealed (written and oral) and the hidden (the `hokhmat nistar` teachings, which gave Judaism the **Zohar** of the Rashbi, the **Torah** of the Ari **haQadosh** and all that is discussed in the Heavenly Yeshiva between the **Ramhal** and his masters).

Arising in part from his age of death **(120 according to Deut. 34:7)** and that **"his eye had not dimmed, and his vigor had not diminished,"** the phrase **"may you live to 120"** has become a common blessing among Jews, especially since 120 is elsewhere stated as the maximum age for Noah's descendants **(one interpretation of Genesis 6:3).**

## Christianity

**Moses is mentioned more often in the New Testament than any other Old Testament figure**. For Christians, **Moses** is often a symbol of God's law, as reinforced and expounded on in the teachings of Jesus. New Testament writers often compared Jesus' words and deeds with **Moses'** to explain Jesus' mission. **In Acts 7:39–43, 51–53**, for example, the rejection of **Moses** by the Jews who worshipped the golden calf is likened to the rejection of Jesus by the Jews that continued in traditional Judaism. **Moses** also figures in several of **Jesus'** messages. In the sixth chapter, Jesus responded to the people's claim that **Moses** provided them *manna* in the wilderness by saying that it was not **Moses**, but God, who provided. Calling himself the **"bread of life"**, Jesus stated that He was provided to feed God's people.

**Moses**, along with **Elijah**, is presented as meeting with Jesus in all three **Synoptic Gospels of the Transfiguration of Jesus in Matthew 17, Mark 9, and Luke 9, respectively. Jesus** refers to the scribes and the Pharisees of the Temple as **"seated in the chair of Moses"**. His relevance to modern Christianity has not diminished. **Moses** is considered to be a saint by several churches; and is commemorated as a prophet **"Holy Prophet and God-seer Moses, on Mount Nebo".**

## Mormonism / *Book of Moses*

Members of **The Church of Jesus Christ of Latter-day Saints** (colloquially called Mormons) generally view **Moses** in the same way that other Christians do. However, in addition to accepting the biblical account of **Moses**, Mormons include Selections from the **Book of Moses** as part of their scriptural canon. This book is believed to be the translated writings of **Moses**, and is included in the **Pearl of Great Price.**

Latter-day Saints are also unique in believing that **Moses was taken to heaven without having tasted death** (translated). In addition, **Joseph Smith and Oliver Cowdery** stated that on April 3, 1836, **Moses** appeared to them in the **Kirtland Temple** (located in Kirtland, Ohio) in a glorified, immortal, physical form and bestowed upon them the **"keys of the gathering of Israel from the four parts of the earth, and the leading of the ten tribes from the land of the north."**

**Moses is mentioned more in the Quran than any other individual and his life is narrated and recounted more than that of any other Islamic prophet**. In general, **Moses** is described in ways which parallel the Islamic prophet Muhammad, and **"his character exhibits some of the main themes of Islamic theology,"** including the **"moral injunction that we are to submit ourselves to God."**

**Moses** is defined in the Quran as both **prophet (*Nabi*)** and **messenger (*Rasul*)**, the latter term indicating that he was one of those prophets who brought a scripture and law to his people. Huston Smith describes an account in the Quran of meetings in heaven between **Moses** and Muhammad, which Huston states were **"one of the crucial events in Muhammad's life,"** and resulted in Muslims observing **5 daily prayers. Moses is mentioned 502 times in the Quran**

In the **Moses** story related by the Quran, **Jochebed is commanded by God to place Moses in an ark and cast him on the waters of the Nile, thus abandoning him completely to God's protection. The Pharaoh's wife Asiya, not his daughter, found Moses floating in the waters of the Nile.** She convinced the Pharaoh to keep him as their son because they were not blessed with any children. The Qur'an's account has emphasized **Moses'** mission to invite the Pharaoh to accept God's divine message as well as give salvation to the Israelites.

According to the Quran, **Moses** encourages the Israelites to enter **Canaan**. The Israelites are made to **wander the Sinai for 40 years. According to Islamic tradition, Moses is buried at Maqam El-Nabi Musa, Jericho.**

## Baha'i Faith

**Moses is one of the most important of God's messengers in the Bahá'í Faith being designated a Manifestation of God.** An epithet of **Moses** in Baha'i scriptures is the **One Who Conversed with God.** He is described as having been **"for a long time a shepherd in the wilderness,"** of having had a stammer, and of being **"much hated and detested"** by the Pharaoh and the ancient Egyptians of his time.

Chief among his achievements was the freeing of his people, the Hebrews, from bondage in Egypt and leading **"them to the Holy Land."** He is viewed as the one who bestowed on Israel 'the religious and the civil law' which gave them **"honour among all nations,"** and which spread their fame to different parts of the world.

Furthermore, through the law, **Moses** is believed to have led the Hebrews 'to the highest possible degree of civilization at that period.' **Abdul'l-Baha asserts that the ancient Greek philosophers regarded "the illustrious men of Israel as models of perfection."** Moses is further described as paving the way for Bahá'u'lláh and his ultimate revelation, and as a teacher of truth, whose teachings were in line with the customs of his time.

## Legacy in politics and law

In a metaphorical sense in the Christian tradition, a **"Moses"** has been referred to as the leader who delivers the people from a terrible situation, who referred to him **"the Moses generation."** In subsequent years, theologians linked the **Ten Commandments** with the formation of early democracy. Pope Francis addressed the United States Congress in 2015 stating that all people need to **"keep alive their sense of unity by means of just legislation... the figure of Moses leads us directly to God and thus to the transcendent dignity of the human being."**

## American history / Pilgrims

References to **Moses** were used by the **Puritans**, who relied on the story of **Moses** to give meaning and hope to the lives of **Pilgrims** seeking religious and personal freedom in America. John Carver wrote in 1620 during the ship *Mayflower's* three-month voyage. He inspired the Pilgrims with a **"sense of earthly grandeur and divine purpose." Next to the fugitives whom Moses led out of Egypt, the little shipload of outcasts who landed at Plymouth are destined to influence the future of the world.**

Bradford evoked the symbol of **Moses** to the weakened and desperate Pilgrims to help calm them and give them hope: **"Violence will break all. Where is the meek and humble spirit of Moses?"** William G. Dever explains the attitude of the Pilgrims: **"We considered ourselves the 'New Israel,' particularly we in America. And for that reason we knew who we were, what we believed in and valued, and what our 'manifest destiny' was."**

## Founding Fathers of the United States

On July 4, 1776, immediately after the **Declaration of Independence** was officially passed, the Continental Congress asked **John Adams, Thomas Jefferson**, and **Benjamin Franklin** to design a seal that would clearly represent a symbol for the new United States. They chose the symbol of **Moses** leading the Israelites to freedom. The Founding Fathers of the United States inscribed the words of **Moses** on the **Liberty Bell: "Proclaim Liberty thro' all the Land to all the Inhabitants thereof." (Leviticus 25).** Upon the death of George Washington in 1799, two thirds of his eulogies referred to him as **"America's Moses,"** with one orator saying that **"Washington has been the same to us as Moses was to the Children of Israel."**

**Benjamin Franklin, in 1788**, saw the difficulties that some of the newly independent American states were having in forming a government, and proposed that until a new code of laws could be agreed to, they should be governed by **"the laws of Moses,"** as contained in the Old Testament.

**John Adams**, 2nd President of the United States, stated why he relied on the laws of **Moses** over Greek philosophy for establishing the United States Constitution: **"As much as I love, esteem, and admire the Greeks, I believe the Hebrews have done more to enlighten and civilize the world. Moses did more than all their legislators and philosophers. Swedish historian Hugo Valentin credited Moses as the "first to proclaim the rights of man."**

## Slavery and civil rights

**Historian Gladys L. Knight** describes how leaders who emerged during and after the period in which slavery in the United States was legal often personified the **Moses** symbol. **"The symbol of Moses was empowering in that it served to amplify a need for freedom."** Therefore, when Abraham Lincoln was assassinated in 1865 after the passage of the **amendment to the Constitution outlawing slavery**, Black Americans said they had lost **"their Moses"**. Lincoln biographer Charles Carleton Coffin writes, **"The millions whom Abraham Lincoln delivered from slavery will ever liken him to Moses, the deliverer of Israel."**

In the 1960s, a leading figure in the civil rights movement was **Martin Luther King Jr., who was called "a modern Moses,"** and often referred to **Moses** in his speeches: **"The struggle of Moses, the struggle of his devoted followers as they sought to get out of Egypt. This is something of the story of every people struggling for freedom."**

## Criticism of Moses

**Thomas Paine and Numbers 31:13–18** in the late eighteenth century, the deist **Thomas Paine** commented at length on **Moses' Laws in *The Age of Reason*** (1794, 1795, and 1807). Paine considered **Moses** to be a **"detestable villain",** and cited **Numbers 31:13–18** as an example of his **"unexampled atrocities".** In the passage, the Jewish army had returned from conquering the Midianites.

The prominent atheist **Richard Dawkins** also made reference to these verses in his 2006 book, *The God Delusion*, concluding that **Moses** was **"not a great role model for modern moralists".** Rabbi Joel Grossman argued that the story is a "powerful fable of lust and betrayal", and that **Moses'** execution of the women was a symbolic condemnation of those who seek to turn sex and desire to evil purposes.

In *Legend of the Jews*, **Phinehas son of Eleazar** defend their innocent action in leaving the women remain alive because **Moses** instructed them to take revenge **"only to the Midianites,"** without mentioning **"Midianite women."** As God had also commanded them to be a holy nation, the **"polluted" or unvirgin** women should not be preferred among sons of Israel, therefore the **"pure"** or virgin women are more sacred for themselves.

# Munich Olympics Massacre

The **Munich massacre** was an attack during the 1972 **Summer Olympics** in Munich, West Germany, at which eleven Israeli Olympic team members were taken hostage and eventually killed, along with a German police officer, by the Palestinian terrorist group **Black September**. Shortly after the crisis began, they demanded 234 prisoners jailed in Israel and the German-held founders of the **Red Army Faction (Andreas Baader and Ulrike Meinhof)** be released. **Black September** called the operation **"Iqrit and Biram"**, after two Palestinian Christian villages whose inhabitants were expelled by the IDF in 1948.

The attack was motivated by secular nationalism, with the commander of the terrorist group, **Luttif Afif,** having been born to Jewish and Christian parents. German neo-Nazis gave the attackers logistical assistance. Police officers killed five of the eight **Black September** members during a failed rescue attempt. They captured the three survivors, whom West Germany released the next month following the hijacking of **Lufthansa Flight 615.**

Mossad responded to the release with the 1973 Israeli raid on Lebanon and **Operation Wrath of God,** tracking down and killing Palestinians suspected of involvement in the massacre. On 3 August 2016, two days prior to the start of the 2016 **Summer Olympics**, the **International Olympic Committee** officially honored the eleven Israelis killed for the first time.

## Prelude

At the time of the hostage-taking, the 1972 **Summer Olympics** was in their second week. The West German Olympic Organizing Committee had hoped to discard the military image of Germany. The Committee was wary of the image portrayed by the 1936 **Summer Olympics**, which Nazi dictator **Adolf Hitler** used for his benefit. Security personnel known as Olys were inconspicuous and only prepared to deal with ticket fraud and drunkenness.

The documentary film *One Day in September* claims that security in the athletes' village was unfit for the Games and that athletes could come and go as they pleased. Athletes could sneak past security, and go to other countries' rooms, by going over the fencing that encompassed the village. The absence of armed personnel had worried Israeli delegation head **Shmuel Lalkin** even before his team arrived in Munich. In later interviews with journalists **Serge Groussard** and **Aaron Klein,** **Lalkin** said that he had also expressed concern with the relevant authorities about his team's lodgings. The team was housed in a relatively isolated part of the **Olympic Village**, on the ground floor of a small building close to a gate, which **Lalkin** felt made his team particularly vulnerable to an outside assault. The West German authorities apparently assured **Lalkin** that extra security would be provided to look after the Israeli team, but **Lalkin** doubts that these additional measures were ever taken.

Olympic organizers asked West German forensic psychologist **Georg Sieber** to create 26 terrorism scenarios to aid the organizers in planning security. His "**Situation 21**" accurately forecast armed Palestinians invading the Israeli delegation's quarters, killing and taking hostages, and demanding Israel's release of prisoners and a plane to leave West Germany.

Organizers balked against preparing for **Situation 21** and the other scenarios, since guarding the Games against them would have gone against the goal of "**Carefree Games**" without heavy security.

## Accusation of German knowledge of the attack

The German weekly news magazine *Der Spiegel* wrote in a cover story in 2012 that the West German authorities had a tip-off from a Palestinian informant in Beirut three weeks before the massacre. The informant told West Germany that Palestinians were planning an "**incident**" at the Olympic Games, and the Foreign Ministry in Bonn viewed the tip-off seriously enough to pass it on to the secret service in Munich and urge that "**all possible security measures**" be taken. However, according to *Der Spiegel,* the authorities failed to act on the tip, and have never acknowledged it in the following 40 years. The magazine further adds that this is only part of a 40-year cover-up by the German authorities of the mishandling of the massacre.

## Hostage-taking

On Monday evening, 4 September, the Israeli athletes enjoyed a night out, watching a performance of *Fiddler on the Roof* and dining with the play's star, Israeli actor **Shmuel Rodensky**, before returning to the **Olympic Village**. On the return trip in the team bus, **Lalkin** denied his 13-year-old son, who had befriended weightlifter **Yossef Romano** and wrestler **Eliezer Halfin**, permission to spend the night in their apartment—an innocent refusal that probably saved the boy's life.

At 4:30 am local time on 5 September, as the athletes slept, eight tracksuit-clad members of the **Black September** faction of the **Palestine Liberation Organization**, carrying duffel bags loaded with **AKM** assault rifles, Tokarev pistols, and grenades, scaled a 2-metre (6 ½ ft.) chain-link fence with the assistance of unsuspecting athletes who were also sneaking into the **Olympic Village**. The athletes were originally identified as Americans, but were claimed to be Canadians decades later.[18] Once inside, the **Black September** members used stolen keys to enter two apartments being used by the Israeli team at Connollystraße 31.

**Yossef Gutfreund**, a wrestling referee, was awakened by a faint scratching noise at the door of Apartment 1, which housed the Israeli coaches and officials. When he investigated, he saw the door begin to open and masked men with guns on the other side. He shouted a warning to his sleeping roommates and threw his 135 kg (300 lbs.) weight against the door in a futile attempt to stop the intruders from forcing their way in. Gutfreund's actions gave his roommate, weightlifting **Coach Tuvia Sokolovsky**, enough time to smash a window and escape.

Wrestling **Coach Moshe Weinberg** fought the intruders, who shot him through his cheek and then forced him to help them find more hostages. Leading the intruders past Apartment 2, **Weinberg** lied by telling them that the residents of the apartment were not Israelis. Instead, **Weinberg** led them to Apartment 3; there, the gunmen corralled six wrestlers and weightlifters as additional hostages. It is possible that **Weinberg** had hoped that the stronger men would have a better chance of fighting off the attackers, but they were all surprised in their sleep.

As the athletes from Apartment 3 were marched back to the coaches' apartment, the wounded **Weinberg** again attacked the gunmen, allowing one of his wrestlers, **Gad Tsobari**, to escape via the underground parking garage.

**Weinberg** knocked one of the intruders unconscious and slashed another with a fruit knife before being shot to death. **Weightlifter Yossef Romano**, a veteran of the **Six-Day War**, also attacked and wounded one of the intruders before being shot and killed. In its publication of 1 December 2015, the New York Times reported that **Yossef Romano was castrated after he was shot.**

The gunmen were left with nine hostages. They were, in addition to **Gutfreund**, sharpshooting coach **Kehat Shorr**, track and field coach **Amitzur Shapira**, fencing master **Andre Spitzer**, weightlifting judge **Yakov Springer**, wrestlers **Eliezer Halfin** and **Mark Slavin**, and weightlifters **David Berger** and **Ze'ev Friedman**. **Berger** was an expatriate American with dual citizenship; **Slavin**, at 18 the youngest of the hostages, had only arrived in Israel from the Soviet Union four months before the **Olympic Games** began.

**Gutfreund**, physically the largest of the hostages, was bound to a chair (Groussard describes him as being tied up like a mummy); the rest were lined up four apiece on the two beds in **Springer** and Shapira's room, and bound at the wrists and ankles and then to each other. **Romano's** bullet-riddled corpse was left at his bound comrades' feet as a warning. **Several of the hostages were beaten during the stand-off, with some suffering broken bones as a result.**

Of the other members of Israel's team, racewalker **Shaul Ladany** had been jolted awake in Apartment 2 by Gutfreund's screams. He jumped from the second-story balcony of his room and fled to the American dormitory, awakening U.S. track coach **Bill Bowerman** and informing him of the attack. **Ladany**, a survivor of the **Nazi Bergen-Belsen concentration camp**, was the first person to spread the alert as to the attack.

The other four residents of Apartment 2 (sharpshooters **Henry Hershkowitz** and **Zelig Shtroch**, and fencers **Dan Alon** and **Yehuda Weisenstein**), plus chef de mission **Shmuel Lalkin** and the two team doctors, managed to hide and later fled the besieged building. The two female members of Israel's Olympic team, sprinter and hurdler **Esther Shahamorov** and swimmer **Shlomit Nir**, were housed in a separate part of the **Olympic Village**. Three more members of Israel's Olympic team, two sailors and their manager, were housed in Kiel, 900 kilometres (600 mi) from Munich.

The attackers were subsequently reported to be part of the Palestinian terrorists from refugee camps in Lebanon, Syria, and Jordan. They were identified as **Luttif Afif** (using the codename Issa), the leader (three of Issa's brothers were also reportedly members of **Black September**, two of them in Israeli jails), his deputy **Yusuf Nazzal** (Tony), and junior members **Afif Ahmed Hamid** (Paolo), **Khalid Jawad** (Salah), **Ahmed Chic Thaa** (Abu Halla), **Mohammed Safady** (Badran), **Adnan Al-Gashey** (Denawi), and his cousin **Jamal Al-Gashey** (Samir).

According to author **Simon Reeve, Afif, Nazzal**, and one of their confederates, had all worked in various capacities in the **Olympic Village**, and had spent a couple of weeks scouting out their potential target. A member of the Uruguayan Olympic delegation, which shared housing with the Israelis, claimed that he found **Nazzal** actually inside 31 Connollystraße less than 24 hours before the attack, but since he was recognized as a worker in the Village, nothing was thought of it at the time.

The other members of the group entered Munich via train and plane in the days before the attack. All of the members of the Uruguay and Hong Kong Olympic teams, which also shared the building with the Israelis, were released unharmed during the crisis.

## International reaction

On 5 September, **Golda Meir**, then Prime Minister of Israel, appealed to other countries to **"save our citizens and condemn the unspeakable criminal acts committed."** She also stated that **"if we [Israel] should give in, then no Israeli anywhere in the world shall feel that his life is safe ... it's blackmail of the worst kind."**

**King Hussein of Jordan—the only leader of an Arab country to denounce the attack publicly—called it a "savage crime against civilization ... perpetrated by sick minds."**

**U.S. President Richard Nixon** privately discussed a number of possible American responses, such as declaring a national day of mourning (favored by Secretary of State **William P. Rogers**), or having Nixon fly to the athletes' funerals. **Nixon** and **Henry Kissinger** decided instead to press the United Nations to take steps against international terrorism.

## Negotiations

The hostage-takers **demanded the release of 234 Palestinians and non-Arabs jailed in Israel**, along with two German insurgents held by the German penitentiary system, **Andreas Baader** and **Ulrike Meinhof,** who were founders of the German **Red Army Faction**. The hostage-takers threw the body of **Weinberg** out the front door of the residence to demonstrate their resolve. Israel's response was immediate and absolute: there would be no negotiation. Israel's official policy at the time was to refuse to negotiate with terrorists under any circumstances, as according to the Israeli government such negotiations would give an incentive to future attacks.

It has been claimed that the German authorities, under the leadership of **Chancellor Willy Brandt** and Minister for the Interior **Hans-Dietrich Genscher**, rejected Israel's offer to send an Israeli special forces unit to Germany. The Bavarian interior minister **Bruno Merk**, who headed the crisis center jointly with **Genscher** and Munich's police Chief **Manfred Schreiber**, denies that such an Israeli offer ever existed.

According to journalist **John K. Cooley**, the hostage situation presented an extremely difficult political situation for the Germans because the hostages were Jewish. **Cooley** reported that the Germans offered the Palestinians an unlimited amount of money for the release of the athletes, as well as the substitution by high-ranking Germans. However, the kidnappers refused both offers.

Munich police chief **Manfred Schreiber** and **Bruno Merk**, interior minister of Bavaria, negotiated directly with the kidnappers, repeating the offer of an unlimited amount of money. According to Cooley, the reply was that **"money means nothing to us; our lives mean nothing to us."** **Magdi Gohary** and **Mohammad Khadif**, both Egyptian advisers to the **Arab League**, and **A.D. Touny**, an Egyptian member of the **International Olympic Committee** (IOC) also helped try to win concessions from the kidnappers, but to no avail. However, the negotiators apparently were able to convince the terrorists that their demands were being considered, as **Issa** granted a total of five extensions to their deadlines.

Elsewhere in the village, athletes carried on as normal, seemingly oblivious of the events unfolding nearby. The Games continued until mounting pressure on the **IOC** forced a suspension some 12 hours after the first athlete had been murdered. United States marathon runner **Frank Shorter**, observing the unfolding events from the balcony of his nearby lodging, was quoted as saying, **"Imagine those poor guys over there. Every five minutes a psycho with a machine gun says, 'Let's kill 'em now,' and someone else says, 'No, let's wait a while.' How long could you stand that?"**

At 4:30 pm, a squad of 38 German police was dispatched to the **Olympic Village**. Dressed in Olympic sweat suits (some also wearing Stahlhelme and carrying Walther MP sub-machine guns), they were members of the German border-police, although according to former Munich policeman **Heinz Hohensinn** they were regular Munich police officers, with no experience in combat or hostage rescue. **Their plan was to crawl down from the ventilation shafts and kill the terrorists**.

The police took up positions awaiting the code word **"Sunshine"**, which upon hearing, they were to begin the assault. In the meantime, camera crews filmed the actions of the officers from the German apartments, and broadcast the images live on television. Thus, the terrorists were able to watch the police prepare to attack. Footage shows one of the kidnappers peering from the balcony door while one of the police officers stood on the roof less than 20 ft. (6 m) from him. In the end, after **Issa** threatened to kill two of the hostages, the police retreated from the premises.

At one point during the crisis, the negotiators demanded direct contact with the hostages to satisfy themselves the Israelis were still alive. Fencing coach **Andre Spitzer**, who spoke fluent German, and shooting **Coach Kehat Shorr**, the senior member of the Israeli delegation, had a brief conversation with German officials while standing at the second-floor window of the besieged building, with two kidnappers holding guns on them. When **Spitzer** attempted to answer a question, he was clubbed with the butt of an **AK-47** in full view of international television cameras and pulled away from the window.

A few minutes later, **Hans-Dietrich Genscher** and **Walter Tröger**, the mayor of the **Olympic Village**, were briefly allowed into the apartments to speak with the hostages. **Tröger** spoke of being very moved by the dignity with which the Israelis held themselves, and that they seemed resigned to their fate. He also noticed that several of the hostages, especially **Gutfreund**, showed signs of having suffered physical abuse at the hands of the kidnappers, and that **David Berger** had been shot in his left shoulder. While being debriefed by the crisis team, **Genscher** and **Tröger** told them that they had seen "**four or five**" attackers inside the apartment. Crucially, these numbers were accepted as definitive.

While **Genscher** and **Tröger** were talking with the hostages, **Kehat Shorr** had told the Germans that the Israelis would not object to being flown to an Arab country, provided that strict guarantees for their safety were made by the Germans and whichever nation they landed in. At 6 pm Munich time, the **Palestinians issued a new dictate, demanding transportation to Cairo.**

## Failed rescue: Ambush plan

The authorities feigned agreement to the Cairo demand (although **Egyptian Prime Minister Aziz Sedki** had already told the German authorities that the Egyptians did not wish to become involved in the hostage crisis). Two **Bell UH-1** military helicopters were to transport the terrorists and hostages to nearby Fürstenfeldbruck, a **NATO** airbase. Initially, the perpetrators' plan was to go to Riem, which was the international airport near Munich at the time, but the negotiators convinced them that Fürstenfeldbruck would be more practical. The authorities, who preceded the **Black September**ists and hostages in a third helicopter, had an ulterior motive: they planned an armed assault at the airport.

Realizing that the Palestinians and Israelis had to walk 200 meters through the underground garages to reach the helicopters, the German police saw another opportunity to ambush the perpetrators, and placed sharpshooters there. But **Issa** insisted on checking the route first. He and some other Palestinians walked pointing their **AK-47s at Schreiber**, **Tröger** and **Genscher**. At that time, the gunmen of the police were lying behind cars in the side streets, and when they approached the latter crawled away, making noise in the process. Thus the terrorists were immediately alerted of the dangerous presence, and they decided to use a bus instead of walking.

The bus arrived at 10:00 pm and drove the contingent to the helicopters. Issa checked them with a flashlight before boarding in groups.

Five German policemen were deployed around the airport in sniper roles—three on the roof of the control tower, one hidden behind a service truck and one behind a small signal tower at ground level. However, none of them had any special sniper training, nor any special weapon (being equipped with the **H&K G3**, the ordinary assault rifle of the **German Armed Forces** without optics or night vision devices). The soldiers were selected because they shot competitively on weekends.

During a subsequent German investigation, an officer identified as **"Sniper No. 2"** stated: **"I am of the opinion that I am not a sharpshooter."** The members of the crisis team—**Schreiber, Genscher, Merk** and **Schreiber's** deputy **Georg Wolf**—supervised and observed the attempted rescue from the airport control tower. Cooley, Reeve and Groussard all place **Mossad chief Zvi Zamir** and **Victor Cohen**, one of Zamir's senior assistants, at the scene as well, but as observers only. Zamir has stated repeatedly in interviews over the years that he was never consulted by the Germans at any time during the rescue attempt and that he thought that his presence actually made the Germans uncomfortable.

A **Boeing 727** jet was positioned on the tarmac with sixteen German police inside dressed as flight crew. It was agreed that **Issa** and **Tony** would inspect the plane. The plan was that the Germans would overpower them as they boarded, giving the snipers a chance to kill the remaining terrorists at the helicopters. These were believed to number no more than two or three, according to what **Genscher** and **Tröger** had seen inside 31 Connollystraße. However, during the transfer from the bus to the helicopters, the crisis team discovered that there were actually eight of them.

## Failure
At the last minute, as the helicopters were arriving at Fürstenfeldbruck, the German police aboard the airplane voted to abandon their mission, without consulting the central command. This left only the five sharpshooters to try to overpower a larger and more heavily armed group.

At that point, Colonel **Ulrich Wegener**, Genscher's senior aide and later the founder of the elite German counter-terrorist unit **GSG 9**, said **"I'm sure this will blow the whole affair!"**

The helicopters landed just after 10:30 pm and the four pilots and six of the kidnappers emerged. While four of the **Black September** members held the pilots at gunpoint (breaking an earlier promise that they would not take any Germans hostage), Issa and **Tony** walked over to inspect the jet, only to find it empty. Realizing they had been lured into a trap, they sprinted back toward the helicopters. As they ran past the control tower, Sniper 3 took one last opportunity to eliminate **Issa**, which would have left the group leaderless. However, due to the poor lighting, he struggled to see his target and missed, hitting **Tony** in the thigh instead. Meanwhile, the German authorities gave the order for snipers positioned nearby to open fire, which occurred around 11:00 pm.

In the ensuing chaos, **Ahmed Chic Thaa** and **Afif Ahmed Hamid**, the two kidnappers holding the helicopter pilots, were killed while the remaining gunmen—possibly already wounded—scrambled to safety, returning fire from behind and beneath the helicopters, out of the snipers' line of sight, shooting out many of the airport lights. A German policeman in the control tower, **Anton Fliegerbauer**, was killed by the gunfire. The helicopter pilots fled; the hostages, tied up inside the craft, could not. During the gun battle, the hostages secretly worked on loosening their bonds and teeth marks were found on some of the ropes after the gunfire had ended.

## Massacre
The Germans had not arranged for armored personnel carriers ahead of time and only at this point where they called in to break the deadlock. Since the roads to the airport had not been cleared, the carriers became stuck in traffic and finally arrived around midnight. With their appearance, the kidnappers felt the shift in the status quo, and possibly panicked at the thought of the failure of their operation. At four minutes past midnight of 6 September, one of them (likely Issa) turned on the hostages in the eastern helicopter and fired at them with a Kalashnikov assault rifle from point-blank range.

**Springer, Halfin** and **Friedman** were killed instantly; **Berger**, shot twice in the leg, is believed to have survived the initial onslaught (as his autopsy later found that he had died of smoke inhalation). **The attacker then pulled the pin on a hand grenade and tossed it into the cockpit**; the ensuing explosion destroyed the helicopter and incinerated the bound Israelis inside.

**Issa** then dashed across the tarmac and began firing at the police, who killed him with return fire. Another, **Khalid Jawad**, attempted to escape and was gunned down by one of the snipers. What happened to the remaining hostages is still a matter of dispute. A German police investigation indicated that one of their snipers and a few of the hostages may have been shot inadvertently by the police. However, a *Time Magazine* reconstruction of the long-suppressed Bavarian prosecutor's report indicates that a third kidnapper (Reeve identifies **Adnan Al-Gashey**) stood at the door of the western helicopter and raked the remaining five hostages with machine gun fire; **Gutfreund, Shorr, Slavin, Spitzer** and **Shapira** were shot an average of four times each. Of the four hostages in the eastern helicopter, only **Ze'ev Friedman**'s body was relatively intact; he had been blown clear of the helicopter by the explosion. In some cases, the exact cause of death for the hostages in the eastern helicopter was difficult to establish because the rest of the corpses were burned almost beyond recognition in the explosion and subsequent fire.

Three of the remaining men lay on the ground, one of them feigning death, and were captured by police. **Jamal Al-Gashey** had been shot through his right wrist, and **Mohammed Safady** had sustained a flesh wound to his leg. **Adnan Al-Gashey** had escaped injury completely. **Tony** escaped the scene, but was tracked down with police dogs 40 minutes later in an airbase parking lot. Cornered and bombarded with tear gas, he was shot dead after a brief gunfight. **By around 1:30 am on 6 September, the battle was over.**

## Criticism

Author **Simon Reeve**, among others, writes that the shootout with the well-trained **Black September** members showed an egregious lack of preparation on the part of the German authorities. They were not prepared to deal with this sort of situation. This costly lesson led directly to the founding, less than two months later, of police counter-terrorism branch **GSG 9.**

It was known a half-hour before the hostages and kidnappers had even arrived at Fürstenfeldbruck that the number of the latter was larger than first believed. Despite this new information, **Schreiber** decided to continue with the rescue operation as originally planned and the new information could not reach the snipers since they had no radios.

The 2006 *National Geographic* Channel's *Seconds from Disaster* profile on the massacre stated that the helicopters were supposed to land sideways and to the west of the control tower, a maneuver which would have allowed the snipers clear shots into them as the kidnappers threw open the helicopter doors. Instead, the helicopters were landed facing the control tower and at the center of the airstrip. This not only gave them a place to hide after the gunfight began, but put Snipers 1 and 2 in the line of fire of the other three snipers on the control tower. The snipers were denied valuable shooting opportunities as a result of the positioning of the helicopters, stacking the odds against what were effectively three snipers versus eight heavily armed gunmen.

As a result, the robbers shot an innocent woman dead. **Schreiber** was consequently charged with involuntary manslaughter. An investigation ultimately cleared him of any wrongdoing, but the program suggested that the prior incident affected his judgment in the subsequent Olympic hostage crisis.

Many of the errors made by the Germans during the rescue attempt were ultimately detailed by **Heinz Hohensinn**, who had participated in Operation Sunshine earlier that day. He stated in *One Day in September* that he had been selected to pose as a crew member. He and his fellow policemen understood that it was a suicide mission, so the group unanimously voted to flee the plane. **None of them were reprimanded for that desertion**.

## Aftermath

The bodies of the five Palestinian attackers—**Afif, Nazzal, Chic Thaa, Hamid** and **Jamal**—killed during the Fürstenfeldbruck gun battle were delivered to Libya, where they received heroes' funerals and were buried with full military honors. On 8 September, Israeli planes bombed ten PLO bases in Syria and Lebanon in response to the massacre. **Up to 200 people were killed.**

The three surviving **Black September** gunmen had been arrested after the Fürstenfeldbruck gunfight, and were being held in a Munich prison for trial. On 29 October, **Lufthansa Flight**

**615** was hijacked and threatened to be blown up if the Munich attackers were not released. Safady and the **Al-Gasheys** were immediately released by West Germany, receiving a tumultuous welcome when they touched down in Libya and giving their own firsthand account of their operation at a press conference broadcast worldwide. Further international investigations into the **Lufthansa Flight 615** incident have produced theories of a secret agreement between the German government and **Black September**- release of the surviving terrorists in exchange for assurances of no further attacks on Germany.

The massacre prompted many European countries to establish permanent, professional, and immediately available counter-terrorism forces, or reorganize already existing units to such purpose. The massacre also prompted prominent arms designers and manufacturers to produce new types of weapons more suitable for counter-terrorism.

## Effect on the Games

In the wake of the hostage-taking, competition was eventually suspended for the first time in modern Olympic history, after public criticism of the **Olympic Committee's** decision to continue the games. On 6 September, **a memorial service attended by 80,000 spectators and 3,000 athletes was held in the Olympic Stadium.** IOC **President Avery Brundage** made little reference to the murdered athletes during a speech praising the strength of the Olympic movement and equating the attack on the Israeli sportsmen with the recent arguments about encroaching professionalism and disallowing Rhodesia's participation in the Games, which outraged many listeners. The victims' families were represented by **Andre Spitzer's** widow **Ankie, Moshe Weinberg's** mother, and a cousin of Weinberg, **Carmel Eliash. During the memorial service, Eliash collapsed and died of a heart attack.**

Many of the 80,000 people who filled the Olympic Stadium for West Germany's football match with Hungary carried noisemakers and waved flags, but when several spectators unfurled a banner reading **"17 dead, already forgotten?"** security officers removed the sign and expelled those responsible from the grounds. During the memorial service, the Olympic Flag was flown at half-staff, along with the flags of most of the other competing nations at the request of **Willy Brandt. Ten Arab nations objected to their flags being lowered to honor murdered Israelis**; their flags were restored to the tops of their flagpoles almost immediately.

**Willi Daume**, president of the Munich organizing committee, initially sought to cancel the remainder of the Games, but in the afternoon Brundage and others who wished to continue the Games prevailed, stating that they could not let the incident halt the Games. Brundage stated **"The Games must go on, and we must ... and we must continue our efforts to keep them clean, pure and honest."** The decision was endorsed by the Israeli government and Israeli Olympic team chef de mission **Shmuel Lalkin**.

Four years later at the 1976 **Summer Olympics** in Montreal, the Israeli team commemorated the massacre: when they entered the stadium at the Opening Ceremony, their national flag was adorned with a black ribbon.

In 2014 the International Olympic Committee agreed to contribute $250,000 towards a memorial to the murdered Israeli athletes. After 44 years, the IOC commemorated the victims of the Munich massacre for the first time in the Rio 2016 **Olympic Village** on 4 August 2016.

## Israeli response: *Operation Wrath of God and 1973 Israeli raid on Lebanon*

**Golda Meir** and the Israeli Defense Committee secretly authorized the Mossad to track down and kill those allegedly responsible for the Munich massacre. The accusation that this was motivated by a desire for vengeance was disputed by **Zvi Zamir**, who described the mission as **"putting an end to the type of terror that was perpetrated"** (in Europe). To this end the Mossad set up a number of special teams to locate and kill these **Fedayeen**, aided by the agency's stations in Europe.

**In a February 2006 interview, former Mossad chief Zvi Zamir answered direct questions:** *Was there no element of vengeance in the decision to take action against the terrorists?* **"No. We were not engaged in vengeance. We acted against those who thought that they would continue to perpetrate acts of terror. I am not saying that those who were involved in Munich were not marked for death. They definitely deserved to die. But we were not dealing with the past; we concentrated on the future."**

The Israeli mission later became known as *Operation Wrath of God* or *Mivtza Za'am Ha'El*. Reeve quotes **General Aharon Yariv**—who, he writes, was the general overseer of the operation—as stating that after Munich the Israeli government felt it had no alternative but to exact justice:

**"We had no choice. We had to make them stop, and there was no other way ... we are not very proud about it. But it was a question of sheer necessity. We went back to the old biblical rule of an eye for an eye ... I approach these problems not from a moral point of view, but, hard as it may sound, from a cost-benefit point of view. If I'm very hard-headed, I can say, what is the political benefit in killing this person? Will it bring us nearer to peace? Will it bring us nearer to an understanding with the Palestinians or not? In most cases I don't think it will. But in the case of Black September we had no other choice and it worked. Is it morally acceptable? One can debate that question. Is it politically vital? It was".**

## Surviving Black September members

Two of the three surviving gunmen, **Mohammed Safady** and **Adnan Al-Gashey**, were allegedly killed by Mossad as part of *Operation Wrath of God*. **Al-Gashey** was allegedly located after making contact with a cousin in a Gulf State, and **Safady** was found by remaining in touch with family in Lebanon. This account was challenged in a book by **Aaron Klein**, who claims that **Al-Gashey** died of heart failure in the 1970s, and that **Safady** was killed by Christian Phalangists in

Lebanon in the early 1980s. However, in July 2005, PLO veteran **Tawfiq Tirawi** told **Klein** that **Safady**, whom **Tirawi** claimed as a close friend, was **"as alive as you are."**

The third surviving gunman, **Jamal Al-Gashey**, was known to be alive as of 1999, hiding in North Africa or in Syria, claiming to still fear retribution from Israel. He is the only one of the surviving terrorists to consent to interviews since 1972, having granted an interview in 1992 to a Palestinian newspaper, and having briefly emerged from hiding in 1999 to participate in an interview for the film *One Day in September*, during which he was disguised and his face shown only in blurry shadow.

## Abu Daoud

Of those believed to have planned the massacre, only Abu Daoud, the man who claims that the attack was his idea, is known to have died of natural causes. Abu Daoud was allowed safe passage through Israel in 1996 so he could attend a PLO meeting convened in the Gaza Strip for the purpose of rescinding an article in its charter that called for Israel's eradication. **Abu Daoud** wrote that funds for Munich were provided by **Mahmoud Abbas**, Chairman of the PLO since 11 November 2004 and President of the Palestinian National Authority since 15 January 2005. In his autobiography, **Abu Daoud writes that Arafat saw the team off on the mission with the words "God protect you."** Daoud died of kidney failure aged 73 on 3 July 2010 in Damascus, Syria.

# Nazirism

In the Hebrew Bible, a **Nazirite** or **Nazarite** is one who voluntarily took a vow described in **Numbers 6:1–21**. "Nazarite" comes from the Hebrew word Nazir meaning **"consecrated" or "separated"**. This vow required the person during this period of time to:

- Abstain from all alcohol derived from grapes. (Traditional Rabbinic authorities state that all other types of alcohol were permitted.)
- Refrain from cutting the hair on one's head; but to allow the locks of the head's hair to grow.
- Not to become ritually impure by contact with corpses or graves, even those of family members.

After following these requirements the person would immerse in a **mikveh** and make three offerings: a lamb as a burnt offering (*olah*), a ewe as a sin-offering (*hatat*), and a ram as a peace offering (*shelamim*), in addition to a basket of unleavened bread, grain offerings and drink offerings, which accompanied the peace offering. **(Numbers 6:18)**

The **Nazirite** is described as being **"holy unto God"**, yet at the same time must bring a sin offering. This has led to divergent approaches to the **Nazirite** in the **Talmud**, and later authorities, with some viewing the **Nazirite** as an ideal, and others viewing him as a sinner.

## Laws of the Nazirite

**Halakha** (Jewish law) has a rich tradition on the laws of the **Nazirite**. These laws were first recorded in the **Mishna**, and in the Talmud in the **tractate *Nazir***. These laws were later codified by **Maimonides** in the *Mishneh Torah Hafla'ah, Nazir.*
**In general there are three types of Nazirites:**

- **A Nazirite for a set time**
- **A permanent Nazirite**
- **A Nazirite like Samson**

A **Samson-like Nazirite** is a permanent **Nazirite**. A person can become a **Nazirite** whether or not the Temple in Jerusalem is standing.

## Redoing the Nazirism

If a **Nazirite** fails in fulfilling these three obligations there may be consequences. A **Nazirite** who becomes defiled by a corpse is obligated to start the entire **Nazirite** period over again. In the **Mishna, Queen Helena** vowed to be a **Nazirite** for seven years, but became defiled near the end of each of two of her first **Nazirite** periods, forcing her to twice start over. **She was a Nazirite for a total of 21 years.**

## Becoming a Nazirite

An Israelite (**Numbers 6:2**) can only become a **Nazirite** by an intentional verbal declaration. A person can specify the duration as an interval of 30 days or more. A person who says **"I am a Nazirite forever"** or **"I am a Nazirite for all my life"** is a permanent **Nazirite**. Likewise if a person says **"I am a Nazirite like Samson,"** the laws of a Samson-like **Nazirite** apply. However, if a person says that he is a **Nazirite** for a thousand years, he is a regular **Nazirite**.

## Being a Nazirite

**This vow required the Nazirite to observe the following:**

- Abstain from all alcohols derived from grapes. (Traditional Rabbinic authorities state that all other types of alcohol are permitted.)
- Refrain from cutting the hair on one's head;
- Avoid corpses and graves, even those of family members, and any structure which contains such.

It is also forbidden for the **Nazirite** to have grape or grape derivatives, even if they are not alcoholic. A **Nazirite** is forbidden to consume any alcohol, and vinegar from such alcohol, regardless of its source. A **Nazirite** cannot use a comb since it is a near certainty to pull out some hair.

A **Nazirite** is not allowed to use a chemical depilatory that will remove hair. A **Nazirite** (except for a Samson-like **Nazirite** as stated above) may not become ritually impure by proximity to a dead body. However a **Nazirite** can contract other kinds of ritual impurity. A **Nazirite** that finds an unburied corpse is obligated to bury it, even though he will become defiled in the process.

## Nazirites in history / Nazirite vows in the Hebrew Bible

Two examples of **Nazirite**s in the Hebrew Bible are **Samson (Judges 13:5), and Samuel (1 Samuel 1:11). In the first case, God sent an angel to make the vow known to the mother for her not-yet-conceived son, Samson, of what He wanted the child to be like in his life. In the second case, the mother (Hannah) made the vow before Samuel was even conceived, because she was barren.**

Samson possessed strength and ability in physical battle against the Philistines, while Samuel became a prophet. Some believe that **Samson** broke his vow by touching the dead body of a lion and drinking wine (**Judges 14:8–10**).

# Neturei Karta

**Neturei Karta** (Jewish Babylonian Aramaic: *nature qarṯā,* literally **"Guardians of the City"**) is a religious group of Haredi Jews, formally created in Jerusalem, British Mandate of Palestine, in 1938, splitting off from **Agudas Yisrael. Neturei Karta** opposes secular **Zionism** and calls for a dismantling of the **State of Israel**, in the belief that Jews are forbidden to have their own state until the coming of the **Jewish Messiah.** While the **Neturei Karta** consider themselves true Jews, the US-based Jewish **Anti-Defamation League** has described them as **"the farthest fringes of Judaism".**

In Israel some members also pray at affiliated *Beit Midrash*, in Jerusalem's **Meah Shearim** neighborhood and in **Ramat Beit Shemesh Bet**. **Neturei Karta** states that no official count of the number of members exists. The **Jewish Virtual Library puts their numbers at 5,000, while the Anti-Defamation League estimates that fewer than 100 members of the community take part in anti-Israel activism.** According to the **Anti-Defamation League**, members of **Neturei Karta** have a long history of extremist statements and support for notable anti-Zionists and Islamists.

**According to the US branch Neturei Karta:**
**"The name Neturei Karta is a name usually given to those people who regularly pray in the Neturei Karta synagogues (Torah Ve'Yirah Jerusalem, Torah U'Tefillah London, Torah U'Tefillah NY, Beis Yehudi Upstate NY, etc.), study in or send their children to educational institutions run by Neturei Karta, or actively participate in activities, assemblies or demonstrations called by the Neturei Karta".**

## Origin of the name

Originally the organization was called **Chevrat HaChayim (Society of Life);** however this name was quickly supplanted in favor of the name **Neturei Karta.** The name *Neturei Karta* literally means **"Guardians of the City"** in Aramaic and is derived from a narrative on page 76c of **Tractate Hagigah** in the Jerusalem **Talmud**. There it is related that **Rabbi Judah haNasi** sent two rabbis on a tour of inspection:

In one town they asked to see the **"guardians of the city"** and the city guard was paraded before them. They said that these were not the guardians of the city but its destroyers, which prompted the citizens to ask who, then, could be considered the guardians. The rabbis answered, **"The scribes and the scholars,"** referring them to *Tehillim* **(Psalms) Chapter 127.** It is this role that **Neturei Karta** see themselves as fulfilling by defending what they believe is **"the position of the Torah and authentic unadulterated Judaism."**

Generally, members of **Neturei Karta** are descendants of Hungarian Jews and Lithuanian Jews who were students of the **Gaon of Vilna** (known as *Perushim*) who had settled in Jerusalem in the early nineteenth century. In the late nineteenth century, their ancestors participated in the creation of new neighborhoods outside the city walls to alleviate overcrowding in the **Old City**, and most are now concentrated in the neighborhood of **Batei Ungarin** and the larger **Meah Shearim** neighborhood.

At the time, they were vocal opponents to the new political ideology of **Zionism** that was attempting to assert Jewish sovereignty in Ottoman-controlled Palestine. They resented the new arrivals, who were predominantly non-religious, while they asserted that **Jewish redemption could be brought about only by the Jewish messiah**.

**Neturei Karta** was founded by **Rabbi Amram Blau and Rabbi Aharon Katzenelbogen. Rabbi Blau** was a native of **Meah Shearim** in Jerusalem and was active in the **Agudat Israel** during the British Mandate era. However, by the 1930s, the **Aguda** began to adopt a more compromising and accommodationist approach to the Zionist movement. This caused **Rabbi Blau** to split with the **Aguda** in 1937 and alongside of **Rabbi Katzenelbogen found Chevrat HaChayim, which was soon to be known thereafter as Neturei Karta.**

Other Orthodox Jewish movements, including some who oppose **Zionism**, have denounced the activities of the radical branch of **Neturei Karta**. According to *The Guardian*, **"Ven among Haredi, or ultra-Orthodox circles, the Neturei Karta are regarded as a wild fringe".** **Neturei Karta** is sometimes confused with Satmar, due to both being **anti-Zionist**. They are separate groups and have had disagreements. **Neturei Karta** asserts that the mass media deliberately downplays their viewpoint and makes them out to be few in number. Their protests in America are usually attended by, at most, a few dozen people. In Israel, the group's protests typically attract several hundred participants, depending on the nature of the protest and its location.

**In July 2013, the Shin Bet arrested a 46-year-old member of Neturei Karta for allegedly attempting to spy on Israel for Iran.** As part of a plea deal, the man was sentenced to $4\frac{1}{2}$ years in prison. **Neturei Karta** has denied that he had ever been a member of their group. **Neturei Karta**'s website states that its members **"frequently participate in public burning of the Israeli flag."** On the Jewish holiday of Purim, **Neturei Karta** members have routinely burned Israeli flags in celebrations in cities such as London, Brooklyn and Jerusalem.

While many in **Neturei Karta** chose to simply ignore the State of Israel, this became more difficult. Some took steps to condemn Israel and bring about its eventual dismantling until the coming of the **Messiah**. Chief among these was **Moshe Hirsch, leader of an activist branch of Neturei Karta, who served in Yasser Arafat's cabinet as Minister for Jewish Affairs.**

**Beliefs**

**Neturei Karta stress what is said in the Mussaf Shemona Esrei ("The Standing Prayer") of Yom Tov, that because of their sins, the Jewish people went into exile from the Land of Israel ("*umipnei chatoeinu golinu meiartzeinu*").** Additionally, they maintain the view – based on the **Babylonian Talmud** – that **any form of forceful recapture of the Land of Israel is a violation of divine will. They believe that the restoration of the Land of Israel to the Jews should happen only with the coming of the Messiah, not by self-determination.**

**Neturei Karta believe that the exile of the Jews can end only with the arrival of the Messiah,** and that human attempts to establish Jewish sovereignty over the Land of Israel are sinful. In **Neturei Karta**'s view, **Zionism is a presumptuous affront against God.** Chief among their arguments against **Zionism** is the **Talmud**ic concept of the so-called **Three Oaths**, extracted from the discussion of certain portions of the Bible. It states that a pact consisting of three oaths was made between God, the Jewish people, and the nations of the world, when the **Jews were sent into exile**.

One provision of the pact was that the Jews would not rebel against the non-Jewish world that gave them sanctuary; a second was that they would not immigrate en masse to the Land of Israel. In return the gentile nations promised not to persecute the Jews. By rebelling against this pact, **they argued, the Jewish people were engaging in rebellion against God.**

The **Neturei Karta** synagogues follow the customs of the **Gaon of Vilna**, due to **Neturei Karta**'s origin within the Lithuanian rather than Hasidic branch of ultra-Orthodox Judaism. **Neturei Karta** is not a Hasidic but a Litvish group; they are often mistaken for **Hasidim** because their style of dress (including a shtreimel on Shabbos) is very similar to that of **Hasidim**. This style of dress is not unique to **Neturei Karta**, but is also the style of other Jerusalem **Litvaks**, such as **Rabbi Yosef Sholom Eliashiv** and his followers.

Furthermore, **Shomer Emunim**, a Hasidic group with a similar anti-Zionist ideology, is often bundled together with **Neturei Karta**. Typically, the Jerusalem **Neturei Karta** will keep the customs of the **"Old *Yishuv"*** of the city of Jerusalem even when living outside of Jerusalem or even when living abroad, as a demonstration of their love for and connection to the **Holy Land**.

**Factionalism**

In the United States, the **Neturei Karta** are led by **Moshe Ber Beck of Monsey, New York**. They affiliate with the radical branch led by **Moshe Hirsch**. Beck has courted controversy by meeting with Nation of Islam leader **Minister Louis Farrakhan**, who has been accused of inciting antisemitism and of describing Judaism as a **"gutter religion"** (although **Farrakhan** insists his words were misinterpreted). In addition, after meeting with the representatives from **Neturei Karta**, **Farrakhan** indicated he would be more cautious in his choice of words in the future.

### Relations with the Palestinians

After two men associated with the **radical branch of Neturei Karta participated in a 2004 prayer vigil for Yasser Arafat outside the Percy Military Hospital in Paris, France**, where he lay on his death bed, the radical branch of **Neturei Karta** was widely condemned by other Orthodox Jewish organizations, including many other **anti-Zionist Haredi organizations** both in New York and Jerusalem. **Moshe Hirsch, and what Hirsch's faction described as an "impressive contingent" of other members, attended Arafat's funeral in Ramallah. Almost a year after the Gaza War a group of Neturei Karta members crossed into Gaza as part of the Gaza Freedom March to celebrate Jewish *Shabbos* to show support for Palestinians in the Hamas ruled enclave.**

### Relations with Iran and President Mahmoud Ahmadinejad

In October 2005, **Neturei Karta** leader Rabbi Yisroel Dovid Weiss issued a statement criticizing Jewish attacks on **Iranian President Mahmoud Ahmadinejad**. Weiss wrote that Ahmadinejad's statements were not **"indicative of anti-Jewish sentiments"**, but rather, **"a yearning for a better, more peaceful world",** and **"re-stating the beliefs and statements of Ayatollah Khomeini, who always emphasized and practiced the respect and protection of Jews and Judaism."**

In March 2006, several members of a **Neturei Karta**'s faction visited Iran where they met with Iranian leaders, including the Vice-President, and praised **Ahmadinejad** for calling for the Zionist regime occupying Jerusalem to vanish from the pages of time. The spokesmen commented that they shared Ahmadinejad's aspiration for **"a disintegration of the Israeli government".**

In an interview with Iranian television reporters, Rabbi Weiss remarked: **"The Zionists use the Holocaust issue to their benefit. We, Jews who perished in the Holocaust, do not use it to advance our interests. We stress that there are hundreds of thousands Jews around the world who identify with our opposition to the Zionist ideology and who feel that Zionism is not Jewish, but a political agenda. ... What we want is not a withdrawal to the '67 borders, but to everything included in it, so the country can go back to the Palestinians and we could live with them ..."**

### Tehran Holocaust Conference

In December 2006, members of **Neturei Karta**, including **Yisroel Dovid Weiss**, attended the **International Conference to Review the Global Vision** of the **Holocaust**, a controversial conference being held in Tehran, Iran that attracted a number of high-profile **Holocaust** deniers.

In his speech, Weiss explained that the occurrence of the **Nazi Holocaust** was irrefutable and spoke about the murder of his own grandparents at **Auschwitz**, but claimed that Zionists had **"collaborated with the Nazis"** and **"thwarted...efforts to save...Jews"** and expressed solidarity with the Iranian position of anti-**Zionism**. **Rabbi Yonah Metzger**, the chief Ashkenazi Rabbi of Israel, immediately called for those who went to Tehran to be put into **'Cherem'**, a form of excommunication. Subsequently, the **Satmar Hassidism** court called on Jews **"to keep away from them and condemn their actions"**.

On 21 December, the **Edah HaChareidis rabbinical council** of Jerusalem also released a statement calling on the public to distance itself from those who went to Iran. The **Edah's** statement followed, in major lines, the **Satmar** statement released a few days earlier. In January 2007, a group of protesters stood outside the radical **Neturei Karta** synagogue in Monsey, New York, demanding that they leave Monsey and move to Iran. **Neturei Karta** and their sympathizers from Monsey's Orthodox community responded with a counter protest.

### 2008 Mumbai attack on Nariman House

One of the targets of the 2008 Mumbai attacks was the Nariman House, which was operated by the Jewish **Chabad** movement. **Neturei Karta** subsequently issued a leaflet criticizing the **Chabad** movement for its relations with **"the filthy, deplorable traitors – the cursed Zionists that are your friends."** It added that the **Chabad** movement has been imbued with **"false national sentiment"** and criticized the organization for allowing all Jews to stay in its centres, without differentiating **"between good and evil, right and wrong, pure and impure, a Jew and a person who joins another religion, a believer and a heretic."**

The leaflet also criticized the invitation of Israeli state officials to the funerals of the victims, claiming that they **"uttered words of heresy and blasphemy."** The leaflet concluded that **"the road have taken is the road of death and it leads to doom, assimilation and the uprooting of the Torah."**

### Sikrikim

A radical breakaway faction called *Sikrikim* is based in Israel, mainly in Jerusalem and **Beit Shemesh.** The group's engagement in acts of vandalism, **"mafia-like intimidation"** and violent protests caused several people, including authority figures, to push for officially labeling them as a terrorist group, along with **Neturei Karta**.

# Noahidism

**Noahidism** or **Noachidism** is a monotheistic ideology based on the **Seven Laws of Noah**, and on their traditional interpretations within **Rabbinic Judaism**. According to Jewish law, non-Jews are not obligated to convert to Judaism, but they are required to observe the **Seven Laws of Noah** to be assured of a place in the **World to Come (Olam Haba)**, the final reward of the righteous. Those who subscribe to the observance of these commandments are referred to as *Bene Noach* (*B'nei Noah*נב), *Children of Noah, Noahides)*, or *Noahites*. Supporting organizations have been established around the world over the past decades, by either Noahides or observant Jews.

## Noahic covenant

According to the **Book of Genesis, Noah and his three sons Shem, Ham, and Japheth** survived the Flood aboard the **Ark**, along with their wives. When **Noah's** family left the **Ark**, God made a covenant with them (**Genesis 9:8–10**) and all the animals they had aboard the **Ark** that He would never again destroy the Earth with a flood, and He set the rainbow in the sky as a symbol of the covenant.

## Maimonides

Maimonides collected all of the Talmudic and halakhic decisions in his time (*c* 1135 AD) and laid them out in his work the *Mishneh Torah*; in addition to Jewish laws and their explanations, the Noahide laws were also collected with their explanation in Maimonides' *Sefer Shoftim* (**Book of Judges**) in the last section *Hilchot Melachim U'Milchamot* ("**The Laws of Kings and Wars**") **8:9–10:12.**

## The Seven Laws of Noah

The seven laws listed by the **Mishnah in Sanhedrin 56a** are: to have laws and courts for the society, and to refrain from blasphemy, idolatry, a set of six forbidden sexual relationships, murder, theft, and eating flesh that was removed from a living animal.

## Modern Noahidism

Some Jewish religious groups have been particularly active in promoting the **Seven Laws**, notably the **Chabad-Lubavitch** movement (whose late leader, **Rabbi Menachem Mendel Schneerson**, launched the global Noahide Campaign), groups affiliated with **Dor Daim**.

**There are two different concepts of Noahidism in Judaism:**
1. Movement *B'nei Noah* that observes 7 Commandments (Seven Laws) only and remaining Commandments do not apply to them". This is the view of Chabad-Lubavitch and few other movements. This means that Noahides may not observe Sabbath, study Torah (except for **Seven Laws**), etc.

2. Movement ***B'nei Noah*** that includes a complete adherence to Judaism as a religion in order to learn from the Jews and together promote the world but without becoming a part of the Jewish people (i.e. without performing a giyur). After ***B'nei Noah*** assume the obligatory seven Commandments, they can, if desired, carry out the rest of the Jewish commandments, including studying the Torah, observing the Sabbath, celebrating Jewish holidays, etc. This view is held, for example, by **Ravi Yoel Schwartz** and Rav Uri Scherki.

In one place of his books, Maimonides writes "**The *goy* must not observe the Sabbath and study the Torah,"** while in another place he says **"If Noahide wants to observe additional commandments besides the 7 basic ones of *B'nei Noah*, he receives a reward from Heaven, and we (the Jews) must support him in this."** Many people quote the first of his statements, not knowing about the existence of the second one.

## High Council of B'nei Noah

A High Council of B'nei Noah, set up to represent B'nei Noah communities around the world, was endorsed by a group that claimed to be the new **Sanhedrin**.

## Acknowledgment

**Rabbi Meir Kahane** organized one of the first Noahide conferences in the 1980s. In 1990, **Kahane** was the keynote speaker at the **First International Conference** of the Descendants of Noah in Fort Worth, Texas. The **Chabad-Lubavitch** movement has been the most active in Noahide outreach, believing that there is spiritual and societal value for non-Jews in at least simply acknowledging the seven laws, and even more so if they accept or observe them.

In April, 2006, the spiritual leader of the **Druze** community in Israel, **Sheikh Mowafak Tarif**, met with a representative of **Chabad-Lubavitch** to sign a declaration calling on all non-Jews in Israel to observe the **Noahide Laws** as laid down in the Bible and expounded upon in Jewish tradition.

In April, **Abu Gosh mayor Salim Jaber** accepted the seven Noahide laws as part of a mass rally by Chabad at the Bloomfield Stadium in Tel Aviv. **""According to Jewish law, it's forbidden for a non-Jew to live in the Land of Israel – unless he has accepted the seven Noahide laws."** The **Anti-Defamation League** issued a strong denunciation of the comments, and called on retracting them.

## Ten Commandments

**Judaism does not require non-Jews to keep all of the Ten Commandments.** Some within Orthodox Judaism view the keeping of certain of the Ten Commandments as being forbidden to non-Jews. The Ten Commandments are actually only **10 from among the total number of 613** Jewish commandments in the Torah. In Biblical Hebrew, the ten commandments that were inscribed by God on the tablets at **Mount Sinai** are called **"the ten sayings,"** because of the **613**

**Jewish commandments ("Mitzvot")**, those 10 are the only ones that were spoken openly by God to the entire Jewish nation when they were assembled at **Mount Sinai**. The rest of the 613 Mitzvot were taught to Moses by God, and Moses taught them to the rest of the Jewish people.

# Nuremberg Trials

The **Nuremberg trials** were a series of military tribunals, held by the Allied forces after World War II, most notable for the prosecution of prominent members of the political, military, and economic leadership of Nazi Germany. The trials were held in the city of Nuremberg, Germany. **Held between 20 November 1945 and 1 October 1946**, the Tribunal was given the task of trying **23** of the most important political and military leaders of the **Third Reich**, though one of the defendants, **Martin Bormann**, was tried in *absentia*, while another, **Robert Ley**, committed suicide within a week of the trial's commencement. Not included were **Adolf Hitler, Heinrich Himmler, and Joseph Goebbels,** all of whom had committed suicide several months before the indictment was signed. (Mussolini was killed 2 days before Hitler committed suicide on April 31, 1945, then Hermann Goring).

## Origin

A precedent for trying those accused of war crimes had been set at the end of **World War I in the Leipzig War Crimes Trials held in Maya to July 1921** before the Reichsgericht (German Supreme Court) in Leipzig, although these had been on a very limited scale and largely regarded as ineffectual. At the beginning of 1940, the Polish government-in-exile asked the British and French governments to condemn the German invasion of their country. The British initially declined to do so; however, in April 1940, a joint British-French-Polish declaration was issued.

Three-and-a-half years later, the stated intention to punish the Germans was much more trenchant. On 1 November 1943, the Soviet Union, the United Kingdom and the United States published their **"Declaration on German Atrocities in Occupied Europe"**, which gave a **"full warning"** that, when the Nazis were defeated, the Allies would **"pursue them to the uttermost ends of the earth...in order that justice may be done. ...**This Allied intention to dispense justice was reiterated at the Yalta Conference and at Berlin in 1945.

British Prime Minister **Winston Churchill** had then advocated a policy of summary execution in some circumstances, with the use of an **Act of Attainder** to circumvent legal obstacles, being dissuaded from this only by talks with US and Soviet leaders later in the war. In late 1943, during the **Tripartite Dinner Meeting at the Tehran Conference**, the Soviet Leader, Joseph **Stalin**, proposed executing 50,000-100,000 German staff officers. US President **Franklin D. Roosevelt** joked that perhaps 49,000 would do. **Churchill was vigorously opposed to executions "for political purposes."** (The U.S. lost about 400,000 in WW-II, the Russian lost 28,000,000).

US Secretary of the Treasury, **Henry Morgenthau, Jr.**, suggested a plan for the total denazification of Germany, this was known as the Morgenthau Plan. The plan advocated the forced de-industrialization of Germany and the summary execution of so-called **"arch-criminals"**, i.e., the major war criminals. Roosevelt initially supported this plan, and managed to convince Churchill to support it in a less drastic form. The demise of the **Morgenthau Plan** created the need for an alternative method of dealing with the Nazi leadership. The plan for the **"Trial of European War Criminals"** was drafted by Secretary of War **Henry L. Stimson** and the War Department. Following Roosevelt's death in April 1945, the new president, **Harry S. Truman**, gave strong approval for a judicial process. The trials were to commence on **20 November 1945, in the Bavarian city of Nuremberg.**

# Creation of the courts

On 14 January 1942, representatives from the nine countries occupied by Germany met in London to draft the **"Inter-Allied Resolution on German War Crimes"**. At the meetings in **Tehran** (1943), **Yalta** (1945) and **Potsdam** (1945), the three major wartime powers, the United Kingdom, United States, and the Soviet Union, agreed on the format of punishment for those responsible for war crimes during World War II. France was also awarded a place on the tribunal, which restricted the trial to "punishment of the major war criminals of the European Axis countries".

**Some 200 German war crimes defendants were tried at Nuremberg, and 1,600 others were tried under the traditional channels of military justice**. Because the court was limited to violations of the laws of war, it did not have jurisdiction over crimes that took place before the outbreak of war on 1 September 1939. **Nuremberg was considered the ceremonial birthplace of the Nazi Party.** It had hosted the Party's annual propaganda rallies and the Reichstag session that passed the Nuremberg Laws. Thus it was considered a fitting place to mark the Party's symbolic demise. Most of the accused had previously been detained at Camp Ashcan, a processing station and interrogation center in Luxembourg, and were moved to Nuremberg for the trial. **Each of the four countries provided one judge and an alternate, as well as a prosecutor.**

# Defense counsel

**The vast majority of the defense attorneys were German lawyers.** The main counsels were supported by a total of 70 assistants, clerks and lawyers. The defense counsel witnesses included several men who took part in the war crimes during World War II, such as **Rudolph Hoess**. The men testifying for the defense hoped to receive more lenient sentences. All of the men testifying on behalf of the defense were found guilty on several counts.

# Trial

The **International Military Tribunal** was opened on November 19, 1945, in the Palace of Justice in Nuremberg. The prosecution entered indictments against 24 major war criminals and seven organizations. These organizations were to be declared **"criminal"** if found guilty. The 24 accused were either indicted but not convicted (I), indicted and found guilty (G), or not charged.

| | | |
|---|---|---|
| 1. | **Hans Frank** | **Hanged 16 October 1946.** |
| 2. | **Wilhelm Frick** | **Hanged 16 October 1946.** |
| 3. | Walther Funk | Died 31 May 1960. |
| 4. | Hermann Goring | Committed suicide the night before his execution. |
| 5. | Rudolf Hess | Committed suicide in 1987. |
| 6. | **Alfred Jodl** | **Hanged 16 October1946.** |
| 7. | **Ernst Kaltenbrunner** | **Hanged 16 October 1946.** |
| 8. | **Wilhelm Keitel** | **Hanged 16 October 1946.** |
| 9. | Gustav Krupp von Bohlen and Halbach | He died in February 1950. |
| 10. | Robert Ley | Committed suicide on 225 October 1945. |
| 11. | Baron Konstantin von Neurath suffering a heart attack. | Released (ill health) 6 November 1954 after Died 14 August 1956. |
| 12. | Franz von Papen | although acquitted and sentenced to eight years. |
| 13. | Erich Raeder | Died 6 November 1960. |
| 14. | **Joachim von Ribbentrop** | **Hanged 16 October 1946.** |
| 15. | **Alfred Rosenberg** | **Hanged 16 October 1946.** |

| | |
|---|---|
| **16. Fritz Sauckel** | **Hanged 16 October 1946.** |
| 17. Dr. Hjalmar Schacht By 1944, he had been imprisoned in a concentration camp by the Nazis. | |
| **18. Arthur Seyss-Inquart** | **Hanged 16 October 1946**. |
| 19. Albert Speer | Expressed repentance. |
| **20. Julius Streicher** | **Hanged 16 October 1946.** |

The accusers were successful in unveiling the background of developments that had led to the outbreak of World War II, which cost at least 40 million lives in Europe alone, as well as the extent of the atrocities committed in the name of the Hitler regime. Twelve of the accused were sentenced to death, seven received prison sentences, three were acquitted, and two were not charged. (57,000,000 died in WW-II, 18,000,000 in WW-I. Total: 75,000,000).

## Executions

**The death sentences were carried out 16 October 1946 by hanging** using the standard drop method instead of long drop. The U.S. army denied claims that the drop length was too short which caused the condemned to die slowly from strangulation instead of quickly from a broken neck. The executioner was **John C. Woods**. Woods had hanged 34 U.S. soldiers during the war, botching several of them. The bodies were taken to **Dachau** and burned there incinerated in a crematorium in Munich, and the ashes scattered over the river **Isar.**

## Nuremberg principles: Subsidiary and related trials

Other trials conducted after the Nuremberg Trials include the following:

- Dachau Trials
- Auschwitz Trial
- Belsen Trial
- Frankfurt Auschwitz Trials
- Mauthausen-Gusen camp trials
- Ravensbruck Trial

## American role in the trial

While **Sir Geoffrey Lawrence** of Britain was the judge chosen as president of the court, the most prominent of the judges at trial arguably was his American counterpart, **Francis Biddle**. Prior to the trial, Biddle had been Attorney General of the United States but had been asked to resign by **Truman** earlier in 1945. Ironically, Biddle was known during his time as Attorney General for opposing the idea of prosecuting Nazi leaders for crimes committed before the beginning of the war, even sending out a **memorandum on January 5, 1945** on the subject. Nuremberg tribunal ruled that any member of an organization convicted of war crimes, such as the **SS** or **Gestapo**, who had joined after 1939 would be considered a war criminal. **Thomas Dodd** was a prosecutor for the United States. There was an immense amount of evidence backing the prosecutors' case, especially since meticulous records of the Nazis' action shad been kept.

There were records taken in by the prosecutors that had signatures from specific Nazis signing for everything from stationery supplies to **Zyklon B gas**, which was used to kill the inmates of the death camps.

## Legacy

The Tribunal is celebrated for establishing that crimes against international law are committed by men, not by abstract entities, and only by punishing individuals who commit such crimes can the provisions of international law be enforced. It served as the model for the International Military Tribunal for the Far East which tried Japanese officials for crimes against peace and against humanity. It also served as the model for the **Eichmann** trial and for present-day courts at **The International Law Commission,** acting on the request of the **United Nations General Assembly**, produced in 1950 the report *Principles of International Law Recognized in the Charter of the Nurnberg Tribunal and in the Judgment of the Tribunal.*

## Establishment of a permanent International Criminal Court

The Nuremberg trials initiated a movement for the prompt establishment of a permanent international criminal court, eventually leading over fifty years later to the adoption of the statute of the **International Criminal Court**.

## Criticism

Critics of the Nuremberg trials argued that the charges against the defendants were only defined as "crimes" after they were committed and that therefore the trial was invalid as a form of "victors' justice". Chief Justice of the United States Supreme Court Harlan Fiske Stone called the Nuremberg trials a fraud. "(Chief U.S. prosecutor) Jackson is away conducting his high-grade lynching party in Nuremberg," he wrote. "I don't mind what he does to the Nazis, but I hate to see the pretense that he is running a court and proceeding according to common law. This is a little too sanctimonious a fraud to meet my old-fashioned ideas.

Jackson, in a letter discussing the weaknesses of the trial, in October 1945 told U.S. President Harry S. Truman that the Allies themselves "have done or are doing some of the very things we are prosecuting the Germans for. Associate Supreme Court Justice William O. Douglas charged that the Allies were guilty of "substituting power for principle" at Nuremberg. "I thought at the time and still think that the Nuremberg trials were unprincipled," Among crimes against humanity stands the offense of the indiscriminate bombing of civilian populations. Can the Americans who dropped the atom bomb and the British who destroyed the cities of western Germany plead 'not guilty' on this count? (Dropping the bombs on Japan saved 1-5 Million people by invasion).

### Introduction of extempore simultaneous interpretation

The Nuremberg Trials employed four official languages: English, German, French, and Russian. Some of the languages heard over the course of the proceedings included **Yiddish, Hungarian, Czech, Ukrainian, and Polish.** The equipment used to establish this system was provided by **IBM**, and included an elaborate setup of cables.

Four channels existed for each working language, as well as a root channel for the proceedings without interpretation. Many were former translators, army personnel, and linguists. Many could not handle the pressure or the psychological strain. Many often had to be replaced. A number of the interpreters following the trials were immediately recruited into the newly formed **United Nations**. Today, all major international organizations, as well as any conference or government that uses more than one official language, uses extempore simultaneous interpretation.

In 1935, **Hitler** introduced the Nuremberg Laws, which prohibited **"Aryans"** from having sexual relations or marriages with Jews, although this was later extended to include **"Gypsies, Negroes or t heir bastard offspring"** stripped German Jews of their citizenship and deprived them of all civil rights.

## Kristallnacht (1938)

On 7 November 1938, Jewish minor **Herschel Grunspan** assassinated Nazi German diplomat **Ernst Vom Rath** in Paris. These pogroms became known as *Kristallnacht* **("Crystal Night" or "Night of Broken Glass").** Jews were attacked and Jewish property was vandalized; over 7,000 Jewish shops and more than 1,200 synagogues. 30, 000 were sent to concentration camps, including **Dachau, Sachsenhausen, Buchenwald**, and **Oranienburg.** The Vichy regime in occupied France actively collaborated in persecuting French Jews.

## In North Africa

In the 1930s, the Fascist Italian regime passed anti-Semitic laws barring Jews from government jobs and government schools, and required them to stamp **"Jewish race"** into their passports. Tunisia, the Nazis arrived in November 1942. The Nazis imposed anti-Semitic policies in Tunisia, including forcing Jews to wear the **Yellow Star**, fines, and property confiscation.

## Death squads (1941-1943)

Germany's invasion of the Soviet Union in June 1941 opened a new phase in the **Holocaust**. Hitler on 30 March 1941 described the war with the Soviet Union as a **"war of annihilation"**. The Soviet territories contained about **3,000,000 Jews** at the start of the war. A mixture of SS, SD, and Security Police, assisted by Ukrainian police, carried out the killings.

### Approx. number killed at each extermination camp

| Camp name | Killed |
|---|---|
| Auschwitz II | 1,000,000 |
| Belzec | 600,000 |
| Chełmno | 320,000 |
| Jasenovac | 97,000 |
| Majdanek | 360,000 |
| Maly Trostinets | 65,000 |
| Sobibor | 250,000 |
| Treblinka | 870,000 |
| **Total** | **3,562,000** |

## Gas chambers

At the extermination camps with gas chambers all the prisoners arrived by train. Usually they were told these were showers or delousing chambers, and there were signs outside saying **"baths"** and **"sauna."** Solid pellets of **Zyklon-B** were dropped into the chambers through vents in the side walls, releasing toxic HCN, or hydrogen cyanide. **As many as 1.4 million Jewish soldiers fought in the Allied armies, including 500,000 in the Red Army, 550,000 in the U.S. Army, 100,000 in the Polish army and 30,000 in the British army.**

## Climax

**Reinhard Heydrich** was assassinated on Prague in June 1942 by soldiers from Czechoslovakia's army-in-exile. On 19 March 1944, **Hitler** ordered the military occupation of Hungary, and **Eichmann** was dispatched to Budapest to supervise the deportation of **Hungary's 800,000 Jews**. Commandant **Rudolf Hoss**, said at his trial that he **killed 400,000 Hungarian Jews** in three months.

## Victims

**The total number of victims is just under six million – around 78 percent of the 7.3 million Jews in occupied Europe at the time.**

## Holocaust: Is a new one possible?

The State of Israel would not have formed without the Holocaust. It was a most unique moment in the history of the world to have enough sympathy for the Jewish people to propose the partition of Palestine between Arabs and Jews. Another Holocaust is not possible anywhere in the world as long as the State of Israel exists. **No Arab country can destroy Israel without it being destroyed.**

But if ever another Holocaust is perpetrated on the Jewish people, the Jews will not climb Masada and commit a communal suicide, nor will they march silently into gas chambers. Like Samson, the Jews will bring the **"House"** down with them. The world should be put on notice:

# No Israel = No Middle East!!!

# October 7<sup>th</sup> (2023) Massacre

On 7 October 2023, the paramilitary wings of **Hamas**, Palestinian **Islamic Jihad**, PRC, PFLP and DFLP launched a series of coordinated armed incursions into the **Gaza** envelope of neighboring Israel, **the first invasion of Israeli home territory since the Arab-Israeli War of 1948.** The attacks, on a Saturday, initiated the Israel–**Hamas** war, almost exactly 50 years after **Operation Badr** and the greater **Yom Kippur War of 6 October 1973**.

**Hamas** and other Palestinian armed groups named the attacks **Operation Al-Aqsa Flood** while in Israel they are referred to as **Black Saturday** or the **Simchat Torah Massacre**, and internationally as the **7 October attack**.

The attacks began in the early morning with a rocket barrage of at least **3,000 rockets** launched against Israel and vehicle-transported and powered paraglider incursions into its territory. **Hamas** fighters breached the **Gaza**–Israel barrier, attacking military bases and massacring civilians in neighboring Israeli communities, including in **Be'eri, Kfar Aza, and Nir Oz**, and at the **Nova Music Festival**. The attacks resulted in **1,139 deaths—695 Israeli civilians (including 36 children), 71 foreign nationals, and 373 members of the security forces. Approximately 250 Israeli civilians and soldiers were taken as hostages to the Gaza Strip, including 30 children**, with the stated goal to force Israel to release Palestinian prisoners. Numerous accounts of rape and sexual assault by **Hamas** fighters have been reported, which **Hamas** has denied.

**Hamas** said its attack was in response to the continued Israeli occupation of the Palestinian territories, the blockade of the **Gaza** Strip, the expansion of illegal Israeli settlements, rising Israeli settler violence, and recent escalations. **At least 44 countries denounced the attack as terrorism**, while some Arab and Muslim countries blamed Israel's occupation of the Palestinian territories as the root cause of the attack. The day was labeled the bloodiest in Israel's history and the deadliest for Jews since the **Holocaust**.

## *Israeli–Palestinian conflict*

Israel has occupied the Palestinian territories, including the **Gaza** Strip, since the **Six-Day War** in 1967. **Hamas, a Palestinian Islamist movement formed in 1987**, is the main Islamist movement in the Palestinian territories. It maintains an uncompromising stance on the **"complete liberation of Palestine",** often using political violence to achieve its goals. **Hamas** has been responsible for numerous suicide bombings and rocket attacks targeting Israeli civilians. In 2017, it adopted a new charter, removing antisemitic language and shifting focus to Zionists rather than Jews.

Before the attack, Saudi Arabia warned Israel of an **"explosion"** as a result of the continued occupation, Egypt had warned of a catastrophe unless there was political progress, and Palestinian

Authority officials gave similar warnings. Less than two months before the attacks, **King Abdullah II of Jordan** lamented that Palestinians had **"no civil rights; no freedom of mobility"**.

## Events leading to the attack

Over the course of 2023, before the attack, increased settler attacks had displaced hundreds of Palestinians, and there were clashes around the Al-Aqsa Mosque, a contested holy site in Jerusalem. Tensions between Israel and **Hamas** rose in September 2023, and *The Washington Post* wrote that the two were **"on the brink of war"**. On 13 September, five Palestinians were killed at the border. Israel said it found explosives hidden in a shipment and halted all exports from **Gaza**; **Hamas** denied this. Reuters quoted Palestinians who said that the several-day ban affected thousands of families.

In response to the ban, **Hamas** put its forces on high alert and conducted military exercises with other groups, including openly practicing storming Israeli settlements. **Hamas** also allowed Palestinians to resume protests at the **Gaza**–Israel barrier. On 29 September, **Qatar**, the UN, and Egypt mediated an agreement between Israel and **Hamas** officials in the **Gaza** Strip to reopen closed crossing points and deescalate tensions; the total number of **Gaza**ns **with work permits in Israel stood at 17,000.**

Egypt said it warned Israel days before the attack that **"an explosion of the situation coming, and very soon, and it would be big."** Israel denied receiving such a warning, although **Michael McCaul,** Chairman of the US House Foreign Relations Committee, said that warnings were given three days before the attack.

## Hamas preparations

**Bedouin clans built smuggling tunnels on the Egypt–Gaza border in 1981**. In 2001, **Hamas** began a vast underground network, initially for smuggling and later serving multiple functions. The tunnels aimed to shift battles underground. According to a 2014 **RAND Corporation** study, **Hamas employed 900 full-time staff for tunnel construction**, each taking three months and costing an average of $100,000. Funding came from commercial schemes via **Gaza**'s mosques.

**Gaza**'s tunnel network, known euphemistically as the "**Gaza metro**", serves **Hamas** for storage, movement, and command. **Hamas** used hardwired phone lines within the tunnels for covert communication over two years, evading Israeli intelligence. This allowed a successful surprise attack on Israel, with specific plans disclosed shortly before the operation, catching intelligence agencies off guard.

In the months preceding the attack, **Hamas** publicly released videos of its militants preparing to attack Israel. A video released in December 2022 showed **Hamas** training to take hostages, while another video showed **Hamas** practicing paragliding. On 12 September, **Hamas** posted a video of its fighters training to blast through the border. After the attack, the **IDF** said that **Hamas** had extensively studied the military bases and settlements near the border. *The Wall Street Journal* has accused Iran of being behind the attack. U.S. officials and Iran have denied this.

The **IDF has reported seizing over 10,000 weapons following the attack**. The arsenal included RPGs, mines, sniper rifles, drones, thermobaric rockets, and other advanced weapons. According to Israeli sources, documents and maps seized from **Hamas** militants indicated that **Hamas** intended a coordinated, month-long operation to invade and occupy Israeli towns, cities, and kibbutzim, including attacking **Ashkelon** by sea and reaching **Kiryat Gat**, 20 miles into Israel. The scale of weapons, supplies, and plans indicated, according to Israel, that **Hamas** intended to inflict mass casualties on Israeli civilians and military forces over an extended period. Western and Middle Eastern security officials gathered evidence suggesting that **Hamas** intended to invade as far as the **West Bank**, had the initial attack been more successful.

## Advance Israeli knowledge

According to *The New York Times*, Israeli officials had obtained detailed attack plans more than a year before the attack. The document described operational plans and targets, including the size and location of Israeli forces, and raised questions in Israel about how **Hamas** learned these details. The document provided a plan that included a large-scale rocket assault before an invasion, drones to knock out the surveillance cameras and automated guns that Israel has stationed along the border, and gunmen invading Israel, including with paragliders.

*The Times* reported, "**Hamas followed the blueprint with shocking precision**." According to *The Times*, the document was widely circulated among Israeli military and intelligence leadership, who largely dismissed the plan as beyond **Hamas**'s capabilities, though it was unclear whether the political leadership was informed. In July 2023, a member of the Israeli signals intelligence unit alerted her superiors that **Hamas** was conducting preparations for the assault, saying, "**I utterly refute that the scenario is imaginary**".

An Israeli colonel ignored her concerns. According to *Haaretz*, Israel's domestic intelligence agency, **Shin Bet,** and **IDF** military commanders discussed a possible threat to the **Nova Music Festival** near **kibbutz Re'im** just hours before the attack, but the festival's organizers were not warned. According to a **BBC** investigation, surveillance reports suggested that **Hamas** was planning a significant operation against Israel, but **senior IDF officers repeatedly ignored the warnings.**

## Attacks

At around 6:30 a.m. Israel Summer Time on Saturday, 7 October 2023, **Hamas** announced the start of the operation, which it called **Operation Al-Aqsa Flood**. **Hamas** commander **Mohammed Deif,** in an audio message, declared the operation was "**to end the last occupation** on Earth". **Deif** said the attack was in response to the 16-year blockade of **Gaza**, Israeli incursions in West Bank cities, violence at **Al-Aqsa mosque**, and Israeli settler violence. Shortly thereafter, **Hamas** Prime Minister **Ismail Haniyeh** made a similar announcement in a televised address.

## Rocket fire

Aftermath of **Hamas** rocket hit on the maternity ward of **Barzilai Medical Center,** a hospital in southern Israel, during the **Hamas**-led attack on Israel. **Deif** said more than 5,000 rockets had been fired from the **Gaza** Strip into Israel in a span of 20 minutes at the start of the operation. Israeli sources reported the launch of 3,000 projectiles from **Gaza**, killing five.

Explosions were reported in areas surrounding **Gaza** and in the **Sharon Plain**, including **Gedera, Herzliyya, Tel Aviv**, and **Ashkelon**. Air raid sirens were activated in Beer Sheva, Jerusalem, Rehovot, Rishon Lezion, and Palmachim Airbase. **Hamas** issued a call to arms, with Deif calling on **"Muslims everywhere to launch an attack".**

Palestinian militants also opened fire on Israeli boats off the **Gaza** Strip, while clashes broke out between Palestinians and the Israel Defense Forces in the eastern section of the **Gaza** perimeter fence. In the evening **Hamas** launched another barrage of about **150 rockets** towards Israel, with explosions reported in **Yavne, Givatayim, Bat Yam, Beit Dagan, Tel Aviv**, and **Rishon Lezion**.

## Incursions into Southern Israel

On 7–8 October **Duration: 1 minute and 45 seconds.1:45** Militants kill Israelis in Sderot Militants killing Israelis in **kibbutz Mefalsim** Blood stain on a house in **Be'eri**. Simultaneously, around **2,900 Palestinian militants infiltrated Israel from Gaza** using trucks, pickup trucks, motorcycles, bulldozers, speedboats, and powered paragliders. The **Sderot** police station was reported to have come under **Hamas** control, with militants killing 30 Israelis, including policemen and civilians. Early in the attack they deliberately destroyed the computer systems at the police station. This disabled communication and delayed the response to the attacks.

Israeli first responders reportedly recovered documents from killed militants' bodies with instructions to attack civilians, including elementary schools and a youth center, to **"kill as many people as possible",** and to take hostages for use in future negotiations. Some of the militants wore body cameras to record the acts, presumably for propaganda purposes. According to reports, some militants used **Captagon** during the attacks—a stimulant produced in Syria and used throughout the Middle East.

The morning of the attack, an Israeli military spokesman said that the militants from **Gaza** had entered Israel through at least seven locations and invaded four small rural Israeli communities, the border city of Sderot, and two military bases from both land and sea. Israeli media reported that seven communities came under **Hamas** control, including **Nahal Oz, Kfar Aza, Magen, Be'eri**, and **Sufa**. The **Erez Crossing** was reported to have come under **Hamas** control, enabling militants to enter Israel from **Gaza**. Israeli Police Commissioner **Kobi Shabtai** said there were 21 active high-confrontation locations in southern Israel.

The *New York Times* reported that an Israeli intelligence document prepared weeks after the attack found that **Hamas** had breached the border fence in over 30 separate locations. Starting at 6.30 a.m. the same day, a massacre unfolded at an outdoor music festival near **Re'im**, resulting in at least 360 dead and many others missing. Witnesses recounted militants on motorcycles opening fire on fleeing participants, who were already dispersing due to rocket fire that had wounded some attendees; some were also taken hostage.

Militants killed civilians at **Nir Oz, Be'eri**, and **Netiv HaAsara**, where they took hostages and set fire to homes, as well as in kibbutzim around the **Gaza** Strip. **Around 50 civilians were killed in the Kfar Aza massacre, 108 in the Be'eri massacre, and 15 people in the Netiv HaAsara massacre. Militants killed 16 or 17 Thai and Nepalese employees during the Kibbutz Alumim massacre.**

Other **Hamas** militants carried out an amphibious landing in **Zikim**. Palestinian sources claim that the local Israeli army base was stormed. The **IDF** said it had killed two attackers on the beach and destroyed four vessels, including two rubber boats. Militants also attacked a military base outside **Nahal Oz**, leaving at least 18 dead and taking seven hostage. An **IDF** fire investigation found that the militants had "**ignited substances... that contain toxic gasses which can cause suffocation within minutes, or even less**" both at the base and in civilian locations.

According to a December 2023 **Ynet** article, there was also an "**immense and complex quantity**" of friendly-fire incidents during the 7 October attack that "**it would not be morally sound to investigate**" given their number and the challenges soldiers were facing at the time. In January 2024, an investigation by Israeli newspaper *Yedioth Ahronoth* concluded that the **IDF** had in practice applied the **Hannibal Directive**, ordering all combat units to stop "**at all costs**" any attempt by **Hamas** militants to return to **Gaza**, even if there were hostages with them. It is unclear how many hostages were killed by friendly fire as a result of the order. According to *Yedioth Ahronoth*, around 70 burnt-out vehicles on roads leading to **Gaza** had been fired on by helicopters or tanks, killing all occupants in at least some cases.

## Re'im music festival massacre

As part of the **Hamas**-led attack, **364 civilians were killed** and many more wounded at the **Supernova Sukkot Gathering**, an open-air music festival celebrating the Jewish holiday of Sukkot near **kibbutz Re'im**. At least 40 hostages were also taken. This mass killing had the largest number of casualties out of a number of massacres targeting Israeli civilians in settlements adjacent to **Gaza** that were part of the 7 October invasion, alongside those at the settlements of **Netiv HaAsara, Be'eri, Kfar Aza, Nir Oz,** and **Holit.**

At 6:30 am, around sunrise, rockets were noticed in the sky. Around 7:00 am, a siren warned of an incoming rocket attack, prompting festival-goers to flee. Subsequently, armed militants, dressed in military attire and using motorcycles, trucks and powered paragliders, surrounded the festival grounds and indiscriminately fired on people attempting to escape. Attendees seeking refuge nearby, in bomb shelters, bushes, and orchards, were killed while in hiding.

Those who reached the road and parking lot were trapped in a traffic jam as militants fired at vehicles. The militants executed some wounded people at point-blank range as they crouched on the ground. The details of the hostages' whereabouts and conditions are not publicly known. The massacre at the festival has been described as the largest terror attack in Israel's history and the worst Israeli civilian massacre ever.

## Kfar Aza massacre

During the **Hamas**-led attack, around **70 Hamas militants attacked Kfar Aza**, a kibbutz about 3 kilometers (1.9 mi) from the border with the **Gaza** Strip, massacring residents and abducting several hostages.

The kibbutz had more than 700 residents, and it took the **IDF** two days to wrest back full control of it. While the exact number of Israelis killed is unknown, as of 15 October, 52 were listed as dead and another 20 or more were missing.

## Be'eri massacre

On the morning of the attack, around **70 Hamas militants carried out a massacre at Be'eri**, an Israeli kibbutz near the **Gaza** Strip. **At least 130 people were killed in the attack, including women (such as peace activist Vivian Silver), children, and infants, claiming the lives of 10% of the community's residents.** Dozens of homes were also burned down. Several newspapers called the massacre an act of terrorism; some compared the brutality of the atrocities to that of ISIS. Hostages were taken, leading to a standoff with the **IDF**. According to survivors, there were also deaths from friendly fire; an Israeli tank fired on a house known to contain around **40 Hamas fighters and 14 hostages, among them two children, killing all hostages in the house but one.**

## Moshav Yakhini

A squad of **Hamas** militants that arrived in a van attacked the **moshav of Yakhini**. There were seven casualties in the **moshav**, including a border police officer. An **IDF** major in the **Maglan** unit was also injured. The community leader's was on holiday in Thailand at the time, and remotely directed the **moshav's** 18-person protection team's response. **YAMAM and Sayeret Matkal IDF units eventually arrived and killed all the attackers.**

## Ein HaShlosha kibbutz

In the **kibbutz Ein HaShlosha**, at least four civilians were killed while defending the kibbutz from militants, and multiple hostages were taken. An 80-year-old Argentinian woman died after her home was set on fire and she was unable to escape. A standoff between the attackers and the residents' security team lasted six hours. The leader of the security team, who was in his sixties, was killed in the firefight. **A 63-year-old grandmother was also among those killed in the attack. A 39-year-old Israeli-Chilean woman was shot eight times.** Thirty survivors were discovered in the kibbutz three days after the massacre, 14 of whom were Thai nationals.

## Psyduck music festival massacre

**Psyduck** was a small trance music festival that took place in the open fields near **kibbutz Nir Oz**, about 2 kilometres (1.2 mi) from the border of **Gaza**. The event drew around 100 participants. **Hamas** militants attacked the festival, killing 17 Israelis. Some were fatally shot at the festival site, while others were killed as they attempted to escape to nearby kibbutzim. Most survivors hid under small bushes until Israel Defense Forces rescued them a few hours later.

## Attack on Re'im military base

At 10 a.m., less than five hours after the attacks began, fighting was reported at **Re'im** military base, headquarters of the **Gaza** Division. It was later reported that **Hamas** took control of the base and took several Israeli soldiers captive before the **IDF** regained control later in the day.

The base was reportedly the location of **IDF** drone and surveillance operations. **Hamas reportedly posted video of dead Israeli soldiers it had killed at the base.**

## Attack on kibbutz Nir Am

**Nir Am** was attacked but no residents were harmed. **Inbal Rabin-Lieberman**, the 25-year-old security coordinator, alongside her uncle **Ami**, led a guard detail that killed multiple militants attempting to infiltrate a nearby chicken farm. They successfully deterred the rest of the invading militants from entering the community.

## Participating and supporting organizations

In addition to **Hamas**, several Palestinian militant groups voiced support for the operation and participated in it to some extent. **The National Resistance Brigades**, the armed wing of the secular-socialist **Democratic Front for the Liberation of Palestine** (DFLP), confirmed their participation in the operation through their military spokesman **Abu Khaled**, saying it had lost three fighters in combat with the **IDF**. The **PFLP** (a Palestinian Marxist-Leninist / Secular

Nationalist political party) and the **Lions' Den group** (a nonpartisan militant group based in the West Bank) voiced support for the operation and declared maximum alertness and general mobilization among their troops. The A**bu Ali Mustafa Brigades**, the **PFLP's** armed wing, published videos of two of their militants storming Israeli watchtowers.

## Hostages taken

Soon after the start of the **Hamas** operation, there were reports that many civilians and soldiers had been taken as captives back to the **Gaza** Strip. Later in the day **Hamas** announced it had captured enough Israeli soldiers to force a prisoner swap, and Israel confirmed hostages had been taken.

In **Be'eri,** up to 50 people were taken hostage; after an 18-hour standoff between militants and **IDF** forces, they were freed. Hostages were also reported taken in **Ofakim**, where policemen led by Chief Superintendent **Jayar Davidov** engaged Palestinian militants in a shootout; **Davidov** and three of his men were killed, and the **IDF** later rescued two Israeli hostages in the suburb of Urim. **There were reports of militants killing and stealing family pets.**

**Hamas** took many hostages back to **Gaza**. On 16 October, they said they were holding **250 hostages** and that it had done so to force Israel to release its Palestinian prisoners. Some of the hostages, including three members of the Bibas family, were subsequently handed over to other militant groups. Palestinian **Islamic Jihad** ended up holding at least 30 of the hostages, but it is unclear whether they or **Hamas** originally kidnapped them.

According to **Ariel Merari**, the raiders **"were ordered to kidnap as many as possible... they intentionally kidnapped a populace that is sensitive from the aspect of Israeli public opinion".** **Merari** doubts that **Hamas** will agree to releasing all of the hostages in **"one go"** regardless of how many of its prisoners are released, since the hostages are its only guarantee against complete destruction at Israel's hands. He believes **Hamas** will try to force a ceasefire and protract the release for weeks or months, until an Israeli offensive is no longer seen as viable.

## Locations of attacks: Contrasting stories about the event

The attacks on 7 October included both civilian and military targets, but the stories told by the different sides of the war show very little overlap. The film **Bearing Witness** depicts the attacks as primary, or solely, an attack on civilians, while **Hamas**'s propaganda videos posted to **Al-Qassam Brigades'** Telegram channel and website depict the operation as primarily, or solely, focused on the destruction of the border fence and other military targets. In the months leading up to 7 October, **Al-Qassam** posted video of themselves and some of their allies training for the attacks against military and ambiguous targets.

## Failed plans

A **Hamas** group carried intelligence information and maps guiding it to the border of the West Bank. **Shikma Prison** was among **Hamas**'s targets, but the group that headed there with the aim to free Palestinian inmates could not find it.

### *Casualties of the 2023 Israel–Hamas war*

**Duration: 2 minutes and 51 seconds. 2:51** Footage of Israeli elite unit clearing after the **Re'im** music festival massacre. The attack is considered the bloodiest day in Israel's history and the deadliest for Jews since the **Holocaust**. Initially up to **1,400 people were reported killed**. As of 10 November the estimate stood at around 1,200. In December this figure was further revised using social security data to 1,139. **This number consists of 766 civilians, including 36 children, and 373 security forces. The youngest person killed was 10 months old, and 25 were people over age 80.**

The attack left over **3,400 wounded, and 247 soldiers and civilians were taken hostage**. On 19 October, Israeli officials reported an additional 100 to 200 missing. By December 2023, the number of missing totalled 5. **Israeli casualties include about 70 Arab Israelis, predominantly from Negev Bedouin communities.** The attack affected a province with a population of 4,000,000 Israelis, while the war displaced 300,000 Israelis.

**On 7 October, over 100 civilians were killed in the Be'eri massacre, including women and children, and over 270 people were killed at a music festival in Re'im**. As of 10 October, over 100 people had been reported killed in the **Kfar Aza** massacre, with the total death toll unknown. Nine people were fatally shot at a bus shelter in Sderot. At least four people were reported killed in **Kuseife**. At least 400 wounded were treated in Ashkelon, while 280 others were reported in Beer Sheva, 60 of whom were in serious condition. In the north, injuries from rocket attacks were reported in Tel Aviv. At least 49 Israeli children and adolescents under the age of 19 were killed in the attack.

**Former Hapoel Tel Aviv F.C. striker Lior Asulin** was among those killed in the **Re'im** music festival massacre. The head of the **Sha'ar HaNegev Regional Council, Ofir Libstein**, was killed in an exchange of fire with the militants. The police commander of **Rahat, Jayar Davidov**, was also killed. The **IDF** confirmed that 247 of its soldiers had been killed. Among those confirmed dead were **Colonel Yonatan Steinberg**, the commander of the **Nahal Brigade**, who was killed near **Kerem Shalom; Colonel Roi Levy, commander of the Multidimensional "Ghost" unit, who was killed near kibbutz Re'im; and Lieutenant Colonel Eli Ginsberg, commander of the LOTAR Counter-terrorism Unit School**.

The **Druze** deputy commander of the 300th **"Baram" Regional Brigade**, Lieutenant Colonel **Alim Abdallah**, was killed in action along with two other soldiers while responding to an infiltration from southern Lebanon on 9 October. Israeli peace activist **Hayim Katsman** was killed in **Holit**. Peace activist **Vivian Silver**, originally thought to be taken hostage, was later confirmed to have been killed during the attack on **Be'eri. Israel Hayom photographer Yaniv Zohar was killed in Nahal Oz.**

The great number and geographical spread of the victims made locating all of their remains difficult. Several weeks after the massacre, once conventional search techniques had been exhausted, the **IDF** approached the **Israel Nature and Parks Authority** for help in tracking the flight paths of vultures, which resulted in the discovery of at least five more bodies. The **IDF** also enlisted the aid of archaeologists from the Israel Antiquities Authority to help recover remains that were so badly burned as to be indistinguishable from the surrounding rubble; the remains of at least ten victims have been recovered this way.

**Hamas** took at least 247 Israelis hostage and transported them to **Gaza**. On 8 October, Palestinian **Islamic Jihad** said it was holding at least 30 captives. At least four people were reportedly taken from **Kfar Aza**. Videos from **Gaza** appeared to show captured people, with **Gaza**n residents cheering trucks carrying dead bodies. Four captives were later reported to have been killed in **Be'eri**, while **Hamas** said that an **IDF** airstrike on **Gaza** on 9 October killed four captives. *Yedioth Ahronoth* photographer **Roy Edan** was reported missing and likely captured alongside his child in **Kfar Aza**. His wife was killed and two of their children were able to hide in a closet until rescued. **Edan's** body was identified ten days later as one of the casualties of the **Kfar Aza massacre.**

American-Israeli **Hersh Goldberg-Polin** was one of the kidnapped. On 11 October, **Hamas's Qassam Brigades** released a video appearing to show the release of three hostages, a woman and two children, in an open area near a fence. Israel dismissed the video as **"theatrics"**. According to **Ynet**, there were also casualties from friendly fire on October 7 which the **IDF** believed **"it would not be morally sound to investigate due to the immense and complex quantity of them that took place in the kibbutzim and southern Israeli communities due to the challenging situations the soldiers were in at the time."**

## Identification of remains

According to **Chen Kugel**, head of the **Abu Kabir Forensic Institute**, hundreds of bodies arrived at the institute in a state **"beyond recognition"**. Pathologists were required to process, among others, bone fragments recovered from fires; a blood-soaked baby mattress; victims who were tied, then executed; and two victims who were tied, then incinerated alive. With hundreds missing and bodies burned beyond recognition, Israeli authorities assembled recovery teams from across society.

This included archaeologists from the **Israel Antiquities Authority**, who identified and removed ancient remains in attempts to sift through ash and rubble for bone fragments other forensic teams overlooked. The sheer number of casualties overwhelmed authorities. Bodies were brought chaotically to the Shura **IDF** base and **Abu Kabir** forensic institute. The different military, police, and civilian teams caused confusion. Archeologists systematically searched rooms, dividing them into grids and carefully extracting bone shards. At one house, the archeology team found a bloodstain under ash that it determined was the outline of a body, later identified by **DNA** analysis as **Meni Godard**.

## Revision of casualty numbers

On 10 November, Israel revised its casualty count from 1,400 to 1,200 after realizing that some bodies that were badly burned were those of **Hamas** fighters. This included 859 civilians, 283 soldiers, 57 policemen, and 10 Shin Bet members. In December 2023, using social security data, this was further revised to 1,139: 695 Israeli civilians (including 36 children), 71 foreign nationals, and 373 security forces. Five people are classed as missing, including four Israelis.

## Israeli response

*2023 Israeli blockade of the Gaza Strip, 2023 Gaza Strip evacuations, 2023 Israeli invasion of the Gaza Strip, and Siege of Gaza City*

After the initial breach of the **Gaza** perimeter by Palestinian militants, it took hours for the Israeli military to respond by sending troops to counterattack. The first helicopters sent to support the military were launched from the north of Israel, and arrived in **Gaza** an hour after fighting began. Israel had difficulty determining which outposts and settlements were occupied, and distinguishing between Palestinian militants and the soldiers and civilians on the ground.

The helicopter crews initially poured down fire at a tremendous rate, attacking about **300 targets** in four hours. Later, the crews began to slow their attacks and carefully select targets. According to *Haaretz* journalist **Josh Breiner**, a police source said that a police investigation found that an **IDF** helicopter that had fired on **Hamas** militants **"apparently also hit some festival participants"** in the **Re'im** music festival massacre. The Israeli police denied **Haaretz's** report.

Subsequent investigation has determined that militants had been instructed not to run so that the air force would think they were Israelis. This deception worked for some time, but pilots began to realize the problem and ignore their restrictions. By around 9 a.m., amid the chaos and confusion, some helicopters started laying down fire without prior authorization. The attack appeared to have been a complete surprise to the Israelis.

The **IDF** launched **Operation Swords of Iron** in **Gaza** and declared a state of emergency for areas within 80 kilometers (50 mi) of the **Gaza** border. It also said that **Hamas "made a grave mistake"** in launching its attack and pledged that **"Israel will win"**. The **IDF** declared a **"state of readiness for war"**, **adding that reservists were to be deployed not only in Gaza but also in the West Bank and along the borders with Lebanon and Syria. Residents in areas near Gaza were asked to stay inside, while civilians in southern and central Israel were** "required to stay next to shelters". Roads around **Gaza** were closed by the **IDF**. Tel Aviv's streets were also locked down.

After the attack, Israel declared a heightened state of preparedness for potential conflict. The **IDF** declared a state of readiness for war, and **Netanyahu** convened an emergency gathering of security authorities. The **IDF** additionally reported that it had begun targeted actions in **Gaza** under what it called *Operation Swords of Iron* (or *Iron Swords*). Israeli Police Commissioner **Kobi Shabtai** announced that a **"state of war"** existed, following what he called **"a massive attack from the Gaza Strip"**. He also announced the closure of all of southern Israel to **"civilian movement"** and the **Yamam** counterterrorism unit's deployment to the area. The **IDF**'s chief spokesperson, **Rear Admiral Daniel Hagari**, said four divisions were deployed to the area, augmenting 31 preexisting battalions.

Israeli **President Isaac Herzog** said the country was facing **"a very difficult moment"**, and offered strength and encouragement to the **IDF**, other security forces, rescue services, and residents who were under attack. In a televised broadcast, Netanyahu said: **"We are at war."** He also said that the **IDF** would reinforce its border deployments to deter others from **"making the mistake of joining this war"**. In a later address, he threatened to **"turn Gaza into a deserted island"** and urged its residents to **"leave now"**.

On 7 October, Israel's Security Cabinet voted to undertake a series of actions to bring about the **"destruction of the military and governmental capabilities of Hamas and Palestinian Islamic Jihad"**, according to a statement by the Prime Minister's Office. The **Israel Electric Corporation**, which supplies up to 80% of **Gaza**'s electricity, cut off power to the area. As a result, **Gaza**'s power supply was reduced from 120 MW to 20 MW, forcing it to rely on power plants paid for by the Palestinian Authority.

**Ben Gurion Airport** and **Ramon Airport** remained operational, but multiple airlines canceled flights to and from Israel. Israel Railways suspended service in parts of the country and replaced some routes with temporary bus routes, and cruise ships removed the ports of Ashdod and Haifa from their itineraries.

## Capture and interrogation of militants

**Hamas Nukhba member recounting the events of the Kfar Aza massacre during interrogation, in a video released by the IDF**

## *Interrogation of militants in the 2023 Israel-Hamas war*

Following the attack, more than **600 militants were captured in Israel**. Israel has claimed that the interrogation of the suspects revealed significant insights into the group's strategies, ideologies, and operational methods that played a crucial role in its military response and in shaping the global understanding of the conflict. Interrogation sessions were held over four weeks, mainly in a southern Israeli prison, and concluded in early November. Interrogation methods used by **Shin Bet** and the **IDF Unit 504** included, based on Israeli sources, psychological engagement in adherence to Israeli law prohibiting physical coercion. Public release of interrogation videos aimed to validate Israeli military actions and counter **Hamas** narratives.

## Israeli Arabs

Arab Israeli politicians, including the United Arab List leader **Mansour Abbas** and Arab Knesset member **Ayman Odeh**, condemned the **Hamas**-led attack on Israel. Israel's **Social Equality Minister Amichai Chikli said, "The Arab population has shown much solidarity and responsibility, and this is especially true for the Bedouin population in the Negev."**

## Palestinian response: Hamas

**Khaled Mashal lauded the Hamas attack**, calling it legitimate resistance to Israeli occupation. He said, **"We know very well the consequences of our operation on Oct. 7"**, emphasizing that Palestinian lives must be sacrificed in the quest for liberation. **Khalil al-Hayya**, a senior member of **Hamas**, said the action was necessary to **"change the entire equation and not just have a clash... We succeeded in putting the Palestinian issue back on the table, and now no one in the region is experiencing calm."** Taher El-Nounou, a **Hamas** media adviser, said that he hoped **"that the state of war with Israel will become permanent on all the borders, and that the Arab world will stand with "**.

**Ghazi Hamad**, a senior **Hamas** official, said in an interview: **"We must teach Israel a lesson, and we will do this again and again. The Al-Aqsa Flood is just the first time, and there will be a second, a third, a fourth. Because we have the determination...to fight."** He emphasized **Hamas**'s willingness to **"pay a price"**, concluding with a call for the elimination of Israel: **"We must remove that country because it constitutes a security, military and political catastrophe to the Arab and Islamic nations"**. These comments came after an incident where Hamad abruptly left a BBC interview when asked about **Hamas**'s killing of civilians in Israel on 7 October.

**Hamas denied killing any civilians in the attack**. Its official announcement referring to the event rejected the **"falsehood of the fabricated allegations"** promoted by some Western media outlets, which unprofessionally adopt the **"Zionist narrative full of lies and slander against our Palestinian people and their resistance, the latest of which was the claim of killing children, beheading them, and targeting civilians"**.

When asked about the **Re'im** music festival massacre, where 260 civilians were murdered, **Hamas** official **Moussa Abu Marzouk** replied that it was a **"coincidence"**, and that the attackers may have thought these were soldiers **"resting"**. In January 2024, **Hamas** released a report titled **"Our Narrative"**, which accepted "some faults" but continued to deny having intentionally targeted civilians, blamed Israel for deaths, and justified the attacks as **"a necessary step and a normal response to confront all Israeli conspiracies against the Palestinian people"**.

## Palestinian Authority

On the eve of the **Hamas** attack at the emergency meeting in Ramallah, Palestinian President **Mahmoud Abbas** said that the Palestinian people had the right to defend themselves against the terror of settlers and occupation troops.

According to Palestinian government agency **WAFA**, Abbas also ordered the government and relevant authorities to immediately send all available resources to alleviate the suffering of Palestinians in **Gaza** under Israeli aggression. On 16 October, he declared that "**Hamas' actions don't represent the Palestinians**". He has yet to condemn the October 7 massacre as of February 2024.

## Palestinian public opinion

In November 2023, as a result of Israeli actions in **Gaza** following the October 7 attacks, **Hamas's** popularity among Palestinians in **Gaza** and the West Bank increased significantly. In a survey conducted on 14 November by the **Arab World for Research and Development (AWRAD)**, a research, consulting and development firm based in Ramallah, Palestinians showed overwhelming support for the attack. It said, **"Palestinians living in the West Bank overwhelmingly answered that they supported the attack to either an extreme or 'somewhat' extent (83.1%)."**

In **Gaza**, Palestinians exhibited lesser consensus, with only 63.6% **"extremely"** or **"somewhat"** supporting the attack. 14.4% answered they neither opposed or supported the attack, and 20.9% opposed the attack to some degree. Only 10% of Palestinians in **Gaza** and the West Bank said they believed **Hamas** committed war crimes during the attack on Israel, and a large majority of Palestinians said they had not seen any videos showing **Hamas** atrocities in Israel.

## *International reactions to the 2023 Israel–Hamas war*

**At least 44 nations denounced Hamas** and explicitly condemned its conduct as terrorism, including a joint statement by the United States, the United Kingdom, France, Italy, and Germany. In contrast, **Arab and Muslim countries including Qatar, Saudi Arabia, Kuwait, Syria, Iran and Iraq blamed Israel for the attack**. The UAE, Bahrain, and China have all amended their initial declarations to expressly denounce the killing and abduction of Israeli civilians. According to a poll conducted by *The Washington Institute for Near East Policy* between 14 November and

6 December 2023, **95% of Saudis did not believe that Hamas had killed civilians in its attack on Israel.**

Over 680 legal experts and 128 human rights experts from Israel and around the world have signed an appeal for the immediate release of all hostages kidnapped by **Hamas**, and for the end of the **"vicious and inhumane capture, violence, torture and other cruel, inhuman or degrading treatment of women and girls, children and infants."** According to the appeal, **"the abductees are defined according to international law as victims of enforced disappearance... blatant violations of international human rights law and humanitarian law, amounting to war crimes and crimes against humanity."**

The **United Nations**, particularly the **United Nations Committee on the Elimination of Discrimination against Women (CEDAW),** faced criticism for failing to condemn **Hamas**'s actions against women and failing to voice disapproval of the **mass rape of Israeli women and girls.**

**The US House of Representatives** overwhelmingly passed a bill to amend the US immigration code and ban people associated with **Hamas**, PIJ, and other perpetrators of the October 7 attacks from seeking immigration-related relief or protections in the United States.

After the attacks, the **Shoah Foundation** said it had gathered over 100 video testimonies of those who experienced the attacks to add them to the collection of **"Holocaust survivor and witness testimony." Shoah Foundation** founder **Steven Spielberg** said of the attacks, **"I never imagined I would see such unspeakable barbarity against Jews in my lifetime"** and that the **Shoah Foundation** project would ensure **"that their stories would be recorded and shared in the effort to preserve history and to work toward a world without antisemitism or hate of any kind."**

### Reported atrocities: *Sexual violence in the 7 October attack on Israel*
**Israeli women and girls were reportedly raped, assaulted, and mutilated by Hamas militants during the incursion, an allegation Hamas denies**. In the months following the attacks, the *The Wall Street Journal* reported on 21 December, there was **"mounting evidence of sexual violence, based on survivor accounts, first responders and witnesses."** These acts were denounced as gender-based violence, war crimes, and crimes against humanity, aligning with the **International Criminal Court's** recognition of sexual violence as such. **Witnesses recounted scenes, including instances of rape, beheadings, and other brutalities.**

**Testimonies described the perpetrators using shovels, beheading victims, and even playing with severed body parts.** The **BBC** reported that **"Videos of naked and bloodied women filmed by Hamas on the day of the attack, and photographs of bodies taken at the sites afterwards,**

**suggest that women were sexually targeted by their attackers."** Forensic examinations showed signs of sexual abuse, mutilations, broken limbs, and broken pelvises, prompting scholars and legal experts to conduct investigations, amassing substantial evidence pointing to crimes against humanity and war crimes. **Hamas was accused of employing rape as a weapon of war**. Some of the released hostages also shared testimonies of sexual violence during their time in **Gaza**. Israel accused international women's rights and human rights groups of downplaying the assaults.

A two-month *New York Times* investigation by **Jeffrey Gettleman, Anat Schwartz**, and **Adam Sella,** released in late December 2023, reported finding at least seven locations where sexual assaults and mutilations of Israeli women and girls were carried out. It concluded that these were not isolated events but part of a broader pattern of gender-based violence during the October 7 massacres.

**The probe was based on video footage, photographs, GPS data from mobile phones, and interviews with more than 150 people**. According to reporting by *The Intercept*, the *New York Times* investigation has been criticized, both externally and internally by other employees, for apparent discrepancies in witness accounts and lax evidentiary standards. On December 30, *The Daily Telegraph* wrote: **"First responders to massacre saw raped and abused bodies, but the rapidity of events—and cultural taboos—may leave the truth uncovered".**

## Torture and mutilation: Dead bodies after the Be'eri massacre

Israeli forces in **Kfar Aza** and **Be'eri** reported that they found bodies of victims mutilated. One **IDF** commander told an **i24 News** reporter that 40 babies had been killed, out of what one estimate described as at least 100 civilian victims.

## Abandoned and damaged cars after the Re'im music festival massacre

Other false reports of this type were spread by **ZAKA** volunteers acting as first responders. In one, a **ZAKA** volunteer said groups of children were found tied up and burned alive. Other reported atrocities included **sexual assaults, rapes, and mutilations**; some victims were reportedly bound, and some victims' bodies desecrated. At the music festival, there was said to be mass killing but less time for torture than at the kibbutz. **About 70% of bodies were reported to have been shot in the back. Graeme Wood** reported that the video footage retrieved from body cameras the attackers wore showed several victims who **"in the beginning of the footage... are alive, by the end they're dead. Sometimes, in fact frequently, after their death their bodies are still being desecrated."**

Other videos show attackers shooting at children, executing men in civilian clothing, throwing grenades into civilian shelters, and an attempted decapitation. First response personnel recovering the bodies reported being extremely distressed by the atrocities they witnessed, and said they placed the bodies of **Hamas** militants in body bags marked with an **"X"** and removed them with a bulldozer.

Israeli security agencies released videos that the *Times of Israel* described as apparent interrogations of **Hamas attackers, in which the subjects said they were ordered to kill, behead, cut off limbs and rape.** A former chief rabbi of the Israeli army, part of the team identifying bodies, said there were many instances of rape and torture, and an Israeli reserve warrant officer said that forensic exams had discovered multiple cases of rape, though neither provided forensic evidence to support the claims. **CNN** has interviewed several Israelis who witnessed the aftermath of the attack, who reported visible signs of rape and excessive violence on the bodies of women and girls from several sites.

A *Ha'aretz* investigation into the claims of mutilation and torture found that "**Members of Hamas and Palestinian Islamic Jihad, as well as other Gazans who entered Israel, committed war crimes and crimes against humanity.**" Regarding "**testimonies about Hamas' atrocities on October 7**", *Ha'aretz* found that "**Most are supported by extensive evidence, but a few have been proved untrue, providing ammunition to deniers of the historic massacre.**" *Ha'aretz* found several cases where Israeli search and rescue units, the army, and politicians disseminated inaccurate information.

An Israeli army officer claimed that babies had been hung on clotheslines; later investigations showed that exactly one infant was killed, alongside her father, and that the reports of groups of children being slaughtered and mutilated were false. **A total of five children under age six were killed, and another 14 between ages 12 and 15 were killed in rocket attacks from Gaza.**

Most of the children were killed alongside family members. *Ha'aretz* **reported that "Hamas terrorists did desecrate corpses during the massacre, especially the bodies of soldiers. There were also beheadings and cases of dismemberment**" but that "**there is no evidence that children from several families were murdered together, rendering inaccurate Netanyahu's remark to U.S. President Joe Biden that Hamas terrorists 'took dozens of children, tied them up, burned them and executed them.'**"

**ZAKA** volunteers shared stories of atrocities, with one repeatedly describing **20 children having been bound and burned at a kibbutz**; the same volunteer said a pregnant woman had her unborn baby cut from her womb and that he had found the woman next to two murdered children aged six and seven. But the list of dead does not correspond to the claims, and no children of that age were killed in the kibbutz; the kibbutz has denied that the story is related to the kibbutz. **Sara Netanyahu**, the Israeli prime minister's wife, sent **U.S. first lady Jill Biden** a letter claiming that a heavily pregnant woman was taken hostage to **Gaza**; the woman was identified as a Thai worker who had been taken hostage and later released. She was not pregnant and had not given birth.

U.S. Secretary of State **Antony Blinken** described some of the evidence given by the same **ZAKA** volunteer: "**a young boy and girl, 6 and 8 years old, and their parents around the breakfast** table. The father's eye gouged out in front of his kids. The mother's breast cut off, the girl's foot amputated, the boy's fingers cut off before they were executed"; and "a baby, an infant, riddled with bullets. Soldiers beheaded. Young people burned alive. I could go on, but it's simply depravity in the worst imaginable way."

## Allegations of beheaded children

In the aftermath of the initial **Hamas** assault, witnesses from the Israeli soldiers, the **Israeli Department Forces,** and the first responder Israeli organization **ZAKA** said on French Israeli TV channel i24news that they had seen the **bodies of beheaded infants at the site of the Kfar Aza massacre**. During **Antony Blinken's** visit to Israel, he said he was shown photos of the massacre by **Hamas** of Israeli civilians and soldiers, and specifically that he saw **beheaded IDF soldiers**. U.S. **President Biden** separately said that he had seen photographic evidence of militants beheading children, but it was not the case; the **White House** subsequently clarified that **Biden** was alluding to news reports of beheadings, which have not contained or referred to photographic evidence.

**NBC** News called reports of **"40 beheaded babies"** unverified allegations, adding that they appeared **"to have originated from Israeli soldiers and people affiliated with the Israel Defense Force"** and that **"an Israeli official told CNN the government had not confirmed claims of the beheadings"**. As of 12 October, CNN had extensively reviewed online media content to verify **Hamas**-related atrocities but found no evidence to support claims of decapitated children.

An Israeli **ZAKA** volunteer reported on 14 October seeing children's bodies with severe injuries and burns. Some of the bodies appeared to have been decapitated, but the exact circumstances were not clear.

According to *The Jerusalem Post*, which reprinted an article from the Israeli website *Themedialine.org* (whose founder, **Felice Friedson**, was praised by *The Jerusalem Post* and is a contributor to it), approximately 200 forensic pathologists and other experts—from Israel, Switzerland, New Zealand, the U.S. and elsewhere—reviewed evidence of the attack at the **National Center of Forensic Medicine (Abu Kabir) in Tel Aviv. Chen Kugel**, head of the center, said that many bodies, including those of babies, were without heads. When asked whether the bodies had been decapitated, Kugel answered yes.

He added that it was difficult to determine whether the dead were decapitated before or after death, or whether their heads had been **"cut off by knife or blown off by RPG"**. On 24 October, Israeli authorities screened bodycam footage of **Hamas** atrocities for journalists, including **"an attempt to decapitate someone who appeared to be still alive using a garden hoe",** as well as a still image of a decapitated **IDF** soldier.

## Immolation

On 20 October, a forensic analysis was presented to the media at **Israel's National Center of Forensic Medicine** that claimed to show evidence of victims burned alive with bound hands. The analysis suggested that one **CT scan** of charred remains showed an adult bound to a child at the time of death. **Many victims had soot in their trachea, indicating that they burned to death**.

## *Allegations of genocide in the 2023 Hamas attack on Israel*

According to several international law and genocide studies experts, **Hamas's assault amounted to genocide**. Legal and genocide experts have condemned the attack, saying it represents a serious violation of international law. They argue that **Hamas** carried out these actions with the intent to destroy the Israeli national group. Some commentators point to **Hamas's founding charter, which advocates for the destruction of Israel,** contains antisemitic language, and, according to certain researchers, implies a call for the genocide of Jews. This has led to suggestions that the October 7 attacks were an effort to fulfill this agenda.

# Operation Entebbe

**Operation Entebbe** was a counter-terrorist hostage-rescue mission carried out by commandos of the Israel Defense Forces (**IDF**) at **Entebbe airport in Uganda on 4 July 1976**. A week earlier, on 27 June, an Air France plane with 248 passengers was hijacked by a hijacker of the **Popular Front for the Liberation of Palestine – External Operations (PFLP-EO**) under orders of **Wadie Haddad**, who had earlier broken away from the mainstream PFLP of **George Habash**. The **PFLP-EO** hijackers consisted of two Palestinians and two members of the **German Revolutionary Cells**. The hijackers had the stated objective to free 40 Palestinian and pro-Palestinian militants imprisoned in Israel and 13 prisoners in four other countries in exchange for the hostages.

The local government supported the hijackers and **Dictator Idi Amin** personally welcomed them. After moving all hostages from the airplane to a disused airport building, the hijackers separated all Israelis from the larger group and forced them into a separate room. Over the following two days, **148 non-Israeli hostages** were released and flown out to Paris. **Some 94 mainly Israeli passengers, along with the 12-member Air France crew, remained as hostages and were threatened with death.** The **IDF** acted on intelligence provided by the Israeli intelligence agency **Mossad**. The hijackers threatened to kill the hostages if their prisoner release demands were not met. This threat led to the planning of the rescue operation.

The operation took place at night. Israeli transport planes carried **100 commandos** over 2,500 miles (4,000 km) to Uganda for the rescue operation. The operation, which took a week of planning, lasted 90 minutes. **102 hostages were rescued**. Five Israeli commandos were wounded and one, the **unit commander, Lt. Col. Yonatan Netanyahu, was killed**. **All the hijackers, three hostages and 45 Ugandan soldiers were killed,** and thirty (some say 11) Soviet-built MiG-17s and MiG-21s of Uganda's air force were destroyed. **Operation Entebbe**, which had the military codename **Operation Thunderbolt**, is sometimes referred to retroactively as **Operation Jonathan** in memory of the unit's leader, **Yonatan Netanyahu**. He was the older brother of **Benjamin Netanyahu**, the current Prime Minister of Israel.

## Hijacking

On 27 June 1976, **Air France Flight 139**, an Airbus A300B4-203, registration F-BVGG (c/n 019), departed from Tel Aviv, Israel, carrying 246 mainly Jewish and Israeli passengers, including four hijackers, waited to board at Athens airport, heading for Paris. Soon after the 12:30 pm takeoff, the flight was hijacked by two Palestinians from the **Popular Front for the Liberation of Palestine – External Operations (PFLP-EO),** and by two Germans, **Wilfried Bose and Brigitte Kuhlmann**, from the **German Revolutionary Cells**. The hijackers diverted the flight to Benghazi, Libya. There it was held on the ground for seven hours for refueling. During that time the hijackers released British-born Israeli citizen **Patricia Martell** who pretended to have a miscarriage. The plane left Benghazi, and at 3:15 pm on the 28th, more than 24 hours after the flight's original departure, it arrived at **Entebbe Airport in Uganda**.

## Hostage situation at Entebbe airport

At Entebbe, the four hijackers were joined by at least four others, supported by the forces of Uganda's President, **Idi Amin**. The hijackers transferred the passengers to the transit hall of the disused former airport terminal where they kept them under guard for the following days. **Amin** came to visit the hostages almost on a daily basis, updating them on developments and promising his efforts in having them freed through negotiations. On 28 June, a **PFLP-EO** hijacker issued a declaration and formulated their demands: In addition to a **ransom of $5 million USD** for the release of the airplane, they demanded the release of 53 Palestinian and Pro-Palestinian militants, 40 of whom were prisoners in Israel. **They threatened that if these demands were not met, they would begin to kill hostages on 1 July 1976.**

## Separation of hostages into two groups

On 29 June, after Ugandan soldiers had opened an entrance to a room next to the crowded waiting hall by destroying a separating wall, the hijackers separated the Israelis and told them to move to the adjoining room.

## Releases of most non-Israeli hostages

On 30 June, the hijackers **released 48 hostages** picked from among the non-Israeli group – mainly elderly and sick passengers and mothers with children. The hostage-takers extended their deadline to 4 July noon and released another group of 100 non-Israeli captives who again were flown out to Paris a few hours later. Among the 106 hostages staying behind with their captors at Entebbe airport were the 12 members of the Air France crew, about ten young French passengers, and the **Israeli group of some 84 people.**

## Operational planning

Many sources indicate that the Israeli cabinet was prepared to release Palestinian prisoners if a military solution seemed unlikely to succeed. The Israeli government also approached the US Government to deliver a message to Egyptian president **Anwar Sadat**, asking him to request **Amin** to release the hostages. This extension of the hostage deadline proved crucial to providing Israeli forces enough time to get to Entebbe. On 3 July at 18:30, the Israeli cabinet approved the rescue mission, presented by **Major General Yekutiel "Kuti" Adam and Brig. Gen. Dan Shomron. Shomron was appointed as the operation commander.**

## Attempts at a diplomatic solution

The Egyptian government under Sadat tried to negotiate with both the **PLO** and the Ugandan government. **PLO** chairman **Yasser Arafat** sent his political aide **Hani al-Hussan** to Uganda as a special envoy to negotiate with the hostage takers and with **Amin**. However, the **PFLP-EO** hijackers refused to see him.

## Raid preparation

When Israeli authorities failed to negotiate a political solution, they decided the only option was an attack to rescue the hostages.

## Aircraft refueling

While planning the raid, the Israeli forces had to figure out how to refuel the Lockheed C-130 Hercules aircraft they intended to use while en route to Entebbe. The Israelis lacked the logistical capacity to aerially refuel four to six aircraft so far from Israeli airspace. The raid could not proceed without assistance from at least one East African government. The Israeli government finally secured permission from **Kenya** for the **IDF** task force to cross Kenyan airspace and refuel at the **Jomo Kenyatta International Airport.**

Kenyan Minister of Agriculture **Bruce MacKenzie** persuaded Kenyan President **Kenyatta** to permit Israeli **Mossad** agents to gather information before the hostage rescue operation in Uganda, and to allow **Israeli Air Force** aircraft to land and refuel at a Nairobi airport after the rescue. In retaliation, Ugandan President **Idi Amin ordered Ugandan agents to assassinate MacKenzie, who was killed on 24 May 1978.** Later, **Mossad** Chief Director **Meir Amit** had a forest planted in Israel in MacKenzie's name.

## Hostage intelligence

**Mossad** built an accurate picture of the whereabouts of the hostages, the number of hijackers, and the involvement of Ugandan troops from the released hostages in Paris. While planning the military operation, the **IDF** erected a partial replica of the airport terminal with the help of civilians who had helped build the original. After **Betzer** collected intelligence and planned for several days, four Israeli Air Force c-130 Hercules transport aircraft secretly flew to Entebbe Airport at midnight without being detected by Entebbe air traffic control. **The Israeli ground task force numbered approximately 100 personnel.**

### Attack route

Taking off from **Sharm al-Sheikh**, the task force flew down the international flight path over the **Red Sea**, mostly flying at a height of no more than 30 m (100 ft) to avoid radar detection by Egyptian Sudanese, and Saudi Arabian forces. Near the south outlet of the Red Sea the C-130s turned south and passed south of **Djibouti**. From there, they went to a point northeast of Nairobi, Kenya, likely across Somalia and the Ogaden area of Ethiopia. They turned west, passing through the African Rift Valley and over **Lake Victoria**.

## Tow Boeing 707 jets followed the cargo planes.

The Israeli forces landed at Entebbe on July 3, at 23:00 IST, with their cargo bay doors already open. A **black Mercedes** that looked like **President Idi Amin**'s vehicle and **Land Rovers** that usually accompanied **Amin**'s Mercedes were brought along. The Israelis hoped they could use them to bypass security checkpoints. When the C-130s landed, Israeli assault team members drove the vehicles to the terminal building at the same fashion as **Amin**. As they approached the terminal, two Ugandan sentries, aware that **Idi Amin** had recently purchased a white Mercedes, ordered the vehicles to stop. The commandos shot the sentries using silenced pistols, but did not kill them. As they pulled away, however, an Israeli commando in one of the following Land Rovers killed them with an unsuppressed rifle.

## Hostage rescue

The Israelis sprang from their vehicles and burst towards the terminal. The hostages were in the main hall of the airport building directly adjacent to the runway. Entering the terminal, the commandos shouted through a megaphone, **"Stay down! Stay down! We are Israeli soldiers,"** in both Hebrew and English. Meanwhile, the other three C-130 Hercules had landed and unloaded armored personnel carriers to provide defense during the anticipated hour of refueling. **The Israelis then destroyed Ugandan MiG fighter planes** to prevent them from pursuing, and conducted a sweep of the airfield for intelligence-gathering.

## Departure

After the raid, the Israeli assault team returned to their aircraft and began loading the hostages. Ugandan soldiers shot at them in the process. The Israeli commandos returned fire with their AK47s, inflicting casualties on the Ugandans. During this brief but intense firefight, Ugandan soldiers fired from the Airport control tower. **Israeli commander Yonatan Netanyahu was shot in the chest and killed during combat with Ugandan soldiers.** He was the only Israeli commando killed in the operation. **At least five other commandos were wounded.**

The Israelis finished evacuating the hostages, loaded Netanyahu's body into one of the plans, and left Entebbe Airport. The entire operation lasted 53 minutes – of which the assault lasted only 30 minutes. All seven hijackers present, and between 33 and 45 Ugandan soldiers were killed. About 11 Ugandan Army Air Forde MiG-17 fighter planes were destroyed on the ground at Entebbe Airport. **The 102 rescued hostages were flown to Israel via Nairobi, Kenya, shortly after the raid.**

## Ugandan reaction

**Dora Bloch**, a 75-year-old Israeli who also held British citizenship, had been released by the hijackers due to illness and taken to Mulago Hospital in Kampala. After the raid she was killed by officers of the Ugandan army, as were some of her doctors and nurses, apparently for trying to intervene. **Amin also ordered the killing of hundreds of Kenyans living in Uganda in retaliation for Kenya's assistance to Israel in the raid.**

## Aftermath

UN Secretary General **Kurt Waldheim** told the Security Council that the raid was **"a serious violation of the sovereignty of a Member State of the United Nations".** The representative of Israel accused Uganda of direct complicity in the hijacking. A second resolution sponsored by Benin, Libya and Tanzania, that condemned Israel, was not put to the vote. Western nations spoke in support of the raid and United States offered significant praise, calling the Entebbe raid **"an impossible operation."** In private conversation with Israeli **Ambassador Dinitz, Henry Kissinger** sounded criticism for Israeli use of US equipment during the operation, but that criticism was not made public.

In the ensuing years, **Betser** and the Netanyahu brothers – **Iddo** and **Benjamin**, all Sayeret Matkal veterans – argued in increasingly public forums about who was to blame for the unexpected early firefight that caused Yonatan's death and partial loss of tactical surprise. As a result of the operation the United States military developed highly trained rescue teams modeled on the Entebbe rescue. **In a letter dated July 13, 1976, the Supreme Commander's Staff of the Imperial Iranian Armed Forces praised the Israeli commandos for the mission and extended condolences for "the loss and martyrdom" of Netanyahu.**

# Operation Wrath of God

**Operation "Wrath of God"** (Hebrew: מבצע זעם האל *Mivtza Za'am Ha'El*), also known as **Operation "Bayonet"**, was a covert operation directed by the **Mossad** to assassinate individuals involved in the **1972 Munich massacre** in which 11 members of the Israeli Olympic team were killed. The targets were members of the Palestinian armed militant group **Black September** and Palestine **Liberation Organization (PLO)** operatives. Authorized by Israeli Prime Minister **Golda Meir** in the autumn of 1972, the operation is believed to have continued for over twenty years. The operation was depicted in the television film *Sword of Gideon* **(1986) and Steven Spielberg's film** *Munich* **(2005).**

## History

Two days after the **Munich massacre** at the 1972 Summer Olympics, Israel retaliated by bombing ten **PLO** bases in Syria and Lebanon. **Prime Minister Golda Meir created Committee X**, a small group of government officials tasked with formulating an Israeli response, with herself and **Defense Minister Moshe Dayan** at the head. She also appointed **General Aharon Yariv** as her Advisor on Counterterrorism; he, along with **Mossad Director Zvi Zamir**, took the principal role in directing the ensuing operation. The committee came to the conclusion that, to deter future violent incidents against Israel, they needed to assassinate those who had supported or carried out the **Munich massacre**, and in dramatic fashion. Pressured by Israeli public opinion and top intelligence officials, **Meir** reluctantly authorized the beginning of the broad assassination campaign.

Yet when the three surviving perpetrators of the massacre were released just months later by **West Germany** in compliance with the demands of the hijackers of a Lufthansa aircraft, any remaining ambivalence she felt was removed. The committee's first task for Israeli intelligence was to draw up an assassination list of all those involved in **Munich**. This was accomplished with the aid of **PLO operatives working for Mossad**, and with information provided by friendly European intelligence agencies. While the contents of the entire list are unknown, reports put the final number of **targets at 20–35, a mix of Black September and PLO** elements. Once this was complete, **Mossad was charged with locating the individuals and assassinating them.**

Critical in the planning was the idea of plausible deniability, that it should be impossible to prove a direct connection between the assassinations and Israel. In addition, the operations were more generally intended to terrorize Palestinian militants. According to **David Kimche**, former deputy head of **Mossad, "The aim was not so much revenge but mainly to make them [the Palestinian terrorists] frightened. We wanted to make them look over their shoulders and feel that we are upon them. And therefore we tried not to do things by just shooting a guy in the street – that's easy...fairly."**

549

It is also known that **Mossad** agent **Michael Harari** led the creation and direction of the teams, although some may not have always been under government responsibility. **Author Simon Reeve** explains that the **Mossad** team – whose squad names are letters of the Hebrew alphabet – consisted of:

**...fifteen people divided into five squads: "Aleph", two trained killers; "Bet", two guards who would shadow the Alephs; "Het", two agents who would establish cover for the rest of the team by renting hotel rooms, apartments, cars, and so on; "Ayin", comprising between six and eight agents who formed the backbone of the operation, shadowing targets and establishing an escape route for the Aleph and Bet squads; and "Qoph", two agents specializing in communications.**

This is similar to former **Mossad** *Katsa* **Victor Ostrovsky's** description of **Mossad's** own assassination teams, the **Kidon**. In fact, **Ostrovsky** says in his book that it was **Kidon** units that performed the assassinations. This is supported by author **Gordon Thomas** who was given access to the debriefing reports submitted by the **eight Kidon and 80 member backup team that were involved in the assassinations.**

Another report by author **Aaron J. Klein** says that these teams were actually part of a unit called **Caesarea**, which would be renamed and reorganized into **Kidon** in the mid-1970s. **Harari** eventually commanded three Caesarea teams of around 12 members each. They were each further divided into logistics, surveillance, and assassination squads.

One of the covert teams was revealed in the aftermath of the **Lillehammer affair** (see **Ali Hassan Salameh** section below), when six members of the **Mossad** assassination team were **arrested by Norwegian authorities**. **Harari** escaped to Israel, and it is possible that others were able to evade capture with him. An article in *Time* **magazine** immediately after the killing put the total number of **Mossad** personnel at 15, which would also be similar to the above descriptions.

A markedly different account comes from the book *Vengeance,* where the author states that according to his source, **Mossad** set up a five-man unit of trained intelligence personnel which he [the source] led in Europe. The book also says that the team operated outside of direct government control, and that its only communications were with **Harari**. Several hours before each assassination, each target's family received flowers with a condolence card reading: **"A reminder we do not forget we do not forgive."**

## Operations: 1972–1988

The first assassination occurred on October 16, 1972, when **Palestinian Wael Zwaiter was killed in Rome. Mossad** agents had been waiting for him to return from dinner, and shot him twelve times. After the shooting, they were spirited away to a safe house. At the time **Zwaiter** was the **PLO** representative in Italy, and while Israel privately claimed he was a member of **Black September** and was involved in a **failed plot against an El Al airliner**, members of the **PLO** argued that he was in no way connected. **Abu Iyad, deputy-chief of the PLO,** stated that Zwaiter was "**energetically**" against terrorism.

The second target of **Mossad** was **Mahmoud Hamshari**, the **PLO** representative in France. Israel believed that he was the leader of **Black September** in France. Using an agent posing as an Italian journalist, **Mossad** lured him from his apartment in Paris to allow a demolition team to enter and install a bomb underneath a desk telephone. On December 8, 1972, the agent posing as a journalist phoned **Hamshari's** apartment and asked if he was speaking to **Hamshari.**

After **Hamshari** identified himself, the agent signaled to other colleagues, who then sent a detonation signal down the telephone line, causing the bomb to explode.

**Hamshari** was mortally wounded in the explosion, but managed to remain conscious long enough to tell Parisian detectives what had happened. **Hamshari died in a hospital several weeks later**. He had given an interview a day after the hostage crisis, saying he was not worried for his life, but did not want to "**taunt the devil.**" **Mossad** did not comment on the fact that **Hamshari** was connected to the attack of Munich. This assassination was the first in a series of **Mossad** assassinations that took place in France. Another assassination took place in London, where a Palestinian activist was pushed under a bus during rush hour.

On the night of January 24, 1973**, Hussein Al Bashir (Jordanian**), the **Fatah** representative in Cyprus, turned off the lights in his Olympic Hotel room in Nicosia. Moments later, a bomb planted under his bed was remotely detonated, killing him and destroying the room. Israel believed him to be the head of **Black September** in Cyprus, though another reason for his assassination may have been for his close ties with the **KGB.**

On April 6, 1973, **Basil al-Kubaissi**, a law professor at the American University of Beirut suspected by Israel of providing arms logistics for **Black September** as well as being involved in other Palestinian plots, was gunned down in Paris while returning home from dinner. As in previous assassinations, he was shot around 12 times by two **Mossad** agents.

Three of the targets on the **Mossad's** list lived in heavily guarded houses in Lebanon that were beyond the reach of previous assassination methods. In order to assassinate them, **Operation Spring of Youth** was launched as a sub-operation of the larger "**Wrath of God**" campaign. On the night of April 9, 1973, **Sayeret Matkal, Shayetet 13**, and **Sayeret Tzanhanim** commandos landed on the coast of Lebanon in Zodiac speedboats launched from Israeli Navy missile boats offshore. The commandos were met by **Mossad** agents, who drove them to their targets in cars rented the previous day, and later drove them back to the beaches for extraction. **The commandos were disguised as civilians, and some were dressed as women.**

In Beirut, they raided guarded apartment buildings and killed **Muhammad Youssef al-Najjar** (Operations leader in **Black September**), **Kamal Adwan** (a Chief of Operations in the **PLO**) and **Kamal Nasser** (**PLO** Executive Committee member and spokesman). During the operation, two Lebanese police officers, an Italian citizen, and **Najjar's** wife were also killed. One Israeli commando was wounded. **Sayeret Tzanhanim** paratroopers raided a six-story building that served as the headquarters of the **Popular Front for the Liberation of Palestine**. The paratroopers met strong resistance and lost two soldiers, but managed to destroy the building. **Shayetet 13** naval commandos and **Sayeret Tzanhanim** paratroopers also raided **PLO** arms-manufacturing facilities and fuel dumps. Some **12–100 PLO and PFLP members were killed during the attacks**.

Three attacks quickly followed the Lebanon operation. **Zaiad Muchasi**, the replacement for **Hussein Al Bashir** in Cyprus, was killed by a bomb in his Athens hotel room on April 11. Two minor **Black September** members, **Abdel Hamid Shibi and Abdel Hadi Nakaa**, were injured in their car in Rome.

**Mossad** agents also began to follow **Mohammad Boudia**, the Algerian-born director of operations for **Black September** in France, who was known for his disguises and womanizing. On June 28, 1973, **Boudia** was killed in Paris by a pressure-activated bomb packed with heavy nuts and bolts placed under his car seat. On December 15, 1979, two Palestinians, **Ali Salem Ahmed and Ibrahim Abdul Aziz**, were killed in Cyprus. According to police, both men were shot with silenced weapons at point-blank range.

On June 17, 1982, two senior **PLO** members in Italy were killed in separate attacks. **Nazeyh Mayer**, a leading figure in the **PLO**'s Rome office, was shot dead outside his home. **Kamal Husain**, deputy director of the **PLO** office in Rome, was killed by a shrapnel bomb placed under the back seat of his car as he drove home, less than seven hours after he had visited the home of Mayer and helped the police in their investigation.

On July 23, 1982, **Fadl Dani**, deputy director of the **PLO** office in Paris, was killed by a bomb that had been placed in his car. On August 21, 1983, **PLO** official **Mamoun Meraish** was killed in his car in Athens by two **Mossad** operatives who shot him from a motorcycle.

On June 10, 1986, **Khaled Ahmed Nazal**, Secretary-General of the **PLO**'s DFLP faction, was gunned down outside a hotel in Athens, Greece. **Nazal** was shot four times in the head. On October 21, 1986, **Munzer Abu Ghazala**, a senior **PLO** official and member of the **Palestinian National Council**, was killed by a bomb as he drove through a suburb of Athens. On February 14, 1988, a car bomb exploded in Limassol, Cyprus, killing Palestinians **Abu Al Hassan Qasim and Hamdi Adwan, and wounding Marwan Kanafami**.

## Ali Hassan Salameh

**Mossad** continued to search for **Ali Hassan Salameh**, nicknamed the **Red Prince**, who was the head of **Force 17 and the Black September** operative believed by Israel to be the mastermind behind the **Munich massacre**. This belief has since been challenged by accounts of senior **Black September** officials, who say that while he was involved in many attacks in Europe, **Salameh** was not at all connected with the events in Munich.

Almost a full year after Munich, **Mossad** believed they had finally located **Salameh** in the small **Norwegian town Lillehammer.** On July 21, 1973, in what would become known as the Lillehammer affair, a team of **Mossad** agents shot and killed **Ahmed Bouchiki**, a Moroccan waiter unrelated to the Munich attack and **Black September**, after an informant mistakenly identified **Bouchiki** as **Salameh**. **Six Mossad agents, including two women**, were arrested by local police, while others, including the team leader, **Michael Harari**, managed to escape back to Israel. Five of the captured were convicted of the killing and imprisoned, but were **released and returned to Israel in 1975**. **Victor Ostrovsky** claimed that **Salameh** was instrumental in leading **Mossad** off course by feeding it false information about his whereabouts.

In January 1974, **Mossad** agents covertly deployed to Switzerland after receiving information that **Salameh** would meet **PLO** leaders in a church on January 12. Two assassins entered the church at the time of the meeting, and encountered three men who appeared to be Arab. One of them made a move for his weapon, and all three were then immediately shot and killed.

The **Mossad** agents continued into the church to search for **Salameh**, but did not find him. In a short time, the decision was made to abort the mission and escape. Shortly afterward, three **Mossad** operatives travelled to London to meet with a source who offered information on **Salameh**. When the source failed to show up, the team members began suspecting they were under surveillance. **A female assassin-for-hire** seduced one of the agents in a hotel, then shot him dead in his hotel room. The **Mossad** team members located the woman in Amsterdam three months later, and she was killed near her home on August 21 after she instinctively reached for a weapon as the team approached her.

Local sources revealed that she was a **freelance assassin**, and it was never learned who exactly contracted her to kill the agent. The **Kidon** team leader was later reprimanded for acting outside the assigned scope of the mission. One of the team members said, **"Most of our victims plead for their lives before being killed but not this woman. She was different. She didn't plead. She looked us all directly in the eye with cold detached hatred. Her face reflected nothing but disdain and defiance before we killed her."**

Following the incident, operation commander **Michael Harari** ordered the mission to kill **Salameh** be aborted. The **Kidon** team, however, elected to ignore the order and try one more time to kill **Salameh**. Intelligence placed **Salameh** at a house in Tarifa, Spain. As three agents moved toward the house, they were approached by an Arab security guard. The guard raised an AK-47 assault rifle, and was immediately shot. The operation was aborted, and the team escaped to a safe house.

In the aftermath of the Lillehammer affair, international outrage prompted **Golda Meir to order the suspension of Operation "Wrath of God"**. The ensuing Norwegian investigation and revelations by the captured agents compromised **Mossad** assets across Europe, including safe houses, agents, and operational methods. **Five years later**, it was decided to recommence the operation under new **Prime Minister Menachem Begin**, and find those on the list still at large.

**Mossad** began surveillance of **Salameh**'s movements after tracking him to Beirut during late autumn of 1978. In November 1978, **a female Mossad agent** identifying herself as **Erika Chambers** entered Lebanon with a British passport issued in 1975, and rented an apartment on the Rue Verdun, a street frequently used by **Salameh**. Several other agents arrived, including two using the pseudonyms **Peter Scriver** and **Roland Kolberg**, traveling with British and Canadian passports respectively. Sometime after their arrival a Volkswagen packed with plastic explosives was parked along Rue Verdun within view of the rented apartment.

At 3:35 p.m. on January 22, 1979, as **Salameh** and four bodyguards drove down the street in a Chevrolet station wagon, the explosives in the Volkswagen were detonated from the apartment with a radio device, killing everyone in the vehicle. **After five unsuccessful attempts, Mossad had assassinated Salameh**. However, the blast also killed four innocent bystanders, including a British student and a German nun, and injured 18 other people in the vicinity. Immediately following the operation the **three Mossad officers fled without trace, as well as up to 14 other agents believed to have been involved in the operation**.

## Munich hostage-takers

Three of the eight terrorists that carried out the Munich massacre survived the botched German rescue attempt at Fürstenfeldbruck airbase on 6 September 1972 and were taken into German custody: **Jamal Al-Gashey, Adnan Al-Gashey, and Mohammed Safady.** On 29 October, they were released in exchange for the hostages onboard hijacked **Lufthansa Flight 615** and travelled to Libya, where they went into hiding.

It had been thought that **Adnan Al-Gashey and Mohammed Safady** were both assassinated by **Mossad** several years after the massacre; **Al-Gashey** was found after making contact with a cousin in a Gulf State, and **Safady** was found by remaining in touch with family in Lebanon. This account was challenged by **Aaron J. Klein**, who wrote that **Adnan** died of heart failure in the 1970s and that **Safady** was killed by Christian Phalangists in Lebanon in the early 1980s. However, in July 2005, **PLO** veteran **Tawfiq Tirawi** told Klein that **Safady**, whom **Tirawi** claimed as a close friend, was **"as alive as you are."** Jamal Al-Gashey went into hiding in North Africa, and is believed to be living in Tunisia; he last surfaced in 1999, when he granted an interview to director **Kevin MacDonald** for the documentary *One Day in September.*

## Other actions

Along with direct assassinations, **Mossad** used a variety of other means to respond to the **Munich massacre** and deter future terrorist action. **Mossad** engaged in a campaign of letter bombs against Palestinian officials across Europe. Historian **Benny Morris** writes that these attacks caused non-fatal injuries to their targets, which included persons in Algeria and Libya, Palestinian student activists in Bonn and Copenhagen, and a Red Crescent official in Stockholm. **Klein** also cites an incident in Cairo where a bomb malfunctioned, sparing the two Palestinian targets.

Former **Mossad** *Katsa* **Victor Ostrovsky** claimed that **Mossad** also used psychological warfare tactics such as running obituaries of still-living militants and sending highly detailed personal information to others. **Reeve** further stated that **Mossad** would call junior Palestinian officials, and after divulging to them their personal information, would warn them to disassociate from any Palestinian cause. British intelligence writer **Gordon Thomas** wrote that hours before each militant was killed, his family would receive flowers and a condolences card bearing the words **"A reminder we do not forget or forgive"**. **Thomas** further claimed that after each killing, **Mossad**'s psychological warfare department leaked notices about the dead militant to Arabic-language newspapers throughout the Middle East.

## Other assassinations

Several assassinations or assassination attempts have been attributed to the **"Wrath of God"** campaign, although doubt exists as to whether **Mossad** was behind them, with breakaway Palestinian factions being suspected of carrying them out. The first such assassination occurred on January 4, 1978, when **Said Hammami**, the **PLO** representative in London, was shot and killed. The assassination is suspected of being the work of either **Mossad** or the **Abu Nidal Organization**. On August 3, 1978, **Ezzedine Kalak**, chief of the **PLO**'s Paris bureau, and his deputy **Hamad Adnan**, were killed at their offices in the **Arab League** building.

Three other members of the **Arab League** and **PLO** staff were wounded. This attack was either the work of **Mossad** or the **Abu Nidal Organization.**

On July 27, 1979. **Zuheir Mohsen**, head of **PLO** military operations, was gunned down in Cannes, France, just after leaving a casino. Responsibility for the attack has been placed by various sources on **Mossad**, other Palestinians, and possibly Egypt. On June 1, 1981, **Naim Khader**, the **PLO** representative in Belgium, was assassinated in Brussels. Officials at the **PLO** information and liaison office in Brussels issued a statement accusing Israel of being behind the killing. **Abu Daoud**, a **Black September** commander who openly claimed to have helped plan the Munich attack, was shot multiple times on August 1, 1981 by a gunman in a Warsaw hotel cafe. **Daoud survived the attack.**

It is unclear whether this was done by **Mossad** or another breakaway Palestinian faction. **Daoud** claimed that the attack was carried out by a Palestinian double agent for **Mossad**, who was killed by the **PLO** ten years later. On March 1, 1982, **PLO** official **Nabil Wadi Aranki** was killed in Madrid. On June 8, 1992 **PLO** head of intelligence **Atef Bseiso** was shot and killed in Paris by two gunmen with suppressed weapons. While the **PLO** and a book by Israeli author **Aaron Klein** blamed **Mossad** for the killing, other reports indicate that the **Abu Nidal Organization** was behind it.

## Black September response

**Black September** did attempt and carry out a number of attacks and hostage takings against Israel. Similar to the **Mossad** letter-bomb campaign, dozens of letter bombs were sent from Amsterdam to Israeli diplomatic posts around the world in September and October 1972. One such attack **killed Ami Shachori, an Israeli Agricultural Counselor in Britain.**

## Attempted assassination of Golda Meir in Rome

A terrorist operation was planned by **Black September** when it learned that **Israeli Prime Minister Golda Meir** would be travelling to Rome to meet with **Pope Paul VI** in January 1973. The planned visit was placed under a regimen of strict secrecy in Israel, and news of the upcoming visit was probably leaked by a pro-Palestinian priest in the **Vatican Secretariat of State**. **Black September** commander **Ali Hassan Salameh began planning a missile attack against Meir's plane as it arrived in Rome**. **Salameh**'s goal was to kill not only **Meir**, but also key cabinet ministers and senior **Mossad** officers accompanying her.

At the time, **Salameh** was negotiating with the **Soviet Union**, asking for safe haven, and he hoped that by the time Israel recovered from this blow, he and his men would be in the Soviet Union and out of Israel's reach. **Black September** smuggled several shoulder-launched Strela 2 missiles to Bari, Italy, from Dubrovnik, Yugoslavia, by boat. The missiles were then smuggled to Rome and positioned around **Fiumicino Airport** shortly before **Meir**'s arrival. To divert **Mossad**'s vigilance away from Rome in the run-up to the attack, **Salameh planned a terrorist attack on the Israeli embassy in Bangkok, Thailand.**

On December 28, 1972, four **Black September** members took over the Israeli embassy in Bangkok, holding 12 hostages. They raised the **PLO** flag over the building, and threatened to kill the hostages unless 36 **PLO** prisoners were released. The building was surrounded by Thai troops and police. The option of a rescue operation was considered in Israel but ruled out. A rescue operation was considered a logistical impossibility, and it was also thought that as the embassy was in busy central Bangkok, the Thai government would never allow the possibility of a shootout to occur. Though their demands were not met, negotiations secured the release of all the hostages and the **Black September militants were given safe passage to Cairo**.

**Mossad** found out about the **plan to assassinate Golda Meir on January 14, 1973**, when a local volunteer informed **Mossad** that he had handled two telephone calls from a payphone in an apartment block where **PLO** members sometimes stayed. The calls were in Arabic, which he spoke. Speaking in code, the caller stated that it was "**time to deliver the birthday candles for the celebration**". **Mossad Director-General Zvi Zamir** was convinced that this was a coded order connected to an upcoming attack. **Zamir** had been convinced that the Bangkok embassy raid was a diversion for a larger attack, due to the participants in the raid having so easily given up, something he did not expect from a group as well-trained, financed, strategically cunning, and motivated as **Black September**.

**Zamir** further interpreted that "**birthday candles**" could refer to weapons, and the most likely one with a candle connotation was a rocket. **Zamir** linked the possible upcoming missile attack with **Meir**'s upcoming arrival, and guessed that **Black September** was planning to shoot down **Meir**'s plane. **Zamir then sent a Mossad *Katsa*,** or field intelligence officer, to Rome, and travelled to the city with a team of **Mossad** officers. **Zamir** met with the head of **DIGOS, the Italian anti-terrorism unit**, and laid out his concerns. **DIGOS** officers raided the apartment blocks from where the calls had been made, and found a Russian instruction manual for launching missiles. Throughout the night, **DIGOS** teams, each accompanied by a **Mossad *Katsa***, raided known **PLO** apartments, but found no evidence of any plot to kill **Meir**. In the morning, a few hours before **Meir**'s plane arrived, **Mossad** agents and Italian police surrounded **Fiumicino Airport**.

A **Mossad *Katsa*** spotted a Fiat van parked in a field close to the flight path. The agent ordered the driver to step out. The back door then flew open, and two militants opened fire. The agent returned fire, severely wounding both of them. The van was found to contain six missiles. The driver escaped on foot, and was pursued by the agent. He was captured as he tried to hijack a car driven by another patrolling **Mossad** operative. The driver was bundled into the car and taken to the truck that served as **Mossad**'s mobile command post, where he revealed the whereabouts of the second missile team after being severely beaten. The truck then sped off, heading north. A cafe-van with three missile launchers protruding from the roof was spotted.

The truck then rammed the van, turning it over, trapping the launch team inside and half-crushing them beneath the weight of the missiles, and turning the van's fixed launchers away from the sky. The unconscious driver was pulled from the van and tossed to the side of the road, and **DIGOS** was alerted that there had been "**an interesting accident they should look into**". **Zamir** briefly considered killing the Palestinian terrorists, but felt that their deaths would serve as an embarrassment to **Golda Meir**'s audience with the pope. The terrorists, who had been involved in the Munich massacre, **were taken to the hospital and eventually allowed to fly to Libya, but within months, all were killed by Mossad.**

## Assassinations of other Israelis and international officials

Two Israelis suspected of being intelligence agents were shot and killed, as well as an Israeli official in Washington. **Baruch Cohen**, a **Mossad** agent in Madrid, was killed on January 23, 1973 by a young Palestinian contact. **Mossad** then conducted a side operation to locate and kill Cohen's assassins, and at least three Palestinians involved in planning and carrying out Cohen's killing were assassinated. **Vittorio Olivares**, an Italian **El Al** employee suspected by **Black September**, was shot and killed in Rome in April 1973. The Israeli military attaché to the United States, **Colonel Yosef Alon**, was assassinated on July 1, 1973 in Chevy Chase, Maryland.

Alon's killer was never officially identified, and the FBI closed its investigation after failing to identify the culprits, but theorized that **Black September** was behind the assassination. **Fred Burton**, former deputy chief of the counterterrorism division of the U.S. State Department's Diplomatic Security Service and Vice-President of the private intelligence and consulting firm **Stratfor,** conducted an investigation and concluded that **Alon's** killer was a **Black September** operative who was killed by **Mossad** in 2011. **Ami Shachori**, an agriculture counselor working at the Israeli Embassy in London, was assassinated by **Black September** on September 19, 1973.

**Black September** conducted several other attacks only indirectly against Israel, including the seizure of Western diplomats in the Saudi embassy in Khartoum but **the group was officially dissolved by al-Fatah in December 1974.**

## Arab reaction

While the first wave of assassinations from October 1972 to early 1973 caused greater consternation among Palestinian officials, it was the raid on Lebanon – **Operation Spring of Youth in April 1973** – that truly shocked the Arab world. The audacity of the mission, plus the fact that senior leaders such as **Yasser Arafat, Abu Iyad and Ali Hassan Salameh** were only yards away from the fighting, contributed to the creation of the belief that Israel was capable of striking anywhere, anytime. It also brought about popular mourning. At the funerals for the victims of the raid, **half a million people came into the streets of Beirut. Nearly six years later, 100,000 people, including Arafat, turned out in the same city to bury Salameh.**

The operation also caused some of the less radical Arab governments to begin putting pressure on Palestinians to stop attacks against Israeli targets and threatened to pull support for the Palestinians if they used their passports during the course of attacks against Israel. As a result, some Palestinian militants began to instead use forged Israeli documents.

## Criticism

In his 2005 book *Striking Back*, author **Aaron Klein** – who says he based his book in large part on rare interviews with key **Mossad** officers involved in the reprisal missions – contends that **Mossad** got only one man directly connected to the massacre. The man, **Atef Bseiso**, was killed in Paris in 1992. Klein goes on to say that the intelligence on **Wael Zwaiter**, the first Palestinian to die, was **"uncorroborated and improperly cross-referenced. Looking back, his assassination was a mistake."** He elaborates, stating that the real planners and executors of Munich had gone into hiding along with bodyguards in the **Eastern Bloc** and Arab world, where Israel could not reach them. Most of those killed were minor Palestinian figures who happened to be wandering unprotected around Western Europe.

"Israeli security officials claimed these dead men were responsible for Munich; **PLO** pronouncements made them out to be important figures; and so the image of **Mossad** as capable of delivering death at will grew and grew." The operation functioned not just to punish the perpetrators of Munich but also to disrupt and deter future terrorist acts, writes Klein. "For the second goal, one dead **PLO** operative was as good as another." Klein quotes a senior intelligence source: **"Our blood was boiling. When there was information implicating someone, we didn't inspect it with a magnifying glass."**

**Abu Daoud**, one of the main planners of the Munich massacre, said in interviews before the release of the movie *Munich* that **"I returned to Ramallah in 1995, and Israel knew that I was the planner of the Munich operation."** The leader of **Black September**, Abu Iyad, was also not killed by Israel, although he was assassinated in 1991 in Tunis by the **Abu Nidal Organization**. Former **Mossad** chief **Zvi Zamir** has countered this in an interview in 2006, when he said that Israel was more interested in striking the **"infrastructure of the terrorist organizations in Europe"** than those directly responsible for Munich. **"We had no choice but to start with preventive measures."**

As the campaign continued, **relatives of the athletes killed at Munich were kept informed**. Simon **Reeve** writes that some felt vindicated, while others, including the wife of fencer **Andre Spitzer**, felt ambivalent. The wife of assassinated **Mossad** agent **Baruch Cohen** called the operation, especially a side operation directed against those who had murdered her husband, sickening. According to **Ronen Bergman** (security correspondent for the Israeli newspaper *Yediot Ahronoth* and expert on **Mossad**): **"This campaign stopped most PLO terrorism outside the borders of Israel. Did it help in any way to bring peace to the Middle East? No. Strategically it was a complete failure."**

Former *Katsa* **Victor Ostrovsky** has said that the direction **Meir** set **Mossad** on, namely that of focusing heavily on the people and operations of the **PLO**, took energy away from intelligence gathering on Israel's neighbors. **This led Mossad to miss the warning signs of the 1973 Yom Kippur War, which caught Israeli defenses by surprise.**

## In popular culture

The 1984 book *Vengeance,* by Canadian journalist **George Jonas**, tells the story of an Israeli assassination squad from the viewpoint of a self-described former **Mossad** agent and leader of the squad, **Avner. Avner** has since been claimed to be a pseudonym for **Yuval Aviv**, an Israeli who now runs a private investigation agency in New York.

However, **Jonas** denies that Aviv was his source for *Vengeance,* although the book has not been independently verified beyond the fact checking Jonas says he has done.

**Jonas** points to a former **Director General of the RCMP Security Service, John Starnes**, who he says believes his source's essential story In spite of this, **Mossad**'s director at the time of the operation, **Zvi Zamir**, has stated that he never knew Aviv. Several former **Mossad** officers who took part in **Operation "Wrath of God"** have also told British journalists that **Yuval Aviv's** version of events is not accurate.

After its 1984 publication the book was listed on the fiction and non-fiction bestseller lists in Britain. Since its release, two films have been based on *Vengeance*. In 1986, **Michael Anderson** directed the **HBO film *Sword of Gideon. ***Steven Spielberg** released a second movie based on the account in December 2005 entitled *Munich*. Both movies use **Yuval Aviv's** pseudonym "**Avner**" and take a certain amount of artistic license with his account.

# Orthodox Judaism

**Orthodox Judaism** is the collective term for the traditionalist branches of contemporary Judaism. Theologically, it is chiefly defined by regarding the **Torah** , both Written and Oral, as revealed by God to **Moses** on Mount Sinai and faithfully transmitted ever since.

**Orthodox Judaism**, therefore, advocates a strict observance of Jewish law, or *Halakha*, which is to be interpreted and determined exclusively according to traditional methods and in adherence to the continuum of received precedent through the ages. It regards the entire *halakhic* system as ultimately grounded in immutable revelation, essentially beyond external influence. Key practices are observing the **Sabbath**, eating kosher, and **Torah** study. Key doctrines include a future **Messiah** who will restore Jewish practice by building the temple in Jerusalem and gathering all the Jews to Israel, belief in a future bodily resurrection of the dead, divine reward and punishment for the righteous and the sinners.

**Orthodox Judaism** is not a centralized denomination. Relations between its different subgroups are sometimes strained, and the exact limits of **Orthodoxy** are subject to intense debate. Very roughly, it may be divided between **Ultra-Orthodox Judaism**, which is more conservative and reclusive; and **Modern Orthodox Judaism**, which is relatively open and to outer society as well as more liberal in practices and customs (The latter is more noticeable among American Jewish communities). These two are largely compared to Israel's Judaism sub-groups **(All-Orthodox affiliated)**: **haredim, datiim, masortiim**, and **hilonim**.

Each of those is itself formed of independent communities. Together, they are almost uniformly exclusionist, regarding **Orthodox** y not as a variety of Judaism, but as Judaism itself. While adhering to traditional beliefs, the movement is a modern phenomenon. It arose as a result of the breakdown of the autonomous Jewish community since the **18th century**, and was much shaped by a conscious struggle against the pressures of secularization and rival alternatives.

## Definitions

The earliest known mention of the term *Orthodox Jews* was made in the *Berlinische Monatsschrift* in 1795. The word *Orthodox* was borrowed from the general **German Enlightenment** discourse, and used not to denote a specific religious group, but rather those Jews who opposed **Enlightenment**. They themselves often disliked the alien, Christian name, preferring titles like **"Torah -true"** (*gesetztreu*), and often declared they used it only for the sake of convenience.

The **German Orthodox leader Rabbi Samson Raphael Hirsch** referred to **"the conviction commonly designated as Orthodox Judaism"**; in 1882, when **Rabbi Azriel Hildesheimer** became convinced that the public understood that his philosophy and Liberal Judaism were radically different, he removed the word *Orthodox* from the name of his **Hildesheimer Rabbinical Seminary**. By the 1920s, the term became common and accepted even in Eastern Europe, and remains as such.

**Orthodox** y perceives itself ideologically as the only authentic continuation of Judaism throughout the ages, as it was until the crisis of modernity; in many basic aspects, such as belief in the unadulterated divinity of the **Torah** or strict adherence to precedent and tradition when ruling in matters of **Jewish Law**, **Orthodox** y is indeed so. Its progressive opponents often shared this view, regarding it as a fossilized remnant of the past and lending credit to their own rivals' ideology.

"**Orthodoxization**" was a contingent process, drawing from local circumstances and dependent on the extent of threat sensed by its proponents: a sharply-delineated **Orthodox** identity appeared in Central Europe, in Germany and Hungary, by the 1860s; a less stark one emerged in Eastern Europe during the Interwar period.

While this was not rarely true, its defining feature was not the forbidding of change and **"freezing"** Jewish heritage in its tracks, but rather the need to adapt to being but one segment of Judaism in a modern world inhospitable to traditional practice. **Orthodox** y developed as a variegated **"spectrum of reactions"** – as termed by **Benjamin Brown** – involving in many cases much accommodation and leniency.

## Modernity crisis: *Jewish emancipation*

Until the latter half of the 18th century, Jewish communities in Central and Western Europe were autonomous entities, another estate in the corporate order of society, with their distinct privileges and obligations. They were led by the affluent wardens' class (*parnasim*), and judicially subject to rabbinical courts, which ruled in most civil matters. The Jews were but one of the groups affected: **Excommunication** was banned, and rabbinic courts lost almost all their jurisdiction. The state, especially since the **French Revolution**, was more and more inclined to tolerate the Jews only as a religious sect, not as an autonomous entity, and sought to reform and integrate them as **"useful subjects"**.

Jewish emancipation and equal rights were also discussed. Thus, the Christian (and especially Protestant) differentiation between **"religious"** and **"secular"** was applied to Jewish affairs, to which these concepts were traditionally alien. By the turn of the century, the weakened rabbinic establishment was facing masses of a new kind of transgressors: They could not be classified as tolerable sinners overcome by their urges (*khote le-te'avon*), or as schismatics like the **Sabbateans** or **Frankists**, against whom all communal sanctions were levied. **Rabbi Elazar Fleckeles**, who returned to Prague from the countryside in 1783, recalled that he first faced there **"new vices"** of principled irreverence towards tradition, rather than "**old vices**" like gossip or fornication.

In Hamburg, **Rabbi RaphaelCohen** attempted to reinforce traditional norms. **Cohen** ordered all the men in his community to grow a beard, forbade holding hands with one's wife in public, and decried women who wore wigs, instead of visible headgear, to cover their hair; **Cohen** taxed and otherwise persecuted members of the priestly caste who left the city to marry divorcees, men who appealed to state courts, those who ate food cooked by **Gentiles**, and other transgressors. Hamburg's Jews repeatedly appealed to the authorities, which eventually justified **Cohen**.

An ideological challenge to rabbinic authority, in contrast to prosaic secularization, appeared in the form of the *Haskalah* (Jewish **Enlightenment**) movement which came to the fore in 1782. **Hartwig Wessely, Moses Mendelssohn**, and other *maskilim* called for a reform of Jewish education, abolition of coercion in matters of conscience, and other modernizing measures. A bitter struggle ensued. Reacting to **Mendelssohn's** assertion that freedom of conscience must replace communal censure, **Rabbi Cohen of Hamburg** commented: The very foundation of the Law and commandments rests on coercion, enabling to force obedience and punish the transgressor. **Denying this fact is akin to denying the sun at noon.**

However, *maskilic'-rabbinic rivalry ended rather soon in most of Central Europe, as governments imposed modernization upon their Jewish subjects, without regard to either party. Schools replaced traditional* cheders, *and standard German began to supplant Yiddish. Differences between the establishment and the Enlightened became irrelevant, and the former often embraced the views of the latter (now antiquated, as more aggressive modes of acculturation replaced the* Haskalahs program). In 1810, when philanthropist Israel Jacobson opened what was later identified as the first **Reform** synagogue in Seesen, with modernized rituals, he encountered little protest.

## Hamburg Temple dispute

It was only the foundation of the **Hamburg Temple** in 1818 which mobilized the conservative elements. The organizers of the new Hamburg synagogue, who wished to appeal to acculturated Jews with a modernized ritual, openly defied not just the local rabbinic court that ordered them to desist but published learned tracts which castigated the entire rabbinical elite as hypocritical and obscurant. The **Temple**'s revised prayer book omitted or rephrased petitions for the coming of the **Messiah** and renewal of sacrifices (post factum, it was considered as the first **Reform** liturgy). Concerted backlash against **Reform** and the emergence of a self-aware conservative ideology, marks the beginning of **Orthodox Judaism**.

The leader and organizer of the **Orthodox camp** during the dispute, and the most influential figure in early **Orthodox** y, was **Rabbi Moses Sofer** of Pressburg, Hungary. Historian **Jacob Katz** regarded him as the first to fully grasp the realities of the modern age. **Sofer** understood that what remained of his political clout would soon disappear, and that he largely lost the ability to enforce observance; as **Katz** wrote, "**obedience to *Halakha* became dependent on recognizing its validity, and this very validity was challenged by those who did not obey**".

**Sofer's** response to the crisis of traditional Jewish society was unremitting conservatism, canonizing every detail of prevalent norms in the observant community lest any compromise legitimize the progressives' claim that the law was fluid or redundant. **Sofer** also awarded customs absolute validity, regarding them as uniformly equivalent to vows; he warned already in 1793 that even the **"custom of ignoramuses"** (one known to be rooted solely in a mistake of the common masses) was to be meticulously observed and revered. **Sofer** was frank and vehement about his conservative stance, stating during the Hamburg dispute that prayers in the vernacular were not particularly problematic, but he forbade them because they constituted an innovation.

He succinctly expressed his attitude in a wordplay he borrowed from the **Talmud**: "**The new (*Chadash*, originally meaning new grain) is forbidden by the Torah anywhere.**" Regarding the new, ideologically-driven sinners, **Sofer** commented in 1818 that they should have been anathemized and banished from the **People Israel** like the heretical sects of yore. But in 1822, three poor (and therefore traditional) members of the community, whose deceased apostate brother bequeathed them a large fortune, rose to the wardens' board. **Breisach** died soon after, and the Pressburg community became dominated by the conservatives. **Sofer** also possessed a strong base in the form of his yeshiva, **the world's largest** at the time, with hundreds of students.

A generation later, a self-aware **Orthodoxy** was already well entrenched in the country. Hungarian Jewry gave rise both to **Orthodoxy** in general, in a sense of a comprehensive response to modernity, and specifically to the traditionalist, militant **Ultra-Orthodoxy.** The 1818–1821 controversy also elicited a very different response, which first arose in its very epicenter. Severe protests did not affect the **Temple's** congregants, eventually leading the wardens of Hamburg's Jewish community to a comprehensive compromise for the sake of unity. They dismissed the elderly, traditional **Chief Dayan Baruch Oser** and appointed **Isaac Bernays**.

He was also forbidden from interfering in the **Temple's** conduct. Though conservative in the principal issues of faith, in aesthetic, cultural, and civil matters, **Bernays** was a reformer and resembled the **Temple** leaders. He forbade the **spontaNeous**, informal character of synagogue conduct typical of **Ashkenazi** tradition, and ordered prayers to be somber and dignified.

The combination of religious conservatism and embrace of modernity in everything else was emulated elsewhere, earning the epithet **"Neo-Orthodox y"**. Bernays and his like-minded followers, such as **Rabbi Jacob Ettlinger**, fully accepted the platform of the moderate *Haskalah*, which now lost its progressive edge. While old-style traditional life was still quite extant in Germany until the 1840s, rapid secularization and acculturation turned **Neo-Orthodox** y into the strict right-wing of German Jewry.

It was fully articulated by Bernays' disciples **Samson Raphael Hirsch** and **Azriel Hildesheimer**, active in mid-century. **Hirsch**, a Hamburg native who was ten during the **Temple** dispute, combined fierce **Orthodox** dogmatism and militancy against rival interpretations of Judaism, with leniency on many modern issues and an elated embrace of German culture. **Neo-Orthodoxy** also spread to other parts and Western Europe.

**Neo-Orthodox** y mostly did not attempt to thoroughly reconcile its conduct and traditional *halakhic* or moral norms (which, among others, banned **Torah** study for women). Rather, it adopted compartmentalization, de facto limiting Judaism to the private and religious sphere, while yielding to outer society in the public sphere. While conservative **Rabbi**s in Hungary still thought in terms of the now-lost communal autonomy, the **Neo-Orthodox** acknowledged, at least de facto, the **confessionalization** of Judaism under emancipation, turning it from an all-encompassing structure defining every aspect of one's life, into a private religious conviction.

## Wissenschaft des Judentums

In the late 1830s, modernist pressures in Germany shifted from the secularization debate, progressing even into the "**purely religious**" sphere of theology and liturgy. A new generation of young, modern university-trained rabbis (many German states already required communal rabbis to possess such education) sought to reconcile Judaism with the historical-critical study of scripture and the dominant philosophies of the day, especially **Kant** and **Hegel**. Influenced by the critical **"Science of Judaism"** (*Wissenschaft des Judentums*) pioneered by **Leopold Zunz**, and often in emulation of the **Liberal Protestant** milieu, they reexamined and undermined beliefs held as sacred in traditional circles, especially the notion of an unbroken chain from Sinai to the Sages. The more radical among the *Wissenschaft* rabbis, unwilling to either limit critical analysis or its practical application, coalesced around **Rabbi Abraham Geiger** to establish the full-fledged **Reform Judaism**. Between 1844 and 1846, Geiger organized three rabbinical synods in Braunschweig, Frankfurt and Breslau, to determine how to refashion Judaism in present times. The tone of the undersigned varied considerably along geographic lines: letters from the traditional societies in Eastern Europe and the **Ottoman Empire**, implored local leaders to petition the authorities and have them ban the movement. Signatories from Central and Western Europe used terms commensurate with the liberal age.

The struggle with *Wissenschaft* criticism profoundly shaped the **Orthodox**. For centuries, **Ashkenazi** rabbinic authorities espoused Nahmanides' position that the **Talmud**ic exegesis, which derived laws from the **Torah** 's text by employing complex hermeneutics, was binding *d'Oraita*. **Geiger** and others presented exegesis as an arbitrary, illogical process, and consequently defenders of tradition embraced **Maimonides'** marginalized claim that the **Sages** merely buttressed already received laws with biblical citations, rather than actually deriving them through exegesis. As **Jay Harris** commented:

**"An insulated orthodox, *or, rather, traditional* rabbinate, feeling no pressing need to defend the validity of the Oral Law, could confidently appropriate the vision of most medieval rabbinic scholars; a defensive German Orthodox y, by contrast, could not. ... Thus began a shift in understanding that led Orthodox rabbis and historians in the modern period to insist that the *entire* Oral Law was revealed by God to Moses at Sinai."**

*Wissenschaft* posed a greater challenge to the modernized **Neo-Orthodox** than to insulated traditionalist. Hirsch and Hildesheimer were divided on the matter, basically anticipating all modernist **Orthodox** attitudes to the historical-critical method. **Hildesheimer** consented to research under limits, subjugating it to the predetermined sanctity of the subject matter and accepting its results only when they did not conflict with the latter.

**Hildesheimer's** approach was emulated by his disciple **Rabbi David Zvi Hoffmann**, who was both a scholar of note and a consummate apologetic. His polemic against the **Graf-Wellhausen** hypothesis (**Hoffman** declared that for him, the unity of the **Pentateuch** was a given, regardless of research) remains the classical **Orthodox** response to Higher Criticism. **Hirsch** often lambasted Hoffman for contextualizing rabbinic literature. All of them stressed ceaselessly the importance of dogmatic adherence to *Torah min ha-Shamayim*, which led them to conflict with **Rabbi Zecharias Frankel,** Chancellor of the **Jewish Theological Seminary** of Breslau.

Unlike the **Reform** camp, **Frankel** both insisted on strict observance and displayed great reverence towards tradition. But though regarded with much appreciation by many conservatives, his keen practice of *Wissenschaft* made him a suspect in the eyes of **Hirsch** and **Hildesheimer**. They demanded again and again that he unambiguously state his beliefs concerning the nature of revelation.

In 1859, **Frankel** published a critical study of the **Mishnah**, and casually added that all commandments classified as "**Law given to Moses at Sinai**" were merely ancient customs accepted as such (he broadened **Asher ben Jehiel's** opinion). **Hirsch** and **Hildesheimer** seized the opportunity and launched a prolonged public campaign against him, accusing him of heresy. Concerned that public opinion regarded both **Neo-Orthodox** y and **Frankel's** "**Positive-Historical School**" centered at Breslau as similarly observant and traditionalist, the two stressed that the difference was dogmatic and not *halakhic.*

They managed to tarnish **Frankel's** reputation in the traditional camp and make him illegitimate in the eyes of many. The **Positive-Historical School** is regarded by **Conservative Judaism** as an intellectual forerunner. While **Hildesheimer** cared to distinguish between **Frankel's** observant disciples and the proponents of **Reform**, he wrote in his diary: *how meager is the principal difference between the Breslau School, who don silk gloves at their work, and Geiger who wields a sledgehammer.*

# Communal schism

During the 1840s in Germany, as traditionalists became a clear minority, some **Orthodox** rabbis, like Salomo Eger of Posen, urged to adopt **Moses Sofer**'s position and anathemize the principally nonobservant. Eating, worshipping or marrying with them were to be banned. **Rabbi Jacob Ettlinger,** whose journal *Treue Zionswächter* was the first regular **Orthodox** newspaper (signifying the coalescence of a distinct **Orthodox** milieu), refused to heed their call. **Ettlinger,** and German **Neo-Orthodox** y in his steps, chose to regard the modern secularized Jew as a transgressor and not as a schismatic.

He adopted **Maimonides'** interpretation of the **Talmud**ic concept *tinok shenishba* (captured infant), a Jew by birth who was not raised as such and therefore could be absolved for not practicing the Law, and greatly expanded it to serve the **Orthodox** need to tolerate the nonobservant majority (many of their own congregants were far removed from strict practice).

The progressives viewed him as too conservative. After just four years of constant strife, he utterly lost faith in the possibility of reuniting the broad Jewish public. In 1851, a small group in Frankfurt am Main which opposed the **Reform** character of the Jewish community turned to **Hirsch**. He led them for the remainder of his life, finding Frankfurt an ideal location to implement his unique ideology, which amalgamated acculturation, dogmatic theology, thorough observance and now also strict secessionism from the **non-Orthodox**. In the very same year, **Hildesheimer** set out for Hungary.

Confounded by rapid urbanization and acculturation – which gave rise to what was known as "**Neology**", a nonobservant laity served by rabbis who mostly favoured the **Positive-Historical** approach – the elderly local rabbis at first welcomed **Hildesheimer**. The rabbi of **Eisenstadt** believed that only a full-fledged modern rabbinical seminary will serve to fulfill his **Neo-Orthodox** agenda. In the 1850s and 1860s, however, a radical reactionary **Orthodox** party coalesced in the backward northeastern regions of Hungary. Led by **Rabbi Hillel Lichtenstein**, his son-in-law **Akiva Yosef Schlesinger** and decisor **Chaim Sofer**, the "**zealots**" were deeply shocked by the demise of the traditional world into which they were born.

**Lichtenstein** ruled out any compromise with modernity, insisting of maintaining **Yiddish** and traditional dress; they considered the **Neologs** as already beyond the pale of Judaism, and were more concerned with **Neo-Orthodoxy,** which they regarded as a thinly-veiled gateway for a similar fate. **Chaim Sofer** summarized their view of **Hildesheimer**: *The wicked Hildesheimer is the horse and chariot of the Evil Inclination... All the heretics in the last century did not seek to undermine the Law and the Faith as he does.*

Michael Silber wrote: *These issues, even most of the religious reforms, fell into gray areas not easily treated within* **Halakha**. *It was often too flexible or ambiguous, at times silent, or worse*

567

*yet, embarrassingly lenient.* Schlesinger was forced to venture outside of normative law, into the mystical writings and other fringe sources, to buttress his ideology. In 1865, the **Ultra-Orthodox** convened in **Nagymihály** and issued a ban on various synagogue reforms, intended not against the **Neologs** but against developments in the **Orthodox** camp, especially after Samuel **Sofer** violated his father's expressed ban and instituted German-language sermons in Pressburg.

The internal **Orthodox** division was conflated by growing tension with the **Neologs.** In 1869, the Hungarian government convened a **General Jewish Congress** which was aimed at creating a national representative body. Fearing **Neolog** domination, the **Orthodox** seceded from the Congress and appealed to Parliament in the name of religious freedom – this demonstrated a deep internalization of the new circumstances; just in 1851, **Orthodo leader Meir Eisenstaedter** petitioned the authorities to restore the coercive powers of the communities. In 1871 the government recognized a separate **Orthodox** national committee.

Adam Ferziger stressed that *membership and loyalty to one of the respective organizations, rather than beliefs and ritual behavior, emerged as the definitive manifestation of Jewish identity.* The Hungarian schism was the most radical internal separation among the Jews of Europe. **Hildesheimer** left back to Germany soon after, disillusioned though not as pessimistic as **Hirsch**. In 1877 **Hirsch** withdrew his congregation from the Frankfurt community and decreed that all the **Orthodox** should do the same. However, even in Frankfurt he encountered dismissal. Unlike the **heteroge Neous** communities of Hungary, which often consisted of recent immigrants, Frankfurt and most German communities were close-knit.

The vast majority of the 15%–20% of German Jews affiliated with **Orthodox** institutions cared little for the polemic, and did not secede due to prosaic reasons of finance and familial relations. Only a handful of Secessionist, *Austrittorthodox*, communities were established in the **Reich**; almost everyone remained as **Communal Orthodox** *Gemeindeortodox,* within Liberal mother congregations.

The organ – a symbol of **Reform** in Germany since 1818, so much that **Hildesheimer** seminarians had to sign a declaration that they will never serve in a synagogue which introduced one – was accepted (not just for weekday use but also on the Sabbath) with little qualm by the French Consistoire in 1856, as part of a series of synagogue regulations passed by **Chief Rabbi Salomon Ulmann.** Even **Rabbi Solomon Klein** of Colmar, the leader of Alsatian conservatives who partook in the castigation of **Zecharias Frankel**, had the instrument in his community.

In England, **Rabbi Nathan Marcus Adler's United Synagogue** shared a very similar approach: It was vehemently conservative in principle and combated ideological reformers, yet served a nonobservant public – as **Todd Endelman** noted, *While respectful of tradition, most English-born Jews were not orthodox in terms of personal practice. Nonetheless they were content to* *remain within an orthodox congregational framework* – **and introduced considerable synagogue reforms.**

## Eastern Europe

The much belated pace of modernization in Russia, Congress Poland and the Romanian principalities, where harsh discrimination and active persecution of the **Jews** continued until 1917. The defining fault-line of Eastern European Jews was between the **Hasidim** and the *Misnagdic* reaction against them. **Reform** attempts by the Czar's government, like the school modernization under **Max Lilienthal** or the foundation of rabbinical seminaries and the mandating of communities to appoint clerks known as **"official rabbis"**, all had little influence.

In 1880, there were only 21,308 Jewish pupils in government schools, out of some **5 million Jews** in total; In 1897, 97% of the 5.2 million Jews in the Pale of Settlement and Congress Poland declared **Yiddish** their mother tongue, and only 26% possessed any literacy in Russian. The leading rabbis maintained the old conception of communal unity: In 1882, when an **Orthodox** party in Galicia appealed for the right of secession, the **Netziv** and other Russian rabbis declared it forbidden and contradicting the idea of Israel's oneness.

While slow, change was by no means absent. In the 1860s and 1870s, anticipating a communal disintegration like the one in the west, moderate *maskilic* rabbis like **Yitzchak Yaacov Reines** and **Yechiel Michel Pines** called for inclusion of secular studies in the *heders* and *yeshivas*, a careful modernization, and an ecumenical attempt to form a consensus on necessary adaptation of *Halakha* to novel times.

The attitude toward Jewish nationalism, particularly **Zionism**, and its nonobservant if not staunchly secularist leaders and partisans, was the key question facing the traditionalists of Eastern Europe. Closely intertwined were issues of modernization in general: As noted by **Joseph Salmon**, the future religious Zionists (organized in the **Mizrahi** since 1902) were not only supportive of the national agenda per se, but deeply motivated by criticism of the prevalent Jewish society, a positive reaction to modernity and a willingness to tolerate nonobservance while affirming traditional faith and practice.

In 1900, the anti-Zionist pamphlet *Or la-Yesharim*, endorsed by many Russian and Polish rabbis, largely demarcated the lines between the **proto-*Haredi*** majority and the **Mizrahi** minority, and terminated dialogue; in 1911, when the 10th **World Zionist Congress** voted in favor of propagating non-religious cultural work and education, a large segment of the **Mizrahi** seceded and joined the **anti-Zionists**.

In 1907, Eastern European **proto-*Haredi*** elements formed the **Knesseth** Israel party, a modern framework created in recognition of the deficiencies of existing institutions. It dissipated within a year. German **Neo-Orthodox** y, in the meantime, developed a keen interest in the traditional Jewish masses of Russia and Poland. The German secessionists already possessed a platform of their own, the *Freie Vereinigung für die Interessen des Orthodox en Judentums*, founded by **Samson Raphael Hirsch** in 1885.

In 1912, two German **FVIOJ** leaders, Isaac Breuer and Jacob Rosenheim, managed to organize a meeting of 300 seceding **Mizrahi**, **proto-*Haredi*** and secessionist **Neo-Orthodox** delegate in Katowice, creating the *Agudath Israel* **party**.

The **Agudah** immediately formed its Council of **Torah** Sages as supreme rabbinic leadership body. Many **Ultra**-traditionalist elements in Eastern Europe, like the Belz and **Lubavitch Hasidim**, refused to join, viewing the movement as a dangerous innovation; and the organized **Orthodox** in Hungary rejected it as well, especially after it did not affirm a commitment to communal secession in 1923. In the 1930s, it was estimated that no more than 20%–33% of Poland's Jews, the last stronghold of traditionalism where many were still living in rural and culturally-secluded communities, could be considered strictly observant.

Eastern European **Orthodox** y, whether **Agudah** or **Mizrahi**, always preferred cultural and educational independence to communal secession, and maintained strong ties and self-identification with the general Jewish public. Within its ranks, the 150-years-long struggle between **Hasidim** and **Misnagdim** was largely subsided; the latter were even dubbed henceforth as "Litvaks", as the anti-Hasidic component in their identity was marginalized. In the interwar period, **Rabbi Yisrael Meir Kagan** emerged as the popular leader of the Eastern European **Orthodox**, particularly the **Agudah-leaning**.

## United States

American Jewry of the 19th century, small and lacking traditional institutions or strong rabbinic presence due to its immigrant-based nature, was a hotbed of religious innovation. In the mid-19th century, **Reform Judaism** spread rapidly, advocating a formal relinquishment of traditions very few in the secularized, open environment observed anyhow; the United States would be derisively named the *Treife Medina*, or **"Profane Country"**, in **Yiddish**.

In 1845 he introduced the words "**Orthodox** " and "**Orthodox** y" into the American Jewish discourse, in the sense of opposing **Reform**; while admiring **Samson Raphael Hirsch**, Leeser was an even stauncher proponent of **Zecharias Frankel,** whom he considered the "**leader of the Orthodox party**" at a time when **Positive-Historical** and **Orthodox** positions were barely discernible from each other to most observers (in 1861, Leeser defended **Frankel** in the polemic instigated by **Hirsch**).

Even before that, in 1897, an old-style *yeshiva*, **RIETS**, was founded in New York. Eventually, its students rebelled in 1908, demanding a modern rabbinic training much like that of their peers in **JTS**. In 1915, **RIETS** was reorganized as a decidedly **Modern Orthodox** institution, and a merger with the JTS was also discussed. In 1923, the **Rabbinical Council of America** was established as the clerical association of the **OU**. Typical of these was **Rabbi Aaron Kotler**, who established Lakewood Yeshiva in New Jersey during 1943.

Lakewood pioneered the **homogeNeous**, voluntary and **enclavist** model of postwar *Haredi* communities, which were independent entities with their own developing subculture. "**Conservative Judaism**", now adopted as an exclusive label by most **JTS** graduates and **RA** members, became a truly distinct movement. In 1950, the Conservatives signaled their break with **Orthodox *halakhic*** authorities, with the acceptance of a far-reaching legal decision, which allowed one to drive to the synagogue and to use electricity on **Sabbath.**

## Theology: Orthodox attitudes

A definite and conclusive credo was never formulated in Judaism; the very question whether it contains any equivalent of dogma is a matter of scholarly controversy. However, while lacking a uniform doctrine, **Orthodox Judaism** is basically united in affirming several core beliefs, disavowal of which is considered major blasphemy. As in other aspects, **Orthodox** positions reflect the mainstream of traditional **Rabbi**nic Judaism through the ages.

Attempts to codify these beliefs were undertaken by several medieval authorities, including **Saadia Gaon** and **Joseph Albo**. Each composed his own creed. Yet, the 13 principles expounded by **Maimonides** in his ***Commentary on the Mishna***, authored in the 1160s, eventually proved the most widely accepted. Albo listed merely three fundamentals, and did not regard the **Messiah** as a key tenet – the exact formulation, and the status of disbelievers (whether mere errants, or heretics who can no longer be considered part of the **People Israel**) were contested by many of **Maimonides'** contemporaries and later sages. But in recent centuries, the **13 Principles** became standard, and are considered binding and cardinal by **Orthodox** authorities in a virtually universal manner.

In the modern era, the prestige of both suffered severe blows, and "**naive faith**" became popular. At a time when excessive contemplation in matters of belief was associated with secularization, luminaries such as **Yisrael Meir Kagan** stressed the importance of simple, unsophisticated commitment to the precepts passed down from the **Beatified Sages**. This is still the standard in the **Ultra-Orthodox** world.

## *God in Judaism*

**Orthodox Judaism adheres to monotheism, the belief in one God**. The basic tenets of **Orthodox** y, drawn from ancient sources like the **Talmud** as well as later sages, prominently and chiefly include the attributes of God in Judaism. This basis is evoked in many foundational texts, and is repeated often in the daily prayers, such as in Judaism's creed-like **Shema Yisrael**: **"Hear, O Israel, the Lord is our God, the Lord is One."**

**Maimonides** delineated this understanding of a monotheistic, personal God in the opening six articles of his thirteen. The six concern God's status as the sole creator, his oneness, his impalpability, that he is first and last, that God alone, and no other being, may be worshipped, and that he is omniscient. **Maimonides** and virtually all sages in his time and since then also stressed that the creator is incorporeal, lacking **"any semblance of a body"**; while almost taken for granted since the Middle Ages, **Maimonides** and his contemporaries noted that anthropomorphic conceptions of God were quite common in their time.

The Kabbalists asserted that while God himself is beyond the universe, he progressively unfolds into the created realm via a series of inferior emanations, or **sefirot**, each a refraction of the perfect godhead. In modern times it is upheld, at least tacitly, in many traditionalist **Orthodox** circles, while **Modern Orthodox** y mostly ignores it without confronting the notion directly.

## Revelation

The defining doctrine of **Orthodox Judaism** is the belief that the **Torah ("Teaching" or "Law"),** both the written scripture of the **Pentateuch** and the oral tradition explicating it, was revealed by God to **Moses** on Mount Sinai, and that it was transmitted faithfully from Sinai in an unbroken chain ever since. One of the foundational texts of rabbinic literature is the list opening the Ethics of the Fathers, enumerating the sages who received and passed on the **Torah** , from **Moses** through **Joshua,** the **Elders,** and **Prophets,** and then onward until **Hillel the Elder** and **Shammai.** This core belief is referred to in classical sources as **"The Law/Teaching is from the Heavens"** (**Torah min HaShamayim**).

One clause in the Jerusalem **Talmud** asserts that anything which a veteran disciple shall teach was already given at Sinai; and a story in the Babylonian **Talmud** claims that upon seeing the immensely intricate deduction of future **Rabbi Akiva** in a vision, **Moses** himself was at loss, until Akiva proclaimed that everything he teaches was handed over to **Moses**. The Written and **Oral Torah** are believed to be intertwined and mutually reliant, for the latter is a source to many of the divine commandments, and the text of the **Pentateuch** is seen as incomprehensible in itself. God's will may only be surmised by appealing to the Oral **Torah** revealing the text's allegorical, anagogical, or tropological meaning, not by literalist reading.

One of the primary intellectual exercises of **Torah** scholars is to locate discrepancies between **Talmud**ic or other passages and then demonstrate by complex logical steps (presumably proving each passage referred to a slightly different situation etc.) that there is actually no contradiction. Like other traditional, non-liberal religions, **Orthodox Judaism** considers revelation as propositional, explicit, verbal and unambiguous, that may serve as a firm source of authority for a set of religious commandments. An important ramification of *Torah min HaShamayim* in modern times is the reserved, and often totally rejectionist, attitude of **Orthodoxy** toward the historical-critical method, particularly higher criticism of the **Bible**.

## *Jewish eschatology*

Belief in a future **Messiah** is central to **Orthodox Judaism**. According to this doctrine, a king will arise from King David's lineage, and will bring with him signs such as the restoration of the **Temple**, peace, and universal acceptance of the God of Israel. The **Messiah** will embark on a quest to gather all Jews to the Holy Land, will proclaim prophethood, and will restore the Davidic Monarchy. Classical Judaism did incorporate a tradition of belief in the resurrection of the dead. There is scriptural basis for this doctrine, quoted by the **Mishnah**: "**All Israelites have a share in the World-to-Come, as it is written:** *And your people, all of them righteous, Shall possess the land for all time; They are the shoot that I planted, My handiwork in which I glory* **(Isa 60:21).**" The **Mishnah** also brands as heretics any Jew who rejects the doctrine of resurrection or its origin from the **Torah**. Those who deny the doctrine are deemed to receive no share in the **World-to-Come.**

There are other passing references to the afterlife in Mishnaic tractates. A particularly important one in *Berakhot* informs that the Jewish belief in the afterlife was established long before the compilation of the **Mishnah** Biblical tradition categorically mentions **Sheol sixty-five** times. Numbers 16:30 states that **Korah went into Sheol alive**, to describe his death in divine retribution. The **Talmud**ic discourse expanded on the details of the **World to Come**. This was to motivate Jewish compliance with their religious codes. In brief, the righteous will be rewarded with a place in **Gan Eden**, the wicked will be punished in **Gehinnom**, and the resurrection will take place in the Messianic age.

## Law, custom, and tradition

As long as both contesting parties base their arguments according to received hermeneutics and precedents and are driven by sincere faith, *both these and those are the words of the Living God* (this **Talmud**ic statement is originally attributed to a divine proclamation during a dispute between the **House of Hillel** and **House of Shammai**). The most basic form of *halakhic* discourse is the **responsa** literature, in which rabbis answered questions directed from commoners or other rabbis, thus setting precedent for the next generations.

The system's oldest and most basic sources are the Mishna and the two **Talmud**s, to which were added the later commentaries and novellae of the **Geonim**. Those were followed by the great codes which sought to assemble and standardize the laws, including **Rabbi Isaac Alfasi's** *Hilchot HaRif*, Maimonides' *Mishneh Torah* , and **Rabbi Asher ben Jehiel's** work (colloquially called *the Rosh*). These three works in particular were the main basis of **Rabbi Jacob ben Asher's**

*Arba'ah Turim*, which in turn became the basis of one of the latest and most authoritative codifications - the 1565 *Shulchan Aruch*, or "Set Table", by **Rabbi Joseph Karo**.

**Maimonides** stated that absolute obedience to rabbinic decrees is stipulated by the verse *and thou shalt observe*, while **Nachmanides** argued that such severeness is unfounded – though such enactments are accepted as binding, albeit less than the divine commandments. A **Talmud**ic maxim states that when in doubt regarding a matter *d'Oraita*, one must rule strenuously, and leniently when it concerns *d'Rabanan.*

Many arguments in *halakhic* literature revolve over whether any certain detail is derived from the former or the latter source, and under which circumstances. Commandments or prohibitions *d'Rabanan*, though less stringent than *d'Oraita* ones, are an equally important facet of Jewish law. They range from the 2nd century BCE establishment of **Hanukkah**, to the bypassing on the Biblical ban on charging interest via the **Prozbul**, and up to the 1950 standardization of marital rules by the **Chief Rabbinate of Israel** which forbade polygamy and levirate marriage even in communities which still practiced those.

**Ashkenazi**m, **Sephardim**, **Teimanim**, and others have different prayer rites, somewhat different kosher emphases (for example, since the 12th century at least, it became an **Ashkenazi** custom not to consume legumes in Passover), and numerous other points of distinction. So do, for example, Hasidic Jews and non-Hasidic (**"Yeshivish"** or **"Litvish"**) ones, though both originate from Eastern Europe. Eating in the **Sukkah** on **Shemini Atzeret** is an area where *Minhag* varies; likewise, how to accommodate the idea of eating some dairy on **Shavuos**. The influence of custom even elicited the complaint of scholars who noted that the common masses observe *Minhag,* yet ignore important divine decrees.

## Rabbinic authority

**Rabbi**nic leadership, assigned with implementing and interpreting the already accumulated tradition, changed considerably in recent centuries, marking a major difference between **Orthodox** and pre-modern Judaism. Since the demise of the **Geonim**, who led the Jewish world up to 1038, *Halakha* was adjudicated locally, and the final arbiter was mostly the **communal rabbi, the** *Mara d'Athra* **(Master of the Area)**.

Their influence varies considerably: In conservative **Orthodox** circles, mainly **Ultra-Orthodox** (**Haredi**) ones, rabbis possess strong authority, and exercise their leadership often. Bodies such as the Council of **Torah** Sages, **Council of Torah Luminaries**, the **Central Rabbinical Congress**, and the **Orthodox Council** of Jerusalem are all considered, at least in theory, as the supreme arbiters in their respective communities.

## Daily life

**Orthodox Judaism** emphasizes practicing rules of **kashrut, Shabbat**, family purity, and **tefilah** (daily prayer). Many **Orthodox** Jews can be identified by their manner of dress and family lifestyle. **Orthodox** men and women dress modestly by keeping most of their skin covered. Married women cover their hair, with scarves (tichel), snoods, turbans, hats, berets, or wigs.

**Orthodox** Jews also follow the **laws of negiah**, which means "**touch**". **Orthodox men and women do not engage in physical contact with those of the opposite sex outside of their spouse,** or immediate family members (such as parents, grandparents, siblings, children, and grandchildren). *Kol Isha* is the prohibition of a woman's (singing) voice to a man (except as per **negiah**).

## Demographics

Professors **Daniel Elazar** and **Rela Mintz Geffen**, according to calculations in 1990, assumed there to be at least 2,000,000 observant **Orthodox** Jews worldwide in 2012, and at least 2,000,000 additional nominal members and supporters who identified as such. These figures made **Orthodoxy** the largest Jewish religious group. Originally, **Elazar** produced an even higher estimate when he considered association by default and assumed higher affiliation rates, reaching a maximum of 5,500,000 that may be considered involved with **Orthodox** y.

In the State of Israel, where the total Jewish population is about 6.5 million, 22% of all Jewish respondents to a 2016 **PEW** survey declared themselves as observant **Orthodox** (9% *Haredim*, or **"Ultra-Orthodox** ", 13% *Datiim*, "**religious**"). 29% described themselves as "**traditional**", a label largely implying little observance, but identification with **Orthodox** y. The second largest **Orthodox** concentration is in the United States, mainly in the Northeast and specifically in New York and New Jersey.

A 2013 PEW survey found that 10% of respondents identify as **Orthodox**, in a total Jewish population of at least 5.5 million. 3% were **Modern Orthodox**, 6% were **Ultra-Orthodox**, and 1% were "**other**" (Sephardic, liberal **Orthodox**, etc.) In Britain, of 79,597 households with at least one Jewish member that held synagogue membership in 2016, 66% affiliated with **Orthodox** synagogues: 53% in "**centrist Orthodox** ", and 13% in "**strictly Orthodox**" (further 3% were Sephardi, which technically eschews the title "**Orthodox** ").

High birth rates are an important aspect of **Orthodox** demographics: They are the most reproductive of all Jews, and **Ultra-Orthodox** communities have some of the highest rates in the world, with 6 children per an average household. While American **Orthodox** are but 10% of all Jews, among children, their share rises immensely: An estimated 61% of Jewish children in New York belong to **Orthodox** households, 49% to **Ultra-Orthodox**.

## Haredi Judaism

**Orthodox Judaism** may be categorized according to varying criteria. The most recognizable sub-group is the *Haredim* (literally, **'trembling' or 'fervent'**), also known as "**strictly Orthodox** ", and the like. They form the most traditional part of the **Orthodox** spectrum. In spite of many differences, *Haredi* rabbis and communities generally recognize each other as such, and therefore accord respect and legitimacy between them.

They are organized in large political structures, mainly **Agudath** Israel of America and the **Israeli United Torah Judaism** party. Other organized groups include the **Anti-Zionist Central Rabbinical Congress** and the Edah HaChareidis. Some *Haredim* also hold a lukewarm or negative assessment of the more modernist **Orthodox**.

## Hasidic Judaism

The **Hasidim** originated in 18th-century Eastern Europe, where they formed as a spiritual revival movement that defied the rabbinical establishment. They exercise tight control over the lives of their followers. Every single one of the several hundreds of independent Hasidic groups/sects (also called "**courts**" or "**dynasties**"), from large ones with thousands of member households to very small, has its own line of *Rebbes*. "**Courts**" often possess unique customs, religious emphases, philosophies, and styles of dress. **As of 2016, there were 130,000 Hasidic households worldwide.**

## Litvaks

The second *Haredi* group are the **Litvaks**, or **Yeshivish**. They originated, in a loose fashion, with the Misnagdim, the opponents of **Hasidim**, who were mainly concentrated in old Lithuania. The confrontation with the **Hasidim** bred distinct ideologies and institutions, especially great *yeshivas*, learning halls, where the study of **Torah** for its own sake and admiration for the scholars who headed these schools was enshrined. With the advent of secularization, the Misnagdim largely abandoned their hostility towards **Hasidim**.

## Sephardic *Haredim*

The third **Ultra-Orthodox** movement is the **Sephardic** *Haredim*, who are particularly identified with the **Shas party** in Israel and the legacy of **Rabbi Ovadia Yosef.** Originating in the **Mizrahi** (Middle Eastern and North African Jews) immigrants to the country who arrived in the 1950s, most of the **Sephardi Haredim** were educated in Litvak yeshivas, both adopting their educators' mentality and developing a distinct identity in reaction to the racism they encountered. **Shas** arose in the 1980s, with the aim of reclaiming Sephardi religious legacy, in opposition to secularism on one hand and the hegemony of European-descended *Haredim* on the other. While living in strictly observant circles (there are several hundreds of **Sephardic-***Haredi* communal rabbis), they, unlike the insular **Hasidim** or Litvaks, maintain a strong bond with the non-Haredi masses of Israeli **Mizrahi society.**

## Modern Orthodox y Judaism

Apart from the *Haredim,* there are other **Orthodox** communities. In the West, especially in the United States, **Modern Orthodoxy**, or **"Centrist Orthodoxy"**, is a broad umbrella term for communities which seek an observant lifestyle and traditional theology, while, at the same time, ascribing positive value to engagement (if not **"Synthesis"**) with the modern world. In the United States, the **Modern Orthodox** form a cohesive community and identity group, highly influenced by the legacy of leaders such as **Rabbi Joseph B. Soloveitchik**, and concentrated around Yeshiva University and institutions like the **Orthodox Union** or **National Council of Young Israel**.

## Religious Zionism

In Israel, **Religious Zionism** represents the largest **Orthodox** public. While Centrist **Orthodox** y's fault-line with the **Ultra-Orthodox** is the attitude to modernity, a fervent adoption of **Zionism** marks the former. **Religious Zionism** not only supports the State of Israel, but it also ascribes an inherent religious value to it; the dominant ideological school, influenced by **Rabbi** Abraham Isaac Kook's thought, regards the state in messianic terms. **Religious Zionism** is not a uniform group, and fragmentation between its strict and conservative flank (often named **"Chardal",** or **"National-*Haredi*"**) and more liberal and open elements has increased since the 1990s. The **National Religious Party**, once the single political platform, dissolved, and the common educational system became torn on issues such as gender separation in elementary school or secular studies.

## Israeli Masorti (traditional) Jews

Another large demographic usually considered aligned with **Orthodox** y are the Israeli *Masortim*, or **"traditional"**. This moniker originated with **Mizrahi** immigrants who were both secularized and reverent toward their communal heritage. However, **Mizrahi** intellectuals, in recent years, developed a more reflective, nuanced understanding of this term, eschewing its shallow image and not necessarily agreeing with the formal deference to **Orthodox** rabbis.

# The Oslo Accord

The **Oslo I Accord** or **Oslo I**, officially called the **Declaration of Principles on Interim Self-Government Arrangements** or short **Declaration of Principles (DOP)**, was an attempt in 1993 to set up a framework that would lead to the resolution of the ongoing Israeli-Palestinian conflict. It was the first face-0to-fce agreement between the government of Israel and the **Palestine Liberation Organization (PLO).**

Negotiations conceding the agreement, an outgrowth of the **Madrid Conference** of 1991, were conducted secretly is Oslo, Norway, hosted by the **Fafo Institute**, and completed on 20 August 1993; the Oslo Accords were subsequently officially signed at a public ceremony I Washington, D.C., on 13 September 1993, in the presence of PLO chairman **Yasser Arafat**, the then Israeli Prime Minister **Yitzhak Rabin** and U.S. President Bill Clinton. The documents themselves were signed by Mahmoud Abbas for the PLO, foreign Minister **Shimon Peres** for Israel, U.S. Secretary of State **Warren Christopher** for the United States and foreign minister **Andrei Kozyrev** for Russia.

The Accord provided for the creation of a Palestinian interim self-government, the Palestinian National Authority (PNA). The Accords also called for the withdrawal of the Israel Defense Forces (IDF) from parts of the Gaza Strip and West Bank.

It was anticipated that this arrangement would last for a five-year interim period during which a permanent agreement would be negotiated (beginning no later than May 1996).

In August 1993, the delegations had reached an agreement which was signed in secrecy by Peres while visiting Oslo. In the Letters of Mutual Recognition, the PLO acknowledged the State of Israel and pledged to reject violence, and Israel recognized the PLO as the representative of the Palestinian people and as partner in negotiations. **Yasser Arafat** was allowed to return to the Occupied Palestinian Territories. In 1995, the Oslo I Accord was followed by Oslo II. Neither promised Palestinian statehood.

## Principles of the Accords

In essence, the accords called for the withdrawal of Israeli forces from parts of the Gaza Strip and West Bank, and affirmed a Palestinian right of self-government within those areas through the creation of a Palestinian Interim Self-Government Authority. Palestinian rule was to last for a five-year interim period during which "permanent status negotiations" would commence in order to reach a final agreement.

The negotiations would cover major issues such as Jerusalem, Palestinian refugees, Israeli settlements, and security and borders were to be decided at these permanent status negotiations (Article V). Israel was to grant interim self-government to the Palestinians in phases.

The Israeli government recognized the PLO as the legitimate representative of the Palestinian people, while the PLO recognized the right of the state of Israel to exist and renounced terrorism as well as other violence, and its desire for the destruction of the Israeli state.

The aim of Israeli-Palestinian negotiations was to establish a Palestinian Interim Self-Government Authority, an elected Council, for the Palestinian people in the West Bank and the Gaza Strip, for a transitional period not exceeding five years, leading to a permanent settlement based on UN Security Council Resolutions 242 and 338, an integral part of the whole peace process.

The two sides viewed the West Bank and Gaza as a single territorial unit.

The Interim period would "begin upon the withdrawal from the Gaza Strip and Jericho area". That withdrawal began with the signing of the Gaza-Jericho Agreement on 4 May 1994, thus the interim period would end on 4 May 1999.

The Council would establish a strong police force, while Israel would continue to carry the responsibility for defending against external threats.

The Declaration of Principles would enter into force one month after its signing.

## Annex 3: Economic cooperation
The two sides agree to establish an Israeli-Palestinian continuing Committee for economic cooperation.

### Permanent status negotiations issues

It was understood that several issues were postponed to permanent status negotiations, including: Jerusalem, refugees, settlements, security arrangements, borders, relations and cooperation with other neighbors, and other issues of common interest.

### Police

It was understood that the Interim Agreement would include arrangements for cooperation and coordination. It was also agreed that the transfer of powers and responsibilities to the Palestinian police would be accomplished in a phased manner. The accord stipulated that Israeli and Palestinian police would do joint patrols.

### Israel's continuing responsibilities

It was understood that, subsequent to the Israeli withdrawal, Israel would continue to be responsible for external security, and for internal security and public order of settlements and Israelis. Israeli military forces and civilians would be allowed to continue using roads freely within the Gaza Strip and the Jericho area.

## Reaction
After a two-day discussion in the Knesset on the government proclamation in the issue of the accord and the exchange of the letters, on 23 September 1993, a vote of confidence was held in which 61 Knesset members voted for the decision, 50 voted against and 8 abstained.

Palestinian reactions were also divided. Fatah, the group that represented the Palestinians in the negotiations, accepted the accords. But Hamas, Palestinian Islamic Jihad and the Popular Front for the Liberation of Palestine objected to the accords.

Jerusalem's new mayor and later Prime Minister Ehud Olmert opposed the agreement and called it a "dark cloud over the city". He favored to bring more Jews to East Jerusalem and expand Jerusalem to the east.

Many Palestinians feared that Israel was not serious about dismantling their settlements in the West Bank, especially around Jerusalem.

## Nobel Peace Prize

In 1994 Israeli Prime Minister **Yitzhak Rabin**, Israeli Foreign Minister Shimon Peres, and PLO Chairman **Yasser Arafat** received the Nobel Peace Prize following the signing on the Oslo Accords.

## Remarks from Benjamin Netanyahu

In a 2001 video, Netanyahu, reportedly unaware he was being recorded, said: Defined military zones are security zones; as far as I'm concerned, the entire Jordan Valley is a defined military zone. Go argue." "Why is that import? Because from that moment on I stopped the Oslo Accords", Netanyahu affirmed. However, this is clearly consistent with **Yitzhak Rabin**'s October 1995 statement to the Knesset on the ratification of the interim Oslo agreement: "B. The security border of the State of Israel will be located in the Jordan Valley, in the broadest meaning of that term."

- The Interim Agreement on the West Bank and the Gaza Strip (also known as Oslo 2), signed on 28 September 1995 gave Palestinians self-rule in Bethlehem, Hebron, Jenin, Nablus, Qalqilya, Ramallah, Tulkarm, and some 450 villages.

# Paradise and Hellfire

**Paradise** (Old Persian: *pairidaeza*) is a place in which existence is positive, harmonious and timeless. It is conceptually a counter-image of the miseries of human civilization, and in **Paradise** there is only peace, prosperity, and happiness. **Paradise** is a place of contentment, often used in the same context as that of utopia.

**Paradise is imagined as an abode of the virtuous dead**. In Christian and Islamic understanding, **Heaven** is a paradisaical relief, evident for example in the **Gospel of Luke** when **Jesus** tells a penitent criminal crucified alongside him that they will be together in **Paradise**.

The **Vedic Indians** held that the physical body was destroyed by fire but recreated and reunited in the **Third Heaven** in a state of bliss. In the **Zoroastrian Avesta**, the "Best Existence" and the "House of Song" are places of the righteous dead. The **Abrahamic faiths** associate **Paradise** with the **Garden of Eden**, that is, the perfect state of the world prior to the fall from grace, and the perfect state that will be restored in the **World to Come**.

## Etymology and semasiology:

By the 6th/5th century BCE, the **Old Iranian** word had been adopted as **Akkadian *pardesu*** and Elamite *partetas* "domain". In Aramaic *pardaysa* reflects "**Royal Park**". Hebrew *pardes* appears thrice in the **Tanakh**; in the **Song of Solomon 4:13, Ecclesiastes 2:5** and **Nehemiah 2:8**. It is from this usage that the use of "**Paradise**" to refer to the **Garden of Eden** derives. This usage also appears in Arabic and the **Qur'an** itself as *Firdaus*.

## Judaism:

The word Pardes, borrowed from the Persian word, occurs in the **Song of Songs 4:13, Ecclesiastes 2:5, and Nehemiah 2:8**, in each case meaning "**park**" or "**garden**", the original Persian meaning of the word, where it describes to the royal parks of **Cyrus the Great** by Xenophon in Anabasis.

Later in **Second Temple era Judaism "Paradise"** came to be associated with the **Garden of Eden** and prophesies of restoration of Eden, and transferred to heaven. In the **Apocalypse of Moses,** Adam and Eve are expelled from **Paradise** (instead of Eden) after having been tricked by the serpent.

Later after the death of Adam, the **Archangel Michael** carries the body of Adam to be buried in **Paradise**, which is in the Third **Heaven**. The **Zohar** gives the word a mystical interpretation, and associates it with the four kinds of Biblical exegesis: *peshat* (literal meaning), *Remez* (allusion), *derash* (anagogical), and *sod* (mystic).

## Christianity:

The New Testament use and understanding of **Paradise** parallels that of contemporary Judaism. The word is used three times in the New Testament writings:
- **Luke 23:43** - by **Jesus** on the cross, in response to the thief's request that **Jesus** remember him when he came in his kingdom.

- **2 Cor.12:4** - in Paul's description of a man's description of a third heaven **Paradise**, which may in fact be a vision Paul himself saw.
- **Rev.2:7** - in a reference to the **Gen.2:8 Paradise** and the tree of life

In the 2nd century AD, Irenaeus distinguished **Paradise** from heaven. In *Against Heresies*, he wrote that only those deemed worthy would inherit a home in heaven, while others would enjoy **Paradise**, and the rest live in the restored Jerusalem.

Origen likewise distinguished **Paradise** from heaven, describing **Paradise** as the earthly **"school"** for souls of the righteous dead, preparing them for their ascent through the celestial spheres to heaven. The Curetonian Gospels read **"Today I tell you that you will be with me in Paradise"**.

## Jehovah's Witnesses:

**Jehovah's Witnesses** believe that **Jehovah**'s purpose from the start was, and is, to have the earth filled with the offspring of **Adam** and **Eve** as caretakers of a global **Paradise**. After God had designed this earth for human habitation, however, **Adam** and **Eve** rebelled against **Jehovah** and so they were banished from the **Garden of Eden**, or **Paradise**. **Jehovah**'s Witnesses also believe that the wicked people will be destroyed at **Armageddon** and that many of the righteous (those faithful and obedient to **Jehovah**) will live eternally in an earthly **Paradise. (Psalms 37:9, 10, 29; Prov. 2:21, 22).**

Joining the survivors will be resurrected righteous and unrighteous people who died prior to Armageddon **(John 5:28, 29; Acts 24:15)**. The latter are brought back because they paid for their sins by their death, **(Rom. 6:23)**. These will be judged on the basis of their post-resurrection obedience to instructions revealed in new **"scrolls" (Rev. 20:12)**. This provision does not apply to those that **Jehovah** deems to have sinned against his holy spirit **(Matt. 12:31, Luke 12:5)**.

One of **Jesus**' last recorded statements before he died were the words to an evildoer hanging alongside him on a torture stake, **"Truly I tell you today, You will be with me in Paradise".—Luke 23:43.**

## Mormonism:

In **Latter Day Saint** theology, **Paradise usually refers to the spirit world**. That is, the place where spirits dwell following death and awaiting the resurrection. In that context, **"Paradise"** is the state of the righteous after death. In contrast, the wicked and those who have not yet learned the gospel of **Jesus Christ** await the resurrection in spirit prison. After the universal resurrection, all persons will be assigned to a particular kingdom or degree of glory. This may also be termed **"Paradise"**.

## Islam:

In the **Qur'an**, **Paradise** is denoted as **"Jannah"** or Garden, with the highest level being called **"Firdaus"**. The word is derived from the original **Avestan** counterpart, and used instead of **Heaven** to describe the ultimate pleasurable place after death, accessible by those who pray, donate to charity, read the **Qur'an**, believe in: **God, the Angels, His revealed books, His prophets and messengers, the Day of Judgement and the Afterlife, and follow God's will in their life.**

**Heaven** in Islam is used to describe the Universe. In Islam, the bounties and beauty of **Heaven** are immense, so much so that they are beyond the abilities of mankind's worldly mind to comprehend.

## The Urantia Book:

The **Urantia** Book portrays **Paradise** as the **"eternal center of the universe of universes,"** and as **"the abiding place of the Universal Father, the Eternal Son, the Infinite Spirit, and their divine co-ordinates and associates**." The book states that **Paradise** is the primal origin and the final destiny for all spirit personalities, and for all the ascending creatures of the evolutionary worlds of time and space.

# Passover

**Passover** ( Hebrew: *Pesakḥ*) is a major Jewish holiday and one of the most widely celebrated Jewish holidays. Together with **Shavuot** and **Sukkot**, **Passover** was one of the **Three Pilgrimage Festivals (*Shalosh Regalim*)** during which the entire population of the kingdom of **Judah** made a pilgrimage to the Temple in Jerusalem.

During the existence of the Temple in Jerusalem, **Passover** was a spring festival that was connected to the offering of the "**first-fruits of the barley**", as barley was the first grain to ripen and to be harvested in the Land of Israel. The festivals now associated with the **Exodus** (**Passover**, **Shavuot,** and **Sukkot**) began as agricultural and seasonal feasts but became completely subsumed into the central narrative of **Israel's deliverance from oppression at the hands of God.**

In the **Book of Exodus**, God helped the Israelites escape from slavery in ancient Egypt by inflicting ten plagues upon the Egyptians before the Pharaoh would release the Israelite slaves. The last of the plagues was the death of the Egyptian first-born. The spirit of the **Lord** knew to *pass over* **the first-born in these homes, hence the English name of the holiday.**

**Passover** commences on the 15th of the Hebrew month of Nisan and lasts for either seven days or eight days for **Orthodox, Hasidic**, and most **Conservative** Jews (in the diaspora). The rituals unique to the **Passover** celebrations commence with the **Passover Seder** **when the 15th of Nisan has begun.**

## Etymology
The verb *Pesach* is first mentioned in the **Torah** 's account of the **Exodus** from Egypt (**Exodus 12:23). "He passed over"** in reference to God **"passing over"** (or **"skipping")** the houses of the Hebrews during the final of the **Ten Plagues of Egypt, in Exodus 12:23, and in Exodus 12:27).**

## The biblical narrative / In the Book of Exodus / *Plagues of Egypt*
**In the Book of Exodus, the Israelites are enslaved in ancient Egypt. Yahweh**, the god of the Israelites, appears to **Moses** in a burning bush and commands **Moses** to confront Pharaoh. To show his power, Yahweh inflicts a series of **10 plagues on the Egyptians**, culminating in the 10th plague, the **death of the first-born**. — *Exodus 11:4–6*

## Other biblical mentions
Called the **"Festival the matzot"** in the Hebrew Bible, the commandment to keep **Passover** is recorded in the **Book of Leviticus:** In the first month, on the fourteenth day of the month at dusk is the **LORD's Passover.** And on the fifteenth day of the same month is the feast of unleavened

bread unto the **LORD (Leviticus 23:5–8). The biblical commandments concerning the Passover (and the Feast of Unleavened Bread) stress the importance of remembering. (Deuteronomy 16:12).**

## Date and duration / *Hebrew calendar and Yom tov sheni shel Galuyot*

The **Passover** begins on the 15th day of the month of Nisan, which typically falls in March or April of the Gregorian calendar. The 15th day begins in the evening, after the 14th day, and the **Seder** meal is eaten that evening. However, due to leap months falling after the vernal equinox, **Passover** sometimes starts on the second full moon after vernal equinox.

## Passover sacrifice

**The main entity in Passover according to Judaism is the sacrificial lamb**. During the existence of the **Tabernacle** and later the Temple in Jerusalem, the focus of the **Passover** festival was the **Passover** sacrifice. **(Numbers 9:11), (Exodus 12:6)**, **(Exodus 23:18), and (Exodus 12:9).** Many Sephardi Jews have the custom of eating lamb or goat meat during the **Seder** in memory of the *Korban Pesach*.

## The Torah commandments regarding *chametz* are:

- To remove all *chametz* from one's home, including things made with **chametz**, before the first day of **Passover** (**Exodus** 12:15). It may be simply used up, thrown out (historically, destroyed by burning), or given or sold to non-Jews (or non-Samaritans, as the case may be).
- To refrain from eating *chametz* or mixtures containing *chametz* during **Passover** (**Exodus** 13:3, **Exodus** 12:20, Deuteronomy 16:3).
- Not to possess *chametz* in one's domain (i.e. home, office, car, etc.) during **Passover** (**Exodus** 12:19, Deuteronomy 16:4).

## Blessing for search of chametz and nullification of chametz

Before the search is begun there is a special blessing. **Blessed are You, Hashem our God, King of the universe, who has sanctified us with his commandments and has commanded us concerning the removal of chametz.**

## *Fast of the Firstborn and siyum*

According to **Exodus 12:29**, God struck down all Egyptian firstborns while the Israelites were not affected. However, it is customary for synagogues to conduct a *siyum* (ceremony marking the completion of a section of **Torah** learning) right after morning prayers, and the celebratory meal that follows cancels the firstborn's obligation to fast.

## Burning and nullification of leaven

On the morning of the 14th of Nisan, any leavened products that remain in the householder's possession, along with the 10 morsels of bread from the previous night's search, are burned (*s'rayfat chametz*).

## Separate kosher for Passover utensils and dishes

Due to the **Torah** injunction not to eat *chametz* (leaven) during **Passover** (**Exodus** 12:15), observant families typically own complete sets of serving dishes, glassware and silverware (and in some cases, even separate dishwashers and sinks) which have never come into contact with *chametz*, for use only during **Passover**.

## Matzah

A symbol of the **Passover** holiday is matzo, an unleavened flatbread made solely from flour and water which is continually worked from mixing through baking, so that it is not allowed to rise. The **Torah** says that it is because the Hebrews left Egypt with such haste that there was no time to allow baked bread to rise; thus flat, **unleavened bread, matzo**, is a reminder of the rapid departure of the **Exodus**. The baking of **matzo** is labor-intensive, as less than 18 minutes is permitted between the mixing of flour and water to the conclusion of baking and removal from the oven. **Some machine-made matzos are completed within 5 minutes of being kneaded.**

## Passover Seder

It is traditional for Jewish families to gather on the first night of **Passover** for a special dinner called a **Seder** (Hebrew *Seder*). Four cups of wine are consumed at various stages in the narrative. The **Seder** is replete with questions, answers, and unusual practices to arouse the interest and curiosity of the children at the table. The children are rewarded with nuts and candies when they ask questions and participate in the discussion of the **Exodus** and its aftermath. The **Seder** concludes with additional songs of praise and faith printed in the Haggadah, including *Chad Gadya* ("One Little Kid" or "One Little Goat").

## The four questions and participation of children

Children have a very important role in the **Passover Seder**. Traditionally the youngest child is prompted to ask questions about the **Passover Seder**, beginning with the words, *Mah Nishtana HaLeila HaZeh* (Why is this night different from all other nights?). **Why is this night different from all other nights? On all other nights, we eat either unleavened or leavened bread, but tonight we eat only unleavened bread? On all other nights, we eat all kinds of vegetables, but tonight, we eat only bitter herbs? On all other nights, we do not dip even once, but tonight we dip twice?** On all other nights, we eat either sitting or reclining, but tonight we only recline?

## Concluding songs

After the **Hallel**, the fourth glass of wine is drunk, and participants recite a prayer that ends in **"Next year in Jerusalem!"** This is followed by several lyric prayers that expound upon God's mercy and kindness, and give thanks for the survival of the Jewish people through a history of exile and hardship.

## Counting of the Omer

Beginning on the second night of **Passover**, the 16th day of Nisan, Jews begin the practice of the Counting of the **Omer**, a nightly reminder of the approach of the holiday of Shavuot 50 days hence. **Since the destruction of the Temple, this offering is brought in word rather than deed.**

## Second Passover

The **"Second Passover" (Pesach Sheni)** on the 14th of Iyar in the **Hebrew Calendar** is mentioned in the **Hebrew Bible's Book of Numbers (Numbers 9:6–13)** as a make-up day for people who were unable to offer the Pesach sacrifice at the appropriate time due to ritual impurity or distance from Jerusalem. **(Numbers 9:12).** There is a custom, though not Jewish law, to eat just one piece of matzo on that night.

## Influence on other religions / Christianity

**The two disciples, Peter and John, were sent by Christ to prepare the Passover** *Easter and Passover (Christian holiday)*

The Christian celebration of **Good Friday** finds its roots in the Jewish feast of **Passover**, the evening on which Jesus was crucified as the **Passover** Lamb.

## Islam / *Day of Ashura § Significance of Ashura for Sunni Muslims*

In the **Sunni** sect of **Islam**, it is recommended to fast on the day of **Ashurah** (10th of Muharram) based on narrations attributed to **Muhammad**. According to Muslim tradition, the Jews of Madinah used to fast on the tenth of Muharram in observance of **Passover**.

In narrations recorded in the **al-Hadith** (sayings of the Islamic **Prophet Muhammad**) of **Sahih al-Bukhari**, it is recommended that Muslims fast on this day. He stated that Muslims should fast for two days instead of one, either on the 9th and 10th day or on the 10th and 11th day of **Muharram**.

# The Patriarchs

The **patriarchs** (Hebrew: אבות *Avot* or *Abot*) of the Bible, when narrowly defined, are **Abraham**, his son Isaac, and Isaac's son Jacob, also named Israel, the ancestor of the Israelites. These three figures are referred to collectively as the patriarchs, and the period in which they lived is known as the patriarchal age. Judaism, Christianity, and Islam hold that the **patriarchs**, along with their primary wives, known as the **matriarchs (Sarah, Rebekah and Leah)** are entombed at the **Cave of the Patriarchs**, a site held holy by the three religions.

**Rachel, Jacob's other wife**, is said to be buried separately at what is known as **Rachel's Tomb**, near Bethlehem, at the site where she is believed to have **died in childbirth.** More widely, the term patriarchs can be used to refer to the twenty male ancestor-figures between **Adam** and **Abraham**. The first ten of these are called the antediluvian patriarchs, because they came before the **Flood**.

## Definition

The patriarchs of the Bible, when narrowly defined, are **Abraham**, his son **Isaac**, and Isaac's son **Jacob**, also named Israel, the ancestor of the Israelites. These three figures are referred to collectively as the patriarchs, and the period in which they lived is known as the patriarchal age. They play significant roles in Hebrew scripture during and following their lifetimes. They are used as a significant marker by God in Revelations and promises, and continue to play important roles in the **Abraham**ic faiths.

Judaism, Christianity and Islam hold that the patriarchs, along with their primary wives, known as the **matriarchs – Sarah** (wife of **Abraham**), **Rebekah** (wife of Isaac) and **Leah** (one of the wives of Jacob) – are entombed at the **Cave of Machpelah** in Hebron, a site held holy by the three religions. **Rachel** is said to be buried separately at what is known as **Rachel's Tomb**, near Bethlehem, at the site where she is believed to have died in childbirth. More widely, the term patriarchs can be used to refer to the twenty male ancestor-figures between **Adam** and **Abraham**. The first ten of these are called the antediluvian patriarchs, because they came before the **Flood**.

## Lifespans

The lifetimes given for the patriarchs in the Masoretic Text of the **Book of Genesis** are: **Adam 930 years, Seth 912, Enos 905, Kenan 910, Mahalalel 895, Jared 962, Enoch 365** (did not die, but was taken away by God), **Methuselah 969, Lamech 777, Noah 950**. The lifespans given have surprising chronological implications, as the following quotation shows. The long lives ascribed to the patriarchs cause remarkable synchronisms and duplications.

Adam lived to see the birth of **Lamech**, the ninth member of the genealogy; **Seth** lived to see the translation of **Enoch** and died shortly before the birth of **Noah**. **Noah** outlived Abram's grandfather, **Nahor**, and died in Abram's sixtieth year. **Shem**, **Noah's son, even outlived Abram. He was still alive when Esau and Jacob were born!**

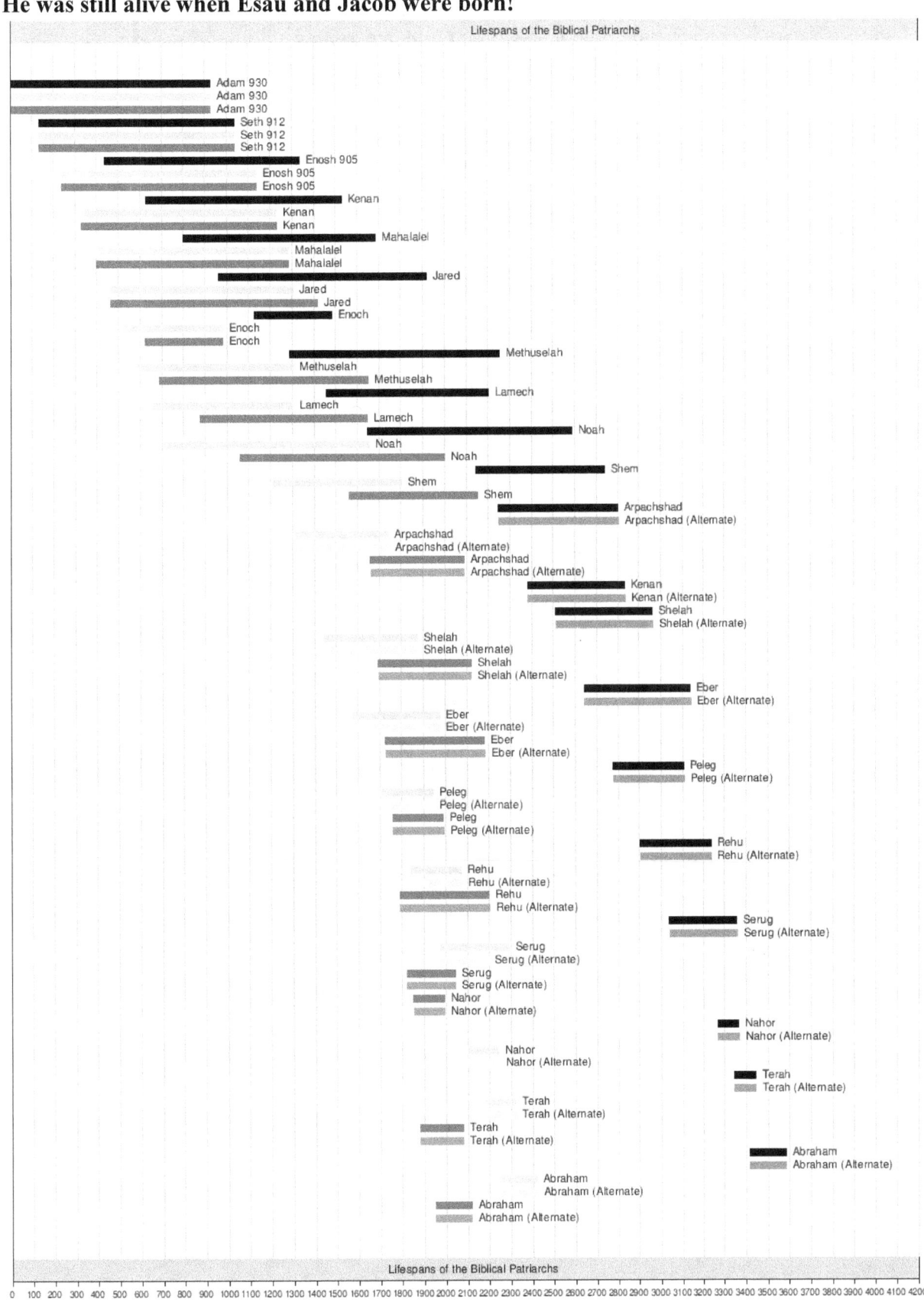

589

## Explanation of color-codes:

- Lifespans recorded in the Septuagint: **Black** and **gray**
- Lifespans recorded in the Syriac Peshitta: **Gold** and **yellow**
- Lifespans recorded in the Masoretic text: **Crimson** and **vermilion**

## Matriarchs

The matriarchs, also known as **"the four mothers"**, are:

- **Sarah**, the wife of Abraham
- **Rebekah**, the wife of Isaac
- **Leah** and **Rachel**, the wives of Jacob

A few Jewish sources list **Bilhah** and **Zilpah** (Jacob's concubines) as additional matriarchs, for a total of six matriarchs.

# Peace: Israel and Palestine

**Israel fought 14 wars since its inception in May 1948.** Five Arab countries have participated in these wars and have been repeatedly defeated. Although Saudi Arabia never engaged directly in any of these wars, it may be said that they have financed all of them. The Palestinians are not united in their leadership and governance. The **West Bank** is controlled by the successors of the P.L.O. while **Gaza** is controlled by **Hamas**. Unless they present a united front with which Israel can negotiate and reach an agreement, **all the peace efforts will be for naught**.

Any Palestinian who signs a true peace agreement with Israel may likely be assassinated by his own people. The Arab insistence on **Jerusalem** being the future capital of Palestine can never be resolved. One city cannot be the capital of 2 countries. The Palestinian question confronting Israel is not left up to the Palestinians to resolve. The **Arab countries (22),** consider the land of Israel a Muslim land. **Jerusalem** is the 3$^{rd}$ holiest city in Islam. This presents a major dilemma without prospects for a long-term peaceful resolution.

**"Peace",** therefore, can only be assured through a strong State of Israel. **Nothing unites the Arabs more than the prospects of Israel's destruction,** now and in the future. A U.N.-established Palestinian State represents a mortal blow to Israel's existence. Presently Israel can restrict offensive material from being acquired by the Palestinians. This will cease the moment a Palestinian State is created. Israel will not be able to prevent the new enemy state from becoming and armed camp, **sworn to destroy Israel no matter how long it will take.**

In my lecture circles, I am often asked **"why do they hate us so much"?** And my answer is that, after 2,000 years of oppression, we have learned to fight back and defend ourselves. **"They"** cannot stomach this. They think Israel arrogant and it should have lost at least one war. The problem is that **Israel can only lose one war and cease to exist. The Arabs can lose 100 wars and still survive.**

## Hamas of Gaza

**Hamas** (Arabic: *Hamas*, an acronym of *Harakat al-Muqāwamah al-Islāmiyyah* ) is a Palestinian Sunni-Islamic fundamentalist militant organization. It has a social service wing, **Dawah**, and a military wing, the **Izz ad-Din al-Qassam Brigades**. It has been the *de facto* **governing authority of the Gaza Strip since its takeover of that area in 2007.** During this period it fought several wars with Israel.

 **Hamas was founded in 1987**, soon after the **First Intifada** broke out, as an offshoot of the **Egyptian Muslim Brotherhood. PLO** Co-founder **Sheik Ahmed Yassin** stated in 1987, and the **Hamas** Charter affirmed in 1988, that **Hamas** was founded to liberate Palestine, including modern-day Israel, from Israeli occupation and to establish an Islamic state in the area that is now Israel, the West Bank and the Gaza Strip. **The group has stated that it may accept a 10-year truce if Israel withdraws to the 1967 borders and allows Palestinian refugees from 1948, including their descendants, to return to what is now Israel. Tactics have included suicide bombings and, since 2001, rocket attacks.**

The attacks on civilians have been condemned as war crimes and crimes against humanity by human rights groups such as **Human Rights Watch.** In the January 2006 Palestinian parliamentary elections, **Hamas won a plurality in the Palestinian Parliament**, defeating the PLO-affiliated **Fatah** party.

## Antisemitism and anti-Zionism / *Racism in the Palestinian territories*

Antisemitism is not the main tenet of **Hamas** ideology. In 2009 representatives of the small **Jewish sect Neturei Karta** met with **Hamas** leader **Ismail Haniyeh** in **Gaza,** who stated that he held nothing against Jews but only against the state of Israel. **Some commentators have pointed out parallels between Hamas's youth organization and Hitler Youth.** In 2006 a spokesman signaled readiness to recognize Israel within the 1967 borders.

## Hamas Charter (1988) / *Hamas Covenant*

- Article 7 of the Hamas Covenant provides the following quotation, attributed to Muhammad:

**"The Day of Judgement will not come about until Moslems fight the Jews (killing the Jews), when the Jew will hide behind stones and trees. The stones and trees will say O Moslems, O Abdulla, there is a Jew behind me, come and kill him. Only the Gharkad tree (evidently a certain kind of tree), would not do that because it is one of the trees of the Jews".**

- Article 22 states that the French revolution, the Russian revolution, colonialism and both world wars were created by the Zionists or forces supportive of Zionism:

**"You may speak as much as you want about regional and world wars. They were behind World War I, when they were able to destroy the Islamic Caliphate, making financial gains and controlling resources. They obtained the Balfour Declaration, formed the League of Nations through which they could rule the world. They were behind World War II, through which they made huge financial gains by trading in armaments, and paved the way for the establishment of their state. It was they who instigated the replacement of the League of Nations with the United Nations and the Security Council to enable them to rule the world through them. There is no war going on anywhere, without having their finger in it."**

- Article 32 of the Covenant refers to an antisemitic forgery, *The Protocols of the Elders of Zion*:

**"Today it is Palestine, tomorrow it will be one country or another. The Zionist plan is limitless. After Palestine, the Zionists aspire to expand from the Nile to the Euphrates. When they will have digested the region they overtook, they will aspire to further expansion, and so on. Their plan is embodied in *The Protocols of the Elders of Zion*, and their present conduct is the best proof of what we are saying".**

## Statements by Hamas members and clerics to an Arab audience

In 2008, **Imam Yousif al-Zahar** of **Hamas** said in his sermon **"Jews are a people who cannot be trusted. They have been traitors to all agreements. Go back to history. Their fate is their vanishing."** Another **Hamas** legislator and imam, **Sheik Yunus al-Astal**, discussed a Koranic verse suggesting that **"suffering by fire is the Jews' destiny in this world and the next."** He concluded **"Therefore we are sure that the Holocaust is still to come upon the Jews."**

**In March 2010**, senior **Hamas** figure **al-Zahar** called on Palestinians everywhere to observe five minutes of silence **"for Israel's disappearance and to identify with Jerusalem and the al-Aqsa mosque"**. He further stated that **"Wherever you have been you've been sent to your destruction. You've killed and murdered your prophets and you have always dealt in loan-sharking and destruction. You've made a deal with the devil and with destruction itself – just like your synagogue."**

On August 10, 2012, **Ahmad Bahr**, Deputy Speaker of the **Hamas** Parliament, stated in a sermon that aired on *Al-Aqsa TV*: **"If the enemy sets foot on a single square inch of Islamic land, Jihad becomes an individual duty, incumbent on every Muslim, male or female. Why? In order to annihilate those Jews. ... O Allah, destroy the Jews and their supporters. O Allah, destroy the Americans and their supporters. O Allah, count them one by one, and kill them all, without leaving a single one."**

In an interview with **Al-Aqsa TV on September 12, 2012, Marwan Abu Ras, a Hamas MP**, who is also a member of the **International Union of Muslim Scholars,** stated (as translated by MEMRI): **"The Jews are behind each and every catastrophe on the face of the Earth. They concocted so many conspiracies and betrayed rulers and nations so many times that the people harbor hatred towards them. ... Throughout history – from Nebuchadnezzar until modern times. ... They slayed the prophets, and so on. ... Any catastrophe on the face of this Earth – the Jews must be behind it."**

On December 26, 2012, Senior **Hamas** official and **Jerusalem** bureau Chief **Ahmed Abu Haliba**, called on **"all Palestinian factions to resume suicide attacks ... deep inside the Zionist enemy"**. On July 28, 2014, **Hamas** spokesman **Osama Hamda**n repeated the **blood libel myth: "We all remember how the Jews used to slaughter Christians, in order to mix their blood in their holy matzos... It happened everywhere.**

## Statements by Hamas members and clerics to an international audience
**In an interview with *CBS This Morning* on July 27, 2014, Hamas leader Khaled Mashaal stated: "We are not fanatics. We are not fundamentalists. We are not actually fighting the Jews because they are Jews per se. We do not fight any other races. We fight the occupiers."**

In May 2009, senior **Hamas MP Sayed Abu Musameh** said, **"in our culture, we respect every foreigner, especially Jews and Christians, but we are against Zionists, not as nationalists but as fascists and racists."** In October 1994, **"Rabin must know that Hamas loves death more than Rabin and his soldiers' love life."**

## Statements on the Holocaust:

**Hamas has been explicit in its Holocaust denial. "This conference bears a clear Zionist goal, aimed at forging history by hiding the truth about the so-called Holocaust, which is an alleged and invented story with no basis. (...) The invention of these grand illusions of an alleged crime that never occurred, ignoring the millions of dead European victims of Nazism during the war, clearly reveals the racist Zionist face, which believes in the superiority of the Jewish race over the rest of the nations. (...) By these methods, the Jews in the world flout scientific methods of research whenever that research contradicts their racist interests".**

**In August 2003, senior Hamas official Dr. Abd Al-Aziz Al-Rantisi wrote in the Hamas newspaper *Al-Risala* that the Zionists encouraged murder of Jews by the Nazis with the aim of forcing them to immigrate to Palestine.** The Europeans had **"created a myth in the name of Holocaust")**

On August 20, 2009, the movement's Popular Committees for Refugees called the Holocaust **"a lie invented by the Zionists, marketing a lie and spreading it"**.

## Violence and terrorism / *Criticism of Hamas*

**"Armed resistance to end the occupation".** From 2000 to 2004, **Hamas** was responsible for killing nearly 400 Israelis and wounding more than 2,000 in 425 attacks. **From 2001 through May 2008, Hamas launched more than 3,000 Qassam rockets and 2,500 mortar attacks into Israel.**

## Attacks on civilians

**After the February 1994 massacre by Baruch Goldstein of 30 Muslim civilians in a Hebron mosque**, the al-Qassam Brigades expanded suicide attacks to target primarily civilians. The most deadly suicide bombing was an attack on a Netanya hotel on March 27, 2002, in which 30 people were killed and 140 were wounded. **Hamas** has defended suicide attacks as a legitimate aspect of its asymmetric warfare against Israel.

**Another Holocaust is not possible anywhere in the world as long as The State of Israel exists.** But if ever another holocaust is perpetrated on the Jewish people, we will not be climbing the Masada to commit communal suicide, nor will we march silently into gas chambers, as we did in WWII.

**Like Samson, we will bring the "House" (The entire Middle East) down with us:**
**NO STATE OF ISRAEL= NO MIDDLE EAST! Remember this!**
**Never Again!!!**

# People of the Book

People of the Book/Scripture (Arabic: 'Ahl al-Kitāb) is an Islamic term which refers to **Jews, Christians and Sabians** and is sometimes applied to members of other religions such as **Zoroastrians**.

The **Qur'an** uses the term in reference to **Jews, Christians and Sabians**. The term was later extended to other religious communities that fell under Muslim rule, including **polytheistic Indians**. Historically, these communities were subject to the **dhimma** contract in an Islamic state.Members of some Christian denominations, such as the **Baptists, Methodists, Seventh-day Adventist Church**, as well as **Puritans** and **Shakers**, have embraced the term **"People of the Book"** in reference to themselves.

## In the Qur'an

In the **Qur'an** the term **"people of the book"** refers to Jews, Christians, and **Sabians**. The scriptures referred to in the **Qur'an** are the **Torah (*at-tawraat*)**, the **Psalms (*az-Zabur*)** and the **Gospel (*al-Injil*)**.

The **Qur'an** emphasizes the community of faith between possessors of monotheistic scriptures, calling on Muhammad to ask them for information. More often, reflecting the refusal of Jews and Christians in Muhammad's environment to accept his message, the **Qur'an** stresses their inability to comprehend the message they possess but do not put into practice and to appreciate that Muhammad's teaching fulfills that message. The **People of the Book** are also referenced in the *jizya* verse (9:29).

## Later Islamic usage

**The use of the term was later extended to Zoroastrians, Samaritans, Mandeans, and even polytheistic Indians.** Islamic scholars differ on whether **Hindus** are **People of the Book**. Most India's inhabitants were followers of the Indian religions. Many of the Muslim clergy of India considered **Hindus** as people of the book. Many Muslims did not treat **Hindus** as pagans or idol-worshipers, although Hinduism does not include **Adam, Eve**, nor the various prophets of Abrahamic religions.

## Dhimmi

*Dhimmi* is a historical term referring to the status accorded to **People of the Book** living in an Islamic state. The word literally means **"protected person."** **Dhimmi**s as citizens in the Islamic state, had certain restrictions, and it was obligatory for them to **pay the jizya tax**, which complemented the **zakat, or alms, paid by the Muslim subjects. Dhimmis** were excluded from specific duties assigned to Muslims, and did not enjoy certain political rights reserved for Muslims, but were otherwise equal under the laws of property, contract, and obligation.

Under sharia, the **Dhimmi** communities were usually subjected to their own special laws, rather than some of the laws which were applicable only to the Muslim community.

For example, the Jewish community in Medina was allowed to have its own **Halakhic** courts, and the **Ottoman** millet system allowed its various **Dhimmi** communities to rule themselves under separate legal courts. **Dhimmi** communities were also allowed to engage in certain practices that were usually forbidden for the Muslim community, such as the **consumption of alcohol and pork.** Historically, **Dhimmi** status was originally applied to **Jews, Christians, and Sabians.** This status later also came to be applied to **Zoroastrians, Hindus, Jains and Buddhists.** Moderate Muslims generally reject the **dhimma** system as inappropriate for the age of nation-states and democracies.

## Judaism

**Thirty-one times in the Qur'an Jews are referred to as "people of the book."** However before the rise of Islam, during Biblical times, **Levitical scribes** redacted and canonized the book of books. The **Babylonian Talmud Baba Batra 14b-14b** describes the order of biblical books. Indeed Rashi himself comments on the **mishnaic statement**, **"Moses received the Torah from Sinai"** by noting since the text does not say **"ha-torah"** (the written torah) but **Torah** (in general) this refers to both the written **torah (24 books of the Old Testament)** and the oral torah.

Scholars of antiquity and the early middle ages do know about the canonization process of the **Tanakh** (the Hebrew Bible) and the redaction processes of the **Talmudim and Midrashim**. Rabbinic tradition has demonstrated a reverence, respect, and love for sacred divinely revealed **"text,"** both written and oral in the process of the chain of transmission **(the Masorah)**. Indeed the metaphor of the book is marshaled in **Talmudic Tractate Rosh Hashanah**, that on **Rosh Hashanah** the fate of each person for the year is written, on **Yom Kippur sealed, and on Hoshanah Rabbah the angels of the heavenly court deliver the verdict to God's archive.**

The **Hai Gaon in 998 in Pumbeditah** comments, **"Three possessions should you prize- a field, a friend, and a book."** The Spanish philosopher, physician, and poet **Rabbi Yehudah HaLevi** writes of the importance of books by commenting, **"My pen is my harp and my lyre, my library is my garden and orchard."**

**Rabbi Yehudah ibn Tibbon** (Adler recension) further elaborates on the importance of his library by commenting, **"Make books your companions; let your bookshelves be your gardens: bask in their beauty, gather their fruit, pluck their roses, take their spices and myrrh. And when your soul be wary, change form one garden to garden, and from one prospect to prospect."**

The Spanish statesman **Rabbi Shmuel ha-Nagid** writes, **"The wise of heart will abandon ease and pleasures for in his library he will find treasures."** **Rabbi Abraham ibn Daud** writes in his **Sefer ha-qabbala** about rabbi **Shmuel ha-Nagid** that he had sofrim who copied **Mishnah** and

**Talmudim**, and he used to donate these commissioned core texts to students who could not afford to purchase them.

**Rabbi Yitzchak ben Yosef of Corbeil** (ca 1280, France) in his **Sefer Mitzvot Qatan** composed in 1276 outlines a detailed strategy for the dissemination of his texts by asserting that every community should finance a copy of his **halakhic** code and keep it for public consultation.

**Rabbi Shimon ben Zemach Duran** (Tashbaz) in his introduction to his halakhic code, **Zohar HaRakiah**, writes, **"When the wise man lies down with his fathers he leaves behind him a treasured and organized blessing: books that enlighten like the brilliance of the firmament (Daniel 12:3) and that extend peace like an eternal flowing river (ISa 66:12)."**

The love and reverence for Jewish books is seen in Jewish law. It is not permissible for a sacred Jewish text to lie on the ground and if by accident a book is dropped to the floor it should be picked up and given a kiss. A Jewish book is not to be left open unless it is being read, nor is it to be held upside down. It is not permitted to place a book of lesser sanctity on top of a book of higher holiness, so for example **one must never place any book on top of the Tanakh.**

## Christian usage

The work of organizations such as the **Wycliffe Bible Translators** and the **United Bible Societies** has resulted in **Bibles being available in 2,100 languages**. Christian converts among evangelized cultures, in particular, have the strongest identification with the term **"People of the Book"**. Many denominations, such as Baptists and the Methodist Church, which are notable for their mission work, have therefore embraced the term **"People of the Book"**.

As stated on its official world website, the **Seventh-day Adventist Church (SDA)** also embraces the term **People of the Book**. It is claimed that prominent Islamic leaders have endorsed Seventh-day Adventists as the **Qur'an**'s true **People of the Book**. The Catholic Church teaches that the Bible is **"one book"** in a dual sense: the Old and New Testaments are the word of God, and **Jesus Christ is the word of God incarnate.**

# Pogroms & persecutions of Jews

A **Pogrom** is a violent riot aimed at the **massacre** or persecution of an ethnic or religious group, particularly a riot aimed at the **massacre** or persecution of Jews. The term originally entered the English language in order to describe 19th and 20th century attacks on Jews in the **Russian Empire** (mostly within the Pale of Settlement, in what would become **Ukraine, Belarus** and **Poland**). Similar attacks against Jews at other times and places also became retrospectively known as **Pogroms**. The word is now also sometimes used to describe publicly sanctioned purgative attacks against non-Jewish ethnic or religious groups.

## Etymology

First recorded in 1882, the Russian word *Pogrom* is derived from the common prefix po- and the verb *Gromit'* (pronounced meaning **"to destroy, to wreak havoc, to demolish violently"**. Its literal translation is **"to harm"**. The noun **Pogrom**, which has a relatively short history, is used in English and many other languages as a loanword, possibly borrowed from **Yiddish** . Its widespread circulation in today's world began with the anti-Semitic excesses in the **Russian Empire** in 1881–1883.

## Historical background

Anti-Jewish riots had already taken place in Europe during the middle Ages. Jewish communities were targeted in the **Black Death** Jewish persecutions of 1348–1350, in Toulon in 1348, in Barcelona as well as in other Catalan cities, during the **Erfurt massacre** (1349), the **Basel massacre, massacres** in Aragon, and in Flanders, as well as the "**Valentine's Day**" Strasbourg **Pogrom of 1349.**

Some 510 Jewish communities were destroyed during this period, extending further to the **Brussels massacre of 1370**. On Holy Saturday of 1389, a **Pogrom** began in Prague that led to the burning of the Jewish quarter, the killing of many Jews, and the suicide of many Jews trapped in the main synagogue; the number of dead was estimated at **400–500 men, women, and children**. The first atrocities against Jewish civilians, on a genocidal scale of destruction, were committed during the Khmelnytsky **Pogroms** of 1648–1657 in present-day Ukraine. The exact number of deaths is unknown, although it is estimated that about 20 percent of the Jews of the entire region were killed. Modern historians give estimates of the scale of the murders by **Khmelnytsky's Cossacks** ranging between **40,000 and 100,000 men, women and children**, or perhaps many more.

## *Anti-Jewish Pogroms in the Russian Empire*

The **Russian Empire**, which previously had very few Jews, acquired territories with the large Jewish populations during the military Partitions of the Polish–Lithuanian Commonwealth in

1772, 1793, and 1795 conducted jointly with the Austrian and Prussian armies, and resulting in Poland's elimination from the geopolitical map of Europe for the next 123 years.

In conquered territories, a new political entity called Pale of Settlement was formed in 1791 by **Catherine the Great**. Most Jewish people from the former Commonwealth were only allowed to reside within the **Pale**, including families expelled by royal decree from St. Petersburg, Moscow, and other big Russian cities. The 1821 **Odessa Pogroms** marked the beginning of the 19th century **Pogroms** in Tsarist Russia; there were four more such **Pogroms** in Odessa before the end of the century. Following the assassination of **Alexander II** in 1881 by **Narodnaya Volya** – blamed on the Jews by the Russian government, anti-Jewish events turned into a wave of **over 200 Pogroms** by their modern definition, which lasted for several years. Jewish self-governing *Kehilla* were abolished by **Tsar Nicholas I** in 1844.

The first, in the 20th century Russia, was the **Kishinev Pogrom** of 1903 in which 47 Jews were killed, hundreds wounded, 700 homes destroyed and 600 businesses pillaged. In the same year, **Pogroms** took place in Gomel (Belarus), Smela, Feodosiya and Melitopol (Ukraine). Extreme savagery was demonstrated with mutilations of the wounded. They were followed by the **Zhitomir Pogrom** (with 29 killed), and the Kiev **Pogrom** of October 1905 resulting in a **massacre of approximately 100 Jews.**

In three years between 1903 and 1906, about **660 Pogroms** were recorded in Ukraine and in Bessarabia; half a dozen more in Belorussia, carried out with the Russian government's complicity. There were no anti-Jewish **Pogroms** recorded in Poland. At about that time, the **Jewish Labor Bund** began organizing armed self-defense units ready to shoot, and the **Pogroms** subsided for a number of years. According to **Professor Colin Tatz**, between 1881 and 1920, there were **1,326 Pogroms in Ukraine which took the lives of 70,000 to 250,000 civilian Jews, leaving half a million homeless.**

## Russian Civil War period

Large-scale **Pogroms**, which began in the **Russian Empire** several decades earlier, intensified during the period of the **Russian Civil War and the Revolution of 1917. Professor Zvi Gitelman** (*A Century of Ambivalence*) estimated that only in 1918–1919 over **1,200 Pogroms took place in Ukraine**, thus amounting to the greatest slaughter of Jews in Eastern Europe since 1648. **Aleksandr Solzhenitsyn** in his book *Two Hundred Years Together* provided additional statistics from research into the **Pogroms** in Ukraine, conducted by **Nahum Gergel** (1887–1931). **Gergel** counted *1,236 incidents of anti-Jewish* violence and estimated that 887 mass **Pogroms** occurred – the remainder being classified as "**excesses**" not assuming mass proportions.

The Kiev **Pogroms** of 1919, according to **Gitelman**, were the first of a subsequent wave of **Pogroms** in which between **30,000 and 70,000 Jews were massacred across Ukraine**. Of all the

**Pogroms** accounted for in Gergel's research, about 40 percent were perpetrated by the **Ukrainian People's Republic** forces led by **Symon Petliura**, 25 percent by the **Ukrainian Green Army** and various Ukrainian nationalist gangs, 17 percent by the **White Army**, especially the forces of **Anton Denikin**. A further 8.5 percent of Gergel's total was attributed to **Pogroms** carried out by men of the **Red Army** – although these **Pogroms** were not sanctioned by the **Bolshevik** leadership; the high command disarmed the regiments which had perpetrated **Pogroms**.

The Ukrainian People's Republic of Symon Petliura did also issue orders condemning **Pogroms**, but it lacked authority to intervene. After May 1919 the Directory lost its role as a credible governing body; almost 75 percent of **Pogroms** occurred between May and September of that year. **Thousands of Jews were killed only for being members of the Jewish faith, without any political affiliations.** The instructions issued from above had only a limited impact on soldiers' attitudes toward violence against Jews, as related by author and future **Nobel laureate Ivan Bunin**. On May 15, 1919, Bunin wrote in his diary about yet another **massacre**:

Members of the **Red Army** in Odessa led a **Pogrom** against the Jewish population in the town of **Big Fountain**. **Ovsyaniko-Kulikovsky** and the writer **Kipen** happened to be there and told me the details. **Fourteen commissars and thirty Jews from among the common people were killed**. Many stores were destroyed. The soldiers tore through the night, dragged the victims from their beds, and killed whomever they met. People ran into the steppe or rushed into the sea. They were chased after and fired upon – a genuine hunt, as it were.

**Kipen** saved himself by accident – fortunately he had spent the night not in his home, but at the **White Flower sanitorium**. At dawn, a detachment of Red Army soldiers appeared 'Are there any Jews here?' they asked the watchman. **'No, no Jews here.'** 'Swear what you're saying is true!' The watchman swore, and they went on farther. **Moisei Gutman**, a cabby, was killed. He was a dear man who moved us from our dacha last fall.

**Gergel's** overall figures, which are generally considered conservative, are based on the testimony of witnesses and newspaper reports collected by the ***Mizrakh-yidish historiche arkhiv,*** which was first based in Kiev, then Berlin and later New York. The English version of Gergel's article was published in 1951 in the YIVO Annual of **Jewish Social Science** titled **"The Pogroms in the Ukraine in 1918–1921"**

In June 1919, the **Jewish First Guard Battalion** from Minsk (at the insistence of its own members) was deployed by the Bolsheviks against the **Polish Army**. According to **Elissa Bemporad,** in August 1919, Polish troops occupied Minsk, murdered thirty-one Jews, beat and attacked many more, looted 377 Jewish-owned shops, and ransacked many private homes. The Polish army also carried out **Pogroms** in Bobruysk, Barysaw, Koidanov and Slutsk. Despite the violence, Jewish political groups, communal institutions, and cultural organizations of all stripes were active under the **Second Polish Republic**. On July 11, 1920, **Rabbi Yechezkel Abramsky** described Polish violence in Minsk as follows:

"Miserable, I walk through the ruined streets, without the strength to keep my head up, buried under the burden of destruction, freshly spilled blood and cries of orphans, theft and murder in every section of the city and in every neighborhood touched by the Polish army. I doubt that the world will ever believe that such horrendous crimes were committed by human beings. Who will believe that the Polish nation began its independent existence with such horrifying actions from the middle ages? Can one believe that people elegantly dressed, with European manners, act like the **Haydamaks** , killing, looting and starting up fires against people, horses and the luggage of those who try to flee Minsk?"

The violence endured by the Jewish population under the Poles encouraged popular support for the **Red Army**, as Jewish public opinion welcomed the establishment of the **Byelorussian Soviet Socialist Republic.**

## Pogroms outside Russia

In the early 20th century the **Pogroms** broke out elsewhere in the world as well. In 1904 in Ireland, the Limerick boycott caused several Jewish families to leave the town. During the 1911 **Tredegar** riot in Wales, Jewish homes and businesses were looted and burned over the period of a week, before the **British Army** was called in by then-**Home Secretary Winston Churchill**, who described the riot as a "**Pogrom**". In 1919, in the Americas, there was a **Pogrom** in Argentina, during the **Tragic Week.**

In the aftermath of the **First World War**, during the localized armed conflicts of independence, 72 Jews were killed and 443 injured in the 1918 Lwów **Pogrom**. The following year, **Pogroms** were reported by the **New-York Tribune** in several cities in the newly reborn Poland, however, the reports were not only exaggerated, but also manufactured by the German legation in Warsaw, quietly opposed to the rebirth of Poland after a century of imperial partitions. The German reports were delivered to **Zionist** headquarters and the foreign press elsewhere by the official services of the **Wihelmstrasse**.

Meanwhile, in the **Mandatory Palestine** under British administration, the Jews have been targeted in the **1929 Hebron massacre and the 1929 Safed Pogrom**. The first **Pogrom** in **Nazi Germany was the *Kristallnacht*,** often called *Pogromnacht*, in which at least 91 Jews were killed, a further 30,000 arrested and incarcerated in Nazi concentration camps, over **1,000 synagogues burned**, and over 7,000 Jewish businesses destroyed or damaged.

## Nazi-occupied Europe

During **World War II,** Nazi German death squads encouraged local populations in German-occupied Europe to commit **Pogroms** against Jews. Brand new battalions of *Volksdeutscher Selbstschutz* (trained by SD agents) were mobilized from among the German minorities, in order to make the local populations share responsibility for the killings. During **Operation Barbarossa** which lasted from June 22 to December 5, 1941, *Reichsfuhrer-SS* **Heinrich Himmler** established the *Schutzmannschaft* collaborationist auxiliary battalions and tasked them with carrying out **Pogroms** behind the front lines.

A large number of **Pogroms** occurred during the **Holocaust** at the hands of non-Germans. Perhaps the deadliest of these Holocaust-era **Pogroms** was the Iasi in Romania, in which as many as **13,266 Jews were killed by Romanian citizens**, police, and military officials. On 1–2 June 1941, the two-day **Farhud Pogrom in Iraq**, in which "**rioters murdered between 150 and 180 Jews, injured 600 others, and raped an undetermined number of women. They also looted some 1,500 stores and homes**". In June–July, 1941, encouraged by the *Einsatzgruppen* in the city of Lviv – location of the Lwów Ghetto – the Ukrainian People's Militia soon reorganized as the Ukrainian Auxiliary Police perpetrated two citywide **Pogroms**, in which around **6,000 Polish Jews were murdered**, in retribution for alleged collaboration with the **Soviet NKVD**; the controversy surrounding the **Lviv Pogroms** of 1941 is still debated today. On 12 October 1941 in **Stanisławów**, some **10,000–12,000 Jewish men, women, and children were shot at the Jewish cemetery by the Germans and the Ukrainian** Auxiliary Police during the so-called "**Bloody Sunday**" (de). The shooters began firing at 12 noon and continued without stopping by taking turns. It was the single largest **massacre** of Jews in General Government prior to mass gassings of *Action Reinhard.*

In Lithuania, some Lithuanian police led by **Algirdas Klimaitis** and the Lithuanian partisans – consisting of **LAF** units reinforced by 3,600 deserters from 29th **Lithuanian Territorial Corps** of the Red Army engaged in anti-Jewish **Pogroms** in Kaunas along with occupying Nazis. **On 25– 26 June 1941 about 3,800 Jews were killed and synagogues and Jewish settlements burned.** During the Jedwabne **Pogrom** of July 1941, some non-Jewish Poles **burned at least 340 Jews in** a barn-house (Institute of National Remembrance) in the presence of **Nazi German** *Ordnungspolizei.* The role of the German *Einsatzgruppe B* remains the subject of debate.

## After World War II

After the end of **World War II**, a series of violent anti-Semitic incidents occurred against returning Jews throughout Europe, particularly in the Soviet-occupied East where Nazi propagandists had extensively promoted the notion of a **Jewish-Communist** conspiracy (see Anti-Jewish violence in Poland, 1944–1946 and Anti-Jewish violence in Eastern Europe, 1944–1946). **Anti-Jewish riots also took place in Britain in 1947.**

In the Arab world, anti-Jewish rioters killed over 140 Jews in the 1945 **Anti-Jewish Riots** in Tripolitania. Following the start of the 1947–48 **Civil War in Mandatory Palestine**, a number of anti-Jewish events occurred throughout the Arab world, some of which have been described as **Pogroms**. In 1947, half of Aleppo's 10,000 Jews left the city in the wake of the Aleppo riots, while other anti-Jewish riots took place in British Aden and the **French Moroccan** cities of Oujda and Jerada.

An early reference to a "**Pogrom**" in The Times, December 1903. Together with the New York Times and the Hearst press, they took the lead in highlighting the **Pogrom** in Kishinev (now Chisinau, Moldova) and other cities in Russia. In May of the same year, The Times' Russian Correspondent **Dudley Disraeli Braham** had been expelled from Russia.

## *Definitions of Pogrom*

According to **Encyclopædia Britannica**, "**the term is usually applied to attacks on Jews in the Russian Empire in the late 19th and early 20th centuries, the first extensive Pogroms followed the assassination of Tsar Alexander II in 1881**", and the *Wiley-Blackwell Dictionary of Modern European History Since 1789* states that **Pogroms "were antisemitic disturbances that periodically occurred within the tsarist empire."** However, the term is widely used to refer to many events which occurred prior to the Anti-Jewish **Pogroms** in the **Russian Empire**.

Historian of Russian **Jewry John Klier** writes in *Russians, Jews, and the Pogroms of 1881– 1882* that "**By the twentieth century, the word 'Pogrom' had become a generic term in English for all forms of collective violence directed against Jews.**" Abramson wrote that "**in mainstream usage the word has come to imply an act of antisemitism**", since whilst "**Jews have not been the only group to suffer under this phenomenon ... historically Jews have been frequent victims of such violence**".

The term is also used in reference to attacks on non-Jewish ethnic minorities, and accordingly some scholars do not include antisemitism as a defining characteristic of *Pogrom*. Reviewing its uses in scholarly literature, historian **Werner Bergmann** proposes that **Pogroms** should be "**defined as a *unilateral, nongovernmental* form of *collective* violence *initiated by the majority population* against a largely defenseless ethnic group, and he states that Pogroms occur when the *majority* expects the state to provide them with no assistance in overcoming a (perceived) threat from the minority,**" but he adds that in western usage, the word's "**anti-Semitic overtones**" have been retained.

Historian **David Engel** supports this, writing that "**there can be no logically or empirically compelling grounds for declaring that some particular episode does or does not merit the label ,**" but he states that the majority of the incidents "**habitually**" described as **Pogroms** took place in societies significantly divided by ethnicity and/or religion where the violence was

603

committed by the higher-ranking group against a stereotyped lower-ranking group against whom they expressed some complaint, and with the belief that the law of the land would not be used to stop them.

There is no universally accepted set of characteristics which define the term **Pogrom**. Klier writes that "**when applied indiscriminately to events in Eastern Europe, the term can be misleading, the more so when it implies that 'Pogroms' were regular events in the region and that they always shared common features.**" Use of the term to refer to events in 1918–19 in Polish cities including Kielce, Pinsk and Lwów was specifically avoided in the 1919 **Morgenthau Report** and the word "**excesses**" was used instead, because the report's authors argued that the use of the term **Pogrom** required a situation to be antisemitic rather than political in nature, which meant that it was inapplicable to the conditions existing in a war zone, and media use of the term **Pogrom** to refer to the 1991 **Crown Heights** riot caused public controversy. **In 2008, two separate attacks in the West Bank by Israeli Jewish settlers on Palestinian Arabs were characterized as Pogroms by then Prime Minister of Israel, Ehud Olmert.**

**Werner Bergmann** suggests a particularly unifying characteristic of all such incidents: "**y the *collective attribution* of a threat, the Pogrom differs from other forms of violence, such as lynchings, which are directed at individual members of a minority group, while the *imbalance of power* in favor of the rioters distinguishes Pogroms from other forms of riot (food riots, race riots, or 'communal riots' between evenly matched groups), and again, the *low level of organization* separates them from vigilantism, terrorism, massacre and genocide**".

## List of events
This is a list of events for which one of the commonly accepted names includes the word "**Pogrom**".

| Date | Pogrom name | Alternative name(s) | Deaths | Description |
|---|---|---|---|---|
| 38 CE | Alexandrian **Pogrom** (name disputed) | Alexandrian riots | | Aulus Avilius Flaccus, the Egyptian prefect of Alexandria appointed by Tiberius in 32 CE, may have encouraged the outbreak of violence; Philo wrote that Flaccus was later arrested and eventually executed for his part in this event. Scholarly research around the subject has |

| Date | Pogrom name | Alternative name(s) | Deaths | Description |
|------|-------------|---------------------|--------|-------------|
| | | | | been divided on certain points, including whether the Alexandrian Jews fought to keep their citizenship or to acquire it, whether they evaded the payment of the poll-tax or prevented any attempts to impose it on them, and whether they were safeguarding their identity against the Greeks or against the Egyptians. |
| 1066 | Granada **Pogrom** | 1066 Granada **massacre** | 4,000 Jews | A mob stormed the royal palace in Granada, which was at that time in Muslim-ruled Al-Andalus, assassinated the Jewish vizier **Joseph ibn Naghrela** and **massacre**d much of the Jewish population of the city. |
| 1096 | 1096 **Pogroms** | Rhineland **massacres** | 2,000 Jews | Peasant crusaders from France and Germany during the Popular Crusade, led by Peter the Hermit (and not sanctioned by the hierarchy of the Catholic Church), attacked Jewish communities in the three towns of Speyer, Worms and Mainz. They were the first Christian **Pogroms** to be officially recorded. |
| 1113 | Kiev **Pogrom** (name disputed) | Kiev revolt | | Rebellion sparked by the death of the Grand Prince of Kiev, in which Jews connected to the prince's economic affairs were among the victims |

| Date | Pogrom name | Alternative name(s) | Deaths | Description |
|---|---|---|---|---|
| 1349 | Strasbourg **Pogrom** | Strasbourg **massacre** | | |
| 1506 | Lisbon **Pogrom** | Lisbon **massacre** | 500 New Christians | After an episode of famine and bad harvests, a **Pogrom** happened in Lisbon, Portugal, in which more than 500 "New Christian" (forcibly converted Jews) people were slaughtered and/or burnt by an angry Christian mob, in the first night of what became known as the "Lisbon Massacre". The killing occurred from 19 to 21 April, almost eliminating the entire Jewish or Jewish-descendant community residing in that city. Even the Portuguese military and the king himself had difficulty stopping it. The event is today remembered with a monument in S. Domingos' church. |
| 1563 | Polotsk **Pogrom** (name disputed) | Polotsk drownings | | Following the fall of Polotsk to the army of Ivan IV, all those who refused to convert to Orthodox Christianity were ordered drowned in the Western Dvina river |
| 1821–1871 | First Odessa **Pogroms** | | | The Greeks of Odessa attacked the local Jewish community, in what began as economic disputes |
| 1881–1884 | First Russian Tsarist **Pogroms** | | 2 Jews | A large-scale wave of anti-Jewish riots swept through south-western Imperial Russia (present-day Ukraine and |

| Date | Pogrom name | Alternative name(s) | Deaths | Description |
|---|---|---|---|---|
| | | | | Poland) from 1881 to 1884 (in that period over 200 anti-Jewish events occurred in the **Russian Empire**, notably the Kiev, Warsaw and Odessa **Pogroms**) |
| 1881 | Warsaw **Pogrom** | | 2 Jews (Included above) | Three days of rioting against Jews, Jewish stores, businesses, and residences in the streets adjoining the Holy Cross Church. |
| 1902 | Czestochowa **Pogrom** (name disputed) | | 14 Jews | A mob attacked the Jewish shops, killing fourteen Jews and one gendarme. The Russian military brought to restore order were stoned by mob. |
| 1903–1906 | Second Russian Tsarist **Pogroms** | | 2,000+ Jews | A much bloodier wave of **Pogroms** broke out from 1903 to 1906, leaving an estimated 2,000 Jews dead and many more wounded, as many Jewish residents took arms to defend their families and property from the attackers. The 1905 **Pogrom** against the Jewish population in Odessa was the most serious **Pogrom** of the period, with reports of up to 2,500 Jewish people killed. |
| 1903 | First Kishinev **Pogrom** | | 47 Jews (Included above) | Three days of anti-Jewish rioting sparked by anti-Semitic articles in local newspapers |
| 1904 | Limerick **Pogrom** (name disputed) | Limerick boycott | None | An economic boycott waged against the small Jewish |

| Date | Pogrom name | Alternative name(s) | Deaths | Description |
|---|---|---|---|---|
| | | | | community in Limerick, Ireland, for over two years |
| 1905 | Second Kishinev **Pogrom** | | 19 Jews (Included above) | Two days of anti-Jewish rioting beginning as political protests against the Tsar |
| 1905 | Kiev **Pogrom** (1905) | | 100 Jews (Included above) | Following a city hall meeting, a mob was drawn into the streets, proclaiming that "all Russia's troubles stemmed from the machinations of the Jews and socialists." |
| 1906 | Siedlce **Pogrom** | | 26 Jews (Included above) | An attack organized by the Russian secret police (Okhrana). Anti-Semitic pamphlets had been distributed for over a week and before any unrest begun, a curfew was declared. |
| 1909 | Adana **Pogrom** | Adana **massacre** | 30,000 Armenians | A **massacre** of Armenians in the city of Adana amidst the Countercoup (1909) resulted in a series of anti-Armenian **Pogroms** throughout the district. |
| 1911 | Tredegar **Pogrom** (name disputed) South Wales | Tredegar riots | None | Jewish shops were ransacked and the army had to be brought in |
| 1914 | Anti-Serb **Pogrom** in Sarajevo | Sarajevo frenzy of hate | 2 Serbs | Occurred shortly after the assassination of Archduke Franz Ferdinand. |
| 1918 | Lwów **Pogrom**(name disputed) | Lemberg **massacre** | 52–150 Jews, 270 Ukrainians | During the Polish-Ukrainian War over three days of unrest in the city, an estimated 52–150 Jewish residents were killed and hundreds more were |

| Date | Pogrom name | Alternative name(s) | Deaths | Description |
|---|---|---|---|---|
| | | | | injured, with widespread looting carried out by Polish soldiers, as well as by lawless civilians, and local criminals. Two hundred and seventy Ukrainians were also killed during this incident. The Poles did not stop the **Pogrom** until two days after it began. The independent investigations by the British and American missions in Poland stated that there were no clear conclusions and that foreign press reports were exaggerated. |
| 1918-1919 | Guba City **Pogrom** | | 3,000-10,000 | Massacre of Mountain Jews in Azerbaijan |
| 1919 | Kiev **Pogroms** (1919) | | 60+ | A series of Jewish **Pogroms** in various places around Kiev carried out by White Volunteer Army troops |
| 1919 | Pinsk **Pogrom** (name disputed) | Pinsk **massacre** | 36 Jews | Mass execution of thirty-five Jewish residents of Pinsk in April 1919 by the Polish Army, during the opening stages of the Polish-Soviet War |
| 1919–20 | Vilna **Pogrom** (name disputed) | Vilna offensive | 65+ Jews and non-Jews | As Polish troops entered the city, dozens of people connected with the Lit-Bel were arrested, and some were executed |
| 1921 | Tulsa **Pogrom** | Tulsa race riot, Little Africa on Fire | Up to 300 Blacks | Destruction of the Greenwood community of Tulsa, the wealthiest black community in the United States, by a white mob with the support of |

| Date | Pogrom name | Alternative name(s) | Deaths | Description |
|---|---|---|---|---|
| | | | | authorities, following an unfounded accusation of sexual assault by a black man against a white woman. |
| 1929 | Hebron **Pogrom** | Hebron **massacre** | 67 Jews | During the 1929 Palestine riots, sixty-seven Jews were killed as the violence spread to Hebron, then part of Mandatory Palestine, by Arabs incited to violence by rumors that Jews were massacring Arabs in Jerusalem and seizing control of Muslim holy places. |
| 1936 | Przytyk **Pogrom**(name disputed) | Przytyk riot | 2 Jews and 1 Polish | Some of the Jewish residents gathered in the town square in anticipation of the attack by the peasants, but nothing happened on that day. Two days later, however, on a market day, as Jewish historians Martin Gilbert and David Vital claim, peasants attacked their Jewish neighbors. |
| 1938 | November **Pogrom** | Kristallnacht | 91 Jews | Coordinated attacks against Jews throughout Nazi Germany and parts of Austria, carried out by SA paramilitary forces and non-Jewish civilians. Accounts from the foreign journalists working in Germany sent shock waves around the world. |
| 1940 | Dorohoi **Pogrom** | | 53 Jews | Romanian military units carried out a **Pogrom** against the local Jews, during which, according to an official |

| Date | Pogrom name | Alternative name(s) | Deaths | Description |
|------|-------------|---------------------|--------|-------------|
| | | | | Romanian report, 53 Jews were murdered, and dozens injured |
| 1941 | Iasi **Pogrom** | | 13,266 Jews | One of the most violent **Pogroms** in Jewish history, launched by governmental forces in the Romanian city of Iasi (Jassy) against its Jewish population. In July 2017, approximately 1000 Jewish survivors of the **Pogrom** became eligible to receive German compensation of $384/month under an agreement between Germany and NY-based Conference on Jewish Material Claims against Germany.[citation needed] |
| 1941 | Antwerp **Pogrom** | | 0 | One of the few **Pogroms** of Belgian history. Flemish collaborators attacked and burned synagogues and attacked a rabbi in the city of Antwerp |
| 1941 | Bucharest **Pogrom** | Legionnaires' rebellion | 125 Jews and 30 soldiers | As the privileges of the paramilitary organization Iron Guard were being cut off by *Conductor* Ion Antonescu, members of the Iron Guard, also known as the Legionnaires, revolted. During the rebellion and **Pogrom**, the Iron Guard killed 125 Jews and 30 soldiers died in the confrontation with the rebels. |
| 1941 | Tykocin **Pogrom** | | 1,400–1,700 Jews | Mass murder of Jewish residents of Tykocin in |

| Date | Pogrom name | Alternative name(s) | Deaths | Description |
|---|---|---|---|---|
| | | | | occupied Poland during World War II, soon after Nazi German attack on the Soviet Union. |
| 1941 | Jedwabne **Pogrom** | | 340 Jews | The local rabbi was forced to lead a procession of about 40 people to a pre-emptied barn, killed and buried along with fragments of a destroyed monument of Lenin. A further 250-300 Jews were led to the same barn later that day, locked inside and burned alive using kerosene |
| 1941 | **Pogrom** in Krnjeuša | | 240 Croats | An organized attack in the territory of the Catholic parish of Krnjeuša in northwestern Bosnia and Herzegovina, carried out by Serb Chetniks against the local Catholic Croat population |
| 1941 | Farhud | | 180 Jewish Iraqis | |
| 1941 | Lviv **Pogroms** | | 4,000–8,000 civilian prisoners and 5,000 Jews | Massacres of civilian prisoners by Soviet forces prior to evacuation, followed by **massacre** of Jews by German and other forces. Subject of a protracted controversy |
| 1946 | Kunmadaras **Pogrom** | | 4 Jews | A frenzy instigated by the crowd's libelous belief that some Jewish people had made sausage out of Christian children |

| Date | Pogrom name | Alternative name(s) | Deaths | Description |
|---|---|---|---|---|
| 1946 | Miskolc **Pogrom** | | 2 Jews | Riots started as demonstrations against economic hardships and later became anti-Semitic |
| 1946 | Kielce **Pogrom** | | 38–42 Jews | Violence against the Jewish community contre, initiated by Polish Communist armed forces (LWP, KBW, GZI WP) and continued by a mob of local townsfolk. |
| 1955 | Istanbul **Pogrom** | Istanbul riots | 13–30 Greeks | Organized mob attacks directed primarily at Istanbul's Greek minority. Accelerated the emigration of ethnic Greeks from Turkey (Jews were also targeted in this event). |
| 1956 | 1956 Ceylonese riots | 1956 anti-Tamil **Pogrom** | 150 Primarily Tamils | 1956 anti-Tamil **Pogrom** or Gal Oya **massacre**/riots were the first ethnic riots that targeted the minority Tamils in independent Sri Lanka. |
| 1958 | 1958 anti-Tamil **Pogrom** | 1958 anti-Tamil **Pogrom** | 300 Primarily Tamils | 1958 anti-Tamil **Pogrom** also known as 58 riots, refer to the first island wide ethnic riots and **Pogrom** in Sri Lanka. |
| 1966 | 1966 anti-Igbo **Pogrom** | | | A series of **massacres** directed at Igbo and other southern Nigerian residents throughout Nigeria before and after the overthrow (and assassination) of the Aguiyi-Ironsi junta by Murtala Mohammed. |
| 1977 | 1977 anti-Tamil **Pogrom** | | 300-1500 Primarily Tamils | The 1977 anti-Tamil **Pogrom** followed the 1977 general elections in Sri Lanka where the Sri Lankan Tamil |

| Date | Pogrom name | Alternative name(s) | Deaths | Description |
|---|---|---|---|---|
| | | | | nationalistic Tamil United Liberation Front won a plurality of minority Sri Lankan Tamil votes in which it stood for secession. |
| 1983 | Black July | 1983 anti-Tamil **Pogrom** | 400–3,000 Tamils | Over seven days mobs of mainly Sinhalese attacked Tamil targets, burning, looting and killing |
| 1984 | 1984 anti-Sikh riots | 1984 anti-Sikh **Pogrom** | 8,000 Sikhs | In October 1984 anti-Sikh **Pogrom** in Delhi, and other parts of India, Sikhs in India were targeted |
| 1988 | Sumgait **Pogrom** | | 26+ (or about 100-300) Armenians and 6+ Azeris (possibly rioters) | Mobs made up largely of ethnic Azeris formed into groups that went on to attack and kill Armenians both on the streets and in their apartments; widespread looting and a general lack of concern from police officers allowed the situation to worsen |
| 1988 | Kirovabad **Pogrom** | | 3+ Soviet soldiers, 3+ Azeris and 1+ Armenian | Ethnic Azeris attacked Armenians throughout the city |
| 1989 | 1989 Bangladesh **Pogroms** | | | Attacks against Bengali Hindus, apparently as a reaction to the laying of the foundation of Ram temple adjacent to the disputed structure in Ayodhya |
| 1990 | Baku **Pogrom** | | 90 Armenians, 20 Russian soldiers | Seven-day attack during which Armenians were beaten, tortured, murdered and |

| Date | Pogrom name | Alternative name(s) | Deaths | Description |
|---|---|---|---|---|
| | | | | expelled from the city. There were also many raids on apartments, robberies and arsons |
| 1991 | Crown Heights **Pogrom** (disputed) | Crown Heights riot | 1 Jew and 1 non-Jew | A three-day riot that occurred in the Crown Heights section of Brooklyn, New York. The riots incited by the death of the seven-year-old Gavin Cato, unleashed simmering tensions within Crown Heights' black community against the Orthodox Jewish community. In its wake, several Jews were seriously injured; one Orthodox Jewish man, Yankel Rosenbaum, was killed; and a non-Jewish man, allegedly mistaken by rioters for a Jew, was killed by a group of African-American men. |
| 1991 | Mława **Pogrom** | | | Five days of rioting in which a mob attacked Roma residents of the Polish town of Mława causing hundreds to flee in terror |
| 2002 | Gujarat **Pogrom** | 2002 Gujarat violence | 790–2,000 Muslims and 254 Hindus | Inter-communal violence in the Indian state of Gujarat which lasted for approximately three days with the state government being accused of supporting or even instigating the riots |
| 2004 | March **Pogrom** | 2004 unrest in Kosovo | 8 ethnic Serbs and 11 ethnic Albanians | Over 4,000 Serbs were forced to leave their homes, 935 Serb houses, 10 public facilities and 35 Serbian Orthodox church- |

| Date | Pogrom name | Alternative name(s) | Deaths | Description |
|------|-------------|---------------------|--------|-------------|
| | | | | buildings were desecrated, damaged or destroyed, and six towns and nine villages were ethnically cleansed according to Serbian media |
| 2013 | 2013 Burma anti-Muslim riots | anti-Rohingya **Pogrom** | Rohingya Muslims | Muslims called the Rohingyas were targeted in the Buddhist-majority Myanmar. |

# Prophet Elijah

Elijah (Hebrew: *Eliyahu*, meaning "My God is Yahweh/YHWH") or Latinized form **Elias** was, according to the **Books of Kings** in the **Hebrew Bible,** a prophet and a miracle worker who lived in the northern kingdom of Israel during the reign of **King Ahab** (9th century BC). In **1 Kings 18**, **Elijah** defended the worship of the Hebrew God over that of the Canaanite deity **Baal** . God also performed many miracles through **Elijah**, including resurrection (raising the dead), bringing fire down from the sky, and entering Heaven alive **"by fire"**. He is also portrayed as leading a school of prophets known as **"the sons of the prophets"**.

Following his ascension, **Elisha**, his disciple and most devoted assistant took over his role as leader of this school. The Book of **Malachi** prophesies **Elijah**'s return **"before the coming of the great and terrible day of the LORD"**, making him a harbinger of the **Messiah** and of the eschaton in various faiths that revere the Hebrew Bible. References to **Elijah** appear in Ecclesiasticus, the New Testament, the **Mishnah** and **Talmud**, the **Qur'an**, the **Book of Mormon**, the Doctrine and Covenants, and **Baha'i** writings.

In Judaism, **Elijah**'s name is invoked at the weekly **Havdalah** ritual that marks the end of **Shabbat,** and **Elijah** is invoked in other Jewish customs, among them the **Passover Seder** and the brit Milah (ritual circumcision). He appears in numerous stories and references in the H**Aggadah** and rabbinic literature, including the Babylonian Talmud.

The Christian New Testament notes that some people thought that **Jesus** was, in some sense, **Elijah**. But **Jesus** makes it clear that **John the Baptist is "the Elijah"** who was promised to come in **Malachi 3:1** in the Septuagint. **(Malachi 4:5) Elijah** appears with **Moses** during the **Transfiguration of Jesus** . **Elijah** is also a figure in various Christian folk traditions, at times identified with earlier pagan thunder or **sky gods**.

In Islam, **Elijah** appears in the **Qur'an** as a prophet and messenger of God, where his biblical narrative of preaching against the worshipers of **Baal** is recounted in a concise form. Due to his importance to Muslims, Catholics and Orthodox Christians, **Elijah** has been venerated as the patron saint of Bosnia and Herzegovina since 1752.

## Biblical accounts

According to the Bible, by the 9th century BC, the **Kingdom of Israel**, once united under **Solomon** , was divided into the northern Kingdom of Israel and southern **Kingdom of Judah,** which retained the historical capital of Jerusalem along with its Temple. However, scholars today are divided as to whether the **United Kingdom** under **Solomon** ever existed. **Omri, King of Israel**, continued policies dating from the reign of Jeroboam, contrary to religious law, that were intended to reorient religious focus away from Jerusalem: encouraging the building of local temple altars for sacrifices, appointing priests from outside the family of the **Levites**, and allowing or encouraging temples dedicated to **Baal** , an important deity in ancient **Canaanite** religion.

**Omri** achieved domestic security with a marriage alliance between his son **Ahab** and princess **Jezebel,** a priestess of **Baal** and the daughter of the **king of Sidon** in Phoenicia. These solutions brought security and economic prosperity to Israel for a time, but did not bring peace with the Israelite prophets, who were interested in a strict **Deuteronomical** interpretation of the religious law.

Under **Ahab's kingship**, these tensions were exacerbated. **Ahab** built a temple for **Baal**, and his wife Jezebel brought a large entourage of priests and prophets of **Baal** and Asherah into the country. It is in this context that **Elijah** is introduced in **1 Kings 17:1 as Elijah "the Tishbite"**. He warns **Ahab** that there will be years of catastrophic drought so severe that not even dew will form, because **Ahab** and his queen stand at the end of a line of kings of Israel who are said to have "done evil in the sight of the Lord."

## 1st and 2nd Kings

No background for the person of **Elijah** is given except for his brief description as being a **"Tishbite."** His name in Hebrew means **"My God is Yahweh",** and may be a title applied to him because of his challenge to worship of **Baal**. As told in the Hebrew Bible, **Elijah**'s challenge is bold and direct. **Baal** was the Canaanite god responsible for rain, thunder, lightning, and dew. **Elijah** not only challenges **Baal** on behalf of God himself, but he also challenges Jezebel, her priests, **Ahab** and the people of Israel.

### *Raising of the son of the widow of Zarephath*

After **Elijah**'s confrontation with **Ahab**, God tells him to flee out of Israel, to a hiding place by the brook Chorath, east of the Jordan, where he will be fed by ravens. When the brook dries up, God sends him to a widow living in the town of **Zarephath** in Phoenicia. When **Elijah** finds her and asks to be fed, she says that she does not have sufficient food to keep her and her own son alive. **Elijah** tells her that God will not allow her supply of flour or oil to run out, saying, **"Do not be afraid ... For thus says the Lord the God of Israel: The jar of meal will not be emptied and the jug of oil will not fail until the day that the Lord sends rain on the earth."**

She feeds him the last of their food, and **Elijah**'s promise miraculously comes true. God gave her **"manna"** from heaven even while he was withholding food from his unfaithful people in the **Promised Land**. Sometime later the widow's son dies and the widow cries, **"You have come to me to bring my sin to remembrance, and to cause the death of my son!"** **Elijah** prays that God might restore her son so that the trustworthiness of God's word might be demonstrated.

**1 Kings 17:22** relates how God **"listened to the voice of Elijah; the life of the child came into him again, and he revived."** This is the first instance of raising the dead recorded in Scripture. This non-Israelite widow was granted the life of her son, the only hope for a widow in ancient society. The widow cried, **"...the word of the Lord in your mouth is truth."** She made a confession that the Israelites had failed to make. After more than three years of drought and famine, God tells **Elijah** to return to **Ahab** and announce the end of the drought: not occasioned by repentance in Israel but by the command of the Lord, who had determined to reveal himself again to his people.

While on his way, **Elijah** meets Obadiah, the head of **Ahab**'s household, who had hidden a hundred Jewish prophets when **Aha** and Jezebel had been killing them. **Elijah** sends Obadiah back to **Ahab** to announce his return to Israel.

## Challenge to Baal

When **Ahab** confronts **Elijah**, he refers to him as the **"troubler of Israel."** **Elijah** responds by throwing the charge back at **Ahab**, saying that it is **Ahab** who has troubled Israel by allowing the worship of false gods. **Elijah** then berates both the people of Israel and **Ahab** for their acquiescence in **Baal** worship. **"How long will you go limping with two different opinions? If the Lord is God, follow him; but if Baal, then follow him."** And the people were silent. The Hebrew for this word, **"go limping"** or **"waver"**, is the same as that used for **"danced" in 1 Kings 18, verse 26,** where the prophets of **Baal** frantically dance. **Elijah** speaks with sharp irony about the religious ambivalence of Israel.

**Elijah** proposes a direct test of the powers of **Baal** and the Jewish God. **The people of Israel, 450 prophets of Baal, and 400 prophets of Asherah are summoned to Mount Carmel.** Two altars are built, one for **Baal** and one for God. Wood is laid on the altars. Two oxen are slaughtered and cut into pieces; the pieces are laid on the wood. **Elijah** then invites the priests of **Baal** to pray for fire to light the sacrifice. They pray from morning to noon without success.

**Elijah** ridicules their efforts. "At noon **Elijah** mocked them, saying, **'cry aloud! Surely he is a god; either he is meditating, or he has wandered away, or he is on a journey, or perhaps he is asleep and must be awakened.'"** They respond by cutting themselves and adding their own blood to the sacrifice (such mutilation of the body was strictly forbidden in the Mosaic Law). **They continue praying until evening without success. Elijah** now orders that the altar of God be drenched with water from **"four large jars"** poured three times. He asks God to accept the sacrifice. Fire falls from the sky, consuming the water, the sacrifice and the stones of the altar itself as well. **Elijah** then orders the deaths of the priests of **Baal**. **Elijah** prays earnestly for rain to fall again on the land. **Then the rains begin, signaling the end of the famine.**

## Mount Horeb

**Jezebel**, enraged that **Elijah** had ordered the deaths of her priests, threatens to kill **Elijah**. Later **Elijah** would prophesize about Jezebel's death, because of her sin. **Elijah** flees to Beersheba in Judah, continues alone into the wilderness, and finally sits down under a shrub, praying for death. He falls asleep under the tree; the angel of the Lord touches him and tells him to wake up and eat. When he awakens he finds bread and a jar of water. He eats, drinks, and goes back to sleep. The angel comes a second time and tells him to eat and drink because he has a long journey ahead of him.

**Elijah** travels for forty days and forty nights to **Mount Horeb, where Moses had received the Ten Commandments**. **Elijah** is the only person described in the Bible as returning to Horeb, after **Moses** and his generation had left Horeb several centuries before. He seeks shelter in a cave. God again speaks to **Elijah**: **"What doest thou here, Elijah?"** **Elijah** did not give a direct answer to the Lord's question but evades and equivocates, implying that the work the Lord had begun centuries earlier had now come to nothing, and that his own work was fruitless. Unlike **Moses**, who tried to defend Israel when they sinned with the golden calf, **Elijah** bitterly complains over the Israelites' unfaithfulness and says he is the **"only one left"**.

Up until this time **Elijah** has only the word of God to guide him, but now he is told to go outside the cave and **"stand before the Lord."** A terrible wind passes, but God is not in the wind. A great earthquake shakes the mountain, but God is not in the earthquake. Then a fire passes the mountain, but God is not in the fire. Then a **"still small voice"** comes to **Elijah** and asks again, **"What doest thou here, Elijah?"** **Elijah** again evades the question and his lament is unrevised, showing that he did not understand the importance of the divine revelation he had just witnessed. God then sends him out again, this time to Damascus to anoint Hazael as king of Aram, Jehu as king of Israel, and **Elisha** as his replacement.

## Vineyard of Naboth

**Elijah** encounters **Ahab** again in **1 Kings 21**, after **Ahab** has acquired possession of a vineyard by murder. **Ahab** desires to have the vineyard of Naboth of Jezreel. He offers a better vineyard or a fair price for the land. But Naboth tells **Ahab** that God has told him not to part with the land. **Ahab** accepts this answer with sullen bad grace. Jezebel, however, plots a method for acquiring the land. She sends letters, in **Ahab**'s name, to the elders and nobles who lived near Naboth. They are to arrange a feast and invite **Naboth**. At the feast, false charges of cursing God and **Ahab** are to be made against him. The plot is carried out and Naboth is stoned to death. When word comes that Naboth is dead, Jezebel tells **Ahab** to take possession of the vineyard.

God again speaks to **Elijah** and sends him to confront **Ahab** with a question and a prophecy: **"Have you killed, and also taken possession?"** and, **"In the place where dogs licked up the blood of Naboth, dogs will also lick up your blood. "Ahab** begins the confrontation by calling

**Elijah** his enemy. **Elijah** responds by throwing the charge back at him, telling him that he has made himself the enemy of God by his own actions. **Elijah** then goes beyond the prophecy he was given and tells **Ahab** that his entire kingdom will reject his authority; that Jezebel will be eaten by dogs within Jezreel; and that his family will be consumed by dogs as well (if they die in a city) or by birds (if they die in the country). When **Ahab** hears this he repents to such a degree that God relents in punishing **Ahab** but will punish Jezebel and their son: Ahaziah.

## Ahaziah

**Elijah**'s story continues now from **Ahab** to an encounter with Ahaziah. The scene opens with Ahaziah seriously injured in a fall. He sends to the priests of **Baal** zebub in Ekron, outside the kingdom of Israel, to know if he will recover. **Elijah** intercepts his messengers and sends them back to Ahaziah with a message **"Is it because there is no God in Israel that you are sending to inquire of Baal -zebub, the god of Ekron?"** Ahaziah asks the messengers to describe the person who gave them this message. They tell him he was a hairy man with a leather belt around his waist and he instantly recognizes the description as **Elijah** the Tishbite. **Ahaziah** sends out three groups of soldiers to arrest **Elijah**. The first two are destroyed by fire which **Elijah** calls down from heaven. The leader of the third group asks for mercy for himself and his men.

**Elijah** agrees to accompany this third group to **Ahaziah**, where he gives his prophecy in person. **Ahaziah** dies without recovering from his injuries in accordance with **Elijah**'s word.

## Departure

According to **2 Kings 2:3–9, Elisha (Eliseus) and "the sons of the prophets"** knew beforehand that **Elijah** would one day be assumed into heaven. **Elisha** asked **Elijah** to **"let a double portion"** of **Elijah**'s **"spirit"** be upon him. **Elijah** agreed, with the condition that **Elisha** would see him be **"taken"**. **Elijah**, in company with **Elisha**, approaches the Jordan. He rolls up his mantle and strikes the water. The water immediately divides and **Elijah** and **Elisha** cross on dry land. **Suddenly, a chariot of fire and horses of fire appear and Elijah is lifted up in a whirlwind.** As **Elijah** is lifted up, his mantle falls to the ground and **Elisha** picks it up.

## Final mention: 2nd Chronicles

**Elijah** is mentioned once more in **2 Chronicles 21:12,** which will be his final mention in the **Hebrew Bible.** A letter is sent under the prophet's name to Jehoram of Judah. It tells him that he has led the people of Judah astray in the same way that Israel was led astray. The prophet ends the letter with a prediction of a painful death. This letter is a puzzle to readers for several reasons. First, it concerns a king of the southern kingdom, while **Elijah** concerned himself with the kingdom of Israel.

Second, the message begins with **"Thus says YHVH, God of your father David..."** rather than the more usual **"...in the name of YHVH the God of Israel."** Also, this letter seems to come after **Elijah's ascension into the whirlwind**. **Michael Wilcock**, formerly of **Trinity College**, **Bristol**, suggests a number of possible reasons for this letter, among them that it may be an example of a better known prophet's name being substituted for that of a lesser known prophet. **John Van Seters,** however, rejects the letter as having any connection with the **Elijah** tradition. However, **Wilcock** argues that **Elijah**'s letter, 'does address a very 'northern' situation in the southern kingdom', and thus is authentic.

## The Christian end of Elijah in Malachi

> "Lo, I will send you the prophet **Elijah** before the great and terrible day of the Lord comes. He will turn the hearts of parents to their children and the hearts of children to their parents, so that I will not come and strike the land with a curse."
>
> — **Malachi 4:5–6,** *New Revised Standard Version*

While the final mention of **Elijah** in the Hebrew Bible is in the **Book of Chronicles**, the Christian Bible's ordering of the books of the Septuagint places the **Book of Malachi** , which prophesies a messiah, before the Gospels and means that **Elijah**'s final Old Testament appearance is in the **Book of Malachi** , where it is written, **"Lo, I will send you the prophet Elijah before the great and terrible day of the Lord comes."** That day is described as the burning of a great furnace, **"... so that it will leave them neither root nor branch."** In Christianity it is traditionally believed that **Elijah**'s appearance during the transfiguration of **Jesus** fulfilled this prophecy. Moreover, in the **Gospel of Matthew**, **Jesus** identifies **John the Baptist** as the spiritual successor to **Elijah**: **"and if you are willing to accept it, he is Elijah who is to come."** Finally, the verses in **Malachi** are believed to indicate that **Elijah** has a role in the end-times, immediately before the **second coming of Jesus**.

## One theory of textual analysis

According to **Susanne Otto**, the **Elijah** stories were added to the **Deuteronomistic History** in four stages. The first stage dates from the final edition of the History, about **560 BC**, when the three stories of **Naboth's** vineyard, the death of **Ahaziah**, and the story of **Jehu's coup** were included to embody the themes of the reliability of God's word and the cycle of **Baal** worship and religious reform in the history of the **Northern Kingdom**. The narratives about the **Omride** wars were added shortly afterwards to illustrate a newly introduced theme, that the attitude of the king towards God determines the fate of Israel.

According to **Otto**, **1 Kings 17–18** was added in early post-Exilic times **(after 538 BC)** to demonstrate the possibility of a new life in community with God after the time of judgment. Additionally, **Otto** suggests that in the fifth century BC, **1 Kings 19:1–18** and the remaining

**Elisha** stories were inserted to give prophecy a legitimate foundation in the history of Israel. The foregoing **Otto** analysis is heavily disputed amongst biblical scholars.

## In the Aggadah, Talmud, and Extra-canonical Books

Jewish legends about **Elijah** abound in the **Aggadah**, which is found throughout various collections of rabbinic literature, including the **Babylonian Talmud**. This varied literature does not merely discuss his life, but has created a new history of him, which, beginning with his death – or "**translation**" – ends only with the close of the history of the human race. The volume of references to **Elijah** in **Jewish Tradition** stands in marked contrast to that in the Canon. As in the case of most figures of Jewish legend, so in the case of **Elijah**, the biblical account became the basis of later legend.

**Elijah** the precursor of the **Messiah**, **Elijah** zealous in the cause of God, **Elijah** the helper in distress: these are the three leading notes struck by the **Aggadah**, endeavoring to complete the biblical picture with the **Elijah** legends. His career is extensive, colorful, and varied. He has appeared the world over in the guise of a beggar and scholar. From the time of **Malachi**, who says of **Elijah** that God will send him before **"the great and dreadful day" (Mal. 3:23)**, down to the later stories of the Chasidic rabbis, reverence and love, expectation and hope, were always connected in the Jewish consciousness with **Elijah**.

## Origin

Three different theories regarding **Elijah**'s origin are presented in the **Aggadah** literature: (1) he belonged to the tribe of Gad, (2) he was a **Benjamite** from Jerusalem, identical with the **Elijah** mentioned in **I Chronicles 8:27**, and (3) he was a priest.

Many Christian Church fathers also have stated that **Elijah was a priest**. Some Rabbis have speculated that he should be identified with Phinehas. According to later Kabbalistic literature, **Elijah was really an angel in human form**, so that he had neither parents nor offspring. The **Midrash Rabbah Exodus 4:2** states "**Elijah** should have revived his parents as he had revived the son of the **Zarephathite**" indicating he surely had parents. The Talmud states "**Said he to him (Elijah): Art thou not a priest: why then dost thou stand in a cemetery?**"

## Elijah's zeal for God

In spite of **Elijah**'s many miracles, the mass of the Jewish people remained as godless as before. A Midrash tells that they even abolished the sign of the covenant, and the prophet had to appear as Israel's accuser before God. In the same cave where God once appeared to **Moses** and revealed Himself as gracious and merciful, **Elijah** was summoned to appear before God. By this summons he perceived that he should have appealed to God's mercy, instead of becoming Israel's accuser. The prophet, however, remained relentless in his zeal and severity, so that God commanded him to appoint his successor.

The vision in which **God revealed Himself to Elijah** gave him at the same time a picture of the destinies of man, who has to pass through **"four worlds."** This world was shown to the prophet by God through symbolism: in the form of the wind, since it disappears as the wind; storm is the day of death, before which man trembles; fire is the judgment in **Gehenna**; and the stillness is the last day.

Three years after this vision **Elijah** was **"translated."** Concerning the place to which **Elijah** was transferred, opinions differ among Jews and Christians, but the old view was that **Elijah** was received among the heavenly inhabitants, where he records the deeds of men, a task which according to the apocalyptic literature is entrusted to **Enoch**. But as early as the middle of the 2nd century, when the notion of translation to heaven underwent divergent possible interpretations by Christian theologians, the assertion was made that **Elijah** never entered into heaven proper. In later literature paradise is generally designated as the abode of **Elijah**, but since the location of paradise is itself uncertain, the last two statements may be identical.

## Ecclesiasticus

In the Wisdom of **Jesus ben Sira (Sirach 48:10)** his tasks are altered to: 1) herald the eschaton, 2) calm God's fury, 3) restore familial peace, and 4) restore the 12 tribes.

## Elijah in Judaism

At Jewish circumcision ceremonies, a chair is set aside for the use of the prophet **Elijah**. **Elijah** is said to be a witness at all circumcisions when the sign of the covenant is placed upon the body of the child. This custom stems from the incident at **Mount Horeb** (1 Kings 19): **Elijah** had arrived at **Mount Horeb** after the demonstration of God's presence and power on **Mount Carmel.** (1 Kings 18) God asks **Elijah** to explain his arrival, and **Elijah** replies: "I have been very jealous for the Lord, the God of hosts; for the people of Israel have forsaken thy covenant, thrown down thy altars, and slain thy prophets with the sword; and I, even I only, am left; and they seek my life, to take it away" **(1 Kings 19:10).** According to Rabbinic tradition, **Elijah**'s words were patently untrue (1 Kings 18:4 and 1 Kings 19:18), and since **Elijah** accused Israel of failing to uphold the covenant, God would require **Elijah** to be present at every covenant of circumcision.

## Elijah's cup / *Passover Seder*

In the Talmudic literature, **Elijah** would visit rabbis to help solve particularly difficult legal problems. **Malachi** had cited **Elijah** as the harbinger of the eschaton. Thus, when confronted with reconciling impossibly conflicting laws or rituals, the rabbis would set aside any decision **"until Elijah comes."** One such decision was whether the **Passover Seder** required four or five cups of wine. Each serving of wine corresponds to one of the **"four expressions of redemption"** in the Book of Exodus:

I am the Lord, and *I will bring you out* from under the burdens of the Egyptians, and *I will deliver you* from their bondage, and *I will redeem you* with an out-stretched arm and with great acts of judgment, and *I will take you* **for my people,** and I will be your God; and you shall know that I am the Lord your God, who has brought you out from under the burdens of the Egyptians" **(Exodus 6:6–7).**

The next verse, **"And *I will bring you* into the land which I swore to give to Abraham, to Isaac, and to Jacob; I will give it to you for a possession. I am the Lord." (Exodus 6:8)** was not fulfilled until the generation following the **Passover** story, and the rabbis could not decide whether this verse counted as part of the **Passover** celebration (thus deserving of another serving of wine). Thus, a cup was left for the arrival of **Elijah.** In practice the fifth cup has come to be seen as a celebration of future redemption. Today, a place is reserved at the Seder table and a cup of wine is placed there for **Elijah.** During the Seder, the door of the house is opened and **Elijah** is invited in. Traditionally, the cup is viewed as **Elijah**'s and is used for no other purpose.

## Havdalah

Havdalah is the ceremony that concludes the **Sabbath Day** (Saturday evening in Jewish tradition). As part of the concluding hymn, an appeal is made to God that **Elijah** will come during the following week. "**Elijah** the Prophet, **Elijah the Tishbite.** Let him come quickly, in our day with the messiah, **the son of David."**

## Elijah in Jewish folklore

The volume of references to **Elijah** in folklore stands in marked contrast to that in the canon. **Elijah**'s miraculous transferal to heaven led to speculation as to his true identity. **Louis Ginzberg** equates him with Phinehas the grandson of Aaron **(Exodus 6:25).** Because of Phinehas' zealousness for God, he and his descendants were promised, **"a covenant of lasting priesthood" (Numbers 25:13).** Therefore, **Elijah** is a priest as well as a prophet. **Elijah** is also equated with the **Archangel Sandalphon,** who four wing beats will carries him to any part of the earth. When forced to choose between death and dishonor, **Rabbi Kahana** chose to leap to his death.

Before he could strike the ground, **Elijah/Sandalphon** had appeared to catch him. Yet another name for **Elijah** is **"Angel of the Covenant"**

## Rabbi Joshua ben Levi

References to **Elijah** in Jewish folklore range from short observations (e. g. It is said that when dogs are happy for no reason, it is because **Elijah** is in the neighborhood) to lengthy parables on the nature of God's justice. One such story is that of **Rabbi Joshua ben Levi**. The rabbi, a friend of **Elijah**'s, was asked what favor he might wish. The rabbi answered only that he be able to join **Elijah** in his wanderings. **Elijah** granted his wish only if he refrained from asking any questions about any of the prophet's actions. He agreed and they began their journey. The first place they came to was the house of an elderly couple who were so poor they had only one old cow. The old couple gave of their hospitality as best they could.

The next morning, as the travelers left, **Elijah** prayed that the old cow would die and it did. The second place they came to was the home of a wealthy man. He had no patience for his visitors and chased them away with the admonition that they should get jobs and not beg from honest people. As they were leaving, they passed the man's wall and saw that it was crumbling. **Elijah** prayed that the wall be repaired and it was so. Next, they came to a wealthy synagogue. They were allowed to spend the night with only the smallest of provisions. When they left, **Elijah** prayed that every member of the synagogue might become a leader.

Finally, they came to a very poor synagogue. Here they were treated with great courtesy and hospitality. When they left, **Elijah** prayed that God might give them a single wise leader. At this Rabbi Joshua could no longer hold back. He demanded of **Elijah** an explanation of his actions. At the house of the old couple, **Elijah** knew that the **Angel of Death** was coming for the old woman. So he prayed that God might have the angel take the cow instead. At the house of the wealthy man, there was a great treasure hidden in the crumbling wall.

**Elijah** prayed that the wall be restored thus keeping the treasure away from the miser. The story ends with a moral: A synagogue with many leaders will be ruined by many arguments. A town with a single wise leader will be guided to success and prosperity. **"Know then, that if thou seest an evil-doer prosper, it is not always unto his advantage, and if a righteous man suffers need and distress, think not God is unjust."**

## Rabbi Eliezer

The **Elijah** of legend did not lose any of his ability to afflict the comfortable. The case of Rabbi Eliezer son of **Rabbi Simon ben Yohai** is illustrative. Once, when walking a beach, he came upon a hideously ugly man—the prophet in disguise. The man greeted him courteously, **"Peace be with thee, Rabbi."** Instead of returning the greeting, the rabbi could not resist an insult, **"How ugly you are! Is there anyone as ugly as you in your town?"** Elijah responded with, **"I don't know. Perhaps you should tell the Master Architect how ugly is this, His construction."** The rabbi realized his wrong and asked for pardon. But **Elijah** would not give it until the entire city had asked for forgiveness for the rabbi and the rabbi had promised to mend his ways.

## Lilith

**Elijah** was always seen as deeply pious, it seems only natural that he would be pitted against an equally evil individual. This was found in the person of **Lilith**. **Lilith in legend was the first wife of Adam**. She rebelled against Adam, the angels, and even God. She came to be seen as a demon and a witch. **Elijah** encountered Lilith and instantly recognized and challenged her, **"Unclean**

one, **where are you going?"** Unable to avoid or lie to the prophet, she admitted she was on her way to the house of a pregnant woman. Her intention was to kill the woman and eat the child.

**Elijah** pronounced his malediction, **"I curse you in the Name of the Lord. Be silent as a stone!"** But, Lilith was able to make a bargain with **Elijah**. She promises to **"forsake my evil ways"** if **Elijah** will remove his curse. To seal the bargain she gives **Elijah** her names so that they can be posted in the houses of pregnant women or new born children or used as amulets. Lilith promises, **"Where I see those names, I shall run away at once. Neither the child nor the mother will ever be injured by me."**

## Elijah in Christianity / References in the New Testament

In the New Testament, **Jesus** would say for those who believed, John the Baptist was **Elijah**, who would come before the **"great and terrible day"** as predicted by **Malachi**. Some English translations of the New Testament use **Elias**, a Latin form of the name. In the **King James Version**, "Elias" appears only in the texts translated from Greek.

## John the Baptist

John the Baptist preached a message of repentance and baptism. He predicted the Day of Judgment using imagery similar to that of **Malachi**. He also preached that the **Messiah** was coming. All of this was done in a style that immediately recalled the image of **Elijah** to his audience. He wore a coat of camel's hair secured with a leather girdle **(Matthew 3:4, Mark 1:6).** He also frequently preached in wilderness areas near the **Jordan River**.

In the **Gospel of John,** when **John the Baptist** was asked by a delegation of priests (present tense) **"Art thou Elias",** he replied **"I am not" (John 1:21). Matthew 11:14 and Matthew 17:10–13** however, make it clear that John was the spiritual successor to **Elijah**. In the **Nativity of St. John the Baptist** in Luke, Gabriel appears to **Zechariah**, John's father, and told him that John **"will turn many of the sons of Israel to the Lord their God,"** and that he will go forth **"in the spirit and power of Elijah" (Luke 1:16–17).**

## Jesus Christ

In the **Gospel of Luke, Herod Antipas** hears some of the stories surrounding **Jesus Christ**. Some tell Herod that **Jesus** is **John the Baptist (whom Herod had executed) come back to life**. Others tell him that **Jesus** is **Elijah**. Later in the same gospel, **Jesus** asks his disciples who the people say that he is. The apostles' answer includes **Elijah** among others. However **Jesus** ' ministry had little in common with that of **Elijah**; in particular, he preached the forgiveness of one's enemies, while **Elijah** killed his. Miracle stories similar to those of **Elijah** were associated with **Jesus** (e. g. raising of the dead, miraculous feeding).

Jesus implicitly separates himself from Elijah when he rebukes James and John for desiring to call down fire upon an unwelcoming Samaritan village in a similar manner to Elijah. Likewise, Jesus rebukes a potential follower who wanted first to return home to say farewell to his family, whereas Elijah permitted this of his replacement Elisha. During Jesus ' crucifixion, some of the onlookers wonder if Elijah will come to rescue him, as by the time of Jesus , Elijah had entered folklore as a rescuer of Jews in distress.

## Transfiguration

Elijah makes an appearance in the New Testament during an incident known as the Transfiguration. At the summit of an unnamed mount, Jesus ' face begins to shine. The disciples who are with Him hear the voice of God announce that Jesus is "My beloved Son." The disciples also see Moses and Elijah appear and talk with Jesus. Peter is so struck by the experience that he asks Jesus if they should build three "tabernacles": one for Elijah, one for Jesus and one for Moses. There is agreement among some Christian theologians that Elijah appears to hand over the responsibility of the prophets to Jesus as the woman by the well said to Jesus (John 4:19) "I perceive thou art a prophet." and Moses also likewise came to hand over the responsibility of the law for the divinely announced Son of God.

## Other references

Elijah is mentioned four more times in the New Testament: in Luke, Romans, Hebrews, and James. In Luke 4:24–27, Jesus uses Elijah as an example of rejected prophets. Jesus says, "No prophet is accepted in his own country," and then mentions Elijah, saying that there were many widows in Israel, but Elijah was sent to one in Phoenicia. In Romans 11:1–6, Paul cites Elijah as an example of God's never forsaking his people (the Israelites).

Hebrews 11:35 ("Women received their dead raised to life again...") refers to both Elijah raising the son of the widow of Zarephath and Elisha raising the son of the woman of Shunem, citing both Elijah and Elisha as Old Testament examples of faith. In James 5:16–18, James says, "The effectual fervent prayer of a righteous man availeth much," and then cites Elijah's prayers which started and ended the famine in Israel as examples.

## Prophet Saint

In Western Christianity, the Prophet Elijah is commemorated as a saint with a feast day on 20 July by the Roman Catholic Church and the Lutheran Church–Missouri Synod. Catholics believe that he was unmarried and celibate. In the Eastern Orthodox Church and those Eastern Catholic Churches which follow the Byzantine Rite, he is commemorated on the same date (in the 21st century, Julian Calendar 20 July corresponds to Gregorian Calendar 2 August). He is greatly revered among the Orthodox as a model of the contemplative life.

He is also commemorated on the Orthodox liturgical calendar on the Sunday of the **Holy Fathers** (the Sunday before the **Nativity of the Lord**). **Elijah** has been venerated as the patron saint of Bosnia and Herzegovina since 26 August 1752, replacing George of Lydda at the request of Bishop Pavao Dragičević. The reasons for the replacement are unclear.

It has been suggested that **Elijah** was chosen because of his importance to all three main religious groups in Bosnia and Herzegovina—Catholics, Muslims and Orthodox Christians. **Pope Benedict XIV** is said to have approved **Bishop Dragičević's** request with the remark that a wild nation deserved a wild patron.

## Carmelite tradition

**Elijah** is revered as the spiritual Father and traditional founder of the Catholic religious Order of Carmelites. In addition to taking their name from Mt. Carmel where the first hermits of the order established themselves, the **Calced Carmelite** and **Discalced Carmelite** traditions pertaining to **Elijah** focus upon the prophet's withdrawal from public life. The medieval **Carmelite Book of the First Monks** offers some insight into the heart of the Orders' contemplative vocation and reverence for the prophet.

In the 17th Century the **Bollandist Society**, who's declared aim was to search out and classify materials concerning the saints venerated by the Church, and to print what seemed to be the most reliable sources of information entered into controversy with the **Carmelites** on this point. In writing of **St. Albert, Patriarch** of Jerusalem and author of the Carmelite rule, the **Bollandist Daniel Papebroch** stated that the attribution of Carmelite origin to **Elijah** was insufficiently grounded.

The Carmelites reacted strongly. From 1681 to 1698 a series of letters, pamphlets and other documents was issued by each side. The **Carmelites** were supported by a Spanish tribunal, while the **Bollandists** had the support of **Jean de Launoy** and the Sorbonne. In November 1698, **Pope Innocent XII** ordered an end to the controversy.

## Liturgical commemorations

Since most Eastern Churches either use Greek as their liturgical language or translated their liturgies from the Greek, *Elias* (or its modern iotacized form *Ilias*) is the form of the prophet's name used among most members of the Eastern Orthodox Church and those Eastern Catholic Churches which follow the **Byzantine Rite.**

The feast day of saint **Elias** falls on July 20 of the Orthodox liturgical calendar (for those churches which follow the traditional Julian Calendar, July 20 currently falls on August 2 of the modern Gregorian Calendar). This day is a major holiday in Lebanon and is one of a handful of holidays there whose celebration is accompanied by a launching of fireworks by the general public.

The full name of **St. Elias** in Lebanon translates to **St. Elias** the Living because it is believed that he did not die but rode his fiery chariot to heaven. The reference to the fiery chariot is likely why the Lebanese celebrate this holiday with fireworks. **Elias** is also commemorated, together with all of the righteous persons of the Old Testament, on the Sunday of the **Holy Fathers** (the Sunday before the **Nativity of the Lord**).

**The Apolytikion in the Fourth Tone for St. Elias:**
The incarnate Angel, the Cornerstone of the Prophets, the second Forerunner of the **Coming of Christ**, the glorious **Elias**, who from above, sent down to **Elisha** the grace to dispel sickness and cleanse lepers, abounds therefore in healing for those who honor him.

**The Kontakion in the Second Tone for St. Elias:**
**O Prophet and foreseer of the great works of God, O greatly renowned Elias, who by your word held back the clouds of rain, intercede for us to the only Loving One.**

## Pagan associations and mountaintops

Starting in the fifth century, **Elias** is often connected with **Helios, the Sun**. The two words have very similar pronunciations in post-classical Greek; **Elijah** rode in his chariot of fire to heaven **(2 Kings 2:11)** just as Helios drove the chariot of the sun across the sky; and the holocaust sacrifice offered by **Elijah** and burned by fire from heaven **(1 Kings 18:38)** corresponds to the sun warming the earth.

**Sedulius** writes poetically in the fifth century that the **"bright path to glittering heaven"** suits **Elias** both **"in merits and name"**, as changing one letter makes his name **"Helios"**; but he does not identify the two. A homily entitled *De ascensione Heliae*, misattributed to Chrysostom, claims that poets and painters use the ascension of **Elijah** as a model for their depictions of the sun, and says that **"Elijah is really Helios"**. **Saint Patrick** appears to conflate **Helios** and **Elias**. In modern times, much Greek folklore also connects **Elias** with the sun.

In Greece, chapels and monasteries dedicated to **Prophet Elias** are often found on mountaintops, which themselves are often named after him. Since **Wachsmuth** (1864), the usual explanation for this has been that **Elias** was identified with Helios, who had mountaintop shrines. But few shrines of Helios were on mountaintops, and sun-worship was subsumed by Apollo-worship by Christian times, and so could not be confused with **Elias**. The modern folklore is not good evidence for the *origin* of the association of the sun, **Elias**, and mountaintops. Perhaps **Elias** is simply a **"natural patron of high places"**.

The association of **Elias** with mountaintops seems to come from a different pagan tradition: **Elias** took on the attributes and the locales associated with Zeus, especially his associations with mountains and his powers over rain, thunder, lighting, and wind. When **Elias** prevailed over the priests of **Baal** , it was on **Mount Carmel (1 Kings 18:38)**, which later became known as **Mount St. Elias.** When he spent forty days in a cave, it was on **Mount Horeb (1 Kings 19:8)**. When **Elias** confronted **Ahab** , he stopped the rains for three years **(1 Kings 17:1-18:1).**

A map of mountain-cults of **Zeus** shows that most of these sites are now dedicated to **Elias**, including **Mount Olympus, Mount Lykaion, Mount Arachnaion, and Mount Taleton** on the mainland, and **Mount Kenaion, Mount Oche, and Mount Kynados** in the islands. Of these, the only one with a recorded tradition of a Helios cult is **Mount Taleton**. **Elias** is associated with pre-Christian lightning gods in many other European traditions. Among Albanians, pilgrimages are made to mountaintops to ask for rain during the summer.

One such tradition that is gaining popularity is the 2 August pilgrimage to Ljuboten on the **Sharr Mountains**. Muslims refer to this day as *Aligjyn* **("Ali Day"),** and it is believed that **Ali becomes Elias at midday.**

As **Elijah** was described as ascending into heaven in a fiery chariot, the Christian missionaries who converted Slavic tribes likely found him an ideal analogy for Perun, the supreme Slavic god of storms, thunder and lightning bolts. In many Slavic countries **Elijah** is known as **Elijah** the Thunderer (*Ilija Gromovnik*), who drives the heavens in a chariot and administers rain and snow, thus actually taking the place of **Perun** in popular beliefs.

Perun is also sometimes conflated with the legendary hero **Elijah of Murom**. The **feast of St. Elias** is known as *Ilinden* in South Slavic, and was chosen as the day of the **Ilinden-Preobrazhenie Uprising** in 1903; it is now the holiday of **Republic Day** in the Republic of Macedonia. In Estonian folklore **Elijah** is considered to be the successor of **Ukko**, the lightning spirit.

## In Georgian mythology, he replaces Elwa. A Georgian story about Elijah:

Once **Jesus**, the prophet **Elijah**, and **St. George** were going through Georgia. When they became tired and hungry they stopped to dine. They saw a Georgian shepherd and decided to ask him to feed them. First, **Elijah** went up to the shepherd and asked him for a sheep. After the shepherd asked his identity **Elijah** said that, he was the one who sent him rain to get him a good profit from farming.

The shepherd became angry at him and told him that he was the one who also sent thunderstorms, which destroyed the farms of poor widows. (After **Elijah, Jesus** and **St. George** attempt to get help and eventually succeed). **Elias** has other pagan associations: a modern legend about **Elias** mirrors precisely the legend of Odysseus seeking a place where the locals would not recognize an oar—hence the mountaintops.

## Elijah and Elias in the Church of Jesus Christ of Latter-day Saints

The Church of **Jesus Christ of Latter-day Saints** acknowledges **Elijah** as a prophet. The Church teaches that the **Malachi** prophecy of the return of **Elijah** was fulfilled on April 3, 1836, when **Elijah** visited the prophet and founder of the church, **Joseph Smith**, along with **Oliver Cowdery**, in the **Kirtland Temple** as a resurrected being. This event is chronicled in **Doctrine and Covenants** 110:13–16. This experience forms the basis for the church's focus on genealogy and family history and belief in the eternal nature of marriage and families.

In Latter-day Saint theology, the name-title **Elias** is not always synonymous with **Elijah** and is often used for people other than the biblical prophet. According to Joseph Smith, The spirit of **Elias** is first, **Elijah** second, and **Messiah** last. **Elias** is a forerunner to prepare the way, and the spirit and power of **Elijah** is to come after, holding the keys of power, building the Temple to the capstone, placing the seals of the Melchizedek Priesthood upon the house of Israel, and making all things ready; then **Messiah** comes to **His Temple**, which is last of all. People to whom the title **Elias** is applied in Mormonism include Noah, the angel Gabriel (who is considered to be the same person as **Noah** in Mormon doctrine), **Elijah**, John the Baptist, **John the Apostle**, and an unspecified man who was a contemporary of **Abraham.** Detractors of Mormonism have often alleged that **Smith**, in whose time and place the King James Version was the only available English translation of the Bible, simply failed to grasp the fact that the **Elijah** of the Old Testament and the **Elias** of the New Testament are the same person. **Latter-day Saints** deny this and say that the difference they make between the two is deliberate and prophetic.

The names **Elias** and **Elijah** refer to one who prepares the way for the coming of the Lord. This is applicable to John the Baptist coming to prepare the way for the Lord and His baptism; it also refers to **Elijah** appearing during the transfiguration to prepare for **Jesus** by restoring keys of sealing power. **Jesus** then gave this power to the twelve saying, **"Verily I say unto you, whatsoever ye shall bind on earth shall be bound in heaven: and whatsoever ye shall loose on earth shall be loosed in heaven."**

## Elijah in Islam

**Elijah** (Arabic: *Ilya*) is also mentioned as a prophet in the **Qur'an, al-An 'am 85**. **Elijah**'s narrative in the Qur'an and later Muslim tradition resembles closely that in the Hebrew Bible and Muslim literature records **Elijah**'s primary prophesying as taking place during the reign of **Ahab** and **Jezebel** as well as **Ahaziah**. He is seen by Muslims to be the **prophetic predecessor to Elisha**. While neither the Bible nor the **Qur'an** mentions the genealogy of **Elijah**, some scholars of Islam believe he may have come from the priestly family of the prophet **Aaron**. **Elijah** is rarely associated with Islamic eschatology and **Islam views Jesus as the Messiah**.

However, **Elijah** is expected to come back along with the mysterious figure known as **Khidr** during the **Last Judgment. Elijah**'s figure has been identified with a number of other prophets and saints, including **Idris**, which is believed by some scholars to have been another name for **Elijah**, and Khidr. Islamic legend later developed the figure of **Elijah**, greatly embellishing upon his attributes, and some apocryphal literature gave **Elijah** the status of a half-human, half-angel. **Elijah** also appears in later works of literature, including the *Hamzanama.*

## Qur'an

**Elijah** is mentioned in the **Qur'an**, where his preaching is recounted in a concise manner. The **Qur'an** narrates that **Elijah** told his people to come to the worship of God and to leave the worship of **Baal**, the primary idol of the area. The **Qur'an** states, **"Verily Elijah was one of the apostles. When he said to his people: "Will you not fear God? "Will ye call upon Ba'al and leave the Best of Creators, God, your LORD and Cherisher and the LORD and Cherisher of your fathers of old?" As-Saaffat 123–126**

The **Qur'an** makes it clear that the majority of **Elijah**'s people denied the prophet and continued to follow idolatry. However, it mentions that a small number of devoted servants of God among them followed **Elijah** and believed in and worshiped God. The **Qur'an** states, **"They denied him (Elijah), and will surely be brought to punishment, except the sincere and devoted Servants of God (among them). And we left his (memory) for posterity." As-Saaffat 127–128**

## In the Qur'an, God praises Elijah in two places:

- **Peace be upon Elijah! This is how we reward those who do good. He is truly among our believing servants.**
— *Qur'an, chapter 37 (As-Saaffat), verse 129–132*

- **And Zachariah and John and Jesus and Elijah, they were all from among the righteous**
— *Qur'an, chapter 6 (Al-An 'am), verse 85*

Numerous commentators, including **Abdullah Yusuf Ali**, have offered commentary on VI: 85 saying that **Elijah, Zechariah, John the Baptist** and **Jesus** were all spiritually connected. **Abdullah Yusuf Ali** says, **"The third group consists not of men of action, but Preachers of Truth, who led solitary lives. Their epithet is: "the Righteous."** They form a connected group round **Jesus. Zachariah** was the father of John the Baptist, who is referenced as **"Elias, which was for to come" (Matt 11:14); and Elias is said to have been present and talked to Jesus at the Transfiguration on the Mount (Matt. 17:3)."**

## Literature and tradition

Muslim literature and tradition recounts that **Elijah** preached to the **Kingdom of Israel**, ruled over by **Ahab** and later his son Ahaziah. He is believed to have been a **"prophet of the desert—like John the Baptist"**. **Elijah** is believed to have preached with zeal to **Ahab** and his wife **Jezebel**, who according to Muslim tradition was partly responsible for the worship of false idols in this area. Muslims believe that it was because the majority of people refused to listen to **Elijah** that **Elisha** had to continue preaching the message of God to Israel after him.

**Elijah** has been the subject of legends and folktales in Muslim culture, usually involving his meeting with **Khidr**, and in one legend, with Muhammad himself. In Islamic mysticism, **Elijah** is associated closely with the sage **Khidr**. One hadith reported that **Elijah** and **Khidr** met together every year in Jerusalem to go on the pilgrimage to Mecca. **Elijah** appears also in the *Hamzanama* numerous times, where he is spoken of as being the brother of **Khidr** as well as one who drank from the **Fountain of Youth.**

Further, it is narrated in **Kitab al-Kafi** that Imam **Ja'far al-Sadiq** was reciting the prostration of **Ilyas** (**Elijah**) in the Syrian language and began to weep. He then translated the supplication in Arabic to a group of visiting scholars: **"O Lord, will I find that you punish me although you know of my thirst in the heat of midday? Will I find that you punish me although you know that I rub my face on Earth to worship you? Will I find that you punish me although you know that I give up sins for you? Will I find that you punish me although you know that I stay awake all night just for you?"** To which Allah then inspired to Ilyas, **"Raise your head from the Earth for I will not punish you".**

Although most Muslim scholars believed that **Elijah** preached in Israel, some early commentators on the **Qur'an** stated that **Elijah** was sent to **Baal** bek, in Lebanon. Modern scholars have rejected this claim, stating that the connection of the city with **Elijah** would have been made because of the first half of the city's name, that of *Baal* , which was the deity that **Elijah** exhorted his people to stop worshiping. Scholars who reject identification of **Elijah**'s town with **Baal** bek further argue that the town of **Baal** bek is not mentioned with the narrative of **Elijah** in either the Qur'an or the Hebrew Bible.

## Elijah in the Baha'i Faith
In the Baha'i, the **Báb**, founder of the Babí Faith, is believed to be the return of **Elijah** and John the Baptist. Both **Elijah** and John the Baptist are considered to be **Lesser Prophets**, whose stations are below that of a Manifestation of God like **Jesus  Christ, Buddha, Muhammad,** the **Báb** or **Bahá'u'llah.** The **Báb** is buried on **Mount Carmel**, where **Elijah** had his confrontation with the prophets of **Baal.**

## Controversies / Miracle of the ravens
That *ravens* fed **Elijah** by the brook Chorath has been questioned. The Hebrew text at **1 Kings 17:4–6** uses the word `*ōrvīm*, which means *ravens*, but with a different vocalization might equally mean *Arabs*. The Septuagint has *ravens,* and other traditional translations followed. Alternatives have been proposed for many years; for example **Adam Clarke** (d. 1832) treated it as a discussion already of long standing. Objections to the traditional translation are that ravens are ritually

unclean (**Leviticus 11:13–17**) as well as physically dirty; it is difficult to imagine any method of delivery of the food which is not disgusting. The parallelism with the incident that follows, where **Elijah** is fed by the widow, also suggests a human, if mildly improbable, agent.

Prof. John Gray chooses *Arabs*, saying **"We adopt this reading solely because of its congruity with the sequel, where Elijah is fed by an alien Phoenician woman."** His translation of the verses in question is: And the word of Jehovah came to **Elijah** saying, go hence and turn eastward and hide thyself in the **Wadi Chorath** east of the Jordan, and it shall be that thou shalt drink of the wadi, and I have commanded the Arabs to feed thee there. And he went and did according to the word of Jehovah and went and dwelt in the **Wadi Chorath** east of the Jordan. And the Arabs brought him bread in the morning and flesh in the evening and he would drink of the wadi.

## Ascension into the heavens

In the Gospel of John, **Jesus** says: **"And no man hath ascended up to heaven, but he that came down from heaven, the Son of man which is in heaven."** **(John 3:13)**. Traditionally Christianity interprets the **"Son of Man" as a title of Jesus**, but this has never been an article of faith and there are other interpretations. Further interpreting this quote, some Christians believe that **Elijah** was not assumed into heaven but simply transferred to another assignment either in heaven or with King Jehoram of Judah. The prophets reacted in such a way that makes sense if he was carried away, and not simply straight up **(2 Kings 2:16)**.

The question of whether **Elijah** was in heaven or elsewhere on earth depends partly on the view of the letter Jehoram received from **Elijah** in **2 Chronicles 21** after **Elijah** had ascended. Some have suggested that the letter was written before **Elijah** ascended, but only delivered later. The rabbinical **Seder Olam** explains that the letter was delivered seven years after his ascension. This is also a possible explanation for some variation in manuscripts of **Josephus'** *Antiquities of the Jews* when dealing with this issue. Others have argued that **Elijah** was only **"caught away"** such as **Philip in Acts 8:39 John Lightfoot** reasoned that it must have been a different **Elijah**. **Elijah's** name typically occurs in Jewish lists of those who have entered heaven alive.

## Return

Centuries after his departure the Jewish nation awaits the coming of **Elijah** to precede the coming of the **Messiah**. For many Christians this prophecy was fulfilled in the gospels, where he appears during the Transfiguration alongside **Moses (Matthew 17:9–13)**. Commentators have said that **Moses'** appearance represented the law, while **Elijah's** appearance represented the prophets. **The Church of Jesus Christ of Latter-day Saints believes that Elijah returned on April 3, 1836 in an appearance to Joseph Smith and Oliver Cowdery, fulfilling the prophecy in Malachi.**

The Baha'i believes **Elijah** returned as the biblical prophet John the Baptist and as the **Báb who founded the Babí Faith in 1844.** The Nation of Islam believes **Elijah** returned as **Elijah**

**Muhammad**, black separatist religious leader (who claimed to be a **"messenger", not a prophet**). This is considered less important than their belief that **Allah** himself showed up in the person of **Fard Muhammad**, the founder of the group. It differs notably from most beliefs about **Elijah**, in that his re-appearance is usually the precursor to a greater one's appearance, rather than an afterthought.

# Prophet Ezekiel

Ezekiel (Hebrew: *Y'ḥezqēl)* is the central protagonist of the **Book of Ezekiel** in the Hebrew Bible. In Judaism, Christianity, and Islam, **Ezekiel** is acknowledged as a Hebrew prophet. In Judaism and Christianity, he is also viewed as the 6th-century BCE author of the **Book of Ezekiel,** which reveals prophecies regarding the destruction of Jerusalem, the restoration to the land of Israel, and what some call the *Millennial Temple* (or Third Temple) visions. The name **Ezekiel means 'God strengthens'.**

## Life

The author of the **Book of Ezekiel** presents himself as **Ezekiel, the son of Buzzi,** born into a priestly (Kohen) lineage. Apart from identifying himself, the author gives a date for the first divine encounter which he presents: **"in the thirtieth year"**. If this is a reference to **Ezekiel**'s age at the time, **he was born around 622 BCE**, about the time of Josiah's reforms. **His "thirtieth year" is given as 5 years after the exile of Judah's king Jehoiachin by the Babylonians.** Josephus claims that **Nebuchadnezzar** of Babylonia's armies exiled three thousand Jews from Judah, after **deposing King Jehoiakim in 598 BCE.**

## Living in Babylon

According to the Bible, **Ezekiel** and his wife lived during the Babylonian captivity on the banks of the **Chebar River, in Tel Abib,** with other exiles from Judah. There is no mention of him having any offspring.

## Prophetic career

Ezekiel describes his calling to be a prophet by going into great detail about his encounter with God and four **"living creatures" with four wheels that stayed beside the creatures.** For the next five years he incessantly prophesied and acted out the **destruction of Jerusalem and its temple**, which was met with some opposition. However, **Ezekiel** and his contemporaries like **Jeremiah,** another prophet who was living in Jerusalem at that time, witnessed the fulfillment of their prophecies with the **siege of Jerusalem by the Babylonians**. On the hypothesis that the **"thirtieth year"** of Ezekiel 1:1 refers to **Ezekiel**'s age, **Ezekiel** was fifty years old when he had his final vision. On the basis of dates given in the **Book of Ezekiel, Ezekiel**'s span of prophecies can be calculated to have occurred over the course of about 22 years. **The last dated words of Ezekiel date to April 570 BCE.**

## World views / Jewish tradition

Ezekiel, like **Jeremiah,** is said by **Talmud and Midrash** to have been a descendant of Joshua by his marriage with the proselyte and former **prostitute Rahab.** Some statements found in rabbinic literature posit that **Ezekiel** was the son of Jeremiah, who was (also) called **"Buzi" because he was despised by the Jews.**

Ezekiel was said to be already active as a prophet while in the Land of Israel, and he retained this gift when he **was exiled with Jehoiachin and the nobles of the country to Babylon**. Rava states in the Babylonian Talmud that although **Ezekiel** describes the **appearance of the throne of God (Merkabah),** this is not because he had seen more than the prophet Isaiah, but rather because the latter was more accustomed to such visions; for the relation of the two prophets is that of a courtier to a peasant, the latter of whom would always describe a royal court more floridly than the former, to whom such things would be familiar. **Ezekiel**, like all the other prophets, has **beheld only a blurred reflection of the divine majesty**, just as a poor mirror reflects objects only imperfectly.

According to the **midrash *Canticles Rabbah***, it was **Ezekiel** whom the three pious men, **Hananiah, Mishael, and Azariah** (also called **Shadrach, Meshach, and Abednego** in the Bible) asked for advice as to whether they should resist Nebuchadnezzar's command and **choose death by fire rather than worship his idol**. At first God revealed to the prophet that they could not hope for a miraculous rescue; whereupon the prophet was greatly grieved, since these three men constituted the **"remnant of Judah"**. But after they had left the house of the prophet, fully determined to sacrifice their lives to God, **Ezekiel** received this revelation: **"Thou dost believe indeed that I will abandon them. That shall not happen; but do thou let them carry out their intention according to their pious dictates, and tell them nothing"**.

## Christianity

**Ezekiel** is commemorated **as a saint** in the liturgical calendar of the **Eastern Orthodox Church**—and those **Eastern Catholic Churches** which follow the **Byzantine Rite**—on July 23 (for those churches which use the traditional Julian Calendar, July 23 falls on August 5 of the modern Gregorian Calendar). **Ezekiel** is commemorated on August 28 on the Calendar of Saints of the **Armenian Apostolic Church**, and on April 10 in the **Roman Martyrology**. Certain Lutheran churches also celebrate his commemoration on July 20.

**Saint Bonaventure** interpreted **Ezekiel's** statement about the **"closed gate"** as a prophecy of the Incarnation: **the "gate" signifying the Virgin Mary and the "prince" referring to Jesus**. This is one of the readings at Vespers on Great Feasts of the Theotokos in the Eastern Orthodox and Byzantine Catholic Churches. This imagery is also found in the traditional Catholic Christmas hymn **"Gaudete"** and in a saying by **Bonaventure**, quoted by **Alphonsus Maria de' Liguori: "No one can enter Heaven unless by Mary, as though through a door."** The imagery provides the basis for the concept that God gave Mary to humanity as the **"Gate of Heaven"** (thence the dedication of churches and convents to the **Porta Coeli**), an idea also laid out in the *Salve Regina* (Hail Holy Queen) prayer.

## Islamic tradition / *Dhul-Kifl*

**Ezekiel** is recognized as a prophet in Islamic tradition. Although not mentioned in the Qur'an by the name, Muslim Scholars, both classical and modern have included **Ezekiel** in lists of the prophets of Islam. The **Qur'an** mentions a prophet called **Zul-Kifl**. This prophet is sometimes identified with **Ezekiel** although **Zul-Kifl's** identity is disputed. **Carsten Niebuhr**, in his *Reisebeschreibung nach Arabian*, says he visited **Al Kifl** in Iraq, midway between Najaf and Hilla and said *Kifl* **was the Arabic form of** *Ezekiel*.

He further explained in his book that **Ezekiel's Tomb** was present in Al Kifl and that the Jews came to it on pilgrimage. The name *Zul-Kifl* would mean **"One of double"**, as *Zul* in Arabic means **"the one of"** and **"Kifl"** means **"double or folded"**. Some Islamic scholars have likened **Ezekiel's** mission to the description of **Dhul-Kifl**. When the exile, monarchy, and state were annihilated, a political and national life was no longer possible. In the absence of a worldly foundation it became necessary to build a spiritual one and **Ezekiel** performed this mission by observing the signs of the time and deducing his doctrines from them.

In conformity with the two parts of his book, his personality and his preaching are alike twofold, and the title *Zul-Kifl* means **"the one of double"** Aside from the possible identification of **Zul-Kifl** with **Ezekiel**, Muslims have viewed **Ezekiel** as a prophet, regardless of his identification with **Zul-Kifl**. **Ezekiel** appears in all Muslim collections of *Stories of the Prophets*. Muslim exegesis further lists **Ezekiel's father as Buzi (*Budhi*)** and **Ezekiel** is given the title *ibn al-adjus*, **denoting "son of the old (man)"**, as his parents are supposed to have been very old when he was born. A tradition, which resembles that of **Hannah** and **Samuel** in the Hebrew Bible, states that **Ezekiel's** mother prayed to God in old age for the birth of an offspring and was given **Ezekiel** as a gift from God.

## Bibliography / Ibn Kutayba, *K. al-Ma'arif* ed. S. Ukasha, 51

**One traditional depiction of the cherubim and chariot vision, based on the description by Ezekiel.**

- Tabari, History of the Prophets and Kings, 2, 53–54
- Tabari, *Tafsir*, V, 266 (old ed. ii, 365)
- Masudi, *Murudj*, i, 103ff.
- *K. al-Badwa l-Ta'rīkh*, iii, 4/5 and 98/100, *Ezechiel*
- Abdullah Yusuf Ali, *Holy Qur'an: Translation and Commentary*, Note. 2473 (cf. index: *Ezekiel*)
- Emil Heller Henning III, "**Ezekiel's** Temple: A Scriptural Framework Illustrating the Covenant of Grace." 2012.

## Tomb

The tomb of **Ezekiel** is a structure located in modern-day south Iraq near **Kefil,** believed to be the final resting place of **Ezekiel**. It has been **a place of pilgrimage to both Muslims and Jews alike**. After the Jewish exodus from Iraq, Jewish activity in the tomb ceased, although a disused synagogue remains in place.

# Prophet Jeremiah

**Jeremiah**, also called the **"weeping prophet"**, was one of the major prophets of the Hebrew Bible (Old Testament of Christian Bible). According to Jewish tradition, **Jeremiah** authored the **Book of Jeremiah**, the **Books of Kings** and the **Book of Lamentations**, with the assistance and under the editorship of **Baruch ben Neriah**, his scribe and disciple.

Greater detail is known about **Jeremiah's** life than for that of any other prophet. However, no biography of him can be written, as there are few facts available. Judaism considers the **Book of Jeremiah** part of its canon, and regards **Jeremiah** as the second of the **Major Prophets**. Christianity and Islam also regard **Jeremiah** as a prophet, and he is respectively quoted in the **New Testament** and his narrative is given in Islamic tradition.

## ⌐ Chronology

**Jeremiah's** ministry was active from the thirteenth year of **Josiah, king of Judah (626 BC)**, until after the fall of Jerusalem and the **destruction of Solomon's Temple in 587 BC. This period spanned the reigns of five kings of Judah: Josiah, Jehoahaz, Jehoiakim, Jehoiachin, and Zedekiah.**

## Biblical narrative / *Book of Jeremiah* / Lineage and early life

**Jeremiah was the son of Hilkiah, a** *Kohen* (Jewish priest) from the **Benjamite** village of **Anathoth**. The difficulties he encountered, as described in the books of **Jeremiah** and **Lamentations**, have prompted scholars to refer to him as **"the weeping prophet"**.

**Jeremiah was called to prophetic ministry c. 626 BC by YHWH to give prophecy of Jerusalem's destruction that would occur by invaders from the north.** This was because Israel had been unfaithful to the laws of the covenant and had forsaken God by **worshiping Baal. Jeremiah condemned people burning their children as offerings to Moloch.** This nation had deviated so far from God that they had broken the covenant, causing God to withdraw his blessings. **Jeremiah** was guided by God to proclaim that the nation of Judah would be faced with famine, plundered and taken captive by foreigners who would exile them to a foreign land. The **prophetess Huldah** was a relative and contemporary of **Jeremiah** while the prophets **Zephaniah** and **Isaiah** were his mentors.

## Calling

**According to Jeremiah 1:2–3, Yahweh called Jeremiah to prophetic ministry in about 626 BC, about five years before Josiah king of Judah turned the nation toward repentance from idolatrous practices (2 Kings 22:3-13).** According to the **Books of Kings**, and **Jeremiah**, Josiah's reforms were insufficient to save Judah and Jerusalem from destruction, because of the sins of **Manasseh, Josiah's** grandfather, and Judah's return to idolatry **(Jeremiah 11:10ff.).** Such was the lust of the nation for false gods that after Josiah's death, the nation would quickly return to the gods of the surrounding nations. **Jeremiah** was said to have been appointed to reveal the sins of the people and the coming consequences.

**Jeremiah** resisted the call by complaining that he was only a child and did not know how to speak. However, the Lord insisted that **Jeremiah** go and speak, and he touched **Jeremiah**'s mouth to place the word of the Lord there. God told **Jeremiah** to **"Get yourself ready!"** The character traits and practices **Jeremiah** was to acquire are specified in **Jeremiah** 1and include not being afraid, standing up to speak, speaking as told, and going where sent. Since **Jeremiah** is described as emerging well trained and fully literate from his earliest preaching, the relationship between him and the **Shaphan** family has been used to suggest that he may have trained at the scribal school in Jerusalem over which **Shaphan** presided.

In his early ministry, **Jeremiah** was primarily a preaching prophet, preaching throughout Israel. **He condemned idolatry, the greed of priests, and false prophets**. Many years later, God instructed **Jeremiah** to write down these early oracles and his other messages.

## Persecution

**Jeremiah**'s ministry prompted plots against him **(Jeremiah 11:21–23)**. Unhappy with **Jeremiah**'s message, possibly for concern that it would shut down the **Anathoth** sanctuary, his priestly kin and the men of **Anathoth** conspired to kill him. However, the Lord revealed the conspiracy to **Jeremiah**, protected his life, and declared disaster for the men of **Anathoth**. When **Jeremiah** complains to the Lord about this persecution, he is told that the attacks on him will become worse. A priest **Pashur** the son of ben Immer, a temple official in Jerusalem, had **Jeremiah** beaten and put in the stocks at the **Upper Gate of Benjamin** for a day. After this, **Jeremiah** expresses lament over the difficulty that speaking God's word has caused him and regrets becoming a laughingstock and the target of mockery. He recounts how if he tries to shut the word of the Lord inside and not mention God's name, the word becomes like fire in his heart and he is unable to hold it in.

## Conflicts with false prophets

**Whilst Jeremiah was prophesying the coming destruction, a number of other prophets were prophesying peace. Jeremiah spoke against these other prophets.** According to the **book of Jeremiah, during the reign of King Zedekiah**, The Lord instructed **Jeremiah** to make a yoke of the message that the nation would be subject to the **king of Babylon**. The prophet **Hananiah** opposed **Jeremiah**'s message.

He took the yoke off of **Jeremiah**'s neck, broke it, and prophesied to the priests and all the people that within two years the Lord would break the yoke of the king of Babylon, but the Lord spoke to **Jeremiah** saying **"Go and speak to Hananiah saying, you have broken the yoke of wood, but you have made instead a yoke of iron." (Jeremiah 28:13)**

## Relationship with the Northern Kingdom (Samaria)

**Jeremiah** was sympathetic to as well as descended from the **Northern Kingdom**. Many of his first reported oracles are about, and addressed to, the **Israelites at Samaria**. He resembles the northern prophet **Hosea**, in his use of language, and examples of God's relationship to Israel. **Hosea** seems to have been the first prophet to describe the desired relationship as an example of ancient Israelite marriage, where a man might be polygynous, while a woman was only permitted one husband. **Jeremiah** often repeats **Hosea's marital imagery (Jeremiah 2:2b–2:3; 3:1–5, 3:19–25; 4:1–2).**

## Babylon

The Biblical narrative portrays **Jeremiah** as being subject to additional persecutions. After **Jeremiah** prophesied that Jerusalem would be handed over to the Babylonian army, the king's officials, including Pashur the priest, tried to convince **King Zedekiah** that **Jeremiah should be put to death** because he was discouraging the soldiers as well as the people. **Zedekiah** answered that he would not oppose them. Consequently, the king's officials took **Jeremiah** and put him down into a cistern, where he sank down into the mud. The intent seemed to be to kill **Jeremiah** by allowing him to starve to death in a manner designed to allow the officials to claim to be innocent of his blood.

A **Cushite rescued Jeremiah** by pulling him out of the cistern, but **Jeremiah remained imprisoned until Jerusalem fell to the Babylonian army in 587 BC. The Babylonians released Jeremiah**, and showed him great kindness, allowing **Jeremiah** to choose the place of his residence, according to a Babylonian edict. **Jeremiah** accordingly went to Mizpah in Benjamin with Gedaliah, who had been made governor of Judea.

## Egypt

**Johanan succeeded Gedaliah, who had been assassinated by an Israelite prince in the pay of Ammon "for working with the Babylonians."** Refusing to listen to **Jeremiah**'s counsel, Johanan fled to Egypt, taking with him **Jeremiah** and **Baruch**, **Jeremiah**'s faithful scribe and servant, and the king's daughters. There, the prophet probably spent the remainder of his life, still seeking in vain to turn the people to God from whom they had so long revolted. **There is no authentic record of his death.**

## Religious views / Judaism

In Jewish rabbinic literature, especially the aggadah, **Jeremiah** and Moses are often mentioned together; their life and works being presented in parallel lines. The following ancient midrash is especially interesting, in connection with **Deuteronomy 18:18**, in which **"a prophet like Moses"** is promised: **"As Moses was a prophet for forty years, so was Jeremiah; as Moses prophesied concerning Judah and Benjamin, so did Jeremiah; as Moses' own tribe rose up against him, so did Jeremiah's tribe revolt against him; Moses was cast into the water, Jeremiah into a** pit; as Moses was saved by a slave (the slave of Pharaoh's daughter); so, Jeremiah was rescued by a slave (Ebed-melech); Moses reprimanded the people in discourses; so did Jeremiah." The prophet Ezekiel was a son of **Jeremiah** according to rabbinic literature.

## Christianity

The **Book of Jeremiah** plays a foundational role in Christian thought as it presages the inauguration of a new covenant **(cf. Jeremiah 31:31ff.)**, to which the New Testament testifies. There are about forty direct quotations of the book in the New Testament, most in **Revelation** in connection with the destruction of Babylon **(e.g., 50:8 in Revelation 18:4; 50:32 in Revelation 18:8; 51:49-50 in Revelation 18:24).** Of the Gospel writers, Matthew is especially mindful of how the events in the life, death and resurrection of **Jesus of Nazareth fulfill Jeremianic prophecies (cf. Matthew 2:17, 27:9).** The writer to the Hebrews also picks up the fulfilment of the prophetic expectation of the new covenant **(Hebrews 8:8-12; 10:16-17).**

## Islam

As with many other prophets of the Hebrew Bible, **Jeremiah** is also regarded as a prophet in Islam. Although **Jeremiah is not mentioned in the Quran**, Muslim exegesis and literature narrates many instances from the life of **Jeremiah** and fleshes out his narrative, which closely corresponds with the account given in the Hebrew Bible. In Arabic, **Jeremiah**'s name is usually vocalized *Irmiyā, Armiyā or Ūrmiyā*, and these forms are occasionally given with **MADD also** (*Irmiyā*).

Classical historians such as Wahb ibn Munabbih gave accounts of **Jeremiah** which turned **"upon the main points of the Old Testament story of Jeremiah: his call to be a prophet, his mission to the king of Judah, his mission to the people and his reluctance, the announcement of a foreign tyrant who is to rule over Judah."** Moreover, some **hadiths** and **Tafsirs** narrate that the Parable of the Hamlet in Ruins is about **Jeremiah**. Also, **in Sura 17(Al-Isra), Ayah 4–7**, that is about the two corruptions of children of Israel on the earth, some hadith and **Tafsir** cite that one of these corruptions is the imprisonment and persecution of **Jeremiah**.

According to Ahmadis the memorization of the Quran fulfills **Jeremiah**'s prophecy, **"I will put my Law within them and I will write it upon their hearts"**. Muslim literature narrates a detailed account of the destruction of Jerusalem, which parallels the account given in the **Book of Jeremiah**.

## Historicity

Scholars differ widely in their views on the likelihood of there being an actual prophet named **Jeremiah**. There is no extra-biblical occurrence of his name. Views differ from the belief that the narratives and poetic sections in **Jeremiah** are contemporary with his life (**W.L. Holladay**), to the view that **Jeremiah** is no more than a fictional character (**R. P. Carroll**).

## Scholarly views

Scholars cannot prove the authorship of **Jeremiah** with any certainty, although consensus has gathered around a thesis of multiple sources, mainly because of the contrast between the poetic discourses and the prose narrative. Some modern scholars think the Deuteronomist edited **Jeremiah** because of the similarity of phrasing between the books of **Jeremiah** and Deuteronomy. For example, Egypt is referred to as an **"iron furnace"** in both **Jeremiah 11:4 and Deuteronomy 4:20**. They also share a similar view of divine justice. **Emanuel Tov** believes that the Septuagint version of **Jeremiah** is earlier, and the **Masoretic Text** version is a later, longer version.

## Nebo-Sarsekim tablet

In July 2007, Assyrologist **Michael Jursa** translated a **cuneiform tablet dated to 595 BC**, as describing a **Nabusharrussu-ukin** as **"the chief eunuch"** of **Nebuchadnezzar II** of Babylon. Jursa hypothesized that this reference might be to the same individual as the **Nebo-Sarsekim** mentioned in **Jeremiah 39:3**.

## Cultural influence

**Jeremiah** inspired the French noun *jérémiade*, and subsequently the English *jeremiad*, meaning **"a lamentation; mournful complaint,"** or further, **"a cautionary or angry harangue."**

**Jeremiah** has periodically been a popular first name in the United States, beginning with the early **Puritan** settlers, who often took the names of biblical prophets and apostles. The names Jeremy and Dermot also derive from **Jeremiah** (the latter by way of Irish *Diarmaid*).

# Prophet Jonah

**Jonah** or **Jonas** (Hebrew: Modern *Yona*; Arabic: *Yunus*, is the name given in the Hebrew Bible (**Tanakh**/Old Testament) to a prophet of the northern kingdom of Israel in about the 8th century BC, the eponymous central character in the **Book of Jonah**, famous for being swallowed by a fish or a whale, depending on translation. The Biblical story of **Jonah** is also repeated, with a few notable differences, in the **Qur'an.**

## The story of Jonah

**Jonah, son of Amittai**, appears in 2 Kings as a prophet from Gath'hepher (a few miles north of Nazareth) active during the reign of **Jeroboam II** (c. 786-746 BC), where he predicts that **Jeroboam** will recover certain lost territories.

**Jonah** is also the central character in the **Book of Jonah**. Ordered by God to go to the city of Nineveh to prophesy against it **"for their great wickedness is come up before me, Jonah seeks instead to flee from "the presence of the Lord"** by going to Jaffa and sailing to **Tarshish**, which, geographically, is in the opposite direction. A huge storm arises and the sailors, realizing this is no ordinary storm, cast lots and learn that **Jonah** is to blame. **Jonah** admits this and states that if he is thrown overboard, the storm will cease.

The sailors try to d ump as much cargo as possible before giving up, but feel forced to throw him overboard, at which point the sea clams. The inspired sailors then offer sacrifices to God. **Jonah** is miraculously saved by being swallowed by a large fish specially prepared by God where he spends three days and three nights. In chapter two, while in the great fish, **Jonah** prays to God in his affliction and commits to thanksgiving and to paying what he vowed. God commands the fish to spew **Jonah** out.

God again orders **Jonah** to visit Nineveh and to prophesy to its inhabitants. This time he goes and enters the city, crying **"In forty days Nineveh shall be overthrown."** After **Jonah** has walked for a day across Nineveh, the people of Nineveh begin to believe his word and proclaim a fast. The king of **Nineveh** puts on sackcloth and sits in ashes, making a proclamation to decree fasting, sackcloth, prayer, and repentance. God sees their works and spares the city at that time. The entire city is humbled and broken with the people (and even the animals) in sackcloth and ashes. Even the king comes off his throne to repent.

Displeased by this, **Jonah** refers to his earlier flight to **Tarshish** while asserting that, since God is merciful, it was inevitable that God would turn from the threatened calamities. He then leaves the city and makes himself a shelter, waiting to see whether or not the city will be destroyed. God causes a plant (in Hebrew a *Kikayon*) to grow over **Jonah**'s shelter to give him some shade from the sun.

And God said to **Jonah**: 'Art thou greatly angry for the **Kikayon?**' And he said: 'I am greatly angry, even unto death.' And the LORD said: 'Thou hast had pity on the gourd, for which thou hast not labored, neither madest it grow, which came up in a night, and perished in a night; and should not I have pit on Nineveh, that great city, wherein are more than **sixscore** thousand persons that cannot discern between their right hand and their left hand, and also much cattle?'

-Book of Jonah, chapter 4, verses 9-11

## Jonah in Christianity

In the New Testament, **Jonah** is mentioned in Matthew 12:38-41, 16:4 and Luke 11:29-32. **"The men of Nineveh shall rise in judgment with this generation, and shall condemn it: because they repented at the preaching of Jonas; and, behold, a greater than Jonas is here."**

-Gospel of Matthew, chapter 12 verses 39-41

**Jonah** is regarded as a saint by a number of Christian denominations. He is commemorated as one of the **Twelve Minor Prophets** in the Calendar of saints of the **Armenian Apostolic Church** on July 31. **Jonah**'s mission to the Ninevites is commemorated by the Fast of Nineveh in Syriac and **Oriental Orthodox Churches**.

## Jonah in Judaism

The **Book of Jonah** is one of the **12 Minor Prophets** included in the **Tanakh**. According to tradition **Jonah** was the boy brought back to life by **Elijah** the prophet, and hence shares many of his characteristics (particularly his desire for 'strict judgment'). The **Book of Jonah** is read every year, in its original Hebrew and in its entirety, on **Yom Kippur** – the **Day of Atonement**, as the **Haftarah** at the afternoon **Mincha prayer**.

Teshuva – the ability to repent and be forgiven by God – is a prominent idea in Jewish thought. This concept is developed in the **Book of Jonah**: **Jonah**, the son of truth, (The name of his father **"Amittai"** in Hebrew means truth,) refuses to ask the people of **Nineveh** to repent. He seeks the truth only, and no forgiveness. When forced to go, his call is heard loud and clear. The people of Nineveh repent ecstatically, **"fasting, including the sheep"**, and the Jewish scripts are critical of this.

## Jonah in Islam

**Jonah** (**Yunus** in Arabic) is highly important in Islam as a prophet who was faithful to God and delivered His messages. In Islam, **Jonah** is also called **Dhul-Nun**, meaning *The One of the Whale*. Chapter 10 of the **Qur'an** is named *Jonah*, although in this chapter only verse 98 refers to him directly. It is said in Muslim tradition that **Jonah** came from the tribe of **Benjamin** and that his father was **Amittai**. **Jonah** is the only one of the **Twelve Minor Prophets** of the Hebrew Bible to be mentioned by name in the **Qur'an**.

**Jonah**'s Qur'anic narrative is extremely similar to the Hebrew Bible story. The **Qur'an** describes **Jonah** as a righteous preacher of the message of God but a messenger who, one day, fled from his mission because of its overwhelming difficulty. The **Qur'an** says that **Jonah** made it onto a ship but, because of the powerfully stormy weather, the men aboard the ship suggested casting lots to throw off the individual responsible. When the lots were cast three times and **Jonah**'s name came out at all three and he was thrown into the open ocean that night. A gigantic fish came and swallowed him, and **Jonah** remained in the belly of the fish repenting and glorifying God to the maximum. As the **Qur'an** says:

"Had it not been that he (repented and) glorified Allah, He would certainly have remained inside the Fish till the Day of Resurrection."

Qur'an, chapter 37 (As-Saaffat), verse 139-144

Therefore, the fish cast Jonah out onto dry land, with Jonah in a state of sickness. After Jonah got up, fresh and well, God told him to go back and preach at his land.

Qur'an, chapter 37 (As-Saaffat), verse 145-148

## Muhammad

**Jonah** is also mentioned in a few incidents during the lifetime of **Muhammad**. After ten years of receiving revelations, **Muhammad** went to the city of **Ta'if** to see if its leaders would allow him to preach his message from there rather than Mecca, but he was cast from the city by the people. He took shelter in the garden of **Utbah** and **Shaybah**, two members, of the **Quraysh** tribe. They sent their servant, **Addas**, to serve him grapes for sustenance. **Muhammad** asked **Addas** where he was from and the servant replied **Nineveh**.

**"The town of Jonah the just, son of Amittai!"** **Muhammad** exclaimed. Addas was shocked because he knew that the pagan Arabs had no knowledge of the prophet **Jonah**. He then asked how **Muhammad** knew of this man. **"We are brothers"** **Muhammad** replied, **"Jonah was a Prophet of God and I, too, am a Prophet of God."** Addas immediately accepted Islam and kissed the hands and feet of **Muhammad**. Thus, **Muhammad**, by saying this, clearly made it a point to the Arabs to not make any distinction between the great apostles of God.

## Shrine at Nineveh
On Nabi Yunus there is a Muslim shrine dedicated to the prophet Jonah.

## Translation
In **Jonah** 2:1 (1:17 in English translation), the original Hebrew text reads *dag gadol*, which literally means **"big fish."** In **Matthew 12:40 as "whale"**. Which states **"For as Jonas was three days and three nights in the whale's belly; so shall the Son of man be three days and three nights in the heart of the earth."** Tyndale's translation was later incorporated into the Authorized Version of 1611. Since then, the **"great fish"** in **Jonah** 2 has been most often interpreted as a whale.

## Suggested literal interpretations
Some believers claim that **Jonah** did die in the belly of the great fish, and was then resurrected by God since **Jesus** himself associated this event in **Jonah**'s life with his own death and resurrection.

## Various locations associated with Jonah
- Place of birth: Mentioned in **2 Kings 14:25**, the town of **Gath-hepher** has saved its name to this day, near the Galilean Arab town of **Mashhad**, where a monument for **Nebi Yunes** still exists. The Israeli **Gath-hepher** industrial zone is erected on that mountain.

- Another sanctuary and mosque called **Nebi Yunes**, is in the Palestinian West Bank town of Halhul, 5 km (3.1 mi) north of Hebron. Muslim tradition has it that this is the burial site of **Jonah** the prophet. A sign erected by the Israeli ministry of religions says that this is **Jonah**'s burial site, but according to Jewish traditions this is the location of the burial of the prophets **Nathan** and **Gad Hahozeh**.

- The sanctuary of **Jama Naballa** Jonas is another place that tradition says is **Jonah**'s grave, near the city of Mosul (today in Iraq), near the ancient remnants of **Nineveh**. On one of the two most prominent mounds of Nineveh ruins, rises the Mosque of the **Prophet Yunus** (previously a Nestorian-Assyrian Church). **Jonah** is believed to be buried here, where **King Esarhaddon** had once built a palace. It is one of the most important mosques in Mosul and one of the few historic mosques that are found on the east side of the city.

- **Jonah**'s grave is also said to be near the city of **Sarafand** (Sarepta) in Lebanon. This is in accordance with several ancient Jewish writings about **Jonah** being the son of the woman from **"Zarephath"** (Sarafand) mentioned in the stories of **Elijah**.

## Connections to other legends

**Joseph Campbell** suggested a parallel between the story of **Jonah** and the epic of **Gilgamesh**, in which **Gilgamesh** obtains a plant from the bottom of the sea. In the **Book of Jonah** a worm (in Hebrew *tola'ath*, "maggot") bites the shade-giving plant's root causing it to wither, while in the **Epic of Gilgamesh**, Gilgamesh plucks his plant from the floor of the sea which he reached by tying stones to his feet. Once he makes it back to the shore, the rejuvenating plant is eaten by a serpent.

**Jonah** is mentioned twice in Chapter 14 of the apocryphal **Book of Tobit**, the conclusion of which finds Tobit's son, **Tobias**, at the extreme age of one hundred and twenty-seven years, rejoicing at the news of Nineveh's destruction by **Nebuchadnezzar** and **Ahasuerus** in apparent fulfillment of **Jonah**'s prophecy against the Assyrian capital.

# Rabbi

A **Rabbi** is a spiritual leader or religious teacher in Judaism. One becomes a **Rabbi** by being ordained by another **Rabbi**, following a course of study of Jewish texts such as the **Talmud.** The basic form of the **Rabbi** developed in the **Pharisaic** and **Talmudic** era, when learned teachers assembled to codify Judaism's written and oral laws. The title "**Rabbi**" was first used in the first century CE. **Orthodox Judaism** does not ordain women as **Rabbi**s. Non-Orthodox movements have chosen to do so for what they view as **halakhic** reasons (**Conservative Judaism**) as well as ethical reasons (**Reform and Reconstructionist Judaism**).

## ☑ Etymology and pronunciation

The Hebrew word רב , which literally means "**great one**" or "**master**", is the original Hebrew form of the title. Sephardic and Yemenite Jews have historically pronounced this word *ribbī* rather than **"Rabbi"**, and this pronunciation also appears in the **Talmud** and in **Ashkenazi** texts prior to the late 18th century.

## Historical overview

A **Rabbi** is not an occupation found in the Hebrew Bible, and ancient generations did not employ related titles such as *Rabban, Rabbi,* **or** *Rav* to describe either the Babylonian sages or the sages in Israel. The title "**Rabbi**" occurs (in Greek transliteration *rhabbi*) in the books of **Matthew, Mark, and John** in the New Testament, where it is used in reference to **"Scribes and Pharisees"** as well as to Jesus. "**Rabbi**" as a religious title does not appear in the Hebrew Bible.

They began the formulation and explication of what became known as Judaism's "**Oral Law**" This was eventually encoded and codified within the **Mishnah** and **Talmud** and subsequent **Rabbinical** scholarship, leading to what is known as **Rabbinic Judaism**.

## Sages

The title "**Rabbi**" was borne by the sages of ancient Israel, who were ordained by the **Sanhedrin** in accordance with the custom handed down by the elders. **Ra***b* was the title of the Babylonian sages who taught in the Babylonian academies. After the suppression of the Patriarchate and Sanhedrin by **Theodosius II** in 425, there was no more formal ordination in the strict sense.

## 18th–19th centuries

Traditionally, **Rabbi**s have never been an intermediary between God and humans. This idea was traditionally considered outside the bounds of Jewish theology. Unlike spiritual leaders in many other faiths, they are not considered to be imbued with special powers or abilities. **Rabbis serve the Jewish community**.

## Judging

Prior to emancipation, rulers delegated discipline and dispute settlement within the Jewish community (*kahal*) to the Jewish community itself. The town **Rabbi**, with his extensive knowledge of **Torah** law (*halakhah*), was expected to preside as **Head of the Court.** The judgments were enforced with fines and various degrees of communal excommunication when necessary. After emancipation, Jews, as citizens of their countries, turned to civil courts for dispute resolution.

## Legislating

The regulations involved matters as diverse as dowries and matrimonial law, relations with gentiles, utilizing civil courts, education of orphans, anti-counterfeiting measures, and the hiring of schoolteachers. **Nn** the modern era **Rabbi**s have enacted *takkanot* in the State of Israel, and the major Jewish movements, such as **Reform**, **Conservative** and **Reconstructionist**, enact *takkanot* for their members. Today most congregational **Rabbi**s are members of a **National Rabbinic Organization.**

## Pastoral counseling

Members of the Jewish community have always turned to **Rabbi**s for advice on personal matters. This is conducted in private on a one-to-one basis. In the pre-modern era, **Rabbi**s had no special training in counseling.

## Leading prayer services

Traditionally **Rabbi**s did not lead prayer services in the modern sense. There is no requirement that a **Rabbi** be present for public prayer. If halakhic questions arose about the prayer service, the **Rabbi** would answer them. In modern synagogues, the **Rabbi** takes a more active role in leading prayer services. At **Sabbat**h and holiday services, the congregational **Rabbi** will deliver a sermon either right before or right after the **Torah** is read.

## Celebrating life's events

**Jewish law does not require the presence of a Rabbi at a marriage, bar or bat mitzvah, circumcision, funeral, house of mourning, or unveiling of a monument at a cemetery**. In the modern era, it is virtually obligatory to have the **Rabbi**'s participation at these events, and ministering to the congregation in these settings has become a major aspect of the modern **Rabbi**nate. Jewish divorce, which requires a **Rabbi**nical court (*beth din*), will always have **Rabbi**s in attendance.

## Charitable works

The synagogue has been a place where charity is collected every weekday after services and then distributed to the needy before Sabbaths and holidays. But it was the **Rabbi**'s task to teach that charity (*tzedakah*) is a core Jewish value.

**Moses Maimonides** formulated a ladder consisting of eight degrees of charity, starting with reluctant giving and ending with teaching someone a trade. Today Jewish federations and foundations collect and distribute most charity within the Jewish community.

## Conversions

Most **Rabbi**s will from time to time encounter someone who is not Jewish seeking information about Judaism or wishing to explore conversion to Judaism. The **Rabbi**'s approach may range from discouragement of the potential convert to mentoring and directing to a conversion class, in accordance with the policy on conversion of the **Rabbi**'s movement. There are no **Rabbi**s serving as "**Jewish missionaries**" per se; there is no parallel in Judaism to the proselytizing of other faiths.

## Chaplaincy

All branches of the U. S. military have Jewish chaplains in their ranks and **Rabbi**s serve in the Israeli Defense Forces. The **Hillel Foundation** provides **Rabbi**s and Jewish services on 550 campuses while **Chabad** operates Jewish centers with a **Rabbi** near 150 college campuses.

## Defending the faith

**Rabbi**s are often called upon to defend the Jewish faith. Mass conversions to Christianity did not take place. One cannot be of the Jewish faith while believing in either the Christian God or the Christian messiah.

## Compensation

In antiquity those who performed **Rabbi**nic functions, such as judging a case or teaching **Torah** to students, did not receive compensation for their services. **Torah** sages were allowed a series of privileges and exemptions that alleviated their financial burdens somewhat. During the period of the **Geonim** (c. 650-1050 CE), opinions on compensation shifted. The Geonim collected taxes and donations at home and abroad to fund their schools (*yeshivot*) and paid salaries to teachers, officials and judges of the Jewish community, whom they appointed.

At the present time, an ordained graduate of a **Rabbi**nical seminary that is affiliated with one of the modern branches of Judaism, **Reform, Conservative, Reconstructionist**, or **modern Orthodox**, will find employment—whether as a congregational **Rabbi**, teacher, chaplain, **Hillel** director, camp director, social worker or administrator—through the placement office of the seminary.

## Authority

Hasidic communities do not have a mere **Rabbi**: they have a **Rebbe**, who plays a similar role but is thought to have a special connection to God. The Rebbes' authority, then, is based on a spiritual connection to God and so they are venerated in a different way from **Rabbi**s.

## Honor

According to the **Talmud**, it is a commandment (*mitzvah*) to honor a **Rabbi** and a **Torah** scholar, along with the elderly, as it is written in **Leviticus 19:32**, **"Rise up before the elderly, and honor the aged."** **Kohanim** (priests) are required to honor **Rabbi**s and **Torah** scholars like the general public. It is also a commandment for teachers and **Rabbi**s to honor their students.

## Ordination / *Semikhah*

A **Rabbi**nical student is awarded *semikhah* (**Rabbi**nic ordination) after the completion of a learning program in a yeshiva or modern **Rabbi**nical seminary or under the guidance of an individual **Rabbi**. Most **Rabbi**nical students will complete their studies in their mid-20s. There is no hierarchy and no central authority in Judaism. Each branch of Judaism regulates the ordination of the **Rabbi**s affiliated with it. The recipient of this ordination can be formally addressed as a *dayan* ("judge") and also retain the title of **Rabbi**.

## Orthodox and Modern Orthodox Judaism

Historically, women could not become **Orthodox Rabbi**s. Starting in 2009, some Modern Orthodox institutions began ordaining women with the title of **"Maharat"**, and later with titles including **"Rabbah"** and **"Rabbi"**. This has met with opposition from many other Orthodox institutions

## Non-Orthodox Judaism / Conservative Judaism

Conservative *semikhah* also requires that its **Rabbi**nical students receive intensive training in **Tanakh**, classical biblical commentaries, biblical criticism, **Midrash, Kabbalah** and **Hasidut**, the historical development of Judaism from antiquity to modernity, Jewish ethics, the halakhic methodology of **Conservative Responsa**. Conservative **Rabbi**nical students earn a **Master of Arts** in **Rabbi**nic Literature in addition to receiving ordination. Most Conservative seminaries ordain women and openly **LGBT** people as **Rabbi**s and cantors.

## Interdenominational recognition

The Orthodox **Rabbi**nical establishment rejects the validity of Conservative, Reform and Reconstructionist **Rabbi**s on the grounds that their movements' teachings are in violation of traditional Jewish tenets. **Orthodox Rabbi**s do not recognize conversions by non-Orthodox **Rabbi**s. Conservative **Rabbi**s recognize all conversions done according to **Halakha**.

## *Women in Judaism and Timeline of women Rabbis*

Women historically have generally not served as **Rabbi**s until the 1970s and the influence of second-wave feminism, when the **Hebrew Union College**-Jewish Institute of Religion first ordained women **Rabbi**s.

# Rastafarianism

**Rastafari**, sometimes termed **Rastafarianism, is an Abrahamic religion** that developed in Jamaica during the 1930s. They are classified it as both a new religious movement and a social movement. They are known as **Rastafari, Rastafarians, or Rastas. Rastas** refer to their beliefs, which are based on a specific interpretation of the Bible, as **"Rastalogy"**. Central is a monotheistic belief in a single God—referred to as **Jah**—who partially resides within each individual. **Haile Selassie,** the **Emperor of Ethiopia** between 1930 and 1974, is given central importance. Many **Rastas** regard him as an incarnation of **Jah** on Earth and as the **Second Coming of JesusChrist**.

Many **Rastas** call for the resettlement of the African diaspora in either **Ethiopia** or Africa more widely, referring to this continent as the **Promised Land of "Zion". Rastafari** originated among impoverished and socially disenfranchised Afro-Jamaican communities in **1930s Jamaica**. Its Afrocentric ideology was largely a reaction against Jamaica's then-dominant British colonial culture. The Movement developed after several Christian clergymen, most notably **Leonard Howell**, proclaimed that **Haile Selassie**'s crowning as emperor in 1930 fulfilled a Biblical prophecy.

In the 1960s and 1970s it gained increased respectability within Jamaica and greater visibility abroad through the popularity of **Rasta**-inspired reggae musicians like **Bob Marley**. Enthusiasm for **Rastafari** declined in the 1980s, following the deaths of **Haile Selassie**. There are an estimated 700,000 to 1 million **Rastas** across the world; the largest population is in Jamaica. The majority of practitioners are of black African descent, although a minority come from other racial groups.

## Definition

Scholars of religion have categorized **Rastafari** as a new religious movement, a new social movement, or as a social movement. Many **Rastas** themselves, however, do not regard it as a religion, instead referring to it as a **"way of life"**. **"Rastafarianism"** is considered offensive by most **Rastafari**, who, being critical of **"isms"** or **"ians"**.

## Beliefs

**Rastas** refer to the totality of their religion's ideas and beliefs as **"Rastalogy"**. It was **"extremely difficult to generalize"** about **Rastas** and their beliefs. The movement has continuously changed and developed over the course of its history. Emphasis is placed on the idea that personal experience and intuitive understanding should be used to determine the truth or validity of a particular belief or practice. No **Rasta** has the authority to declare what beliefs and practices are orthodox and which are heterodox.

**Rastafari** belief is deeply influenced by **Judeo-Christian religion**. It accords the Bible a central place in its belief system, regarding it as a holy book, and adopts a literalist interpretation of its contents. The religion being "**highly Protestant in outlook**".

They believe that the Bible was originally written on stone in the **Ethiopian** language of Amharic. The Bible's final book, the **Book of Revelation**, is widely regarded as the most important part for **Rastas**, having a particular significance for their situation.

## Jah Rastafari and Jesusof Nazareth

**Rastafari** are monotheists, worshiping a singular God whom they call **Jah**. The term "**Jah**" is a shortened version of "**Jehovah**", the name of God in English translations of the Old Testament. **Rastas** also believe that **Jah** is inherent within each human individual. This belief is reflected in the aphorism, often cited by **Rastas** that "**God is man and man is God**".

In believing that **human beings have an inner divinity within themselves**, **Rastas** help to cultivate a bastion against the uncertainty and insecurity that exists within society and societal institutions. **Jesusof Nazareth** is an important figure in **Rastafari**. However, practitioners reject the traditional depiction of **Jesus**present in Christianity, particularly the depiction of him as a white European. They believe that **Jesus**was a black African and that he was a **Rasta**. Many **Rastas** taking the view that **the God worshipped by most white Christians is actually the Devil.**

One recurring saying among **Rastafari** is that "**The Pope is Satan**". Jesus is given particular prominence among a **Rastafari** denomination known as the **Twelve Tribes of Israel**. **Rastas** believe that his second coming is imminent. **Accordingly, they do not share the view of other Rastas that Haile Selassie was the second coming of Jesus. Haile Selassie's body had been buried beneath a toilet in his palace, remaining undiscovered there until 1992.** During his life, Selassie described himself as a devout Christian.

## Afrocentrism, Babylon, and Zion

Practitioners of **Rastafari** identify themselves with the ancient **Israelites—God's chosen people in the Old Testament.** **Rastafari** teaches that the black African diaspora are exiles living in "**Babylon**," a term applied to Western society. In the **Old Testament, Babylonians** the Mesopotamian city which conquered and deported the Israelites from their homeland **between 597 and 586 BCE.**

**Rastas** believe that the slavery, exile, and exploitation of black Africans was punishment for failing to live up to their status as **Jah**'s chosen people. During the first three decades of the **Rastafari** movement, it placed strong emphasis on the need for the African diaspora to be repatriated to Africa. There is no uniform **Rasta** view on race. **Rastas** typically believe that black

Africans are God's chosen people, meaning that they made a deal with him and thus have a special responsibility. **This is similar to beliefs in Judaism**.

## Salvation and paradise

**Rastafari** has been characterized as a millenarianist movement, for it espouses the idea that the present age will come to an apocalyptic end. With Babylon destroyed, **Rastas** believe that humanity will be ushered into a "**new age**".

In this Day of Judgement, Babylon will be overthrown, and **Rastas** would be the chosen few who survive. They argue is prophesied in **Daniel 2: 31–32**. The righteous will live in paradise in Africa. **Rastas** do not believe that there is a specific afterlife to which human individuals go following bodily death. **They believe in the possibility of eternal life, and that only those who shun righteousness will actually die.**

## Morality, ethics, and gender roles

Most **Rastas** share a pair of fundamental moral principles: These are love of God and love of neighbor. Most of Jamaican practitioners have rejected both capitalism and socialism as models of economic development. Many **Rastas** joined the **People's Revolutionary Government which was formed in 1979**, although **Marxist-Leninist** factions later turned against them.

## Gender roles and sexuality

**Rastafari** promotes the idea that women should submit to male leadership. External observers—have claimed that **Rastafari** accords women an inferior position to men. **Rasta** discourse often presents women as morally weak and susceptible to deception by evil, and claims that they are impure during their period of menstruation. **Rastas** legitimize these gender roles by citing Biblical passages, particularly those in the **Book of Leviticus**, and in the writings of **Paul the Apostle.**

As it existed in Jamaica, **Rastafari** was not monogamous. **Rasta men are permitted to have multiple female sex partners, while women are expected to reserve their sexual activity for their one male partner**. **Rastafari** places great importance on family life and the raising of children, with reproduction being encouraged.

Both contraception and abortion are usually censured by **Rastas**. **Rastas** also typically express hostile attitudes to **homosexuality**, regarding homosexuals as evil and unnatural; this attitude derives from references to **same-sex sexual activity in the Bible**. **Rastas** see the growing **acceptance of birth control and homosexuality in Western society as evidence of the degeneration of Babylon as it approaches its apocalyptic end.**

## Use of cannabis / *Cannabis and religion*

**Rastas** argue that the use of **ganja** is promoted in the Bible, specifically in **Genesis 1: 29, Psalms 18:8, and Revelation 22:2. Rastas** portray cannabis as the supreme herb, and regard it as having healing properties. The pipe is passed in a counter-clockwise direction around the assembled circle of **Rastas**.

## History

The **Rastafari** movement developed out of the legacy of the Atlantic slave trade, in which over ten million Africans were enslaved and transported from Africa to the Americas between the sixteenth and nineteenth centuries. Here, they were sold to European planters and forced to work on the plantations. Around a third of these transported Africans were relocated in the Caribbean, with under **700,000 being settled in Jamaica.**

In 1834, slavery in Jamaica was abolished after the British government passed the **Slavery Abolition Act 1833**. Many Afro-Jamaicans joined Christian churches during the **Great Revival of 1860–61.**

## Haile Selassie and the early Rastas: 1930–1949

Emperor **Haile Selassie** was crowned **Emperor of Ethiopia** in 1930. A number of Christian clergymen, claimed that Selassie's coronation was evidence that he was the **black messiah** that they believed was prophesied in the **Book of Revelation (5:2–5; 19:16), the Book of Daniel (7:3),** and the **Book of Psalms (68:31). Emperor Haile Selassie, considered by Rastas to be the reincarnation of Christ.**

## International spread and decline: 1970–present

In the mid-1970s, reggae's international popularity exploded. The most successful reggae artist was **Bob Marley**, who **"more than any other individual, was responsible for introducing Rastafarian themes, concepts and demands to a truly universal audience".**

## Organization

**Rastafari** is not a homogeneous movement and has no single administrative structure, nor any single leader. The structure of **Rastafari** groups is less like those of Christian denominations and is instead akin to the cellular structure of other African diasporic traditions like **Haitian Vodou, Cuban Santeria**, and **Jamaica's Revival Zion**.

## Twelve Tribes of Israel

**The Twelve Tribes of Israel sect was founded in 1968 in Kingston by Vernon Carrington**. He regarded himself as the reincarnation of the **Old Testament prophet Gad, one of Jacob's twelve sons,** and his followers thus refer to him as **"Prophet Gad", "Brother Gad", or "Gadman".**

"Only a thin line dividing the sect from true Christianity". Practitioners are often dubbed "Christian Rastas" because they believe Jesusis the messiah and only savior.

## Demographics

**As of 2012, there were an estimated 700,000 to 1 million Rastas worldwide.** The **Rasta** message resonates with many people who feel marginalized and alienated by the values and institutions of their society. In valorizing Africa and blackness, **Rastafari** provides a positive identity for youth in the African diaspora by allowing them to psychologically reject their social stigmatization.

# Reform Judaism

**Reform Judaism** (also known as **Liberal Judaism** or **Progressive Judaism**) is a major Jewish denomination that emphasizes the evolving nature of the faith, the superiority of its ethical aspects to the ceremonial ones, and a belief in a continuous revelation, closely intertwined with human reason and intellect, and not centered on the theophany at **Mount Sinai**.

The origins of **Reform Judaism** lie in 19th-century Germany, where its early principles were formulated by **Rabbi Abraham Geiger** and his associates; since the 1970s, the movement adopted a policy of inclusiveness and acceptance, inviting as many as possible to partake in its communities, rather than strict theoretical clarity. It is strongly identified with progressive political and social agendas, mainly under the traditional Jewish rubric *Tikkun Olam*, or "Repairing of the World".

The various regional branches sharing these beliefs, all united within the international **World Union for Progressive Judaism. Founded in 1926, the WUPJ estimates it represents at least 1.8 million people in 50 countries.**

## Definitions

Its inherent pluralism and great importance placed on individual autonomy impede any simplistic definition of **Reform Judaism**. They warrant and obligate further modification and reject any fixed, permanent set of beliefs, laws or practices.

## Theology / God

In regard to God both among clergy and constituents, leading to broader, dimmer definitions of the concept – **the movement had always officially maintained a theistic stance, affirming the belief in a personal God. The 1885 Pittsburgh Platform described the "One God... The God-Idea as taught in our sacred Scripture"** as consecrating the Jewish people to be its priests. So was the **1937 Columbus Declaration of Principles, which spoke of "One, living God who rules the world".** The 1999 Pittsburgh Statement of Principles declared the **"reality and oneness of God". "Jewish conception of God: One and indivisible, transcendent and immanent, Creator and Sustainer".**

## Revelation

**The basic tenet of Reform theology is a belief in a continuous, or progressive, revelation, occurring continuously and not limited to the theophany at Sinai, the defining event in traditional interpretation.** According to this view, all **Holy Scripture** of **Judaism**, including the Pentateuch, were authored by human beings who, although under divine inspiration. The chief promulgator of this concept was **Abraham Geiger**, generally considered the founder of the movement. This highly rationalistic view virtually identified human reason and intellect with divine action, leaving little room for direct influence by God.

In the decades around World War II, this rationalistic and optimistic theology was challenged and questioned. It was gradually replaced, mainly by the Jewish existentialism of **Martin Buber** and **Franz Rosenzweig**, centered on a complex, personal relationship with the creator.

## Ritual, autonomy and law

**Reform Judaism** emphasizes the ethical facets of the faith as its central attribute, superseding the ceremonial ones. The postwar **"New Reform"** lent renewed importance to practical, regular action as a means to engage congregants, abandoning the sanitized forms of the **"Classical"**. The notion of an intervening, commanding God remained foreign to denominational thought. The **"New Reform"** approach to the question is characterized by an attempt to strike a mean between autonomy and some degree of conformity, focusing on a dialectic relationship between both. The movement never entirely abandoned *halakhic* (traditional jurisprudence), but had largely made ethical considerations or the spirit of the age the decisive factor in determining its course.

## Messianic age and election

**Reform sought to accentuate and greatly augment the Universalist traits in Judaism, turning it into a faith befitting the Enlightenment ideals ubiquitous at the time it emerged**. Its earliest proponents rejected **Deism** and the belief that all religions would unite into one, and it later faced the challenges of the Ethical movement and Unitarianism.

One major expression of that, which is the first clear **Reform** doctrine to have been formulated, is the idea of universal **Messianism**. The belief in redemption was unhinged from the traditional elements of return to Zion and restoration of the Temple and the sacrificial cult therein, and turned into a general hope for salvation. The considerable loss of faith in human progress around **World War II** greatly shook this ideal, but it endures as a precept of **Reform**.

The movement maintained the idea of the **Chosen People of God**, but recast it in a more universal fashion: that the mission of Israel was to spread among all nations and teach them divinely-inspired ethical monotheism, bringing them all closer to the **Creator**. Like the **Orthodox**, they insisted that the People Israel was created by divine election alone, and existed solely as such. The 1999 Pittsburgh Platform and other official statements affirmed that the **"Jewish people is bound to God by an eternal *B'rit*, covenant"**.

## Soul and afterlife

**Reform** anchored reason in divine influence, accepted scientific criticism of hallowed texts and sought to adapt **Judaism** to modern notions of rationalism. They also denied the belief in the future bodily resurrection of the dead. Notions of afterlife were reduced merely to the immortality of the soul. **The 1999 Pittsburgh Statement of Principles**, for example, used the somewhat ambiguous formula **"the spirit within us is eternal"**.

The concept of reward and punishment in the world to come was abolished as well. The only perceived form of retribution for the wicked, if any, was the anguish of their soul after death, and vice versa, bliss was the single accolade for the spirits of the righteous. Angels and heavenly hosts were also deemed a foreign superstitious influence.

## Practice / Liturgy

Vernacular segments were added alongside or instead of the **Hebrew and Aramaic text**, to ensure the congregants understood the petitions they expressed; and some new prayers were composed to reflect the spirit of changing times. Blessings and passages referring to the coming of **the Messiah, return to Zion**, renewal of the sacrificial cult, resurrection of the dead, reward and punishment and overt particularism of the People Israel were replaced, recast or excised altogether.

## Observance

An official rescheduling of Sabbath to Sunday was advocated by **Kaufmann Kohler** for some time, though he retracted it eventually. Religious divorce was declared redundant and the civil one recognized as sufficient by American **Reform**. From 1890, converts were no longer obligated to be circumcised. **Circumcision** or Letting of Blood for converts and newborn babies became virtually mandated in the 1980s; ablution for menstruating women gained great grassroots popularity at the turn of the century, and some synagogues built **mikvehs** (ritual baths). Confirmation for girls eventually developed into the **Bat Mitzvah**, now popular among all except strictly **Orthodox** Jews.

## Openness

**Tolerance for LGBT and ordination of LGBT rabbis were also pioneered by the movement.** Intercourse between consenting adults was declared as legitimate by the **Central Conference of American Rabbis** in 1977, and openly gay clergy were admitted by the end of the 1980s. Same-sex marriage were sanctioned by the end of the following decade. From the second half of the 20th Century, it employed the old rabbinic notion of *Tikkun Olam*, **"repairing the world"**, as a slogan under which constituents were encouraged to partake in various initiatives for the betterment of society. The **Religious Action Center** of **Reform Judaism** became an important lobby in service of progressive causes such as the rights of women, minorities, **LGBT**, and the like.

## Jewish identity

While opposed to interfaith marriage in principle, officials of the major **Reform** rabbinical organization, the **Central Conference of American Rabbis (CCAR)**, estimated in 2012 that about half of their rabbis partake in such ceremonies. **In American Reform, 17% of synagogue-member households have a converted spouse, and 26% unconverted one.**

## Organization and demographics

The **WUPJ** established further branches around the planet, alternatively under the names **"Reform"**, **"Liberal"** and **"Progressive**. In 1990, Reconstructionist **Judaism** entered the WUPJ as an observer. **The WUPJ claims to represent a total of at least 1.8 million people.** Worldwide, the movement is mainly centered in North America. The largest **WUPJ** constituent by far is the Union for **Reform Judaism** (until 2003: **Union of American Hebrew Congregations**) in the United States and Canada. As of 2013, the **Pew Research Center** survey calculated it represented about 35% of all 5.3 million Jews in the U.S., making it the single most numerous Jewish religious group in the country. **Steven M. Cohen** deduced there were 756,000 adult Jewish synagogue members – about a quarter of households had an unconverted spouse (according to 2001 findings), adding some 90,000 non-Jews and making the total constituency roughly 850,000 – and further 1,154,000 **"Reform-identified non-members"** in the United States.

## The New Reform Judaism

On 26 May 1999, after a prolonged debate and six widely different drafts rejected, a **"Statement of Principles for Reform Judaism"** was adopted in Pittsburgh. It affirmed the **"reality and oneness of God"**, the Torah as **"God's ongoing revelation to our people"**, and committed to the **"ongoing study of the whole array of Commandments and to the fulfillment of those that address us as individuals and as a community. Some of these sacred obligations have long been observed by Reform Jews; others, both ancient and modern, demand renewed attention."**

While the wording was carefully crafted in order not to displease the estimated 20%–25% of membership that retained Classicist persuasions, it did raise condemnation from many of them. In 2008, the Society for Classical **Reform Judaism** was founded to mobilize and coordinate those who preferred the old Universalist, ethics-based and less-observant religious style, with its unique aesthetic components.

# Rosh Hashanah

**Rosh Hashanah**, literally meaning **"head of the year"**, is the Jewish New Year. The biblical name for this holiday is **Yom Teruah**, literally **"day of shouting or blasting"**. It is the first of the Jewish **High Holy Days** *Yamim Nora'im.* "Days of Awe") specified **by Leviticus 23:23–32** that occur in the early autumn of the **Northern Hemisphere**.

**Rosh Hashanah** is a two-day celebration that begins on the first day of **Tishrei**, which is the seventh month of the ecclesiastical year. In contrast to the ecclesiastical year, where the first month Nisan, the **Passover** month, marks **Israel's exodus from Egypt**, **Rosh Hashanah** marks the beginning of the civil year, according to the teachings of Judaism, and is the traditional anniversary of the creation of **Adam and Eve**, the first man and woman according to the Hebrew Bible, and the inauguration of humanity's role in God's world.

**Rosh Hashanah** customs include sounding the shofar (a cleaned-out ram's horn), as prescribed in the **Torah**, following the prescription of the Hebrew Bible to **"raise a noise"** on *Yom Teruah*. Eating symbolic foods is now a tradition, such as apples dipped in honey, hoping to evoke a sweet new year.

## Etymology

The term "**Rosh Hashanah**" in its current meaning does not appear in the **Torah**. **Leviticus 23:24** refers to the festival of the first day of the seventh month as *zikhron teru'ah* ("a memorial of blowing "). It is also referred to in the same part of Leviticus as (*shabbat shabbaton*) or ultimate Sabbath or meditative rest day, and a **"holy day to God"**. The term *rosh hashanah* appears once in the Bible **(Ezekiel 40:1**

In the Jewish prayer-books **Rosh Hashanah** is also called *Yom Hazikaron* (the day of remembrance), not to be confused with the modern Israeli remembrance day of the same name. **Rosh Hashanah** is the New Year for people, animals, and legal contracts. The **Mishnah** also sets this day aside as the new year for calculating calendar years, **shmita and yovel** years. **Rosh Hashanah commemorates the creation of man.**

## Origin

The Semites generally set the beginning of the new year in autumn, while other ancient civilizations chose spring for that purpose, such as the Persians or Greeks; the primary reason was agricultural in both cases, the time of sowing the seed and bringing in the harvest. In the Hebrew Bible: **"Three times in the year you shall keep a feast unto me… the feast of unleavened bread (Passover)… the feast of harvest (Shavuot)… and the feast of ingathering (Sukkot) which is** *at the departing of the year*" **(Exo. 23:14–16). "At the departing of the year"** implies that the New Year begins here.

## Religious significance

The **Mishnah** contains the second known reference to **Rosh Hashanah** as the **"day of judgment"** In the **Talmud** tractate on **Rosh Hashanah**, it states that three books of account are opened on **Rosh Hashanah**, wherein the fate of the wicked, the righteous, and those of the intermediate class are recorded. The names of the righteous are immediately inscribed in the book of life and they are sealed **"to live"**. The intermediate class is allowed a respite of ten days, until **Yom Kippur**, to reflect, repent and become righteous; the wicked are **"blotted out of the book of the living forever"**.

**"The Holy One said, 'on Rosh Hashanah recite before Me Sovereignty, Remembrance, and Shofar blasts The assumption is that everyone was sealed for life and therefore the next festival is Sukkot (Tabernacles) that is referred to as "the time of our joy".**

## Shofar blowing / Rosh Hashana, Ashkenaz version

The best-known ritual of **Rosh Hashanah** is the blowing of the shofar, a musical instrument made from an animal horn. The shofar is blown at various instances during the **Rosh Hashanah** prayers, with a total of 100 blasts over the day. It is a symbolic **"wake-up call,"** stirring Jews to mend their ways and repent. The shofar blasts call out: **"Sleepers, wake up from your slumber! Examine your ways and repent and remember your Creator."**

## Prayer service

On **Rosh Hashanah** day, religious poems, called *piyyutim*, are added to the regular services. Biblical verses are recited at each point. According to the **Mishnah**, 10 verses (each) are said regarding kingship, remembrance, and the shofar itself, each accompanied by the blowing of the shofar.

The **Mussaf Amidah** prayer on **Rosh Hashanah** is unique in that apart from the first and last 3 blessings, it contains 3 central blessings making a total of 9. The verses are 3 from the **Torah**, 3 from the **Ketuvim**, 3 from the **Nevi'im**, and one more from the **Torah**. Recitation of these three blessings is first recorded in the **Mishna**, though writings by **Philo** and possibly even **Psalms 81**.

## Customs / The days before Rosh Hashanah

The sound of the *shofar* is intended to awaken the listeners from their **"slumbers"** and alert them to the coming judgment. **The shofar is not blown on Shabbat.** The Sephardic tradition is to start at the beginning of Elul, while the **Ashkenazi** practice is to start a few days before **Rosh Hashanah**.Many Orthodox men immerse in a mikveh in honor of the coming day.

## Symbolic foods / *Rosh Hashanah Seder*

**Rosh Hashanah** meals usually include apples dipped in honey to symbolize a sweet new year. The blessings have the incipit "*Yehi ratzon*", meaning "**May it be Thy will.**" Pomegranates are used in many traditions, to symbolize being fruitful like the pomegranate with its many seeds. The use of apples dipped in honey, symbolizing a sweet year, is a late medieval Ashkenazi addition, though it is now almost universally accepted. Typically, round challah bread is served, to symbolize the cycle of the year.

## Tashlikh

The ritual of **tashlikh** is performed on the afternoon of the first day of **Rosh Hashanah** by Ashkenazic and most Sephardic Jews (but not by Spanish & Portuguese Jews or some Yemenites). **"Who is like unto you, O God...And You will cast all their sins into the depths of the sea"**, and Biblical passages including **Isaiah 11:9 ("They will not injure nor destroy in all My holy mountain, for the earth shall be as full of the knowledge of the Lord as the waters cover the sea")** and Psalms 118:5–9, Psalms 121 and Psalms 130.

## Greetings

The Hebrew common greeting on **Rosh Hashanah** is *Shanah Tovah* which translated from Hebrew means "**good year**". The formal Sephardic greeting is "M**ay you merit many years**", to which the answer is **"pleasant and good ones"**.

## Duration and timing

The **Torah** defines **Rosh Hashanah** as a one-day celebration, and since days in the Hebrew calendar begin at sundown, the beginning of **Rosh Hashanah** is at sundown at the end of **29 Elul**. Since the time of the **destruction of the Second Temple of Jerusalem in 70 CE** and the time of **Rabban Yohanan ben Zakkai**, normative Jewish law appears to be that **Rosh Hashanah** is to be celebrated for two days.

Orthodox and Conservative Judaism now generally observe **Rosh Hashanah** for the first two days of **Tishrei**, even in Israel where all other Jewish holidays dated from the new moon last only one day. **Karaite Jews**, who do not recognize Rabbinic Jewish oral law and rely on their own understanding of the **Torah**, observe only one day on the first of **Tishrei**, since the second day is not mentioned in the Written **Torah**. **The first day of Rosh Hashanah never falls out on Sunday, Wednesday, or Friday.**

# Sabbateans

The **Sabbateans** (or **Sabbatians**) were a variety of followers of disciples and believers in **Sabbatai Zevi (1626–1676),** a Jewish rabbi who was proclaimed to be the **Jewish Messiah** in 1666 by **Nathan of Gaza**. Vast numbers of Jews in the Jewish diaspora accepted his claims, even after he became a Jewish apostate with his conversion to Islam in the same year.

**Sabbatai Zevi**'s followers, both during his **"Messiahship"** and after his conversion to Islam, are known as **Sabbateans**. They can be grouped into three: **"Maaminim"** (believers), **"Haberim"** (associates), and **"Ba'ale Milhamah"** (warriors). Part of the **Sabbateans** lived on until well into the 20th century as **Dönmeh** (turkey).

## Sabbateans who remained Jews

In Jewish history many Jews after **Sabbatai Zevi's apostasy**, although horrified, clung to the belief that **Zevi** could still be regarded as the true Jewish messiah. They constituted the largest number of **Sabbateans** during the seventeenth and eighteenth centuries. These very Jews fell under the category of **Sectarian Sabbateans** which was born when **many Sabbateans refused to accept that Zevi's apostasy might have been indicative of the fact that their faith was genuinely an illusion.**

Polemics against Islam erupted directly after **Zevi's conversion**. Some of these attacks were considered part of a largely Anti-Sabbatean agenda. Accusations coming from Anti-**Sabbateans** revolved around the idea that **Sabbatai Zevi's conversion to Islam was rightfully an indicator of a false claim of Messianism.**

## Sabbatai Zevi's conversion to Islam

**Sabbatai Zevi had officially abandoned his faith for Islam.** However, the fact remains that **Zevi is the most famous Jew to have become a Muslim. Nathan of Gaza**, the scholar closest to **Zevi**, who had caused **Zevi** to reveal his Messiahship and in turn became his prophet, **never followed his master into Islam but remained a Jew,** albeit **excommunicated by his Jewish brethren.**

## Sabbatean – Sufi similarities

Claims of ties between **Sabbatean Kabbalah** and **Sufism** go back to the days of **Sabbatai Zevi**. **Zevi**'s exile in the Balkans brought him into close contact with several forms of unorthodox **Sufi**sm which existed in the region. The **Dönme** community of Salonika came to play a significant role in the **Sufi** life, of the region and its members actively involved with a number of **Sufi** orders, particularly the **Mevlevi**.

The often claimed connection between the movement and **Bektashi Sufism** relies merely on circumstantial evidence and coincidence rather than any concrete substantiation. There were a number of other heterodox **Sufi** movements in the region in the mid-17th century, including the **Hamzevis, Melamis and Qalandars**.

## The Dönme

Inside the **Ottoman Empire**, those followers of **Zevi** who had converted to Islam but who secretly continued Jewish observances and Brit Mila became known as the *Dönme* **(Turkish:** *dönme* **"convert").**

## Sabbatean-related controversies in Jewish history

The controversy was a momentous incident in Jewish history of the period, involving both **Rabbi Yechezkel Landau and the Vilna Gaon**, and may be credited with having crushed the lingering belief in **Sabbatai** current even in some Orthodox circles.

## Sabbateans and early Hasidism

Some scholars see seeds of the **Hasidic** movement within the Sabbatean movement. When Hasidism began to spread its influence, a serious schism evolved between the Hasidic and non-Hasidic Jews. **Those who rejected the Hasidic movement dubbed themselves as** *Misnagdim* **("opponents").**

Critics of Hasidic Judaism expressed concern that **Hasidism** might become a messianic sect as had occurred among the followers of both **Sabbatai Zevi** and **Jacob Frank**. However *The Baal Shem Tov*, **the founder of Hasidism**, came at a time when the Jewish masses of Eastern Europe were reeling in bewilderment and disappointment engendered by the two **Jewish false messiahs Sabbatai Zevi (1626–1676) and Jacob Frank (1726–1791) in particular.**

## Disillusioned Jewish Sabbateans

Sabbatai's conversion to Islam was extremely disheartening for the world's Jewish communities. Muslims and Christians jeered at and scorned the credulous and duped Jews. In spite of Sabbatai's apostasy, many of his adherents still tenaciously clung to him, claiming that his conversion was a part of the Messianic scheme.

## Jacob ben Aaron Sasportas

**Rabbi Jacob ben Aaron Sasportas** (1610–1698) was one of the fiercest opponents of the Sabbatean movement. He wrote many letters to various communities in Europe, Asia, and Africa, exhorting them to unmask the impostors and to warn the people against them. He documented his struggle in his book *Tzitzat Novel Tzvi*, the title being based on **Isaiah 28:4.**

# Sabians (Judeo-Christian)

The **Sabians** (Arabic: *al-Ṣābi'ah or al-Ṣābi'ūn*) of Middle Eastern tradition were a religious group mentioned three times in the **Qur'an** as a **People of the Book,** along with the Jews and the Christians. In the *hadith*, they were described simply as **converts to Islam.** The **Sabians** were identified by early writers with the ancient Jewish Christian group the **Elcesaites**, and with gnostic groups such as the **Hermeticists** and the **Mandaeans**. Today, the **Mandaeans** are still widely identified as **Sabians**.

## Etymology

The Arabic root (*ṣ-b-'*), means to grow forth or rise out of. When said of a star it means to rise, which may explain the association with star-worshippers. When relating to a religion it means one who left his former religion and was even a title of Muhammad for not being part of his tribe's faith. All people who leave their faiths, finding fault in them, but have yet to come to Islam, related to the **Hanif.** The word **Sabians** or *Ṣubba* is also said to be derived from the Aramaic root related to baptism.

## In the Qur'an

The **Qur'an** briefly mentions the **Sabians** in three places, with hadith providing additional details as to who they were: Indeed, the believers, Jews, Christians, and **Sabians**—whoever ˹truly˺ believes in God and the Last Day and does good will have their reward with their Lord. And there will be no fear for them, nor will they grieve. [Qur'an 2:62]

Indeed, the believers, Jews, **Sabians** and Christians—whoever ˹truly˺ believes in God and the Last Day and does good, there will be no fear for them, nor will they grieve. [Qur'an 5:69] Indeed, the believers, Jews, **Sabians**, Christians, Magi, and the polytheists—God will judge between them ˹all˺ on Judgment Day. Surely God is a Witness over all things. [Qur'an 22:17]

## In later Islamic sources

**"The Sabians believe they belong to the prophet Noah, they read Zabur, and their religion looks like Christianity." "they worship the angels"**. Many modern scholars identify the *Zabur* as the Psalms.

**Al-Biruni** (writing at the beginning of the eleventh century CE) said that the **'"real Sabians'"** were **"the remnants of the Jewish tribes who remained in Babylonia when the other tribes left it for Jerusalem in the days of Cyrus and Artaxerxes.**

Caliph **al-Ma'mun** of Baghdad in 830 CE stood with his army at the gates of Harran and questioned the Harranians about what protected religion they belonged to. As they were neither Muslim, Christian, Jewish or Magian, the caliph told them they were non-believers.

He said they would have to become Muslims, or adherents of one of the other religions recognized by the Qur'an by the time he returned from his campaign against the Byzantines or he would kill them. In the **Qur'an II.59**, said that **Sabians** were tolerated. The Harranian **Sabians** played a vital role in **Baghdad** and in the rest of the Arab world from 856 until about 1050; serving as the main source of ancient Greek philosophy and science as well as shaping intellectual life. **The most prominent of the Harranian Sabians was Thabit ibn Qurra**.

## Non-Islamic sources / Maimonides

The Jewish scholar **Maimonides** (1125–1204) translated the book *The Nabataean Agriculture*, which he considered an accurate record of the beliefs of the **Sabians**, who believed in idolatrous practices **"and other superstitions mentioned in the Nabatean Agriculture."** He provided considerable detail about the **Sabians** in his *Guide for the Perplexed* **(completed 1186–1190)**.

## Modern identification / In Bahá'í writings

The **Sabians** are also mentioned in the literature of the **Bahá'í Faith:** Those **"who worship idols in the name of the stars, who believed their religion derived from Seth and Idris",** and others **"who believed in the son of Zechariah (John the Baptist) and didn't accept the advent of the son of Mary (Jesus Christ)".**

## 21st century scholars

21st century scholars have possibly identified the **Sabians as Mandaeans or Harranians**. In the marsh areas of **Southern Iraq**, there was a continuous tradition of Mandaean religion, and that another pagan, or **"Sabian"**, center in the tenth-century Islamic world centered on Harran. These pagan **"Sabians"** are mentioned in the **Nabataean** corpus of **Ibn Wahshiyya**.

A group of modern-day people based in Iraq call themselves **Sabians** and **follow the teachings of John the Baptist**. They are **Mandaeans (or *Sabian Mandaeans*).** Due to their faith, pacifism and lack of tribal ties, they have been vulnerable to violence since the 2003 invasion of Iraq, and **numbered fewer than 5,000 in 2007. They primarily live around Baghdad**, where the last sheik resides who conducts services and baptisms. Many from the sect have moved from Baghdad to Kurdistan where it is safer.

# Salvation

**Salvation** is being saved or protected from harm or being saved or delivered from a dire situation. In religion, **Salvation** is stated as the saving of the soul from sin and its consequences. The academic study of **Salvation** is called **soteriology.**

## Meaning: *Redemption (theology)*

In religion, **Salvation** is the saving of the soul from sin and its consequences. It may also be called **"deliverance"** or **"redemption"** from sin and its effects. **Salvation** is considered to be caused either by the grace of a deity, by free will and personal efforts through prayer and **asceticism**, or by some combination of the two. Religions often emphasize the necessity of both personal effort—for example, repentance and asceticism—and divine action (e.g. **grace).**

## Abrahamic religions: *Atonement in Judaism*

In contemporary Judaism, redemption (Hebrew *ge'ulah*), refers to God redeeming the people of Israel from their various exiles. This includes the final redemption from the present exile. Judaism holds that adherents do not need personal **Salvation** as Christians believe. **Jews do not subscribe to the doctrine of original sin.** Instead, they place a high value on individual morality as defined in the law of God — embodied in what Jews know as the **Torah** or The Law, given to **Moses** by God on biblical Mount Sinai, the summary of which is comprised in the **Ten Commandments.**

In Judaism, **Salvation** is closely related to the idea of redemption, a saving from the states or circumstances that destroy the value of human existence. God as the universal spirit and **Creator** of the World, is the source of all **Salvation** for humanity, provided an individual honors God by observing his precepts. So redemption or **Salvation** depends on the individual. The Jewish concept of **Messiah** visualizes the return of the prophet **Elijah** as the harbinger of one who will redeem the world from war and suffering, leading mankind to universal brotherhood under the fatherhood of one God. The **Messiah** is not considered as a future divine or supernatural being but as a dominating human influence in an age of universal peace, characterized by the spiritual regeneration of humanity.

In Judaism, **Salvation** is open to all people and not limited to those of the Jewish faith; the only important consideration being that the people must observe and practice the ethical pattern of behavior as summarized in the **Ten Commandments**. Live a holy and righteous life dedicated to Yahweh, the God of Creation. Therefore, **Salvation** has been primarily conceived in terms of the destiny of Israel as the elect people of Yahweh (often referred to as "**the Lord**"), the God of Israel.

In the biblical text of Psalms, there is a description of death, when people go into the earth or the **"realm of the dead"** and cannot praise God. The first reference to resurrection is collective in **Ezekiel's** vision of the dry bones, when all the Israelites in exile will be resurrected. There is a reference to individual resurrection in the **Book of Daniel (165 BCE),** the last book of the Hebrew Bible. It was not until the 2nd century BCE that there arose a belief in an afterlife, in which the dead would be resurrected and undergo divine judgment.

The **Salvation** of the individual Jew was connected to the **Salvation** of the entire people. The concept of **Salvation** was tied to that of restoration for Israel. During the **Second Temple Period**, the Sadducees, High Priests, denied any particular existence of individuals after death because it wasn't written in the Torah, while the Pharisees, ancestors of the rabbis, affirmed both bodily resurrection and immortality of the soul, most likely based on the influence of **Hellenistic** ideas about body and soul and the Pharisaic belief in the **Oral Torah**. The Pharisees maintained that after death, the soul is connected to God until the messianic era when it is rejoined with the body in the land of Israel at the time of resurrection.

## Christianity: *Salvation and Atonement in Christianity*

Christianity's primary premise is that the incarnation and death of **Jesus Christ** formed the climax of a divine plan for humanity's **Salvation**. This plan was conceived by God consequent on **the Fall of Adam,** the progenitor of the human race, and it would be completed at the **Last Judgment**, when the **Second Coming of Christ** would mark the catastrophic end of the world. For Christianity, **Salvation** is only possible through **Jesus Christ**. Christians believe that Jesus' death on the cross was the once-for-all sacrifice that atoned for the sin of humanity.

According to Christian belief, sin as the human predicament is considered to be universal. In **Romans 1:18-3:20** the **Apostle Paul** declared everyone to be under sin—Jew and Gentile alike. **Salvation** is made possible by the life, death, and resurrection of Jesus. The overwhelming majority agrees that **Salvation** is made possible by the work of **Jesus Christ**, the Son of God, dying on the cross.

**"At the heart of Christian faith is the reality and hope of Salvation in Jesus Christ. Christian faith is faith in the God of Salvation revealed in Jesus of Nazareth. His plan includes the promise of blessing for all nations through Abraham and the redemption of Israel from every form of bondage. This role was fulfilled by Jesus, who will ultimately destroy all the devil's work, including suffering, pain, and death."**

**Salvation** is believed to be a process that begins when a person first becomes a Christian, continues through that person's life, and is completed when they stand before Christ in judgment. **"I *have been* saved; I *am being* saved; and I *will be* saved."** The overwhelming majority agrees that **Salvation** is made possible by the work of **Jesus Christ**, the **Son of God**, dying on the cross.

Since human existence on Earth is said to be **"given to sin",** **Salvation** also has connotations that deal with the liberation of human beings from sin, and the suffering associated with the punishment of sin—i.e., **"the wages of sin are death**." **Salvation** must be concerned with the total person. **"It must offer redemption from bondage, forgiveness for guilt, reconciliation for estrangement, renewal for the marred image of God"**.

## *Islam and Jannah*

In Islam, **Salvation** refers to the eventual entrance to heaven. Islam teaches that people who die disbelieving in the God do not receive **Salvation**. It also teaches that non-Muslims who die believing in the God but disbelieving in his message (Islam), are left to his will. **Those who die believing in the One God and his message (Islam) receive Salvation.**

**Narrated Anas that Muhammad said,**
**"None has the right to be worshipped but Allah" and has in his heart good (faith) equal to the weight of a wheat grain will be taken out of Hell."**
— *Muhammad Sahih al-Bukhari, 1:2:43*

Islam teaches that all who enter into Islam must remain so in order to receive **Salvation**. **"If anyone desires a religion other than Islam (submission to Allah), never will it be accepted of him; and in the Hereafter He will be in the ranks of those who have lost (all spiritual good)."**
— *Quran, Sura 3 (Al Imran), ayat 85*

## *Tawhid and Shirk (Islam)*

Belief in the "One God", also known as the *Tawhid* in Arabic, consists of two parts (or principles):
1. **Tawḥīdu r-Rubūbiyya**: Believing in the attributes of God and attributing them to no other but God. Such attributes include Creation, having no beginning, and having no end. These attributes are what make a God. **Islam also teaches 99 names for God**, and each of these names defines one attribute. No intercession is required to communicate with, or worship, God.
2. **Tawḥīdu l-'ilūhiyya**: Directing worship, prayer, or deed to God, and God only. For example, worshiping an idol or any saint or prophet is also considered **Shirk**, though prophets and saints may be asked for guidance or to pray for them.

## *Repentance in Islam and Islamic views on sin*

Islam acknowledges the inclination of humanity towards sin. Therefore, Muslims are constantly commanded to seek God's forgiveness and repent. Islam teaches that no one can gain **Salvation** simply by virtue of their belief or deeds, instead it is the Mercy of God, which merits them **Salvation**. Islam teaches that God is Merciful. Of no effect is the repentance of those who continue to do evil, until death faces one of them.
— *Qur'an, Sura 4 (An-Nisa), ayat 17*

Islam describes a true believer to have **Love of God and Fear of God**. No bearer of burdens can bear the burden of another. In the end, to your Lord is your Return, when He will tell you the truth of all that ye did (in this life), for He knoweth well all that is in (men's) hearts.
— *Qur'an, Sura 39 (Az-Zumar), ayat 7*

Islam teaches that a child is born sinless, regardless of the belief of his parents, dies a Muslim; he enters heaven, and does not enter hell. **Sahih al-Bukhari, 2:23:467**

## *Five Pillars of Islam*
There are acts of worship that Islam teaches to be mandatory. Islam is built on five principles.
1. To testify that none has the right to be worshipped but Allah and Muhammad is Allah's Apostle.
2. To offer the compulsory prayers dutifully and perfectly, five times a day.
3. To pay Zakat to poor and needy (i.e. obligatory charity of 2.5% annually of surplus wealth).
4. To perform Hajj. (I.e. Pilgrimage to Mecca) if you can.
5. To observe fast during the month of Ramadhan. **Sahih al-Bukhari, 1:2:7**

**Not performing the mandatory acts of worship may deprive Muslims of the chance of Salvation.**

## Indian religions: *Moksha and Nirvana*
**Hinduism, Buddhism, Jainism** and **Sikhism** share certain key concepts, which are interpreted differently by different groups and individuals. In those religions one is not liberated from sin and its consequences, but from the **samsara** (cycle of rebirth) perpetuated by passions and delusions and its resulting karma. **Salvation** is called *moksha* or *mukti* which mean liberation and release respectively.

This state and the conditions considered necessary for its realization is described in early texts of Indian religion such as the Upanishads and the Pali Canon, and later texts such the Yoga Sutras of Patanjali and the Vedanta tradition. *Moksha* can be attained by **sadhana**, literally **"means of accomplishing something"**.

Nirvana is the profound peace of mind that is acquired with **moksha** (liberation). In Buddhism and Jainism, it is the state of being free from suffering. In **Hindu philosophy**, it is union with the **Brahman** (Supreme Being). Blowing out of the fires of desire, aversion, and delusion, and the imperturbable stillness of mind acquired there-after. **In Theravada Buddhism the emphasis is on one's own liberation from samsara.**

The Mahayana traditions emphasize the bodhisattva path, in which **"each Buddha and Bodhisattva is a redeemer"**, assisting the Buddhist in seeking to achieve the redemptive state. To achieve total detachment from worldly concerns, but have instead chosen to remain engaged in the material world to the degree that this is necessary to assist others in achieving such detachment.

## *Moksha (Jainism)*

In Jainism, ***Salvation, moksa*** **and** *nirvana* are one and the same. When **a soul (*atman*)** achieves moksa, it is released from the cycle of births and deaths, and achieves its pure self. It then becomes a *siddha* (literally means one who has accomplished his ultimate objective). **Attaining Moksa requires annihilation of all *karmas*, good and bad, because if karma is left, it must bear fruit.**

# Samaritansism

The **Samaritanss** (**Samaritans** Hebrew: translit. *Shamerim*, **"Guardians/Keepers/Watchers (of the Torah)"** are an ethnoreligious group of the Levant originating from the Israelites (or Hebrews) of the Ancient Near East. Ancestrally, **Samaritanss** claim descent from the tribe of **Ephraim** and **tribe of Manasseh** (two sons of **Joseph**) as well as from the **Levites**, who have links to ancient **Samaria** (now constituting the majority of the territory known as the West Bank) from the period of their entry into **Canaan**, while some suggest that it was from the beginning of the Babylonian captivity up to the **Samaritans** polity under the rule of **Baba Rabba**. **Samaritanss** used to include descendants who ascribed to the **Benjamin tribe, but this line became extinct in the 1960s.**

In the **Talmud**, a central post-exilic religious text of Rabbinic Judaism, the **Samaritanss** are called *Cutheans* (Hebrew: *Kutim*), referring to the ancient city of **Kutha**, geographically located in what is today Iraq. In the biblical account, however, Kuthah was one of several cities from which people were brought to **Samaria**, and they worshiped **Nergal**. **Samaritanss** believe that their worship, which is based on the **Samaritans Pentateuch**, is the true religion of the ancient Israelites from before the Babylonian captivity, preserved by those who remained in the **Land of Israel**, as opposed to Judaism, which they see as a related but altered and amended religion, brought back by those returning from the **Babylonian Captivity**.

Conversion to Christianity under the Byzantines also reduced their numbers. Conversions to Islam took place as well, and by the mid–Middle Ages, estimated only around 1,900 **Samaritanss** remained in Palestine and Syria. **As of January 1, 2017, the population was 796**, divided between **Qiryat Luza** on Mount Gerizim and the city of **Holon**, just outside Tel Aviv. For liturgical purposes, **Samaritans** Hebrew, **Samaritans** Aramaic, and Arabic are used, all written with the **Samaritans** alphabet. While the Israeli Rabbinic authorities consider **Samaritans**ism to be a branch of Judaism, the Chief Rabbinate of Israel requires **Samaritanss** to officially go through a formal conversion to Judaism in order to be recognized as **Halakhic Jews**. While those with dual Israeli-Palestinian citizenship (living in **Qiryat Luza**) are generally exempted.

## ⌐ Origins / Samaritans sources

According to **Samaritans** tradition, **Mount Gerizim** was the original **Holy Place** of the Israelites from the time that **Joshua** conquered Canaan and the tribes of Israel settled the land. The reference to **Mount Gerizim** derives from the biblical story of **Moses** ordering Joshua to take the **Twelve Tribes of Israel,** to the mountains by **Shekhem** (Nablus) and place half of the tribes, six in number, on **Mount Gerizim**, the **Mount of the Blessing**, and the other half on **Mount Ebal**, the **Mount of the Curse. Deut. 11:29; 27:12; Josh. 8:33).** **Samaritanss** claim they are Israelite descendants of the Northern Israelite tribes of **Ephraim and Manasseh**, who survived the destruction of the Kingdom of Israel (**Samaria**) by the Assyrians in 722 BCE. After **Joshua**'s death, **Eli** the priest left the **Tabernacle** which **Moses** erected in the desert and established on **Mount Gerizim** and built another one under his own rule in the hills of **Shiloh.**

## Jewish sources

The emergence of the **Samaritanss** as an ethnic and religious community distinct from other Levant peoples appears to have occurred at some point after the **Assyrian conquest of the Israelite Kingdom of Israel in approximately 721 BCE.** The records of **Sargon II of Assyria** indicate that he deported 27,290 inhabitants of the former kingdom. According to 2 Kings and **Josephus,** the people of Israel were removed by the king of the Assyrians (**Sargon II**) to **Halah,** to Gozan on the **Khabur River** and to the towns of the Medes. The king of the Assyrians then brought people from Babylon, Cuthah, Avah, Emath, and Sepharvaim to place in **Samaria.** The king of the Assyrians sent one of the priests from Bethel to teach the new settlers about God's ordinances.

Dates the Assyrian onslaught at **721 BCE to 647 BCE.** Mesopotamian pottery in **Samaritans** territory cluster around the lands of **Menasheh** and that the type of pottery found was produced around 689 BCE. Some date their split with the Jews to the time of **Nehemiah, Ezra**, and the building of the **Second Temple** in Jerusalem after the Babylonian exile. **To this day the Samaritanss claim descent from the tribe of Joseph.**

## Dead Sea scrolls

The **Dead Sea scroll 4Q372** hopes that the northern tribes will return to the **land of Joseph**. However, they are not referred to as foreigners. It goes on to say that the **Samaritanss** mocked Jerusalem and built a temple on a high place to provoke Israel.

## Assyrian account of the conquest and settlement of Samaria

The account of the Assyrian kings, which was among the archaeological discoveries in Babylon, differs from the **Samaritans** account, and confirms much of the Jewish biblical account but may differ in regard to the ethnicity of the foreigners settled in **Samaria** by the Assyrians. **"The inhabitants of Samaria/Samerina, who agreed with a king  me, not to do service and not to bring tribute and who did battle, I fought against them with the power of the great gods, my lords. I counted as spoil 27,280 people, together with their chariots, and gods, in which they trusted."**
— *Nimrud Prisms, COS 2.118D, pp. 295–296*

## History / Iron Age

The narratives in Genesis about the rivalries among the twelve sons of Jacob are viewed by some as describing tensions between north and south. They were temporarily united in the United Monarchy, but after the death of Solomon, the kingdom split in two, the **Kingdom of Israel** with its last capital city **Samaria** and the Kingdom of Judah with its capital Jerusalem. The

Deuteronomistic history, portrayed Israel as a sinful kingdom, divinely punished for its idolatry and iniquity by being **destroyed by the Assyrians in 720 BCE.** The **Samaritanss** claimed that they were the true Israel who were descendants of the **"Ten Lost Tribes" taken into Assyrian captivity**. Moreover, they claimed that their version of the Pentateuch was the original and that the Jews had a falsified text produced by **Ezra** during the Babylonian exile.

## Persian period

Throughout the Persian Period, Judeans and **Samaritanss** fought periodically with one another. The **Samaritanss** were a blend of all kinds of people—made up of Israelites who were not exiled when the **Northern Kingdom was destroyed in 722 BCE.** When the **Judean exile ended in 539 BCE** and the exiles began returning home from Babylon, **Samaritanss** found their former homeland of the north populated by other people who claimed the land as their own and Jerusalem, their former glorious capital, in ruins. The inhabitants worshiped the **Pagan gods**, but when the then-sparsely populated areas became infested with dangerous wild beasts, they appealed to the king of Assyria for Israelite priests to instruct them on how to worship the **"God of that country."**

According to **Chronicles 36:22–23**, the Persian emperor, **Cyrus the Great (reigned 559–530 BCE)**, permitted the return of the exiles to their homeland and ordered the rebuilding of the Temple (Zion). **The prophet Isaiah identified Cyrus as "the Lord's Messiah". Ezra 4** says that the local inhabitants of the land offered to assist with the building of the new Temple during the time of **Zerubbabel**, but their offer was rejected. Following Solomon's death, sectionalism formed and inevitably led to the division of the kingdom. This division lead to the Judeans rejecting the offer made by the **Samaritanss** to centralize worship at the Temple.

**The rebuilding of the Jewish Temple in Jerusalem took several decades**. The project was first led by **Sheshbazzar** (ca. 538 BCE), later by **Zerubbabel** and **Jeshua**, and later still by **Haggai** and **Zechariah** (520–515 BCE). **The work was completed in 515 BCE.** Archaeological excavations at Mount Gerizim indicate that a **Samaritans** temple was built there in the first half of the 5th century BCE. The date of the schism between **Samaritanss** and Jews is unknown.

## Hellenic era / Antiochus IV Epiphanes and Hellenization

**Antiochus IV Epiphanes** was on the throne of the **Seleucid Empire from 175 to 163 BCE.** His policy was to Hellenize his entire kingdom and standardize religious observance. According to 1 **Maccabees 1:41-50** he proclaimed himself the incarnation of the **Greek god Zeus** and mandated death to anyone who refused to worship him. In the 2nd century BCE, a series of events led to a revolution by a faction Judeans against **Antiochus IV**.

**During the reign of Antiochus IV (175–164 BCE):** The **Samaritans** temple was renamed either **Zeus Hellenios** (willingly by the **Samaritanss** according to Josephus) or, more likely, **Zeus Xenios**, (unwillingly in accord with **2 Macc. 6:2**). Shortly afterwards, the Greek king sent

Gerontes the Athenian to force the Jews of Israel to violate their ancestral customs and live no longer by the laws of God; and to profane the Temple in Jerusalem and dedicate it to **Olympian Zeus**, and the one on Mount Gerizim to Zeus.

## Hasmonean influence

During the Hellenistic period, **Samaria** was largely divided between a Hellenizing faction based in **Samaria** (Sebastaea) and a pious faction, led by the **High Priest** and based largely around Shekhem and the rural areas. **Samaria** was a largely autonomous state nominally dependent on the **Seleucid Empire until around 113 BCE**, when the Jewish **Hasmonean ruler John Hyrcanus** destroyed the **Samaritans** temple and devastated **Samaria**. **The Hellinized Samaritans Temple at Mount Gerizim was destroyed by John Hyrcanus in 113 BC, having existed about 200 years.**

## Early Roman era

Under the Roman Empire, **Samaria** became a part of the **Herodian Kingdom**, Herodian Tetrarchy and with deposition of the Herodian ethnarch **Herod Achelaus** in early 1st century CE, **Samaria** became a part of the province of Judaea. The Temple of Gerizim was rebuilt after the **Bar Kokhba revolt against the Romans, around 136 CE**. Much of **Samaritans** liturgy was set by the high priest **Baba Rabba** in the 4th century. There were some **Samaritanss** in the Sasanian Empire, where they served in the army.

## Byzantine times / *Samaritans Revolts*

This period is considered as something of a golden age for the **Samaritans** community, the population thought to number up to a million. According to **Samaritans** sources, **Eastern Roman emperor Zeno (who ruled 474–491** and whom the sources call **"Zait the King of Edom")** persecuted the **Samaritanss**. The Emperor went to Neapolis (Shechem), gathered the elders and asked them to convert; when they refused, **Zeno** had many **Samaritanss** killed.

Later, in 484, the **Samaritanss** revolted. The rebels attacked **Sichem**, burned five churches built on **Samaritans** holy places and cut the finger of bishop Terebinthus, who was officiating the ceremony of Pentecost. Under a charismatic, messianic figure named **Julianus ben Sabar** (or ben Sahir), the **Samaritanss** launched a war to create their own independent state in 529. With the help of the Ghassanids, **Emperor Justinian I** crushed the revolt; tens of thousands of **Samaritanss** died or were enslaved. The **Samaritans** community dwindled to tens of thousands.

## Middle Ages

**Though initially guaranteed religious freedom after the Muslim conquest of Palestine, Samaritans numbers dropped further as a result of massacres and conversions.** By the time of the early Muslim conquests, apart from Palestine, small dispersed communities of **Samaritanss** were living also in Arab Egypt, Syria, and Iran. Like other non-Muslims in the empire, such as

Jews, **Samaritanss** were often considered to be **People of the Book.** They had the right to practice their religion, but, as **dhimmi**, adult males had to pay the **jizya or "protection tax"**. The tradition of men wearing a red tarboosh may go back to an order by the Abbasid Caliph al-Mutawakkil (847-861 CE) that required non-Muslims to be distinguished from Muslims. During the Crusades, **Samaritanss**, like the non-Latin Christian inhabitants of the Kingdom of Jerusalem, were second-class citizens.

## Ottoman rule

While the majority of the **Samaritans** population in Damascus was massacred or converted during the reign of the **Ottoman Pasha Mardam Beq** in the early 17th century, the remainder of the **Samaritans** community there, in particular, the **Danafi** family, which is still influential today, moved back to Nablus in the 17th century. In 1624, the last **Samaritans** High Priest of the line of **Eleazar** son of Aaron died without issue, but according to **Samaritans** tradition, descendants of **Aaron's** other son, Ithamar, remained and took over the office. By the late Ottoman period, the **Samaritans** community dwindled to its lowest. In 19th century, with pressure of conversion and persecution from the local rulers and occasional natural disasters, the community fell to just over 100 persons.

## British Mandate

The situation of the **Samaritans** community improved significantly during the British Mandate of Palestine. The censuses of 1922 and 1931 recorded 163 and 182 **Samaritanss** in Palestine, respectively. The majority of them lived in Nablus.

## Israeli, Jordanian and Palestinian rule

By the late 1950s, around 100 **Samaritanss** left the West Bank for Israel under an agreement with the Jordanian authorities in the West Bank. Until the 1990s, most of the **Samaritanss** resided in the West Bank city of (Nablus) below **Mount Gerizim**. They relocated to the mountain itself near the Israeli village **Har Brakha** as a result of violence during the First Intifada (1987–1990).

## Demographics

**As of January 1, 2017, there were 796 Samaritanss,** half of whom reside in their modern homes at **Kiryat Luza** on Mount Gerizim, which is sacred to them, and the rest in the city of Holon, just outside Tel Aviv. There are also four **Samaritans** families residing in Binyamina-Giv'at Ada, Matan, and Ashdod.

## Samaritans origins of Palestinian Muslims in Nablus

Much of the local Palestinian population of Nablus is believed to be descended from **Samaritanss** who had converted to Islam. The **Samaritanss** themselves describe the Ottoman period as the worst period in their modern history, as many **Samaritans** families were forced to convert to Islam during that time. The passing of the **al-Hakim Edict** by the Fatimid Caliphate in 1021, under which all Jews and Christians in the Fatimid ruled southern Levant were ordered to either convert to Islam or leave, along with another notable forced conversion to Islam imposed at the hands of the rebel **ibn Firāsa**, would contribute to their rapid unprecedented decrease, and ultimately almost complete extinction as a separate religious community.

As a result, they had decreased from nearly a million and a half in late Roman (Byzantine) times to 146 people by the end of the Ottoman Era.In the Christian Bible, the **Gospel of John** relates an encounter between a **Samaritans** woman and Jesus in which she says that the mountain was the center of their worship. She poses the question to Jesus when she realizes that he is the **Messiah**. Jesus affirms the Jewish position, saying **"You (that is, the Samaritanss) worship what you do not know"**.

# The Samson Option

According to the biblical narrative, **Samson** died when he grasped two pillars of the Temple of Dagon, and **"bowed himself with all his might"** (**Judges 16:30, KJV**). This has been variously interpreted as **Samson** pushing the pillars apart.

The **Samson Option** is the name that some military analysts and authors have given to Israel's deterrence strategy of massive retaliation with **nuclear weapons** as a **"last resort"** against a country whose military has destroyed much of Israel. Commentators also have employed the term to refer to situations where non-nuclear, non-Israeli actors, have threatened conventional weapons retaliation, such as **Yasser Arafat** and **Hezbollah.**

The name is a reference to the biblical Israelite judge **Samson** who pushed apart the pillars of a Philistine temple, bringing down the roof and killing himself and thousands of Philistines who had captured him, crying out **"Let me die with the Philistines!"** (*Judges 16:30*).

## Nuclear ambiguity

Israel refuses to confirm or deny it has nuclear weapons or to describe how it would use them, an official policy of nuclear ambiguity, also known as **"nuclear opacity."** This has made it difficult for anyone outside the Israeli government to describe the country's true nuclear policy definitively, while still allowing Israel to influence the perceptions, strategies and actions of other governments. However, over the years, some Israeli leaders have publicly acknowledged their country's nuclear capability: **Ephraim Katzir** in 1974, **Moshe Dayan** in 1981, **Shimon Peres** in 1998, and **Ehud Olmert** in 2006.

During his 2006 confirmation hearings before the United States Senate regarding his appointment as George W. Bush's Secretary of Defense, **Robert Gates** admitted that Israel had nuclear weapons. In his 2008 book *The Culture of War*, **Martin van Creveld**, a professor of military history at Israel's Hebrew University, wrote that since **Gates** admitted that Israel had nuclear weapons, any talk of Israel's nuclear weapons in Israel can lead to **"arrest, trial, and imprisonment."** Thus Israeli commentators talk about **"doomsday weapons"** and the **Samson Option**.

Nevertheless, as early as 1976, the **CIA believed that Israel possessed 10 to 20 nuclear weapons. By 2002 it was estimated that the number had increased to between 75 and 200 thermonuclear weapons**, each in the multiple-megaton range. **Kenneth S. Brower has estimated as many as 400 nuclear weapons.** These can be launched from land, sea and air. **This gives Israel a second strike option even if much of the country is destroyed.**

## *Nuclear strategy, Deterrence theory, and Assured destruction*

Although nuclear weapons were viewed as the ultimate guarantor of Israeli security, as early as the 1960s the country avoided building its military around them, instead pursuing absolute conventional superiority so as to forestall a last resort nuclear engagement. The original conception of the **Samson Option** was only as deterrence.

According to United States journalist **Seymour Hersh** and Israeli historian **Avner Cohen**, Israeli leaders like **David Ben-Gurion, Shimon Peres, Levi Eshkol** and **Moshe Dayan** coined the phrase in the mid-1960s. They named it after the biblical figure **Samson**, who pushed apart the pillars of a Philistine temple, bringing down the roof and killing himself and thousands of Philistines who had captured him, mutilated him, and gathered to see him further humiliated in chains. They contrasted it with ancient **siege of Masada where 936 Jewish Sicarii committed mass suicide rather than be defeated and enslaved by the Romans.**

In what they called the **"Last Secret of the Six Day War"** the New York Times reported that in the days before the **1967 Six Day War** Israel planned to insert a team of paratroopers by helicopter into the Sinai. Their mission was to set up and remote detonate a nuclear bomb on a mountaintop as a warning to belligerent surrounding states. The greatly outnumbered Jewish state in a surprising turn of events effectively eliminated the **Egyptian Air Force** and occupied the Sinai winning the war before the test could even be set up. Retired Israeli brigadier general **Itzhak Yaakov** referred to this operation as the **Israeli Samson Option**.

In the **1973 Yom Kippur War**, Arab forces were overwhelming Israeli forces and Prime Minister **Golda Meir** authorized a nuclear alert and ordered **13 atomic bombs** be readied for use by missiles and aircraft. The Israeli Ambassador warned **President Nixon of "very serious conclusions"** if the United States did not airlift supplies. Nixon complied. This is seen by some commentators on the subject as the first threat of the use of the **Samson Option**.

**Seymour Hersh** writes that the **"surprising victory of Menachem Begin's Likud Party in the May 1977 national elections... brought to power a government that was even more committed than Labor to the Samson Option and the necessity of an Israeli nuclear arsenal."**

**Louis René Beres,** a professor of Political Science at Purdue University, chaired **Project Daniel,** a group advising Prime Minister **Ariel Sharon**. He argues in the **Final Report of Project Daniel** and elsewhere that the effective deterrence of the **Samson Option** would be increased by ending the policy of nuclear ambiguity. In a 2004 article he recommends Israel use the **Samson Option** threat to **"support conventional preemptions"** against enemy nuclear and non-nuclear assets because **"without such weapons, Israel, having to rely entirely upon non-nuclear forces, might not be able to deter enemy retaliations for the Israeli preemptive strike."**

## Authors' opinions

**Ari Shavit** writes of Israel's nuclear strategy: **"Concerning anything and everything nuclear, Israel would be much, much more cautious than the United States and NATO. Concerning anything and everything nuclear, Israel would be the responsible adult of the international community. It would well understand the formidable nature of the demon and keep it locked in the basement"**.

Some have written about the **"Samson Option"** as a retaliation strategy. In 2002, the *Los Angeles Times* published an opinion piece by Louisiana State University professor **David Perlmutter** which the American Jewish author **Ron Rosenbaum** writes **"goes so far as to justify"** a **Samson Option** approach:

Israel has been building nuclear weapons for 30 years. The Jews understand what passive and powerless acceptance of doom has meant for them in the past, and they have ensured against it. **Masada was not an example to follow**—it hurt the Romans not a whit, but **Samson in Gaza**? What would serve the Jew-hating world better in repayment for thousands of years of massacres but a **Nuclear Winter**? Or invite all those tut-tutting European statesmen and peace activists to join us in the ovens? For the first time in history, a people facing extermination while the world either cackles or looks away—**unlike the Armenians, Tibetans, World War II European Jews or Rwandans—have the power to destroy the world. The ultimate justice?**

**Rosenbaum** writes in his 2012 book *How the End Begins: The Road to a Nuclear World War III* that, in his opinion, in the **"aftermath of a second Holocaust"**, Israel could **"bring down the pillars of the world (attack Moscow and European capitals for instance)"** as well as the **"holy places of Islam."** He writes that "**abandonment of proportionality is the essence**" of the **Samson Option**.

In 2003, a military historian, **Martin van Creveld**, thought that the **Al-Aqsa Intifada** then in progress threatened Israel's existence. Van Creveld was quoted in **David Hirst's** *The Gun and the Olive Branch* (2003) as saying:

**"We possess several hundred atomic warheads and rockets and can launch them at targets in all directions, perhaps even at Rome. Most European capitals are targets for our air force. Let me quote General Moshe Dayan: 'Israel must be like a mad dog, too dangerous to bother.' I consider it all hopeless at this point. We shall have to try to prevent things from coming to that, if at all possible. Our armed forces, however, are not the thirtieth strongest in the world, but rather the second or third. We have the capability to take the world down with us. And I can assure you that that will happen before Israel goes under"**.

However, it was unlikely Israel could have even targeted Europe as according to **Brig. Gen. Yitzhak Yaakov**, who was the mastermind behind the "**Samson Option**", Israel did not yet have other measures like bombs or missiles to carry the nuclear payload.

In 2012, in response to **Günter Grass's** poem **"Was gesagt werden muss"** (**"What Must Be Said"**) which criticized Israel's nuclear weapons program, Israeli poet and Holocaust survivor **Itamar Yaoz-Kest** published a poem entitled **"The Right to Exist: a Poem-Letter to the German Author" which addresses Grass by name. It contains the line: "If you force us yet again to descend from the face of the Earth to the depths of the Earth — let the Earth roll toward the Nothingness."** *Jerusalem Post* journalist **Gil Ronen** saw this poem as referring to the **Samson Option**, which he described as the strategy of using Israel's nuclear weapons, **"taking out Israel's enemies with it, possibly causing irreparable damage to the entire world."**

# Sanhedrin

The **Sanhedrin** (Hebrew and Jewish Palestinian Aramaic: **"sitting together,"** hence **"assembly"** or **"council"**) was an assembly of **twenty-three or seventy-one** rabbis appointed to sit as a tribunal in every city in the ancient **Land of Israel .**

There were two classes of rabbinical courts called **Sanhedrin**, the **Great Sanhedrin** and the **Lesser Sanhedrin**. A **lesser Sanhedrin of 23 judges** was appointed to each city, but there was to be only one **Great Sanhedrin of 71 judges**, which among other roles acted as the Supreme Court, taking appeals from cases decided by lesser courts. The *Av Beit Din* or chief of the court, who was second to the *nasi*; and sixty-nine general members (*Mufla*). In the **Second Temple** period, the **Great Sanhedrin** met in the Temple in Jerusalem, in a building called the **Hall of Hewn Stones**. The **Great Sanhedrin** convened every day except festivals and the Sabbath day (**Shabbat**).

After the destruction of the **Second Temple** and the failure of the **Bar Kokhba Revolt,** the **Great Sanhedrin** moved to Galilee, which became part of the Roman province of Syria Palaestina. The last universally binding decision of the **Great Sanhedrin** appeared in 358 CE, when the Hebrew Calendar was abandoned. The **Great Sanhedrin** was finally disbanded in 425 CE after continued persecution by the **Eastern Roman Empire.**

## History / Precursors

In the Hebrew Bible, Moses and the Israelites were commanded by God to establish courts of judges who were given full authority over the people of Israel, who were commanded by God to obey every word the judges instructed and every law they established. The **Mishnah** arrives at the number twenty-three based on an exegetical derivation: it must be possible for a "**community**" to vote for both conviction and exoneration. The minimum size of a "**community**" is 10 men (10 vs 10).

## Early Sanhedrin

The Hasmonean court in the **Land of Israel** , presided over by Alexander Jannaeus, king of Judea until 76 BCE, followed by his wife, was called *Synhedrion or Sanhedrin*. Only after the destruction of the **Second Temple** was the **Sanhedrin** made up only of sages.

## Herodian and early Roman rule

The first historic mention of a **Synhedrion** occurs in the **Psalms of Solomon (XVII: 49)**, a Jewish religious book written in Greek. A *Synhedrion* is mentioned 22 times in the Greek New Testament, including in the Gospels in relation to the trial of Jesus, and in the *Acts of the Apostles,* which mentions a *"Great Synhedrion"* in chapter 5 where **Rabbi Gamaliel** appeared, and also in chapter 7 in relation to the stoning death of **Saint Stephen.**

## During Jewish–Roman Wars

After the **destruction of the Second Temple in 70 CE**, the **Sanhedrin** was re-established in Yavneh with reduced authority. The seat of the **Patriarchate** moved to **Usha** under the presidency of **Gamaliel II in 80 CE**. In 116 it moved back to Yavneh, and then again back to **Usha.**

## After Bar Kokhba Revolt

Following the **Bar Kokhba revolt**, southern Galilee became the seat of rabbinic learning in the **Land of Israel**. This region was the location of the court of the Patriarch which was situated first at Usha, then at **Bet Shearim**, later at Sepphoris and finally at Tiberias. Finally, it moved to Tiberias in 193, under the presidency of **Gamaliel III** (193–230) ben **Judah haNasi.**

During the presidency of **Gamaliel IV** (270–290), due to Roman persecution, it dropped the name **Sanhedrin**; and its authoritative decisions were subsequently issued under the name of *Beth HaMidrash*. **Sanhedrin** demise begun in 313 with the **Edict of Milan** regarding religious tolerance and marking the end of the persecutions against Christians, thus seen as the first step towards Christianity becoming the official state religion of the **Roman Empire.**

As a reaction against Julian's pro-Jewish stance, the later emperor **Theodosius I** (r. 379–392 CE) forbade the **Sanhedrin** to assemble and declared ordination illegal. **Capital punishment** was prescribed for any Rabbi who received ordination, as well as complete destruction of the town where the ordination occurred. **Rabbi Hillel II** recommended change to a mathematically based calendar that was adopted at a clandestine, and maybe final, meeting in 358 CE. **This marked the last universal decision made by the Great Sanhedrin.**

**Gamaliel VI** (400–425) was the **Sanhedrin**'s last president. With his death in 425, **Theodosius II** outlawed the title of **Nasi**, the last remains of the ancient **Sanhedrin**. An imperial decree of 426 diverted the patriarchs' tax (*post excessum patriarchorum*) into the imperial treasury. Thereafter, Jews were gradually excluded from holding public office.

## Function and procedures

The **Sanhedrin** as a body claimed powers that lesser Jewish courts did not have. As such, they were the only ones who could try the king, extend the boundaries of the Temple and Jerusalem, and were the ones to whom all questions of law were finally put. The second highest-ranking member of the **Sanhedrin** was called the **Av Beit Din**, or **"Head of the Court".**

During **Second Temple** era, the **Sanhedrin** met in a building known as the **Hall of Hewn Stones (*Lishkat ha-Gazit*),** which has been placed by the Talmud and many scholars as built into the north wall of the **Temple Mount**, half inside the sanctuary and half outside, with doors providing access both to the Temple and to the outside. It was only necessary for a 23-member panel (functioning as a Lesser **Sanhedrin**) to convene. In general, the full panel of 71 judges was only convened on matters of national significance (e.g., a declaration of war) or in the event that the 23-member panel could not reach a conclusive verdict.

Due to Christian persecution, **Hillel II** was obliged to fix the calendar in permanent form in 359 CE. This institution symbolized the passing of authority from the Patriarchate to the **Babylonian Academies.**

## Presidents / *Nasi (Hebrew title) / Tannaim*

Before 191 BCE the **High Priest** acted as the *ex officio* head of the **Sanhedrin**, but in 191 BCE, when the **Sanhedrin** lost confidence in the **High Priest**, the office of **Nasi** was created. The **Sanhedrin** was headed by the chief scholars of the great **Talmudic Academies** in the **Land of Israel** . Being a member of the house of **Hillel** and thus a descendant of **King David**, the Patriarch, known in Hebrew as the *Nasi* (prince), enjoyed almost royal authority. The Patriarchate attained its zenith under **Judah ha-Nasi** who compiled the **Mishnah**, a compendium of views from Judean thought leaders of Judaism other than the Torah.

## Revival attempts

Since its **dissolution in 358 CE by imperial decree**, there have been several attempts to re-establish this body either as a self-governing body, or as a puppet of a sovereign government. None of these attempts were given any attention by Rabbinic authorities and little information is available about them.

## Napoleon Bonaparte's "Grand Sanhedrin"

The **"Grand Sanhedrin"** was a Jewish high court convened by **Napoleon I** to give legal sanction to the principles expressed by the **Assembly of Notables** in answer to the twelve questions submitted to it by the government. On October 6, 1806, the **Assembly of Notables** issued a proclamation to all the Jewish communities of Europe, inviting them to send delegates to the **Sanhedrin**, to convene on October 20. This proclamation, written in Hebrew, French, German, and Italian. When in the war against Prussia (1806–07) the emperor invaded Poland and the Jews rendered great services to his army, he remarked, laughing, **"The Sanhedrin is at least useful to me."**

## *Modern attempts to revive the Sanhedrin*

Since the dissolution of the **Sanhedrin** in 358 CE, there has been no universally recognized authority within **Halakha. Maimonides** (1135–1204) was one of the greatest scholars of the Middle Ages, and is arguably one of the most widely accepted scholars among the Jewish people since the closing of the Talmud in 500. **Maimonides** proposed a rationalist solution for achieving the goal of re-establishing the highest court in Jewish tradition and reinvesting it with the same authority it had in former years. **There have been several attempts to implement Maimonides' recommendations, the latest being in modern times.**

# Second Temple

The **Second Temple** was the Jewish holy temple which stood on the **Temple Mount** in Jerusalem during the **Second Temple** period, **between 516 BCE and 70 CE**. It replaced **Solomon's Temple** (the **First Temple**), which was **destroyed by the Neo-Babylonian Empire in 586 BCE**, when Jerusalem was conquered and part of the population of the **Kingdom of Judah** was taken into exile to Babylon.

The **Second Temple** was originally a rather modest structure constructed by a number of Jewish exile groups returning to the Levant from Babylon under the **Achaemenid-appointed governor Zerubbabel**. However, during the reign of **Herod the Great, the Second Temple was completely refurbished**. Much as the Babylonians destroyed the **First Temple, the Romans destroyed the Second Temple and Jerusalem in 70 CE** as retaliation for an ongoing Jewish revolt. The **Second Temple** lasted for a total of 585 years. (516 BC to 70 AD). Jewish eschatology includes a belief that the **Second Temple** will be replaced by a future **Third Temple.**

## Biblical narrative

The accession of **Cyrus the Great** of the **Achaemenid Empire** in 559 BCE made the re-establishment of the city of Jerusalem and the rebuilding of the Temple possible. According to the **books of Ezra and Nehemiah**, the Jewish exiles returned to Jerusalem following a decree from **Cyrus the Great (Ezra 1:1–4, 2 Chron 36:22–23),** construction started at the original site of the altar of **Solomon's Temple**. The original core of the **book of Nehemiah**, may have been combined with the core of the **Book of Ezra** around 400 BCE. After 12 years, the Israelites have been backsliding and taking non-Jewish wives.

After the return from Babylonian captivity, arrangements were immediately made to reorganize the desolated **Yehud Province** after the demise of the **Kingdom of Judah** seventy years earlier. The body of pilgrims, forming a band of **42,360**, having completed the long and dreary journey of some four months, from the banks of the **Euphrates to Jerusalem**. The people poured their gifts into the sacred treasury with great enthusiasm. First they erected and dedicated the **altar of God** on the exact spot where it had formerly stood. And in the second month of the second year (**535 BCE**), amid great public excitement and rejoicing, the foundations of the **Second Temple** were laid.

Seven years later, **Cyrus the Great**, who allowed the Jews to return to their homeland and rebuild the **Second Temple**, died (2 Chronicles 36:22–23) and was succeeded by his son **Cambyses**. Seven or eight months, **Darius** became king (**522 BCE**). It was ready for consecration in the spring of **516 BCE**, more than twenty years after the return from captivity. The Temple was completed on the third day of the month Adar, in the sixth year of the reign of **Darius**, amid great rejoicings on the part of all the people (**Ezra 6:15.16**). The Jews were no longer an independent people, but were subject to a foreign power. The **Book of Haggai** includes a prediction that the glory of the second temple would be greater than that of the **first (Haggai 2:9).**

## The Second Temple lacked the following holy articles:
- The Ark of the Covenant containing the Tablets of Stone, before which were placed the pot of manna and Aaron's rod
- The Urim and Thummim (divination objects contained in the **Hoshen**)
- The holy oil
- The sacred fire.

In the **Second Temple**, the **Kodesh Hakodashim (Holy of Holies)** was separated by curtains rather than a wall as in the **First Temple**. Still, as in the **Tabernacle**, the **Second Temple** included:
- The Menorah (golden lamp) for the *Hekhal*
- The Table of Showbread
- The golden altar of incense, with golden censers.

According to the Mishnah, the "**Foundation Stone**" stood where the **Ark** used to be, and the **High Priest** put his censer on it on **Yom Kippur.** The **Second Temple** also included many of the original vessels of gold that had been taken by the Babylonians but restored by **Cyrus the Great**. According to the Babylonian **Talmud**, however, the Temple lacked the *Shekinah*, the dwelling or settling divine presence of God, and the *Ruach Hakodesh*, the **Spirit of Holiness**, present in the first.

## Rabbinical literature
Traditional rabbinic literature state that **the Second Temple stood for 420 years. The Second Temple destruction was in 70 CE.**

## Rededication by the Maccabees
Following the conquest of Judea by **Alexander the Great**, it became part of the **Ptolemaic Kingdom of Egypt** until 200 BCE, when **King Antiochus III the Great** of Syria defeated **King Ptolemy V Epiphanes** of Egypt at the **Battle of Paneion**. Judea became at that moment part of the **Seleucid Empire of Syria. Judaism was effectively outlawed.**

In 167 BCE, **Antiochus IV Epiphanes** ordered an altar to **Zeus** erected in the Temple. He also banned circumcision and ordered pigs to be sacrificed at the altar of the Temple. Following the **Maccabean Revolt** against the **Seleucid Empire**, the **Second Temple** was rededicated and became the religious pillar of the Jewish **Hasmonean kingdom**, as well as culturally associated with the Jewish holiday of **Hanukkah**.

## Hasmonean dynasty and Roman conquest

**Salome Alexandra**, the queen of **Hasmonean Kingdom** appointed her elder son **Hyrcanus II** as the high priest of Judaea. Her younger son **Aristobulus II** was determined to have the throne, and as soon as she died he seized the throne. **Hyrcanus**, who was in line to be the king, agreed to be contented with being the high priest.

**Antipater**, the governor of Idumæa, encouraged **Hyrcanus** not to give up his throne. Eventually **Hyrcanus** fled to **Aretas III**, **king of the Nabateans**, and returned with an army to take back the throne. He defeated **Aristobulus** and besieged Jerusalem. The Roman general **Pompey**, who was in Syria fighting against the **Armenians** in the **Third Mithridatic War**, sent his lieutenant to investigate the conflict in Judaea. The Romans besieged and took the city in 63 BCE. The temple was not looted or harmed by the Romans. **Pompey** himself, perhaps inadvertently, went into the **Holy of Holies** and the next day ordered the priests to repurify the Temple and resume the religious practices.

## Herod's Temple

Reconstruction of the temple under **Herod** began with a massive expansion of the **Temple Mount.** When the Roman emperor **Caligula** planned to place his own statue inside the temple, Herod's grandson **Agrippa I** was able to intervene and convince him against this.

## Construction

**Herod's Temple** was one of the larger construction projects of the 1st century BCE. **Josephus** records that this was his masterpiece. The old temple built by **Zerubbabel** was replaced by a magnificent edifice. The Temple itself would be constructed by the priests. Later the **Exodus 30:13** sanctuary shekel was reinstituted to support the temple as the temple tax.

## Platform

It was Herod's plan that the entire **Mt. Moriah** be turned into a giant square platform. The Temple Mount was originally intended to be 1600 feet wide by 900 feet broad by 9 stories high, with walls up to 16 feet thick, but had never been finished. A trench was dug around the mountain, and huge stone **"bricks"** were laid. Some of these weighed well over **100 tons. King Herod** had architects from Greece, Rome and Egypt plan the construction.

## Second Temple Judaism

The period between the construction of the **Second Temple in 515 BCE** and its destruction by the Romans in 70 CE witnessed major historical upheavals and significant religious changes that would affect most subsequent **Abrahamic religions.**

# Sephardi Jews

**Sephardi Jews**, also known as **Sephardic Jews** or simply **Sephardim**, are a Jewish ethnic division whose ethnogenesis and emergence as a distinct community of Jews coalesced in the **Iberian Peninsula** around the start of the 2$^{nd}$ millennium (i.e., about the year 1000). They established communities throughout **Spain and Portugal**. Their millennial residence as an open and organized Jewish community in Iberia was brought to an end starting with the **Alhambra Decree** by Spain's Catholic Monarchs in the late 15$^{th}$ century, which resulted in a combination of internal and external migrations, **mass conversions and executions**.

## Narrow ethnic definition: Sephardim Tehorim
A **Sephardi** Jew is a Jew descended from the Jews who lived in the **Iberian Peninsula** in the late 15$^{th}$ century, immediately prior to the issuance of the **Alhambra Decree** of 1492 by order of the Catholic Monarchs in Spain, and the decree of 1496 in Portugal by order of **King Manuel I**.

## Divisions
Both the Spanish and Portuguese edicts ordered their respective Jewish populations to choose from one of **three options**: 1) convert to Catholicism to be allowed to remain within the kingdom, 2) remain Jews and be expelled by the stipulated deadline, or 3) be subjected to death without trial for any Jew who did not convert of leave by the deadline. In Spain, the **Jews were only given four months from the time the decree was issued before the expiry of the set deadline.**

Jews were promised royal "**protection and security**" for the effective three-month window before the deadline. They were permitted to take their belongings with them – except "**gold or silver or minted money**". The real purpose of the 1492 edict likely was not expulsion, but compulsory conversion of all **Spanish Jews**. Many opted to leave the country rather than convert. This failure to leave Portugal was then reasoned by the king to signify a default acceptance of Catholicism by the Jews, proclaiming them **New Christians**. Actual physical forced conversions, however, were also experienced throughout Portugal.

## Sephardic Bnei Anusim
The **Sephardic Bnei Anusim** consists of the contemporary and largely nominal Christian descendants of assimilated 15$^{th}$ century **Sephardic Anusim**. These descendants of Spanish and Portuguese Jews forced or coerced to convert to Catholicism remained, as **converses**, in Iberia. **Sephardic Bnei Anusim** had not been able to return to the Jewish faith over the last five centuries. The Jewish Agency for Israel estimates the **Sephardic Bnei Anusim** population to number in the millions. The **Inquisition** itself was only finally formally disbanded in the 19$^{th}$ century.

Recent revelations as a result of modern **DNA** evidence and newly discovered records in Spain. Overall, it is now estimated that up to 10% of colonial Latin America's Iberian settlers may have been of **Sephardic** origin. With Latin America's current population standing at close to 590 million people the bulk of which consists of persons of full or partial Iberian ancestry. **It is estimated that up to 50 million of these possess Sephardic Jewish ancestry to some degree.**

## Neo-Western Sephardim

**Neo-Western Sephardim** refers to a small but growing population among the **Sephardic Bnei Anusim** in Iberia and **Ibero-America** who in the late 20th and early 21st centuries have recently begun returning to Judaism.

## Post-1492

Following the 1492 edict of expulsion from Spain, **Sephardic** Jews settled mainly in the **Ottoman Empire,** Morocco and Algeria, and other areas of Middle East, like Israel, Lebanon, Syria, Iraq and Iran. In the migrations subsequent to the deadline established by the **edict in Portugal (1497),** **Sephardic**-descended New Christians fled to southern France, Italy, and most notably the Netherlands. Here they reverted to Judaism and migrated once again to the Americas. As a result of the more recent Jewish exodus from Arab lands, many of the **Sephardim Tehorim** from the Middle East and North Africa relocated to either Israel or France.

## Sephardim in modern Spain and Portugal

**Today, around 50,000 recognized Jews live in Spain**, according to the Federation of Jewish communities in Spain. The Jewish community in Portugal is considerably smaller. A community of 600 **Sephardic** Jews lives in Gibraltar.

## Spanish citizenship by Spanish Sephardic descent

In 2014, it was reported that **Spain's Cortes Generales** had begun legislating to establish a new right of return process to grant Spanish citizenship to the descendants of **Spanish Sephardic** Jews who were expelled or fled from the country five centuries ago following the **Spanish Inquisition**. Very few of the estimated **3.5 million Sephardic** Jews in the world qualifying and the economic filter ensures that only people with high purchasing power can apply.

## Portuguese citizenship by Portuguese Sephardic descent

In April 2013 Portugal amended its **Law on Nationality** to make way for legislation conferring citizenship to descendants of **Portuguese Sephardic Jews** who were expelled from the country five centuries ago following the **Portuguese Inquisition**. Portugal would thus become the first country after Israel to enact a **Jewish Law of Return**.

## Early history

Barbarian invasions brought most of the **Iberian Peninsula** under **Visigothic** rule by the early 5th century. Arians, the **Visigoths** were largely uninterested in the religious creeds within their kingdom. Under successive Visigothic kings and under ecclesiastical authority, many orders of expulsion, forced conversion, isolation, enslavement, execution, and other punitive measures were made. By 612-621, the situation for Jews became intolerable and many left Spain for nearby northern Africa.

In 711, thousands of Jews from North Africa accompanied the Moslems who invaded Spain, subsuming Catholic Spain and turning much of it into an Arab state. The Jews of Hispania had been utterly embittered and alienated by Catholic rule by the time of the Muslim invasion. Wherever they went, the Muslims were greeted by Jews eager to aid them in administering the country. This began two centuries of Muslim rule in the **Iberian Peninsula**, which became known as the **"Golden Age"** of **Sephardi** Jewry.

## Jews in Muslim Iberia

With the victory of **Tariq ibn Ziyad** in 711, the lives of the **Sephardim** changed dramatically. Though Islamic law placed restrictions on *dhimmis* the coming of the **Moors** was by and large welcomed by the Jews of Iberia. Jews provided valuable aid to the Muslim invaders. Once captured, the defense of Cordoba was left in the hands of Jews, and **Granada, Malaga, Seville**, and **Toledo** were left to a mixed army of Jews and **Moors**.

In spite of the restrictions placed upon the Jews as *dhimmis,* life under Muslim rule was one of great opportunity and Jews flourished as they did not under the **Christian Visigoths**. Many Jews came to Iberia, seen as a land of tolerance and opportunity, from the Christian and Muslim worlds. Following initial Arab victories, and especially with the establishment of **Umayyad** rule by **Abd al-Rahman I** in 7 55, the native Jewish community was joined by Jews from the rest of Europe, as well as from Arab lands, from Morocco to Babylon. Jewish communities were enriched culturally, intellectually, and religiously by the commingling of these diverse Jewish traditions.

Arabic culture, also made a lasting impact on **Sephardic** cultural development. General re-evaluation of scripture was prompted by Muslim anti-Jewish polemics and the spread of rationalism. The cultural and intellectual achievements of the Arabs, and much of the scientific and philosophical s peculation of Ancient Greek culture, which had been best preserved by Arab scholars, was made available to the educated Jew. Arabic became the main language of **Sephardic** science, philosophy, and everyday business, as had been the case with **Babylonian** *Geonim*.

The **Golden Age** is most closely identified with the reign of **Abd al-Rahman III** (882-942), the first independent **Caliph of Cordoba**, and in particular with the career of his Jewish councilor, **Hasdai ibn Shaprut** (882-942). In translating the great works of Arabic, Hebrew, and Greek into Latin, Iberian Jews were instrumental in bringing the fields of science and philosophy, which formed much of the basis of **Renaissance** learning, into the rest of Europe. **Rabbi Samuel ha-Nagid (ibn Naghrela)** was the **Vizier of Granada**. He was succeeded by his son **Joseph ibn Naghrela** who was slain by an incited mob along with most of the Jewish.

A major persecution was the **1066 Granada massacre, which occurred on December 30**, when a Muslim mob stormed the royal palace in Granada, **crucified Jewish vizier Joseph ibn Naghrela** and massacred most of the Jewish population of the city. **"More than 1,500 Jewish families, numbering 4,000 persons, fell in one day."** The decline of the **Golden Age** began before the completion of the **Christian** *Reconquista*. When the **Almohads** gave the Jews a choice of either death or conversion to Islam, many Jews emigrated. Some, such as the family of **Maimonides**, fled south and east to the more tolerant Muslim lands, while others went northward to settle in the growing Christian kingdoms.

In 1497 the Decree ordering the expulsion or forced conversion of all the Jews was passed, and the **Sephardim** either fled or went into secrecy under the guise of **"Cristaos Novos"**, i.e. New Christians (this Decree was symbolically revoked in 1996 by the Portuguese Parliament). Those who were fortunate enough to reach the **Ottoman Empire** had a better fate: the **Sultan Bayezid**

II sarcastically sent his thanks to **Ferdinand** for sending him some of his best subjects, thus **"impoverishing his own lands while enriching his (Bayezid's)"**.

This was followed by a great massacre of Jews in the city of Lisbon in 1506 and the establishment of the **Portuguese Inquisition** in 1536. This caused the flight of the Portuguese Jewish community, which continued until the extinction of the **Courts of Inquisition** in 1821; by then there were very few Jews in Portugal. A sizable **Sephardic** community had settled in Morocco and other Northern African countries, which were colonized by France in the 19th century. **Jews in Algeria were given French citizenship in 1870 by the** *decret Cremieux.*

## The Holocaust

On the eve of **World War II**, the European **Sephardi** community was concentrated in Southeastern Europe countries of Greece, Yugoslavia, and Bulgaria. Its leading centers were in Salonika, Sarajevo, Belgrade, and Sofia. The Jewish communities of Serbia and northern Greece, including the 50,000 Jews of Salonika, fell under direct German occupation in April 1941 and bore the full weight and intensity of **Nazi** repressive measures from dispossession, humiliation, and forced labor to hostage taking, and finally deportation to the death camp **Auschwitz-Birkenau**.

During WWII and until **Operation Torch,** the Jews of pro-Nazi **Vichy** Morocco/Algeria/Tunisia suffered the same anti-Semitic legislation that Jews suffered in France metropole. **Operation Torch therefore saved more than 400,000 Jews in European North Africa**.

## Later history and culture

As of April 2013, **Sephardim** who are descendants of those expelled in the inquisition are entitled to claim Portuguese citizenship. The amendment to Portugal's "**Law on Nationality**" was approved unanimously on 11 April 2013. A similar law was approved in Spain in 2014.

## Genetics

**Sephardic** Jews are very closely related to Ashkenazi Jews, and both diverged from Iraqi and Iranian Jews approximately 2,500 years ago.

## List of Nobel laureates (Sephardi Jews):

- 1911 – Tobias Asser, 1958 – Boris Pasternak, 1959 – Emilio G. Segre, 1968 – Rene Cassin, 1969 – Salvador Luria, 1980 – Baruj Benacerraf, 1981 – Elias Canetti, 1985 – Franco Modigliani, 1986 – Rita Levi-Montalcini, 1997 – Claude Cohen-Tannoudji, 2012 – Serge Haroche, 2014 – Patrick Modiano.

# Shekhinah

The **Shekhinah** (Biblical Hebrew: *šekīnah*; also Romanized *Shekina(h)*, *Schechina(h)*, *Shechina(h)*) is the English transliteration of a Hebrew word meaning **"dwelling"** or **"settling"** and denotes the dwelling or settling of the divine presence of God. **This term does not occur in the Bible, and is from rabbinic literature.**

## In Judaism

In classic Jewish thought, the **Shekhinah** refers to a dwelling or settling in a special sense, a dwelling or settling of divine presence, to the effect that, while in proximity to the **Shekhinah**, the connection to God is more readily perceivable. The **Shekhinah represents the feminine attributes of the presence of God,** *Shekhinah* being a feminine word in Hebrew, based especially on readings of the **Talmud.**

## Manifestation

The prophets made numerous references to visions of the presence of God, particularly in the context of the **Tabernacle or Temple**, with figures such as thrones or robes filling the Sanctuary. These visions have traditionally been attributed to the presence of the **Shekhinah.** The **Shekhinah** is referred to as manifest in the **Tabernacle** and the Temple in Jerusalem throughout rabbinic literature.

The Talmud states that **"the Shekhinah rests on man neither through gloom, nor through sloth, nor through frivolity, nor through levity, nor through talk, nor through idle chatter, but only through a matter of joy in connection with a mitzvah."** There is no occurrence of the word "Shekhinah" in pre-rabbinic literature such as the **Dead Sea Scrolls.**

## Targum

In the **Targum** the addition of the noun term **Shekhinah** paraphrases Hebrew verb phrases such as **Exodus 34:9 "let the Lord go among us"** (a verbal expression of presence) which **Targum** paraphrases with God's **"Shekhinah"** (a noun form). In the post-temple era usage of the term **Shekhinah** may provide a solution to the problem of God being omnipresent and thus not dwelling in any one place.

## Jewish prayers

The 17th blessing of the daily *Amidah* prayer concludes with the line **"who returns His Presence (*shekhinato*) to Zion"**. The Liberal Jewish prayer-book for **Rosh Hashanah** and **Yom Kippur** (*Machzor Ruach Chadashah*) contains a creative prayer based on **Avinu Malkeinu**, in which the feminine noun *Shekhinah* is used in the interests of gender neutrality.

## Sabbath Bride

The theme of the **Shekhinah** as the **Sabbath Bride** recurs in the writings and songs of 16th century Kabbalist, **Isaac Luria**. The *Asader Bishvachin* song, written in Aramaic by **Luria** (his name appears as an acrostic of each line) and sung at the evening meal of **Shabbat** is an example of this. **The song appears in particular in many siddurs in the section following Friday night prayers and in some Shabbat song books.**

A paragraph in the **Zohar** starts: **"One must prepare a comfortable seat with several cushions and embroidered covers, from all that is found in the house, like one who prepares a canopy for a bride. For the Shabbat is a queen and a bride. This is why the masters of the Mishna used to go out on the eve of Shabbat to receive her on the road, and used to say:** *'Come, O bride, come, O bride!'*

**And one must sing and rejoice at the table in her honor ... one must receive the Lady with many lighted candles, many enjoyments, beautiful clothes, and a house embellished with many fine appointments ..."** The tradition of the **Shekhinah** as the Shabbat Bride, the *Shabbat Kallah*, continues to this day.

## As feminine aspect

**Kabbalah** associates the **Shekhinah** with the female. **"The introduction of this idea was one of the most important and lasting innovations of Kabbalism. ...no other element of Kabbalism won such a degree of popular approval."** The feminine Jewish divine presence, the **Shekhinah**, distinguishes Kabbalistic literature from earlier Jewish literature.

**"In the imagery of the Kabbalah the Shekhinah is the most overtly female *Sefirah*, the last of the ten Sefirot, referred to imaginatively as 'the daughter of God'. ... The harmonious relationship between the female Shekhinah and the six Sefirot which precede her causes the world itself to be sustained by the flow of divine energy. She is like the moon reflecting the divine light into the world."**

## Nativity and life of Moses

The *Zohar*, a foundation book of kabbalah, presents the **Shekhinah** as playing an essential role in the conception and birth of Moses. Later during the Exodus on the **"third new moon"** in the desert, **"*Shekhinah* revealed Herself and rested upon him before the eyes of all."**

## The Tenth *Sefirah*

In **Kabbalah**, the **Shekhinah is the tenth *Sefirah*,** and the source of life for humans on earth below the **Sefirotic** realm. **Shekhinah** is sometimes seen as a divine winged being, dwelling with the people of Israel and sharing in their struggles. Moses is the only human considered to have risen beyond **Shekhinah** into the Sefirotic realm, reaching the level of *Tiferet,* or the bridegroom of the **Shekhinah**.

## In Christianity

The concept is similar to that in the **Gospel of Matthew 18:20**, **"Where two or three are gathered together in my name there am I in their midst."** Some Christian theologians have connected the concept of **Shekhinah** to the Greek term *Parousia*, **"presence"** or **"arrival,"** which is used in the New Testament in a similar way for **"divine presence".**

## Branch Davidians

Lois Roden, whom the original **Branch Davidian Seventh-Day Adventist Church** acknowledged as their teacher/prophet from 1978 to 1986, laid heavy emphasis on women's spirituality and the **feminine aspect of God**. She published a magazine, *Shekinah*, often rendered *SHEkinah*, in which she explored the concept that the **Shekhinah** is the **Holy Spirit**.

## Islam / In the Qur'an

*Sakinah* signifies the **"presence or peace of God"**. As **"support and reassurance"** it was **"sent by God into the hearts"** of Muslims and Muhammad. In the Qur'an, the **Sakinah** is mentioned six times, in **Surat *al-Baqara, at-Tawba* and *al-Fath*.**

Sakinah means **"tranquility"**, **"peace"**. **"Calm"**, from the Arabic root *sakana*: **"to be quiet"**, **"to abate"**, **"to dwell"**. In Islam, *Sakinah* "designates a special peace, the **"Peace of God"**. Although related to Hebrew *Shekhinah*, the spiritual state is not an **"indwelling of the Divine Presence"** The ordinary Arabic use of the word's root is **"the sense of abiding or dwelling in a place"**. *Sakinahhh* **in Islamic mysticism signifies an interior spiritual illumination."**

## Comments regarding Sakinahh

*Sakinahh* in the **Qur'an** can refer to God's blessing of solace and succour upon both the Children of Israel and Muhammad. **Sakinahhh** is a spirit from God that speaks. **"Sakinahhh is a sweet breeze/wind, whose face is like the face of a human"**. **"When Sakinahhh glanced at an enemy, they were defeated"**, the **Ark of the Covenant (*at-Tabut*),** to which the Sakinahh was associated, that souls found therein peace, warmth, companionship and strength.

## Gnosticism

*Shekhinah,* often in plural, is also present in some gnostic writings written in Aramaic, such as the writings of the Manichaeans and the Mandaeans, as well as others. In these writings, *shekinas* **are described as hidden aspects of God, somewhat resembling the *Amahrāspandan* of the Zoroastrians.**

# Shema Yisrael

*Shema Yisrael* (*Shema Israel* or *Sh'ma Yisrael*; Hebrew: **"Hear, O Israel"**) is a Jewish prayer, and is also the first two words of a section of the **Torah**, and is the title (better known as **The Shema**) of a prayer that serves as a centerpiece of the morning and evening Jewish prayer services. The first verse encapsulates the monotheistic essence of Judaism: **"Hear, O Israel: the LORD our God, the LORD is one"**, found in **Deuteronomy 6:4**. Observant Jews consider the **Shema** to be the most important part of the prayer service in Judaism, and its twice-daily recitation as a *mitzvah* (religious commandment). Also, it is traditional for Jews to say the **Shema** as their last words, and for parents to teach their children to say it before they go to sleep at night.

The verse is sometimes alternatively translated as **"The LORD is our God; the LORD is one"** or "**The LORD is our God, the LORD alone.**" (Biblical Hebrew rarely used a copula in the present tense, so it has to be inferred; in the **Shema**, the syntax behind this inference is ambiguous.) The word used for **"the LORD"** is the tetragrammaton YHWH. The term "**Shema**" is used by extension to refer to the whole part of the daily prayers that commences with *Shema Yisrael* and comprises Deuteronomy 6:4–9, 11:13–21, and Numbers 15:37–41. These sections of the **Torah** are read in the weekly **Torah** portions *Va'etchanan, Eikev,* and *Shlach*, respectively.

## History

Originally, the *Shema* consisted of only one verse: Deuteronomy 6:4 (see **Talmud Sukkah** 42a and Berachot 13b). The recitation of the **Shema** in the liturgy, however, consists of three portions: Deuteronomy 6:4–9, 11:13–21, and Numbers 15:37–41. The three portions are mentioned in the **Mishnah** (Berachot 2:2). The three portions relate to central issues of Jewish belief. In the **Mishnah** (Berakhot 2:5) the reciting of the **Shema** was linked with re-affirming a personal relationship with God's rule. Literally, reciting the **Shema** was stated as **"receiving the kingdom of heaven."**

Additionally, the **Talmud** points out that subtle references to the **Ten Commandments** can be found in the three portions. As the **Ten Commandments** were removed from daily prayer in the Mishnaic period (70–200 CE), the **Shema** is seen as an opportunity to commemorate the **Ten Commandments.**

There are two larger-print letters in the first sentence (**'ayin ע and daleth ד**) which, when combined, spell "**עד**". In Hebrew this means "**witness**". The idea thus conveyed is that through the recitation or proclamation of the **Shema** one is a living witness testifying to the truth of its message. Modern Kabbalistic schools, namely that of the **Ari**, teach that when one recites the last letter of the word "'**echad**'" (אחד), meaning **"one"**, he is to intend that he is ready to "**die into God"**.

## Content / *Shema Yisrael*

The first, pivotal, words of the **Shema** are, in the original Hebrew: שְׁמַע יִשְׂרָאֵל יְהֹוָה אֱלֹהֵינוּ יְהֹוָה אֶחָד,
which can be transliterated: *Sh'ma Yisra'el, YHWH 'eloheinu, YHWH 'eḥad.*

Rabbinic Judaism teaches that the Tetragrammaton (י-ה-ו-ה), **YHWH**, is the ineffable and actual
name of God, and as such is not read aloud in the **Shema** but is traditionally replaced with אדני,
Adonai ("LORD"). For that reason, the **Shema** is recited aloud as: *Sh'ma Yisrael Adonai
Eloheinu Adonai Eḥad*: "Hear, O Israel: the LORD is our God, the LORD is One."

## The literal word meanings are roughly as follows:

*Sh'ma*: literally means *listen*, *heed*, or *hear and do* (according to the Targum, *accept*) *Yisrael*:
**Israel, in the sense of the people or congregation of Israel.** *Adonai*: often translated as
**"LORD"**, it is read in place of the **YHWH** written in the Hebrew text; Samaritans say **Shema**,
which is Aramaic for "**the Name**" and is the exact equivalent of the Hebrew "**ha-Shem**", which
Rabbinic Jews substitute for "**Adonai**" in a non-liturgical context such as everyday speech.

*Eloheinu*: the plural 1st person possessive of אֱלֹהִים *Elohim*, meaning "our God". *Echad*: the
**unified and cardinal number** *One* אֶחָד. This first verse of the **Shema** relates to the kingship of
God. The first verse, **"Hear, O Israel: the LORD our God is One LORD",** has always been
regarded as the confession of belief in the One God. Due to the ambiguity of the possible ways to
translate the Hebrew passage, there are several possible renderings:

**"Hear, O Israel! Adonai is our God! Adonai is One!"** and, **"Hear, O Israel! Adonai is our
God – Adonai alone."** Many commentaries have been written about the subtle differences
between the translations. There is an emphasis on the oneness of God and on the sole worship of
God by Israel. There are other translations, though most retain one or the other emphases.

## *Baruch Shem*

**"Blessed be the name of His glorious kingdom for ever and ever"** The second line is a rabbinic
addition and is recited silently during congregational worship (except on **Yom Kippur**, when it is
recited aloud). In Reform and Conservative Judaism, it is recited aloud, but in a quieter voice than
the rest of the prayer. It was originally a liturgical response in use in the Temple when the name
of God was pronounced and took the form of *Baruch shem k'vod l'olam*, **"Blessed be his glorious
name forever"** (Psalm 72:19). However, in time the words *malchuto* ("His kingdom") and
*va'ed* ("for ever and ever") were added. *Malchuto* was introduced by the rabbis during
Roman rule as a counter to the claim of divine honors by Roman emperors. *Va'ed* was introduced
at the time of the **Second Temple** to contrast the view of the *minim* (heretics) that there is no life
after death.

## V'ahavta

The following verses are commonly referred to as the *V'ahavta* according to the first word of the verse immediately following the *Shema*, or in Classical Hebrew *V'ahav'ta* meaning **"and you shall love..."**. They contain the command to love God with all one's heart, soul, and might (Deuteronomy 6:5). The **Talmud** emphasizes that you will, at some point, whether you choose to or not, and therefore uses **"shall"** - future tense - love God. Then verse 7 goes on to remind the community to remember all the commandments and to **"teach them diligently to your children and speak of them when you sit down and when you walk, when you lie down and when you rise",** to recite the words of God when retiring or rising; to bind those words **"on thy arm and thy head"** (classically Jewish oral tradition interprets as *tefillin*), and to **"inscribe them on the door-posts of your house and on your gates"** (referring to *mezuzah*).

## Summary

In summary, the content flows from the assertion of the oneness of God's kingship. Thus, in the first portion, there is a command **to love God with all one's heart, soul, and might**, and to remember and teach these very important words to the children throughout the day. Obeying these commands, says the second portion, will lead to rewards, and disobeying them will lead to punishment. To ensure fulfillment of these key commands, God also commands in the third portion a practical reminder, wearing the *tzitzit*, **"that ye may remember and do all my commandments, and be holy unto your God."** The full content verse by verse, in Hebrew, English transliteration, and English translation, can be found on the **jewfaq.org** website.

The second line quoted, **"Blessed be the Name of His glorious kingdom for ever and ever",** was originally a congregational response to the declaration of the Oneness of God; it is therefore often printed in small font and recited in an undertone, as recognition that it is not, itself, a part of the cited Biblical verses. The third section of the **Shema** ends with **Numbers 15:41**, but traditional Jews end the recitation of the **Shema** by reciting the first word of the following blessing, *Emet,* or **"Truth"** without interruption.

## Jewish women and the Shema

In **Orthodox Judaism**, women are not required to daily recite the **Shema** (as a command from the **Torah**), as with other time-bound requirements which might impinge on their traditional familial obligations, although they are obligated to pray at least once daily without a specific liturgy requirement, and many fulfill that obligation through prayers like the **Shema**. **Conservative Judaism** generally regards Jewish women as being obligated to recite the **Shema** at the same times as men. Reform and Reconstructionist Judaism do not regard gender-related traditional Jewish ritual requirements as necessary in modern circumstances, including obligations for men, but not women, to pray specific prayers at specific times. Instead, both genders may fulfill all requirements.

## Accompanying blessings

The blessings preceding and following the *Shema* are traditionally credited to the members of the **Great Assembly**. They were first instituted in the liturgy of the Temple in Jerusalem. According to the **Talmud**, the reading of the **Shema** morning and evening fulfills the commandment **"You shall meditate therein day and night"**. As soon as a child begins to speak, his father is directed to teach him the verse **"Moses commanded us a law, even the inheritance of the congregation of Jacob"**, and teach him to read the **Shema**. The reciting of the first verse of the **Shema** is called "**the acceptance of the yoke of the kingship of God**" (*kabalat ol malchut shamayim*). **Judah ha-Nasi**, who spent all day involved with his studies and teaching, said just the first verse of the **Shema** in the morning "**as he passed his hands over his eyes**", which appears to be the origin of the custom to cover the eyes with the right hand while reciting the first verse.

## Blessings

During *Shacharit*, two blessings are recited before the **Shema** and one after the **Shema**. There is a question in Jewish law as to whether these blessings are *on* the **Shema**, or *surrounding* the **Shema**. The conclusion that has been drawn is that they are *surrounding* the **Shema**, because the structure is similar to that of blessings of the **Torah**, and there is doubt as to whether such blessings would actually *enhance* the **Shema**. The two blessings that are recited before the **Shema** are **Yotzer ohr and Ahava Rabbah/Ahavat Olam**. The blessing after is known as **Emet Vayatziv.**

During *Maariv*, there are two blessings before the **Shema** and two after. The two before are **HaMaariv Aravim** and **Ahavat Olam**. The two after are **Emet V'Emunah and Hashkiveinu**. Ashkenazim add Baruch Hashem L'Olam outside of Israel on weekdays. Overall, the three blessings in the morning and four in the evening which accompany the **Shema** sum to seven, in accordance with the verse in Psalms: **"I praise You seven times each day for Your just rules."**

## Bedtime Shema

Before going to sleep, the first paragraph of the **Shema** is recited. This is not only a commandment directly given in the Bible (in Deuteronomy 6:6–7), but is also alluded to from verses such as **"Commune with your own heart upon your bed" (Psalms 4:4).** Some also have the custom to read all three paragraphs, along with a whole list of sections from **Psalms, Tachanun**, and other prayers. Altogether this is known as the *K'riat Shema she-al ha-mitah*. According to **Arizal**, reading this prayer with great concentration is also effective in cleansing one from sin. This is discussed in the **Tanya.**

## Other instances

The exhortation by the **Kohen** in calling Israel to arms against an enemy (which does not apply when the Temple in Jerusalem is not standing) also includes **Shema** Yisrael. According to the **Talmud, Rabbi Akiva** patiently endured while his flesh was being torn with iron combs, and died

702

reciting the **Shema**. He pronounced the last word of the sentence, *Eḥad* (**"one"**) with his last breath. Since then, it has been traditional for Jews to say the **Shema** as their last words. In 2006 **Roi Klein**, a major in the Israel Defense Forces, said the **Shema** before jumping on a live grenade and dying to save his fellow soldiers.

## In later Jewish Scripture:
- **2 Kings 19:19: "And now, O Lord our God, please deliver us from his hand, so that all the kingdoms of the earth may know that You are the Lord God alone."**
- **Zechariah 14:9: "And the Lord shall become King over all the earth; on that day shall the Lord be one, and His name one."**
- **Malachi 2:10: "Have we not all one father? Has not one God created us? Why should we betray, each one his brother, to profane the convenant of our forefathers?"**

## In Second Temple Literature:
- *Letter of Aristeas* **132:** "But first of all he taught that God is one, and that his power is made manifest in all things, and that every place is filled with his sovereignty, and that nothing done by men on earth secretly escapes his notice, but that all that anyone does and all that is to be is manifest to him."
- **2 Maccabees 7:37-38**: "I, like my brothers, give up body and life for the laws of our fathers, appealing to God to show mercy soon to our nation and by afflictions and plagues to make you confess that he alone is God, and through me and my brothers to bring to an end the wrath of the Almighty which has justly fallen on our whole nation."
- **Philo, *On Special Laws* 1.30:** "This lesson he continually repeats, sometimes saying that God is one and the Framer and Maker of all things, sometimes that He is Lord of created beings, because stability and fixity and lordship are by nature vested in Him alone."
- **Josephus, *Antiquities of the Jews* 4.199:** "And let there be neither an altar nor a temple in any other city; for God is but one, and the nation of the Hebrews is but one."
- **Josephus, *Against Apion* 2.193:** "There ought also to be but one temple for one God; for likeness is the constant foundation of agreement. This temple ought to be common to all men, because he is the common God of all men."

## In the New Testament:
- **Mark 12:28-29 (NASB):** One of the scribes came and heard them arguing, and recognizing that He had answered them well, asked Him, "What commandment is the foremost of all?" Jesus answered, "The foremost is, 'Hear, O Israel! The Lord our God is one Lord'
- **Romans 3:29-30 (NASB):** "Or is God the God of Jews only? Is He not the God of Gentiles also? Yes, of Gentiles also, since indeed God who will justify the circumcised by faith and the uncircumcised through faith is one."
- **James 2:19 (NASB):** "You believe that God is one. You do well; the demons also believe, and shudder."

## Music and film

Arnold Schoenberg used it as part of the story to his narrative orchestral work *A Survivor from Warsaw* (1947).

## Divine unity of the Shema in Hasidic philosophy / *Jewish philosophy, Kabbalah, and Hasidic philosophy*

The second section of the Tanya brings the mystical panentheism of the founder of Hasidic Judaism, the **Baal Shem Tov**, into philosophical explanation. It outlines the Hasidic interpretation of God's Unity in the first two lines of the **Shema**, based upon their interpretation in **Kabbalah**.

The emphasis on **Divine Omnipresence** and immanence lies behind Hasidic joy and *devekut*, and its stress on transforming the material into spiritual worship. In this internalisation of Kabbalistic ideas, the Hasidic follower seeks to reveal the Unity and hidden holiness in all activities of life. Medieval, rationalist Jewish philosophers (exponents of *Hakirah*–rational "investigation" from first principles in support of Judaism), such as **Maimonides**, describe Biblical monotheism to mean that there is only one God, and his essence is a unique, simple, infinite Unity. Jewish mysticism provides a philosophic paradox, by dividing God's Unity into God's essence and emanation. In **Kabbalah** and especially Hasidism, God's Unity means that there is nothing independent of his essence.

The new doctrine in Lurianic **Kabbalah** of God's *tzimtzum* ("withdrawal") received different interpretations after Isaac Luria, from the literal to the metaphorical. To Hasidism and **Schneur Zalman**, it is unthinkable for the **"withdrawal"** of God that **"makes possible"** Creation, to be taken literally. The paradox of *Tzimtzum* only relates to the Ohr Ein Sof ("**Infinite Light**"), not the **Ein Sof** (Divine essence) itself. God's infinity is revealed in both complementary infinitude (infinite light) and finitude (finite light). The **"withdrawal"** was only a concealment of the Infinite Light into the essence of God, to allow the latent potentially finite light to emerge after the God limiting *tzimtzum*.

God himself remains unaffected (**"For I, the Lord, I have not changed" Malachi 3:**6). His essence was **One**, alone, before Creation, and still One, alone, after Creation, without any change. As the *tzimtzum* only limits God to a concealment, therefore God's Unity remains Omnipresent. In the **Baal Shem Tov's** interpretation, Divine providence affects every detail of Creation. The **"movement of a leaf in the wind"** is part of the unfolding Divine presence, and is a necessary part of the complete *Tikkun* (Rectification in **Kabbalah**). This awareness of the loving Divine purpose and significance of each individual and his free will, awakens mystical love and awe of God.

**Schneur Zalman** explains that God's divided Unity has two levels, an unlimited level and a limited one, that are both paradoxically true. The main text of medieval **Kabbalah**, the **Zohar**, describes the first verse of the **Shema** ("Hear O Israel, the Lord is God, the Lord is One") as the "**Upper level Unity**", and the second line ("**Blessed be the Name of the Glory of His Kingdom forever**") as the limited "**Lower level Unity**". **Schneur Zalman** gives the Chabad explanation of this. In his **Kabbalah** philosophy, all Creation is dependent on the limited, immanent, potentially finite, "**Light that Fills all Worlds**", that each Creation receives continually.

All is *bittul*–nullified to the light, even though in our realm this complete dependence is hidden. From this perspective, of God knowing the Creation on its own terms, Creation exists, but the true essence of anything is only the **Divine spark** that continuously recreates it from nothing. God is One, as nothing has any independent existence without this continual flow of **Divine Will** to Create. **This is the pantheistic Lower Level Unity.** In relation to God's essence, Creation affects no change or withdrawal. All Creation takes place "**within**" God. "**There is nothing but God**". The ability to create can only come from the infinite Divine essence, represented by the Tetragrammaton name of God. However, "**It is not the essence of the Divine, to create Worlds and sustain them**", as this ability is only external to the Infinite essence "**outside**" God. Creation only derives from God's revelatory antropomorphic "**speech**" (as in Genesis 1), and even this is unlike the external speech of Man, as it too remains "**within**" God. From this upper perspective of God knowing himself on his own terms, the created existence of Creation does not exist, as it is as nothing in relation to **Zalman's** philosophically constructed concept of God's essence. This monistic acosmism is the "**Upper Level Unity**", as from this perspective, **only God exists.**

## The *Shahadah* is "a declaration of belief" in Islam.

The words used in the **Shema** prayer are similar to the words of Sura 112 (**Al-Tawhid or Monotheism**) in **Qur'an**. The words "أَحَدٌ" in Arabic is taken from the word "אֶחָד" in Hebrew.

Arabic: ("**Say, He is Allah the One**")

### *Christian views on the Old Covenant*

The *Shema* is one of the Old Testament sentences quoted in the New Testament. The Gospel of **Mark 12:29–31** mentions that Jesus of Nazareth considered the opening exhortation of the **Shema** to be the first of his two greatest commandments and linked with a second (based on Leviticus 19:18b): "**The first of all the commandments is, Hear, O Israel; The Lord our God is one Lord: And thou shalt love the Lord thy God with all thy heart, and with all thy soul, and with all thy mind, and with all thy strength: this is the first commandment. And the second is like, namely this, Thou shalt love thy neighbor as thyself.**"

In **Luke 10:25–27** the **Shema** is also linked with **Leviticus 19:18**. The verses **Deuteronomy 6:5** and **Leviticus 19:18b** both begin with *ve'ahavta*, "**and you shall love**". In Luke's Gospel, it appears that this connection between the two verses was already part of cultural discussion or practice.

Theologians **Carl Friedrich Keil and Franz Delitzsch** noted that **"the heart is mentioned first (in Deuteronomy 6:5), as the seat of the emotions generally and of love in particular; then follows the soul (*nephesh*) as the centre of personality in man, to depict the love as pervading the entire self-consciousness; and to this is added, "with all the strength", i.e. of body and soul.**

The *Shema* has also been incorporated in Christian liturgy, and is discussed in terms of the Trinity. In the Catholic Liturgy of the Hours, the *Shema* is read during the **Night Prayer** or *Complines* every Saturday, thereby concluding the day's prayers. The **Anglican Book of Common Prayer** in use in Canada since 1962, has included the **Shema** in its Summary of the Law. Since 2012, when the Anglican Use version of the BCP was adapted for use in Canada, it has been recited by Roman Catholics as well.

**The Orthodox Church of the Culdees utilize the Shema in the Daily Services.**

# Sheol (Hades)

Sheol (*SHEE-ohl*, Hebrew: שְׁאוֹל *Šə'ōl*), in the Hebrew Bible, is a place of darkness to which the dead go. When the Hebrew scriptures were translated into Koine Greek in ancient Alexandria around 200 BC, the word *Hades* (the Greek underworld) was substituted for **Sheol**. While the Hebrew Bible describes **Sheol** as the permanent place of the dead, in the **Second Temple** period (roughly 500 BC – 70 AD) **Sheol** is considered to be the home of the wicked dead, while Paradise is the home of the righteous dead until the **Last Judgement** (e.g. **1 Enoch 22; Luke 16:19–31**). In some texts, **Sheol** was considered a place of punishment, meant for the wicked dead, and is equated with **Gehenna** in the **Talmud**. This is reflected in the New Testament where Hades is both the underworld of the dead and the personification of it.

## Judaism

The family tomb is the central concept in understanding biblical views of the afterlife. It is **"not mere sentimental respect for the physical remains that is...the motivation for the practice, but rather an assumed connection between proper sepulture and the condition of happiness of the deceased in the afterlife"**.

The early Israelites apparently believed that the graves of family, or tribe, united into one and that this, unified collectively, is to what the Biblical Hebrew term **Sheol** refers: the common grave of humans. Although not well defined in the **Tanakh, Sheol** in this view was a subterranean underworld where the souls of the dead went after the body died.

The Babylonians had a similar underworld called **Aralu** and the Greeks had one known as **Hades**. Other biblical names for **Sheol** were: **Abaddon** (ruin), found in **Psalm 88:11, Job 28:22** and **Proverbs 15:11;** *Bor* **(the pit), found in Isaiah 14:15 and Isaiah 24:22, Ezekiel 26:20;** and *Shakhat* (corruption), found in **Isaiah 38.17, and Ezekiel 28:8**. The Tanakh has few references to existence after death. The notion of resurrection of the dead appears in two biblical sources, **Daniel (Daniel 12) and Isaiah (Isaiah 25–26 ).**

## Personification in the Hebrew Bible

**Sheol** in the Hebrew Bible refers to an underworld deity. The Akkadian plates mention the name *shuwalu* **or** *suwala* in reference to a deity responsible for ruling the abode of the dead. What is more, some scholars argue that **Sheol** understood anthropomorphically fits the semantic complex of the other ancient Near Eastern death deities such as **Nergal, Ereshkigal or Mot**.

## Hebrew Bible

A number of biblical texts reference **Sheol**. The following is a selection: **Numbers 16:31–34:** As soon as he finished saying all this, the ground under them split apart and the earth opened its mouth and swallowed them and their households, and all those associated with **Korah**, together with their possessions. They went down alive into the realm of the dead, with everything they owned; the earth closed over them, and they perished and were gone from the community. At their cries, all the Israelites around them fled, shouting, **"The earth is going to swallow us too!"**

**Job 7:7–10**: Remember, O God, that my life is but a breath; my eyes will never see happiness again. The eye that now sees me will see me no longer; you will look for me, but I will be no more. As a cloud vanishes and is gone, so one who goes down to the grave does not return. He will never come to his house again; his place will know him no more.

**Psalm 88:2–10**: May my prayer come before you; turn your ear to my cry. I am overwhelmed with troubles and my life draws near to death. I am counted among those who go down to the pit; I am like one without strength. I am set apart with the dead, like the slain who lie in the grave, whom you remember no more, who are cut off from your care. You have put me in the lowest pit, in the darkest depths. Your wrath lies heavily on me; you have overwhelmed me with all your waves. You have taken from me my closest friends and have made me repulsive to them. I am confined and cannot escape; my eyes are dim with grief. I call to you, Lord, every day; I spread out my hands to you. Do you show your wonders to the dead? Do their spirits rise up and praise you?

**Ecclesiastes 9:7–10**: Go, eat your bread joyfully and drink your wine with a merry heart, for God has already accepted your deeds. At all times, let your garments be white, and let oil not be wanting on your head. Enjoy life with the wife whom you love all the days of the life of your vanity, whom He has given you under the sun, all the days of your vanity, for that is your portion in life and in your toil that you toil under the sun. Whatever your hand attains to do with your strength, do; for there is neither deed nor reckoning, neither knowledge nor wisdom in the grave, where you are going.

## New Testament

In the New Testament there are also passages describing **Hades**, such as the story of the rich man and Lazarus in **Luke 16:19–31.**

# The Six-Day War (1967)

The **Six-Day War** (Hebrew: *Milhemet Sheshet Ha Yamim*; Arabic *Naksah*, **"The Setback"** , also known as the **June War**, **1967 Arab–Israeli War**, or **Third Arab–Israeli War**, was fought between June 5 and 10, 1967 by Israel and the neighboring states of Egypt (known at the time as the United Arab Republic), Jordan, and Syria.

Relations between Israel and its neighbors had never fully normalized following the **1948 Arab–Israeli War**. In 1956 Israel invaded the Egyptian Sinai, with one of its objectives being the reopening of the **Straits of Tiran** which Egypt had blocked to Israeli shipping since 1950. Israel was subsequently forced to withdraw, but won a guarantee that the **Straits of Tiran** would remain open. While the **United Nations Emergency Force** was deployed along the border, there was no demilitarization agreement.

In the period leading up to June 1967, tensions became dangerously heightened. Israel reiterated its post-1956 position that the closure of the straits of Tiran to its shipping would be a *casus belli*. In May Egyptian **President Gamal Abdel Nasser** announced that the straits would be closed to Israeli vessels and then mobilized its Egyptian forces along its border with Israel. On 5 June Israel launched what it claimed were a series of preemptive airstrikes against Egyptian airfields. Claims and counterclaims relating to this series of events are one of a number of controversies relating to the conflict.

The Egyptians were caught by surprise, and nearly the entire Egyptian air force was destroyed with few Israeli losses, giving the Israelis air supremacy. Simultaneously, the Israelis launched a ground offensive into the **Gaza Strip** and the Sinai, which again caught the Egyptians by surprise. After some initial resistance, Egyptian leader **Gamal Abdel Nasser** ordered the evacuation of the Sinai. Israeli forces rushed westward in pursuit of the Egyptians, inflicted heavy losses, and conquered the Sinai.

**Nasser** induced Syria and Jordan to begin attacks on Israel by using the initially confused situation to claim that Egypt had defeated the Israeli air strike. Israeli counterattacks resulted in the seizure of East Jerusalem as well as the **West Bank** from the Jordanians, while Israel's retaliation against Syria resulted in its occupation of the **Golan Heights**.

**On June 11, a ceasefire was signed**. In the aftermath of the war, Israel had crippled the Egyptian, Syrian and Jordanian militaries, **having killed over 20,000 troops while only losing less than 1,000 of their own**. The Israeli success was the result of a well-played and prepared strategy, the poor leadership of the Arab states and their poor military leadership and strategy. **Israel seized the Gaza Strip and the Sinai Peninsula from Egypt, the West Bank from Jordan and the Golan Heights from Syria.** Israel's international standing greatly improved in the years after and their victory humiliated Egypt, Jordan and Syria, leading **Nasser** to resign in shame; he was later reinstated after protests in Egypt against his resignation occurred.

However, the speed and ease of Israel's victory would lead to a dangerous overconfidence within the ranks of the **Israel Defense Forces (IDF)**, contributing to initial Arab successes in the subsequent **1973 Yom Kippur War**; another Israeli success occurred in the **Yom Kippur War** and the Arab militaries were again crushed. The displacement of civilian populations resulting from the war would have long-term consequences, as **300,000 Palestinians fled the West Bank and about 100,000 Syrians left the Golan Heights to become refugees**. Across the Arab world, Jewish minority communities fled or were expelled, with refugees going mainly to Israel or Europe.

## Background / *Origins of the Six-Day War*

After the 1956 Suez Crisis, Egypt agreed to the stationing of a **United Nations Emergency Force (UNEF)** in the Sinai to ensure all parties would comply with the 1949 Armistice Agreements. In the following years there were numerous minor border clashes between Israel and its Arab neighbors, particularly Syria. In early November 1966, Syria signed a mutual defense agreement with Egypt. Soon after this, in response to **Palestine Liberation Organization (PLO)** guerilla activity, including a mine attack that left three dead, the Israeli Defence Force (**IDF**) attacked the village of as-Samu in the Jordanian-occupied **West Bank**. Jordanian units that engaged the Israelis were quickly beaten back. **King Hussein of Jordan criticized Egyptian President Gamal Abdel Nasser for failing to come to Jordan's aid, and "hiding behind UNEF skirts".**

In May 1967, **Nasser** received false reports from the Soviet Union that Israel was massing on the Syrian border. **Nasser** began massing his troops in two defensive lines in the Sinai Peninsula on Israel's border (May 16), expelled the **UNEF** force from Gaza and Sinai (May 19) and took over UNEF positions at Sharm el-Sheikh, overlooking the **Straits of Tiran**. Israel repeated declarations it made in 1957 that any closure of the Straits would be considered an act of war, or justification for war, but **Nasser** closed the Straits to Israeli shipping on May 22–23. After the war, U.S. **President Lyndon Johnson** commented:

**"If a single act of folly was more responsible for this explosion than any other, it was the arbitrary and dangerous announced decision that the Straits of Tiran would be closed. The right of innocent, maritime passage must be preserved for all nations". On May 30, Jordan and Egypt signed a defense pact**. The following day, at Jordan's invitation, the Iraqi army began deploying troops and armored units in Jordan. They were later reinforced by an Egyptian contingent. On June 1, Israel formed a **National Unity Government** by widening its cabinet, and on **June 4** the decision was made to go to war. The next morning, Israel launched **Operation Focus**, a large-scale surprise air strike that was the opening of the **Six-Day War**.

## Military preparation

Before the war, Israeli pilots and ground crews had trained extensively in rapid refitting of aircraft returning from sorties, enabling a single aircraft to sortie up to four times a day (as opposed to the norm in Arab air forces of one or two sorties per day). This enabled the **Israeli Air Force (IAF)** to send several attack waves against Egyptian airfields on the first day of the war, overwhelming the **Egyptian Air Force**, and allowed it to knock out other Arab air forces on the same day. This has contributed to the Arab belief that the **IAF** was helped by foreign air forces.

Pilots were extensively schooled about their targets, and were forced to memorize every single detail, and rehearsed the operation multiple times on dummy runways in total secrecy. The Egyptians had constructed fortified defenses in the Sinai. These designs were based on the assumption that an attack would come along the few roads leading through the desert, rather than through the difficult desert terrain. The Israelis chose not to risk attacking the Egyptian defenses head-on, and instead surprised them from an unexpected direction.

**James Reston**, writing in *The New York Times* on May 23, 1967, noted, **"In discipline, training, morale, equipment and general competence his [Nasser's] army and the other Arab forces, without the direct assistance of the Soviet Union, are no match for the Israelis. ... Even with 50,000 troops and the best of his generals and air force in Yemen, he has not been able to work his way in that small and primitive country, and even his effort to help the Congo rebels was a flop."** On the eve of the war, Israel believed it could win a war in 3–4 days. The United States estimated Israel would need 7–10 days to win, with British estimates supporting the U.S. view.

## Armies and weapons

The Israeli army had a total strength, including **reservists, of 264,000**, though this number could not be sustained, as the reservists were vital to civilian life. Against Jordan's forces on the **West Bank**, Israel deployed about 40,000 troops and 200 tanks (eight brigades). Israeli Central Command forces consisted of five brigades. The first two were permanently stationed near Jerusalem and were the **Jerusalem Brigade** and the mechanized **Harel Brigade**. **Mordechai Gur's** 55th Paratroopers Brigade was summoned from the Sinai front. The 10th Armored Brigade was stationed north of the **West Bank**. The **Israeli Northern Command** comprised a division of three brigades led by **Major General Elad Peled** which was stationed in the Jezreel Valley to the north of the **West Bank**.

On the eve of the war, **Egypt massed approximately 100,000 of its 160,000 troops in the Sinai**, including all seven of its divisions (four infantry, two armored and one mechanized), four independent infantry brigades and four independent armored brigades. Over a third of these soldiers were veterans of Egypt's continuing intervention into the **North Yemen Civil War** and another third were reservists. **These forces had 950 tanks, 1,100 APCs, and more than 1,000 artillery pieces.**

**Syria's army had a total strength of 75,000** and was deployed along the border with Israel. **The Jordanian Armed Forces included 11 brigades, totaling 55,000 troops.** Nine brigades (45,000 troops, 270 tanks, 200 artillery pieces) were deployed in the **West Bank**, including the elite armored 40th, and two in the Jordan Valley. They possessed sizable numbers of **M113 APCs** and were equipped with some 300 modern Western tanks, 250 of which were U.S. **M48 Pattons**. They also had 12 battalions of artillery, six batteries of 81 mm and 120 mm mortars, a paratrooper battalion trained in the new U.S.-built school and a new battalion of mechanized infantry.

The Jordanian Army, then known as the **Arab Legion**, was a long-term-service, professional army, relatively well-equipped and well-trained. Israeli post-war briefings said that the Jordanian staff acted professionally, but was always left "**half a step**" behind by the Israeli moves. The small **Royal Jordanian Air Force** consisted of only 24 British-made **Hawker Hunter** fighters, six transports, and two helicopters. According to the Israelis, the **Hawker Hunter** was essentially on par with the French-built Dassault **Mirage III** – the **IAF**'s best plane. 100 Iraqi tanks and an infantry division were readied near the Jordanian border. Two squadrons of Iraqi fighter-aircraft, **Hawker Hunters** and **MiG 21s**, were rebased adjacent to the Jordanian border.

**The Arab air forces were reinforced by some aircraft from Libya, Algeria, Morocco, Kuwait, and Saudi Arabia** to make up for the massive losses suffered on the first day of the war. They were also aided by **volunteer pilots from the Pakistan Air Force acting in an independent capacity. PAF pilots shot down several Israeli planes.**

## Weapons

With the exception of Jordan, the Arabs relied principally on Soviet weaponry. Jordan's army was equipped with American weaponry, and its air force was composed of British aircraft. Egypt had by far the largest and the most modern of all the Arab air forces, consisting of about **420 combat aircraft, all of them Soviet-built and with a heavy quota of top-of-the-line MiG-21s.** Of particular concern to the Israelis were the **30 Tu-16 "Badger"** medium bombers, capable of inflicting heavy damage on Israeli military and civilian centers. Israeli weapons were mainly of Western origin. Its air force was composed principally of French aircraft, while its armored units were mostly of British and American design and manufacture. Some infantry weapons, including the ubiquitous Uzi, were of Israeli origin.

## Preemptive air attack / *Operation Focus*

**Israel's first and most critical move was a surprise attack on the Egyptian Air Force.** Initially, both Egypt and Israel announced that they had been attacked by the other country. On June 5 at

7:45 Israeli time, as civil defense sirens sounded all over Israel, the **IAF** launched **Operation Focus (*Moked*).** All but 12 of its nearly 200 operational jets launched a mass attack against Egypt's airfields. The Egyptian defensive infrastructure was extremely poor, and no airfields were yet equipped with hardened aircraft shelters capable of protecting Egypt's warplanes. **Most of the Israeli warplanes headed out over the Mediterranean Sea, flying low to avoid radar detection, before turning toward Egypt. Others flew over the Red Sea.**

Meanwhile, the Egyptians hindered their own defense by effectively shutting down their entire air defense system: they were worried that rebel Egyptian forces would shoot down the plane carrying **Field Marshal Abdel Hakim Amer** and **Lt-Gen. Sidqi Mahmoud,** who were en route from al Maza to Bir Tamada in the Sinai to meet the commanders of the troops stationed there. In any event, it did not make a great deal of difference as the Israeli pilots came in below Egyptian radar cover and well below the lowest point at which its **SA-2 surface-to-air missile** batteries could bring down an aircraft.

Although the powerful Jordanian radar facility at Ajloun detected waves of aircraft approaching Egypt and reported the code word for "**war**" up the Egyptian command chain, Egyptian command and communications problems prevented the warning from reaching the targeted airfields. The Israelis employed a mixed-attack strategy: bombing and strafing runs against planes parked on the ground, and bombing to disable runways with special tarmac-shredding penetration bombs developed jointly with France, leaving **surviving aircraft unable to take off.**

The runway at the Arish airfield was spared, as the Israelis expected to turn it into a military airport for their transports after the war. Surviving aircraft were taken out by later attack waves. The operation was more successful than expected, catching the Egyptians by surprise and destroying virtually all of the Egyptian Air Force on the ground, with few Israeli losses. Only four unarmed Egyptian training flights were in the air when the strike began. **A total of 338 Egyptian aircraft were destroyed and 100 pilots were killed**, although the number of aircraft lost by the Egyptians is disputed.

**Among the Egyptian planes lost were all 30 Tu-16 bombers, 27 out of 40 Il-28 bombers, 12 Su-7 fighter-bombers, over 90 MiG-21s, 20 MiG-19s, 25 MiG-17 fighters, and around 32 assorted transport planes and helicopters.** In addition, Egyptian radars and SAM missiles were also attacked and destroyed. **The Israelis lost 19 planes**, including two destroyed in air-to-air combat and 13 downed by anti-aircraft artillery. One Israeli plane, which was damaged and unable to break radio silence, was shot down by Israeli Hawk missiles after it strayed over the **Negev Nuclear Research Center**. Another was destroyed by an exploding Egyptian bomber.

**The attack guaranteed Israeli air supremacy for the rest of the war**. Attacks on other Arab air forces by Israel took place later in the day as hostilities broke out on other fronts. The large numbers of Arab aircraft claimed destroyed by Israel on that day were at first regarded as **"greatly exaggerated"** by the Western press. However, the fact that the **Egyptian Air Force**, along with other Arab air forces attacked by Israel, made practically no appearance for the remaining days of the conflict proved that the numbers were most likely authentic. Throughout the war, Israeli aircraft continued strafing Arab airfield runways to prevent their return to usability. Meanwhile, **Egyptian state-run radio had reported an Egyptian victory, falsely claiming that 70 Israeli planes had been downed on the first day of fighting.**

## Gaza Strip and Sinai Peninsula

The Egyptian forces consisted of seven divisions: four armored, two infantry, and one mechanized infantry. Overall, Egypt had around 100,000 troops and 900–950 tanks in the Sinai, backed by 1,100 APCs and 1,000 artillery pieces. This arrangement was thought to be based on the Soviet doctrine, where mobile armor units at strategic depth provide a dynamic defense while infantry units engage in defensive battles. Israeli forces concentrated on the border with Egypt included six armored brigades, one infantry brigade, one mechanized infantry brigade, three paratrooper brigades, giving a total of around 70,000 men and 700 tanks, who were organized in three armored divisions. They had massed on the border the night before the war, camouflaging themselves and observing radio silence before being ordered to advance.

The Israeli plan was to surprise the Egyptian forces in both timing (the attack exactly coinciding with the **IAF** strike on Egyptian airfields), location (attacking via northern and central Sinai routes, as opposed to the Egyptian expectations of a repeat of the 1956 war, when the **IDF** attacked via the central and southern routes) and method (using a combined-force flanking approach, rather than direct tank assaults).

## Northern (El Arish) Israeli division

On June 5, at 7:50 a.m., the northernmost Israeli division, consisting of three brigades and commanded by **Major General Israel Tal,** one of Israel's most prominent armor commanders, crossed the border at two points, opposite **Nahal Oz** and south of **Khan Yunis**. They advanced swiftly, holding fire to prolong the element of surprise. Tal's forces assaulted the "**Rafah Gap**", a seven-mile stretch containing the shortest of three main routes through the Sinai towards **El-Qantarah el-Sharqiyya and the Suez Canal**. The Egyptians had four divisions in the area, backed by minefields, pillboxes, underground bunkers, hidden gun emplacements and trenches. The terrain on either side of the route was impassable. The Israeli plan was to hit the Egyptians at selected key points with concentrated armor.

Tal's advance was led by the 7th Armored Brigade under **Colonel Shmuel Gonen**. The Israeli plan called for the 7th Brigade to outflank **Khan Yunis** from the north and the 60th Armored Brigade under **Colonel Menachem Aviram** would advance from the south. The two brigades would link up and surround **Khan Yunis**, while the paratroopers would take **Rafah**. Gonen entrusted the breakthrough to a single battalion of his brigade.

Initially, the advance was met with light resistance, as Egyptian intelligence had concluded that it was a diversion for the main attack. However, as Gonen's lead battalion advanced, it suddenly came under intense fire and took heavy losses. A second battalion was brought up, but was also pinned down. Meanwhile, the **60th Brigade** became bogged down in the sand, while the paratroopers had trouble navigating through the dunes. The Israelis continued to press their attack, and despite heavy losses, cleared the Egyptian positions and reached the **Khan Yunis** railway junction in little over four hours.

Gonen's brigade then advanced nine miles to Rafah in twin columns. Rafah itself was circumvented, and the Israelis attacked **Sheikh Zuweid**, eight miles to the southwest, which was defended by two brigades. Though inferior in numbers and equipment, the Egyptians were deeply entrenched and camouflaged. The Israelis were pinned down by fierce Egyptian resistance, and called in air and artillery support to enable their lead elements to advance. **Many Egyptians abandoned their positions after their commander and several of his staff were killed.**

The Israelis broke through with tank-led assaults. However, Aviram's forces misjudged the Egyptians' flank, and were pinned between strongholds before they were extracted after several hours. By nightfall, the Israelis had finished mopping up resistance. Israeli forces had taken significant losses, with **Colonel Gonen** later telling reporters that **"we left many of our dead soldiers in Rafah, and many burnt-out tanks."** The Egyptians suffered some 2,000 casualties and lost 40 tanks.

## Advance on Arish

On June 5, with the road open, Israeli forces continued advancing towards Arish. Already by late afternoon, elements of the **79th Armored Battalion** had charged through the seven-mile long Jiradi defile, a narrow pass defended by well-emplaced troops of the **Egyptian 112th Infantry Brigade.** In fierce fighting, which saw the pass change hands several times, the Israelis charged through the position. The Egyptians suffered heavy casualties and tank losses, while Israeli losses stood at 66 dead, 93 wounded and 28 tanks. Emerging at the western end, Israeli forces advanced to the outskirts of Arish. **As it reached the outskirts of Arish, Tal's division also consolidated its hold on Rafah and Khan Yunis.**

The following day, June 6, the Israeli forces on the outskirts of Arish were reinforced by the 7th Brigade, which fought its way through the Jiradi pass. After receiving supplies via an airdrop, the Israelis entered the city and captured the airport at 7:50 am. The Israelis entered the city at 8:00 am. **Company commander Yossi Peled** recounted that **"Al-Arish was totally quiet, desolate.**

Suddenly, the city turned into a madhouse. Shots came at us from every alley, every corner, every window and house."

An **IDF** record stated that **"clearing the city was hard fighting. The Egyptians fired from the rooftops, from balconies and windows. They dropped grenades into our half-tracks and blocked the streets with trucks. Our men threw the grenades back and crushed the trucks with their tanks."** Gonen sent additional units to Arish, and the city was eventually taken.

**Brigadier-General Avraham Yoffe**'s assignment was to penetrate Sinai south of **Tal's** forces and north or Sharon's. **Yoffe's** attack allowed Tal to complete the capture of the Jiradi defile, **Khan Yunis.** All of them were taken after fierce fighting. **Gonen** subsequently dispatched a force of tanks, infantry and engineers under **Colonel Yisrael Granit** to continue down the Mediterranean coast towards the Suez Canal, while a second force led by **Gonen** himself turned south and captured **Bir Lahfan and Jabal Libni**.

## Mid-front (Abu-Ageila) Israeli division

Further south, on June 6, the Israeli 38th Armored Division under **Major-General Ariel Sharon** assaulted Um-Katef, a heavily fortified area defended by the Egyptian 2nd Infantry Division under **Major-General Sa'adi Nagib**, and consisting of some 16,000 troops. The Egyptians also had a battalion of tank destroyers and a tank regiment, formed of **Soviet World War II** armor, which included **90 T-34-85 tanks, 22 SU-100 tank** destroyers, and about 16,000 men. The Israelis had about 14,000 men and 150 post-World War II tanks including the AMX-13, **Centurions**, and **M50 Super Shermans** (modified M-4 Sherman tanks).

Two armored brigades in the meantime, under **Avraham Yoffe**, slipped across the border through sandy wastes that Egypt had left undefended because they were considered impassable. Simultaneously, **Sharon's** tanks from the west were to engage Egyptian forces on **Um-Katef** ridge and block any reinforcements. Israeli infantry would clear the three trenches, while **Heliborne paratroopers** would land behind Egyptian lines and silence their artillery. An armored thrust would be made at al-Qusmaya to unnerve and isolate its garrison.

As Sharon's division advanced into the Sinai, Egyptian forces staged successful delaying actions at **Tarat Umm, Umm Tarfa, and Hill 181**. An Israeli jet was downed by anti-aircraft fire, and Sharon's forces came under heavy shelling as they advanced from the north and west. The Israeli advance, which had to cope with extensive minefields, took a large number of casualties. A column of Israeli tanks managed to penetrate the northern flank of **Abu Ageila**, and by dusk, all units were in position. The Israelis then brought up ninety 105 mm and 155 mm artillery guns for a preparatory barrage, while civilian buses brought reserve infantrymen under **Colonel Yekutiel Adam** and helicopters arrived to ferry the paratroopers. These movements were unobserved by the Egyptians, who were preoccupied with Israeli probes against their perimeter.

As night fell, the Israeli assault troops lit flashlights, each battalion a different color, to prevent friendly fire incidents. At 10:00 pm, Israeli artillery began a barrage on **Um-Katef**, firing some 6,000 shells in less than twenty minutes, the most concentrated artillery barrage in Israel's history. Israeli tanks assaulted the northernmost Egyptian defenses and were largely successful, though an entire armored brigade was stalled by mines, and had only one mine-clearance tank. Israeli infantrymen assaulted the triple line of trenches in the east.

To the west, paratroopers commanded by **Colonel Danny Matt** landed behind Egyptian lines, though half the helicopters got lost and never found the battlefield, while others were unable to land due to mortar fire. Those that successfully landed on target destroyed Egyptian artillery and ammunition dumps and separated gun crews from their batteries, sowing enough confusion to significantly reduce Egyptian artillery fire.

Egyptian reinforcements from Jabal Libni advanced towards **Um-Katef** to counterattack, but failed to reach their objective, being subjected to heavy air attacks and encountering Israeli lodgments on the roads. Egyptian commanders then called in artillery attacks on their own positions. The Israelis accomplished and sometimes exceeded their overall plan, and had largely succeeded by the following day. The Egyptians took heavy casualties, while **the Israelis lost 40 dead and 140 wounded**.

**Yoffe's** attack allowed **Sharon** to complete the capture of the **Um-Katef**, after fierce fighting. The main thrust at **Um-Katef** was stalled due to mines and craters. After **IDF** engineers had cleared a path by 4:00 pm, Israeli and Egyptian tanks engaged in fierce combat, often at ranges as close as ten yards. The battle ended in an Israeli victory, with **40 Egyptian and 19 Israeli tanks destroyed**. Meanwhile, Israeli infantry finished clearing out the Egyptian trenches, with Israeli casualties standing at 14 dead and 41 wounded and Egyptian casualties at 300 dead and 100 taken prisoner.

## Other Israeli forces

Further south, on June 5, the 8th Armored Brigade under **Colonel Albert Mandler**, initially positioned as a ruse to draw off Egyptian forces from the real invasion routes, attacked the fortified bunkers at **Kuntill**a, a strategically valuable position whose capture would enable Mandler to block reinforcements from reaching Um-Katef and to join **Sharon'**s upcoming attack on **Nakhl**. The defending Egyptian battalion, outnumbered and outgunned, fiercely resisted the attack, hitting a number of Israeli tanks. However, most of the defenders were killed, and only three Egyptian tanks, one of them damaged, survived. **By nightfall, Mendler's forces had taken Kuntilla.**

With the exceptions of **Rafah** and **Khan Yunis**, Israeli forces had initially avoided entering the **Gaza Strip**. Israeli **Defense Minister Moshe Dayan had expressly forbidden entry into the area**. After Palestinian positions in Gaza opened fire on the Negev settlements of **Nirim** and **Kissufim, IDF Chief of Staff Yitzhak Rabin overrode Dayan's instructions and ordered the**

**11th Mechanized Brigade under Colonel Yehuda Reshef to enter the Strip.** The force was immediately met with heavy artillery fire and fierce resistance from Palestinian forces and remnants of the Egyptian forces from **Rafah**.

By sunset, the Israelis had taken the strategically vital **Ali Muntar ridge**, overlooking Gaza City, but were beaten back from the city itself. Some 70 Israelis were killed, along with Israeli journalist **Ben Oyserman** and American journalist **Paul Schutzer**. **Twelve members of UNEF were also killed.** On the war's second day, June 6, the Israelis were bolstered by the 35th Paratroopers Brigade under **Colonel Rafael Eitan, and took Gaza City along with the entire Strip. The fighting was fierce, and accounted for nearly half of all Israeli casualties on the southern front.** However, Gaza rapidly fell to the Israelis.

Meanwhile, on June 6, two Israeli reserve brigades under **Yoffe**, each equipped with 100 tanks, penetrated the Sinai south of Tal's division and north of **Sharon's**, capturing the road junctions of **Abu Ageila, Bir Lahfan**, and **Arish**, taking all of them before midnight. Two Egyptian armored brigades counterattacked, and a fierce battle took place until the following morning. The Egyptians were beaten back by fierce resistance coupled with airstrikes, sustaining heavy tank losses. They fled west towards **Jabal Libni**.

## The Egyptian Army

During the ground fighting, remnants of the **Egyptian Air Force** attacked Israeli ground forces, but took losses from the **Israeli Air Force** and from Israeli anti-aircraft units. Throughout the last four days, Egyptian aircraft flew 150 sorties against Israeli units in the Sinai. Many of the Egyptian units remained intact and could have tried to prevent the Israelis from reaching the Suez Canal or engaged in combat in the attempt to reach the canal.

However, when the **Egyptian Field Marshal Abdel Hakim Amer heard about the fall of Abu-Ageila, he panicked and ordered all units in the Sinai to retreat. This order effectively meant the defeat of Egypt.** Meanwhile, **President Nasser**, having learned of the results of the Israeli air strikes, decided together with **Field Marshal Amer** to order a **general retreat from the Sinai within 24 hours**. No detailed instructions were given concerning the manner and sequence of withdrawal.

## Next fighting days

As Egyptian columns retreated, Israeli aircraft and artillery attacked them. Israeli jets used napalm bombs during their sorties. The attacks destroyed hundreds of vehicles and caused heavy casualties. At **Jabal Libni**, retreating Egyptian soldiers were fired upon by their own artillery. At **Bir Gafgafa**, the Egyptians fiercely resisted advancing Israeli forces, knocking out three tanks and eight half-tracks, and killing 20 soldiers.

Due to the Egyptians' retreat, the Israeli High Command decided not to pursue the Egyptian units but rather to bypass and destroy them in the mountainous passes of West Sinai. Therefore, in the following two days (June 6 and 7), all three Israeli divisions (**Sharon** and **Tal** were reinforced by an armored brigade each) rushed westwards and reached the passes. Sharon's division first went southward then westward, via **An-Nakhl**, to **Mitla Pass** with air support.

It was joined there by parts of **Yoffe's** division, while its other units blocked the **Gidi Pass**. These passes became killing grounds for the Egyptians, who ran right into waiting Israeli positions and suffered heavy losses. According to Egyptian diplomat **Mahmoud Riad, 10,000 men were killed in one day alone, and many others died from hunger and thirst. Tal's units stopped at various points to the length of the Suez Canal.**

Israel's blocking action was partially successful. Only the **Gidi pass** was captured before the Egyptians approached it, but at other places, Egyptian units managed to pass through and cross the canal to safety. Due to the haste of the Egyptian retreat, soldiers often abandoned weapons, military equipment, and hundreds of vehicles. Many Egyptian soldiers were cut off from their units had to walk about 200 kilometers on foot before reaching the Suez Canal with limited supplies of food and water and were exposed to intense heat.

**Thousands of soldiers died as a result**. Many Egyptian soldiers chose instead to surrender to the Israelis. However, the Israelis eventually exceeded their capabilities to provide for prisoners. As a result, they **began directing soldiers towards the Suez Canal** and only taking prisoner high-ranking officers, who were expected to be exchanged for captured Israeli pilots.

During the offensive, the Israeli Navy landed six combat divers from the **Shayetet 13** naval commando unit to infiltrate Alexandria harbor. The divers sank an Egyptian minesweeper before being taken prisoner. **Shayetet 13** commandos also infiltrated into **Port Said harbor**, but found no ships there. A planned commando raid against the Syrian Navy never materialized. Both Egyptian and Israeli warships made movements at sea to intimidate the other side throughout the war, but did not engage each other. However, **Israeli warships and aircraft did hunt for Egyptian submarines throughout the war.**

On June 7, Israel began the conquest of **Sharm el-Sheikh**. The Israeli Navy started the operation with a probe of Egyptian naval defenses. An aerial reconnaissance flight found that the area was less defended than originally thought. At about 4:30 am, three Israeli missile boats opened fire on Egyptian shore batteries, while paratroopers and commandos boarded helicopters and **Nord Noratlas** transport planes for an assault on **Al-Tur**, as **Chief of Staff Rabin was convinced it was too risky to land them directly in Sharm el-Sheikh.**

However, the city had been largely abandoned the day before, and reports from air and naval forces finally convinced **Rabin** to divert the aircraft to **Sharm el-Sheikh**. There, the Israelis engaged in a pitched battle with the Egyptians and took the city, killing 20 Egyptian soldiers and taking 8 prisoner. At 12:15 pm, **Defense Minister Dayan announced that the Straits of Tiran constituted an international waterway open to all ships without restriction.**

On June 8, Israel completed the capture of the Sinai by sending infantry units to **Ras Sudar** on the western coast of the peninsula. Several tactical elements made the swift Israeli advance possible: first, the surprise attack that quickly gave the **Israeli Air Force** complete air superiority over the Egyptian Air Force; second, the determined implementation of an innovative battle plan; third, the lack of coordination among Egyptian troops. These factors would prove to be decisive elements on Israel's other fronts as well.

## West Bank / *Jordanian campaign (1967)*

**Jordan was reluctant to enter the war**. **Nasser** used the confusion of the first hours of the conflict to convince King **Hussein** that he was victorious; he claimed as evidence a radar sighting of a squadron of Israeli aircraft returning from bombing raids in Egypt, which he said was an Egyptian aircraft en route to attack Israel. One of the Jordanian brigades stationed in the **West Bank** was sent to the Hebron area in order to link with the Egyptians. **Hussein decided to attack. The IDF's strategic plan was to remain on the defensive along the Jordanian front, to enable focus in the expected campaign against Egypt.**

Intermittent machine-gun exchanges began taking place in Jerusalem at 9:30 am, and the fighting gradually escalated as the Jordanians introduced mortar and recoilless rifle fire. Under the orders from **General Narkis**, the Israelis responded only with small-arms fire, firing in a flat trajectory to avoid hitting civilians, holy sites or the **Old City**. At 10:00 am on June 5, the Jordanian Army began shelling Israel. Two batteries of **155 mm Long Tom** cannons opened fire on the suburbs of Tel Aviv and **Ramat David Airbase**. The commanders of these batteries were instructed to lay a two-hour barrage against military and civilian settlements in central Israel. **Some shells hit the outskirts of Tel Aviv.**

By 10:30 am, **Eshkol had sent a message via Odd Bull to King Hussein promising not to initiate any action against Jordan if it stayed out of the war. King Hussein replied that it was too late, "the die was cast".** At 11:15 am, Jordanian howitzers began a 6,000-shell barrage at Israeli Jerusalem. The Jordanians initially targeted **kibbutz Ramat Rachel** in the south and Mount Scopus in the north, then ranged into the city center and outlying neighborhoods. Military installations, the Prime Minister's Residence, and the Knesset compound were also targeted. Israeli civilian casualties totaled 20 dead and about 1,000 wounded. **Some 900 buildings were damaged, including Hadassah Ein Kerem Hospital.**

At 11:50 am, sixteen Jordanian **Hawker Hunters** attacked **Netanya, Kfar Sirkin and Kfar Saba**, killing one civilian, wounding seven and destroying a transport plane. Three **Iraqi Hawker Hunters** strafed civilian settlements in the Jezreel Valley, and an **Iraqi Tupolev Tu-16** attacked Afula, and was shot down near the Megiddo airfield. The attack caused minimal material damage, hitting only a senior citizens' home and several chicken coops, but sixteen Israeli soldiers were killed, most of them when the **Tupolev** crashed.

## Israeli cabinet meets

When the Israeli cabinet convened to decide what to do, **Yigal Allon and Menahem Begin argued that this was an opportunity to take the Old City of Jerusalem**, but **Eshkol** decided to defer any decision until **Moshe Dayan** and **Yitzhak Rabin** could be consulted. **Uzi Narkiss** made a number of proposals for military action, including the capture of Latrun, but the cabinet turned him down. **Dayan** rejected multiple requests from **Narkiss** for permission to mount an infantry assault towards **Mount Scopus**. However, **Dayan** sanctioned a number of more limited retaliatory actions.

## Initial response

Shortly before 12:30 pm, the **Israeli Air Force** attacked Jordan's two airbases. The Hawker Hunters were refueling at the time of the attack. The Israeli aircraft attacked in two waves, the first of which cratered the runways and knocked out the control towers, and the second wave **destroyed all 21 of Jordan's Hawker Hunter fighters, along with six transport aircraft and two helicopters**. One Israeli jet was shot down by ground fire.

**Israeli aircraft also attacked H-3, an Iraqi Air Force base in western Iraq**. During the attack, 12 MiG-21s, 2 MiG-17s, 5 Hunter F6s, and 3 Il-28 bombers were destroyed or shot down. **A Pakistani pilot stationed at the base shot down an Israeli fighter and a bomber during the raid.** The Jordanian radar facility at Ajloun was destroyed in an Israeli airstrike. Israeli **Fouga Magister jets** attacked the Jordanian 40th Brigade with rockets as it moved south from the **Damiya Bridge**. Dozens of tanks were knocked out, and a convoy of 26 trucks carrying ammunition was destroyed. In Jerusalem, Israel responded to Jordanian shelling with a missile strike that devastated Jordanian positions. **The Israelis used the L missile, a surface-to-surface missile developed jointly with France in secret.**

## Jordanian battalion at Government House / *Battle of Ammunition Hill*

A Jordanian battalion advanced up **Government House** ridge and dug in at the perimeter of **Government House**, the headquarters of the **United Nations** observers, and opened fire on **Ramat Rachel, the Allenby Barracks** and the Jewish section of **Abu Tor** with mortars and recoilless rifles. UN observers fiercely protested the incursion into the neutral zone, and several manhandled a Jordanian machine gun out of **Government House** after the crew had set it up in a second-floor window. After the Jordanians occupied **Jabel Mukaber**, an advance patrol was sent out and approached **Ramat Rachel**, where they came under fire from four civilians, including the wife of the director, who were armed with old Czech-made weapons.

The immediate Israeli response was an offensive to retake **Government House** and its ridge. The Jerusalem **Brigade's Reserve Battalion 161**, under **Lieutenant-Colonel Asher Dreizin**, was given the task. Dreizin had two infantry companies and eight tanks under his command, several of which broke down or became stuck in the mud at **Ramat Rachel**, leaving three for the assault. The Jordanians mounted fierce resistance, knocking out two tanks.

The Israelis broke through the compound's western gate and began clearing the building with grenades, before **General Odd Bull, commander of the UN observers**, compelled the Israelis to hold their fire, telling them that the Jordanians had already fled. The Israelis proceeded to take the **Antenna Hill**, directly behind **Government House**, and clear out a series of bunkers to the west and south.

The fighting, often conducted hand-to-hand, continued for nearly four hours before the surviving Jordanians fell back to trenches held by the **Hittin Brigade**, which were steadily overwhelmed. By 6:30 pm, the Jordanians had retreated to Bethlehem, having suffered about 100 casualties. **All but ten of Dreizin's soldiers were casualties, and Dreizin himself was wounded three times**.

## Israeli invasion

During the late afternoon of June 5, the Israelis launched an offensive to encircle Jerusalem, which lasted into the following day. During the night, they were supported by intense tank, artillery and mortar fire to soften up Jordanian positions. Searchlights placed atop the **Labor Federation** building, then the tallest in Israeli Jerusalem, exposed and blinded the Jordanians. The Jerusalem Brigade moved south of Jerusalem, while the mechanized **Harel Brigade** and 55th Paratroopers Brigade under **Mordechai Gur** encircled it from the north.

A combined force of tanks and paratroopers crossed no-man's land near the **Mandelbaum Gate**. One of **Gur**'s paratroop battalions approached the fortified **Police Academy**. The Israelis used **Bangalore** torpedoes to blast their way through barbed wire leading up to the position while exposed and under heavy fire. With the aid of two tanks borrowed from the **Jerusalem Brigade**, they captured the **Police Academy**. After receiving reinforcements, they moved up to attack **Ammunition Hill.**

The Jordanian defenders, who were heavily dug-in, fiercely resisted the attack. All of the Israeli officers except for two company commanders were killed, and the fighting was mostly led by individual soldiers. The fighting was conducted at close quarters in trenches and bunkers, and was often **hand-to-hand**. The Israelis captured the position after four hours of heavy fighting. During the battle, **36 Israeli and 71 Jordanian soldiers were killed**.

The battalion subsequently drove east, and linked up with the Israeli enclave on **Mount Scopus** and its **Hebrew University** campus. **Gur's** other battalions captured the other Jordanian positions around the **American Colony**, despite being short on men and equipment and having come under a Jordanian mortar bombardment while waiting for the signal to advance.

At the same time, the mechanized **Harel Brigade** attacked the fortress at **Latrun**, which the Jordanians had abandoned due to heavy Israeli tank fire. The brigade attacked **Har Adar,** but seven tanks were knocked out by mines, forcing the infantry to mount an assault without armored cover. The Israeli soldiers advanced under heavy fire, jumping between stones to avoid mines. **The fighting was conducted at close-quarters, often with knives and bayonets.**

The Jordanians fell back after a battle that left two Israeli and eight Jordanian soldiers dead, and Israeli forces advanced through **Beit Horon** towards Ramallah, taking four fortified villages along the way. By the evening, the brigade arrived in Ramallah. Meanwhile, the **163rd Infantry Battalion** secured **Abu Tor** following a fierce battle, severing the **Old City** from **Bethlehem and Hebron.** Meanwhile, **600 Egyptian commandos stationed in the West Bank** moved to attack Israeli airfields. Led by Jordanian intelligence scouts, they crossed the border and began infiltrating through Israeli settlements towards **Ramla** and **Hatzor.**

They were soon detected and sought shelter in nearby fields, which the Israelis set on fire. **Some 450 commandos were killed, and the remainder escaped to Jordan.** From the **American Colony**, the paratroopers moved towards the **Old City**. Their plan was to approach it via the lightly defended **Salah al-Din Street**. However, they made a wrong turn onto the heavily defended **Nablus Road**. The Israelis ran into fierce resistance. Their tanks fired at point-blank range down the street, while the paratroopers mounted repeated charges. Despite repelling repeated Israeli charges, the Jordanians gradually gave way to Israeli firepower and momentum. The Israelis suffered some 30 casualties – half the original force – while the Jordanians lost 45 dead and 142 wounded.

Meanwhile, the Israeli **71st Battalion** breached barbed wire and minefields and emerged near **Wadi Joz**, near the base of **Mount Scopus**, from where the **Old City** could be cut off from Jericho and East Jerusalem from **Ramallah**. Israeli artillery targeted the one remaining route from Jerusalem to the **West Bank**, and shellfire deterred the Jordanians from counterattacking from their positions at **Augusta-Victoria**. An Israeli detachment then captured the **Rockefeller Museum** after a brief skirmish.

Afterwards, the Israelis broke through to the Jerusalem-Ramallah road. At **Tel al-Ful**, the Israelis fought a running battle with up to thirty Jordanian tanks. The Jordanians stalled the advance and destroyed a number of half-tracks, but the Israelis launched air attacks and exploited the vulnerability of the external fuel tanks mounted on the Jordanian tanks. The Jordanians lost half their tanks, and retreated towards Jericho. Joining up with the 4th Brigade, the Israelis then descended through **Shuafat** and the site of what is now **French Hill**, through Jordanian defenses at **Mivtar**, emerging at **Ammunition Hill**.

With Jordanian defenses in Jerusalem crumbling, elements of the **Jordanian 60th Brigade** and an infantry battalion were sent from Jericho to reinforce Jerusalem. Its original orders were to repel the Israelis from the Latrun corridor, but due to the worsening situation in Jerusalem, the brigade was ordered to proceed to Jerusalem's Arab suburbs and attack **Mount Scopus**. Parallel to the brigade were infantrymen from the **Imam Ali Brigade**, who were approaching Issawiya. The brigades were spotted by Israeli aircraft and decimated by rocket and cannon fire. Other Jordanian attempts to reinforce Jerusalem were beaten back, either by armored ambushes or airstrikes.

Fearing damage to holy sites and the prospect of having to fight in built-up areas, **Dayan ordered his troops not to enter the Old City.** He also feared that Israel would be subjected to a fierce international backlash and the outrage of Christians worldwide if it forced its way into the **Old City**. Privately, he told **David Ben-Gurion** that he was also concerned over the prospect of Israel capturing Jerusalem's holy sites, only to be forced to give them up under the threat of international sanctions.

## The West Bank (June 7)

On June 7, heavy fighting ensued. **Dayan had ordered his troops not to enter the Old City**; however, upon hearing that the UN was about to declare a ceasefire, he changed his mind, and without cabinet clearance, decided to capture it. Two paratroop battalions attacked **Augusta-Victoria Hill**, high ground overlooking the **Old City** from the east.

One battalion attacked from **Mount Scopus**, and another attacked from the valley between it and the **Old City**. Another paratroop battalion, personally led by **Gur**, broke into the **Old City**, and was joined by the other two battalions after their missions were complete. The paratroopers met little resistance. **The fighting was conducted solely by the paratroopers;** the Israelis did not use armor during the battle out of fear of severe damage to the **Old City**.

In the north, one battalion from **Peled's** division was sent to check Jordanian defenses in the Jordan Valley. A brigade belonging to **Peled's** division captured the western part of the **West Bank**. One brigade attacked Jordanian artillery positions around Jenin, which were shelling **Ramat David Airbase**. The **Jordanian 12th Armored Battalion**, which outnumbered the Israelis, held off repeated attempts to capture Jenin. However, Israeli air attacks took their toll, and the **Jordanian M48 Pattons**, with their external fuel tanks, proved vulnerable at short distances, even to the Israeli-modified Shermans. Twelve Jordanian tanks were destroyed, and only six remained operational.

Just after dusk, Israeli reinforcements arrived. The Jordanians continued to fiercely resist, and the Israelis were unable to advance without artillery and air support. One Israeli jet attacked the Jordanian commander's tank, wounding him and killing his radio operator and intelligence officer. The surviving Jordanian forces then withdrew to Jenin, where they were reinforced by the **25th Infantry Brigade.** The Jordanians were effectively surrounded in Jenin.

Jordanian infantry and their three remaining tanks managed to hold off the Israelis until 4:00 am, when three battalions arrived to reinforce them in the afternoon. The Jordanian tanks charged, and knocked out multiple Israeli vehicles, and the tide began to shift. After sunrise, Israeli jets and artillery conducted a two-hour bombardment against the Jordanians. The Jordanians lost 10 dead and 250 wounded, and had only seven tanks left, including two without gas, and sixteen **APCs.** The Israelis then fought their way into Jenin, and captured the city after fierce fighting.

After the **Old City** fell, the Jerusalem Brigade reinforced the paratroopers, and continued to the south, capturing Judea and **Gush Etzion**. Hebron was taken without any resistance. Fearful that Israeli soldiers would exact retribution for the **1929 massacre of the city's Jewish community,** Hebron's residents flew white sheets from their windows and rooftops, and voluntarily gave up their weapons. The **Harel Brigade** proceeded eastward, descending to the **Jordan River.**

On June 7, Israeli forces seized Bethlehem, taking the city after a brief battle that left some 40 Jordanian soldiers dead, with the remainder fleeing. On the same day, one of **Peled's** brigades seized Nablus; then it joined one of **Central Command's** armored brigades to fight the Jordanian forces; as the Jordanians held the advantage of superior equipment and were equal in numbers to the Israelis.

Again, the air superiority of the **IAF** proved paramount as it immobilized the Jordanians, leading to their defeat. One of Peled's brigades joined with its **Central Command** counterparts coming from Ramallah, and the remaining two blocked the Jordan River crossings together with the **Central Command's 10th.** Engineering Corps sappers blew up the **Abdullah** and **Hussein** bridges with captured Jordanian mortar shells, while elements of the **Harel Brigade** crossed the river and occupied positions along the east bank to cover them, but quickly pulled back due to American pressure. The Jordanians, anticipating an Israeli offensive deep into Jordan, assembled the remnants of their army and Iraqi units in Jordan to protect the western approaches to **Amman** and the southern slopes of the **Golan Heights.**

No specific decision had been made to capture any other territories controlled by Jordan. After the **Old City** was captured, **Dayan** told his troops to dig in to hold it. When an armored brigade commander entered the **West Bank** on his own initiative, and stated that he could see Jericho, **Dayan** ordered him back. It was only after intelligence reports indicated that **Hussein** had withdrawn his forces across the **Jordan River** that **Dayan** ordered his troops to capture the **West Bank**. According to **Narkis**:

**"First, the Israeli government had no intention of capturing the West Bank. On the contrary, it was opposed to it. Second, there was not any provocation on the part of the IDF. Third, the rein was only loosened when a real threat to Jerusalem's security emerged. This is truly how things happened on June 5, although it is difficult to believe. The end result was something that no one had planned."**

## Golan Heights

In May–June 1967, the Israeli government did everything in its power to confine the confrontation to the Egyptian front. **Eshkol** and his colleagues took into account the possibility of some fighting on the Syrian front.

## Syria's attack

**False Egyptian reports of a crushing victory against the Israeli army and forecasts that Egyptian forces would soon be attacking Tel Aviv influenced Syria's decision to enter the war.** Syrian artillery began shelling northern Israel, and twelve Syrian jets attacked Israeli settlements in the Galilee. Israeli fighter jets intercepted the Syrian aircraft, shooting down three and driving off the rest. In addition, two **Lebanese Hawker Hunter** jets, two of the twelve Lebanon had, crossed into Israeli airspace and began strafing Israeli positions in the Galilee. They were intercepted by Israeli fighter jets, and one was shot down.

A minor Syrian force tried to capture the water plants at **Tel Dan** (the subject of a fierce escalation two years earlier), **Dan**, and **She'ar Yashuv**. These attacks were repulsed with the loss of twenty soldiers and seven tanks. An Israeli officer was also killed. But a broader Syrian offensive quickly failed. Syrian reserve units were broken up by Israeli air attacks, and several tanks were reported to have sunk in the **Jordan River**. Other problems included tanks being too wide for bridges, lack of radio communications between tanks and infantry, and units ignoring orders to advance. **A post-war Syrian army report concluded**:

**"Our forces did not go on the offensive either because they did not arrive or were not wholly prepared or because they could not find shelter from the enemy's planes. The reserves could not withstand the air attacks; they dispersed after their morale plummeted."** The Syrians abandoned hopes of a ground attack and began a massive bombardment of Israeli communities in the **Hula Valley** instead.

## Israeli Air Force attacks the Syrian airfields

On the evening of June 5, the **Israeli Air Force attacked Syrian airfields. The Syrian Air Force lost some 32 MiG 21s, 23 MiG-15 and MiG-17 fighters, and two Ilyushin Il-28**

**bombers, two-thirds of its fighting strength.** The Syrian aircraft that survived the attack retreated to distant bases and played no further role in the war. Following the attack, **Syria realized that the news it had received from Egypt of the near-total destruction of the Israeli military could not have been true.**

## Israelis debate whether the Golan Heights should be attacked

On June 7 and 8, the Israeli leadership debated about whether to attack the **Golan Heights** as well. Syria had supported pre-war raids that had helped raise tensions and had routinely shelled Israel from the **Heights**, so some Israeli leaders wanted to see Syria punished. Military opinion was that the attack would be extremely costly, since it would entail an uphill battle against a strongly fortified enemy. The western side of the **Golan Heights** consists of a rock escarpment that rises 500 meters (1,700 ft.) from the Sea of Galilee and the Jordan River, and then flattens to a gently sloping plateau. **Dayan opposed the operation bitterly at first, believing such an undertaking would result in losses of 30,000 and might trigger Soviet intervention.**

**Prime Minister Eshkol**, on the other hand, was more open to the possibility, as was the head of the **Northern Command, David Elazar**, whose unbridled enthusiasm for and confidence in the operation may have eroded **Dayan**'s reluctance. Eventually, the situation on the Southern and Central fronts cleared up, intelligence estimated that the likelihood of Soviet intervention had been reduced, reconnaissance showed some Syrian defenses in the **Golan** region collapsing, and an intercepted cable revealed that **Nasser was urging the President of Syria to immediately accept a cease-fire.** At 3 am on June 9, Syria announced its acceptance of the cease-fire. Despite this announcement, **Dayan** became more enthusiastic about the idea and four hours later at 7 am, **"gave the order to go into action against Syria" without consultation or government authorization.** The Syrian army consisted of about 75,000 men grouped in nine brigades, supported by an adequate amount of artillery and armor. Israeli forces used in combat consisted of two brigades (the 8th Armored Brigade and the **Golani Brigade**) in the northern part of the front at **Givat HaEm**, and another two (infantry and one of **Peled's** brigades summoned from Jenin) in the center. The **Golan Heights'** unique terrain (mountainous slopes crossed by parallel streams every several kilometers running east to west), and the general lack of roads in the area channeled both forces along east-west axes of movement and restricted the ability of units to support those on either flank.

Thus the Syrians could move north-south on the plateau itself, and the Israelis could move north-south at the base of the **Golan** escarpment. An advantage Israel possessed was the **excellent intelligence collected by Mossad operative Eli Cohen (who was captured and executed in Syria in 1965)** regarding the Syrian battle positions. Syria had built extensive defensive fortifications in depths up to 15 kilometers, comparable to the **Maginot Line**.

As opposed to all the other campaigns, **IAF** was only partially effective in the **Golan** because the fixed fortifications were so effective. However, the Syrian forces proved unable to put up effective defense largely because the officers were poor leaders and treated their soldiers badly; often officers would retreat from danger, leaving their men confused and ineffective. The Israelis also had the upper hand during close combat that took place in the numerous Syrian bunkers along the **Golan Heights**, as they were armed with the **Uzi**, a submachine gun designed for close combat, while Syrian soldiers were armed with the heavier **AK-47** assault rifle, designed for combat in more open areas.

## Israeli attack: first day

On the morning of June 9, Israeli jets began carrying out dozens of sorties against Syrian positions from **Mount Hermon to Tawfiq**, using rockets salvaged from captured Egyptian stocks. The airstrikes knocked out artillery batteries and storehouses and forced transport columns off the roads. The Syrians suffered heavy casualties and a drop in morale, with a number of senior officers and troops deserting. The attacks also provided time as Israeli forces cleared paths through Syrian minefields. However, the airstrikes did not seriously damage the Syrians' bunkers and trench systems, and the bulk of Syrian forces on the **Golan** remained in their positions.

About two hours after the airstrikes began, the **8th Armored Brigade**, led by **Colonel Albert Mandler**, advanced into the **Golan Heights** from **Givat HaEm**. Its advance was spearheaded by Engineering Corps sappers and eight bulldozers, which cleared away barbed wire and mines. As they advanced, the force came under fire, and five bulldozers were immediately hit. The Israeli tanks, with their maneuverability sharply reduced by the terrain, advanced slowly under fire toward the fortified village of **Sir al-Dib**, with their ultimate objective being the fortress at **Qala**. Israeli casualties steadily mounted. Part of the attacking force lost its way and emerged opposite **Za'ura**, a redoubt manned by Syrian reservists.

With the situation critical, **Colonel Mandler** ordered simultaneous assaults on **Za'ura** and **Qala**. Heavy and confused fighting followed, with Israeli and Syrian tanks struggling around obstacles and firing at extremely short ranges. Mandler recalled that **"the Syrians fought well and bloodied us. We beat them only by crushing them under our treads and by blasting them with our cannons at very short range, from 100 to 500 meters."** The first three Israeli tanks to enter **Qala** were stopped by a Syrian bazooka team, and a relief column of seven Syrian tanks arrived to repel the attackers.

The Israelis took heavy fire from the houses, but could not turn back, as other forces were advancing behind them, and they were on a narrow path with mines on either side. The Israelis continued pressing forward, and called for air support. A pair of Israeli jets destroyed two of the Syrian tanks, and the remainder withdrew. The surviving defenders of **Qala** retreated after their commander was killed. Meanwhile, **Za'ura** fell in an Israeli assault, and the Israelis also captured the **'Ein Fit fortress**.

In the central sector, the Israeli 181st Battalion captured the strongholds of **Dardara** and **Tel Hillal** after fierce fighting. Desperate fighting also broke out along the operation's northern axis, where **Golani Brigade** attacked thirteen Syrian positions, including the formidable **Tel Fakhr** position. Navigational errors placed the Israelis directly under the Syrians' guns. In the fighting that followed, both sides took heavy casualties, with the Israelis losing all nineteen of their tanks and half-tracks.

The Israeli battalion commander then ordered his twenty-five remaining men to dismount, divide into two groups, and charge the northern and southern flanks of **Tel Fakhr**. The first Israelis to reach the perimeter of the southern approach laid bodily down on the barbed wire, allowing their comrades to vault over them. From there, they assaulted the fortified Syrian positions. **The fighting was waged at extremely close quarters, often hand-to-hand.**

On the northern flank, the Israelis broke through within minutes and cleared out the trenches and bunkers. During the seven-hour battle, the Israelis lost 31 dead and 82 wounded, while the Syrians lost 62 dead and 20 captured. Among the dead was the Israeli battalion commander. The **Golani Brigade's 51st Battalion took Tel 'Azzaziat**, and **Darbashiya** also fell to Israeli forces. By the evening of June 9, the four Israeli brigades had all broken through to the plateau, where they could be reinforced and replaced. Thousands of reinforcements began reaching the front, those tanks and half-tracks that had survived the previous day's fighting were refueled and replenished with ammunition, and the wounded were evacuated. By dawn, the Israelis had eight brigades in the sector.

Syria's first line of defense had been shattered, but the defenses beyond that remained largely intact. **Mount Hermon** and the **Banias** in the north, and the entire sector between **Tawfiq** and **Customs House Road** in the south remained in Syrian hands. In a meeting early on the night of June 9, Syrian leaders decided to reinforce those positions as quickly as possible, and to maintain a steady barrage on Israeli civilian settlements.

## Israeli attack: the next day

Throughout the night, the Israelis continued their advance. Though it was slowed by fierce resistance, an anticipated Syrian counterattack never materialized. At the fortified village of Jalabina, a garrison of Syrian reservists, leveling their anti-aircraft guns, held off the **Israeli 65th Paratroop Battalion** for four hours before a small detachment managed to penetrate the village and knock out the heavy guns.

Meanwhile, the 8th Brigade's tanks moved south from **Qala**, advancing six miles to **Wasit** under heavy artillery and tank bombardment. At the **Banias** in the north, Syrian mortar batteries opened fire on advancing Israeli forces only after **Golan**i **Brigade** sappers cleared a path through a minefield, killing sixteen Israeli soldiers and wounding four.

On the next day, June 10, the central and northern groups joined in a pincer movement on the plateau, but that fell mainly on empty territory as the Syrian forces retreated. At 8:30 am, the Syrians began blowing up their own bunkers, burning documents and retreating. Several units joined by **Elad Peled's** troops climbed to the **Golan** from the south, only to find the positions mostly empty. When the 8th Brigade reached **Mansura**, five miles from Wasit, the Israelis met no opposition and found abandoned equipment, including tanks, in perfect working condition.

In the fortified Banias village, **Golan**i Brigade troops found only several Syrian soldiers chained to their positions. During the day, the Israeli units stopped after obtaining maneuver room between their positions and a line of volcanic hills to the west. In some locations, Israeli troops advanced after an agreed-upon cease-fire to occupy strategically strong positions. To the east, the ground terrain is an open gently sloping plain. This position later became the cease-fire line known as the **"Purple Line"**.

*Time* **magazine** reported: **"In an effort to pressure the United Nations into enforcing a ceasefire, Damascus Radio undercut its own army by broadcasting the fall of the city of Quneitra three hours before it actually capitulated. That premature report of the surrender of their headquarters destroyed the morale of the Syrian troops left in the Golan area."**

## Conclusion / *Israeli Military Governorate*

By June 10, Israel had completed its final offensive in the **Golan Heights**, and a ceasefire was signed the day after. Israel had seized the **Gaza Strip**, the **Sinai Peninsula**, the **West Bank** of the Jordan River (including East Jerusalem), and the **Golan Heights**. **About one million Arabs were placed under Israel's direct control in the newly captured territories**. Israel's strategic depth grew to at least 300 kilometers in the south, 60 kilometers in the east, and 20 kilometers of extremely rugged terrain in the north, a security asset that would prove useful in the **Yom Kippur War six years later**.

Speaking three weeks after the war ended, as he accepted an honorary degree from Hebrew University, **Yitzhak Rabin gave his reasoning behind the success of Israel: "Our airmen, who struck the enemies' planes so accurately that no one in the world understands how it was done and people seek technological explanations or secret weapons; our armored troops who beat the enemy even when their equipment was inferior to his; our soldiers in all other branches ... who overcame our enemies everywhere, despite the latter's superior numbers** and fortifications—all these revealed not only coolness and courage in the battle but ... an understanding that only their personal stand against the greatest dangers would achieve victory for their country and for their families, and that if victory was not theirs the alternative was annihilation."

In recognition of contributions, **Rabin** was given the honor of naming the war for the Israelis. From the suggestions proposed, including the **"War of Daring", "War of Salvation", and "War of the Sons of Light"**, he **"chose the least ostentatious, the Six-Day War, evoking the days of creation"**. **Dayan**'s final report on the war to the Israeli general staff listed several shortcomings in Israel's actions, including misinterpretation of **Nasser**'s intentions, overdependence on the United States, and reluctance to act when Egypt closed the Straits. He also credited several factors for Israel's success: **Egypt did not appreciate the advantage of striking first** and their adversaries did not accurately gauge Israel's strength and its willingness to use it.

In Egypt, according to **Heikal**, **Nasser** had admitted his responsibility for the military defeat in June 1967. According to historian **Abd al-Azim Ramadan**, **Nasser**'s mistaken decisions to expel the international peacekeeping force from the **Sinai Peninsula** and close the **Straits of Tiran** in 1967 led to a state of war with Israel, despite Egypt's lack of military preparedness. After the **1973 Yom Kippur War**, Egypt reviewed the causes of its loss of the 1967 war. Issues that were identified included "**the individualistic bureaucratic leadership**"; "**promotions on the basis of loyalty, not expertise, and the army's fear of telling Nasser the truth**"; lack of intelligence; and better Israeli weapons, command, organization, and will to fight.

## Israeli casualties of war

**Between 776 and 983 Israelis were killed and 4,517 were wounded. Fifteen Israeli soldiers were captured. Arab casualties were far greater. Between 9,800 and 15,000 Egyptian soldiers were listed as killed or missing in action. An additional 4,338 Egyptian soldiers were captured. Jordanian losses are estimated to be 700 killed in action with another 2,500 wounded. The Syrians were estimated to have sustained between 1,000 and 2,500 killed in action. Between 367 and 591 Syrians were captured.**

## USS *Liberty* incident

On June 8, 1967, **USS *Liberty***, a United States Navy electronic intelligence vessel sailing 13 nautical miles (24 km) off Arish (just outside Egypt's territorial waters), was attacked by Israeli jets and torpedo boats, nearly sinking the ship, **killing 34 sailors and wounding 171**. Israel said the attack was a case of mistaken identity, and that the ship had been misidentified as the **Egyptian vessel *El Quseir*. Israel apologized for the mistake, and paid compensation to the victims or their families, and to the United States for damage to the ship.**

The war inspired the Jewish diaspora, which was swept up in overwhelming support for Israel. According to **Michael Oren**, the war enabled American Jews to **"walk with their backs straight and flex their political muscle as never before. American Jewish organizations which had previously kept Israel at arms-length suddenly proclaimed their Zionism."** Thousands of Jewish immigrants arrived from Western countries such as the United States, United Kingdom, Canada, France, and South Africa after the war. **From 1970 to 1988, some 291,000 Soviet Jews were granted exit visas, of whom 165,000 immigrated to Israel and 126,000 immigrated to the United States.**

## Jews in Arab countries-Pogroms and expulsion / *Jewish exodus from Arab and Muslim countries*

**According to historian and Ambassador Michael B. Oren:**

**"Mobs attacked Jewish neighborhoods in Egypt, Yemen, Lebanon, Tunisia, and Morocco, burning synagogues and assaulting residents. A pogrom in Tripoli, Libya, left 18 Jews dead and 25 injured; the survivors were herded into detention centers. Of Egypt's 4,000 Jews, 800 were arrested, including the chief rabbis of both Cairo and Alexandria, and their property sequestered by the government. The ancient communities of Damascus and Baghdad were placed under house arrest, their leaders imprisoned and fined. A total of 7,000 Jews were expelled, many with merely a satchel."**

**In September, the Khartoum Arab Summit resolved that there would be "no peace, no recognition and no negotiation with Israel"**. On November 22 Egypt and Jordan accepted **United Nations Security Council Resolution 242**. **Nasser** posited the equation that any direct peace talks with Israel were tantamount to surrender.

Resolution 242 recognized the right of **"every state in the area to live in peace within secure and recognized boundaries free from threats or acts of force." Israel returned the Sinai to Egypt in 1978, after the Camp David Accords, and disengaged from the Gaza Strip in the summer of 2005.** Perhaps as many as **70,000 people emigrated from the Gaza Strip to Egypt and elsewhere in the Arab world.**

In addition, **between 80,000 and 110,000 Syrians fled the Golan Heights**, of which about 20,000 were from the city of Quneitra. A total of 130,000 Syrian inhabitants fled or were expelled from the territory, most of them pushed out by the Israeli army. **The Israeli settlements in Gaza were evacuated and destroyed in August 2005 as a part of Israeli disengagement from Gaza.**

# Sodom and Gomorrah

**Sodom** and **Gomorrah** were cities mentioned in the **Book of Genesis** and throughout the Hebrew Bible, the New Testament and in deuterocanonical sources, as well as in the Qur'an and hadith.

According to the **Torah**, the kingdoms of **Sodom** and **Gomorrah** were allied with the cities of **Admah, Zeboim** and **Bela**. These five cities, also known as the **"cities of the plain"**, were situated on the **Jordan River** plain in the southern region of the land of **Canaan**. The plain, which corresponds to the area just north of the modern-day **Dead Sea**, was compared to the **Garden of Eden** as being a land well-watered and green, suitable for grazing livestock.

Divine judgment by God was then passed upon **Sodom** and **Gomorrah** and two neighboring cities, which were completely consumed by fire and brimstone. Neighboring **Zoar (Bela)** was the only city to be spared. In **Abraham**ic religions, **Sodom** and **Gomorrah** have become synonymous with impenitent sin, and their fall with a proverbial manifestation of divine retribution. **Sodom** and **Gomorrah** have been used as metaphors for **vice and homosexuality** viewed as a deviation. The story has therefore given rise to words in several languages, including the English word *sodomy*, used in sodomy laws to describe a sexual **"crime against nature" consisting of anal or oral sex, either homosexual or heterosexual, or sexual activity between a person and a non-human animal (bestiality)**. Some Islamic societies incorporate punishments associated with **Sodom** and **Gomorrah** into **Sharia**.

## Historicity

In 1976 **Giovanni Pettinato** claimed that a cuneiform tablet that had been found in the newly discovered library at **Ebla** contained the names of all five of the cities of the plain (**Sodom, Gomorrah, Admah, Zeboim**, and **Bela**), listed in the same order as in Genesis. Today, the scientific consensus is that **"Ebla has no bearing on … Sodom and Gomorra."**

If the cities actually existed, they might have been destroyed as the result of a natural disaster. One theory says that the **Dead Sea** was devastated by an earthquake between **2100 and 1900 BC**, which could have unleashed showers of steaming tar. It is possible that the towns were destroyed by an earthquake in the region, especially if the towns lay along a major fault, the **Jordan Rift Valley**. Some people claims the area was destroyed by the plume of a meteor that impacted in the Alps, based on a cuneiform tablet called the Planisphere, which they claim represents the sky around the time of the supposed disaster and shows a moving object that could be seen from Earth.

Possible candidates for **Sodom** or **Gomorrah** are the sites discovered or visited by **Walter E. Rast and R. Thomas Schaub** in 1973, including **Bab edh-Dhra**, which was originally excavated in 1965 by archaeologist **Paul Lapp**, and later finished by **Rast** and **Schaub** following his death. All sites were located near the **Dead Sea**, with evidence of burning and traces of sulfur. Archaeological remains excavated from **Bab edh-Dhra** are currently displayed in **Karak Archaeological Museum** (Karak Castle), **Amman Citadel Museum**, and the **British Museum**.

Another possible candidate for **Sodom** is the **Tall el Hammam** dig site which began in 2006 under the direction of **Steven Collins**. **Tall el Hammam** is located in the southern **Jordan River** valley approximately 14 kilometers northeast of the **Dead Sea**, and seemingly fits the biblical descriptions of the **lands of Sodom**. Analysis of the findings indicates that the site was occupied from the **Chalcolithic period** on up to the **Iron Age** along with evidences of glazed artifacts – such as potter and rocks, and destruction. The researchers claim to have discovered an ash layer containing human bone fragments, which they believe indicates a meteor airburst and sudden end to the civilization in this area. Recently, desert glass had been found among the glazed pottery shards. It is also evident that the area was not occupied for several centuries afterward. The Jewish historian **Josephus** identifies the **Dead Sea** in geographic proximity to the ancient biblical city of **Sodom**. However, he refers to the lake by its Greek name, **Asphaltites.**

### Biblical narratives

The **Book of Genesis** is the primary source that mentions the cities of **Sodom** and **Gomorrah**. Major and minor prophets in the Hebrew Bible have also referred to **Sodom** and **Gomorrah** to parallel t heir prophetic events. The **New Testament** also contains passages of parallels to the destruction and surrounding events that pertained to these cities and those who were involved.

### Battle of Siddim

In **Genesis Chapter 14 Sodom** and **Gomorrah**'s political situation is described during the time biblical **Lot** had encamped in **Sodom**'s territory. Genesis 13:13 indicates that at that time, **"the men of Sodom *[were]* wicked and sinners before the LORD exceedingly."** **Sodom** was ruled by **King Bera** while **Gomorrah** was ruled by **King Birsha**. Their kingship, however, was not sovereign because all of the river Jordan plain was under **Elamite** rule for twelve years. The **kingdom of Elam** was ruled by **King Chedorlaomer**.

They waged war in the **Vale of Siddim** in the fourteenth year. The battle was brutal with heavy losses in the cities of the plain, with t heir resultant defeat. **Sodom** and **Gomorrah** were spoiled of t heir goods, and captives were taken, including **Lot**. The tide of war turned when **Lot**'s uncle **Abram** gathered an elite force that slaughtered **King Chedorlaomer's** forces in **Hobah**, north of Damascus. The success of his mission freed the cities of the plain from under **Elam's** rule.

### Judgment

In **Genesis 18** three men, thought by most commentators to have been angels appearing as men, came to **Abraham** in the plains of Mamre. After the angels received the hospitality of **Abraham** and **Sarah**, his wife, "the Lord" revealed to **Abraham** that he would destroy **Sodom** and **Gomorrah**, because their cry was great, **"and because their sin is very grievous."** [Gen. 18:20]

In response, **Abraham** inquired of the **Lord** if he would spare the city if 50 righteous people were found in it, to which the **Lord** agreed he would not destroy it for the sake of the righteous yet dwelling therein. **Abraham** then inquired of God for mercy at lower numbers (first 45, then 40, then 30, then 20, and finally at 10), with the **Lord** agreeing each time. [**Gen. 18:22-33, 35**] Two angels were sent to **Sodom** to investigate and were met by **Abraham**'s nephew **Lot**, who convinced the angels to lodge with him, and they ate with **Lot**.

> **Genesis 19:4-5 – And they called unto Lot, and said unto him, Where *[are]* the men which came in to thee this night? bring them out unto us, that we may know them. (NRSV: know them, NIV: can have sex with them, NJB; can have intercourse with them).**

**Lot** refused to give his guests to the inhabitants of **Sodom** and, instead, offered them his two virgin daughters **"which have not known man"** and to **"do ye to them as /is/ good in your eyes"**. **[Gen. 19:8]** However, they refused this offer, complained about this alien, namely **Lot**, giving orders, and then came near to break down the door. **Lot**'s angelic guests rescued him and struck the men with blindness and they informed **Lot** of their **mission to destroy the city. [Genesis 19:9-13]**

Then (not having found even 10 righteous people in the city), they commanded **Lot** to gather his family and leave. As they made their escape, one angel commanded **Lot** to **"look not behind thee"** (singular **"thee"**). **[Genesis 19:17]** However, as **Sodom** and **Gomorrah** were destroyed with brimstone and fire from the **Lord**, **Lot**'s wife looked back at the city, and she became a pillar of salt. **[Genesis 19:23-26]**

### Jewish

**Rictor Norton** views classical Jewish texts as stressing the cruelty and lack of hospitality of the inhabitants of **Sodom** to the "**stranger**". The people of **Sodom** were seen as guilty of many other significant sins Rabbinic writings affirm that the **Sodom**ites also committed economic crimes, blasphemy and bloodshed. A modern orthodox position is one that holds, **"The paradigmatic instance of such aberrant behavior is found in the demand of the men of Sodom to 'know' the men visiting Lot, the nephew of Abraham, thus lending their name to the practice of 'sodomy'."**

The scholar and activist **Jay Michaelson** proposes a reading of the story of **Sodom** that emphasizes the violation of hospitality as well as the violence of the **Sodom**ites. **"Homosexual rape is the way in which they violate hospitality – not the essence of their transgression**. The verses cited by **Michaelson** include **Jeremiah 23:14**, where the sins of Jerusalem are compared to **Sodom** and are listed as adultery, lying, and strengthening the hands of evildoers; **Amos 4:1-11** (oppressing the poor and crushing the needy); **[Amos 4:1-11]** and **Ezekiel 16:49-50, [Ezekiel 16:49-50]** which defines the sins of **Sodom** as **"pride, fullness of bread, and abundance of idleness was in her and in her daughters, neither did she strengthen the hand of the poor and needy. And they were haughty, and did** *toevah* **before me, and I took them away as I saw fit."**

### Christian

Several theories have been advanced in Christian thought concerning the sin of **Sodom**. One area of dispute is whether the mob was demanding the homosexual rape of **Lot**'s guests. A second area of dispute is whether the act of **homosexuality** or the act of inhospitality and violence toward foreigners is the more significant ethical downfall of **Sodom**.

**King James Version:**

> **And they called unto Lot, and said unto him, Where [are] the men which came in to thee this night? bring them out unto us, that we may know them. – Gen. 19:5**

However, the word **"know"** in the King James Version has been used as referred to **sexual intercourse**. One example can be found in **Genesis 4:1** between **Adam** and **Eve**:

**And Adam knew Eve his wife; and she conceived, and bare Cain, and said, I have gotten a man from the Lord. – Gen. 4:1**

For this reason, many of the most popular of the 20ᵗʰ century translations, including the New International Version, the New King James Version, and the New Living Translation, translate *yada* as **"have sex with"** or **"know…carnally"** in Gen. 19:5. The observation that one of the examples of *know* meaning to know sexually occurs when **Lot** responds to the **Gen. 19:5** request, only there verses later in the same narrative:

**Behold now, I have two daughters which have not known man, let me, I pray you, bring them out unto you, and do ye to them as is good in your eyes: only unto these men do nothing… - Genesis 19:8**

**The apocryphal Second Book of Enoch (different from the one Jude quotes from) condemns "sodomitic" sex (Enoch 10:3, 34:1), thus indicating that homosexual relations was the prevalent *physical* sin of Sodom.**

### Islamic

The Qur'an contains twelve references to **"the people of Lot",** the biblical **Lot**, but meaning the residents of **Sodom** and **Gomorrah** (references 6:86-90, 7:80-84; 11:74-83, 15:58-77; 21:74-75; 26, 160-173; 27:54-58; 29:28-30, 33-35; 37:133-138; 51:32-37; 54:33-38 and 66:10), and their destruction by God is associated explicitly with their **sexual practices**.

The 'people of Lot' transgressed consciously against the bounds of God. Their avarice led to inhospitality and robbery, which in turn led to the humiliation of strangers by mistreatment and rape. It was their abominable sin of **homosexual sex** which was seen as symptomatic of their attitudes and upon **Lot**'s exhorting them to abandon their transgressions against God; they ridiculed him, and threatened him with dire consequences. **"The location remains unnamed in the Qur'an."**

# Solomon's Temple

According to the Hebrew Bible, **Solomon's Temple, also known as the First Temple, was the Holy Temple (Hebrew: *Bet HaMikdash*) in ancient Jerusalem, on the Temple Mount (also known as Mount Zion), before its destruction by Nebuchadnezzar II after the Siege of Jerusalem of 587 BCE.**

The Hebrew Bible states that the temple was constructed under **Solomon, King of the United Kingdom of Israel and Judah.** This would date its construction to the 10th century BCE. During the kingdom of Judah, the temple was dedicated to **Yahweh**, and is said to have housed the **Ark of the Covenant. The First Temple stood for 410 years.**

## The Temple according to the Bible

According to the biblical sources, the temple was constructed under **King Solomon** during the united monarchy of Israel and Judah. This puts the date of its construction in the **mid-10th century BCE.** The following is a summary of the history according to **Book of Samuel** and **Book of Kings**, with notes on the variations to this story in the later **Book of Chronicles**.

The *Mishkan* (dwelling place) of the god of Israel was originally the portable shrine called the **Ark of the Covenant**, which was placed in the **Tabernacle** tent. **King David**, having unified all Israel, brought the **Ark** to his new capital, Jerusalem, intending to build there a temple in order to house the **Ark** in a permanent place. The task of building passed to **David's** son and successor **Solomon, 1 Kings 6:1-38**.

**King Solomon** requested the aid of **King Hiram of Tyre** to provide both the quality materials and skilled craftsmen. During the construction, a special inner room, named in Hebrew *Kodesh Hakodashim* (Holy of Holies), was prepared to receive and house the **Ark of the Covenant** (1 Kings 6:19); and when the Temple was dedicated, the **Ark** – containing the **Tablets of Stone** – was placed therein (**1 Kings 8:6-9**).

The exact location of the **First Temple** is unknown: it is believed to have been situated upon the hill which forms the site of the 1st century Second Temple and present-day Temple Mount, where the **Dome of the Rock** is situated. **2 Chronicles 12:9 and 1 Kings 14:26** describes the Sack of Jerusalem by the **Pharaoh Shishaq**, who **"took away the treasures of the house of the LORD, and the treasures of the king's house."**

According to **2 Kings 14:14**, the Temple was looted by **Jehoash** of Israel in the early 8th century and again by **King Ahaz** in the late 8th century (2 Kings 16:8). **King Josiah**, the grandson of **Manasseh**, refurbished and made changes to the Temple by removing idolatrous vessels and destroying the idolatrous priesthood c. **621 BCE (2 Kings 22:3-9; 23:11-12).**

The Temple was plundered by the **Babylonian King Nebuchadnezzar** when the Babylonians attacked Jerusalem during the brief reign of **Jehoiachin c.598 (2 Kings 24:13), Josiah's** grandson., A decade later, **Nebuchadnezzar** again besieged Jerusalem and after 30 months finally **breached the city walls in 587 BCE, subsequently burning the Temple**, along with most of the city (2 Kings 25). According to Jewish tradition, **the Temple was destroyed on *Tisha B'Av*, the 9<sup>th</sup> day of Av (Hebrew calendar).**

## Most Holy Place

The ***Kodesh Hakodashim***, or **Holy of Holies**, (1 Kings 6:19; 8:6), also called the "**Inner House**" (6:27), (Heb. 9:3) was 20 cubits in length, breadth, and height. It was floored and wainscoted with cedar of Lebanon (1 Kings 6:16), and its walls and floor were overlaid with gold (6:20, 21, 30).

The color scheme of the veil was symbolic. Blue represented the heavens, while red or crimson represented the earth. Purple, a combination of the two colors, represents a meeting of the heavens and the earth. **"In the year that King Uzziah died, I saw the Lord sitting upon a throne high and lifted up, and His train filled the *hekhal* (sanctuary)." Isaiah 6:1**

## The Jerusalem Temple

Scholars and archeologists generally agree on the structure of **Solomon**'s Temple as described in **1 Kings 6:3-5**, with the main building, the *hekhal*, in English now sometimes called **"the sanctuary,"** the *devir*, the inner sanctuary, and finally the **Holy of Holies**. This main building of the Temple is depicted on coins from the **Bar Kokhba revolt**.

## Brazen Sea

The large basin known as the "**Brazen Sea**" measured 10 cubits wide brim to brim, 5 cubits deep and with a circumference of 30 cubits around the brim, rested on the backs of twelve oxen (1 Kings 7:23-26). The **Book of Kings** gives its capacity as **"2,000 baths"** (90 cubic meters), but Chronicles (2 Chr. 4:5-6) inflates this to three thousand baths (136 cubic meters).

**Josephus** reported that the vessels in the Temple were composed of **Orichalcum** in *Antiquities of the Jews*. According to **1 Kings 7:48** there stood before the **Holy of Holies** a golden altar of incense and a table for showbread. This table was of gold, as were also the five candlesticks on each side of it.

## Archaeology

Because of the religious and political sensitivities involved, no archaeological excavations and only limited surface surveys of the **Temple Mount** have been conducted since Warren's expedition of 1867-70. **There is no direct archaeological evidence for the existence of Solomon's Temple.**

# Solomon's Song of Songs

The **Song of Songs** also known as the **Song of Solomon, Canticles**, or the **Canticle of Canticles**, is one of the **"scrolls"** (*Megillot*) of the **Writings** (*Ketuvim*), the last section of the **Tanakh** or Hebrew Bible. It is also the fifth book of Wisdom in the Old Testament of the Christian Bible. In Sephardic Jewish tradition, The **Song of Songs** is read every Friday night for the divine loving union they see in it; Ashkenazim chant it on the **Sabbath** during **Passover**, marking the beginning of the grain harvest and commemorating the **Exodus** from Egypt.

Scripturally, the **Song of Songs** is unique in its celebration of sexual love. It gives **"the voices of two lovers, praising each other, yearning for each other, proffering invitations to enjoy"**. The two each desire the other and rejoice in their **sexual intimacy**. The **"daughters of Jerusalem"** form a chorus to the lovers, functioning as an audience whose participation in the lovers' erotic encounters facilitates the participation of the reader. Jewish tradition reads it as an allegory of the relationship between God and Israel. Christian tradition, in addition to appreciating the literal meaning of a romantic song between man and woman, has read the poem as an allegory of Christ and his **"bride"**, the Christian Church.

## Structure

There is widespread consensus that, although the book has no plot, it does have what can be called a framework, as indicated by the links between its beginning and end. Beyond this, however, there appears to be little agreement: attempts to find a chiastic structure have not been compelling, and attempts to analyze it into units have used differing methods and arrived at differing results. The following schema from **Kugler & al.** Must therefore be taken as indicative rather than determinative:

- Introduction (1:1–6)
- Dialogue between the lovers (1:7–2:7)
- The woman recalls a visit from her lover (2:8–17)
- The woman addresses the daughters of Zion (3:1–5)
- Sighting a royal wedding procession (3:6–11)
- The man describes his lover's beauty (4:1–5:1)
- The woman addresses the daughters of Jerusalem (5:2–6:4)
- The man describes his lover, who visits him (6:5–12)
- Observers describe the woman's beauty (6:13–8:4)
- Appendix (8:5–14)

## Summary

The introduction calls the poem **"the song of songs"**, a superlative construction commonly used in Scriptural Hebrew to show something as the greatest and most beautiful of its class (as in **Holy of Holies**). The poem proper begins with the woman's expression of desire for her lover and her self-description to the **"daughters of Jerusalem"**: she insists on her blackness, likening it to the **"tents of Kedar"** (nomads) and the **"curtains of Solomon"**.

A dialogue between the lovers follows: the woman asks the man to meet; he replies with a lightly teasing tone. The two compete in offering flattering compliments **("my beloved is to me as a cluster of henna blossoms in the vineyards of En Gedi", "an apple tree among the trees of the wood", "a lily among brambles**", while the bed they share is like a forest canopy). The section closes with the woman telling the daughters of Jerusalem not to stir up love such as hers until it is ready.

The woman recalls a visit from her lover in the springtime. She uses imagery from a shepherd's life, and she says of her lover that **"he pastures his flock among the lilies".** The woman again addresses the daughters of Jerusalem, describing her fervent and ultimately successful search for her lover through the night-time streets of the city. When she finds him she takes him almost by force into the chamber in which her mother conceived her. She reveals that this is a dream, seen on her **"bed at night"** and ends by again warning the daughters of Jerusalem **"not to stir up love until it is ready".**

The next section reports a royal wedding procession. **Solomon** is mentioned by name, and the daughters of Jerusalem are invited to come out and see the spectacle.

The man describes his beloved: Her hair is like a flock of goats, her teeth like shorn ewes, and so on from face to breasts. Place-names feature heavily: her neck is like the **Tower of David**, her smell like the scent of Lebanon. He hastens to summon his beloved, saying that he is ravished by even a single glance. The section becomes a **"garden poem",** in which he describes her as a **"locked garden"** (usually taken to mean that she is chaste). **The woman invites the man to enter the garden and taste the fruits.** The man accepts the invitation, and a third party tells them to eat, drink, **"and be drunk with love".**

The woman tells the daughters of Jerusalem of another dream. She was in her chamber when her lover knocked. She was slow to open, and when she did, he was gone. She searched through the streets again, but this time she failed to find him and the watchmen, who had helped her before, now beat her. She asks the daughters of Jerusalem to help her find him, and describes his physical good looks. Eventually, she admits her lover is in his garden, safe from harm, and committed to her as she is to him.

The man describes his beloved; the woman describes a rendezvous they have shared. (The last part is unclear and possibly corrupted.) The people praise the beauty of the woman. The images are the same as those used elsewhere in the poem, but with an unusually dense use of place-names, e.g., pools of Hebron, gate of **Bath-rabbim**, tower of Damascus, etc.

The man states his intention to enjoy the fruits of the woman's garden. The woman invites him to a tryst in the fields. She once more warns the daughters of Jerusalem against waking love until it is ready. The woman compares love to **death and Sheol**: love is as relentless and jealous as these two, and cannot be quenched by any force. She summons her lover, using the language used before: he should come **"like a gazelle or a young stag upon the mountain of spices"**.

## Composition

**The Song** offers no clue to its author or to the date, place, or circumstances of its composition. The superscription states that it is "**Solomon**'s", but even if this is meant to identify the author, it cannot be read as strictly as a similar modern statement. The most reliable evidence for its date is its language: Aramaic gradually replaced Hebrew after the end of the Babylonian exile in the late 6th century BCE, and the evidence of vocabulary, morphology, idiom and syntax clearly points to a late date, centuries after King **Solomon** to whom it is traditionally attributed.

It has parallels with **Mesopotamian and Egyptian** love poetry from the first half of the 1st millennium BCE, and with the pastoral idylls of **Theocritus**, a Greek poet who wrote in the first half of the 3rd century BCE; as a result of these conflicting signs, speculation ranges from the 10th to the 2nd centuries BCE, with the cumulative evidence supporting a later **Hellenistic** period date. Debate continues on the unity or disunity of the Song. Those who see it as an anthology or collection point to the abrupt shifts of scene, speaker, subject matter and mood, and the lack of obvious structure or narrative. Those who hold it to be a single poem point out that it has no internal signs of composite origins, and view the repetitions and similarities among its parts as evidence of unity. Some claim to find a conscious artistic design underlying it, but there is no agreement among them on what this might be. The question therefore remains unresolved.

The setting in which the poem arose is also debated. Some academics posit a ritual origin in the celebration of the sacred marriage of the **god Tammuz** and the **goddess Ishtar**. Whether this is so or not, the poem seems to be rooted in some kind of festive performance. External evidence supports the idea that the Song was originally recited by different singers representing the different characters, accompanied by mime.

## Judaism

**The Song** was accepted into the Jewish canon of scripture in the 2nd century CE, after a period of controversy in the 1st century. It was accepted as canonical because of its supposed authorship by **Solomon** and based on an allegorical reading where the subject-matter was **taken to be not sexual desire but God's love for Israel.** For instance, the famed first and second century **Rabbi Akiva** forbade the use of the **Song of Songs** in popular celebrations. He reportedly said, **"He who sings the Song of Songs in wine taverns, treating it as if it were a vulgar song, forfeits his share in the world to come".**

However, **Rabbi Akiva** famously defended the canonicity of the **Song of Songs**, reportedly saying when the question came up of whether it should be considered a defiling work, **"God forbid!**

**"For all of eternity in its entirety is not as worthy as the day on which Song of Songs was given to Israel, for all the Writings are holy, but Song of Songs is the Holy of Holies."**

It is one of the overtly mystical Biblical texts for the **Kabbalah,** which gave esoteric interpretation on all the Hebrew Bible. Following the dissemination of the **Zohar** in the 13th century, Jewish mysticism took on a metaphorically anthropomorphic erotic element, and **Song of Songs** is an example of this. In **Zoharic Kabbalah**, God is represented by a system of ten **sephirot** emanations, each symbolizing a different attribute of God, comprising both male and female.

The **Shechina** (indwelling Divine presence) was identified with the **feminine sephira Malchut, the vessel of Kingship**. This symbolizes the Jewish people, and in the body, the female form, identified with the woman in **Song of Songs**. Her beloved was identified with the male **sephira Tiferet**, the **"Holy One Blessed be He"**, central principle in the beneficent Heavenly flow of Divine emotion. In the body, this represents the male torso, uniting through the **sephira Yesod** of the male sign of the covenant organ of procreation.

Through beneficent deeds and Jewish observance, the Jewish people restore cosmic harmony in the Divine realm, healing the exile of the **Shechina** with God's transcendence, revealing the essential **Unity of God**. This elevation of the World is aroused from Above on the **Sabbath**, a foretaste of the redeemed purpose of **Creation**. The text thus became a description, depending on the aspect, of the creation of the world, the passage of *Shabbat*, the covenant with Israel, and the coming of the Messianic age. **"Lecha Dodi"**, a 16th-century liturgical song with strong Kabbalistic symbolism, contains many passages, including its opening two words, taken directly from **Song of Songs**.

In modern Judaism, certain verses from the Song are read on *Shabbat* eve or at **Passover**, which marks the beginning of the grain harvest as well as commemorating the Exodus from Egypt, to symbolize the love between the **Jewish People** and their God. Jewish tradition reads it as an allegory of the relationship between God and Israel. **Solomon B. Freeh of writes of the Song**:

As revealed in numerous Talmudic passages, in the **Targum** and in the **Midrash**, this biblical book is interpreted as referring to God's love for Israel. This interpretation (evidently the one ascribed to the *Keneset Hagdola* in Abot d'R. **Nathan, Schechter**, A #1) soon became official. In fact, anyone quoting verses from the **Song of Songs** giving them the *literal* meaning was declared a heretic who had forfeited his portion in **Paradise** (Tos. Sanh. XII, 10). This symbolic interpretation of the book was, with some re-interpretation, carried over into Christianity and there, too, it became official.

## Christianity

Christians admitted the canonicity of the **Song of Songs** from the beginning, but after Jewish exegetes began to read the Song allegorically, as having to do with God's love for his people, Christian exegetes followed suit, treating the love that it celebrates as an analogy for the love between God and the Church. Over the centuries the emphasis of interpretation shifted, the 11th century adding a moral element and the 12th century understanding the Bride as the **Virgin Mary**, each new reading absorbing rather than simply replacing earlier ones, so that the commentary became ever more complex, with multiple layers of meaning. This approach leads to conclusions not found in the more overtly theological books of the Bible, which consider the relationship between God and man as one of inequality. In contrast, reading the **Song of Songs** as an allegory of God's love for his Church suggests that the two partners are equals, bound in a freely consented emotional relationship.

## Feminism

In modern times, the poem has attracted the attention of feminist Biblical critics. *The Feminist Companion to the Bible* **series**, edited by **Athalya Brenner,** has two volumes (1993, 2001) devoted to the Song, the first of which was actually the first volume of the whole series. **Phyllis Trible** had earlier published **"Depatriarchalizing in Biblical Interpretation"** in 1973, offering a reading of the Song with a positive representation of sexuality and egalitarian gender relations, which was widely discussed, notably (and favorably) in **Marvin Pope's** major commentary for the **Anchor Bible.**

# State of Israel

**Israel**, officially the **State of Israel**, is a country in the Middle East, on the southeastern shore of the Mediterranean Sea and the northern shore of the Red Sea. It has land borders with Lebanon to the north, Syria to the northeast, Jordan on the east, the Palestinian territories of the West Bank and Gaza Strip to the east and west, respectively, and Egypt to the southwest. The population of Israel was estimated in 2017 to be 8,786,860 people, of whom 74.7% were Jewish, 20.8% Arab and 4.5% others.

The Kingdoms of Israel and Judah emerged during the Iron Age. The **Neo-Assyrian Empire** destroyed Israel around 720 BCE. Judah was later conquered by the Babylonian, **Persian** and **Hellenistic** empires and had existed as Jewish autonomous provinces. The successful **Maccabean Revolt** led to an independent Jewish kingdom in 110 BCE, which came to an end in 63 BCE when Judea became a client state of the Roman Republic. Judea lasted as a Roman province until the failed Jewish revolts resulted in widespread destruction, expulsion of Jewish population and the renaming of the region from *Judaea* to *Syria Palaestina*.

Jewish presence in the region has persisted to a certain extent over the centuries. In the 7th century Palestine was taken from the **Byzantine Empire** by the Arabs and remained in Muslim control until the **First Crusade of 1099, followed by the Ayyubid conquest of 1187**. The Egypt extended its control over the Levant in the 13th century until its defeat by the **Ottoman Empire** in 1517. During the 19th century, national awakening among Jews led to the establishment of the **Zionist movement** in the diaspora followed by waves of immigration to **Ottoman** and later **British Palestine.**

**In 1947, the United Nations adopted a Partition Plan for Palestine** recommending the creation of independent Arab and Jewish states and an internationalized Jerusalem. The plan was accepted by the **Jewish Agency for Palestine**, and rejected by Arab leaders. The following year, the Jewish Agency declared the independence of the State of Israel, and the subsequent **1948 Arab–Israeli War** saw Israel's establishment over most of the former Mandate territory, while the West Bank and Gaza were held by neighboring Arab states.

Israel has since fought several wars with Arab countries, and it has since 1967 occupied territories including the West Bank, Golan Heights and the Gaza Strip (still considered occupied after 2005 disengagement). Efforts to resolve the Israeli–Palestinian conflict have not resulted in peace. However, peace treaties between Israel and both Egypt and Jordan have been signed.

In its **Basic Laws,** Israel defines itself as a Jewish and democratic state. Israel is a representative democracy with a parliamentary system, proportional representation and universal suffrage. The prime minister is head of government and the **Knesset** is the legislature. Israel is a developed country and an **OECD** member, with the 34th-largest economy in the world by nominal gross domestic product as of 2016. Israel has the highest standard of living in the Middle East, and has one of the highest life expectancies in the world.

## Etymology

Upon independence in 1948, the country formally adopted the name **"State of Israel"** after other proposed historical and religious names including *Eretz Israel* ("**the Land of Israel**"), **Zion**, and Judea, were considered but rejected. In the early weeks of independence, the government chose the term **"Israeli"** to denote a citizen of Israel, with the formal announcement made by **Minister of Foreign Affairs Moshe Sharett**.

**Jacob's twelve sons** became the ancestors of the Israelites, also known as the *Twelve Tribes of Israel* or *Children of Israel*. Jacob and his sons had lived in **Canaan** but were forced by famine to go into Egypt for four generations, lasting 430 years, until **Moses**, a great-great grandson of Jacob, led the Israelites back into **Canaan** during the **"Exodus"**. The area is also known as the **Holy Land**, being holy for all Abrahamic religions including **Judaism, Christianity, Islam** and the **Baha'i Faith**.

## *Prehistory of the Levant*

The oldest evidence of early humans in the territory of modern Israel, **dating to 1.5 million years ago**, was found in **Ubeidiya near the Sea of Galilee**. Other notable Paleolithic sites include caves **Tabun, Qesem** and **Manot**. The oldest fossils of anatomically modern humans found outside Africa are the **Skhul** and **Qafzeh hominins**, who lived in the area that is now northern Israel 120,000 years ago. Around 10th millennium BCE, the **Natufian** culture existed in the area.

## Antiquity: *History of ancient Israel and Judah*

The **Exodus**, and the conquest described in the **Book of Joshua**, and instead views the narrative as constituting the Israelites' inspiring national myth. Ancestors of the Israelites may have included ancient Semitic-speaking peoples native to **Canaan**. The Israelites and their culture, according to the modern archaeological account, did not overtake the region by force, but instead branched out of the **Canaan**ite peoples and culture through the development of a distinct monolatristic—and later monotheistic—religion centered on **Yahweh.**

### Map of Israel and Judah in the 9th century BCE

While it is unclear if there was ever a **United Monarchy**, there is well accepted archeological evidence referring to **"Israel"** in the **Merneptah Stele** which dates to about 1200 BCE; and the **Canaan**ites are archeologically attested in the **Middle Bronze Age**. A **Kingdom of Israel existed by ca. 900 BCE** and a **Kingdom of Judah existed by ca. 700 BCE**. The Kingdom of Israel was destroyed around 720 BCE, when it was conquered by the **Neo-Assyrian Empire.**

In 586 BCE, **King Nebuchadnezzar II** of Babylon conquered Judah. According to the Hebrew Bible, he destroyed **Solomon's Temple** and exiled the Jews to Babylon. The defeat was also recorded in the **Babylonian Chronicles.** The Babylonian exile ended around 538 BCE under the rule of the **Persian Cyrus the Great** after he captured Babylon. The **Second Temple** was constructed around 520 BCE.

The population of the province was greatly reduced from that of the kingdom, archaeological surveys showing a population of around 30,000 people in the 5th to 4th centuries BCE.

## Classical period: *Second Temple period*

With successive Persian rule, the autonomous province **Yehud Medinata** was gradually developing back into urban society, largely dominated by Judeans. Incorporated into Ptolemaic and finally **Seleucid** empires, the southern Levant was heavily **Hellenized**, building the tensions between Judeans and Greeks. The conflict erupted in 167 BCE with the **Maccabean Revolt**, which succeeded in establishing an independent **Hasmonean Kingdom** in Judah, which later expanded over much of modern Israel, as the Seleucids gradually lost control in the region.

The **Roman Empire** invaded the region in 63 BCE, first taking control of Syria, and then intervening in the **Hasmonean Civil War**. With the decline of the **Herodian dynasty**, Judea, transformed into a Roman province, became the site of a violent struggle of Jews against Greco-Romans, culminating in the **Jewish–Roman wars**, ending in wide-scale destruction, expulsions, and genocide. Jewish presence in the region significantly dwindled after the failure of the **Bar Kokhba** revolt against the Roman Empire in 132 CE.

The **Mishnah** and part of the **Talmud,** central Jewish texts, were composed during the 2nd to 4th centuries CE in Tiberias and Jerusalem. Christianity was gradually evolving over Roman paganism, when the area stood under Byzantine rule. After the Persian conquest and the installation of a short-lived **Jewish Commonwealth in 614 CE, the Byzantine Empire reconquered the country in 628.**

## Middle Ages and modern history

In 634–641 CE, the region, including Jerusalem, was conquered by the Arabs who had just recently adopted Islam. Control of the region transferred between the **Rashidun Caliphs, Umayyads, Abbasids, Fatimids, Seljuks, Crusaders**, and **Ayyubids** throughout the next three centuries.

During the siege of Jerusalem by the **First Crusade in 1099,** the Jewish inhabitants of the city fought side by side with the **Fatimid** garrison and the Muslim population who tried in vain to defend the city against the **Crusaders.** When the city fell, about **60,000 people were massacred,**

**including 6,000 Jews seeking refuge in a synagogue**. At this time, a full thousand years after the fall of the Jewish state, there were Jewish communities all over the country.

In 1165, **Maimonides** visited Jerusalem and prayed on the Temple Mount, in the **"great, holy house."** In 1141 the Spanish-Jewish poet **Yehuda Halevi** issued a call for Jews to migrate to the Land of Israel, a journey he undertook himself. In 1187 **Sultan Saladin**, founder of the **Ayyubid Dynasty**, defeated the Crusaders in the **Battle of Hattin** and subsequently captured Jerusalem and almost all of Palestine. In time, **Saladin** issued a proclamation inviting Jews to return and settle in Jerusalem, and according to **Judah al-Harizi**, they did: **"From the day the Arabs took Jerusalem, the Israelites inhabited it."**

**Al-Harizi** compared **Saladin**'s decree allowing Jews to re-establish themselves in Jerusalem to the one issued by the **Persian king Cyrus the Great over 1,600 years earlier. Nahmanides (Ramban)**, the 13th-century Spanish rabbi and recognized leader of Jewry greatly praised the land of Israel and viewed its settlement as a positive commandment incumbent on all Jews. He wrote **"If the gentiles wish to make peace, we shall make peace and leave them on clear terms; but as for the land, we shall not leave it in their hands, nor in the hands of any nation, not in any generation."**

In 1260, control passed to the **Mamluk sultans of Egypt**. The country was located between the two centers of Mamluk power, Cairo and Damascus, and only saw some development along the postal road connecting the two cities. Jerusalem, although **left without the protection of any city walls since 1219**, also saw a flurry of new construction projects centered around the **Al-Aqsa Mosque** compound on the Temple Mount. In 1266 the **Mamluk Sultan Baybars** converted the **Cave of the Patriarchs** in Hebron into an exclusive Islamic sanctuary and banned Christians and Jews from entering, which previously would be able to enter it for a fee. **The ban remained in place until Israel took control of the building in 1967.**

In 1516, the region was conquered by the **Ottoman Empire**; it remained under Turkish rule until the end of the **First World War**, when Britain defeated the **Ottoman** forces and set up a military administration across the former **Ottoman Syria**. In 1920 the territory was divided between Britain and France under the mandate system.

## Zionism and British mandate: Theodor Herzl

Since the existence of the earliest Jewish diaspora, many Jews have aspired to return to **"Zion"** and the **"Land of Israel"**. After the Jews were expelled from Spain in 1492, some communities settled in Palestine. During the 16th century, Jewish communities struck roots in the **Four Holy Cities—Jerusalem, Tiberias, Hebron,** and **Safed**—and in 1697, **Rabbi Yehuda HeHasid** led a group of 1,500 Jews to Jerusalem. In the second half of the 18th century, Eastern European opponents of Hasidism, known as the **Perushim**, settled in Palestine.

The first wave of modern Jewish migration to **Ottoman-ruled Palestine**, known as the **First Aliyah, began in 1881**, as Jews fled pogroms in Eastern Europe. Although the Zionist movement already existed in practice, **Austro-Hungarian journalist Theodor Herzl** is credited with founding political Zionism, a movement which sought to establish a Jewish state in the Land of Israel. In 1896, **Herzl** published *Der Judenstaat (The Jewish State)*, offering his vision of a future Jewish state; the following year he presided over the **First Zionist Congress.**

**The Second Aliyah (1904–14),** began after the Kishinev pogrom; some 40,000 Jews settled in Palestine, although nearly half of them left eventually. Both the first and second waves of migrants were mainly Orthodox Jews, although the **Second Aliyah** included socialist groups who established the *kibbutz* **movement.** During World War I, British Foreign Secretary **Arthur Balfour** sent the **Balfour Declaration of 1917** to **Baron Rothschild** a leader of the British Jewish community, that stated that Britain intended for the creation of a Jewish "**national home**" within the Palestinian Mandate.

In 1918, the Jewish Legion, a group primarily of Zionist volunteers, assisted in the British conquest of Palestine. Arab opposition to British rule and Jewish immigration led to the 1920 Palestine riots and the formation of a Jewish militia known as the **Haganah ("The Defense")**, from which the **Irgun and Lehi**, or the **Stern Gang**, paramilitary groups later split off. In 1922, the League of Nations granted Britain a mandate over Palestine under terms which included the **Balfour Declaration** with its promise to the Jews, and with similar provisions regarding the Arab Palestinians.

**The Third (1919–23) and Fourth Aliyahs (1924–29)** brought an additional 100,000 Jews to Palestine. The rise of **Nazism** and the increasing persecution of Jews in 1930s Europe led to the **Fifth Aliyah**, with an influx of a quarter of a million Jews. This was a major cause of the **Arab Revolt** of 1936–39 during which the British Mandate authorities alongside the **Zionist militias of Haganah and Irgun killed 5,032 Arabs and wounded 14,760**, resulting in over ten percent of the adult male Palestinian Arab population killed, wounded, imprisoned or exiled.

The British introduced restrictions on Jewish immigration to Palestine with the **White Paper of 1939**. With countries around the world turning away Jewish refugees fleeing the **Holocaust**, a clandestine movement known as **Aliyah Bet** was organized to bring Jews to Palestine. By the end of World War II, the Jewish population of Palestine had increased to 33% of the total population.

## After World War II

After World War II **The Haganah joined Irgun and Lehi** in an armed struggle against British rule. At the same time, hundreds of thousands of Jewish **Holocaust** survivors and refugees sought a new life far from their destroyed communities in Europe. The **Yishuv** attempted to bring these refugees to Palestine but many were turned away or rounded up and placed in **detention camps in Atlit and Cyprus by the British**.

On 22 July 1946, **Irgun** attacked the British administrative headquarters for Palestine, which was housed in the southern wing of the **King David Hotel** in Jerusalem. A total of 91 people of various nationalities were killed and 46 were injured. The attack initially had the approval of the **Haganah**. In 1947, the British government announced it would withdraw from Palestine, stating it was unable to arrive at a solution acceptable to both Arabs and Jews.

On 15 May 1947, the General Assembly of the newly formed United Nations resolved that the **United Nations Special Committee on Palestine be created "to prepare for consideration at the next regular session of the Assembly a report on the question of Palestine." In the Report of the Committee dated 3 September 1947** to the General Assembly, the majority of the Committee in Chapter VI proposed a plan to replace the British Mandate with **"an independent Arab State, an independent Jewish State, and the City of Jerusalem ... the last to be under an International Trusteeship System."** On 29 November 1947, the General Assembly adopted **Resolution 181 (II)** recommending the adoption and implementation of the *Plan of Partition with Economic Union.*

The Jewish Agency, which was the recognized representative of the Jewish community, accepted the plan. The **Arab League** and **Arab Higher Committee of Palestine** rejected it, and indicated that they would reject any other plan of partition. On the following day, 1 December 1947, the **Arab Higher Committee** proclaimed a three-day strike, and Arab gangs began attacking Jewish targets. The Jews were initially on the defensive as civil war broke out, but in early April 1948 moved onto the offensive. **The Arab Palestinian economy collapsed and 250,000 Palestinian Arabs fled or were expelled.**

**On 14 May 1948, the day before the expiration of the British Mandate, David Ben-Gurion, the head of the Jewish Agency, declared "the establishment of a Jewish state in Eretz-Israel, to be known as the State of Israel."** The only reference in the text of the Declaration to the borders of the new state is the use of the term *Eretz-Israel* (**"Land of Israel"**). The following day, **the armies of four Arab countries—Egypt, Syria, Transjordan and Iraq—**entered what had been **British Mandatory Palestine**, launching the **1948 Arab–Israeli War; contingents from Yemen, Morocco, Saudi Arabia and Sudan joined the war.**

After a year of fighting, a ceasefire was declared and temporary borders, known as the **Green Line**, were established. Jordan annexed what became known as the West Bank, including East Jerusalem, and Egypt took control of the Gaza Strip. The United Nations estimated that more than **700,000 Palestinians were expelled by or fled from advancing Israeli forces during the conflict**—what would become known in Arabic as the *Nakba* (**"catastrophe"**).

## Early years of the State of Israel: *Arab–Israeli conflict*

**Israel was admitted as a member of the United Nations by majority vote on 11 May 1949.** In the early years of the state, the **Labor Zionist** movement led by **Prime Minister David Ben-Gurion** dominated Israeli politics. The **Kibbutzim,** or collective farming communities, played a pivotal role in establishing the new state.

Immigration to Israel during the late 1940s and early 1950s was aided by the Israeli Immigration Department and the non-government sponsored **Mossad LeAliyah Bet ("Institution for Illegal Immigration").** **Mossad LeAliyah Bet** was disbanded in 1953. The immigration was in accordance with the One Million Plan.

An **influx of Holocaust survivors and Jews from Arab and Muslim countries** to Israel during the first three years increased the number of **Jews from 700,000 to 1,400,000.** By 1958, the population of Israel rose to two million. Between 1948 and 1970, approximately 1,150,000 Jewish refugees relocated to Israel. Some new immigrants arrived as refugees with no possessions and were housed in temporary camps known as *ma'abarot*; by 1952, **over 200,000 people were living in these tent cities.**

The need to solve the crisis led **Ben-Gurion** to sign a reparations agreement with West Germany that triggered mass protests by Jews angered at the idea that Israel could accept monetary compensation for the Holocaust. In 1956, Great Britain and France aimed at regaining control of the **Suez Canal**, which the Egyptians had nationalized. The continued blockade of the **Suez Canal** and Straits of Tiran to Israeli shipping, together with the growing amount of Fedayeen attacks against Israel's southern population, and recent Arab grave and threatening statements, prompted Israel to attack Egypt.

Israel joined a secret alliance with Great Britain and France and overran the Sinai Peninsula but was pressured to withdraw by the United Nations in return for guarantees of Israeli shipping rights in the **Red Sea** via the **Straits of Tiran** and the Canal. The war, known as the **Suez Crisis**, resulted in significant reduction of Israeli border infiltration. In the early 1960s, Israel captured **Nazi** war criminal **Adolf Eichmann** in Argentina and brought him to Israel for trial. The trial had a major impact on public awareness of the **Holocaust. Eichmann remains the only person executed in Israel by conviction in an Israeli civilian court.**

## After the war: The Sinai Peninsula was returned to Egypt in 1982.

Arab nationalists led by **Egyptian President Gamal Abdel Nasser** refused to recognize Israel, and called for its destruction. By 1966, Israeli-Arab relations had deteriorated to the point of actual battles taking place between Israeli and Arab forces. In May 1967, Egypt massed its army near the border with Israel, expelled UN peacekeepers, stationed in the **Sinai Peninsula** since 1957, and blocked Israel's access to the Red Sea.

Israel, on 5 June, launched a pre-emptive strike against Egypt. Jordan, Syria and Iraq responded and attacked Israel. In a **Six-Day War,** Israel defeated Jordan and captured the West Bank, defeated Egypt and captured the Gaza Strip and Sinai Peninsula, and defeated Syria and captured the **Golan Heights**. Jerusalem's boundaries were enlarged, incorporating East Jerusalem, and the **1949 Green Line** became the administrative boundary between Israel and the occupied territories. Most important among the various Palestinian and Arab groups was the **Palestinian Liberation Organization (PLO)**, established in 1964, which initially committed itself to **"armed struggle as the only way to liberate the homeland".** Palestinian groups launched a wave of attacks against Israeli and Jewish targets around the world, including a massacre of Israeli athletes at the **1972 Summer Olympics in Munich**. The Israeli government responded with an assassination campaign against the organizers of the massacre, a bombing and a raid on the PLO headquarters in Lebanon.

On 6 October 1973, as Jews were observing **Yom Kippur,** the Egyptian and Syrian armies launched a surprise attack against Israeli forces in the Sinai Peninsula and Golan Heights, that opened the **Yom Kippur War**. The war ended on 25 October with Israel successfully repelling Egyptian and Syrian forces but **having suffered over 2,500 soldiers killed in a war which collectively took 10–35,000 lives in about 20 days.**

An internal inquiry exonerated the government of responsibility for failures before and during the war, but public anger forced **Prime Minister Golda Meir** to resign. In July 1976 an airliner was hijacked during its flight from Israel to France by Palestinian guerrillas and landed at **Entebbe, Uganda**. Israeli commandos carried out an operation in which **102 out of 106 Israeli hostages were successfully rescued.**

### *Israeli–Palestinian peace process: One-state solution, Two-state solution*

The 1977 **Knesset** elections marked a major turning point in Israeli political history as **Menachem Begin's Likud party** took control from the Labor Party. Later that year, **Egyptian President Anwar El Sadat** made a trip to Israel and spoke before the **Knesset** in what was the first recognition of Israel by an Arab head of state. In the two years that followed, **Sadat** and **Begin signed the Camp David Accords (1978)** and the **Israel–Egypt Peace Treaty (1979).** In return, Israel withdrew from the Sinai Peninsula and agreed to enter negotiations over an autonomy for Palestinians in the West Bank and the Gaza Strip.

On 11 March 1978, a PLO guerilla raid from Lebanon led to the **Coastal Road massacre**. Meanwhile, **Begin's government provided incentives for Israelis to settle in the occupied West Bank**, increasing friction with the Palestinians in that area. **The Basic Law: Jerusalem, Capital of Israel, passed in 1980**, was believed by some to reaffirm Israel's 1967 annexation of Jerusalem by government decree, and reignited international controversy over the status of the city.

**In 1981 Israel annexed the Golan Heights**, although annexation was not recognized internationally. Israel's population diversity expanded in the 1980s and 1990s. Several waves of **Ethiopian Jews** immigrated to Israel since the 1980s, while between 1990 and 1994, immigration from the **post-Soviet** states increased Israel's population by twelve percent.

On 7 June 1981, **the Israeli air force destroyed Iraq's sole nuclear reactor under construction just outside Baghdad**, in order to impede Iraq's nuclear weapons program. An Israeli government inquiry—the **Kahan Commission—would later hold Begin, Sharon and several Israeli generals as indirectly responsible for the Sabra and Shatila massacre.**

The **First Intifada,** a Palestinian uprising against Israeli rule, broke out in 1987, with waves of uncoordinated demonstrations and violence occurring in the occupied West Bank and Gaza. Over the following six years, the **Intifada** became more organized and included economic and cultural measures aimed at disrupting the Israeli occupation. More than a thousand people were killed in the violence. During the **1991 Gulf War**, the PLO supported **Saddam Hussein** and Iraqi Scud missile attacks against Israel.

In 1992, **Yitzhak Rabin became Prime Minister** following an election in which his party called for compromise with Israel's neighbors. The following year, **Shimon Peres** on behalf of Israel, and **Mahmoud Abbas** for the PLO, **signed the Oslo Accords**, which gave the Palestinian National Authority the right to govern parts of the West Bank and the Gaza Strip. **The PLO also recognized Israel's right to exist and pledged an end to terrorism**.

In 1994, the **Israel–Jordan peace treaty** was signed, making Jordan the second Arab country to normalize relations with Israel. Arab public support for the Accords was damaged by the continuation of Israeli settlements and checkpoints, and the deterioration of economic conditions. Israeli public support for the Accords waned as Israel was struck by Palestinian suicide attacks. **In November 1995, while leaving a peace rally, Yitzhak Rabin was assassinated by Yigal Amir, a far-right-wing Jew who opposed the Accords.**

Under the leadership of **Benjamin Netanyahu** at the end of the 1990s, Israel withdrew from Hebron, and signed the **Wye River Memorandum**, giving greater control to the **Palestinian National Authority**. **Ehud Barak**, elected Prime Minister in 1999, began the new millennium by withdrawing forces from Southern Lebanon and conducting negotiations with **Palestinian Authority Chairman Yasser Arafat** and **U.S. President Bill Clinton** at the **2000 Camp David Summit**. During the summit, Barak offered a plan for the establishment of a Palestinian state. The proposed state included the entirety of the Gaza Strip and over 90% of the West Bank **with Jerusalem as a shared capital.**

Each side blamed the other for the failure of the talks. After a controversial visit by **Likud leader Ariel Sharon** to the Temple Mount, the **Second Intifada** began. Some commentators contend that the uprising was pre-planned by Arafat due to the collapse of peace talks. **Sharon** became prime minister in a 2001 special election. During his tenure, **Sharon** carried out his plan to unilaterally withdraw from the Gaza Strip and also spearheaded the construction of the **Israeli West Bank barrier**, ending the **Intifada**. By this time 1,100 Israelis had been killed, mostly in suicide bombings. The Palestinian fatalities, from 2000 to 2008, reached 4,791 killed by Israeli security forces, 44 killed by Israeli civilians, and 609 killed by Palestinians.

In July 2006, a **Hezbollah** artillery assault on Israel's northern border communities and a cross-border abduction of two Israeli soldiers precipitated the month-long **Second Lebanon War**. On 6 September 2007, the Israeli Air Force destroyed a nuclear reactor in Syria. The **2008–09 Gaza War** lasted three weeks and ended after Israel announced a unilateral ceasefire.

**Hamas** announced its own ceasefire, with its own conditions of complete withdrawal and opening of border crossings. In what Israel described as a response to more than a hundred Palestinian rocket attacks on southern Israeli cities, Israel began an operation in Gaza on 14 November 2012, lasting eight days. Israel started another operation in Gaza following an escalation of rocket attacks by **Hamas** in July 2014.

## *Demographics of Israel and Israelis*

In 2017, Israel's population was an estimated 8,680,600 people, of whom 6,484,000 (74.7%) were recorded by the civil government as Jews. 1,808,000 Arabs comprised 20.8% of the population, while non-Arab Christians and people who have no religion listed in the civil registry made up 4.5%. **By June 2012, approximately 60,000 African migrants had entered Israel. About 92% of Israelis live in urban areas.**

## *Religion in Israel and Abrahamic religions*

Israel comprises a major part of the **Holy Land**, a region of significant importance to all **Abrahamic religions – Judaism, Christianity, Islam, Druze and** Baha'i. The religious affiliation of Israeli Jews varies widely: a social survey indicates that 49% self-identify as **Hiloni** (secular), 29% as **Masorti** (traditional), 13% as Dati (religious) and 9% as **Haredi** (ultra-Orthodox). **Haredi Jews are expected to represent more than 20% of Israel's Jewish population by 2028.**

Making up 17.6% of the population, Muslims constitute Israel's largest religious minority. About 2% of the population is Christian and 1.6% is Druze. **Out of more than one million immigrants from the former Soviet Union, about 300,000 are considered not Jewish by the Chief Rabbinate of Israel.**

## Education in Israel

Many international business leaders such as **Microsoft founder Bill Gates** have praised Israel for its high quality of education in helping spur Israel's economic development and technological boom. In 2015, the country ranked third among OECD members (after Canada and Japan) for the percentage of 25–64 year-olds that have attained tertiary education with 49% compared with the OECD average of 35%. **In 2012, the country ranked third in the world in the number of academic degrees per capita (20 percent of the population).** Israel has a school life expectancy of 16 years and a **literacy rate of 97.8%.**

*Maariv* described the Christian Arabs sectors as **"the most successful in education system"**, since Christians fared the best in terms of education in comparison to any other religion in Israel. Israel has **nine public universities** that are subsidized by the state and **49 private colleges**. The **Hebrew University** of Jerusalem, Israel's second-oldest university after the **Technion**, houses the **National Library of Israel, the world's largest repository of Judaica and Hebraica.**

## Politics of Israel and Israeli system of government

Parliamentary elections are scheduled every four years, but unstable coalitions or a no-confidence vote by the **Knesset** can dissolve a government earlier. In 2003, the **Knesset** began to draft an official constitution based on these laws. The president of Israel is head of state, with limited and largely ceremonial duties. **Israel has no official religion**, but the definition of the state as **"Jewish and democratic"** creates a strong connection with Judaism, as well as a conflict between state law and religious law.

## Judiciary of Israel and Israeli law

Israel has a three-tier court system. At the lowest level are magistrate courts, situated in most cities across the country. Above them are district courts, serving as both appellate courts and courts of first instance; they are situated in five of Israel's six districts. **The third and highest tier is the Supreme Court, located in Jerusalem**; it serves a dual role as the highest court of appeals and the High Court of Justice.

The election of judges is carried out by a committee of two **Knesset** members, three Supreme Court justices, two Israeli Bar members and two ministers (one of which, Israel's justice minister, is the committee's chairman). The committee's members of the **Knesset** are secretly elected by the **Knesset**, and one of them is traditionally a member of the opposition, the committee's Supreme Court justices are chosen by tradition from all Supreme Court justices by seniority, the **Israeli Bar** members are elected by the bar, and the second minister is appointed by the Israeli cabinet.

**Israel's Basic Law: Human Dignity and Liberty seeks to defend human rights and liberties in Israel.**

## Israeli-occupied territories

Most negotiations relating to the territories have been on the basis of **United Nations Security Council Resolution 242**, which emphasizes **"the inadmissibility of the acquisition of territory by war",** and calls on Israel to withdraw from occupied territories in return for normalization of relations with Arab states, a principle known as **"Land for peace".**

Following the 2007 **Battle of Gaza**, when **Hamas** assumed power in the Gaza Strip, Israel tightened its control of the Gaza crossings along its border, as well as by sea and air, and prevented persons from entering and exiting the area except for isolated cases it deemed humanitarian. Gaza has a border with Egypt and an agreement between Israel, the European Union and the PA governed how border crossing would take place (it was monitored by European observers).

## Military: *Israel Defense Forces and Israeli security forces*

The Israel Defense Forces is the sole military wing of the Israeli security forces, and is headed by its **Chief of General Staff, the *Ramatkal*,** subordinate to the Cabinet. The IDF consist of the army, air force and navy. It was founded during the 1948 Arab–Israeli War by consolidating paramilitary organizations—chiefly the **Haganah**—that preceded the establishment of the state. The IDF also draws upon the resources of the **Military Intelligence Directorate (*Aman*), which works with Mossad and Shabak.**

**Most Israelis are drafted into the military at the age of 18**. Men serve two years and eight months and women two years. Following mandatory service, Israeli men join the reserve forces and usually do up to several weeks of reserve duty every year until their forties. Most women are exempt from reserve duty. Arab citizens of Israel(except the Druze) and those engaged in full-time religious studies are exempt from military service, although the exemption of yeshiva students has been a source of contention in Israeli society for many years. **The IDF maintains approximately 176,500 active troops and an additional 445,000 reservists.**

The **Israeli Navy's Dolphin submarines are believed to be armed with nuclear Popeye Turbo missiles, offering second-strike capability**. Since the **Gulf War in 1991**, when Israel was attacked by Iraqi Scud missiles, all homes in Israel are required to have a reinforced security room, **Merkhav Mugan**, impermeable to chemical and biological substances.

## Economy

Israel is considered the most advanced country in Southwest Asia and the Middle East in economic and industrial development. The country is ranked 16th in the **World Economic Forum's *Global Competitiveness Report*** and 54th on the **World Bank's *Ease of Doing Business*** index. It has **the**

**second-largest number of startup companies in the world** after the United States, and the third-largest number of NASDAQ-listed companies after the U.S. and China. Israel was also ranked 4th in the world by share of people in high-skilled employment.

**Imports to Israel, totaling $57.9 billion in 2016,** include raw materials, military equipment, investment goods, rough diamonds, fuels, grain, and consumer goods. In 2016, **Israeli exports reached $51.61 billion.**

## Science and technology

**Israel boasts 140 scientists, technicians, and engineers per 10,000 employees,** the highest number in the world (in comparison, the same is 85 for the U.S.). Israel has produced **six Nobel Prize-winning scientists since 2004** and has been frequently ranked as one of the countries with the highest ratios of scientific papers per capita in the world. In 2012 Israel was ranked ninth in the world by the **Futron's Space Competitiveness Index**. **In 2003, Ilan Ramon became Israel's first astronaut, serving as payload specialist of STS-107, the fatal mission of the Space Shuttle** *Columbia.*

**The Sorek desalination plant is the largest seawater reverse osmosis (SWRO) desalination facility in the world**. The country hosts an annual **Water Technology and Environmental Control Exhibition & Conference (WATEC)** that attracts thousands of people from across the world. **Over 90% of Israeli homes use solar energy for hot water**, the highest per capita in the world.

**Krav Maga**, a martial art developed by Jewish ghetto defenders during the struggle against fascism in Europe, is used by the Israeli security forces and police. Its effectiveness and practical approach to self-defense, have won it widespread admiration and adherence around the world.

# Suez War Crisis (1956)

The **Suez Crisis**, also referred to as the **Tripartite Aggression** or **Suez War** was a diplomatic and military confrontation in late 1956 between **Egypt** on one side, and **Britain, France** and **Israel** on the other, with the United States, the **Soviet Union** and the **United Nations** playing major roles in forcing **Britain, France** and **Israel** to withdraw. Less than a day after **Israel** invaded **Egypt**, **Britain** and **France** issued a joint ultimatum to **Egypt** and **Israel**, and then began to bomb Cairo.

Despite the denials of the **Israel**i, British and French governments, evidence began to emerge that the invasion of **Egypt** had been planned beforehand by the three powers. **Anglo-French** forces withdrew before the end of the year, but **Israel**i forces remained until March 1957, prolonging the crisis. **In April, the canal was fully reopened to shipping.**

The attack followed the President of **Egypt Gamal Abdel Nasser's** decision of 26 July 1956 to nationalize the **Suez Canal**, after the withdrawal of an offer by **Britain** and the United States to fund the building of the Aswan Dam, which was in response to **Egypt**'s new ties with the **Soviet Union** and recognizing the **People's Republic of China** during the height of tensions between China and Taiwan. The aims of the attack were primarily to regain Western control of the canal and to remove **Nasser** from power.

The three allies, especially **Israel**, were mainly successful in attaining their immediate military objectives, but pressure from the United States and the **USSR** at the **United Nations** and elsewhere forced them to withdraw. As a result of the outside pressure **Britain** and **France** failed in their political and strategic aims of controlling the canal and removing **Nasser** from power. **Israel** fulfilled some of its objectives, such as attaining freedom of navigation through the **Straits of Tiran.** As a result of the conflict, the **UNEF** would police the **Egypt**ian–**Israel**i border to prevent both sides from recommencing hostilities.

## Background

The **Suez Canal** was opened in 1869, after ten years of work financed by the French and **Egypt**ian governments. The canal was operated by the **Universal Company of the Suez Maritime Canal,** an **Egypt**ian-chartered company; the area surrounding the canal remained sovereign **Egypt**ian territory and the only land-bridge between Africa and Asia. The canal instantly became strategically important; it provided the shortest ocean link between the Mediterranean and the Indian Ocean. The canal eased commerce for trading nations and particularly helped European colonial powers to gain and govern their colonies.

In 1875, as a result of debt and financial crisis, the **Egypt**ian ruler was forced to sell his shares in the canal operating company to the British government of **Benjamin Disraeli.** They were willing buyers and obtained a 44% share in the canal's operations for less than £4 million; this maintained the majority shareholdings of the mostly French private investors. With the 1882 invasion and occupation of **Egypt**, the United Kingdom took *de facto* control of the country as well as the canal proper, and its finances and operations. The 1888 **Convention of Constantinople** declared the canal a neutral zone under British protection. In ratifying it, the **Ottoman Empire** agreed to permit international shipping to pass freely through the canal, in time of war and peace. The Convention came into force in 1904, the same year as the *Entente cordiale*, between **Britain** and **France**.

Despite this convention, the strategic importance of the **Suez Canal** and its control were proven during the **Russo-Japanese War of 1904—1905,** after Japan and Britain entered into a separate bilateral agreement. Following the Japanese surprise attack on the **Russian Pacific Fleet** based at **Port Arthur** the Russians sent reinforcements from their fleet in the Baltic Sea. The British denied the Russian fleet use of the canal and forced it to steam around the entire continent of Africa, giving the Japanese forces time to solidify their position in the **Far East.**

The importance of the canal as a strategic intersection was again apparent during the **First World War,** when **Britain** and **France** closed the canal to non-Allied shipping. The attempt by **German-Ottoman** forces to storm the Canal in February 1915 led the British to commit 100,000 troops to the defense of **Egypt** for the rest of the **First World War**. The canal continued to be strategically important after the **Second World War** as a conduit for the shipment of oil. Petroleum business historian **Daniel Yergin** wrote of the period:

**"In 1948, the canal abruptly lost its traditional rationale.... [British] control over the canal could no longer be preserved on grounds that it was critical to the defense either of India or of an empire that was being liquidated. And yet, at exactly the same moment, the canal was gaining a new role – as the highway not of empire, but of oil.... By 1955, petroleum accounted for half of the canal's traffic, and, in turn, two thirds of Europe's oil passed through it."** By 2000, only 8% of the imported oil in **Britain** arrived via the **Suez Canal** with the rest coming via the Cape route.

## Events leading to the Suez Crisis: Post-war years

In the aftermath of the **Second World War**, **Britain** was reassessing its role in the region in light of the severe economic constraints and its colonial history. The economic potential of the Middle East, with its vast oil reserves, as well as the **Suez Canal**'s geo-strategic importance against the background of the **Cold War,** prompted **Britain** to consolidate and strengthen its position there. **The kingdoms of Egypt and Iraq were seen as vital to maintaining strong British influence in the region.**

**Britain**'s military strength was spread throughout the region, including the vast military complex at **Suez** with a garrison of some 80,000, making it one of the largest military installations in the world. The **Suez** base was considered an important part of **Britain**'s strategic position in the Middle East; however, increasingly it became a source of growing tension in **Anglo-Egypt**ian relations. Unrest began to manifest itself in the growth of radical political groups, such as the **Muslim Brotherhood** in **Egypt**, and an increasingly hostile attitude towards **Britain** and her presence in the country. Added to this anti-British fervor was the role **Britain** had played in the creation of **Israel**.

In October 1951, the **Egypt**ian government unilaterally abrogated the **Anglo-Egypt**ian **Treaty** of 1936, the terms of which granted **Britain** a lease on the **Suez** base for 20 more years. **Britain** refused to withdraw from **Suez**, relying upon its treaty rights, as well as the sheer presence of the **Suez garrison**. The price of such a course of action was a steady escalation in increasingly violent hostility towards **Britain** and British troops in **Egypt**, which the **Egypt**ian authorities did little to curb.

On 25 January 1952, British attempts to disarm a troublesome auxiliary police force barracks in Ismailia resulted in the **deaths of 41 Egypt**ians. This in turn led to anti-Western riots in Cairo resulting in heavy damage to property and the deaths of several foreigners, including 11 British citizens. This proved to be a catalyst for the removal of the **Egypt**ian **monarchy**. On 23 July 1952 a military coup by the 'Free Officers Movement'—led by **Muhammad Neguib** and future **Egypt**ian President **Gamal Abdul Nasser**—overthrew **King Farouk** and established an **Egypt**ian republic.

Since the establishment of **Israel** in 1948, cargo shipments to and from **Israel** had been subject to **Egypt**ian authorization, search and seizure while attempting to pass through the **Suez Canal**. On 1 September 1951, the **United Nations** Security Council **Resolution 95** called upon **Egypt**: "... to **terminate the restrictions on the passage of international commercial ships and goods through the Suez Canal, wherever bound, and to cease all interference with such shipping.**" This interference and confiscation, contrary to the laws of the canal (Article 1 of the 1888 **Suez Canal** Convention), increased following the coup.

## Post-revolution period

**Britain**'s desire to mend Anglo-**Egypt**ian relations in the wake of the coup saw her strive for rapprochement throughout 1953 and 1954. Part of this process was the agreement, in 1953, to terminate British rule in Sudan by 1956 in return for Cairo's abandoning of its claim to suzerainty over the Nile Valley region. In October 1954, **Britain** and **Egypt** concluded an agreement on the phased evacuation of British troops from the **Suez** base, the terms of which agreed to withdrawal of all troops within 20 months, maintenance of the base to be continued, and for **Britain** to hold the right to return for seven years. The **Suez Canal Company** was not due to revert to the **Egypt**ian government until 16 November 1968 under the terms of the treaty.

Despite the establishment of such an agreement with the British, **Nasser**'s position remained tenuous. The loss of **Egypt**'s claim to Sudan, coupled with the continued presence of **Britain** at **Suez** for a further two years, led to domestic unrest including an assassination attempt against him in October 1954. The tenuous nature of **Nasser**'s rule caused him to believe that neither his regime, nor **Egypt**'s independence would be safe until **Egypt** had established itself as head of the Arab world. This would manifest itself in the challenging of British Middle Eastern interests throughout 1955.

At the same time, **the United States was attempting to woo Nasser into an alliance**. The central problem for American policy in the Middle East was that this region was perceived as strategically important due to its oil, but the United States, weighed down by defense commitments in Europe and the Far East, lacked sufficient troops to resist a Soviet invasion of the Middle East. As a consequence, American diplomats favored the creation of a **NATO**-type organization in the Near East to provide the necessary military power to deter the Soviets from invading the region.

A major dilemma for American policy was that the two strongest powers in the Near East, **Britain** and **France**, were also the ones that many local nationalists objected to the most. From 1953 onwards, American diplomacy had attempted unsuccessfully to persuade the powers involved in the Near East, both local and imperial to set aside their differences and unite against the **Soviet Union**. The Americans took the view that just as fear of the **Soviet Union** had helped to end the historic Franco-German enmity that so, too, could anti-Communism end the more recent **Arab-Israel**i dispute. In May 1953, during a meeting with the American Secretary of State, **John Foster Dulles**, who asked **Egypt** to join an **anti-Soviet Alliance**.

Dulles informed **Nasser** of his belief that the **Soviet Union** was seeking world conquest, that the principal danger to the Near East came from the Kremlin, and urged **Nasser** to set aside his differences with **Britain** to focus on countering the **Soviet Union**. In this spirit, **Dulles** suggested that the **Nasser** negotiate a deal that would see **Egypt** assume sovereignty over the **Canal Zone** base, but then allow the British to have "**technical control**" in the same way that Ford auto company provided parts and training to its **Egypt**ian dealers. **The CIA offered Nasser a \$3 million bribe if he would joined the proposed Middle East Defense Organization; Nasser took the money, but then refused to join.**

The **Soviet Union** under the new leadership of **Nikita Khrushchev** was making a major effort to win influence in the so-called **"third world".** As part of the diplomatic offensive, **Khrushchev** had abandoned Moscow's traditional line of treating all non-communists as enemies and adopted a new tactic of befriending so-called "**non-aligned**" nations, which often led by leaders who were non-Communists, but in varying ways and degrees were hostile towards the West.

The Chinese Premier **Zhou Enlai** who met **Nasser** at the 1955 **Bandung Summit** and was impressed by him, recommended that **Khrushchev** treat **Nasser** as a potential ally. **Zhou** described **Nasser** to **Khrushchev** as a young nationalist, who though no Communist, could if used correctly do much damage to Western interests in the Middle East. Marshal **Josip Broz Tito** of Yugoslavia, who also come to know **Nasser** at Bandung told **Khrushchev** in a 1955 meeting that "**Nasser** was a young man without much political experience, but if we give him the benefit of the doubt, we might be able to exert a beneficial influence on him, both for the sake of the Communist movement, and...The **Egypt**ian people". **Nasser had first broached the subject of buying weapons from the Soviet Union in 1954.**

Instead of siding with either super-power, **Nasser** took the role of the spoiler and tried to play off the super-powers in order to have them compete with each other in attempts to buy his friendship. **Nasser**'s first choice for buying weapons was the United States, but his frequent anti-**Israel**i speeches and his sponsorship for the *Fedayeen* who were making raids into **Israel** had made it difficult for the **Eisenhower** administration to get the approval of Congress to sell weapons to **Egypt**. **Nasser**'s hope was that faced with the prospect of **Egypt** buying Soviet weapons, and thus coming under Soviet influence the **Eisenhower** administration would be forced to sell **Egypt** the weapons he wanted. **Khrushchev**, who very much wanted to win the **Soviet Union** influence in the Middle East, was more than ready to arm **Egypt** if the Americans proved unwilling.

**Britain**'s close relationship with the two **Hashemite kingdoms** of Iraq and Jordan were of particular concern to **Nasser**. In particular, Iraq's increasingly amicable relations with **Britain** were a threat to **Nasser**'s desire to see **Egypt** as head of the Arab world. The creation of the **Baghdad Pact in 1955** seemed to confirm **Nasser**'s fears that **Britain** was attempting to draw the **Eastern Arab World** into a bloc centered upon Iraq, and sympathetic to **Britain**. **Nasser**'s response was a series of challenges to British influence in the region that would culminate in the **Suez Crisis**.

## Frustration of British aims

He also began to align **Egypt** with the kingdom of **Saudi Arabia**—whose rulers were hereditary enemies of the Hashemites—in an effort to frustrate British efforts to draw Syria, Jordan and Lebanon into the orbit of the **Baghdad Pact**. **Nasser** frustrated British attempts to draw Jordan into the pact by sponsoring demonstrations in Amman, leading **King Hussein** to dismiss the British commander of the **Arab Legion Glubb Pasha** in March 1956 and throwing **Britain**'s Middle Eastern security policy into chaos.

**Nasser** struck a further blow against **Britain** by negotiating an arms deal with communist Czechoslovakia in September 1955 thereby ending **Egypt**'s reliance on Western arms. Later, other members of the **Warsaw Pact** also sold arms to **Egypt** and Syria. In practice, all sales from the Eastern Bloc were authorized by the **Soviet Union**, as an attempt to increase Soviet influence over the Middle East.

This caused tensions in the United States because **Warsaw Pact** nations now had a strong presence in the region. At the same time, the French Premier **Guy Mollet,** who facing an increasing serious war in Algeria, where the rebels of the **FLN** were being supported by **Egypt**, had come to perceive **Nasser** as a major threat During a visit to London in March 1956, **Mollet** told **Eden** that his country was faced with an Islamic threat to the very soul of **France** supported by the **Soviet Union**.

## Nationalization of the Suez Canal and the road to crisis

**Britain** was eager to tame **Nasser** and looked towards the United States for support. However, **President Eisenhower** strongly opposed British-French military action. America's closest Arab ally, **Saudi Arabia**, was just as fundamentally opposed to the **Hashemite-dominated Baghdad Pact** as **Egypt**, and the U.S. was keen to increase its own influence in the region. The events that brought the crisis to a head occurred in the spring and summer of 1956.

On 16 May, **Nasser** officially recognized the **People's Republic of China**, a move that angered the U.S. and its secretary of state, **John Foster Dulles**, a keen sponsor of Taiwan. This move, coupled with the impression that the project was beyond **Egypt**'s economic capabilities, **caused Eisenhower to withdraw all American financial aid for the Aswan Dam project on 19 July.**

Finally, the **Eisenhower** administration had become very annoyed at **Nasser**'s efforts to play the United States off against the **Soviet Union**, and decided to call **Nasser**'s bluff by refusing to finance the **Aswan** high dam with the intention of teaching **Nasser** a lesson. As early as September 1955, when **Nasser** announced the purchase of the Soviet military equipment via Czechoslovakia, Dulles had written that competing for **Nasser**'s favor was probably going to be **"an expensive process"**, one that Dulles wanted to avoid as much as possible.

### *Nationalization*

**Nasser**'s response was the nationalization of the **Suez Canal**. On 26 July, in a speech in Alexandria, **Nasser** gave a riposte to **Dulles**. During his speech he deliberately pronounced the name of **Ferdinand de Lesseps,** the builder of the canal, a code-word for **Egypt**ian forces to seize control of the canal and implement its nationalization.

He announced that the **Nationalization Law** had been published, that all assets of the **Suez Canal Company** had been frozen, and that stockholders would be paid the price of their shares according to the day's closing price on the **Paris Stock Exchange**. That same day, **Egypt closed the canal to Israeli shipping. Egypt** also closed the Straits of Tiran to **Israeli** shipping, and blockaded the **Gulf of Aqaba**, in contravention of the **Constantinople Convention** of 1888. Many argued that this was also a violation of the **1949 Armistice Agreements.**

The nationalization of the **Suez Canal** hit British economic and military interests in the region. Prime Minister **Anthony Eden** was under immense domestic pressure from Conservative MPs who drew direct comparisons between the events of 1956 and those of the **Munich Agreement** in 1938. Since the US government did not support the British protests, the British government decided in favor of military intervention against **Egypt** to avoid the complete collapse of British prestige in the region.

**Eden** was hosting a dinner for **King Feisal II** of Iraq and his Prime Minister, **Nuri as-Said,** when he learned the Canal had been nationalized. They both unequivocally advised **Eden** to "**hit Nasser hard, hit him soon, and hit him by yourself**" – a stance shared by the vast majority of the British people in subsequent weeks. If **Nasser** went unchallenged the whole Middle East would go his way.

The French Premier **Guy Mollet** was outraged by **Nasser**'s move, and was utterly determined that **Nasser** would not be allowed to get away with it. During an interview with **Henry Luce, Mollet** held up a copy of **Nasser**'s book *The Philosophy of the Revolution* and said: **"This is Nasser's *Mein Kampf.* If we're too stupid not to read it, understand it and draw the obvious conclusions, then so much the worse for us".** On July 29, 1956, the French Cabinet had decided upon military action against **Egypt** in alliance with **Israel**, and Admiral **Nomy** of the French Naval General Staff was sent to **Britain** to inform the leaders of that country of what **France** had decided to and to invite them to join if they were interested.

 Given the way that the Algeria (which was considered to be integral part of **France**) had become engulfed in a spiral of increasing savage violence that French leaders longed to put an end to, the **Mollet** cabinet had been tempted by **Molotov's** offer, but in the end, **Mollet** who was a firm Atlanticist had chosen to remain faithful towards **NATO**. Direct military intervention, however, ran the risk of angering Washington and damaging Anglo-Arab relations. As a result, the British government concluded a **secret military pact with France and Israel** that was aimed at regaining control over the **Suez Canal**. An alliance was soon formed between **Eden** and **Guy Mollet**, French Prime Minister, with headquarters based in London.

General **Hugh Stockwell** and Admiral **Barjot** were appointed as Chief of Staff. International conferences were organized to secure agreement on **Suez Canal** operations but all were ultimately fruitless.

## The Menzies Committee

The Australian Prime Minister, **Robert Menzies,** was dispatched to Cairo to act as chairman of a committee charged with leading negotiations with **Nasser**. **Menzies'** September 7 official communiqué to **Nasser** presented a case for compensation for the **Suez Canal Company** and the "establishment of principles" for the future use of the Canal. **Nasser** saw such measures as "derogation" and rejected **Menzies'** proposals. **Menzies** hinted to **Nasser** that **Britain** and **France** might use force to resolve the crisis, but United States **President Eisenhower openly opposed the use of force and Menzies left Egypt without success.**

## Protocol of Sèvres

Three months after **Egypt**'s nationalization of the **Suez Canal Company**, a secret meeting took place at Sèvres, outside Paris. **Britain** and **France** enlisted **Israeli** support for an alliance against **Egypt**. The parties agreed that **Israel** would invade the Sinai. **Britain** and **France** would then intervene, purportedly to separate the warring **Israeli** and **Egypt**ian forces. **David Ben-Gurion** did not trust the British in view of their treaty with Jordan and he was not initially in favor of the plan, since it would make **Israel** alone look like the aggressor; however he soon agreed to it since such a good opportunity to strike back at **Egypt** might never again present itself.

## Motivation of the involved states

The interests of the parties were various. **Britain** was anxious lest it lose efficient access to the remains of its empire. Both the French and the British felt that **Nasser** should be removed from power. The French **"held the Egyptian president responsible for assisting the ant colonial rebellion in Algeria."** **Israel** wanted to reopen the **Straits of Tiran** leading to the **Gulf of Aqaba** to **Israeli** shipping, and saw the opportunity to strengthen its southern border and to weaken what it saw as a dangerous and hostile state. This was particularly felt in the form of attacks injuring approximately 1,300 civilians emanating from the **Egypt**ian-held **Gaza Strip**.

The **Israel**is were also deeply troubled by **Egypt**'s procurement of large amounts of Soviet weaponry that included 530 armored vehicles, of which 230 were tanks; 500 guns; 150 **MiG 15** jet fighters; 50 **Iluyshin-28** bombers; submarines and other naval craft. The influx of this advanced weaponry altered an already shaky balance of power. Additionally, **Israel** believed **Egypt** had formed a secret alliance with Jordan and Syria.

The United States worked hard through diplomatic channels to resolve the crisis without resorting to conflict. The British, Washington's closest ally, ignored **Eisenhower**'s pointed warning that the American people would not accept a military solution. The **American Central Intelligence Agency** (CIA) was taking high-altitude photos of the allied activities, and more details came from human sources in London, Paris and Tel Aviv.

## Israel

American military historian **Derek Varble** called the **Israel Defense Forces (IDF)** the "best" military force in the Middle East while at the same time suffering from "deficiencies" such as "immature doctrine, faulty logistics, and technical inadequacies". The **IDF**'s Chief of Staff, Major General **Moshe Dayan**, encouraged aggression, initiative, and ingenuity amongst the **Israel**i officer corps while ignoring logistics and armored operations. **Most of the IDF weapons in 1956 came from France.** The main **IDF** tank was the **AMX-13** and the main aircraft were the Dassault **Mystère IVA** and the **Ouragan**. **Superior pilot training was to give the Israeli Air Force an unbeatable edge over their Egyptian opponents.**

## Egypt

In the **Egypt**ian military, politics rather than military competence were the main criterion for promotion. The **Egypt**ian commander, **Field Marshal Abdel Hakim Amer**, was a purely political appointee who owed his position to his close friendship with **Nasser**. A heavy drinker, he would prove himself grossly incompetent as a general during the Crisis. In 1956, the **Egypt**ian military was well equipped with weapons from the **Soviet Union** such as **T-34** and **JS-3 tanks, MiG-15 fighters, Ilyushin Il-28 bombers, SU-100** self-propelled guns and assault rifles. **Egypt**ian troops were excellent in defensive operations, but had little capacity for offensive operations owning to the lack of "rapport and effective small-unit leadership".

## Planning

In July 1956, **Eden** ordered his Chiefs of Staff to begin planning for an invasion of **Egypt. Eden**'s plan called for the Cyprus-based 16th Independent Parachute Brigade Group to seize the **Canal Zone**. The Prime Minister's plan was rejected by the Chiefs of Staff. In early August, the Contingency Plan was modified by including a strategic bombing campaign that was intended to destroy **Egypt**'s economy, and thereby **hopefully bring about Nasser's overthrow**.

## *Operation Musketeer*

**Stockwell** offered up **Operation Musketeer**, which was to begin with a two-day air campaign that would see the British gain air superiority. To destroy the 300,000-strong **Egypt**ian Army in his planned battle of annihilation, Stockwell estimated that he needed 80,000 troops, while at most the British Army could spare was 50,000 troops; the French could supply the necessary 30,000 troops to make up the shortfall.

On 11 August 1956 **General Keightley** was appointed commander of **Musketeer** with the French Admiral **Jobert** as Deputy-Commander. A major problem both politically and militarily with the planning for **Musketeer** was the one-week interval between sending troops to the eastern Mediterranean and the beginning of the invasion. In late August 1956, the French Admiral **Pierre Barjot** suggested that **Port Said** once again be made the main target, which lessened the number of troops needed and thus reduced the interval between sending forces to the eastern Mediterranean and the invasion.

## *Operation Revise*

On 8 September 1956 **Revise** was approved by the British and French cabinets. Both **Stockwell** and **Beaufre** were opposed to revise as an open-ended plan with no clear goal beyond seizing the **Canal Zone**, but were embraced by **Eden** and **Mollet** as offering greater political flexibility and the prospect of lesser **Egypt**ian civilian casualties. At the same time, **Israel** had been working on **Operation Kadesh** for the invasion of the Sinai. **Dayan's** plan put an emphasis on air power combined with mobile battles of encirclement.

**Kadesh** called for the **Israel**i air force to win air superiority, which was to be followed up with **"one continuous battle"** in the Sinai. **Israel**i forces would in a series of swift operations encircle and then take the main **Egypt**ian strongpoints in the Sinai.

Thus, the 202nd Paratroop Brigade commanded by **Colonel Ariel Sharon** was to land in the far-western part of the Sinai to take the **Mitla Pass**, and thereby cut off the **Egypt**ian forces in the eastern Sinai from their supply lines. In October 1956, **Eden**, after two months of pressure, finally and reluctantly agreed to French requests to include **Israel** in **Operation Revise**. The British alliances with the Hashemite kingdoms of Jordan and Iraq had made the British very reluctant to fight alongside **Israel**, lest the ensuing backlash in the Arab world threaten London's friends in Baghdad and Amman. **Under the Protocol of Sèvres**, the following was agreed to:

- 29 October: **Israel** to invade the Sinai.
- 30 October: Anglo-French ultimatum to demand both sides withdraw from the **Canal Zone**.
- 31 October: **Britain** and **France** begin **Revise**.

## Invasion

### Operation Kadesh: The Israeli operation in the Sinai Peninsula

**Operation Kadesh** received its name from ancient **Kadesh**, located in the northern Sinai and mentioned several times in the **Hebrew Pentateuch**. The **Egypt**ian blockade of the Tiran Straits was based at **Sharm el-Sheikh** and, by capturing the town; **Israel** would have access to the Red Sea for the first time since 1953, which would allow it to restore the trade benefits of secure passage to the Indian Ocean.

The **Gaza Strip** was chosen as another military objective because **Israel** wished to remove the training grounds for Fedayeen groups, and because **Israel** recognized that **Egypt** could use the territory as a staging ground for attacks against the advancing **Israel**i troops. On 24 October, **Dayan** ordered a partial mobilization. When this led to a state of confusion, **Dayan** ordered full mobilization, and chose to take the risk that he might alert the **Egypt**ians.

The conflict began on 29 October 1956. At about 3: 00 pm, **Israel**i **Air Force Mustangs** launched a series of attacks on **Egypt**ian positions all over the Sinai Because **Israel**i intelligence expected Jordan to enter the war on **Egypt**'s side, **Israel**i soldiers were stationed along the **Israeli-Jordanian** frontier. **Israeli-Arab** villages along the Jordanian border were placed under curfew, and orders were given to shoot curfew violators. This resulted in the killings of 48 civilians in the Arab village of **Kafr Qasim** in an event known as the **Kafr Qasim massacre**. The border policemen involved in the killings were later tried and imprisoned, with an **Israel**i court finding that the order to shoot civilians was **"blatantly illegal"**.

### *Early actions in Southern Sinai*

On 29 October, Operation **Kadesh** – the invasion of the Sinai, began when an **Israel**i paratrooper battalion was air-dropped into the Sinai Peninsula, east of the **Suez Canal** near the Mitla Pass. In conjunction with the para drop, four **Israel**i P-51 Mustangs using their wings and propellers, cut all overhead telephone lines in the Sinai, severely disrupting **Egypt**ian command and control.

At the same time, **Colonel Sharon's 202nd Paratroop Brigade raced out towards the Mitla Pass**. A major problem for **Sharon** was vehicle break-down.

### *Early actions along the Gulf of Aqaba, and the central front*

As the paratroopers were being dropped into the Sinai, the **Israel**i 9th Infantry Brigade captured **Ras an-Naqb**, an important staging ground for that brigade's later attack against **Sharm el-Sheikh. The Egyptians surrendered, with no Israeli casualties sustained.**

## Battle of Jebel Heitan, Paratroop Brigade under attack

The portion of the Paratroopers under **Sharon**'s command continued to advance to meet with the 1st Brigade. En route, **Sharon** assaulted Themed in a dawn attack, and was able to storm the town with his armor through the Themed Gap. **Sharon** routed the Sudanese police company, and captured the settlement. On his way to the **Nakla**, **Sharon**'s men came under attack from **Egypt**ian **MIG-15s**. On the 30th, **Sharon** linked up with **Eytan** near **Nakla**.

**Dayan** had no more plans for further advances beyond the passes, but **Sharon** decided to attack the **Egypt**ian positions at **Jebel Heitan**. **Sharon** sent his lightly armed paratroopers against dug-in **Egypt**ians supported by aircraft, tanks and heavy artillery. **Sharon** sent two infantry companies, a mortar battery and some **AMX-13** tanks under the command of **Mordechai Gur** into the **Heitan Defile** on the afternoon of 31 October 1956.

The **Egypt**ian forces occupied strong defensive positions and brought down heavy anti-tank, mortar and machine gun fire on the **IDF** force. Gur's men were forced to retreat into the **"Saucer"**, where they were surrounded and came under heavy fire. Hearing of this, **Sharon** sent in another task force while Gur's men used the cover of night to scale the walls of the **Heitan Defile.** During the ensuing action, the **Egypt**ians were defeated and forced to retreat. A total of 260 **Egypt**ian and 38 **Israel**i soldiers were killed during the battle.

**Dayan** himself maintained that **Sharon** was correct to order the attack without orders, and that under the circumstances, **Sharon** made the right decision; instead he criticized **Sharon** for his tactics of attacking the **Egypt**ians head-on, which **Dayan** claimed led to unnecessary casualties. **Most of the deaths sustained by the Israelis in the entire operation were sustained at Jebel Heitan.**

## Air operations, first phase

From the outset, the **Israel**i Air Force flew paratroop drops, supply flights and medevac sorties. **Israel**'s new French-made Dassault **Mystere IV** jet fighters provided air cover for the transport aircraft. In air combat, **Israel**i aircraft shot down between seven and nine **Egypt**ian jets with the loss of one plane, but **Egypt**ian strikes against the ground forces continued through to 1 November. With the attack by the British and French air forces and navies, President **Nasser** ordered his pilots to disengage and fly their planes to bases in Southern **Egypt**. The **Israel**i **Air Force** was then free to strike **Egypt**ian ground forces at will, as **Israel**i forces advanced into the Western Sinai.

## Naval operations

On 30 October, the **Egypt**ian Navy dispatched the *Ibrahim el Awal*, an ex-British Hunt class destroyer, to Haifa with the aim of shelling that city's coastal oil installations. On 31 October the *Ibrahim el Awal* reached Haifa and began bombarding the city with its four 102mm (4-inch) guns. The **Israel**i destroyers **INS** *Eilat* and **INS** *Yaffo* then gave chase and caught up with the **Egypt**ian warship. The **Israel**i destroyers, together two **Israel**i Air Force Dassault **Ouragans**, succeeded in damaging the destroyer's turbo generator, rudder and antiaircraft guns. Left without power and unable to steer, the *Ibrahim el Awal* surrendered to the **Israel**i destroyers. The **Egypt**ian destroyer was subsequently incorporated into the **Israel**i Navy and renamed **INS** *Haifa* **(K-38).**

## The Hedgehog-Abu Uwayulah operations

The village of **Abu Uwayulah** in the central Sinai served as the road center for the entire Sinai, and thus was a key **Israeli** target. To the east of **Abu Uwayulah** were several ridges that formed a natural defensive zone known to the **Israelis** as the "Hedgehog". Led by Colonel **Avraham Adan,** an **IDF** force entered the **al-Dayyiqa** and at dawn on 31 October attacked **Abu Uwayulah**. After an hour's fighting, **Abu Uwayulah** fell to the **IDF**. At the same time, another **IDF** battalion attacked the **Ruafa ridge.**

After taking **Abu Uwayulah, Adan** committed all of his forces against the **Ruafa ridge** of the "Hedgehog". **Adan** began a three-pronged attack with one armored force striking northeastern edge of **Ruafa**, a mixed infantry/armored force attacking the north edge and a feint attack from a neighboring knoll. During the evening attack on 31 October, a chaotic battle raged on **Ruafa** ridge with much **hand-to-hand fighting**. Through every **IDF** tank involved was destroyed, after a night's fighting, **Ruafa** had fallen to the **IDF**.

**Dayan**, who had grown impatient with the failure to storm the "Hedgehog", sacked the 10th Brigade's commander Colonel **Shmuel Golinda** and replaced him with Colonel **Israel Tal**. However, the ferocity of the **IDF** assault combined with rapidly dwindling stocks of water and ammunition caused **Colonel Mutawally** to order a general retreat from the "Hedgehog" on the evening of 1 November.

## The Gaza Strip operations

The city of **Rafah** was strategically important to **Israel** because control of that city would sever the **Gaza Strip** from the Sinai and provide a way to the main centers of the northern Sinai, **al-Arish and al-Qantarah.** Assigned to capture **Rafah** were 1st Infantry Brigade led by Colonel **Benjamin Givli** and 27th Armored Brigade commanded by Colonel **Haim Bar-Lev** of the **IDF**. In the morning of 1 November, **Israeli AMX-13s** encircled and took **Hills 34** and **36** At that point, General **al-Abd** ordered his forces to abandon their posts outside of **Rafah** and retreat into the city.

With **Rafah** more or less cut off and **Israeli** forces controlling the northern and eastern roads leading into the city, **Dayan** ordered the **AMX-13s** of the 27th Armored Brigade to strike west and take **al-Arish**. By this point, **Nasser** had ordered his forces to fall back towards the **Suez Canal**, so at first the Bar-Lev and his men met little resistance as they advanced across the northern Sinai. **Three hours later, the Israelis took Rafah. On 2 November, Bar-Lev's forces took al-Arish.**

Meanwhile, the **IDF** attacked the **Egypt**ian defenses outside of **Gaza City** late on 1 November. After breaking through the **Egypt**ian lines, the **Israeli** tanks headed into **Gaza City**. Joined by infantry, the armor attacked the **al-Muntar** fortress outside of **Gaza City**, **killing or capturing 3,500 Egyptian National Guard troops.** By noon of 2 November, there was no more **Egypt**ian opposition in the **Gaza City** area. On 3 November, the **IDF** attacked **Egypt**ian and Palestinian forces at **Khan Yunis**. After a fierce battle, the **Israeli** 37th Armored Brigade's Sherman tanks broke through the heavily fortified lines outside of **Khan Yunis** held by the 86th Palestinian Brigade.

After some street-fighting with **Egypt**ian soldiers and **Palestinian Fedayeen, Khan Yunis** fell to the **Israeli**s. There are claims that after taking **Khan Yunis**, the **IDF** committed a massacre. In both **Gaza City** and **Khan Yunis**, street-fighting led to the deaths of **"dozens, perhaps hundreds, of non-combatants"**. By noon of 3 November, the **Israel**is had control of almost the entire **Gaza Strip** save for a few isolated strongpoints, which were soon attacked and taken. The UN estimated that in total **447 to 550 Palestinian civilians were killed** by **Israel**i troops during the first weeks of **Israel**i occupation of the strip.

## *The Sharm el-Sheikh operations*

By 3 November, with the **IDF** having successfully taken the **Gaza Strip**, Arish, the **Hedgehog**, and **Mitla Pass, Sharm el-Sheikh** was the last **Israel**i objective The main difficulty faced by Colonel **Abraham Yoffe's** 9th Infantry Brigade was logistical. There were no good roads linking **Ras an-Naqb** to **Sharm el-Sheikh**. After taking the border town of **Ras an-Naqb** on 30 October, Daylan ordered **Yoffe** to wait until air superiority was ensured. **Yoffe** set out for **Sharm el-Sheikh** on 2 November, and his major obstacles were the terrain and vehicle break-down. **Israel**i Navy ships provided support to the 9th Division during its advance.

After numerous skirmishes on the outskirts of **Sharm el-Sheikh**, H ordered an attack on the port around midnight on 4 November. After four hours of heavy fighting, **Yoffe** ordered his men to retreat. On the morning of 5 November, **Israel**i forces launched a massive artillery barrage and napalm strikes against **Egypt**ian forces defending **Sharm el-Sheikh**. At 9:30 am on 5 November, the **Egypt**ian commander, Colonel **Raouf Mahfouz Zaki**, surrendered **Sharm el-Sheikh**.

## Anglo-French task force

To support the invasion, large air forces had been deployed to Cyprus and Malta by **Britain** and **France** and many aircraft carriers were deployed.

## *Revise: Phases I and II*

In the morning of 30 October **Britain** and **France** sent ultimatums to **Egypt** and **Israel**. They initiated **Operation Musketeer** on 31 October, with a bombing campaign. **Nasser responded by sinking all 40 ships present in the canal closing it to all shipping** – shipping would not move again until early 1957. Not until late on October 31, did **Nasser** disregard **Amer's** rosy assessment and ordered his forces to disengage in the Sinai and to retreat back to the **Canal Zone** to face the expected Anglo-French invasion.

**Eden** and **Mollet** ordered **Phase I** of **Operation Revise** to begin 13 hours after the Anglo-French ultimatum. British bombers based in Cyprus and Malta took off to Cairo with the aim of destroying Cairo airport, only to be personally ordered back by **Eden** when he learned that American civilians were being evacuated at Cairo airport.

Starting on the morning of 1 November, carrier-based **de Havilland Sea Venoms, Chance-Vought Corsairs and Hawker Sea Hawks** began a series of daytime strikes on **Egypt**. By the night of 1 November the **Egyptian Air Force had lost 200 planes**. With the destruction of **Egypt's** air force, **Keightley** ordered the beginning of **Revise Phase II**. As part of **Revise Phase II,** a wide-ranging interdiction campaign began. On 3 November **F4U-7 Corsairs** from the 14.F and 15.F *Aéronavale* taking off from the French carriers *Arromanches* and *La Fayette*, attacked the aerodrome at Cairo. The very aggressive French **General Beaufre** suggested at once that Anglo-

French forces seize the **Canal Zone** with airborne landings instead of waiting the planned ten days for **Revise** II to be worked through.

## *Telescope Modified: the Paratroops land*

On late 5 November, an advance element of the 3rd Battalion of the British Parachute Regiment dropped on **El Gamil Airfield**, a narrow strip of land, led by **Brigadier M.A.H. Butler** The "**Red Devils**" could not return **Egypt**ian fire while landing, but once the paratroopers landed, they used their Sten guns, three-inch mortars and anti-tank weapons with great effect.

Having taken the airfield with a dozen casualties, the remainder of the battalion flew in by helicopter. The Battalion then secured the area around the airfield. The British forces moved up towards **Port Said** with air support before digging in at 13:00 to hold until the beach assault. **Egypt**ian resistance varied, with some positions fighting back until destroyed, while others were abandoned with little resistance. The French paratroopers stormed and took **Port Said's** waterworks that morning, an important objective to control in a city in the desert.

**Chateau-Jobert** followed up this success by beginning an attack on **Port Fuad**. During the fighting in the **Canal Zone**, the French paratroopers often practiced their "**no-prisoners'**" **code and executed Egyptian POWs**. The **Egypt**ian commander at Port Said, General **Salahedin Moguy** then proposed a truce. His offer was taken up, and in the ensuring meeting with General **Butler, Chateau-Jobert** and **General Massu**, was offered the terms of surrendering the city and marching his men to the Gamil airfield to taken off to POW camps in Cyprus.

## *The Royal Marines come ashore at Port Said*

At first light on 6 November, commandos of No. 42 and **40 Commando Royal Marines** stormed the beaches, using landing craft of **World War II** vintage (Landing Craft Assault and Landing Vehicle Tracked). The battle group standing offshore opened fire, giving covering fire for the landings and causing considerable damage to the **Egypt**ian batteries and gun emplacements. The town of Port Said sustained great damage and was seen to be alight. Upon entering downtown **Port Said**, the Marines became engaged in fierce urban combat as the **Egypt**ians used the Casino Palace Hotel and other strongpoints as fortresses.

**Nasser** proclaimed the **Suez** War to be a "**people's war**". As such, **Egypt**ian troops were ordered to don civilian clothes while guns were freely handed out to **Egypt**ian civilians. From **Nasser's** point of view, a "**people's war**" presented the British and French with an insolvable dilemma. If the Allies reacted cautiously to the "**people's war**", than that would result in Allied forces becoming bogged down by sniper attacks, who had the advantage of attacking "**...with near impunity by hiding among crowds of apparent non-combatants**". These tactics worked especially well against the British. British leaders, especially **Eden** and the **First Sea Lord Admiral Sir Louis Mountbatten** were afraid of being labeled "**murderers and baby killers**", and sincerely attempted to limit **Egypt**ian civilian deaths.

At **Port Said**, the heavy fighting in the streets and the resulting fires destroyed much of the city, killing thousands of civilians. While clearing **Port Fouad**, the Ier *Regiment Etranger Parachutiste* killed 100 **Egypt**ians without losing a man in return. In total, 10 French soldiers were killed and 30 injured during the landing and the subsequent battles. The helicopter borne assault of 45 Commando was the first time helicopters were used by UK Forces to lift men directly into a combat zone.

Especially fierce fighting took place at the **Port Said's Customs House** and **Navy House**. The **Egypt**ians destroyed **Port Said's** Inner Harbor, which forced the British to improvise and use the **Fishing Harbor** to land their forces. Rather than focusing on breaking out to take **al-Qantarah**, the Royal Marines became bogged down in clearing every building in **Port Said** of snipers. The Centurions of the **Royal Tank Regiment** supported by the paratroopers of 2 RPC began a slow advance down to **al-Qantarah** on the night of 6 November.

## Casualties

Total British dead were 16, with 96 wounded. French casualties stood at 10 dead and 33 wounded. **The Israeli losses were 177 dead and 899 wounded**. The number of **Egypt**ians killed was **"never reliably established"**. **Egypt**ian casualties to the **Israel**i invasion were estimated at **1,000-3,000 dead and 4,000 wounded**, while losses to the Anglo-French operation were estimated at 650 dead and 900 wounded.

## End of hostilities
### Anti-war protests in Britain

Protests against the war occurred in **Britain** after the invasion began. The angry, passionate, much-watched debates about the **Suez war** on *Free Speech* mirrored the divided public response to the war.

> **The bitter division in public opinion provoked by the British intervention in the Middle East has already had one disastrous consequence. It has deflected popular attention from the far more important struggle in Hungary. Hungary has appealed to the West...It is the first, and perhaps will prove the only opportunity to reverse the calamitous decisions of Yalta.**

According to public opinion polls at the time, 37% of the British people supported the war while 44% were opposed. Inspired by Bevan's speech, the crowd at Trafalgar Square then marched on 10 Downing Street chanting "**Eden Must Go!**", and attempted to storm the Prime Minister's residence.

## International reaction

Along with the **Suez** crisis, the United States was also dealing with the near-simultaneous **Hungarian Revolution**. While **Israel** refused to withdraw its troops from the **Gaza Strip** and **Sharm el-Sheikh**, **Eisenhower** declared, "**We must not allow Europe to go flat on its back for the want of oil.**" Senate Majority Leader **Lyndon B. Johnson** and minority leader **William Knowland** objected to American pressure on **Israel**. Johnson told the Secretary of State **John Foster Dulles** that he wanted him to oppose "**with all its skill**" any attempt to apply sanctions on **Israel**.

**Eisenhower** was "**insistent on applying economic sanctions**" to the extent of cutting off private American assistance to **Israel** which was estimated to be over $100 million a year. In the early hours of 2 November, the **General Assembly** adopted the United States' proposal for **Resolution**

**997 (ES-I);** the vote was 64 in favor and 5 opposed (Australia, New Zealand, **Britain**, **France**, and **Israel**) with 6 abstentions. It called for an immediate ceasefire, the withdrawal of all forces behind the armistice lines, an arms embargo, and the reopening of the **Suez Canal**, which was now blocked.

Nehru achieved his objective of protecting **Egypt**'s sovereignty and **Nasser**'s honor; the **Suez** War ended in **Britain**'s humiliation and **Eden** later resigned. **Britain** and **France** agreed to withdraw from **Egypt** within a week; **Israel did not**. Meanwhile on 7 November in **Israel**, **David Ben-Gurion** addressed the Knesset in a victory speech that would set **Israel** on a collision course with the UN, the US and others. He declared a great victory and that the 1949 armistice agreement with **Egypt** was dead and buried.

Later on 7 November in New York, the emergency session passed **Resolution 1002**, again calling for the immediate withdrawal of **Israel**i troops to behind the armistice lines, and for the immediate withdrawal of British and French troops from **Egypt**ian territory. **Eisenhower** immediately ordered the **U-2s** into action over Syria and **Israel** to search for any Soviet air forces on Syrian bases, so the British and French could destroy them. **Bulganin** accused **Ben-Gurion** of supporting European colonialism, and **Mollet** of hypocrisy for leading a socialist government while pursuing a right-wing foreign policy.

## Cease fire

The British government faced political and economic pressure. **Sir Anthony Eden**, the British Prime Minister, announced a cease fire on 6 November, warning neither **France** nor **Israel** beforehand. The **Israel**is refused to host any UN force on **Israel**i controlled territory and left the Sinai in March, 1957.

## Aftermath

The imposed end to the crisis signaled the definitive weakening of the United Kingdom and **France** as global powers. Middle-sized powers were no longer free to act independently. **Nasser**'s standing in the Arab world was greatly improved, with his stance helping to promote pan-Arabism. The **Suez** Crisis may have directly led to the **14 July Revolution in Iraq**. **King Faisal II** and Prime Minister **Nuri-as-Said** were murdered within two years of their advice to **Eden** to "**hit Nasser hard and quickly**".

The fight over the canal also laid the groundwork for the **Six Day War in 1967** due to the lack of a peace settlement following the 1956 war. The Soviets got away with their violent suppression of the rebellion in Hungary, and were able to pose at the **United Nations** as a defender of small powers against imperialism.

> **The fact that the Eisenhower administration itself applied crushing economic pressure to the British and French to disengage from Suez, and that it subsequently forced an Israeli pull-back from the Sinai as well-all of this, one might thought, would won the United States the lasting gratitude of Nasser, the Egyptians and the Arab world. Instead, the Americans lost influence in the Middle East as a result of Suez, while the Russians gained it.**

Nikita Khrushchev's much publicized threat expressed through letters written by **Nikolai Bulganin** to begin rocket attacks on November 5 on **Britain**, **France** and **Israel** if they did not withdraw from **Egypt** was widely believed at the time to have forced a ceasefire. It was **Khrushchev**, not **Eisenhower**, whom **Nasser** publicly thanked as **Egypt**'s savior and special friend.

Thus began a long period of crises starting with the **Berlin crisis** of 1958 and culminating in the **Cuban Missile Crisis** of 1962, where **Khrushchev** threatened to start **World War III** if he did not get his way. The **Eisenhower** Doctrine was regarded by **Nasser** as a heavy-handed American attempt to dominate the Middle East (a region that **Nasser** believed he ought to dominate), and led him to swinging behind the **Soviet Union** as the best counter-weight.

## Egypt

In October 1956, when the **Suez** Crisis erupted, 1,000 Jews were arrested and 500 Jewish businesses were seized by the government. A statement branding the Jews as **"Zionists and enemies of the state"** was read out in the mosques of Cairo and Alexandria. Jewish bank accounts were confiscated and many Jews lost their jobs. Lawyers, engineers, doctors and teachers were not allowed to work in their professions. Thousands of Jews were ordered to leave the country. They were allowed to take only one suitcase and a small sum of cash and forced to sign declarations **"donating"** their property to the **Egypt**ian government.

By 1957 the Jewish population of **Egypt** had fallen to 15,000. Despite the **Egypt**ian defeat, **Nasser** emerged as an enhanced hero in the Arab world. Many Arabs saw **Nasser** as the conqueror of European colonialism and Zionism, simply because **Britain**, **France** and **Israel** left the Sinai and the northern **Canal Zone**". **Eisenhower** himself later stated privately that he regretted his opposition to the combined **British, French** and **Israel**i response to the Crisis. After retiring from office **Eisenhower** came to see the **Suez** Crisis as perhaps his biggest foreign policy mistake.

### France

**Franco-American ties never recovered from the Suez crisis.** Paris considered U.S. betrayal of the French war effort in Indochina at **Dien Bien Phu** in 1954. From the point of view of **General de Gaulle**, the **Suez** events demonstrated to **France** that it could not rely on its allies. The damage to the ties between Paris and Washington D.C.

**"culminated in President de Gaulle's 1966 decision to withdraw from the military integration of NATO."** According to the protocol of Sèvres agreements, **France secretly transmitted parts of its own atomic technology to Israel, including a detonator.**

### Israel

Israel emerged victorious from the war. Its forces executed a military campaign that leading military theorist **B.H. Liddell Hart** termed **"brilliant."** The **Israel** Defense Forces gained confidence from the campaign. **David Ben-Gurion**, reading on 16 November that 90,000 British and French troops had been involved in the **Suez** affair, wrote in his diary, **'If they had only appointed a commander of ours over this force, Nasser would have been destroyed in two days.'**

Israel escaped the political humiliation that befell **Britain** and **France** following their swift, forced withdrawal. In October 1965 **Eisenhower** told Jewish fundraiser and Republican party supporter **Max M. Fisher** that he greatly regretted forcing **Israel** to withdraw from the Sinai peninsula.

## Other parties

After **Suez, Cyprus, Aden** and **Iraq** became the main bases for the British in the region while the French concentrated their forces at **Bizerte** and **Beirut**. **UNEF** was placed in the Sinai (on **Egypt**ian territory only) with the express purpose of maintaining the cease-fire. The Soviets' burgeoning influence in the Middle East, although it was not to last, included acquiring Mediterranean bases, introducing multipurpose projects, supporting the budding Palestinian liberation movement and penetrating the Arab countries.

## Commanders and leaders

| | |
|---|---|
| Moshe **Dayan** | Abdel Hakim Amer |
| Ariel **Sharon** | Saadedden Mutawally |
| Rafael Eitan | Sami Yassa |
| Haim Bar-Lev | Jaafar al-Abd |
| Avraham **Yoffe** | Salahedin Moguy |
| **Israel** Tal | Raouf Mahfouz Zaki |
| Mordechai Gur | |
| Avraham Adan | |

## Casualties and losses

| Israel: | Egypt: |
|---|---|
| 231 killed | 1,650 – 3,000 |
| 899 wounded | killed |
| 4 captured | 1,000 civilians |
| | Killed |
| | 4,900 wounded |

# Tabernacle

According to the Hebrew Bible, the **Tabernacle** (Hebrew, *mishkān,* meaning **"residence"** or **"dwelling place"**), also known as the **Tent of the Congregation** was the portable earthly dwelling place of **Yahweh** (the God of Israel) used by the Israelites from the **Exodus** until the conquest of **Canaan. Moses** was instructed at **Mount Sinai** to construct and transport the **Tabernacle** with the Israelites on their journey through the wilderness and their subsequent conquest of the **Promised Land. After 440 years, Solomon's Temple in Jerusalem superseded it as the dwelling-place of God.**

The main source describing the **Tabernacle** is the biblical **Book of Exodus,** specifically **Exodus 25–31 and 35–40.** Those passages describe an inner sanctuary, the **Holy of Holies,** created by the veil suspended by four pillars. This sanctuary contained the **Ark of the Covenant,** with its cherubim-covered mercy seat. Traditional scholars contend that it describes an actual **Tabernacle** used in the time of **Moses** and thereafter.

## Description

Historical criticism has identified two accounts of the **Tabernacle** in **Exodus**, a briefer **Elohist** account and a longer Priestly one. Traditional scholars believe the briefer account describes a different structure, perhaps **Moses'** personal tent.

### Elohist account

**Exodus 33:7–10** refers to **"the Tabernacle of the congregation"** (in some translations, such as the **King James Version**) or **"the tent of meeting"** (in most modern translations), which was set up outside of camp with the **"cloudy pillar"** visible at its door. The people directed their worship toward this center. Attributes this description to the **Elohist** source (E), which is believed to have been written about **850 BCE or later.**

### Priestly account

The more detailed description of a **Tabernacle,** located in **Exodus chapters 25–27 and Exodus chapters 35–40,** refers to an inner shrine (the most holy place) housing the ark and an outer chamber (holy place), with a **six-branch seven-lamp menorah** (lampstand), table for showbread, and altar of incense. An enclosure containing the sacrificial altar and bronze laver for the priests to wash surrounded these chambers. This view is based on **Exodus 36, 37, 38** and **39** that describe in full detail how the actual **construction of the Tabernacle took place during the time of Moses.**

## Tent of the Presence

According to **Exodus 33:7-11**, this tent was for communion with **Yahweh**, to receive oracles and to understand the divine will. The people's elders were the subject of a remarkable prophetic event at the site of this tent in **Numbers 11:24-30.**

## Builders

In **Exodus 31**, the main builder and maker of the priestly vestments is specified as **Bezalel**, son of **Uri son of Hur** of the tribe of **Judah**, who was assisted by **Oholiab** and a number of skilled artisans.

## Holy of Holies

Beyond this curtain was the cube-shaped inner room, the *Qŏḏeš HaQŏḏāšîm* (Holy of Holies). This area housed the **Ark of the Covenant**, inside which were the two stone tablets brought down from **Mount Sinai** by **Moses** on which were written the **Ten Commandments**, a golden urn holding the *manna*, and Aaron's rod which had budded and borne ripe almonds. **(Exodus 16:33–34, Numbers 17:1–11, Deuteronomy 10:1–5; Hebrews 9:2–5)**

## Restrictions

There is a strict set of rules to be followed for transporting the **Tabernacle** laid out in the Hebrew Bible. For example: **"You must put the Levites in charge of the Tabernacle of the Covenant, along with its furnishings and equipment. They must carry the Tabernacle and its equipment as you travel, and they must care for it and camp around it. Whenever the Tabernacle is moved, the Levites will take it down and set it up again. Anyone else who goes too near the Tabernacle will be executed."**
*— Numbers 1:48-51 NLT*

## Rituals / *Korban, Animal sacrifice § Judaism, and Holocaust (sacrifice)*

Twice a day, a priest would stand in front of the golden prayer altar and burn fragrant incense. Other procedures were also carried out in the **Tabernacle**:

- The daily meal offering: **Leviticus 6:8–30**
- Guilt offerings and peace offerings: **Leviticus 7**
- Ceremony of Ordination: **Leviticus 8**
- Octave of Ordination: **Leviticus 9**
- Yom Kippur: **Leviticus 16**
- Ordeal of the bitter water for suspected adulteresses: **Numbers 5:11-29**
- Dedication of Nazirites: **Numbers 6:1-21**
- Preparation of the ashes of a red heifer for the water of purification: **Numbers 19**

An Israelite healed of *tzaraath* would be presented by the priest who had confirmed his healing **"at the door of the Tabernacle of meeting"**, and a woman healed of prolonged menstruation would present her offering (two turtledoves or two young pigeons) to the priest **"at the door of the Tabernacle of meeting"**. It was at the door of the **Tabernacle** that the community wept in sorrow when all the chiefs of the people were impaled and the men who had joined in worship to the **Baal of Peor were killed on God's orders.**

## Subsequent history

During the conquest of **Canaan**, the main Israelite camp was at **Gilgal (Joshua 4:19; 5:8–10)** and the **Tabernacle** was probably erected within the camp: **Joshua 10:43ESV "...and returned into the camp"** (*see* **Numbers 1:52–2:34 "...they shall camp facing the tent of meeting on every side").** After the conquest and division of the land among the tribes, the **Tabernacle** was moved to **Shiloh** in Ephraimite territory (Joshua's tribe) to avoid disputes among the other tribes **(Joshua 18:1; 19:51; 22:9; Psalm 78:60).** It remained there during the 300-year period of the biblical judges (the rules of the individual judges **total about 350 years [1 Kings 6:1; Acts 13:20],** but most ruled regionally and some terms overlapped).

After the **Ark** was captured by the Philistines, **King Saul** moved the **Tabernacle** to Nob, near his home town of Gibeah, but after he massacred the priests there **(1 Samuel 21–22)**, it was moved to Gibeon, a Yahwist hill-shrine **(1 Chronicles 16:39; 21:29; 2 Chronicles 1:2–6, 13)**. Just prior to David's moving the ark to Jerusalem, the ark was located in **Kiriath-Jearim (1 Chronicles 13:5–6).**

The **Ark** was eventually brought to Jerusalem, where it was placed **"inside the tent David had pitched for it" (2 Samuel 6:17; 1 Chronicles 15:1),** not in the **Tabernacle**, which remained at Gibeon. The altar of the **Tabernacle** at **Gibeon** was used for sacrificial worship **(1 Chronicles 16:39; 21:29; 1 Kings 3:2–4),** until **Solomon** finally brought the structure and its furnishings to Jerusalem to furnish and dedicate the Temple. **(1 Kings 8:4).**

## Relationship to the golden calf

Some rabbis have commented on the proximity of the narrative of the **Tabernacle** with that of the episode known as the sin of the golden calf recounted in **Exodus 32:1-6.** Maimonides asserts that the **Tabernacle** and its accoutrements, such as the golden **Ark of the Covenant** and the golden Menorah were meant as **"alternates"** to the human weakness and needs for physical idols as seen in the golden calf episode.

## Blueprint for synagogues

Every synagogue has at its front an ark, *aron kodesh*, containing the Torah scrolls, comparable to the **Ark of the Covenant** which contained the tablets with **Ten Commandments**. This is the holiest spot in a synagogue, equivalent to the **Holy of Holies. (Numbers 6:22–27).**

## New Testament references

The **Tabernacle** is mentioned several times in the **Epistle to the Hebrews** in the New Testament. For example, according to **Hebrews 8:2–5 and 9:2–26** Jesus serves as the true climactic high priest in heaven, the true **Tabernacle**, to which its counterpart on earth was a symbol and foreshadow of what was to come (**Hebrews 8:5**).

# The Talmud

The **Talmud**; Hebre: *talmud* **"instruction, learning", "teach, study"**) is a central text of Rabbinic Judaism. It is also traditionally referred to as *Shas*, a Hebrew abbreviation of *shisha sedarim*, the **"six orders",** a reference to the six orders of the **Mishnah**. The term "**Talmud**" normally refers to the collection of writings named specifically the **Babylonian Talmud (*Talmud Bavli*)**, although there is also an earlier collection known as the **Jerusalem Talmud**, or **Palestinian Talmud (*Talmud Yerushalmi*).**

The **Talmud** has two components: the **Mishnah** (Hebrew: c. 200 CE), a written compendium of Rabbinic Judaism's **Oral Torah** (**Talmud** translates literally as **"instruction"** in Hebrew); and the **Gemara** (c. 500CE), an elucidation of the **Mishnah** and related Tannaitic writings that often ventures onto other subjects and expounds broadly on the **Hebrew Bible**.

The entire **Talmud** consists of **63 tractates, and in standard print are over 6,200 pages long**. It is written in Tannaitic Hebrew and **Jewish Babylonian Aramaic** and contains the teachings and opinions of thousands of rabbis (dating from before the Common Era through the fifth century CE) on a variety of subjects, including **Halakha** (law), Jewish ethics, philosophy, customs, history, lore and many other topics. The **Talmud** is the basis for all codes of Jewish law, and is widely quoted in rabbinic literature.

## History

**Originally, Jewish scholarship was oral**. Rabbis expounded and debated the **Torah** (the written **Torah** expressed in the **Hebrew Bible**) and discussed the **Tanakh** without the benefit of written works (other than the Biblical books themselves). This situation changed drastically, mainly as the result of the destruction of the Jewish commonwealth and the **Second Temple in the year 70 CE** and the consequent upheaval of Jewish social and legal norms. As the Rabbis were required to face a new reality – mainly Judaism without a Temple, it is during this period that rabbinic discourse began to be recorded in writing.

An alternative form, organized by subject matter instead of by biblical verse, became dominant about the year 200 CE, when **Rabbi Judah the Prince** redacted the **Mishnah**. The most famous two were the **School of Shammai and the School of Hillel**. In general, all valid opinions, even the non-normative ones, were recorded in the **Talmud**.

## Structure

General subject matter are divided into 60 or 63 tractates (**masekhtot**; singular: *masekhtot*) of more focused subject compilations, though not all tractates have **Gemara**. Each tractate is divided into chapters (*perakim*; singular: *perek*), 517 in total, that are both numbered according to the Hebrew alphabet and given names, usually using the first one or two words in the first **Mishnah**.

## Mishnah

The *Mishnah* is a compilation of legal opinions and debates. Statements in the **Mishnah** are typically terse, recording brief opinions of the rabbis debating a subject; or recording only an unattributed ruling, apparently representing a consensus view.

The rabbis recorded in the **Mishnah** are known as the **Tannaim**. Since it sequences its laws by subject matter instead of by biblical context, the **Mishnah** discusses individual subjects more thoroughly than the **Midrash**. The **Mishnah**'s topical organization thus became the framework of the **Talmud** as a whole.

## Gemara

In the three centuries following the redaction of the **Mishnah**, rabbis in Israel and Babylonia analyzed, debated, and discussed that work. These discussions form the **Gemara**. *Gemara* means **"completion"** (from the Hebrew *gamar*: **"to complete"**) or **"learning"** (from the Aramaic: **"study"**). The **Gemara** mainly focuses on elucidating and elaborating the opinions of the Tannaim. **The rabbis of the Gemara are known as Amoraim.**

Much of the **Gemara** consists of legal analysis. The starting point for the analysis is usually a legal statement found in a **Mishnah**. Another important function of **Gemara** is to identify the correct Biblical basis for a given law presented in the **Mishnah** and the logical process connecting one with the other: this activity was known as *talmud* long before the existence of the "**Talmud**" as a text.

### Halakha and Aggadah

The **Talmud** is a wide-ranging document that touches on a great many subjects. Traditionally **Talmud**ic statements are classified into two broad categories, *halakhic* and *aggadic* statement. Halakhic statements directly relate to questions of Jewish law and practice (**Halakha**). **Aggadic** statements are not legally related, but rather are exegetical, homiletical, ethical, or historical in nature.

## Bavli and Yerushalmi

The older compilation is called the Jerusalem **Talmud** or the *Talmud Yerushalmi*. It was compiled in the 4th century CE in Galilee. The **Babylonian Talmud** was compiled about the year 500, although it continued to be edited later. The word "**Talmud**", when used without qualification, usually refers to the **Babylonian Talmud**.

## *Talmud Yerushalmi* (Jerusalem Talmud)

The **Jerusalem Talmud**, also known as the **Palestinian Talmud**, or **Talmuda de-Eretz Yisrael** (**Talmud** of the Land of Israel), was one of the two compilations of Jewish religious teachings and commentary that was transmitted orally for centuries prior to its compilation by Jewish scholars in the **L** and of **Israel**. It is written largely in Jewish **Palestinian Aramaic**

By this time Christianity had become the state religion of the **Roman Empire** and Jerusalem the holy city of Christendom. In 325, **Constantine the Great,** the first Christian emperor, said **"let us then have nothing in common with the detestable Jewish crowd."** This policy made a Jew an outcast and pauper.

The apparent cessation of work on the **Jerusalem Talmud** in the 5th century has been associated with the decision of **Theodosius II in 425** to sup press the **Patriarchate** and put an end to the practice of **semikhah**, formal scholarly ordination.

Despite its incomplete state, the Jerusalem **Talmud** remains an indispensable source of knowledge of the development of the **Jewish Law** in the **Holy Land**.

## Babylonian Talmud

The **Babylonian Talmud** (*Talmud Bavli*) consists of documents compiled over the period of Late Antiquity ($3^{rd}$ to $5^{th}$ centuries). During this time the most important of the Jewish centers in Mesopotamia, a region called "**Babylonia**" in Jewish sources and later known as Iraq, were **Nehardea, Nisibis** (modern Nusaybin), **Mahoza** (**al-Mada'in**, just to the south of what is now Baghdad).

**Pumbedita** (near present-day al Anbar Governorate), and the **Sura Academy**, probably located about 60 km south of Baghdad. The Babylonian **Talmud** comprises the **Mishnah** and the **Babylonian Gemara,** the latter representing the culmination of more than 300 years of analysis of the **Mishnah** in the **Talmud**ic Academies in Babylonia.

## Comparison of style and subject matter

The language of the **Jerusalem Talmud** is a western Aramaic dialect, which differs from the form of Aramaic in the **Babylonian Talmud**.

Neither the Jerusalem nor the Babylonian **Talmud** covers the entire **Mishnah**: for example, a **Babylonian Gemara** exists only for 37 out of the 63 tractates of the **Mishnah**. The influence of the **Babylonian Talmud** has been far greater than that of the *Yerushalmi*. According to **Maimonides** (whose life began almost a hundred years after the end of the **Gaonic era**), all Jewish communities during the Gaonic era formally accepted the **Babylonian Talmud** as binding upon themselves.

## Geonim

The earliest **Talmud** commentaries were written by the **Geonim** (c. 800 – 1000, CE) in Babylonia. After the death of **Hai Gaon**, however, the center of **Talmud** scholarship shifts to Europe and North Africa.

## Commentaries

The **Talmud** is often cryptic and difficult to understand. Its language contains many Greek and Persian words that became obscure over time. A major area of **Talmud**ic scholarship developed to explain these passages and words. Another important work is the *Sefer ha-Mafteah* (**Book of the Key**) by **Nissim Gaon**, which contains a preface explaining the different forms of **Talmud**ic argumentation. **Rabbi Nathan b. Jechiel** created a lexicon called the *Arukh* the $11^{th}$ century to help translate difficult words.

By far the best known commentary on the **Babylonian Talmud** is that of **Rashi (Rabbi Solomon ben Isaac, 1040-1105)**. The commentary is comprehensive, covering almost the entire **Talmud**. Medieval Ashkenazic Jewry produced another major commentary known as **Tosafot ("additions" or "supplements")**. The *Tosafot* are collected commentaries by various medieval Ashkenazic Rabbis on the **Talmud (known as *Tosafists* or Ba'alei *Tosafot*)**. Unlike **Rashi**, the *Tosafot* is not a running commentary, but rather comments on selected matters.

Over time, the approach of the **Tosafists** spread to other Jewish communities, particularly those in Spain. Among these are the commentaries of **Nachmanides (Ramban), Solomon ben Adret (Rashba), Yom Tov of Seville (Ritva) and Nissim of Gerona (Ran).** Two of the most significant of these are the **Yad Ramah** by **Rabbi Meir Abulafia** and *Bet Habechirah* by **Rabbi Menahem haMeiri**, commonly referred to as "Meiri".

## Pilpul

During the 15th and 16th centuries, a new intensive form of **Talmud** study arose. Complicated logical arguments were used to explain minor points of contradiction within the **Talmud**. The term *pilpul* was applied to this type of study. **Pilpul** practitioners posited that the **Talmud** could contain no redundancy or contradiction whatsoever.

## Role in Judaism

The **Talmud** represents the written record of an oral tradition. It became the basis for many rabbinic legal codes and customs, most importantly for the **Mishneh Torah** and for the **Shulchan Aruch.** Orthodox and, to a lesser extent.

## Karaism

Another movement that rejected the oral **Torah** was **Karaism**. It arose within two centuries of the completion of the **Talmud**. **Karaism** developed as a reaction against the **Talmud**ic Judaism of Babylonia. The central concept of **Karaism** is the rejection of the **Oral Torah**, as embodied in the **Talmud**, in favor of a strict adherence to the **Written Torah** only. This opposes the fundamental Rabbinic concept that **the Oral Torah was given to Moses on Mount Sinai together with the Written Torah.**

## Reform Judaism

The rise of Reform Judaism during the 19th century saw more questioning of the authority of the **Talmud**. Reform Jews saw the **Talmud** as a product of late antiquity, having relevance merely as a historical document.

## Present day

Orthodox Judaism continues to stress the importance of **Talmud** study as a central component of Yeshiva curriculum, in particular for those training to become Rabbis.

## Conservative Judaism:

Conservative Judaism similarly emphasizes the study of **Talmud** within its religious and rabbinic education. Generally, however, Conservative Jews study the **Talmud** as a historical source-text for **Halakha.**

# Tanakh

The **Tanakh,** also *Tenakh, Tenak, Tanach*), or *Mikra* or **Hebrew Bible** is the canonical collection of Jewish texts, which is also a textual source for the **Christian Old Testament**. These texts are composed mainly in Biblical Hebrew, with some passages in **Biblical Aramaic** (in the books of **Daniel, Ezra** and a few others). The traditional Hebrew text is known as the **Masoretic Text. The Tanakh consists of twenty-four books.** The books of the **Tanakh** were passed on by each generation, and according to rabbinic tradition were accompanied by an oral tradition, called the **Oral Torah.**

## *Development of the Hebrew Bible canon*

There is no scholarly consensus as to when the **Hebrew Bible** canon was fixed: some scholars argue that it was fixed by the **Hasmonean Dynasty**, while others argue it was not fixed until the second century CE or even later. According to the **Talmud**, much of the **Tanakh** was compiled by the men of the **Great Assembly (*Anshei Knesset HaGedolah*),** a task completed in 450 BCE, and it has remained unchanged ever since. The **twenty-four book canon** is mentioned in the **Midrash Koheleth 12:12**: *Whoever brings together in his house more than twenty four books brings confusion.*

## Language and pronunciation

During the early Middle Ages scholars known as the **Masoretes** created a single formalized system of vocalization. This was chiefly done by **Aaron ben Moses ben Asher,** in the **Tiberias School**, based on the oral tradition for reading the **Tanakh**, hence the name **Tiberian Vocalization.**

It also included some innovations of **Ben Naftali** and the Babylonian exiles. Some Orthodox Jews hold the pronunciation and cantillation to derive from the revelation at Sinai. The combination of a text (***Mikra***), pronunciation (***Niqqud***) and cantillation (***Te`amim***) enable the reader to understand both the simple meaning and the nuances in sentence flow of the text.

## Books of the Tanakh

**The Tanakh consists of twenty-four books**: it counts as one book each **Samuel, Kings, Chronicles** and **Ezra–Nehemiah** and counts the **Twelve Minor Prophet**s as a single book. In Hebrew, the books are often referred to by their prominent first word(s).

## Torah

The Torah (literally **"teaching"**), also known as the **Pentateuch**, or as the **"Five Books of Moses"**. Printed versions (rather than scrolls) of the Torah are often called *Chamisha Chumshei Torah.*

("five fifth-sections of the Torah"), and informally a *Chumash*.

- Bereshit (literally **"In the beginning"**)—Genesis
- Shemot (literally **"Names"**)—Exodus
- Vayikra (literally "**And He called**")—Leviticus
- Bəmidbar (literally "**In the desert** ")—Numbers
- Devarim (literally "**Things"** or "**Words**")—Deuteronomy

## Nevi'im

*Nevi'im* (Hebrew: *Nəḇî'îm,* "**Prophets**") is the second main division of the **Tanakh**, between the **Torah** and **Ketuvim**. It contains two sub-groups, the Former Prophets (*Nevi'im Rishonim,* the narrative books of **Joshua, Judges, Samuel** and **Kings**) and the **Latter Prophets** (*Nevi'im Aharonim,* the books of **Isaiah, Jeremiah** and **Ezekiel** and the **Twelve Minor Prophets**). These three books are also the only ones in **Tanakh** with a special system of cantillation notes that are designed to emphasize parallel sticks within verses. However, the beginning and end of the book of Job are in the normal prose system.

## Five scrolls (*Hamesh Megillot*)

The five relatively short books of the Song of Songs, the Book of Ruth, the Book of Lamentations, Ecclesiastes and the Book of Esther are collectively known as the *Hamesh Megillot* (Five Megillot).

The Five Megillot (*Hamesh Megillot*). These books are read aloud in the synagogue on particular occasions, the occasion listed below in parenthesis.

- **Shir Hashīrīm** (Song of Songs) or (Song of Solomon) (Passover)
- **Ruth** (Book of Ruth) (Shavuot)
- **Eikhah** (Lamentations) (Tisha B'Av)
- **Koheleth** (Ecclesiastes) (Sukkot)
- **Ester** (Book of Esther) (Purim)

## Other books

- **Daniel** (Book of Daniel)
- **'Ezra** (Book of Ezra—Book of Nehemiah)
- **Divrei ha-Yamim** (Chronicles)

The Jewish textual tradition never finalized the order of the books in **Ketuvim**. The **Babylonian Talmud** (Bava Batra 14b — 15a) gives their order as **Ruth, Psalms, Job, Proverbs, Ecclesiastes, Song of Solomon, Lamentations of Jeremiah, Daniel, Scroll of Esther, Ezra, Chronicles.** In Tiberian Masoretic codices, including the **Aleppo Codex** and the **Leningrad Codex**, and often in old Spanish manuscripts as well, the order is **Chronicles, Psalms, Job, Proverbs, Ruth, Song of Solomon, Ecclesiastes, Lamentations of Jeremiah, Esther, Daniel, Ezra.**

- **613 mitzvot, formal list of Jewish 613 commandments**

# The Tannaim

*Tannaim* (Hebrew: **"repeaters"**, **"teachers"**) were the **Rabbi**nic sages whose views are recorded in the **Mishnah**, from approximately 10-220 CE. The period of the *Tannaim*, also referred to as the Mishnaic period, lasted about 210 years. It came after the period of the *Zugot* ("pairs"), and was immediately followed by the period of the *Amoraim* ("interpreters").

The Mishnaic period is commonly divided up into five periods according to generations. There are approximately **120 known *Tannaim*.** The *Tannaim* lived in several areas of the Land of Israel. The spiritual center of Judaism at that time was Jerusalem, but after the destruction of the city and the **Second Temple**, **Rabbi Johanan ben Zakai** and his students founded a new religious center in **Yavne**. Other places of Judaic learning were founded by his students in Lod and in **Bnei Brak**.

## History

The *Tannaim* operated under the occupation of the **Roman Empire**. During this time, the *Kohanim* (priests) of the **Temple** became increasingly corrupt and were seen by the Jewish people as collaborators with the Romans, whose mismanagement of Iudaea province (composed of **Samaria, Idumea and Judea** proper) led to riots, revolts and general resentment.

Until the days of **Hillel and Shammai** (the last generation of the *Zugot*), there were few disagreements among **Rabbi**nic scholars. After this period, though, the "**House of Hillel**" and the "**House of Shammai**" came to represent two distinct perspectives on Jewish law.

The *Tannaim,* as teachers of the Oral Law, are said to be direct transmitters of an oral tradition passed from teacher to student that was written and codified as the basis for the **Mishnah**, **Tosefta**, and Tannaitic teachings of the **Talmud**. According to rabbinic tradition, the *Tannaim* were the last generation in a long sequence of oral teachers that began with Moses.

## Language of the Mishnah

The language in which the **Tannaim** of Palestine and Babylonia wrote is referred to as **Mishnaic Hebrew (MH)**, or in Hebrew **Lešon hakhamim, meaning "the language of the Sages."** Texts were written in MH between roughly 70 CE to 500 CE. Tannaitic literature, which includes the **Mishnah**, the **Tosefta**, the halachic **Midrashim**, and **Seder** ʻolam Rabba was redacted between roughly 70 CE to 250 CE. Research has demonstrated that Hebrew was spoken in Palestine until about 200 CE.

## Prominent *Tannaim* / Titles

The *Nasi* (plural *Nesi'im*) was the highest-ranking member and presided over the **Sanhedrin**. *Rabban* was a higher title than *Rabbi*, and it was given to the *Nasi* starting with **Rabban Gamaliel Hazaken** (Gamaliel the Elder). The title *Rabban* was limited to the descendants of **Hillel,** the sole exception being **Rabban Yochanan ben Zakai**, the leader in Jerusalem during the siege, who safeguarded the future of the Jewish people after the **Great Revolt** by pleading with **Vespasian**. **Rabbi Eleazar ben Azariah**, who was also *Nasi*, was not given the title *Rabban*, perhaps because he only held the position of *Nasi* for a short while and it eventually reverted to the descendants of **Hillel**.

For this reason **Hillel** has no title before his name: his name in itself is his title, just as **Moses** and **Abraham** have no titles before their names. Examples include *Avraham Avinu* (**Abraham our father**) and *Moshe Rabbeinu* (**Moses our teacher**).) Starting with **Rabbi Judah haNasi** (**Judah the *Nasi***), often referred to simply as "**Rabbi**".

## Nesi'im
**The following were *Nesi'im*, that is to say presidents of the Sanhedrin.**
- Hillel
- Shammai
- Shimon ben Hillel, about whom very little is known
- Gamaliel Hazaken (Gamaliel the Elder)
- Shimon ben Gamliel
- Yochanan ben Zakai
- Gamaliel of Yavne
- Eleazar ben Azariah, who was *Nasi* for a short time after Rabban Gamliel was removed from his position
- Shimon ben Gamliel of Yavne
- Judah HaNasi (Judah the *Nasi*), known simply as "**Rabbi**", who compiled the **Mishnah**

## Generations
**The Mishnaic period is commonly divided into five periods according to generations of the Tannaim.**

**The generations of the Tannaim included:**
1. **First Generation**: Rabban Yohanan ben Zakkai's generation (c. 40 BCE-80 CE).
2. **Second Generation**: Rabban Gamaliel II of Yavneh, **Rabbi** Eliezer and **Rabbi** Yehoshua's generation, the teachers of **Rabbi** Akiva.
3. **Third Generation**: The generation of **Rabbi** Akiva and his colleagues.
4. **Fourth Generation**: The generation of **Rabbi** Meir, **Rabbi** Yehuda and their colleagues.
5. **Fifth Generation**: **Rabbi** Judah haNasi's generation.
6. **Sixth Generation**: The interim generation between the **Mishnah** and the **Talmud**: **Rabbi**s Shimon ben Judah HaNasi and Yehoshua ben Levi, etc.

## Before the destruction of the Temple
- Hillel

- Shammai
- Gamliel Hazaken (Gamliel the Elder)

## Generation of the destruction (1st generation of Tannaim)
- Shimon ben Gamliel
- Yochanan ben Zakai
- Yehuda ben Baba

## Between the destruction of the Temple and Bar Kokhba's revolt (2nd generation)
- Rabbi Joshua ben Hannania
- Eliezer ben Hurcanus
- Gamaliel of Yavne
- Eleazar ben Arach

## Generation of Bar Kokhba's revolt (3rd generation of Tannaim)
- Rabbi Akiva
- Rabbi Tarfon
- Ishmael ben Elisha
- Eleazar ben Azariah
- Yose HaGelili
- Elisha ben Abuyah (the "Other" or apostate)

## After the revolt
- Shimon ben Gamliel of Yavne
- Meir
- Shimon bar Yochai, who, according to traditional lore, wrote the Zohar
- Yose ben Halafta
- Yehuda ben Ilai
- Rabbi Nehemiah

## Compilers of the Mishnah (5th generation of Tannaim)
- Rabbi Yose
- Rabbi Yishmael
- Rabbi Shimon
- Rabbi Nathan
- Rabbi Hiyya
- Judah HaNasi (known simply as *Rabbi* or *Rebbi*); compiled the **Mishnah**

# Tefillin

**Tefillin** or **phylacteries**, is a set of small black leather boxes containing scrolls of parchment inscribed with verses from the **Torah**. **Tefillin** is worn by observant adult Jews during weekday morning prayers. In **Orthodox** communities, it is only worn by men, while in non-**Orthodox** communities, it may be worn by men and women.

The arm-tefillah is placed on the upper arm, and the strap wrapped around the arm, hand and fingers; while the head-tefillah is placed above the forehead. It is intended to fulfill the **Torah**'s instructions to keep as a "**sign**" and "**remembrance**" of the **Exodus**, signifying that God brought the children of Israel out of Ancient Egypt.

## Biblical source
**The obligation of Tefillin is mentioned four times in the Torah:**
Twice when recalling The **Exodus** from Egypt: **13:9, 13:16, 6:9, & 11:18**.

## Etymology
The word "**Tefillin**" is not found in the Bible, which calls them *ot* **(sign)**, *zikaron* (memorial), or *totafot*. The **Talmud** explains that the word *totafot* is combination of two foreign words: *Tot* means "**two**" in the "**Caspi**" language and *Fot* means "**two**" in the "**Afriki**" language. **"for when one sees the Tefillin it causes him to remember and speak about the Exodus from Egypt".** "**Tefillin**" is derived from the Hebrew *pelilah*, "**justice, evidence**", for **Tefillin** act as a sign and proof of God's presence among the Jewish people.

## Purpose
The **Tefillin** are to serve as a reminder of God's intervention at the time of the **Exodus** from Egypt. **Maimonides** details of the sanctity of **Tefillin** and writes that **"as long as the Tefillin are on the head and on the arm of a man, he is modest and God-fearing and will not be attracted by hilarity or idle talk; he will have no evil thoughts, but will devote all his thoughts to truth and righteousness".** "**This is my God and I will glorify Him**" (Exodus 15:2). **Numbers Rabbah 12:3** presents **Tefillin** as capable of defeating **"a thousand demons"** emerging on **"the left side"**. **Tefillin** are believed to possess life-lengthening qualities.

In earlier **Talmud**ic times, **Tefillin** were either cylindrical or cubical, but later the cylindrical form became obsolete. Nowadays the boxes should be fashioned from a single piece of animal hide and form a base with an upper compartment to contain the parchment scrolls. The straps must be black on their outer side, but may be any color except red on their inner side. The **Shulchan Aruch** states that the custom is to wind six or seven times around the forearm.

## Parchment scrolls

The passages are written by a scribe with special ink on parchment scrolls (*klaf*). These are: **"Sanctify to me ..."** (**Exodus** 13:1–10); **"When YHWH brings you ..."** (**Exodus** 13:11–16); **"Hear, O Israel ..."** (Deuteronomy 6:4–9); and **"If you observe My Commandments ..."** (Deuteronomy 11:13-21). **The passages contain 3,188 letters, which take a sofer (scribe) between 10–15 hours to complete.**

## Obligation and gender

The duty of laying **Tefillin** rests upon Jews after the **age of thirteen years**. Although women were traditionally exempt from the obligation, some early codifiers allowed them to do so. It has been claimed **Rashi's daughters** and the **wife of Chaim ibn Attar** wore **Tefillin**, but there is no historical evidence for these claims. In modern times, people of both genders choose to wear **Tefillin**, and are encouraged to do so by some. **Women affiliated with the Conservative movement wrap Tefillin.**

## Laws and customs regarding putting on Tefillin

**Ashkenazi** practice is to put on and remove the arm **Tefillin** while standing in accordance to the *Shulchan Aruch*, while most **Sephardim** do so while sitting in accordance with the **Ari**. All, however, put on and remove the head **Tefillin** while standing. The **arm-Tefillin** is laid on the inner side of the bare left arm, right arm if one is left handed, two finger breadths above the elbow, so that when the arm is bent the **Tefillin** faces towards the heart. Then the **head-Tefillin** is placed on the middle of the head just above the forehead, so that no part rests below the hairline. **A bald or partially bald person's original hairline is used.**

# Ten Commandments

## The Ten Commandments

- I am the **LORD** thy God
- No other gods before me
- No graven images or likenesses
- Not take the **LORD**'s name in vain
- Remember the Sabbath day
- Honor thy father and thy mother
- Thou shalt not kill
- Thou shalt not commit adultery
- Thou shalt not steal
- Thou shalt not bear false witness
- Thou shalt not covet

The **Ten Commandments** also known as the **Decalogue**, are a set of biblical principles relating to ethics and worship, which play a fundamental role in Judaism and Christianity. The commandments include instructions to worship only God, to honor one's parents, and to keep the Sabbath, as well as prohibitions against idolatry, blasphemy, murder, adultery, theft, dishonesty, and coveting. The **Ten Commandments** appear twice in the **Hebrew Bible**, in the **books of Exodus and Deuteronomy.**

## Terminology

In biblical Hebrew, the **Ten Commandments** are called עשרת הדברים and in Rabbinical Hebrew עשרת הדברות, both translatable as **"the ten words", "the ten sayings",** or **"the ten matters"**. Most major English versions use **"commandments."** The English name **"Decalogue"** is derived from Greek, *dekalogos*, the latter meaning and referring to the Greek translation **"ten words",** found in the Septuagint (or **LXX**) at **Exodus 34:28 and Deuteronomy 10:4.** The stone tablets, are called *HaBrit*, meaning **"the tablets of the covenant".**

## The Ten Commandments

Different religious traditions divide the seventeen verses of **Exodus 20:1–17** and their parallels at **Deuteronomy 5:4–21** into ten **"commandments"** or **"sayings"** in different ways. All scripture quotes above are from the **King James Version** unless otherwise stated.

## Traditions:

The biblical narrative of the revelation at Sinai begins in **Exodus 19** after the arrival of the children of Israel at Mount Sinai (also called **Horeb**). On the morning of the third day of their encampment, **"there were thunders and lightnings, and a thick cloud upon the mount, and the voice of the trumpet exceeding loud"**, and the people assembled at the base of the mount. After **"the LORD came down upon mount Sinai"**, **Moses** went up briefly and returned and prepared the people, and then in **Exodus 20 "God spoke"** to all the people the words of the covenant, that is, the "**Ten Commandments**" as it is written.

The people were afraid to hear more and moved **"afar off"**, and **Moses** responded with **"Fear not."** Nevertheless, he drew near the **"thick dArkness"** where "**the presence of the Lord**" was to hear the additional statutes and **"judgments"**, all which he **"wrote"** in the **"book of the covenant"** which he read to the people the next morning, and they agreed to be obedient and do all that the **LORD** had said.

**Moses** escorted a select group consisting of Aaron, Nadab and Abihu, and **"seventy of the elders of Israel"** to a location on the mount where they worshipped **"afar off"** and they "**saw the God of Israel**" above a "**paved work**" like clear sapphire stone. And the **LORD** said unto **Moses**, **"Come up to me into the mount, and be there: and I will give thee tablets of stone, and a law, and commandments which I have written; that thou mayest teach them"**. And **Moses** rose up, and his minister Joshua: and **Moses** went up into the mount of God.
— *First mention of the tablets in Exodus 24:12–13*

The mount was covered by the cloud for six days, and on the seventh day **Moses** went into the midst of the cloud and was **"in the mount forty days and forty nights."** And **Moses** said, **"the LORD delivered unto me two tablets of stone written with the finger of God; and on them was written according to all the words, which the LORD spake with you in the mount out of the midst of the fire in the day of the assembly."** …And the people "**worshipped**" the calf. After the full forty days, **Moses** and Joshua came down from the mountain with the tablets of stone: **"And it came to pass, as soon as he came nigh unto the camp, that he saw the calf, and the dancing: and Moses' anger waxed hot, and he cast the tablets out of his hands, and brake them beneath the mount."**

According to Jewish tradition, **Exodus 20:1–17** constitutes God's first recitation and inscription of the **Ten Commandments** on the two tablets, which **Moses** broke in anger with his rebellious nation, and were later rewritten on replacement stones and placed in the **Ark** of the covenant; and **Deuteronomy 5:4–25** consists of God's re-telling of the **Ten Commandments** to the younger generation who were to enter the **Promised Land**.

## Religious interpretations

The **Ten Commandments** concern matters of fundamental importance in Judaism and Christianity: the greatest obligation (to worship only God), the greatest injury to a person (**murder**), the greatest injury to family bonds (adultery), the greatest injury to commerce and law (bearing false witness), the greatest inter-generational obligation (honor to parents), the greatest obligation to community **(truthfulness),** the greatest injury to moveable property (theft). The **Ten Commandments** are written with room for varying interpretation. They do not specify punishments for their violation.

## Judaism

The **Ten Commandments** form the basis of Jewish law, stating God's universal and timeless standard of right and wrong – unlike the rest of the **613 commandments in the Torah**, which include, for example, various duties and ceremonies such as the **kashrut dietary laws.** The traditional Rabbinical Jewish belief is that the observance of these commandments and the other *mitzvot* are required solely of the Jewish people and that the laws incumbent on humanity in general are outlined in the **seven Noahide laws**, several of which overlap with the **Ten Commandments. In the era of the Sanhedrin transgressing any one of six of the Ten Commandments theoretically carried the death penalty.**

## Two tablets / *Tablets of Stone*

According to the **Talmud,** the compendium of traditional **Rabbinic Jewish law**, tradition, and interpretation, one interpretation of the biblical verse **"the tablets were written on both their sides",** is that the carving went through the full thickness of the tablets, yet was miraculously legible from both sides.

## Use in Jewish ritual

The **Mishna** records that during the period of the **Second Temple**, the **Ten Commandments** were recited daily, before the reading of the **Shema Yisrael,** but that this practice was abolished in the synagogues so as not to give ammunition to heretics who claimed that they were the only important part of **Jewish law**, or to dispute a claim by early Christians that *only* the **Ten Commandments** were handed down at Mount Sinai rather than the whole **Torah**.

Today, the **Ten Commandments** are heard in the synagogue three times a year: as they come up during the readings of **Exodus** and **Deuteronomy**, and during the festival of **Shavuot**. **Maimonides** has opposed this custom since one may come to think that the **Ten Commandments** are more important than the rest of the **Mitzvot.**

## Roman Catholicism / *Ten Commandments in Catholic theology*

In Roman Catholicism, **Jesus freed Christians from the rest of Jewish religious law, but not from their obligation to keep the Ten Commandments**. It has been said that they are to the moral order what the creation story is to the natural order.

The Commandments are considered essential for spiritual good health and growth, and serve as the basis for social justice. Summarized by **Jesus** into two **"great commandments"** that teach the love of God and love of neighbor, they instruct individuals on their relationships with both.

## Main points of interpretative difference / Sabbath day

**All Abrahamic religions observe a weekly day of rest, called the Sabbath**. Saturday in Judaism (both reckoned from dusk to dusk), and Sunday, from midnight to midnight, in Christianity. Most dictionaries provide both first-day and seventh-day definitions for "**Sabbath**" and "**Sabbatarian**".

## Killing or murder / *Thou shalt not kill*

Multiple translations exist of the **fifth/sixth commandment**; the Hebrew words לא תרצח are variously translated as **"thou shalt not kill"** or **"thou shalt not murder"**. The imperative is against unlawful killing resulting in bloodguilt. The Hebrew Bible contains numerous prohibitions against unlawful killing, but **does not prohibit killing in the context of warfare (1Kings 2:5–6), capital punishment (Leviticus 20:9–16)** and **self-defence (Exodus 22:2–3),** which are **considered justified.**

## Theft / *Thou shalt not steal*

**"thou shalt not steal"** was originally intended against stealing people—against abductions and slavery, in agreement with the Talmudic interpretation of the statement as **"thou shalt not kidnap" (Sanhedrin 86a).**

## *Idolatry, Idolatry in Judaism, and Idolatry in Christianity*

**Idolatry is forbidden in all Abrahamic religions**. In Judaism there is a prohibition against *worshipping* an idol or a representation of God, but there is no restriction on art or simple *depictions.* **Islam** has a stronger prohibition, banning representations of God, and in some cases of **Muhammad**, humans and, in some interpretations, any living creature. In **Gospel of Barnabas, Jesus** stated that **idolatry is the greatest sin** as it divests a man fully of faith, and hence of God. The controversy reached crisis level in the 8th century, during the period of iconoclasm: the smashing of icons.

In 726 **Emperor Leo III** ordered all images removed from all churches; in 730 a council forbade veneration of images, citing the **Second Commandment**; in 787 the **Seventh Ecumenical Council** reversed the preceding rulings, condemning iconoclasm and sanctioning the veneration of images; in 815 **Leo V** called yet another council, which reinstated iconoclasm; in 843 **Empress Theodora again reinstated veneration of icons.**

## Adultery

Originally this commandment forbade male Israelites from having sexual intercourse with the wife of another Israelite; the prohibition did not extend to their own slaves. **Sexual intercourse between an Israelite man, married or not, and a woman who was neither married nor betrothed was not considered adultery.**

## Dating

**If the Ten Commandments are based on Hittite forms**, it would date them to somewhere between the 14th-12th century BCE.

## The Ritual Decalogue

Some proponents of the Documentary hypothesis have argued that the biblical text in **Exodus 34:28** identifies a different list as the **Ten Commandments**, that of **Exodus 34:11–27**. Since this passage does not prohibit murder, adultery, theft, etc., but instead deals with the proper worship of **Yahweh**, some scholars call it the **"Ritual Decalogue"**, and disambiguate the **Ten Commandments** of traditional understanding as the **"Ethical Decalogue"**.

The **Decalogue** and the book of the covenant represent two ways of manifesting God's presence in Israel: the **Ten Commandments** taking the archaic and material form of stone tablets kept in the **Ark** of the covenant, while the book of the covenant took oral form to be recited to the people. **Qur'anic reference** to the **Ten Commandments** can be found in **chapter 2 verses 83 and 84** " **"And when We took the covenant from the Children of Israel… And when We took your covenant, "Do not shed each other's blood (9) or evict one another from your homes (10)." Then you acknowledged while you were witnessing"**

## Display on public property:

The United States Constitution forbids establishment of religion by law; however images of **Moses** holding the tablets of the Decalogue, along other religious figures including **Solomon, Confucius**, and **Mohamed** holding the **Qur'an**, are sculpted on the north and south friezes of the pediment of the **Supreme Court** building in Washington. Images of the **Ten Commandments** have long been contested symbols for the relationship of religion to national law. By the beginning of the twenty-first century in the U.S organizations such as the **American Civil Liberties Union** (ACLU) and Americans United for Separation of Church and State launched lawsuits **challenging the posting of the Ten Commandments in public buildings.**

Many Christian conservatives have taken the banning of officially sanctioned prayer from public schools by the U.S. **Supreme Court** as a threat to the expression of religion in public life. In response, they have successfully lobbied many state and local governments to display the **Ten Commandments** in public buildings. Those who oppose the posting of the **Ten Commandments** on public property argue that it violates the establishment clause of the **First Amendment to the Constitution of the United States.** Some argue that prohibiting the public practice of religion is a violation of the first amendment's guarantee of freedom of religion.

# Ten Lost Tribes of Israel

The **Ten Lost Tribes** of Israel refers to those tribes of ancient Israel that formed the **Kingdom of Israel,** after the kingdom was destroyed in about 722 BCE by Assyria. No record exists of the Assyrians having exiled people from **Dan, Asher, Issachar, Zebulun or western Manasseh.**

Descriptions of the deportation of people from **Reuben, Gad, Manasseh in Gilead, Ephraim and Naphtali** indicate that only a portion of these tribes were deported. The deported communities are mentioned as still existing at the time of the composition of the books of **Kings** and **Chronicles,** and not wholly assimilated into the Assyrian populace. **DNA studies have found no evidence of the existence of any lost tribes,** with the exception of the **Lemba,** for whom a Y-chromosome connection has been confirmed, but no maternal **DNA.**

## The Bible: The Twelve Tribes
According to the Hebrew Bible, **Jacob** (who was later named Israel; **(Gen. 35:10)** had 12 sons and at least one daughter (**Dinah**) by two wives and two concubines. **The twelve sons fathered the twelve Tribes of Israel.**

| Traditional division: Israel: | Division according to apportionment of land in |
|---|---|
| 1. Reuben | 1. Reuben |
| 2. Simeon | 2. Simeon |
| 3. Levi | 3. Judah |
| 4. Judah | 4. Issachar |
| 5. Issachar | 5. Zebulun |
| 6. Zebulun | 6. Dan |
| 7. Naphtali | 7. Naphtali |
| 8. Gad | 8. Gad |
| 9. Asher | 9. Asher |
| 10. Joseph | 10. Benjamin |
| 11. Benjamin | 11. Ephraim (son of Joseph) |
| | 12. Manasseh (son of Joseph) |

According to the Bible, the **Kingdom of Israel** (or Northern Kingdom) was one of the successor states to the older **United Monarchy** (also called the **Kingdom of Israel**), which came into existence in about the 930s BCE after the northern **Tribes of Israel** rejected Solomon's son **Rehoboam** as their king. Nine landed tribes formed the Northern Kingdom: the tribes of **Reuben, Issachar, Zebulun, Dan, Naphtali, Gad, Asher, Ephraim and Manasseh.** In addition, some members of **Tribe of Levi**, who had no land allocation, were found in the **Northern Kingdom.**

The **Tribes of Judah** and **Benjamin** remained loyal to **Rehoboam** and formed the **Kingdom of Judah** (or Southern Kingdom). Members of **Levi** and the remnant of Simeon were also found in the **Southern Kingdom.** In 732 BCE, the Assyrian king, **Tiglath-Pileser III** sacked Damascus and Israel, annexing Aramea and territory of the tribes of **Reuben, Gad and Manasseh.**

People from these tribes including the **Reubenite** leader, were taken captive and resettled in the region of the **Khabur River** system in Assyria/Mesopotamia. According to **2 Kings 16:9**, the population of Aram and the annexed part of Israel was deported to Assyria. Israel continued to exist within the reduced territory as an independent kingdom subject to Assyria until around 720 BCE, when it was again invaded by Assyria and the rest of the population deported. However, it is estimated that only a f fifth of the population (about 40,000) were actually resettled out of the area during the two deportation periods under **Tiglath-Pileser III and his successor Sargon II.**

**2 Chronicles 30:1-11** explicitly mentions northern Israelites who had been spared by the Assyrians in particular members of **Dan, Ephraim, Manasseh, Asher and Zebulun** and how members of the latter three returned to worship at the Temple in Jerusalem at that time. The Jewish tradition held until modern times that all the population of the kingdom was deported by Assyria, never to be heard of again. They are considered the **Ten Lost Tribes**. In **Luke 2:36** of **the New Testament, an individual is identified with the tribe of Asher.**

However in **2 Kings 17:34** it says of the newly exiled Israelites that were in Assyria; to this day they persist in their former practices. They neither worship **Yahweh** nor adhere to the decrees and regulations, the laws and commands that **Yahweh** gave the descendants of **Jacob, whom he named Israel**. The Hebrew Bible does not use the phrase **"Ten Lost Tribes"**. However, **1 Kings 11:31** states that the kingdom would be taken from Solomon and give ten tribes to Jeroboam.

## Religious Beliefs

There are numerous references in biblical writings. In **Ezekiel 37:16-17,** the prophet is told to write on one stick: **"For Judah..."** and on the other (quoted here in part), **"For Joseph..."** (The main Lost Tribe). The prophet is then told that these two groups shall be someday reunited. **Ezekiel 37:16-17**

The **Church of Jesus Christ of Latter-day Saints** (LDS) has extensive teachings regarding the gathering of Israel and the restoration of the ten tribes. One of their main **Articles of Faith** written by Joseph Smith, Jr. is as follows: **"We believe in the literal gathering of Israel and in the restoration of the Ten Tribes; that Zion (the New Jerusalem) will be built upon the American continent; that Christ will reign personally upon the earth; and, that the earth will be renewed and receive its paradisiacal glory." (LDS Articles of Faith #10)**

Regarding the **Ezekiel 37** prophecy, the **LDS Church** teaches that the **Book of Mormon** is the stick of **Ephraim** mentioned and that the Bible is the stick of Judah, thus comprising two witnesses for **Jesus Christ**. The **LDS Church** considers the **Book of Mormon** one of the main tools for the spiritual gathering of Israel. There are also discussions in the **Talmud** as to whether the **Ten Lost Tribes** will eventually be reunited with the **Tribe of Judah**, that is, with the Jewish people.

**Historians have generally arrived at the conclusion that the Lost Tribes merged with the local population. While others were presumably absorbed by the last Judean exiles who in 597-586 BC were deported to Assyria...Unlike the Judeans of the southern Kingdom, who survived a similar fate 135 years later, they soon assimilated..."**

## Beta Israel of Ethiopia

The **Beta Israel** (also known derogatorily as Falashas) are **Ethiopian** Jews. Some members of the **Beta Israel** as well as several Jewish scholars believe that they are descended from the lost Tribe of **Dan**, as opposed to the traditional story of their descent from the **Queen of Sheba.**

## Lemba

The **Lemba people** (Vhalemba) from Southern Africa claim to be descendants of several Jewish men who traveled from what is now Yemen to Africa in search of gold, where they took wives and established new communities. **DNA** testing has genetically linked the Lemba with modern Jews and **Muslim Semites**.

## Persian Jews

Persian Jews claim descent from the **Tribe of Ephraim**. Persian Jews (also called Iranian Jews) are members of Jewish communities living in Iran and throughout the former greatest extent of the **Persian Empire**.

## Bukharian Jews

There has been speculation that the **Bukharian Jews** are related to the **Tribe of Issachar** because a common surname among them is **Issacharoff.**

## China: Kaifeng Jews

The discovery of a Jewish community by a Jesuit missionary in the early 17th century to have been an important factor leading to the increased currency of theories and tales related to the **Lost Tribes**. In 1605, **Jesuit missionary Matteo Ricci** discovered a small community consisting of approximately ten to twelve families of Chinese Jews in Kaifeng, China. According to historical records, a Jewish community in Kaifeng built a synagogue in 1163, during the **Southern Song Dynasty**, which existed until the late nineteenth century.

## The United States, American Indians

In 1650, a British divine named "Thomas Thorowgood, who was a preacher in Norfolk, published a book entitled *Jews in America or Probabilities that the Americans are of that Race*, which he had prepared for the New England missionary society. Thorowgood's tract argued that the native population of North America were descendants of the **Ten Lost Tribes**.

## British Israelism variant

British Israelism (also known as Anglo-Israelism) espouses a theory that people of Western European descent, especially Britain and the United States, are descended from the lost tribes of Israel. Tudor Parfitt, author of *The Lost Tribes: The History of a Myth*, states that the proof cited by adherents of British Israelism is **"of a feeble composition even by the low standards of the genre."**

## Brit-Am variant

**Brit-Am**, sometimes confused with British Israelism, is an organization centered in Jerusalem, and composed of Jews and non-Jews, **Brit-Am**, like British Israel, identifies the **Lost Ten Tribes** with peoples of West European descent, but does so from a Jewish perspective. It uses Rabbinical

Commentary supplemented by secular theories that posit the **Lost Tribes Scythian/Cimmerian** connection, which are believed to have been ancestors of current Western European cultures and nations.

An example of **Brit-Am** scholarship may be seen from its treatment of **Obadiah 1:20**. In Hebrew **Obadiah** mentions the Sepharad, believed by some to refer to **Iberian Jews**, where the original Hebrew as understood by **Rabbinical Commentators** such as **Rashi** and **Don Isaac Abrabanelas** referring to the Lost Ten tribes in France and England. **"The Tribe of Dan is to be found amongst part of the Danish, Irish, and Welsh."**

## Other variants

The lost Israelites can be defined by the **Y-DNA** haplogroup R, which makes up much of the population of Europe and Russia, which is in contract to British Israelism and **Brit-Am**, which believe that the Israelites became only Western Europeans.

## Japanese

Some writers have speculated that the Japanese people may be direct descendants of part of the **Ten Lost Tribes**.

> **"It is in fact in Japan that we can trace the most remarkable evolution in the Pacific of an imagined Judaic past. As elsewhere in the world, the theory that aspects of the country were to be explained via an Israelite model was introduced by Western agents."**

# Tetragrammaton

The **Tetragrammaton** in Phoenician (12th century BCE to 150 BCE), Paleo-Hebrew (10th century BCE to 135 CE), and square Hebrew (3rd century BCE to present) scripts. The **Tetragrammaton** or **Tetragram** (from Greek , meaning "**four letters**") is the four-letter Hebrew word יהוה, the name of the biblical God of Israel. The name, **"the form *Yahweh* is now accepted almost universally"**.

The books of the Torah and the rest of the Hebrew Bible except **Esther, Ecclesiastes**, and (with a possible instance in **verse 8:6**) the **Song of Songs** contain this Hebrew name. Observant Jews and those who follow **Talmud**ic Jewish traditions do not pronounce יהוה nor do they read aloud proposed transcription forms such as *Yahweh* or *Yehovah*; instead they replace it with a different term, whether in addressing or referring to the God of Israel. Common substitutions in Hebrew are **Adonai ("My Lord")**, *HaShem* ("**The Name**") and *hakadosh baruch hu* ("**The Holy One, Blessed Be He")**.

## Four letters

Modern scholars generally agree that **YHWH** is derived from the Hebrew triconsonantal root היה (h-y-h), **"to be, become, come to pass"**, an archaic form of which is הוה (**h-w-h**), with a third person masculine y- prefix, equivalent to English "**he**". They connect it to **Exodus 3:14**, where the divinity who spoke with Moses responds to a question about his name by declaring: "**I am that I am**" or "**I will be what I will be**".

## Vocalization / YHWH and Hebrew script

Like all letters in the Hebrew script, the letters in **YHWH** originally indicated consonants. Therefore it can be difficult to deduce how a word is pronounced from its spelling, and the **Tetragrammaton** is a particular example: all four of its letters can be *matres lectionis.* One of the frequent cases was the **Tetragrammaton**, which according to later Jewish practices should not be pronounced but read as "**Adonai**" ("**My Lord**"), or, if the previous or next word already was **Adonai,** as "**Elohim**" ("**God**"). Writing the vowel diacritics of these two words on the consonants **YHVH** produces יְהֹנָה and יֱהֹוָה respectively, non-words that would spell "**Yehovah**" and "**Yehovih**" respectively.

The oldest complete or nearly complete manuscripts of the Masoretic Text with **Tiberian Vocalization**, such as the *Aleppo Codex* and the *Leningrad Codex,* both of the 10th or 11th century, mostly write יְהֹוָה (*yhwah*), with no pointing on the first *h*. It could point to the *qere* being **Shema,** which is Aramaic for "**the Name**".

## Uncertainty in the first half of the nineteenth century

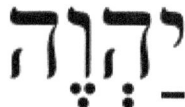

**Theoretical Hebrew punctuation for *Yahweh*, if this were used instead of those of *Adonai* and *Elohim*.** Most commentators favoured *Yahwoh*, in line with the statement by several ancient writers that the Jews called their **God IAΩ**. This form has the same vowel structure as in the Hebrew names of **Jacob** and **Pharaoh.**

## Yahweh

In spite of the uncertainties that exist, there is now strong scholarly consensus that the original pronunciation of the **Tetragrammaton** is *Yahweh* (יַהְוֶה): **"The strong consensus of biblical scholarship is that the original pronunciation of the name YHWH that God goes on to use in verse 15 was Yahweh. Non-Jews later combined the vowels of Adonai with the consonants of the Tetragrammaton and invented the name "Jehovah". "Whatever, therefore, be the true pronunciation of the word, there can be little doubt that it is not *Jehovah*."**

## Non-biblical Texts / Texts with Tetragrammaton

The oldest known inscription of the **Tetragrammaton** dates to 840 BCE: the **Mesha Stele** mentions the Israelite god *Yahweh*. Also a wall inscription, dated to the late 6th century BCE, with mention of **Yahweh** had been found in a tomb at **Khirbet Beit Lei**. **Yahweh** is mentioned also in the **Lachish** letters (587 BCE) and the slightly earlier Tel Arad ostraca, and on a stone from **Mount Gerizim** (III or beginning of II century BCE).

## The Tetragrammaton in the Hebrew Bible

In the Hebrew Bible, the **Tetragrammaton** occurs 6828 times, as can be seen in **Kittel's** *Biblia Hebraica* and the *Biblia Hebraica Stuttgartensia*. In addition, the marginal notes or *masorah* indicate that in another 134 places, where the received text has the word *Adonai*, an earlier text had the **Tetragrammaton**, which would add up to 142 additional occurrences. The first appearance of the **Tetragrammaton** in the Hebrew Bible is in the **Book of Genesis 2:4**. **The only books it does not appear in are Ecclesiastes, the Book of Esther, and Song of Songs.**

## Dead Sea Scrolls

In the **Dead Sea Scrolls** and other Hebrew and Aramaic texts the **Tetragrammaton** and some other names of God in Judaism (such as **El or Elohim**) were sometimes written in paleo-Hebrew script, showing that they were treated specially. Most of God's names were pronounced until about the 2nd century BCE. The 4Q120, a Greek fragment of **Leviticus (26:2–16)** discovered in the **Dead Sea scrolls (Qumran)** has ιαω ("**Iao**"), the Greek form of the Hebrew **Trigrammaton YHW.**

## Septuagint

Scholars differ on whether in the original Septuagint translations the **Tetragrammaton** was represented by **Κύριος, by ΙΑΩ**, by the **Tetragrammaton** in either normal or Paleo-Hebrew form, or whether different translators used different forms in different books. While some interpret the presence of the **Tetragrammaton** in **Papyrus Fouad 266**, the oldest Septuagint manuscript in which it appears, as an indication of what was in the original text, others see this manuscript as **"an archaizing and Hebraizing revision of the earlier translation κύριος"**. In the **Book of Exodus** alone, represents the **Tetragrammaton** 41 times.

## Usage in religious traditions / Judaism / *Genizah*

Especially due to the existence of the **Mesha Stele**, the Jahwist tradition found in **Exod. 3:15**, and ancient Hebrew and Greek texts, biblical scholars widely hold that the **Tetragrammaton** and other names of God were spoken by the ancient Israelites and their neighbors. Sometime after the destruction of **Solomon's Temple**, the spoken use of God's name as it was written ceased among the people, even though knowledge of the pronunciation was perpetuated in rabbinic schools. The **Talmud** relays this occurred after the death of **Simeon the Just.**

Rabbinic sources suggest that the name of God was pronounced only once a year, by the high priest, on the **Day of Atonement.** Others, including **Maimonides**, claim that the name was pronounced daily in the liturgy of the Temple in the priestly benediction of worshippers (Num. vi. 27), after the daily sacrifice; in the synagogues, though, a substitute (probably **"Adonai"**) was used. Since the **destruction of Second Temple of Jerusalem in 70 CE**, the **Tetragrammaton** has no longer been pronounced in the liturgy. However the pronunciation was still known in Babylonia in the latter part of the 4th century.

## Spoken prohibitions

The vehemence with which the utterance of the name is denounced in the **Mishnah** suggests that use of **Yahweh** was unacceptable in rabbinical Judaism. **"He who pronounces the Name with its own letters has no part in the world to come!"** It is sometimes called the **"Ineffable"**, **"Unutterable", or "Distinctive Name".** When someone wants to refer in third person to either the written or spoken Name, the term *HaShem* **"the Name"** is used; and this handle itself can also be used in prayer. The traditional phrase used in **sitting Shiva** and **"Raḥmana l'tzlan"** (**"may the Merciful save us" i.e. "God forbid").**

## Written prohibitions

Writing the **Tetragrammaton** (or these other names) unnecessarily is prohibited, so as to avoid having them treated disrespectfully, an action that is forbidden.

## *Kabbalah and Hasidic philosophy*

There are two main schools of **Kabbalah** arising in 13th century Spain. These are called **Theosophic Kabbalah** represented by **Rabbi Moshe De leon** and the **Zohar**, and the **Kabbalah** of Names or Prophetic **Kabbalah** whose main representative is Rabbi **Abraham Abulafia** of Saragossa. **Rabbi Abulafia** wrote many wisdom books and prophetic books where the name is used for meditation purposes from 1271 onwards.

**Abulafia** put a lot of attention on Exodus 15 and the **Songs of Moses**. In this song it says **"Yehovah is a Man of War, Yehovah is his name"**. He prophesied in his book **"The Sign"**, **Therefore, thus said YHWH, the God of Israel: Have no fear of the enemy"**. **Moshe Chaim Luzzatto**, says that the tree of the **Tetragrammaton "unfolds"** in accordance with the intrinsic nature of its letters, **"in the same order in which they appear in the Name, in the mystery of ten and the mystery of four."** It unfolds in this aforementioned order and **"in the mystery of the four expansions"**.

Luzzatto summarises, **"In sum, all that exists is founded on the mystery of this Name and upon the mystery of these letters of which it consists. This means that all the different orders and laws are all drawn after and come under the order of these four letters. This is not one particular pathway but rather the general path, which includes everything that exists in the Sefirot in all their details and which brings everything under its order."** It has been argued that the Kabbalistic **Tree of Life**, with its ten spheres of emanation, is in some way connected to the tetractys, but its form is not that of a triangle.

## Christianity

It is assumed that early Jewish Christians inherited from Jews the practice of reading "**Lord**" where the **Tetragrammaton** appeared in the Hebrew text, or where a **Tetragrammaton** may have been marked in a Greek text. Gentile Christians, primarily non-Hebrew speaking and using Greek texts, may have read "**Lord**" as it occurred in the Greek text of the New Testament and their copies of the Greek Old Testament.

## Christian translations

Use of the Septuagint by Christians in polemics with Jews led to its abandonment by the latter, making it a specifically Christian text. From it Christians made translations into Coptic, Arabic, Slavonic and other languages. Christian translations of the Bible into English commonly use "**LORD**" in place of the **Tetragrammaton** in most passages, often in small capitals (or in all caps), so as to distinguish it from other words translated as **"Lord"**.

## Catholicism

On 29 June 2008, the **Holy See** reacted to the then still recent practice of pronouncing, within Catholic liturgy, the name of God represented by the **Tetragrammaton**. The early Christians, it said, followed the example of the Septuagint in replacing the name of God with "**the Lord** for their use of "**the Lord**" in reference to Jesus, as in **Philippians 2:9–11** and other New Testament texts. It therefore directed that, ""**in liturgical celebrations, in songs and prayers the name of God in the form of the *Tetragrammaton* YHWH is neither to be used or pronounced**.

# Tikkun Olam

***Tikkun olam***, (*literally*, **"repair of the world"**, *alternatively*, **"construction for eternity"**) is a concept in Judaism interpreted in Orthodox Judaism as the prospect of overcoming all forms of idolatry. Documented use of the term dates back the Mishnaic period. Since medieval times, kabbalistic literature has broadened use of the term. To the ears of contemporary pluralistic Rabbis, the term connotes "**the establishment of Godly qualities throughout the world.**"

### History
The phrase ***tikkun olam*** is included in the ***Aleinu***, part of Jewish congregational prayer. The ***Aleinu*** beseeches God:

> "**To speedily see Your mighty splendor, to remove detestable (idolatry) from the land, and the (false) gods will be utterly 'cut off', to *tahken olam* in God's kingdom**"

In other words, when all the people of the world abandon false gods and recognize God, the world will have been perfected. Being that we share a partnership with God, humanity is instructed to take the steps towards improving the state of the world and helping others, which simultaneously brings more honor to God's sovereignty.

The **American Conservative Movement's** prayer book, ***Siddur Sim Shalom***, published by the Rabbinical Assembly and the United Synagogue of Conservative Judaism, **"A Prayer for Our Country"** includes the verses, **"May citizens of all races and creeds forge a common bond in true harmony to banish all hatred and bigotry"** and uniting all people in peace and freedom and helping them to fulfill the vision of your prophet: **'Nation shall not lift up sword against nation, neither shall they experience war anymore.'** **"Both lines express wholeheartedly the idea of universal equality, freedom, and peace for all."**

## Lurianic Kabbalah
Lurianic **Kabbalah** dwells on the role of prayer and ritual in ***tikkun olam***. According to this vision of the world, God contracted part of God's self into vessels of light – partly limiting himself – to create the world. These vessels shattered and their shards became sparks of light trapped within the material of creation. Prayer, especially contemplation of various aspects of the divinity (***sephirot***), releases these sparks of god's self and allows them to reunite with God's essence, bringing them closer to a fixed world.

According to **Moshe Chaim Luzzatto**, in his book ***Derech Hashem***, the physical world is connected to spiritual realms above that influence the physical world, and furthermore, Jews have the ability, through physical deeds and free will, to direect and control these spiritual forces. God's desire in creation was that God's creations ultimately will recognize God's unity and overcome evil; this will constitute the perfection (***tikkun***) of creation.

The association between the **Lurianic conception of *tikkun olam*** and ethical action assigns an ultimate significance to even small acts of kindness and small improvements of social policy.

Lurianic **Kabbalah** saw itself as repairing God and the world to come rather than this world and its social relations.

A generation recovering from the tragedy of the **Holocaust** resonates with the imagery of shattered vessels. Both Lurianic **Kabbalah** and ethical understandings of *tikkun olam* emphasize the role of human responsibility and action.

### Performance of *mitzvot*

Jews believe that performing of ritual mitzvot (good deeds, commandments, connections, or religious obligations) is a means of *tikkun olam,* helping to perfect the world, and that the performance of more *mitzvot* will hasten the coming of the **Messiah** and the **Messianic Age**. This belief dates back at least to the early Talmudic period.

### Observing Shabbat

Some explain the power of **Shabbat** by its effect on the other six days of the week and their role in moving society towards the Messianic Age. **Shabbat** helps being about the Messianic Age because Shabbat rest energizes Jews to work harder to bring the Messianic Age nearer during the six working days of the week.

### Ethical behavior

Maimonides writes that *tikkun olam* requires efforts in all three of the great **"pillars"** of Judaism: Torah study, acts of kindness, and the ritual commandments.

### Tzedakah

*Tzedakah* is a central theme in Judaism and serves as one of the **613 commandments**. **Tzedakah** is used in common parlance as charitable giving. *Tzedek*, the root of *tzedakah*, means justice or righteousness. Acts of *tzedakah* are used to generate a more just world. Philanthropy is defined as giving money in order to **"promote the common good."** Philanthropy is an effective tool in performing *tikkun olam* as it supports the organizations that perform direct service.

### Building a model society

By performing the *mitzvot*, it is believed that the Jewish people will become a model society. This idea sometimes is attributed to Biblical verses that describe the Jews as **"a kingdom of priests and a holy nation" (Exodus 19:5-6)** and **"a light of the nations"** or **"a light to the nations" (Isaiah 42:6 and Isaiah 49:6).**

Thus, the ultimate goal of *mitzvot* is for moral and religious values and deeds to permeate the Jewish people and ultimately the entire world, but the ritual *mitzvot* nevertheless play a vital role in this model of *tikkun olam*, strengthening what is accomplished by the ethical.

### Improving the world

The conservative position is that individuals and communities should not use government efforts as a substitute for the individual and collective responsibility for these *mitzvot.*

# Timeline of Jewish history

This is a list of notable events in the development of Jewish history. All dates are given according to the Common Era, not the Hebrew calendar.

**1312 BCE**
Moses and the Exodus from Egypt

**c. 1250 BCE–c. 1025 BCE**
Biblical judges lead the people

**c. 1025 BCE–c. 1010 BCE**
King Saul

**c. 1010 BCE–c. 970 BCE**
King David

**c. 970 BCE–c. 931 BCE**
King Solomon

**c. 960 BCE**
Solomon's Temple in Jerusalem completed

**c. 931 BCE**
Split between Kingdom of Israel (Samaria) and the Kingdom of Judah

**c. 931 BCE–c. 913 BCE**
King Rehoboam of Judah

**c. 931 BCE–c. 910 BCE**
King Jeroboam of Israel

**840 BCE**
Mesha inscription describes Moabite victory over a son of King Omri of Israel.

**c. 740 BCE–c. 700 BCE**
prophecy of Isaiah

**c. 740 BCE–c. 722 BCE**
Kingdom of Israel falls to Neo-Assyrian Empire

**c. 715 BCE–c. 687 BCE**
King Hezekiah of Judah

**c. 649 BCE–c. 609 BCE**
King Josiah of Judah institutes major reforms

**c. 626 BCE – c. 587 BCE**
prophecy of Jeremiah

**c. 600 BCE**
Ketef Hinnom scrolls

**597 BCE**
first deportation to Babylon

**586 BCE**
Jerusalem falls to Nebuchadnezzar and Solomon's Temple destroyed

Second Temple period[edit]

*Main articles: Second Temple period, Yehud (Persian province), Maccabean Revolt, Hasmonean dynasty, Herodian kingdom, and Jewish-Roman Wars*

**539 BCE**

Jews allowed to Return to Zion, by permission of Cyrus.

**520 BCE**

Prophecy of Zechariah

**c. 520 BCE**

Zerubbabel leads the first group of Jews from captivity back to Jerusalem

**516 BCE**

Second Temple consecrated

**c. 475 BCE**

Often associated with Xerxes I of Persia, Queen Esther revealed her identity to the king and began to plead for her people, pointing to Haman as the evil schemer plotting to destroy them.

**c. 460 BCE**

Seeing anarchy breaking out in Judea, Xerxes' successor Persian King Artaxerxes sent Ezra to restore order.

**332 BCE**

Alexander the Great conquers Phoenicia and Gaza.

**332 BCE?**

According to Josephus, Alexander visits Judea and seeks out the high priest Jaddus. He shows Alexander the prophecy of Alexander's own life and conquests found in the Book of Daniel. This story is considered apocryphal and created centuries later, perhaps in the early Hasmonean period, though.

**167–140 BCE**

The Maccabean Revolt against the Greek Syrian Seleucid Empire, led by Judas Maccabeus, resulting in victory and installation of the Hanukkah holiday.

**150 BCE–100 CE**

At some point during this era the Tanakh (Hebrew Bible) is finalized and canonized. Jewish religious works that were explicitly written after the time of Ezra were not canonized, although many became popular among many groups of Jews. Later works that were included in the Greek translation of the Bible (the Septuagint) become known as the deuterocanonical books.

**140–63 BCE**

The Hasmonean dynasty rules Judea. The Hasmonean kingdom expands outward to Idumea, Samaria, Perea, Galilee, and Gilead due to weakness and dissolution within the Seleucid Empire.

**63 BCE**

Pompey lay siege to and entered the Temple, Judea became a client kingdom of Rome.

**40 BCE–4 BCE**

Herod the Great appointed King of the Jews by the Roman Senate, replacing the Hasmonean dynasty with the Herodian dynasty.

**1st century CE**

**6–4 BCE**

Jesus of Nazareth was born in Bethlehem, Herodian Kingdom.

**6 CE**

Province of Roman Judea created by merging Judea proper, Samaria and Idumea.

**10 CE**

Hillel the Elder, considered the greatest Torah sage, dies, leading to the dominance of Shammai till 30 CE, see also Hillel and Shammai.

**26–36 CE**

Sanhedrin trial of Jesus, Roman trial of Jesus, and the crucifixion of Jesus.

**30 CE**

Helena of Adiabene, a vassal Parthian kingdom in Mesopotamia, converts to Judaism. Significant numbers of Adiabene population follow her, later also providing limited support for Jews during Jewish-Roman wars. In the following centuries the community mostly converts to Christianity.

**30–70 CE**

Schism within Judaism during the Second Temple period. A sect within Hellenised Jewish society starts Jewish Christianity, see also Rejection of Jesus. Siege and Destruction of Jerusalem by the Romans (1850 painting by David Roberts)

**66–70**

The First Jewish–Roman War ended with destruction of the Second Temple and the fall of Jerusalem. 1,100,000 people are killed by the Romans during the siege, and 97,000 captured and enslaved.[citation needed] The Sanhedrin was relocated to Yavne by Yochanan ben Zakai, see also Council of Jamnia. Fiscus Judaicus levied on all Jews of the Roman Empire whether they aided the revolt or not.

**70–200**

Period of the *Tannaim*, rabbis who organized and elucidated the Oral Torah. The decisions of the *Tannaim* are contained in the Mishnah, Beraita, Tosefta, and various Midrash compilations.

**73**

Final events of the First Jewish–Roman War – the fall of Masada. Christianity starts off as a Jewish sect and then develops its own texts and ideology and branches off from Judaism to become a distinct religion.

**2nd century**

**115–117**

Kitos War (Revolt against Trajan) – a second Jewish-Roman War initiated in large Jewish communities of Cyprus, Cyrene (modern Libya), Aegipta (modern Egypt) and Mesopotamia (modern Syria and Iraq). It led to mutual killing of hundreds of thousands Jews, Greeks and Romans, ending with a total defeat of Jewish rebels and complete extermination of Jews in Cyprus and Cyrene by the newly installed Emperor Hadrian.

**131–136**

The Roman emperor Hadrian, among other provocations, renames Jerusalem "Aelia Capitolina" and prohibits circumcision. Simon bar Kokhba (Bar Kosiba) leads a large Jewish revolt against Rome in response to Hadrian's actions. In the aftermath, most Jewish population is annihilated (about 580,000 killed) and Hadrian renames the province of Judea to Syria Palaestina, and attempts to root out Judaism.

**136**

Rabbi Akiva is martyred.

**138**

With Emperor Hadrian's death, the persecution of Jews within the Roman Empire is eased and Jews are allowed to visit Jerusalem on Tisha B'av. In the following centuries the Jewish center moves to Galilee.

**3rd century**

**200**

The Mishnah, the standardization of the Jewish oral law as it stands today, is redacted by Judah haNasi in the land of Israel.

**259**

Nehardea in Babylonia destroyed by the Palmyrenes, which destruction caused the widespread dispersion of Jews in the region.

**220–500**

Period of the *Amoraim*, the rabbis of the Talmud.

**4th century**

**315–337**

Roman Emperor Constantine I enacts new restrictive legislation. Conversion of Christians to Judaism is outlawed, congregations for religious services are curtailed, but Jews are also allowed to enter Jerusalem on the anniversary of the Temple's destruction.

**351–352**

Jewish revolt against Constantius Gallus is put down. Sepphoris is razed to the ground.

**358**

Because of the increasing danger of Roman persecution, Hillel II creates a mathematical calendar for calculating the Jewish month. After adopting the calendar, the Sanhedrin in Tiberias is dissolved.

**361–363**

The last pagan Roman Emperor, Julian, allows the Jews to return to "holy Jerusalem which you have for many years longed to see rebuilt" and to rebuild the Second Temple. Shortly after, the Emperor is assassinated, and the plan is dissolved.

**363**

Galilee earthquake of 363

**379**

In India, the Hindu king Sira Primal, also known as Iru Brahman, issued what was engraved on a tablet of brass, his permission to Jews to live freely, build synagogue, own property *without conditions attached* and *as long as the world and moon exist*.

**5th century**

**438**

The Empress Eudocia removes the ban on Jews' praying at the Temple site and the heads of the Community in Galilee issue a call "to the great and mighty people of the Jews": "Know that the end of the exile of our people has come"!

**450**

Redaction of the Jerusalem Talmud

**6th century**

**500–523**

Yosef Dhu Nuwas, King of Himyarite Kingdom (Modern Yemen) converting to Judaism, upgrading existing Yemenese Jewish center. His kingdom falls in a war against Axum and the Christians.

**550**

The main redaction of Babylonian Talmud is completed under Rabbis Ravina and Ashi. To a lesser degree, the text continues to be modified for the next 200 years.

**550–700**

Period of the *Savoraim,* the sages in Persia who put the Talmud in its final form.

**555–572**

The Fourth Samaritan Revolt against Byzantium results in great reduction of the Samaritan community, their Israelite faith is outlawed. Neighbouring Jews, who mostly reside in Galilee, are also affected by the oppressive rule of the Byzantines.

**7th century**

**610–628**

Jews of Galilee led by Benjamin of Tiberias gain autonomy in Jerusalem after revolting against Heraclius as a joint military campaign with ally Sassanid Empire under Khosrau II and Jewish militias from Persia, but are subsequently massacred.

**612**

Sisebut, king of the Visigoths, forces his Jewish subjects to convert to Christianity.

**7th century**

The rise and domination of Islam among largely pagan Arabs in the Arabian Peninsula results in the almost complete removal and conversion of the ancient Jewish communities there, and sack of Levant from the hands of Byzantines.

Middle Ages

**8th century**

**700–1250**

Period of the Gaonim (the Gaonic era). Jews in southern Europe and Asia Minor lived under the often intolerant rule of Christian kings and clerics. Most Jews lived in the Muslim Arab realm

(Andalusia, North Africa, Palestine, Iraq and Yemen). Despite sporadic periods of persecution, Jewish communal and cultural life flowered in this period. The universally recognized centers of Jewish life were in Jerusalem and Tiberias (Syria), Sura and Pumbeditha (Iraq). The heads of these law schools were the *Gaonim*, who were consulted on matters of law by Jews throughout the world. During this time, the Niqqud is invented in Tiberias.

## 711

Muslim armies invade and occupy most of Spain (At this time Jews made up about 8% of Spain's population). Under Christian rule, Jews had been subject to frequent and intense persecution, which was formalized under Muslim rule due to the dhimmi rules in Islam. Jews and Christians had to pay the jizya. Some sources mark this as the beginning of the Golden age of Jewish culture in Spain, although most mention 912.

## 740

The Khazar (a Turkic semi-nomadic people from Central Asia) King and members of the upper class adopt Judaism. The Khazarate lasts until 10th century, being overrun by the Rus, and finally conquered by Rus and Byzantine forces in 1016.

## 760

The Karaites reject the authority of the oral law, and split off from rabbinic Judaism.

## 9th century

## 807

Abbasid Caliph Harun al-Rashid orders all Jews in the Caliphate to wear a yellow belt, with Christians to wear a blue one.

## 846

In Sura, Iraq, Rav Amram Gaon compiles his siddur (Jewish prayer book.)

## 850

al-Mutawakkil made a decree ordering dhimmi Jews and Christians to wear garments distinguishing them from Muslims, their places of worship to be destroyed, and allowing them little involvement in government or official matters.

## 871

An incomplete marriage contract dated to October 6 of this year is the earliest dated document found in the papers of the Cairo Geniza.

## 10th century

## 912–1013

The Golden age of Jewish culture in Spain. Abd-ar-Rahman III becomes Caliph of Spain in 912, ushering in the height of tolerance. Muslims granted Jews and Christians exemptions from military service, the right to their own courts of law, and a guarantee of safety of their property. Jewish poets, scholars, scientists, statesmen and philosophers flourished in and were an integral part of the extensive Arab civilization. This period ended with the Cordoba massacre in 1013.

## 940

In Iraq, Saadia Gaon compiles his siddur (Jewish prayer book).

## 945

In the Serenissima Repubblica di Venezia, the Senate forbids sea captains from accepting Jewish passengers.

**11th century**

**1008–1013**

Caliph Al-Hakim bi-Amr Allah ("the Mad") issues severe restrictions against Jews in the Fatimid Caliphate. All Jews are forced to wear a heavy wooden "golden calf" around their necks. Christians had to wear a large wooden cross and members of both groups had to wear black hats.

**1013**

During the fall of the city, Sulayman's troops looted Córdoba and massacred citizens of the city, including many Jews. Prominent Jews in Córdoba, such as Samuel ibn Naghrela were forced to flee to the city in 1013.

**1013–1073**

Rabbi Yitchaki Alfassi (from Morocco, later Spain) writes the *Rif*, an important work of Jewish law.

**1016**

The Jewish community of Kairouan, Tunisia is forced to choose between conversion and expulsion.

**1033**

Following their conquest of the city from the Maghrawa tribe, the forces of Tamim, chief of the Zenata Berber Banu Ifran tribe, perpetrated a massacre of Jews in Fez.

**1040–1105**

Rabbi Shlomo Yitzhaki (Rashi) writes important commentaries on almost the entire Tanakh and Talmud.

**1066 December 30**

Granada massacre: Muslim mob stormed the royal palace in Granada, crucified Jewish vizier Joseph ibn Naghrela and massacred most of the Jewish population of the city. "More than 1,500 Jewish families, numbering 4,000 persons, fell in one day."

**1090**

Granada was captured by Yusuf ibn Tashfin, King of the Almoravides. The Jewish community, believed to have sided with the Christians, was destroyed. Many fled, penniless, to Christian Toledo.

**1095–1291**

Christian Crusades begin, sparking warfare with Islam in Palestine. Crusaders temporarily capture Jerusalem in 1099. Tens of thousands of Jews are killed by European crusaders throughout Europe and in the Middle East.

**12th century**

**1100–1275**

Time of the *tosafot*, Talmudic commentators who carried on Rashi's work. They include some of his descendants.

**1107**

Moroccan Almoravid ruler Yusuf ibn Tashfin expels Moroccan Jews who do not convert to Islam.

**1135–1204**

Rabbi Moses ben Maimon, aka Maimonides or the Rambam is the leading rabbi of Sephardic Jewry. Among his many accomplishments, he writes one of the most influential codes of law (The Mishneh Torah) in Jewish History as well as, in Arabic, many philosophical works including the (Guide for the Perplexed).

**1141**

Yehuda Halevi issues a call to the Jews to emigrate to Palestine. He is buried in Jerusalem.

**1148**

Berbers oblige Jews to convert in Cordoba. Maimonides leaves Cordoba

**1176**

Maimonides completed his Introduction to the *Mishneh Torah*.

**1187**

Upon the capture of Jerusalem, Saladin summons the Jews and permits them to resettle in the city. In particular, the residents of Ashkelon, a large Jewish settlement, respond to his request.

**1189**

Jacob of Orléans slain in antisemitic riots that swept through London during the coronation of King Richard I. The king later punished the perpetrators of the crime.

**1190**

150 Jews of York, England, killed in a pogrom, known as the *York Massacre*.

**13th century**

**1240**

Jews living in England, under King Henry III, were blamed for counterfeiting the money and when the local citizens began to exact revenge on them, the king expelled his Jewish subjects in order to save them from harm.

**1250–1300**

The life of Moses de Leon, of Spain. He publishes to the public the Zohar the 2nd century CE esoteric interpretations of the Torah by Rabbi Shimon bar Yochai and his disciples. Thus begins the evolution of modern Kabbalah (esoteric Jewish mysticism).

**1250–1550**

Period of the *Rishonim*, the medieval rabbinic sages. Most Jews at this time lived in lands bordering the Mediterranean Sea or in Western Europe under feudal systems. With the decline of Muslim and Jewish centers of power in Iraq, there was no single place in the world which was a recognized authority for deciding matters of Jewish law and practice. Consequently, the rabbis recognized the need for writing commentaries on the Torah and Talmud and for writing law codes that would allow Jews anywhere in the world to be able to continue living in the Jewish tradition.

**1267**

Nachmanides (Ramban) settles in Jerusalem and builds the Ramban Synagogue.

**1270–1343**

Rabbi Jacob ben Asher of Spain writes the *Arba'ah Turim* (Four Rows of Jewish Law).

**1276**

Massacre in Fez to kill all Jews stopped by intervention of the Emir.

**1290**

Jews are expelled from England by Edward I after the banning of usury in the 1275 *Statute of Jewry*.

**14th century**

**1300**

Rabbi Levi ben Gershom, aka Gersonides. A 14th-century French Jewish philosopher best known for his *Sefer Milhamot Adonai* ("The Book of the Wars of the Lord") as well as for his philosophical commentaries.

**1304–1394**

Jews are repeatedly expelled from France and readmitted, for a price.

**1343**

Jews persecuted in Western Europe are invited to Poland by Casimir the Great.

**1346–1353**

Jews scapegoated as the cause of the growing Black Death. See also Medieval antisemitism

**1348**

Pope Clement VI issued two papal bulls in 1348 (6 July and 26 September), the latter named *Quamvis Perfidiam*, which condemned the violence and said those who blamed the plague on the Jews had been "seduced by that liar, the Devil." He urged clergy to take action to protect Jews as he had done.

**1349**

Several hundred Jews are publicly burned to death in the Strasbourg massacre.

**1350s**

Genetic testing conducted on Ashkenazi Jews has pointed to a bottleneck in the 1300s in the Ashkenazi Jewish population where it dwindled down to as few as 250–420 people.

**1369–70**

Civil war in Spain, between brothers Peter of Castile (Pedro) and Henry II of Castile (Enrico), leads to the deaths of 38,000 Jews, embroiled in the conflict.

**15th century**

**1478**

King Ferdinand and Queen Isabella of Spain institute the Spanish Inquisition.

**1486**

First Jewish prayer book published in Italy.

**1488–1575**

Rabbi Yosef Karo spends 20 years compiling the Beit Yosef, an enormous guide to Jewish law. He then writes a more concise guide, the Shulkhan Arukh, that becomes the standard law guide for the next 400 years. Born in Spain, Yosef Karo lives and dies in Safed.

**1488**

Obadiah ben Abraham, commentator on the Mishnah, arrives in Jerusalem and marks a new epoch for the Jewish community.

## 1492

The Alhambra Decree: Approximately 200,000 Jews are expelled from Spain, The expelled Jews relocate to the Netherlands, Turkey, Arab lands, and Judea; some eventually go to South and Central America. However, most emigrate to Poland. In later centuries, more than 50% of Jewish world population lived in Poland. Many Jews remain in Spain after publicly converting to Christianity, becoming Crypto-Jews.

## 1492

Bayezid II of the Ottoman Empire issued a formal invitation to the Jews expelled from Spain and Portugal and sent out ships to safely bring Jews to his empire.

## 1493

Jews expelled from Sicily. As many as 137,000 exiled.

## 1496

Jews expelled from Portugal and from many German cities.

Early Modern Era

### 16th century

### 1501

King Alexander of Poland readmits Jews to Grand Duchy of Lithuania.

### 1506

Lisbon massacre: Dominican friars promised absolution for sins committed over the previous 100 days to those who killed the Jews of Lisbon, and a crowd of more than 500 people (many of them sailors from the counties of Holland and Zeeland, and the Kingdom of Germany) gathered, persecuted, tortured, killed, and burnt at the stake hundreds of Jews. Women and children were beaten to death. Some Portuguese families saved their Jewish neighbors by hiding them.

### 1511

Printing of Jewish books by mechanical press began by Daniel Bomberg.

### 1516

Venetian Ghetto established, the first Jewish ghetto in Europe. Many others follow.

### 1525–1572

Rabbi Moshe Isserles (The Rema) of Kraków writes an extensive commentary to the Shulkhan Arukh called the *Mappah*, extending its application to Ashkenazi Jewry.

### 1534

King Sigismund I of Poland abolishes the law that required Jews to wear special clothes.

### 1534

First Yiddish book published, in Poland.

### 1534–1572

Isaac Luria **("the Arizal")** teaches Kabbalah in Jerusalem and (mainly) Safed to select disciples. Some of those, such as Ibn Tebul, Israel Sarug and mostly Chaim Vital, put his teachings into writing. While the Sarugian versions are published shortly afterwards in Italy and Holland, the Vitalian texts remain in manuscripti for as long as three centuries.

**1547**

First Hebrew Jewish printing house in Lublin.

**1550**

Jews expelled from Genoa, Italy.

**1550**

Moses ben Jacob Cordovero founds a Kabbalah academy in Safed.

**1567**

First yeshiva is founded in Poland.

**1577**

A Hebrew printing press is established in Safed, the first press in Palestine and the first in Asia.

**1580–1764**

First session of the Council of Four Lands (*Va'ad Arba' Aratzot*) in Lublin, Poland. 70 delegates from local Jewish **kehillot** meet to discuss taxation and other issues important to the Jewish community.

**17th century**

**1621–1630**

Shelah HaKadosh writes his most famous work after emigrating to the Land of Israel.

**1623**

First time separate (*Va'ad*) Jewish Sejm for Grand Duchy of Lithuania.

**1626–1676**

False Messiah Sabbatai Zevi.

**1627**

Kingdom of Beta Israel in what is now modern day Ethiopia collapses and loses autonomy.

**1633**

Jews of Poznań granted a privilege of forbidding Christians to enter into their city.

**1648**

Jewish population of Poland reached 450,000 (i.e., 4% of the 1,1000,000 population of Polish–Lithuanian Commonwealth is Jewish), Bohemia 40,000 and Moravia 25,000. Worldwide population of Jewry is estimated at 750,000.

**1648–1655**

The Ukrainian Cossack Bohdan Chmielnicki leads a massacre of Polish gentry and Jewry that leaves an estimated 65,000 Jews dead and a similar number of gentry. The total decrease in the number of Jews is estimated at 100,000.

**1655**

Jews readmitted to England by Oliver Cromwell.

**1660**

1660 destruction of Safed.

**1679**

Jews of Yemen expelled to Mawza

## 18th century

**1700–1760**

Israel ben Eliezer, known as the Baal Shem Tov, founds Hasidic Judaism, a way to approach God through meditation and fervent joy. He and his disciples attract many followers, and establish numerous Hasidic sects. The European Jewish opponents of Hasidim (known as Misnagdim) argue that one should follow a more scholarly approach to Judaism. Some of the more well-known Hasidic sects today include Bobover, Breslover, Gerer, Lubavitch (Chabad) and Satmar Hasidim.

**1700**

Rabbi Judah HeHasid makes **aliyah** to Palestine accompanied by hundreds of his followers. A few days after his arrival, Rabbi Yehuda dies suddenly.

**1700**

Sir Solomon de Medina is knighted by William III, making him the first Jew in England to receive that honour.

**1720**

Unpaid Arab creditors burn the synagogue unfinished by immigrants of Rabbi Yehuda and expel all Ashkenazi Jews from Jerusalem. *See also Hurva Synagogue*

**1720–1797**

Rabbi Elijah of Vilna, the Vilna Gaon.

**1729–1786**

Moses Mendelssohn and the Haskalah (Enlightenment) movement. He strove to bring an end to the isolation of the Jews so that they would be able to embrace the culture of the Western world, and in turn be embraced by gentiles as equals. The Haskalah opened the door for the development of all the modern Jewish denominations and the revival of Hebrew as a spoken language, but it also paved the way for many who, wishing to be fully accepted into Christian society, converted to Christianity or chose to assimilate to emulate it.

**1740**

Parliament of Great Britain passes a general act permitting Jews to be naturalized in the American colonies. Previously, several colonies had also permitted Jews to be naturalized without taking the standard oath "upon the true faith of a Christian."

**1740**

Ottoman authorities invite Rabbi Haim Abulafia (1660–1744), renowned Kabbalist and Rabbi of Izmir, to come to the Holy Land. Rabbi Abulafia is to rebuild the city of Tiberias, which has lain desolate for some 70 years. The city's revival is seen by many as a sign of the coming of the Messiah.

**1740–1750**

Thousands immigrate to Palestine under the influence of Messianic predictions. The large immigration greatly increases the size and strength of the Jewish Settlement in Palestine.

**1747**

Rabbi Abraham Gershon of Kitov (Kuty) (1701–1761) is the first immigrant of the Hasidic Aliyah. He is a respected Talmudic scholar, mystic, and brother-in-law of Rabbi Israel Baal Shem Tov (founder of the Hasidic movement). Rabbi Abraham first settles in Hebron. Later, he relocates to Jerusalem at the behest of its residents.

**1759**

Followers of Jacob Frank joined ranks of Polish szlachta (gentry) of Jewish origins.

**1772–1795**

Partitions of Poland between Russia, Kingdom of Prussia and Austria. Main bulk of World Jewry lives now in those 3 countries. Old privileges of Jewish communities are denounced.

**1775–1781**

American Revolution; guaranteed the freedom of religion.

**1775**

Mob violence against the Jews of Hebron.

**1789**

The French Revolution. In 1791 France grants full right to Jews and allows them to become citizens, under certain conditions.

**1790**

In the US, President George Washington sends a letter to the Jewish community in Rhode Island. He writes that he envisions a country "which gives bigotry no sanction...persecution no assistance". Despite the fact that the US was a predominantly Protestant country, theoretically Jews are given full rights. In addition, the mentality of Jewish immigrants shaped by their role as merchants in Eastern Europe meant they were well-prepared to compete in American society.

**1791**

Russia creates the Pale of Settlement that includes land acquired from Poland with a huge Jewish population and in the same year Crimea. The Jewish population of the Pale was 750,000. 450,000 Jews lived in the Prussian and Austrian parts of Poland.

**1798**

Rabbi Nachman of Breslov travels to Palestine.

**1799**

While French troops were in Palestine besieging the city of Acre, Napoleon prepared a Proclamation requesting Asian and African Jews to help him conquer Jerusalem, but his unsuccessful attempt to capture Acre prevented it from being issued.

**1799**

Mob violence on Jews in Safed.

19th century

**1800–1900**

The Golden Age of Yiddish literature, the revival of Hebrew as a spoken language, and the revival of Hebrew literature.

**1808–1840**

Large-scale aliyah in hope of Hastening Redemption in anticipation of the arrival of the Messiah in 1840.

**1820–1860**

The development of Orthodox Judaism, a set of traditionalist movements that resisted the influences of modernization that arose in response to the European emancipation and Enlightenment movements; characterized by continued strict adherence to Halakha.

**1830**

Greece grants citizenship to Jews.

**1831**

Jewish militias take part in the defense of Warsaw against Russians.

**1834–1835**

Muslims, Druze attack Jews in Safed, Hebron & in Jerusalem. (See related: Safed plunder).

**1837**

Moses Haim Montefiore is knighted by Queen Victoria

**1837**

Galilee earthquake of 1837 devastates Jewish communities of Safed and Tiberias.

**1838–1933**

Rabbi Yisroel Meir ha-Kohen (Chofetz Chaim) opens an important yeshiva. He writes an authoritative Halakhic work, Mishnah Berurah.

**Mid-19th century**

Beginning of the rise of classical Reform Judaism.

**Mid-19th century**

Rabbi Israel Salanter develops the Mussar Movement. While teaching that Jewish law is binding, he dismisses current philosophical debate and advocates the ethical teachings as the essence of Judaism.

**Mid-19th century**

Positive-Historical Judaism, later known as Conservative Judaism, is developed.

**1841**

David Levy Yulee of Florida is elected to the United States Senate, becoming the first Jew elected to Congress.

**1851**

Norway allows Jews to enter the country. They are not emancipated until 1891.

**1858**

Jews emancipated in England.

**1860**

Alliance Israelite Universelle, an international Jewish organization is founded in Paris with the goal to protect Jewish rights as citizens.

**1860–1875**

Moshe Montefiori builds Jewish neighbourhoods outside the Old City of Jerusalem starting with Mishkenot Sha'ananim.

**1860–1864**

Jews are taking part in Polish national movement, that was followed by January rising.[citation needed]

**1860–1943**

Henrietta Szold: educator, author, social worker and founder of Hadassah Women's Zionist Organization of America.

**1861**

The Zion Society is formed in Frankfurt am Main, Germany.

**1862**

Jews are given equal rights in Russian-controlled Congress Poland. The privileges of some towns regarding prohibition of Jewish settlement are revoked. In Leipzig, Moses Hess publishes the book Rome and Jerusalem, the first book to call for the establishment of a Jewish socialist commonwealth in Palestine. The book is also notable for giving the impetus for the Labor Zionist movement.

**1867**

Jews emancipated in Hungary.

**1868**

Benjamin Disraeli becomes Prime Minister of the United Kingdom. Though converted to Christianity as a child, he is the first person of Jewish descent to become a leader of government in Europe.

**1870–1890**

Russian Zionist group Hovevei Zion (Lovers of Zion) and Bilu (est. 1882) set up a series of Jewish settlements in the Land of Israel, financially aided by Baron Edmond James de Rothschild. In Rishon LeZion Eliezer ben Yehuda revives Hebrew as spoken modern language.

**1870**

Jews emancipated in Italy.

**1871**

Jews emancipated in Germany.

**1875**

Reform Judaism's Hebrew Union College is founded in Cincinnati. Its founder was Rabbi Isaac Mayer Wise, the architect of American Reform Judaism.

**1877**

New Hampshire becomes the last state to give Jews equal political rights.

**1878**

Petah Tikva is founded by religious pioneers from Jerusalem, led by Yehoshua Stampfer.

**1880**

World Jewish population around 7.7 million, 90% in Europe, mostly Eastern Europe; around 3.5 million in the former Polish provinces.

**1881–1884, 1903–1906, 1918–1920**

Three major waves of pogroms kill tens of thousands of Jews in Russia and Ukraine. More than two million Russian Jews emigrate in the period 1881–1920.

**1881**

On December 30–31, the First Congress of all Zionist Unions for the colonization of Palestine was held at Focşani, Romania.

**1882–1903**

The First Aliyah, a major wave of Jewish immigrants to build a homeland in Palestine.

**1886**

Rabbi Sabato Morais and Alexander Kohut begin to champion the Conservative Jewish reaction to American Reform, and establish The Jewish Theological Seminary of America as a school of 'enlightened Orthodoxy'.

**1890**

The term "Zionism" is coined by an Austrian Jewish publicist Nathan Birnbaum in his journal *Self Emancipation* and was defined as the national movement for the return of the Jewish people to their homeland and the resumption of Jewish sovereignty in the Land of Israel.

**1895**

First published book by Sigmund Freud.

**1897**

In response to the Dreyfus affair, Theodor Herzl writes Der Judenstaat (The Jewish State), advocating the creation of a free and independent Jewish state in Israel.

**1897**

The Bund (General Jewish Labour Bund) is formed in Russia.

**1897**

First Russian Empire Census: 5,200,000 of Jews, 4,900,000 in the Pale. The lands of former Poland have 1,300,000 Jews or 14% of population.

**1897**

The First Zionist Congress was held at Basel, which brought the World Zionist Organization (WZO) into being.

20th century

**1902**

Rabbi Dr. Solomon Schechter reorganizes the Jewish Theological Seminary of America and makes it into the flagship institution of Conservative Judaism.

**1903**

St. Petersburg's *Znamya* newspaper publishes a literary hoax *The Protocols of the Elders of Zion*. Kishinev Pogrom caused by accusations that Jews practice cannibalism.

**1905**

1905 Russian Revolution accompanied by pogroms.

**1915**

Yeshiva College (later University) and its Rabbi Isaac Elchanan Rabbinical Seminary is established in New York City for training in a Modern Orthodox milieu.

**1916**

Louis Brandeis, on the first of June, is confirmed as the United States' first Jewish Supreme Court justice. Brandeis was nominated by American President Woodrow Wilson.

The Balfour Declaration which supported the establishment of a Jewish homeland in Palestine and protected the civil and religious rights of existing non-Jewish communities.

## 1917

The British defeat the Turks and gain control of Palestine. The British issue the Balfour Declaration which gives official British support for "the establishment in Palestine of a national home for the Jewish people ... it being clearly understood that nothing shall be done which may prejudice the civil and religious rights of existing non-Jewish communities in Palestine". Many Jews interpret this to mean that all of Palestine was to become a Jewish state.

## 1917 February

The Pale of Settlement is abolished, and Jews get equal rights. The Russian Civil War leads to over 2,000 pogroms with tens of thousands murdered and hundreds of thousand made homeless.

## 1918–1939

The period between the two World Wars is often referred to as the "golden age" of *hazzanut* (cantors). Some of the great Jewish cantors of this era include Abraham Davis, Moshe Koussevitzky, Zavel Kwartin (1874–1953), Jan Peerce, Josef "Yossele" Rosenblatt (1882–1933), Gershon Sirota (1874–1943), and Laibale Waldman.

## 1919

February 15: Over 1,200 Jews killed in Khmelnitsky pogrom.

March 25: Around 4,000 Jews killed by Cossack troops in Tetiev.

June 17: 800 Jews decapitated in assembly-line fashion in Dubova [uk].

## 1920

At the San Remo conference Britain receives the League of Nations' British Mandate of Palestine.

April 4–7: Five Jews killed and 216 wounded in the Jerusalem riots

## 1920s–present

A variety of Jewish authors, including Gertrude Stein, Allen Ginsberg, Saul Bellow, Adrienne Rich and Philip Roth, sometimes drawing on Jewish culture and history, flourish and become highly influential on the Anglophone literary scene.

## 1921

British military administration of the Mandate is replaced by civilian rule.

## 1921

Britain proclaims that all of Palestine east of the Jordan River is forever closed to Jewish settlement, but not to Arab settlement.

**1921**

Polish–Soviet peace treaty in Riga. Citizens of both sides are given rights to choose the country. Hundred thousands of Jews, especially small businesses forbidden in the Soviets, move to Poland.

**1922**

Reform Rabbi Stephen S. Wise established the Jewish Institute of Religion in New York. (It merged with Hebrew Union College in 1950.)

**1923**

Britain gives the Golan Heights to the French Mandate of Syria. Arab immigration is allowed; Jewish immigration is not.

The First World Congress of Jewish Women is held 6–11 May in Vienna.

**1924**

2,989,000 Jews according to religion poll in Poland (10.5% of total). Jewish youth consisted 23% of students of high schools and 26% of students of universities.

**1926**

Prior to World War I, there were few Hasidic yeshivas in Europe. On Lag BaOmer 1926, Rabbi Shlomo Chanoch Hacohen Rabinowicz, the fourth Radomsker Rebbe, declared, "The time has come to found yeshivas where the younger generation will be able to learn and toil in Torah", leading to the founding of the Keser Torah network of 36 yeshivas in pre-war Poland.

**1929**

A long-running dispute between Muslims and Jews over access to the Western Wall in Jerusalem escalates into the 1929 Palestine riots. The riots included attacks by Arabs on Jews, resulting in massacres in Hebron and Safed, and violence against Jews in Jerusalem.

**1930**

World Jewry: 15,000,000. Main countries USA (4,000,000), Poland (3,500,000 11% of total), Soviet Union (2,700,000 2% of total), Romania (1,000,000 6% of total). Palestine 175,000 or 17% of total 1,036,000.

**1933**

Hitler takes over Germany; his anti-Semitic sentiments are well-known, prompting numerous Jews to emigrate.

**1935**

Regina Jonas became the first woman to be ordained as a rabbi.

**1937**

Adin Steinsaltz born, author of the first comprehensive Babylonian Talmud commentary since Rashi in the 11th century.

**1939**

The British government issues the 'White Paper'. The paper proposed a limit of 10,000 Jewish immigrants for each year between 1940 and 1944, plus 25,000 refugees for any emergency arising during that period.

**1938–1945**

The Holocaust (Ha Shoah), resulting in the methodical extermination of nearly 6 million Jews across Europe.

**1940s–present**

Various Jewish filmmakers, including Billy Wilder, Woody Allen, Mel Brooks and the Coen Brothers, frequently draw on Jewish philosophy and humor, and become some of the most artistically and popularly successful in the history of the medium.

**1941**

The Muslim residents of Baghdad carried out a savage pogrom against their Jewish compatriots. In this pogrom, known by its Arabic name *al-Farhud*, about 200 Jews were murdered and thousands wounded, on June 1–2. Jewish property was plundered and many homes set ablaze.

**1941**

The Lubavitcher Rebbe, Rabbi Menachem Schneerson, arrives in New York after escaping Nazi Europe. Along with his father-in-law, the previous Rebbe, he builds one of the largest worldwide movements (Chabad-Lubavitch) aimed at inspiring Jews to return to their heritage and Torah observance.

**1945–1948**

Post-Holocaust refugee crisis. British attempts to detain Jews attempting to enter Palestine illegally.

**1946–1948**

The violent struggle for the creation of a Jewish state in the British mandate of Palestine is intensified by Jewish defense groups: Haganah, Irgun, and Lehi (group).

**November 29, 1947**

The United Nations approves the creation of a Jewish State and an Arab State in the British mandate of Palestine.

**May 14, 1948**

The State of Israel declares itself as an independent Jewish state hours before the British Mandate is due to expire. Within eleven minutes, it is de facto recognized by the United States. Andrei Gromyko, the Soviet Union's UN ambassador, calls for the United Nations to accept Israel as a member state. The UN approves.

**May 15, 1948**

1948 Arab–Israeli War: Syria, Iraq, Transjordan, Lebanon and Egypt invade Israel hours after its creation. The attack is repulsed, and Israel conquers more territory. A Jewish exodus from Arab and Muslim lands results, as up to a million Jews flee or are expelled from Arab and Muslim nations. Most settle in Israel. See also 1949 Armistice Agreements.

**1948–1949**

Almost 250,000 Holocaust survivors make their way to Israel. "Operation Magic Carpet" brings thousands of Yemenite Jews to Israel.

**1956**

The 1956 Suez War Egypt blockades the Gulf of Aqaba, and closes the Suez canal to Israeli shipping. Egypt's President Gamal Abdel Nasser calls for the destruction of Israel. Israel, England,

and France go to war and force Egypt to end the blockade of Aqaba, and open the canal to all nations.

**1964**

Jewish-Christian relations are revolutionized by the Roman Catholic Church's Vatican II.

**1965**

Los Angeles Dodgers pitcher Sandy Koufax refuses to pitch Game 1 of the 1965 World Series because it fell on Yom Kippur.

**1966**

Shmuel Yosef Agnon (1888–1970) becomes the first Hebrew writer to win the Nobel Prize in literature.

**May 16, 1967**

Egyptian President Nasser demands that the UN dismantle the UN Emergency Force I (UNEF I) between Israel and Egypt. The UN complies and the last UN peacekeeper is out of Sinai and Gaza by May 19.

**1967 May**

Egyptian President Gamal Abdel Nasser closes the strategic Straits of Tiran to Israeli shipping. Egyptian troops replace the United Nations in the Sinai Peninsula.

**June 5–10, 1967**

The Six-Day War. Israel launches a pre-emptive strike against Egypt, Jordan, and Syria. Israeli aircraft destroy the bulk of the Arab air forces on the ground in a surprise attack, followed by Israeli ground offensives which see Israel decisively defeat the Arab forces and capture the Sinai Peninsula, the West Bank, and the Golan Heights.

**September 1, 1967**

The Arab Leaders meet in Khartoum, Sudan. The Three No's of Khartoum: No recognition of Israel. No negotiations with Isracl. No pcacc with Israel.

**1968**

Rabbi Mordechai Kaplan formally creates a separate Reconstructionist Judaism movement by setting up the Reconstructionist Rabbinical College in Philadelphia.

**1969**

First group of African Hebrew Israelites begin to migrate to Israel under the leadership of Ben Ammi Ben Israel.

**Mid-1970s to present**

Growing revival of Klezmer music (The folk music of European Jews).,

**1972**

Sally Priesand became the first female rabbi ordained in the US, and is believed to be only the second woman ever to be formally ordained in the history of Judaism.

**1972**

Mark Spitz sets the record for most gold medals won in a single Olympic Games (seven) in the 1972 Summer Olympics. The Munich massacre occurs when Israeli athletes are taken hostage by Black September terrorists. The hostages are killed during a failed rescue attempt.

**October 6–24, 1973**

The Yom Kippur War. Egypt and Syria, backed up by expeditionary forces from other Arab nations, launch a surprise attack against Israel on Yom Kippur. After absorbing the initial attacks, Israel recaptures lost ground and then pushes into Egypt and Syria. Subsequently, OPEC reduces oil production, driving up oil prices and triggering a global economic crisis.

**1975**

President Gerald Ford signs legislation including the Jackson–Vanik amendment, which ties US trade benefits to the Soviet Union to freedom of emigration for Jews.

**1975**

United Nations adopts resolution equating Zionism with racism. Rescinded in 1991.

**1976**

Israel rescues hostages taken to Entebbe, Uganda.

**September 18, 1978**

At Camp David, near Washington D.C., Israel and Egypt sign a comprehensive peace treaty, The Camp David Accord, which included the withdrawal of Israel from the Sinai.

**1978**

Yiddish writer Isaac Bashevis Singer receives Nobel Prize

**1979**

Prime Minister Menachem Begin and President Anwar Sadat are awarded Nobel Peace Prize.

**1979–1983**

Operation Elijah: Rescue of Ethiopian Jewry.

**1982 June–December**

The Lebanon War. Israel invades Southern Lebanon to drive out the PLO.

**1983**

American Reform Jews formally accept patrilineal descent, creating a new definition of who is a Jew.

**1984–1985**

Operations Moses, Joshua: Rescue of Ethiopian Jewry by Israel.

**1986**

Elie Wiesel wins the Nobel Peace Prize

**1986**

Nathan Sharansky, Soviet Jewish dissident, is freed from prison.

**1987**

Beginning of the First Intifada against Israel.

**1989**

Fall of the Berlin Wall between East and West Germany, collapse of the communist East German government, and the beginning of Germany's reunification (which formally began in October 1990).

**1990**

The Soviet Union opens its borders for the three million Soviet Jews who had been held as virtual prisoners within their own country. Hundreds of thousands of Soviet Jews choose to leave the Soviet Union and move to Israel.

**1990–1991**

Iraq invades Kuwait, triggering a war between Iraq and Allied United Nations forces. Israel is hit by 39 Scud missiles from Iraq.

**1991**

Operation Solomon: Rescue of the remainder of Ethiopian Jewry in a twenty-four-hour airlift.

**October 30, 1991**

The Madrid Peace Conference opens in Spain, sponsored by the United States and the Soviet Union.

**April 22, 1993**

The United States Holocaust Memorial Museum dedicated.

Yitzhak Rabin and Yasser Arafat shake hands at the signing of the Oslo Accords, with Bill Clinton behind them, 1993

**September 13, 1993**

Israel and PLO sign the Oslo Accords.

**1994**

The Lubavitcher (Chabad) Rebbe, Menachem Mendel Schneerson, dies.

**October 26, 1994**

Israel and Jordan sign an official peace treaty. Israel cedes a small amount of contested land to Jordan, and the countries open official diplomatic relations, with open borders and free trade.

**December 10, 1994**

Arafat, Rabin and Israeli Foreign Minister Shimon Peres share the Nobel Peace Prize.

**November 4, 1995**

Israeli Prime Minister Yitzhak Rabin is assassinated.

**1996**

Peres loses election to Benyamin (Bibi) Netanyahu (Likud party).

**1999**

Ehud Barak elected Prime Minister of Israel.

21st century

**May 24, 2000**

Israel unilaterally withdraws its remaining forces from its security zone in southern Lebanon to the international border, fully complying with the UN Security Council Res. 425.

**2000 July**

Camp David Summit.

**2000, Summer**

Senator Joseph Lieberman becomes the first Jewish-American to be nominated for a national office (Vice President of the United States) by a major political party (the Democratic Party).

**September 29, 2000**

The al-Aqsa Intifada begins.

**2001**

Election of Ariel Sharon as Israel's Prime Minister.

**2001**

Jewish Museum of Turkey is founded by Turkish Jewry

**2004**

Avram Hershko and Aaron Ciechanover of the Technion win the Nobel Prize in Chemistry. The Jewish Autonomous Oblast builds its first synagogue, Birobidzhan Synagogue, in accordance with halakha. Uriyahu Butler became the first member of the African Hebrew Israelite community to enlist in the Israel Defense Forces (IDF)

**March 31, 2005**

The Government of Israel officially recognizes the Bnei Menashe people of Northeast India as one of the Ten Lost Tribes of Israel, opening the door for thousands of people to immigrate to Israel.

**2005 August**

The Government of Israel withdraws its military forces and settlers from the Gaza Strip.

**2005 December**

Prime Minister Ariel Sharon falls into a coma; Deputy Premier Ehud Olmert takes over as Acting Prime Minister

**2006 March**

Ehud Olmert leads the Kadima party to victory in Israeli elections, becomes Prime Minister of Israel.

**2006 July–August**

A military conflict in Lebanon and northern Israel started on July 12, after a Hezbollah cross-border raid into Israel. The war ended with the passage of United Nations Security Council Resolution 1701 after 34 days of fighting. About 2,000 Lebanese and 159 Israelis were killed, and civilian infrastructure on both sides heavily damaged.

**2008 December**

The Israel Defense Forces (IDF) launches Operation Cast Lead (מבצע עופרת יצוקה) against Hamas in the Gaza Strip.

**2009 March**

Benjamin Netanyahu becomes Prime Minister of Israel (also, continues as the Chairman of the Likud Party).

**2014 January**

Ariel Sharon dies, after undergoing a sudden decline in health, having suffered renal failure and other complications, after spending 8 years in a deep coma due to his January 2006 stroke, on January 11, 2014.

**2016 March**

The Jewish Agency declares an end to immigration from Yemen, following the successful conclusion of a covert operation that brought 19 people to Israel over several days. The last 50 Yemenite Jews refuse to leave Yemen.

**2017 December**

The United States extends formal recognition of Jerusalem as the capital of Israel.

**2019 March**

The United States became the first country to recognize Israeli sovereignty over the Golan Heights territory which it held since 1967.

**2020 August**

Israel and the United Arab Emirates sign a peace treaty.

**30 April 2021**

45 people are killed in the 2021 Meron stampede during Lag BaOmer.

**7 October 2023**

In the day considered the deadliest for Jews since the Holocaust, as well as deadliest day in Israel's history, 1,390 people are killed in the 2023 Hamas attack on Israel.

# Torah (Pentateuch)

The **Torah (Hebrew: "instruction, teaching")** is the central reference of Judaism. It can most specifically mean the **first five books (*Pentateuch= Genesis, Exodus, Leviticus, Numbers, Deuteronomy*),** of the **twenty-four books of the Tanakh,** and it usually includes the rabbinic commentaries (*perushim*). It can mean the continued narrative from **Book of Genesis** to the end of the **Tanakh**

**Torah** consists of the origin of Jewish peoplehood: their call into being by God, their trials and tribulations, and their **covenant with their God,** which involves following a way of life embodied in a set of moral and religious obligations and civil laws (*halakha*). In rabbinic literature the word **"Torah"** denotes both the five books and the **Oral Torah ("Torah that is spoken").** The Oral **Torah** consists of interpretations and amplifications and are now embodied in the **Talmud** and **Midrash.**

According to rabbinic tradition, all of the teachings found in the **Torah**, both written and oral, were given by God through the prophet **Moses**, some at Mount Sinai and others at the **Tabernacle,** and all the teachings were written down by **Moses**, which resulted in the **Torah** that exists today. According to the **Midrash, the Torah was created prior to the creation of the world,** and was used as the blueprint for Creation.

The majority of Biblical scholars believe that the written books were a product of the **Babylonian captivity (c. 600 BCE),** based on earlier written and oral traditions, and that it was completed by the period of **Achaemenid rule (c. 400 BCE).**

The term **"Torah"** is used in the general sense to include both Rabbinic Judaism's written law and **Oral Law,** serving to encompass the entire spectrum of authoritative Jewish religious teachings throughout history, including the **Mishnah,** the **Talmud,** the **Midrash** and more. The earliest name for the first part of the Bible seems to have been **"The Torah of Moses".** It appears in **Joshua (8:31–32; 23:6) and Kings (I Kings 2:3; II Kings 14:6; 23:25).**

## Contents
The **Torah** starts from the beginning of God's creating the world, through the beginnings of the people of Israel, their descent into Egypt, and the giving of the **Torah** at Mt. Sinai. It ends with the death of **Moses**, just before the people of Israel cross to the promised land of Canaan.

## In Hebrew, the five books of the Torah:
- **Bereshit** (literally "In the beginning")—Genesis
- **Shemot** (literally "Names")—Exodus
- **Vayikra** (literally "And He called")—Leviticus

- **Bəmidbar** (literally "In the desert [of]")—Numbers
- **Devarim** (literally "Things" or "Words")—Deuteronomy

## Bereshit/Genesis

*Genesis* begins with the so-called "**primeval history**" (Genesis 1–11), the story of the world's beginnings and the descent from Adam. This is followed by the story of the three patriarchs (**Abraham, Isaac** and **Jacob**), **Joseph** (Genesis 12–50) and the four matriarchs (**Sarah, Rebekah, Leah and Rachel).**

God gives to the patriarchs a promise of the land of Canaan, but at the end of Genesis the sons of Jacob end up leaving Canaan for Egypt due to a regional famine. They had heard that there was a grain storage and distribution facility in Egypt.

## Shemot/Exodus

**Exodus** begins the story of God's revelation to his people of Israel through **Moses**, who leads them out of Egypt (**Exodus 1–18**) to Mount Sinai. There the people accept the covenant with God, agreeing to be his people and abide by his holy Law, in return for his agreeing to be their God, and protect and defend them from their enemies, and provide for and prosper them.

**Moses** receives the **Torah** from God, and teaches His laws and **Covenant** (**Exodus 19–24**) to the people of Israel. It also talks about the first violation of the covenant when the **Golden Calf** was constructed (Exodus 32–34). Exodus includes the instructions on building the **Tabernacle** and concludes with its actual construction **(Exodus 25–31; 35–40).**

## Vayikra/Leviticus

*Leviticus* begins with instructions to the Israelites on how to use the Tabernacle, which they had just built (**Leviticus 1–10**). This is followed by rules of **clean and unclean** (**Leviticus 11–15**), which includes the laws of slaughter and animals permissible to eat, the **Day of Atonement (Leviticus 16)**, and various moral and ritual laws sometimes called the **Holiness Code (Leviticus 17–26). Leviticus 26** provides a detailed list of rewards for following God's commandments and a detailed list of punishments for not following them.

## Bəmidbar/Numbers

*Numbers* tells how Israel consolidated itself as a community at Sinai (**Numbers 1–9**), set out from Sinai to move towards Canaan and **spied out the land** (Numbers 10–13). Because of unbelief at various points, but especially at **Kadesh Barnea (Numbers 14)**, the Israelites were condemned to wander for **forty years** in the desert instead of immediately entering the **Promised Land**. Even **Moses** sins and is told he would not live to enter the land (**Numbers 20**). At the end of Numbers (**Numbers 26–35**) Israel is ready to enter the **Promised Land**.

## Devarim/Deuteronomy

*Deuteronomy* is a series of speeches by **Moses** on the plains of **Moab** opposite Jericho. **Moses** proclaims the Law (Deuteronomy 12–26), gives instruction concerning covenant renewal at **Shechem** (Deuteronomy 27–28) and gives Israel new laws (the **"Deuteronomy Code"**). At the end of the book (Deuteronomy 34) **Moses** is allowed to see the **Promised Land** from a mountain, and then dies.

The text emphasizes that **no one knows where Moses was finally buried** (34:6). Knowing that he was nearing the end of his life, **Moses** had appointed **Joshua** his successor, bequeathing to him the mantle of leadership. Soon afterwards Israel begins the conquest of **Canaan**.

The modern scholarly consensus is that the **Pentateuch** was composed in the late 7th or the 6th century BC. The **Pentateuch** (or **Torah**, as it is known by Jews) comprises material taken from six centuries of human history, which has been put together to give a comprehensive picture of the creation of the world and of God's dealings with his peoples, specifically with the people of Israel.

## Torah and Judaism

The **Oral Torah** was given to **Moses at Mount Sinai**, which, according to the tradition of **Orthodox Judaism**, occurred in **1312 BC**. The **Written Torah** has multiple authors and was written over centuries. The Talmud (**Menachot 30a**) says that the last eight verses of the **Torah** that discuss the death and burial of **Moses** could not have been written by **Moses**, that they were written after his death by **Joshua**. All classical rabbinic views hold that the **Torah** was entirely **Mosaic and of divine origin**.

## Ritual use

Regular public reading of the **Torah** was introduced by **Ezra the Scribe** after the return of the Jewish people from the **Babylonian captivity** (c. 537 BCE), as described in the **Book of Nehemiah**. The **Torah** remained unchanged in the **two thousand years since the destruction of the Temple in Jerusalem (70 CE, by the Romans)**. Jews observe an annual holiday, **Simchat Torah**, to celebrate the completion and new start of the year's cycle of readings.

## The Oral Torah

Rabbinic tradition holds that **Moses** learned the whole **Torah** while he lived on Mount Sinai for 40 days and nights and both the oral and the written **Torah** were transmitted in parallel with each other. The **Oral Law** was committed to writing. Lectures and traditions only alluded to in the few hundred pages of **Mishnah**, became the thousands of pages now called the *Gemara*.

Gemara is written in Aramaic, having been compiled in Babylon. The **Mishnah and Gemara together are called the Talmud**. The Rabbis in Israel also collected their traditions and compiled them into the **Jerusalem Talmud**. Since the greater number of Rabbis lived in Babylon, the **Babylonian Talmud** was adapted.

## Production and use of a Torah scroll: *Sefer Torah*

The fidelity of the Hebrew text of the **Tanakh**, and the **Torah** in particular, is considered paramount, down to the last letter. An error of a single letter, ornamentation, or symbol of the **304,805** stylized letters that make up the text renders a **Torah** scroll unfit for use, hence a special skill is required and a scroll takes considerable time to write and check.

Written entirely in Hebrew, a *Sefer Torah* contains **304,805** letters, all of which must be duplicated precisely by a trained *sofer* **("scribe"),** an effort that may take as long as approximately one and a half years. **Torah** scrolls are stored in the holiest part of the synagogue in the Ark known as the **"Holy Ark".**

## Torah translations: Aramaic/ *Targum*

The **Book of Ezra** refers to translations and commentaries of the Hebrew text into Aramaic. These translations would seem to date to the 6th century BCE. The Aramaic term for *translation* is *Targum*.

## Greek: *Septuagint*

One of the earliest known translations of the first **five books of Moses** from the Hebrew into Greek was the **Septuagint**. This Greek version of the **Hebrew Scriptures** dates from the 3rd century BCE, originally associated with **Hellenistic Judaism.**

## Arabic

From the eighth century AD, the cultural language of Jews living under Islamic rule became Arabic rather than Aramaic. **"Around that time, both scholars and lay people started producing translations of the Bible into Judeo-Arabic using the Hebrew alphabet."** The best known was produced by **Saadiah**, and continues to be in use today, **"in particular among Yemenite Jewry."**

## Modern languages: Jewish translations

While Christianity includes the **five books of Moses (the *Pentateuch*)** among their sacred texts in its Old Testament, Islam states that only the original **Torah** was sent by God. In neither religion does the **Torah** retain the religious legal significance that it does in **Orthodox Judaism.**

The **Quran** refers heavily to **Moses** to outline the truth of his existence and the religious guidelines that God had revealed to the Children of Israel. According to the **Qur'an**, Allah says **"It is He Who has sent down the Book (the Qur'an) to you with truth, confirming what came before it. And He sent down the Taurat (Torah) and the Injeel (Gospel)." [3:3]**

Muslims call the **Torah** the *Taurat* and consider it the word of God given to **Moses**. However, Muslims also believe that **this original revelation was corrupted (*Tahrif*)** over time by Jewish scribes, (**Qur'an 7:144–144**)

According to the text of the Hebrew **Torah**, from the creation of **Adam** until Noah's flood the elapsed time is recorded as **one thousand six hundred and fifty-six years.**

# Twelve Tribes of Israel

In the Hebrew Bible, the **Twelve Tribes of Israel** or **Tribes of Israel** descended from the 12 sons of the patriarch Jacob (who was later named Israel) and his two wives, **Leah and Rachel**, and two concubines, **Zilpah and Bilhah**.

## Biblical (Torah) narrative

The tribes of Israel are described in the books of the **Torah** (Pentateuch), accounts written in the 8th–6th centuries BCE in Hebrew.

## Tribes

The Israelites were the twelve sons of the biblical patriarch Jacob. Jacob also had one daughter, **Dinah**, whose descendants were not recognized as a separate tribe.

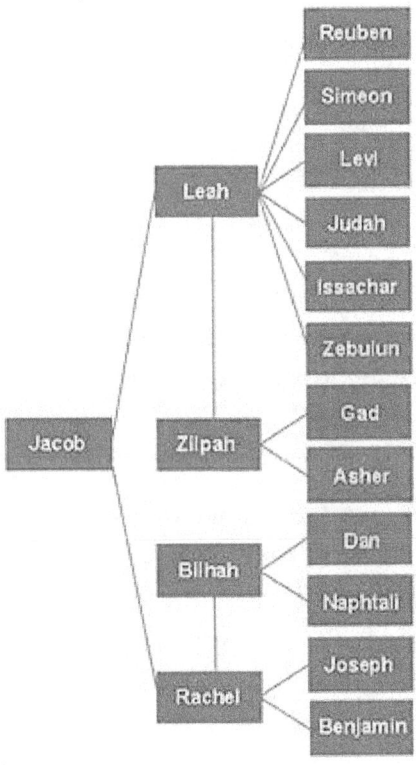

## Parentage of Jacob's twelve sons, per Genesis 35

The sons of Jacob were born in **Padan-aram** from different mothers, as follows:

- **The sons of Leah**; Reuben (Jacob's firstborn), Simeon, Levi, Judah, Issachar, & Zebulun
- **The sons of Rachel**; **Joseph**, and Benjamin
- **The sons of Bilhah**, Rachel's handmaid; Dan, and Naphtali
- **The sons of Zilpah**, Leah's handmaid; Gad, and Asher

## Deuteronomy 27:12–13 lists the twelve tribes:

- **Reuben** (Hebrew ראובן *Rə'ûḇēn*)

- **Simeon** (שמעון *Šimʿôn*)
- **Levi** (לוי *Lêwî*)
- **Judah** (יהודה *Yehuḏā*)
- **Issachar** (יששכר *Yiśśāḵār*)
- **Zebulun** (זבולון *Zəḇūlun*)
- **Dan** (דן *Dān*)
- **Naphtali** (נפתלי *Nap̄tālî*)
- **Gad** (גד *Gāḏ*)
- **Asher** (אשר *ʾĀšêr*)
- **Benjamin** (בנימין *Binyāmîn*)
- **Joseph** (יוסף *Yôsēp̄*), later split into two "half-tribes":
  - **Ephraim** (אפרים *ʾEp̄rayim*)
  - **Manasseh** (מנשה *Mənaššeh*)

Jacob elevated the descendants of **Ephraim and Manasseh** (the two sons of **Joseph** and his Egyptian wife **Asenath**) to the status of full tribes in their own right due to **Joseph** receiving a double portion after **Reuben** lost his birth right because of his transgression with **Bilhah.** In the biblical narrative, the period from the conquest of Canaan under the leadership of **Joshua** until the formation of the first **Kingdom of Israel**, passed with the tribes forming a loose confederation, described in the **Book of Judges**.

The extent to which a **United Kingdom of Israel** ever existed is a matter of ongoing dispute. Living in exile in the sixth century BCE, the prophet **Ezekiel** has a vision for the restoration of Israel, of a future utopia in which the twelve tribes of Israel are living in their land again.

## Land allotment

The Land of Israel was divided into twelve sections corresponding to the twelve tribes of Israel. The Tribe of **Levi** had no land appropriation but had six Cities of Refuge under their administration as well as the Temple in Jerusalem. There was no land allotment for the **Tribe of Joseph,** but **Joseph**'s two sons, **Ephraim** and **Manasseh**, received their father's land portion.

## In Christianity

In the Christian New Testament, the twelve tribes of Israel are referred to twice in the gospels and twice in the **Book of Revelation**. In **Matthew**, paralleled by **Luke**, Jesus anticipates that in the **Kingdom of God**, his followers will **"sit on thrones, judging the twelve tribes of Israel"**. The **Epistle of James** is addressed to the twelve tribes who are dispersed abroad. The dying Jacob blesses his twelve sons.

## In Islam

The **Qur'an** (7th century CE) states that the people of **Moses** were split into twelve tribes. **Surah 7 (Al-A'raf) verse 160** says:

"We split them up into twelve tribal communities, and We revealed to Moses, when his people asked him for water, 'Strike the rock with your staff,' whereat twelve fountains gushed forth from it. Every tribe came to know its drinking-place. And We shaded them with clouds, and We sent down to them manna and quails: 'Eat of the good things We have provided you.' And they did not wrong Us, but they used to wrong themselves."

## Historicity

For thousands of years, Christians and Jews accepted as fact the history of the twelve tribes. Similarly, the notion that all twelve tribes are descended from the twelve sons of **Jacob** appears to have emerged late: **"almost no tribal lists, and virtually none outside of the books of Genesis and Chronicles, mention Jacob or present him as the literal ancestor of the tribes."**

# Tzimtzum

The *Tzimtzum* or *tsimtsum* (Hebrew *ṣimṣūm* "contraction/constriction/condensation") is a term used in the **Lurianic Kabbalah** to explain **Isaac Luria's** doctrine that God began the process of creation by "**contracting**" his *Ohr Ein Sof* (infinite light) in order to allow for a "**conceptual space**" in which finite and seemingly independent realms could exist.

This primordial initial contraction, forming a *ḥālāl happānuy* "vacant space" into which new creative light could beam, is denoted by general reference to the *Tzimtzum*. In Kabbalistic interpretation, *Tzimtzum* gives rise to the paradox of simultaneous Divine presence and absence within the vacuum and resultant Creation.

## Function

Because the *Tzimtzum* results in the "**empty space**" in which spiritual and physical Worlds and ultimately, free will can exist, God is often referred to as "**Ha-Makom**" ("**the Place**", "**the Omnipresent**") in Rabbinic literature (**"He is the Place of the World, but the World is not His Place"**). Relatedly, *Olam* — the Hebrew for "**World/Realm**" — is derived from the root עלם meaning "**concealment**". The subsequent spiritual realms and the ultimate physical universe conceal to different degrees the infinite spiritual lifeforce of creation.

Their progressive diminutions of the **Divine Ohr (Light)** from realm to realm in creation are also referred to in the plural as secondary *Tzimtzumim* (**innumerable "condensations/veilings/constrictions"** of the lifeforce). However, these subsequent concealments are found in earlier, **Medieval Kabbalah**. The new doctrine of **Luria** advanced the notion of the primordial withdrawal (**a** *dilug* – radical "leap") in order to reconcile a causal creative chain from the Infinite with finite Existence.

**Prior to Creation, there was only the infinite Or Ein Sof filling all existence**. When it arose in G-d's Will to create worlds and emanate the emanated ... He contracted (in Hebrew "**Tzimtzum**") Himself in the point at the center, in the very center of His light. He restricted that light, distancing it to the sides surrounding the central point, so that there remained a void, a hollow empty space, away from the central point ... After this **Tzimtzum** ... He drew down from the Or **Ein Sof** a single straight line from His light surrounding from above to below, and it chained down descending into that void. ... In the space of that void He emanated, created, formed and made all the worlds.

## Inherent paradox / *Apophatic theology § Judaism*

A commonly held understanding in **Kabbalah** is that the concept of *Tzimtzum* contains a built-in paradox, requiring that God be simultaneously transcendent and immanent. Viz.: On the one hand, if the "**Infinite**" did not restrict itself, then nothing could exist—everything would be overwhelmed by God's totality. Existence thus requires God's transcendence, as above. On the other hand, God continuously maintains the existence of, and is thus not absent from, the created universe.

The Divine life-force which brings all creatures into existence must constantly be present within them ... were this life-force to forsake any created being for even one brief moment, it would revert to a state of utter nothingness, as before the creation.

**Rabbi Nachman of Breslav discusses this inherent paradox as follows:**
**"Only in the future will it be possible to understand the *Tzimtzum* that brought the "Empty Space" into being, for we have to say of it two contradictory things ... the Empty Space came about through the *Tzimtzum*, where, as it were, He 'limited' His Godliness and contracted it from there, and it is as though in that place there is no Godliness ... the absolute truth is that Godliness must nevertheless be present there, for certainly nothing can exist without His giving it life."**

## Science and Kabbalah / *Hyle*

The fundamental difference between modern science and traditional **Kabbalah** is the "post-Aristotelian scientific doctrine" about that space would be first created while in the Jewish religion of the Bible the faith considers that light was created before anything else.

### *Lurianic Kabbalah*

Isaac **Luria** introduced four central themes into kabbalistic thought, *Tzimtzum*, **Shevirat HaKelim (the shattering of the vessels), Tikkun (repair), and Partzufim**. These four are a group of interrelated, and continuing, processes. *Tzimtzum* describes the first step in the process by which God began the process of creation by withdrawing his own essence from an area, creating an area in which creation could begin.

**Shevirat HaKelim** describes how, after the *Tzimtzum*, God created the vessels (**HaKelim**) in the empty space, and how when God began to pour his **Light** into the vessels they were not strong enough to hold the power of God's **Light** and shattered (**Shevirat**). The third step, **Tikkun**, is the process of gathering together, and raising, the sparks of God's **Light** that were carried down with the shards of the shattered vessels.

Since *Tzimtzum* is connected to the concept of exile, and **Tikkun** is connected to the need to repair the problems of the world of human existence, **Luria** unites the cosmology of **Kabbalah** with the practice of Jewish ethics, and makes ethics and traditional Jewish religious observance the means by which God allows humans to complete and perfect the material world through living the precepts of a traditional Jewish life. Thus, in contrast to earlier, **Medieval Kabbalah**, this made the first creative act a concealment/Divine exile rather than unfolding revelation. This dynamic crisis-catharsis in the Divine flow is repeated throughout the **Luria**nic scheme.

## Chabad view

In **Chabad Hassidism** the concept of *Tzimtzum* is understood as not meant to be interpreted literally, but rather to refer to the manner in which God impresses his presence upon the consciousness of finite reality: thus *Tzimtzum* is not only seen as being a real process but is also seen as a doctrine that every person is able, and indeed required, to understand and meditate upon. In the **Chabad** view, the function of the *Tzimtzum* was **"to conceal from created beings the activating force within them, enabling them to exist as tangible entities, instead of being utterly nullified within their source"**. The *Tzimtzum* produced the required **"vacated space"**, devoid of direct awareness of God's presence.

## Vilna Gaon's view

The Vilna Gaon held that *Tzimtzum* was not literal, however, the **"upper unity"**, the fact that the universe is only illusory, and that *Tzimtzum* was only figurative, was not perceptible, or even really understandable, to those not fully initiated in the mysteries of **Kabbalah**.

## History and Hester Panim

In the modern era, **Shoah** has been the subject of discussion about theological thinking: the **Hester Panim** is a part of modern exegesis. **Tzimtzum** is a process before Creation but during history the same **"structure"** is even present, as modern philosophy like to know. The characteristic of **Shoah** is part of individual life and a part of this structure of history.

## Application in clinical psychology

An Israeli professor, **Mordechai Rotenberg**, believes the Kabbalistic-Hasidic *Tzimtzum* paradigm has significant implications for clinical therapy. According to this paradigm, God's **"self-contraction"** to vacate space for the world serves as a model for human behavior and interaction. The *Tzimtzum* model promotes a unique community-centric approach which contrasts starkly with the language of Western psychology.

# Wars of Israel

This is a **list of wars and other major military engagements involving Israel**. Since its declaration of independence in May 1948, the State of Israel has fought various wars with its neighboring Arab states, two major Palestinian Arab uprisings known as the First Intifada and the Second Intifada (see Israeli–Palestinian conflict), and a broad series of other armed engagements rooted in the Arab–Israeli conflict.

**Israel has been involved in a number of wars and large-scale military operations, including**:

- **1948 Arab–Israeli War** (November 1947 – July 1949) – Started as 6 months of civil war between Jewish and Arab militias when the mandate period in Palestine was ending and turned into a regular war after the establishment of Israel and the intervention of several Arab armies. In its conclusion, a set of agreements were signed between Israel, Egypt, Jordan, Lebanon, and Syria, called the 1949 Armistice Agreements, which established the armistice lines between Israel and its neighbours, also known as the *Green Line*.

- **Palestinian Fedayeen insurgency** (1950s–1960s) – Palestinian attacks and reprisal operations carried out by the Israel Defense Forces during the 1950s and 1960s. These actions were in response to constant fedayeen incursions during which Arab guerrillas infiltrated from Syria, Egypt, and Jordan into Israel to carry out attacks against Israeli civilians and soldiers. The policy of the reprisal operations was exceptional due to Israel's declared aim of getting a high 'blood cost' among the enemy side which was believed to be necessary in order to deter them from committing future attacks.

- **Suez Crisis** (October 1956) – A military attack on Egypt by Britain, France, and Israel, beginning on 29 October 1956, with the intention to occupy the Sinai Peninsula and to take over the Suez Canal. The attack followed Egypt's decision of 26 July 1956 to nationalize the Suez Canal after the withdrawal of an offer by Britain and the United States to fund the building of the Aswan Dam. Although the Israeli invasion of the Sinai was successful, the United States and USSR forced it to retreat. Even so, Israel managed to re-open the Straits of Tiran and pacified its southern border.

- **Six-Day War** (June 1967) – Fought between Israel and Arab neighbors Egypt, Jordan, and Syria. The nations of Iraq, Saudi Arabia, Kuwait, Algeria, and others also contributed troops and arms to the Arab forces. Following the war, the territory held by Israel expanded significantly ("The Purple Line"): The West Bank (including East Jerusalem) from Jordan, Golan Heights from Syria, Sinai and Gaza from Egypt.

- **War of Attrition** (1967–1970) – A limited war fought between the Israeli military and forces of the Egyptian Republic, the USSR, Jordan, Syria, and the Palestine Liberation Organization from 1967 to 1970. It was initiated by the Egyptians as a way of recapturing the Sinai from the Israelis, who had been in control of the territory since the mid-1967 Six-Day War. The hostilities ended with a ceasefire signed between the countries in 1970 with frontiers remaining in the same place as when the war began.

- **Yom Kippur War** (October 1973) – Fought from 6 to 26 October 1973 by a coalition of Arab states led by Egypt and Syria against Israel as a way of recapturing part of the territories which they lost to the Israelis back in the Six-Day War. The war began with a surprise joint attack by Egypt and Syria on the Jewish holiday of Yom Kippur. Egypt and Syria crossed the cease-fire lines in the Sinai and Golan Heights, respectively. Eventually Arab forces were defeated by Israel and there were no significant territorial changes.

- **Palestinian insurgency in South Lebanon** (1971–1982) – The PLO relocated to South Lebanon from Jordan, staged attacks on the Galilee, and used South Lebanon as a base for international operations. In 1978, Israel launches Operation Litani – the first Israeli large-scale invasion of Lebanon, which was carried out by the Israel Defense Forces in order to expel PLO forces from the territory. Continuing ground and rocket attacks, and Israeli retaliations, eventually escalate into the 1982 War.

- **1982 Lebanon War** (1982) – Began on 6 June 1982, when the Israel Defense Forces invaded southern Lebanon to expel the PLO from the territory. The Government of Israel ordered the invasion as a response to the assassination attempt against Israel's ambassador to the United Kingdom, Shlomo Argov, by the Abu Nidal Organization and due to the constant terror attacks on northern Israel made by the Palestinian guerrilla organizations which resided in Lebanon. The war resulted in the expulsion of the PLO from Lebanon and created an Israeli Security Zone in southern Lebanon.

- **South Lebanon conflict** (1985–2000) – Nearly 15 years of warfare between the Israel Defense Forces and its Lebanese Christian proxy militias against Lebanese Muslim guerrilla, led by Iranian-backed Hezbollah, within what was defined by Israelis as the "Security Zone" in South Lebanon.

- **First Intifada** (1987–1993) – First large-scale Palestinian uprising against Israel in the West Bank and the Gaza Strip.

- **Second Intifada** (2000–2005) – Second Palestinian uprising, a period of intensified violence, which began in late September 2000.

- **2006 Lebanon War** (summer 2006) – Began as a military operation in response to the abduction of two Israeli reserve soldiers by the Hezbollah. The operation gradually strengthened, to become a wider confrontation. The principal participants were Hezbollah paramilitary forces and the Israeli military. The conflict started on 12 July 2006 and continued until a United Nations-brokered ceasefire went into effect on 14 August 2006, though it formally ended on 8 September 2006, when Israel lifted its naval blockade of Lebanon. The war resulted in a stalemate.

- **Gaza War** or **Operation Cast Lead** (December 2008 – January 2009) – Three-week armed conflict between Israel and Hamas during the winter of 2008–2009. In an escalation of the ongoing Israeli–Palestinian conflict, Israel responded to ongoing rocket fire from the Gaza Strip with military force in an action titled "Operation Cast Lead". Israel opened the attack with a surprise air strike on 27 December 2008. Israel's stated aim was to stop such rocket fire from and the import of arms into Gaza. Israeli forces attacked military and civilian targets, police stations, and government buildings in the opening assault. Israel declared an end to the conflict on 18 January and completed its withdrawal on 21 January 2009.

- **2012 Israeli operation in the Gaza Strip** or **Operation Pillar of Defense** (November 2012) – Military offensive on the Gaza Strip.[1]

- **2014 Gaza War** or **Operation Protective Edge** (July–August 2014) – Military offensive on the Gaza Strip as a response to the collapse of American-sponsored peace talks, attempts by rival Palestinian factions to form a coalition government, the kidnapping and murder of three Israeli teenagers, the subsequent kidnapping and murder of a Palestinian teenager, and increased rocket attacks on Israel by Hamas militants.[2]
- **Syrian Civil War** and the Iran–Israel conflict during the Syrian civil war.
- **2021 Israel–Palestine crisis** or **Operation Guardian of the Walls** (May 2021) – Riots between Jews and Arabs in Israeli cities. Hamas fired rockets into Israel, with Iron Dome intercepting the most dangerous projectiles. Israel began airstrikes in Gaza.
- **Israel–Hamas war** (October 2023- ). **Operation Swords of Iron**

# Yahweh

**Yahweh** was the national god of the kingdoms of Israel (**Samaria**) and **Judah**, with origins reaching at least to the early **Iron Age** and apparently to the **Late Bronze Age**. In the oldest biblical literature he is a **storm-and-warrior deity** who leads the heavenly army against Israel's enemies; at that time the Israelites worshipped him alongside a variety of Canaanite gods and goddesses, including **El**, Asherah and **Baal**, but in later centuries **El** and **Yahweh** became conflated and **El**-linked epithets such as **El Shaddai** came to be applied to **Yahweh** alone, and other gods and goddesses such as **Baal** and Asherah were absorbed into the Yahwistic religion.

From the 9th into the 6th centuries BCE the Yahwistic religion separated itself from its Canaanite heritage as **Yahweh** became the main god of the **Kingdom of Israel** (Samaria) and of Judah, and over time the royal court and Temple in Jerusalem promoted **Yahweh** as the god of the entire cosmos, possessing all the positive qualities previously attributed to the other gods and goddesses. By the end of the Babylonian captivity (6th century BCE), the very existence of foreign gods was denied, and **Yahweh** was proclaimed as the creator of the cosmos and the **one true God of all the world.**

During the **Second Temple** period, speaking the name of **Yahweh** in public became regarded as taboo. Jews began to substitute the divine name with the word, meaning **"Lord"**, and after the Temple was destroyed in 70 CE the original pronunciation was forgotten.

## Bronze Age origins

There is almost no agreement on the meaning and origins of the name **Yahweh**. *Ehyeh ašer ehyeh* **("I Am that I Am")**, the explanation presented in **Exodus 3:14**, appears to be a late theological gloss invented to explain **Yahweh**'s name at a time when the original meaning had been forgotten. The heavenly host accompanying **El**, the chief god of the Canaanites, as he marched beside the earthly armies of Israel.

He does not appear to have been a Canaanite god, although the Israelites were originally Canaanites. **Yahweh** was originally a **"divine warrior from the southern region associated with Seir, Edom, Paran and Teman"**. A plausible etymology for the name could be from the root *HWY*, which would yield the meaning **"he blows"**, appropriate to a weather divinity.

## Iron Age I (1200–930 BCE): El, Yahweh, and the origins of Israel

Israel emerges into the historical record in the last decades of the 13th century BCE, at the very end of the **Late Bronze Age** when the Canaanite city-state system was ending, and the milieu from which Israelite religion emerged was accordingly Canaanite. **El**, **"the kind, the compassionate"**, **"the creator of creatures"**, was the chief of the Canaanite gods, and he, not **Yahweh**, was the original **"God of Israel"**—the word **"Israel"** is based on the name **El** rather than **Yahweh**. He

844

lived in a tent on a mountain from whose base originated all the fresh waters of the world, with the goddess **Asherah** as his consort.

Prominent in this group was **Baal,** who had his home on **Mount Zaphon**; over time **Baal** became the dominant Canaanite deity, so that **El** became the executive power and **Baal** the military power in the cosmos. **Baal**'s sphere was the thunderstorm with its life-giving rains, so that he was also a fertility god. Below the seventy second-tier gods was a third tier made up of comparatively minor craftsman and trader deities, with a fourth and final tier of divine messengers and the like. **El** and his sons made up the **Assembly of the Gods**, each member of which had a human nation under his care, and a textual variant of **Deuteronomy 32:8–9** describes **El** dividing the nations of the world among his sons, with **Yahweh** receiving Israel.

The Israelites initially worshipped **Yahweh** alongside a variety of Canaanite gods and goddesses, including **El**, Asherah and **Baal**. In the period of the Judges and the first half of the monarchy, **El** and **Yahweh** became conflated in a process of religious syncretism. Features of **Baal**, **El**, and **Asherah** were absorbed into the Yahwistic religion, Asherah possibly becoming embodied in the feminine aspects of the **Shekhinah** or divine presence, and **Baal**'s nature as a storm and weather god becoming assimilated into **Yahweh**'s own identification with the storm.

In the earliest literature such as the **Song of the Sea (Exodus 15:1–18**, celebrating **Yahweh**'s victory over Egypt at the exodus), **Yahweh** is a warrior for his people, a storm-god typical of ancient Near Eastern myths, marching out from a region to the south or south-east of Israel with the heavenly host of stars and planets that make up his army. Israel's battles are **Yahweh**'s battles, Israel's victories are his victories, and while other peoples have other gods, Israel's god is **Yahweh**, who will procure a fertile resting-place for them:

**There is none like God, O Jeshurun (i.e., Israel)**
**who rides through the heavens to your help ...**
**he subdues the ancient gods, shatters the forces of old ...**
**so Israel lives in safety, untroubled is Jacob's abode ...**
**Your enemies shall come fawning to you,**
**and you shall tread on their backs.**
**— *Deuteronomy 33:26–29***

## Iron Age II (1000–586 BCE): Yahweh as God of Israel / *Yahwism*

Iron Age **Yahweh** was the national god of the **kingdoms of Israel and Judah,** and appears to have been worshipped only in these two kingdoms; the god , for example, was worshipped only by the Assyrians.

After the 9th century BCE the tribes and chiefdoms of Iron Age I were replaced by ethnic nation states, Israel, Judah, Moab, Ammon and others, each with its national god, and all more or less equal. Thus **Chemosh** was the god of the Moabites, Milcom the god of the **Ammonites, Qaus** the god of the Edomites, and **Yahweh** the "God of Israel" (no "God of Judah" is mentioned anywhere in the Bible).

In each kingdom the king was also the head of the national religion and thus the viceroy on Earth of the national god; in Jerusalem this was reflected each year when the king presided over a ceremony at which **Yahweh** was enthroned in the Temple.

The centre of **Yahweh**'s worship lay in three great annual festivals coinciding with major events in rural life: **Passover** with the birthing of lambs, **Shavuot** with the cereal harvest, and **Sukkot** with the fruit harvest. They became linked to events in the national mythos of Israel: **Passover** with the exodus from Egypt, Shavuot with the law-giving at Biblical **Mount Sinai**, and **Sukkot** with the wilderness wanderings. **Yahweh**'s worship presumably involved sacrifice, but many scholars have concluded that the rituals detailed in **Leviticus 1–16**, with their stress on purity and atonement, were introduced only after the **Babylonian exile.**

**Yahweh**-worship was famously aniconic, meaning that the god was not depicted by a statue or other image. This is not to say that he was not represented in some symbolic form. But according to the Biblical texts the temple in Jerusalem featured **Yahweh**'s throne in the form of two **cherubim**, their inner wings forming the seat and a box (the **Ark of the Covenant**) as a footstool, while the throne itself was empty.

## Yahweh and the rise of monotheism

Pre-exilic Israel, like its neighbors, was polytheistic, and Israelite monotheism was the result of unique historical circumstances. The original god of Israel was **El**, as the name demonstrates—its probable meaning is "**may El rule**". In the early tribal period, each tribe would have had its own patron god; when kingship emerged, the state promoted **Yahweh** as the national god of Israel, supreme over the other gods, and gradually **Yahweh** absorbed all the positive traits of the other gods and goddesses. **Yahweh** and **El** merged at religious centres with **El**'s name becoming a generic term for "god" and **Yahweh**, the national god, appropriating many of the older supreme god's titles such as **El Shaddai** (Almighty) and **Elyon** (Most High).

**Asherah**, formerly the wife of **El**, was worshipped as **Yahweh**'s consort or mother. **Yahweh** may also have appropriated **Anat, the wife of Baal,** as his consort, as **Anat-Yahu** ("Anat of Yahu", i.e., **Yahweh**) is mentioned in 5th century BCE records from the Jewish colony at **E**lephantine in Egypt.

A goddess called the **Queen of Heaven** was also worshipped, probably a fusion of **Astarte** and the Mesopotamian goddess **Ishtar**, possibly a title of **Asherah**. Worship of **Baal** and **Yahweh** coexisted in the early period of Israel's history, but they were considered irreconcilable after the 9th century BCE, following the efforts of **King Ahab** and his queen Jezebel to elevate **Baal** to the status of national god.

The worship of **Yahweh** alone began at the earliest with **Elijah in the 9th century BCE**, but more likely with the prophet **Hosea** in the 8ᵗʰ· gaining ascendancy in the Babylonian exile and early post-exilic period. They did not believe **Yahweh** was the only god in existence, but instead believed he was the only god the people of Israel should worship.

## Second Temple Judaism

In 539 BCE Babylon itself fell to the Persian conqueror **Cyrus**, and in 538 BCE the exiles were permitted to return to **Yehud Medinata**, as the Persian province of Judah was known.

The Temple is commonly said to have been rebuilt in the period 520–515 BCE, so that 70 years to have passed between the destruction and the rebuilding, fulfilling a prophecy of **Jeremiah.** Much of the Hebrew Bible was assembled, revised and edited in the 5th century BCE to reflect the realities and challenges of the Persian era. The returnees had a particular interest in the history of Israel: the written **Torah (the books of Genesis, Exodus, Leviticus, Numbers and Deuteronomy)**, may have existed in various forms during the Monarchy (the period of the kingdoms of **Israel** and **Judah**), but it was in the **Second Temple** that it was edited and revised into something like its current form.

In the Persian-era authors, with some works being composed at this time (the last ten chapters of Isaiah and the books of **Haggai, Zechariah, Malachi** and perhaps **Joel**) and the older prophets edited and reinterpreted. The corpus of **Wisdom books** saw the composition of **Job**, parts of Proverbs, and possibly **Ecclesiastes**, while the book of **Psalms** was possibly given its modern shape and division into five parts at this time.

**Torah**, or ritual law, was also important, and the Temple priests were responsible for teaching it, but the concept of scripture developed only slowly. While the written **Torah** (the Pentateuch) and the Prophets were accepted as authoritative by the 1st century CE, beyond this core the different Jewish groups continued to accept different groups of books as authoritative.

During the **Second Temple** period, speaking the name of **Yahweh** in public became regarded as taboo. Jews began to substitute the divine name with the word *adonai,* meaning **"Lord".** The **High Priest** of Israel was permitted to speak the name once in the Temple during the **Day of Atonement,** but at no other time and in no other place. **After the Temple was destroyed in 70 CE, the original pronunciation of the Tetragrammaton was forgotten**.

The period of Persian rule saw the development of expectation in a future human king who would rule purified Israel as **Yahweh**'s representative at the end of time—a messiah. The first to mention this were **Haggai** and **Zechariah**, both prophets of the early Persian period. They saw the messiah in **Zerubbabel,** a descendant of the **House of David**. The first **High Priest**, **Joshua** (**Zechariah** writes of two messiahs, one royal and the other priestly). **From these ideas, Christianity, Rabbinic Judaism, and Islam would later emerge.**

## Graeco-Roman syncretism

The archangels **Michael, Gabriel, Raphael, and Ouriel** and Jewish cultural heroes such as **Abraham, Jacob**, and **Moses** are also invoked frequently. **Tacitus, John the Lydian,** and **Cornelius Labeo** all identify **Yahweh** with the Greek god **Dionysus**. In his *Quaestiones Convivales*, the Greek writer Plutarch writes that the Jews hail their god with cries of "**Euoi**" and "**Sabi**", phrases associated with the worship of **Dionysus**.

# Yeshiva: Beth Midrash

A **yeshiva** is a Jewish educational institution that focuses on the study of traditional religious texts, primarily the **Talmud** and the **Torah.** The studying is usually done through daily *shiurim* (lectures or classes) as well as in study pairs called *chavrutas* (Aramaic for **'friendship' or 'companionship'**). Historically, yeshivas were attended by males only. Today, all non-Orthodox and a few **Modern Orthodox yeshivas are open to females.**

## Etymology

The transference in meaning of the term from the learning session to the institution itself appears to have occurred by the time of the great **Talmudic Academie**s in Babylonia, **Sura** and **Pumbedita,** which were known as *shte ha-yeshivot* (the two colleges).

## History / Origins

The **Mishnah** tractate **Megillah** mentions the law that a town can only be called a **"city"** if it supports ten men (*batlanim*) to make up the required quorum for communal prayers.

## Geonic Period

The Geonic period takes its name from *Gaon,* the title bestowed on the heads of the three yeshivas in existence from the third to the thirteenth century. Throughout the **Geonic Period** there were three yeshivot. These were named for the cities in which they were located: **Jerusalem, Sura, and Pumbedita**; the yeshiva of Jerusalem would later relocate to Cairo.

The yeshiva served as the highest educational institution for the Rabbis of this period. In addition to this, the yeshiva wielded immense power as the principal body for interpreting Jewish law. In this regard, the community saw the **Gaon** of a yeshiva as the highest judge on all matters of Jewish law. The yeshiva of Jerusalem was finally forced into exile in Cairo in 1127, and eventually dispersed entirely. Likewise, the yeshivot of **Sura** and **Pumbedita** were dispersed following the Mongol invasions of the 13th century.

## Lithuanian yeshivas

Organized **Torah** study was revolutionized by **Rabbi Chaim Volozhin**, a disciple of the **Vilna Gaon** (an influential 18th-century leader of Judaism). The **Volozhin yeshiva** was closed some 60 years later due to the Russian government's demands for the introduction of certain secular studies. Many prominent contemporary *yeshivot* in the United States and Israel are continuations of these institutions and often bear the same name.

In the 19th century, **Rabbi Israel Salanter** initiated the **Mussar** movement in non-Hasidic Lithuanian Jewry, which sought to encourage yeshiva students and the wider community to spend regular times devoted to the study of Jewish ethical works. The masters of **Mussar** saw a need to augment **Talmud**ic study with more personal works. **Hasidism** began previously, in the 18th Century, within traditional Jewish life in the Ukraine, and spread to Hungary, Poland and Russia.

## Hasidic yeshivas

With the success of the yeshiva institution in Lithuanian Jewry, the Hasidic world developed their own yeshivas, in their areas of Eastern Europe. Examples of these Hasidic yeshivas are the **Chabad Lubavitch** yeshiva system of **Tomchei Temimim, founded by Sholom Dovber Schneersohn in Russia in 1897**, and the **Chachmei Lublin Yeshiva** established in Poland in 1930 by **Meir Shapiro**, who is renowned in both Hasidic and Lithuanian Jewish circles for initiating the **Daf Yomi** daily cycle of **Talmud** study.

These paths see **Hasidism** as a means to the end of inspiring emotional *devekut* (spiritual attachment to God) and mystical enthusiasm. The works of the Rebbes of **Chabad**, initiated by its founder **Schneur Zalman of Liadi**, to systematically investigate and articulate the **"Torah of the Baal Shem Tov"** in intellectual forms.

## Sephardi yeshivas

Although the yeshiva as an institution is in some ways a continuation of the **Talmudic Academies in Babylonia**, large scale educational institutions of this kind were not characteristic of the North African and Middle Eastern Sephardi Jewish world in pre-modern times. In 19th-century Jerusalem, early educational institutions on the European model were **Midrash Bet Zilkha founded in 1870s Iraq and Porat Yosef Yeshiva founded in Jerusalem in 1914**.

Also notable is the **Bet El yeshiva** founded in 1737 in Jerusalem for advanced Kabbalistic studies. With the establishment of Sephardi yeshivas in Israel, after the immigration of the Arabic Jewish communities there, some Sephardi yeshivas incorporated study of more accessible Kabbalistic texts into their curriculum.

## Conservative movement yeshivas

In 1854, the **Jewish Theological Seminary of Breslau** was founded. It was headed by **Zecharias Frankel,** and was viewed as the first educational institution associated with **"positive-historical Judaism"** (the predecessor of **Conservative Judaism**).

## Reform and Reconstructionist seminaries

**Hebrew Union College (HUC)**, affiliated with Reform Judaism, was founded in 1875 under the leadership of **Rabbi Isaac Mayer Wise** in Cincinnati, Ohio. **HUC** later opened additional locations in New York, Los Angeles, and Jerusalem. Similarly, the **Reconstructionist Rabbinical College** of **Reconstructionist Judaism**, founded in Pennsylvania in 1968, functions to train its future clergy.

## Contemporary Orthodox yeshivas

Traditionally, religious girls' schools are not called **"yeshiva."** The **Bais Yaakov** system was started in 1918 under the guidance of **Sarah Schenirer**. This system provided girls with a **Torah** education, more toward practical **Halakha** and the study of **Tanakh**, rather than **Talmud. Bais Yaakovs are strictly Haredi schools**.

## Curriculum

In some institutions, classical Jewish philosophy texts or **Kabbalah** are studied, or the works of individual thinkers (such as **Abraham Isaac Kook**). The curriculum focuses on classical Jewish subjects, including **Talmud, Tanakh, Midrash, Halacha, and Philosophy,** with an openness to modern scholarship.

## Chavruta-style learning

**Chavruta**-style learning tends to be loud and animated. In the heat of discussion, they may even wave their hands, pound the table, or shout at each other. One of the skills of chavruta-style learning is the ability to block out all other discussions in the study hall and focus on one's *chavruta* alone.

## Jewish law

Generally, a period is devoted to the study of practical *Halacha* (Jewish law). The text most commonly studied in Ashkenazic Yeshivot is the *Mishnah Berurah* written by **Rabbi Yisrael Meir Kagan**, the **Chofetz Chaim**. The *Mishnah Berurah* is a compilation of *halachic* opinions rendered after the time of the writing of the *Shulchan Aruch*.

## Ethics, mysticism and philosophy

**Hasidic yeshivot** study the mystical, spiritual works of Hasidic philosophy (*Chassidus*). This draws on the earlier esoteric theology of **Kabbalah**, but articulates it in terms of inner psychological awareness and personal analogies. This makes Jewish mysticism accessible and tangible, so that it inspires emotional **dveikus** (cleaving to God) and spiritual contribution to daily Jewish life.

## Torah and Bible study

Intensive study of the **Torah (Genesis, Exodus, Leviticus, Numbers and Deuteronomy** with the commentary of **Rashi (Rabbi Shlomo Yitzhaqi** 1040 - 1105) is stressed and taught in all elementary grades, often with Yiddish translations and more notes in Haredi yeshivas.

## Languages

In most Lithuanian and Hasidic yeshivot throughout the world, classes are taught in **Yiddish**; **Modern Orthodox, Zionist**, or *Baal teshuvah* yeshivot may use Modern or Israeli Hebrew or the local language.

# YHWY (Elohim)

In the **Hebrew Bible**, the word *elohim* (Hebrew: אֱלֹהִים) sometimes refers to a single deity, particularly (but not always) the **Jewish God**, at other times it refers to deities in the plural. The word is identical to the usual plural form of the word *el,* which means gods or magistrates, and it is cognate to the word *'l-h-m* which is found in Ugaritic, where it is used as the pantheon for Canaanite gods, the children of **El,** and conventionally vocalized as **"Elohim"**. Rabbinic scholar **Maimonides** wrote that the various other usages are commonly understood to be homonyms.

The ambiguity of the term *elohim* is the result of such changes, cast in terms of **"vertical translatability"**, i.e. the re-interpretation of the gods of the earliest recalled period as the national god of monolatrism as it emerged in the 7th to 6th century BCE in the **Kingdom of Judah** and during the Babylonian captivity, and further in terms of monotheism by the emergence of Rabbinical Judaism in the 2nd century CE.

## Grammar and etymology / *El (deity), Ilah, and Allah*

The word *elohim or 'elohiym* (*elohiym*) is a grammatically plural noun for **"gods" or "deities"** or various other words in Biblical Hebrew. However, when referring to the Jewish **God,** *Elohim* is usually understood to be grammatically singular. It is generally thought that **Elohim** is derived from *Eloah*, the latter being an expanded form of the Northwest Semitic noun *'IL*. The related nouns *Eloah* (אלוה) **and** *el* (אֵל) are used as proper names or as generics, in which case they are interchangeable with *elohim*.

An exact cognate outside of Hebrew is found in **Ugaritic** *lhm*, the family of **El,** the creator god and chief deity of the Canaanite pantheon, in **Biblical Aramaic** *Elahi* and later **Syriac** *Alaha* ("God"), and in Arabic *'ilāh* ("god, deity") (or *Allah* as "The God"). "El" is usually derived from a root meaning **"to be strong" and/or "to be in front"**.

### *Ancient Canaanite religion*

The word *el* (singular) is a standard term for **"god"** in Aramaic, paleo-Hebrew, and other related Semitic languages including **Ugaritic**. The Canaanite pantheon of gods was known as *'ilhm,* **the Ugaritic equivalent to** *elohim.* In the Ugaritic Baal cycle we read of **"seventy sons of Asherah"**. Each **"son of god"** was held to be the originating deity for a particular people.

### Usage / *Hebrew grammar / Names of God in Judaism*

*Elohim* occurs frequently throughout the **Torah**. In some cases **(e.g. Exodus 3:4, "*Elohim* called unto him out of the midst of the bush ...")**, it behaves like a singular noun in Hebrew grammar, and is then generally understood to denote the **single God of Israel**. (for example, **Exodus 20:3, "You shall have no other gods before me")**. The word *Elohim* occurs more than 2500 times

**in the Hebrew Bible**, with meanings ranging from **"gods"** in a general sense (as in **Exodus** 12:12, where it describes **"the gods of Egypt"**), to specific gods (e.g., 1 Kings 11:33, where it describes **Chemosh "the god of Moab"**, or the frequent references to **Yahweh** as the **"elohim"** of Israel), to the spirits of the dead brought up at the behest of **King Saul** in **1 Samuel 28:13**. **Maimonides said: "I must premise that every Hebrew knows that the term Elohim is a homonym, and denotes God, angels, judges, and the rulers of countries,"**

## With plural verb

In **1 Samuel 28:13**, *elohim* is used with a plural verb. In **Genesis 20:13**, **Abraham**, before the polytheistic Philistine king **Abimelech**, says that **"Elohim (translated as God) caused) me to wander"**.

## With singular verb

*Elohim*, when meaning the God of Israel, is mostly grammatically singular, and is commonly translated as **"God"**, and capitalized. In **Genesis 1:26**, it is written**: "Then Elohim (translated as God) said (singular verb), 'Let us (plural) make (plural verb) man in our (plural) image, after our (plural) likeness'"**. *Elohim* singular is to be distinguished from *elohim* plural gods. In **1 Samuel 19:13, 16** only one image is intended; in most other places a single image may be intended; in **Zechariah 10:2** alone is it most naturally taken as a numerical plural.

## Sons of God

The Hebrew word for **"son"** is *ben*; plural is *bānim*. The Hebrew term *benei elohim* (**"sons of God"** or **"sons of the gods"**) in Genesis 6:2 compares to the use of **"sons of gods"**. Gods can be referred to collectively as *bene Elim*, *bene Elyon*, or *bene elohim*.

## Elohist

There may be a theological point, that God did not reveal his name, *Yahweh*, before the time of Moses, though **the Jahwist was aware of the prophetic books from the 7th and 8th centuries BCE.** Walking through the **Garden of Eden** looking for **Adam** and **Eve**. The Elohist often presents **Elohim** as in the Elohist version of the tale of **Jacob's ladder**, in which there is a ladder to the clouds, with angels climbing up and down, with **Elohim** at the top. **Yahweh** is simply stationed in the sky, above the clouds without the ladder or angels. **Likewise, the Elohist describes Jacob wrestling with an angel.**

## Latter Day Saint Movement / *God in Mormonism*

In **Mormonism**, **Elohim** refers to **God the Father**. **Elohim** is the father of **Jesus** in both the physical and the spiritual realms, whose name before birth is said to be **"Jehovah"**. To indicate a **"plurality of excellence or intensity, rather than distinctively of number"**.

# The Yom Kippur War (Oct 6<sup>th</sup>, 1973)

The history books say that **Israel**i intelligence broke down in the 1970s and allowed the Arabs to launch a simultaneous sneak attack in 1973. The invasion on **Yom Kippur**, **Israel**'s most holy day, caught the entire country unawares. Only the heroic intervention of an American Jew, Secretary of State **Henry Kissinger**, saved the tiny nation from destruction. Some of the **"old spies"** make gagging noises when presented with this version of history. Others pretend to be convulsed with laughter. **Kissinger** was a military incompetent, whose petty intrigues and dabbling in covert operations nearly caused the destruction of **Israel**.

- In order to curry favor with the Arabs, the White House ordered the National Security Agency to suppress information that a sneak attack against **Israel** would take place on October 6, 1973.
- **Kissinger**'s strategy was to let **Israel** get **"bloodied"** a bit and then force both sides to the peace table.
- The man who saved **Israel** from **Kissinger**'s blunders was the White House chief of staff, **Alexander Haig**.
- The man who became the scapegoat for **Kissinger**'s blunders was the CIA counterintelligence chief, **James Jesus Angleton**.

**Israel**'s old nemesis, **Nasser**, was dead, but his successor, **Anwar Sadat**, was not considered an improvement by Prime Minister **Golda Meir**, who recalled his pro-Nazi stance during World War II as evidence of his hatred for Jews. But **Sadat** was more than just another Nazi in Arab clothing. He was a brilliant politician. In fact, **Sadat**'s initiative was a missed opportunity, a tragic blunder. If **Sadat** could not persuade **Israel** to negotiate for the return of Egyptian land, he would force **Israel** to meet his terms.

**Sadat** had turned to the Soviets for military support. The Soviets had taken the Arab military commanders under their wing and explained that it was the lack of Egyptian intelligence security, not the failure of Soviet arms, which accounted for the 1967 debacle. **Hundreds of Soviet Military Intelligence (the GRU) agents** poured into **Israel**. Between 1967 and 1973 the **GRU** had penetrated **Israel**'s most secret communications channels, identified **Israel**i sources in Arab countries, and probed for weak points in **Israel**i electronic surveillance.

After 1967 the **Israel**is had grown overconfident. The **Mossad** was blinded. Arab agents were equipped with the best communications gear available – ironically, American-made satellite communication sets developed by the **NSA**. For the first time, the **Israel**is could not listen in to Arab war plans. In 1972 **Sadat** threw the Soviets out and told both superpowers that they had squandered his peace initiatives. **He would redeem Egyptian honor by force of arms**.

No one took him seriously. They should have anticipated that **Saudi Arabian** oil was crucial to American interests, and that **President Sadat** of Egypt was putting immense pressure on **King Faisal,** head of the Saudi royal family. Not that there was any real political difference between the two leaders – both were Arab nationalists. In fact, **King Faisal** was even more emphatic than **Sadat** about the need to destroy the **State of Israel**. The **Wahhabi** tradition of ignorant racism was alive and well.

In 1973, **Faisal** announced that he was changing his mind about an oil embargo. For a start, the oil marketplace had changed radically. The United States was already dependent on **Saudi oil**, twelve years before the previously predicted date of 1985. **Sadat**'s repudiation of **Nasser's** pro-Soviet stance also weighed heavily in the king's deliberations.

The **Saudis** geared up for economic war against the Jewish patrons in the West. The oil men could see billions of dollars of profits going down the drain, and all because of **Israel**. This time the king meant business. He took the propaganda offensive in a series of media interviews that made it clear that by supporting **Israel**, the United States was placing its oil supplies at risk. **On August 23, 1973, Sadat told Faisal that he intended to attack Israel**. The king promised his support, financially and by way of the **"oil weapon."**

A few days later the powerful Saudi oil minister, **Sheik Ahmed Yamani**, began dropping hints to the oil companies about a cutback in production that would affect the United States. The United States must change its policy of supporting **Israel** or suffer the consequences. This time they got their message through: **Bashing Jews was good for business**. The **Nixon** administration realized that a new policy was needed to avert a potential disaster. By the fall of 1973 U.S. consumers were on the brink of panic, and gas prices had begun their steep rise.

The **Organization of Petroleum Exporting Countries (OPEC)** demanded a new deal from the oil companies, and a showdown was set for October 6, in Vienna. The companies chose **John J. McCloy** as their lawyer to push their case for a counter-cartel against the Arabs. **McCloy was not well disposed to Israeli interests.** As previously discussed, **McCloy** was the U.S. official during World War II who ordered, in writing, that no American planes be diverted to bomb the gas chambers and then **released Nazi war criminals imprisoned at Nuremberg.**

However, the American response for a counter-cartel was too little too late. The **Moslem** world had been preparing secretly for battle. When the Egyptian army began its military buildup in the Sinai, the **CIA** passed a new estimate to the **Israel**is on September 26 that war was growing more likely. By the end of the first week of October, everyone was relaxed. **The Israelis were blissfully ignorant of the storm building around them**. On October 1 only ten people in Egypt knew that their training exercise was about to be converted into a genuine attack. On October 3 the date and hour of the attack was agreed upon with the Syrians: 2:00 P.M. October 6. The Syrians then briefed their Soviet advisers. **It was the best-kept secret in the Arab world.**

On October 3 and 4 the **NSA** decoded several messages from the Soviet embassy about the evacuation of personnel. **By October 4 the NSA knew beyond a shadow of a doubt that an attack on Israel would take place on the afternoon of October 6.** The **Nixon** White House ordered the NSA to sit on the information. **"We knew where. We were told to shut up and let it happen."** American intelligence was helping Israel's enemies in time of war.

The **Israeli** mobilization plan requires sixteen hours to call up its reserves for war. In wartime, everyone in **Israel** uses their own cars to transport hitchhiking soldiers to their positions. This quaint mobilization plan works well, with sixteen hours' notice. **Eight hours' warning causes chaos in Israel. Two hours' notice is a disaster.**

One **NSA** official later confirmed publicly that he knew of the planned attack on **Israel** by Syria and Egypt thirty hours before the United States notified **Israel**. **The NSA's warning was not circulated to the Israelis or to other members the U.S. intelligence community.**

On the same day **Israel**i intelligence continued to rate the risk of attack as a **"very low probability."** In fact, only the **NSA** knew that the Arab version of **Pearl Harbor** was about to happen. Dozens of summaries based on electronic intercepts were sent on a restricted channel to the **Nixon** White House. As one source admitted, **Nixon's staff had at least two days' advance warning that an attack was coming on October 6.**

*But no one in the Nixon White House warned the Jews until the last few hours on the day of the attack.* **Nixon certainly had a motive for revenge.** **Nixon** was well aware that, apart from **J. Edgar Hoover**, only the **Israel**is knew enough about his past to cause him major political damage. As the **Watergate** tape-recordings show, **Nixon was terribly afraid of the Jews**. He made lists of his enemies and kept track of Jewish Americans in his administration. **Nixon knew that Jews didn't vote for him anyway.**

During September and October 1973 the **Nixon** White House turned a blind eye toward **Sadat**'s plans for a consolidated sneak attack against the Jews. Not one word of the **NSA**'s information leaked out until the morning of the attack. Egypt and Syria had attacked **Israel**, and the **Yom Kippur War** had started. If **Israel** wanted American support, **Kissinger** warned, it could not even begin to mobilize until the Arabs invaded. **No general mobilization was issued after the warning from the United States.** The cabinet was still in emergency session when the attack came. Prime Minister **Golda Meir** was supposedly the person who overruled all entreaties from Defense Minister **Moshe Dayan** for immediate offensive action. **She cited Kissinger's threats as the major reason.**

The **Israel**i front-line units were crushed as the Egyptian army used high-powered water cannon to blast down **Israel**i sand forts and then cross the **Suez**. In the north, Syrian tank brigades obliterated significant sections of the **Israel**i battle line within hours. **Kissinger was conveniently absent on the day the war broke out, sitting "incommunicado at the Waldorf Astoria in New York".**
**Kissinger had set up the Jews.** He sat on the **NSA**'s information, disappeared on the day of the invasion, and waited three days before convening the **Security Council** at the UN. **Kissinger** was eager that **Israel** should be forced to comply with **UN Resolution 242**, which would reverse all the territorial gains that **Israel** had made in 1967. Instead of rushing arms to **Israel**, Defense Secretary **James Schlesinger** cautioned that the United States had to keep a **"low profile in order not to create an Arab reaction"** in the oil markets.

The outbreak of hostilities gave the Arabs at the Vienna oil negotiations a great morale boost. The oil companies offered a 15 percent price increase, but the Arabs wanted to double their take. The time was ripe to squeeze the West. Any country that helped **Israel** in the war faced an oil embargo. The oil men wanted their political masters to abandon the Jews. The economy and national security of the United States were at stake. **The Israeli ambassador called Kissinger hourly to complain: "These delays are costing lives. Who's playing games?"**

By Monday, October 8, the third day of the war, **the American games had cost Israel heavily. Several thousand soldiers had died, more in the first day than had died in the entire 1967 war**. **Over 500 tanks were destroyed. The Israeli air force had been crippled by Soviet SAM missiles.** At the start of the war, the **Israel**is had had only a seven-day supply of ammunition for some units.

For once **Moshe Dayan** was despondent. He said sadly: **"The situation is desperate. Everything is lost. We must withdraw."** The end of **Israel** seemed imminent and **Meir**'s friend made plans for the two of them to commit suicide. Only when **Israel**i ammunition was almost exhausted did the Americans act. The war had been going for six days, and the Arabs continued to inflict huge casualties on the Jews. **The secret architect of this "let Israel come out ahead, but bleed" strategy was none other than Henry Kissinger.**

But six days into the **Yom Kippur War**, the White House was beginning to realize that it might be much worse than a small **"nosebleed"** for the Jews. On October 12 **Nixon** received **Meir**'s desperate plea for assistance. The Soviets had started a massive resupply operation to Syria and Egypt; without a similar response from the United States for the Jews, **Israel would surely be destroyed.**

Henry **Kissinger** allegedly told **Nixon**, in no uncertain terms, that the country could not stand by and allow **Israel** to be defeated by Soviet arms. When Prime Minister **Meir** secretly wrote to **Nixon "warning that Israel was being overwhelmed and might soon be destroyed,"** Washington gave her some comfort. The Americans told the **Israel**is they could have supplies for the war, as long as it was done secretly.

The arms were to be shipped by plane, and only at night. **Nixon** personally leaned on Portugal to supply a refueling base in the Azores, and the operations were timed to land in **Israel** under cover of darkness. The American cargo planes landed in broad daylight on October 14. The very next day, October 15, the **Israel**is did exactly that, launching a successful counteroffensive that threw back the Egyptians just as they seemed likely to destroy **Israel**. **The man they blame for betraying Israel in 1973 is Henry Kissinger. Many of the American comments about Kissinger are unprintable. He was an intelligence professional for the Dulles brothers. In fact, Allen Dulles thought quite highly of him.**

In 1946-47, just as **Dulles** was putting together his OPC network to recruit e x-Nazi **"freedom fighters,"** Captain **Kissinger** suddenly became a civilian instructor at the intelligence school in Germany, which coincidentally also became a cover for OPC agents. The 1947 version of the army's *Consolidated Orientation and Guidance Manual* listed the various war criminals living in the U.S. zone, indexed them by atrocity, and cross-referenced them to their various employers in Western intelligence. This top-secret manual was considered basic reference for intelligence officers at the time **Kissinger was teaching intelligence courses. If Kissinger knew about the OPC's Nazi recruiting, he kept his mouth shut.**

In 1952 **Kissinger** became a consultant for the **National Security Council's Psychological Strategy Board,** which supported **Dulles'** entire program of covert paramilitary operations. This office consulted on the employment of Nazis as **"freedom fighters"** behind the **Iron Curtain** for the rest of the **Eisenhower-Nixon** administration. In 1954 **Nelson Rockefeller** took over as **Cold War** coordinator for the White House. **Shortly thereafter Kissinger was promoted to consultant to the NSC's "highest policy-making board for implementing clandestine operations against foreign governments."**

By the time **Nixon** ran for president in 1968, **Kissinger was an old professional in spy work.** A few days after the election, **Nixon** asked him to head his NSC, setting up a new organization **"to exclude the CIA from the formulation of policy."** **Kissinger** has always denied involvement with **Dulles'** Nazis. From the **Israeli** point of view, **Kissinger might as well have been an Arab.** **Israel**i intelligence remembered that **it was Kissinger who told them not to mobilize and wait for the Arabs to fire the first shot. It was Kissinger who went into hiding on the first day of the war.**

Instead of standing by the only democracy in the Middle East, **Kissinger had sold the Jews out for Arab oil.** Then, as the new secretary of state, he wanted to take the credit for **"peace"** negotiations in which **Israel** would have to give back the territory it had won in 1967. **Kissinger never meant to do as much harm as he did. The problem was incompetence, not bigotry.** His aim was to let the Jews win the war, but to wound them a little in the process.

However, **his scheme nearly destroyed Israel.** The Soviets, who had completely penetrated **Israel**i communications, were relaying to the Arabs the despair within the inner circle of **Golda Meir**'s advisers. With Soviet prompting, other Arab nations had jumped into the war. **Two Iraqi tank divisions, with 30,000 men and 1,200 armed vehicles, had suddenly appeared on the Golan Heights.**

Just as **President Nixon** was considering **Meir**'s desperate plea, which reached him on October 12, **Israel** had some help from the White House chief of staff, **General Alexander Haig. Haig** held up the oil companies' letter recommending a price increase for Arab oil producers for several crucial days. **Haig**'s action helped **Israel**, by allowing time for **Meir**'s dramatic plea to have its effect on **Nixon** and for the cold hard facts of the Arab and Soviet threats to sink in at the White House.

But **Al Haig** did much more for **Israel**. In fact, he was making policy behind **Kissinger**'s back. Defense Secretary **Schlesinger** had dragged his feet too long on military supplies. The U.S. airlift did not even commence until Sunday, October 14. **Haig** realized that there was a good chance that the **Israel**i Army would be crushed before the bulk of the supplies reached the front. The logistics loop was too long. On Saturday, October 6, **Alexander Haig told Israeli intelligence that there was a new weapon that could stop the Arab tank onslaught. If they could get a team to the United States, he would give it to them.**

The U.S. Army had just developed the tube-launched, optically tracked, wire-guided (**TOW**) missile and so far had shared it only with Britain and West Germany. The **TOW** could be fired from a foxhole and destroy a moving tank three kilometers away. As the missile was flying, it unreeled three kilometers of cable behind it, connected to a steering telescope.

As the enemy tank moved, trying to get away from the missile, the missile followed, even up and downhill. **The "kill ratio" for the TOW was 97 percent.** The **Israel**i captains and majors had long hair, mustaches, and wore hippie-style civilian clothes. The **Israel**is disappeared the next day for training. The **Israel**is were back in **Israel** by October 14, just in time to repulse a massive Egyptian armored attack in the Sinai. **It was the turning point of the war.**

**Al Haig** was stripping every **TOW** missile off the eastern seaboard of the United States and from Germany and shipping them to **Israel**. A number of histories of the **Yom Kippur War** have made a great deal of the **Israeli threat to use the atomic bomb.** On the other hand, four thousand **TOW** missiles could make quite an impact. They did just that. **Al Haig**'s missiles arrived in time to blunt the next Egyptian offensive. The opening of the final Egyptian assault on **Israel** turned into a rout as the Arabs' tank force was cut to ribbons.

**Haig had saved Kissinger's reputation by giving Israel the TOWs.** If the vital **Mitla Pass** had fallen, **Israel**'s fate would have been sealed. It is no coincidence that the **Israel**is put their atomic bombs back into storage on October 14, the day the **TOW** s were first tried out in **Israel**. On October 15 the **Israeli** army counterattacked, crossed the **Suez Canal**, and began to drive toward Cairo. **By October 16 the Soviet premier Kosygin flew to Cairo and advised Sadat to call for a cease-fire.**

The **Israel**is kept quiet about the **TOW** missiles. As a young Army captain in the late 1940s, **Haig** had served briefly in **General Gehlen's** Nazi base and hated what he saw. **Gehlen's** recruitment of Nazis as **Cold War "freedom fighters,"** the revival of anti-Semitism, and programs aimed directly at the new **State of Israel**, and was sickened by the hypocrisy and cynicism of his superiors. As cogently argued by **Len Colodny** and **Robert Gettlin, it was Haig who became "Deep Throat" in the Watergate Affair. Haig vehemently denies that he was the source of the leaks against Nixon.**

Bad intelligence about Soviet actions and intentions probably caused **Kissinger** to hit the panic button and put American forces on full alert. **Seymour Hersh** documented that it was **Kissinger himself who first leaked word to the Egyptians that Israel had three nuclear missiles.** The Arabs were not impressed. They had a more powerful weapon: oil. On October 16 the Arab members of OPEC unilaterally announced a 70 percent oil price rise.

They threatened the president with an oil embargo unless the American resupply of **Israel** was stopped, but **Nixon**, to his credit, refused to back down. **Nixon** and **Kissinger** argued that the supplies to **Israel** were anti-Soviet, not anti-Arab. **Nixon made some gratuitous comments about Kissinger's Jewish origins and pledged Kissinger's absolute neutrality.**

In fact, Iraq wanted to nationalize all U.S. interests in the Middle East. On October 19 **Nixon announced a $2.2 billion military aid package for Israel.** The Arab response was entirely predictable to everyone except **Kissinger**. Libya immediately announced a total embargo on the United States. Saudi Arabia had done likewise. Further, the Saudi cutback in production was increased from 5 to 10 percent each month, and then to 20. Once again the **House of Saud** was trying to blackmail an American president over **Israel**. As usual, profit triumphed over principle and **Aramco** cut off oil supplies to the **U.S. Navy**.

Washington actually had to turn to London to ask if it could supply the **Sixth Fleet**, much as Britain had been forced to turn to the United States in 1956. For a few hours on October 25, it even seemed as if the two superpowers were squaring off for a nuclear confrontation, but then **Kissinger pressured the Jews to allow the Arab armies to retreat unmolested.** The cease-fire held. **By October 26 the Yom Kippur War was over.** Soon thereafter **Israel** and Egypt began their first direct talks in a quarter of a century. The first priority for the **White House** was to find a scapegoat for the failure to give **Israel** timely intelligence. By throwing **James Angleton** to the wolves, the White House could kill two investigations with one stone.

**Golda Meir** wanted to know why their trusted source, **James Jesus Angleton**, had not given them any warning of the Arab attack. It was perhaps fitting that Angleton's failure helped end his longstanding liaison with **Israel.** **His iron grip on the CIA's Israeli desk was being questioned.** **Schlesinger** later told Angleton's biographers, **Tom Mangold**, that **"he was unhappy at the intimacy that had developed . . . between the Counterintelligence chief and the Israelis."** However, after only five months in the job, **Schlesinger** left the CIA and became defense secretary in July 1973. **Angleton's control of the Israeli account was given a reprieve with William Colby, the new CIA head.**

**Angleton** had become quite obsessive and paranoid and, although only 66, was long overdue for retirement. **Angleton became the major fall guy for all the failures of U.S. intelligence during the 1973 war.** Angleton resisted all attempts at his removal in a most ferocious manner. Perhaps **Colby feared that Angleton, like James Forrestal, would have committed suicide.** In December 1974 Colby finally acted.

After twenty-three years of officially holding the **Israeli** account, and nearly thirty since he first seized de factor control over it with his Zionist intelligence forgery, **Angleton was removed as the Israeli liaison.** **Colby** transferred responsibility for **Israeli** matters to the Near East Division. A few days after **Angleton** lost his last remaining job as head of counterintelligence. **After his death in 1986, his friends in Israeli intelligence gathered to dedicate a memorial to his memory.**

**There was hardly a Jew in the American government whom Angleton had not bugged.** Angleton's secret files on the Jews were discovered during the investigation of **Operation Chaos.** Later it was revealed that Angleton also was instrumental in using **Chaos** to spy on both the **Israeli** embassy in Washington and domestic Jewish groups. This covert operation involved the **CIA** buying a trash collection company to collect the garbage of both the **Israeli** embassy and the **B'Nai Brith** for intelligence purposes.

**The Nixon White House was a circle of snakes swallowing each other's tails.** When the dust had finally settled on the 1973 war, **Nixon** had resigned. **Angleton had been fired, Kissinger was discredited, but Israel had received more arms in three months than from all previous U.S. presidents combined.**

## Casualties
**Israel suffered between 2,521 and 2,800 killed in action.** An additional 7,250 to 8,800 soldiers were wounded. Some 293 **Israel**is were captured.

Approximately 400 **Israel**i tanks were destroyed. Another 600 were disabled but returned to service after repairs. The **Israel**i Air Force lost 102 airplanes: 32 F-4s, 53 A-4s, 11 Mirages and 6 Super Mysteres. Two helicopters, a Bell 205 and a CH-53, were also lost.

Egypt and Syria never disclosed official figures. *The Sunday Times* combined Egyptian and Syrian losses of 16,000 killed, and yet another source citing a figure of some 15000 dead and 35,000 wounded. U.S. estimates placed Egyptian casualties at 13,000. Iraq lost 278 killed and 898 wounded, while Jordan suffered 23 killed and 77 wounded.

Some 8,372 Egyptians, 392 Syrians, 13 Iraqis and 6 Moroccans were taken prisoner. Arab tank losses amounted to 2,250. 400 of these fell into **Israel**i hands in good working order and were incorporated into **Israel**i service. **Between 341 and 514 Arab aircraft were shot down**. Arab naval vessels, including 10 missile boats, were sunk for no **Israel**i losses.

- **On a visit to Israel on December 17th, 1973, Kissinger refused to visit Yad-Vashem Holocaust Museum.**

- **Israel** cannot trust America or any other ally; it must be able to defend itself. Lesson learned!

# Yom Kippur (Holiday)

**Yom Kippur**, also known as the **Day of Atonement**, is the holiest day of the year in Judaism. Its central themes are atonement and repentance. Jews traditionally observe this holy day with an approximate 25-hour period of fasting and intensive prayer, often spending most of the day in synagogue services.

## ☑ Etymology

*Kippur* can also mean to cleanse, with the **Yom Kippur** procedures in the Temple cleansing the people of sin.

## Roch Hashanah and Yom Kippur

**Yom Kippur** is "**the tenth day of seventh month**" (Tishrei) and is regarded as the "**Sabbath of Sabbaths**". **Roch Hashanah** (referred to in the **Torah** as *Yom Teruah*) is the first day of that month according to the Hebrew calendar. On this day forgiveness of sins is also asked of God. **Yom Kippur** completes the annual period known in Judaism as the **High Holy Days** or *Yamim Nora'im* ("Days of Awe") that commences with **Roch Hashanah.**

## Heavenly books opened

According to Jewish tradition, God inscribes each person's fate for the coming year into a book, the **Book of Life**, on **Roch Hashanah**, and waits until **Yom Kippur** to "seal" the verdict. During the **Days of Awe**, a Jew tries to amend their behavior and seek forgiveness for wrongs done against God (*bein adam leMakom*) and against other human beings (*bein adam lechavero*). At the end of **Yom Kippur**, one hopes that they have been forgiven by God.

## Prayer service

Unlike a regular day, which has three prayer services (*Ma'ariv,* the evening prayer; *Shacharit,* the morning prayer; and *Mincha,* the afternoon prayer), or a Shabbat or **Yom Tov**, which have four prayer services (*Ma'ariv; Shacharit; Mussaf,* the additional prayer; and *Mincha*), **Yom Kippur has five prayer services** (*Ma'ariv; Shacharit; Musaf; Mincha;* and *Ne'ilah,* **the closing prayer**).

## Observance

As one of the most culturally significant Jewish holidays, **Yom Kippur** is observed by many secular Jews who may not observe other holidays. Many secular Jews attend synagogue on **Yom Kippur**—for many secular Jews the **High Holy Days** are the only times of the year during which they attend synagogue—causing synagogue attendance to soar.

## General observances

**Leviticus 16:29** mandates establishment of this holy day on the 10th day of the 7th month as the day of atonement for sins. It calls it the **Sabbath of Sabbaths** and a day upon which one must afflict one's soul.

## The prohibitions are the following:
1. No eating and drinking
2. No wearing of leather shoes
3. No bathing or washing
4. No anointing oneself with perfumes or lotions
5. No marital relations

A parallel has been drawn between these activities and the human condition according to the Biblical account of the expulsion from the **Garden of Eden**. The soul is considered to be the life force in a body. By feeling pain one can feel how others feel when they are in pain. This is the purpose of the prohibitions.

## In order to gain atonement from God, one must:
1. Pray
2. Repent of one's sins
3. Give to charity

## Eve / *Kol Nidre*

Before sunset on **Yom Kippur** eve, worshipers gather in the synagogue. The **Ark** is opened and two people take from it two **Sifrei Torah** (**Torah scrolls**). Then they take their places, one on each side of the **Hazzan**, and the three recite (in Hebrew):

In the tribunal of Heaven and the tribunal of earth, we hold it lawful to pray with transgressors. The cantor then chants the **Kol Nidre** prayer (Aramaic: **"All vows"**). It is recited in Aramaic. The leader and the congregation then say together three times **"May all the people of Israel be forgiven, including all the strangers who live in their midst, for all the people are in fault."** The **Torah** scrolls are then placed back into the **Ark**, and the **Yom Kippur** evening service begins.

## Prayer services

The morning prayer service is preceded by litanies and petitions of forgiveness called *selichot*; on **Yom Kippur**, many *selichot* are woven into the liturgy of the **mahzor** (prayer book. This is followed by *Mincha* (the afternoon prayer) which includes a reading (**Haftarah**) of the entire **Book of Jonah**, which has as its theme the story of God's willingness to forgive those who repent. **Yom Kippur** comes to an end with a recitation of *Shema Yisrael* and the blowing of the *shofar*, which marks the conclusion of the fast.

## Reform Judaism

Reform synagogues generally experience their largest attendance of the year on **Yom Kippur** and **Roch Hashanah** for worship services. A central feature of **Reform** these services is the rabbinic sermon. **"For more than a century and a half in the Reform Movement," "High Holiday sermons were among the most anticipated events in synagogue life, especially on the eve of Roch Hashanah and Kol Nidre night."**

## Repentance (*Teshuva*) and confessional (*Vidui*)

The **Talmud** states, **"Yom Kippur atones for those who repent and does not atone for those who do not repent".** Repentance in Judaism is done through a process called **Teshuva**, which in its most basic form consists of regretting having committed the sin, resolving not to commit that sin in the future and to confess that sin before God.

## Avodah: remembering the Temple service

This traditional prominence is rooted in the **Babylonian Talmud**'s description of how to attain atonement following the destruction of the Temple. According to **Talmud** tractate **Yom**a, in the absence of a Temple, Jews are obligated to study the **High Priest's** ritual on **Yom Kippur**, and this study helps achieve atonement for those who are unable to benefit from its actual performance.

## In the Torah

The **Torah** calls the day *Yom HaKippurim* and in it Leviticus 23:27 decrees a strict prohibition of work and affliction of the soul upon the tenth day of the seventh month, later known as **Tishrei**.

## Midrashic interpretation

Traditionally, **Yom Kippur** is considered the date on which **Moses** received the second set of **Ten Commandments.** It occurred following the completion of the second 40 days of instructions from God. At this same time, the Israelites were granted atonement for the sin of the **Golden Calf**; hence, its

The **Kohen Gadol** wore five sets of garments (three golden and two white linen), immersed in the *mikvah* five times, and washed his hands and feet ten times. Sacrifices included two (daily) lambs, one bull, two goats, and two rams, with accompanying *mincha* (meal) offerings, wine libations, and three incense offerings (the regular two daily and an additional one for **Yom Kippur**). The **Kohen Gadol** entered the **Holy of Holies** four times.

## Observance in Israel

**Yom Kippur** is a legal holiday in the modern state of Israel. There are no radio or television broadcasts, airports are shut down, there is no public transportation, and all shops and businesses are closed.

# Zionism

**Theodor Herzl** was the founder of the Modern **Zion**ist movement. In his 1896 pamphlet *Der Judenstaat,* he envisioned the founding of a future independent Jewish state during the 20th century. **Zionism** is an ideology and nationalist movement that espouses the establishment of, and support for a Jewish state centered in the area roughly corresponding to **Canaan**, the **Holy Land**, the region of **Palestine** or **Eretz Israel** on the basis of a long Jewish connection and attachment to that land.

**Modern Zionism** emerged in the late 19th century in Central and Eastern Europe as a national revival movement, both in reaction to newer waves of antisemitism and as a response to **Haskalah,** or **Jewish Enlightenment**. Soon after this, most leaders of the movement associated the main goal with creating the desired state in **Palestine**, then an area controlled by the **Ottoman Empire.**

**Zionism** posited a negation of Jewish life in the diaspora and, until 1948 perceived its primary goal as an ideal ingathering of exiles (*kibbutz galuyot*) in the ancient heartland of the Jewish people, and, through the establishment of a state, the liberation of Jews from the persecutions, humiliations, discrimination and antisemitism they had been subject to. Since the establishment of the State of Israel in 1948, **Zionism** has continued primarily to advocate on behalf of Israel and to address threats to its continued existence and security.

A variety of **Zionism**, called **cultural Zionism**, founded and represented most prominently by **Ahad Ha'am**, fostered a secular vision of a Jewish **"spiritual center"** in Israel. Unlike **Herzl**, the founder of political **Zionism**, Ahad Ha'am strived for Israel to be **"a Jewish state and not merely a state of Jews"**. **Critics of Zionism for the exodus of Palestinians, and the subsequent denial of their right to return to lands and property lost during the 1948 and 1967 wars.**

## Terminology

The term "**Zionism**" is derived from the word *Zion*, referring to Jerusalem. These groups were collectively called the "**Lovers of Zion**" and were seen as countering a growing Jewish movement toward assimilation.

## Overview

The common denominator among all **Zionists** has been a claim to the land historically known as **Palestine**, and in Jewish writings as **Eretz Israel** as a national homeland of the Jews and as the legitimate focus for Jewish national self-determination. After almost two millennia of the Jewish diaspora residing in various countries without a national state, the **Zionist** movement was founded in the late 19th century by secular Jews, largely as a response by **Ashkenazi** Jews to rising antisemitism in Europe, exemplified by the **Dreyfus Affair** in France and the anti-Jewish pogroms in the **Russian Empire**. The political movement was formally established by the Austro-Hungarian journalist **Theodor Herzl** in 1897 following the publication of his book *Der Judenstaat* (*The Jewish State*).

At that time, the movement sought to encourage Jewish migration to **Ottoman Palestine**. "**I believe that a wondrous generation of Jews will spring into existence. The Maccabeans will rise again... The Jews who wish for a State will have it. We shall live at last as free men on our own soil, and die peacefully in our own homes. The world will be freed by our liberty, enriched by our wealth, magnified by our greatness. And whatever we attempt there to accomplish for our own welfare, will react powerfully and beneficially for the good of humanity.**" (**Theodore Herzl**, concluding words of *The Jewish State*, 1896).

Creating an alliance with **Great Britain** and securing support for some years for Jewish emigration to **Palestine**. The movement was eventually successful in establishing **The State of Israel on May 14, 1948**, as the homeland for the Jewish people. By the early 21st century, more than 40% of the world's Jews lived in Israel, more than in any other country. In 1975, the United **Nations General Assembly** passed **Resolution 3379**, which designated **Zionism** as "**a form of racism and racial discrimination**". The resolution was repealed in 1991 by **replacing Resolution 3379 with Resolution 46/86**.

**Theodor Herzl,** the ideological father of **Zionism**: "**Let them give us sovereignty over a piece of the Earth's surface, just sufficient for the needs of our people, then we will do the rest!**" **Herzl** considered two possible destinations to colonize, **Argentina** and **Palestine**. But conceded that **Palestine** would have greater attraction because of the historic ties of Jews with that area. Major aspects of the **Zion**ist idea are represented in the **Israeli Declaration of Independence**: The **Land of Israel** was the birthplace of the Jewish people. Here their spiritual, religious and political identity was shaped. Here they first attained to statehood, created cultural values of national and universal significance and gave to the world the eternal **Book of Books.**

## History

The delegates at the **First Zionist Congress**, held in Basel, Switzerland (1897). Following the destruction of the **Second Temple** and the massacre of the Jews in Jerusalem. Of the 600,000 (Tacitus) or 1,000,000 (**Josephus**) Jews of Jerusalem, all of them either died of starvation, were killed or were sold into slavery.

According to the **Tanakh**, God had assigned Canaan to the Jews as a **Promised Land**, a belief conserved also in the **Septuagint** and both Christian and Islamic tradition. **The Diaspora began in 586 BCE during the Babylonian occupation of Israel.** The Babylonians destroyed the **First Temple,** which was central to Jewish culture at the time. After the 1st-century **Great Revolt** and the 2nd-century **Bar Kokhba** revolt, the **Roman Empire** banned Jews from Jerusalem and called the territory *Syria Palaestina.*

In the middle of the 16th century, the Portuguese Sephardi **Joseph Nasi**, with the support of the Ottoman Empire, tried to gather the Portuguese Jews, first to migrate to Cyprus, then owned by the **Republic of Venice**, and later to resettle in Tiberias. Nasi – who **never converted to Islam** – eventually obtained the highest medical position in the empire, and actively participated in court life. He convinced **Suleiman I** to intervene with the **Pope** on behalf of Ottoman-subject Portuguese Jews imprisoned in Ancona.

In the 17th century **Sabbatai Zevi** (1626–1676) announced himself as the **Messiah** and gained many Jews to his side, forming a base in Salonika. He first tried to establish a settlement in Gaza, but moved later to Smyrna. The bloody pogroms of **Bohdan Khmelnytsky** had wiped out one-third of the Jewish population and destroyed many centers of Jewish learning and communal life. Individual efforts supported the emigration of groups of Jews to **Palestine, pre-Zionist Aliyah,** even before 1897, the year considered as the start of practical **Zionism**. The **Reformed** Jews rejected this idea of a return to **Zion**. "T**he union of all the children of God in the confession of the unity of God"**.

**Sir Moses Montefiore**, famous for his intervention in favor of Jews around the world, including the attempt to rescue **Edgardo Mortara**, established a colony for Jews in **Palestine**. In 1854, his friend **Judah Touro** bequeathed money to fund Jewish residential settlement in **Palestine**. The official beginning of the construction of the **New Yishuv** in **Palestine** is usually dated to the arrival of the **Bilu group** in 1882, who commenced the **First Aliyah.** Most immigrants came from the **Russian Empire**, escaping the frequent pogroms and state-led persecution in what are now Ukraine and Poland. Additional **Aliyahs** followed the **Russian Revolution** and its eruption of violent pogroms. At the end of the 19th century, Jews were a small minority in **Palestine**.

In the 1890s, **Theodor Herzl** infused **Zionism** with a new ideology and practical urgency, leading to the **First Zionist Congress** at Basel in 1897, which created the **World Zionist Organization** (WZO). The **Russian Empire**, with its long record of state-organized genocide and ethnic cleansing **("pogroms"),** was widely regarded as the historic enemy of the Jewish people.

## Territories considered

Throughout the first decade of the **Zion**ist movement, there were several instances where **Zion**ist figures supported a Jewish state in places outside **Palestine**, such as **Uganda** and **Argentina.** However, other **Zion**ists emphasized the memory, emotion and tradition linking Jews to the Land of Israel. In 1903, British Colonial Secretary **Joseph Chamberlain** offered **Herzl** 5,000 square miles in the **Uganda Protectorate** for Jewish settlement. The area was populated by a large number of **Maasai**, who did not seem to favor an influx of Europeans. After **Herzl died in 1904,** the Congress decided on July 1905 to decline the British offer and, **"direct all future settlement efforts solely to Palestine"**.

## Balfour Declaration and the Palestine Mandate 1917

**"His Majesty's government view with favor the establishment in Palestine of a national home for the Jewish people, and will use their best endeavors to facilitate the achievement of this object, it being clearly understood that nothing shall be done which may prejudice the civil and religious rights of existing non-Jewish communities in Palestine, or the rights and political status enjoyed by Jews in any other country"**.

In 1922, the **League of Nations** adopted the declaration, and granted to Britain the **Palestine** Mandate: **"The Mandate will secure the establishment of the Jewish national home ... and the development of self-governing institutions, and also safeguard the civil and religious rights of all the inhabitants of Palestine, irrespective of race and religion."**

**Weizmann**'s role in obtaining the **Balfour Declaration** led to his election as the **Zion**ist movement's leader. He remained in that role until 1948, and then was elected as the first President of Israel after the nation gained independence. Riots erupted in **Palestine** in 1920, 1921 and 1929, in which both Jews and Arabs were killed. In response to the violent events noted above, the **Peel Commission** published a report proposing new provisions and restrictions in **Palestine**.

## Rise of Hitler

**In 1933, Hitler came to power in Germany**, and in 1935 the **Nuremberg Laws** made German Jews stateless refugees. The subsequent growth in Jewish migration and the impact of Nazi propaganda aimed at the Arab world led to the 1936–1939 Arab revolt in **Palestine**. Britain established the **Peel Commission** to investigate the situation. The commission did not consider the situation of Jews in Europe but called for a **two-state solution**. It implemented the **White Paper of 1939.** This planned to end Jewish immigration by 1944 and to allow no more than 75,000 additional Jewish migrants.

The **Jewish Agency** for **Palestine** under the leadership of **David Ben-Gurion** increasingly dictated policy with support from **American Zionists** who provided funding and influence in Washington. Following the end of the war, a massive wave of stateless Jews, mainly **Holocaust** survivors, began migrating to **Palestine** in small boats in defiance of British rules. The British either imprisoned these Jews in Cyprus or sent them to the British-controlled **Allied Occupation Zones** in Germany. Following the failure of the **1946–47 London Conference on Palestine,** at which the United States refused to support the British leading to both the **Morrison–Grady Plan** and the **Bevin Plan** being rejected by all parties, **the British decided to refer the question to the UN on February 14, 1947.**

**Post-World War II**

With the German invasion of the **USSR** in 1941, Stalin reversed his long-standing opposition to **Zionism**, and tried to mobilize worldwide Jewish support for the Soviet war effort. In May 1947 Soviet Deputy Foreign Minister **Andrei Gromyko** told the United Nations that the USSR supported the partition of **Palestine** into a Jewish and an Arab state. However once Israel was established, Stalin reversed positions, favored the Arabs.

In 1947, the **United Nations Special Committee** on **Palestine** recommended that western **Palestine** should be partitioned into a Jewish state, an Arab state and a **UN-controlled territory**, *Corpus separatum,* around Jerusalem. This partition plan was adopted on November 29, 1947, with UN **GA Resolution 181**, 33 votes in favor, 13 against, and 10 abstentions.

**Jewish-Arab fighting spiraled into the 1947–1949 Palestine war**. The conflict led to an exodus of about 711,000 Palestinian Arabs, known in Arabic as *al-Nakba* (**"the Catastrophe"**). More than a quarter had already fled prior to the declaration of the State of Israel and the start of the 1948 Arab–Israeli War. The exodus of 850,000 Jews from the Arab world, mostly to Israel. In 1944–45, **Ben-Gurion** described the **One Million Plan** to foreign officials as being the "**primary goal and top priority of the Zionist movement.**"

The immigration restrictions of the **British White Paper of 1939 the Israeli Declaration of Independence in May 1948.**

## Liberal Zionism

**General Zionists** identified with the liberal European middle class to which many **Zion**ist leaders such as **Herzl** and **Chaim Weizmann** aspired. Liberal **Zion**ists see that "**Jewish history shows that Jews need and are entitled to a nation-state of their own. But they also think that this state must be a liberal democracy, which means that there must be strict equality before the law independent of religion, ethnicity or gender.**"

## Revisionist Zionism

**Revisionist Zionists**, led by **Ze'ev Jabotinsky**, developed what became known as **Nationalist Zionism,** whose guiding principles were outlined in the 1923 essay *Iron Wall.* In 1935 the Revisionists left the **World Zionist Organization** because it refused to state that the creation of a Jewish state was an objective of **Zionism**.

## Religious Zionism

**Religious Zionism** is an ideology that combines **Zionism** and observant Judaism. Before the establishment of the State of Israel, **Religious Zionists** were mainly observant Jews who supported **Zion**ist efforts to build a Jewish state in the Land of Israel. After the **Six-Day War** and the capture of the West Bank, a territory referred to in Jewish terms as Judea and Samaria, right-wing components of the **Religious Zionist** movement integrated nationalist re-vindication and evolved into **Neo-Zionism. Their ideology revolves around three pillars: the Land of Israel, the People of Israel and the Torah of Israel.**

## Green Zionism

**Green Zionism** is a branch of **Zionism** primarily concerned with the environment of Israel. The only specifically environmentalist **Zion**ist party is the **Green Zionist Alliance**.

## Christian Zionism

Some Christians actively supported the return of Jews to **Palestine** even prior to the rise of **Zionism**, as well as subsequently. **Evangelical Christian restorationists** of the 1840s anticipation of and political lobbying within the UK for **Restorationism**. **John Nelson Darby's** doctrine of **dispensationalism** is credited with promoting **Zionism**, following his 11 lectures on the hopes of the church, the Jew and the gentile given in Geneva in 1840.

Christian **Zionism** strengthened significantly after the **Six-Day War** of 1967, and many dispensationalist and non-dispensationalist evangelical Christians, especially Christians in the United States, now strongly support **Zionism. Martin Luther King Jr**. was a strong supporter of Israel and **Zionism**. In the last years of his life, the founder of the **Latter Day Saint movement, Joseph Smith**, declared, **"The time for Jews to return to the land of Israel is now."**

## Muslim Zionism

While most Israeli **Druze** identify as ethnically Arab, today, tens of thousands of Israeli Druze belong to "**Druze Zionist**" movements.

## Anti-Zionism

**Zionism** is opposed by a wide variety of organizations and individuals. The preamble of the **African Charter on Human and Peoples' Rights**, which has been ratified by 53 African countries as of 2014, includes an undertaking to eliminate **Zionism**. In 1945 US **President Franklin D Roosevelt** met with **King Ibn Saud** of Saudi Arabia. Ibn Saud pointed out that it was Germany who had committed crimes against the Jews and so Germany should be punished. **Roosevelt** concluded that Israel "**could only be established and maintained by force."**

## Haredi Judaism and Zionism

Many **Haredi Orthodox** organizations oppose **Zionism**; they view **Zionism** as a secular movement. Many Hasidic groups in Jerusalem, most famously the **Satmar Hasidim**, as well as the larger movement they are part of, the **Edah HaChareidis**, are strongly anti-**Zion**ist. They were in apparent violation of the traditional notion that **Jews should wait for the Jewish Messiah.** The **Neturei Karta,** an **Orthodox Haredi** religious movement, strongly oppose **Zionism,** considering Israel a **"racist regime"**. They are viewed as a cult on the **"farthest fringes of Judaism"** by most mainstream Jews; the Jewish **Virtual Library** puts their numbers at 5,000.

## Anti-Zionism or antisemitism

Criticism of Israel may be used as an excuse to express viewpoints that might otherwise be considered antisemitic. Other scholars argue that certain forms of opposition to **Zionism** constitute antisemitism. To avoid accusations of antisemitism, the **Palestine Liberation Organization** has historically avoided using the word **"Jewish"** in favor of using **"Zionist."**